Short Story Criticism

Guide to Gale Literary Criticism Series

For criticism on	Consult these Gale series
Authors now living or who died after December 31, 1959	*CONTEMPORARY LITERARY CRITICISM (CLC)*
Authors who died between 1900 and 1959	*TWENTIETH-CENTURY LITERARY CRITICISM (TCLC)*
Authors who died between 1800 and 1899	*NINETEENTH-CENTURY LITERATURE CRITICISM (NCLC)*
Authors who died between 1400 and 1799	*LITERATURE CRITICISM FROM 1400 TO 1800 (LC)* *SHAKESPEAREAN CRITICISM (SC)*
Authors who died before 1400	*CLASSICAL AND MEDIEVAL LITERATURE CRITICISM (CMLC)*
Authors of books for children and young adults	*CHILDREN'S LITERATURE REVIEW (CLR)*
Dramatists	*DRAMA CRITICISM (DC)*
Poets	*POETRY CRITICISM (PC)*
Short story writers	*SHORT STORY CRITICISM (SSC)*
Black writers of the past two hundred years	*BLACK LITERATURE CRITICISM (BLC)*
Hispanic writers of the late nineteenth and twentieth centuries	*HISPANIC LITERATURE CRITICISM (HLC)*
Native North American writers and orators of the eighteenth, nineteenth, and twentieth centuries	*NATIVE NORTH AMERICAN LITERATURE (NNAL)*
Major authors from the Renaissance to the present	*WORLD LITERATURE CRITICISM, 1500 TO THE PRESENT (WLC)*

ISSN 0895-9439

Volume 33

Short Story Criticism

Criticism of the
Works of Short Fiction Writers

Anna Sheets Nesbitt
Editor

The Gale Group

DETROIT • SAN FRANCISCO • LONDON • BOSTON • WOODBRIDGE, CT

Library of Congress Catalog Card Number 88-641014
ISBN 0-7876-3079-9
ISSN 0895-9439

Printed in the United States of America

10   9   8   7   6   5   4   3   2   1

Contents

Preface   vii

Acknowledgments   xi

Preface

A Comprehensive Information Source
on World Short Fiction

Short Story Criticism (SSC) presents significant criticism of the world's greatest short story writers and provides supplementary biographical and bibliographical materials to guide the interested reader to a greater understanding of the authors of short fiction. This series was developed in response to suggestions from librarians serving high school, college, and public library patrons, who had noted a considerable number of requests for critical material on short story writers. Although major short story writers are covered in such Gale series as *Contemporary Literary Criticism (CLC), Twentieth-Century Literary Criticism (TCLC), Nineteenth-Century Literature Criticism (NCLC),* and *Literature Criticism from 1400 to 1800 (LC),* librarians perceived the need for a series devoted solely to writers of the short story genre.

Coverage

SSC is designed to serve as an introduction to major short story writers of all eras and nationalities. Since these authors have inspired a great deal of relevant critical material, *SSC* is necessarily selective, and the editors have chosen the most important published criticism to aid readers and students in their research.

Approximately eight to ten authors are included in each volume, and each entry presents a historical survey of the critical response to that author's work. The length of an entry is intended to reflect the amount of critical attention the author has received from critics writing in English and from foreign critics in translation. Every attempt has been made to identify and include the most significant essays on each author's work. In order to provide these important critical pieces, the editors sometimes reprint essays that have appeared elsewhere in Gale's Literary Criticism Series. Such duplication, however, never exceeds twenty percent of an *SSC* volume.

Organization

An *SSC* author entry consists of the following elements:

- The **Author Heading** cites the name under which the author most commonly wrote, followed by birth and death dates. If the author wrote consistently under a pseudonym, the pseudonym will be listed in the author heading and the author's actual name given in parentheses on the first line of the biographical and critical introduction.

- The **Biographical and Critical Introduction** contains background information designed to introduce a reader to the author and the critical debates surrounding his or her work.

- A **Portrait of the Author** is included when available. Many entries also contain illustrations of materials pertinent to an author's career, including holographs of manuscript pages, title pages, dust jackets, letters, or representations of important people, places, and events in the author's life.

- The list of **Principal Works** is chronological by date of first publication and lists the most important works by the author. The first section comprises short story collections, novellas, and novella collections. The second section gives information on other major works by the author. For foreign authors, the editors have provided original foreign-language publication information and have selected what are considered the best and most complete English-language editions of their works.

- **Criticism** is arranged chronologically in each author entry to provide a useful perspective on changes in critical evaluation over the years. All short story, novella, and collection titles by the author featured in the entry are printed in boldface type to enable a reader to ascertain without difficulty the works discussed. Also for purposes of easier identification, the critic's name and the publication date of the essay are given at the beginning of each piece of criticism. Unsigned criticism is preceded by the title of the journal in which it appeared.

■ Critical essays are prefaced with **Explanatory Notes** as an additional aid to students and readers using SSC. An explanatory note may provide useful information of several types, including: the reputation of the critic, the intent or scope of the critical essay, and the orientation of the criticism (biographical, psychoanalytic, structuralist, etc.).

■ A complete **Bibliographical Citation,** designed to help the interested reader locate the original essay or book, precedes each piece of criticism.

■ The **Further Reading List** appearing at the end of each author entry suggests additional materials on the author. In some cases it includes essays for which the editors could not obtain reprint rights. Boxed material following the further reading list provides references to other biographical and critical sources on the author in series published by Gale.

Beginning with volume six, SSC contains two additional features designed to enhance the reader's understanding of short fiction writers and their works:

■ Each SSC entry now includes, when available, **Comments by the Author** that illuminate his or her own works or the short story genre in general. These statements are set within boxes or bold rules to distinguish them from the criticism.

■ A **Select Bibliography of General Sources on Short Fiction** is included as an appendix. This listing of materials for further research provides readers with a selection of the best available general studies of the short story genre.

Other Features

A **Cumulative Author Index** lists all the authors who have appeared in *SSC, CLC, TCLC, NCLC, LC,* and *Classical and Medieval Literature Criticism (CMLC),* as well as cross-references to other Gale series. Users will welcome this cumulated index as a useful tool for locating an author within the Literary Criticism Series.

A **Cumulative Nationality Index** lists all authors featured in SSC by nationality, followed by the number of the SSC volume in which their entry appears.

A **Cumulative Title Index** lists in alphabetical order all short story, novella, and collection titles contained in the SSC series. Titles of short story collections, separately published novellas, and novella collections are printed in italics, while titles of individual short stories are printed in roman type with quotation marks. Each title is followed by the author's name and corresponding volume and page numbers where commentary on the work is located. English-language translations of original foreign-language titles are cross-referenced to the foreign titles so that all references to discussion of a work are combined in one listing.

Citing Short Story Criticism

When writing papers, students who quote directly from any volume in the Literary Criticism Series may use the following general forms to footnote reprinted criticism. The first example pertains to material drawn from periodicals, the second to material reprinted from books:

¹Henry James, Jr., "Honoré de Balzac," *The Galaxy* 20 (December 1875), 814-36; reprinted in *Short Story Criticism,* Vol. 5, ed. Thomas Votteler (Detroit: The Gale Group, 1990), pp. 8-11.

²F. R. Leavis, *D. H. Lawrence: Novelist* (Alfred A. Knopf, 1956); reprinted in *Short Story Criticism,* Vol. 4, ed. Thomas Votteler (Detroit: The Gale Group, 1990), pp. 202-06.

Comments

Readers who wish to suggest authors to appear in future volumes, or who have other suggestions, are invited to contact the editors by writing to The Gale Group, Literary Genres Division, 27500 Drake Rd., Farmington Hills, MI 48331-3535.

Acknowledgments

The editors wish to thank the copyright holders of the excerpted criticism included in this volume and the permissions managers of many book and magazine publishing companies for assisting us in securing reproduction rights. We are also grateful to the staffs of the Detroit Public Library, the Library of Congress, the University of Detroit Mercy Library, Wayne State University Purdy/Kresge Library Complex, and the University of Michigan Libraries for making their resources available to us. Following is a list of the copyright holders who have granted us permission to reproduce material in this volume of *SSC*. Every effort has been made to trace copyright, but if omissions have been made, please let us know.

COPYRIGHTED MATERIAL IN *SSC*, VOLUME 33, WERE REPRODUCED FROM THE FOLLOWING PERIODICALS:

AJS Review: The Journal of the Association for Jewish Studies, v. XIII, Spring-Fall, 1988. © 1989 by the Association for Jewish Studies. Reproduced by permission.—*Ariel: A Review of International English Literature,* v. 20, July, 1989 for "John Fowles's Variation on Angus Wilson's Variation on E. M. Forster: 'The Cloud,' 'Et Dona Ferentes,' and 'The Story of a Panic'" by Frederick M. Holmes. Copyright © 1989 The Board of Governors, The University of Calgary. Reproduced by permission of the publisher and the author.—*Book Week--The Washington Post,* December 8, 1963 for "They're Human Too" by Haskel Frankel. © 1963, The Washington Post. Copyright © 1963 by Haskel Frankel. Reproduced by permission of Brandt & Brandt Literary Agents, Inc.—*The Canadian Forum,* v. 36, 1956.—*The Classical Journal,* v. XXIX, December, 1985. Reproduced by permission of the publisher. —*College Literature,* v. XI, 1984. Copyright © 1984 by West Chester University. Reproduced by permission.—*Commonweal,* v. XCIX, February 8, 1974. Copyright © 1974 Commonweal Publishing Co., Inc. Reproduced by permission of Commonweal Foundation.—*Critique: Studies in Modern Fiction,* v. XXV, Fall, 1983; v. XXXVI, Spring, 1995. Copyright © 1983, 1995 Helen Dwight Reid Educational Foundation. Both reproduced with the permission of the Helen Dwight Reid Educational Foundation, published by Heldref Publications, 1319 18th Street, N.W., Washington, DC 20036-1802.—*English Journal,* v. 60, September, 1971 for "Alienation and Isolation in Nelson Algren's `A Bottle of Milk for Mother'" by Daniel R. Silkowski. Copyright © 1971 by the National Council of Teachers of English. Reproduced by permission of the publisher and the author.—*The Georgia Review,* v. XV, Summer, 1961; v. XXI, Fall, 1967. Copyright, © 1961, 1967, by the University of Georgia. Both reproduced by permission.—*German Life and Letters,* v. 19, 1966. © 1966. Reproduced by permission of Blackwell Publishers.—*The International Fiction Review,* v. 6, Summer, 1979. © copyright 1979 International Fiction Association. Reproduced by permission.—*Judaism: A Quarterly Journal,* v. 35, Fall, 1986. Copyright © 1986 by the American Jewish Congress. Reproduced by permission.—*Kirkus Reviews,* v. LXIII, October 15, 1995. Copyright © 1995 The Kirkus Service, Inc. All rights reserved. Reproduced by permission of the publisher, *Kirkus Reviews* and Kirkus Associates, L.P.—*Library Journal,* v. 120, November 1, 1995 for a review of "The Texas Stories of Nelson Algren" by Albert E. Wilhelm. Copyright © 1995 by Reed Publishing, USA, Division of Reed Holdings, Inc. Reproduced by permission of the author.—*Modern Fiction Studies,* v. 31, Spring, 1985. Copyright © 1985 by Purdue Research Foundation. Reproduced by permission of The Johns Hopkins University Press.—*Modern Languages,* v. 55, March, 1974. Reproduced by permission.—*Negro American Literature Forum,* v. 4, July, 1970 for "'Sonny's Blues': James Baldwin's Image of Black Community" by John M. Reilly; v. 8, Fall, 1974 for "James Baldwin's 'Sonny's Blues': A Message in Music" by Suzy Bernstein Goldman. Copyright © 1970, 1974 by the respective authors. Both reproduced by permission of the publisher and the respective authors.—*Neophilologus,* v. LVIII, October, 1974 for "Ironic Reversal in the Short Stories of Siegfried Lenz" by Brian Murdoch; v. LXVI, January, 1982 for "'Don't Force Me to Tell You the Ending': Closure in the Short Fiction of Sh. Rabinovitsh (Sholem-Aleykhem)" by David Neal Miller. © 1974, 1991 by H. D. Tjeenk Willink. Both reproduced by permission of the respective authors.—*The New Leader,* v. LVII, December 9, 1974. © 1974 by The American Labor Conference on International Affairs, Inc. Reproduced by permission.—*The New Republic,* v. 170, January 19, 1974. © 1974 The New Republic, Inc. Reproduced by permission of *The New Republic.*—*The New York Times Book Review,* February 2, 1947; November 11, 1973; November 4, 1974; November 26, 1989. Copyright 1947, © 1973, 1974, 1989 by The New York Times Company. All reproduced by permission.—*Orbis Litterarum,* v. XXIX, 1974. Reproduced by permission.—*Papers on Language and Literature,* v. 23, Winter, 1987. Copyright © 1987 by The Board of Trustees, Southern Illinois University . Reproduced by permission.—*Philosophy and Literature,* v. 1, Fall, 1977. Copyright © 1977 by The University of Michigan-Dearborn. Reproduced by permission.—*Prooftexts,* v. 1, May, 1981; v. 6, January, 1986. Copyright © 1981, 1986 by The Johns Hopkins University Press. All rights reserved. Both reproduced by permission of The Johns Hopkins University Press.—*The Saturday Review,* v. 30, February 8, 1947. 1947, renewed 1975 *Saturday Review* Magazine, © 1979 General Media Communications, Inc. Reproduced by permission of Saturday Review Publications, Ltd.—*South Atlantic Quarterly,* v. 73, Summer, 1974. Copyright © 1974 by Duke University Press, Durham, NC. Reproduced by permission.—*The South Carolina Review,* v. 18, Fall, 1985; v. 20, Fall, 1987. Copyright © 1985, 1987 by Clemson University. Both reproduced by permission.—*The Southern Humanities Review*, v. XXVII, Spring, 1993. Copyright (c)1993 by Auburn University. Reproduced by permission.—*The Southern Literary Journal*, v. XIII, Fall, 1980. Copyright © 1980 by the Department of English, University of North Carolina at Chapel Hill. Reproduced by permission.—*Southern Quarterly*, v. 31, Spring, 1993. Copyright © 1993 by the University of Southern Mississippi. Reproduced by permission.—*Southern Studies*, v. XIX, Winter, 1980 for "The Ebb and Flow of Time and Place in 'The Lost Boy'" by Timothy Dow Adams. Reproduced by permission of the author.—*Soviet Literature*, n. 1, 1979.—*Studies in Short Fiction*, v. 14, Fall, 1977; v. 19, Fall, 1982; v. 30, Winter, 1993; v. 31, Spring, 1994. Copyright 1977, 1982, 1993, 1994 by Newberry College. All reproduced by permission.—*Texas Studies in Literature and Language*, v. 23, Spring, 1981. Copyright © 1981 by the University of Texas Press. All rights reserved. Reproduced by permission.—*The Thomas Wolfe Review*, v. 7, Fall, 1983; v. 13, Fall, 1989. Both reproduced by permission.—*The University of Mississippi Studies in English*, v. IX, 1991. Copyright © 1991 The University of Mississippi. Reproduced by permission.—*Twentieth Century Literature*, v. 28, Fall, 1982; v. 42, Spring, 1996. Copyright 1982, 1996 Hofstra University Press. Both reproduced by permission.

COPYRIGHTED MATERIAL IN *SSC*, VOLUME 33, WERE REPRODUCED FROM THE FOLLOWING BOOKS:

Aarons, Victoria. From *Author as Character in the Works of Sholom Aleichem*. Edwin Mellen Press, 1985. Copyright © 1985, Victoria Aarons. All rights reserved. Reproduced by permission.—Abood, Edward F. From *Underground Man*. Chandler & Sharp Publishers, Inc., 1973. Copyright © 1973 by Chandler & Sharp Publishers, Inc. All rights reserved. Reproduced by permission.—Bloom, Edward. From "Critical Commentary on 'Only the Dead Know Brooklyn'" in *The Order of Fiction: An Introduction*. The Odyssey Press, 1964. Reproduced by permission of the Literary Estate of Edward A. Bloom.—Boyarin, Jonathan. From "Sholem-Aleykhem's 'Stantsye Baranovitsh'" in *Identity and Ethos: A Festschrift for Sol Liptzin on the Occasion of His 85th Birthday*. Edited by Mark H. Gelber. Peter Lang, 1986. © Peter Lang Publishing, Inc., New York 1986. All rights reserved. Reproduced by permission.— Briggs, Julia. From *Night Visitors: The Rise and Fall of the English Ghost Story*. Faber and Faber Limited, 1977. Copyright © 1977 by Julia Briggs. All rights reserved. Reproduced by permission of Faber & Faber Ltd.—Broich, Ulrich. From "John Fowles, 'The Enigma' and the Contemporary British Short Story" in *Modes of Narrative, Approaches to American, Canadian and British Fiction*. Edited by Reingard M. Nischik and Barbara Korte. Königshausen & Neumann, 1990. © Verlag Dr. Johannes Königshause and Dr. Thomas Neumann, Würzburg 1990. Reproduced by permission.—Brown, J. Brooks. From *The Empathic Reader: A Study of the Narcissistic Character and the Drama of the Self*. Amherst: The University of Massachusetts Press, 1989. Copyright © 1989 by The University of Massachusetts Press. All rights reserved. Reproduced by permission.—Butwin, Joseph and Frances Butwin. From *Sholom Aleichem*. Twayne Publishers, 1977. Copyright © 1977 by G. K. Hall & Co. All rights reserved. Reproduced by permission of the Joseph Butwin and the Literary Estate of Frances Butwin.—Clute, John. From "Vernon Lee" in *Supernatural Fiction Writers: Fantasy and Horror, Volume 1, Apuleius to May Sinclair*. Edited by E. F. Bleiler. Charles Scribner's Sons, 1985. Copyright © 1985 Charles Scribner and Sons. All rights reserved. Reproduced with the permission of Macmillan Library Reference USA, a division of Ahsuog, Inc.—Cox, Martha Heasley and Wayne Chatterton. From *Nelson Algren*. Twayne Publishers, 1975. Copyright © 1975 by G. K. Hall & Co., a division of Twayne Publishers, Inc., an imprint of Macmillan Library Reverence. All rights reserved. Reproduced with the permission of Macmillan Library Reference USA, a division of Ahsuog, Inc.—Drew, Bettina. From the introduction to *The Texas Stories of Nelson Algren*. Edited by Bettina Drew. University of Texas Press, 1995. Copyright © 1995 by the University of Texas Press. All rights reserved. Reproduced by permission of the author.—Evans. Elizabeth. From *Thomas Wolfe*. Frederick Ungar Publishing Co., 1984. Copyright © 1984 Frederick Ungar Publishing Co., Inc. Reproduced by permission.—Foster, Thomas C. From *Understanding John Fowles*. University of South Carolina Press, 1994. Copyright © 1994 University of South Carolina Press. Reproduced by permission.—Geismar, Maxwell. From *American Moderns: From Rebellion to Conformity*. Hill and Wang, 1958. Copyright © 1958 by Maxwell Geismar. Renewed 1986 by Anne Geismar. All rights reserved. Reproduced by permission of the Literary Estate of Maxwell Geismar.—Gibson, A. Boyce. From *The Religion of Dostoevsky*. SCM Press Ltd., 1973. © SCM Press Ltd. Reproduced by permission.—Gittlemann, Sol. From *Sholom Aleichem: A Non-Critical Introduction*. Mouton, 1974. © Copyright 1974 Mouton & Co. N. V. Publishers, The Hague. Reproduced by permission of Mouton de Gruyter. A Division of Walter de Gruyter & Co.—Goodheart, Eugene. From "Dostoevsky and the Hubris of the Immoralist" in *The Cult of the Ego: The Self in Modern Literature*. University of Chicago Press, 1968. © 1968 by The University of Chicago. All rights reserved. Reproduced by permission of the publisher and the author.—Gurko, Leo. From *Thomas Wolfe: Beyond the Romantic Ego*. Thomas Y. Crowell, 1975. Copyright © 1975 by Leo Gurko. All rights reserved. Used by permission of HarperCollins Publishers.—Gutierrez, Donald. From *The Dark and Light Gods: Essays on the Self in Modern Literature*. The Whitston Publishing Company, 1987. Copyright 1987 The Whitston Publishing Company. Reproduced by permission of the author.—Halberstam-Rubin, Anna. From *Sholom Aleichem: The Writer as Social Historian*. Peter Lang, 1989. © Peter Lang Publishing, Inc., New York 1989. All rights reserved. Reproduced by permission.—Holman, C. Hugh . From the introduction to *The Short Novels of Thomas Wolfe*. Charles Scribner's Sons, 1961. Copyright © 1961 by Charles Scribner's Sons. Renewed 1989 by Verna McLeod Holman. Reproduced by permission of the Literary Estate of C. Hugh Holman. In North American and the

PHOTOGRAPHS AND ILLUSTRATIONS APPEARING IN *SSC,* VOLUME 33, WERE RECEIVED FROM THE FOLLOWING SOURCES:

Sholom Aleichem
1859-1916

(Also transliterated as Sholem-Aleykhem; pseudonym of Solomon Rabinowitz, also transliterated as Rabinovich, Rabinovitsh, and Rabinovitch) Ukrainian-born Yiddish short story writer, novelist, and dramatist.

INTRODUCTION

One of the founding authors of Yiddish literature, Sholom Aleichem's reputation is based primarily on humorous short stories, such as those adapted for the musical *Fiddler on the Roof,* in which he depicted the Jewish Pale of Settlement, those areas in Russia to which Jews were restricted during the nineteenth century. While other Russian Jews of his era wrote in either Hebrew or Russian, Sholom Aleichem chose to write in Yiddish, a language spoken by eastern European Jews that is derived from High German but usually written with Hebrew characters. His stories reflect the determined optimism and faith of Jewish people amid poverty and persecution, bringing humor to this grim setting through absurd situations and revealing monologues. Sholom Aleichem used the literary forms of the monologue and the epistle to present his characters in their own idiom with no intervention from a narrator, a method that led to his fame as the "folk voice" of Ukrainian Jewry.

Biographical Information

The son of a prosperous, educated merchant, Sholom Aleichem was born in the Ukrainian city of Pereyaslav and spent his early years in a shtetl, a small, impoverished Jewish community that functioned much like a medieval town. His early proclivity for writing so impressed his father that he sent him to a Russian secondary school, where he would receive a secular education, rather than to a yeshiva, the traditional Jewish religious academy for advanced studies. After graduation, Sholom Aleichem moved to Kiev and took a job as a government rabbi and began to publish articles in Hebrew and Russian on educational and liturgical reform. Wanting to reach the large audience of shtetl Jews who could not read Hebrew, he decided to write in Yiddish, a language then derided by educated Jews. Protecting his professional reputation by adopting the pseudonym Sholom Aleichem (a Hebrew greeting meaning "peace be with you"), he published his first short story, "The Two Stones," in 1883. Over the next few years, Sholom Aleichem wrote critically acclaimed short stories and several novels, hoping to provide more serious and artistic examples of Yiddish writing in contrast with the frivolous romances that prevailed in Yiddish literature of that time. Having established himself as a respectable Yiddish author, he encouraged other Yiddish writers by founding and editing *Di yidishe folksbiblyotek,* an annual devoted to Yiddish literature.

Throughout the 1890s, Sholom Aleichem wrote stories incessantly. The immensely popular Tevye stories and Menachem Mendl series date from this period, and their success gave Sholom Aleichem's family enough security to enable him to devote himself entirely to writing. In 1905 pogroms, in which thousands of Jews were massacred, forced the family to flee into exile. Despite his immense popularity, Sholom Aleichem soon found himself in financial trouble. Having sold his copyrights to unscrupulous publishers years before, he received no royalties from the sales of his works. He traveled constantly, giving lectures and readings in Europe and America, until he collapsed from tuberculosis in Russia in 1908. While Sholom Aleichem recovered in Italy, unable to pay his debts, some friends raised money by sponsoring a twenty-fifth anniversary jubilee in honor of his first story. They received donations from all over the world and arranged to reclaim his copyrights from publishers. Financially secure and having recovered his health by 1913, Sholom Aleichem resumed his lecture and reading tours. However, the outbreak of World War I in 1914 drove him and his family once more into exile. They moved to New York, where he died in 1916.

Major Works of Short Fiction

Sholom Aleichem's fame rests primarily on his short stories, which were among the first Yiddish works to be accepted as serious literature. In their detailed representation of shtetl life, these stories successfully reflect the chaotic world of eastern European Jews. As well as documenting the Jews' daily suffering from hunger and persecution, he addressed the problem of changing values among the younger generation, particularly their increasing secularization and disregard for tradition. Sholom Aleichem's stories never follow a conventional plotline: they begin in the midst of trouble, more disasters occur, then they break off without resolution. However, instead of focusing on the disruption and calamity that provide much of the substance for his short stories, he maintained a tone of humor and optimism. For example, Tevye the dairyman, one of Sholom Aleichem's most popular characters, distracts the reader from the tragedy of his stories through his audacious challenges to God and his humorous misquotations of religious verses. Menachem Mendl, the fast-talking dreamer who fails in every business venture he attempts, amuses the reader with his outrageous plans and his frenzied pace. Presenting himself as a listener in his stories and allowing his characters to speak without authorial intervention, Sholom Aleichem added to the humor by having his characters inadvertently reveal their attitudes and faults.

Critical Reception

Despite the careful craftsmanship of Sholom Aleichem's narratives, the naturalness of his characters' speech and the accuracy of his descriptions of shtetl life led to his initial reputation as simply a "recorder" of Jewish life. Early critics focused on the cheerfulness of the characters, on their "laughter through tears" as a way of coping with the endless adversity in their lives. More recent critics have noted a tragic side to Sholom Aleichem's stories, maintaining that his works inspire sympathy as well as laughter. Significant change has occurred in the critical estimates of Tevye: once seen as a cheerful but naïve character who inadvertently misquotes scripture through his ignorance, he has recently been described as a perceptive man who consciously manipulates religious quotations to comment on his life and on God. While Sholom Aleichem's writing is now considered more complex than it was previously, his importance as a founder of Yiddish literature has never been disputed. Likewise, critics and readers have consistently appreciated the humorous and poignant stories in which he masterfully evoked the resiliency and hopefulness of shtetl Jews.

PRINCIPAL WORKS

Short Fiction

Tevye der milkhiger [*Tevye's Daughters*] 1894
Menakhem-Mendl [*The Adventures of Menakhem-Mendl*] 1895

Mottel Peyse dem khazns [*Adventures of Mottel, the Cantor's Son*] 1907-16
The Old Country 1946
Inside Kasrilevke 1948
Stories and Satires 1959
Old Country Tales 1966
Some Laughter, Some Tears 1968
The Best of Sholom Aleichem 1979
Holiday Tales 1979

Other Major Works

Stempenyu [*Stempenyu*] (novel) 1889
Yosele Solovey (novel) 1890
Tsezeyt un tseshpreyt (drama) 1905
In shturm (novel) 1907
Samuel Pasternak (drama) 1907
*Stempenyu (drama) 1907
Blondzhnde shtern [*Wandering Stars*] (novel) 1912
Shver tsu zayn a yid (drama) 1914
Dos groyse gevins (drama) 1916
Ale verk fun Sholom Aleichem. 28 vols. (short stories, novels, dramas, and unfinished autobiography) 1917-25
The Great Fair (unfinished autobiography) 1955

*This work is an adaptation of the novel *Stempenyu.*

CRITICISM

Ba 'Al-Makhshoves (essay date 1908)

SOURCE: "Sholem Aleichem: A Typology of His Characters," in *Prooftexts*, Vol. 6, No. 1, January, 1986, pp. 7-15.

[*In the following essay, which was originally published in 1908, the critic examines prominent character types in Sholom Aleichem's stories and how they reflect Jewish reaction to life in exile.*]

Sholem Aleichem is one of the fortunate Yiddish writers who does not have to wait for an anniversary celebration to publicize his name among the broad masses of our people; his name was a household word before the critics even began to take notice of him. It was not unusual for an entire town to wait with baited breath for a new issue of *Der yid* in which Sholem Aleichem, with a broad grin, lambasted a certain class of speculators and stock market sharpies. Among the folk, there is hardly a celebration or gathering where the guests are not asked: "Would you care to hear some Sholem Aleichem read aloud?" as one would offer a good glass of wine with a piece of cake. The folk has long since discovered the delicious flavor of Sholem Aleichem's works. Thanks to this Jew from *Volin,* the saddened, oppressed people, with its embittered heart and caustic tongue, has learned how to laugh.

And this is no small achievement. Laughter means the ability to see oneself and the world through the eyes of a stranger, to free oneself momentarily from the material world, from the "ego," and to view God's creation with the eyes of a newborn babe. To laugh is to be able to feel innocent, free of sins against oneself and others; it is a brief experience of freedom from the historical, everlasting transgressions that defile our souls with greasy stains. The person who laughs rises to the height of a miniature God who is briefly able to transcend and annul his own creation.

Each of us has experienced that difficult state when we imagine ourselves to have committed a terrible sin or to have just experienced a terrible catastrophe. In these heavy moments, we are seized by the fleeting hope that this is nothing but a dream, that any minute we'll snap out of it and all the fears will trickle away, like water in sand. Now imagine that one of us had the power to render the *real* world into a dream. Such a one appears before us, and lo—all our mistakes and experiences, all the repressions we suffer, all the evils we perpetrate on others and that others perpetrate upon us—all this becomes only an awkward nightmare from which we will soon awaken, the ugly vision dissipating before our very eyes. Imagine how thankful we would be to this sorcerer. Well, each and every divinely inspired poet is just such a sorcerer, transforming our actual, physical existence into a dream.

Sholem Aleichem is just such an artist. Thanks to his hearty laughter, our real world becomes a fairy tale. The Jewish petty merchant in the figure of Menakhem-Mendl becomes some kind of fantastic being. The average middle class Jew who commits as many follies in his life as the hero of the monologue "Gimmazye" ("Gymnasium"), laughs at his mirror image, the poor fool in the story who tries so hard to break through the *numerous clausus* of the Russian high school, getting involved in a whole array of crooked deals, destroying himself and his profession and in sum, only trading in his shoe for a slipper. The reader laughs at this fool as heartily as if the story had nothing whatsoever to do with him. Sholem Aleichem has temporarily freed him from his foolish day-to-day existence by transforming it into a caricature, a dream.

This phenomenon becomes even clearer when we take a closer look at Sholem Aleichem's major hero, Menakhem-Mendel of Yehupets. For Menakhem-Mendl is a parable, an analogue of the Jewish merchant and *luftmentsh,* a living symbol of the vast majority of the Jewish people. Examine this character carefully through Sholem Aleichem's perspective and you can barely restrain yourself from laughing. Yesterday he was a stock broker, today he is a matchmaker, tomorrow he'll be a wood merchant and the day after an insurance agent. You can find him on the steps of every stock exchange, in each and every marketplace, his spirit hovering over each minute transaction. A wagonload of wheat passes by and Menakhem-Mendl gets to finger two or three stalks: presto—he's a grain expert. He sees a nobleman whose estate includes a forest and by morning he is the agent for the forest which the nobleman never intended to sell. No sooner does he see a widow or a divorcee, than he drags a prospective groom to meet her. An item in the paper on some crazy Rothschild collecting fleas propels him straightaway into the flea busi-

ness. Thousands of plans, angles and deals flit through his mind like evil spirits, and if Menakhem-Mendl stops for a split second to think, you can be sure that he has just come up with a new and grander lunacy to add to the thousands already in his head. Menakhem-Mendl is always in a fever. In his hallucinatory world, butter and leather, wheat and needles, are indistinguishable, and he is capable of matching up two boys as bride and groom or of sending logs down a river that dried up ages ago.

Menakhem-Mendl of Yehupets is the madness of the Jewish people embodied in the figure of the Jewish petty merchant. Try compiling the biographies of several hundred Jewish *luft*-merchants and you will be astounded. You'll think you fell into an asylum where behind every Menakhem-Mendl of Yehupets, scratching the back of his neck with his walking stick as he prepares for some new undertaking, there hovers the pale and drawn demonic figure of madness.

Menakhem-Mendl is a product of the Jewish condition in exile. Constant persecution has made him into a weird creature. The Jew, always isolated from the normal and typical sources of livelihood, had to make a living on side roads, searching out the unusual and exceptional so as to keep alive. The ordinary and typical occupations were not for him. He had always had to discover the loopholes that were of no concern to the rulers of the land because their wealth did not depend on them. As a result, a penchant for all kinds of exceptions, fantastic deals, and unusual undertakings was nurtured in the soul of the Jewish merchant. The Jew was in the same situation as the Spanish or Portuguese adventurer of the sixteenth century who was always dreaming of discovering new and unexplored territories, a kind of Pizarro or Vasco da Gama who discovered every now and then a new remote source of income. Today thousands of Jewish merchants are Menakhem-Mendls who inherited their parents' appetite for outlandish undertakings but lack their depth of judgment, their purposefulness or calm. Menakhem-Mendl, the Jewish counterpart of Khlestakov, the scatterbrained hero of Gogol's *Inspector General,* is a national type, a figure who is everywhere to be seen, a living embodiment of Jewish foolishness.

God created the world in sets of opposites and the artist practices an *imitatio Dei.* Sholem Aleichem's Tevye is the exact opposite of his Menakhem-Mendl. If one can compare Menakhem-Mendl's head and heart to a roadside inn open to all traffic, then Tevye's heart would be a backwoods hut where a stranger rarely appears. Menakhem-Mendl is by nature a transitional type. He is constantly on the move, but his movement lacks a clear goal. Menakhem-Mendl is the Jew who threw off the Jewish gaberdine in the late 1870s and 80s and began to assume European manners. He symbolizes the first signs of assimilation among the middle merchant class, the largest class among Jews. Tevye, to the contrary, is the old Jewish quarter that resists all change and holds firm to the old customs till death do them part. Menakhem-Mendl is *modern* Jewry of the street while Tevye is *conservative* Jewry.

Actually, Tevye is sooner a female type than a male. His wife wears the pants while he takes on the lighter chores—delivering butter and cheese on his wagon to various customers. As a representative type of the old Jewish masses, his head is full of various scriptural passages, snatches of Psalms, preachers' parables and quotations from the study house which are half-understood and distorted. But despite his ignorance, he is still something of a scholar among his own kind. Once upon a time such people were the folk intellectuals. Although his use of scriptural citations is always wrong and he never knows the correct interpretation of the words, he grasps their inner meaning nonetheless. If you collect all his sayings you notice that they are totally imbued with the spirit of the House of Study. He is a great believer and man of faith, observing all worldly pleasures with a grownup's smile. Goodness and gentleness thrive in his heart. He is free of jealousy and hatred and is extremely hospitable. He has no profound dealings with people but he values highly each and every Jew (Jews being the only category of people he knows), if for no other reason than that he *is* a Jew, one of the millions of the chosen whose fate has been so intimately intertwined with his since the time of Abraham. Tevye's soul knows no hastiness or sudden impulse; it is a quiet and settled soul which becomes all the more peaceful and joyous with each Sabbath or festival.

Menakhem-Mendl is surrounded by a whole array of demons who toss him back and forth all week long. He does not rest even on the Sabbath, when his son, the *Gymnasium* student, opens his mail for him and lest his bill of exchange be refused, off he rushes to the bank with his *shabes-goy,* as if possessed by demons, when necessary, even signing his name on the Sabbath. Tevye, on the other hand, is surrounded by angels of peace. All week long they keep at a distance and accompany his wagon on the road to Boyberik. Come Sabbath, they take up prominent positions at his table and add splendor to his Sabbath songs and dishes. Tevye the milkman possesses the peace and calm of men of the soil. It is as if Tevye were the owner of a plot of land situated in some far-off Jewish country that is guarded and protected by King David's bodyguard and that this Jewish kingdom sees to it that no harm befalls him. But a closer look reveals that Tevye's landed property is actually the House of Study and his restful nature stems from the fact that he, pauper and milkman though he be, will ultimately inherit the worlds of the just; that in the world to come, a golden chair with four solid legs (such as never need a carpenter) has been prepared for him.

But he who lives in the next world is blind and foolish in this world. Tevye's eye never catches what is happening around him. The Lord has blessed him with a pack of daughters, one more attractive and talented than the next, hard-working, industrious and lively—it's a pleasure to watch them. And Tevye is grateful to the Lord of His providence. In the long summer days, as he rattles along the road in his wagon and he and his horse take a comfortable summer nap, Tevye maps out all kinds of plans for his daughters and imagines all kinds of good fortune. In the end, all these plans are completely foiled. Each of his

daughters abandons him in turn. One falls in love with a young tailor; a second drowns herself because of a love affair with a rich man's son and a third gets married to some "Feferl"—a thin young man in a black shirt—and goes off with him to Siberia bearing his child. Tevye's mind does not begin to grasp all this. He cannot comprehend how a person could take his very own life. And what is all this business about falling in love? There he stands blinking his tear-filled eyes and shrugging his shoulders. He is completely convinced of his own wisdom, that only he knows how life should be lived and that these young upstarts are clearly out of their minds. By nature a good and mild-mannered person, Tevye bears no grudge against anyone and his inner piety and steadfastness unto God keep him from despair. He absorbs the blows of Fate just as his nag absorbs the strokes of his whip. He revives with a proverb, with a scriptural passage and on he drives in his wagon of dairy goods to the wealthy customers of Boyberik who often have outstanding debts on their purchases of summer cheese, eggs and butter.

Menakhem-Mendl and Tevye are the two poles of the Jewish masses. One is momentum, the other is static tranquility. The momentum has no goal and lives from day to day while the tranquility has once and for all established its goal which has no connection whatsoever to *this* world. Both types embody the disintegration of Jewish folk life. Were the Jewish people's will to be reduced to these two alternatives, nothing would remain of the Jewish collective other than a ruin, a pile of sand at the shores of human existence.

But both types, despite the distance between them, share a common ground—both are connected to the social processes going on around them. Menakhem-Mendl and Tevye are obviously both Jews living in exile who are subjected to a double yoke: the yoke imposed by the ruling classes and the specific Jewish edicts. Here we discover that the Jewish masses, embodied by Menakhem-Mendl and Tevye, never wage war against this external pressure. Each of them views these hardships as a law of nature which cannot be countered. Is it possible to combat the power of gravity? The only possible solution is to avoid the effects of the natural law: bricks come tumbling down from the roof—take shelter in a cellar; there's a terrible cold spell—don't show your face out of doors.

The masses, as described by Sholem Aleichem through his major characters, are anything but revolutionary: they are totally unaware that the revolt of a large collective can have a significant social impact. They view the life around them as a fixed entity, a set frame, that cannot and will not be altered. Since it is impossible to break out of it, every conceivable trick must be used to stretch out one's body in the narrow, stifling frame. And if you can't stretch out, you squeeze in and manage—somehow.

Take one look at the life of these masses and you realize that there exists no bridge to unite Sholem Aleichem's generation with that of its children. Severed from their parents, the latter grow up with contempt or at best, with a pitying, sardonic smile for the human bodies who brought this new generation into the world. Tevye's children can only feel sorry for their good father whom life deceives every step of the way leaving him orphaned in his old age, devoid of pleasure and devoid of children. The children of the Menakhem-Mendls, however, cannot even stand the sight of their father. At best, they can pity him for living a life which is as confused, lightless, poor and troubled as the life of a worm.

Sholem Aleichem has himself become so much a part of his generation, that he does not get around to showing us the offspring of the Menakhem-Mendls. On the rare occasions that he does mention them, they appear as shadows, as portraits standing remotely in the background whose features are barely visible. He himself, being a child of his time, has no eye for the younger generation—he sees them, as it were, through a veil and does not understand them. His artistry holds back his pen whenever he begins to portray the Feferls, the Josephs, the generation of the children. He senses that he lacks the means to make them emerge as clearly and boldly as his Tevyes and Menakhem-Mendls.

Sholem Aleichem the humorist and caricaturist is also the unadulterated naturalist: there is not the slightest hint of romanticism, sentimentalism or vague idealism. His descriptions have the effect of coarse and unadorned life itself, and if we were to sum up the world which he depicts, we, the later generation, would be perfectly justified in pronouncing the verdict of—good riddance. But who knows if we are really rid of the world in which Tevye and Menakhem-Mendl are the leading players? I have my strong doubts on the matter. There is, however, one segment of Sholem Aleichem's creitivity in which he is less of a naturalist and more of a poet, nore sentimental and warm-hearted. I am referring to his *Mayses far yidishe kinder (Stories for Jewish Children)*.

The world of the Jewish child is cramped and dark. Before he can even walk properly, his father wraps him in a sweaty, dirty prayershawl and the parents carry the infant off to neder, to his teacher Reb Yisroel the Angel of Death. Two inimical forces surround him from his early years: an angry, morose father instructs him every step of the way, and if his father lets go for a moment, he falls into the hands of wicked Reb Yisroel. The patriarchal world of Christians as of Jews does not recognize the concept of childhood. The child is not an end in himself. Only at the point when he begins to adopt the traditions of his father and grandfather is he conceded any value. In the pious world of old, as in medieval Europe, no distinction is drawn between a child and an adult. Likewise, they know of no transition from childhood to adolescence. On that day when the child first puts on the tassled undergarment and pronounces a blessing over the *tsitses,* he is already likened unto his elders. He spends his childhood in a double prison: the home is one, the heder another. The melancholy which so imbues the Jewish spiritual heritage overlays the Jewish school and home. The child is forcibly kept from fresh air, light and children's games. Each step he takes is predetermined and he is caged in by thousands of pedagogical rules that trans-

form his childhood into a trying and gloomy period of life.

Only on selected days of the year, during festivals when fathers and grandfathers themselves become children for a while and make merry in front of the Lord with cups of wine, lulabim, ethrogim, myrtle branches, *homen-tashn,* Torah scrolls and the like, only then is the child freed from his prison. Now the Jewish youngster who was bewitched all year long into being a caricature of an adult Jew, is transformed into a natural, loving and lively Jewish child.

In Sholem Aleichem's *Mayses far yidishe kinder* which are always associated with one of the Jewish festivals, the Jewish child appears before us in all his virtues and charms. The Jewish festivals are the *benevolent* force which allows the child to catch his breath for a while and prevent him from succumbing altogether under the dry and clumsy tutelage of his fathers and teachers.

In addition to the festivals, there are two other benevolent forces that prevent the Jewish child from becoming completely crushed under the severe supervision of the father and the teacher.

Jews were providential in that a half of their population was exempted from the 613 commandments. Only three positive commandments were conferred upon the woman, and so her soul was less burdened by the spiritual heritage than was her husband's. Except for the fact that the woman is also a mother to her children in the Jewish home, she is otherwise free of the burdensome religious duties and her emotional life is therefore more natural and freer. Behind their mothers' aprons, the Yoseles and Moteles take refuge from the fathers and teachers, and whatever is rained out of them during the day under male supervision, begins to flow once again under the warm gaze of the kindly mother.

Then too, there are simple folk as well as scholars, among the Jews. The great Jewish masses, though deeply influenced by the dry and morose bookmen, were far too ignorant to become as arid and as alienated from the world as their benchwarmers and clergymen. Among the Jewish masses, the desire for a good laugh, for enjoying a more cheerful and more natural life has not yet been extinguished. And Sholem Aleichem's children often flee from their fathers and teachers to the uncouth simple folk, to some musician or other in a back street or simply to a jolly simpleton. The two forces of darkness are confronted by *three* forces of light and if a Jewish child of old managed to grow up more naturally, better and freer than the others, it was thanks to his mother, to the carefree ignorance of the masses and to the Jewish holidays.

Sholem Aleichem's stories for Jewish children are also epic portraits of the manner in which our fathers lived. Menakhem-Mendl and Tevye are complete in themselves; the writer does not depict the background from which they came, but assumes that the reader will provide this from his own imagination. In the children's stories, however, we see the still life and the animate phenomena surrounding the life of a Jew from birth on. And if you were to add Sholem Aleichem's sketches **Kleyne mentshelekh mit kleyne hasoges** (**Little People with Little Minds**) to his children's stories, you would have a complete and clear portrait of the Jewish material environment, beginning with a Jewish festival and ending with a Jewish funeral.

In the pages of his storybooks, Sholem Aleichem has captured an entire culture which is receding further and further from us. If we wish to have a deeper and clearer understanding of the roots from which we came, we must draw upon Sholem Aleichem's stories as reliable sources that depict the old Jewish world. Into the children's stories he introduced much life, joy and natural charm, creating the illusion of some temporary home, and causing us briefly to forget that the present generation grew up *doubly homeless* on account of their fathers and teachers. History robbed the people of its land and the severe patriarchal education robbed it of the home of *childhood.*

In his children's stories, Sholem Aleichem is no longer the dry naturalist of his monologues. Putting aside the inimical forces in the Jewish home, he allows the friends of the Jewish child to come forward: the mothers, the jolly simple folk and especially the Jewish festivals. He immerses the life of the Jewish child in the poetry of a Jewish festival, which explains why his children's stories have a completely different quality. They radiate life, fresh air and sunshine. A moist, jovial eye peers out of them at the reader.

The creator of Tevye and Menakhem-Mendl longs for some kind of home; a home which is free of Tevye's inertia and the wild momentum of a crazy Menakhem-Mendl. He finds such a home in the lovely holiday of a Jewish child.

Meyer Wiener (essay date 1941)

SOURCE: "On Sholem Aleichem's Humor," in *Prooftexts,* Vol. 6, No. 1, January, 1986, pp. 41-54.

[*In the following excerpt, which was originally published in 1941, Wiener discusses Aleichem's unique brand of humor.*]

The Victory over Human Fear

Brave children, when fearful upon entering a dark room at night, sing cheerful songs to themselves. Like most metaphors, this one is only partially applicable, but there is a kind of humor that depends, in part, on this sort of spunky singing in the dark. So too, in Sholem Aleichem's humor we find not only laughter and tears, but the sort of merriment that comes from having overcome and tamed the fear of chaos, the fear of a maimed, confused and falsely-ordered life. This conquest of fear of the tragic in life ennobles and deepens humor, lending it an aspect of nobility.

Sholem Aleichem presented the poverty of the great masses of Jews in the shtetl and the city during the period of imperialistic capitalism, but without yielding to the spirit of depression and lament. When Motl Peysi's impoverished family reached the point of having to sell all of its possessions, Sholem Aleichem had Motl describe this in the following way: "Of all the household things we sold, none gave me more pleasure than the glass cupboard." After this cupboard was sold, there were some "technical problems" in removing it from the house. Motl says: "For a moment I was afraid for the cupboard"—he is actually afraid that it may remain in the house!

> Sholem Aleichem's humor constitutes a unique category in world literature: it is possible to locate the various influences on the development of his style of humor, but with Sholem Aleichem, a new division of the poetics of comedy begins, a category known as "Sholem Alechemian humor" to go alongside Aristophenian laughter, Dickensian humor, Heinesque irony, Gogolesque satire, and so on.
>
> —*Meyer Wiener*

Motl describes his mother crying because everything was being sold. His sick, dying father calls from the next room to ask what is going on. "'Nothing,' mother answers, wiping her red eyes, and the way her lower lip and her whole face quiver you'd have to be made of stone not to burst out laughing." When everything is sold, and they are down to their last possessions, Motl [looking forward to rolling about on the floor] says, "the joy of joys was when they got to my brother Elye's sofa and to my cot."

The tsarist pogroms were the culmination of horror and dread in the lives of the Jewish masses. Sholem Aleichem was very shaken by these occurrences; it is, therefore, remarkable to note how he handled this subject in his work. The tragedy of the pogroms is frequently dealt with, yet in his literary works he avoided direct descriptions as much as possible, and rendered them, when he did, in an oddly "lighthearted," almost humorous manner.[1]

There were not a few writers who relished and lingered over the horror of pogrom descriptions. Certain passages of Bialik's work set the tone for this; its end-product was Lamed Shapiro's pogrom story "The Cross." But at whom was their rage directed? On close consideration, it is clear that to a large degree, it was directed at the victims of the pogroms themselves. This sort of Bialikian "Pain and Outrage" emphasizes the national contradictions. Sholem Aleichem's art, on the other hand, stirs the conscience, because it is addressed to that which is most human in our humanity, and is imbued with faith in man and his future. It diverts us from a fruitless, misanthropic fear and guides us towards a purer vital spirit, toward that crucial striving for a better sort of life. Here, too, Sholem Aleichem's humor is ennobling and purifying.

Motl says: "At first when I heard people talking about 'a pogrom' I was all ears. Now when I hear the word 'pogrom,' I run! I prefer happy stories." Sholem Aleichem says "I dislike sad stories. My muse does not wear a black veil; she is poor but happy." There is so much love for the oppressed in this "hatred of the black veil," and so much sadness in this "happiness in poverty."

Sholem Aleichem reports a conversation between two children emigrating to America with their parents after a pogrom:

> I ask him, what's a pogrom? I hear all the emigrants talking about 'pogrom' but I have no idea what it is. Kopl gloats over me:

> "You don't know what a pogrom is? Gee, are you dumb! Pogroms are everywhere these days. They start from nothing, but once they start, they go on for three days."

> "But what is it," I ask, "a fair?"

> "Some fair! They break windows, smash furniture, tear up pillows—feathers fly like snow."

> "What for?"

> "What for? For nothing! A pogrom isn't only against houses, it's against stores too. They smash all the stores, throw everything out into the streets or steal it, push things around, douse everything with kerosene, strike a match, and burn it up."

> "Don't be funny."

> "What do you mean, y'think I'm kidding? Then, when there's nothing left to steal, they go from house to house with axes and sticks, followed by the police. They sing and whistle and shout 'Hey, guys, kill the dirty Jews!' They smash, kill, stab with spears . . .'"

> "Who?"

> "What do you mean who? Jews!"

> "What for?"

> "What for? 'Cause it's a pogrom!"

> "So it's a pogrom, so what?"

> "Get away, you're an ass. I don't want to talk to you," Kopl says to me, pushes me away, and puts his hands in his pockets like a grownup.

These are supposedly children talking like children, but the words are pure Sholem Aleichem. And the proof of

this is his treatment of the subject of the pogroms in other works, for example in his study **"Digroyse behole fun di kleyne mentshelekh"** (**"The Great Hulabaloo of the Small Folk"**). The story's bitter irony borders on the grotesque: the inhabitants of Kasrilevke escape from a pogrom to Kozodoyevke, and those of Kozodoyevke to Kasrilevke, because where else should they run? (It is interesting to note, that in his final version of this story Sholem Aleichem omitted or softened those parts that had provided a more detailed realistic treatment of the pogroms.)

The same motif reappears some years later (1906) in the chapter **"Shprintse"** of *Tevye.* "It seems that the 'Constitution' [an ironic euphemism for the pogroms—MV] must be more powerful there than here in Yehupetz, because they are on the run, they are all on the run. You may ask: why are they running to us? But then, why do we run to them? It has become a local custom, praise God, that at the first rumor of pogroms, Jews start running from one place to another, as it says in the Scriptures: And they set forth, and they encamped, and they encamped and they set forth—which means, 'you come to me, I'll go to you.'"

And then, years later, we find the same tone in the cited pogrom passage of *Motl, Son of Peysi, the Cantor,* where the seemingly naive, childish conversation exposes the senseless brutality of the murderous Black Hundreds with much greater bitterness than in the "prophetic" ranting of Bialik. There is also more anguish in these words, more love for the folk and more attachment to it.

The assumption behind Bialik's censure is a belief in a "Black-Hundred"-quality of mankind, a belief that the reactionary forces constitute an eternal law of nature. Bialik's censure-and-insult pathos leads ultimately to petty nationalism, to a gloomy, pessimistic view of the world.

Sholem Aleichem's comical-ironic pathos is immeasurably more realistic and more humane. Its deepest assumption is a faith in the progress of the human race, a hope for a better, more intelligent social order. He exhorted his readers to strive hopefully, not to submit to the obstacles before them, but to grasp hold of life, to work and demand their due.

Remarks about Tevye

At first glance, the subject of *Tevye the Dairyman* is a homey Jewish one, "the problem of child-rearing." Actually, this cycle of "portraits from private life" depicts not simply the misfortunes of one family, and the conflicts between generations, but also the very way in which the foundations of society are eroded in a period of transition from one historical age to another.

The family here is simply a microcosm of the basic characteristics of contemporary society as a whole. Family feelings play a large part in this work, "because the curse of children is the worst of the biblical litany of curses," (**"Shprintse"**), but the ideals of the family do not stem from the normal bourgeois tendency toward individualization and atomization of society; they are the historic consequences of persecutions and oppression which have persisted through the generations and have resulted in a withdrawal to the family as the sole source of consolation. Tevye's life, which forces him out of his family and back into the real world in violent and tragic fashion, reflects the fundamental social forces of that period.

The plot of *Tevye* is simple enough, even transparent. Collisions and catastrophes occur, but never any complicated events or actions: great humor cannot support oversubtlety. The end of each chapter is fairly predictable from the beginning; there are no great surprises. After the first half of this unique poem there is no doubt about how it will end, and yet there is so much innovation, so much of the unexpected. The great classical outline of the work is discernable in the simplicity of its construction.

The basic plots, from the chapter **"Modern Children,"** to the end, are not new. A daughter chooses a husband against the wishes of her parents (the obstacles are social or ideological); the conflict with her parents ensues with tragic results. This subject is varied five times.

The narrative core of these variations is also not new: misalliance (Tseytl, Shrpintse, Beylke); difference in background and even religion, between parents and the daughters' beloved (Hodel and Khave). By the time Sholem Aleichem wrote these chapters, all these subjects had already been treated by others. Even the motif of wandering, **"Lekh-lekh" ("Go Forth")**, written in 1914, was familiar in Yiddish literature.

This did not bother Sholem Aleichem: his purpose was not to invent new plots. Certain plots are almost unavoidable and self-evident if one wants to depict the primary characteristics of an age, and not its secondary features. They are so typical, that simply finding them is no accomplishment; they are, as it were, the natural plots of the time. The challenge is to treat these plots in a lively and profound manner. Otherwise, the result is banal, although in real life these issues are far from banal. Raising these run-of-the-mill stories to such a magnificent level, risking five variations on the same theme in a single work—this required Sholem Aleichem's plain genius.

Tevye is a solemn work, yet it exudes a high degree of lyricism. Amazing how Sholem Aleichem leads Tevye into the woods, against a background of "nature," a forest landscape, hardly a typical setting for the Jewish man of the soil. This poor shred of an idyll is indispensable to the characters of Tevye and his daughters.

Sholem Aleichem treated the old subject of the ignorant, hardworking hick in an extremely novel manner. What Sholem Aleichem saw in him! Who else could see these things? Incidentally, it often appears to me that Tevye's proverbs and biblical quotations are not as ignorant as he pretends, that his "translations" are purposefully contorted, in a sort of spirited wittiness. It often seems as if Sholem Aleichem himself was stylizing the matter here.

Description

Dickens and Mendele had a great influence on Sholem Aleichem's style, but when we compare their work, certain differences are obvious. Dickens loved description and portraiture; Mendele indulged in it willingly, occasion permitting; Sholem Aleichem rarely paints or describes and then only in hasty strokes.

Details interested Sholem Aleichem too, but from an acoustic rather than an optic point of view: how does a character respond verbally to a private or social event.

It is widely acknowledged that Sholem Aleichem in two or three strokes can sketch a character with complete accuracy. It used to be said that he could do portraits, but not landscapes. That is not so:

> And the wagon, as if out of spite, crept slowly along. Before you can reach the Dnieper you have to cross one sand dune and then another, thick yellow sand, knee-deep; slowly, step by step, the horses drag themselves forward, barely able to pull their legs out of the sand. The wheels sink and the wagon groans, as the Dnieper appears closer and closer, in all its breadth and beauty.

> On the banks of the river tall green rushes, speckled with yellow, spread their long, sharp leaves, which are reflected in the water, lending the old river a special charm. All is still.

> The river spreads far and wide, like the sea, in all directions: the waters flow quietly by. Where to? It's a secret. The blue sky looks down from above and catches its reflection in the water along with the sun, which is not about to set. The sky is clear. The water clear. The sand clear, and the air. And a divine stillness reigns, reminiscent of the Psalms: "The expanse is the Lord's." Suddenly, a bird streaks from the rushes with a cry, cuts like an arrow through the pure still air, soaring away in a zigzag. But then, apparently, thinking better of it, the bird zigzags back and disappears once more into the yellow-green rushes.

(*From the Fair,* chap. 37)

This is a very delicate and beautiful landscape, a sort of Japanese graphic. Sholem Aleichem could paint and describe nature as well, but did so seldom, it was not his style. Sholem Aleichem shared Dickens's passion for description only with regard to speech; his artistic attention concentrated for the most part on the nuances of emotions as expressed in words.

The Garrulousness of Sholem Aleichem's Characters

Sholem Aleichem's humor constitutes a unique category in world literature: it is possible to locate the various influences on the development of his style of humor, but with Sholem Aleichem, a new division of the poetics of comedy begins, a category known as "Sholem Alechemian humor" to go alongside Aristophenian laughter, Dickensian humor, Heinesque irony, Gogolesque satire, and so on.

If the reflection of reality in art is connected in some way with imitating and reproducing reality, then Sholem Aleichem's style, both directly and indirectly, is extremely mimetic in all its details, even to the gesticulations which are hinted at by the words themselves.[2] In every successful story of Sholem Aleichem, an actor is there, playing his part, even when the story is read silently.

Sholem Aleichem has a special sort of "comic" prose style. All the usual poetic devices are transformed into elements of verbality: the comedy derives not so much from the stories as from the style in which they are recounted—from the various styles of garrulousness of the characters. These are, so to speak, his metaphors, tropes, stylizations, and so forth.

His sentences are directed in the first place not to the eye, but to the ear; dialogues or monologues are his favorite forms. His stories are comedies in prose, and are easily transformed into stage comedies.

In "If I Were Rothschild" (1902), Sholem Aleichem even inserted two bits of stage directions, "comes to a halt," and "reflects for a moment," which are aimed at the reader as well as the recitateur. These stage directions are vestigial remnants of the umbilical cord which links Sholem Aleichem's prose style to comedy itself.

No Yiddish writer has a style as close to the language and narrative manner of the "ordinary Jew" as Sholem Aleichem. No one so accurately reproduced the language of the toiler, the common man, the artisan, coachman, pauper, maid, all the varied inhabitants of Kasrilevke, the bohemian *luftmentsh* and the ordinary *luftmentsh*; the speech of the Menakhem-Mendlian maniac, the happy pauper, the bitter, oppressed housewife, the feverish, nervous talk of the market women and the sedate, tranquil talk of intelligence and experience: Tevye's language; the language of little children, unhappy mothers, actors, pious Jews, cardplayers, the talk of all sorts of professions, districts, dialects: tremendous treasures of language, reflecting the enormous diversity of life.

This is one side of the issue. It is quite wrong to assume, however, that Sholem Aleichem actually reproduced the language of "real life" in its raw form. His language so closely resembles colloquial speech that the "experts" were led to conclude that this was not literature at all, but something simultaneously greater and less than literature, something "snatched" from life and therefore, life itself. Because of this claim, naive people think that there is nothing simpler than writing like Sholem Aleichem, record what you hear, and there you have it. The results of such limitations are well known.

Actually, the transformation of language in Sholem Aleichem's works occurred by means of an extension of the idiosyncrasies in the styles of the real Menakhem-Mendl, the real Tevye, the actual prototypes of various groups and regions, etc. to their logical conclusions, the point at which they assume the form which they would have taken had they existed in the exact same circumstances for many more generations. In this sharpened state, their speech is transmuted by the author's affectionate and poetic personality until they assume a lyrical smoothness, an artistic polish, charm and beauty, and became Sholem Aleichem's own style.

The characters and events decribed in Sholem Aleichem's *From the Fair* are in effect, prototypes of characters and events *in many* of his other depictions of Kasrilevke and Mazepevke. But although this fictional autobiography is very far from historical accuracy, there is nonetheless a very definite difference between these characters and events and those in his other works. This same difference applies between actual, colloquial speech and Sholem Aleichem's style.

Wordplays

Sholem Aleichem's humor is linked with "speech" to a greater degree than that sort of humor which emphasizes the comedy of antics or events. The essence and meaning of Sholem Aleichem's characters also emerges, of course, from the facts and situations in which they operate, but these are for the most part more tragic than comic. The comic situation is less compelling than the words in which it is related. Sholem Aleichem humorized mostly through speech, or more precisely by allowing his characters to speak. The funniest situations in his works achieve their comic appeal mostly through the way in which they are related by his characters, by their verbal reaction to events.

The social and economic rootedness of Sholem Aleichem's characters is illusory, the entire milieu, its behavior, psychology, its mode of thinking and of feeling are affected by this illusoriness. Thus the verbosity, the talkativeness of his characters—as opposed to their actual deeds—assumes a special significance (as a substitute) for their actions.

This verbosity, with all the by-products of such intense speech, repetition, and digression—gesticulation, voice modulation, facial expression—has no effect in actual life and is rather "unreal" or "fantastic." These elements, which Sholem Aleichem noted and absorbed, were singularly important in the formation of his style. When he attempted to exceed the limits of this style—especially in his novels—he fell short of mastery; only when he himself adopted the tone of one of his characters did he make even the most "imaginary" facts, events and situations become compelling and realistic.

It is not paradoxical, therefore, to claim that the reality which Sholem Aleichem portrayed was "imaginary": his realism consisted of discovering the "imaginary" aspects of the life he describes, as well as its objective bases and ideas.

This explains Sholem Aleichem's proclivity for dialogue, monologue and for the verbal, essentially comic form. It also accounts for his attraction to the would-be feuilletons, in which the conversations of his characters are supposedly overheard by the author. Even his true feuilletons, where he takes a direct stand on contemporary problems, were generally not written in a direct, fully personal manner, but were stylized, composed of various narrative mannerisms of his different characters. Style is not simply a means, but an integral part of the subject matter itself: it reflects the subtleties of life.

The modulation and intonation of words is therefore as crucial to his style as their meaning: the words must themselves indicate how to reproduce the entire illusorily-expressive, artful wordplay of busy self-importance. Correctly understood, the words of the text signal the intonation and gesticulations that should accompany them. Sholem Aleichem constructed his sentences so that the naked words would project how everything should look and sound.

This Sholem Aleichem did *consciously.* As early as 1884 he wrote: "Our jargon has more scope for satire than other languages: with a small shrug, an aside, a nickname, the slighest stroke of emphasis, a sentence turns satirical and evokes a spontaneous smile from the reader. Not to mention imitations of the individual speaker (practically every Jew has his own language with all his varied gesticulations)."[3]

Here Sholem Aleichem attributes to the language his own artistic skill, and substitutes the speaking-style of his major characters for that of the Yiddish language itself. But these words clearly show that even at this early stage Sholem Aleichem realized the possibility of transmitting with the word, *through* the word, the entire range of accompanying gestures to suggest the emotional impulse that called the word forth.

Sholem Aleichem wanted to present speech in its full dramatic scope, in order to communicate its illusory sources. The act of speaking, after all, plays such a major role in this life, where a Menakhem-Mendl can do and accomplish so little. The comedy of Sholem Aleichem's stories derives not only from the meaning of the words, but also from the gesticulations with which the reader associates them.

For this reason Sholem Aleichem's masterpeices do not have their greatest impact when read, but rather when declaimed: Sholem Aleichem's works are directed, in fact, not only to the factual imagination but to the verbal "imagination," if such imprecise terminology may be used. (It is imprecise because both forms of imagination proceed from a concrete, essentially similar basis in the "facts of reality.")

Speech, as such, can only be appreciated aurally, just as dramatic works must be staged, so Sholem Aleichem's stories must be declaimed, acted out. Sholem Aleichem himself made a habit of reading his stories publicly, and it is no coincidence that of all the Yiddish writers (and certainly most of the non-Yiddish writers), his works are most often publicly recited and read.

Sholem Aleichem's works, even the smallest of his master-stories are therefore a sort of wordplay, depicting an illusory, playacting world. This is a new genre in world literature. On the surface it appears to be prose, but in essence, it resembles high comedy.

The Tragedy of Illusions

"What is there about Jewish singing and playing, that always evokes only sad thoughts?" It embodies the life of the people.

Sholem Aleichem's "happy stories" are one large satirical elegy on the oppressed nature of man, his abasement through hunger, through the hatred of one people for another, the backwardness of life and thought, and the disablement of his creative powers, all of which results from the cruel order of things which condemns one man to be exploited by another. The free creative spirit thrives only from plenty; when subject to exploitation, people sink into pettiness; they become "little people with little notions."

Even the bodily movements of such "little people" are funny, they seek and strive and bustle about, show the most strenuous exertions, work themselves to death—over a trivial, joyless shred of "bliss" which is either fabricated or worthless. These figures are far from heroic, but they proceed along their quixotic adventures with unusual, almost heroic courage.

The pettiness of their ideas is tragic in itself, but more tragic is the fact that their superhuman energies are expended in vain. The comedy lies in their external appearance, in the movements, words the details of their predicaments; the tragedy lies in the content, in the conclusion which in the works of Sholem Aleichem is almost always tragic.

In Sholem Aleichem's major characters there is always a bit of the shlimazl: sometimes the character is good-hearted, charming, decent and sometimes simply sad and foolish, but he is always a shlimazl. Sholem Aleichem almost never depects happiness, fulfilled goals.

Tevye's nobility raises him qualitatively above anything laughable: certain deliberately humorous aspects of his garrulousness are only meant to intensify the tragic essence of the story. Here too the laughter does not derive from plenty, because there is not the smallest measure of joy, of happiness.

No one evoked as much laughter as Sholem Aleichem, and yet no one so exclusively chose the joylessness of Jewish life as the subject of his work. Perhaps this is why Peretz disliked Sholem Aleichem, while admitting his artistic power. Peretz praised Sholem Aleichem for this ability to "scrape off the mould," that is, educate through satire, or more specifically, to destroy illusions.

Sholem Aleichem was constantly demonstrating to the masses that their happiness in their social condition was illusory, that this sort of life was itself almost illusory. In his works he always asked the seemingly "happiest people" of all the "Kodnis": What are you so happy about? The illusoriness of their entire luftlife, of their crippled and damaged existence, is the main theme of his work.

Sholem Aleichem's humor is based on a profoundly accurate idea: that the prevailing social conditions oppressed and cripped man until he became not only miserable but ridiculous.

—*Meyer Wiener*

Sholem Aleichem disliked "happy endings," they would be a distortion, contradicting the essence of his work, they would trivialize his humor.

The story of the bewitched tailor, which is constructed like a sunny joke, and suffused with a lyrical, idyllic tone is actually a melancholic, marvellous poem with an infinitely tragic ending, or more precisely, with no ending at all, for the tragedy is limitless. It ends with the poet's shrug.

> The reader will ask, "And the fate of the tailor? the moral? The purpose of the story?" Don't make me continue, children! The ending was not a happy one. The story began well enough, but ended, as most happy stories do, alas, very sadly . . . and because you know that the author of this story is not given to bouts of sadness in fact you know how he hates to "point a moral" and prefers jolly tales to gloomy plaints, he therefore bids you farewell with a smile, and blesses both Jews and people at large with more of laughter than tears. Laughter is healthy, doctors prescribe laughter.

The bitter irony of this last, famous dictum of Sholem Aleichem must be evident from its context, even to the most thick-skinned reader. . . .

Sholem Aleichem's critics have made intelligent but also some foolish observations about him. Once I wrote that Sholem Aleichem was a "consoler." What nonsense! How simple it would have been for him to round out at least some of his works with happy endings, instead of with misery, and often crude misery to boot. This would not have detracted from the comedy of the works, and would have soothed and comforted the spirits of his readers. But it would have banalized his work, being more suitable for the role of a great jester, which several of his critics have attempted to apply to him, but which is as completely foreign and contrary to his tragic consciousness. It would have been more genial, but not realistic—it would have undermined the truth about the life of the masses at that time, that their desires, lusts, dreams, had to remain unful-

filled and unrealized in those given social conditions. The oppressed classes *were* always abused, aggrieved, deceived; so it was and so Sholem Aleichem depicted it.

Characters and Passions

Comic genres generally deal with fools, shlimazls, dreamers, maniacs: with miserable, unsuccessful, false, or evil people and deeds. As soon as the characters or their deeds cease to exhibit such qualities, they also cease being comical. One might therefore assume that there is nothing much to seek in the satiric-comic genres, no meaningful figures, no heroic passions, and of course, no problems. The truth is very different of course: in Aristophanes' comedy even philosophical themes were broached; Don Quixote is a fool, a shlimazl, a dreamer, a maniac, but it cannot be denied that apart from these comic elements of his character, there are qualities that command respect. In his crazy actions we catch glimpses of "heroic" passions, and in his striving we can see, as in a crooked mirror, something approaching lofty goals and spiritual concerns.

Our Mendele's Benjamin III is an unfortunate fool, a shlimazl, a dreamer and maniac: his behavior is clumsy, his goal is delusional, but one cannot dispute the nobility of his intention, and the existence of distinct—though convoluted and comical—elements of the "heroic" in his quixotic striving. All these and similar comic-satiric characters are more or less broken and crippled, but they nonetheless possess significant qualitities of character and something oddly heroic in their passions and quests.

A character normally attains significance through *passions* which exhibit something of greatness, albeit in a comical-distorted, contradictory form. Tevye is a character of significance,[4] but we see in him more pathos than passion— the pathos of a bitter, wise, passive resistance to raging forces of life.

Sholem Aleichem's artistic heroes, Stempenyu, Yosele Solovey, Rafalesko, all possess some sublime qualities, but they are not Sholem Aleichem's master characters, nor are they developed comically.

In general, Sholem Aleichem did not encourage the contradictory play of loftiness and worthlessness in his *characters:* the situation, the event rather than the individual stands at the center of Sholem Aleichem's stories. His characters—usually some variation of the Menakhem-Mendl type—are invidivualized only as much as is necessary to vary his eternal theme.

Whether it is a fault or not, Sholem Aleichem did not imbue his characters with sublime passions, which echo— accurately or distortedly—ideological battles of the time; he did not give us characters who could be spokesmen for the contemporary world-views.

Sholem Aleichem's humor is based on a profoundly accurate idea: that the prevailing social conditions oppressed and cripped man until he became not only miserable but ridiculous. The comedy inherent in the senseless and passive suffering during the period of imperialism is depicted through characters who, with the exception of Tevye, are so crushed by the old and new economic, social and national oppression and so removed from normal consciousness that the roar of the struggle for the liberation of the world does not even reach them.

The tragedy of the Menakhem-Mendl type lies also in the absence of noble—be they illusory or convoluted—strivings: the mad hustling and get-rich scheming is not a passion in the true sense of the word. Menakhem-Mendl is actually a slight though fanatic competitor, and if by some chance he were to meet with success, we know from the monologue, "If I were Rothschild," what he would be likely to do. Nervous zest is not the same thing as passion.

Passions must somehow be rooted in real life: they may be mistaken, confused or confounded, but unless they have some basis in reality, they are simply madness. Don Quixote's fantasies are *no longer* realistic, at least they were once so, in part: a hundred or two hundred years earlier he would have been much less comical. The distance between Don Quixote's fantasies and reality is much smaller than in the case of Menakhem-Mendl; Don Quixote's mistaken judgment in his ideals is considerably less than that of Menakhem-Mendl.

From the the very outset, Menakhem-Mendl's goal lacked even a grain of realism. But beyond that, the goal itself was so very pitiful. The fate of all of the Menakhem-Mendls evokes in the reader, among other responses, a gnawing dissatisfaction with the immensity of the effort, the fervency of the enthusiasm, that have been expended in the pursuit of such a negligible goal, one which is not even achieved as the character loses everything he has. The reader, too, feels somewhat cheated in his expectations.

At first glance, there is nothing to be regretted in the frustration of such a goal, nor anything tragic in itself. Even the comedy remains superficial until we grasp its essence, the conditions which condemned people to such fates. Only at that point can we be moved by the wretched sort of life which turns people into Menakhem-Mendls, and only at that point can we discern the writer's full intent, the comic tragedy of his characters.

The presence of sublime qualities in his comic figures would have destroyed the uniqueness of Sholem Aleichem's humor. The tragedy of Menakhem-Mendl would not emerge as graphically were he imbued with "tragic" (heroic) qualities. In humor, every minor sin against realism is much more serious, and is punished much more swiftly, than in any other genre: it loses its humor. An essential feature of Menakhem-Mendl's comedy is the fact that both his ambition and his goal are so dismal and trivial, that he lacks any lofty goals. Sholem Aleichem told things as they were, and this gives no joy to a poet. The misfortunes of the groups which Sholem Aleichem depicted extended to some extent to his own creation: we detect in them something of the petit-bourgeois outlook on life.

Notes

First published in 1941, *Vegn Sholem-Aleykhems humor* was reprinted in vol. 2 of Wiener's *Tsu der geshikhte fun der yidisher literatur in 19tn yorhundert* [On the History of Nineteenth-Century Yiddish Literature] (New York, 1946), pp. 281-378. The translation is from chaps. 5-10, 12, and was done by Ruth R. Wisse.

[1] He did write publicistic "letters" with detailed descriptions, but refused to lecture about the pogroms. See *Dos Sholem-Aleykhem-bukh*, ed. Y. D. Berkovitsh (New York, 1926), p. 213.

[2] The words "mime," "mimical" etc. come from the Greek "mimesis," i.e., imitation, and relate to any artistic reproduction, but most particularly to that of the actor.

[3] "In the Junkheap—Among the Rags" [Yiddish], an unpublished review, in *Dos Sholem-Aleykhem-bukh*, p. 326.

[4] Sholem Aleichem tried to create a sort of scholarly variation of Tevye in the character of Reb Yuzifl. This poor, oppressed, hurt and deeply wounded creature crawls into a deep lair—the "other world"—no longer wants to see the sunshine, and exhibits much senseless courage, extraordinary stubbornness and quiet but wild determination in his withdrawal from life. "There is nothing funny about us," says Reb Yuzifl. "My God, one must cry and learn our lesson about what we are and what we have become."

Saul Bellow comments on Aleichem's achievement:

Sholom Aleichem wrote for the family circle and his attitude was that of an entertainer. Hebrew was the language of serious literature among the Jews of the Pale; Yiddish the secular language and the language of comedy. A popular writer, a caricaturist and sentimentalist, Sholom Aleichem had much more in common with Dickens than he had with Mark Twain, to whom he has often been compared. He was a great ironist—the Yiddish language has an ironic genius—and he was a writer in whom the profoundly sad, bitter spirit of the ghetto laughed at itself and thereby transcended itself.

Saul Bellow, "Laughter in the Ghetto" in
Saturday Review, *May 30, 1953, p. 15.*

Alfred Kazin (essay date 1956)

SOURCE: "Sholom Aleichem: The Old Country," in *Contemporaries,* Atlantic-Little, Brown & Company, 1962, pp. 271-78.

[*In the following excerpt, which was originally published in 1956 as an introduction to* Selected Stories of Sholom Aleichem, *Kazin assesses Aleichem's treatment of Jewish people and the Yiddish language.*]

The way to read Sholom Aleichem is to remember from the outset that he is writing about a people, a folk: the

Yiddish-speaking Jews of Eastern Europe. There are a great many Jews and non-Jews who resent the idea that the Jews are a people, for they think this requires all Jews to speak the same language and to live in the same territory. But Sholom Aleichem's characters already are a people. They are a people not merely because they speak the same language, Yiddish, or because they live in the Pale of settlement that the Czarist government kept Jews in. They are a people because they think of themselves as a people. And what is most important, they are a people because they enjoy thinking of themselves as a people.

This is the great thing about the Jews described by Sholom Aleichem. They enjoy being Jews, they enjoy the idea of belonging to the people who are called Jews—and "their" Sholom Aleichem, perhaps more than any other Jewish writer who has ever lived, writes about Jewishness as if it were a gift, a marvel, an unending theme of wonder and delight. He is one of those writers whose subject is an actual national character, a specific type—the Jew as embodied in the poor Jew of Eastern Europe. In a way he does remind us of Mark Twain, [As Kazin observes in a footnote: "Sholom Aleichem was so often called 'the Jewish Mark Twain' that Mark Twain on meeting him, referred to himself as 'the American Sholom Aleichem'."] who was so entranced with a new character, the Western American, that he was always trying to weigh him, to describe him, as if he, Mark Twain, had discovered a new chemical element. . . .

It is this European, seasoned, familiar pleasure in the national circle of one's own people, that lies behind Sholom Aleichem's stories. But what kind of enjoyment can these people derive from being Jews, since they are incessantly harassed by the Russian government and surrounded by peasants who are usually anti-Semitic and can easily be goaded, with the help of the usual encouragement from the government itself and a lot of vodka, into making pogroms? What is it, in short, that makes for *enjoyment* in these local terms? The answer is that one enjoys being a member of a people because one shares in the feast of their common experience. You share in something that is *given* to you instead of having to make every institution and every habit for yourself, out of nothing, in loneliness and with exertion. The secret of this enjoyment consists not so much in physical solidarity and "togetherness," in the absence of loneliness, as in the fact that a deep part of your life is lived below the usual level of strain, of the struggle for values, of the pressing and harrowing need—so often felt in America—to define your values all over again in each situation, where you may even have to insist on values themselves in the teeth of a brutish materialism. . . .

This is the fabled strength of "the old country," which deprived the Jews of Eastern Europe of every decency that we take for granted, but allowed them to feast unendingly on their own tradition—and even to enjoy, as an unconscious work of art, their projection of their fiercely cherished identity. The very pen name "Sholom Aleichem" is an instance of this. . . . *Sholom aleichem* is the Hebrew greeting, "Peace be unto you," that is technically exchanged

between Jews. It is said with more lightness and playfulness than you would guess from the literal translation. Its chief characteristic, as a greeting, is the evidence it gives of relatedness. Now Solomon Rabinowitz, who actually belonged to the prosperous and more "emancipated" middle class of Russian Jewry (he even married into its landed gentry), took this pen name precisely because he found in the phrase an image of the sweet familiarity, the informality, the utter lack of side, that is associated with the Yiddish-speaking masses of Eastern Europe. A Yiddish writer who calls himself *Mister* Sholom Aleichem tells us by this that he has chosen cannily to picture himself as one of the people and, modestly, to be a register or listening post for his people. Sholom Aleichem! The name's as light as a feather, as "common" as daylight, as porous to life as good Yiddish talk: it is the very antithesis of the literary, the mannered, the ornate. If you didn't know anything else about Mister Sholom Aleichem (several of his characters address him so when they bring their stories to him) you should be able to guess from the name the role that he has chosen to play in his own work. He is the passer-by, the informal correspondent, the post office into which Jews drop their communications to the world. All he does, you understand, is to write down stories people bring him. He invents nothing. And need one say—with that name, with that indescribably dear, puckish, wrinkled face of his—that you will never learn from him *what* he has invented, that he has all Yiddish stories in his head, that any one story people bring him will always be capped with another?

In the world of Sholom Aleichem, nothing has to be made up, for the life of the Jews, to say nothing of the Jewish character, is an unending drama. Nor can it be said of anything that it's never been seen or heard of before. The Jews have lived with each other for a very long time, and they know each other through and through—and this, often enough, is what they enjoy. Their history, alas, has too often been the same, and everything that you see in Kasrilevka (the little Jewish town which is all little Jewish towns) or Yehupetz (Kiev, the big city) can be matched from something in Mazeppa's time, which is late seventeenth century, or that of Haman, who tried to kill all the Jews in Persia in the fifth century B.C. Nor, indeed, is anything ever said just *once*. Everything is real, everything is typical, and everything is repeated.

You must understand, first, that Sholom Aleichem's characters possess almost nothing except the world—the holy word, which is Hebrew, and the word of everyday life, which is Yiddish. They are "little" people, not in the sense that they are poor little victims, but in the sense that they are unarmed, defenseless, exiled, not in the world, not in *their* kind of world. All they have is the word. They talk as poor people always talk—because poor people live near each other, and so have a lot of opportunity to talk. They talk the way the European poor always talk—Cockneys or Neapolitans or Provençals: they talk from the belly; they roar, they bellow, they grunt, they scream. They imitate the actual sounds that life makes, and they are rough and blunt. But most of all, they are poor Jews talking, i.e., they find an irony in language itself. Their words strive after the reality, but can never adequately express the human situation. . . .

Yiddish is the poor Jew's everyday clothes rather than his Sabbath garment, Hebrew. But in the Jewish consciousness it is precisely the life of everyday that is contrasted with the divine gift of the Sabbath, and it is this awareness of what life is actually like (seen always against the everlasting history of this people and the eternal promise) that makes the very use of Yiddish an endless commentary on the world as found.

And it is a commentary on the spirit of language itself. One of the things you get from Sholom Aleichem is this mockery of language, a mockery which—need I say it?—carries a boundless pleasure in language and a sense of the positive strength that goes with mighty talk.

Irving Howe (essay date 1963)

SOURCE: "Sholom Aleichem: Voice of Our Past," in his *A World More Attractive: A View of Modern Literature and Politics,* Horizon, 1963, pp. 207-15.

[*In the following excerpt, Howe discusses Aleichem's significance within the Jewish literary tradition, asserting "He is, I think, the only modern writer who may truly be said to be a culture-hero."*]

Fifty of sixty years ago the Jewish intelligentsia, its head buzzing with Zionist, Socialist and Yiddishist ideas, tended to look down upon Sholom Aleichem. His genius was acknowledged, but his importance skimped. To the intellectual Jewish youth in both Warsaw and New York he seemed old-fashioned, lacking in complexity and rebelliousness—it is even said that he showed no appreciation of existentialism. . . .

The conventional estimate—that Sholom Aleichem was a folksy humorist, a sort of jolly gleeman of the *shtetl*—is radically false. He needs to be rescued from his reputation, from the quavering sentimentality which keeps him at a safe distance.

When we say that Sholom Aleichem speaks for a whole culture, we can mean that in his work he represents all the significant levels of behavior and class in the *shtetl* world, thereby encompassing the style of life of the east European Jews in the nineteenth century. In that sense, however, it may be doubted that he does speak for the whole *shtetl* culture. For he does not command the range of a Balzac or even a Faulkner, and he does not present himself as the kind of writer who is primarily concerned with social representation. The ambition, or disease, of literary "scope" leaves him untouched. . . .

Sholom Aleichem speaks for the culture of the east European Jews because he embodies—not represents—its essential values in the very accents and rhythm of his speech, in the inflections of his voice and the gestures of his hands,

in the pauses and suggestions between the words even more than the words themselves. To say that a writer represents a culture is to imply that a certain distance exists between the two. But that is not at all the relationship between Sholom Aleichem and the culture of the east European Jews: it is something much more intimate and elusive, something for which, having so little experience of it, we can barely find a name. In Sholom Aleichem everything that is deepest in the ethos of the east European Jews is brought to fulfillment and climax. He is, I think, the only modern writer who may truly be said to be a culture-hero, a writer whose work releases those assumptions of his people, those tacit gestures of bias, which undercut opinion and go deeper into communal life than values.

In his humorous yet often profoundly sad stories, Sholom Aleichem gave to the Jews what they instinctively felt was the right and true judgment of their experience: a judgment of love through the medium of irony. Sholom Aleichem is the great poet of Jewish humanism and Jewish transcendence over the pomp of the world. For the Jews of Eastern Europe he was protector and advocate; he celebrated their communal tradition; he defended their style of life and constantly underlined their passionate urge to dignity. But he was their judge as well: he ridiculed their pretensions, he mocked their vanity, and he constantly reiterated the central dilemma, that simultaneous tragedy and joke, of their existence—the irony of their claim to being a Chosen People, indeed, the irony of their existence at all.

Sholom Aleichem's Yiddish is one of the most extraordinary verbal achievements of modern literature, as important in its way as T. S. Eliot's revolution in the language of English verse or Berthold Brecht's infusion of street language into the German lyric. Sholom Aleichem uses a sparse and highly controlled vocabulary; his medium is so drenched with irony that the material which comes through it is often twisted and elevated into direct tragic statement—irony multiples upon itself to become a deep winding sadness. Many of his stories are monologues, still close to the oral folk tradition, full of verbal by-play, slow in pace, winding in direction, but always immediate and warm in tone. His imagery is based on an absolute mastery of the emotional rhythm of Jewish life; describing the sadness of a wheezing old clock, he writes that it was "a sadness like that in the song of an old, worn-out cantor toward the end of Yom Kippur"—and how sad that is only someone who has heard such a cantor and therefore knows the exquisite rightness of the image can really say.

The world of Sholom Aleichem is bounded by three major characters, each of whom has risen to the level of Jewish archetype: Tevye the Dairyman; Menachem Mendel the *luftmensch*; and Mottel the cantor's son, who represents the loving, spontaneous possibilities of Jewish childhood. Tevye remains rooted in his little town, delights in displaying his uncertain Biblical learning, and stays close to the sources of Jewish survival. Solid, slightly sardonic, fundamentally innocent, Tevye is the folk voice quarreling with itself, criticizing God from an abundance of love, and realizing in its own low-keyed way all that we mean, or should mean, by humaneness.

The stories Sholom Aleichem told his readers were often stories they already knew, but then, as the Hasidic saying goes, they cared not for the words but the melody.

—Irving Howe

Tevye represents the generation of Jews that could no longer find complete deliverance in the traditional God yet could not conceive of abandoning Him. No choice remained, therefore, but to celebrate the earthly condition: poverty and hope. . . .

Menachem Mendel, Tevye's opposite, personifies the element of restlessness and soaring, of speculation and fancyfree idealization, in Jewish character. He has a great many occupations: broker, insurance agent, matchmaker, coal dealer, and finally—it is inevitable—writer; but his fundamental principle in life is to keep moving. The love and longing he directs toward his unfound millions are the love and longing that later Jews direct toward programs and ideologies. He is the utopian principle of Jewish life; he is driven by the modern demon. Through Tevye and Menachem Mendel, flanked by little Mottel, Sholom Aleichem creates his vision of the Yiddish world. . . .

Sholom Aleichem came at a major turning point in the history of the east European Jews: between the unquestioned dominance of religious belief and the appearance of modern ideologies, between the past of traditional Judaism and the future of Jewish politics, between a totally integrated culture and a culture that by a leap of history would soon plunge into the midst of modern division and chaos. Yet it was the mark of Sholom Aleichem's greatness that, coming as he did at this point of transition, he betrayed no moral imbalance or uncertainty of tone. . . .

The world he presented was constantly precarious and fearful, yet the vision from which it was seen remained a vision of absolute assurance. It was a vision controlled by that sense of Jewish humaneness which held the best of—even as it transcended—both the concern with the other world that had marked the past and the eagerness to transform this world that would mark the future. His work abounds in troubles, but only rarely does it betray anxiety. . . .

Sholom Aleichem believed in Jews as they embodied the virtues of powerlessness and the healing resources of poverty, as they stood firm against the outrage of history, indeed, against the very idea of history itself. Whoever is unable to conceive of such an outlook as at least an ex-

treme possibility, whoever cannot imagine the power of a messianism turned away from the apocalyptic future and inward toward a living people, cannot understand Sholom Aleichem or the moment in Jewish experience from which he stems. . . .

The stories Sholom Aleichem told his readers were often stories they already knew, but then, as the Hasidic saying goes, they cared not for the words but the melody. What Sholom Aleichem did was to give back to them the very essence of their life and hope, in a language of exaltation: the exaltation of the ordinary. . . .

Sholom Aleichem did not hesitate to thrust his barbs at his readers, and they were generous at reciprocating. Having love, they had no need for politeness. But the love of which I speak here is sharply different from that mindless ooze, that collapse of will, which the word suggests to Americans. It could be argumentative, fierce, bitter, violent; it could be ill-tempered and even vulgar; only one thing it could not be: lukewarm. . . .

[The] power to see the world as it is, to love it and yet not succumb to it . . . , that is the power one finds in Sholom Aleichem.

Sol Gittleman   (essay date 1974)

SOURCE: "Stories for Jewish Children," in *Sholom Aleichem: A Non-Critical Introduction,* Mouton, 1974, pp. 143-60.

[*In the following essay, Gittleman examines Aleichem's portrayals of Jewish mothers and sons in his short fiction and finds similarities in Philip Roth's novel* Portnoy's Complaint.]

"If only you realize what we're
doing for you. Do him a favor and he
doesn't appreciate it. Don't jump, don't
run. Walk like a human being."

—Mother to her child in
"The Ruined Passover"

1. PORTNOY IN KASRILEVKE

It may seem somewhat strained . . . to make reference to a rather sensational bestseller in America which appeared in 1969, but, for better or worse, there is no denying that Philip Roth's *Portnoy's Complaint*[1] has a certain attraction to the student of Sholom Aleichem who has had the opportunity to consider the image of the Jewish child, particularly the son, in the collected works. Roth's now infamous hero, Alexander Portnoy, is the *ne plus ultra* of Jewish sons, or at least that is his own opinion of his situation. In the novel, Portnoy is going through analysis with a psychiatrist, in an effort to explain his particular neurosis. He has all sorts of problems, some sexual, some social, but all, he claims, have their roots in the same source: his mother. Portnoy (and Roth) analyse what he considers to be the trauma of being the son of a Jewish mother. Now, it would be a self-defeating effort if we were to take a detour and consider the merits of Roth's novel as literature. What *is* of some interest to us is the nature of the characterization of Mrs. Portnoy, her son's relationship to her, and the extent to which Roth's novel is a statement which has its inspiration from the same taproot which Sholom Aleichem drew upon in creating characters remarkably similar to Mrs. Portnoy.

Roth, in effect, attempts to describe what it is like to be a Jewish child in America. Of the hundreds of stories which Sholom Aleichem wrote, the largest proportion were tales about children, and most interestingly, the majority of these were narrated in 'Portnoy fashion', by an adult seemingly unburdening himself of a particularly important incident in his early life which he only much later comes to recount. Two volumes were entitled **Stories for Jewish Children** (*Mayses far yidishe kinder*), but it is more accurate to say that the majority are stories *about* Jewish children. Sholom Aleichem goes into considerable detail to analyse what it was like to be a Jewish child, and particularly a Jewish child who happened to be a son, born and raised in the *shtetl* atmosphere of Czarist Russia. The Jewish male child of the *shtetl* represented "the family's opportunity to be as good as anybody—our chance to win honor and respect".[2] In theological terms, each male child was a potential Messiah, and was treated accordingly. The upbringing, cultural education, and general welfare of this potentially important little creature was naturally enough the responsibility primarily of his mother. It is at this point, remarkably, that a gap of a chronological century and a thousand years of civilized progress appear to be insignificant, as Roth and Sholom Aleichem converge on a strikingly similar characterized stereotype—or archetype—in the Jewish mother.

The mothers in Sholom Aleichem's stories are variations on a theme, differing in degree, never in kind. Some are brutal, others extraordinarily kind and self-sacrificing, none are indifferent to their children's needs; but all of them are alike in the total belief in the infallability of their techniques of child-rearing, as well as their possession of an instinct which was to guarantee no resistance whatsoever from the young men who were their subjects. It is rare to find such a consistent delineation of character in any one writer's corpus as one does of the mother-matriarch in Sholom Aleichem's writings. She displays a singlemindedness and dedication to her task—producing the perfect child—which quite obviously impressed the author. Perfection in the child meant, in terms of the Jewish communal structure, honor for the family, for the parents, and the only certain way, even for the impoverished, of gaining status in the community. It was in terms of the methodology employed to attain this status that Sholom Aleichem makes his criticism.

"'Look at that pair of hands!' And she slapped me smartly across my wrists to make me drop them. 'When you sit at Uncle Hertz's table remember to keep your hands down, do you hear me? And don't let your face get as red as Yadwocha the peasant girl's. And don't roll your eyes like a tomcat. Do you hear what I'm telling you? And sit up like a human being. And the main thing is—your nose. Oh that nose of yours. Come here, let me put your nose in order.'" Throughout this story, **"The Purim Feast"**, a young boy is shoved, pushed, and generally abused by a mother who is "trying to make a *mentsh* out of him".[3] Clearly the author is in a way attempting a subtle characterization. He presents a selfish, domineering, coarse, and thoroughly unsympathetic picture devoid of even a hint of genuine maternal instincts. The boy is abused during preparations for the family Purim festival, at which the young man is to shine, in order to impress Uncle Hertz, the *nogid* of the family circle, and in doing so will shed honor and glory on his mother and father, as well as on himself. Thus, when the party ends in disaster (he was overcome by a fit of uncontrollable laughter and beaten black and blue by his mother for this behavior), he is made to feel an assortment of guilts, having betrayed the larger family, his parents, and himself. Years later, when he discusses the event (the occasion for the story itself), we can sense the extraordinary humiliation which he must have felt on that occasion, as well as the guilt which no doubt marked him for life: "That night I cursed my own bones and I cursed Purim and the Purim feast . . . and more than anyone else I cursed Uncle Hertz, may he forgive me, for he has long since passed on to his reward. On his grave stands a tombstone, the most imposing tombstone on the whole cemetery, and on it in gold letters are engraved the virtues in which he excelled during his life . . ."

There is one other dimension to this particular type of hard-driving Jewish mother, and that is her relationship with her husband. Before the big event, he asks his wife if Uncle Hertz, who is her brother, has arrived yet from out-of-town:

> "'Well, what's the news? Has your Hertz arrived yet?' And she gave him such a fare-thee-well that my father didn't know whether to stand up or to sit down. 'What do you mean by *my* Hertz? What sort of expression!' 'Whose is he if not yours? Is he mine?' said my father trying to do better. But he didn't advance far . . . My mother attacked him on all sides at once. 'Well, if he is mine, what of it? You don't like it? His ancestry isn't good enough for you? You had to divide your father's inheritance with him, is that it? You never got any favors from him, is that it?' 'Who says I didn't' my father offered in a milder tone, ready to surrender himself. But it didn't do any good. My mother wasn't ready to make a truce yet. 'You have better brothers than I have? Is that it? Finer men, more important, more prosperous, more respectable ones, is that it? 'Quiet now. Let there be an end to this. Leave me alone', said my father, pulling his cap over his eyes and running out of the house. My father lost the battle and my mother remained the victor. She is always the victor."

Sholom Aleichem is obviously dealing with a situation he finds abnormal, that of a family of emotionally emasculated males, dominated by a female force which is, to the writer, unacceptable within the structure of the Jewish family, with its strict sense of role-playing. In terms of the female liberationists, Jewish family life played into the hands of male chauvinism. Perhaps sensing the fundamental frustrations of the female, Sholom Aleichem created a whole range of basically unhappy Jewish women whose sole gratification derives from the success of their child-rearing. Perhaps this accounts in part for the extraordinary amount of energy which his mother figures generate toward this end.

Clearly nothing outraged Sholom Aleichem so much as this brutalization of children. He dedicated the two volumes of children's stories to them, while hoping that the adults might at least become enlightened as to their responsibilities as parents.

—Sol Gittleman

What is also noteworthy about Sholom Aleichem's matriarchs is that they are almost totally lacking in the sensibility to understand the individual emotional needs and problems of their children. There is *never* any of the modern psychological rhetoric about inhibitions, fixations, sensitivity, and never any understanding of these issues by the mother, although Sholom Aleichem makes it quite clear that the lack of this understanding has caused the narrator—rarely himself in these children's stories—abundant mental stress. The characteristic which Sholom Aleichem finds particularly distressing is the regular use of the device of maternal self-sacrifice in order to create guilt feelings in the young child and a sense of dedication to fulfilling the program which the family has in mind. In **"The Dreydl"** there is no physical punishment inflicted upon the young child, and the mother is utterly kind-hearted and warmly affectionate. The story, like so many others, is in the form of a reminiscence.

The young boy in this case was an orphan, which in the *shtetl* social structure meant without both parents, or also solely without a father. In that case, the education of the child was taken over by a committee of elders, for above all, regardless of status, a Jewish male had to be educated in the Law. Everything was done to stimulate a boy's interest in the Talmud; no single idea dominated the family as much. To have a *talmid khokhem,* a prodigiously bright young scholar, was the ultimate goal of every *shtetl* family. And for an widowed mother, the mandate was the same, the responsibility even greater, perhaps. This explains in part the description of the mother taking her son to *kheder*—elementary school—in **"The Dreydl"**: "'Remember now, study diligently', Mama said, standing by the door. She turned to look at me with a feeling of mingled joy, love, and compassion. I understand Mama's look quite well. She was happy that I was studying in the company of respectable children, but her heart ached that she

had to part with me."[4] Yet soon, the narrator detected a pressure which left him as a child puzzled, but which as an adult he has come to understand: "I couldn't understand why Mama always complained that she barely made enough to pay for the store rent and for the *kheder* tuition. Why did she single out tuition? What about food, clothing, shoes, etc? All she thought about was tuition." The psychological offensive by the mother here is non-violent, but very effective. There is no more than the innuendo of self-sacrifice on her part and endurance of hardship, in order that he might get an education. When summer came, our young student had a difficult time concentrating:

> Who could even think of praying or studying then? But had you spoken to Mama, she would have told you that her husband, may he rest in peace, was not like that. He was a different sort of person. May he forgive me for saying this, but I don't know what sort of person he was. I only know that Mama constantly badgered and reminded me that I had had a father, threw up to me a dozen times a day that she was paying *kheder* tuition for me, and asked only two things of me: to put my mind to studies and my heart to prayers.

The mother's prime means of motivating the boy is by underlining strongly what she is willing to give up for him, and the effect on the mind of the seven- or eight-year-old boy is predictable, even in retrospect: "She froze, she went hungry, never had sufficient sleep or enough to eat. She suffered all this for my sake. Only for me. Why? Didn't she deserve to have a little pleasure, too? Everyone has his own criterion for joy. For my mother there was no greater pleasure in the world than my chanting the Sabbath and holiday *Kiddush* over the wine for her, or my conducting the Passover Seder, or lighting the Hanuka candles for her." The young man's reaction to his mother's total dedication to her goals is, within the framework of the *shtetl* world, understandable. As an adult he is now puzzled by his guilt feelings, but not particularly resentful or defensive. In terms of the communal structure, his mother's techniques, if we may call them that, have been developed over perhaps centuries, and the young man's cultural memory, within the traditions of the Jewish family and its ritual of child-rearing, allows for a highly developed sense of guilt toward the sacrificing matriarch to have a positive effect on the infant, child, adolescent, and man. The guilt feelings are put to good use, the Jewish child was generally highly motivated towards those goals established by his parents; down through the centuries of the *shtetl,* stability became the keynote of Jewish family life. The son did *not* rebel against his parents, and it was not until the *shtetl* itself was undermined that these tried and true methods of guilt attachment began to cause real emotional problems. The further the disintegration of the secure *shtetl* world proceeds, the more neurotic becomes the reaction of maternal attachment on the part of the child.

The most bizarre, and perhaps ridiculous, expression of this is in Roth's *Portnoy's Complaint.* Since we only experience Portnoy's mother through his own distorted view, we can only be certain of the effect that she has had on the young man, not of what she was really like as a person. What we have here is a *shtetl* mother attempting to use her instinctive equipment for child-rearing, on a young man who no longer has the *shtetl* security to wrap himself in. Alexander Portnoy is no longer a Kasrilevkite. He is two generations removed from Eastern Europe, and his reaction to a mother almost entirely identical to the mother of Sholom Aleichem's **"The Dreydl"** is to become a neurotic, with a wildly exaggerated mother fixation.

In other Sholom Aleichem stories the lack of psychological compassion takes on an almost unreal dimension. In **"Pity for Living Creatures"** one is astonished (as is clearly Sholom Aleichem himself) at the adult reaction to what must have been a relatively standard problem: the reaction of a young child to the religious ritual of animal slaughter as proscribed by Jewish Law. A young boy observes a fish swimming in the family bathtub, a carp which is intended for the Friday night Sabbath feast: "The poor thing desperately wanted to return to the river . . . 'It's a pity', I told Mama, 'a pity for living creatures.'" The mother and cook discover that this compassion comes from discussions with the rabbi, whereupon she bursts out laughing and dismisses her son: "You're a fool, but your rabbi is a bigger one. Just keep grating the horseradish."[5] Later he observes a *shokhet* slitting the throats of chickens and weeps. When he admonishes the cook for beating a cat who stole, she thinks, from the kitchen, she throws him out: "Get out of here, of I'll smack your face. God almighty, where do such foolish children come from?" He is beaten by two gentile boys when he interferes with their killing of fallen birds; then he is beaten by his father for being with gentiles. He is the only person in the village who cares for a terribly ill and deformed little child, who soon dies. Whenever the child's mother sees him, she thinks of her child and weeps "Then Mama chased me away. 'If you wouldn't be underfoot and go where you're not supposed to go, then people wouldn't remember things they ought not to remember.'" Whenever he thinks of the little child, he cries, and his mother replies with laughter: "Did the horseradish get into your eyes? Wipe your eyes, you foolish boy . . . Wipe your nose, too." In a day and age when we are accustomed to trying to understand the nature of a child's emotional needs and responses, the adult reacton to this young boy's particular fixation—the suffering of animals—seems cruel and unjust. However, there was no room for sentiment and sensitivity which did not conform to the normal, acceptable standards of the *shtetl,* and children—boys in particular—who manifested such feelings received no consideration and, as in the case of our young friend in **"Pity for Living Creatures"**, beatings and scoldings.

If anyone has suffered under the delusion that all of Sholom Aleichem's stories are filled with gentle humor, the few we have so far considered in this [essay] should give cause for reconsideration. Clearly, there are aspects of the Jewish "Mutter Gestalt" which Sholom Aleichem did not find appealing. These few stories, and another dozen like them, are not funny, specifically because of an all-consuming mother. Yet, there are others which project the same mother figure, but emphasize the positive rather than the negative. **"Gitl Purishkevitch"** is the name of one such delightful mother, who is no less forceful in her domination of her son: "He's a good boy, sound as an apple, handsome and plain as can be. He's got all the virtues, but learning he didn't like. What am I saying—didn't like? Beat him, smash him to smithereens, but still he refused to study. 'What's going to be with you, Moishe,' says I, 'if you say no to reading, writing, and praying? You'll only be fit to be a dogcatcher!'" The widowed Gitl does everything she can to give her son respectability, and is fairly satisfied with her efforts. She is a door-to-door *shtetl* saleswomen for Wissotsky's Tea. This hard-working, every-day *mentsh* is given the added positive touch by Sholom Aleichem by being placed in a frame much like that which gave Tevye his opportunity to shine: a meeting with the author: "They told me that there's a writer chap here named Sholom Ilikem. Is that you himself, the Sholom Ilikem that writes?" Old Gitl then relates her tale of woe, which turns out to be a paean for motherhood, and a perfectly convincing one, at that. One day, she suddenly finds her son threatened by the draft. In terms of *shtetl* life, the Jew's relationship to military service was always traumatic. There was no way which could satisfy the Jew's particular needs of daily life and his obligation to serve a government which was openly anti-Semitic. As a result, the Jews did everything they could to avoid military life, and numerous Sholom Aleichem stories deal with this theme, as well as with the theme of Jewish patriotism and bravery in combat for Czarist Russia.[6] In Gitl's case, however, a rank injustice was about to be done:

> Draft? What draft? He's a one-and-only child, an only son to his widowed mother that owes everything she is to God and then Wissotsky. Has such a thing ever been heard of? Is there no God? Where's your sense of justice? But when the cards say trouble, you can go knock your head against the wall! It turned out that my Moishe was the exact same age as the three sons of our rich man's three daughters, may three well-placed boils prevent them from being able to stand, lie and sit.

Gitl's son is about to become the scapegoat for the *nogid's* grandsons. Sholom Aleichem, always on the look-out for treacherous *negidim,* now moralizes on how the rich keep their progenies out of the armed forces, while the poor are forced to serve. In Sholom Aleichem's Kasrilevke, there is always a doctor ready to certify a bad back, or a fever which is undiagnosible. She appeals to the draft board and is thrown out. She goes to the regional governor and is thrown out. Then, as she describes it, "she straight off sold everything she had and set out to seek the truth right in Petersburg itself . . . and if I had to get hold of the Czar himself, don't you think I could have found him? When it comes to the truth I could even reach God himself." What it has come to is her son, Moishe, and Gitl will not give him up, not even to the army. She enters the chambers of the Duma, Russia's parliament, to hear the debate on the draft laws, which turn out to be strongly anti-Jewish, but worse still, discriminatory against the poor. It is suggested that Jews be permitted to buy their way out of the army, all of which is too much for Gitl: "Expect me to keep still? So I called out from the gallery and screamed loud enough for the entire Duma to hear: 'What about Moishe?' The police throw her out, but a sympathetic deputy hears her case, and miracle of miracles, Moishe is released from his military obligation, which, by the way, he was enjoying.

In this story, a mother's dogged determination to find justice and her belief in a righteous cause finally triumph. Ironically, Sholom Aleichem subtly suggests that perhaps the young man would have been better off had he accepted military duty. Still, he revels in Gitl's victory and does not harshly undermine the triumph of motherhood.

Sholom Aleichem had a particular spot of affection for the widowed woman who, like Gitl, sacrifices and saves for her son. **"The Little Pot"**, like **"Gitl Purishkevitch"**, is in the form of a Chekhovian monologue in which the central character is permitted to reveal herself in her own words, in this case, to her rabbi. Yenta the Poultrywoman is one of Sholom Aleichem's most stereotyped and yet most extraordinary character. She embodies almost all the clichés which have been associated with, in a larger sense, motherhood in general even in America. She is the type of caricatured matriarch favored by mass media humorists: doting, kind but singleminded, and inevitably associated with chicken soup:

> So every day I make him a chicken soup out of a quarter of a chicken, and every night when he comes home from *cheder* he eats it. And I sit across the table from him with some work in my hands and rejoice at the sight. I pray to God that He should help me so that tomorrow I should be able to make him another soup out of another quarter of a chicken. 'Mother', he asks me, 'why don't you eat with me?' 'Eat', I said, 'eat all you want. I ate already.' 'What did you eat?' 'What did I eat? What difference does it make what I ate, as long as I ate?' And when he is through reading or studying, I take a couple of baked potatoes out of the oven, or rub a slice of bread with onion and make myself a feast. And I swear to you by all that is holy, that I get more enjoyment and satisfaction out of that onion than I would out of the finest roast or the richest soup, because I remember that my Dovidl, may the evil eye spare him, had some chicken soup and that tomorrow he will have chicken soup again.[7]

In the above passage one senses a balanced harmony, an understanding between mother and son which has a heritage as old as the *shtetl*. There is a distinct ritualization to the mother-son relationship which in the Old World provided a framework which proved to be acceptable to all parties. However, the structure proved to be non-adaptable. The very same mother, with the same expectations and hopes, when transferred to a suburb of Newark, New Jersey and doting over a son with an Ivy League education, becomes, at least in the eyes of this son, a figure who totally dominates his existence and inculcates such extraordinary guilt feelings that only psychoanalysis can relieve the oppression from his psyche. This is the problem of Alexander Portnoy, who represents in every respect the traditional Jewish son, but now lacking one major and totally determining factor: the cultural memory of the

shtetl. Along with Portnoy's emancipation came the loss of a certain part of his Jewish identity which permitted the male youth to accept somewhat benignly the feelings of total immersion in the matriarchal will which Sholom Aleichem's male children somehow accept, with more or less resignation. The mother of Alexander Portnoy is no different from the mother of the young man in **"The Little Pot"**. Her reactions, her instincts are exactly the same as her *shtetl* antecedent. What has changed is the world in which she had operated over the centuries, the world of the accepted norms of mother-son relationships within the tight confines of the Jewish family.

Yet, Portnoy cannot break loose cleanly, without a residue. Although he has moved to suburbia and appears totally Americanized, there lingers in him this five-hundred-year-old accumulation of Jewish consciousness, a faint remembrance, a reflex action which unfortunately manifests itself as an abnormality of behavior which fixates him. He is a typical Sholom Aleichem character, but living in another time and in another world.

2. THE BRUTALIZATION OF THE CHILD

One extremely unexpected aspect of the child in Sholom Aleichem—and by extrapolation in the *shtetl* itself—is his brutalization by parents, peers, and particularly teachers. The young man of the story **"The Flag"** experiences general mockery and physical punishment because of a speech impediment: "Everyone under the sun thought it a good deed to beat me: my father, my mother, my sisters, my teacher, my classmates. They all tried to get me to talk properly."[8] Furthermore, it was the birthright of the rich child to beat up the poor or orphaned child.[9] Any young boy could expect a whipping if he expressed interest in an occupation or activity which was not in keeping with the *yikhus,* the status of his parents.[10]

But in general, the great sadism was demonstrated by the elementary school teachers. Study for the Jewish child began at age three, when he was carried off by the *belfer,* the teaching assistant, to the *dardeki melamed,* the elementary teacher, who enjoyed absolutely no status in the community, because he "lives by selling what he should be giving."[11] Goaded by this lack of respect from his peers, the teacher traditionally lashed out at his young pupils, who were, moreover, the victims of some of the most antiquated teaching methods conceived of by men. Three-year-old children were forced to memorize the Hebrew letters, then by rote learn passages of the Bible, which were recited endlessly, while the *melamed* marched up and down the aisles, with whip in hand.

In Sholom Aleichem's writings, these teachers are without exception misfits and failures who vent their frustration by "beating, flogging, and crippling Jewish children".[12] None is more devastating than **"Boaz the Teacher"**.[13] The narrator remembers "the day Mama took me by the hand and brought me to Boaz's *cheder* for the first time; I felt like a young chicken on its way to the *shokhet.* It flutters with fright, poor thing—not comprehending, but sensing that the future isn't all chicken feed." The teacher himself is as demonic as the child had sensed and as the adult could reflect on: the only pedagogic device was the whip. "A child must fear—God, the rebbi, his parents, sins, and evil thoughts. In order for a child to be imbued with the correct amount of fear, he must be laid down properly, with pants lowered, and given two dozen lashes." Sholom Aleichem underscores a sense of genuine perversion beyond this apparent morality of abuse: "He was never in a rage when he dispensed the whippings. Boaz was not the sort to get angry . . . He considered laughing something terrible. Boaz had never laughed in his life and hated to see others laughing . . . Sometimes we got a whipping just for the fun of it. 'Let's see how a little boy lets himself be whipped.'" Nowhere is there justice, nowhere reason. In **"Robbers!"** the teacher Mazeppa, a small, thin tyrant, "hated lengthy chitchats. Even for the slightest incident— whether you were guilty or not—he ordered you to lie down for a whipping. 'Rebbi, Yosl-Yakov hit me.' 'Lie down.' 'Rebbi, that's a lie. He kicked me first.' 'Lie down.' 'Rebbi, Chaim-Berl stuck his tongue out at me.' 'Lie down.' 'Rebbi, that's a downright lie. It was *he* who thumbed his nose at *me*.' 'Lie down . . .'" Everyone was whipped, the poor more than the rich, the small more than the big. It was no wonder that the children themselves turned brutal to one another and to other things. In **"Methuseleh, a Jewish Horse"**, Ruvele, a ruthless, cynical Jewish youth, gets his pleasure out of tormenting a horse. Sholom Aleichem, in an effort to justify this distorted vision of a Jewish boy, informs us that Ruvele himself was beaten by his parents because he had the temerity to want to be a violinist.

Although the poor suffered more than the rich, the *nogid*'s son did not escape. In the Purim story **"Visiting with King Ahasuerus"**, Sholom Aleichem plays with the prince and the pauper theme. The rich lad, who tells the story, is the traditional have-not: He cannot participate in the Purim play "because I came from a rich and prominent family".[14] The object of his regret is the poorest child of the village: "But most of all I was jealous of Feivel the orphan who would don a red shirt and masquerade as Joseph the Righteousness for the troupe's performance of *The Sale of Joseph.*" But he was the grandson of Reb Meir, the richest man in town and has "his own personal Angel of Death" to guard over his morality: Reb Itzi, his tutor. For a moment he escapes the family's net and joins the troupe of actors, until his Angel of Death catches him and turns him over to his father:

> Once outside, my father stopped, took one look at me, and briskly slapped me twice. 'That's just a prelude. Once we get home, your tutor will really give it to you. Now listen here, Reb Itzi, I'm turning him over to you, and I want you to whip the daylights out of him. Til he's black and blue. A boy going on nine! Let him remember what it is to run off with the Purim players, those low-down, low-class, third-rate clowns, those down-at-the-heel tramps. Let him remember what it means to ruin everyone's holiday.

Clearly nothing outraged Sholom Aleichem so much as this brutalization of children. He dedicated the two vol-umes of children's stories to them, while hoping that the adults might at least become enlightened as to their responsibilities as parents. Yet in spite of the apparent hopelessness of the plight of these children, they somehow manage to survive. After all, they all narrate their own stories, and these narrations take on a quality of reminiscence which is strangely devoid of bitterness or resentment. In fact, although he clearly marks 'the good guys and the bad guys' in these children's stories, Sholom Aleichem at least tacitly stresses the durability of the Jewish child 'to make it' while growing up in what normally might be described as a psychologically debilitating environment. And as if to re-assure us completely, he permits us to follow the history of one of these children from his earliest years until young manhood (in that world, somewhere around twelve!), and shows him triumphant in spite of every possible disruption and lack of consideration. It is only fitting that Sholom Aleichem's most durable, even most honest creation should be such a child, Mottel, the orphaned son of an impoverished cantor.

3. "HOORAH, I'M AN ORPHAN"

For Sholom Aleichem, Mottel was someone special. A draft of a Mottel-story was on the table next to his death-bed, and over a period of almost twenty-five years spanning two continents, Mottel remained at the center of Sholom Aleichem's thoughts. More than Tevye, more than Menachem-Mendel, he represents the Jewish spirit as Sholom Aleichem saw it, both in Europe and in America. Of his three major characters, only Mottel is described in The New World. He belongs in America, and is as much at home on the East Side of New York as he was back in Kasrilevke. Fortunate for us, Mottel is an excellent observer of his surroundings, for he tells his own story, a Jewish picaro who gets himself involved in every enterprise of his family, grows up through the forced feeding of events which shook Europe, travels across half the world, and comes out underneath the Delancey Street Bridge as stable as one could hope for.[15]

Mottel's adventures constitute thirty-nine interrelated chapters, a perpetual serialization in episodic form which involves, besides Mottel, his widowed mother ("She's doing what she always does—she's crying"); his brother Eli, a serious, responsible young man who inherits the role of head of the family and who invests in a series of outrageously funny business enterprises; his wife, pock-marked Brocha with the bass voice; Eli's best friend Pinney, always with a cuff rolled up, or a sock falling down, Pinney with the long, skinny body, a *schlimazl* who somehow manages in a world not made for *schlimazls*. The adventures of Mottel present the most comprehensive chronicle of Jewish life at the turn of the century. After experiencing little success in a variety of legal and illegal business ventures, the group, a sort of Jewish commune at that point, decides that they have had enough of Europe, and that the land of the future is America. So, amidst total confusion and mother's wailing over the grave of her husband, the families (there are Eli's and Pinney's) head for an illegal border crossing at the frontier of Russia and the Austro-Hungarian Empire. Confrontations with Austrians, Germans, Jews of all descriptions telling hair-raising stories ("If you compare her bad luck with my bad luck, you'll realize that she's lucky!"). As they travel closer and closer to the western coast of Europe for the hoped-for trip to America, their problems become more complex and Mottel's mother's tears more copious, until her crying becomes a cause for serious concern: it could keep them out of the United States, if she develops trachoma from crying. When she hears this, of course she bursts out crying. In Antwerp they wait for mother's condition to improve, and pass the time observing the German Jews who also are waiting for the boat: "All Jews on 'the other side' hate Yiddish, and love German. Even beggars talk German. They're ready to die of starvation, as long as they do it in German." Finally, they manage to get to London, and Brocha, who hates the city, wails from one end of town to the other: "London, why don't you burn?"

But by far the most exciting part of their exodus involves the trip across the ocean and their arrival in New York. There is a most moving description of the *Yom Kippur* services on the high seas, as the elegant Jews of first class come down to steerage to mourn and to worship with the common Jews. Ad for Mottel's mother, on the saddest of all the days of the Jewish year, "Mother is happy—this is *her* day!"

Everything comes to a near disaster on Ellis Island, as the travellers wait to go through the immigration process. Sholom Aleichem's description of the situation is perhaps the most definitive statement ever made in literature on the subject of Ellis Island, now a relic of history and a permanent part of the Age of Immigration. Pinney, who is a rabid pro-American throughout the book, is crushed by "Elie's Island" and its inhumanity. Families are permanently separated, people are locked up, deported, there are pitiful scenes of desperate peasants, unable to communicate in English, making futile efforts to join their loved ones. Sholom Aleichem in a rare departure includes peoples from all lands in these Ellis Island scenes and condemns the whole system out of hand.

But in spite of these vicissitudes, they finally plant themselves on the piers of New York, and Pinney turns to Europe for the extraordinary speech which was quoted earlier, addressed to a decadent Old World which will someday regret the loss of its Jews. Not everywhere is the image of America so overwhelmingly positive as it is in Pinney's speech on the banks of the Hudson River, and certainly Sholom Aleichem's own experiences had a great deal to do with this mixed reaction.[16] But Pinney's message ("You murderers, we have to thank you for having reached this haven, this refuge, this great and blessed land") is clear; for the *proste Yidn* of Kasrilevke, for the Jewish down-and-outers, America was indeed the land of the free.

America works wonders on 'the gang'. Feivel soon becomes Philip; Mendel is called Mike, and everybody is 'making a living'. Furthermore, they are not even strangers in a strange land, for soon after their departure, Kasrilevke burned to the ground, and the survivors came to America. Former *negidim* now find themselves working on pushcarts on Second Avenue. Others work in factories, take part in workers' rallies, go out on strike, and participate in the tremendous excitement of life on the Lower East Side of New York around the turn of the century.[17] All of this is seen through the eyes of a delightfully realistic young boy growing up in the midst of a world teeming with new experiences. At this point, with Mottel's life still before him and an unfinished story on his bed table, Sholom Aleichem died.

The direction he would have taken, had he lived to continue Mottel's adventures, was clear. He had a definite problem in mind for future stories: how would the Jew face Americanization, the threat of assimilation in a land which gave the Jew relative freedom of choice. Although he himself did not live to confront this challenge, Sholom Aleichem left a rich enough heritage, so that others, some far removed from Kasrilevke, were able to continue. But clearly, Sholom Aleichem the realist recognized the way of the future for the Jew. Kasrilevke was no more. Sholom Aleichem, the town's architect, benefactor, and major citizen, burned it to the ground in a symbolic gesture of finality. It is somewhat foreboding to note how, almost twenty years before Adolf Hitler's rise to power, Sholom Aleichem signaled the end of European Jewry.

Notes

[1] (New York: Random House, 1969).

[2] *Portnoy's Complaint*, 5.

[3] In *The Tevye Stories and Others*, 111-117.

[4] In *Some Laughter Some Tears*, 65-82.

[5] In *Some Laughter Some Tears*, 101-106.

[6] See, for example, "The First Passover Night of the War", in *Old Country Tales*, 259-265. A Jewish soldier says the following: "Just three things are enough to make me happy. That a Jew like me is equal to everyone else; that a Jew like me is one of the Czar's men; that a Jew like me can show his loyalty to the entire world. Let our enemies see that a Jew too can serve faithfully and well, and that a Jew also can hold his head high with honor of the land where his ancestors' bones lie buried, and where his bones too will lie." "Gitl Perushkevitch", is to be found in *Old Country Tales*, 139-148.

[7] "The Little Pot", in *Tevye's Daughters*, 180-191.

[8] "The Flag", in *Old Country Tales*, 73-84.

[9] See "The Esrog" in *Some Laughter Some Tears*, 26-36.

[10] See "Methuseleh, A Jewish Horse", in *Old Country Tales*, 87-97; and "From the Riviera", in *Stories and Satires*, 303-307; also, "The Fiddle", in *Selected Stories of Sholom Aleichem*, 307-323.

[11] Zborowski and Herzog, 89.

[12] "The Little Redheaded Jews", in *Some Laughter Some Tears*, 191-230. This is one of Sholom Aleichem's hardest-hitting satires on Jewish obstinacy in accepting Zionism.

[13] "Boaz the Teacher", in *Some Laughter Some Tears*, 161-168.

[14] In *Old Country Tales*, 51-64.

[15] The English title is *Adventures of Mottel the Cantor's Son*, translated by Tamara Kahana (New York: Collier Books, 1961). The original Yiddish mentions Mottel's father in the title: *Motl Peyse dem khazns*, in two volumes of the *Ale verk* twenty-eight volumes of 1917-25 (vols. 17 and 18).

[16] Besides being a haven where the Menachem-Mendels flee to, America is the setting for several non-Mottel stories, with a definite bias on the part of the author evident. See "Mr. Green has a Job" in *Some Laughter Some Tears*, 233-236; and the devastating "Story of a Greenhorn", 243-248 in the same volume.

[17] See, most notably, Hutchins Hapgood, *The Spirit of the Ghetto*, Paperback edition (New York: Schocken Books, 1966).

Joseph Butwin and Frances Butwin
(essay date 1977)

SOURCE: "The Speaking Voice," in *Sholom Aleichem*, Twayne Publishers, 1977, pp. 95-124.

[*Frances Butwin is a Polish-born American translator and critic. With Julius Butwin, she selected and translated a collection of stories by Sholom Aleichem, which was published in 1946 as* The Old Country. *She has since translated several other volumes of Sholom Aleichem's works. Joseph Butwin is an American educator and critic who has published articles on English, French, and Yiddish literature. In the following essay from their biographical and critical study of Sholom Aleichem, the authors explore Aleichem's use of* skaz—*the spoken tale—and compare it to American examples from Mark Twain and Ring Lardner.*]

In his essay on Nikolai Leskov, Walter Benjamin describes the historical process that "has quite gradually removed narrative from the realm of living speech and at the same time is making it possible to see a new beauty in what is vanishing."[1] The printing press and the vast expansion of its use along with other advances of industrialism had already made storytelling obsolete along the Atlantic fringe of Europe and North America toward the end of the nineteenth century. On the fringes of this world, in Russia and in frontier America, several writers found ways of telling stories in print without losing the charm of "living speech." Benjamin discusses Leskov. Mark Twain is another and so is Sholom Aleichem.

Storytelling was still very much alive among Jews of the Russian Pale in Sholom Aleichem's time, and many of his own stories take the form of a spoken tale. In **"On Account of a Hat"** the writer, Sholom Aleichem, listens while another man, a Kasrilevkite, tells him the story of Sholom Shakhnah. Continual interjections—"do you hear me?"—remind us that the Kasrilevkite and not Sholom Aleichem is responsible for the story. At the end when the

man asks his question—"You think it's so easy to put one over on Kasrilevke?"—we are left with the final reminder that what we have read is a spoken communication between two people and that one of them, the speaker, lives on the same plane with everyone else in Kasrilevke, including the subject of his story, Sholom Shakhnah. It is only the speaker's arrogance that separates him from the *shlimazl* in the story. Otherwise he is one of the people, speaking with the identifiable voice of the people. The identification of the speaker in the frame and the way he speaks when he takes over combine to place the story within the circle of folk culture. He tells Sholom Aleichem that he has "bushels and baskets of stories" about Sholom Shakhnah. His story emerges from a folk anthology available to any citizen of Kasrilevke. The verbal tics of the speaker do not give the story a particular style or signature by which we generally identify writers. Rather these tics are the earmarks of a typical storyteller who relates his stories aloud without benefit of correction or "style." He is, as Sholom Aleichem assures us in the frame, "no *litterateur*." A story belongs to literature when "an author puts down his completed piece of writing." It belongs to folklore "from the moment it is adopted by the community."[2] Even while Sholom Aleichem was in the act of making Yiddish into a vehicle for a written literature, he deliberately left the impression of the opposite process in his stories. The apparent dominance of the speaking voice constitutes an escape from literature into folkways through a mode of narration well known to Russian writers and best identified by Russian critics as *skaz*, a word meaning "to say, speak, relate."

As a form *skaz* creates the illusion of speech in stories where a large part of what we read is given over to what appears to be the transcription of one voice speaking. It is to be distinguished from literary I-narration by the presence of a listener within the frame of the story. When the second person is used it is this listener, not a vague reading public, that is intended. In what follows it will be convenient to refer to the literary, first-person narration as "narration" and to *skaz* as "speech." We are constantly made aware that what we read is intended to be speech by the way language is used, by the word order, the spelling, and the vocabulary. Often *skaz* is marked as speech and not narration by the use of dialect. Spelling can be made to indicate special pronunciation, though eccentric spelling is less frequent among the early Yiddish writers who were also charged with the standardization of the printed language. Word order and vocabulary are marked by their departure from standard usage. In what the speaker says the rigorous control of plot that we often associate with the short story gives way to the rambling and digressive patterns of natural speech, often in excess. The result is less a story than a characterization. The character of the speaker comes to us as it does in drama, through speech without benefit of authorial interpretation. If the author can be said to exist in the text of *skaz*, he resides in the second person, the listener, called by Mikhail Baxtine the "compositional equivalent" of the author, present perhaps in a frame story. Otherwise the author is effaced from the monologue, and yet we are aware of his shadowy presence as a listener and as an enlarged consciousness that allows us to judge the necessarily limited perspective of the speaker. This narrowness may simply be the limitation placed on a single point of view; it may also be a function of the geographical, social, and educational level implied by the use of dialect. Whatever the cause, the effect is ironic. Our bird's-eye view corrects what Victor Erlich calls the "worm's eye view" of the speaker. Erlich discusses *skaz* in a short article where he suggests that this notion could be fruitfully applied to the monologues of Sholom Aleichem. Earlier Russian critics studied Leskoy and Gogol. American readers have met *skaz* in Mark Twain's "Celebrated Jumping Frog" and in Ring Lardner's "Haircut."[3]

Sholom Aleichem's sense of himself as an artist in a popular rather than strictly literary tradition helps to explain his affinity for this form of storytelling. The reason for this affinity is especially clear in the light of comments of Baxtine:

> The element of *skaz* in the direct sense (an orientation toward oral speech) is a factor necessarily inherent in any storytelling. Even if the narrator is represented as writing his story and giving a certain literary polish to it, all the same he is not a literary professional; what he commands is not a specific style but only a socially or individually defined manner of storytelling, a manner that gravitates toward oral *skaz*. . . . We believe that in the majority of cases *skaz* is brought in precisely for the sake of a different voice, one which is socially distinct and carries with it a set of viewpoints and evaluations which are just what the author needs. In point of fact, it is a storyteller who is brought in, and a storyteller is not a literary man; he usually belongs to a lower social strata, to the common people (precisely the quality the author values in him), and he brings with him oral speech.[4]

The nonliterary orientation of *skaz* eases the transition from folkways into literary conventions for the Yiddish writer, and the oral presentation gives the Yiddish writer a vehicle that is especially appropriate to his language. Max Weinreich explains the use of Yiddish among Russian Jews in a way that shows how natural it is for this language to be assimilated into literature through the vehicle of *skaz*. He distinguishes the traditional literary language, Hebrew, from Yiddish:

> Ashkenazic bilingualism, definitely, is not founded on the dichotomy of sacred versus profane. The difference it stresses is that between oral language and the language of recording. . . . Just as Hebrew was the language of recording, Yiddish was the language of speech. As soon as the businessmen, or the rabbis for that matter, met and went on discussing the issues raised in their [Hebrew] correspondence, the erstwhile Hebrew writers at once switched to Yiddish. Oral communication, except for passages from the sacred texts repeated verbatim, was firmly linked with the vernacular.[5]

Sholom Aleichem would exploit the illusion of oral speech to lay the base for the rise of a secular, vernacular literature among the Jews of eastern Europe.

I *The American Example*

The characteristic features of *skaz* are dependent on features of language and style which are difficult to penetrate in a foreign language and even more difficult to translate. For this reason we will precede our study of Sholom Aleichem's use of this form with a look at two American examples. The style is most clearly identified and understood by the native speaker. It is our belief that a reader trained in native examples is then prepared to appreciate the foreign.

The American reader has been prepared for a reading of Sholom Aleichem's monologues by humorists whose work is allied to an oral, folk tradition. Mark Twain, the most notable American practitioner, was fully aware of the difficulties in translating the form that we are calling *skaz*. For the 1875 edition of "The Celebrated Jumping Frog" he affixed a French translation in order to prove this point. Translation into standard French flattens all that is distinct in Simon Wheeler's monologue. Mark Twain's deliberately maladroit retranslation of the French back into English is an amusing exercise, but it misrepresents the problems of translation. Wheeler's first words are:

> "Rev. Leonidas W. H'm, Reverend Le—well, there was a feller once by the name of *Jim* Smiley, in the winter of '49—or maybe it was the spring of '50—I don't recollect exactly, somehow . . ."

In the French:

> "Il y avait une fois ici un individu connu sous le nom de Jim Smiley: c'était dans l'hiver de 49, peut-être bien au printemps de 50, je ne me rappelle pas exactement."

And back into English:

> "It there was one time here an individual known under the name of Jim Smiley; it was in the winter of '49, possibly well at the spring of '50, I no me recollect not exactly."

What is to be done? A word for word translation of Simon Wheeler's speech is impossible; the rendition in standard French is dull, and a French equivalent may not exist.

The translator of Sholom Aleichem into English faces many of the problems of the foreign translator of Mark Twain, especially when he sets out to translate writing that purports to represent speech. The sense that the speaker is using Yiddish, often in an idiosyncratic way, must be retained without giving way to the parody suggested by the faithful recreation of Yiddish syntax in English. The reader of the Yiddish text will only find Yiddish syntax amusing in certain instances, and it is these instances that the translator must try to render. Similar problems accompany the other features of speech.

We can appreciate the problems faced by a foreign translator of "The Celebrated Jumping Frog." For Mark Twain the story came directly out of the oral, folk milieu. He first heard the story of the jumping frog as a tale told around a tavern stove in a mining camp. He told the story to a friend who recommended that he "write it down," as his biographer says.[6] A story that is "written down" instead of "written" suggests dictation, a transcription of a spoken tale in this case. "The Celebrated Jumping Frog" retains that quality in its final form. The narrator of the frame story acts as a listener and then as a recorder of Simon Wheeler's tale, which he hears without interruption and, we are to assume, records verbatim. The difference between a conventional first person or I-narration and *skaz* should be evident in a comparison of the first words of the narrator and the first words of the speaker: "In compliance with the request of a friend of mine, who wrote me from the East, I called on good-natured, garrulous old Simon Wheeler, and inquired after my friend's friend, Leonidas W. Smiley, as requested to do, and I hereunto append the results." After several paragraphs of explanation, Simon Wheeler begins with the words already quoted: "Rev. Leonidas W. H'm, Reverend Le—well . . ." Wheeler is allowed to pause and reflect and correct himself. Unfinished words and sentences, indications of pronunciation and vocal emphasis as well as the deictic "here" pointing to an immediate location of the speaker all depart from the standard first-person narration and contribute to the impression of speech.

The writing of *skaz* corresponds in some ways to the collecting of folksongs and folktales insofar as collection generally begins when the folk tradition is dying out. It is an attempt to salvage what is all but lost to modernism.

*—James Butwin and
Frances Butwin*

Throughout his tale Simon Wheeler wanders through the same maze indicated by his first sentence. A more direct response would have been: "Leonidas W. Smiley. Never heard of him." Instead Wheeler comes up with a *Jim* Smiley and sets out to prove that "he was the curiousest man about always betting on anything." A number of examples of Smiley's obsessive gambling lead to the story of the jumping frog. The proof is serial; that is, it takes the form of a list with digressions. A list of this kind need never end. In this case the monologue ends when Wheeler is called away and the listener makes his getaway. Thus if we simplify Wheeler's digression we have two stories represented by two distinct uses of language. The story of the jumping frog exists within the frame of a story about a man who is trapped by an incorrigible raconteur. The frame is a first-person narration written in no particular place for no particular audience in a language reserved for written expression. Smiley speaks to a particular listener within the boundaries of a particular time and place. The fact that from what he says we could not then say where or when he is speaking does not contradict our sense that he is speaking at a definite location and at a certain time: "Just set where you are, stranger, and rest easy—I ain't going to be gone a second." We locate the scene from within. "Where you are" becomes the place; "a second" is the time; "You . . . stranger" is the listener. It is just these intimate indications of the immediate scene that limit the perspective and make explicit indications of historical time and geographical place unlikely. The difference between a broad perspective and the narrow perspective of the speaker within the scene makes room for the irony characteristic of this form.

The double vision required by irony is first provided by the relation of frame and monologue. Even in the absence of an actual frame story, as in Ring Lardner's "Haircut," the implied prescience of a listener adds another consciousness and with it the other mentality that stands between us and speaker and makes for irony. Frequently we are made to understand that this consciousness resides in the listener, the "compositional equivalent" of the author within the story.

The listener, though frequently silent, has an important role to play in the monologue. He is frequently a stranger. In Mark Twain's story he has connections in "the East," and in Lardner's story the listener is recognized as an outsider: "You're a newcomer, ain't you? I thought I hadn't seen you round before. I hope you like it good enough to stay. As I say, we ain't no New York City or Chicago, but we have pretty good times." He is a stranger, but he must in no way inhibit the loquaciousness of the speaker. He is enough of an insider to inspire confidence and enough of an outsider to require explanation. A complete insider would reduce the monologue to the inscrutable local code that passes for communication within a household or within the most intimate communities. The complete outsider would not understand the dialect or, in the case of Yiddish, the language. Our recognition of linguistic peculiarity creates boundaries between the speaker's world and our own. A person may be very much within the geographic and linguistic range of the speaker and still recognize peculiarities, which will create a sense of distance and, with it, a sense of irony. If we allow the idea of boundary to be represented by geography, the world that is familiar to the speaker in "Haircut" is limited to a few small towns in Michigan. Whitey refers to Detroit and "the Northern Penninsula" as the outer rim of his world. Beyond that rim are New York and Chicago, which are made to seem as familiar as the local towns mentioned in the monologue are unfamiliar. The microscopic geography that is known to the little people in the story is largely hidden to the outside world, and this difference is the difference in perspective that guides the irony of the story. From our vantage point we are allowed to be amused by the way local people talk, and we assume the enlarged moral stature that allows us to censure their moral pettiness.

Small-town Michigan was the place of Ring Lardner's youth. By the time he wrote "Haircut" he had moved away from Michigan, in fact, to Chicago and New York. It is not uncommon for the masters of this style to recreate the language and location known to their youth from the vantage point of maturity. Sholom Aleichem did the same in Odessa and Kiev and eventually in New York. In the 1920s American writers from the Middle West were still engaged in the critical judgment of small-town life that began in Hannibal, Missouri, and had been going on as long in the Russian Pale. At the same time the American small towns were diminishing into railway stops on the way to big cities, and local dialects were giving way to the uniformity of mass communication. Ring Lardner would live to be the satirist of the radio voice. With the diminution of regional differences in America and the urbanization of the *shtetl* in Russia, writers in both countries began "to see a new beauty in what [was] vanishing" and to record it for the amusement as well as for the budding nostalgia of their readers. This, to extend Benjamin's point, is when "living speech" and storytelling work their way into written literature.

The writing of *skaz* corresponds in some ways to the collecting of folksongs and folktales insofar as collection generally begins when the folk tradition is dying out. It is an attempt to salvage what is all but lost to modernism. Some Yiddish writers—Peretz and Ansky—engaged in the collection of folklore that definitely enters their art. But can we say of Sholom Aleichem and Mark Twain that they wrote folktales? Certainly characters like Tevye and Tom Sawyer have entered folk tradition. If the stories themselves seem to be folktales it is because they are framed and spoken in such a way that they seem to emanate directly from the folk. Within explicit or implicit frames we meet nonliterary people who spin yarns in a voice that we associate with speech and communication rather than with literary narration. But the key to the folkloric quality of a story is found in the form that it takes in repetition. A folktale is retellable. Now when a story like "The Celebrated Jumping Frog" is retold the qualities that are most likely to be lost are precisely those that give us the impression that it comes to us directly from the folk. The frame will be forgotten, and it is unlikely that the dialect will be reproduced. For one thing dialect does not survive indirect quotation. We may say:

"Wheeler says, 'He ketched a frog one day.'"

But we cannot say:

"Wheeler said that he ketched a frog one day."

Only a person who actually speaks Wheeler's dialect would report his speech in the second way. Otherwise the folk dialect only survives direct quotation, which is the way that oral *skaz* can survive intact. Thus its survival has more in common with the survival of a literary work than with the continuity of folklore:

> A literary work is objectivized, it exists concretely apart from the reciter. Each subsequent reader or reciter returns directly to the work. Although the interpretation of previous reciters can be taken into account, this is only one of the components in the reception of the work; whereas for a folklore work the only path leads from implementer to implementer.[7]

So say Roman Jakobson and Petr Bogatyrev, writing in the wake of the formalist interest in a Russian literature that draws heavily on folklore. Sholom Aleichem and Mark Twain are not to be considered collectors of folklore nor are they what Jakobson and Bogatyrev call "implementers." Their stories often include folktales and they preserve the folk voice. For both the imitation of folklore is the triumph of art.

II *The Yiddish Example*

Sholom Aleichem, like Mark Twain, was fond of reading his stories aloud. Both writers understood that the special quality of what they had written could best be conveyed with the speaking voice. Early in his career Mark Twain wrote to his wife that the "Jumping Frog" was "the best humorous sketch America has produced yet, and I must read it in public some day, in order that people may know what there is in it." For both writers the power of a story is in the presence of a speaking voice and much of what they write is geared to promote the conviction in the reader that he is not reading but listening.

Sholom Aleichem often seems to be telling rather than writing a story: "Listen, Jewish children, I will tell you a story about a little knife. . . ." Not only among children but among adults he repeatedly demonstrates the function of the storyteller. Storytelling is not reserved for specialists. We are reminded many times that anyone Sholom Aleichem meets is a possible raconteur, and in a number of stories he includes the telling of a tale in a way that shows the importance of storytelling among Jews of the Pale. For this he frequently adopts the format of the spoken tale implanted within a narrative. In addition to providing the occasion for the interior tale, the narrative frame is itself a story about what happens when a story is told. The teller of tales exercises definite powers over people, powers that may or may not be benign. As readers we are obliged to look closely at the act of storytelling within the stories of Sholom Aleichem.

In **"The Tenth Man"** a group of nine Jews in a railway car seeks the participation of a tenth to complete the *minyan* required for one of their number to say a mourner's prayer for his dead son.[8] The tenth man is an assimilated Jew, reluctant to join, but convinced to do so by another who says he will reward him with a good story. When the prayer is completed the storyteller tells three brief anecdotes that shame the tenth man and drive him out of the car at the next stop. The storyteller is especially important in the railway car, the forum *par excellence* in Sholom Aleichem. The railway brings a mixing of strangers, enforced idleness, a necessary suspension of business, and the convenient punctuation of stops. As we have seen, travel away from home is the frequent occasion of adventure. At the very least people meet, speak, and respond to each other in a way that is itself the action of a story.

In the **Railway Stories** the train brings the familiar author-listener together with the speakers whose stories he records. In **"The Station at Baranovitch"** the general chatter of disasters cited at the beginning of chapter 3 resolves itself into the telling of a single tale. The voice of a speaker interrupts the summary of the narrator. The long list of problems ends with the infamous name of Azev, the revolutionary terrorist and police agent known to English readers as Razumov in Conrad's *Under Western Eyes*. The interrupting voice picks this name out of the air and repeats it with his own eccentric pronunciation, "Aszhev." He has a tale of treachery that puts Azev in the shade. His pronunciation and his pauses remind us that we are reading the story of a man speaking to a crowd of Jews on a train as well as listening to a story about an innkeeper who is helped to escape from prison and punishment by his generous townsmen. From abroad the innkeeper sends more and more outrageous requests for help, finally blaming his benefactors for his exile. Chief among these benefactors is the speaker's grandfather whose plight is the subject of the story. Eventually the ingrate, having received money at every request, tries outright blackmail. He will tell the officials how he escaped if the grandfather does not send more money. At each stage of the storytelling, as the tension mounts with every request, the speaker tantalizes his listeners by pausing for a cigarette or leaving the car for something to eat at a station buffet. During these pauses we return to the narrator who describes the tension among the anxious audience. As readers we respond both to the speech act that takes place on the train as an event in itself and to the series of events that the speaker describes. Both are exasperating. When and how will it end? Finally in the station at Baranovitch, when the story seems to have reached its crisis, the speaker jumps up, announces that he has reached his destination, and leaves the train with his story unfinished and his audience unsatisfied. We have come to regard storytelling in two ways, but on reflection we see that both stories are essentially the same. It is as if a con man for reasons of his own were to tell a story about a con man.

In **"The Station at Baranovitch"** part of the confidence trick lies in the speaker's ability to convince his audience that only he could finish the story. When he begins to speak everyone in the car is sure he has heard the story before, that it had happened in his town, but the speaker assures them that it is all historical fact, once recorded in his town hall which, unfortunately, burned down with all of its records. The kind of story told by the traveler is a familiar folktale which really belongs to the community of listeners. What the listeners do not know is how it will be concluded in this case, and before they can find out, this story gives way to another story, the story of how a trainload of Jews was cheated of a conclusion. The story reminds its readers of the place the storyteller takes in the community of Jews. It was certainly part of Sholom Aleichem's sense of his own place among his listeners that Baranovitsh is the town where his own reading tour was cut short by his illness in 1908 shortly before the story was written.

"Sixty-six," written a year later, is a story told in the same form. The title refers to a card game favored by a stranger, described by the narrator as "a respectable man, a traveling salesman like me."[9] In the course of describing his own addiction to cards the stranger tells a number of anecdotes about other addicts who have been fleeced by strangers on trains. Finally, he describes the time that he himself was the victim of a team that pretended to be a father and a son. In the story the son plays foolishly at first, draws the speaker in, and then takes him for all he has. When they arrive in Odessa and the speaker realizes that he has been duped, the young man disappears and the old man remains to deny every claim of the victim who is made to seem mad. The story has by this time taken so many turns that we may have forgotten the brief frame in which it is lodged. We may be reading the story on only one level, attending only to the frustration and loss of the speaker, until we return to the frame narration at the very end. Having finished his series of stories, the speaker pulls out a deck of cards and suggests a game. The narrator, noting the ease with which his companion handles cards, brushes him off. The storytelling was the ploy of a con man softening up a victim. The reader is consciously or unconsiously obliged to anatomize the act of storytelling, to disengage the constituent parts of the story. The fact that both **"Sixty-six"** and **"The Station at Baranovitch"** point to a confidence game serves to emphasize both the doubleness and the possible duplicity of stories that divide themselves into two verbal acts, one that we are calling speech, the other narration.

The doubleness of these two stories can be seen simply as a division of intention. The speaker within the story has one intention or outright design on his listeners. He is prepared to trick them in one way or another with his storytelling. *Skaz* becomes performance. However repetitious and wayward the telling, we come to recognize the design of the speaker. This recognition becomes part of a second intention, that of the author speaking through his "compositional equivalent," the listener and recorder. The author's intention is to tell a story about a certain act of storytelling. In the stories collected under the heading *Monologn* (*Monologues*) this doubleness is less obviously a question of the speaker's malign intention. The speakers in the monologues have no conscious design on their listeners. They are not tricksters. To start with they may be seeking advice, as in **"The Little Pot"** and **"A Bit of Advice,"** though it becomes clear that they do not mean to take it. Mostly they speak from a compulsion to speak. Speech takes the form of complaint. The obvious self-interest of the speaker in **"Sixty-six"** becomes a less conscious urge toward self-esteem. The speakers grope through indirection and repetition toward a recuperation of losses. They aim vaguely at self-aggrandizement, and they never succeed. **"Gitl Purishkevitch"** is trapped in the endless maze of czarist bureaucracy in an attempt to free her only son from the draft; the man in **"A Predestined Disaster"** is the victim of what appears to be appalling ingratitude from a family whose troubles he has inherited. Both defend themselves to the point where we as readers lose patience and turn our criticism away from the inequity that is being described to the process by which it is being described. In the end the speaker may force us to adopt the position of an absent antagonist, the bureaucrat, the neighbor, the child who is the apparent occasion of the complaint. From the point of view of original intention, the speech backfires; it has no other effect than to confirm and compound the predicament of the speaker. In two stories where advice is sought the supplicants succeed only in antagonizing their potential benefactors, a rabbi in **"The Little Pot"** and Sholom Aleichem, the author, in **"A Bit of Advice."**[10]

In **"The Little Pot"** Yente goes to the rabbi to ask if the pot that she has reserved for the cooking of meat has been made nonkosher by the spilling of a pot of milk in the same oven. She arrives at her question only after a long series of seemingly unrelated complaints and observations, bits of gossip and recrimination and, for her son, undiluted praise—all that has made the name Yente synonymous with talk. The rabbi is overwhelmed. Although we do not hear a word from him, he finally faints and the monologue ends with Yente's cry for the *rebbetzin* and water. We have here the characteristic double-story line, but the emphasis in **"The Little Pot"** falls squarely on the speech act itself. Neither the frame story of a rabbi who is talked to distraction nor the speaker's story of a contaminated pot is particularly important to the reader's response to the monologue. The pot is barely mentioned, and the fainting fit is just a convenient way to turn off what could be an endless flow of speech. The speech is everything, and it is the peculiar progress within Yente's sentences and then from subject to subject that draws and keeps the reader's attention.

The speech that overwhelms the rabbi is a rapid patter of language back and forth through repetitions and inversions that turn nearly every sentence into a pattern of balanced phrases that mount and progress through the addition of more words. She begins by introducing her problem in a forthright way: "Rabbi! Ikh vill aykh fregen a shalleh vill ikh aykh" (Rabbi! I want to ask you a question want I to [ask] you). Already we note a dangerous tendency to prolixity. The balanced parentheses of pronoun-verb-verb-pronoun betray her natural tendency toward a rhythm of speech that approaches song and demands return and repetition. She continues:

Ikh bin Yente bin ikh, Yente di Kurelapnitshke.
Ikh handel mit eyer handel ikh,
mit eyfes, mit genz, un mit katshkes.
Ikh hob mir mayne shtendige kaynetes, hob ikh mir.

I am Yente am I, Yente the Poultrywoman.
I deal in eggs deal I,
in chickens, in geese, in ducks.
I have my regular customers have I.

Each additional line continues the pattern of redundancy. Yente is Yente the Poultrywoman; by definition pountrywomen deal in eggs, chickens, geese, and ducks. Yente's life is like her speech in that a great deal of energy is expended with little to show for it. Her speech is a treadmill made to work double time:

Khap ikh a dreyerel, khap ikh,
a mol do a mol dorten
do genumen, dort gegeben, dort gegeben, do genumen—
me' drayt zikh . . .

Grab I three kopeks grab I,
sometimes here sometime there,
here take, there give, there give, here take—
one turns about . . .

Repetitive phrases grow by the accretion of new words that stimulate new associations. Having introduced herself and described the way she makes a living and what kind of a living she makes she explains that she must work double time because she is a widow, but she knows what work is because when she was young she worked with her mother who was called Basheh, Basheh the Candlemaker, she was a candlemaker: "Meyn mama . . . Basheh hot zi gehaysen, Basheh di Lekhtsiherin, zi iz geven a lekhtsiherin. . . ." In those days candles were used and not these new lamps with the faulty chimneys which reminds her of the chimney she cracked last week. So it goes. She catches herself: "Yo, akegen vos iz dos gekumen tsu der?" (O, how did we get around to that?). This is the habitual phrase by which she recalls herself to what she believes to be her subject. Speakers in *skaz* are incorrigible wanderers whose most familiar verbal ties are the phrases by which they get back on the track.

Once back on the track Yente returns to the early death of her husband, which followed a cough that was very poorly diagnosed by the doctors who were also mistaken in the case of Yokel, son of Aaron the *Shokhet.* She, to return to the subject, is a widow left with a house to share with tenants, one a deaf old man and the other a flour dealer named Gnessi and her husband and children. Gnessi is a shrew who nags her husband and keeps a sloppy house, *fartiopet un farshliopet,* a real mess. Proverbial and homely speech makes this frequent appeal to rhyme. Her own cleanliness merits more emphatic rhyme:

bay mir iz reyn, bay mir is sheyn,
bay mir iz tsikhtig, bay mir iz likhtig

which shorn of rhyme means clean, lovely, immaculate, bright.

Gnessi's children are uncontrollable rascals, always clambering about the oven, just the opposite of her own Dovidl, the orphan, a scholar and sickly. The boy is the image of his father. He studies and coughs. She lists all of his accomplishments and all of his ailments. Once he was sick for six weeks when he was frightened by what he took to be a ghost but what turned out to have been Lippa the Water Carrier coming home at dusk in a white fur coat. Yente exercised all the folk customs that are known to prevent death—she spoke magic words over him, sold him and bought him back again, changed his name with the addition of Chaim, meaning life. Her account is passionate and pathetic. Here her propensity for crude rhythm and rhyme takes a sad, lyric turn: "un treren—treren, ver redt fun treren?" (and tears—tears, who speaks of tears?) After his sickness Yente is required by the doctor to give Dovidl hot chicken soup made from at least a quarter of a chicken every day. The heroic acquisition of this quarter chicken brings to mind the books that she also gets for him in spite of the doctor's recommendation that he read less. Clearly something is happening that Yente does not understand. David goes to *kheder* all day and reads all night. But what does he read? She does not know. She cannot read. He gives her lists of books to borrow from her rich customers. The doctor tells her that the boy must not stay up all night with these books. "If he is fated to be a doctor, tell him he'll become a doctor a few years later." "What kind of a nightmare is that?" Yente asks herself. "Why not a governor?" When she tells her son what the doctor has said, he blushes fiercely and asks that they change doctors. "Don't even talk to him anymore." As far as Yente knows, her boy is bound for the yeshiva and religious study. But the doctor has seen David's books and knows otherwise. Again a new world creeps in, children change, and parents are left in the dark. The basic irony that surrounds *skaz* resides in the limited information of the speaker and the absence of any other point of view but for what enters through oblique allusion.

In spite of the apparent digression and repetition Yente is beginning to advance on her subject. It is the making of David's soup that is the occasion for the visit to the rabbi. One day Gnessi chooses to make dumplings—*balabekhkes*—with milk on the shared stove. Yente pauses for a little disquisition on Gnessi's cooking before she returns to the fatal hour. Gnessi's husband returns home early, they quarrel, and in the middle of things, the milk is spilt. A flurry of curses follows. David's soup is ruined. No great loss. Yente has a few other things around the house. But what of the pot? She has only one. Once she had three. She is in the act of describing the demise of the other two when the rabbi faints.

It is clear that Yente's case could be stated more simply. She emits a full-scale *apologia pro sua vita* where a brief statement would have been sufficient. It is characteristic of Sholom Aleichem's monologists that they reach toward broad confession or complaint no matter what the occasion. And yet the selection is not entirely random. Yente's speech is a thesis without a thesis sentence; it is an argument that hinges on hidden principles. In "Haircut" every detail contributes to an explanation of Jim Kendall's death, and yet it is not clear that the speaker fully understands what he has said. He gives us all the information that we need to know that Paul Dickson killed Kendall as punishment for shaming Julie Gregg and that Doc Stair uses his job as coroner to cover up the murder. Similarly all of Yente's digressions contribute to an explanation of the domestic chaos in which the crisis occurs. Extenuating circumstances may influence the rabbi's decision. She certainly wants to hear that her pot can be used again. Even if the pot has been contaminated, the process by which it can be made kosher again is not difficult.[11] But, as Zborowski and Herzog add, "running to the rabbi is time consuming and difficult." Surely Yente is seeking a favorable judgment, and yet we cannot be sure that she has exercised any conscious control over what she has said. As to her son, she says more than she fully understands. Ultimately a sense of order may be shared by the author and the reader but it is not known to the speaker and may be lost on the listener. The listener may know better, but the speaker is lost in a maze, and we are above

it. The difference between the speaker's knowledge and ours is a condition of the irony that controls Sholom Aleichem's monologues.

When we speak of an author and a reader of *skaz* we refer to creatures whose existence cannot be inferred from the text. What the text gives us instead is a dialogue where one person assumes the role of speaker and the other of listener. We have said that in this process the effaced author becomes something more akin to the listener than the speaker. Sholom Aleichem assumes that role in one of the monologues and in the Tevye stories.

In **"A Bit of Advice"** a young man comes to Sholom Aleichem precisely because he is "such a prolific writer." As it happens, the advice that he seeks is not literary. He assumes rather naively that a prolific writer will know everything there is to know about life, and it is about his life that he wishes to be advised. But before Sholom Aleichem comes to understand the nature of the visit, he assumes that the young man is a writer with a manuscript in hand. The frame of a *skaz* narrative becomes a vehicle for explicit literary criticism. The beleaguered writer guesses that he will be subjected to a novel in three parts, "as long as the Jewish Exile," or a drama in four acts with characters who bear conveniently allegorical names, or an elevated ode to Zion with a quatrain that he offers up as parody. In other words, he names everything but the short story that adheres to everyday experience written in everyday Yiddish. This event, Sholom Aleichem seems to say, is the source of his own stories. Storytellers come to him like uninvited guests; they hail him on the road; they sit down next to him on railway trains. They speak to him, and he writes down what he hears.

In the course of asking whether or not he should divorce his wife, the young man in **"A Bit of Advice"** reveals all of his own snobbery, jealousy, and avarice and most of all his inability to accept advice or make a decision. The young man's chronic indecision is reflected by his inability as a speaker to say what he means: "I happen to be a young man from a little village. I mean, the village isn't such a little village, it's a rather good-sized village, one could very well say a town—but on the other hand, compared to your town, it is still a village." All this goes into the choice of *shtetl* or *shtodt,* a distinction that might be important if he were discussing rights of residence with a Russian official but which means nothing here. This indecision follows him through the story. When Sholom Aleichem gives him the advice that he has sought, the young man cannot follow it and reverses his position. Sholom Aleichem tries to accommodate him and is met with another reversal and then another and another until the writer rises in a fury and tries to throw his visitor out.

The narrator of this story is the listener but he is not simply the "compositional equivalent" of the author. Insofar as the story is by Sholom Aleichem we are to think of the narrator as the author or at least as a writer. In that case what the persistent speaker interrupts is the proper work of the writer which is not the giving of marital advice but the writing of stories. The young man's misconception of that task constitutes an impertinent imposition which he prolongs with his exasperating tendency to digress and his inability to make a decision. Several times Sholom Aleichem tries to force the young man to come to the point: "'If you don't mind, young man,' I interrupted him in midsentence." This variation of the uninterrupted speech is the author's joke at the expense of his own favored medium. His art is no contrivance; it is the irrepressible popular voice that accosts him and imposes itself upon him through no fault of his own.

In his best known sequence of stories Sholom Aleichem describes a far more congenial relation with his equally irrepressible friend Tevye. Little need be said about the relationship of Tevye and Sholom Aleichem in these stories. The frames are of very little importance as stories; the authorial figure, Sholom Aleichem, is almost totally effaced. His shadowy, silent presence and his identification as a writer of books account for the form of the stories. In the early stories the two men meet in vaguely specified or unspecified places and Tevye begins to speak. Tevye uses their infrequent and accidental meetings as the occasion for an explanation of what has happened in the interval. As the stories become more gloomy Tevye's premature aging is what requires explanation. When he comes to the story of Chava, the apostate, Tevye enjoins his friend not to repeat what he is about to tell him:

> I would not repeat it to anyone else, for while the pain is great, the disgrace is even greater. But how is it written? *"Shall I conceal it from Abraham—Can I keep any secrets from you?"* Whatever is on my mind I shall tell you. But one thing I want to ask you. Let it remain between you and me. For I repeat: the pain is great, but the disgrace—the disgrace is even greater.

When he has concluded his story he repeats his request: "Be as silent as the grave concerning this. Don't put what I told you into a book." It may be a sign of Tevye's utter desolation at this point that even his confidential friend betrays him by recording his shame, but we would not say that **"Chava"** is the story of that betrayal. Sholom Aleichem's candor is at best a minor confirmation of the impression that the story derives from an extraliterary source. The last two stories are in part travel stories. Sholom Aleichem and Tevye meet while traveling, and Tevye must describe the events that uprooted him. **"Tevye Goes to Palestine,"** written in the period of the *Railway Stories,* brings them together in a train compartment, but unlike **"The Station at Baranovitch"** and **"Sixty-six"** the encounter contributes very little to the total effect of the story. If the frames are unimportant in the Tevye stories, the fact that there is a listener is very important. The Tevye stories are to be regarded as speech; speech requires a listener. In order to give the impression of locution one must preserve the idea of an interlocutor, however silent. The presence of the listener is the occasion for the speaking voice, and it is through the preservation of the speaking voice that Sholom Aleichem was able to make a living literature out of the "jargon."

Nearly every sentence in the Tevye stories is impressed with the rhythm of spoken Yiddish and the peculiar wealth of allusion that characterizes the speaker. Tevye is fond of quotation, and his speech is most lively when he is quoting himself. Throughout the stories Tevye speaks to Sholom Aleichem, and much of what he says is quotation of what he has said at other times. When he tells Sholom Aleichem how he first gained the thirty-seven rubles from the grateful family in Boyberik, he recreates the scene outside the *datcha* where they live. The rich man turns to Tevye and asks who he is. "Where do you live. What do you do for a living? Do you have any children? How many?" Naturally Tevye lights on the last question. His reply is filled with proverbs, unfinished Hebrew phrases, quotations from prayer and from his wife put side by side, all punctuated by the habitual "ikh zog . . . zog ikh" (I say).

> Kinder? zog ikh. Nit tsu farzindiken. Oyb itlikher kind, zog ikh, iz verteh, vi meyn Golde vill mir eynreden, a milyon, bin ikh reykher fun'm gresten g'vir in Yehupetz. Der khesoren, zog ikh, vos orem iz nit reykh, krum iz nit gleykh, azoi vi in posak shteyt: ha-mavdil bein koydish la-khoyl. Ver es hot di klinger dem iz voyl.

> Children? I say. Not to commit a sin [but] if each child, I say, is worth, as my Golde wants to convince me, a million, I am richer than the richest man in Yehupetz. The fault, I say, is that poor is not rich, crooked is not straight, as it is written, "He who separates the sacred from the profane . . ." for the one with the coins things go well.

Tevye's response is never direct. In this case the abundance of children is immediately associated with his poverty, the degree of which is supported by a typically rhymed Yiddish proverb, the truth of which is confirmed by the greater authority of a phrase from Hebrew prayer. *Hamavdil bein koydish la-khoyl* comes from the final prayer of the Sabbath, the *Havdalah,* marking the division between the holy Sabbath and the profane week. This division is now compared to the division of rich and poor, crooked and straight, but the Hebrew phrase also reaches forward by rhyme into the next phrase for *la-khoyl* in the Ashkenazic pronunciation rhymes with the Yiddish *voyl.* In Tevye's speech sacred and profane are rarely divided. One flows into the other in fragments often drawn together, as they are here, by rhythm and rhyme and free association. Further along in the same speech he talks himself into resignation: "God is a father. He has his way, that is, he sits above and we suffer below. We labor, we drag logs; do we have any choice?" "Vi di gemorah zogt: bamakom she-ein ish—iz a hering fish." (As the gemorah says: in a place where no man is—herring is a fish.) It is true that gemorah refers to the place where no man is as a place where whoever is there will have to serve, that is, have to become a man. Similarly wherever no other fish is available—that is, among poor people—"herring is a fish," herring will do. Elliptical phrases and eccentric connections draw the sacred and the profane together continually in Tevye's speech.

Tevye's insistent "zog ikh" calls repeated attention to the fact that this is speech, that this gymnastic verbosity is the result of a man speaking. We are reminded with every attribution of himself and every *b'kitzur* ("in short") that we are overhearing actual, extemporized speech. It is the total impression left by this style that makes it "hard to think of [Sholom Aleichem] as a 'writer'."

III *Written* Skaz

Skaz is, by definition, speech, and when we read it we read a text that pretends to be a transcription of speech and thus creates what Boris Eixenbaum called "the illusion of *skaz*." An earlier approach to an authentic use of language unmediated by the presence of an author created the epistolary novel, a form that has been given special favor by writers of *skaz*. Epistolary *skaz* differs very little from the speech act that it generally echoes. Much of the humor of the letter lies in the writer's inability to distinguish between written and spoken language. Words are spelled the way they sound. No concessions are made to prose style. Epistles in this style generally flow between two of a kind. Thus the characteristic silent listener in oral *skaz* is eliminated. The form continues to recreate an act of communication between a first and a second person, but the second person is allowed to respond in kind and is also subject to our sense of ironic distance.

Ring Lardner's "Some Like Them Cold" is a correspondence between a Mr. Lewis and a Miss Gillespie following a brief meeting at the train station in Chicago.[12] The letters pass between Chicago where she stays and New York where he has gone. We infer from the letters the story of their relationship which rises through a series of lures and flirtations and then vanishes when Mr. Lewis, who has become "Dear Mr. Man," finds another woman in New York and becomes "Dear Mr. Lewis" again. In the last letter she rebuffs him in a way that clearly terminates the series. It is amusing to see the way the relationship develops without narrative interpretation. Soon we project upon the letters our own sense of their direction and wait for the correspondents to catch on and adjust. What we see is two people pluming themselves with words, often falling flat in ways that neither recognizes. The writers characterize themselves through a series of written tics comparable to the repeated earmarks of oral *skaz*. Miss Gillespie uses quotation marks when she wishes to call attention to words that are not quite in her vocabulary: "Don't you love Service or don't you care for 'highbrow' writings?" The marks seem to mean that the word is on loan from somebody else; she is not entirely responsible for what she says within those marks. They never mean that she is quoting her correspondent. When she does cite something that he has said she expurgates it in a way that recommends her gentility. His comment on the heat of New York: "The reason why New Yorkers is so bad is because they think they are all ready in H——" meets her qualified approval: "I laughed when I read what you said about New York being so hot that people thought it was the 'other place.'" In his letters "girlies" or "pips" try to "make me" but he resists. She is "glad you have not 'fallen' for the 'ladies' who have tried to make your acquain-

tance in New York." When Mr. Lewis describes the woman that he is about to marry it is clear that he was not looking for the kind of refinement advertised by Miss Gillespie. In this case, "distants," as Mr. Lewis would write it, does not make the heart grow fonder, and letters are not enough.

Sholom Aleichem appeals to an audience that recognizes popular locution and is amused by it in a way that people who are completely bound within the style of life and speech are not.

—James Butwin and Frances Butwin

The fragility of the epistolary relationship in Lardner's story is a function of the characteristic deviations from the standards of written prose. That is, both writers show that they would be more at home talking than writing. Mr. Lewis spells as he speaks, and Miss Gillespie requires quotation marks to render the tone of what she wants to say. The letters will not last. They should be talking to each other, not writing. Miss Gillespie is, by her own admission, "a great talker." Her sister "would be perfectly satisfied to just sit in the apartment and listen to me 'rattle on.'" Here the quotation marks seem to represent her sister's part in the dialogue. Written *skaz* records a yearning for speech.

Sholom Aleichem's Menakhem-Mendl stories take the form of several series of letters that pass between the husband who has taken temporary residence first in Odessa and then in Kiev and his wife Sheyne-Sheyndl in Kasrilevke.[13] We are not surprised to find that Mendl is first of all a talker. He describes his qualifications as an insurance salesman: "The most important thing is—language, the gift of speech. An agent has to know the language. That is to say, he has to know how to talk. Talk against time; talk at random; talk glibly, talk himself out of breath; talk you into things; talk in circles." For both husband and wife the will to speak overflows the boundaries of the letter into inevitable postscripts, and what they say poses obvious contradictions to the conventions of letter-writing. Both observe conventional salutations and valedictions of the kind that we also find in the correspondence between Sholom Aleichem and his father. Menakhem-Mendl begins:

> To my dear, wise, and modest helpmeet, Sheyne-Sheyndl, long may she live!
>
> Firstly, I am come to inform you that I am, by the grace of God, well and in good cheer. May the Lord, blessed be His name, grant that we always hear from one another none but the best, the most comforting, and the happiest of tidings—amen.

Often as not what follows is the report of an utter disaster, the happy tidings of another failure. Similarly Sheyne-Sheyndl begins: "To my dear, esteemed, renowned, and honored husband, the wise and learned Menakhem-Mendl, may his light shine forever." And she proceeds to decry him as an idiot. Her salutation continues: "In the first place, I want to let you know that we are all, praise the Lord, perfectly well, and may we hear the same from you, please God, and never anything worse." What she then says seems to exist in spite of what she has just said as a formal letter writer: "In the second place, I am writing to say that the children are down with the measles, all three of them, and I don't sleep nights, while he is sitting there drinking vinegar with licorice." Sometimes her habitual valediction is appropriate; sometimes it is not.

> So please dash a telegram off to me, come home as soon as possible, and put an end to all this, which is the heartfelt wish of your really devoted wife, Sheyne-Sheyndl.

> Rest assured that before you have time to look around, your partners will swindle you from head to foot, because you've always been a *shlimazl* and will remain a *shlimazl,* which is the heartfelt wish of your really devoted wife. . . .

What she really wants to say remains peculiarly detached from what she is obliged to write.

Sandwiched between the formal pieties of the introductions and conclusions are all of the peculiar tics and locutions that characterize the correspondents. Sheyne-Sheyndl calls attention to her husband's willful separation from his family by speaking to him as if she were speaking about him. "He is living happily ever after in Odessa; he is riding around on springs, bathing in big and little fountains. . . . What else does he want!" Her use of the third person recreates her own greatest fear, that other people are talking about them. It is also a way of recreating the conversations that go on between her and her mother whose responses to Mendl are constantly quoted by her daughter. "Vi zogt di Mama" (as mother says), is the phrase that repeatedly opens the maternal store of proverbs.

Phrases that recur in Menakhem-Mendl's letters all serve to reflect the conditions of his life. He is what is called a *luftmensh,* he lives on air, especially in Yehupetz where his aerial existance is enforced by police restrictions which do not allow him as a Jew to reside within the city. Every night he disappears to Boyberik or, later, to a rooming house where frequent raids send him into hiding. During the day he lives on the streets, harassed by the police when he cannot afford to sit in a cafe and be harassed by impatient waiters. He chases after a living on the fringe of the bourse, does his business on the streets and at cafe tables; he is constantly on the move. He lives among a whole population of Jews whose basic instability draws them to fly-by-night schemes. One must get rich quick or not at all. The speed and mobility of the life accounts for the haste in which the letters are written. "And since I am pressed for time, I must cut this short," he writes toward the conclusion of each, before the valediction and the inevitable postscript.

All of Mendl's schemes begin with high hopes and end in disaster. We are given a foretaste of the fall with the phrases that accompany every dream vision: "eyn khesoren iz nokh; iz ober di tsoreh . . ." (There's only one problem, one drawback . . .). In one letter both phrases appear and thus impose two conditions that would make a deal impossible if it were not already a swindle. He has a chance to sell some valuable land. The first problem is that it is somewhere in Siberia—"Simber" to Mendl—beyond the reach of railroads; the second problem is the want of a customer. Only Brodsky could afford it, and Brodsky is unapproachable. The role that Mendl is to take in these recurrent pipedreams is that of the middleman, and it is in the middle that he is always caught, "un ikh oykh b'sukhm" (and I among them): "Manufacturers are pining away for a penny, capitalists are holding back, and brokers are out of a job, *un ikh oykh b'sukhm.*"

Menakhem-Mendl and Sheyne-Sheyndl are bound to repeat the pattern of their letters through each cycle of adventures. Mendl's hopes are high; his wife is skeptical; Mendl's hopes are crashed to bits; his wife's fears are confirmed and she admonishes him to give up and come home. Sometimes he heads for Kasrilevke, but generally even before that he has landed on another opportunity. He speculates in the fluctuation of currency; he is a broker in houses and forests and oil fields; he tries to be a writer, a marriage broker and an insurance agent. Mendl's Messiah is money, and his Messianic vision is definitely apocalyptic. Therefore nothing can destroy his hopes. His great expectations seem to thrive on destruction, and in his letters the exaggeration of one spawns the other. The letters are an exercise in superlative despair and its twin, hope:

> I want you to know, my dearest wife, that the end of the world has come! The rates of exchange which arrived from Petersburg are so terrible that everything went dark before our eyes. It hit us like a bolt of lightning, like a bomb. . . . The speculators have fled, disappeared into thin air, *un ikh oykh b'sukhm.* The stock market is finished! . . . It's like the destruction of the Temple!

By the postscript of the same letter despair is turned about: "After your house burns down, you're bound to get rich. I believe that's true, and after the kind of catastrophe we've had, one could do wonderful business." As readers we tend to correct Mendl's turbulent flights. The letters are written with an imperfect knowledge of the world. When he writes he does not know the sequel of the events that he describes. He is in the middle of them. Only the amusing story of his career as a matchmaker is told as one long narrative where he, as both the teller of the tale and its protagonist, must withold the surprise ending. Otherwise the stories are split into letters written during the course of the events they describe. The timing of events within this format limits his knowledge of a sequel that is perpetually hidden in the future and therefore subject to blind hope. The biographical fact of his Kasrilevkite education insures the further limitation of his knowledge of the great world into which he is thrown. Mendl's misconception of the world gives way to double irony when it is filtered through the mind of his wife and returned to him, transformed again, in the next letter.

Menakhem-Mendl is a familiar type of comic figure, the innocent cast into the great world where he immediately but only partially absorbs its ways and its language. He relays this new information to his wife who throws it back in his face transformed by her own combination of shrewd criticism and innocence. Mendl announces that he has become *a shrayber*; to her he is a *rayber*; he describes the process that will make his fortune in the money market as *stalazhen,* a concept that neither he nor the reader can ever thoroughly grasp but which apparently means that he will buy foreign currency cheap and sell it dear after this "stallage." For his wife *stalazhen* become *delezhansen,* and he patiently explains her mistake:

> Stalazhen iz nit, vi du rufst es, delezhansen. Delezhansen iz dos, vos me' fort oif dem keyn Radomishl un keyn Zhitomir.

> Stallages are not, as you call them, diligences. Diligences are the things one rides to Radomishl and to Zhitomir.

When Mendl stops dealing with "London" in Odessa—that is, speculating on the difference between the ruble and the English pound—and moves to Yehupetz where he deals in "papers"—that is, speculates on the stock exchange—and then decides to become a broker, Sheyne-Sheyndl recalls for him his failures "mit London, mit di papierlikh—papers—mit di pipernotes." This last, an outgrowth of *papierlekh* grafted onto the stocks which he calls *liliputz* comes out meaning "vipers"—"papers and vipers," she gives him.

The imperfect absorption of foreignisms into written or spoken monologue is a further reflection of the amusing smallness of the world familiar to the speaker or writer. For Menakhem-Mendl the little bits of English, French, and German that he meets on the market are all transformed, and what he leaves unchanged comes back to him remade according to the lights of Kasrilevke. His description of Semedeni's Cafe—a real establishment in Kiev, owned by an Italian and frequented by Sholom Aleichem—returns to him as "Simi-Dina's"—"who in the world is she? In our town there used to be a midwife called Sima-Dina, but she passed away long ago." Foreign or otherwise unfamiliar words suffer a similar fate when put at the mercy of the speaker of oral *skaz.* Either they are reduced to nonsense or they are converted into something familiar.

It is Sheyne-Sheyndl's innocence and invective that combine to remake the world according to her own lights, and it is the medium of written *skaz* that allows Sholom Aleichem to exploit the irony of this transformed speech act. One person addresses another without the intervention of the greater intelligence conventionally associated with a narrator. The innocence of the husband and wife locked in

garbled communication is generally amusing and benign. It is just as well that they do not quite understand the full extent of the depravity of the cities. Elsewhere their limitations are more serious and, from the point of view of history, more exasperating. People can be made conscious of their time and place without the benefit of hindsight or travel. The unconsciousness of Menakhem-Mendl and Sheyne-Sheyndl is a source of comedy but it is also a serious limitation that they share with all of Sholom Aleichem's "kleyneh menshelekh mit kleyneh h'shages" (little people with little ideas).

For more than a decade after 1894 the Dreyfus Affair shook the French Republic and drew the attention of the world. Among Jews the accusation of Dreyfus and the public response that first brought the slogan "Death to the Jews" onto the streets of modern Europe had a profound effect. "I was transformed into a Zionist by the Dreyfus Affair," Theodor Herzl recalled shortly before his death in 1904.[14] When he began to organize the settlement of a Jewish state from the diaspora, Herzl, a Viennese journalist working in Paris, knew very little about the Jewish population of Russia and Poland, and he knew nothing of earlier attempts to develop the Zionist idea. Soon eastern Europe would know the case of Dreyfus and the ideas of Herzl well. The way these events and ideas filtered down to the likes of Menakhem-Mendl and his "wise and modest helpmeet" became a source of comedy for Sholom Aleichem. At the same time Kasrilevkite intransigence became a subject of wry satire.

Dreyfus is the subject of a joke told, but not entirely understood, by Sheyne-Sheyndl. Like most digressions from the main events of their lives, the exchange on the subject of Dreyfus is carried out in postscripts. First Sheyne-Sheyndl tells her husband the story of the local "mademoiselle" who has rejected every suitor until she is finally brought one that seems to her liking. The young people are left alone:

> Says the bride to the fiancé, "What are they saying about Dreyfus in your town?" Says he, "Which Dreyfus?" Says she to him, "You don't know which Dreyfus?" Says he, "No, what does he deal in? . . ." So she burst out of the room and faints, and the poor fiancé has to return to his town in disgrace. . . .

> And by the way, since you are among people of the world, will you please explain to me who is this Dreyfus, and why is the whole world making such a fuss over him?

One would think that the telling of this little story would require that the teller understand the allusion. But Paris is outside the boundaries of Sheyne-Sheyndl's world. She knows just enough to know that Dreyfus is not a local businessman. Beyond that she refers to her worldly husband in Yehupetz. Menakhem-Mendl's clarification of the case makes it even more complicated than it really was, if that is possible. To the intrinsic difficulties of the facts Menakhem-Mendl adds the twists and turns of uncorrected speech that are associated with *skaz* as a form:

This is how it goes. It seems that in Paris there was a Captain Dreyfus; that is, a captain who was called Dreyfus. There was also Esterhazy who was a major. (A major is bigger than a captain, or maybe it's the other way around—a captain is bigger than a major.) Anyhow, he was a Jew—Dreyfus, I mean. And Esterhazy, the major, was not a Jew. So he went and wrote a *bordereau*.

He follows the story through the comings and goings of Zola and the generals and the lawyers until it begins to sound very much like one of his own business deals. Finally "he was judged guilty and not guilty—make of that what you will. . . . Is the story of Dreyfus quite clear to you now?"

Sheyne-Sheyndl responds from Kasrilevke with questions which are really quite reasonable if we consider the clarity of the report and the narrowness of the world in which she lives. "How can a Jew become a captain?" she asks, since in the Russian Army promotion was impossible for a Jew. "And what is that *bondero* which they keep tossing from one to another?" The event itself diminishes into trivia and is never fully understood. Sholom Aleichem would repeat the ironic reception of "Dreyfus in Kasrilevke" in a story of that name written two years later (1902) and collected under the heading "Little People with Little Ideas."[15] Kasrilevke receives news of the world through Zeydl, the one man in town who subscribes to a newspaper. The first response to the arrest is simple: "What won't a Jew do to make a living?" But when they discover that Dreyfus was falsely accused and when the case is reopened, Kasrilevke rises to the occasion. How then do "little people" assimilate the news of the world? By translating it into local and domestic terms:

"Ah, I would have liked to have been there when he met his wife."

"And I would have liked to see the children when they were told, 'Your father has arrived.'"

When Zeydl is forced to report the ambiguous verdict—guilty and not guilty—his townsmen do not blame the judges or the generals or the French people but Zeydl himself, because he is closest at hand. They do not believe him.

Zionism meets the same skeptical reception in Kasrilevke. It must be remembered that this cycle of Menakhem-Mendl letters was written only two years after the first Zionist Congress at Basel in 1897. The movement was not new, but the international organization was. The impact was immense and immediate throughout eastern Europe. Sholom Aleichem was already contributing stories to the Zionist journal *Der Yid,* and he later attended several of the International Congresses. The new movement enters the letters through the limited vision of the protagonists. Sheyne-Sheyndl asks Mendl for more information: "They say that in Yehupetz people are getting registered for the Holy Land. Anybody who pays a deposit for forty kopeks will go. . . ." Presumably the forty kopeks represents a donation rather than a registration, but put in Sheyne-Sheyndl's

way it sounds like the kind of lunatic scheme that might engage her husband who nonetheless recognizes that she is describing Zionism. "This is a very noble idea, even though they don't seem to think much of it on the Yehupetz exchange." He would prefer that the Zionists spoke Yiddish and not Russian at their meetings. This Zionist tendency to abjure the use of the language of the Exile often alienated Yiddishists, and Mendl's position may reflect Sholom Aleichem's early uncertainty. But on the whole it is clear that the unspoken authorial sympathy rests with the new movement. Mendl admits that he has raised the subject with several companions at the exchange. They scoff. "Zionism! Doctor Herzl! What kind of business is that!"

America, no doubt, would be more to their liking, the land where business was known to thrive and whither one by one businessmen disappear. When we last hear from Menakhem-Mendl he too is going to America:

Why America all of a sudden? Because they say that in America life is good for Jews. They say that gold is rolling in the streets, yours for the picking. Their money is reckoned in dollars, and people—people are held above rubies. . . . Everybody assures me that in America I'll make good, please God—and they mean *good.* Everyone is going to America these days because there is nothing to do here. Absolutely nothing. All business is finished. Well, if everybody is going why shouldn't I go, too? What have I got to lose?

This is Mendl's last flight, and we are left to assume the usual conclusion. The American dream is for Sholom Aleichem the last fantasy of the Jewish *luftmensh.* A *boydem,* he would say, an empty attic, dreams returned to dust.

Irony in Sholom Aleichem begins as an attitude toward language. The choice to hold the spoken language up for inspection as something worthy of special attention already implies the distance required by irony. Sholom Aleichem appeals to an audience that recognizes popular locution and is amused by it in a way that people who are completely bound within the style of life and speech are not. Sholom Aleichem wrote for a society that was already uprooted, no longer living in the villages, rarely in the small towns, but mostly in big cities both within the Pale and beyond, in Warsaw and in America. Millions of his readers had been born in the world that he describes; most had left it, and it itself had changed. We look to his novels and his plays for a record of that change. In drama and long narration Sholom Aleichem steps out of the world in which he writes, the small world bound by the range of one voice speaking.

Notes

[1] Walter Benjamin, "The Story Teller," in *Illuminations: Essays and Reflections,* edited with an introduction by Hannah Arendt, trans. H. Zohn (New York: Schocken Books, 1969), p. 87.

[2] Roman Jakobson and Petr Bogatyrev, "On the Boundary Between Studies in Folklore and Literature," in *Readings in Russian Poetics:*

Formalist and Structuralist Views, ed. L. Matejka and K. Pomorska (Cambridge, Mass.: The MIT Press, 1971), p. 91.

³ Mixail Baxtine, "Discourse Typology in Prose," in *Readings in Russian Poetics,* pp. 176-96. Victor Erlich, "A Note on the Monologue as a Literary Form: Sholom Aleichem's *Monologn*—A Test Case," in *For Max Weinreich on his Birthday: Studies in Jewish Languages, Literature, and Society* (The Hague: Mouton & Co., 1964), pp. 44-50. For the entire discussion of *skaz* the authors are indebted to Professor Ann Banfield of the University of California at Berkeley. See her "Narrative Style and the Grammar of Direct and Indirect Speech," *Foundations of Language* 10 (1973), 1-39.

⁴ Baxtine, *Readings in Russian Poetics,* p. 186.

⁵ Max Weinreich, "Yiddishkayt and Yiddish: On the Impact of Religion on Language in Ashkenazic Jewry," in *Mordecai M. Kaplan Jubilee Volume* (New York: Jewish Theological Seminary of America, 1953), p. 512.

⁶ Justin Kaplan in the introduction to *Great Short Stories of Mark Twain* (New York: Harper and Row, 1967), p. vii. "The Celebrated Jumping Frog" appears on pp. 79-95 of that edition. Ring Lardner's "Haircut" appears in *"Haircut" and Other Stories* (New York: Charles Scribner & Sons, 1954), pp. 9-21.

⁷ Jakobson and Bogatyrev, *Readings in Russian Poetics,* pp. 91-92.

⁸ "The Tenth Man," in *Some Laughter, Some Tears,* pp. 153-57.

⁹ "Sixty-six," in *Old Country Tales,* pp. 214-25.

¹⁰ "The Little Pot," in *Tevye's Daughters,* pp. 180-91. "A Bit of Advice," in *Some Laughter, Some Tears,* pp. 131-44.

¹¹ *Life is With People,* p. 370.

¹² "Some Like Them Cold," in *"Haircut" and Other Stories,* pp. 169-90.

¹³ *The Adventures of Menahem-Mendl,* trans. T. Kahana (New York: G. P. Putnam's Sons, 1969). Yiddish examples come from the Morgnfrayhayt edition, II.

¹⁴ Quoted in Dubnow, *History of the Jews,* V, 671.

¹⁵ "Dreyfus in Kasrilevke," in *The Old Country,* pp. 260-64.

Hana Wirth-Nesher (essay date 1981)

SOURCE: "Voices of Ambivalence in Sholem Aleichem's Monologues," in *Prooftexts,* Vol. 1, No. 2, May, 1981, pp. 158-71.

[*In the following essay, Wirth-Nesher discusses the paradoxical nature of the monologue form in Aleichem's short fiction.*]

It is generally recognized that Sholem Aleichem's success as a writer rests upon an almost mystical intermingling of laughter and trembling, the combination of traits that Bellow singled out as characteristic of Jewish literature in general.¹ Since the appearance of his fiction in the 1880s, generations of readers have been asking themselves just how Sholem Aleichem manages to both move and amuse them simultaneously. A quick review of his most memorable characters—Motl the cantor's son, Tevye the dairyman, Menakhem-Mendl the *luftmentsh*—demonstrates that the human voice is the medium of his great achievement, for in spoken language he found his vehicle for expressing Jewish life in Eastern Europe at the turn of the century.² The best works of Sholem Aleichem are his first person addresses, sometimes delivered directly to the mediator-author seated in a third class train compartment or under a tree, or written compulsively to an unreceptive wife. In all cases, the variety and perfection of idiosyncrasy in each individual voice earn our admiration. It is the monologue, therefore, that gives shape to all of his work and any attempt to understand his art must address itself to the nature of that form. Moreover, Sholem Aleichem's monologues are some of the finest expressions of the general preoccupation with spokenness and the human voice in Yiddish literature.

Sholem Aleichem inherited the monologue form both from the general European literary tradition, where it is known specifically in Russian literary scholarship as the *skaz,*³ and from the Yiddish literary tradition, where the Maskilim deliberately used uncultivated Yiddish voices to underscore their satirical and didactic intent and to keep their Hebraist authorial personae well distanced from what they considered to be jargon.⁴ Dov Sadan has argued that Sholem Aleichem freed the monologue from its original purpose of satirizing and turned it into a vehicle for idiomatic Yiddish, thus making it an embodiment of the people themselves. As a result, the monologue enabled Sholem Aleichem to identify with a great variety of individualized types. Sadan is right to see in Sholem Aleichem's monologues a departure from satire and strict social criticism, but his monologues are more complex than their function as a vehicle for idiomatic Yiddish suggests. Dan Miron's recent theory that the monologues are really an idealized form of spoken Yiddish qualifies that of Sadan by taking it an important step further.⁵ As conscious artistic constructs that are decidedly not at one with the people uttering them, Miron observes, the voices are critical while also verging on parody. It is Miron's insistence on the artistic consciousness here that is valuable in understanding the force of the monologues.

Victor Erlich has pointed out that the best definition of the *skaz* is that offered by Hugh McLean, "a stylistically individualized inner narrative placed in the mouth of a fictional character and designed to produce the illusion of oral speech,"⁶ and by eliminating "inner," Erlich adds, we have a workable description of Sholem Aleichem's monologues. Erlich goes on to discuss how the monologue, as an anomalous verbal interaction, accounts for some of Sholem Aleichem's telling comic effects. The preposterousness of an interminable monologue where a dialogue would be normal, Erlich writes, always calls attention to the limitations of the monologist. As a result, we get a "worm's-eye view of reality." Sholem Aleichem's monologues, he concludes, exhibit a solipsistic world view, verbal isolation. While Erlich helps place Sholem Aleichem's monologues in a broad formal literary context, his theory of solipsism contributes to our understanding of only the comic effects of the monologues, not their tragic side. They are tragic, as I will discuss later, because they are attempts at communication, often failed attempts.

Looking beyond the comic dimension to the pathological, I. J. Trunk claims that Sholem Aleichem's monologists want to hear their own voices in order to objectify their own sense of self in reality.[7] Because speech is the only reality in which they can be free, they reach out to their own self-created illusions. The work, he says, reflects their desire and becomes a substitute for action; by talking, they "do." Trunk's assessment of the speakers' insecurity is borne out by the monologues, but his further Jungian conclusions about the "feminine" nature of the monologists resulting from their emotionalism and hypersubjectivity and hence expressing the "feminine" nature of the Jewish people in Eastern Europe are far less convincing. As I plan to point out, it is not just the garrulousness of the speakers that is unnerving; it is the hidden substance of their speech, which occasionally the listeners, and we the readers, are able to detect. As Dan Miron has noted, the comedy of the monologues depends on the reader's being superior in intellect to the speaker. In other words, a gap exists between the cultivated and uncultivated mind, the former seeing history in an ordered cause-and-effect relationship and the latter seeing it as random, disconnected and illogical.[8] The distinction is a valuable one and, I believe, confirms the point that the monologues are critical artistic fabrications and not the product alone of a sensitive literary stenographer rendering the voice of the people. But while our superiority as listeners may indeed contribute to our laughter, it does not account for our sense of dread at the darker side of the monologues. They are not all comic in tone, and the ironic distance created by what Miron has accurately called the cultivated mind's view of the uncultivated one results in pathos and despair as often as it does in comedy. Moreover, the listener and reader are not always synonymous, as in **"Dos tepl"** (**"The Pot"**) and **"An eytse"** (**"A Piece of Advice"**), where a rabbi and the author's persona respectively are the listeners. The rabbi in **"Dos tepl"** may be more cultivated than the speaker, but he does not necessarily share our perspective.

In place of an emphasis on either comedy or pathology, I would suggest that there exists a general tension in all of the monologues, at times surfacing as comedy, at other times surfacing as pathos, and that this tension results not so much from cultivated listeners and uncultivated speakers as it does from a collision of traditionalists and secularists, conservatives and radicals, or a collective world view of absolutes coming up against an individualistic skeptical view. Since the speaker is usually a traditionalist of one type or another, he or she feels like an outsider to a changing world they no longer understand. Thus, comic techniques that are frequently repeated and that are applied to ambivalent subjects which have deeper meanings than appear on the surface can disturb as well as amuse

us. It is the relationship of this darker side to the comic, of the trembling to the laughter, that I wish to explore.

In all of the monologues collected in one volume by that name,[9] with the exception of the two set in America, there is a basic situation. A monologist lodges a complaint with the listener, who is either the reader or a specific implied persona, concerning an injustice which he or she has suffered and which threatens the speaker's traditional view of the world. If society would conform to what the speakers believe (or still want to believe) is a true world order, then their sufferings would cease. As I will attempt to demonstrate, these complaints against society and even against God are not always conscious. Frequently, there is a manifest content which is practical and prosaic in tone and conveys genuine protest only metaphorically, as in **"Dos tepl,"** for example, where the broken pot of a poor woman is really a vehicle for lamenting the unjust fatal illness of an only son. It is this contrast between form and content that may be comic at times, but the grievance is ultimately what is left with the reader.

Written between 1901 and 1916, the monologues range widely in voices of the Jewish community: men and women, rural and urban, poor, middle class, and wealthy, modest and proud, insecure and bold. What they have in common is dissatisfaction, a complaint that is almost a serious protest, and their garrulousness. The latter is their defense mechanism as it helps them avoid confrontation with their real criticism of their society and even of God's dealings with his people. Too terrified to follow their surface grievances to their logical conclusions because they might destroy the beliefs that define them and without which they cannot imagine life, the monologists intermittently retreat back into the homespun truths and familiar phrases of their collective world. They must do so to protect themselves, and they most often do so unconsciously. This movement between the individual's urge to cry out and his culture's role as both comfort and gag is expressed in the speaker's shifts in language, shifts that often seem illogical and comic, but are coherent on a deeper level. As a result, we have the familiar paradoxical response to Sholem Aleichem's monologues of laughter and sorrow.

To test this thesis about the dynamic of Sholem Aleichem's style, it is necessary to read one or two representative monologues. I have avoided selecting a monologue from one of the longer works, because a reading of one of the Tevye monologues, for example, necessitates an examination of the entire series. Instead, I have chosen "pure" monologues, each a piece that stands alone and yet appeared in a volume of monologues as part of Sholem Aleichem's collected works. Of these monologues, I have chosen **"Dos tepl"** and **"An eytse"** because they are expertly crafted and because Sholem Aleichem's male and female speakers differ in their concerns and it is worthwhile to look at one of each. In **"Dos tepl"** a widow appeals to a rabbi for advice about a pot that is no longer kosher, but what she actually wants is an answer to a question for more profound than that concerning dietary laws—the incapacitated pot is really her son and she wants to know why an only son of a widow should be stricken with an incurable disease. In **"An eytse"** a traditional young husband supported by his wife's family so that he can devote himself to religious study is threatened by a young doctor whose secular knowledge has made him prestigious, powerful, and, to the scholar's misery, more manly in the eyes of his young wife. Each monologue is addressed to an appropriate authority for the obvious problem facing the speaker—the *yidene* speaks to a rabbi about a possible violation of dietary law, the now unkosher pot, and the young man tells his tale to a writer, the persona Sholem Aleichem, because "you write about everything, therefore you must know everything." And as I will demonstrate, in both cases the authority figure and listener, when he can no longer bear the monologue, acts irrationally to put it and its threatening implications to an end.

An examination of the speech patterns of **"Dos tepl"** will reveal the polarity of formulaic phrases expressing customary thoughts and unconscious forbidden feelings. At first glance there may appear to be no pattern in the ramblings of the *yidene's* monologue, yet a close look reveals a regular set of transformations from latent meaning, a preoccupation with meaningless death or suffering, to manifest meaning, a practical reference to the community's events, values, and rituals; in other words, from the individual to the collective. The speaker is a widow whose only son seems to have inherited his father's fatal cough. She begins by telling the rabbi of her daily struggle to provide him with the chicken broth prescribed by the doctor. But the presence of her neighbor Gnese, her husband, and her brood, with whom she shares a room and stove, perpetually mocks her existence, for our speaker can find no justice in the blessings of a large family for a slovenly and inept housekeeper like Gnese, and widowhood with a sickly son for a diligent self-sacrificing woman like herself. Ostensibly, she has come to the rabbi because Gnese's negligence and untamed brood have caused some of the milk in the pot to spill onto the widow's only meat kettle, the one she uses for David's daily broth.

She begins in the rambling style common to many of the monologues by identifying herself: she is the wife of a scholar who died young and the daughter of Basye, the candlemaker, candles reminding her of more modern gas lights, reminding her of two lamps she broke recently. "O, akegn vos iz dos gekumen tsu reyd? Akegn dos vos ir zogt: yung geshtorbn," i.e. "Yes, how did this come up? Because of what you said: 'Died young.'"

In this opening digression, the tone of the entire monologue is set, but the order here is the reverse of what will occur from this point on. Here, the widow's digression has linked a broken glass with someone who died young, a foreshadowing of the broken pot as a metaphor for her dying son. In this instance, she goes from practical mundane reference, the broken lamp, to her real concern— premature death. In all of the following references she will allude to her genuine fears first and then rapidly shift to the practical. Yekl's sister died in childbirth, she remarks in one of her so-called digressions, always ending in suggestive ellipses at the end of a paragraph with the

formulaic, "Now how did this come up?—Oh, being a widow," that is, from mention of senseless death to her own practical problems. In discussing her tenants, one of these an old man mistreated by his children, she ends bitterly about old age. "How did this come up?" she asks, "Oh, neighbors" which brings her back to daily life again.

In Sholem Aleichem's monologues we recognize what is unique to his style; from Sholem Aleichem's voices emanate the laugher and trembling that we associate with his fiction.

—Hana Wirth-Nesher

In other such instances she goes from the death of a friend's wife, and an obligatory aside to the rabbi about God giving and God taking, to mention of her only son. By this time, the pattern has emerged and the reader can sense beneath the story of her neighbors and her pot the obsession with her child's health. In telling the story of David's serious fright from a ghost, actually caused by the innocent water carrier dressed in white, she goes from the shroud allusion to what she calls her real subject, health. Her bitter outcry against doctors, who won't or can't prescribe medication for David's cough, is really only an aside, she says, from her real subject, the famous chicken broth. But when she finally discusses her hated neighbor Gnese, the pattern surfaces most clearly. Gnese's children, she says, cough all day from their mother's bad cooking, specifically her excessive use of pepper. What she means, the widow assures us, is that Gnese is a *shlimazl,* can't do anything right. But the cough reference has alerted us. The inexplicable injustice suffered by the widow is now everywhere. The implication here is that while the widow slaves over her chicken broth in order to *prevent* her only son's cough, God has given many children to Gnese who actually *causes* them to cough. When the widow reports Gnese's screams that David should be a scapegoat for them all, being only one and therefore less important than her own children— "Zayn zol Dovidl di kapore far undz alemen"—she immediately leaves the topic of scapegoats and death for what she contends, once more, is her main concern—Jewish ritual and law—"from milk and meat on one oven, no good can come." ("Fun milkhiks mit fleyshiks in eyn oyvn kon keyn guts nisht aroys.") The metaphor of pot for son is made explicit in the widow's warning to Gnese before the disastrous damage to the vessel. "If you make this pot treyf, I shall be left without a pot at all, and without the pot I'm like a person without hands, because I have only *one* pot, that's all." Moreover, the use of the endearing diminutive *tepl* rather than *top* is another indication of the association between the pot and her children.

By the time the widow curses her neighbor for having ruined her pot, we know that she is cursing her as a mocking emblem of the great injustice she feels but dares not express openly. "How did this come up?" she asks, slipping right back into a proverb about Jewish domestic life, "Because pots and good housekeeping you can never have enough of."

The question that she poses to the rabbi is finally a thinly veiled protest about God's justice in the world. "When a pot breaks," she asks, "why is it always the whole one, the good one?" And then the veil drops. "I want to ask you, rabbi, why something is as it is. Picture two people walking, one is an only son, a one and only, a mother's source of trembling, and the other is. . . ." But the rabbi can bear no more, and the monologue ends with the widow calling for the rebbetzin to help revive her unconscious husband who has fainted, we now understand, before the desperate question to which he had no answer could be uttered, before the metaphor could be explicitly revealed.

The young man in **"An eytse"** is in a similar situation. His tale of indecisiveness and impotence is so powerfully threatening that the listener abandons his usual stance as observer and resorts to violence in order to terminate the monologue. Like the widow, the young man sees himself as the victim of injustice, not through enduring hunger or death, but through social humiliation. He is caught between two social norms: the traditional honored position of being a "kept" son-in-law by wealthy in-laws and the newer social system which permits a young doctor, because of his secular scientific knowledge, to examine and stimulate his wife who, in turn, regularly calls for him to relieve her anxiety attacks. And this while her parents generally assume that the depression and hysteria suffered by their daughter results from mistreatment by her husband. The young man curses a world that presents him with two equally disastrous alternatives: (1) the "modern" one: he can demand an end to the visits, thereby risking a divorce and a merciless reentry into the struggle for existence, attendant upon losing the wealth and honor that the marriage has given him; (2) or the "traditional" one: he can do nothing, retaining dignity at the price of daily humiliation. Just as the widow's monologue is marked by repeated references to death, this monologue contains repeated repressed desires for violence. Like a bull with a red mantle before him, the young man is incited to violence whenever he sees his mother-in-law's Turkish shawl as the woman runs in to comfort her only child and to call for the doctor. Each time he begins to fantasize violent action (physical or verbal)—to stamp on and tear the shawl to pieces, to defame the doctor with the truth about his practice, or to stab or drown himself—the author/listener interrupts in order to get him *back* to his subject. He is caught, as is the widow, between what he *should* feel, expressed in customary phrases such as the one about his in-laws, "May they live to be a hundred," and what he does feel, which he cannot express except as forbidden fantasy. This vacillation is more apparent whenever he attempts to qualify his statements: "I myself am from a small town . . . that is, the town isn't actually small" or "She [his wife] isn't exactly overly bright . . . that is, she's not a fool." One of the ironies of this monologue is that Sholem Aleichem the listener, who actually appears a few

times unlike the rabbi in the previous one, is originally relieved to discover that his visitor is not a writer, believing that an actual case history will be less troublesome than dealing with a manuscript of fiction. But the young man has come to Sholem Aleichem because he thinks writing about life makes one an expert on living, and it is this very inability to distinguish between action and fantasy that accounts for his anguished indecisiveness, and that threatens the listener who has before him a case of passive observation carried to an extreme. His only response, at the end, is itself violent—he wants to strangle the speaker.

In each of these two monologues, a grievance about the real world seethes below a manner of speech and a context that represents proper behavior, custom, and resignation to the rules of that society. And in each case, an inability to express this "why?" openly because it means accusing God or society, results in a double story and a tension that finally threatens the listener. In each of them, a personal grief gives way to collective reasoning, but the need to express that individual pain persists. Moreover, apart from the fear of heretical social outcry, both the *yidene* and the young man are afraid to face basic psychological truths about themselves—the mother is unable to face her imminent loss and the young husband is unable to face his humiliation. Their speech is an indicator of constant avoidance of such personal pain, for in each to face the psychological problem would entail admission of personal weakness. This is a step they cannot afford, because their sense of personal self apart from society is so undeveloped that without a social or cultural complaint they are left with nothing. Their grief must be the result of society's or God's injustice because they do not see themselves as individual beings. Sholem Aleichem depicts this avoidance of what they suspect is true in techniques that have frequently been singled out as the bases of his humor—garrulity, verbosity, repetitions, digressions, and a confusion of the literal and figurative.[10]

A close look at a passage from **"Dos tepl"** should illustrate how some of this works. The following excerpt is the penultimate paragraph of the monologue. It is immediately preceded by Gnese's outburst, "Your Dovidl should be sacrificed for all of us—he's only one!" and Yente's response, "What do you say to a slut like that? Shouldn't she have her mouth slapped shut with a wet towel?" It is followed by Yente's halting and indirect attempt to ask the rabbi her real question with her analogy of the two sons—"One is an only son, his mother trembles over him. . . ." The rabbi's fainting at this point ends the monologue.

> What were we saying? Yes, you said, *from dairy and meat on the same oven, no good can come.* . . . So there was the pot, see, upside-down, and the milk spilled all over the oven. Rabbi, I'm afraid that (God forbid) it may *just* have touched my pot, and then I'm a lost soul! Comes to think of it, though, how could the milk have reached it? My pot was standing there in a far corner, shoved away somewhere at the opposite end of the oven. But it's the old story—the chicken or the egg? Anything's possible; how can I be sure? Just

my rotten luck! What if . . . ? Rabbi, I'll tell you the honest truth, see. Never mind the broth. A broth is a broth. Of course, it breaks my heart—what will Dovidl eat, poor thing? But I'll probably think up something, probably. Yesterday, I bought some geese at the market, made some roasts to sell, so there are a few giblets left for Saturday—heads, innards, this, that. You can make something from it! But woe is me, Rabbi, how *can* I, if I don't have a pot? I'm afraid if you say the pot is *treyf*, I'm left without a pot, see; and without a pot, it's like I'm without a hand, because I've got only one pot. That is, as for pots, I used to have three meat pots. But then Gnese (may she sink into the earth) once borrowed a pot from me, a brand new pot, and then she goes and gives me back a crippled pot. So I said to her, "What kind of pot is this?" So she said, "It's your pot." So I said, "How come I get back a crippled pot when I gave you a brand new pot?" So she said, "Shut it. Don't yell like that, who needs your things? First of all, I gave you back a brand new pot. Second, the pot I took from you was a crippled pot. And third, I never even took a pot from you. I have my own pot, so get off my back!" There's a slut for you. . . .[11]

It begins with what has already been established throughout the monologue as a rhetorical strategy of avoidance, the shift from Gnese's allusion to David's death to the practical and proverbial advice about the dairy and meat dishes on one oven. Yente has once again avoided voicing her complaint and facing loss of life by retreating into the laws of her tradition. The illogical statement about what really worries her in the middle of the paragraph is also a rhetorical decoy. "Never mind the broth," she says, or for that matter what Dovidl will eat. What she fears is that she will be left without a pot, "because I've got only one pot." Here the pot is both a literal means of saving Dovidl's life, for without it she can't cook him his essential food, and the symbol of the boy himself, an only son who is marked for death. Her circular reasoning contributes to the motif: I'm not really worried about the broth; I'm actually worried about the pot because without it I can't cook the broth which I'm worried about not having. The missing assumption, of course, is that broth keeps David alive. On a manifest level, the pot is important, not David's broth. On a deep level they're the same thing.

The tone of this passage, characteristic of Sholem Aleichem's tone in almost all of the monologues, is simultaneously comic and tragic, the "laughter and trembling" that has become common coin in recent discussions of his fiction. But exactly how does the darkness seep through the comic voice? The comedy here is largely a result of faulty reasoning and inappropriate emphasis, but the particular logical flaws ironically reinforce the darker main theme of the work, as seen in the example of the broth. In other words, the repetition of rhetorical devices, which are initially enjoyed only for their comic effect, eventually strike the reader as also neurotic linguistic twitches, speech patterns that reflect social dislocation. They're still comic, but their cumulative effect is unsettling and disturbing as well. For example, by the time the reader laughs at Yente's report of Gnese's series of excuses about the pot, each cancelling out the previous one, the pot has already accrued meaning as a symbol of David. We are amused by

the illogic[12] but restrained by the vehicle of that illogical progression. The same is true for another comic technique in this passage, an inappropriate emphasis or displacement of serious comments in what appear to be light contexts. In the passage "Rabbi, I'm afraid (God forbid) it may *just* have touched my pot, and then I'm a lost soul!", the expletive "God forbid" in the context of the drop of milk on the meat pot appears to be a habitual aside, comic evidence of Yente's garrulousness. But in the context of the pot as David and his mother's fear of death, the expletive takes on ominous nuances. The same is true for "I'm a lost soul!" which is comic over-statement on the level of ritual matters, but serious confession on the level of her personal tragedy. In this, the penultimate paragraph, tragic echoes trail behind all of the comic devices. "A broth is a broth," says Yente, and then in a stale and overstated aside she admits that losing it "breaks my heart." We are amused at her flip exaggeration while also being moved by her careful skirting of her real heartbreak.

These two monologues are typical of the entire monologue collection which, in turn, embodies some of the general characteristics of Sholem Aleichem's writings. First, they demonstrate the differing concerns of men and women, a result of the division of labor and assigned roles in Jewish communal life. The women, bound to the daily chores of physical survival, concern themselves with practical issues (excluding, of course, women of wealth). The men, generally or at least ideally protected from the market place and the kitchen, are more concerned with social standing or moral issues. In a well-known longer work, for example, Menakhem-Mendl the luftmentsh fantasizing about the future and his practical mundane wife Sheyne Sheyndl are the archetypal characters of this world view. Of the monologues in the volume in which **"Dos tepl"** and **"An eytse"** appear, five of the monologists, for example, are women who tend to express themselves in culinary terms: **"Gitl Purishkevitch"** (1911), **"Gendz"** (1902), **"Der yontefdiker tsimes"** (1904), **"A vayse kapore"** (1904), **"Dos tepl"** (1901). The names of two of them are pejorative: Yente, meaning a vulgar or sentimental woman, and Gitl Purishkevitsh, who shares the name of the leading antisemite in the Duma. For all five, the buying, selling, and preparation of food for either nourishment or ritualistic purposes all become metaphors of social maladies.

In addition to the symbolic kitchen utensil in **"Dos tepl,"** in **"Gendz"** ("Geese") a poor woman who raises geese for a living begins with complaints about individuals in her town and ends in a general lament about the rich townspeople's neglect of the poor and starving. Eventually the geese, because they are flexible and hardy, become a symbol of her own children, then only of her daughters, and finally of herself—the life of a woman in the shtetl, haunted by the cries of her hungry family. Another voice of a simple Jewish woman complaining about the greed of others occurs in **"Der yontefdiker tsimes"** ("The Holiday Stew") where food, the specially prepared tsimmes, is stolen, while the speaker is away visiting a crippled sister. The tsimmes, a kind of potpourri of ingredients, can be understood also to refer to her motley group of neighbors and, in its idiomatic sense, to the whole sorry business. Because she directs her complaints against the *hayntike* (moderns, literally "those of today") who want to divide goods among all people communally, she is really protesting socialism with a practical example of greed.

In a direct appeal to the author/listener Sholem Aleichem, Gitl Purishkevitsh, the name of another monologist and also the title of the monologue, wants revenge and justice for her sufferings with the help of the writer's pen. Like the widow in **"Dos tepl,"** she too is a widow with an only son, and like the former, she too pays lip service to God with a hint of cynicism, "First God and then Wissotzky," the latter providing her with a livelihood since she is a seller of tea. But being poor, neither God nor Wissotzky come to her aid when her only son is drafted after the three sons of the rich merchant are exempted from duty. Sholem Aleichem gives us an entirely different voice in **"A vayse kapore"** (**"The White Scapegoat"**), the monologue of a simple bourgeoise, assimilated, pretentious, and stereotypical with her gambling unfaithful husband (complete with perfumed rose-colored stationery), her Chopin-loving mother, and her jaded flirtations. In the monologue she appeals to a traditional listener who will appreciate her sense of responsibility in annually ordering a *kapore-hindl* for each member of her household and will understand her pride in being the only member of her home with a sense of *yidishkayt*. In this monologue, the rooster is an item of ritual, the only symbol of traditional Judaism which is the speaker's source of pride, and idiomatically, again, another ironic source of pride, as she characterizes her romantic parlor room success with "Zey zenen ale geven nokh mir a kapore," i.e., "They were all after me like scapegoats." In other words, "they had a crush on me," implying the indifference one feels toward any scapegoat.

With the exception of **"Vayse kapore,"** the four *yidenes* who speak in these monologues are pleading for justice on a very elementary level—they want food. Several speak of husbands too preoccupied with study to concern themselves with physical sustenance, a task left to the Jewish woman. And in each case, the topic of food is both literal and metaphorical, for the buying, selling, and preparing of food is both a vehicle and an avoidance strategy for condemning their society and even their God. Because the monologist in **"Vayse kapore"** does not have to worry about acquiring food for her family, her complaint concerns changing mores and deteriorating tradition, similar to the complaints of the male monologists in this collection.

Just as this *yidene* feels that she is an outsider because she occasionally maintains a tradition that everyone in her assimilated circle has entirely discarded, these male speakers all feel like outsiders, but to different systems.

In addition to antagonism between religious and secular values, as in **"An eytse,"** there are also conflicts between business and professional values and between the bourgeois community and a loose community of political radicals, students, and artists. To cite but one example, **"Yoysef,"** told by a "gentleman" to the author, gives us the voice of a smug "modern" bachelor who sees himself as a rake but winces at being called "bourgeois." The monologue ostensibly relates the love and unsuccessful courtship of a young woman, whom he loses to a young socialist leader named Yoysef who is blessed with the power of eloquent speech. Yoysef's apprehension, imprisonment, and execution and the disappearance of the beautiful young woman along with the restaurant that served as a meeting place for the young socialists reveal that the "gentleman" was really in love with the Left, and that this is a monologue about the romanticism of conspiracy as seen through the eyes of an alienated bourgeois.

Despite the differing concerns of the men and women monologists, they share what is common to all of the characters in Sholem Aleichem's fictional world—the victimizing of traditional men and women by historical change and forces of modernism. Perhaps the monologues of Tevye the diaryman constitute Sholem Aleichem's greatest achievement in the genre because he combined the concerns of both men and women and the succession of one man's personal sorrows with a corresponding succession of collective beliefs all in one eloquent voice. Tevye is profoundly moved at the sight of his hungry children while he also weeps at their moral choices, for they betray views of the world unlike his own. He, too, would like to openly challenge God and he, too, backs away into Yiddish folk sayings and idioms that, by their very communality, protect him from modernism by offering momentary comfort.

No speaker in these collected monologues is as endearing as Tevye, Menakhem-Mendl, Motl the cantor's son, or many other Sholem Aleichem characters, perhaps because a single appearance deprives us of the cumulative effect that often induces reader empathy. Nor are there any child protagonists, whom Sholem Aleichem so skillfully presented elsewhere. What unites these disparate voices is their lack of occasion for rejoicing, their extreme restlessness, and their faltering belief in anything. In fact, from 1901 to 1916, there is an increasing incursion of modernism, a gradual shift from doubting a traditional god and the justice of a traditional way of life to doubting the new god of secular capitalism, culminating in the most vulgar embrace of materialism in the least successful monologues the two set in America. The most masterful of these monologues is **"Dos tepl,"** for it is an intricately structured muffled cry of pain.

By far the most successful monologues in this collection are those in which language patterns—clichés, homespun truths, well-worn phrases—mediate between the wavering believer and his or her despair but cannot heal or entirely console, as in **"Dos tepl"** and **"An eytse."** The linguistic disguises which Sholem Aleichem has draped around his speakers, according to M. Viner, permit the writer to escape from making the moral choices that his mutually contradictory and eclectic petit bourgeois social views would have eventually necessitated. [13] So, mirrored in the vacillation of the monologists is the uncertainty of the author himself, who, like his speakers, releases a flood of language to remove him from crisis.

In Sholem Aleichem's monologues we recognize what is unique to his style; from Sholem Aleichem's voices emanate the laughter and trembling that we associate with his fiction. Furthermore, because they are carefully crafted patterns of speech often directed at particular listeners, these monologues offer interesting models of how language can be both imprisoning and comforting. The essentially public and social nature of language mediates between an individual and his or her direct experience of life, and it is this mediating function of words that has been at the center of both literary and critical writings in recent times. And the monologue serves well as a means of expressing the limits of language. At the far end of Sholem Aleichem's monologues, in a distilled form, is the hysterical voice of Beckett's neurotic woman in *Not I,* a voice that addresses the audience uninterruptedly and, in a recent New York production, is seen only as a pair of lips in space, or the lone voice of Kasper in Peter Handke's play by that name, trying desperately to retain some independent identity amid the robot-like broadcasted voices mouthing all of the clichés of the culture. [14] Sholem Aleichem never attempted to express such nausea about language because he had not discarded all of the collective truths of his society. Instead, his own ambivalence about individual expression and societal identity and obligation speaks through the confused voices of his monologists, for whom the Yiddish idiom and the truths it had so long expressed were both a shelter and a prison, a place of warmth and consolation and a place of deceit. And in that tension, a drama of recent Jewish history is enacted, its comic ironies and genuine despair.

Notes

[1] Saul Bellow, "Introduction" to *Great Jewish Short Stories* (New York, 1963).

[2] For a discussion of his voices see Ruth R. Wisse, *Sholem Aleichem and the Art of Communication,* The B. G. Rudolph Lectures in Judaic Studies (Syracuse University, 1979).

[3] Victor Erlich, "A Note on the Monologue as a Literary Form: Sholem Aleichem's *'Monologn'*—A Test Case," *For Max Weinreich on his Seventieth Birthday: Studies in Jewish Language, Literature, and Society* (The Hague, 1964), p. 45.

[4] Dov Sadan, "Three Foundations" [Yiddish], *Di goldene keyt,* 34 (1959), p. 53.

[5] Dan Miron, *Shalom Aleykhem: pirkey masa* [S.A.: Critical Essays] (Ramat-Gan, 1970). See also his "Bouncing Back: Destruction and Recovery in Sholem Aleykhem's *Motl Peyse dem Khazns,*" *VIVO Annual of Jewish Social Science,* 18 (1978), pp. 119-84.

[6] Hugh McLean, "On the Style of Leskovian Skaz," *Harvard Slavic Studies,* 2 (Cambridge, Mass., 1954), p. 299.

[7] Y. Y. Trunk, *Sholem Aleykhem—zayn vezn un zayne verk [Sholem Aleichem—His Essence and His Works]* (Warsaw, 1937), pp. 167-207.

[8] Miron, *Shalom Aleykhem.*

[9] All quotations from the monologues are taken from *Ale verk fun Sholem-Aleykhem* (The Collected Works of Sholem Aleichem), (New York: Folksfond edition, 1917-25), vol. 21.

[10] For a discussion of his humorous techniques see Rhoda S. Kachuk, "Sholom Aleichem's Humor in English Translation," *YIVO Annual of Jewish Social Science,* 11 (1956-57), pp. 39-81.

[11] Translation by Sacvan Bercovitch in *The Best of Sholom Aleichem,* ed. by Irving Howe and Ruth Wisse (Washington, 1979), p. 80.

[12] For an interesting analysis of this humor see Sigmund Freud, *Jokes and Their Relation to the Unconscious* (New York, 1969), chap. 2.

[13] M. Viner, *Tsu der geshikhte fun der yidisher literatur in 19tn yorhundert* [On the History of Yiddish Literature in the Nineteenth Century] (New York, 1946), p. 2, p. 260-64.

[14] For a most recent clever use of the monologue form see Susan Sontag's story "Baby" in *I, etcetera* (New York, 1978).

David Neal Miller (essay date 1982)

SOURCE: "'Don't Force Me to Tell You the Ending': Closure in the Short Fiction of Sh. Rabinovitsh (Sholem-Aleykhem)," in *Neophilologus,* Vol. LXVI, No. 1, January, 1982, pp. 102-10.

[*In the following essay, Miller considers the problematic endings of Aleichem's short fiction.*]

The nonspecialist (I shall use a none-too-hypothetical undergraduate student as example) comes to the works of Rabinovitsh unaided by a sense of the world, or rather worlds, portrayed in his fictions: holidays, rituals, customs, folkways—the common cultural coin of Eastern European Jewry—all must be glossed and explained. If the student comes to these texts unaided, however, he or she also comes unburdened: the name Sholem-Aleykhem no longer conjures up visions of the public persona which Rabinovitsh labored so long to establish—the genial, wise, invariably middle-aged folk humorist and consoler of his people. To the contemporary student, the stories are but stories, to be approached with the same attitudes and with the same critical tools as any others; and Sholem-Aleykhem is but a name.

However distressing this state of affairs must be to the committed advocate of Yiddish culture (and I, for one, find it very distressing indeed), it does, somewhat paradoxically perhaps, lead to more sophisticated readings of the stories themselves. This occurs in several ways: first, the student is unaware that Rabinovitsh's fiction is generally considered genial, humorous, consoling, and can approach the texts without predisposition; second, the student in this age of rhetorical criticism is well equipped to deal with what Dan Miron has aptly termed the presence of Sholem-Aleykhem, that is, with a narrative consciousness representing "neither the author, nor a full-fledged fictional character"[1]—this is, after all, a rather characteristic narrative mode in twentieth-century fiction; third, Rabinovitsh's stories are quite naturally regarded as fictional constructs, rather than as personal documents belonging to the public persona of Sholem-Aleykhem. In fact, many students are as unwilling to be caught in an intentional fallacy as they are to be caught cheating on a final examination.

How, precisely, do my students' readings of Rabinovitsh differ from the critical—one is tempted to say, from the uncritical—mainstream of Rabinovitsh scholarship? The most frequently voiced comment is that the stories end so unusually: either the narrator refuses to complete his chosen narrative, or one turns the page, expecting to continue reading a story, and finds to one's surprise a new title with a new story; often, as in **"Oysgetreyslt"** (Shaken Out),[2] the characters in the frame story itself express their perplexity with the non-endings of stories told by character-narrators, and this, of course, sensitizes the reader to problematic endings in stories without narrative frames. More perceptive students add to these comments a remark to the effect that the narrator—perhaps also the historical author—finds his material all but impossible to control, and that such control which is placed upon the material proves insufficient to bring the narrative to a successful conclusion.

Interestingly, for the literature on Rabinovitsh is comparatively sophisticated, the problematic nature of his fictional closure has hardly been noticed.[3] There has, to be sure, been mention that the endings are not often unambiguously happy. Meyer Viner, though neither the first nor the most subtle critic to address himself to this question, put the matter plainly in his monograph "Vegn Sholem-Aleykhems humor" (On Sholem-Aleykhem's Humor):

> Di tragik (ligt) inem inhalt, inem ruzultat: in der fabule, in der leyzung fun der suzhet, inem sof, vos iz bay Sholem-Aleykhemen kimat shtendik a troyeriker. (The tragedy lies in the content, in the result, in the plot and its resolution, in the ending, which is, in Sholem-Aleykhem, almost always unhappy).[4]

Additionally, Miron has noted that Rabinovitsh's narratives often group themselves by thematic/structural pattern, and that one such pattern begins with optimistic anticipation and, predictably, ends with disillusioned resignation.[5] The problem here under consideration, however, is not whether the endings are happy or unhappy, but rather why the narrators so frequently avoid endings altogether. Our first step will be to examine the concluding paragraphs of two rather well known and often translated works from the canon, **"Shir-hashirim"** (The Song of Songs) and **"Der farkishefter shnayder"** (The Enchanted Tailor).

"Shir-hashirim: a yugnt-roman in fir teyl" (The Song of Songs: A Novel of Youth (or, with delightful ambiguity, A Youthful Romance in Four Parts) was published in periodical installments from 1909 through 1911, and collected without major revision in the *Folksfond* edition of 1917.[6] It is a first-person narrative at times purporting to

be direct transcription of a child's (later, a young man's) thoughts, at times a retrospective account by an intrusive author-narrator. The stories recount the growing affection between Shimek, a child of about nine, and Buzi, the approximately eleven-year-old daughter of his deceased older brother—that is, his niece. The first and last pair of stories are separated by an *erzaehlte Zeit* of an unspecified, but substantial number of years, during which the young man had left the shtetl, as well as his childhood friend, to seek a secular education. A letter from his father mentioning Buzi's engagement drives Shimek home, leads him to an awareness and, finally, to a declaration of his love for Buzi. Both have come too late. Buzi runs away from the narrator who, after a page or so of procrastination, addresses the reader directly as follows:

> Tsvingt mikh nit, ikh zol aykh dertseyln dem sof fun mayn roman. Der sof, er meg zikh zayn der bester, iz er a troyeriker akord. Der onheyb, der ergster onheyb, iz beser funem bestn sof. Es iz mir deriber a sakh gringer un a sakh mer ongenem tsu dertseyln aykh di dozike geshikhte nokh a mol funem onheyb. Nokh a mol un nokh a mol un nokh hundert mol. Un mitn eygenem loshn vos ale mol . . . Der onheyb, der ergster onheyb, iz beser funem shenstn sof. Der onheyb, loz zayn der sof, der epilog fun mayn nit-oysgetrakhtn, nor emesn, shmertslekhn roman, vos ikh hob mir derloybt tsu kroynen mitn nomen: Shir-hashirim. (Don't force me to tell you the ending of my novel. An ending, even the very best, strikes an unhappy note. But a beginning, even the very worst, is better than the finest ending. For this reason, I find it easier and more comfortable to tell you the same story once more from the beginning. Once more and twice more and a hundred times more. And in the same words each time. . . . A beginning, even the very worst, is better than the most beautiful ending. So let the beginning also be the ending, the epilogue to a novel which is not dreamt-up but true and painful, and which I've permitted myself to crown with the title: The Song of Songs).[7]

The narrator has, as we have seen, refused to complete his narrative, although, by repeating the initial paragraph—a paragraph which had already been repeated near the beginnings of the second, third, and fourth installments[8]—he has given **"Shir-hashirim"** a coda of sorts. The narrator's reasons for his refusal are, for the most part, personal, rather than literary: the narrative is not a *mayse* (tale), but rather a *geshikhte* (history); it is, furthermore, "nit oysgetrakht, nor emes" (not dreamt-up but true). History cannot responsibly be altered to suit purely literary demands, yet this particular history is simply too painful for the narrator to recount. There is, however, a suggestion that the non-ending of **"Shir-hashirim"** is itself artistically desirable: beginnings are more beautiful than endings, presumably also for the reader. And, of course, the historical Rabinovitsh must take responsibility for the shape of his constructs, even if his narrators are allowed to plead extenuating circumstances.

The justly-famous concluding paragraph of **"Der farkishefter shnayder"** (The Enchanted Tailor), a story written in 1900 and collected in the *Folksfond* edition,[9] makes a less ambiguous aesthetic assertion. We may remember that the story recounts the misadventures of one Shimen-Eli Shma-Koleynu, whose inkeeper-relative exchanged his newly-purchased female goat for a male, the male for a female when Shimen-Eli returns to the town of the woman from whom he had purchased the goat, and the female for a male again on the hero's journey home. What we are not apt to remember—a number of adaptations, including the scandalously inaccurate *World of Sholom Aleichem* adaptation by Arnold Perl,[10] take liberties with the conclusion—is that Shimen-Eli suffers a nervous breakdown and perhaps worse as a result of his relative's prank, that the artisans of his town form a mob to exact blood vengeance from the neighboring townspeople, that the goat is irretrievably lost. The narrator concludes as follows:

> Un der shnayder nebekh? . . . Un der hayoytse-lanumaze? . . . Un der may-ko mashme-lon fun der maysevet fregn der lezer. Tsvingt mikh nisht, kinder! Der sofiz geven nisht keyn guter sof. Ongehoybn hot zikh di mayse zeyer freylekh, un oysgelozt hot zi zikh, vi dos rov freylekhe geshikhtes, oy-vey, zeyer troyerik. . . . Un makhmes ir kent dem mekhaber fun der geshikhte, az er iz beteve nit keyn moyre-shkhoyrenik un hot faynd klogedike un hot lib beser lakhndike mayses, un makhmes ir kent im un veyst, az er hot faynd "moral" un zogn muser iz nit zayn derekh—lokhn gezegnt zikh mit aykh der farfaser mitokh skhok, lakhndik, un vintsht aykh, az yidn, un glat mentshn oyf der velt, zoln mer lakhn eyder veynen. Lakhn iz gezunt. Doktoyrim heysn lakhn. . . . (And the unfortunate tailor? What became of him? And what does the story mean, the reader will ask. Don't press me, children. The end was not a happy one. The story began happily enough, but it ended like most cheerful stories, very unhappily. And since you know that I am not a gloomy soul who prefers tears to laughter and likes to point a moral and teach a lesson, let us part as cheerfully as we can. And I wish that all Jews and everybody else in the world may have more opportunities to laugh than to cry. Laughter is healthful. The doctors bid us laugh).[11]

The abrupt conclusion of **"Der farkishefter shnayder"** is, in its general conceit, not unlike that of **"Shir-hashirim"**: in both cases, the narrator interrupts the narrative before its action has concluded, begs the reader's indulgence, and explains that his purpose has been to avoid an unpleasant ending. There are, however, important if subtle differences in the narrative situations of the two texts. Unlike the character-narrator of **"Shir-hashirim,"** the narrator of **"Der farkishefter shnayder"** does not himself take part in the action, and accordingly does not have a direct personal stake in its outcome. He is not even its purported author: the half-title carries the annotation: "aroysgenumen fun an altn pinkes un baputst" (taken from an old communal register and embellished).[12] Thus avoidance of painful recollection cannot have been a factor in the narrator's decision to truncate the story's ending.

If the narrator stands at some remove from his material, so does the reader, who is carefully distanced from the world of the inset story. For one thing, little information is proffered about the prehistories of the characters, or of their activities which do not impinge on the immediate story—

a perfectly legitimate narrative option but, interestingly, one which Rabinovitsh condemns in *Shomers mishpet* (*The Trial of Shomer*): "Ver," he asks of the main character in Shaykevitsh's *Dos antikl oder di koshere meydl* (The Precious Thing, or the Virtuous Maiden), "is Izak, vos iz er geven, vos iz er haynt? Dos vil undz der farfaser nit oyszogn." (Who is Izak? What was he once? What is he now? We don't know; the author won't tell us.)[13] The narrator—although not, of course, the historical author—would have recourse to the conceit of retelling a story found in an old communal register; data not present in the register would not be accessible to the narrator.

The *pinkes* (register) is not meant to lend veracity to the narrative, but only to distance the reader from it, since the geography it details is so clearly fictitious: "Zlodeyevke, a shtetl, vos ligt in der svive fun Mazepevke, nisht vayt fun Khaplapovitsh un Kozodoyevke, tsvishn Yampeli un tsvishn Strishtsh, punkt oyf dem veg, vos me fort fun Pishi-Yabede durkh Petshi-Khvost keyn Tetrevets un fun dortn keyn Yehupets."[14] The mock-Biblical chapter introductions and transitions (e.g. "ish hoyo beZlodyuvki" (there dwelt a man in Zlodeyevke) or "haboyker or" (and it was morning))[15] similarly do not lend historical veracity, but, quite on the contrary, force the reader to consider **"Der farkishefter shnayder"** in apposition to canonized texts the literal historicity of which no orthodox believer may permit him- or herself to question. That the characters are referred to—by the narrator, as well as by their contemporaries—only in epithetic *redende Namen* is a further attempt to insulate the readership from the intrinsically engaging, and often quite moving, events of the story.

There is, lastly, a third kind of distancing present—not of narrator from narrative, nor of reader from narrative, but of reader from narrator. In contrast to the narrator-confidant of **"Shir-hashirim,"** whom, if the ontology of fiction would permit, a hypothetical reader might well sway to complete his history, the narrator of **"Der farkishefter shnayder"** is clearly in control both of himself and of the narrative act; the readers are more than once addressed, and simultaneously dismissed, as *kinder* (children).

Why, then, should this narrator decline to complete his narrative, since he is motivated neither to spare his own feelings nor to protect his readership? The reason, I believe, resides not in this particular fiction, but, rather, in Rabinovitsh's theory of fiction. The assertion, here made by the narrator of **"Der farkishefter shnayder"** but elsewhere, as we shall see, made by Rabinovitsh, is not that real-world beginnings are better/happier/prettier than are endings (the assertion made my the narrator of **"Shir-hashirim"**), but rather that literary beginnings are happier than literary endings, that happy beginnings lead inevitably to unhappy endings, and that this is true of "dos rov freylekhe geshikhtes" (most happy stories).[16] The storyteller's prerogatives are limited, then, to the decision to attempt happy stories, despite foreknowledge of their inevitable outcome: the logic of fiction insists upon unhappy endings, the vocation of the storyteller upon happy ones.

One might well ask why Rabinovitsh chose to adopt a theoretical position which would apparently preclude successful narration a priori. The answer, I believe, lies in two imperatives, both of which he acknowledged and neither of which he was willing to forgo: a realistic imperative and a humoristic imperative.

We may reconstruct Rabinovitsh's realistic imperative syllogistically. The first premise is that literature must reflect the life of the people for whom it is written. "A hayntiker roman muz undz gebn nor dos, vos dos lebn git undz" (A contemporary novel must give us only what life gives us), he writes in **"A briv tsu a gutn fraynd"** (A Letter to a Good Friend).[17] And again in *Shomers mishpet*: "Der srayber . . . der folksshrayber, der kinstler, der poet, der virklekher poet iz far zayn epokhe, in zayne yorn, a shpigl, in velkhn se tut zikh opbildn, opshaynen di shtraln funem lebn, vi in a reynem kval vaser" (The writer, the popular writer, the artist, the poet, the true poet is in his time, for his epoch, in his years a mirror in which the rays of life are reproduced and reflected as in a pure pool of water).[18]

The conclusion is inescapable: a true poet, at least at that particular moment in history, was obliged to reflect a bitter and unhappy reality. In his article on "Der yidisher dales in di beste verke fun undzere folks-shriftshteler" (Jewish Poverty in the Best Works of Our Popular Writers),[19] Rabinovitsh suggests that, empirically, those writers who have been closest to the condition of the least privileged Jewish classes—Abramovitsh (Mendele Moykher-sforim) and Linetski, in particular—have also produced the artistically most satisfying works.

Rabinovitsh's realistic imperative is unambiguous and clearly stated. The concurrent humoristic imperative is less easily located in the critical writings, although it is touched on obliquely in *Shomers mishpet* and **"A briv tsu a gutn fraynd."** (Of course, an author's fictional practice, and not his criticism, must be the ultimate arbiter of all observations). Rabinovitsh does seem to equate the creating of fictions with the creating of humorous fictions:

Tsu zayn a folksshrayber darf men zayn a talantfuler shrayber un a patriot, a mentshnfraynd, me darf lib hobn dos folk, un shtrofndik un lakhndik, darf men dem zayn getray, ibergebn un lib hobn, azoy vi Abramovitsh, vos lakhndik un shpetndik, zet men, vi es trift zikh im dos blut. (In order to be a popular writer, one must be a talented craftsman and a patriot, a humanist and lover of the people, and, chastising and laughing, remain devoted to them and love them, like Abramovitsh, who, though laughing and mocking, is also—we see—dripping blood).[20]

Closeness to the people, a desire to serve them, seems to imply the necessity of humor—or at least of a humorous front: "Nito . . . keyn troyerikere zakh oyf der velt, az me darf lakhn beys se glust zikh veynen . . . (There's nothing sadder in the world than having to laugh while longing to weep).[21]

We shall return later to the "laughter through tears" cliché, and direct our attention for the moment only to the notion that good (i.e. responsible) writers must be capable of laughter and, presumably, of writing texts which provoke laughter.

Rabinovitsh's obliqueness about the matter of humor is—and here I am obligated to Nokhem Oyslender's excellent article on "Der yunger Sholem-Aleykhem un zayn roman *Stempenyu*" (The Young Sholem-Aleykhem and His Novel, *Stempenyu*),[22]—to a very great extent, conditioned by the severe criticism of works which appeared in the Yiddish and Hebrew-language press in 1887 and 1888. Accused of *letsones* (buffoonery, mockery, clowning), a young Rabinovitsh apparently took the criticism to heart and even commissioned an introduction to his *Folks-biblyotek* by Y. Kaminer, one of his more rigorous critics:

In itsiker kalter geshikhte-tsayt darf men undzer folk gebn mer varemes, varemes fun a refue vegn, tsu biselekh vayn oykh. Nishkoshe, mit vayn—mit fantazye, mit poezye, mit hofenung kon men a bisl shtarkn dos shvakhe farkhlinet harts. Hit aykh op fun kalte maykholim, ayz-kalte kritik iber a yidisher zakh—got zol aykh hitn! Es iz nit di tsayt atsind. Oykh zoyers zol nit kumen in ayer mogn: zoyere satire iber a yidisher kapote, zoyere vitsn iber yidishn limed, nit atsind! Afile ot di vaynike tsukerlekh, di reformes mit di formes, nit atsind, nit atsind! (In the present cold times, we must give our people more warm foods with curative powers, and also a bit of wine. Wine isn't bad: imagination, poetry, and hope can strengthen a weak, irregularly beating heart. But watch out for cold foods: sour satires of orthodox mores, sour jokes about Jewish pedagogy—now now! Even those little sugarcakes filled with wine: the forms and reforms—not now, not now!)[23]

In a letter to Shimen Dubnov of 1889, Rabinovitsh abjures humor, a vow that we may be happy to see honored in the breach. "Bay mayn gantser noygung," Rabinovitsh writes, "tsum freydlekhn humor, felt mir oys mut in der itstiker undzerer sotsyaler lage tsu traybn letsones" (Despite my powerful leanings toward upbeat humor, in the present social situation I simply do not have the courage to clown around).[24]

One needn't sympathize with this rather curious rejection of humor—and even of the satire so tied to the maskilic (Jewish Englightenment) tradition—to see that Rabinovitsh's dual predilections could not possibly coexist without creating serious structural problems in his narratives, the problems which led inevitably to the truncated endings of the two stories which we have previously examined. How was Rabinovitsh to reconcile the two imperatives?

The notion of laughter through tears, though formulated by Rabinovitsh himself (the earlier citations from *Shomers mishpet* are, I believe, their first appearance), is clearly inadequate to explain the dynamic of Rabinovitsh's fiction: it would, for example, be cruel to laugh at the misfortunes of Shimen-Eli or at the lost love of Shimek. Nor, conversely, must all laughter be tear-tinged: even a predominantly oppressive social reality admits a modicum of uncomplicated jest. In fact, the model of laughter through tears was offered to describe the dilemma of the *folksshray-*

ber himself, rather than his fiction or the reader's reaction to it; as such, it is not without merit.

The solution was, I would suggest, a good deal more subtle—sufficiently subtle, in fact, to have hitherto escaped detection: Rabinovitsh reserved the realistic imperative for himself, and ascribed the humoristic imperative to his Sholem-Aleykhem persona. On the one hand, the oeuvre is consistently realistic and Oyslender is quite correct in asserting that "Vi shtark er iz nit ibergetsaygt in dem, az di 'letsones' . . . hot ibergelebt ir tsayt—dem gebot fun realizm farblaybt er dokh af vayter oykh getray" (No matter how shaken he was by the accusation of buffoonery, how firmly persuaded that clowning had outlived its usefulness, to the commandment of realism he remained ever faithful).[25] On the other hand, the humoristic imperative was clearly more attractive to the historical author: not only was it, too, retained, but Rabinovitsh did his very best to become his fictional persona.

Miron is thus uncharacteristically inaccurate in suggesting that Rabinovitsh was

> perhaps even a little too successful. For such was the vitality and suggestiveness of this presence that Sholem-Aleykhem not only dispossessed the author's real name of its reputation, . . . but also overwhelmed, to a certain extent, his private personality, blurring the dividing line between his public role, as the national comedian, and his private life. Moreover, one can sense how, more than one time along his career, the presence of Sholem-Aleykhem constrained the author.[26]

The data do not bear this out, but, rather, lead to a contrary conclusion: both textual and extra-textual evidence lead me to believe that the Sholem-Aleykhem persona was consciously and thoroughly cultivated—from the earliest barrage of pseudonymous correspondence in the *Yidishes folksblat* to the double signature on Rabinovitsh's testament—that Rabinovitsh strove to become Sholem-Aleykhem, much as Samuel Clemens strove to become Mark Twain or, in our day, Ian Fleming strove to become James Bond. This is, I should add, not offered as a means of understanding Rabinovitsh's very interesting psychological makeup—a literary theoretician hardly has the tools to undertake such a task—but rather as a means of understanding the dynamics of specific literary texts.

To summarize, then, texts can contain mutually contradictory imperatives when these are ascribed to discrete loci—in this case, the realistic imperative to Rabinovitsh as implied author, and the humoristic imperative to the Sholem-Aleykhem persona.[27] That this makes the stories unstable and difficult to conclude with grace is apparent to students unburdenend by acquaintance with the public persona which Rabinovitsh labored a lifetime to construct.

Finally, I would like to suggest that this instability, this lack of graceful accommodation of imperatives makes Rabinovitsh's fiction more, rather than less, successful: it is emblematic of the modern temper that ideologies equally attractive but mutually incompatible demand simulta-

neous loyalty. If this renders Rabinovitsh's oeuvre unusually complex, it is only because of the complexity of the societal demands which inform it and which it reflects, in Rabinovitsh's words, "vi in a reynem kval vaser" (as in a pure pool of water).

Notes

* This is a revised version of a paper delivered at the 1977 Colloquium in Yiddish Studies sponsored by the YIVO Institute for Jewish Research, New York.

[1] Dan Miron, *Sholem Aleykhem: Person, Persona, Presence* (New York: YIVO Institute for Jewish Research, 1972), p. 42. Cf. also p. 8 et passim.

[2] Sh. Rabinovitsh, *Ale verk fun Sholem-Aleykhem* (Complete Works of Sholem-Aleykhem), VI (Kleyne mentshelekh mit kleyne hasoges (Little People with Little Frailties); New York: Sholem-Aleykhem folksfond, 1918), 211-21.

[3] Ruth Wisse and Irving Howe touch briefly on the question of closure in their epistolary "Hevenu Sholom Aleichem: New Interpretations of Sholom Aleichem", *Moment*, 4, No. 3 (Jan.-Feb. 1979), 44 et passim.

[4] Meyer Viner, *Vegn Sholem-Aleykhems humor* (On Sholem-Aleykhem's Humor) (Moscow: Melukhe-farlag "Der emes," 1940). Rpt. in his *Tsu der geshikhte fun der yidisher literatur in 19-tn yorhundert (Etyudn un materyaln)* (On the History of Nineteenth-Century Yiddish Literature (Studies and Materials)), II (New York: YKUF, 1946), 304.

[5] Dan Miron, Seminar in Sholem-Aleykhem, Max Weinreich Center for Advanced Jewish Studies, 1977.

[6] Sh. Rabinovitsh, *Ale verk fun Sholem-Aleykhem* (Complete Works of Sholem-Aleykhem), II (Fun peysekh tsu peysekh (From Passover to Passover); New York: Sholem-Aleykhem folksfond, 1917), 7-74.

[7] *Ale verk*, II, 74.

[8] *Ale verk*, II, 22, 32-33, 54-55.

[9] Sh. Rabinovitsh, *Ale verk fun Sholem-Aleykhem* (Complete Works of Sholem-Aleykhem), XVI (Oreme un freylekhe, Ershtes bukh (Poor People and Happy People, First Book); New York: Sholem-Aleykhem folksfond, 1919), 9-69.

[10] Arnold Perl, *The World of Sholom Alechem: A Play* (New York: Dramatists Play Service, 1953).

[11] *Ale verk*, XVI, 68. The translation has been adapted from that of Julius and Frances Butwin, "The Enchanted Tailor," in *The Old Country* (New York: Crown, 1946), pp. 136-37.

[12] *Ale verk*, XVI, 7.

[13] Sh. Rabinovitsh, *Shomers mishpet, oder der sud prisyashnykh oyf ale romanen fun Shomer, stenografirt vort am vort fun Sholem-Aleykhem* (The Trial of Shomer, Literally Recorded by Sholem-Aleykhem) (Barditshev: Yankev Sheftil, 1888), p. 18.

[14] Zlodeyevke, a shtetl in the vicinity of Mazepevke, not far from Khaplapovitsh and Kozodoyevke, between Yampeli and Strishtsh, right

on the road which leads from Pishi-Yabede through Petshi-Khvost to Tetrevets and from there to Yehupets. *Ale verk*, XVI, 9. The town names are fanciful and often describe their inhabitants (e.g. Zlodeyevke (Thieves' Town), Kozodoyevke (Goat Milkers' Town)) or characteristic lifestyles (e.g. Khaplapovitsh (Helter-Skelter Town)). This onomastic device was familiar to readers of nineteenth- and twentieth-century literature of the Jewish Enlightenment (*Haskole*) in both Hebrew and Yiddish. Cf. Abramovitsh's Glupsk (Sillytown), Kaptsansk (Paupers' Town), or Tuneyadevke (Idlers' Town). The narrator's insistent geographic specificity in the first paragraph of "Der farkishefter shnayder" claims both aesthetic license and, somewhat paradoxically, extraliterary veracity. As such, it draws the reader's attention not only to the inhabitants' difining characteristics, but also to the recurring literary matrix of which they are a part; Mazepevke, for example, had made the first of several appearances as early as 1893 ("Stantsye Mazepevke" (Mazepevke Station), *Hoyzfraynt*, 3, 15). On the other hand, the extraliterary historicity of Rabinovitsh's *neshome-landshaft* is reinforced by mention of fictitious town names whose real-world analogues are unambiguously established in the corpus (e.g. Yehupets (Kiev)), as well as by a non-Jewish and pre-Enlightenment tendency toward self-deprecatory, descriptive town naming in Byelorussia and the Northern Ukraine (e.g. Zmievka (Snakes' Town) near Oryel). Maskilic (Jewish Enlightenment) onomastic strategies are, it seems, more complex than has been acknowledged, and would merit more detailed examination.

[15] *Ale verk*, 9 and 15, resp.

[16] *Ale verk*, XVI, 68.

[17] Sh. Rabinovitsh, "A briv tsu a gutn fraynd" (A Letter to a Good Friend), in *Di yudishe folks-biblyotek*, 2 (1889), 309.

[18] *Shomers mishpet*, p. 67.

[19] Sh. Rabinovitsh, "Der yidisher dales in di beste verke fun undzere folks-shriftshteler" (Jewish Poverty in the Best Works of Our Popular Writers), in *Dos yidishe folksblat*, Suppl. to no. 39, passim.

[20] *Shomers mishpet*, p. 57.

[21] *Shomers mishpet*, p. 58.

[22] Nokhem Oyslender, "Der yunger Sholem-Aleykhem un zayn roman *Stempenyu*" (The Young Sholem-Aleykhem and His Novel, *Stempenyu*), in *Shriftn fun der katedre far yidisher kultur ba der alukrainisher visnshaftlekher akademye, literarishe un filologishe sektsye*, 1 (1928), 5-72.

[23] Yitskhok Kaminer, "A briv tsum heroysgeber fun Dr. Y. Kaminer" (A Letter to the Editor from Dr. Y. Kaminer), in *Di yudishe folks-biblyotek*, 1 (1888), III.

[24] Cited by Oyslender, "Der yunger Sholem-Aleykhem," p. 31.

[25] Oyslender, "Der yunger Sholem-Aleykhem," p. 32.

[26] Dan Miron, *Sholem Aleykhem*, p. 8.

[27] I use *persona* to denote both *implied author*, which inheres in the text (cf. Wayne Booth, *The Rhetoric of Fiction* (Chicago: Univ. of Chicago Press, 1961), pp. 71-76; Wolfgang Kayser, "Kleist als Erzaehler," in his *Die Vortragsreise: Studien zur Literatur* (Berne: Francke, 1958), p. 169), and *putative author*, which inheres in its packaging (i.e. the Sholem-Aleykhem cited on by-line and title page). I exclude from consideration that Sholem-Aleykhem who appears as character-narrator in

certain of Rabinovitsh's texts—especially, though not exclusively, early ones; cf. Dan Miron, *Sholem Aleykhem*, 24 et passim.

Victoria Aarons (essay date 1985)

SOURCE: "Authorial Voice in the Kasrilevke Stories," in *Author as Character in the Works of Sholom Aleichem*, The Edwin Mellen Press, 1985, pp. 73-99.

[*In the following excerpt, Aarons examines the defining characteristics of Aleichem's* shtetl *stories.*]

At the heart of Sholom Aleichem's short stories, monologues and feuilletons lies Kasrilevke, the fictionalized shtetl, representative of the small villages at the outskirts of the cities where Jews were forced to live. In one of the Kasrilevke stories, **"The Town of the Little People,"** Sholom Aleichem explains the origin of the name, Kasrilevke:

> The town of the little people into which I shall now take you, dear reader, is exactly in the middle of that blessed Pale into which Jews have been packed as closely as herring in a barrel and told to increase and multiply. The name of the town is Kasrilevka. How did this name originate? I'll tell you:

> Among us Jews poverty has many faces and many aspects. A poor man is an unlucky man, he is a pauper, a beggar, a schnorrer, a starveling, a tramp, or a plain failure. A different tone is used in speaking of each one, but all these names express human wretchedness. However, there is still another name—*kasril*, or *kasrilik*. That name is spoken in a different tone altogether, almost a bragging tone. For instance, "Oh, am I ever a kasrilik!" A kasrilik is not just an ordinary pauper, a failure in life. On the contrary, he is a man who has not allowed poverty to degrade him. He laughs at it. He is poor, but cheerful.[1]

These two elements, poverty and the unfaltering attitudes of the Kasrilevkites, characterize Sholom Aleichem's stories of the shtetl prior to its destruction. These shtetl Jews were self-sufficient and isolated from the rest of the world, a condition which allowed them to maintain their religious customs and values.

Although Menakhem-Mendl is distanced physically from the shtetl, for the most part the characters in both the monologues and in *The Adventures of Menakhem-Mendl* share these characteristics. Isolated and unnoticed by the rest of the world, the shtetl Jews, as Sholom Aleichem depicts them, were immune to change and relatively untouched by events in the outside world. Menakhem-Mendl, for instance, the writer of the letter collection considered in the previous chapter, becomes almost a figure of myth because he is impervious to events. His foredoomed attempts to find a place in the economic world outside the shtetl become heroic, paradoxically, by his failure to be daunted by a situation he does not understand. When, for instance, Mendl fails to prosper in the refinery business he writes to his wife, Sheyne-Sheyndl:

. . . The business has bit the dust. Manufacturers are pining away for a penny, capitalists are holding back, and brokers are out of a job, with not a thing to do, and me in the middle.

You probably think it's the end of the world? Oh, no, you are not to worry, my dearest wife. God is eternal, . . . People like me don't go under, heaven forbid. On the contrary, only now do I feel confident that, God willing, I am bound to rise in the world because I am now working on a deal which must bring, as my share, almost one hundred thousand rubles![2]

Menakhem-Mendl, like the majority of Sholom Aleichem's Kasrilevke characters, is endowed with an unwavering optimistic good-nature. He accepts disaster because he is accustomed to it, and does not let it affect his spirits. Instead of succumbing to the multitude of disasters he encounters on his travels outside of the safe confines of the shtetl, he always survives, essentially undaunted by each near escape, either from absolute poverty or from the hands of the authorities.

When Aleichem made the decision to write fiction in Yiddish instead of in Hebrew and to legitimize the language as an effective literary medium he ran up against the bias that Yiddish was only useful in its ability to express old world values and superstitions, and therefore was an illegitimate literary medium.

—Victoria Aarons

Sholom Aleichem never seems entirely comfortable with this kind of character in his early works, but by and large his stance is one of sympathetic distance, as we have seen in the previous chapters. This position of detached amusement is an acceptable attitude for Sholom Aleichem's audience of Europeanized Jews. Menakhem-Mendl, for example, is doomed to failure because of external circumstances barring his way, but primarily because of his own internal limitations, which are presented to us in a comic, sympathetic and non-threatening manner. Because these characters are essentially isolated from the rest of the world, and unnoticed in Mendl's case, even when they find their way out of the shtetl confines, they pose no real problem for the Europeanized intellectual audience that Sholom Aleichem so clearly intended to reach.

However, when the shtetls begin to open themselves up to the outside world the nature of the Jewish problem widens. The rhetorical problem for the author in the monologues and letters was one of advancing a comfortable attitude toward one's heritage. A similar attitude carries over to the stories of the pre-Enlightenment Kasrilevke

and the host of characters that react comically to all kinds of situations. While these characters complicate matters and fare precariously through life, the author and reader observe them from an amused and sympathetic distance.

Sholom Aleichem wrote during a time of great upheaval in the shtetls. The Enlightenment, and perhaps even more, the twentieth century in Europe in general, brought about the gradual loosening and finally the disintegration of the old world villages. A large number of the Kasrilevke stories are devoted to this change in the life and customs of the shtetls. I devote this [essay] to these Kasrilevke stories that mark the changes in shtetl life because they demonstrate a drastic shift in authorial voice and stance from that in the earlier stories, monologues and letters.

The writer seems to have changed his mind in these stories. He no longer looks back at the shtetl and the shtetl Jew with nostalgia. In fact, when Sholom Aleichem enlarges his canvas by discussing Kasrilevke in light of its changes and in relation to Eastern Europe at large, we discover him searching for an appropriate stance all over again, as he begins to reflect upon the new dramatic situation.

Sholom Aleichem was also perhaps forced, in a sense, to make the transition in his stories to include the historical changes taking place in the shtetls in particular and in Eastern Europe at large. When he made the decision to write fiction in Yiddish instead of in Hebrew and to legitimize the language as an effective literary medium he ran up against the bias that Yiddish was only useful in its ability to express old world values and superstitions, and therefore was an illegitimate literary medium. It was perhaps necessary for Sholom Aleichem, if he were to successfully prove the potential for Yiddish as transcending its prescribed biases, to place his works within the current literary trends and topics of other Russian—not necessarily Jewish—writers. In other words, Sholom Aleichem may have felt that he would defeat his purpose, and the purpose for Yiddish, if Yiddish was only appropriate in the expression of old world shtetl stories. The author, on the contrary, perhaps felt compelled to incorporate the historical changes as they took place, because although not chronicles, his stories were always characterized by those elements of realism that make them so vivid. In fact, to successfully break from the prescribed satiric and comic narrative methods imposed upon Yiddish fiction writers by the maskilim, discussed in my opening chapter, Sholom Aleichem had to broaden not only his literary techniques but his subject matter as well. Otherwise, Yiddish literature faced the possibility of dying out with that culture.

The stance embraced in these past works is no longer acceptable when the shtetl, as Sholom Aleichem once knew it, disintegrates, because, although the situation changes, the characters do not. The shtetl folk in these stories share the same characteristics as do the shtetl Jews in the previous monologues, stories and letters. They continue to be restricted by their limited emotional and intellectual faculties while optimistically struggling through life. The problem for the writer rests on this precise point. That is, while the rigid old world shtetl breaks down and opens itself up to outside culture and education, the shtetl inhabitants do not. They, in effect, remain the same. Therefore, when we regard the shtetl Jews within the enlarged canvas of European tradition, they appear in a very different light. Instead of adjusting to the changes imposed upon them, the shtetl Jews are hopelessly unable to cope with the sophisticated world and their very characters become an impediment to change.

For example, the shtetl where we found Sheyne-Sheyndl, Menakhem-Mendl's wife, was a place isolated from the outside world and suspended in time. The only incidents of importance were those events that affected them directly within their own homes or towns, where everyone knew everyone else, and made it a point to be involved in the business of his neighbor. The majority of Jews who inhabited the shtetls did not speak the language of their host country, but rather communicated almost solely in Yiddish, the *mame-loshn.* They were, thus, for the most part, unaware of the events happening outside of their immediate surroundings. They instead were governed by ritual activities, religious customs and superstitions which the maskilim (the Jewish intellectuals of the Enlightenment) felt were responsible for their continued isolationism.[3] As members of the shtetls were forced by poverty or restlessness to leave the confines of the shtetls, more and more of the outside world inevitably entered into their lives. However, when confronted with news of the rest of the world the shtetl Jews respond to it in the only way they know how. In the story, **"Dreyfus in Kasrilevke,"** Sholom Aleichem comically describes the manner in which events from the big cities were brought inside the shtetl communities and the peculiarly insular way the shtetl folk understood the news.

> I doubt if the Dreyfus case made such a stir anywhere as it did in Kasrilevka . . .
>
> How did Kasrilevka get wind of the Dreyfus case? Well, how did it find out about the war between the English and the Boers, or what went on in China? What do they have to do with China? Tea they got from Wisotzky in Moscow. . . .
>
> So how did Kasrilevka learn about the Dreyfus case? From Zeidel.
>
> Zeidel, Reb Shaye's son, was the only person in town who subscribed to a newspaper, and all the news of the world they learned from him, or rather through him. He read and they interpreted. He spoke and they supplied the commentary. He told what he read in the paper, but they turned it around to suit themselves, because they understood better than he did.[4]

The authorial tone in the above passage is unmistakably sarcastic, and marks a distinctive change in authorial voice and judgment.

Sholom Aleichem may in fact be responding to the maskilic argument that the shtetl Jews should shed their medieval and superstitious customs and attitudes in order to become assimilated into European life. It is perhaps the case that Sholom Aleichem, in these stories that mark the transitional stages of the shtetl, indicates his attitude against the contemporary Jewish critics who demanded an end to isolationism, and exposed the small-town Jew to the world at large. What Sholom Aleichem seems to find is that exposure doesn't necessarily mean assimilation; it can, rather, reveal the common Jew's inadequacies before the world.

The entire rhetorical situation thus changes in these Kasrilevke stories that mark the transitional stages of shtetl life, and the critic must ask a new set of questions of the writer and of the stories themselves. What happens to the shtetl Jew when forced to become a part of European culture? What attitude must the reader, in this instance, adopt toward a people and a culture no longer mythical or suspended in time, but in the midst of a larger controlling culture? Finally, what questions must the critic ask of the writer in terms of the changes he is forced to make in his attempts to come to terms with an entirely different, and essentially more problematic situation? It is one thing to come to terms with an isolated culture, existing in the past. It is quite another issue to regard those same people in relation to the rest of the world as it approaches the twentieth century.

A Singular Authorial Voice

When the traditional standards of the shtetl break down, the ironic distance between the implied author and the persona that characterized Sholom Aleichem's past works, no longer functions as a major narrative technique. In both the monologues and *The Adventures of Menakhem-Mendl* the writer created a narrator who, because of his limitations and short-sighted vision of the world, was unreliable. His values and attitudes therefore differed, in varying degrees, from those of the author and the reader. Through the establishment of two voices, the persona's and the implied author's, the judgments of the author are developed, and he is set apart from the material by his ironic posture. The biographical author further distanced himself from his subject by creating the authorial figure of Sholom Aleichem who claimed responsibility for gaining access to the stories and letters.

In a large number of the Kasrilevke stories, unlike the previous works, we hear one narrating voice and experience little, if any, distinction between the figure of Sholom Aleichem and the writer, Sholem Rabinovitsh. In the story, **"The Great Panic of the Little People,"** for example, the fictionalized Sholom Aleichem merges with the author as narrator and writer.

> Heaven has apparently decreed that Kasrilevke's Jews are destined to have more woes than anyone else in the world. Wheresoever there was calamity, misfortune, troubles and misery, trials and tribulations, they sought to sympathize, taking each affliction to heart more than anyone the world over. . . . by what stretch of the imagination could you reasonably account for the Kasrilevkites' involvement with the Boers, whom the English conquered and wiped out? In Kasrilevke that

war, too, caused a hullabaloo. . . . I mean pain, heartache, and humiliation. . . .

Moreover, please tell me, my dear Kasrilevkites, why you have to break your heads over Serbia, where in the middle of one fine night some officers killed the Czar and his wife and chucked them out the window? Why should all these things worry you more than anyone else? Don't you have anything else to worry about? Have you already married off and provided for all your children? What sort of habit is it, I ask you, to stick your nose into every pot? Believe me, the world will get along very nicely without you, and everyone will undoubtedly manage to take care of himself.

The author begs his reader's pardon for addressing such cutting remarks to his fellow Kasrilevkites. But please understand, dear friends, that I myself am a Kasrilevkite. Born and bred in Kasrilevke, I was educated in its Talmud Torahs and schools and was even married there. But then I set my little ship adrift in the great and tempestuous sea of life whose waves are high as houses. And despite the fact that one is perpetually in a tumult and on the go, I have never ever forgotten either my beloved home town Kasrilevke, may it thrive and prosper to ripe old age, or my dear brethren, the Kasrilevkite Jews, may they be fruitful and multiply. When we experience violence, disaster or calamity *here,* far away from Kasrilevke, I immediately ask myself: What's happening *there,* in my home town?[5]

The entire manner of narration in the above passage is significantly distinct from the rambling, illogical catalogue of complaints that characterized the narrators in the monologues and the letters. The narrator in the monologue, **"A Predestined Disaster,"** for example, connected his tale not with a logical progression of ideas, but with a series of disasters connected by the statement, "to make a long story short,. . . ."[6] But he never managed to state anything briefly; his endless circling was terminated only by exhaustion. Although the voice of the author is silent throughout the monologue, his judgments, which are also those of Sholom Aleichem, the fictionalized recipient of the tales, are made clear to us by his development of the persona.

In the Kasrilevke stories . . . however, there is little distinction between the speaker and the author. The narrator is generally *not* a persona, and we must assume that his voice is the same as the author's. This narrator, as the above citation demonstrates, is learned and eloquent (e.g., his use of metaphors). Even the diction in the above example is elevated in a fashion impossible earlier. The humor is a conscious stance on the part of the narrator, Sholom Aleichem, as contrasted to the inadvertent humor of the narrators in the earlier works.

And this technique of creating a pseudonym which becomes both narrator and dramatized character in his own right perhaps marks Sholom Aleichem's greatest achievement. Sholom Aleichem, fictionalized character-narrator, allows the writer an enormous amount of literary freedom. As Dan Miron so aptly demonstrates in *A Traveler Disguised* and in *Sholem Aleykhem: Person, Persona, Presence,* the figure of Sholom Aleichem functions as both

insider and outsider. He is at once a member of the shtetl community, privy to the confidences of the other Jews as well as maintaining a posture of distanced observer of those experiences related to him. The writer, Sholom Aleichem, by assuming the name of his main narrator-character calls attention to his complex relationship to his own material. He can be a critical observer of that which is closest to him, his people and his heritage.

In many of these Kasrilevke stories Sholom Aleichem appears as not merely a silent recipient of the tales but as an active participant in the stories themselves. This role results in a dramatic shift in the tone of the narrative. In the Kasrilevke stories that mark the end of the pre-Enlightenment shtetl life, we are not distanced from the speaker by his intellectual limitations, but rather, we are able to identify with his speech, diction and word choice. The Kasrilevke Jews are not viewed with the sympathetic detachment of the letters and the monologues; they are still undaunted, but their attempt to understand the non-shtetl world is viewed with a kind of objectivity which slides, over and over, into criticism. Sholom Aleichem even apologizes to the reader for his critical remarks on the grounds that he is "a Kasrilevkite" himself. Yet the establishment of his identity with the shtetl folk in no way serves to temper the overt criticism his words confer. Although he has put a physical distance between himself and the shtetl, it is clear by his tone that he has not found a comfortable perspective from which he can view his heritage. He is haunted by the shtetl and criticises the Kasrilevkites for their naive involvement and excessive reactions to incidents that do not even remotely affect them, resulting in a masked self-criticism.

The critical voice of the author in this respect is perhaps a response to those of his contemporaries who advocated the shtetl Jew's involvement with the outside world. Not only does their child-like provincialism and limited world view prevent them from understanding and appropriately reacting to world-wide events, but Sholom Aleichem clearly satirizes the events themselves. His comparison of the Boer War and the assassination of the Czar and his family in Serbia to the problem of marrying off one's children in the small shtetls undermines the enormity of those events in the national news, and implies the essential question of the reasons for their involvement in world-wide affairs. Why should the shtetl Jew become educated to a world that offers merely more trouble and inadequacies? Although the narrator has escaped the problems and restrictions of the shtetl, he finds himself in the midst of far greater disasters. Sholom Aleichem may also be making distant events human, as seen through the eyes of those who are too "naive" to regard war and politics as mere abstractions.

In the letters and the monologues, Sholom Aleichem clearly thought that he could define a stance toward the shtetls of Europe, a satisfactory stance, that did not involve much of an actual relationship. But when he comes face to face with the Kasrilevkites' confrontation with the contemporary culture, his involvement is very apparent. The following paragraph is an attack:

For your information, no matter how small, forlorn, and castaway Kasrilevke may be, it is connected to the rest of the world by a sort of wire which if tapped at one end delivers a message at the other. Let me put it another way. Kasrilevke can be compared to a unborn child, tied to its mother's umbilical cord, that feels everything the mother feels. The mother's pain is the child's pain and vice versa. The only thing that puzzles me is why Kasrilevke feels the troubles and woes of the entire world while absolutely no one cares about Kasrilevke, or sympathizes with its afflictions. Kasrilevke is a kind of step-child of the world. The first to react to a misfortune, Kasrilevke scurries about more than anyone else and goes without sleep till it practically knocks at death's door.

Yet—oh blast those anti-Semites!—should this stepchild fall ill and collapse in a corner, burning feverishly like an oven, wasting away for lack of food, and thirsting for lack of water, you may be sure that not a soul would even cast a glance in its direction.[7]

The controlling tone of the narrative becomes primarily argumentative, because the author is not separated aesthetically or emotionally from the situation he describes by another narrating figure. The tone is pathetic and the irony suggests a tragic mask of human concern, anger and a provincial compassion that tries to compass the world. As I have indicated, Sholom Aleichem the character-narrator did not manifest norms and judgments significantly different from those of the author in the previously discussed works. However, Sholom Aleichem was never a mere nominal replacement for the author. Rather Sholom Aleichem is created to function as an intermediary figure, one that stands between the author and the character-narrator. However, his function in the monologues and letters has been minimal, defined primarily as the vehicle through which the stories are made accessible to us.

In these Kasrilevke stories, however, Sholom Aleichem, narrator, is too close to the author to function as an intermediary figure. Instead of a narrator telling his story to Sholom Aleichem, it is Sholom Aleichem's story that we hear directly from him. When the narrative is governed by one voice instead of two, the authorial judgments are presented to the reader *explicity* instead of *implicitly*. Sholom Aleichem here serves as the narrating voice through which the author makes what was once implicit now explicit; his role is no longer minimal. When Sholom Aleichem, the author, introduces a narrator who reminds his audience that he is a writer, it is not merely an act of playful self-indulgence on his part, nor a stylistic technique. Rather, it provides an opening in the narrative for direct authorial intervention which previously was indirect, implied through the establishment of dramatic irony and distance.

For example, Sholom Aleichem, in one series of stories, returns to Kasrilevke, his home town, as satirist and author, in order to write a **"Guide to Kasrilevke"**:

Of recent years all sorts of books about cities and lands and similar useful subjects have made their appearance in other languages. So I've said to myself, 'We imitate

other peoples in everything: they print newspapers—so do we; they have Christmas trees—so have we; they celebrate New Year's—so do we. Now, they publish guide books to their important cities (they have "A Guide to St. Petersburg," "A Guide to Moscow," "A Guide to Berlin," "A Guide to Paris," and so on)—why shouldn't we get out "A Guide to Kasrilevke"?[8]

As the analysis of previous works has shown, Sholom Aleichem is generally defined by his profession, and it is the fact that he is a writer that has distinguished him from the monologists and has provided the justification for the acquisition of Menakhem-Mendl's letters. In the Kasrilevke stories Sholom Aleichem's profession is at once the source of comedy and the main aspect of his character that distinguishes him from the shtetl "folk" and binds him to the biographical author. When this change from two voices to one controlling voice occurs the reader is thus asked to accept the posture of that speaker in a different way. The author loses the distance he once had in relation to his subject because he no longer has an intermediary figure to bridge the gap between the two worlds. There is, in fact, no longer this physical separation because the shtetl Jew is becoming a part of that larger world. As Sholom Aleichem tells us in the passage cited above, the shtetl Jews imitate the rest of the world. When the shtetl attempts to copy the standards of the outside world, it loses its traditional values and practices.

His question, "Why shouldn't we get out 'A Guide to Kasrilevke'?" is, of course, rhetorical and serves to emphasize by contrast the disparity between the small shtetl and the big cities. Although Sholom Aleichem continues to be funny, more than anything else, the reader is presented with an overt indictment of the current trends and values which override the potential comic situation for the work. Instead of laughing at the limitations of the shtetl folk, Sholom Aleichem involves himself directly in the text as he proposes to comment on the changes that have occurred in the shtetls.

The Argument

The complex argument in the Kasrilevke stories is directed toward a diverse audience, and the effect is that of an author attempting to discover a suitable channel to direct the blame for an increasingly hopeless set of events, circumstances and attitudes.

Sholom Aleichem cannot maintain an adequate amount of distance from the material; his anger extends in many directions. The attitudes and capabilities of the shtetl folk are no longer a source of amusement for the writer. They are depicted as a source of bitter sorrow and embarrassment for the Jewish intellectual who has left the shtetl. The Kasrilevkites are depicted as always on the fringes of life, always missing. Their predicament is caused, in part, by their own internal restrictions, and also by the indifference, as well as overt hostility, on the part of the outside world. Sholom Aleichem describes the shtetl "folk" in hopeless terms: "This has ever been the fate of the little folk of Kasrilevke: when they dream of good things to eat—they haven't a spoon; when they have a spoon—they don't dream of good things to eat."[9]

Sholom Aleichem is, of course, one of the great Jewish humorists. What gives his fiction such strength and stylistic merit, however, is his flexibility of form. Like a magician, he is able to conjure up voices to fit the changing ethos of his time.

—*Victoria Aarons*

When the shtetl Jews are required to assimilate into European culture they simply cannot adapt, and thus are shown to the outside world as an embarrassment to those Enlightenment intellectuals who advocated assimilation, or at least change. When Sholom Aleichem, for example, returns to his home town to compose the guide book to Kasrilevke he does so in order to measure the shtetl's progress. The voice of the author is sarcastic and judgmental:

> In conceiving this project I have, of course, been swayed more by considerations of public service than by personal motives. My book will serve as a guide to strangers visiting Kasrilevke. It will tell them where to get off the train; what transportation to use; where to get a tasty meal or good glass of wine; or where to enjoy an amusing play and other such wholesome fun of which there is much in Kasrilevke. For Kasrilevke is no longer the town it used to be. The great progress of the world has made inroads into Kasrilevke and turned it topsy-turvy. It has become a different place.[10]

When Sholom Aleichem refers to the "wholesome fun of which there is much in Kasrilevke" we are drawn to the sarcastic voice of the author by the disparity between what we know of Kasrilevke, a poor ghetto, and the attempt to emulate the wealth and culture of the big cities. The author here can no longer show the shtetl as a place with its own rich culture and traditions. The changes, "inroads," that have occurred require the loss of the old world culture.

Sholom Aleichem's position concerning the "progress" made in the shtetl is clear. He satirizes the kinds of progress made in Kasrilevke by the common folk, and the changes which are characterized by imitation. When the shtetl attempts to imitate the advancements of the big cities it fails. Of its hotels, he writes: "Noiach the doorman showed me into a dark room, reeking of freshly tanned leather, decayed pickles, and stale cheap tobacco"; of restaurants: "The smells that assailed my nostrils as I mounted the stairs were not especially fragrant, but an empty stomach doesn't pick and choose."[11]

The attempts of the Kasrilevkites to imitate progressiveness in the cities are thwarted by the inherent old world provincialism and limited resources that characterize the

shtetl folk in general in Sholom Aleichem's earlier stories. Instead of advancing, the shtetl loses its own traditions and becomes merely a parody of European culture. For Sholom Aleichem, the loveable shtetl characters become a problem that he cannot resolve. The authorial voice is thus no longer objective and datached. His previous intention to reconcile a distanced audience to its heritage is impossible because the heritage of which he once spoke sympathetically no longer exists as he knew it.

The collection of vignettes in "Progress In Kasrilevke," for example, introduces the final phase in the upheaval within the small Eastern European shtetls. Sholom Aleichem returns to his home town (a recurring situation in these transitional stories), to discover drastic changes in the entire environment and lives of the shtetl Jews. He no longer recognizes the people who once inhabited Kasrilevke. Both external appearances and internal values have changed, and these Jews seem to have lost all those qualities which made them acceptable to an outside audience.

> It's amazing what can happen to a village! You know, my old home town has undergone such changes I can't even recognize it any more. After being away for ages, I came back to Kasrilevke for a few weeks and wandered around its streets, spoke to the people, and looked for old friends. But how? Where? For whom? Most of them had gone the way of all flesh, a few, had gone to America, and the newly-rich weren't the ones I was looking for. It was a topsy-turvy world. Where did the famous little people with their little ideas disappear to? Where were all those know-it-all, bearded Jews who poked fun at everything? Where were those young people with canes who used to wander around the marketplace looking for business in vain, who out of depths of despair ribbed one another and then the whole world?
>
> Now, I saw dandies strolling through the streets, staid people with homburgs and pince-nez. Of the once slovenly women with their white stockings and red garters, and of the girls with their colorful kerchiefs— not a trace remained. Ladies with chapeaus now walked past me. Matrons with parasols. Chic young ladies wearing gloves. New People. A new world. . . .
>
> . . . That's the external picture, so to speak. But, under the surface Kasrilevke had changed even more. I just couldn't believe I was home. As I walked through the village, I looked for at least one of the old clubs. I remember there used to be clubs to the point of excess here. And I'm not talking about the Psalms and Mishna Clubs. I mean societies like the Free-Loan, the Free-Kitchen, the Visit-the-Sick, the Clothe-the-Poor, the Help-the-Needy, the Medical-Aid, the Relieve-the-Oppressed. It seemed that all these groups had gone the way of their founders. They passed on like most of the little people, like lonely old Rabbi Yozifl, may the fruits of Paradise be his. Thinking of him brought tears to my eyes.[12]

The narrator, Sholom Aleichem, continues to be the mouthpiece for the author. That is, there is no noticeable distance between his voice and the biographical author's, and the voice we hear is saddened and embittered by the changes that have taken place in Kasrilevke. Sholom Aleichem complains that the humor and sense of community have disappeared from the shtetl as a result of European influence. He describes the pre-Enlightenment shtetl, its limitations and infirmities, in relation to the changes it has made. These negative aspects of the pre-Enlightenment shtetl serve as a foil, and we would expect that the modern changes would strengthen the shtetl and make life easier for its inhabitants. What the reader expects, however, fails to materialize and the changes that occur prove to be even worse than the previously existing conditions. The reader perceives Sholom Aleichem's nostalgia as ironic; the narrator misses those poverty-stricken conditions that once held the shtetl community together. Instead he finds the community at odds with itself:

> . . . there was a Yiddish Club and a Hebrew Society. One couldn't bear the sight of the other, or stand mention of the other's name. Then there was the Choral Society which had split into two. One group was now called "The Flute," the other, "The Trumpet." They were quite ready to eliminate each other. Then there were two progressive schools—aggressive, really—each with murder in its eye. . . .[13]

Sholom Aleichem contrasts these new groups to the organizations of old, such as "Clothe-the-Poor" and "Free-Loan." The "progress" that has infiltrated the shtetls manifests itself by the Kasrilevkites' imitation of all the negative facets of big city life and values, demonstrated above by the competition and lack of community which existed in the previous Kasrilevke stories.

Sholom Aleichem clearly loses the distance he once had as author. He further places his audience of Jewish intellectuals in a tenuous position because his attacks and disappointments are directed toward them as well as toward the inadequacies of the shtetl folk. The expectations of the Enlightenment intellectuals for the shtetl Jews are unreasonable and self-serving.

Sholom Aleichem's argument is structured in analogous terms, demonstrated by the previous example of the comparative changes that occurred in the shtetls. He now compares life in the shtetl to life in the outside world, and finds both lacking. Sholom Aleichem shows the shtetl to be a microcosm of the larger world. He describes Europe as a country riddled with problems, from the "Dreyfus affair" in particular to isolationism and anti-semitism in general. To paraphrase Sholom Aleichem; if the larger, more experienced, "enlightened" world cannot handle its own problems, then the Kasrilevkites certainly cannot. Within that overall structure lies another argument: if the Kasrilevkites can barely perform basic survival tasks, such as securing adequate food, maintaining comfortable living conditions, and resolving their own internal conflicts, then it is absurd to assume that the shtetl can become like modern Europe.

As we can see, Sholom Aleichem's anger becomes explicit because he fails to maintain an objective distance from

his material; he cannot. He is, in fact, directly inside the shtetl in these stories and his stance thus changes. When Sholom Aleichem, the biographical author, breaks down the distance between himself and his spokesman, Sholom Aleichem, narrator-character, his perspective toward the subject inevitably changes. He expresses anger at the shtetl Jews, and at Jewish intellectuals. Sholom Aleichem, in fact, fails to resolve the dilemma that he discovers when the shtetls are exposed to the rest of the world. The narrative consequences reflect this new authorial stance and perhaps Sholom Aleichem's own sense that he has essentially complicated his audience's reaction to the fiction.

Narrative Structure

The major difference between the Kasrilevke stories and Sholom Aleichem's earlier works lies in the function of comedy. Humor, as I discussed earlier, served this writer as a means of escape from the essential tragedy of the situation he described. Humor made the material more acceptable for a removed reading audience. His Kasrilevke Jews, although hungry, maintained their sense of humor. When Sholom Aleichem was comically ironic the reader was allowed to view the characters from the author's distanced yet sympathetic stance. Humor for the author thus established the necessary distance from which he could respond to and regard his characters.

In these later Kasrilevke stories the function of comedy changes. Here the comic situations and characters reflect the author's despair. His voice is sarcastic rather than ironic. Irony implied more ambiguity; sarcasm is in many ways an assault, and cannot be regarded by the reader as ambiguous. Because the author is directly inside these stories as an embittered and indignant commentator, the comic elements appear intrusive and thus much less effective, less interesting, in fact. The comic structure in the story **"Bandits,"** for example, reflects the writer's own sense that he no longer provides them with a stance of ironic distance.

In **"Bandits"** Sholom Aleichem is both protagonist and narrator-author. He enters his hotel room in Kasrilevke only to discover "three queer-looking men whom I had never seen before rummaging about with a candle. My bed was upset, my clothes-press was open, my suitcase lay in the middle of the room, and my papers and manuscripts were scattered helter-skelter on the floor."[14] The robbers demand money from Sholom Aleichem and a bantering cross-examination ensues:

> 'Where are you from?'
>
> 'From Yehupetz.'
>
> 'What's your name?'
>
> 'Sholom Aleichem.'
>
> Mistaking my name for the customary Yiddish greeting, they returned the compliment by saying, 'Aleichem Sholom,' adding, 'your name please.'
>
> 'Sholom Aleichem.'

'Aleichem Sholom.' We're asking you what they call you.'

'Sholom Aleichem—that's what they call me.'

'An odd name. What do you do?'

'I'm a writer.' (Pp. 99-100)

Clearly Rabinovitsh's choice of "Sholom Aleichem" as a pseudonym functions as a source of humor in itself, since it is the traditional formal greeting between Jews,[15] and its comic nature and use cannot be denied. The audience in this case is no longer allowed an ironic vision of the events, but laughs because of the play on words and the virtually slap-stick humor of the situation. The dialogue continues along these same lines as the bandits attempt to understand Sholom Aleichem's profession:

'So what do you write? Petitions or documents or denunciations?'

'I write articles and story books for Jewish children.'

'In other words, you're a book vendor, an author.'

. . . 'Write where?'

'In the papers.'

'What papers?'

'Yiddish papers.'

'Are there Yiddish papers?'

'What do you suppose?'

'What do they do with them?'

'They print them.'

. . . 'What are they good for?'

'For reading.'

'Who reads them?'

'Jews.' . . . (Pp. 100-103)

The entire narrative is structured around this kind of comic bantering and while funny and essentially light-hearted it lacks the stylistic eloquence achieved through the dramatic irony of his earlier stories. This kind of humorous play on the language might well be effective for an immediate audience of Yiddish-speaking shtetl Jews, but for an extended audience of Jewish intellectuals, this narrative form falls into the early maskilic notion of the function of Yiddish as a literary medium, discussed earlier, that is, that Yiddish is used primarily to satirize itself by emphasizing its inferiority to other languages.

When Sholom Aleichem structures his story around these comic lines the narrative loses its dramatic movement and the design of the story is circular, lacking the tension he developed in the earlier works through the reader's ironic understanding of the texts. Instead of an ironic authorial tone, in fact, the comedy leads to a tone of indignation on the part of author. Sholom Aleichem laments the fact that he is forced to write in a language that is considered illegitimate, and to write for a limited audience. The humor here serves as a veil through which tragic implications are filtered. The closeness between the narrator and the author prevents any distance Sholom Aleichem might otherwise achieve. This kind of satire introduces an element of self-criticism into the work, resulting in Sholom Aleichem's sense that he too is by no means exempt from the blame he places on the European intellectuals.

I am not suggesting that this is the only case in which Sholom Aleichem ironizes his profession. On the contrary, writing in Yiddish, the frequent misunderstanding of his audience, and the poverty that a Yiddish writer experienced are common topics in his repertoire of short works. For example, in the monologue, **"An eytse,"** a young man has been waiting three days to discuss an urgent matter with the writer, Sholom Aleichem. As soon as the writer takes a glimpse of the young man he assumes his visitor must be a potential writer himself.

I looked the odd creature over. A typical small-town intellectual—a writer. A pale young man with huge, black, sad eyes, the sort of eyes that plead with you to have pity on a lost lonely soul. I don't like such eyes. I'm afraid of them. They never laugh; they never smile. They're always looking inward, immersed in their own ego. I despise such eyes.[16]

The author in this example laughs at himself and asks his audience to do the same. In **"Bandits,"** however, the author fails to distance himself sufficiently from his narrator in order to laugh at Sholom Aleichem, the writer, with his intended audience. Furthermore, Sholom Aleichem directs his anger at those who have placed the nineteenth century Yiddish fiction writer in such a position; his tone indicates self-pity. When, for example, Sholom Aleichem responds to the bandits' demands for money, he informs them: "Where do I get money? God has spared me from it." (P. 98) The irony that characterized his previous works turns to indignation, and the humor does not temper the overt criticism and hostility demonstrated in his tonal shift.

Although Sholom Aleichem concludes the dialogue on this note, he never entirely loses the eloquence of the previous works. Sholom Aleichem, given his ability to change his position at will, becomes like the rest of the shtetl folk. When the bandits leave his room the writer loses his calm demeanor and runs screaming into the streets:

"Help! Help! Help!" I let out the weirdest shrieks when the prowlers had left, and roused the entire house. There was wild scramble from every part of the hotel. Women jumped out of beds in their petticoats, and the menfolk—if you will pardon me—in just their drawers. They thought there was a fire. . . .

"Hush, hush, nobody's house is on fire," Noiach the doorman cried out. He turned to me. "I'd like to know why you're shrieking like a lunatic calf. Why are you bawling like in a madhouse? You're liable to wake up all the yactors!"

"Robbers, murderers! Bandits have just set upon me and robbed me!"

On hearing the word "robbers," the entire crowd was horror-stricken and raised a wild rumpus, all talking at the same time. (Pp. 104-105)

Sholom Aleichem, the author, appears to try out various postures as he once again distances himself from his narrator, Sholom Aleichem, who becomes a persona, one of the shtetl folk. The narrator's once learned, removed position as visitor-writer gives way and he is totally enmeshed in the actions and misconceptions of the other characters.

Here the author regains complete control once again and the story is brought to an appropriate closure. We hear a different authorial tone from the anger displayed earlier. The disjointed and disoriented voice of the narrator-persona abruptly shifts to the stylistic eloquence that clearly suggests the earlier voice of Sholom Aleichem:

I stood alone in the midst of the mud, bewildered by the night and its terrors and alarms. A dank chill gripped my body and penetrated every limb. Here and there a faint light loomed in a window. Blue wreaths of smoke curled up out of a stray chimney. A bright streak appeared above the horizon. From a number of places rose the crowing of roosters, which were tuning up their throats and vocalizing in every imaginable pitch and style: 'Cock-a-doodle-doo!'

It was getting light now. (Pp. 109-110)

Sholom Aleichem returns at the end of the story to his distanced position of observer. He paints a picture of a frightened people, unable to cope with even the slightest conflict. It is when the author distances himself from the text that he is most effective. Sholom Aleichem, by his very nature, can stand between the biographical author and the subject, allowing him that distanced perspective, or step aside, as it were, and allow for direct authorial intrusion. However, Sholom Aleichem's role as persona in the later Kasrilevke stories is rare, and usually we find the author directly inside the texts and his judgment and indictment override the essential humor of his works.

When Sholom Aleichem explicitly addresses himself to life outside of the shtetl he is perhaps the most bitter. There is little trace of ironic humor in these stories, and the irony gives way to overt anger, unmasked.

Outside The Shtetl

When the dramatic situation in the later Kasrilevke stories moves from the confines of the shtetl to the outside world, Sholom Aleichem's anger is intensified because he is forced to view the shtetl Jews through the eyes of outsiders. He depicts the shtetl Jew's exposure to overt-anti-semitism in the large European cities. The hopelessness of the situation of the Jews in Europe is finally confronted by the author, and his stance is only barely disguised. Sholom Aleichem demonstrates no restraint of authorial voice as he describes the shtetl Jews in the outside world, and his angry attacks extend to intellectual Jews and non-Jews alike.

In "The Poor and the Rich" section within *Inside Kasrilevke,* the controlling authorial voice is bitterly satiric as Sholom Aleichem describes the anti-semitic responses toward the shtetl Jews as they are forced into the big cities in search of assistance. The attitudes of the non-Jews in the cities suggest the enormous gap between the two worlds and emphasize the impossibility of assimilation or acceptance. The stories in this collection are entirely satiric in nature and the anger displayed by the author increases as the reactions of the non-Jews to the homeless shtetl inhabitants are judged.

The dramatic situation in these stories arises from a disaster that struck Kasrilevke. The shtetl is virtually burned to the ground, leaving people homeless and hungry. A delegation of Kasrilevke Jews is sent to Yehupetz, "the great and beautiful Gentile City," to solicit contributions for the desperate Kasrilevkites.

The authorial tone as exemplified by the description of Yehupetz as the gentile city, cited above, is immediately satiric, and Sholom Aleichem's argument is for perhaps the first time didactic and moralistic:

Now you mustn't suppose that there is a dearth of Jews in this non-Jewish town. Quite the contrary. As is well known, Yehupetz has had Jews in its midst from the days of antiquity on; and, it should be added, it craves them about as much as a man craves a headache.

For no matter when you come to Yehupetz and no matter what newspaper of theirs you pick up, the first thing that strikes your eye is the word 'Jews.' Thus you will read that such and such a number of them have applied for admission to the university but were not taken in; such and such a number of them were caught in a nightly raid (aimed to ferret out non-resident Jews) and *were* taken in. The reverse has never been known to happen: that Jews seeking admission to the university should be accepted and those caught in a raid should be rejected. This is about as possible as it is for a famished man to mistake another man's mouth for his own and to cram food into it by error.[17]

Sholom Aleichem is no longer laughing at the Jewish situation in Europe and the narrative essentially becomes overridingly didactic and tragic. I doubt if either an audience of European intellectuals or an audience of shtetl Jews would find the above description funny. As a result of this drastic tonal shift from his earlier stories about the Kasrilevkite Jews, Sholom Aleichem complicates the rhetorical, literary, and aesthetic situation that controls his narrative. Consider the tone in the following excerpts: "They feel their best only when they are all together. The non-Jewish world is quite willing to please them and keeps on telling them: 'You like to be together, don't you—Well, stick together then,'"[18] The writer's sarcastic tone is really an attack on the myths and attitudes of the Europeans: "It's a known fact that every Jew takes along on the road no fewer than two or three bundles, . . . Hence, when traveling, Jews don't look so much like travelers as like wanderers, emigrants going to some faraway country where you simply can't get either pillows or quilts or rags—not at any price."[19]

The final result of Sholom Aleichem's didactic and moralistic tone in these Kasrilevke stories is that he fails to find a resolution to a dynamic situation. There is, in fact, no viable solution to the problem of the world's acceptance of the shtetl Jew, and the Jew's ability to survive in such a hostile environment. The problem is far too deeply rooted for change. As a result the author is angry and bitterly sorrowful. His anger appears to be directed against Jews and non-Jews alike and the causes of the problem are like the various links in a chain. Sholom Aleichem is no longer comfortable with, nor amused by the shtetl Jews because of their inability to adapt to the changes that confront them. He is further bitter towards those Jewish intellectuals who unrealistically insist that the shtetl folk come out in the open and gracefully merge into European culture. These demands and the subsequent thwarted attempts to fulfill them only intensify anti-semitism because the difference between the shtetl Jews, gentiles and intellectual Jews are magnified when the shtetl Jews find themselves out of their protective—albeit ambiguous—environment. Sholom Aleichem loses control of the narrative because he really cannot find an appropriate target for the blame. Perhaps what he cannot come to terms with in these stories is that there is no one particular group to blame, and no definitive resolution to the problem. The situation itself, finally, seems to have been an inevitable culmination of the changes which occurred throughout history, and I think we find a writer struggling to find an acceptable stance toward an entirely hopeless situation.

Because the author lacks a suitable stance, he begins to weaken his hold on the reader. That is, his audience remains in an uncomfortable position throughout these stories. When, for example, in the story **"In High Places,"** the shtetl Jews in the city finally find the only place that will accept them, Sholom Aleichem tells us that place is jail:

> Unfortunately, however, none of the high-born were looking down, and our delegates, the most prominent citizens of Kasrilevke, headed by their rabbi, Reb Yozifl, were led away with great pomp to a place which is rent-free and where no racial and social distinctions exist—one place where Jews, even if they come from Kasrilevke, can stay as long as they live, if only the Lord will grant them length of life.[20]

I think that the above citation speaks for itself. Sholom Aleichem attacks his European audience for their neglect of the shtetl Jews and thus fails to draw the reader inside the text. He is, instead, in a position where he stands on the side of his characters against the reader. Therefore, instead of persuading his audience to change their attitudes toward the old world shtetl and the shtetl folk, he alienates his audience even further from their heritage and from the dynamic situation that existed at the turn of the century.

This is by no means to imply that Sholom Aleichem's mastery as a fiction writer is lessened by the narrative structure and tone in these stories. I think, however, that this aspect of his fiction has been neglected, perhaps even denied. Sholom Aleichem is, of course, one of the great Jewish humorists. What gives his fiction such strength and stylistic merit, however, is his flexibility of form. Like a magician, he is able to conjure up voices to fit the changing ethos of his time. He limits himself to no one form. Sholom Aleichem constructs comic caricatures, sympathetic types, tragic figures in a humorous vein that shifts in degree and in visibility.

Clearly, the shtetl was never glamorized or made the object of sentimental attachment. In fact, Sholom Aleichem has portrayed the shtetl as isolated, destitute, and its inhabitants as often petty, illogical, constantly disoriented. However, the sincerity and genuine feelings displayed by the old world shtetl Jews are replaced in these later stories by artificial adaptation of values and appearances foreign to those same Jews. These transitional Kasrilevke stories were written in 1914-1915 when Sholom Aleichem himself had immigrated to New York and had optimistic hopes of a successful literary career and a supportive intellectual community.[21] In these expectations he was severely disappointed and as a result, perhaps his bitter tone is much more apparent in these stories than ever before. The negative conclusion reached in the stories of the changing shtetl and the outcome of its inhabitants extends to the immigrants who have fled European persecution and even to the modernization of the shtetl itself. Hence, the tone of utter despair in the narration of the later Kasrilevke stories. If hope was suggested before, it is entirely abandoned here. The author is unable to come to terms with the hopeless situation he perceives so acutely.

The complete hopelessness of the situation for the shtetl Jews extends beyond the confines of the ghetto, into an Enlightened Europe, and the land of promise itself. Persecution and isolation, on a far greater level, await them in the outside world when they must abandon their values and adapt themselves to an unfamiliar and unaccepting environment. The problem for Sholom Aleichem, the writer, I think, is how to come to terms with the hopeless situation and not to despair, not to lose his aesthetic distance. He is unable to accomplish this in these Kasrilevke stories because his anger and disappointment made it impossible for him to maintain the level of detachment, sophistication and obvious artistic skill he demonstrates in so many of his other works. In most of Sholom Aleichem's works, when the author is not distanced from the text by another narrating voice the result is satiric, didactic and denunciatory.

Notes

1 Sholom Aleichem, "The Town of the Little People," in *Selected Stories of Sholom Aleichem,* trans., Julius and Frances Butwin, Alfred Kazin, ed., (New York: Random House, 1956), p. 28.

2 Sholom Aleichem, *The Adventures of Menahem-Mendl,* trans., Tamara Kahana (New York: Paragon Books, 1979), pp. 134-135.

3 Refer to footnote 22 in Chapter I.

4 Sholom Aleichem, "Dreyfus in Kasrilevka," in *Collected Stories of Sholom Aleichem: The Old Country,* trans., Julius and Frances Butwin (New York: Crown Publishers, Inc., 1946), pp. 260-261.

5 Sholom Aleichem, "The Great Panic of the Little People," in *Old Country Tales,* trans., Curt Leviant, (New York: Paragon Books, 179), pp. 98-100.

6 Sholom Aleichem, "A Predestined Disaster," in *Old Country Tales,* pp. 149-160.

7 Sholom Aleichem, "The Great Panic of the Little People," in *Old Country Tales,* p. 100.

8 Sholom Aleichem, "A Guide to Kasrilevke, Author's Foreword," in *Inside Kasrilevke,* trans., Isidore Goldstick (New York: Schocken Books, Inc., 1948), p. 7.

9 Sholom Aleichem, "Reb Yozifl and the Contractor," in *Inside Kasrilevke,* p. 222.

10 Sholom Aleichem, "A Guide to Kasrilevke, Author's Foreword," in *Inside Kasrilevke,* pp. 7-8.

11 Sholom Aleichem, excerpts from "A Guide to Kasrilevke," in *Inside Kasrilevke,* pp. 27-28 and p. 44.

12 Sholom Aleichem, "Progress in Kasrilevke," in *Stories and Satires,* trans., Curt Leviant (New York: Sagamore Press, Inc., 1959), pp. 17-18.

13 Sholom Aleichem, "Progress in Kasrilevke," in *Stories and Satires,* p. 18.

14 Sholom Aleichem, "Bandits," in *Inside Kasrilevke,* p. 97. All further references to this story are from this edition and will be noted in the body of my study.

15 Dan Miron discusses the use of Sholom Aleichem as a comic element in the stories:

> By choosing a formal greeting for a name, the author was first and foremost asserting the comic, prankish, and "contrary" nature of his persona. A being, whose very name consists in an incongruity or in a pun-like misuse of language, is bound to be "funny." Thus the name Sholem-Aleykhem, appearing under the title of a feuilleton or a story, conditions the reader's reading of the work and directs his expectations from it. . . . One suspects that most people who wrote on Yiddish literature became so familiar with the name Sholem-Aleykhem that they altogether lost the sense of its original absurdity. . . . In order to recharge its waning comic potential and refresh the reader's perception of its preposterousness, he employed various

gimmicks, such as that of comic misunderstanding, the recurrent employment of such gimmicks should not be interpreted as a mere recourse to easy techniques of getting a laugh from an audience ready to laugh almost at anything, but rather as the author's persisting intention to protect the basic comic feature of his persona, . . . from fading.

(Miron, "Sholem Aleykhem: Person, Persona, Presence," in *The Uriel Weinreich Memorial Lecture I,* [New York: Yivo Institute for Jewish Research, 1972], pp. 32-34.)

16 Sholom Aleichem, "A Bit of Advice," in *Some Laughter, Some Tears: Tales From the Old World and the New,* trans., Curt Leviant (New York: Paragon Books, 1979), pp. 131-132.

17 Sholom Aleichem, "The Delegation," in "The Poor and the Rich" section of *Inside Kasrilevke,* pp. 115-116.

18 Sholom Aleichem, "Among Their Own," in *Inside Kasrilevke,* pp. 165-166.

19 Sholom Aleichem, "Among Their Own" in *Inside Kasrilevke,* p. 165.

20 Sholom Aleichem, "In High Places," in *Inside Kasrilevke,* p. 193.

21 See Rabinovitsh's biography, *My Father, Sholom Aleichem,* by Marie Waife-Goldberg (New York: Simon and Schuster, 1968), "In America," Chapter XVII, pp. 278-317.

Emanuel S. Goldsmith   (essay date 1986)

SOURCE: "The Divine Humor of Sholom Aleichem," in *Judaism,* Vol. 35, No. 4, Fall, 1986, pp. 391-401.

[*In the following essay, Goldsmith contends that Aleichem's "humor is a unique phenomenon in the history of Jewish culture and a surprising mutation in the evolution of the Jewish spirit."*]

The basic attitude of traditional Judaism towards humor is expressed in the Talmudic injunction that "it is forbidden to make fun of anything except idolatry."[1] It was the ethical earnestness, ritual strictness, other-worldliness and asceticism of the Talmud, the Midrash and later rabbinic literature which set the tone for Jewish life until modern times. Despite the fact that the Talmud and Midrash contain a few humorous attacks on super-piety and overzealousness in the interpretation of Scripture and tradition, the rabbis knew that humor could also be used against their own religious teachings and, consequently, they opposed it.[2]

In the Middle Ages, rabbis sought to restrict revelry on the merry festival of Purim as well as at weddings and other celebrations.[3] For many centuries they also opposed the establishment of the happy *Simhat Torah* holiday as a recognized festival. The revelry permitted in the Christian world probably smacked too much of paganism for them to seek to emulate it in the Jewish community.

> Medieval drama never excluded the comic from its religious ritual . . . near the season of Lent the monks

used to appoint one of their number to be Lord of Unreason and chant the liturgy of Folly, during which an Ass was worshipped and the Mass parodied in a ceremony no less religious, in its profane way, than the Dionysian and Saturnalian revels of Greece and Rome.[4]

In light of this, the merry-making of the *Purim-shpielers* and of the *badkhonim* or Jewish wedding-jesters, from the middle ages to the eighteenth century, seems very tame indeed.

The emergence of Jewish humor, as we know it today, coincides with the proliferation of ideological diversity in Eastern European Jewish society, on the one hand, and with the triumph of the Yiddish language as a major written and oral medium of Jewish culture, on the other.[5] Modern Jewish humor is essentially "the spiritual laughter of a people which laughed in order not to always have to cry"[6] and is inextricably linked to the traditional Jewish way of life with its interweaving of poverty, ritualism, intellectualism, and wit.

Modern Jewish humor is an expression of the national character of the Jewish people. Its primary characteristic is the ridicule of idolatry and all man-made gods.

> A Jew does not laugh simply because he loves a punchline or a trick. A Jew laughs because there resides within him the ancient irony of the Psalms which he adapts to the constantly new manifestations of paganism everywhere and of idolatry in his own communal life.[7]

Other characteristic elements of Jewish humor are the love of Torah and learning, opposition to ignorance, and a deep sense of justice which refuses to recognize differences between rich and poor. According to Aaron Zeitlin, the democratic spirit of Jewish humor is rooted in Jewish religious ethics. "It is a democratic spirit which draws sustenance from a faith which makes all persons equal not before a civil law but before the Creator of the world." A good deal of Jewish humor revolves around the eternal Jewish complaint expressed by Sholom Aleichem's Tevye, "where is God and where is justice?" "For the authentic Jew justice and God necessarily go together."[8]

Sholom Aleichem's humor is a unique phenomenon in the history of Jewish culture and a surprising mutation in the evolution of the Jewish spirit. When one takes into account that for many centuries non-religious literature was viewed as alien to Judaism and that the very reading of such literature was a sin (*bittul Torah*), the novelty of Sholom Aleichem's achievement becomes even more remarkable. While scattered examples of wit and humor may be found in the Bible, the Talmud and medieval Hebrew writings, the higher reaches of humor such as one finds in Sholom Aleichem are almost completely absent from Jewish literature before he made his appearance. Yet even he must be viewed within the context of the evolution of Judaism and the history of the Jewish people. Biblical monotheism discovered God's presence in history and the

purpose of human life in ethical behavior. It held up to ridicule the meaninglessness and immorality of paganism and created a context of optimism which fostered confidence and hope for human life.

In the eighteenth century two revolutionary movements in Jewish thought prepared the ground for the flowering of Jewish humor in the years to come. Hasidism, in fostering joy as the proper mood for religious life and worship, criticized the strictness and rigidity of traditional Jewish religion. It viewed the religious leadership and accepted standards of piety with contempt and could not help but make fun of conventional religious standards and values. The Haskalah, or Jewish enlightenment movement, on the other hand, held both the Hasidim and their opponents up to rational scrutiny and found them wanting. Haskalah gave birth to a relatively large body of satirical writing in Hebrew and Yiddish which sought to wean Jews away from the excesses of religious tradition and the narrowness of isolation and exclusivism.

In his classical study of Sholom Aleichem, Meir Wiener characterizes the humor which enables us to transcend misfortune as a "noble, gracious way to overcome an unpleasant situation in which one finds oneself through no fault of his own." Without self-respect, purity of the spirit, and wisdom of the heart, no such humor is possible. "It soothes the pain of a perplexing, degrading situation with inner spiritual power derived from faith in the dignity of man and in the principle of justice and its ultimate victory."[9] Even in the most hopeless of situations, such humor playfully feigns victory in order to emphasize the meaninglessness, evil, and unnaturalness of our predicament. It protects sarcastically and gives one the courage to endure. For students of literature and philosophy, this positive laughter is divine comedy.

Sholom Aleichem's writings are the highest expression of such divine comedy.

> I wasn't worried about God so much, (says Tevye, the epitome of Sholom Aleichem's characters.) I could come to terms with Him one way or another. What bothered me was people. Why should people be so cruel when they could be so kind? Why should human beings bring suffering to one another as well as to themselves, when they could all live together in peace and good will?[10]

Sholom Aleichem's laughter is philosophical, creative, affirmative and healthful. It is provoked primarily by the discrepancy and the distance between what is and what ought to be. It helps in a rational and realistic evaluation of the world and it encourages improvement.[11] It is laughter that "triumphs over pain and hardship in the passion for an enduring ideal, the joy of bringing the light of happiness, of truth and beauty into a dark world."[12] It inculcates love for the Jewish people and its heritage of history, culture and religion. On the day before Yom Kippur, Sholom Aleichem tells us, we would hardly recognize Noah-Wolf the butcher. "He stops fighting with the other butchers, becomes soft as butter toward his customers, is considerate to the servant girls, becomes so unctuous you could almost spread him over a boil." He puts on his holiday garment, goes from house to house, to all his customers and neighbors, to ask for pardon for the sins he may have committed during the past year. "If anything I have said offended you, I want to apologize, and wish you a happy New Year." "The same to you, Noah-Wolf," they respond. "May God pardon us all."[13]

Divine comedy "criticizes almost with love, and at a very high level. . . . It has judgment without criticism; laughter but above the battle, and an affirmation which is almost direct. It takes all actuality to be its province and contrasts this with the whole of the logical order. . . ."[14] Where Dante's *Divine Comedy* describes Hell, Purgatory, and Paradise, Sholom Aleichem describes Kasrilevka. "His great love for the Jewish people stood by him when he accepted the challenge to complete his own 'Divine Comedy,'" writes Jacob Glatstein. "It was not God's laughing at his little human creatures but a Jewish 'Divine Comedy,' in the sense of God's dwelling with Jews, participating day-by-day in the tragicomedy of their life."[15] Sholom Aleichem's humor opens a window on the enduring values and traditions of the Jewish people. It possesses broad humanity and profound faith in man's unconquerable spirit. In trying times, it sweetened the bitterness of a difficult existence. During the Holocaust, it brought comfort to the Jews locked in ghettos and annihilation camps.

The primary characters of Sholom Aleichem's three major works—*Tevye, Menahem-Mendl* and *Mottel, the Cantor's Son*—are humorous variations on the theme of the indefatigable optimism of the Jewish people. Mottel's motif is "Hurray for me! I'm an orphan!" Menahem-Mendl will not permit his constant failures at earning a livelihood to dissuade him from trying something new. Tevye, like Job of old, refuses to permit adversity to turn him from the path of faith. Unlike Job, however, Tevye is able to transcend tribulation through humor as well as through religion.

> I say that the main thing is faith (proclaims Tevye). A Jew must hope. What if we work ourselves to the bone? That's why we're Jews. . . . As you know, I'm a great believer. I never have any complaints against the Almighty. Whatever he does is good. As Scripture says, "Trust in the Lord"—Put your faith in God and he'll see to it that you lie six feet under, bake bagels and still thank him. . . . I say that we have a great God and a good God but, nevertheless, I say, I would like a blessing for every time God does something the likes of which should happen to our enemies.[16]

Sholom Aleichem's humor is the kind of divine gift and stratagem for personal and national survival which may yet save mankind from itself. Today, the inherent decency and goodness of people is almost ignored. "Our ideological confusion presents a tremendous challenge for all idealists, creative writers, and thinkers to recognize and confront these evils with their opposites: oppression . . . with freedom . . . , lies and deceit with truth; fanaticism with reason; terrorism with peace; arrogance . . . with humility; . . . ugliness with beauty.[17]

The kind of laughter that Sholom Aleichem evokes—the laughter of acceptance, friendship, sympathy and contentment—is essential to human dignity and sanity. "Laughter," writes Wylie Sypher, "is a tactic for survival, a mark of 'superior adaptation' among gregarious animals."[18] Sholom Aleichem's laughter "is born out of the pure joy of living, the spontaneous expression of health and energy—the sweet laughter of the child . . . the warm laughter of the kindly soul which heartens the discouraged, gives health to the sick and comfort to the dying."[19] In the Bible, Abraham is willing to sacrifice the beloved son of his old age in order to demonstrate his faith. In a Sholom Aleichem story, the "happiest man" in Kodno is the poor man who risks his life to save his dying son by throwing himself before the carriage of the physician who may be able to save him. "I would have liked to take a picture of him," writes Sholom Aleichem, "to let the whole world see what a really happy man looked like, the happiest man in Kodno."[20]

Eric Bentley writes about receiving joy, the higher pleasure of comedy, only from an author in whom we sense joy's opposite. "The comic dramatist's starting point is misery; the joy at his destination is a superb and thrilling transcendence."[21] Sholom Aleichem concludes his travelogue of Kasrilevka with a description of the town's two cemeteries—the old and the new. "The new one is old enough and rich enough in graves. Soon there will be no place to put anyone, especially if a pogrom should break out or any of the other misfortunes which befall us in these times." The Kasrilevkites take special pride in the old cemetery both because famous people are buried in it and because it is "the only piece of land of which they are the masters, the only bit of earth they own where a blade of grass can sprout and a tree can grow and the air is fresh and one can breathe freely."[22] "The secret source of humor," wrote Mark Twain, "is not joy but sorrow."[23]

Five years before Sholom Aleichem's death in 1916, in a letter of consolation to friends who were mourning the death of a child, he revealed the deepest secret of his humor.

> It's an ugly, evil world, (he wrote). I say to you that just to spite the world one must not cry. If you want to know, this is the true source, the real reason for my usually good mood, for my "humor," as they call it. Just to spite the world don't cry! Just to spite the world—only laugh, only laugh! . . .[24]

It took many years of privation, hardship and artistic struggle for Sholom Aleichem to come to that realization. The little boy who had delighted in mimicking his elders and whose first literary work was an alphabetical list of his stepmother's curses, developed his understanding of the function of laughter and the nature of humor only gradually. Slowly he overcame the natural tendency to provoke laughter by telling jokes and pointing out the grotesque and incongruous and, instead, explored the healing powers of understanding, acceptance, and compassion. By that time he had become the Columbus of Jewish laughter and the discoverer of the power of the Jewish smile. He became the physician with an effective balm for his people's wounds, the engineer capable of tapping its hidden well-springs of joy and comfort.

Sholom Aleichem's humor was suffused with a deep love for his people, committed to the alleviation of its suffering and determined to record for posterity the radiance of a way of life based on humanity and kindness.

—Emanuel S. Goldsmith

The tremendous adulation which Sholom Aleichem achieved from all segments of Yiddish-speaking Jewry during his lifetime and which continued unabated until the Holocaust, is one of the truly remarkable phenomena in the history of Jewish culture. Once, during a reading tour in Warsaw, a pious young man ran up to him on the street and kissed his hand. Although the young man belonged to a sect of Jewry for whom the reading of secular literature was a sacrilege, he could not help saying, "You are our comfort. You sweeten for us the bitterness of exile."[25] As early as 1908, Ba'al Makhshoves, the literary critic, began an essay with the words: "Sholom Aleichem is one of those fortunate Yiddish writers who need not wait for a literary anniversary to make their names known among the broad masses. Even before the critics took to Sholom Aleichem, he was well-known in almost every Jewish home."[26] S. Niger, a literary critic who took many years to warm up to Sholom Aleichem, eventually admitted that "no one thing in Jewish life affected the westernized Jew in Eastern Europe so much as these stories—except, perhaps, pogroms. Just as pogroms brought to the surface his repressed fears and tears, so Sholom Aleichem evoked his less profound but equally suppressed laughter and raillery at the world."[27]

Sholom Aleichem seems to have rediscovered two insights of the biblical Book of Proverbs: "A joyful heart makes for good health; despondency dries up the bones" (17:22) and "If there is anxiety in a man's mind let him quash it and turn it into joy with a good word." (12:25) The traditional rendering of the last verse was "if there is anxiety in a man's mind let him talk it out of his mind." An awareness of the powers of laughter and speech was Sholom Aleichem's most important contribution to Jewish literature. But he modified these two insights in the light of East European Jewish life. Laughter was not to mock, but to encourage, and speech had to involve movements, facial expressions and vocal intonations, so that in his writings he includes comically detailed descriptions of facial movements and physical gestures. This technique was a major departure in Jewish writing.

Verbal play with logic is another characteristic of Sholom Aleichem's humor. His characters often sacrifice the rules of sound reasoning for considerations of humanity and kindness. They even find it impossible to conceive that their persecutors are impervious to the cause of justice and the cry of the oppressed. His "little people" "will take things for granted without warrant; they will count their chickens before they are hatched; they will commit regularly the chief fallacies known to every elementary student of logic. Rules do not appeal to them; they are creatures of the heart."[28]

> If I were Goethe, (Sholom Aleichem tells us in his autobiography), I would not describe the sorrows of young Werther, I would describe the sorrows of a poor Jewish lad who was madly in love with the cantor's daughter. If I were Heine, I would not sing of Florentine nights; I would sing of the night of *Simhat Torah,* when Jews make the rounds of *Hakafot* and when young women and pretty girls mingle with the men in the synagogue—the one night when this is permitted. The women kiss the Scroll of the Law. They jump up and down squeaking in every key. "Long life to you!" The answer is "Same to you, same to you!"[29]

Sholom Aleichem's real artistic purpose, for all the irony and humor, was "to portray the ordinary Jew, outwardly crushed by his depressing conditions but inwardly glowing with a majestic sense of his past and his future."[30] On *Simhat Torah,* he tells us, even the grouchy Jew who disapproves of everything and is critical of everything is proud of his heritage. Though he be a man whom nothing can satisfy and no one can please, on this festival he too feels that it is good to be a Jew. Joyously he shouts: "Friends! I want to know, is there anything better than to be a Jew? I ask you one thing: What can be finer than to be a Jew on *Simhat Torah?*"[31] To laugh with Sholom Aleichem is to experience the joy of Jewishness.

The natural breeding ground for responsible behavior and loyalty to mankind is the civilization and tradition into which one is born.[32] The contradictions which Sholom Aleichem points out and utilizes to make us laugh are the contradictions inherent in Jewish life. At a time when Jewish life seemed threatened with extinction because of immigration, religious and cultural erosion and other factors, Sholom Aleichem's writings—which reached more Jews than those of any other author—gave a sense of reality and concreteness to a community in transition. "Is there a Jewish people in the world?" asked Y. H. Brenner, an important Hebrew writer, at the turn of the century. "Is there a specific character to these transports which come and go? Do these wandering groups possess an approach of their own to the world? Can they laugh and cry about life in their own way? Has the Jewish street any vital strengths, any talent for living at all? Yes indeed! The answer is affirmative because there is a Sholom Aleichem!"[33]

One of Sholom Aleichem's major contributions to Yiddish literature was this conferring of an "illusion of territoriality" on the homeless Jewish people. His characters are presented in universal dimensions and bear resemblance to the non-Jewish characters of "normal" nations whom one finds in world literature. This legitimized Yiddish creative writing for a people which had hitherto sought hidden, esoteric meanings—religious, ethical, mystical, didactic, tendentious—in its writings. "Reading Sholom Aleichem, the Jew began to look at himself with a sympathetic, understanding smile as if he were viewing himself from afar. He could laugh through tears at his own misfortunes. This was indeed the liberation and redemption effecting complete transcendence—the highest achievement of belles-lettres."[34]

To be properly understood, Sholom Aleichem's popularity must be viewed partly in terms of the position that he attained relatively early in his career as one of the three founding fathers of Yiddish literature, the two others being Mendele Mocher Seforim and Yitzchok Leybush Peretz. These three, all of whom passed away between 1915 and 1917, played a crucial role in the emergence of modern Jewish culture and self-consciousness. They wrote when the great masses of Eastern European Jewry (which, at the time, constituted, by far, the overwhelming majority of the Jews) were emerging from their medieval status as a segregated pariah people, leaving their traditional little towns or *shtetlekh* and becoming part of Western culture. Mendele, Sholom Aleichem and Peretz belonged to those small circles of *maskilim* or idealistic intellectuals who were at once committed to both the modernization of Jewry and the conscious preservation and furtherance of Jewish distinctiveness and identity. As East European Jews moved into the large cities of Europe and America, they took with them feelings of inadequacy which stemmed from their lack of familiarity with Gentile languages and culture and from the inferior role which Jews had traditionally been forced to play in Christian mythology. These founding fathers of Yiddish literature urged their people to step proudly into the modern world as heirs of a great culture which had much to contribute. While repudiating Jewish isolationism and cultural backwardness, they pointed with pride to the humanistic impulses of the Jewish tradition and the superiority of Jewish ethical standards. For them, the solidarity and spiritual unity of Jewry were inviolate and were to be preserved at all costs. These concerns, popularly referred to, from the early days of the Hasidic movement, as *Ahavat Yisrael,* or love of the Jewish people, constituted a modern, non-theological version of the doctrine of Jewish chosenness, albeit without overtones of chauvinism or exclusiveness.

Mendele, Sholom Aleichem and Peretz became culture-heroes who had a far greater impact on the lives of their readers than did any of the characters whom they created in their fiction. Mendele was the wise, knowledgeable Jew, rooted in the tradition but aware of new winds blowing in the Jewish community. Sholom Aleichem was the happy-go-lucky storyteller who made his readers marvel at the poor but cheerful characters of his tales and take pride in their traditional values and ideals. Peretz was the voice of Jewish humanism and the modern teacher of national ethics and Hasidic idealism.

Sholom Aleichem drew freely on the writings of Mendele for plots, characters, ambiance. He succeeded, however, in transcending the predominantly critical approach to

Jewish life in many of Mendele's works by transmuting the latter's satire and irony into the language of joy and laughter. He replaced the latter's sadness and seriousness with compassion and humor. Mendele had spoken of his own writings as expressing the very core of a Jew "who, even when he does sing a merry tune, sounds from afar as if he were sobbing and weeping."[35] His view of Jewish life was trenchantly conveyed in the names that he chose for the three towns in which his major stories take place: Idlersville, Foolstown, and Paupersville. Sholom Aleichem, on the other hand, described the *shtetl* whose little people refused to allow poverty to depress them and the name of the town became a synonym for people who are "poor but cheerful." That town is Kasrilevka—a derivative of the Hebrew name Kasriel, meaning "crown of God."

There is a direct line from the Yiddish folk tales of the "wise men" of Chelm through Mendele's Kabtzansk or Paupersville to Sholom Aleichem's Kasrilevka or Cheerfultown. In the Chelm tales, wit dominates; in the Kabtzansk stories, satire reigns; in the Kasrilevka adventures, pathos and humor have the day. "The town into which I shall now take you, dear reader," Sholom Aleichem writes, "is exactly in the middle of that blessed Pale [of Settlement] into which Jews have been packed as closely as herring in a barrel and told to increase and multiply. The name of the town is Kasrilevka." The Pale of Settlement, the restricted area of Czarist Russia in which Jews were permitted to live, was a symbol of Jewish degradation and oppression and could hardly be called blessed. Yet, although Jews there were packed as tightly as herring in a barrel, they managed to reproduce themselves like fish in water, as if they had been commanded to do so by their enemies who instituted the Pale of Settlement and promulgated other decrees against them. Or was the act of proliferation perhaps the *shtetl*-dwellers' only way of getting back at their oppressors? It is significant that the town's name is Kasrilevka—a happy name, a joyous name. "A *kasrilik* is not just an ordinary pauper, a failure in life. On the contrary, he is a man who has not allowed poverty to degrade him. He laughs at it. He is poor, but cheerful."

When a *kasrilik* finally reaches Paris and manages to visit a famous fellow Jew, he convinces Rothschild that he has brought with him something that the latter cannot buy in Paris for any amount of money: eternal life. Upon hearing how much eternal life will cost him, the banker says no more, but counts out three hundred rubles, one by one. The Kasrilevkite slips the money into his pocket, and says: "If you want to live forever, my advice to you is to leave this noisy, busy Paris and move to our town of Kasrilevka. There you can never die, because since Kasrilevka has been a town, no rich man has ever died there."[36]

Sholom Aleichem also wrote of the Kasrilevka *melamed* or school-teacher who fantasizes about what he would do if he were Rothschild:

> This is the life! No more worries about making a living. No more headaches about where the money for the Sabbath is coming from. My daughters are all married off—a load is gone from my shoulders.

After taking care of the needs of his family and his town, the *melamed* extends his philanthropic efforts to his brothers and sisters all over the world. In his daydreams, he brings an end to the persecution of his people and to wars throughout the earth.

> Do you understand what I've done? I have not only put over a business deal, but people have stopped killing each other in vain, like oxen. And since there will be no more war, what do we need weapons for? The answer is that we don't. And if there are no more weapons and armies and bands and other trappings of war, there will be no more envy, no more hatred, no Turks, no Englishmen, no Frenchmen, no Gypsies, and no Jews. The face of the earth will be changed. As it is written: "Deliverance will come—" The Messiah will have arrived.[37]

Sholom Aleichem's writings possess a strong spiritual dimension which qualifies them to be considered part of the Torah tradition of the Jewish people. Kierkegaard spoke of religious faith as beginning with a sense of "the discrepancy, the contradiction, between the infinite and the finite, the eternal and that which becomes."[38] He felt that "the religious individual has, as such, made the discovery of the comical in the largest measure."[39] In his autobiography, Sholom Aleichem describes his Uncle Pinney as an extremely observant Jew for whom

> another person's business, anything that smacked of communal affairs, everything that constituted helping a fellow Jew took precedence . . . he would hurry off to arrange the wedding of a poor orphan and dance all night long with her poor relatives—here surely was an opportunity to be kindly which did not often present itself. . . . The poorer the wedding, the greater the merrymaking. That is, the poorer the bride, the wilder Uncle Pinney danced. . . . Ecstasy and inspiration would illuminate his face as at prayer. The musicians would play a Jewish tune; everybody would clap to the rhythm; the circle would gradually widen; and the dancer, balancing among the burning lights, became more ecstatic and more inspired as he proceeded. . . . It was not dancing. Rather, it ws a kind of divine service, a holy rite.[40]

Sholom Aleichem's humor, like his Uncle Pinney's dancing, was a divine service and a holy rite. Association with others is as necessary for laughter as it is for worship. If joke-telling requires a teller, subject-matter and an audience, Sholom Aleichem's humor also requires an awareness of the presence of the God of Israel who is the subjective and objective representation of the Spirit of the Jewish people. In his will, Sholom Aleichem warned his descendants not to forsake their people or their faith and commanded them to bear with honor his hard-earned Jewish name. In the dedication of his autobiography to his children, he wrote: "Read it from time to time. Perhaps you or your children will learn something from it—to love our people and to appreciate their spiritual treasures which lie scattered in all the corners of our great Exile, in this great world."[41] Sholom Aleichem's humor was suffused with a deep love for his people, committed to the alleviation of its suffering and determined to record for posterity the radiance of a way of life based on humanity and kindness. In his legacy of divine laughter the Jewish peo-

ple lives. In his affirmative humor it confronts itself and, getting to know itself and its heritage with a spoonful of sugar, is forever reborn with a chuckle and a smile.

Notes

[1] *Megillah* 25b.

[2] Y. Ovsay, *Ma'amarim Urshimot* (New York, 1946), p. 10.

[3] Cf. Y. Lifshitz, *"Badkhonim un Leytsim bay Yidn,"* *Arkiv far der Geshikhte fun Yidishn Teater un Drame,* ed. J. Shatzky (Vilna-New York: 1930), pp. 38-74.

[4] W. Sypher, "The Meanings of Comedy" in *Comedy,* ed. W. Sypher (Baltimore, 1980), p. 221.

[5] Cf. B.J. Bialostotzky, *Yidisher Humor un Yidishe Leytsim* (New York, 1963), pp. 53-56.

[6] A. Zeitlin, *Literarishe un Filosofishe Eseyen* (New York, 1980), p. 178.

[7] Bialostotzky, *Op. cit.,* p. 59.

[8] Zeitlin, *Op. cit.,* p. 182.

[9] M. Wiener, *Tsu der Geshikhte fun der Yidisher Literatur in Nayntsnin Yorhundert* (New York, 1946), Vol. II, p. 287.

[10] Sholom Aleichem, *Tevye's Daughters,* tr. F. Butwin (New York, 1949), p. 160.

[11] Cf. J.O. Hertzler, *Laughter* (New York, 1970), p. 216.

[12] J.E. Boodin, *God: A Cosmic Philosophy of Religion* (New York, 1934), p. 212.

[13] Sholom Aleichem, *The Old Country,* tr. J. and F. Butwin (New York, 1946), p. 321.

[14] J. Feibelman, *In Praise of Comedy* (New York, 1939), p. 206.

[15] J. Glatstein, *Af Greyte Temes* (Tel Aviv, 1967), p. 31f.

[16] Quoted in I.I. Trunk, *Tevye un Menakhem-Mendl in Yidishn Velt-Goyrl* (New York, 1944), p. 31.

[17] J. Eccles and D. Robinson, *The Wonder of Being Human* (New York, 1984), p. 178.

[18] Sypher, *Op. cit.,* p. 204.

[19] Boodin, *Op. cit.,* p. 212.

[20] Sholom Aleichem, *Tevye's Daughters,* pp. 69-77.

[21] E. Bentley, *The Life of Drama* (New York, 1964), p. 302.

[22] Sholom Aleichem, *The Old Country,* p. 6f.

[23] Mark Twain, *Following the Equator,* 1897; cf. *The International Thesaurus of Quotations,* ed. R.T. Tripp (New York, 1970), p. 293.

[24] Quoted in I.D. Berkowitz, *Undzere Rishoynim* (Tel Aviv, 1966), vol. 4, p. 168.

[25] Quoted in *Dos Sholom Aleykhem Bukh*, ed. I.D. Berkowitz, second edition (New York, 1958), p. 355.

[26] Ba'al Makhshoves, *Geklibene Verk* (New York, 1953), p. 172.

[27] S. Niger, "The Gift of Sholom Aleichem," *Commentary*, (August 1946): 119.

[28] A.A. Roback, "Sholom Aleichem's Humor," *Congress Bi-Weekly*, vol. 26, no. 6 (March 16, 1959): 9.

[29] Sholom Aleichem, *The Great Fair*, tr. T. Kahana (New York, 1955), p. 295f.

[30] I. Rabinovich, *Major Trends in Modern Hebrew Fiction* (Chicago, 1968), p. 19.

[31] Sholom Aleichem, *Tevye's Daughters*, p. 170.

[32] Cf. L. Mumford, *The Transformations of Man* (New York, 1956), pp. 197-199.

[33] Y.H. Brenner, *Kol Kitvey Y.H. Brenner*, vol. 3 (Tel Aviv, 1967), p. 106. The essay was written in 1905.

[34] B. Rivkin, *Grunt-Tendentsn fun der Yidisher Literatur in Amerike* (New York, 1948), p. 14f.

[35] Mendele Mocher Seforim, *Fishke the Lame*, tr. G. Stillman (New York, 1960), p. 13.

[36] Sholom Aleichem, *The Old Country*, pp. 1-6.

[37] Sholom Aleichem, *Tevye's Daughters*, pp. 16-19.

[38] Quoted in Sypher, *Op. cit.*, p. 196f.

[39] Ibid., p. 234.

[40] Sholom Aleichem, *The Great Fair*, p. 61f.

[41] Sholom Aleichem, *The Great Fair*, dedication.

Jonathan Boyarin   (essay date 1986)

SOURCE: "Sholem-Aleykhem's 'Stantsye Baranovitsh'," in *Identity and Ethos: A Festschrift for Sol Liptzin on the Occasion of His 85th Birthday*, edited by Mark H. Gelber, Peter Lang, 1986, pp. 89-99.

[*In the following essay, Boyarin discusses Aleichem's narrative technique as evinced in his short story "Stantsye Baranovitsh."*]

Sholem-Aleykhem's works bridge the gulf between us and the world he evokes. That gulf, immeasurably deepened by the Holocaust, was already evidenced by the distinc-

tion between the Russian-speaking author, Sholem Rabinovitsh, and the Yiddish persona "Sholem-Aleykhem." One aspect of Rabinovitsh's enduring genius may be identified as the awareness of the break between the world in which live storytelling was commonplace and the world in which Rabinovitsh lived, and his consequent creation of unique artifices—such as the Sholem-Aleykhem persona[1]—to bridge the gap without denying it.

Walter Benjamin's essay on "The Storyteller"[2] may help a reader to appreciate Sholem Rabinovitsh's art. Perhaps central therein is Benjamin's observation that "[one] listening to a story is in the company of the storyteller." The auditor is thus linked to the characters, setting, and events of the story by the narrator. The narrator shares something of himself as he tells the story. A live storyteller may use rhetorical devices to place himself within his tale as much as do those who "write stories." His account of the world within the tale is not marred thereby. His presence as a sharer of meaning helps to make a story out of an unconnected series of events. Furthermore, it is a commonplace that "a story need not have happened to be true." For a story to be true, the storyteller must create confidence in the *intent* of his narration. For Benjamin, the ability to share this kind of truth is exceedingly rare at "the present time," which he dates from World War I.

A second characteristic of a story, according to Benjamin, is its longevity: "It preserves and concentrates its strength and is capable of releasing it even after a long time." For him, part of this economy is the freedom of the story from the burden of explicit social or psychological analysis. By this open-endedness stories invite reflection, retelling, and reinterpretation. They are irreducible, in the sense that their essence cannot be separated from their expression. They are also inexhaustible, receiving new energy each time they are told.

Benjamin contrasts these aspects of the story with what he calls "information," the predominant mode of communication in the present. Where the story is evocative, information is explicit. Where the story retains its power far from its place and time of origin, information rapidly loses its significance. Most important, whereas the story stands or falls on the basis of who tells it and how, the accuracy of information is defined as its independence from the judgment of the one who conveys it.

Throughout his career, Rabinovitsh wrote for newspapers. His early feuilletons were surrounded by the kind of "information" that Benjamin deplores; they provided stuff for the mundane conversation of the passengers who appear in Sholem-Aleykhem's *Railroad Stories*. This volume contains, along with **"Stantsye Baranovitsh,"**[3] nineteen other stories written in 1902 and 1909. The framing device for all the stories is a railroad car full of Jews.

The frame narrator of the entire volume is a travelling salesman, a *komivoyazher*, who "explains" in an introductory note that he has decided to occupy his time on trains writing down the stories he hears there. In the brief preface to the volume, Rabinovitsh uses two devices to make his readers feel they know this narrator. First, he deflates the artistic pretensions of the Yiddish writer, the "Mr. Sholem-Aleykhem" to whom the Tevye stories are respectfully recounted:

> Vey-vey, vos me zet zikh on untervegns! A shod, vos ikh bin nit keyn shrayber. Dos heyst, az me vil tsurik, mist vos bin ikh nit keyn shrayber? Vos iz azelkhes, eygentlekh, a shrayber? Yeder mensh kon zayn a shrayber. Ubefrat nokh—of idish. "Zhargon"—oykh mir an eysek! Me nemt a pen un me shraybt.

> [The things you see when you're travelling! It's a pity I'm not a writer. On the other hand, why should I say I'm no writer? After all, what's a writer? Anybody can be a writer. Especially in Yiddish. "Zhargon"—big deal! You pick up a pen and you write . . .]

The author thus creates a narrator who accords perfectly with the merchants from whom he is to hear most of the tales he records, by thinking of his stories as goods:

> yeder geshikhte hob ikh gegebn an andern nomen, fayntshik, vi es geher tsu zayn—mayse soykher. Ikh vays nit, tsi vel ikh inem gesheft fardinen, tsi ikh vel brekhen ruk un lend. Halevy zol ikh khotsh aroys mit mayn keren.

> [. . . I gave every story its own name, the way one is supposed to—like a salesman. I don't know whether I'll make money on the deal or lose my shirt. I hope I'll get out with my capital intact . . .]

The concerns of the narrator's travelling companions are stock market and grain prices and the social advancement and protection of their children. They are anything but fanatics, either of the religious or revolutionary type. They are "regular Jews."

In addition to the immediate effect of simply reading or hearing **"Stantsye Baranovitsh,"** we can reinforce our connection to the time the story was written by reviewing the relevant criticism. This helps us move beyond the most common American-Jewish response to Sholem-Aleykhem's genius: a somewhat bizarre nostalgia for the sentimental powerlessness of Jews in the Russian Empire, combined with admiration for verbal techniques seen as "quintessentially Yiddish," rather than distinctive to Rabinovitsh.

The only essay devoted solely to the **Railroad Stories**[4] argued that the author depicts therein a class trapped in self-delusion. Maks Erik, the eminent Soviet Yiddish critic, emphasized the immediate historical situation and the class character of the passengers in the train, and identified two main themes in the volume. The first was the hopelessness of the Russian Jewish petit-bourgeoisie in the aftermath of the failed revolution of 1905 and the repression attendant on it; the second was what he called the *idiotizm* of the petit-bourgeoisie as a result of their hopeless situation.

While praising Sholem-Aleykhem's art and humor along the way, Erik ultimately accused the author of the same narrow vision shared by his characters. He identified the absence of historical analysis in the stories with the "limitations" of Sholem-Aleykhem's world view: "Sholem-Aleykhem's humor is incapable of freeing itself from the nightmare of Tsarist Russia." Whether Erik actually believed this, or intended to satisfy the censors, is uncertain. The fact is that it is precisely the hapless autonomy of Sholem-Aleykhem's characters that is so striking. They are indeed buffeted by history, but not by the didactic concerns of their creator. For that reason, they continue to live long after the specific historical situation has disappeared.

After World War II, a new generation of critics attempted to understand the ability of the "comic writer" Sholem-Aleykhem to move those who had no living memory of the world he describes. The considerations elaborated in various essays by Walter Benjamin on the relations between language, history, and the sharing of personal experience are quite evident in this recent work. Ruth Wisse, for instance, has discussed the central theme of successful and failed communication in Sholem-Aleykhem's work.[5] The shared language of the Jews is celebrated but also shown as dangerous. It can create a false sense of insulation from the outside; it can be manipulated by unscrupulous people within the community. This ambiguity is evident in several titles within the **Railroad Stories**: **"The Luckiest Man in Kodny"** is so because he has managed to get a great doctor to see his deathly-ill son; three men discuss their sons' being "Taken"—into the gymnasium or into the army; and **"The Hoshane Rabe"** is an averted disaster.

Dan Miron has analyzed Sholem Rabinovitsh's creation of the Sholem-Aleykhem persona as a versatile artistic device, bridging the social and geographical gap between author and reader, who meet via the Yiddish newspaper.[6] The term "Sholem-Aleykhem," as Miron notes, is used between two fellow Jews who are either strangers, or who have not seen each other for a long time, or who wish to express respect and welcome. In Yiddish, it is thus used to reduce distance. Here again, the author takes the technology of "information"—the newspaper—and creates a successful imitation of the storytelling situation. It is worth adding that he manages to personalize even the newspaper, breaking through the reification of the medium and fancifully reminding his readers that the link between them and himself is actually a human one:

> Sholem-aleykhem!
> Aleykhem-sholem!
> Fun vanen fort men?
> Fun varshe.
> Vos iz ayer gesheft?
> Ikh bin a idishe tsaytung.
> Ma shmeykhem?
> *Idishe folkstsay tung.*

> (Sholem-aleykhem!
> Aleykhem-sholem!
> Where are you travelling from?

From Warsaw.
What do you do?
I am a Jewish newspaper.
What's your name?
Yidishe Folkstsay tung.)[7]

In this way, the reader is allowed to eavesdrop on the private affairs on the writer and his publisher, so to speak. "Sholem-Aleykhem" is here the writer on the train doing business, the mirror of the *Railroad Stories'* *komivoyazher,* whose persona is that of a business man trying his hand at writing. In this early quotation, we see the author in the process of establishing a common world with his readers through the semblance of dialogue.

In the pages David Roskies devotes to the *Railroad Stories,*[8] he notes that, along with increasing desperation, the allusive resources of Jewish language still seem to hold their own in this volume written in the first decade of the century. That was just before the Great War, from which, as Benjamin wrote, "men returned . . . grown silent—not richer, but poorer in communicable experience."[9] Roskies corroborates the identification of that war with a collapse of communication, observing that it was not until the outbreak of World War I that one of Sholem-Aleykhem's characters was reduced to helpless silence. Roskies goes on to explain the significance of such a silence:

> These unredeemed moments are the very ones that etch themselves into the collective memory, for a silence beyond prayer is the ultimate dead end . . . such breakdowns do irreparable damage unless they are remembered. The act of remembering draws the broken links into a chain. . . .[10]

Sholem Rabinovitsh's act of genius in **"Stantsye Baranovitsh"** was to create such an unredeemed moment in fiction. Today, the story serves us as a sort of prescient *kapore,* an artificial and controllable version of the actual historical disaster which affords us a sense of connection to that earlier time.

The train is, of course, representative both of the intimacy of the "shtetl" and of its dislocation. Likewise, it is both a new form of the classic storytelling situation—in which people's hands were busy and their minds were free—and a perversion of that situation, since on a train, the passengers are actually harnessed to technology, rather than being in control of it. The schedule of the train will, therefore, both provide time for the story-within-the-story to develop and ultimately cause its interruption. A brief summary of the plot will allow me to detail the written and "oral" rhetorical heightening of narrative which is necessary for the missing conclusion to have its full force.

Like many of the stories in the volume, the bulk of **"Stantsye Baranovitsh"** consists of a narrative recounted by one of the passengers in the third-class carriage. In this case, the encapsulated monologue is sparked by mention of Azev, a famous *agent-provocateur* who infiltrated the Social Revolutionary party around the time of the 1905 Revolution. The speaker announces that in his home town of Kaminke, in his own grandfather's time, there was a traitor who could have put Azev to shame. His name was Kivke, and he was an innkeeper. Once Kivke got into an argument with some peasants about theology, and the upshot of it was his being sentenced to run the gauntlet. The Jewish community was outraged, and led by the narrator's grandfather, Reb Nisl Shapiro, hit on a plan to save Kivke: They had him fake a heart attack in prison, staged a burial (bribing the proper authorities), and secretly got him across the border to Brody in the Austro-Hungarian Empire. They celebrated properly but soon a letter came from Kivke asking for money. The money was collected and sent, but requests for increasing amounts were repeated at various intervals over the next few years. The narrator's grandfather found it more and more difficult to collect the money requested, and when it was not forthcoming, Kivke replied by making explicit the threat of blackmail implied from the start. If the money did not come soon, he would have no choice other than to return to Kaminke (thus spelling disaster for the entire community) or commit suicide. Reb Nisl Shapiro thereupon wrote a letter to Kivke, in which he asserted that absolutely no more money would be sent. At that, Kivke wrote back that if the money was not sent, he would write to the governor explaining the whole story, and include Reb Nisl Shapiro's signed letter as evidence. At this point in the account of Reb Nisl Shapiro's troubles with Kivke, the train on which the story is being told reaches Baranovitsh, where the narrator has to change trains, and he departs.

The abrupt ending of even such a summary paragraph is a bit shocking. Throughout **"Stantsye Baranovitsh,"** the author is successful (more, I would suggest, than in any of the other *Railroad Stories*) at playing off the train situation against the rhythm of the Kaminker Jew's monologue. He thus heightens the spiralling tension of the Jewish community held hostage from across the border with sardonic allusions to the dialectic of story and information.

Before the monologue begins, everyone in the car is talking about nothing in particular: "everybody was talking. All at once. As usual." The pace of these sentences already suggests the wheels of a train, rolling fast and jerky. No one, however, commands the crowd's attention. Everything about the cacophany suggests lack of control and lack of genuine dialogue:

> Ot redt men, dakht zikh, funem "urozhay," a geret of veyts un of hober, un ot iz men ariber (a smikhes haparshe!) of milkhome. Nisht gehalten zikh bay der milkhome keyn finf minut, tut men a shprung-ariber glaykh tsu der revolutsye. Fun der revolutsye git men zikh a vorf in der konstitutsye, un fun der konstitutsye falt men shoyn bemeyle arayn in di pogromen, mit di retsikhes, redeyfes un naye gzeyres of iden, miten traybenish fun di derfer, mitn loyfenish keyn amerike. . . .

> [Here we are talking, one would think, of the harvest, chatting about wheat and oats, and then we switch (some connection!) to the war. We don't keep talking about the war five minutes before we jump over to the revolution. From the revolution we throw ourselves

into the constitution, and from the constitution we somehow fall into the pogroms, with the murder, harrassment, and new anti-Jewish proclamations, with the expulsion from the villages, with the race to America. . . .]

The verbs "switch," "jump," "throw," "fall" suggest purposeless motion, lack of self-direction. The phonic association between *revolutsye* and *konstitutsye* implies the language of modernity controlling its users. From the references to the "expulsion" and the "race"—Erik's complaint notwithstanding—we sufficiently infer the historical helplessness of the Jews of Russia in 1909.

Relief only comes with the mention of Azev and the Kaminker Jew's cry: "A - zh - e - v!" To signal that a tale is about to be told "orally," the author has the *komivoyazher* explain that the Jew from Kaminke pronounces "z" as "zh," because he is missing teeth in front. The *komivoyazher* adds: "I immediately took a liking to this character. I liked his openness, his language, his calling us all cows. I enjoy, I envy that sort of person." This last passage is cited by Maks Erik in defense of his thesis about the "idiocy" of petit-bourgeois life as a theme in the **Railroad Stories.** In this crowd of potential competitors, the Kaminker's contempt for his audience perversely reinforces his charisma; Benjamin remarks that the main contribution of traders (read *komivoyazher*) as storytellers was "to refine the tricks with which the attention of the listener was captured."

In any case, everyone is eager to hear the story, and the Kaminker begins, making assurances that what he will relate is no *"bovemayse fun toyzent un eyn nakht,"* no mere fantasy. Rather, he has heard it from his father, whose father in turn told it "countless times." Two more characteristics of stories—their repetition and their transmission from generation to generation—are thus cited. Furthermore, "the whole story was written down in an old chronicle, which was burned a long time ago." Such a reference, of course, adds mystery as well as authority; but it also prefigures the disruption of memory.

At the point in the Kaminker story where Reb Nisl Shapiro decides on his plan to rescue Kivke—but has not divulged it to the community—the Kaminker decides to pause for effect (and for a cigarette). Thus his monologue is broken, and the reader is drawn into the circle of listeners. At various points further along the Kaminker will pause with rhetorical comments such as: "Good, no? . . . Take your time . . . These things are easier said than done."

The story continues with Kivke's feigned "death," parodying the enchantment customary in a fairy tale. The potency of the mention of death is underlined when the narrator describes it as "aza min apopleksye ["a sort of apoplexy"], nit do gedakht." "Nit do gedakht" is one of several phrases employed in Yiddish to ensure that reference to evil does not bring it closer. Here, in addition to the obvious irony that even Kivke in distant Kaminke two generations earlier had suffered no apoplexy, the

warning reinforces the sense of connection between the characters of the monologue and the audience in the train, and between all these and the Yiddish reader. (That the average Yiddish reader would hardly make such an analysis merely reinforces the point that the author's art focused on brilliant manipulation of an intimately shared idiom.)

At the exact midpoint of **"Stantsye Baranovitsh,"** there is an "intermission"; the train pulls into a station, and the Kaminker checks with the stationmaster to find out how far they are from Baranovitsh. Aside from adding suspense again, this affords the chorus of passengers time to comment:

"Creative."

"Has what to say."

When the Kaminker returns, he relates the second letter from Kivke. The letters reveal the ornamental Hebrew which Rabinovitsh uses elsewhere in his characters' letters.[11] The first letter, announcing Kivke's safe arrival, begins with the words: *"Bokashti lehodiye, az ikh bin in Brod"* ("I beg to inform you that I am in Brod"); on receiving it, the community rejoices. The second begins identically, but continues *"Bokashti leshloyekh"* ("I beg you to send"). The contrast between the two captures in a nutshell the theme of blackmail from afar; language subverts as well as celebrates. Indeed, when this letter is ignored, it is followed by another, "without an 'I beg to inform you,' but with an 'I beg you to send,' all by itself," and ending with the first threat to return to Kaminke.

This perverse power of language goes hand-in-hand with the helplessness of the Jewish community. When the money is finally sent for Kivke to get married, traditional greetings go along with it, together with the wish that: "It will make him forget that there's a Kaminke in the world." Could anything be more of a sign of despair than this desire to be forgotten? The subsequent attempt at silence, a decision "not to respond at all" to Kivke's next letter, is consistent.

When Kivke repeats his threat of blackmail, Reb Nisl Shapiro decides to give language one more try, writing a letter to Kivke (and signing it). Even the proud Jew from Kaminke is forced to admit: "he should pardon me, it was his greatest foolishness" (incidentally suggesting that his references to his grandfather's wisdom were all made tongue in cheek). Signature is thus cited as the most dangerous form of language. The fact that the climax of the story hinges on writing adds another term to the play of oral and written elements in **"Stantsye Baranovitsh."**

The last moments of the monologue are Kivke's threatening reply, and Reb Nisl Shapiro's panic upon receiving it. The ensuing catastrophe is, however, far worse than anything the Kaminker Jew's narrative could have held on its own: The train pulls in at Baranovitsh, and the speaker interrupts himself: "Jews, we're stopping? Where are we?"

A voice from the platform answers, as impersonal as the tolling of a bell:

"Stantsye Baranovitsh, Stantsye Baranovitsh." At this, the Kaminker jumps out, and asks everyone on the platform:

> Baranovitsh?
> Baranovitsh.
> It looks like the scene when we bless the New
>   Moon:
> 'Sholem-Aleykhem?
> Sholem-Aleykhem.'

Here we have reached the sharpest of contrasts between the exchange of information and the communication of self. The fact that this is indeed Baranovitsh can only be requestioned and reconfirmed; the repetition of the formula of greeting, on the contrary, contains reaching, emotion, and personality, and the exchange is a new experience each time as different Jews repeat it. It also is the author's by-line.

This is not quite the end of **"Stantsye Baranovitsh,"** however. There is still time for the passengers to demand the end of the tale, and for the Kaminker to respond impatiently, "What ending? It's just the beginning!" We readers are won over, but not so the *komivoyazher,* who has the last word:

"May the station at Baranovitsh burn to the ground!"

Notes

¹ Dan Miron, "Sholem-Aleykhem: Person, Persona, Presence," *The Uriel Weinreich Memorial Lecture I* (New York: YIVO Institute for Jewish Research, 1972).

² Walter Benjamin, *Illuminations* (New York: Schocken, 1969), pp. 83-109.

³ Sholem-Aleykhem, *Ayznban-geshiktes (Ksovim fun a komivoyazher)* (New York: *Spetsyele morgn-fruyhuyt oysgabe,* 1937), pp. 41 59.

⁴ Maks Erik, "Vegn Sholem-Aleykhem's 'ksovim fun a komivoyazher,'" *Afn visnshaftlekhn front,* 1935, 161-172.

⁵ Ruth Wisse, "Sholem Aleichem and the Art of Communication," (Syracuse: The B.G. Rudolph Lectures in Judaic Studies, 1979).

⁶ Miron, *ibid.*

⁷ Sholem-Aleykhem, *Idishe shrayber* (New York: *Spetsyele morgn-frayhayt oysgabe,* 1937), pp. 41-59.

⁸ David Roskies, *Against the Apocalypse: Responses to Catastrophe in Modern Jewish Culture* (Cambridge and London: Harvard University Press, 1984).

⁹ Benjamin, p. 84.

¹⁰ Roskies, p. 181.

¹¹ *Ibid.*

David G. Roskies (essay date 1988)

SOURCE: "Sholem Aleichem: Mythologist of the Mundane," in *AJS Review,* Vol. XIII, Nos. 1-2, Spring-Fall, 1988, pp. 27-46.

[*In the following essay, Roskies examines Aleichem's use of mythology in his short fiction and places his work within the context of Yiddish literature.*]

What could be more obvious for a writer who called himself How-Do-You-Do than to place folklore and folkspeech at the center of his work? After all, it was his childhood friend Shmulik who had inducted him into the world of storytelling; ever since then, the celebrated author could have mined the treasures of Jewish myth and legend as his natural legacy. But Shmulik's formative role in *From the Fair* was as much a fiction as the name Sholem Aleichem itself, which masked the true beginnings of a typical Russian-Jewish maskil named Rabinovitsh.¹ Everything in the program of the Haskalah, as in Sholem Rabinovitsh's early career, militated against the discovery of folklore: the overwhelming antipathy of the Jewish Enlightenment to fantasy, superstition, and folk custom;² Rabinovitsh's concern for fostering a highbrow literary culture in Yiddish based on the realistic portrayal of poverty, on social satire and stylistic discipline;³ and, perhaps most importantly, the young writer's adulation for the arch-maskil Abramovitsh-Mendele, who embodied this new critical standard.⁴ When, along with other of his contemporaries, Sholem Aleichem finally overcame these formidable obstacles and negotiated his way back to the folk, readers were so taken by his reinvention of Jewish folklore that they mistook it for the real thing.

In the heyday of maskilic rationalism, the fledgling group of secular East European Jewish writers had striven for a negotiated settlement with the sources of fantasy. Miracles in the Bible, especially such epoch-making events as the Splitting of the Sea of Reeds, were still to be credited, but the purveyors of contemporary miracle tales—the Hasidim—were to be laughed off the stage of history.⁵ The dichotomy in Abraham Mapu's fiction between biblical romance (*Ahavat Zion,* 1853) and social satire (*'Ayyit Zavu'a,* 1857) epitomized this divide-and-conquer strategy. According to Abramovitsh, writing in 1860, fantasy was legitimate in works of fiction so long as it was governed by logic, morality, and the laws of grammar.⁶ In general, fantasy was best relegated to dreams or prophetic visions, and even then, was best understood in an allegorical vein.

By the time the young Sholem Aleichem entered the literary scene, a new period of Jewish self-determination had begun, ushered in by Leo Pinsker's *Auto-Emancipation* (1882). Answering Pinsker's call, intellectuals were now expected to serve the "folk" by depicting its socioeconomic life in a critical, realistic manner.⁷ The main measure of change, however, was in the treatment of the past; a sense of a common past, the argument went, would generate a common purpose. History, heretofore seen as the realm of madness (most notably, in Abramovitsh's *Di klyatshe / Susati,* 1873), was now rehabilitated as a source of national pride. Midrash, which the maskilim had viewed as the repository of canonized falsehood, was selectively reclaimed as a legitimate source of postbiblical fantasy. Dreams and nightly visions proliferated, especially in Hebrew narrative poetry.

Still, history, midrash, and hallucination were hardly the stuff of everyday life. The problem for Sholem Aleichem, as for all the other lapsed positivists, was finding a believable this-worldly setting for fantasy. The shtetl, or East European Jewish market town, while ideally situated to provide the requisite social panorama, had long since been discredited among the maskilim as a hotbed of superstition and exaggerated response.[8] True son of the Haskalah, and a loyal disciple of Abramovitsh, Sholem Aleichem, too, wrote comic exposés of shtetl foibles in the requisite satiric style—a pastiche of biblical Hebrew.[9] To be sure, if one went back far enough in the East European Jewish past, one could find a marvelous tale or two. Why, even Ayzik-Meyer Dik, that died-in-the-wool Litvak, had allowed for legendary exploits in the Vilna and Poland of old.[10] Everything was possible *before* the partitions of Poland. In the dreary, industrialized present, however, with Jews flocking en masse to the big cities, or farther still, where it was every man and woman for themselves—from this rocky terrain no marvelous waters could flow.

In 1897, the inchoate yearnings of the 1880s coalesced into the two great political movements of Jewish eastern Europe—Zionism and the Bund. This politization process freed the creative writers—as opposed to the journalists and ideologues—to steer an independent course, to look inward and to more fully explore the internal resources of their culture. The first point on the unexplored map of Jewish culture was the world of fantasy that was situated in the *heder,* in the house of study *bein minhah le-ma'ariv,* in the hasidic *shtibl,* or closer still—in the realm of the human conscious. So close, and yet, so far. It was easier, in fact, for this generation of moderns to drain swamps in Palestine or to organize tallith weavers into a labor union than to turn folklore and fantasy into the substance of their art. No wonder, then, that two writers who successfully remade themselves into modern Jewish storytellers became canonical figures on the strength of their stylized fictions. As different as Zionism was from the Bund, that is how differently Peretz and Sholem Aleichem negotiated the perilous terrain of Jewish fantasy.

Peretz, who quickly emerged as a chief exponent of Jewish neoromanticism, used every trick in the book to bracket the experience and expression of the folk: in particular, through his choice of setting and speakers, and through a strict separation between fact and fancy. As the maskilim had done before him, Peretz continued to relegate folklore and fantasy to the legendary past. "There once dwelt in Safed a Jew of great wealth and good fortune," began his most perfect romance, *Mesires-nefesh* ("Devotion Without End"), "who traded in jewels, diamonds, and other precious stones. He was truly a man of great wealth, not like the upstarts of our day."[11] To such marvelous settings as Safed and Prague, the old stand-bys of the magical

itinerary, Peretz now added the shtetl—a prelapsarian shtetl of his own making, where every water carrier was a hidden saint and every traveling magician could be Elijah in disguise.

Just as the shtetl was close enough to be believable and far enough to allow free rein to fantasy, so the speakers in these stories had to combine faith and a certain level of sophistication. For if Peretz didn't believe in the miracle himself, he had to keep inventing narrators who did. In his celebrated hasidic monologues, the miracle existed only in the eyes of the beholder. To narrate the romances and folktales, Peretz created a slightly bookish, slightly playful voice, modulating between them as the occasion required.

Finally, by an elaborate use of supernatural props, Peretz preserved the distinction between illusion and reality. Through a bureaucratic heaven where even the Devil was subject to protocol. Peretz made it perfectly clear that his real subject was the world of human strivings and human failings.[12]

In contrast, Sholem Aleichem never abandoned his commitment to critical realism. Throughout his career, he stuck to observable reality and drew, wherever possible, on first-hand experience. Fortunately, during the period of his debut, a simple technique was introduced into Hebrew literature that allowed for a recreated—but safely distanced—world of fantasy. All one needed was to conjure up the experience of a child, for whom, presumably, marvelous things were an everyday occurrence.[13] For Sholem Aleichem, the experiment proved that recreating the myth from a child's point of view was as difficult as from a Hasid's.

"Dos meserl" ("The Penknife," subtitled "A Foolish But a Sad Story from My Childhood") was Sholem Aleichem's first little masterpiece.[14] It tells the story of a Jewish boy from a "good home" who has a passion for penknives that ultimately leads him to an act of theft. First written in 1886, the story suffered from two conflicting agenda: an exposé of the *heder* and its debilitating effect on the body and soul of Jewish boys, and a universal tale of initiation. To achieve the first, Sholem Aleichem addressed his adult male readers (*mayne lezer, mayne brider*) in a modern European diction, complete with Russian proverbs. At the same time, through dramatic vignettes, he tried to vivify the child's world from within. The story turns mythic when, on a midsummer's night, the moon intrudes upon the hero as he fondles his stolen treasure. Suddenly, images of hellfire crowd his mind, destroying the idyllic mood. Then, the next day in *heder* he has to witness a poverty-stricken boy being brought to trial for stealing money from a charity-box. This is enough to unhinge our hero completely and he falls into a delirium. Upon awakening, the hero's mother tells him what actually happened.

> vi azoy me hot mikh oyfgehoybn fun der erd kimat a toytn; vi azoy ikh bin gelegn tsvey vokhn keseyder in a helish fayer un hob nor gekvaket, vi a zhabe, un epes keseyder geredt fun shmits un fun meserlekh . . . me

hot shoyn gerekhnt, az ikh bin shoyn kholile geshtorbn
. . . un nokh dem, plutsem, hob ikh a nis gegebn zibn
mol, mamesh fun toyt lebedik gevorn . . .

how they picked me up from the floor half-dead; how
I lay in bed for two weeks on end croaking like a frog,
and kept on babbling something about lashes and
penknives . . . people thought that I was already dead,
God forbid . . . and then, suddenly, I sneezed seven
times, and came to, as if arisen from the dead . . .

Through the seven-fold sneeze, the hero's fate is linked to
that of the Shunammite woman's only son whom Elisha
miraculously resusitates in 2 Kings 4. Though there is no
Man of God to effect the birth and rebirth of the son, the
courageous and God-fearing Shunammite woman is implicitly figured in the hero's mother. Thus, Sholem Aleichem superimposed two complementary layers of myth—
one emanating from the child, the other from the adult
(the hero's mother and the adult male reader). It is one
thing for a child to translate his naive conception of reward and punishment into mythic terms, but quite another
when life itself replays one of the most poignant scenes in
the Bible. The child's myth of good and evil is reinforced
by the adult myth of death and resurrection.

Were it not for the young Sholem Aleichem's overriding
need to be useful, to press for educational reform, to tell
rather than to show, he might have been able to exploit
this myth of death and resurrection—so subtly played out
on a realistic plane—by allowing for some catharsis, some
reconciliation between the son and the adult world. (That
catharsis is precisely what resolves the second version of
the story, written in 1901-3, for children.) In the 1880s,
the time had not yet come for rehabilitating the experience
of childhood for its own sake or for properly integrating
the mythic component into one's fictional world. Nevertheless, with this modest beginning Sholem Aleichem had
already laid the groundwork for a particular use of myth.

Myth, for Sholem Aleichem, came to mean two different
but complementary things. (1) It was the belief system of
the Jews, the stories they actually lived by, that structured
their perceptions of reality. As he later developed it, that
myth was accessible to all Jews, inasmuch as every Jew
had once been a child, celebrated some festival or other in
one way or another, and knew how to talk. Myth was the
source of hope and of transcendence. (2) Myth was also
the deep structure of Jewish experience, a fixed number of
archetypal plots that were embedded not in one's individual psychology but in Jewish history itself. Myth was fate
and it was inescapable.

When, to return to our exercise in Jewish literary history,
the rediscovery of myth and fantasy in the last decade of
the nineteenth century irrevocably changed the form and
content of Jewish writing in Eastern Europe, Sholem Aleichem had already crossed the threshold on his own terms.
The most innovative writers—Peretz and Berdichewsky in
prose, Bialik and Tchernichowsky in poetry—began to seek
the sources of renewal not horizontally, in the latest developments in European culture, but vertically, in the

medieval, ancient, and folk strata of Jewish and (in Tchernichowsky's case) pagan culture.[15] Though Sholem Aleichem, too, embarked on a period of internal renewal, the
Bible and midrashim, the medieval romance, the stories of
Nahman of Bratslav and of *Shivhei ha-Besht* exerted no
special attraction for him. He did not cultivate them as the
buds of Jewish efflorescence.[16] What captured his imagination instead were the contemporary, often secular, forms
of Jewish folk expression: how young lovers in the shtetl
reenacted the Song of Songs; how the Jewish holidays
brought momentary relief to an otherwise unbearable existence; how the folksong idiom was updated to comment
on current affairs.

At a time when Jewish students at the Moscow Conserva-
tory went slumming in the small towns to collect authentic
Jewish folksongs,[17] Sholem Aleichem was doing the lecture circuit with his own local find—a lawyer and amateur
songwriter from Kiev, Mark Warshawski.[18] Sholem Aleichem maintained that these newly composed songs, often
set to well-known Slavic melodies or dance tunes, could
legitimately be called Yiddish *folksongs.* "Folksongs," he
instructed Joel Engel, the pioneer of Jewish ethnomusicol-
ogy in Eastern Europe, were "all songs written in the simple Jewish folk language [*proster yidisher folksshprakhe*]
. . . that are put out for the sake of the folk."[19] As proof
that the function of a cultural artifact was more important
than its origins, Sholem Aleichem pointed to his own song
on the mass immigration to America, *Shlof mayn kind*
("Sleep, My Child"). Published in 1892, it was already
incorporated as a traditional lullaby in the Ginsburg-Marek
collection of 1901.[20] While Sholem Aleichem certainly
did not disparage the work of retrieving and preserving
the Yiddish folk heritage,[21] his own concern was for the
varied manifestations of Jewish popular culture—those
hybrid forms that were being adapted by and for the folk
in the here-and-now of everyday life. This dynamic approach to the materials of the folk turned Sholem Aleichem's oeuvre into the source of a new popular culture.
Some 200,000 copies of his stories were to circulate in
chapbook form; on the eve of World War I, they would be
available on newsstands from Warsaw to New York.[22]

The neoromantic writers in Yiddish and Hebrew could
appropriate folklore, fantasy, and storytelling only as something bracketed in time, something removed from the industrial present by virtue of its style, simplicity, marvelous occurrences, dualistic schemes, and heroic struggles.
All these bespoke an act of noblesse oblige on the part of
the sophisticated minds that worked so hard to adopt a
"lower" form of literature and raise it to the status of
Western art. Only Sholem Aleichem achieved a true synthesis of storytelling and contemporary life: something so
subtly stylized that it didn't sound like "literature" at all;
something so spontaneous and real that it all but covered
its anecdotal and mythic tracks; something so normative
and commonplace that it appealed to every kind of reader—except the highbrow intellectual.

In the typical dialectic of literary evolution, Sholem Aleichem sought to carry out his new agenda by looking to
the "periphery" of the Jewish literary "system," that is, to

those genres that he and the other innovators had hereto-fore considered hackneyed, conservative, and outdated.[23] Unlike the others, however, Sholem Aleichem went back only one generation, to the discarded elements of Haskalah literature itself: the monologue, the epistle, and the maskilic chapbook.[24] In his first Tevye story (1894), he revived a particular type of monologue—the pseudo-maggidic ser-mon, complete with scriptural epigraphs, a homiletic struc-ture, and a dazzling array of proverbial sayings.[25] In his first Menakhem-Mendl series (1892), he revived the whole *brivn-shteler* ("letter-writer") with its archaic formulae at beginning and end and its inflated diction throughout.[26] For his first and only stylized chapbook, *A mayse on an ek* (1901), later retitled *Der farkishefter shnayder,* he chose a *mayse-bikhl* written by Ayzik-Meyer Dik as his model, with its invented Hebrew captions, farcical plot, and gro-tesque characters.[27]

What these three forms had in common was that they were "closed": closed by virtue of their stylized language, their rigid formal conventions, and their personal mode of nar-ration.[28] In all three there was a fixed, predictable struc-ture that allowed only for repetition, not for significant change, and the human experience was conveyed through clichéd speech by a totally subjective and presumably unsophisticated narrator. In contrast, the feuilleton and novel genres that he had just spent a decade trying to master were "open" forms in which an omniscient narrator was expected to use a modern, fluid diction to represent the linear course of life in its social causality. Though Sholem Aleichem continued writing feuilletons and nov-els for the rest of his life, this retrieval of very old-fash-ioned genres was to finally unlock the source of his ge-nius.

In the maggidic monologue, the letter-writer, and the chap-book, Sholem Aleichem discovered an objective correla-tive for an alternate approach to human existence itself. These closed narrative forms would not serve him merely as a naive folk vehicle which he could then subvert or allegorize to his heart's content, the way Peretz and Ber-dichewsky creatively betrayed the hasidic tale and mono-logue. Like Gogol, his new literary idol, Sholem Aleichem discovered a natural affinity between his own imagination and that of the folk. The patterns of experience that he drew from his own psyche he found to be identical to those of Jewish folklife.[29] By appropriating the literary genres most recently rendered obsolete, he could now explore for the first time the interplay of stasis and change, fate and free will, myth and the mundane. And that explo-ration would corroborate the experience of the folk from below and from within.

Few works in Sholem Aleichem's oeuvre stand in such glorious isolation as **"A Tale Without an End."**[30] Though originally conceived as one in a series of endless tales, only one other, **"Oylem-habe"** ("**Eternal Life,**" 1902), was ever written, and that story, narrated in a leisurely style in the first person, moved realistically from inno-cence to experience. In contrast, the tale of the frenetic tailor rushing to and from the neighboring town in search of the she-goat his wife sends him out to buy is a self-

consuming artifact. It stands alone because fantasy goes berserk here. The myth remains unchecked and unmediat-ed. It is as if, in this one-time experiment in stylized folk narrative, Sholem Aleichem let fantasy loose and watched it wreak havoc in the world of experience. Still, it taught him everything he needed to know.

> Sholem Aleichem never abandoned his commitment to critical realism. Throughout his career, he struck to observable reality and drew, wherever possible, on firsthand experience. Fortunately, during the period of his debut, a simple technique was introduced into Hebrew literature that allowed for a recreated—but safely distanced—world of fantasy.
>
> —*David G. Roskies*

(1) Through its famous opening line, *Ish hoyo beZlodi-evke,* with its comic allusion to Job and its friendly jab at Ayzik-Meyer Dik, he signaled to the reader that the story was a foregone conclusion, that the hapless hero would never be able to escape his tragicomic fate. (2) He then proceeded to situate the hero within a charmed circle of like-sounding towns: "there was a man in Zlodeyevke, a shtetl near Mazepevke, not far from Khaplapovitsh and Kozodoyevke, between Yampoli and Strishtsh, just on the way from Pishi-Yabede to Petshi-Khvost to Tetrevits and from there to Yehupets." This was a fictional geography redolent with legends (of Mazepa, the Robin Hood of Russia), with he-goats (*kozes*) and scoundrels (*zlodeyi*), with Slavic sounds and Slavic humor. (3) For all the he-ro's confidence that his voice would finally be heard, whence his nickname, Shimen-Elye Shma Koleynu, Sholem Aleichem endowed him and everyone around him with repetitive, parasitic speech patterns, the product of limited minds that could not cope with the slightest change, let alone with the inscrutable forces conspiring against them. (4) Then, at the center of this grotesque little world, our storybook narrator introduced a she-goat, the symbol of desire, the mythic creature that was supposed to mediate the polarities between husband and wife, rich and poor, town and country, but would, through its constant trans-formations, turn the hero into a scapegoat and drive him mad. (5) Finally, the most difficult part of Sholem Ale-ichem's exercise was figuring out how it should end, since, by definition, it was a story never destined to end. At first, as Uri Eisenzweig argued in a brilliant exposition of the story,[31] Sholem Aleichem tried to resolve the plot on the plane of history: the workers of Zlodeyevke take up Shi-men-Elye's cause and set out in protest for the neighbor-ing town. But in the final version of 1909-11, Sholem Aleichem introduced the storyteller himself as a *deus ex machina* who alone could rescue the narrative from its

subversive indeterminacy and, by extension, save the world from its inevitable fate.

Laid bare, as the formalists would say, in this one-of-a-kind stylized chapbook, were the main elements of Sholem Aleichem's storytelling art: the reuse of anecdotes or well-worn plots that allowed for few structural changes; a self-contained symbolic landscape that was both nurturing and claustrophobic; a gallery of characters whose sole means of escaping disaster was to talk their way out of it; a mythic presence or ideal derived exclusively from the realm of everyday life and all this within a larger contest between the destructive force of history and the redemptive power of the storyteller.

The chapbook format allowed Sholem Aleichem to play with the stylistic and structural conventions of Yiddish popular fiction in such a way as to underline—and undermine—the workings of myth and fantasy. Stylistically, one of two choices was open to him: either to write in *daytshmerish*, the Germanic syntax and vocabulary used to situate a Yiddish narrative in the European romance tradition, or to adopt a more learned, Hebrew-Aramaic style that situated a work within a canon of Jewish sacred legends. (Ayzik-Meyer Dik, the great Yiddish popularizer of the 1850s and 1860s, had cultivated both styles, depending on his subject matter.) In **"A Tale Without an End,"** Sholem Aleichem brilliantly exploited the latter possibility by playing *two different* Hebrew-Aramaic styles off one another: that of the storybook narrator and that of the central male characters.[32] Mythic and mock-mythic allusions abounded in their language, beginning, as we have already seen, in the opening sentence of the story.

The problem with Shimen-Elye, however, is that his pastiche of Scripture, liturgy, and life is the ossified product of a mind that cannot generate anything new.[33] Like Major Kovaliov, the collegiate assessor who wakes up one morning in St. Petersburg to find himself without a nose, Shimen-Elye is a man of limited psychological resources who is trapped by the world of experience.[34] Which is too bad, because Shimen-Elye's favorite slogans—*hayom haras oylem,* "today the world was created," and *undzer folk sher un ayzn—amkho,* "steam-iron and shears, our people Israel!"—bespeak an optimistic outlook on life and a concern with the commonweal. Among his own—the other laborers and guildsmen of town—Shimen Elye is looked upon as something of a scholar, but his verbal skills carry little weight with Tsipe-Beyle-Reyze, his wife. All he can offer in defense on that score is the biblical prooftext *hu yimshol bakh,* "he shall rule over thee" (Gen. 4:16). Would that it were so!

Now when myth functions properly, according to Lévi-Strauss, its purpose is to mediate the binary oppositions of life and death, heaven and earth, purity and pollution.[35] Precisely because Shimen-Elye's world is structured in so binary a fashion—husbands vs. wives, rich vs. poor, town vs. countryside—his failure to see the discrepancy between the ideal and the real, the sacred text and actual experience, is that much more apparent. For Shimen-Elye is a man hemmed in on all sides: tyrannized by a super-regi-

mented, emasculating, and impoverished society and trapped by metaphysical forces outside of his control. On one occasion alone, when released into the great outdoors for the first and only time in his life (the beginning of chapter 2), does he use the liturgy to express the ironic distance between the biblical promise and shtetl reality. Immediately thereafter, buoyed up by his newfound sense of autonomy, he locks horns with his great adversary, Dodi the Innkeeper. And that is Shimen-Elye's undoing.

Dodi is the very embodiment of myth. He is the lord of enchantment, "a hairy, thickset Jew with a big belly and a potato nose and the voice of a wild ox," i.e., an ogre. Dodi is the perfect foil to our curly black-haired hero Shimen-Elye with his goatee and flattened nose and groove down his lower lip, all of which make him look like a goat even before his trials begin. And the setting for this battle between ogre and man-goat is equally fantastical: an enchanted inn situated midway between the poles of desire. This enchanted setting is what characterized both of Sholem Aleichem's "Tales Without an End" and would later resurface in many different guises.[36]

Just as Dodi's Oak Tavern exerts an ambiguous pull on all travelers—whether for good or for evil is still uncertain—the goal of Shimen-Elye's expedition is a town of appearances. How, for instance, can one expect to find a she-goat in a town called He-Goatsville, where peasant women in the market confuse a rooster with a hen, and where people's nicknames mask what they really are: Khayim-Khone the Wise is anything but, and his wife, Teme-Gitl the Silent, never shuts up? Indeed, what Shimen-Elye discovers in Khayim-Khone the *melamed* is his exact counterpart—another henpecked husband who operates with a fixed repertoire of religious formulae.[37] No chance to redeem one's manhood here!

The selfsame Khayim-Khone, however, first calls attention to the goat as a multidetermined mythic figure. Through his discussion of the Gemara which Shimen-Elye happens to walk in on, the reader is warned that goats beget sorrow, because as symbols of human desire they are bound to incur double damages.

> Az der shnayder iz arayngekumen tsu reb Khayim-Khone dem klugn, hot er im getrofn bay der arbet, vu er iz gezesn . . . iber der gemore un gelernt mit di talmidim mit a nign af koley-koyles di gemore Bove kame: "*Hahu barkho* di dozike tsig, vos zi hot derzen a min esnvarg fun oybn afn fesl, hot zikh di tsig tsugekhapt tsum esnvarg. . . . *Khayvo Rovo*, hot Rovo gepasknt, az zi darf batsoln farn esnvarg un farn fesl dem gantsn hezek . . ."

> When the tailor entered the house of Reb Khayim-Khone the Wise, he found him at work . . . bent over the Gemara, leading his pupils at the tops of their voices through the Talmud passage "On Damages": "Now that goat, when it saw that there was food on the top of the barrel, that same goat leaped toward that same food . . . Rabbah said 'Guilty,' and set it down that she must pay for the fodder and the barrel that was damaged." (Y 14-15, 16, E 14, 15)

Hebrew-Aramaic, the language of Jewish learning and rational discourse, becomes instead the main repository of the myth, at least for the male members of shtetl society. It is more than these hapless henpecked husbands can bear. Whereas Shimen-Elye uses ineffectual mantras lifted from the liturgy, Khayim-Khone the *melamed* drills his unfortunate charges in a seemingly irrelevant passage from the Talmud. But the tailor's mythic quest for the nurturing she-goat seems to have disturbed the status quo and endowed all the goat-texts with a power of their own that cannot be domesticated by traditional means.

Henceforth, many voices try to interpret the role of the goat—as goblin, as *gilgul,* as the kid of the Khad Gadya—but none dares verbalize its true mythic function: Having failed to reconcile the polarities of life, the goat should serve as biblical scapegoat and be cast into the wilderness, thus expiating the failings of a very flawed society. Instead, in the story's ultimate transformation, Shimen-Elye himself becomes the sacrificial victim, while the goat runs wild and disappears.

In this way Sholem Aleichem introduced a Jewish mythic component as a tragic subtext to a comic folktale plot. In the parodic folktale, the hero's back-and-forth movement between two essentially identical towns could conceivably go on forever, gaining in comic momentum as more people are drawn into the act. But through the biblical-talmudic-haggadic goat, Sholem Aleichem injected the fatalistic themes of thwarted desire, victimization, and vicarious sacrifice. The goat that was to provide the milk for Shimen-Elye's starving family causes his blood to be spilt instead.[38]

On every conceivable level, then, the **"Tale Without an End"** tells of failed mediation: of a traditional society that could not even resolve the petty rivalry between two neighboring towns; of a traditional language that did more to obfuscate and mystify reality than to break it down into manageable parts; of a mythic force let loose by the tailor's innocent quest that destroys him, his family, and the equilibrium of his town. Never before had a stylized Jewish folktale been used to expose so much dissolution. Never would Sholem Aleichem use this genre to do so again.

Instead, there emerged out of the crucible of the **"Tale Without an End"** a new, normative mythology such as Jewish literature had not seen before, a humanistic myth that was both profoundly consolational and deeply ironic. On the simplest level, what made it normative was that Sholem Aleichem conjured up a world of mainstream, proto-misnagdic, East European Judaism: Hasidism, Kabbalah, demonology, heaven and hell—the stock-in-trade of Jewish neoromanticism—figured in these stories hardly at all. Dodi the innkeeper, who keeps switching the goats on poor Shimen-Elye, is the most demonic character in Sholem Aleichem's storytelling corpus, just as the motif of the *gilgul* is about the closest that Sholem Aleichem ever came to Kabbalah. Even the Sabbath, so central to Heine, Bialik, and Asch, played no role in Sholem Aleichem's search for Jewish myth. (According to Berkovitsh, Sholem Aleichem probably remembered the Sabbath

as a time of boredom and intolerable restrictions.[39]) Rather, it was material culture, in the main, that mediated the myth.

Sholem Aleichem understood that the folk apprehended the great myths of creation, revelation, and redemption through ritual objects and local custom. In particular, it was the holiday cycle—building a sukkah, buying an esrog, dancing with a flag on Simkhes Torah, leading the children through hakofes, lighting candles and playing cards on Hanukkah, delivering *shalekhmones* on Purim or putting on a *purim-shpil,* and above all, preparing for and celebrating the seder—it was on these communal and familial occasions that the ordinary Jew, rich or poor, male or female, experienced the transcendent power of Jewish myth. It was the time, to use Bakhtin's now-famous term, that the carnival aspect of life broke through the everyday routine. (To be sure, the Jewish "carnival" was a far cry from the Bacchanalia, or even from Breughel; still, in the relative asceticism of the shtetl, a few good drinks could go a long way!)

Through his emphasis on material culture and the carnival, Sholem Aleichem expressed his egalitarian and humanistic bias. This was a Judaism equally accessible to all and not limited to the formal religious institutions. Though Shimen-Elye, the liturgical voice of the shtetl artisans, fails to use his modicum of learning to achieve a balance between myth and reality, other nonclerical figures in Sholem Aleichem's stories succeed. By making creative use of Jewish sacred texts they form a kind of folk aristocracy: Tevye the dairyman, Fishl the melamed, Berl Vinegar, Yankl Yunever, and more.

Thus the myth could also be mediated by a certain type of folk hero who was situated outside the synagogue, the studyhouse, and the yeshiva, and got his hands dirty in the mud and muddle of everyday life. To a greater or lesser degree these characters had their own ironic sense of the discrepancy between the real and the ideal. Through them, as through the celebration of the holidays, the myth was invoked as a foil to reality.

Nowhere was the gap between present reality and future promise drawn so precisely and so poignantly as in the holiday stories that Sholem Aleichem began writing in earnest after 1900. What made them so poignant—and so true to the folk conception of life—was that they showed how fleeting was the moment of transcendence, if achieved at all.[40] For the plot of these stories, such as it was, presented one of two alternatives: either the King-for-a-day motif or the Marred Holiday (*der farshterter yontef*). In either event, whether Yuzik the Orphan becomes king of the seder or Leybl bites off the *pitom* of the coveted esrog before it can be used, the celebrant has to return to the grind, to a life that is unredeemed. "My heart is shattered," says the child-narrator at the end of **"The Guest,"** the story of an exotic visitor who absconds with the family silver, jewelry, and maid.[41]

> nisht af di zilberne koyses mit di zilberne lefl, goplen
> un mesers, vos zenen nem gevorn, un nisht af der

mames tsirung, un nisht afn mezumen gelt, un nisht af
Rikl di moyd—khapt zi der ruekh!—nor af dem
gliklekhn-gliklekhn land, vos se valgern zikh dortn
brilyantn, perlen, dimentn, un af dem beysamigdesh,
mit di kehanim, mit di leviyim, mitn orgl, mitn
mizbeyakh, mit di korbones un mit di ale iberike gute
zakhn, vos me hot bay mir avekgeroybt, tsugenumen,
tsugenumen, tsugenumen.

But not on account of the loss of our goblets and
silverware or of my mother's scanty jewelry and the
money. Not on account of Rickel the maid—the devil
take her! But because now I will never see that happy,
happy land where precious stones lie carelessly about
in the streets, where there is a holy temple with priests,
Levites, an organ, and an ancient altar with sacrifices.
All these marvelous things cruelly, wantonly stolen
from me . . .

Here, unlike **"The Penknife,"** the child is transported into
the world of myth as a matter of course; yet even so normative a dream cannot be sustained for more than a few
hours. That is because the myth in Sholem Aleichem's
stories now functioned as an ironic foil even when it was
ostensibly most potent. Sometimes the glass was half-full
and sometimes it was half-empty, but never was a state of
permanent fullness held out as a realistic possibility.

One way, then, that the great myths operated in Sholem
Aleichem's stories was through the actual behavior and
speech of very ordinary Jews. On the one hand, myth
allowed them a momentary reprieve from the pain and
drugery of life, and on the other, it underlined the un-
bridgeable gap between transcendence and life's inherent
constraints.

In the folklore of the nations, the operative myth was
heroic; it was a tale of conquest and happy endings. Among
Jews, the best that could be hoped for was a tale of averted disaster. In contemporary Jewish folklore Sholem Aleichem found the one recurrent plot that confirmed his
innermost sense of life: "Ale yidishe mayses," he wrote in
1903, "ale umglikn bay undz heybn zikh on fun a kleyni-
kayt" ("all Jewish tales, all disasters among us begin with
a trivial occurrence"). And as for the endings: "Yidishe
mayses lozn zikh oys, tsum maynstn, troyerik" ("Jewish
stories end, for the most part, on a sad note").[42] As a
writer of sentimental novels, as a so-called realist, Sholem
Aleichem always bowed to convention by ending his well-
made plots on a more-or-less happy note. As a storyteller,
Sholem Aleichem tried as best he could to mitigate the
tragic ending that all Jewish stories had to end with.[43] He
did it most boldly in the final version of **"A Tale Without
an End."** The new ending deserves to be quoted in full
even though everyone has heard parts of it before.

Un der hayoytsey lonu mize? Un der may-ko-mashmo-
lon fun der mayse?—vet fregn der lezer. Tsvingt mikh
nisht, kinder! Der sof iz geven nisht geyn guter sof.
Ongehoybn hot zikh di mayse zeyer freylekh, un
oysgelozt hot zi zikh, vi dos rov freylekhe geshikhtes,
oy-vey, zeyer troyerik. Un makhmes ir kent dem

mekhaber fun der geshikhte, az er iz beteve nit keyn
morye-shkhoyrenik un hot faynt klogedike un hot lib
beser lakhndike mayses, un makhmes ir kent im un
veyst, az er hot faynt "moral" un zogn muser iz nit
zayn derekh—lokheyn gezegnt zikh mit aykh metokh
skhok der farfaser, lakhndik, un vintsht aykh, az yidn,
un glat mentshn af der velt, zoln mer lakhn eyder
veynen. Lakhn iz gezunt. Doktoyrim heysn lakhn . . .

"What is the moral of this tale?" the reader will ask.
Don't press me, friends. It was not a good ending. The
tale began cheerfully enough, and it ended as most
such happy stories do—badly. And since you know
the author of the story—that he is not naturally a
gloomy fellow and hates to complain and prefers
cheerful stories—and you know that he hates insisting
on a story's "moral," and that moralizing is not his
manner. . . . Then let the maker of the tale take his
leave of you smiling, and let him wish you, Jews—and
all mankind—more laughter than tears. Laughter is
good for you. Doctors prescribe laughter.

This statement could not have been written in 1901, for
then, at the beginning of his career as master storyteller,
Sholem Aleichem was still looking to history to provide
him with an ending. Now, in 1909-11, it was after the
failed revolution of 1905; after his permanent exodus from
Russia; after his near-fatal attack of tuberculosis in the
midst of a triumphal return visit; after years of recuperation in this spa and that; and after he had composed the
bulk of his major story-cycles, none of which, as yet, had
actually ended.[44] It was also during this period of enforced
exile that Sholem Aleichem returned repeatedly to the
figure of Shmulik the orphan, ever enhancing his status in
the author's fictional autobiography so as to portray the
Sholem Aleichem persona as a traditional storyteller.[45]

As opposed to the comic Hebrew-Yiddish glosses with
which the story began, this author's finale was written in
a weighty, repetitive, heavily Hebraized style, suggesting
the importance the author himself attached to these
thoughts. It was the closest he ever came to an explication
of his story-telling art. The "closed" form of the story, he
might have been saying, in anticipation of Umberto Eco,
was addressed to Everyman ("Jews—and all mankind"),
and therefore could yield as many potential meanings as
there were readers. Unlike the novels that he was forced
to write at the behest of his newspaper bosses, stories did
not require of an Ideal Reader to respond in a prescribed
way; and so, the "moral" be damned.

Secondly, the storyteller was the doctor of the soul. He
alone knew the diagnosis, having laid bare the recurrent
pattern underlying the vagaries of life. He alone could
describe the myth as actually lived—truncated, ironic, tragic. He alone could piece it back together again by playing
the different forces off one another: language against life,
stasis against historical change, fate against free will.

In the end, it was the story itself that kept hope alive, or
more precisely, the ability of Jews to reconstitute themselves wherever they were into a community of listeners—
whether as third-class passengers on a Russian train or

on board a ship bound for America or even as a one-time audience to hear the famous Sholem Aleichem himself read aloud from his works. And the story they heard, as told to them by a master raconteur, an expert in Jewish life and lore, was a story that could happen to anyone precisely because versions of it had already happened countless times before: in the home of a Shunammite woman, in the land of Uz, or in some enchanted forest.

Notes

1 David G. Roskies, "Unfinished Business: Sholem Aleichem's *From the Fair*," *Prooftexts* 6 (1986): 73-74; Dan Miron, *Sholem Aleykhem: Person, Persona, Presence* (New York, 1971).

2 Dan Miron, "Folklore and Antifolklore in the Yiddish Fiction of the *Haskalah*," in *Studies in Jewish Folklore*, ed. Frank Talmage (Cambridge, Mass., 1980), pp. 219-249.

3 Sholem Aleichem. "Der yidisher dales in di beste verke fun undzere folks-shriftshteler," supplement to *Yudishes folksblat* (St. Petersburg), 1888, pp. 1075-1090, 1101-1110, 1149-1157, 1183-1189, 1205-1216; idem, *Shomers mishpet, oder der sud prisyazhnik af ale romanen fun Shomer* (Bardichev, 1888); H. Reminik, "Sholem-Aleykhem in kampf far realizm in di 80er yorn," *Shtern* (Minsk), nos. 5-6 (1938): 122-148.

4 Dan Miron, *A Traveler Disguised: A Study in the Rise of Yiddish Fiction in the Nineteenth Century* (New York, 1971), chap. 2.

5 The following survey of myth and fantasy in Hebrew literature from the Haskalah until the turn of the century is based on Dan Miron, *Bo'ah, laylah: ha-sifrut ha-'ivrit bein higayyon l'ee-gayyon be-mifneh ha-me'ah ha-'esrim* (Tel Aviv: Dvir, 1987), esp. pp. 11-22, 86-96.

6 S. Y. Abramovitsh, *Mishpat Shalom* (Vilna: Rom, 1860), pp. 9-10, as quoted by Miron, *Bo'ah, laylah*, p. 89.

7 How the ideological shift of the 1880s affected Yiddish literature has been covered most extensively by Nokhem Oyslender in "Der yunger Sholem-Aleykhem un zayn roman 'Stempenyu,'" in *Shriftn fun der katedre far yidisher kultur bay der alukrainisher visnshaftlekher akademye* 1 (1928): 5-72.

8 Dan Miron, "Batrakhtungen vegn klasishn imazh fun shtetl in der yidisher beletristik," in *Der imazh fun shtetl: dray literarishe shtudyes* (New York, 1981), pp. 19-138.

9 Sholem Aleichem, "Tmunot u-tslalim mihayyei hayehudim bi-Mazepevka" (1889-1890), in *Ktavim ivriyim*, ed. Chone Shmeruk (Jerusalem, 1976), pp. 87-156. Most relevant to my thesis is the story called "Ha'otsar" (pp. 106-115), in which Sholem Aleichem burlesques the legend of the lost treasure. On this, see Dan Miron, "Otsarot muqdamim," in *Shalom Aleichem: Masot meshulavot*, 2d rev. ed. (Ramat Gan, ca. 1980), pp. 244-256.

10 See, for example, AMaD (Ayzik-Meyer Dik), *Yudis di tsveyte: ayn herlekhe royber geshikhte in Vilne* (Vilna, 1875) and *Sholem der karabelnik* (Vilna, 1877). In contrast, Dik's *Di gayster geshikhtn* (Vilna, 1871) recounts incidents from the author's life in Vilna and Nesvizh which appeared to be supernatural but whose rational cause was eventually revealed.

11 *Mesires-nefesh*, in *Ale verk fun Y. L. Perets*, 11 vols. (New York, 1947-48), 5:207-251. Trans. as "Devotion Without End" in *A Treasury of Yiddish Stories*, ed. Irving Howe and Eliezer Greenberg (New York, 1954), pp. 118-148.

12 For more on Peretz's reinvention of Jewish folk narrative, see Gershon Shaked, *Hasipporet ha-'ivrit 1880-1970*, vol. 1 (Israel, 1977), pp. 140-160; David G. Roskies, "Peretses shaferisher farrat fun der yidisher folks-mayse," in *Proceedings of the Eighth World Congress of Jewish Studies*, Division C (Jerusalem, 1982), pp. 349-355.

13 Miron, *Bo'ah, laylah*, pp. 91-92.

14 All references are to the critical ed. of *"Dos meserl"* prepared by Chone Shmeruk (Jerusalem and Cincinnati, 1983) as a sample text of the Complete Edition of Sholem Aleykhem's Works.

15 On the reappropriation of traditional narratives, see David C. Jacobson, *Modern Midrash: The Retelling of Traditional Jewish Narratives by Twentieth-Century Hebrew Writers* (Albany, 1987).

16 Analyzing Sholem Aleichem's attitudes towards Yiddish and Hebrew, Abraham Novershtern arrives at a similar conclusion. See "Sholem-Alyekhem un zayn shtelung tsu der shprakhn-frage," *Di goldene keyt* 74 (1971): 167.

17 Albert Weisser, *The Modern Renaissance of Jewish Music: Events and Figures [in] Eastern Europe and America* (New York, 1954), chap. 3.

18 Nachman Meisel, "Sholem Aleichem and His 'Find'," in *Sholem Aleichem Panorama*, ed. Melech Grafstein (London, Ont., 1948), p. 46-50.

19 Sholem Aleichem, "A briv tsum h' Engel fun'm 'Voskhod'," *Der yid* 3, no. 24 (June 13, 1901): 14-16.

20 *Evreiskie narodniye pesni v Rossi*, ed. S. M. Ginsburg and P. S. Marek (St. Petersburg, 1901), no. 82.

21 On Sholem Aleichem's interest in folklore, see I. Mitlman and Kh. Nadel, "Sholem-Aleykhem der redaktor-aroysgeber," in *Sholem-Aleykhem: zamlung fun kritishe artiklen un materyaln* (Kiev, 1940), p. 191.

22 Y. D. Berkovitsh, *Undzere rishoynim*, 5 vols. (Tel Aviv, 1966), 4:70.

23 See Itamar Even-Zohar, "The Relations between Primary and Secondary Systems in the Literary Polysystem" (1973), in *Papers in Historical Poetics* (Tel Aviv, 1978), pp. 14-20.

24 This is an adaptation of Dov Sadan's thesis outlined in his seminal essay "Three Foundations [Sholem Aleichem and the Yiddish Literary Tradition]" (1959), trans. in *Prooftexts* 6 (1986): 55-63.

25 The precise genealogy of Sholem Aleichem's monologues has never been established. Sadan (ibid.) argues for a direct link with the "naive" and "satiric" monologues of the Galician Haskalah. Victor Erlich implies a connection to the Russian *skaz* in "A Note on the Monologue as a Literary Form: Sholem Aleichem's 'Monolgn'—A Test Case," in *For Max Weinreich on His Seventieth Birthday: Studies in Jewish Languages, Literature, and Society*, ed. Lucy Dawidowicz (The Hague, 1964), pp. 44-50. In "Magidishe maskes fun Markuze biz Mendele" (Paper read at the Second International Conference on Research in Yiddish Language and Literature, Oxford, July 11, 1983), I first suggested that the Tevye monologues be read in the context of "maggidic masks" in Yiddish Haskalah literature.

[26] Surprisingly little work has been done on the epistolary genre in nineteenth-century Yiddish literature. The only studies I know of are Yehude Elzet [Judah Loeb Zlotnick], *Mit hundert yor tsurik: Shtudien in dem amolikn inerlekhn yidishn lebn* (Montreal, 1927) and Max Weinreich, "Lewin Liondor's brivn-shteler," *YIVO-bleter* 18 (1941): 109-112. Prior to writing *Menakhem-Mendl*, Sholem Aleichem experimented with the epistolary form in "Di ibergekhapte briv af der post" (1883-1884). See the Soviet ed. of *Ale verk* (Moscow, 1948), 1:54-155, 487-511.

[27] *Oyzer Tsinkes un di tsig* (Vilna, 1868), described by Haim Liberman in "La-bibliografia shel A. M. Dik," *Ohel RaHeL* (Brooklyn, 1980), pp. 498-499. The only extant copy of this chapbook is in the private library of the Lubavitsher Rebbe. All my efforts since 1971 to secure a Xeroxed copy of this book have failed.

[28] On the concepts of "closed" and "open" forms, see Umberto Eco, *The Role of the Reader: Explorations in the Semiotics of Texts* (Bloomington, 1984).

[29] Donald Fanger, *The Creation of Nikolai Gogol* (Cambridge, Mass., 1979), p. 100. For more on the Gogol connection, see I. J. Trunk, *Sholem-Aleykhem: zayn vezn un zayne verk* (Warsaw, 1937), pp. 41-47, and David G. Roskies, "The Storyteller as Hero," *The New Republic*, 9 November 1987.

[30] Sholem Aleichem, *A mayse on an ek* (Warsaw, 1901). The caption to this first version reads: "Aroysgenumen fun an altn pinkes un baputst." References to the Yiddish text (Y) are from "Der farkishefter shnayder" in *Mayses un monologn*, vol. 13 of the Progres ed. (Warsaw, 1913), pp. 3-51. The English trans. (E) by Leonard Wolf is in *The Best of Sholom Aleichem*, ed. Irving Howe and Ruth R. Wisse (New York, 1982), pp. 3-46.

[31] Uri Eisenzweig, "Le Chtettl, Retroactivement (*le Tailleur ensorcelé*, de Cholem Aleichem)," *Territoires occupés de l'imaginaire juif* (Paris, 1980), pp. 196-198.

[32] On this, see Dov Sadan, "Kmo shekosuv: araynfir-bamerkn tsu Tevye dem milkhikers toyres," in *Tsvishn vayt un noent: eseyen, shtudyes, briv* (Tel Aviv, 1982), pp. 9-23.

[33] The satiric use of parasitic speech patterns in nineteenth-century Yiddish fiction and drama has occupied all of the major scholars in the field. For the most seminal statements, some of which have a direct bearing on Sholem Aleichem, see Meyer Wiener, "Di rol fun shprakhfolkor in der yidisher literature," *Shriftn* (Kiev) 1 (1928): 73-129; Miron, *A Traveler Disguised*, esp. pp. 169-179; and Benjamin Hrushovski, "Dekonstruktsiah shel dibbur: Shalom Aleichem veha-semiotika shel ha-folklor ha-yehudi," afterword to his trans. of *Tevye hahalhan ve-monologim* (Tel Aviv, 1983), pp. 195-212.

[34] Cf. Fanger, *The Creation of Nikolai Gogol*, p. 236.

[35] Claude Lévi-Strauss, "The Structural Study of Myth," in *Myth: A Symposium*, ed. Thomas A. Sebeok (Bloomington and London, 1970), pp. 81-106.

[36] For an analysis of this motif in *Oylem-habe*, see Ruth R. Wisse, *Sholem Aleichem and the Art of Communication* (Syracuse, 1979), pp. 19-21. Cf. also *Iber a hitl* ("On Account of a Hat"), where the train station in Zlodeyevke functions as an enchanted setting.

[37] Eisenzweig, "Le Chtettl," p. 149.

[38] Cf. the following in Stith Thompson's *Motif-Index of Folk Literature*, rev. ed., 6 vols. (Bloomington and London, 1966): man transformed into a goat (D 134), goat's milk is inexhaustible (D 1652.3.2), revenant as goat (E 423.1.9), the devil in the form of a goat (G 303.3.3.1.6), and esp. tailor associated with a goat (X 222).

[39] *Undzere rishoynim*, 2:73.

[40] These are collected in the following volumes of *Ale verk* in the Folksfond ed.: *Fun peysekh biz peysekh* (vol. 2); *Lekoved yontef* (vols. 22-23), as well as in many of the *Mayses far yidishe kinder* (Vols. 8-9) which also double as holiday tales.

[41] Sholem Aleichem, "Der oyrekh" (1906), in vol. 2 of *Lekoved yontef*, vol. 18 of *Ale verk* in the Folksfond ed. (New York, 1925), pp. 114-115. Etta Blum's trans., quoted here from *The Best of Sholom Aleichem*, p. 288, does not quite capture the incantation of loss.

[42] The first quotation is from "Konkurentn" (1903), *Fun peysekh biz peysekh*, vol. 2 of *Ale verk* (New York, 1925), p. 140. The second is from "Di fon" (1900), *Felitonen* (Tel Aviv, 1976), p. 25.

[43] Here I take issue with David Neal Miller, who argued: "the logic of fiction insists upon unhappy endings, the vocation of the storyteller upon happy ones." See "'Don't Force Me to Tell You the Ending': Closure in the Short Fiction of Sh. Rabinovitsh (Sholem-Aleykhem)," *Neophilologus* (Amsterdam) 66 (1982): 106.

[44] In a letter of 1 May 1909 to his Yiddish publisher Y. Lidsky, Sholem Aleichem wrote: "Neither you nor I should publicize the 'Tale Without an End,' because what you have is the revised copy ('The Haunted Tailor')." Two years later he instructed his son-in-law Berkovitsh to publish the story with its new ending (letters of 10 and 24 March 1911, in Russian). I am indebted to Dr. Abraham Novershtern for this information. As mentioned earlier, this new ending did not appear in print until 1913.

[45] Roskies, "Unfinished Business," pp. 73-74.

Anna Halberstam-Rubin   (essay date 1989)

SOURCE: "Extra-Legal Disabilities, Raids, Pogroms and Other Forms of Hostility," in *Sholom Aleichem: The Writer as Social Historian*, Peter Lang, 1989, pp. 65-84.

[*In the following excerpt, Halberstam-Rubin asserts that Aleichem's short stories demonstrate how ignorance, prejudice, and violent physical attacks affected the day-to-day lives of the Jewish people in his time.*]

The focus of this [essay] is the illustration of the ways Sholom Aleichem captured and illuminated such historical phenomena as raids, pogroms, the blood-libel and other forms of Jew-baiting. These "extra-legal" hostilities paralleled and were related to the formal, anti-Jewish legislation such as the residential and occupational restrictions. As in the case of the legal problems, the author enables us to "participate" in some of these events and to gain an understanding of their impact upon all concerned, especially the victims. The most detailed account of the developments surrounding the phenomenon of the pogroms is given by Dubnov to whose evidence of the reigns of Alexander III and Nicholas II we shall return.[1]

Raids—expeditions to catch and deport illegal residents in the large cities after the May Laws of 1882—were frequent occurrences. Thousands were caught and expelled from the cities.[2] The passage below describes a raid probably witnessed by Sholom Aleichem who himself lived illegally in the city of Kiev following his marriage in 1883. That circumstance caused him untold grief and inspired his many stories of oblavy, or raids.

The account that follows is number eighteen of the author's collection known as ***Railroad Stories.*** The title of this particular tale is **"Call Me Knacknissel."**[3] The literal translation of the term "Knacknissel" is "nutcracker," but it connotes a character with an I-don't-care-what-you-think-of-me attitude. The setting is on a train where a particular traveler is relating to an individual, a kind of traveling salesman, one of his personal experiences.

The traveler is on the way to Yehupetz (the author's fictional name for Kiev) to see a physician. Since he has no Pravozhitel'stvo, he cannot stay in any of the hotels. His brother-in-law, an otherwise unsuccessful individual, was in the employ of the local dignitary Brodsky who obtained for his employee the required residence permit. The latter (the employee of Brodsky) is a pauper and glad to earn a few rubles by putting up his brother-in-law whenever he came to town, though he had to break an official law to get these extra earnings. Thus the narrator is assured that he has a place where he can be relatively safe while in Yehupetz:

> This time, however, I arrive and see—my people . . . are running around without heads. "What is the matter?" "It is bad." "What do you mean?" "*Oblaves.*" Feh, I thought who knows what! Oblaves—that is, after all, an old sickness from way back then. . . . "No," say they . . . now there isn't a night without a raid. And if they catch a Jew . . . it is . . . one, two, three, with the *etap* [caravan to Siberia]. "Nu, and money?" "Dust." "A ruble?" "Blah." "A three ruble note?" "Not even a million!" "In that case," say I "it really is misery."[4]

The local authorities not only fine the victims, but they send them to Siberia as well. The accompanying scandal affects local people like Brodsky, who are used to getting their way with bribes when necessary. Our man, however, is concerned with himself, not with Brodsky. He must remain in town for a number of days. What is he going to do? Come evening, he retires to sleep. The moment he falls asleep he hears: "Trach, ta-re-rach! I open my eyes. 'Who is there?' 'We are lost!' says my brother-in-law, the *shlimazel* [a ne-er-do-well individual] . . . who is shaking like a leaf."[5]

Suddenly our man has an idea. He proposes to his brother-in-law, who is a bit of a fool, that they exchange documents. Not realizing the implication of the proposal (that he give up his legal residence permit) his brother-in-law agrees and the deed is done. In the meantime the rapping

on the door gets louder, the police threaten to bring the house down. The children wake up and cry and his brother-in-law becomes very frightened. Our man, on the other hand, assumes an air of confidence and opens the door. Because of his confident manner, backed up by the papers, a handout (always expected in addition to the documents) and his brother-in-law's fear, the police arrest the wrong man and send him off to Siberia.

In the end the fellow succeeds in liberating his kinsman from exile. To this day, however, he continues to gloat over his successful "combination"—the plan that got him off the hook. His brother-in-law was in Siberia, while he was able to come and go in Yehupetz. There is only one thing you can do about it all, he continues: "You can call me Knacknissel!"

Unscrupulous as his behavior was, the follow did come up with unusual resourcefulness. It was the kind of resourcefulness, moreover, that required split-second thinking and decision-making. The entire "devilish" plan, however, the author demonstrates, was not premeditated, but was elicited by the pressure of dire personal need. Under similar circumstances there are always a few willing to save their own skins by whatever means available—including the sacrifice of their kin.

In this story the author does more than describe a raid. He gives us evidence of the influence of hostility, or outside pressure, on the behavior of Jews. He also provides some evidence of the motivations for corruption. In the case of the brother-in-law it is poverty that induces him to violate a law in order to make a few rubles. He shows us the police organizing harrassing raids in order to collect bribes from the victims. They not only take, but expect money to be offered by Jews. We see a hostile world which requires any means if one is to survive, including cheating and escaping. We also find here references to unequal treatment given to different classes. People like Brodsky, the rich, had recourse to permits and other privileges not enjoyed by the poor. It was the latter upon whom hostilities such as deportation and pogroms were likely to be inflicted (see note 5). Finally, we are shown the conditions which can produce a character who makes evasion of the law into an art, and who cares little that he nearly destroyed his brother-in-law. All of it, the author seems to be saying, is a logical development flowing from the circumstances.

The author's first encounter with the city of Kiev, described in his autobiography, took place prior to his marriage (probably in 1881) during the period that followed his banishment from the household of his future father-in-law Loyev. The passages that follow are instructive not only because we find here evidence of a raid experienced by the author, but because of other historical details of a non-fictitious nature. The place he selected as lodging during that particular stay in the city was the Jewish inn that belonged to Reb Alter Koniever. This inn was located, we are told, in the lower part of the city known as *Podol* in which Jews were able to reside. Here is the way the author describes it:

I say that Jews are allowed to live there, but I hasten to correct myself, so that no one will gain the notion that all Jews, God forbid, were allowed there. Not so. Only those Jews are allowed there who have obtained the required residence permit—"pravozhitel'stvo." For instance: craftsmen, members of the first guild, *Nicholaievske* soldiers [those who had gone through the service of Nicholas I] and those who have children in secondary schools. All other Jews found are illegal, there for only a short period of time, and living in great fear at the mercy of the janitor and of the . . . local officials.[6]

Such toleration by local officials of "contraband" Jews lasts only until the next oblava, during which they are rounded up and exiled from the city. That fact, however, does not inhibit those who need to be there from coming to Kiev. The innkeeper sees to it that each *revisie* [inspection; the official term for the raid] should take place smoothly. This is accomplished by making sure beforehand that no illegal residents are found on the premises. He makes sure that he knows when a raid is expected by "delivering" wherever it is necessary.[7] Recalling his own experience Sholom Aleichem says:

> The author of these events had the honor to experience the pleasure of hiding in the attic during his first stay in the large, holy city of Kiev, and to tremble in fear together with several other of his compatriots. The event transpired during a dark, winter night. Since the raid was a sudden, unexpected one, there was no time for the males to get—I beg your pardon—their pants, nor the women their undergarments on. It was fortunate that the "inspection" was a short one, otherwise the victims would have expired from the cold. . . .[8]

This particular raid turned out well, since no one was found. In addition to having seen to it that the relevant officials were bribed, the innkeeper had also managed to hide his illegal guests. Some, as we saw, in the attic, some in the basement, others in closets and crates. Some were forced into places inconceivable as hideouts for human beings.

This passage from the author's experience, like the one above, indicates the indignities of persecution in the form of raids and the consequent corruption that accompanied them.

Pogroms

It is instructive before turning to the fiction of Sholom Aleichem to bring some sample selections from Dubnov who devotes considerable space to these events.

The selection below is from his description of the first pogrom of 1881 which Sholom Aleichem's fiction echoes. It took place in the city of Yelizavetgrad [Kirovo] in the south.

> On the night of the 15th of April [the fourth day of the Easter holiday] there occurred an attack upon Jews in the side-streets of the city. The dwellings affected were mainly those that contained taverns. One Jew was killed. Around seven . . . in the morning, on the 16th of April, the unrest was renewed and it spread with unusual force to the rest of the city. Employees of restaurants and hotels, master-craftsmen, foremen, lackeys, valets of officers, soldiers out of service—all of these elements took part in the movement. The city presented an unusual sight: The streets were covered with feathers and filled with broken, scattered furniture. Doors and windows were broken . . . an excited throng is rushing about in every direction shouting and whistling and engaging, unopposed, in its destructive work. As an aside to that picture—there is total indifference on the part of the surrounding, non-Jewish inhabitants to the ongoing pogrom.[9]

Dubnov points out that the police and military units, called in to restore order, were given no definite instructions and did not move to prevent the attacks on Jews. Their failure to do so served as a sign to the "pogromtchiks" [perpetrators] that they were free to do as they pleased. It was not until the 17th that the authorities halted the violence.[10]

The pogroms of 1881 culminated with a three-day pogrom in the city of Warsaw. As above, the disorder broke out during the celebration of a holiday, this time Christmas. A false fire alarm in a church created a panic in which twenty-nine people were trampled to death. Jews were blamed for the incident. The mob ran wild, rampaging and looting Jewish houses with impunity. It was only after the third day, according to an established pattern, that the authorities bethought themselves to intervene, having allowed the lesson to sink in.

> On the 27th of December an order was issued by the governor general of Warsaw, forbidding the assembly of looters . . . it came too late, after the destruction and looting in the city of 4,500 Jewish dwellings, businesses and synagogues. Twenty-four people were wounded and several million rubles were lost.[11]

Dubnov also relates the pogroms that began a few days following the coronation of Alexander III. In the large city of Rostov-on-the-Don, close to a hundred Jewish establishments were robbed and the Russian masses availed themselves of all that could be removed. Two months later an even larger pogrom occurred in the northern city of Yekaterinoslav [Dnepropetrovsk]. Dubnov points out that the "wholesome" element of the population were represented, including women and children. In this particular pogrom a number of synagogues were destroyed and the looters desecrated a number of Torah scrolls. Five hundred families were ruined.[12]

Though the pogroms of the 1880's were marked by initial indifference, the government eventually did move to stop them. During 1903-1907, however, the period when the worst kinds of violence against Jews occurred, a new element appears to have entered the situation. This time the government made it a matter of policy to instigate against Jews in order to deflect the wrath of the masses from themselves. Pointing to the many Jews in the ranks of revolutionary leadership, they declared the entire revolutionary idea as a Jewish affair—alien to the Russian people.

In the forefront of such instigation was the notoriously influential Bessarabian official Krushevan, editor of the newspaper *Bessarabetz*. Seeking to make a name for himself, he openly advocated violence against Jews. His campaign of several years culminated, in the spring of 1903, in an open call for the Christian community to take revenge for the Jewish "ritual murder" of that year. The result of that instigation was the pogrom in Kishenev, the capital city of Bessarabia, during Passover, April 6, 1903. The pogrom was carefully planned by the officials of the province, who had encouragement from the central government, and carried out with their assistance. In the words of Dubnov:

> When the church bells began to ring [on the first day of Easter and the sixth day of Passover] several gangs, groups of citizens and workers, began simultaneously to destroy Jewish dwellings and stores. Police and soldiers, stationed in the streets, did not disperse the . . . looters.[13]

Arrests were rare, and those taken into custody were immediately released, reinforcing the prevailing notion that it was permissible to rob and kill Jews.

> In the evening the killing began: the murderers, armed with clubs, axes and knives killed Jews in their houses and in the streets. Even then, however, the authorities remained silent. On the other hand, when a group of Jews, armed with clubs, attempted to chase away the murderers, the police disarmed them. . . .[14]

The organizers of the violence decided to give the murderers free reign. Consequently, the murders also continued the next day, April 7.

> Entire families were wiped out. Many individuals were left at the point of death, . . . in their last agony. Some had nails driven into their heads, others had their eyes picked out. Little children were thrown down from upper floors. . . .[15]

Concerning the numerous pogroms during October 1905, Dubnov renders the following insights:

> As if a signal had been given, there rose everywhere the "Black Hundreds," pogrom-gangs under the mask of "patriots," and there ensued a horrible blood-orgy which lasted an entire week, 18-25 of October. The main victims of that long "Bartholomew night" were Jews. . . . All were astonished at the systematic and uniform manner in which this bloody work was carried out. The picture that presented itself . . . was as follows: Due to the Manifesto of October 17, the progressive part of the population march through the streets with their emblems and speeches. . . . At the same time participants of "patriotic demonstrations" pour out from every corner, consisting of the rabble of the population—spies, police in civilian dress; they carry the tsar's picture under the national flag . . . they sing the hymn of the tsar, accompanied by cries: "Hurrah, beat the Jews. . . ." (see note 17).

Sholom Aleichem's demonstration pogrom is in his work *In the Storm*.[16] In this major work the author captures many aspects of the process of change unleashed by the clash between old and new forces in Russia on the threshold of the twentieth century. He pays special attention to the turbulence in thought and in action that ushered in the Revolution of 1905 and its aftermath.

Among the poignant glimpses of the tragic incidents of that period there is a description in this work of a pogrom to which the very elements in the nation demanding social change—liberals and revolutionaries alike—are indifferent. The author also emphasizes participation by the local people—men, women, and children—in the atrocities. He carefully describes the background against which the events take place in order to drive home the fact that they indeed occurred during a period of demand for liberal reform. Sholom Aleichem captures the mood of the nation: "With giant strides did the movement spread . . . over all cities and villages—leaving behind the resonant echo in which the word *freedom* [emphasis added] rang out."[17]

Sholom Aleichem stresses that all the "wheels" of the governmental system ceased to turn; the entire social network and its machinery came to a halt, and the nation was held in a trance of silence and of expectation—in a kind of "natural celebration, a big festival; not of the sort handed down by tradition, but one . . . brought about by the efforts of man . . ." after generations of struggle. An atmosphere of rest and repose descended upon all, uniting them under one idea, that the day of rest and repose is here (the day of the approach of human rights).[18]

The author describes the throngs of people filling the streets and their elation at the promise of freedom and of a constitutional state. He relates the immediate reaction to the Manifesto given by Nicholas II in October of 1905, which had raised such great hopes for a new era:

Itzikl Shostopol was still asleep when there came the knock on his door.

> —Who is it? was heard from Itzikl.
>
> —It is I, Safranovitch.
>
> —Sasha? What is it?
>
> —[Mazel Tov], Constitution!
>
> —What?
>
> —A constitution was given us . . . get up, the world is in an uproar![19]

In the midst of all this rejoicing Sholom Aleichem injects a very somber note. An individual enters the stage: he is a Jew who has gone berserk as a result of a life of poverty and degradation; the final blow that sends him into madness is the imprisonment and death of his revolutionary daughter. He is a prophet, predicting retribution in the form of a blood bath. His outcry is heartrending, but also descriptive of what is to come:

> —Can't you see how the stones are falling from the heavens? Fiery stones . . . and feathers . . . without end? Can't you hear the cries of the raped women, the torn-up children, the old . . . people? Don't you see the ripped open bellies filled with live cats . . . ?[20]

This tragic apparition is given us in the midst of a description of the revolutionary events that led to the Manifesto of 1905. What is especially noteworthy is the author's juxtaposition of *freedom* and *oppression* occurring at the same time and being actuated by the same people. The rejoicing on the part of Sasha Safranovitch does not last long. Doubts, reflecting the feeling of liberal forces in the land, begin to reassert themselves almost instantly. Sasha, on the way home from the Shostopols, meets with his father:

> —Sasha? From where are you coming?
>
> —From the Shostopols.
>
> —Did you tell them the news?
>
> —Nu. of course.
>
> —What did I tell you?
>
> —What did you tell me?
>
> —Constitution! . . .
>
> —Wait papa, you are not yet finished.
>
> —What are you talking about, Sasha, God help you! Here is the newspaper, here, read!
>
> —I already read, read.
>
> —Nu?
>
> —Nu—nu![21]

The father understands his son's meaning—that there wasn't really going to be a truly constitutional state. Sholom Aleichem, in this instance, places himself with those Russian historians who claim that, from the outset, Nicholas did not intend to grant what he had promised.[22]

Several other historians deal with the attempt to close the gap between the socioeconomic and political conditions in Russia during the decade preceding World War I. Most of them find the Constitutional experiment to have been too limited and the leadership insufficiently enlightened to have ushered in the necessary modern state (see notes 17, 22). His description of the events shows that repression began without any provocation by the revolutionary forces.

The throng, the author writes, is moving spontaneously, in unison. Above all the other noises of their celebration there rises the single word: *Constitution.* In the midst of their enthusiasm, a speaker emerges to remind them of the martyrs whose blood made the present events possible. They must also remember those still alive but behind bars, and so the entire throng moves to free the prisoners.

Among the prisoners is Tamara, the daughter of Shostopol, whom Sasha expects to marry. Shostopol, Sasha and his father are all in the throng. The latter is filled with glee. "It is all true then? There is to be a constitution, all to be equal—even Jews? The political prisoners will gain their freedom . . . ? Jews and Christians are seen to embrace each other, and it seems like the Messianic age. Prisoners are being freed and, among them, Tamara. They see her mount the rostrum and her father stretches out his arms toward her. Suddenly, shots are heard, the firing of many rifles. People begin to fall and are trampled underfoot. Blood flows and the mass is moving again, this time gripped by the urgency of the new developments.[23]

The reaction begins with fear and repression of the revolutionaries and soon spreads to the Jewish quarter. What follows is a glimpse of the events:

> —Proprietor! On the Jewish street, they say, it is merry!
>
> —Sh . . . what do you mean merry? asks Itzikl.
>
> —A pogrom, they say. All jump from their seats.
>
> —A what?
>
> —A pogrom—Don't you know? A Jewish pogrom. The same as in Kishenev. . . .[24]

The feelings of Jews that accompany the word "pogrom," Sholom Aleichem tells us, cannot be described; they are known only to Jews. The "harshness" of that term is increased tremendously by its utterance on that day. "Today a pogrom? How is that possible?! . . . All sit . . . frozen. Sasha sat up . . . and his eyes met those of Tamara. In that encounter there was expressed all that had never been uttered between them." Tamara is a young revolutionary with cosmopolitan, socialist views. Sasha is a Jewish nationalist, or Zionist. Their arguments are utilized by the author to reflect the ongoing debate among intellectuals on the question of "what is to be done" in terms of solutions to the Jewish problems. Here he gives us a bit of the rationale of young Jews caught in differing loyalties. Tamara breaks out, suddenly:—It is a lie! It is not possible, it cannot be . . . !

> —Why can't it be? It can very well be! says Sasha. This is the logical epilogue which should have been expected. . . .[25] [Sholom Aleichem's opinion concerning the pogroms of 1905 and 1906]

Tamara leaves the room and runs into the street; the author is making her a witness to the events. Along with the fleeing Jews from the poor quarter she encounters a policeman who is engaged in turning back the exiles. She confronts this official and asks how he can "allow" such things to happen? He counsels her to leave, at once, if she does not want to share the fate of these Jews.

> —Why Jews? Tamara asks.

> —Because today is such a day . . . answers the policeman . . . with indifference as if he were talking about cleaning the streets, or other such mundane matters.[26]

She runs further and witnesses the following scene: A young woman is running and is being pursued by two women. She is pulling along her two little children. In her hand is a small basket with all the possessions left to her. The women catch up with her and are in the process of tearing her kerchief off her head, when Tamara arrives and confronts them: "What are you doing?" "Today we are allowed!" they say . . . but walk away merrily.[27]

The young woman tells her of the terrible things going on the *Zhidovska* [Jewish] street—of people being beaten, murdered and trampled underfoot. This theme of brutality—of rape, murder, beheadings, the ripping apart of women, the tearing asunder of children while still alive and throwing them on a dunghill—is echoed in a poem written by the contemporary poet Chaim Nachman Bialik. The work, which Sasha reads to Tamara in order to impress upon her the need for a Jewish homeland, is titled "In the City of Murder." Sholom Aleichem utilizes Bialik's description of these horrible details, based on fact, to heighten our awareness of what a pogrom was really like.[28]

The young woman pleads with Tamara to take her to the home of a "good" Christian, someone willing to hide her and her children. Tamara agrees, and reflects for a moment, attempting to come up with a suitable place. She decides to take her charges to Romanenko, the progressive high school teacher who is the father of her dear friend and companion of all the liberal elements in town with faith in progressive education. Tamara, like thousands of other young people barred from the schools of higher learning since the ordinance of July 1887,[29] was in need of a tutor. Romanenko, to whom her father turned for advice, recommended the services of his own son, a serious scholar, who not only prepared Tamara for university entrance, but inducted her into the revolutionary movement.

> Tamara continues walking and sees a procession, from afar, with "Nationalist" flags. What does it mean? . . . She sees . . . a pretty sight. Doors are being broken down, windows smashed, there is throwing, beating and smashing. Little Gentile boys . . . men and girls participate and someone is being beaten. She sees people fall and being trampled by horses. . . . The procession . . . comes to a halt in front of the high school. . . . The elder Romanenko is standing on the balcony and is taking bows. From the crowd emanates a thunderous "Hoorah!" "Down with the Constitution!" Death to the Jews!!! Hoorah! Death to the Jews!!. . . .[30]

Tamara sees, is a witness herself, and becomes aware that the perpetrators of this pogrom are not merely the passive soldiers of an authoritarian government; they are not merely the tsar's bureaucracy, but men, women and children, the Russian people themselves. The name Romanenko, chosen by Sholom Aleichem for the above liberal-turned-reactionary, is significant. The author, no doubt, is pointing his finger at the real Romanenko and other radicals like him, who instigated against Jews. As one of the leaders of the radical party *Narodnaya Volia,* Romanenko signed his name to literature calling for violence against Jews.[31] The author is pointing his finger at the anti-Semitism that went hand-in-hand with parts of the liberal-revolutionary movements.

Other Forms of Hostility

Among the ways in which Jews were kept in their place and made to feel their low civic status was the use of speech—they were addressed in a contemptuous manner. This hostility was manifested both on the official level, in the way Jews were dealt with by various governmental officials, and by the general Christian population. It was commonplace for Christians to scorn, ridicule and shout at Jews, and to call them derogatory names. It was a technique intended to assail their dignity as human beings, a technique vastly perfected in the Nazi concentration camps. . . . Other facts of this nature will be reflected in the pages that follow, wherever they form part of the plot of a given story, or are relevant parts of the discussion.

The novel *Nostalgia,*[32] contains a description of contemptuous treatment of Jews at the hands of a local official. . . . In their effort to raise funds for the purchase of land in Palestine, the leaders of a Jewish community encounter obstruction from the postmaster who is a known anti-Semite. Among the behavioral features exhibited by this individual are contempt, name-calling, threats and other forms of harrassment calculated to delay the sending of the funds. Public humiliation of Jews became state policy under Nicholas II, when special distortions of their Jewish names were insisted upon.

The by now familiar character Ivanov, from *It is Hard to Be a Jew,* was subjected to a great deal of hostility of this kind. He was called in repeatedly to appear before the local authorities who found some reason to harrass him. In the excerpt that follows he is confronted, for the first time in his experience, with the kind of language Jews had to endure as a matter of course:

> Shapiro: Why don't you ask him, for instance, what he said . . . when the old official called out to him: "Hey, Hershko, come here" [he used the informal speech reserved for children and other inferiors].

> Ivanov: [Turning to his friend with whom he made the wager.] Do you understand? The old drunkard dares to address me familiarly, should I have ignored him?

> Schneierson: [Smiling at his friend] So what did you tell him?

Ivanov: I didn't tell him anything. I merely asked him since when are we so close that we address each other by the familiar "thou" . . . ?

Schneierson: [Laughing] Well, and what followed?

Ivanov: He turns to me and snaps: "Shut your Jewish trap!" I nearly let him have it.[33]

There are countless examples throughout the works of Sholom Aleichem that could be given as evidence of the treatment of Jews as less than human. The attempt, however, is to illustrate, and not to exhaust this point. The selection chosen to close this section reflects not only utter contempt of Christians for Jews, but also the tragic resignation of the latter in Jewish lore. The hero of the story **"The Jew Who Became a Bird,"** is unusually humble and pious. The nobleman's treatment of the Jew, on the other hand, though given by the author as an example of events from the remote past, is typical of the "sport" the gentry in the territories of the Pale were accustomed to having with their Jewish tenants in the annals of Jewish lore.[35] If we accept the proposition that the lore of a people springs from deeply rooted perceptions of reality, and I am inclined to do so, then this story does tell us something about the conditions of life, the fear of arbitrary cruelty, the author wishes to illustrate.

The story concerns an impoverished individual with a houseful of children who is a rather simple soul. Therefore, it is the lot of his wife, a capable woman, to run the tavern they are renting from the nobleman in their region. The husband's job consists of periodically renewing the contract with the estate owner, or landlord, and it is on such an errand that he is engaged in this story.

He enters the landlord's premises and finds an assembly of guests. They have just risen from the table and are preparing for the hunt. Not a good time for his business, reflects our man, but it turns out that he is mistaken. The Lord, well into his cups, is rather eager to conduct business. He approaches the Jew with elation and asks him for how long he wishes to rent the tavern. The Jew replies that he would like it for a few years, but will accept whatever he is given. Before he is able to conclude his statement, he is interrupted by the gentleman who says: "Good, this time I shall give you the tavern for the usual period of ten years, but under one condition: you must turn yourself into a bird for me." The Jew looks at him and asks: "What do you mean I should turn myself into a bird for you?" The Lord replies:

It is simple. You will climb up on the roof of that stable over there, do you see? There you will pretend that you are a bird and I shall aim and try to get you straight in your head. Did you understand?[36]

This was greeted by a burst of laughter and the Jew, thinking that the man is jesting, asked him how long he has to make up his mind. He is given one minute to reflect about the matter and is told that either he goes through with the deal, or he must vacate the tavern tomorrow. It dawns on

him that the Lord is not jesting and he asks him, "And what will happen in case your aim should succeed?" This causes even greater merriment among the assembled guests, but the Jew remains standing in stupefaction.

He realizes the gravity of the situation and wants to go home, but remembers his wife and children and the need to vacate the business. He decides that there is no way out, that it must be a test from God. He obtains an additional minute of reprieve in order to make peace with his maker, but he can do no more than call out the traditional Hear O Israel and begins climbing on the roof, while tears are streaming from his eyes. In his heart there glimmers the hope that God will save him: "God if he only wants to—knows how. He had great faith . . ."

The Lord put him through the various motions necessary to approximate a bird after which he took aim and fired. He shot the poor fellow through the middle of his forehead and the Jew flew off the roof like a dead bird.[37]

The author distinguishes the above story, which appears in the middle of his autobiography, from experiences he personally lived through by indicating that it is a tale from the past told by his grandfather. The tale is intended, in his own phrase, to illustrate "Jews of yore" and "lords of yore."[38] The emphasis on past brutalities in this instance appears to be intended to point out that the quality of life, resulting from capricious, arbitrary cruelty experienced by Jews of his own generation, goes back to the remote past. The particulars of this story are not important; they may well be fiction invented by the author to illustrate the "general" quality of life—the cruel conditions under which Jews in the Russian Pale were forced to live for centuries.

The Blood Libel

That Sholom Aleichem was greatly concerned about the renewed blood libel and the form it took in Russia during the progressive twentieth century is evident from several contexts. We saw that Tevyeh referred to this charge—mentioning Mendel Beilis by name and emphasizing that this victim was forced to "cleanse his soul" for sins that were not his.

The play *It is Hard to Be a Jew,* referred to above, is also relevant in this context. In it, Sholom Aleichem refers to the fear of a pogrom by a Jewish community, during which the reprehensible blood libel also plays a role. Moreover, the selection chosen also illustrates the degree of helplessness of the Jews because the author makes it clear that not only were the innocent victims inadequately protected, but that the authorities actually conspired against them by manipulating events in such a way as to create an atmosphere in which a pogrom could be precipitated.

The facts were as follows: shortly before Passover a Christian boy disappeared. He turned up murdered in the Jewish section of town where most of the Jews lived. This was construed to be evidence that the Jews murdered him. The authorities then looked around for a religious Jew, preferably one without money or connections, on whom to pin the charge. To find the victim and to arrest him would have resulted in an atmosphere in which the entire community of Jews would be vulnerable. The plan which the local authorities carefully prepared, to stage an unexpected raid during the Seder ceremony in order to arrest the victim, was only accidentally foiled. They had singled out Ivanov for this honor, who was, however, really a Christian. Had he been a Jew, there would have been little he or other Jews could have done to avert a tragedy to the entire community. The dialogue below refers to the plotting by local officials to manufacture victims and evidence for an accusation that would bring a pogrom in its wake:

> Katz: You ask what is new in town? The news is not good. It is bitter in town. . . .
>
> David: What is the matter?
>
> Katz: I am talking about the tragedy . . . the murdered Gentile boy who was found here. They are planning to make a pogrom . . . there will almost certainly be a pogrom. . . . It is being planned for Passover. . . .
>
> David: On Passover, and you know all that?
>
> Katz: Of course I know, I also know that they intend to implicate certain people in this affair . . . a certain Schneierson. . . .
>
> David: What connections does Schneierson have with this affair?
>
> Katz: That I don't know. All I know is that they intend to implicate him. . . . They are in need of a pious individual . . . who is supposed to have collected the blood of all the murdered Christian children and to have distributed it among the Jews for Passover. Since the Schneiersons are descended from pious stock, they want one of them, a Schneierson.[39]

Schneierson was the assumed name of Ivanov. He was new in the community, had no previous connections to the authorities, and, most important, he appeared to be poor and helpless.

In part of the play the leaders of the Jewish community meet with their rabbi deliberating the situation. The rabbi expresses the hope that the governor's promise that there will be no pogrom will prove true. The governor, they repeat to each other, said: "be calm" and "accept peace," as well as "don't agitate others." One of the representatives present observes sarcastically: "he-he- that means . . . that we shouldn't stage a pogrom ourselves, he-he-he."[40] Those present at this meeting also mention that the governor, in spite of his "calming" promise, asked each of them individually what information they can give him about the Schneiersons.[41]

The above passage and this entire section of the play expose the treachery and the deliberate lies of the local officials who in spite of their promises planned to have the pogrom as the Jews suspected that they would. Such treachery on the part of local authorities is no figment of the author's imagination but well-documented historical fact. Dubnov, for example, claims that what occurred in a given region during the pogroms in the 1880's was largely colored by attitudes of regional . . . officials.[42]

Sholom Aleichem is evidently reproducing here some of the details of the pogrom in Balta in 1882, inspired by and carried out with the collaboration of the authorities. That pogrom, like the one described above, occurred during Passover. In it, as in the fiction of Sholom Aleichem, the governor and local police conspired to trap the Jews and actively participated in the atrocities. Even the blood libel occurred at Balta. Unlike the fiction of Sholom Aleichem, however, the story in Balta did not have a happy ending. The Balta pogrom was gruesome in the horror it left in its wake at home and the cruelty it inspired in other localities.[43]

As the selections [in this essay show] Sholom Aleichem leaves us with the feeling that hostilities such as raids were a direct result of the legal restrictions on mobility. If no special permits had been necessary for residence in certain areas, there would have been no illegal residents whom it was necessary to find and deport. Hostilities such as ridicule, contempt, false accusations and other Jew-baiting practices, of which the pogrom was the extreme expression, were developments elicited by the separate, low civic status of the Jews. Ignorance and prejudice against them, filtering down from the highest levels, created a climate in which persecution of Jews was not merely ignored but took on elements of social sanction. As we have seen, these facts are known to historians of the Russian scene of the period. Sholom aleichem is showing us the phenomena as they affected the day-to-day life of the Jews.

Notes

[1] Simon Dubnov, *World History of the Jewish People From the Earliest Times to the Present,* trans. Ch. S. Kazdan, 10 vols. (New York: Congress for Jewish Culture, 1953) 98-186.

[2] Dubnov 109. Instead of aiding the victims of the pogrom, a function the government was expected to render, administrative harrassments were instituted in the form of raids which Dubnov designates by the term "legalized pogroms," 109-10.

[3] *Railroad Stories* 273-82.

[4] *Railroad* 278.

[5] *Railroad* 279. Dubnov 305, 138, claims that it was mainly the poor who were slaughtered at Kishinev; the rich were able to obtain protection. As far as bribing the authorities is concerned, he calls the legislation that made bribes an absolute necessity if one were to survive and the ways Jews found to circumvent these laws "the Russian Constitution."

[6] *Back From the Fair* 228.

[7] *Fair* 229.

[8] *Fair* 230.

[9] Dubnov 103-04.

[10] Dubnov 103-04.

[11] Dubnov 117-18.

[12] Dubnov 134.

[13] Dubnov 304.

[14] Dubnov 305.

[15] Dubnov 305.

[16] Vol. 24.

[17] *Storm* 184. For a description of that "liberal" feeling in the land during the period in question see Dubnov, 302-332. Like Sholom Aleichem, Dubnov sees the irony of parallel development of liberalism and persecution. Thus, pogroms and persecution are discussed under the heading: "Pogroms and Revolution in Russia." It is in this chapter that he relates the pogroms of October 1905, pp. 322-326. During the week of October 18-25, there were some 50 pogroms in most major cities. See also his discussion of pogroms and liberal trends under the title: "The Government Duma and the Pogroms of 1906," 327-332. See also Sidney Harcave, *First Blood: The Russian Revolution of 1905* (New York: Macmillan, 1964). Harcave documents the spontaneous nature of the strikes during January through October of 1905 and the demands for reform which brought to a halt economic and social life, culminating in the Manifesto issued by the tsar on October 17. Harcave sees Nicholas II as having missed his chance to prevent revolution in Russia by failing to carry out the promise of the Manifesto. The pogroms against Jews are seen as evidence that the government was looking for scapegoats.

[18] *Storm* 184; Dubnov 35-322. Dubnov views the reaction of the masses in 1905 expressive of the conviction that revolutionary measures are necessary if basic change is to come about.

[19] *Storm* 189.

[20] *Storm* 187-88.

[21] *Storm* 190.

[22] Harcave, *First Blood,* see note 17. The system of the Duma instituted in Russia in June of 1907 was merely a shadow of a Western style parliamentary system. The first and second Dumas, which would have given a measure of civic freedom and political participation to classes not previously admitted, were terminated very rapidly. On the failure of the third and fourth Dumas which made revolution inevitable, see Geoffrey Hosking, *The Russian Constitutional Experiment: Government and Duma 1907-1914* (Cambridge: Cambridge UP, 1973). See also Alfred Levin, *The Second Duma: A Study of the Social Democratic Party and the Russian Constitutional Experiment* (New Haven: Yale UP, 1940). Levin feels that the second Duma was a genuine opportunity to create a constitutional government on the European model. He sees government obstruction among the major reasons why this Duma failed. Levin sees the third Duma to have greatly curtailed representation of liberal forces. See his "June 3, 1907: Action and Reaction" in A.D. Ferguson and A. Levin, eds. *Essays in Russian History* (Hamden, Conn.: Archon, 1964). On the chances of evolutionary democracy in Russia and the role of WWI, see also Leopold Haimson, "The Problem of

Social Stability in Urban Russia, 1905-1917," *Slavic Review,* Part 1 in 23 (December 1964): 619-642; Part 2 in 24 (January 1965): 122. Haimson sees radicalization in Russia with or without the war. See also Harcave, *The Years of the Golden Cockerel: The Last Romanov Tsars 1814-1917* (New York: Crowell, 1962), in which Harcave ascribes Russian failure to develop a modern constitutional state to the ineptitude of its ruling men. Dubnov claims that the violence against Jews in 1905 can be traced to the tsar, pp. 223-224.

[23] *Storm* 193-99.

[24] *Storm* 202.

[25] *Storm* 203.

[26] *Storm* 205.

[27] *Storm* 205.

[28] *Storm* 94-99.

[29] *Storm* 140-41.

[30] *Storm* 206-07.

[31] *Storm* 206-07; Dubnov 117-20.

[32] Vol. 3: 113-26.

[33] *Hard* 78.

[34] *Fair* 241-46.

[35] There exists an entire literature, much of it concerned with Chassidic themes and stories, in which the Chassidic rebbe renders assistance, both material and spiritual, to the victims of persecution at the hands of the gentry. The atrocities encountered in these tales are typical of the story described by the author.

[36] *Fair* 245.

[37] *Fair* 245.

[38] *Fair* 245-46. One of the persistent problems of imperial Russia was the failure of its rulers to do away with arbitrary authority and to institute a rule of law. See Hans Kohn, *Basic History of Modern Russia Political Cultural and Social Trends* (Princeton: Nostrand, 1957) 12, 18-19, 49-52, 56-57. For a discussion of the *arbitrary brutality* of the Russian nobleman toward his inferiors see Edward Daniel Clarke, "Russian Nobility in 1800," reprinted in Kohn, *Basic History* 122-26.

[39] *Hard* 99.

[40] *Hard* 114.

[41] *Hard* 115.

[42] Dubnov 109-14. Dubnov shows that though the decrees and circulars of Alexander III and his officials created panic throughout the Pale, the greatest excesses took place in the south. Much depended on the attitudes of local officials. Thus, the public prosecutor of Kiev, Strelnikov, was responsible for great excesses there. On the other hand, an indi-

vidual such as Count E. I. Toteleben, governor of a northwestern province, was able to minimize brutalities by his categorical refusal to allow pogroms under his jurisdiction.

[43] Dubnov 125-26.

V. S. Pritchett (essay date 1990)

SOURCE: "Sholom Aleichem: Pain and Laughter," in *Lasting Impressions: Selected Essays,* Chatto & Windus, 1990, pp. 11-15.

[*In the following essay, Pritchett favorably assesses Aleichem's humor and storytelling ability.*]

Sholom Aleichem is one of the prolific masters of Yiddish comic storytelling, an art springing from the oral folk traditions of Eastern Europe and crossed by the pain and laughter of racial calamity. Like all comics he is serious, has one foot in the disorder and madness of the world and, as a Jew, the other foot in the now perplexing, now exalted, adjuration of the Law and the Prophets. Did God really choose their fate for the Jewish people? If so, was He being irresponsible, or why doesn't He make it clear? There is no answer. The oppressed stick to their rituals and are obliged to perfect the delights of cunning, the consolations of extravagant fantasy, the ironies and pedantries of the moralist who is privately turning his resignation into a weapon. With so many insoluble dilemmas on his hands, Aleichem developed that nimbleness of mind and fancy, those skills of masking and ventriloquism, that made him the prolific 'natural' in short tales drawn partly from the remaking of folk tradition, a juggler of puns, proverbs, and sudden revealing images caught from the bewildered tongues of his people.

There are certain distinctions to be noted when we speak of the general Jewish gift for anecdote. These are made clear in the exchange of letters between Irving Howe and Ruth Wisse which introduce their selection from a striking variety of Aleichem's best work and discuss the growth of mind it reveals. Mr Howe points out that Aleichem is not a 'folksy tickler of Jewish vanities' and the Yiddish folk material he uses is not as cosy 'as later generations of Jews have liked to suppose'. Under the laughter is fright and the old driving forces of anxiety and guilt: if Aleichem is close to folk sources he escapes the collective claustrophobia of a folk tradition that was broken by the pogroms and wars that drove the Eastern European Jews to flight or death; he has let in the light of 'a complicated and individual vision of human existence. That means terror and joy, dark and bright, fear and play.'

Ruth Wisse points to Aleichem's position in the period when the Jewish moral crisis came to a head in Eastern Europe. Writing of his contemporaries, the classical masters Mendele Mocher Sforim and I. L. Peretz, she says that they are embattled writers, 'fiercely critical of their society', strong in dialectical tendency, pitting old against new; whereas Aleichem, who also felt the break in the

Jewish tradition and in his own life, 'makes it his artistic business to *close* the gap. In fact, wherever the danger of dissolution is greatest, the stories work their magic in simulating or creating a *terra firma.*' I do not know the work of these writers but it is certainly true of Aleichem's work that it shows his balance and poise in tales like '**A Yom Kippur Scandal**', '**Station Baranovich**', the terrifying '**Krushniker Delegation**', '**Eternal Life**', and above all in the four grave Tevye tales. As he tries to face his daughters' rebellion against tradition Tevye becomes, tragically, something more than a folk figure: he becomes a man.

One can see Aleichem's instant, restless eye unfitted him for the novel. As the Tevye stories show, he could be grave without encumbering himself with novelistic architecture.

—V. S. Pritchett

Aleichem has the style of the spontaneous talker, at home in many garrulous idioms; it is a style that plays as it moves forward dramatically and then, hit by an image or a proverb, circles back. The narrator's mind is continually split between what is happening and something else, some fear, some scheme, some hope that is going on in his mind. He acts on impulse and regrets at once; always escaping from his situation, he is back in it only to find it changed, usually for the worse. He writes as a man backing away from the next minute and going headlong into it. Nearly all of Aleichem's people are whirled around by their imaginations, addressing fate, knocked this way and then that by scripture or the proverbs—'When a soup bone is stuck in somebody's face who doesn't give it a lick?' On second thoughts, 'You can skin a bear in the forest but you still can't sell its hide there.' Speculation is their anguish. They burn with a fever. 'My blood began to whistle like a teakettle.' Aleichem's powers of invention pour out of the language he utters. The innumerable surprises of language so entangle us that we are caught out by the vaster surprises of the tale. In catching us out, his art shows its depth.

Aleichem's people themselves belong to a storytelling culture. He is as astonished and disturbed by his bizarre tales as we are and uses the device of not bringing them to an end, sometimes in order to show that the meaning of the tale has been hidden and we must work it out for ourselves or go on making it up on our own. This is evidence of a very self-conscious art, as Mr Howe says.

A clear example is '**A Yom Kippur Scandal**'. A stranger comes to the synagogue and overcomes mistrust by handing out silver coins, but when the rituals are over, he suddenly screams out that he has been robbed of 1800 roubles, on the holiest day of the year. He had put the money into the praying stand and it has gone. The rabbi and his congregation turn out their pockets. Only one person refuses. He is a young man notorious for knowing the Talmud by heart, for being a master of Hebrew, arithmetic, algebra, unequalled in chess—perfection. The congregation argue with him, he begs to be spared, but they throw him to the ground and, going through his pockets discover only a couple of gnawed chicken bones and a dozen plum pits still wet from chewing.

> You can imagine what an impression this made—to discover food in the pockets of our prodigy on this holiest of fast days. Can you imagine the look on the young man's face, and on his father-in-law's? And on that of our poor rabbi?

But what about the 1800 roubles? Never found. Gone forever, says the storyteller, and never explains. We can suspect, if we like, that the stranger had invented the drama, to cover up the fact that he had stolen his employer's money. But Aleichem does not explain. Why not? Because the deeper sin than the sin of theft is the sin against God and His Law? Aleichem still doesn't say. We are perhaps left to search our own souls. Who knows?

'Station Baranovich' is another tale that stops short of its ending. It is told by a Jewish stranger on a train and is an event that occurred in czarist times. A loose-tongued bartender called Kivke starts a religious argument with peasants on a Sunday. He is reported to the police and is sentenced to be stripped naked and to run a gauntlet of cavalry officers, who will whip him. The Jews unite to plot his escape. They fake the death of Kivke in prison, arrange a mock funeral, and get him out of the country. He shows his gratitude by blackmailing them for larger and larger sums of money now that he is free. The final threat is to report the whole thing to the Russian Commissioner. But at this point the train stops at Baranovich and the teller of the story jumps out. What happened next, what is the end? the listeners shout. All they get is

> 'What end? It was just the beginning!'

and he is gone. Aleichem says

> May Station Baranovich burn to the ground!

What does he mean? Ruth Wisse says it sounds like a protest against his own art or a defence of it. More likely it seems to me that the end being 'just the beginning' evokes the only too familiar frightful prospect that awaited the Jews of that village, a further test of their emotions, their ingenuity as an oppressed people.

Aleichem's humour has a double edge; it is concerned with a good deal of trickery or with efforts to bring off a successful or kind action which come to disaster because of some helpless absent-mindedness. In 'Eternal Life' the green young theological student who lives under the thumb of his mother-in-law volunteers, out of a desire to do a good deed that will win him Eternal Life, to take the body of a dead mother to the burial ground, because the father cannot leave the house and has no sleigh. The jour-

ney through the blizzard is terrible, so terrible that he cannot remember the name of the dead woman. So he is mad enough to make up the tale that the body is his mother-in-law's; she has died of fright. The inspector of the Burial Society asks, What sort of fright?

> My tongue seemed to stick to my palate. I decided that, since I had begun with lies, I might as well continue with lies, and I made up a long tale about my mother-in-law sitting alone, knitting a sock, forgetting that her son Ephraim was there, a boy of thirteen, overgrown and a complete fool. He was playing with his shadow. He stole up to her, waved his hands over her head and uttered a goat cry, *Mehh!* He was making a shadow goat on the wall. And at this sound my mother-in-law fell from her stool and died.

Again and again, the storyteller invents other selves when he dramatises a dilemma. Yet this story is not mechanical farce; it passes through the moods of youthful exultation and sorrow, and as the blizzard drives him almost into sleep on the sleigh, the idea of Eternal Life has the sweetness of death and then turns to terror, for the wind seems to be the voice of the dead woman on the sleigh. She seems to accuse him and say, What are you doing to me, young man? Destroying a daughter of Israel who has died?

In this story we move through joy, exaltation, fear, and farce, as if these were a weather in which the people live. Indeed in all the stories, the feelings bound from one to another. The characters repeat themselves with comic fervour, as if searching for guarantees; they dramatise themselves as if they were momentary universes. Each in turn is the only one who loves, hates, scolds, whines, tricks or believes. In their voices these people, who have no land, have their territory and thus Aleichem has written its history.

Irving Howe notes that the Mottel farces introduce a Tom Sawyer-like note, which one does not hear in the adult stories. I notice something like a theme of Flann O'Brien's in one of them, **'My Brother Elye's Drink'**—in *Mottel the Cantor's Son*. It is about a boy out to make a fortune from homemade kvass and ink, and who even offers to rid his town of mice. One can see Aleichem's instant, restless eye unfitted him for the novel. As the Tevye stories show, he could be grave without encumbering himself with novelistic architecture. One surprise is the almost complete lack of erotic or mystical fantasy, such as we find in I. B. Singer.

FURTHER READING

Aarons, Victoria. *Author as Character in the Works of Sholom Aleichem.* New York: Edward Mellen Press, 1985, 176 p.
  Examines thematic and stylistic aspects of Sholom Aleichem's work.

Butwin, Joseph, and Frances Butwin. *Sholom Aleichem.* Boston: Twayne Publishers, 1977, 173 p.

Full-length biographical and critical study focusing on Sholom Aleichem's work.

Gittleman, Sol. "Sholom Aleichem's 'Tevye Stories': The Crisis of Family Life." In *From Shtetl to Suburbia: The Family in Jewish Literary Imagination,* pp. 54-85. Boston: Beacon Press, 1978.
    Discusses the traditional values present in Sholom Aleichem's *Tevye's Daughters* stories.

————. *Sholom Aleichem: A Non-Critical Introduction.* The Hague: Mouton, 1974, 203 p.
    Survey of Sholom Aleichem's works, including biographical background, discussion of major themes, and analysis of their influence on later writers.

Grafstein, Melech, ed. *Sholom Aleichem Panorama.* London, Ontario: The Jewish Observer, 1948, 415 p.
    Collection of essays on Sholom Aleichem's life and work, and translations of his stories, plays, letters, and memoirs.

Halberstam-Rubin, Anna. *Sholom Aleichem: The Writer as Social Historian.* New York: Peter Lang, 1989, 165 p.

Places Sholom Aleichem's work within a historical context and discusses how historical events impacted his fiction, drama, and novels.

Kaufman, Bel. "Sholom Aleichem." In *Abroad in America: Visitors to the New Nation,* edited by Marc Prachter, pp. 270-78. Reading, Mass.: Addison-Wesley Publishing Co., 1976.
    Biographical sketch written by Sholom Aleichem's granddaughter, which is followed by a presentation of Sholom Aleichem's views on America as expressed in his writing and through the characters in his stories.

Miron, Dan. *Sholem Aleykhem: Person, Persona, Presence.* New York: Walden Press, 1972, 45 p.
    Investigates the function of the pseudonym "Sholom Aleichem" and the effect of the fictional author on the text of the stories.

Samuel, Maurice. *The World of Sholom Aleichem.* New York: Alfred A. Knopf, 1945, 331 p.
    Description of the culture and language of the Jewish Pale of Settlement, using Sholom Aleichem's stories as illustrations.

Additional coverage of Sholom Aleichem's life and career is contained in the following sources published by The Gale Group: *Contemporary Authors,* **Vol. 104; and** *Twentieth-Century Literary Criticism,* **Vols. 1, 35.**

Nelson Algren
1909–1981

(Born Nelson Ahlgren Abraham) American novelist, short story writer, journalist, poet, and essayist.

INTRODUCTION

Algren lived most of his life in Chicago and often explored in his fiction the gritty underworld of Chicago's impoverished neighborhoods. Called the "poet of the Chicago slums" by American critic Malcolm Cowley, Algren often addressed such subjects as poverty, drug addiction, violence, oppression, and social injustice in his novels and short stories. Many critics have described his work as social protest fiction and have aligned him with the realistic or naturalistic literary traditions because of his frank and passionate depiction of the underdogs in American society and his use of unsentimental prose and authentic street dialect. Although Algren is known primarily for his novels, in particular *The Man with The Golden Arm* (1949), winner of the National Book Award and the basis for a well-known film of the same name, his short stories have been lauded for the precision and control some critics find lacking in his longer works. Some of Algren's best-known short stories include "So Help Me," "Design for Departure," and "A Bottle of Milk for Mother," the latter of which has been widely studied and anthologized.

Biographical Information

Algren was born in Detroit and grew up in a working-class Polish neighborhood of Chicago. He graduated with a degree in journalism from the University of Illinois in 1931 but was unable to find work during the Depression. Travelling to New Orleans and later to the Southwest, Algren worked odd jobs, including carnival worker, salesman, migratory worker, and gas station attendant. His experiences at a gas station in Rio Hondo, Texas, in 1933 led to his writing his first short story, "So Help Me," published in *Story* magazine that same year. Algren became involved in the Communist Party and, with Jack Conroy, edited a leftist magazine called *The New Anvil*. In the late 1930s, he joined the Federal Writers Project, which gave him a chance to write full time. From 1941 until his death, Algren worked as a journalist, often reporting on the victims of poverty and crime. He also served in the U.S. Army from 1942 to 1945 as a medical corpsman. The decade following his discharge was his most productive as a writer; Algren published two novels, the short story collection *The Neon Wilderness* (1947), and the prose poem *Chicago: City on the Make* (1951). Algren knew many important writers of the period, including Ernest

Hemingway, Richard Wright, James T. Farrell, Jean-Paul Sartre, and Simone de Beauvoir. He also traveled extensively throughout Europe, Asia, Central America, and the United States. Algren left Chicago in 1975 and moved to New Jersey and later to Long Island. He died of a heart attack in Sag Harbor, New York, in 1981.

Major Works of Short Fiction

Many of Algren's short stories were first published in such magazines as *Nation, Life, Atlantic, Partisan Review, Playboy,* and *Rolling Stone,* and were later collected in *The Neon Wilderness, The Last Carousel* (1973), and *The Texas Stories of Nelson Algren* (1995). *The Neon Wilderness* contains twenty-four stories, with all but eight of them set in Chicago. "So Help Me" tells the story of Homer, a young uneducated man who is apprehended for the murder of a Jewish boy named David. This work is written as an extended dramatic monologue and reveals Homer's emotions and state of mind as he recounts his story to a lawyer. "A Bottle of Milk for Mother" centers on Lefty Bicek, a Polish-American youth living in Chicago. Lefty, who is a pitcher in a Polish baseball league and an aspiring boxer, is caught robbing a drunkard. As he flees the scene, Lefty accidentally shoots his gun. He is unaware, however, until he is interrogated by Captain Kozak at the police station, that the man he robbed has died. During the questioning, Lefty acts defiant and tough, but by the end of the interrogation, he has been dismissed and degraded by the police officers. Another story in the volume, "Depend on Aunt Elly," focuses on a young woman who cannot escape prostitution and her relationship with a boxer. "Design for Departure" is the story of Mary, a frightened young woman who, neglected by her father and his girlfriend, decides to make a life of her own. She finds work in a packinghouse but eventually turns to prostitution. Shortly after, Mary meets Christy, who sexually abuses her but then becomes her lover and drug supplier. When Christy is sentenced to jail for three years, Mary becomes distraught and, upon his release, asks Christy to give her a lethal dose of drugs. *The Last Carousel,* in addition to including some of Algren's short stories, contains sketches, reminiscences, essays, and unpublished portions of his novels. The title story of the volume, "The Last Carousel," depicts the seedy atmosphere of carnival life in Texas, and "The Captain Has Bad Dreams" is the account of a police captain who confronts feelings of despair and nihilism as he deals with nightly lineups of burglars, drug addicts, and alcoholics. *The Texas Stories of Nelson Algren* features stories that are set in Texas during the Depression. Centering on migrant workers, vagrants, and impoverished Mexicans, these stories were gleaned from Algren's experiences in the Southwest during the 1930s and address such themes as corruption, racism, and anti-Semitism.

Critical Reception

Critical reaction to Algren's fiction has been mixed, with some suggesting that he never received sufficient critical attention during his lifetime. Many have noted that after Algren earned acclaim in the 1950s for such works as *The Neon Wilderness* and *The Man with the Golden Arm,* he virtually stopped writing fiction, focusing instead on journalism and travel writing. Some have also suggested that he alienated himself from the literary establishment by decrying critics for placing more emphasis on literary analysis than on writing itself. For example, Algren once stated: "I don't read [critics]. I doubt anyone does, except other critics. It seems like a sealed-off field with its own lieutenants, pretty much preoccupied with its own intrigues." Critic George Bluestone unsuccessfully attempted to redeem Algren's reputation in a 1957 essay in *Western Review,* in which he provided a thoughtful scholarly analysis of Algren's fictional works and refuted most commentators by stating that "to read [Algren] in the naturalist tradition is to misread him." Although many literary critics overlooked or shunned Algren, such notable authors as Ernest Hemingway, Carl Sandburg, and Richard Wright lauded Algren's contribution to contemporary American fiction. Hemingway once called Algren

one of the most notable authors of his generation, and writers and critics alike praised his realistic depiction of the underside of American society and his emphasis on social concerns. Others, however, have faulted Algren for what they call his recycling of material; many of Algren's short stories became episodes in his novels, and portions of his novels were later changed and published separately as short stories. Despite the ambivalence and controversy Algren's work has generated, he is remembered as a highly influential writer who addressed such subjects as poverty, oppression, and drug addiction before it was fashionable to do so. Concerning Algren's legacy, R. W. Lid has stated, "Algren saw and felt and responded in literary works of magnitude and distinction to the cultural and social forces that aggravate poverty and lead to the denial of human rights long before such inequities created an awakened national conscience."

PRINCIPAL WORKS

Short Fiction

The Neon Wilderness 1947
Nelson Algren's Own Book of Lonesome Monsters [editor] 1962
The Last Carousel (short stories, essays, sketches) 1973
The Texas Stories of Nelson Algren 1995

Other Major Works

Somebody in Boots (novel) 1935
Never Come Morning (novel) 1942
The Man with the Golden Arm (novel) 1949
Chicago: City on the Make (prose poem) 1951
A Walk on the Wild Side (novel) 1956
A Walk on the Wild Side (play) 1960
Who Lost an American? (nonfiction) 1963
Notes from a Sea Diary: Hemingway All the Way (nonfiction) 1965
Calhoun: Roman eines Verbrechens [*The Devil's Stocking*] (novel) 1981
Nonconformity: Writing on Writing (nonfiction) 1996

*Algren wrote the introduction and contributed one short story, "The House of the Hundred Grassfires," to this work.

CRITICISM

John Woodburn (review date 1947)

SOURCE: "People of the Abyss," in *The New York Times Book Review,* February 2, 1947, p. 16.

[*In the following review of* The Neon Wilderness, *Woodburn states that the collection is uneven but praises Algren's sympathetic characterization.*]

The world of Nelson Algren's *The Neon Wilderness* is like James T. Farrell's, one he never made. It is not the same world as Farrell's, however, despite the fact that all but eight of these twenty-four brutal, pitiful and piteous stories occur in Chicago, among the streets and alleyways where Studs Lonigan and Danny O'Neill traced their wayward patterns. For Algren's is an Existential world, a sunless place of whispering, tangible shadows, where nightmare becomes a dense reality, and the future is slain by the intolerable present.

Algren's people are residents of the abyss. They are the ones who came to the end of the road and did not stop, and are now too damaged to return. Outlawed and lost, their lives, if they may be said to be alive, have become feral and instinctual, and their acts seem more the convulsive reflexes of dangling men than gestures of volition. A starved alley-cat, spitting with a broken back, is as sensible of its predicament as are these cornered ones. They share with the alley-cat a kind of animal innocence, and it is this, and only this, which elevates them to moments of simple tragedy, all other dignity being denied them.

As a collection, *The Neon Wilderness* has its mountains and valleys; it is both monotonous and uneven. There is so little light here, one story throwing its thick shadow on another, that some of the individual impact is lost. But a few of the stories rise strongly above the monotone and leave a scar on the memory. The best of these, in my opinion, is **"Design for Departure,"** which tells in one story of a frightened girl a whole life that was never lived. Then, as among the mountains, I shall remember **"A Bottle of Milk for Mother,"** and the Polish-American hoodlum chattering with hopeless, braggart cunning in the police station; and the almost unbearable scorn and pity of **"The Children,"** in which sniggering, vicious adolescents prance through a Hiawatha pageant in a House of Correction.

I wish Mr. Algren had not fallen in love with the compound adjective "pavement-colored," and did not strive so hard for arresting titles. But, uneven as this collection is, it shows Nelson Algren's power, the magnificent anger and indignation with which he articulates the lives of these ruined and invalidated people. He is deeply and pitifully concerned with them, and he is determined that we should be aware of them, that we should see, as he sees, the personal delinquency of his characters dissolve within the greater, more terrible delinquency of our synthetic society.

Catherine Meredith Brown (review date 1947)

SOURCE: "Chicago without Tears or Dreams," in *The Saturday Review,* Vol. 30, February 8, 1947, p. 14.

[*In the review of* The Neon Wilderness *below, Brown praises Algren's portrayal of the downtrodden and discusses the plots of various stories.*]

The challenge of the short story must be infinitely compelling to those writers willing to meet it. The demands of a limited scope make incident, character, and mood tight and tellingly heightened. Economy of things said, of those things left unsaid, can be memorable when practised well. Chekhov in three pages paints a portrait; Hemingway does an entire underworld story in not many words; O. Henry gives us middle-class goodness; and Saroyan makes man's loneliness a poignant dream. It is the author's undercurrent theme in any good collection of short stories that serves to unite the whole.

> **Mr. Algren is a definite apostle of amorality. Either through environment or inheritance, his people are completely devoid of any ability to recognize, let alone live by, conventional standards of so-called good citizenship.**
>
> **—Catherine Meredith Brown**

In [*The Neon Wilderness*] Mr. Algren cries out for the under-dog. It is, in a quote from "The City" by David Wolff, "the usurpation of man over man" with which he deals. It is the dregs, the underprivileged, the eternally downtrodden, who people his pages. Some of them scarcely dream; they only live in fear of arrest, starvation, or sudden death. Their city is Chicago. It is the great throbbing city of Whitman painted by Reginald Marsh. The men are tough-fibered, living by lies, their wits, or their fists. Their women love them and are loyal to whatever profession they serve. There is no justice, no hope for any, nor is there much joy. By the same token, there is no judgment on these poor lost souls. Walt Whitman's attitude, "I feel I am of them—I belong to those convicts and prostitutes myself and henceforth I will not deny them—for how can I deny myself?" represents Mr. Algren's approach.

Each of the twenty-four stories creates its own mood. Except for three of them, the plots are played in taverns, cheap hotels; and city streets. In "that's the way it's always been" the scene shifts to war's theatre and a bitter Willie-and-Joe indictment of a despicable brass hat. **"The Heroes"** is also a war story, the most humorous of the entire lot. Here is an American-born Indian who patterns himself on the Hollywood conception of the red man. His dialogue is perfect; he typecasts his comrades, his enemies, and his commanders. He feels Custer made a mistake in taking his last stand; he actually does not think he would have gone West "because who'd want to leave Olivia De Havilland to all those Washington wolves?" I think Corporal Hardheart, affectionately known as Chief Booze-heart, is one of the happier figures. Another is the Negro who finds his longing for home satisfied in Algiers. He goes there AWOL, content with his Algerienne, "and across the waters . . . he heard the great bell tolling, tolling from the lion-colored hills of home." He has found peace.

For the others there is drink, dope, and jail. Unforgettable and powerful is the fearful story of the legless man, his burlesque queen mistress, and his fight to the finish with Fancy, the bartender, in "the face on the bar-room floor." This is Mr. Algren's strongest moment. There is enough horror, ugliness, and ghoulishness in it to satify Sartre. In another vein we get evil fantasy and a logical motive for degradation in "how the devil came down division street." Then there is bitterness in "the children"; poetry and faith in "poor man's pennies"; terrible conquest in "depend on aunt elly"; and, in the first story, "the captain has bad dreams," a nightmare line-up of what is to follow.

Mr. Algren is a definite apostle of amorality. Either through environment or inheritance, his people are completely devoid of any ability to recognize, let alone live by, conventional standards of so-called good citizenship. Conditioned by struggle, their instincts are all for the end, without even a passing nod to the means.

The e.e. cummings trick of no capital letters seems a slight irritant to me. The sometimes special phrases of prize-fighting or of the gangster world make for effortful reading. However, after the initial shudder, the staccato precision of the writing must be read, remembered, and admired.

George Bluestone (essay date 1957)

SOURCE: "Nelson Algren," in *Western Review,* Vol. 22, No. 1, Autumn, 1957, pp. 27-44.

[*In the following excerpt taken from an essay in which Bluestone primarily discusses Algren's novels, the critic provides a mixed assessment of* The Neon Wilderness, *focusing on the story "Design for Departure."*]

It is true that the stories [in *The Neon Wilderness*], like meditative finger exercises, explore situations and characters that have already become familiar. The drug addicts, petty thieves, prison inmates, small-time fighters, corrupt police, dypsos, winos, hobos and prostitutes—all are here. The boy in **"The Brother's House"** who discovers that he cannot return home looks back to Cass McKay; the drugged prostitute in **"Is Your Name Joe?"** to Steffi R. The fight between Legless Railroad Shorty and the bartender Fancy in **"The Face on the Barroom Floor"** will appear in *A Walk on the Wild Side;* **"The Captain Has Bad Dreams"** in *The Man With the Golden Arm.* As in Balzac's world, or Faulkner's, a character, once created, can crop up anywhere. But the stories, like the novels, are bound not so much by a common cast of characters as by a general background of disorder. The characters have a curious kind of horizontal mobility, capable of changing their physical location without ever changing their status. What makes this change impossible is less the entrapment of poverty than the destructive forces unleashed by the failure of love. Almost always there follows the kind of shocked somnambulism which is equivalent to living death. Sometimes the destruction is due to a moral weakness in the

character (Baby Needles' rejection of Wilma in **"Depend on Aunt Elly"**), sometimes to caprice or bad luck (Mary's loss of Deaf Christiano in **"Design for Departure"**). But whatever the origin, love's destruction breeds a terrible kind of spiritual stasis, a curious kind of dreamlike, empty marking time for which terminal death is the only cure.

Interesting as exceptions, these pieces are not entirely convincing as stories. They lack the sustained narrative power of Algren's best prose, the felt starkness of his urban imagery.

—George Bluestone

In two of these stories, however, the dominant pattern is reversed. Instead of love's annihilation ensuring death, redemptive love saves the characters from utter defeat. In **"Stickman's Laughter,"** Banty Longobardi, after coming home to find his wife away, loses his entire paycheck in a night of drunken gambling. When he comes home shamed, he finds his wife ready to forgive him, ready to share responsibility for the loss. "My fault," she says, "I knew it was payday but I went out just the same." The love between them is still the crucial thing: "So nothing important had been lost after all." A similar situation is worked out in **"He Swung and He Missed."** In a sad, bitter-sweet kind of way, love salvages something for Young Rocco and Lili after their ironic defeat.

Interesting as exceptions, these pieces are not entirely convincing as stories. They lack the sustained narrative power of Algren's best prose, the felt starkness of his urban imagery. In their own way, they are as dissatisfying as the stories which, despite effective passages, exhibit no central development. Vignettes like **"The Children"** and **"Pero Venceremos"** are not so much organic narratives as elucidations of frozen situations. A merely static sketch remains impersonal.

On the other hand, the most successful stories are those which carry out Algren's obsessive pattern. In a world where social relations are based on parasitic oppression and brute survival, love is the only way in which human beings may meaningfully relate. Nothing else is finally reliable. That is why the ruin of love is inevitably disastrous. **"Depend on Aunt Elly," "So Help Me,"** and **"Design for Departure"** are satisfying stories not because they are longest (they are that), but because they work out the pattern which consistently elicits Algren's verbal passion. In **"Design for Departure,"** for example, the girl Mary spends her life searching for some human Christ to deliver her from lovelessness. Neglected by her father, and the harridan widow who lives with him, Mary leaves to make her way alone "in a twilit world between sleep and waking," first by working in a packinghouse, then by prostitution. Her first moment of human communion comes from Deaf Christiano, who first conquers her sexually and then makes her his mistress. Mary allows herself to be taken because, like Steffi, she cannot fight; she can only whimper and submit. But her submission turns to genuine love in response to Christy's unexpected kindness. The fact that Christy is an underworld character is not at all relevant for Mary. That he returns her love is all that really counts. Even Christy's act of feeding Mary drugs stems from a desire to keep her happy, to relieve her from the daily misery of their marginal lives. When Christy is taken away by the police, Mary cannot survive without him. During Christy's three year sentence, Mary becomes totally helpless and hopelessly degenerate. When Christy returns after his release, he finds her too far gone to save. Mary pleads for a dosage of narcotics strong enough to kill her, and Christy, after some hesitation, accedes to her wishes. In inverted Christian terms, Christy knows he is performing an act of mercy. Mary knows it too: "Then, like a bearer of peace, she heard Deaf Christiano's shuffling ascent up the Golgotha of the stairs." Without the single thread of love that has held her to this life, Mary is incapable of going on.

The denouement is terrible enough, but Algren's symbolism and imagery have carefully prepared it. In the birth-scar which Mary perpetually tries to hide ("that side of her face had a curiously dead aspect"); in her habit of sleeping in the foetal position; in the palpable doom of city imagery, Mary's fate becomes—except for her brief interlude with Christy—a kind of elaborate preparation for death. The best passages suggest this: "The night wind wandered past each night. The years closed in like a fog bank. Till the wind felt like someone crying, and the fog felt like a wall. While overhead, the city nights, above the endless maze of telephone wires, an ancestral moon looked calmly down, like the great moon of forever." It is an almost apocryphal vision of a timeless universe in which the only hope for a loveless life is the deliverance of death.

The fact remains, however, that most of the stories fall short of **"Design for Departure."** The total effect is a curious amalgam, reminiscent of the static, even paralytic, action that occurs between the novels' key events. The impression is uneven, like a fabric in which separate pieces of cloth have been loosely stitched together.

Maxwell Geismar (essay date 1958)

SOURCE: "Nelson Algren: The Iron Sanctuary," in *American Moderns: From Rebellion to Conformity,* Hill and Wang, 1958, pp. 187-94.

[In the following excerpt, Geismar comments on Algren's focus on character development in The Neon Wilderness.*]*

The stories in *The Neon Wilderness* (1948) are in a softer vein [than Algren's other books]. For the first time women appear here, not only as credible human beings, but as a source of comfort and aid, however briefly, in the fast run between the womb and the grave. There is the sketch,

reminiscent of Sherwood Anderson's Midwestern vein, of the workingman who gambles and drinks his week's pay away on Saturday night because his wife had not been home to meet him; but she comforts him with her flesh at the end. "So nothing important has been lost after all." There is the stupid miserable creature who calls herself "the girl that men forgot awright," but there is also Wilma who gave all her love to another of Algren's boxers, and kept him straight, until her past caught up with her. There is the gambler who believes in "lucky bucks, fast money, and good women"—this glittering vista of Algren's Chicago slum world at its highest peak. And there is the tale of Railroad Shorty—a "halfy" or legless man—who clubs a young bartender to death in a casual brawl.

Algren's powerful effects are usually in his big scenes rather than in the portrayal or development of character. He is almost at his best in this volume of short stories where he can suggest the whole contour of a human life in a few terse pages. There is more warmth and humor here, too, than in the earlier books. It is, all in all, an excellent collection of short stories, perhaps one of the best we had in the 1940's.

Algren on learning to write:

Nobody yet ever learned to write at a writers' conference. For these are social occasions; while writing, always and everywhere, is as secret and antisocial as safecracking. All you can possibly learn here is what other men's lights are.

You have to have your own lights to go by, and your own fences for leaping. And these you find only off by yourself. Off on your own where you learn to set your own pace, take your own chances, and your own sweet time as well.

For in the end it is only in the impartial practise of life itself that the writer finds the promise of perfection for his art. It is only among the things of the earth that he may mature the strength of his imagination. In the end it is only his life that counts.

Nelson Algren, in "Things of the Earth: A Groundhog view," in The California Quarterly, *Vol. 2, No. 1, Autumn, 1952.*

Haskel Frankel (review date 1963)

SOURCE: "They're Human Too," in *Washington Post Book Week,* Vol. 1, December 8, 1963, p. 20.

[In the following excerpt from a review of the anthology Nelson Algren's Own Book of Lonesome Monsters, *Frankel discusses Algren's introduction to the work and the one story he contributed, "The House of the Hundred Grassfires."]*

In his introduction to this anthology of 15 stories [*Nelson Algren's Own Book of Lonesome Monsters*], Nelson

Algren refers to the 1959 murder of a 3½-year-old Philadelphia girl. Her father wrote a letter to the citizenry which concluded with the statement: "Let no feeling of vengeance influence us. Let us rather help him who did so human a thing." Algren uses this murder and other references to evolve the point he wishes to make: "The stories that follow have the common hope that every man, no matter how lonesome nor what a monster, is deserving of understanding by us other lonesome monsters."

The plight of the lonesome monster has long engaged Mr. Algren's interest and sympathies. **"The House of the Hundred Grassfires,"** a section of *A Walk on the Wild Side* and the editor-author's only contribution to the anthology aside from his introduction, is a case in point. His story of one night in the business life of a brothel offers more lonesome monsters a page than the other 14 stories combined. There are the girls and the madam, of course, a priest who is both defrocked and deranged, a nasty 6-year-old and a masochistic naval lieutenant who seeks to recreate the pleasure of the whippings he received as a child from his mammy. That Mr. Algren can create sympathy even as he builds revulsion is a reminder of his impressive talents.

Algren on America:

It is not in the great cities of Europe nor in the lion-colored villages on the Sahara's edge, not in the terrible slums of Naples, nor in the half-sunk huts along the ruined walls of ancestral cities in Yucatan, that one sees the most dehumanized faces of our time. Not in the backwash of time and poverty or war, but in Los Angeles and Muncie and Chicago and New York, in the backwash of the American Century, that one discovers the most harried, intense, debauched, irresponsible faces in the world; full of an astonished good faith and an incredulous disappointment.

Nelson Algren, in "Things of the Earth: A Groundhog view," in The California Quarterly, *Vol. 2, No. 1, Autumn, 1952.*

R. W. Lid (essay date 1966)

SOURCE: "A Commentary on Algren's 'A Bottle of Milk for Mother,'" in *The Short Story: Classic and Contemporary,* J. B. Lippincott Company, 1966, pp. 504-12.

[*In the following essay, Lid discusses the primary conflicts in the short story "A Bottle of Milk for Mother" by examining Algren's use of detail, character, and symbolism.*]

In **"A Bottle of Milk for Mother,"** Bruno Lefty Bicek, the young pitcher of the Polish Warriors S.A.C., and an aspiring boxer, makes his descent, step by step, into hell. At the beginning of the story he stands, a shorn Samson (the Warriors have all had their heads shaved), in the query room of the Racine Street police station before his accus-

ers—Milano and Comiskey, the arresting officers; Sergeant Adamovitch, the fatherly turnkey; and Captain Kozak, "eleven years on the force and brother to an alderman." A prim-faced reporter in a raccoon coat from the *Dziennik Chicagoski* is also present. Lefty has been caught robbing a drunk of his pay in a precinct captain's hallway. The bullet he fired into the floor to scare the "boobatch" accidentally hit the old man in the groin, and he is dead; but at the beginning of the story Lefty doesn't know this. It is only revealed to him in the course of the interrogation, which takes the form of an impersonally cruel cancelling out of every one of the boy's hopes and dreams, his defenses.

Algren's story is built around several related conflicts which only gradually emerge in the course of the action. On the simplest level, perhaps, is the conflict between Lefty Bicek and Captain Kozak. In the course of the interrogation the Captain tries to make the boy confess his role in the robbery of the old man and also to implicate various members of the Polish Warriors S.A.C. We watch the Captain persist until he has enough to convict the boy, if not the others.

On a more complex level, and partly revealed by the lines from Whitman which Algren has chosen as an epigraph for his story, is the conflict between the author and his society. It is clear that the indictment returned by Nelson Algren in **"A Bottle of Milk for Mother"** is not against Lefty Bicek but against a society which, failing to realize and accept the full measure of its responsibility, has turned its back on the boy and others like him. This is relatively easy to see from even a casual reading of the story, but to gather the full implication of what Algren is saying, and the full force of his art, we have to pay attention to his use of detail, character, and symbolic devices—as well as to the larger pattern of his fable.

As the interrogation of Lefty proceeds, and as it becomes more and more difficult for the youth to smile, the symbolic configuration of Algren's world emerges. For all the story's seeming realism, Algren uses reality as Dante did, and in some ways his effects are as startling as Dante's. Like Dante, Algren possesses an infernal vision.

Algren's figures, one should point out, are largely Roman Catholics, and the author uses Christian imagery to articulate the pattern of guilt which he sees behind the corruption of society. Social commentary and Christian motif are so interwoven in Algren's fiction as to be almost inseparable. This can be seen in the basic pattern which underlies **"A Bottle of Milk for Mother,"** the symbolic reenactment of a portion of the Christ story, his denial and descent into hell. It is made explicit by the story's ending. His confession elicited and the questioning over, Lefty Bicek remains standing before the Captain's desk. The arresting officers have slipped out. The reporter, his notebook put away, is buttoning his coat. Captain Kozak is "studying the charge sheet as though Bruno Lefty Bicek were no longer in the room. Nor anywhere at all."

"I'm still here," the boy said wryly, his lip twisting into a dry and bitter grin.

Kozak looked up, his big, wind-beaten, impassive face looking suddenly to the boy like an autographed pitcher's mitt he had once owned. His glance went past the boy and no light of recognition came into his eyes. Lefty Bicek felt a panic rising in him: a desperate fear that they weren't going to press him about the rod, about the old man, about his feelings. "Don't look at me like I ain't nowheres," he asked. And his voice was struck flat by fear.

"'Your case is well disposed of,' Kozak said, and his eyes dropped to the charge sheet forever." Lefty Bicek's earthly life is over. He will be led out of the interrogation room, into the corridor, and through the open door to the winding steel staircase and the cells below. Algren's Christ-figure begins his spiral descent down into the tiers of hell.

Algren's hero is a figure of adolescent mind and limited emotional experience. His mind is a hodge podge of dreams, schemes, plans: a cluster of tawdry hopes and aspirations pulled from the rag bag of American culture. Even the possibility of escape is conceived by him in terms of a crude B-grade movie, with his friends appearing in front of the police station with a sub-machine gun in a cream-colored roadster, while he makes a melodramatic run for it, zigzagging through the building and down a fire escape three stories into the roadster below. "Like that George Raft did that time he was innocent at the Chopin. . . ." Throughout **"A Bottle of Milk for Mother"** Lefty's thoughts are cast in a similar vernacular, revealing the fantasy world in which he privately lives, particularly his yearnings for recognition as ball player and boxer. He is secretly gratified that Captain Kozak seems to know that he is the Warrior's first-string pitcher, and he wonders if the Captain saw him play the Sunday he finished his own game and then relieved Dropkick Kodadek in the sixth inning of the second game. "Why hadn't anyone called him 'Iron-Man Bicek' or 'Fireball Bruno' for that one?" If Lefty is reluctant to discuss his occasional boxing career, it is only because he is aware that Captain Kozak is trying to link his handler, Benkowski, with the hold-up. At various times in the course of the story he goes into a boxer's shuffle. Once he is on the verge of unbuttoning his shirt to show off his chest; Adamovitch puts one hand on his shoulder and slaps the boy's hand down. But Lefty's irrepressible ego cannot really be beaten down. At once boyish and inoffensive, it keeps breaking in upon the awareness of the officers and the Captain, who would much rather dismiss the boy out of mind than have to acknowledge his humanity. In a profoundly moving way Lefty is Algren's symbolic reminder of the sanctity of the individual; he represents Algren's affirmation of the inviolable human spirit.

Like Fitzgerald's Jay Gatsby, Algren's Bruno "Lefty" Bicek is an essential innocent (it is surely the deliberate author who makes George Raft an innocent figure in the gangster film at the Chopin Theater), and like Gatsby he is caught up in the national dream, though in **"A Bottle of Milk for Mother"** its form is somewhat cruder and its underlying realities are given more explicit statement than in *The Great Gatsby*. Lefty dreams of success by the traditional

routes open to the newly arrived and the poor and the ill-educated, the fight ring and the ball park. In Algren's version of the story there is no fetching symbol, no Daisy Buchanan, to embody the Dream; there is no green light at the end of the dock to beckon romantically in the dark, no cascade of expensive and "beautiful shirts" for a Daisy to sob over. The overriding symbol is Lefty's shriven head, ready to receive its crown of thorns, while the symbolic objects of Lefty's world are a worn and sleeveless blue work shirt too tight across the shoulders, a pair of square-toed boy's shoes laced with a buttonhook, a pair of trousers with ragged, turn-up cuffs, and a frayed greenish cap which once had bright checks and earlaps (the crown of thorns).

In the course of Algren's story Lefty Bicek seems only dimly aware of the difference between right and wrong; he seemingly has no sense of guilt. (At the end of the story Sergeant Adamovitch—the name is symbolic—locks the boy in his cell. He asks him in his most fatherly voice, "Feel all right, son?" In his mind he is thinking: "The kid don't *feel* guilty is the whole trouble. You got to make them *feel* guilty or they'll never go to church at all. A man who goes to church without feeling guilty for *something* is wasting his time, I say.") Lefty makes no overt comment, either to the men in the police station or in his mind, to indicate that he understands such distinctions. Like Gatsby, he seems lacking in rudimentary moral knowledge. But Lefty does have an essential if limited understanding of how society operates in his world. One catches a reflection of this in his account of what he told his victim in Polish when he strong-armed him in the precinct captain's hallway. "I told him polite-like, like a Polish-American citizen, this was Chiney-Eye-a-Friend-of-Mine's hallway. 'No more after this one,' I told him. 'This is your last time gettin' rolled, old man. After this I'm pertectin' you, I'm seein' to it nobody touches you. . . .'" The Captain exchanges glances with the reporter from the *Chicagoski,* who nervously turns to cleaning his glasses, which depend from a black ribbon (and which impress the naïve Lefty). Both Kozak and the reporter understand what lies behind the boy's imitation of his elders.

The reporter is an important figure in Algren's world, not in himself, but for what he represents. A bored observer of the scene, he is the representative of the outside world, of all clean-living, right-thinking Poles. In the query room his major concern is his own comfort, particularly the chair he is sitting in, which he finds "a pretty comfy old chair for a dirty old police station." But the chair is too close to the wall radiator, the reporter is uncomfortably warm. He simply doesn't have the energy to move the heavy chair. Just how close he is to seeing the brinks of hell, he never realizes, and the true meaning of the events which transpire in the police station passes him by. He fails to appreciate the innocent nature of the bluff behind Lefty's refusal to involve his buddies. "I was singlin'. Lone-wolf stuff," the boy tells the Captain. At which the reporter, thinking out his news story in advance, writes in his mind: "This correspondent has never seen a colder gray than that in the eyes of the wanton killer who arrogantly styles himself *the lone wolf of Potomac Street.*" The reporter's disavowal of Lefty, his dismissal of the boy as a human being, is all the more obvious for being implied rather than stated. It is this evasion of responsibility, the denial of the boy's humanity, that lies at the root of Algren's indictment of society.

Ultimately Lefty Bicek's defiance, his tough but faked exterior, his opposition to authority, is based on Algren's profound awareness of the complicity of society in the criminal act. It is also based on his radical vision of the nature of authority. Like Dante, who placed his simonists in the reaches of hell, he is aware of the corruption at the heart of authority. In the climactic scene in **"A Bottle of Milk for Mother"** this becomes increasingly clear. Lefty makes his final appeal.

> "Captain, I ain't been in serious trouble like this before . . ." he acknowledged, and paused dramatically. He'd let them have it straight from the shoulder now: "So I'm mighty glad to be so close to the alderman. Even if he is indicted."
>
> There. Now they knew. He'd told them.
>
> "You talkin' about my brother, Bicek?"
>
> The boy nodded solemnly. Now they knew who they had hold of at last.

Lefty's appeal, of course, is greeted with derision. Significantly it is Sergeant Adamovitch who leads in the mockery of the boy. (He has already denied him in his mind: "He didn't like this kid. This was a low-class Polak. He himself was a high-class Polak because his name was Adamovitch and not Adamowski.") Adamovitch guffaws.

> The boy jerked toward the officer: Adamovitch was laughing openly at him. Then they were all laughing openly at him. He heard their derision, and a red rain danced one moment before his eyes; when the red rain was past, Kozak was sitting back easily, regarding him with the expression of a man who has just been swung at and missed and plans to use the provocation without undue haste.

Lefty then loses his composure, turns to the reporter ("Hey, Stingy-whiskers!") and yells: "Write down I plugged the old rumpot, write down Bicek carries a rod night 'n day 'n don't care where he points it. You, I go around slappin' the crap out of whoever I feel like—." He fails to provoke them, they all remain unmoved. The Captain resumes his questioning, but Lefty's mind has set against them all.

"A Bottle of Milk for Mother" ends with Lefty Bicek in his cell on his knees, his head a pious oval in the cell's gray light. Adamovitch thinks the boy is praying and he takes off his hat. Lefty responds: "This place'll rot down 'n mold over before Lefty Bicek starts prayin', boobatch. Prays, squeals, 'r bawls. So run along 'n I'll see you in hell with your back broke. I'm lookin' for my cap I dropped is all." Adamovitch watches Lefty grope for his cap, then leaves.

He did not stay to see the boy, still on his knees, put his hand across his mouth and stare at the shadowed wall.

Shadows were there within shadows.

"I knew I'd never get to be twenty-one anyhow," Lefty told himself softly at last.

In achieving something like tragic eloquence for his now muted hero, Algren suggests a knowledge of good and evil, of guilt and punishment, which transcends the complacent proscriptions of society.

It could be said that Algren writes in what he has called "the antilegalistic tradition toward society which . . . distinguished Chicago writers since the early years of the century." Both *The American Tragedy* and *Native Son,* Algren points out in *Who Lost an American?,* were written in that tradition.

> Dreiser's method of challenging the legal apparatus and Wright's method were different, but the purpose of both was to demand that those economically empowered disprove their complicity in the crimes for which Clyde Griffiths and Bigger Thomas stood accused. Both writers made literature by demanding that the prosecuting attorney show his hands.

Yet neither this tradition, nor the broader one of American naturalism, in which his writing is usually placed, explains Algren's originality or the powerful effects he achieves with the sparsest of materials. The major source of his power lies elsewhere, as I have already suggested: in Algren's infernal vision and its radical use of the resources of Christian tradition. The epigraph to **"A Bottle of Milk for Mother"** is the lines from Whitman that run

> I feel I am of them—
> I belong to those convicts and prostitutes myself—
> And henceforth I will not deny them—
> For how can I deny myself?

If the idiom is highly personal (as is Algren's), the thoughts are nevertheless those of basic Christianity. They echo the New Testament and the words of Barabbas's and Mary Magdalene's Christ—just as Algren's stories and novels embody Christian themes and rework in various patterns fragments of the Christ story. In the closing scene of **"A Bottle of Milk for Mother,"** Algren's universal manchild, his suffering god, overtly suggests Christ in Gethsemane. I am not maintaining for a minute that Algren writes systematic allegory, but I am suggesting that the symmetry of pattern in Algren's fiction has its roots in a deeper cultural source than the traditional underdog bias of social realism.

Finally, there is the form of **"A Bottle of Milk for Mother"**: a spiralling form, an intense tiering downward. This Dantesque spiralling is symbolically mirrored at the end of the story in Lefty Bicek's descent down the winding steel staircase to the cells below; but throughout the story something like this spiral has operated in the narrative, providing pattern and depth to the seemingly random interrogation in the police station query room. The questioning circles and circles around the circumstances of the shooting of the old man, driving the boy inward and downward, alienating him from those in the room, placing him solely on his own limited resources.

We watch Lefty as he first reacts to the prodding of Captain Kozak, who, his lips barely moving, remarks that Lefty will be held on open charge until he talks. "The boy licked his own lips, feeling a dryness coming into his throat and a tightening in his stomach." He begins to talk about seeing the old man cash his paycheck, stops as if he has finished his story, then resumes hurriedly as Kozak glances over the boy's shoulder at the arresting officer. Soon he realizes that his tongue is going faster than his brain, and he pauses. The Captain begins to question him about his friends, Benkowski and Nowogrodski and Idzikowski, with the obvious intention of making Lefty admit that one or more of them was in with him on the stickup. We become conscious of a small clock or a wrist watch somewhere in the room ticking away distinctly. Kozak tells the boy "to get ahead with your lyin' a little faster." Lefty then describes the scene in the hallway. The Captain asks him about the gun and Lefty feels "a single drop of sweat slide down his side from under his armpit. Stop and glide again down to the belt." A minute later and he is told that the old man is dead. Then the Captain returns relentlessly to the question of who was with him. Lefty replies that he was alone. But his voice has taken on "the first faint touch of fear." The questioning goes on, the Captain again probing for a way to make the boy admit that others were with him: Lefty feints and dodges, deflecting the questions as best he can, pretending he barely knows Benkowski, bluffing that he's not afraid of prison, yawning in their faces: each time more desperate, more naked, more empty inside—until the men in the query room are no longer interested in him. They have what they need to convict him, if not the others.

The questioning has swiftly carried the boy toward the pit from which there is no hope of deliverance. Lefty will never see his twenty-first birthday.

Daniel R. Silkowski (essay date 1971)

SOURCE: "Alienation and Isolation in Nelson Algren's 'A Bottle of Milk for Mother'," in *English Journal*, Vol. 60, No. 6, September, 1971, pp. 724-27.

[*In the following essay, Silkowski discusses themes of identity and isolation in "A Bottle of Milk for Mother," focusing on how to make the story meaningful to students.*]

Sue came to school each day in a canary yellow Mustang; Leslie wore clothes right out of the pages of a fashion magazine; Gary wanted to be sure I had filled out his recommendation for Yale.

Our next short story was to be Nelson Algren's **"A Bottle of Milk for Mother."** I had spent part of my childhood

in the areas described by Lefty Bicek. I was moved by my recollections of those neighborhoods. My problem, however, was not only how to convey the appreciation of realistic detail, but also how to make the theme of the story relevant to my class of fairly well-to-do suburban students.

I relied on the fact that, having lived in the area, I could personally attest to the accuracy of some of Algren's comments and descriptions. Happily, as we worked through the story, my class and I discovered that the themes of identity and isolation were, like all good themes, universally applicable, and not at all peculiar to the setting in which Algren presented them.

> Two months after the Polish Warriors S.A.C. had had their heads shaved, Bruno Lefty Bicek got into his first difficulty with the Racine Street police. The arresting officers and a reporter from the *Dziennik Chicagoski* were grouped about the captain's desk when the boy was urged forward into the room by Sergeant Adamovitch. . . .

Thus, in his first "difficulty," Lefty finds himself under the scrutiny of the watchdog of public morality (the reporter) and the guardian of public morality (the police). The first conversation between Lefty and Captain Kozak reveals that certain attitudes and conflicts are already existent.

> "Let the jackroller tell us how he done it hisself."
>
> "I ain't no jackroller."
>
> ". . . you one of them Chicago Av'noo moll-buzzers?"
>
> "I ain't that neither."
>
> "C'mon, c'mon, I seen you in here before—what were you up to, followin' that poor old man?"
>
> "I ain't been in here before."

The captain's opening remarks reveal that he already has a predisposition about Lefty; his impartiality is as faulty as his grammar. The captain knows Lefty; he speaks to him at his own level, in his own terms. But Lefty will not accept the categories which the captain tries to impose upon him; Lefty is neither a "jackroller" nor a "moll-buzzer."

Kozak's next words, "What were you doin' on Chicago Av'noo in the first place when you live up around Division? Ain't your own ward big enough you have to come down here to get in trouble," try to place Lefty geographically, and carry with them the implication that Lefty does not belong here in the Racine Street district. He is thus an intruder, an outsider.

Lefty's defense, "I was just walkin' down Chicago like I said to get a bottle of milk for Mother, when the officers jumped me," has two objectives: first, he offers a plausible excuse for being out of his territory, and second, it puts him in the class of "good boys who do errands for their mothers."

Again Kozak removes Lefty from the class of "good boys" by displaying the spring-blade knife, Lefty's own "double-edged double-jointed spring-blade cuts-all genuine Filipino twisty-handled all-American gut-ripper." Breaking the five-inch blade, Kozak says, "C'mon, Lefty, tell us about it. 'N it better be good."

> The boy began slowly, secretly gratified that Kozak appeared to know he was the Warriors' first-string left-hander: maybe he'd been out at that game against the Knothole Wonders the Sunday he'd finished his own game and then had relieved Dropkick Kodadek in the sixth in the second. Why hadn't anyone called him "Iron-Man Bicek" or "Fire-ball Bruno" for that one?

"Iron-Man Bicek," "Fire-ball Bruno": those were names a talent scout or college coach could conjure with. Why hadn't *Dziennik Chicagoski* sent a reporter out to cover that one?

Kozak's admonitions about Lefty's rights, "Everythin' you say can be used against you," and "Don't talk unless you want to," are warnings given to any member of our society, but his threat to hold Lefty on an open charge until he does talk at once removes Lefty from the common citizenry. Perhaps aware of the implications of that threat, Lefty begins his explanation, describing how he followed the man "just to break the old monotony. Just a notion, you might say. . . ."

Then comes the first of many comments by Lefty, all indicative of his awareness of alienation. "I'm just a neighborhood kid, Captain." Here is Lefty's attempt to place himself back into a sphere where he will be recognized.

When Kozak says nothing, Lefty continues his narrative, going to another tack. "Has the alderman been in to straighten this out, Captain?" Of course, he wants to imply that anyone who is "just a neighborhood kid" is known in his own community, has friends who will come to his aid.

Commenting on the old man he followed, Lefty points out, with some scorn, that "he was a old guy, a dino you. He couldn't speak a word of English." If anyone were the outsider, the foreigner, it was the old man. Again Lefty seeks to establish his own identity at the expense of the old man: "I don't like to see no full grown man drinkin' that way. A Polak hillbilly he was, 'n certain'y no citizen."

Even when describing how difficult it was for him to get the money from the old man, Lefty inserts the comment, "I'm just a neighborhood fella." Whatever advantage Lefty had hoped to gain from these references to neighborhood and friends is negated by the admission that he did fire the pistol.

> "I didn't really fire, though. Just at his feet. T' scare him so's he wouldn't jump me. I fired in self-defense. I just wanted to get out of there. . . . You do crazy things sometimes, fellas—well, that's all I was doin'."

Perhaps realizing that his crime, as all crimes, has already separated him from the community at large, Lefty "added aloud, before he could stop himself: "'N beside I had to show him—"

"Show him what, Left-hander?"

"That I wasn't just another greenhorn sprout like he thought."

And further: "Lot of people think I'm just a green kid. I showed 'em. I guess I showed 'em now all right."

Yet he immediately tries to reestablish his image.

> "I'm just a neighborhood kid. I belonged to the Keep-Our-City-Clean Club at St. John Cant'us. I told him polite-like, like a Polish-American citizen, this was Chiney-Eye-a-Friend-of-Mine's hallway."

To no avail. Kozak informs Lefty that the old man was killed. And just as Lefty had changed the conversation before, Kozak now inquires about some of Lefty's friends, bringing up the topic of boxers at the local arena, the City Gardens. As with the baseball game, Lefty warms enthusiastically to the topic, happy that Kozak seems to recognize something distinctive about Lefty. But Kozak is merely doing his job, gathering all the information he can about the robbery, even about Lefty's shaved head.

Once again Lefty tries to turn this fact to his favor, relating how the first haircut led to others, eventually to the formation of the Baldhead S.A.C. "They thought it was a club you." As with any club, unity, solidarity, and identity are established. "So that's why we changed our name then, that's why we're not the Warriors any more, we're the Baldhead True American Social 'n Athletic Club."

Even though Sergeant Adamovitch thinks of Lefty as a "low class Polak," Lefty is persistent in his attempt to establish his identity and be a typical useful member of society.

> "That's why I want to get out of this jam. So's it don't ruin my career in the rope arena. I'm goin' straight. This has sure been one good lesson fer me. Now I'll go to a big-ten collitch 'n make good you."

But Kozak once more removes Lefty from that society. "What do you think we ought to do with a man like you, Bicek?" Lefty catches the shift in meaning: not a "neighborhood boy" who might be in some minor trouble for doing something "crazy," but a "man" who has committed murder and thereby alienated himself from society. He tries not to let the threat of a long term at the local reformatory upset him. He says:

> "I wouldn't wait that long. Hungry Piontek-from-by-the-Warehouse you, he lammed twice from that St. Charles farm. 'N Hungry don't have all his marbles even. He ain't even a citizen."

And once again Lefty's reference to his friendship with the alderman is an attempt to be identified with the community.

Of course, all these attempts are useless.

"I don't want to tell you anything." His mind was setting hard now, against them all. Against them all in here and all like them outside. And the harder it set, the more things seemed to be all right with Kozak. . . .

Lefty tries once more to fit in.

"I ain't mad, Captain. I don't blame you men either. It's your job, it's your bread 'n butter to talk tough to us neighborhood fellas. . . ." But Kozak was studying the charge sheet as though Bruno Lefty Bicek were no longer in the room. Nor anywhere at all.

"I'm still here," the boy said wryly. . . .

[Kozak's] glance went past the boy and no light of recognition came into his eyes.

"Don't look at me like I ain't nowheres. I was born in this country. I'm educated here—."

But no one was listening to Bruno Lefty Bicek any more.

The last scene, Lefty in his cell, shows how far the alienation, rejection, and isolation have gone. In the gloom, Sergeant Adamovitch sees Lefty pause and go down on his knees.

"This place'll rot down 'n mold over before Lefty Bicek starts prayin', boobatch. Prays, squeals, 'r bawls. So run along 'n I'll see you in hell with yer back broke. I'm lookin' for my cap I dropped is all."

This is Lefty's last significant act. Alienated from his society, he tries to salvage at least some shred of his identity by an act of defiance, an utterance against the society that has so effectively shut him out. Even this act is a failure.

[Adamovitch] did not stay to see the boy, still on his knees, put his hands across his mouth and stare at the shadowed wall.

Shadows were there within shadows.

"I knew I'd never get to be twenty-one anyhow," Lefty told himself softly at last.

James R. Frakes (review date 1973)

SOURCE: "Something of Algren for Everyone," in *The New York Times Book Review*, November 11, 1973, p. 20.

[*In the following review of* The Last Carousel, *Frakes comments on Algren's use of humor in the stories.*]

It's about time! When we've got a living American writer as sure-footed and as fast off the mark as Nelson Algren, it's almost criminal not to have something of his in hard covers at least once a year, to heft and roar at and revel in. Having, early in his career, ceded the Chicago territory to Sandburg, Farrell and Algren, Ernest Hemingway later paid our man the ultimate tribute: "Mr. Algren can hit with both hands and move around and he will kill you if you are not awfully careful." Was he, like Seymour Glass, *never wrong?*

Mr. Algren hates waste, finds nothing dispensable. When he latches on to a snappy line or anecdote, he really milks it, even throws it into his nonfiction to hype the action or distract attention from his greased deal.

—*James R. Frakes*

What we have here in this big fat volume [*The Last Carousel*] is a cockeyed chrestomathy of 37 Algren pieces from 1947 to 1972, reprinted from such journals as *The Chicago Sunday Tribune* and *Chicago Sun-Times, Rolling Stone, The Dude, Commentary, The Atlantic* and *Playboy.* Short fiction, travel sketches, reminiscences, character assassinations, pop history material deleted from *A Walk on the Wild Side,* odes to Chicago springs. Even occasional lapses into poetry. (Oh hell! Henry James wrote some rotten plays; Lardner ended his career censoring song lyrics; Brando played Napoleon; Billie Holiday liked banked strings behind her singing; and Louis Armstrong recorded with Andy Iona and His Islanders.)

Mr. Algren hates waste, finds nothing dispensable. When he latches on to a snappy line or anecdote, he really milks it, even throws it into his nonfiction to hype the action or distract attention from his greased deal. "I've always thought," he confesses, "I could make it as a standup comic." I guess he figures that the guys he breaks up in the Carefree Corner Bar aren't likely to catch his act the next month at Caesar's Palace. But I suspect he just doesn't give a damn, or else he'd have edited out the repeats and overlappings in this catch-all volume. It's a mistake and a dilution to read this collection from beginning to end, because then you can see the invisible wires, watch the lips move, spot the palmed ace. Skipping pays off here. I don't think you have to be, *pace* Papa, "awfully careful," just picky enough to be sure you're witnessing Algren at the top of his form, with his hallmark stamped on every link.

My own tip-sheet would read like this: Start with **"Dark Came Early in That Country,"** as authentic a boxing story as I've ever read—the voice, sounds, smells, textures, everything. Then to **"Bullring of the Summer Night,"** where jockey Hollis Floweree gets caught with an electrified whip and dwindles (in **"Moon of the Arfy Darfy"**) into a grandstand "stooper"—stooping for winning tickets people throw away by mistake. A couple of saloon stories next—**"A Ticket on Skoronski,"** where perfect dialogue lifts a cardiac death to raw, wrenching comedy; and **"Come in if You Love Money,"** a consummate juggling act in which the action is split and bounced back and forth between a draw-poker game in the foreground and the 1964 Derby on the tube in the background.

Follow with the definitive account of the 1919 White Sox caper (**"Ballet for Opening Day"**), the demythologized version of Chicago journalism (**"Different Clowns for Different Towns"**), and maybe **"Previous Days,"** a handful of memories that Algren somehow never got around to developing—about Blanche Sweet under the tapioca, a Catholic stereopticon ("I saw Christ make Calvary four times"), how to spot feelers and jumpers, a stomach stab-wound sealed with Mystic Tape (it didn't hold), a Willow Springs whorehouse run by an ex-Rams football player who roused the women with a referee's whistle for morning workout ("He made us practice everything but passing").

As you make the turn for home, even off with **"The Mad Laundress of Dingdong-Daddy-land,"** wherein you'll view the archetypal Algren characters in action: "a pair of sexless wrecks—two long-ruined hero-in-heads—were drying contraceptives on a shoerack above a gas stove." And fly under the wire with **"Watch Out for Daddy,"** a gruesomely hilarious saga of a hooker-addict and her pimp. ("Poor useless boy—I'd rather have his hate than some fat square-fig's love. Love or hate, whatever, it don't matter so long as it's real.")

The also-ran material consists of a dozen or so toss-offs, which you can ignore. It's your money. I purely howled at the one about Nijinsky, Diaghilev and a nine-pound mackerel, though I squirmed a little at the plodding narrative of **"The Cortez Gang"** and the environmental justification of Bonnie and Clyde as outlaw-heroes navel-deep in American tradition. To offset the moony lovesongs to San Francisco and Tokyo, we're treated to lip-smacking hatchet-jobs on Otto Preminger, Alfred Kazin, Writers Workshops, Norman Podhoretz, Jacques Barzun, and academics in general. Though he doesn't seem to care a lot for Kim Novak, Allen Ginsberg or Tony Martin, he does like Carol Channing. The bloodiest St. Valentine's Day Massacre is performed on Simone de Beauvoir ("her sense of personal responsibility for the world had overwhelmed her responses to it") during a Tunisian travelogue.

On his trip to the Orient, Algren managed to record a junior-welterweight title match in Tokyo and a cricket fight in Saigon, as well as to observe how happy women are when they submit gracefully to male dominance. And after nine months in the mysterious East, he emerges with a single aphorism: "Never eat in a place with sliding doors unless you're crazy about raw fish." These nuggets are tossed off like Necco wafers: "Never date a girl vocalist whose favorite song is 'Somewhere Over the Rainbow'—there'll always be a dude in the lobby wearing long sideburns and green eyeshades waiting to take over her check"; "Any time you get into a town where the cops don't have uniforms, you can be sure the chow is going to be lousy."

Okay, but what about all the familiar complaints about Algren's work—his pretending to be a tough-minded naturalist when he's really a closet transcendentalist, his sentimentalizing of the world's losers as if only the fringe-people retained freedom and purity, his shameless exploitation of the dispossessed for easy laughs from the coupon-clippers? Well, all of these charges can be documented from *The Last Carousel.* Admitted. Lots of chocolate-covered cherries ooze through these pages: "a thousand heartbroken dawns," "dimly fell the shadows, one by one, of bars," "memory ties rainbows of forgetfulness about old lost years," "the fly-a-kite spring," "the broken-handled cups of hopes that had never come true."

The eschatological imagery wears thin: merry-go-rounds going around for the last time, the golden arm failing at last, the ferris-wheel sinking forever downward into dust, toteboard lights going blind with dusk. And you'll recognize the cast of old sad scufflers, dread-the-dawn dingbats, hustlers, nabs, fireships, boothbroads, bings and finks. "You *like* underdogs?" Preminger wanted to know. To him Algren: "I like some people who are under, but not *because they're under.* Under is just where they happen to be."

No plea-copping, but the truth is that these drifters are out for everyone's blood; if they're "lovable," it's for reasons Runyon never dreamt of. Algren once pointed out that the great thing about Hemingway's books is their sympathy for those unworthy of it, and that may be the word on Algren himself. Like Howard Hawks, he has deep respect for professionalism, even if the American know-how is applied only to con-jobs, to techniques for moving the minches and flapping the jays. Because he moved fastest and most evasively around the periphery of the White Sox scandal, Abe Attell "survives best of all."

Anyone daring to review Nelson Algren today stands in grave danger of being a "past-poster"—a party who puts down a heavy bet on a horse that has already won.

Saul Maloff (review date 1974)

SOURCE: "Maverick in American Letters," in *The New Republic,* Vol. 170, January 19, 1974, pp. 23-4.

[*In the following review of* The Last Carousel, *Maloff faults Algren's overblown prose, his self-indulgence, and the repetitive nature of the stories in the volume.*]

No writer has been more relentlessly faithful to his scene and cast of characters than Nelson Algren. His scene is the "wild side," the "neon wilderness," the seamier sprawls of Chicago and its spiritual extensions across this broad land—America as Chicago. And his characters are the drifters and grifters, clowns and carnies, pimps and pushers, hustlers and hookers, gamblers and touts, junkies and lushes, marks and victims, conmen and shills, freaks and grotesques—the born losers who constitute a half-world, an anti-society to the society that never appears, not even as a sensed or felt presence, in Algren's work. Over the four decades of his life as a writer, scene and characters have never changed. Atmosphere, obsessions, talk, ways of putting in the time—all are fixed, held in suspension, dreamed and long after hazily recalled, caught not as they once were but as they are remembered, just as they are about to dissolve and become ballads. The mythical time, whatever the calendar reads, is always the '30s, somewhere around the longest year of 1935.

**Algren, in his best moments, is
incomparably if lachrymosely good.**

—Saul Maloff

Except when it's time for settling old scores. Since *The Last Carousel* is for the most part an ingathering of magazine pieces, many of them from the pages of *Playboy,* anything goes. So Algren allows himself yet another unpleasant portrait of Simone de Beauvoir and some small diversions in the form of vendettas—against Alfred Kazin in particular and critics in general; the University of Iowa Writers' Workshop in particular and, in general, workshops and other forms of corrupting the young and suspectible. As these and some other self-indulgent pieces do evident violence to the prevailing unity of tone and subject, the internal pressure to include them must have been tremendous. They succeed largely in getting off some cheap shots, though some of the objects so richly deserve savaging, one can't wholly begrudge the author these incidental pleasures, any more than one can deny him the pleasures of some fine childhood reminiscence, or of recording racetrack, baseball and boxing lore, in which Algren, in his best moments, is incomparably if lachrymosely good.

But the book takes its echoing tone from Algren's chronic weakness for "fine" writing, the kind of overblown elegaic lyricism—tremulous, quivering, cadenced, or wistful, celebratory, nostalgic, poignant—that used to be called prose-poetry. It was widely practiced by sensitive young writers in conscious quest of an American demotic voice some suitable song for the open road—the endless, receding plains, prairies, rivers of the imagined West. Of that chorus, Algren's voice was the most prominent and is the longest lasting, the others have long since faded. Decidedly a literary manner, it came on aggressively anti-literary: tough-tender and bittersweet, sentimental and swaggering, robust, keen-eyed, sprung from the soil, epic, open to the full spectrum of American experience, defiantly outside the mainstream of literary modernism and contemptuous of it, a strong dose of salts for the university wits and nancies—in short a species of literary populism and native romanticism, a nervously American preoccupation of the '30s.

The trouble with "style," with any strongly marked literary manner, is that it can become its own object of con-

templation. Algren has always been a gifted yarn-spinner, a teller of tall tales and manner as to be finally strangled by them. Helplessly our sorely strained attention shifts from story and character. Typically the story outgrows its limits, expands, without warrant, toward legend. Characters degenerate into "colorful characters"; and our attention, having been thus wrenched from its ostensible objects, centers on the evocative voice of the poet singing of summer with full-throated ease. Not a page is free of it.

Even in self-mockery it is enamored of itself. Take a random example. In **"Come In If You Love Money,"** a piece set in Butte—which is, and always has been, more legend than city—and populated with appropriately colorful characters (bawdy, colorful madame and her girls, beery pokerplayers and such central-casting types) we get

> a place where winds blow all day beneath the earth; where narrow rails cut through volcanic rock, bearing drivers, begoggled and gaunt, whose only light is borne by a battery attached to a helmet of steel. Five thousand feet beneath the Butte Country Club, blood-colored streams stagnate between automatic ramps. A spatter of copper sulphate, in the ominous overhand, winks in the gloom like a handful of mischievous stars.

A colorful background and underground for colorful characters; and soon after a full bursting into rollicking ballad:

> As I walked out on the night-streets of Montana, as I walked out in old Butte one foul night, I saw more dread-the-dawn dingbats looking for a doorway . . . more quivering, quaking, transfixed and trembling, catatonic, stoned and zonkified drunks looking for a park bench than I'd ever seen on Chicago's North Clark Street. I saw more pensionless and emphysemized voyeurs kibitzing the lightless corners than I'd ever seen on West Division Street.

In passages of recitative, strewn among the arias, the throttled narrative somehow advances, haltingly. The game of poker is played out; the chips are gathered in. But if song not story is the point of all this, how else to end it save with a cadenza:

> Deadpan Jack murdered me and Deadpan Jack will murder you. / And Butte, Montana, is a town where everyone finds his own Deadpan Jack. / Since the times when the gold came easy. And flesh was still not dear. When fists were the thing that mattered most. / Yet money mattered more.

The collection includes actual quasiballadic verse: "Epitaph: *The Man with the Golden Arm,*" "Ode to an Absconding Bookie," "Tricks Out of Times Long Gone"; but always the prose aspires to that state, so that, disconcertingly, the movement from time to time comes to a full stop to allow space for the insertion of verses before movement toward status can be resumed. Or, as in **"Moon of the Arfy Darfy,"** a racetrack piece (a literary subject solely owned by Algren), the prose ends, or runs out, and is transmuted or consummated in a verse or doggeral equivalent:

> When toteboard lights go blind with dusk / And other losers have gone home / Above the grandstand's damps and glooms / A moon of the backstretch on the wane / Sees a rider whose silks are long outworn.

Riding into the neon sunset, dissolving into the gloaming of legend.

Algren is a maverick of American letters: a solitary, impervious writer in possession of a true though narrow talent whose feeling runs richest only when it is touched by

> all those whose lives were lived by someone else / Come once again with palms outstretched to claim / What never rightly was their own;

by the

> tarts out of times long gone, [by] Boothbroad, bluemoon cruiser, coneroo / Drifters of no trade whose voices, unremembered / Complain continually among the cables overhead. . . .

Now tarts, with all due respect, may have hearts of gold, and no doubt they—together with drifters of *no* trade— have stories to tell; but their stories are few in number, drab in texture, small in scope—and, in the nature of things, somewhat similar in tone and substance. Algren, our only poet of the lumpen proletariat, is the rambling minstrel of times that never were and are now long gone. He alone has remembered their voices and restored their lives. In order to make them memorable, the stuff of lore, figures in the American landscape, he provides the amplification, with reedy winds, often one lonesome oboe, off-key, and augmented strings, some of them snapped.

Commonweal (review date 1947)

SOURCE: A review of *The Last Carousel*, in *Commonweal*, Vol. XCIX, No. 18, February 8, 1974, pp. 467-69.

[*In the following excerpt, the critic praises the short stories in* The Last Carousel *and discusses the similarities between Algren's fiction and nonfiction.*]

Nelson Algren hasn't written any novels for going on 20 years now—which is sad in a way. But it's not like he's been exactly idle in the years between: *The Last Carousel* is the third collection of short pieces he has published since his last novel. Unlike the other two (*Who Lost an American?* and *Notes from a Sea Diary*), this one contains a lot of short fiction. There is a sad-funny section on whore-house life that had been cut from *A Walk on the Wild Side*, titled **"The House of the Hundred Grass-fires."** And there are a good-sized handful of short stories that have appeared over the years in *Playboy* and some other places. What can I say? They are very good. I could

insert some specifics at this point, and maybe I should. The title story, **"The Last Carousel,"** for instance, perfectly captures the seedy atmosphere of the carnival. **"Watch Out for Daddy"** and **"The Mad Laundress of Ding Dong Daddyland"** treat addictions of different sorts. And **"Dark Came Early in That Country,"** the first story in the book and my favorite of the lot, is as good as anything I've read on the crummy world of boxing since *Fat City*. There are more, and I wonder why he didn't make a separate book of them. One that could carry the label, "Short Fiction by Nelson Algren," would have far greater impact, I should think, than this big bag of mixed pieces.

One reason he may have decided to put them all together is that Algren's journalism is a little hard to tell from his fiction. They look a lot alike. Algren puts himself right in the middle of his non-fiction, too, sets scenes beautifully, and tells it all with dialogue and colorful details interwoven through the narrative. In other words, to give it a recently-stylish label, it's New Journalism—and Nelson Algren was writing it this way whem Tom Wolfe was still at Yale working on his PhD in American Studies. This being the case and with journalism being exalted today in some quarters high above fiction as a mode of serious expression, I can't for the life of me figure out why he hasn't retained greater eminence. The feeling persists that if he lived someplace else he would be one of the Great Men of American Letters, holder of fellowships, dispenser of wisdom.

For that vast indifference felt in Chicago for the rest of the country, is very widely reciprocated. In good circles, Chicago has the reputation of being a smelly place populated by rude people. This it largely deserves. But it is more than only that, and if you want to find out how much more, you might start out by reading Mike Royko and Nelson Algren.

R. W. Lid (essay date 1975)

SOURCE: "A World Imagined: The Art of Nelson Algren," in *American Literary Naturalism: A Reassessment,* Carl Winter Universitätsverlag, 1975, pp. 176-96.

[*In the following excerpt, Lid provides an overview of Algren's career and critical reaction to his works. He also discusses the short story "A Bottle of Milk for Mother."*]

> It is but nature to be shy of a mortal who declares that a thief in jail is as honorable a personage as Gen. George Washington.
>
> —Melville to Hawthorne

It is not so long ago, as literary history goes, that it was convenient to speak of Nelson Algren as a literary naturalist. It gave us direction in reading his works, and provided rubrics by which to measure his achievements. In addition, Algren himself felt a kinship with such writers as Dreiser and Wright, and such personal identification made easy a view of his writings as belonging in the naturalistic tradition. No one questioned much what it meant precisely to see Algren in this light, or pondered the ways in which his writings were unique and different from those of others in the same tradition, because to speak of him as a naturalist was to speak honorifically.

There the matter pretty much rested. Algren was known as the author of *Somebody in Boots* (1935) and *Never Come Morning* (1942); also **The Neon Wilderness** (1947), a collection of short stories, and *The Man with the Golden Arm* (1949), which won him the National Book Award and brought him national prominence. In general he was thought of as an author who revealed great heart in his portrayal of the underdog in American society. More aptly, he wrote compassionately, honestly, and skillfully about a world of poverty and oppression, of social ills and injustices within American society that needed correction.

Not surprisingly, in the early 50's Algren was much in the public eye. He made good newspaper copy. There aren't many winners in American literature—and Algren looked for the moment a winner, perhaps even destined to join Faulkner and Hemingway in literary legend. Like them his personality appeared to be as much an extension of his work as his work was a replication of his character and temperament. He bore the same indelible mark of originality as they did.

To most who read about him he appeared to be a somewhat lonely and romantic figure. His personal turf was the near north side of Chicago, which included the Polish American neighborhood surrounding the triangle where Milwaukee Avenue and Ashland and Division Streets come together, and the Clark Street of honky-tonks and cheap bars. In this locale he deliberately chose to live, openly identifying with those he wrote about—the poor, the downtrodden, the losers in American society. He was insider to the mysteries of tenement life, of jails, prisons, whorehouses. He was the all-night poker player, the high roller, the nameless man on the bar stool nursing a beer. Alternately he appeared as tough guy and sentimentalist in remarks reporters picked up and quoted. Sometimes he was irrepressibly the clown, as if for the moment he had become a character from one of his own novels. But at all times he was the omnipresent participant-observer, a role the public gradually became conscious of and which was reinforced by his long essay of 1951, *Chicago: City on the Make*. It is only in retrospect that the public figure of Algren of these years appears to have been the alter ego of a man in serious trouble.

Algren's 1951 Whitmanesque essay on Chicago marked a turning point in his career. From this point on he was seemingly to be more and more on the outs with American society. Critics were to become chary of praising him, readers were to become skeptical of the value of what he had to tell them. He was to grow frustrated with both, and after he published *A Walk on the Wild Side* in 1956, he was to cease to write serious fiction. The novels and stories of his early years were replaced by travel books and collections of essays such as *Who Lost an American?* and

Notes from a Sea Diary: Hemingway All the Way. The Algren of *Never Come Morning* and *The Man with the Golden Arm* had opted out of American society. What continued to attract readers to his new works was a distinctive voice—one that revealed many of the features of the voice of the novels but was qualitatively different. It was more strident, more wise-cracking, more contentious, as if the speaker did not expect to be listened to seriously.

During these years Algren began a flamboyant quarrel with the critics, attacking well-known figures under such thinly disguised pseudonyms as Leslie Fleacure, Elvis Zircon, Lionel Thrillingly, and Justin Poddlespitz. They were the "new owners" of American literature, having arrived "directly from their respective campuses armed with blueprints to which the novel and short story would have to conform, were a passing grade to be awarded." They made criticism the focus of American writing, "and that," Algren remarks, "was a pretty shrewd move right there, as neither Elvis nor Leslie nor Justin could write fiction." In retrospect Algren's Chicago-style attack would appear merely ludicrous, if it weren't for the serious alienation of the author it reveals.

It is obvious that Algren felt some sort of conspiracy was going on in American letters in the late fifties and early sixties, though today it appears that what he was really commenting upon and sensitively reacting to was at least in part the growth of a college educated audience and the widening split in the reading public which accompanied it. In effect the literary critics moved in to fill what could be called a print gap. At the same time these critics represented a new force in literature as the universities they were so frequently part of underwent a curriculum revolution in literary study. More and more the scholarly pursuit in literature became a pursuit of the living author, the contemporary figure. For various reasons Algren did not appear to qualify as a subject for study.

Algren's open hostility to criticism could perhaps be viewed as in part responsible for the neglect he suffered during these years. Yet in the end this is not very plausible. Hemingway and Faulkner were just as hostile to criticism, and perhaps even more contemptuous. It is likely that Algren's identification by him self and by the critics with a seemingly dying literary tradition played a larger and more significant role. Perhaps for this reason George Bluestone, writing sympathetically about Algren in the late fifties, declared that "to read him in the naturalistic tradition is to misread him." Bluestone went on to try to define Algren's originality, but in doing so he ingeniously made him into an intellectual puzzle, finding, for example, inverted Christian symbolism in his use of traditional imagery. In the end Bluestone's attempt to redeem Algren in the eyes of the critics was unsuccessful.

To suggest as some have done that naturalism and Algren's reputation died together is a gross simplification as well as a misstatement of fact. Both seem well and assured of long life. Naturalism took a new direction, even as Philip Rahv announced its decline. As for Algren, his reputation can only rise as readers rediscover his works and come to find in them not merely the only serious literary voice that spoke with passion of the poor during a long, lonely decade but a prophetic voice: one that dealt with social issues which were to be important for the next two decades in American life: with drug addiction, of course, as in *The Man with the Golden Arm,* but also with the climate of poverty and the conditions of mind it breeds, with the responsibility of all of society for these conditions, with the culpability of the police and the denial of life represented by our penal institutions, by all our institutions.

Algren saw and felt and responded in literary works of magnitude and distinction to the cultural and social forces that aggravate poverty and lead to the denial of human rights long before such inequities created an awakened national conscience—a conscience which was to coalesce, first in SNCC and the civil rights march on Washington in 1963, then move through segments of American society in the form of student protests and sit-ins, demands for minority and ethnic studies within the universities, the Third World movements, anti-Vietnam peace marches, the Poor People's Freedom Train, the woman's liberation movement. While Algren may not share a belief in all the notions of these diverse groups, or the alternative life style some call for, his work derives from the same radical roots: from the call for justice and the demand for social change, from the belief that man's institutions are ill-equipped to meet the needs of man. To some our institutions seem perversely designed to prevent man from achieving his humanity—or, as Algren demonstrated through his moving story of Lefty Bicek, from even reaching manhood.

At the beginning of **"A Bottle of Milk for Mother"** Algren's adolescent hero stands in the query room of the Racine Street police station before his accusers—Milano and Comiskey, the arresting officers; Sergeant Adamovitch, the fatherly turnkey; and Captain Kozak, "eleven years on the force and brother to an alderman." A prim-faced reporter in a raccoon coat from the *Dziennik Chicagoski* is also present. Lefty has been caught robbing a drunk of his pay in a precinct captain's hallway. The bullet he fired into the floor to scare the "boobatch" accidentally hit the old man in the groin, and he is dead; but at the beginning of the story Lefty doesn't know this. It is only revealed to him in the course of the interrogation, which takes the form of an impersonally cruel cancelling out of every one of the boy's hopes and dreams, his defenses.

Algren's hero is a ghetto youth dressed in a worn and sleeveless blue work shirt too tight across the shoulders, a pair of square-toed boy's shoes laced with a buttonhook, a pair of trousers with ragged, turned-up cuffs, and a frayed cap which once had earlaps. His range of experience is severely limited by his environment and by the confinement it produces. He dreams, as all ghetto youth do, of escaping his surroundings, of sudden riches and overnight success. His mind is a hodge podge of schemes and plans: a cluster of tawdry hopes and aspirations pulled from the rag bag of American culture. Even the possibility of es-

cape from the police is conceived by him in terms of a crude B-grade movie, with his friends appearing in front of the station with a sub-machine gun in a cream-colored roadster, while he makes a melodramatic run for it, zig-zagging through the building and down a fire escape three stories into the roadster below. "Like that George Raft did that time he was innocent at the Chopin. . . ."

Throughout **"A Bottle of Milk for Mother"** Lefty's thoughts are cast in a similar vernacular, revealing the fantasy world in which he privately lives, particularly his yearning for recognition. A pitcher for the Polish Warriors S.A.C. and an aspiring boxer, Lefty dreams of success by the traditional routes open to the newly arrived and the poor and the ill-educated: the fight ring and the ball park. If Lefty is reluctant to discuss his occasional boxing career, it is only because he is aware that Captain Kozak is trying to link his handler Benkowski with the hold-up. At various times in the course of the story he goes into a boxer's shuffle. Once he is on the verge of unbuttoning his shirt to show off his chest; Adamovitch puts one hand on his shoulder and slaps the boy's hand down. But Lefty's irrepressible ego cannot really be beaten down. At once boyish and inoffensive, it keeps breaking in upon the awareness of the officers and the Captain, who would much rather dismiss the boy out of mind than have to acknowledge his humanity. In a profoundly moving way Lefty represents Algren's affirmation of the inviolable human spirit.

Bruno Lefty Bicek is essentially an innocent (it is surely the deliberate author who makes George Raft an innocent figure in the gangster film at the Chopin Theater), even though in the course of Algren's story he seems only dimly aware of the difference between right and wrong and has no sense of guilt. (At the end of the story Sergeant Adamovitch—the name is symbolic—locks the boy in his cell. He asks him in his most fatherly voice, "Feel all right, son?" In his mind he is thinking: "The kid don't *feel* guilty is the whole trouble. You got to make them *feel* guilty or they'll never go to church at all. A man who goes to church without feeling guilty for *something* is wasting his time, I say.") Lefty makes no overt comment, either to the men in the police station or in his mind, to indicate that he understands such distinctions. But Lefty does have an essential if limited understanding of how society operates in his world. One catches a reflection of this in his account of what he told his victim in Polish when he strongarmed him in the precinct captain's hallway. "I told him polite-like, like a Polish-American citizen, this was Chiney-Eye-a-Friend-of-Mine's hallway. 'No more after this one,' I told him. 'This is your last time gettin' rolled, old man. After this I'm pertectin' you, I'm seein' to it nobody touches you. . . .'" The Captain exchanges glances with the reporter from the *Chicagoski,* who nervously turns to cleaning his glasses, which depend from a black ribbon (and which impress the naive Lefty). Both Kozak and the reporter understand what lies behind the boy's imitation of his elders.

The reporter is an important figure in Algren's world, not in himself, but for what he represents. A bored observer of the scene, he is the representative of the outside world, of all clean-living, right-thinking Poles. In the query room his major concern is his own comfort, particularly the chair he is sitting in, which he finds "a pretty comfy old chair for a dirty old police station." But the chair is too close to the wall radiator, the reporter is uncomfortably warm. He simply doesn't have the energy to move the heavy chair. Just how close he is to seeing the brink of hell, he never realizes, and the true meaning of the events which transpire in the police station pass him by. He fails to appreciate the innocent nature of the bluff behind Lefty's preposterous alibi: that he "was just walkin' down Chicago . . . to get a bottle of milk for mother." The reporter also fails to see the courage of Lefty's refusal to involve his buddies. "I was singlin'. Lonewolf stuff," the boy tells the Captain. At which the reporter, thinking out his news story in advance, writes in his mind: "This correspondent has never seen a colder gray than that in the eyes of the wanton killer who arrogantly styles himself *the lone wolf of Potomac Street.*" The reporter's disavowal of Lefty, his dismissal of the boy as a human being, is all the more obvious for being implied rather than stated. It is this evasion of responsibility, the denial of the boy's humanity, which Algren develops into a general indictment of society.

Algren on writers and writing:

I just don't like the writing racket nowadays. You know—you get yourself an office, good connections, and then you write yourself a memorandum, with questions like "What's going good this year? What's the contemporary formula?" Then you just follow the party line and you make a lot of money. I'll tell you exactly what I don't like about our literary set, our arbiters, our critics. There's a big boycott operates against the man who wears brown shoes after six in the evening.

That's the way the New York critics look at my writing. They don't *like* it. They say: "We're tired of Cannery Row people." They want novels about their own kind. They don't believe that people live in America as they do live. They say that we've had enough of writing about the antisocial and the criminal. But this has always been the function of the writer, to find out what a human being is. I have always felt that the writing man is on the side of the defendant, the accused. But all those critics take the policeman's attitude.

I believe that corruption begins at the top. I know a lot of racket people and people who have done time, mostly people who have a legitimate front but with something else going on underneath it. I just like them better than the so-called good people. My friends have a different set of values: they are generous in personal relationships and they are less hypocritical. Morally they are sounder than the "good" people who run Chicago by complicity. But too many writers are eager to enter into the complicity.

Nelson Algren, in an interview in The Spectator,
Vol. 203, No. 6851, October 16, 1959.

Martha Heasley Cox and Wayne Chatterton (essay date 1975)

SOURCE: "The Contour of Human Life," in *Nelson Algren,* Twayne Publishers, 1975, pp. 39-58.

[*In the essay below, Cox and Chatterton provide an overview of Algren's short stories, stating that critical focus on his novels has minimized "Algren's considerable achievement in the [short story] genre."*]

Critics such as Chester Eisinger, George Bluestone, Maxwell Geismar, and Leslie Fiedler, who have assessed Algren's fiction comprehensively, have approached the major works chronologically, but they have usually ignored his early stories and have discussed some others only as they have appeared between the publications of the novels. Such treatment has tended to minimize Algren's considerable achievement in the genre: he has written more than fifty substantial short stories, including his first work, during his career as novelist, poet, reviewer, and travel-book writer.

Algren considered the short story important. In 1945, when he decided to settle in Chicago and to become "serious about writing," he concentrated on the short stories which were included in his only collection of the genre, **The Neon Wilderness.** A number of his short stories, little altered, have become episodes in the novels; a number of episodes from the novels, just as slightly changed, have been published separately as short stories. Algren admits, in fact, that the only way he knows to write a novel is "just to keep making it longer and longer." These tendencies suggest that, in some important ways, the short stories rather than the novels might be a clearer index to Algren's talent.

Algren's first short story, **"So Help Me,"** is an extended dramatic monologue, a precursor of the highly charged interrogation scenes containing the long and often subtle confessionals which become some of the most effective sections in Algren's later work. In **"So Help Me,"** the speaker-narrator is a somewhat garrulous, uneducated young man. A Depression-era roustabout, he tells his story, after having been apprehended for murder, as a deposition to a "big-league lawyer." The story he tells is a straight-line and uncomplicated one: Homer, the speaker, tells of seeing a lost-looking but well-dressed Jewish boy, David, standing with a suitcase on a New Orleans wharf, of befriending him in hopes of getting some of his money, of their chance meeting with an ex-convict named Fort in a hobo jungle, of the trio's migrant jobs while Homer and Fort slyly try to con David out of his possessions, and of the actual robbing of the Jitney Jungle store in Texas and the subsequent flight, which is successful until Fort is so panicked by one of David's screaming nightmares that he shoots him.

The story-telling is immature in many ways. Though the monologue form is required perhaps because of the deposition frame and because it is useful for sustaining the character of the speaker, dialogue seems essential in some sections as the story develops; and its avoidance suggests the author's lack of technique or control. Sometimes, too, the almost breathless panoramic paragraphs are broad narratives that hurry the reader across seemingly unnecessary movements and incidents. **"So Help Me,"** however, is a remarkable first story and a foretaste of much that is to become important in Algren's later fiction.

The story's overtone, its density of implication, its texture, and its solidity of detail are noteworthy. The recurrent phrase "so help me"—which appears at least twice at crucial moments during Homer's recounting of the events leading to the impulsive shooting, and again as the last line of the narrative—becomes both a desperate avowal of Homer's sincerity and a plea for assistance. From time to time, Homer unwittingly reveals that he is pathetically unaware of his own obsessions or twisted values, as when, after Homer tricks David into pawning the suitcase until money comes from Homer's mythical brother in Apalachicola, Homer refuses to let Fort accompany him to the pawnshop because his friend "has very deceptive ways sometimes." Moreover, Algren's use of the key phrase "We're cut apart—cut apart!", one which David screams in his walking nightmares, is particularly effective; for it gradually increases the tension until the outcry trips the trigger-finger of the unnerved Fort, and it serves as a recurrent thematic statement of the psychological and spiritual isolation of the characters themselves.

Between **"So Help Me"** and his collection of short stories, *The Neon Wilderness,* Algren had written his two earliest novels, *Somebody in Boots* and *Never Come Morning.* The first novel was unsuccessful; the second, successful enough to be encouraging without being a bestseller. But, by the author's own admission, he had written both novels during a long period of random, youthful, and largely rootless wandering and army service. By 1945, convinced that, if his writing were to be taken seriously, he had to become serious about writing, he began work on his volume of short stories, only a few of which he had written previously. In his Preface to the American Century Series Edition of *The Neon Wilderness* (1960), he suggests that he was aware that he was herding his career into a new direction: "I made a U-turn in 1946 and ran down several memories I had been haunting before they could start haunting me." These memories were a composite of all his experiences—real, literary, and imaginary.

One of the first and most revealing lessons Algren learned was the difference between the ultra-conscious, the laboriously researched, the over-planned story, and the "accidental" product of his spontaneity and his already fully stocked warehouse of key-phrases, character traits, and informing motifs. Two of the stories in *The Neon Wilderness,* in particular, demonstrate the superiority of Algren's "accidental" story over the "self-conscious" one. **"Design for Departure,"** the principal thematic story of the collection, emphasizes the jungle motif and contains the phrase "the neon wilderness" as part of its narrative. It was carefully researched and "self-conscious." The accidental story, which is one of the real triumphs in Algren's career, is **"How the Devil Came Down Division Street."**

No writer was ever more determined to make all the "standard" preparations for creating a short story masterpiece than was Algren from the moment he began planning **"Design for Departure"**:

> I had a very ambitious hope of writing a really great story, and I went about that in a very determined way. I slept in bum hotels and talked to prostitutes, and I knocked around State and Harrison Streets, tried to hear conversations going on in the next room—picked up, you know, bits of actual conversation. I worked very hard on that. I worked on it off and on for years. That was to be such a great story. Nobody wanted to publish it.

"Design for Departure," which was originally intended as the title for the whole collection, bears a marked resemblance to Stephen Crane's short novel *Maggie: A Girl of the Streets* (1893). The similarity between the two stories is particularly remarkable in the early scenes of **"Design for Departure"** where the young girl, Mary, blossoms in an environment similar to that which spawned Crane's Maggie; and Mary blossoms there despite what Crane would have called "lurid altercations" between her drunken guardians—her real father, Sharkey, and his common-law wife, the "dead-picker" widow, who exist in avid mutual destructiveness. But, unlike her predecessor, Mary is not that "most rare and wonderful production of a tenement district, a pretty girl," but a blemished one, for her face has a birthmark.

Though Mary's tenement world is not quite the purgatory of Maggie's, it has the more modern trappings of the same dungheap: "Kleenex, fifty-cent horse tickets, and cigarette snipes . . . stamped and trampled into the floor's ancient cracks," a subterranean cave like Crane's "dark region," where she "screamed in sleep without waking at all: as though the fear she felt in her dream was less than the fear she would know upon waking."

These similarities are not surprising since Algren has frequently acknowledged his debt to Crane, once saying "I know him so well I sometimes think I wrote him myself." Parallels with other Naturalist pioneers, particularly with Dreiser's *Sister Carrie,* would be easy to make; but such comparisons tend to diminish a talent whose strengths are more unique than derivative. The "work-monotony" syndrome of Naturalist fiction, for instance, could be traced to Emile Zola, but is a too unavoidable observation of life to charge authors with borrowing it from one another. The kindred monotonies of the sewing-machine jobs of Dreiser's Carrie and Crane's Maggie, the packing-house jobs of Upton Sinclair's Jurgis Rudkus in *The Jungle,* and the bacon-wrapping job of Algren's Mary are all manifestations of a universal condition more than of a literary convention.

In **"Design for Departure,"** the time comes when Mary moves away from Sharkey and from the widow's proud boast, "Sometimes I fall down. But I don't stagger." Alone in the dreadful, impersonal isolation of "one of those cheap caverns which are half way between a rooming house and a cheap hotel," Mary becomes an automaton at her bacon-wrapping job and otherwise occupies "a twilit land between sleep and waking"—always sleeping in the foetal position as an envelope against the void of her life. Into this vacuum comes deaf Christiano, the sweeper of halls, who waits in Mary's room to seduce her; and she succumbs with only a whimper. After she has become a partner in the badger game with Christy and Ryan, the proprietor of the Jungle Club, a victim calls the police, who take Christy, "the one human being who had been kind to her," away in handcuffs. During his imprisonment, Mary turns to prostitution and drug addiction, and becomes diseased. When Christy returns, she warns him away, performing in her disease and despair the inevitably appropriate act demanded by circumstance—the request that Christy give her the last, lethal dose of narcotics to ease them both from a life become irrevocably intolerable.

With the appearance of deaf Christiano the uniqueness of Algren's jungle world becomes unmistakable; it is no longer the same as Crane's or Dreiser's. Mary is not, like Maggie, "pounced upon by the first wolf in this jungle and seduced" [Charles Child Walcutt, *American Literary Naturalism: A Divided Stream,* Minneapolis, 1956]. Instead, both Mary and Christy are victims of psychological and spiritual starvation. She is seduced by a deeply flawed jungle humanoid whose very incompleteness helps to explain, within the only framework possible to those who must survive in a jungle metropolis, not only his capacity for true if primitive kindness but also his ultimate fidelity to her. And, by the same token, Mary's only resistance is the whimper of one who, knowing nothing but defeat, must accept her seduction as the established pattern of her existence.

But even in Algren's special universe of crime, prostitution, drunkenness, and drug addiction, Mary finds with Christy the only human rapport she has ever known—in its way a genuine love which exists independent of all that is otherwise sordid and degraded. With Christy's imprisonment, however, all hope disappears. In her narcotic degeneracy and disease, she counts it an act of Christian mercy that Christy will, on his return, perform the last narcotic ritual necessary to round out the "elaborate preparation for death" [George Bluestone, "Nelson Algren," *Western Review,* Vol. XXII, Autumn 1957] which has been her life.

With the infusion of human sensibility and Christian mythos into the jungle world, Algren achieves a trademark of his contribution to American Naturalistic fiction: deep compassion for the fallen and degraded. In this story, Algren makes his most obvious excursion into Christian allegory; for he makes Christy a half-brother to those pseudonyms of Christ produced by Joseph Conrad, Fyodor Dostoevsky, Ivan Turgenev, Faulkner, Albert Camus, and Hemingway. Though somewhat inverted, the allegory is plain not only in the names of Mary and Christy themselves but also in Mary's search for deliverance from a lost world through the sacrificial act of a mortal Christ. The Christian mythos, a symptom of unremitting seriousness in Algren's early work, is perhaps too weighty for the basic subject matter in **"Design for Departure."** Nonetheless, perceptive critics like George Bluestone have recognized it as one of the most admirable stories in the collection.

Part of the lesson which Algren learned from writing **"Design for Departure"** was that he could not immerse himself too early and too painstakingly in serious preparation without stifling life-giving properties which a greater reliance upon intuition could preserve. The value of the lesson has been proved by the continued popularity of a story which he wrote in one afternoon and revised only once, a basically serious study of Division Street life told with the bizarre lightness of much of his best work since that time. Needing some money in a hurry, Algren fictionized a Pole's account of a neighborhood family that was convinced that its house was haunted. The result was **"How the Devil Came Down Division Street,"** a story which "is still brand new," though so often anthologized (even in foreign languages) that Algren now denies reprint permission since he fears its over-publication.

The narrative begins as a frame story in which Roman Orlov accepts a double-shot of whiskey from the narrator in return for an explanation of how he became the acknowledged prince of Division Street drunks. The immediate scene is the Polonia Bar on Division Street where Roman spends his life declaring that "The devil lives in a double-shot" and pleading with his friends to help him "drown the worm" which, though drowned each day, nonetheless gnaws incessantly. Long in the telling, broken by curses and sobs, Roman's tale is founded upon a narrative irony in which the miraculous saving of a totally derelict drunken father creates a totally derelict drunken son.

The machinery by which Algren achieves this switching of positions appears slight and perhaps too ingenious at first glance; but, viewed in environmental terms, it is ultimately defensible: one of the crucial conditions of the family's existence is sleeping accommodations which force one or another of the family to sleep under rather than in a bed. Papa Orlov, in whose head "many strange things went on," earns pennies at night by playing his accordion in Division Street taverns. By day, he sleeps in the tenement apartment, but never in Mama O's bed. It is as though, "having given himself all night to his accordion, he must remain true to it during the day." The apartment contains only two beds—one is for eleven-year-old Teresa and Mama Orlov, who "cooked in a Division Street restaurant by day and cooked in her own home at night"; the other bed is shared by thirteen-year-old Roman and the seven-year-old twins. Slumber is so precarious that "nobody encouraged Papa O. to come home at all"; but, when he does, he sleeps under Roman's bed until the children go to morning Mass.

The problem is a simple one of domestic geometry. And, since the solution works, there is no difficulty until the terms of the problem require substitutions. Trouble begins when the family is upset by a ghostly knocking at the door: first, on a Sunday with only Papa O. at home; again, that evening; again, in the middle of the night. A dream of a blood-spattered young man waiting in the hall convinces Mama O. that some change is coming; therefore, she is not surprised when Papa O. comes home inexplicably without his accordion. Implored for an explanation of the knocking and the dream, neighbors tell of the brutal murder there in which a young man crazed by drink had beaten to death his unwed mate and had then hanged himself in the closet. They had been buried together in unsanctified ground, and he is now returning in search of peace.

For a writer both celebrated and condemned for his sympathy with the underdog, the downbeaten, the oppressed and cornered, Algren has shown a surprising sympathy with the haunted and spiritually oppressed law officer.

—Martha Heasley Cox and
Wayne Chatterton

The priest proclaims it the "will of God that the Orlovs were chosen to redeem the young man through prayer and that Papa O. should have a wife instead of an accordion." So, deprived of an accordion through God's will, Papa stays home, sleeps in his proper place beside Mama, and soon becomes the best janitor on Noble Street. As a result, the haunting ceases. By and large, this miracle saves the Orlov family; it brings from the landlord a surcease of rent and makes the previously retarded Teresa the most important person in her class. But for Roman, the miracle is only that of the change-ling; for, with Papa sleeping in Mama's bed, Teresa must take Roman's place beneath the bed. Unable to sleep there at night, Roman haunts Papa's well-worn paths to the taverns to drown the worm each night until that bitterest hour, dawn, when "he must go home though he has no home." That is why, as the biggest drunk on Division Street, Roman insists that the devil lives in a double-shot.

In **"How the Devil Came Down Division Street"** Algren added a dimension which characterizes most of his later work: the bizarre, flamboyant, and sometimes grim humor. And nowhere has he more successfully combined the elements of the modern gothic, the comic ghost story, and meaningful social commentary.

The charge most frequently leveled against Algren's short fiction is that it consists of sketches rather than of fully formed short stories. He concentrated upon what Bluestone calls moments of "frozen change before a death or final loss" which characterize passages in the early novels, especially in *Never Come Morning*. Most of Algren's short fiction substitutes for conventional rounding-out of action a deliberately static framework in which the very lack of action emphasizes the paralysis of characters who must be brought to the full realization of their paralysis,

as in the last line of **"A Bottle of Milk for Mother"**—"I knew I'd never get to be twenty-one anyhow."

"A Bottle of Milk for Mother" is the most widely anthologized of three dramatized sketches which are among Algren's most effective contributions to modern short story craft: the "interrogation stories." Some of these are elaborate verbal exchanges drawn from official police "line-ups"; others are more fully narrated adaptations of the "third degree." At some time between 1935 and 1941, in an attempt to recover a stolen wallet, Algren received a card admitting him to regular police line-ups. For years thereafter he haunted these ceremonials where he observed, absorbed, and learned to interpret stance, glance, gesture, facial and auditory inflection, and the dialectal thrust typical of reactions between accuser and accused.

The respect and popularity accorded **"A Bottle of Milk for Mother"** are the result of the directness and penetration with which Algren manages a verbal duel between a suspect and a police captain. The young Polish baseball-pitcher-turned-prize-fighter, Bruno "Lefty" Bicek, possesses slow-witted street cunning. The precinct police captain Kozak (called Tenczara in *Never Come Morning*) is an omniscient nemesis figure whose weary cynicism camouflages an intimate knowledge of the criminal mind and a solid expertise in the ploys of interrogative suggestion, innuendo, and snare. From the beginning, the game is hopeless for the cornered suspect; but in the long run, Captain Kozak proves himself even the better gambler.

The story opens in Captain Kozak's office into which Bruno, charged with the fatal robbery-shooting of an old man in a tenement hallway, is ushered by Sergeant Adamovitch. With dramatic irony, the opening sentence tells the reader something Bruno himself does not know: this is his "final difficulty" with the police. From the moment Bruno enters, he is subjected to the expert terrorizing of the official team composed of two sergeants, a plain-clothes man, and a reporter. The story is an advanced form of the deposition, but the unbroken monologue of **"So Help Me"** becomes in this story an elaborate pattern of move and countermove, one always controlled by the cynical though sphinx-like captain, and one always edging the suspect inexorably toward final revelations which he does not know he is making.

The crucial turns are often very delicate, as when Kozak virtually ignores the pathetically naive alibi that Bruno was only on an errand to get a bottle of milk for his mother, or when Bruno is rattled by Kozak's abrupt shift from the familiar "Lefty" to the austere and threatening "Bicek." Each time the suspect feels that he has managed to gloss his own portrait, he finds it looking more and more like a prison photo. Finally, on his knees in a cell in an accidental attitude of prayer as he looks for his pavement-colored cap, he mutters to impersonal walls, "I knew I'd never get to be twenty-one anyhow."

Captain One-Eye Tenczara of *Never Come Morning* is the first of Algren's weary, burdened, but sardonic and wily cops. After conducting the interrogation which is the basis of **"A Bottle of Milk for Mother."** Tenczara also presides over the first important line-up scene in Algren's stories, a scene which is the progenitor of **"The Captain Has Bad Dreams,"** which in turn became the germinal idea for **"The Captain Is Impaled."** In this evolution lies one of the remarkable paradoxes in Algren's fiction: for a writer both celebrated and condemned for his sympathy with the underdog, the downbeaten, the oppressed and cornered, Algren has shown a surprising sympathy with the haunted and spiritually oppressed law officer.

The interrogation stories reveal the development of this broader recognition in Algren's writing. At first, with One-Eye Tenczara's interrogations, the focus is upon the criminal and the crime. The officer's function is largely that of a medium through which the reader can perceive the complexity of the sub-legal, sub-social, sometimes even subhuman activities which persist behind the city's respectable façades. But from story to story, as lost soul follows lost soul across a platform under spotlights, the focus shifts from the accused to the accuser. The guilt of the criminal becomes, at last, that of the oppressor also.

Together, the stories **"The Captain Has Bad Dreams"** and **"The Captain Is Impaled"** serve as the final stages in this evolution; but the difference lies chiefly in the greater intensity with which the later story shifts guilt to the interrogator. These veteran police captains with at least eleven years' service are jaded, disillusioned, hardened officers—ones as hard as the hardened criminals they interrogate interminably. Haunted by the creeping erosion of their rightness and assurance, they become at last compassionate in their cynicism; identifiable with those they oppress, they are cognizant that they, too, are implicitly guilty of the wrongs they condemn eternally in others.

Both stories share the same subject, one that is perhaps best capsulized by Algren himself in a passage from **"The Captain Is Impaled,"** in which he tells whom the "snickerers" are waiting in the darkened auditorium to identify: "the man who'd slugged the night watchman and the one who'd snatched the imported purse through the window of the Moving El; for him who'd chased somebody's sister down a dead-end alley or forged her daddy's signature; tapped a gas main or pulled a firebox; slit the janitor's throat in a coal-bin or performed a casual abortion on the landlord's wife in lieu of the rent." Others are also there, to be identified or charged not by the victimized public but by the police themselves. Like spirits in a latter-day *Divine Comedy,* these are malefactors who do violence not upon others but upon themselves—the drunks, hopheads, loiterers, attempted suicides.

The setting is minimal in **"The Captain Has Bad Dreams"**: "They come off the streets for a night or a week and pause before the amplifier with a single light, like a vigil light, burning high overhead. Each pauses, one passing moment, to make his brief confessional." Though essentially the same, the setting is elaborated upon in **"The Captain Is Impaled"** in which the time is "that loneliest of all jailhouse hours, the hour between the evening chow-cart's passing and Lights On." The reader is with the prisoners in a jail cell, and the auditorium is "just the other side of that green steel door." Furthermore, the reader is painfully aware that those who lurk nightly in the dark auditorium are now coming in. These are the "snickerers," who come every night to point their fingers at the accused, even though the accused can admit no fear. Everybody is "in on a bad rap. So how could anyone get fingered?"

In **"The Captain Has Bad Dreams,"** the identification of the accuser with the sufferers is vague. Some nights the captain "was all for hanging the lot of them at 11 P.M. On other evenings he advised them to take turns throwing themselves under the El, which roared regularly past." But at home he is plagued by dreams with mystic overtones—dreams in which "they passed and repassed him restlessly, their faces half averted, forever smiling uneasily as though sharing some secret and comforting knowledge of evil which he could never know." The lost ones have given him his own cross; and, like them, he is impaled upon it. The impalement image itself, when it first occurs in **"The Captain Has Bad Dreams,"** applies not to the captain but to an addict who has given himself up voluntarily and stands against the lighted wall "as though impaled, an agonized Jesus in long-outgrown clothes."

By the time **"The Captain Is Impaled"** appeared, two years later, Algren had transfered the impalement from the tortured addict to the tortured captain. Though the story is only an episode in the career of Frankie Machine in *The Man with the Golden Arm,* it is a satisfactory short story which achieves fullest irony and mature thematic force. Understanding the indictment leveled at him by a defrocked priest, "We are all members of one another," the captain watches the "snickerers" leave the line-up room; but he stays behind with his prisoners "to follow each man to a cell all his own, there to confess the thousand sins he had committed in his heart . . . for there was no priest to wash clean the guilt of the captain's darkening spirit nor any judge to hear his accusing heart." He warns himself to come off his own cross, but he cannot, for "the Captain was impaled."

Algren's stories are highly homogeneous. As has been noted, his subjects are dope addiction, prostitution, incarceration, gambling, prize-fighting, horse racing, and army life, one or more of which predictably appears in most of his work. Nonetheless, certain stories have similarities which differentiate them from others. Three, for instance, are related to the interrogation group because they deal with conditions which drive suspects into police offices or line-ups and because they reflect the value-deterioration and the rationalizing of the confessionals.

"Poor Man's Pennies" is built almost entirely upon the "transparent alibi" typical of the line-up confessionals. Here the alibis help create a narrative that explores the reasons for a nice girl's involvement with a worthless fabricator. Gladys, understanding that Rudy's compulsive lies "are a poor man's pennies," manages to marry him to get him paroled to her; and she spends ten trouble-free years in probationary bliss. **"Poor Man's Pennies"** has moments of broad farce or even burlesque, and it ends in at least temporary salvation; but it is, nevertheless, "a saga of organized stumbling by born incompetents toward a palpably impossible end" [Chester E. Eisinger, "Nelson Algren: Naturalism as the Beat of the Iron Heart," *Fiction of the Forties,* Chicago, 1963].

The other two stories of this group, **"A Lot You Got to Holler"** and **"Please Don't Talk About Me When I'm Gone,"** are more serious sagas of organized stumbling; both are told in first person as forms of the confessional. The first story is an indictment of a brutal, unfeeling father who deprives his son of his mother, marries the mother's sister, and punishes the boy indiscriminately for becoming an inveterate thief and con-boy. Searching for the lost warmth of his mother and adopting all forms of subterfuge because of his fear of his father, the boy finds himself in a fierce paternal feud. Like Huckleberry Finn, he ponders the morality of adult society; he finds its values so inverted that he concludes "I was always in the clear so long as I was truly guilty. But the minute my motives were honest someone would finger me." The story is a handbook of petty thievery, short-change artistry, and con-methods through which the boy progresses until he is jailed and then paroled to his father, whom he baits until the old man is glad to be rid of him.

"Please Don't Talk About Me When I'm Gone," a somewhat rambling story, begins at the moment when Rose, a prostitute who is arrested for murder, is ushered into the police wagon. As the crowd pulls back, she thinks, "My whole life it's the first time anyone made room for me. And now just look what for." Told in retrospect, the story ends at the same moment and with the same words.

Clearly related to the stealing, con-game, and interrogation stories is another three-tale cluster representing the legal retribution which society imposes upon the caught and convicted. These stories, identifiable as studies of incarceration and release, explore in turn early confinement in a juvenile detention home, adult confinement in a southern jail, and the disillusionment of release. **"The Children"** is a devastating treatment of the stupidity of professional "do-gooders" who smugly minister to budding hoods without the remotest perception of what is happening inside their heads. The detention home or "reformatory" does no reforming but serves as a centralized criminal-information exchange where the inmates' appearance of docility toward over-dressed women benefactors is their cover for an esoteric underworld education.

"El Presidente de Méjico," an adaptation of the Texas jailhouse episode in *Somebody in Boots,* is the most effective of the "tank stories." Though the title focuses attention upon Portillo the Mexican, a six-week bridegroom with a pregnant wife, the story really concerns the jailhouse world in which a young man learns the world's cruelties. Portillo, detained for questioning about the location of a still, is kept outside the cell-block to protect him from Jesse Gleason, the "bad-man" of the tank. Gleason, who had killed Mexicans on both sides of the border, had returned for justice to the American side where "he had

more relatives than the sheriff and was confident of beating the rap." Without explanation, Portillo is released; but he is dragged back at nightfall with a great bullet hole in his stomach, a result of his having tried to run from the sheriff. Too nearly dead to be able to grant permission for surgery, he dies on the floor, never to know whether his unborn son becomes President of Mexico. Later, after Gleason is acquitted, he is endowed with Spanish boots and Portillo's sombrero.

Slight but poignant, **"The Brother's House"** probes into that overwhelming longing for release which all prisoners must outlast. David survives by dreaming of his return to the house where he had lived with his brothers. The beatings they gave him cannot be admitted into his dreams; he has nowhere else to go. Released, he trudges homeward for eighteen days, only to be met at the gate with the query, "What do you want?"

Two stories, **"Stickman's Laughter"** and **"Katz,"** concern loss by gambling. In both stories, the losing-formula is classic and the same: a mounting pile of winnings, then suddenly—nothing. **"Stickman's Laughter,"** however, has one of the few near-redemptive conclusions in all of Algren's fiction. Like the good husband he is, Banty Longobardi takes his pay home to an equally good wife who, though rarely away, has not returned from visiting her mother. Lonely and disappointed, Banty resorts to a crap game; wins forty dollars; and, even more bitterly disappointed when his wife is not yet home to share his good fortune, gets drunk and loses all his money at the same crap table. Ashamed and fearful, he goes home again and finds his wife willing to take blame for being away and even to sympathize with "poor Banty" for missing dinner and the movies. "So nothing important had been lost after all."

Such a salvation is impossible for Katz, the young poker player whose name is the title of his story. With sixty-five dollars in his pocket, he runs the win-then-lose route until he has only eight quarters left. In a five-dollar-start game, he pretends to have more in a closed fist and calls that he has "threes" to make the dealer think he has three threes instead of two. He is caught and thrown down the stairs in disgrace. Unlike Banty, who gambles only from loneliness, Katz feels that money makes him important, invincible: "Katz believed in lucky bucks, fast money, and good women." His defeat is ignominious; his character makes it impossible for him to know the redeeming love to which Banty returns.

In both stories, much depends upon the ironic twists of the parrotlike cry of stickman and dealer, "Tell 'em where you got it and how easy it was." The cry has a literal meaning when Banty wins but an ironic one when he loses; it is ironic on one level when Katz loses the first time; but, as a sneering phrase directed at an inept cheater, it means something altogether different the second time.

As concrete and authoritative as the gambling tales but even more sordid and hopeless in outlook are several stories dealing with prostitution and drug addiction. The slightest of the group, **"Is Your Name Joe?"**, is the half-demented monologue of a simple-minded prostitute to whom all men are "Joe" because "Joes" have been the only ones important enough in her life to drive her steadily into perdition. Two other stories, written in the late 1960's, return to the successful addiction-prostitution themes of the two major novels. **"All Through the Night"** probes once more the faith which the prostitute has in the "Daddy" whose only real aim is to gain all he can from her. As a graphic revisitation to the addict world of *The Man with the Golden Arm,* the story is effective; but the use of names with biblical vibrations, Beth-Mary and Christian, is not as well integrated with the thematic values as in **"Design for Departure."**

In **"Decline & Fall of Dingdong-Daddyland"** (1969), Algren amplifies the kitchen condom-factory episode from *A Walk on the Wild Side.* Essentially a story of mutual entrapment in which an old ex-con provides the heroin for two addicted ex-hookers in return for their help in manufacturing garish condoms, Dingdong Daddies and their variations, it is a terrifying tale despite the gloss of broad humor with which it is told. These derelicts exist in hateful interdependence until the old man dies, leaving a hundred-thousand dollars worth of heroin in the brass bedposts, where it remains to this day safe and dry in some forgotten dump underneath an El.

Two stories in *The Neon Wilderness* are only peripherally prostitution stories. **"Kingdom City to Cairo"** is a first-person story told by a young hitch-hiker picked up by a former Seventh-Day Adventist minister. The minister has been deprived of his credentials for making a bawdy house of an historic hotel he owns in a neighboring town, where he also goes to pick up mail from his brother's wife with whom he is having an affair. He keeps telling the young man, "You see, I have a weakness"; but, even after the young man accepts a free bed and escapes an army of bed-bugs in the ancient bawdy house, he is still unsure "whether the Reverend's weakness was women, whisky, his single kidney, or practical joking."

A more substantial prostitution-prize-fighting tale, **"Depend on Aunt Elly,"** is one of the most ironically bitter stories in *The Neon Wilderness.* In addition to developing the theme that a girl can never escape prostitution after she has adopted the profession, the story also successfully combines Algren's interest in official graft, entrapment, incarceration, and prize fighting. The title, lifted from the context, is biting in its implications: "Aunt" turns out to be a proprietary rather than a familial term, and Elly herself is truly dependable but only in collecting a monthly fee from Wilma, the small-time prostitute, whom she had bilked into spending all of her money to buy a furlough instead of the promised commutation from the prison farm. A part-Indian prize fighter, Baby Needles, rescues Wilma from a whorehouse, marries her unaware of her perpetual debt to Elly, derives from the marriage courage to develop his "bolo punch" into near-championship form, but then finds and reads one of Elly's dunning letters, loses heart, returns to liquor, and rejects his wife for not being honest with him. He is left alone with only Wilma's lucky-piece,

a pathetic rabbit's foot, that is "clutched in his hand, the great knuckles showing white and helplessly through the copper skin." Altogether, the story is one of Algren's most effective efforts to depict the luckless, accidental fashion in which desperate people are deprived of mutually redeeming love.

> Nowhere outside the short stories has Algren been so free to exercise his ability to construct a tale from the single, self-revelatory catch-phrase which often becomes the essence of theme.
>
> —*Martha Heasley Cox and Wayne Chatterton*

Baby Needles is typical of the second- and third-rate prize fighters who appear in Algren's fiction; all of them yearn for fame and money, and sometimes they approach both, but they see them fade mirage-like. This syndrome reaches its lowest depths in *The Neon Wilderness* story **"Million-Dollar Brainstorm"** where the brainstorm is not the million-dollar one which the mountainous pug Tiny Zion dreams of, but his own literally scrambled brains. After bringing Tiny home from his last knockout and a messy binge, his manager knows by looking at his eyes that Tiny will be throwing his mother out the window next, "Or jumpin' outa it hisself."

Though the prize fight stories always deprive the fighter of fighter's dreams, they sometimes allow him to settle for something else, or even for something more meaningful and permanent. Two progressive phases of such settlement appear in a 1968 *Atlantic* story, **"Home to Shawneetown,"** and in **"He Swung and He Missed,"** which was part of *The Neon Wilderness.* **"Home to Shawneetown"** is the saga of a better-than-average itinerant fighter who meets and beats good opposition all over the country but who sees clearly in time that a swab stick, a roll of gauze, and a vaseline jar are his total reward for getting his "face punched in for fourteen years." So he accepts his wife's long-standing suggestion that they open a diner, and with the first-night customers he contentedly watches a televised fight between two of his old opponents.

The last of the three prize fight stories, **"He Swung and He Missed,"** reflects Algren's admiration for Hemingway's classic story "Fifty Grand." Though Young Rocco is not championship material, he gives everything to every fight and never considers taking a dive—until the last fight of his career, which he agrees to throw because he cannot stand seeing his wife without decent shoes. But he finds when in the ring that he cannot willingly lose; "his own pride" is "double-crossing him." Solly knocks him out, however—in a prolonged and graphic fight sequence as specific as the best blow-by-blow commentary. In the dressing room, his wife confronts him fearfully, saying she had bet all his advance on him and now they have nothing. But he is able to grin "a wide white grin," and "that was all she needed to know it was okay after all."

Since Algren had little rapport with the manufactured society of military life, his five army stories are not among his best. Though they have all the concreteness and specificity of his other works—intimate knowledge of the mystique behind hierarchies of rank, command of black-market angles, perception of the enlisted man's view of military punishment and reward—the characterizations seldom achieve the keenness of Algren's dope addicts, jailbirds, and prize fighters. In **"That's the Way It's Always Been"** and in **"The Heroes,"** the real war is not with the Germans but with American officers, both commissioned and "numcum," including the chaplain. The commanding officer, a superb incompetent, devotes his energies to prolonging the war, to delivering marathon lectures, and, like the chaplain, to cornering expensive war souvenirs in the field and nurses in bed. To the plain soldier, even God is a grafter; for His vice-regent the chaplain preserves the profitable status quo with glib wisdom, "That's the way it's always been." The relentless war between enlisted man and commanding officer is a landlubber's *Mr. Roberts* in which a major victory is achieved when the medics have the Colonel himself as a pneumonia patient; and the Mexican-Osage Corporal Hardheart of **"The Heroes"** is a character not far removed from the half-insane aspect of the military establishment later chronicled by Joseph Heller in *Catch-22.* Many soldiers flee such insanity, as does the Negro soldier of **"He Couldn't Boogie-Woogie Worth a Damn,"** who holes up in Marseilles with a lovely Algerienne prostitute who promises to smuggle him into Africa as her Algerien. The story is interesting partly as an early Marseilles version of *Chicago: City on the Make,* for it penetrates the heart and spirit of the great French industrial metropolis: "a worker's city, a dirty dockside mechanic sprawling, in a drunken sleep, his feet trailing the littered sea."

In **"No Man's Laughter,"** an air-force cousin of *What Makes Sammy Run?,* a young habitual delinquent, who develops into the best "wheelman" on Chicago's Near Northwest Side, becomes an air-force hero by diving his plane into an enemy cruiser because he cannot tolerate imaginary mocking laughter from the decks below. In **"Pero Venceremos,"** a tale of reminiscence, a man wounded during the Spanish war relives the experience incessantly in bars and saloons and bores his friends and acquaintances, most of them veterans of World War II. The pathetic punch-line comes when, after remarking that "it's just like yesterday," the wounded veteran O'Connor shakes his head "like a man recalling an endless dream" and murmurs in self-contradiction, "It feels more like tomorrow."

Algren has produced only one short story which can be legitimately labeled a barroom story, **"The Face on the Barroom Floor,"** one of the most convincing and hard-hitting pieces of fiction in *The Neon Wilderness.* Remarkable for its introduction of the early prototype of Schmidt, the awesome legless man of *A Walk on the Wild Side,*

"The Face on the Barroom Floor" successfully communicates the pride and strength of the great torso on a wheeled platform, Railroad Shorty, who even on his wheels can beat anybody at anything. Venus Darling, the little peep-show peeler, boasts of his love-prowess and is offended at the bartender's joke, "Is that where he gets his money then?" Bound to refute the intolerable suggestion that he takes money from women, "Halfy" challenges young Fancy and, at the ghoulish urging of bar patrons, pounds his face "to a scarlet sponge" on the barroom floor, wheels away "like Jesus Christ ridin' his cross," and leaves Brother B. to close his bar forever. The fight is as senseless as the one in Crane's *The Blue Hotel;* but it is more bestial and is given point by the same kind of ironic signs, here NO CREDIT and NO SALE, which make all necessary comment.

During the 1960's, Algren, a lifelong horseplayer, worked somewhat desultorily on a "racetrack novel." This material supplied a few short stories, such as **"The Moon of the Arfy Darfy"** and **"A Ticket on Skoronski"** which appeared in the *Saturday Evening Post* in 1964 and 1966, respectively. **"The Moon of the Arfy Darfy"** is the first-person account of Floweree, an unlucky jockey who, at the suggestion of a bar proprietor, impersonates the famous jockey Willie Hartack so that a "big-hand, big-belly, big-laugh, old jolly-boy" from Omaha can bribe him to throw a race. With the real Hartack riding, the horse wins as expected; and "It looked like a rainy day in Omaha." Only partly a racing story, **"A Ticket on Skoronski"** uses a racing dream as extra-sensory prognosticator and mood builder.

Through the 1960's, Algren's short pieces attracted the attention of men's magazines like *Playboy* and *Dude,* a market which has been receptive not only to fiction but also to mood and occasional pieces, adventure, autobiography, and the highly personal essay. Much of Algren's later work falls into these categories, and **"God Bless the Lonesome Gas Man"** is typical of these later works. Drawing rather lightly upon the army-prize-fighting-barroom materials of previous stories, it is the slight but ingenious tale of Chester, who becomes a "smeller" for the "mighty utility," Some People's Gas. His nose was so often broken during an army boxing career that a necessary operation had given him the olfactory sensitivity of a bloodhound. Night or day he is on call to smell for gas leaks in endless miles of tubing. He is so good at his job that he predicts an explosion where the company has no records of gas lines. But the smell of gas gets into his skin; his cherished wife and his best friends cannot be near him; "he wasn't wanted anywhere but where gas was leaking." He goes to seed and loses weight, but he cannot quit his job because he will get his pension in twenty years.

Among these later efforts are also mood pieces like **"The Unacknowledged Champion of Everything"** (*Noble Savage,* 1960), autobiographical studies like **"The Father and Son Cigar"** (*The Playboy Reader*), and several reprints of adaptations of sections from *Who Lost an American?*—**"Down with All Hands"** (*Atlantic* [Dec., 1960]),

"The Peseta with the Hole in the Middle" (*Kenyon Review,* Part I [Autumn, 1961]; Part II [Winter, 1962]), and **"They're Hiding the Ham on the Pinball King, or, Some Came Stumbling"** (*Contact* [Sept., 1961]).

Altogether, the published short stories of Algren are a considerable achievement. Though somewhat uneven, "a curious amalgam" [as stated by Bluestone], the stories of *The Neon Wilderness* have elicited unexpected discipline from an author so often charged with looseness and with over-rhapsodizing in his novels. Catherine Meredith Brown justifiably says of the short stories what has rarely if ever been claimed for the novels: "the staccato precision of the writing must be read, remembered, and admired" ["Chicago without Tears or Dreams," *Saturday Review of Literature,* Vol. XXX, Feb. 8, 1947]. In contending that Algren "is almost at his best" in the short stories, Maxwell Geismar may have been nearer the truth than many other critics have recognized.

In the short stories, where Algren "can suggest the whole contour of human life in a few terse pages," he has demonstrated the complete range of his literary attainments. In them was born his distinctive comic sense—the light irony of **"How the Devil Came Down Division Street,"** the satire against mock-respectability in **"Kingdom City to Cairo,"** the broadside against stumbling incompetence in the army stories, and the almost slapstick but sympathetic comedy of **"Poor Man's Pennies"**—all a prelude to the "Rabelaisian humor" of *A Walk on the Wild Side,* all early evolutionary stages of a comic sense which has dominated Algren's later work.

Nowhere outside the short stories has Algren been so free to exercise his ability to construct a tale from the single, self-revelatory catch-phrase which often becomes the essence of theme: "So help me"; "Sometimes I stagger. But I don't fall down"; "The devil lives in a double-shot"; "I knew I'd never get to be twenty-one anyhow"; "We are all members of one another"; "Lies are a poor man's pennies"; "Tell 'em where you got it and how easy it was"; "I'm the girl that men forget." Nowhere else has he controlled so stringently his tendency to blend the sordid and the poetic; as a result, the short stories have largely escaped the adverse reaction which such a controversial mixture has brought against the novels.

Otherwise, however, the short stories are almost indistinguishable from the novels. In each genre are the same twilit shadow-world of alley, bar, brothel, jail, cave-like tenement, and flea-bag hotel room; the same maudlin and monotonous juke-box tunes punctuated by the rattling of the El above its thousand columns; the same hopheads, drunks, mackers, outworn prostitutes, sharpies, and general losers; the same grotesqueries of tone and situation; the same concrete and specific insights; the same entrapments, vague unrest, and futile striving. Above all, these stories, despite their shortcomings, are a monument to the honesty, directness, and authority of a writer who has depicted a nightmare society which its parent world would rather disown but which Algren knows too well to let it endure unsung.

Tom Carson (essay date 1986)

SOURCE: An introduction to *The Neon Wilderness,* Writers and Readers Publishing, Inc., 1986, pp. 7-11.

[*In the following introduction to the 1986 edition of* The Neon Wilderness, *Carson calls the collection "the pivotal book of Nelson Algren's career" and comments on Algren's writing style and the relationship between his short stories and his novels.*]

The Neon Wilderness, first published in 1947, is the pivotal book of Nelson Algren's career—the one which bid a subdued but determined farewell to everything that had earlier made him no more than just another good writer, and inaugurated the idiosyncratic, bedevilled, cantankerously poetic sensibility that would see him ranked among the few literary originals of his time. With *The Neon Wilderness,* Algren turned into one of the few American writers, increasingly uncommon since Dreiser, in whom compassion for the dispossessed does not involve a sort of mental portage to reach them. The great revelation for him had been that deprivation was not an abnormal social category but a human absolute, and the pressure in *Neon Wilderness* comes from a writer trying to measure up to the people he's writing about.

He had begun as a Depression novelist, albeit one whose conventionally patterned outrage at social injustice felt more like a fence around his material than a key to its meaning. Traces of the attitude can be found in some of the earlier pieces in this collection. But while a novel can be written to back up a thesis, the short story is more resistant to that. Its equivalent tendency is toward parable—a harder version of the truth, poetic and ineluctable rather than sociological and circumstantial. So even **"A Bottle of Milk for Mother,"** included here, is in some ways more resonant than the novel (*Never Come Morning,* Algren's second) for which it provided the seed. In this version, he doesn't have to explain the interlock of events leading up to Lefty Bicek's arrest for the most useless imaginable homicide, much less stage-manage them into spelling out any acceptable sort of message, either of pity or condemnation. He can simply present Bicek, in all his terrified terribleness, as a random window on humanity.

There's an implicit condescension in most fiction about the lower depths, starting with that term for them. The writer's typical rejection of artfulness, of all literary lilt and sensuality, however manfully meant as an indictment, ends up slipping you the hint that beauty and grace are qualities somehow beyond the class of people in question. Not so for Algren, once he'd found himself. He cultivated every quicksilver ravishment of language that he knew, flinting it with a colloquialism no longer merely mimetic—although Algren could be a fictional ventriloquist of unusual attentiveness and tact, as several stories here display—but metaphorically charged, because he knew that nothing less multilayered and fine-tuned would do justice to the complicated nuance and subtle play of inner awareness that his characters were otherwise presumed to lack only because they were unable to articulate them. The best mature stories in **Neon Wilderness** move on a river of such openness to the details of experience, and perception so unmarred by preconception, that pigeonholing them according to their subject matter ends up seeming like a form of evasion.

> **In Algren's telling, even anger ultimately gets subsumed within a sense of all-abiding mystery.**
>
> —*Tom Carson*

Which is why the style is one of the few genuinely poetic prose styles that can also be called genuinely accurate. Once he'd learned to fly, Algren took chances with his material that no conventional proletarian writer would dare. When his people con outrageously, or blunder into the same emotional manhole they've blundered into a hundred times before, he derides them like the wised-up barkeep down the block; and the intimacy telegraphed by his humor makes those fouled-up barterings with existence painful in a way that neither he nor his readers can exclude themselves from. And it's another mark of Algren's singularity that though his characters' destiny may be tragic, the best ones' behavior isn't always seen as pathetic. Trapped they may be—but their various delusions, eccentricities, addictions and other skewings of reality are often made to appear not as symptoms but active responses, survival strategies, necessarily inventive ways of coping and sustaining some sense of self in the trap. This is understanding on a uniquely humane and unmediated level.

It seems fitting that two of the most striking stories here anticipate crucial elements of Algren's two enduring novels. In plot, **"The Captain Has Bad Dreams"** is no more than a circumstantial account of the nightly lineup in a Chicago precinct house. A recidivist procession of burglars, drunks, junkies, and would-be rapists, never more haunting than in their sly awareness of their own failure, play out ritualistic maneuvers of chicanery and bluff before the captain, as if in a chess tournament where each piece equals a new game. In meaning, the story is a set of freeze-frames of a man trying to make logical what could only be expressed as inchoate despair: the tension between the captain's struggle to deny that he is as much part of the wreckage as the debris before him, and his yearning to give in like them to a nihilism that seems less compromised than his own existence, has made him near to mad. It's Dostoevsky shorn of metaphysics, and all the more monstrous for being mundane. And the captain will reappear in *The Man With the Golden Arm*, the book acknowledged as Algren's idiosyncratic masterpiece—obsessed, by then, by a furtive lust to write his own name on the list of the guilty, even as he stalks the junkie Frankie Machine.

Meanwhile, *A Walk On the Wild Side*—a masterpiece so idiosyncratic that it's never been properly acknowledged at all—is foreshadowed in **"The Face On the Barroom Floor."** The story's Railroad Shorty, like the novel's Legless Schmidt, is an ex-fighter who's been cut in half by a train, and now wheels himself around on a leather-strapped handmade platform. Under either name, he's a great creation—a cripple that you can't feel sorry for. His massive self-sufficiency commands only apprehensive respect; it's the most massively admirable quality he has, and yet it's what turned him into the monster that his deformity alone never could. A younger man (the novel's hero Dove Linkhorn, in the story a bespectacled bartender nicknamed "Fancy"), as determined to break free of callowness as the cripple is of ever being seen as weak, challenges the latter's authority by attempting to sever his one human link, the hooker whose bed he shares while refusing to do the same with her money. In the brutality that ensues, Fancy is beaten to a pulp, and the cripple loses his human connection anyway—he recoils, not in disgust but in self-disgust, from the woman's delight in the reason for the beating. But none of them could have acted in any other way—at least not without relinquishing their struggle for an identity of their own, the only battlefield where the outcome is still open for them. Futile, and awful, it may be; but meaningless—no.

But the claim for **Neon Wilderness** doesn't rest only on the preludes it offers to Algren's subsequent work. Look, for instance, at the desperate, wondrously written **"Design For Departure."** A rather ordinary young woman slips, less down than sideways, into hooking and addiction—dreamily, but her dreaminess long outlasts her hopes. Finally, she comes to see herself as the Virgin Mary, and her lover-connection as Christ. But her insanity, instead of being characterized as pathetic, is merely witnessed: it's the thing that lets her go on living in an unbearable situation. Or else read, in **"Depend On Aunt Elly,"** about another woman submitting to a scheming jailer's blackmail in order to regain her freedom after being unjustly sent to prison, and fatalistically accepting her lover's leaving her when he finds out about it; and notice how, in Algren's telling, even anger ultimately gets subsumed within a sense of all-abiding mystery. There is, in this book, a great deal of wonderful writing; and a number of people, places, feelings, and truths that you may never have met, seen, or known, but that you'll never be able to stop yourself from recognizing once the book is closed.

Kirkus Reviews (review date 1995)

SOURCE: A review of *The Texas Stories of Nelson Algren*, in *Kirkus Reviews*, Vol. LXIII, No. 20, October 15, 1995, p. 1457.

[*Below, the critic provides a positive review of* The Texas Stories of Nelson Algren.]

Usually thought of as an urban midwestern realist, Algren (1909-81) also wrote gritty, cynical accounts of rural poverty and crime set in Texas during, and as transformed by, the Depression years. The stories [in *The Texas Stories of Nelson Algren*] are set in tank towns and hobo jungles and jails, and comprise a virtual sociology of life on the bum (where "God help you if you run and God help you if you fight; God help you if you're broke and God help you if you're black"). The best of these pieces, chosen by editor [Bettina] Drew (*Nelson Algren: A Walk on the Wild Side,* 1989), include several harsh excerpts from Algren's first novel, *Somebody in Boots* (1934), most notably the violent "**Thundermug,**" and two stories from his famous collection *The Neon Wilderness* (1951)—the more compelling of which is "**Depend on Aunt Elly,**" the gritty tale of a luckless whore's relationship with a traveling boxer. The standout later work is "**The Last Carousel,**" a wonderfully detailed picture of carnival life that effectively showcases the hard-boiled lyricism for which this often underrated writer deserves to be better remembered.

Albert E. Wilhelm (review date 1995)

SOURCE: A review of *The Texas Stories of Nelson Algren,* in *The Library Journal,* Vol. 120, No. 18, November 1, 1995, p. 108.

[*Below, Wilhelm comments favorably on* The Texas Stories of Nelson Algren.]

Best known for his tales of urban slums, Algren also wrote eloquently about the Rio Grande Valley of Texas. He first experienced this region in 1932 as a wandering college graduate who could find no job. Surrounded by desperation and casual violence, Algren produced semi-autobiographical stories like "**So Help Me,**" which dramatizes brutal exploitation. Set apart by his Jewishness, Algren also observed and recorded episodes of racism and discrimination. After stealing a typewriter, Algren spent several weeks in jail, and this experience provided impetus for his pervasive theme of the individual oppressed by corrupt authority. Later works in this collection [*The Texas Stories of Nelson Algren*], like "**The Last Carousel,**" provide more detached and bemused treatments of Algren's Texas experiences. Spanning more than four decades, these 12 stories display nicely the evolution of Algren's style.

Bettina Drew (essay date 1995)

SOURCE: An introduction to *The Texas Stories of Nelson Algren,* University of Texas Press, 1995, pp. ix-xviii.

[*In the following introduction to* The Texas Stories of Nelson Algren, *Drew provides an overview of the time Algren spent in Texas during the 1930s and discusses how the author incorporated his experiences in the Southwest into his short stories.*]

This slender volume [*The Texas Stories of Nelson Algren*] preserves a unique and devastating view of the Lone Star State during the Depression, a melancholy and explosive world of hoboes, migrant workers, ranch hands, penniless Mexicans, carnival roustabouts, and the dangerous and helpless inhabitants of county jails. These firsthand impressions of impoverished lives formed the philosophical and moral foundation for all of Nelson Algren's later work. Though dubbed "the poet of the Chicago slums" and long known as a naturalistic urban writer, the author of *The Man with the Golden Arm* and *A Walk on the Wild Side* actually began his career at the very bottom of the United States in 1932, in the Rio Grande Valley in Texas. The journalism degree he'd earned the year before hadn't helped him find a job in Chicago or Minneapolis or anywhere else in the Midwest in those stagnant days before Roosevelt, so when the cold weather came on, he hitchhiked south to continue his search for newspaper work. He drifted down to New Orleans and spent a few months living in cheap rooms selling coffee and beauty products door-to-door; then he rode a long string of boxcars to Texas.

Decades later Algren would remember Texas as "an empty room furnished with the fixtures of another day," but its heat and light and open land offered his first experience of the American West: vast and compelling and a million miles away from the industrialized confines of Chicago. In the Rio Grande Valley huge grapefruit and orange groves were flanked by palms lazily brushing an ever-blue sky; bougainvillea bloomed; bamboo and wild cane hugged the irrigation canals. Once a chaparral wilderness, the Valley had boomed during the twenties, attracting people from all over the country, and it was, in its way, one of the state's most cosmopolitan regions.

On the surface. Below it, in the summer of 1932, was desperation. Amid the poor farmers and transient fruit bums harvesting crops for sixty to seventy-five cents a day, Algren saw a simmering, almost casual violence: the everyman-for-himself philosophy reigned. "Don't ever show *any*one that money," he warned his friend Ben Curtis, who, joining him from Chicago, still had a few funds. "If anybody discovers you've got any money they'll kill you for it." They were living in a Sinclair gas station between Rio Hondo and Harlingen with an ex-con from New Orleans named Luther, selling a little gas each week and trying to make their fortune packing the black-eyed peas Luther picked up from local farmers. One night Luther failed to return to the station. When Algren heard him, very late, drive up and fill his tank, he realized the man was going to skip town without paying the farmers and that he and Ben would end up with knives in their backs if they didn't clear out. He was, quite simply, living in a world where human life had lost its value. "I'd been assured it was a strive and succeed world," he said later. "You got yourself an education and a degree and then you went to work for a family newspaper and then married a nice girl and raised children and this was what America was. But this was not what America was." And in "**So Help Me,**" the story Algren wrote almost immediately about a naked Valley exploitation that ends in death, the nightmare cries of the victim, David—"We're cut apart—cut apart—cut apart!" punctuate the narrative like a shocked, futile refrain in a landscape of overwhelming spiritual desolation.

The Texas stories provide a revealing overview-in-microcosm of Algren's writing career. . . . He always treated themes suited to his own emotional needs, but his work nearly always focused on the outside world and depicted characters who were very, very different from himself.

—*Bettina Drew*

Algren wandered aimlessly around the Valley. He lived briefly in a friendly boardinghouse, worked as a shill at a carnival wheel of chance. He crossed the border to Matamoros and came back again, ate in missions, slept in hobo jungles, lost in crap games, rode in cattle or refrigerated boxcars, was sometimes arrested for vagrancy. He met men whose eyes were rimmed with grime and dust or whose mouths were covered in sores, one who'd spent five months at Huntsville for stealing a chicken, another who went about on all fours like an animal, men who were starving, men who had lost legs or arms in accidents on the tracks. Around Christmas of 1932 he headed home to Chicago, emotionally and physically exhausted. There, he rode the streetcar downtown to write in the office of a friend who owned a typewriter and sought out the literary arm of the Communist Party.

When **"So Help Me"** appeared in *Story* magazine in 1933, an editor from Vanguard Press asked if he were working on a novel. Algren said yes, secured a $100 advance, and returned, by boxcar, to the Lone Star State.

For no apparent reason, Algren began the novel *Somebody in Boots* (1935) in the West Texas town of Alpine, a railway switching point for migrants riding the rails to the California fruit fields and a shipping center for a vast ranching area controlled by legendary Texas land barons. Hoping to make himself "the American Gorky" and dedicating his novel to the homeless, Algren planned to tell the story of Cass McKay, a shoeless, hollow-chested, illiterate youth "utterly displaced, not only from society but from himself . . . adrift in a land that no longer had any use for him." A man without responsibility even to himself, McKay appears in portions of **The Texas Stories** as he wanders aimlessly through life being brutalized. Algren created him on a typewriter in an empty roomful of them at Sul Ross Teachers College.

Algren lived in a boardinghouse frequented by railroad hands and cowboys; he claims, quite plausibly, to have met Frank James's widow. When it was time to get back to Chicago, however, he couldn't bear the thought of leaving all those idle typewriters. So he stole one, packed it off to his parents' house in Chicago, and caught an eastbound freight thinking he'd committed the perfect crime. But the forces of the law merely called ahead to the next town: he was taken back to Alpine's Brewster County jail to await the circuitriding judge, likely to face two years' hard labor at Huntsville.

The month he spent in the Brewster County jail—which he later remembered as five—had an incalculable, lifelong effect on his work: there is a long jail sequence in every novel he wrote, and the individual alone against the law became a familiar Algren theme. Algren witnessed rapes, beatings, sadistic games. The lockup was cold in midwinter, and a "wet filth" soaked the floor; since the guards' take came from how much they could save on the prisoners' meals, the inmates grew thin on cornbread and mush. Fortunately for the cause of literature, at Algren's trial his lawyer, in a surprisingly literary plea, compared him to Jean Valjean of *Les Misérables,* and, though convicted, Algren was given mercy and twenty-four hours to get out of the state.

"Had I been black, of course, I would have gone to Huntsville," he knew all too well. A pecking order based on race had naturally reigned in the jail: blacks and Mexicans were the lowest of the low, and Algren, still going by his given name of Nelson Algren Abraham, was the Jew. But Algren understood intuitively that this hierarchy merely reflected the institutionalized racism of the Texas state. He had seen, in any group of hoboes, that blacks were invariably shipped off to jail; he'd watched a Mexican prisoner, shot by the sheriff's men, die on the cell-block floor without medical treatment. Themes of racism and anti-Semitism resonate in most of **The Texas Stories**; and they were crucial to Algren's conception of the state.

Algren's awareness of state power was hardly diminished when he found himself forcibly obliged to return to Texas to join the army at Camp Maxey, near Paris, in late 1943. Even at that late date a sense of the old pioneer life could still be glimpsed in rural Texas, but while Algren was always deeply affected by the state's stark landscape, his evocations of it have little to do with the celebrations of nature and open spaces that Texas chroniclers J. Frank Dobie and Walter Prescott Webb were writing during the same era. Instead, the land Algren saw mirrored the moral indifference he found there. The wide open spaces only illusorily suggested an untamed land; the forces of authority were firmly entrenched. Even in the late 1960s, when he went to Dallas to speak against Lyndon Johnson's Vietnam policies, Texas always seemed to give him a heightened sense of being a radical in a conservative country. The Texas that Algren understood was one in which the law—racist, abusive, and corrupt—ruled with an utter ruthlessness and power. It was the man or woman caught hopelessly by the law that attracted Algren as subjects for stories—the young prostitute paying too high a price to avoid hard labor, the mythologized Bonnie and Clyde, the hungry man in a West Texas jail looking at four years on the pea farm at Huntsville. The instinctive need to speak for the powerless, the driving force behind all Algren's work, began in Texas. Later he would sum up this literary vision succinctly: "Literature," he wrote in the early days of the Cold War, "is made upon any occasion when a challenge is put to the legal apparatus by conscience in touch with humanity."

The Texas stories provide a revealing overview-in-microcosm of Algren's writing career. The first seven pieces, written in the 1930s, find our young author attempting various literary devices and innovations in search of his strengths: his assessment that *Somebody in Boots* was "an uneven novel written by an uneven man in a most uneven of American times" can easily apply to many of these early pieces. Originally appearing in the long-forgotten Texas literary magazine *Calithump,* **"Lest the Traplock Click"** is both a gem of boxcar lore never reprinted elsewhere and a fascinating study in techniques that Algren almost immediately abandoned. The narrative itself shows a verbal gift not yet shaped and controlled; the point of view of the college man, expressing impatience with the uneducated hobo, was a mistake Algren would never repeat. Most significantly, the story is overtly autobiographical: the hero, Jonathan, is a college-educated vagabond like Algren himself, who is finally able to return to a hot bath in his family's middle-class home; Algren learned almost immediately to disguise such obviously autobiographical elements in his fiction. He always treated themes suited to his own emotional needs, but his work nearly always focused on the outside world and depicted characters who were very, very different from himself.

"So Help Me," his first success, was another matter. Although the victim, David, was similar to Algren—a young Jewish man from the North carrying a watch and a suitcase—there autobiography ceased. A monologue told in a Southern transient vernacular, the story reveals David only from the point of view of his companions—as someone to be used and then killed when he gets in the way. The narrator's shrewdness in structuring his tale to gain the sympathy of the big-league lawyer Breckenridge and to shift blame onto his partner suggests the subtlety of vision that Algren later brought to his portraits of lost people in his finest work. Algren would often return to the dilemma of the man who must choose between informing or being sent up himself. **"So Help Me"** is one of Algren's finest stories, easily a great part of the reason that Larry McMurtry wrote some thirty-five years after it appeared that Algren still held the best literary claim on the Rio Grande Valley.

But to judge from handwritten drafts **"So Help Me"** was written quickly, in an uninterrupted stream, and Algren was not, in the 1930s, able to regularly conjure up such impressive narrative feats. The following year in Alpine he wrote a number of third-person narratives that he later worked into the novel: **"Kewpie Doll,"** included here more for its portrait of West Texas townspeople looting the freight trains than for its mastery of the short story genre, has the feeling of a folk tale, while the glimpse into the lives of ranch hands in **"Holiday in Texas"** includes a direct attempt to inject the rhetoric of proletarian realism into his fiction. Algren quickly abandoned this rhetoric as an impediment to his art—but not before publishing relat-

ed ideas in *Somebody in Boots,* which may help to explain, to a small degree, his lifelong dissatisfaction with the book.

Yet that novel, and its excerpts **"If You Must Use Profanity," "A Place to Lie Down,"** and **"Thundermug"** in *The Texas Stories,* provide an important record of the outcasts' daily experiences in the 1930s—a relentless struggle to keep clean, avoid violence, sleep unmolested, and eat something better than garbage. In response to the despair wrought by the Depression, American writers actively articulated the experiences of the dispossessed, from the plight of the migrant workers in James Agee's *Let Us Now Praise Famous Men* and Steinbeck's *The Grapes of Wrath* to the jobless people dancing for a living in *They Shoot Horses, Don't They?* by Horace McCoy. The era's economic victims occupied a generation of writers from Caldwell and Cantwell to Herbst and Hemingway; in Texas, Edward Anderson left *Hungry Men* and *Thieves Like Us.* But with the notable exceptions of Edward Dahlberg's *Bottom Dogs,* Edwin Newhouse's *You Can't Sleep Here,* and Tom Kromer's forgotten period classic, *Waiting for Nothing,* relatively few unflinchingly and graphically depicted the gruesome conditions endured by the human beings who made up the bottommost level of society. Today, when homelessness has been accepted as a fact of life rather than as widespread evidence of a societal breakdown, it can only be hoped that writers of our era will document the wretched existences of the hundreds of thousands of homeless Americans as vividly and sensitively as Algren did in *Somebody in Boots.*

Algren continued to write about people from the lower tier of society throughout his career, and by the late forties, settled in Chicago, he had won a number of literary awards for short fiction and had masterfully explored the violent underworld of juvenile delinquency and prostitution in *Never Come Morning* (1942). *The Texas Stories* includes two stories of this period, taken from the successful collection *The Neon Wilderness* (1947). Written shortly before Algren began work on the National Book Award-winning *Man with the Golden Arm* (1949), **"Depend on Aunt Elly,"** springing from his army days near Paris, evokes the long-fingered hand of Texas authority reaching even into the love relationship of the outcast woman, Wilma; **"El Presidente de Méjico"** was a late reworking of the prisoner's death in the Brewster County jail that shows Algren as a first-person narrator with the role of the victim—as well as the hapless Jewish Wolfe—assigned to someone else, in the author's now-characteristic habit. Both of these stories are excellent examples of the thoroughly modern and poetic naturalism for which Algren is most widely known and celebrated.

After the publication of *A Walk on the Wild Side* in 1956, Algren took a twenty-year break from the novel form. During that time, he described himself as a journalist, pursuing travel writing, criticism, short fiction, book introductions, and essays. The last two pieces in *The Texas Stories,* written during the late sixties and early seventies, are evocations of the Texas past that illustrate Algren's continuing affinity with the state over the decades. In

"After the Buffalo," which originally appeared as the introduction to *The True Story of Bonnie and Clyde,* Algren again displays his fascination with characters from uprooted and displaced social groups. Describing the historical and social context of the outlaws, Algren sees them as relatives of Cass McKay and Dove Linkhorn from *A Walk on the Wild Side,* "outcasts of the cotton frontier," descendants of fiddle players who drank from the jug and either fought for the Confederacy or sat out the Civil War in their backwater cabins because they didn't want to work for the man on either side. To Algren, Bonnie and Clyde were anachronistic bank robbers, misplaced in an era when the really big bucks came out of perfectly legitimate transactions with the fountain pen, and he takes pleasure in showing that the public response to these two products of the dust bowl was in many ways as outrageous and mean-spirited as the hunted themselves.

"The Last Carousel," which earned second prize in *Playboy*'s annual fiction contest in 1972, brings this small collection full circle, for **The Texas Stories** moves from the intense anger of Algren's proletarian writings to the controlled naturalism that he practiced so brilliantly during the forties, to the lyric nostalgia, laced with absurdist humor, that was so uniquely Algren in his later years. In this last evocation of the gas station and his travels through Texas, Algren looked back with a gentle humor and a kind of awe for a world long past that he had been permitted to experience. The looming horror of death that once haunted **"So Help Me"** was gone. In Algren's final vision, at the end, there is only a long figure, poised above a crowded backwater carnival, riding a Ferris wheel in a swirling Texas dust storm.

In the more than sixty years since Algren first visited Texas, the ranches and stockyards and railways have given way to skyscrapers and airports and freeways and brand-new subdivisions. The state has in many ways completely re-invented itself in the national imagination, gaining an updated urban image as hundreds of thousands have come from out of state to take advantage of its easy business climate and Sunbelt living. Conditions in the jails are reported, fortunately, to have improved. Texas has long been a land known for both its millionaires and its grinding poverty, however, and a modern landscape of private shopping malls and underground downtown walkways and gate-guarded communities and the individualized transport of the automobile has served ingeniously to keep the people without plumbing or sanitation in shacks along the Rio Grande, or the thousands in Texas cities who have no place to lie down or rest, from entering meaningfully into the public view or consciousness. Their continued presence in a land of such plenty, however, suggests that the desperation Algren was writing about hasn't really changed, in human terms, that much at all.

FURTHER READING

Criticism

Edwards, Thomas R. "Underground Man." *New York Review of Books* XXXVII, No. 11 (June 28, 1990): 22-4.

> Provides an overview of Algren's life and career and discusses mixed critical reaction to his work.

Harkness, James David. "Nelson Algren: 60 Years from Mack Avenue, He Still Likes 'The People Underneath'." *Detroit Free Press* (May 26, 1974): 6-9.

> Feature article based on an interview with Algren in which Harkness discusses Algren's life and career.

Leonard, John. "Monsters, Butter-Pastry, Saltines." *National Review* 15, No. 26 (December 31, 1963): 571.

> Negative review of *Nelson Algren's Own Book of Lonesome Monsters.* Leonard states that four stories, including Algren's, do not belong in the anthology and the remaining pieces are "severely flawed."

Interviews

Baker, John F. Interview with Nelson Algren. *Publishers Weekly* 204, No. 26 (December 31, 1973): 12-13.

> Interview conducted following the publication of Algren's *The Last Carousel.* The author discusses such topics as critical reception to his works in Europe and contemporary American writers he admires.

Perlongo, Robert A. Interview with Nelson Algren. *Chicago Review* II, No. 3 (Autumn 1957): 92-8.

> Algren discusses such subjects as *The Man with the Golden Arm,* meeting Ernest Hemingway, contemporary American fiction, and his writing technique.

Ray, David. "A Talk on the Wild Side: A Bowl of Coffee with Nelson Algren." *The Reporter* 20, No. 12 (June 11, 1959): 31-3.

> Interview in which Algren discusses his association with Ernest Hemingway, whether academic studies are necessary to be a writer, and characters in *The Neon Wilderness.*

Additional coverage of Algren's life and career is contained in the following sources published by The Gale Group: *Contemporary Authors,* Vols. 13-16, 103, rev. ed.; *Contemporary Authors New Revision Series,* Vol. 20; *Contemporary Literary Criticism,* Vols. 4, 10, 33; *Dictionary of Literary Biography,* Vol. 9; *Dictionary of Literary Biography Yearbook: 1981, 1982*; and *Major 20th-Century Writers,* Vol. 1.

"Sonny's Blues"
James Baldwin

The following entry presents criticism on Baldwin's short story "Sonny's Blues." For a discussion of Baldwin's complete short fiction, see *Short Story Criticism,* Volume 10.

INTRODUCTION

One of the most eminent writers in post-World War II American literature, Baldwin garnered widespread critical acclaim for his story "Sonny's Blues," which was published in the collection *Going to Meet the Man.* Set in the early 1950s in New York City, the story is narrated by an unnamed man who relates his attempts to come to terms with his long estranged brother Sonny, a jazz musician. In this work, Baldwin drew on many of his own experiences to explore the issues of racial conflict, individual identity, and the complexity of human motivations.

Plot and Major Characters

In "Sonny's Blues" a conservative black teacher narrates his attempts to comprehend the alienated perspective of his brother Sonny, an unemployed jazz pianist and occasional heroin user. Upon hearing that Sonny has been arrested for possession of narcotics, the unnamed teacher refuses to become involved. As the story proceeds, he is led to a personal awareness of human frailty through the death of his young daughter. Recalling how his mother sympathetically comforted his father when his father's brother was intentionally hit and killed by a car driven by a drunken white man, the narrator acts on his mother's request that he offer the same sympathy to Sonny in times of duress. Listening to Sonny's jazz solo at a bar in Greenwich Village, the narrator is finally led to an understanding of universal suffering and of his brother's attitudes.

Major Themes

In "Sonny's Blues" Baldwin presents an existential world in which suffering characterizes man's basic state. The story's principal characters, in addition to struggling through an absurd world devoid of inherent meaning, must also persevere in a society that tolerates racism. Baldwin addresses these issues by employing metaphors of darkness and anxiety, incorporating images of confinement, and offering portraits of life in contemporary Harlem. Music in "Sonny's Blues," specifically jazz music, is likewise utilized as a controlling metaphor to examine questions of heritage, society, and racial relations in America. Music as a means of communication between people is

also considered a meaningful theme in "Sonny's Blues." Additional themes include brotherly love, familial relationships, and, as with Baldwin's longer works, the search for identity, specifically what it means to be an African-American male in mid-twentieth century American society.

Critical Reception

"Sonny's Blues" is considered one of Baldwin's most compelling and effective pieces of short fiction, as well as a deft portrayal of the substantial role jazz music has played in American society in general and in the African-American community in particular. Many critics have evaluated "Sonny's Blues" against Baldwin's longer works, focusing on the themes of suffering and redemption. A few critics have noted inconsistencies in the story's tone; others have argued that Baldwin's treatment of social and political issues is too heavy-handed. Even so, "Sonny's Blues" is considered one of Baldwin's finest works, a succinct and moving exploration of familial and racial relations in modern American society.

CRITICISM

John M. Reilly (essay date 1970)

SOURCE: "'Sonny's Blues': James Baldwin's Image of Black Community," in *Negro American Literature Forum,* Vol. 4, No. 2, July, 1970, pp. 56-60.

[*In the following essay, which is generally regarded as among the most influential treatments of "Sonny's Blues," Reilly examines Baldwin's sympathetic evocation of black community.*]

A critical commonplace holds that James Baldwin writes better essays than he does fiction or drama; nevertheless, his leading theme—the discovery of identity—is nowhere presented more successfully than in the short story **"Sonny's Blues."** Originally published in *Partisan Review* in 1957 and reprinted in the collection of stories *Going to Meet the Man* in 1965, **"Sonny's Blues"** not only states dramatically the motive for Baldwin's famous polemics in the cause of Black freedom, but it also provides an esthetic linking his work, in all literary genres, with the cultures of the Black ghetto.

The fundamental movement of **"Sonny's Blues"** represents the slow accommodation of a first-person narrator's consciousness to the meaning of his younger brother's way of life. The process leads Baldwin's readers to a sympathetic engagement with the young man by providing a knowledge of the human motives of the youths whose lives normally are reported to others only by their inclusion in statistics of school dropout rates, drug usage, and unemployment.

The basis of the story, however, and its relationship to the purpose of Baldwin's writing generally, lies in his use of the Blues as a key metaphor. The unique quality of the Blues is its combination of personal and social significance in a lyric encounter with history. "The Blues-singer describes first-person experiences, but only such as are typical of the community and such as each individual in the community might have. The singer never sets himself against the community or raises himself above it." Thus, in the story of Sonny and his brother an intuition of the meaning of the Blues repairs the relationship between the two men who have chosen different ways to cope with the menacing ghetto environment, and their reconciliation through the medium of this Afro-American musical form extends the meaning of the individual's Blues until it becomes a metaphor of Black community.

Sonny's life explodes into his older brother's awareness when the story of his arrest for peddling and using heroin is reported in the newspaper. Significantly the mass medium of the newspaper with the impersonal story in it of a police bust is the only way the brothers have of communicating at the opening of the story. While the narrator says that because of the newspaper report Sonny "became real to me again," their relationship is only vestigially personal, for he "couldn't find any room" for the news "anywhere inside . . .".

In the story of Sonny and his brother an intuition of the meaning of the Blues repairs the relationship between the two men who have chosen different ways to cope with the menacing ghetto environment.

—John M. Reilly

While he had had his suspicions about how Sonny was spending his life, the narrator had put them aside with rationalizations about how Sonny was, after all, a good kid. Nothing to worry about. In short, the storyteller reveals that along with his respectable job as an algebra teacher he had assumed a conventional way of thinking as a defense against recognizing that his own brother ran the risk of "coming to nothing." Provoked by the facts of Sonny's arrest to observe his students, since they are the same age as Sonny must have been when he first had heroin, he notices for the first time that their laughter is disenchanted rather than good-humored. In it he hears his brother, and perhaps himself. At this point in the story his opinion is evidently that Sonny and many of the young students are beaten and he, fortunately, is not.

The conventionality of the narrator's attitude becomes clearer when he encounters a nameless friend of Sonny's, a boy from the block who fears he may have touted Sonny onto heroin by telling him, truthfully, how great it made him feel to be high. This man who "still spent hours on the street corner . . . high and raggy" explains what will happen to Sonny because of his arrest. After they send him someplace and try to cure him, they'll let Sonny loose, that's all. Trying to grasp the implication the narrator asks: "You mean he'll never kick the habit. Is that what you mean?" He feels there should be some kind of renewal, some hope. A man should be able to bring himself up by his will, convention says. Convention also says that behavior like Sonny's is deliberately self-destructive. "Tell me," he asks the friend, "why does he want to die?" Wrong again. "Don't nobody want to die," says the friend, "ever."

Agitated though he is about Sonny's fate the narrator doesn't want to feel himself involved. His own position on the middle-class ladder of success is not secure, and the supporting patterns of thought in his mind are actually rather weak. Listening to the nameless friend explain about Sonny while they stand together in front of a bar blasting "black and bouncy" music from its door, he senses something that frightens him. "All this was carrying me some place I didn't want to go. I certainly didn't want to know how it felt. It filled everything, the people, the houses, the music, the dark, quicksilver barmaid, with menace; and this menace was their reality."

Eventually a great personal pain—the loss of a young daughter—breaks through the narrator's defenses and makes him seek out his brother, more for his own comfort than for Sonny's. "My trouble made his real," he says. In that remark is a prefiguring of the meaning the Blues will develop.

It is only a prefiguring, however, for the time Sonny is released from the state institution where he had been confined, the narrator's immediate need for comfort has passed. When he meets Sonny he is in control of himself, but very shortly he is flooded with complex feelings that make him feel again the menace of the 110th Street bar where he had stood with Sonny's friend. There is no escaping a feeling of icy dread, so he must try to understand.

As the narrator casts his mind back over his and Sonny's past, he gradually identifies sources of his feelings. First he recalls their parents, especially concentrating on an image of his family on a typical Sunday. The scene is one of security amidst portentousness. The adults sit without talking, "but every face looks darkening, like the sky outside." The children sit about, maybe one half asleep and another being stroked on the head by an adult. The darkness frightens a child and he hopes "that the hand which strokes his forehead will never stop." The child knows, however, that it will end, and now grown-up he recalls one of the meanings of the darkness is in the story his mother told him of the death of his uncle, run over on a dark country road by a car full of drunken white men. Never had his companion, the boy's father, "seen anything as dark as that road after the lights of the car had gone away." The narrator's mother had attempted to apply her tale of his father's grief at the death of his own brother to the needs of their sons. They can't protect each other, she knows, "but," she says to the narrator about Sonny, "you got to let him know you's *there*."

Thus, guilt for not fulfilling their mother's request and a sense of shared loneliness partially explain the older brother's feeling toward Sonny. Once again, however, Baldwin stresses the place of the conventional set of the narrator's mind in the complex of feelings as he has him recall scenes from the time when Sonny had started to become a jazz musician. The possibility of Sonny's being a jazz rather than a classical musician had "seemed—beneath him, somehow." Trying to understand the ambition, the narrator had asked if Sonny meant to play like Louis Armstrong, only to be told that Charlie Parker was the model. Hard as it is to believe, he had never heard of Bird until Sonny mentioned him. This ignorance reveals more than a gap between fraternal generations. It represents a cultural chasm. The narrator's inability to understand Sonny's choice of a musical leader shows his alienation from the mood of the post-war bebop sub-culture. In its hip style of dress, its repudiation of middle-brow norms, and its celebration of esoteric manner the bebop sub-culture made overtly evident its underlying significance as an assertion of Black identity. Building upon a restatement of Afro-American

music, bebop became an expression of a new self-awareness in the ghettos by a strategy of elaborate non-conformity. In committing himself to the bebop sub-culture Sonny attempted to make a virtue of the necessity of the isolation imposed upon him by his color. In contrast, the narrator's failure to understand what Sonny was doing indicates that his response to the conditions imposed upon him by racial status was to try to assimilate himself as well as he could into the mainstream American culture. For the one, heroin addiction sealed his membership in the exclusive group; for the other, adoption of individualistic attitudes marked his allegiance to the historically familiar ideal of transcending caste distinctions by entering into the middle class.

Following his way Sonny became wrapped in the vision that rose from his piano, stopped attending school, and hung around with a group of musicians in Greenwich Village. His musical friends became Sonny's family, replacing the brother who had felt that Sonny's choice of his style of life was the same thing as dying, and for all practical purposes the brothers were dead to each other in the extended separation before Sonny's arrest on narcotics charges.

The thoughts revealing the brothers' family history and locating the sources of the narrator's complex feelings about Sonny all occur in the period after Sonny is released from the state institution. Though he has ceased to evade thoughts of their relationship, as he had done in the years when they were separated and had partially continued to do after Sonny's arrest, the narrator has a way to go before he can become reconciled to Sonny. His recollections of the past only provide his consciousness with raw feeling.

The next development—perception—begins with a scene of a revival meeting conducted on the sidewalk of Seventh Avenue, beneath the narrator's window. Everyone on the street has been watching such meetings all his life, but the narrator from his window, passersby on the street, and Sonny from the edge of the crowd all watch again. It isn't because they expect something different this time. Rather it is a familiar moment of communion for them. In basic humanity one of the sanctified sisters resembles the down-and-outer watching her, "a cigarette between her heavy, chapped lips, her hair a cuckoo's nest, her face scarred and swollen from many beatings. . . . Perhaps," the narrator thinks, "they both knew this, which was why, when, as rarely, they addressed each other, they addressed each other as Sister." The point impresses both the narrator and Sonny, men who should call one another "Brother," for the music of the revivalists seems to "soothe a poison" out of them.

The perception of this moment extends nearly to conception in the conversation between the narrator and Sonny that follows it. It isn't a comfortable discussion. The narrator still is inclined to voice moral judgments of the experiences and people Sonny tries to talk about, but he is making an honest effort to relate to his brother now and reminds himself to be quiet and listen. What he hears is that Sonny equates the feeling of hearing the revivalist sister sing with the sensation of heroin in the veins. "It makes you feel—in control. Sometimes you got to have that feeling." It isn't primarily drugs that Sonny is talking about, though, and when the narrator curbs his tongue to let him go on, Sonny explains the real subject of his thoughts.

Again, the facts of Sonny's experience contradict the opinion of "respectable" people. He did not use drugs to escape from suffering, he says. He knows as well as anyone that there's no way to avoid suffering, but what you can do is "try all kinds of ways to keep from drowning in it, to keep on top of it, and to make it seem . . . like *you*." That is, Sonny explains, you can earn your suffering, make it seem "like you did something . . . and now you're suffering for it."

The idea of meriting your suffering is a staggering one. In the face of it the narrator's inclination to talk about "will power and how life could be—well, beautiful," is blunted, because he senses that by directly confronting degradation Sonny has asserted what degree of will was possible to him, and perhaps that kept him alive.

At this point in the story it is clear that there are two themes emerging. The first is the theme of the individualistic narrator's gradual discovery of the significance of his brother's life. This theme moves to a climax in the final scene of the story when Sonny's music impresses the narrator with a sense of the profound feeling it contains. From the perspective of that final scene, however, the significance of the Blues itself becomes a powerful theme.

The insight into suffering that Sonny displays establishes his priority in knowledge. Thus, he reverses the original relationship between the brothers, assumes the role of the elder, and proceeds to lead his brother, by means of the Blues, to a discovery of self in community.

As the brothers enter the jazz club where Sonny is to play, he becomes special. Everyone has been waiting for him, and each greets him familiarly. Equally special is the setting—dark except for a spotlight which the musicians approach as if it were a circle of flame. This is a sanctified spot where Sonny is to testify to the power of souls to commune in the Blues.

Baldwin explicates the formula of the Blues by tracing the narrator's thoughts while Sonny plays. Many people, he thinks, don't really hear music being played except so far as they invest it with "personal, private, vanishing evocations." He might be thinking of himself, referring to his having come to think of Sonny through the suffering of his own personal loss. The man who makes the music engages in a spiritual creation, and when he succeeds, the creation belongs to all present, "his triumph, when he triumphs, is ours."

In the first set Sonny doesn't triumph, but in the second, appropriately begun by "Am I Blue," he takes the lead and begins to form a musical creation. He becomes, in the

narrator's words, "part of the family again." What family? First of all that of his fellow musicians. Then, of course, the narrator means to say that their fraternal relationship is at last fulfilled as their mother hoped it to be. But there is yet a broader meaning too. Like the sisters at the Seventh Avenue revival meeting Sonny and the band are not saying anything new. Still they are keeping the Blues alive by expanding it beyond the personal lyric into a statement of the glorious capacity of human beings to take the worst and give it a form of their own choosing.

At this point the narrator synthesizes feelings and perception into a conception of the Blues. He realizes Sonny's Blues can help everyone who listens be free, in his own case free of the conventions that had alienated him from Sonny and that dimension of Black culture represented in Sonny's style of living. Yet at the same time he knows the world outside of the Blues moment remains hostile.

The implicit statement of the esthetics of the Blues in this story throws light upon much of Baldwin's writing. The first proposition of the esthetics that we can infer from **"Sonny's Blues"** is that suffering is the prior necessity. Integrity of expression comes from "paying your dues." This is a point Baldwin previously made in *Giovanni's Room* (1956) and which he elaborated in the novel *Another Country* (1962).

The second implicit proposition of the Blues esthetics is that while the form is what it's all about, the form is transitory. The Blues is an art in process and in that respect alien from any conception of fixed and ideal forms. This will not justify weaknesses in an artist's work, but insofar as Baldwin identifies his writing with the art of the singers of Blues it suggests why he is devoted to representation, in whatever genre, of successive moments of expressive feeling and comparatively less concerned with achieving a consistent overall structure.

The final proposition of the esthetics in the story **"Sonny's Blues"** is that the Blues functions as an art of communion. It is popular rather than elite, worldly rather than otherwise. The Blues is expression in which one uses the skill he has achieved by practice and experience in order to reach toward others. It is this proposition that gives the Blues its metaphoric significance. The fraternal reconciliation brought about through Sonny's music is emblematic of a group's coming together, because the narrator learns to love his brother freely while he discovers the value of a characteristically Afro-American assertion of life-force. Taking Sonny on his own terms he must also abandon the ways of thought identified with middle-class position which historically has signified for Black people the adoption of "white" ways.

An outstanding quality of the Black literary tradition in America is its attention to the interdependence of personal and social experience. Obviously necessity has fostered this virtue. Black authors cannot luxuriate in the assumption that there is such a thing as a purely private life. James Baldwin significantly adds to this aspect of the tradition in **"Sonny's Blues"** by showing that artful expression of personal yet typical experience is one way to freedom.

Sherley Anne Williams (essay date 1972)

SOURCE: "The Black Musician: The Black Hero as Light Bearer," in *Give Birth to Brightness: A Thematic Study in Neo-Black Literature,* The Dial Press, 1972, pp. 135-52.

[*In the following essay, Williams analyzes the figure of the musician in African-American literature, concluding that in Baldwin's fiction it functions as "the embodiment of alienation and estrangement, which the figure of the artist becomes in much of twentieth century literature."*]

The Drifters are in the fetid bosom of Manhattan
Rocking the Apollo like an exploding battleship:
The bobbing Black crowd reach long upward
The short-skirted young girls dog in the aisles . . .
    The Drifters are in the big Apple tonight
sing us a song . . . SANG!

     . . . . .

When I see them strut to the foot lights, faintly
smiling amongst themselves, giving measured "cool"
    response
to the screaming, the dancing, the reaching, and then
    looking
into the crowd and darkness, swagger a retreat with
    that
Elemental sexuality (that has been our only hope for
    so long)
I love those black bastards with all the heart I dare.

               David Henderson
            from "Neon Diaspora"
                Black Fire

The conflict with whites over rights, privileges and status has played a large and important part in the history of Black people in this country. This is a commonplace among historians, sociologists, political scientists and others who deal with the negro problem. It has been often and, sometimes, unfortunately, a commonplace among Black writers. The racial conflict in its many ramifications—what racial oppression has done to Blacks and whites, the ways in which Blacks confront and seek to overcome that oppression, etc.—narrows the perspective from which one can view literary characters. For, as a major theme, racial conflict, no matter how radical or startling the situations or solutions, limits even multidimensional characters to roles as either part of the solution or part of the problem. The history of Blacks, and whites, also, is used as a prism which refracts in virtual isolation only a small part of the experience which has gone into making those much entwined histories.

The complexities of the collective Black experience have always had their most valid and moving expression in Black music; music is the chief artifact created out of that experience. Where Black music and Black musicians are used in literature as vehicles for thematic development or as subject matter, however, they are generally touched upon lightly and rarely explored as a theme deserving of individual and primary treatment. Most often, the Black musician and the music he creates are allied with a hedonistic, often raffish, sometimes shiftless way of life which is in conflict with or depicted in contrast to conventional morality and respectability. In novels published during the first three decades of the twentieth century by James Weldon Johnson, Claude McKay and Langston Hughes, the Black music of the period provides a picturesque backdrop, an exotic framework within which the characters attempt to work out their individual destinies.

McKay in *Home to Harlem* (1928) and Hughes in *Not Without Laughter* (1930) make use of the "jazz life"—the rowdy subculture of lower-income Black communities—first characterized by Johnson in *The Autobiography of an Ex-Colored Man* (1912) and popularized by the white negrophile, Carl Van Vechten, in *Nigger Heaven* (1926) as a demi-world where music, dancing, violence and crime rage rampant. Black music becomes, in McKay and Hughes, a symbol of liberation from a stifling respectability and materialistic conventionality which have an odor of decay about them. McKay is content with implying this conflict through the use of the jazz life as a framework for depicting the central characters, Jake and Ray, in *Home to Harlem.*

Unlike McKay's novel, Hughes's *Not Without Laughter* makes a very direct use of music as a symbol of contention, personifying the struggle in the characters of Harriett and Jimboy whose love of secular Black music estranges them from the pious Hagar and the materialistic Tempy, to whom the blues is a godless, vulgar music. Caught between these opposing forces are the young protagonist, Sandy, and his mother, Anjee. Jimboy and Harriett, Sandy's father and his maternal aunt, are laughter and singing; they act out their belief that there is more to life than working for the white man and praising God. This makes them, in the view of Hagar, Sandy's grandmother, and Tempy, another maternal aunt, shiftless and immoral. Hagar's religion is based on forgiveness and turning the other cheek. Heaven is for her the ultimate happiness; she looks for neither happiness nor fun in the earthly world. The gaiety and desire to be near bright lights and laughter, which is so much a part of the nature of her youngest daughter, Harriett, finds no echoing response in her. For Tempy, religion is a means of expressing her rising status in the world; "refinement" in deportment, dress and worship is her way of signaling her economic distance from her rural, poverty-stricken origins. Blues and ragtime are not so much immoral as niggerish, manifestations of the very characteristics which Tempy thinks are uncultured and ignorant and from which, in her upward climb, she disassociates herself. Both Hagar and Tempy believe that only in work can Black people find salvation; for Hagar, salvation is spiritual, for Tempy it is material.

Anjee, Hagar's second daughter, is, in nature, somewhat like her mother. She is pious and generous, but more phlegmatic and less far seeing. She yearns toward the gaiety and laughter of her husband, is in fact fascinated by them, and can no more stop loving Jimboy than she can willingly stop breathing. Despite the fact that, after almost ten years of being left behind as Jimboy wanders from town to town and job to job, she does pack up and join him, her own nature remains unchanged by her contact with the flame that is Jimboy. She is, if anything, duller, more plodding at the novel's end than at its beginning.

Sandy is influenced by the opposing forces and he achieves a synthesis which allows him to take the best from the warring life styles. Despite the hardships involved, he decides to return to school. Hughes, however, makes it clear that it is not a step in the status-seeking climb toward white respectability which motivates Sandy's choice:

> ' . . . I'm going back to my classes in September. . . . I'm through with elevators.'

> Jimboy! Jimboy! Like Jimboy! something inside him warned, quitting work with no money, uncaring.

> 'Not like Jimboy,' Sandy countered against himself. 'Not like my father, always wanting to go somewhere. I'd get as tired of traveling all the time as I do of running this elevator up and down day after day. . . . I'm more like Harriett—not wanting to be a servant at the mercies of white people forever. . . . I want to do something for myself, by myself. . . . Free. . . . I want a house to live in, too, when I'm older—like Tempy and Mr. Sile's. . . . But I wouldn't want to be like Tempy's friends—or her husband, dull and colorless, putting all his money away in a white bank, ashamed of colored people.'

Characteristically, Hughes amplifies Sandy's decision through a further use of the symbol of Black music.

> Clowns! Jazzers! Band of dancers! . . . But was that why Negroes were poor, because they were dancers, jazzers, clowns? . . . The other way round would be better: dancers because of their poverty; singers because they suffered; laughing all the time because they must forget. . . . It's more like that, thought Sandy.

> A band of dancers. . . . Black dancers—captured in a white world. . . . Dancers of the spirit, too. Each Black dreamer a captured dancer of the spirit.

Music is refuge, release, expression. But Hughes and McKay make no attempt to go beyond the relatively simple equation that Black music is Black escape from the deadening restraints of white civilization. They make no further attempt to explore the themes presented by the Black musician or his music. In this, they depart from the path first tentatively explored in Johnson's novel. For Johnson, in the fictional *Autobiography of an Ex-Colored Man,* depicts the losing battle of a half-white musician turned businessman who struggles to affirm himself in the heritage and culture of his mother's people. His hope of creating a place for Black music among serious Western classical music is not enough to compensate for his own

lack of strength. The nameless central character finally trades his Black musical heritage with its attendant pain, suffering and humiliation for the less terrifying but more profitable life of a white businessman. For the character, this retreat into passing for white is a defeat which he recognizes as his own willingness to accept the non-threatening aspects of his heritage—Black music and the supposed Black exoticism—and his lack of the psychological and physical strength to withstand the terrifying forms which racism often takes, even though these forms are also a part of the Black heritage. Music is a metaphor and symbol standing in both its secular and sacred forms not only for the immediate Black experience as in McKay and Hughes, but for history and heritage and the acceptance of one's self in a positive and regenerating relationship to that heritage. The protagonist in attempting to garner serious attention and respect for the music seeks to add another dimension to the image of a rude boisterous music created by a poverty-stricken, ignorant people.

It is again tempting to try to fit these novels completely within the Western literary tradition of the literature of roguery—the picaresque. Certainly there are elements which might be termed picaresque in all three novels: the episodic plots, the characters of uncertain or nameless origins from the lowest strata of society, the alienation from the larger society which is inherent in their skin color and the chaotic nature of the society, symbolized in the supposed chaos of the music's structure and more accurately suggested by the fact that the music is itself a way of structuring, ordering or relieving the pressures of society's chaos. But to confine the Black musician to the picaresque mode as a means of interpretation is to obscure an essential quality of his image. The Black musician, the jazz, blues or gospel artist, in crystallizing and synthesizing his own experience and that of his listeners, exemplifies unity and community rather than the alienation and isolation of the picaro.

The character of the Black musician must be viewed as a figure in the modern Black parallel to the picaresque existence, street life—the jazz life in the novels of Hughes, McKay and Johnson. Even here, in a world pervaded by various types of hustlers and con men, the Black musician stands in a unique light. Although he, like the other figures in the street life, deals in dreams, he is not a hustler for he also deals in love. When he touches, both in technique and emotion, the roots of his own past and the past of his Black listeners, putting them all in touch with the heart's ache and the heart's ease of that group experience, he makes a black light to shine within himself and within them. And it is that light, transitory as it is, which binds them all together.

But what happens in the dance hall, night club, church sanctuary or theatre stage seldom finds a parallel in the outside world. The power and cathartic effect which he has been able to exercise through the use of his instrument or his voice rarely holds sway there. Off the bandstand or outside the church, the musician becomes just another Black who can be messed over, messed with and messed up just like anybody else—perhaps more so. For the sensitivity to emotions, situations and their nuances, which allows him to transmute his life experience into music, also makes him more vulnerable to the more painful and abrasive aspects of that experience. And when he has been rubbed so raw that pain and joy can no longer be translated or transmuted into art, he is very much in trouble.

The Black musician in trouble is the figure which most often appears in Black literature. This growing body of work extends the theme first broached in the novels of Johnson and McKay, the poetry of Sterling Brown and the poetry and fiction of Langston Hughes. In their tentative explorations of the relationship between Black life and Black music—the trials and joys of being Black in the white man's world—they lay the foundation for the portrayal of the musician who brings together the sublime and beautiful, the complex and brutal pieces of his experience in his music and finally is torn apart himself by the very complexity and brutality which he has helped to ameliorate. Clay, the protagonist in *Dutchman,* gives a beautiful summation of this theme when he tells his white antagonist Lula: "If Bessie Smith had killed some white people, she wouldn't have needed that music. She could have talked very straight and plain about the world. No metaphors. No grunts. No wiggles in the dark of her soul. Just straight two and two are four. Money. Power. Luxury. Like that."

There is truth in this view, a limited truth. That pain plays a large part in Black music is evident in the lyrics of the blues, the spirituals, the gospels, in the raw harshness which has been such an important aspect in the development of jazz. Yet, there is the beautiful lyricism of Charlie Parker and John Coltrane which also expresses triumph and transcendence, the sly humor and laughing confidence, the will to make it on through, to work it on out which are also expressed in blues, gospels and spirituals. The former view is predicated upon two assumptions: the first that had the Emancipation Proclamation and the amendments which broadened its effects and meaning been followed in spirit and letter, that ragtime, blues and jazz would never have been created. It sees Black music primarily as a response to an outside stimulus rather than to an inner drive which would have found expression no matter what the circumstance. The second assumption is perhaps more serious for it strikes at the very basis of Black music, its communal roots. It assumes that the music is more an affirmation of self than an affirmation of self in relation to group, that the musician creates an interior monologue rather than a dialogue between and about himself and the group and their past and present. Thus to concur wholeheartedly in Clay's solution is to overlook the fact that killing white people will not necessarily make a Black person love himself or others. A part of the lesson of Clay and Walker is that whatever the relationship between Blacks and whites, Black people must still deal with each other and themselves.

Recognizing that Black life is, in large measure, Black music, several writers have used the musician as a symbol of the centuries of culture and tradition which stand behind American Blacks. The musician, then, becomes a heightened example of what can and does happen to Black people, and his salvation perhaps points the way to theirs. Unlike the other figures in the Life, the musician does not need to be told that his source is the group, the Black context; his music already provides that model. In being recalled to the group, his need is for a spiritual or physical bridge to span the gulf between his music and his life.

The musician in the works of James Baldwin is more than a metaphor; he is the embodiment of alienation and estrangement, which the figure of the artist becomes in much of twentieth century literature.

—Sherley Anne Williams

In Blacksnake Brown, Jane Phillips (*Mojo Hand,* 1965) creates a shamanesque figure who initiates the heroine into the deeper meanings of Black life and experience. The crude vulgar musician, Richie, depicted in *Night Song* (Williams, 1962) is akin to the tortured musical genius described by Clay, as is Ludlow Washington, the blind saxophonist in William Melvin Kelley's *A Drop of Patience* (1965). The latter two are driven in part by a self-hatred which wars with their love of music, that is, their love of Blackness. Richie's personal dilemma is finally resolved in death, a death which is largely predicated upon his own self-destructive traits. Ludlow returns to the group experience which produced him, realizing at the novel's end that the pursuit of fame as a jazz artist in night clubs and concert halls is unimportant compared to the need of Black people for Black musicians who will speak to them and for them in the forums of their own communities. It is also his need, for in order to be at peace with himself he has to be with his own people.

The musician in the works of James Baldwin is more than a metaphor; he is the embodiment of alienation and estrangement, which the figure of the artist becomes in much of twentieth century literature. Most of his characters have at the center of their portrayal an isolation from the society, the culture, even each other. They are also commentaries upon the brutal, emasculating, feared—and fearing—land from which they are so estranged. The musician is also for Baldwin an archetypal figure whose referent is Black lives, Black experiences and Black deaths. He is the hope of making it in America and the bitter mockery of never making it well enough to escape the danger of being Black, the living symbol of alienation from the past and hence from self and the rhythmical link with the mysterious ancestral past. That past and its pain and the transcendence of pain is always an implicit part of the musician's characterization in Baldwin. Music is the medium through which the musician achieves enough under-standing and strength to deal with the past and present hurt.

The short story, **"Sonny's Blues,"** sketches this kind of relationship between the individual and his personal and group history. Sonny is a jazz pianist who has recently returned from a drug cure. The story is set in New York, Harlem, and seems at first glance merely another well-written story about a young Black man trying to become himself, to attain his majority and retain his humanity amid all the traps which have been set to prevent just that. But the simplicity of the tale is only surface deep; in a rising crescendo of thematic complexity, the present struggle is refracted through the age-old pain, the age-old life force. The story is narrated by Sonny's older brother who has found it difficult to understand what music means to Sonny. Sonny's desire to be a jazz musician, which his broth-er associates with the "good-time" life, has created a schism between himself and his more orthodox brother. And be-cause the brother cannot understand what lies between himself and Sonny, he cannot forgive Sonny for Sonny's own pain, which he, for all his seniority, is powerless to ease, or for the pain which their ruptured relationship has caused him. The closing pages of the story are a descrip-tion of the brother's reaction as he listens to Sonny play for the first time.

> All I know about music is that not many people ever really hear it. And even then, on the rare occasions when something opens within, and the music enters, what we mainly hear, or hear corroborated, are personal, private, vanishing evocations. But the man who creates the music is hearing something else, is dealing with the roar rising from the void and imposing order on it as it hits the air. What is evoked in him, then, is of another order, more terrible because it has no words, and triumphant, too, for that same reason. And his triumph, when he triumphs, is ours. I just watched Sonny's face. His face was troubled, he was working hard, but he wasn't with it.

The attempt to once again make it through music brings no instant transformation. Sonny is approaching the center of his life and he cannot know what he will find there. But he understands that if he is to live, he must deal with that dread, that terror, chance the terrifying in order to tri-umph.

> And I had the feeling that, in a way, everyone on the bandstand was waiting for him, both waiting for him and pushing him along. But as I began to watch Creole, I realized that it was Creole who held them all back. He had them on a short rein. Up there, keeping the beat with his whole body, wailing on the fiddle, with his eyes half closed, he was listening to everything, but he was listening to Sonny. He was having a dialogue with Sonny. He wanted Sonny to leave the shoreline and strike out for the deep water. He was Sonny's witness that deep water and drowning were not the same thing—he had been there, and he knew. And he wanted Sonny to know. He was waiting for Sonny to do the things on the keys which would let Creole know that Sonny was in the water.

The musical group, Ellison's "marvel of social organiza-tion," is the catalyst which makes it possible for Sonny to begin to see himself through the music, to play out his own pain through the expression of it.

> And Sonny hadn't been near a piano for over a year. And he wasn't on much better terms with his life, not the life that stretched before him now. . . . And the face I saw on Sonny I'd never seen before. Everything had been burned out of it, and, at the same time, things usually hidden were being burned in, by the fire and fury of the battle which was occurring in him up there.

> Yet, watching Creole's face as they neared the end of the first set, I had the feeling that something had happened, something I hadn't heard. . . . Creole started into something else, it was almost sardonic, it was *Am I Blue.* And, as though he commanded, Sonny began to play. Something began to happen. And Creole let out the reins. The dry, low, black man said something awful on the drums. Creole answered, and the drums talked back. Then the horn insisted, sweet and high, slightly detached perhaps, and Creole listened, commenting now and then, dry, and driving, beautiful and calm and old. Then they all came together again, and Sonny was part of the family again. I could tell this from his face. He seemed to have found, right there beneath his fingers, a damn brand-new piano. It seemed that he couldn't get over it. Then, for awhile, just being happy with Sonny, they seemed to be agreeing with him that brand-new pianos certainly were a gas.

Sonny's music and his life become one and he is fused with the musical group in a relationship which sustains one because it sustains all. And finally, through the music, Sonny's brother begins to understand not so much Sonny, as himself, *his* past, *his* history, *his* traditions and that part of himself which he has in common with Sonny and the long line of people who have gone before them.

> Then Creole stepped forward to remind them that what they were playing was the blues. He hit something in all of them, he hit something in me, myself, and the music tightened and deepened, apprehension began to beat the air. Creole began to tell us what the blues were all about. They were not about anything very new. He and his boys up there were keeping it new, at the risk of ruin, destruction, madness, and death, in order to find new ways to make us listen. For, while the tale of how we suffer, and how we are delighted, and how we may triumph is never new, it always must be heard. There isn't any other tale to tell, it's the only light we've got in all this darkness.

> And this tale, according to that face, that body, those strong hands on those strings, has another aspect in every country, and a new depth in every generation. Listen, Creole seemed to be saying, listen. Now these are Sonny's blues. He made the little black man on the drums know it, and the bright, brown man on the horn. Creole wasn't trying any longer to get Sonny in the water. He was wishing him Godspeed. Then he stepped back, very slowly, filling the air with the immense suggestion that Sonny speak for himself.

Then they all gathered around Sonny, and Sonny played. Every now and again one of them seemed to say, amen. Sonny's fingers filled the air with life, his life. But that life contained so many others. And Sonny went all the way back, he really began with the spare, flat statement of the opening phrase of the song. Then he began to make it his. It was very beautiful because it wasn't hurried and it was no longer a lament. I seemed to hear with what burning he had made it his, with what burning we had yet to make it ours, how we could cease lamenting. Freedom lurked around us and I understood, at last, that he could help us to be free if we would listen, that he would never be free until we did. Yet, there was no battle in his face now. I heard what he had gone through, and would continue to go through until he came to rest in earth. He had made it his: that long line, of which we knew only Mama and Daddy. And he was giving it back, as everything must be given back, so that, passing through death, it can live forever.

It is this then, this intense, almost excruciating, but always sustaining relationship among musicians and between them and their audiences which the musician is meant to evoke. The emphasis is gradually transformed from pain to survival to life. All are linked together by invisible webs, indestructible bonds of tradition and history, and this heritage, once revealed, becomes the necessary regenerative power which makes life possible. One senses this in Rufus, the drummer and central character in the first Book of *Another Country,* for as Baldwin says in describing the last set of Rufus's last gig:

> . . . during the last set, [Rufus] came doubly alive because the saxophone player, who had been way out all night, took off on a terrific solo.
>
> . . . . .
>
> The men on the stand stayed with him, cool and at a little distance, adding and questioning and corroborating, holding it down as well as they could with an ironical self-mockery, but each man knew that the boy was blowing for every one of them

But this relationship is subverted and eventually destroyed by Rufus's involvement with a Southern white woman, Leona, a poor, plain girl-woman whom Baldwin seems to posit as one part of the reality behind the myth of sacred Southern white womanhood. But in grappling with her, Rufus is hedged about by the brutality of the past and his own slender personal resources. The integration of past and present is always on the level of pain and never that of life. The strength which made it possible for his ancestors to endure and to survive that pain is buried somewhere within Rufus, in a place which he does not even realize exists. He becomes more entangled with Leona, wallowing in an ancient source of pain, but never calls upon his family, or his music, the symbols of life, the talismen against death which might have been his salvation—and Leona's. He attempts to use sex as a weapon against her in the same way in which white society has used sex as a weapon against him. The "terrible muscle"

and the "violent deep," the male and female sexual organs in Baldwin's works, are always, when used as weapons, self-destructive. Leona is driven insane by Rufus's brutal treatment of her. Rufus, weighted down with guilt and the pain of both past and present, commits suicide.

Baldwin attempts to establish a contrasting structure between this relationship and the relationship which develops between Vivaldo, the white boy who had been his best friend, and Ida, his beloved younger sister. Rufus and Leona end their lives in despair and death, while Vivaldo and Ida, drawn together at first by the love they both had for Rufus, finally achieve an uneasy peace with each other. It is a peace, which, though hard won and perhaps easily lost, is based on a deeper understanding of themselves and each other and their relationship. Rufus returns to the past and cannot find his way out again. But Vivaldo, in his relationship with Ida, tries to move into the future, to break the mold of degradation and humiliation which has usually characterized the relationship of white men with Black women.

Rufus's struggle informs the other two Books in the novel, and the characters are defined and distinguished through their relationship to him. The strength of the first Book, however, its technical and thematic brilliance, finds only dim echoes in these later portions and it is the agony of Rufus as he seeks to reconcile the past hate with the present love and his tragic failure which dominates the novel.

In *Blues for Mister Charlie,* the outline sketched in **"Sonny's Blues"** becomes a tumultuous and vivid portrayal of that history and tradition which has made Black experience Black life. Richard has lost touch with the group, abused himself and his tradition and fallen back on drugs as a means of making it through the world. Because of his drug thing, he is out of step, out of time and the play, in part, deals with Richard's attempt to get back in step, to find that lost group rhythm.

Suzy Bernstein Goldman (essay date 1974)

SOURCE: "James Baldwin's 'Sonny's Blues': A Message in Music," in *Negro American Literature Forum,* Vol. 8, No. 3, Fall, 1974, pp. 231-33.

[*In the following essay, Goldman examines Baldwin's use of musical structure and leitmotifs in the narrative and dialogue of "Sonny's Blues."*]

In **"Sonny's Blues"** theme, form, and image blend into perfect harmony and rise to a thundering crescendo. The story, written in 1957 but carrying a vital social message for us today, tells of two black brothers' struggle to understand one another. The older brother, a straight-laced Harlem algebra teacher, is the unnamed narrator who represents, in his anonymity, everyman's brother; the younger man is Sonny, a jazz pianist who, when the story opens, has just been arrested for peddling and using heroin. As in so much of Baldwin's fiction, chronological time is upset.

Instead the subject creates its own form. In this story of a musician, four time sequences mark four movements while the leitmotifs of this symphonic lesson in communication are provided by the images of sound. Musical terms along with words like "hear" and "listen" give the title a double meaning. This story about communication between people then reaches its climax when the narrator finally hears his brother's sorrow in his music, hears, that is, Sonny's blues.

The story begins when the narrator learns of Sonny's arrest in a most impersonal manner—by reading the newspaper. Yet this rude discovery sounds the initial note in these two brothers' growing closeness. The shock of recognition forces the narrator to confront his past refusal to accept the miserable truths around him. For too long, he admits, he had been "talking about algebra to a lot of boys who might, every one of them . . . be popping off needles every time they went to the head." He completes his own first lesson in understanding and takes his first step towards Sonny when he begins to hear his own students:

> I listened to the boys outside. . . . Their laughter struck me for perhaps the first time. It was not the joyous laughter which . . . one associates with children. It was mocking and insular, its intent to denigrate. It was disenchanted, and in this, also, lay the authority of their curses. Perhaps I was listening to them because I was thinking about my brother and in them I heard my brother. And myself.

> One boy was whistling a tune, at once very complicated and very simple, it seemed to be pouring out of him as though he were a bird, and it sounded very cool and moving through that harsh, bright air, only just holding its own through all those other sounds.

This last boy particularly suggests Sonny, the young man who makes himself heard and transcends the disenchantment, the darkness, with his song. Then immediately the narrator encounters another surrogate brother in Sonny's old friend who has come to the school to bring the news. Conversation between the two is guarded and hostile until the narrator, although he has never liked his brother's friend, begins to hear the boy and to feel guilty for never having heard him before, "for never having supposed that the poor bastard had a story of his own, much less a sad one." Standing together outside a bar while a juke box sounds from within, the friend confesses that he first described to Sonny the effects of heroin. Again the narrator psychologically retreats. Fearful of learning about heroin and too anxious himself to help Sonny, he timidly asks what the arrest means. The friend's reply is telling. "Listen," he shouts. "They'll let him out and then it'll just start all over again. That's what I mean." The two part after the friend, pretending to have left all his money home, plays upon the narrator's guilt and basic kindness to the tune of five dollars. Thus the first movement ends.

The second movement opens with the narrator's first letter to Sonny. Sonny's answer, equating drug addiction with prison and both with Harlem, shows his need to reach his brother. Finally the two men have begun to communicate with one another. The letters continue until Sonny's return to New York when the narrator, who has started at last "to wonder about Sonny, about the life that Sonny lived inside," takes him home. The narrator is awkward here, wanting only to hear that Sonny is safe and refusing to accept the fact that he might not be. He is still unwilling to see Sonny on Sonny's terms; like an overly anxious parent he must make Sonny conform to his own concepts of respectability.

The word "safe" is the note that takes us into the third movement, to time past when Sonny's father claimed there was "no place safe." In the flashbacks the narrator recalls events that fuse past, present, and future. Parallels are drawn between the father and Sonny, between the Harlem of one generation and the Harlem of the other. Images of darkness mingle with those of sound. For each generation, however, the tragedy is new, for the older people are reluctant to inform the young ones of the condition of the Black race. The old folks who sit in the dark quit talking, because if the child "knows too much about what's happened to *them,* he'll know too much too soon about what's going to happen to him." Thus even in the past, silence was preferable to expression.

We learn also of another pair of brothers, Sonny's father and uncle. The uncle, like Sonny, was a musician, but he got killed one night when some drunk white men ran him over in their car. The narrator's mother tells her older son this story to make him look after his brother, but her death, occurring shortly after this conversation, only shows the immeasurable gulf between the two boys. The narrator, recently married, thinks he is taking care of Sonny by forcing him to live with his wife's family, but Sonny, already on drugs though unable to admit it, could not want anything less. Their failure to communicate is at its peak. When Sonny announces his ambition "to play jazz," the appalled narrator is totally unresponsive. The most he can promise is to buy Charlie Parker's records, although Sonny insists he doesn't care what his brother listens to. Certainly he doesn't listen to Sonny, urging him only to be respectable and stay in school:

> "You only got another year. . . . Just try to put up with it till I come back. Will you please do that? For me?"

> He didn't answer and he wouldn't look at me.

> "Sonny, you hear me?"

> He pulled away. "I hear you. But you never hear anything *I* say."

The narrator, though he didn't know what to say to that, reminds Sonny of the piano at his in-laws, and Sonny gives in. Later we learn of Sonny's obsession with the piano. Because he has no one to communicate with, the piano becomes his only source of expression:

> As soon as he came in . . . , until suppertime. And, after supper, he went back to that piano and stayed

there until everybody went to bed. He was at the piano all day Saturday and all day Sunday. . . .

Isabel finally confessed that it wasn't like living with a person at all, it was like living with sound. And the sound didn't make any sense to her, didn't make any sense to any of them—naturally. . . . He moved in an atmosphere which wasn't like theirs at all. . . . There wasn't any way to reach him. . . .

They dimly sensed, as I sensed, . . . that Sonny was at that piano playing for his life.

They succeed in reaching him, however, when they discover he has not been in school but in a white girl's Greenwich Village apartment playing music. After that Sonny enlists. When he returns, a man, although the narrator "wasn't willing to see it," the brothers fight, for to the narrator Sonny's "music seemed to be merely an excuse for the life he led. It sounded just that weird and disordered."

At this point they cut off all contact.

The fourth movement begins by recapitulating and developing the first. "I read about Sonny's troubles in the spring. Little Grace died in the fall." We move through time easily now, perceiving the connection between the narrator's first letter to Sonny and his daughter's death: "My trouble made his real." He has begun, finally, to sympathize, to understand.

The last movement then begins its own theme, the new relationship between the brothers. A subtly presented but major change in this relationship occurs when they watch a street revival meeting:

The revival was being carried on by three sisters in black, and a brother. All they had were their voices and their Bibles and a tambourine. . . .

"Tis the old ship of Zion," they sang. . . . Not a soul under the sound of their voices was hearing this song for the first time, not one of them had been rescued. . . . The woman with the tambourine, whose voice dominated the air, whose face was bright with joy, was divided by very little from the woman who stood watching her, a cigarette between her heavy, chapped lips, her hair a cuckoo's nest, her face scarred and swollen from many beatings, and her black eyes glittering like coal. Perhaps they both knew this, which was why, when, as rarely, they addressed each other, they addressed each other as Sister.

There is a greater brotherhood among people than mere kinship. Moreover, the narrator realizes that their music saves them, for it "seemed to soothe a poison out of them." The narrator's simultaneous recognition of the meaning of brotherhood and the power of music leads directly to Sonny's invitation. He asks his brother to listen, that night, to his own music. That street song is thus a prelude to the brothers' first honest talk and carries us to the finale when Sonny plays for the narrator.

Sonny now tells his brother that the woman's voice reminded him "of what heroin feels like." This equation of music and drugs, recalling the narrator's discussion with Sonny's friend outside a bar, explains why the one could be a positive alternative to the other. We better understand Sonny's desperate commitment to the piano. Sonny is "doing his best to talk," and the narrator knows that he should "listen." He realizes the profundity of Sonny's suffering now and sees also his own part in it: "There stood between us, forever, beyond the power of time or forgiveness, the fact that I had held silence—so long!—when he had needed human speech to help him."

The narrator's epiphany allows Sonny to continue, and he makes explicit now the connection between music and his own need to be heard:

There's not really a living ass to talk to, . . . and there's no way of getting it out—that storm inside. You can't talk it and you can't make love with it, and when you finally try to get with it and play it, you realize *nobody's* listening. So *you've* got to listen. You got to find a way to listen.

Playing his own song, Sonny finds a way to listen, though he confesses that heroin sometimes helped him release the storm. Now he wants his brother to hear the storm too.

And he finally does. When Sonny, his voice barely audible, says of heroin "It can come again," the brother replies, "All right . . . so it can come again. All right." For that first true acceptance of himself, Sonny tells the narrator, "You're my brother."

The finale brings our two themes of interpersonal communication and music together. Baldwin arranges a discussion between the musicians and their instruments using the language of ordinary conversation. Creole, the leader of the group, is guiding Sonny as they begin to play. "He was listening to Sonny. He was having a dialogue with Sonny." Then they work towards the climax:

The dry, low, black man said something awful on the drums, Creole answered, and the drums talked back. Then the horn insisted, . . . and Creole listened, commenting now and then. . . . Then they all came together again, and Sonny was part of the family again. . . .

Creole began to tell us what the blues were all about. . . . He and his boys up there were keeping it new, at the risk of ruin, destruction, madness, and death, in order to find new ways to make us listen. For, while the tale of how we suffer, and how we are delighted, and how we may triumph is never new, it always must be heard. There isn't any other tale to tell, it's the only light we've got in all this darkness.

Finally Creole steps back to let Sonny speak for himself:

Listen, Creole seemed to be saying, listen. Now these are Sonny's blues. . . .

Sonny's fingers filled the air with life, his life. . . .
Sonny . . . really began with the spare, flat statement
of the opening phrase of the song. . . . I understood,
at last, that he could help us to be free if we would
listen, that he would never be free until we did.

Sonny's music stirs special memories in the brothers' lives,
but these blues belong to all of us, for they symbolize the
darkness which surrounds all those who fail to listen to
and remain unheard by their fellow men.

Donald C. Murray (essay date 1977)

SOURCE: "James Baldwin's 'Sonny's Blues': Complicated and Simple," in *Studies in Short Fiction,* Vol. 14, No.
4, Fall, 1977, pp. 353-57.

[*In the following essay, Murray explores themes of self-
identity, escape, loss, and transcendence in "Sonny's
Blues."*]

One boy was whistling a tune, at once very complicated
and very simple, it seemed to be pouring out of him as
though he were a bird, and it sounded very cool and
moving through all that harsh, bright air, only just
holding its own through all those other sounds.

In the world of **"Sonny's Blues,"** the short story by James
Baldwin, the author deals with man's need to find his
identity in a hostile society and, in a social situation which
invites fatalistic compliance, his ability to understand himself through artistic creation which is both individual and
communal. **"Sonny's Blues"** is the story of a boy's growth
to adulthood at a place, the Harlem ghetto, where it's
easier to remain a "cunning child," and at a time when
black is not beautiful because it's simpler to submerge
oneself in middle-class conformity, the modish antics of
the hipster set, or else, at the most dismal level, the limbo
of drug addiction, rather than to truly find oneself. Sonny's brother, the narrator of the story, opts for the comforts of a respectable profession and his specialty, the
teaching of algebra, suggests his desire for standard pro-
cedures and elegant, clear-cut solutions. On the other hand,
Sonny at first trafficks with the hipster world; yet not
without imposing "his own halfbeat" on "the way the
Harlem hipsters walk." Eventually, however, as if no longer
able to hold his own through all those other sounds of
enticement and derision, Sonny is sentenced to a government institution due to his selling and using heroin.

With his brother in a penal establishment and himself a
member of the educational establishment, it's fitting that
the narrator would learn of Sonny's imprisonment while
reading the newspaper, probably an establishment press,
and while riding in a subway, an appropriate vehicle for
someone who hasn't risen above his origins so far as he
hopes. The subway world of roaring darkness is both the
outside world of hostile forces and the inner heart of
darkness which we encounter at our peril, yet encounter
we must. The narrator at first cannot believe that Sonny

has gone "down" ("I had kept it outside me for a long
time."), but he is forced to realize that it has happened,
and, thinking of heroin, he suspects that perhaps "it did
more for [Black boys like Sonny] than algebra could.
Playing upon the homonym of Sonny, Baldwin writes that,
for the narrator's brother, "all the light in [Sonny's] face"
had gone out.

**To be aware of oneself, Baldwin believes,
is to feel a sense of loss, to know where we
are and what we've left behind.**

—Donald C. Murray

Images of light and darkness are used by Baldwin to illustrate his theme of man's painful quest for an identity.
Light can represent the harsh glare of reality, the bitter
conditions of ghetto existence which harden and brutalize
the young. Early in the story the narrator comes upon a
boy in the shadow of a doorway, a psychologically stunted creature "looking just like Sonny," "partly like a dog,
partly like a cunning child." Shortly thereafter he watches
a barmaid in a dingy pub and notes that, "When she smiled
one saw the little girl, one sensed the doomed, still-struggling woman beneath the battered face of the semi-whore."
Both figures will appear again, in other forms, during the
revival meeting later in the story. At this point, however,
the narrator turns away and goes on "down the steps" into
the subway. He retreats from the light, however dim.

Another kind of light is that of the movie theater, the light
which casts celluloid illusions on the screen. It is this
light, shrouded in darkness, which allows the ghetto-dwell-
ers' temporary relief from their condition. "All they really
knew were two darknesses," Baldwin writes, "the darkness of their lives, which was now closing in on them, and
the darkness of the movies, which had blinded them to
that other darkness." This image of the movie theater neatly
represents the state of people who are at once together
and alone, seated side-by-side yet without communication.
Baldwin deftly fuses the theater and subway images: "They
were growing up with a rush and their heads bumped
abruptly against the low ceiling of their actual possibilities." The realities are far different from the idealistic
dreams of the cinema; as outside the subway window, so
behind the cinema screen there is nothing but roaring
darkness.

There is no escape from the darkness for Sonny and his
family. Dreams and aspirations are always dispelled, the
narrator comments, because someone will always "get up
and turn on the light." "And when light fills the room," he
continues, "the child is filled with darkness." Grieved by
the death of his child, fortuitously named Grace, and aware
of the age difference between himself and Sonny, the
narrator seems unconsciously to seek out the childlike

qualities of everyone he meets. He is not quite the self-satisfied conformist which some critics have made him out to be. He looks back toward a period in the lives of others when they presumably were not tormented by the need to choose between modes of living and to assert themselves. To the extent that he is given to this psychological penchant, the narrator is close in age to Sonny and **"Sonny's Blues"** is the story of the narrator's dawning self-awareness. The revelation of his father's brother's murder and the fact of Grace's death make Sonny's troubles real for the narrator and prompt the latter's growth in awareness.

To be aware of oneself, Baldwin believes, is to feel a sense of loss, to know where we are and what we've left behind. Sonny's presence forces the narrator to examine his own past; that is, the past which he left behind in the ghetto ("the vivid, killing streets of our childhood") and, before that, in the South. "Some escaped the trap," the narrator notes, "most didn't." "Those who got out always left something of themselves behind," he continues, "as some animals amputate a leg and leave it in the trap." The image is violent and is in keeping with the narrator's tendency to see people "encircled by disaster." The violence reminds us of the fate of the narrator's uncle, a kind of black Orpheus who, carrying his guitar, was deliberately run-down by a group of drunken whites. The narrator's father, we are told, was permanently disturbed by the slaughter of his brother. The age difference between the narrator and Sonny, like that between the narrator and his uncle and that between Sonny and his fellow musician Creole, all suggest that the fates of the generations are similar, linked by influences and effects. "The same things happen," the narrator reflects, "[our children will] have the same things to remember."

So, too, the story is cyclical. We begin in the present, move into the immediate past, then into the more remote past of the narrator's family, then forward to the time of the narrator's marriage and his early conversations with Sonny about his proposed career as a musician, thereafter to Sonny's release from prison and his most recent discussion of music ("It makes you feel—in control"), and finally to the night club episode in the immediate present. Similarities in characters and events link the various sections of the story. The barmaid in the opening section, who was "still keeping time to the music," and the boy whose birdlike whistling just holds its own amid the noise, are linked to the revivalists, whose "singing filled the air," and to Sonny, whose culture hero is "Bird" Parker and whose role is to create music rather than merely keep time. The revivalists are singing near the housing project whose "beat-looking grass lying around isn't enough to make [the inhabitants'] lives green." Looking like one of the narrator's schoolboys, Sonny watches the three sisters and brother in black and carries a notebook "with a green cover," emblematic of the creative life he hopes to lead. Unlike his brother's forced payment to the indigent, childlike man, Sonny drops change into the revivalists' tambourine and the instrument, with this gratuitous gift, turns into a "collection plate." The group has been playing "*If I could only hear my mother play again!*" and Sonny, after "faintly

smiling," returns to this brother's home, as if in response to the latter's promise to their mother that he will safeguard Sonny. Recognizing Sonny as both a creative individual and a brother, the narrator is "both relieved and apprehensive."

The narrator's apprehension is justified in that he is about to witness Sonny's torturous rebirth as a creative artist. "'But I can't forget—where I've been,'" Sonny remarks to his brother and then adds: "'I don't mean just the physical place I've been, I mean where I've *been*. And *what* I've been'." In terms which might recall Gerard Manley Hopkins' anguished sonnet "I wake and feel the fell of darkness," Sonny goes on to describe his own dark night of the soul: "'I was all by myself at the bottom of something, stinking and sweating and crying and shaking, and I smelled it, you know? *my* stink, and I thought I'd die'." Because of the enormous energy and dedication involved in his role as Blues musician, Sonny is virtually described as a sacrificial victim as well as an initiate into the mysteries of creativity. Somewhat like the Christ of *noli me tangere,* Sonny's smile is "sorrowful" and he finds it hard to describe his own terrible anguish because he knows that it can come again and he almost wonders whether it's worth it. Yet his anguish is not only personal but representative, for as he looks down from the window of his brother's apartment he sees "'all that hatred and misery and love,'" and he notes that, "'It's a wonder it doesn't blow the avenue apart'." As the pressure mounts within Sonny, the author sets the scene for the final episode of the story.

Befitting the special evening which ends **"Sonny's Blues,"** the locale shifts to the "only night club" on a dark downtown street. Sonny and the narrator pass through the narrow bar and enter a large, womblike room where Sonny is greeted with "'Hello, boy'" by a voice which "erupted out of all that atmospheric lighting." Indeed the atmosphere is almost grandly operatic in its stage quality. The booming voice belongs to the quasi-midwife, Creole, who slaps Sonny "lightly, affectionately," as if performing the birth rite. Creole is assisted by a "coal-black" demiurge, "built close to the ground," with laughter "coming up out of him like the beginning of an earthquake." As if to underscore the portentousness of this evening in Sonny's "kingdom," the narrator thinks that, "Here it was not even a question that [Sonny's] veins bore royal blood." The imagery of light now blends with that of water as the narrator, describing the light which "spilled" from the bandstand and the way in which Sonny seems to be "riding" the waves of applause, relates how Sonny and the other musicians prepare to play. It is as if Sonny were about to undergo another stage in his initiation into mature musicianship, this time a trial by fire. "I had the feeling that they, nevertheless, were being most careful not to step into that circle of light too suddenly," the narrator continues, "that if they moved into the light too suddenly, without thinking, they would perish in flame." Next the imagery suggests that Sonny is embarking upon a sacred and perilous voyage, an approach to the wholly other in the biblical sense of the phrase; for the man who creates music, the narrator observes, is "hearing something else, is dealing with the roar rising from the void and imposing order on it as it hits the air." The roaring darkness of the subway is transformed into something luminous. Appropriately, the lighting turns to indigo and Sonny is transfigured.

Baldwin is no facile optimist. The meaning of "Sonny's Blues" is not, to use the glib phrase, the transcendence of the human condition through art. Baldwin is talking about love and joy, tears of joy because of love.

—Donald C. Murray

Now the focus again shifts to Creole, who seems to hold the musicians on a "short rein": "He wanted Sonny to leave the shore line and strike out for the deep water. He was Sonny's witness that deep water and drowning were not the same thing—he had been there, and he knew." Creole now takes on the dimensions of the traditional father-figure. He is a better teacher than the narrator because he has been in the deep water of life; he is a better witness than Sonny's father because he has not been "burned out" by his experiences in life. Creole's function in the story, to put it prosaically, is to show that only through determination and perseverance, through the taking of a risk, can one find a proper role in life. To fail does not mean to be lost irretrievably, for one can always start again. To go forward, as Sonny did when Creole "let out the reins," is to escape the cycle which, in the ghetto of the mind, stifles so many lives, resulting in mean expectations and stunted aspirations. The narrator makes the point that the essence of Sonny's blues is not new; rather, it's the age-old story of triumph, suffering, and failure. But there is no other tale to tell, he adds, "it's the only light we've got in all this darkness."

Baldwin is no facile optimist. The meaning of **"Sonny's Blues"** is not, to use the glib phrase, the transcendence of the human condition through art. Baldwin is talking about love and joy, tears of joy because of love. As the narrator listens to his brother's blues, he recalls his mother, the moonlit road on which his uncle died, his wife Isabel's tears, and he again sees the face of his dead child, Grace. Love is what life should be about, he realizes; love which is all the more poignant because involved with pain, separation, and death. Nor is the meaning of **"Sonny's Blues"** the belief that music touches the heart without words; or at least the meaning of the story is not just that. His brother responds deeply to Sonny's music because he knows that he is with his black brothers and is watching his own brother, grinning and "soaking wet." This last physiological detail is important, not just imagistically, because Baldwin is not sentimentalizing his case in **"Sonny's Blues."** The narrator is well aware, for example, that his profound response to the blues is a matter of "only a moment, that the world waited outside, as hungry as ti-

ger"—a great cat ready to destroy the birdlike whistling— "and that trouble stretched above us, longer than the sky." The final point of the story is that the narrator, through his own suffering and the example of Sonny, is at last able to find himself in the brotherhood of man. Such an identification is an act of communion and **"Sonny's Blues"** ends, significantly, with the image of the homely Scotch-and-milk glass transformed into "the very cup of trembling," the Grail, the goal of the quest and the emblem of initiation.

Edward Lobb (essay date 1979)

SOURCE: "James Baldwin's Blues and the Function of Art," in *The International Fiction Review,* Vol. 6, No. 2, Summer, 1979, pp. 143-48.

[*In the following essay, Lobb discusses Baldwin's exploration of the nature and purpose of art.*]

James Baldwin's short story **"Sonny's Blues,"** first published in 1957, has been anthologized several times since its inclusion in Baldwin's *Going to Meet the Man* (1965). It is a fine and immediately appealing story, but it has never received critical treatment adequate to its complexity. The best analysis—an essay by John M. Reilly [in *Negro American Literature Forum,* 1970]—rightly asserts the centrality of the blues in the story as a means of personal and social communication. In the last scene, Reilly sees the reconciliation of the narrator and his brother (which certainly does occur) and an affirmation of the blues as "a metaphor of Black community." But the meaning of the blues is, as I hope to show, rather wider than Reilly seems to think, and is part of a larger theme which is conveyed almost wholly through the story's images. **"Sonny's Blues"** is Baldwin's most concise and suggestive statement about the nature and function of art, and is doubly artful in making that statement through life situations.

Throughout most of the story, the narrator is unable to understand his younger brother Sonny, who is a jazz pianist. He feels guilt at not having looked after Sonny, but is really incapable of understanding what has driven Sonny to heroin. Sonny himself is not too articulate on the subject when he writes to his brother from prison: he says "I guess I was afraid of something or I was trying to escape from something and you know I have never been very strong in the head (smile)." This "something" is never precisely defined, but it is always associated with darkness. Sonny writes that he feels "like a man who's been trying to climb up out of some deep, real deep and funky hole and just saw the sun up there, outside," and the temptation is to suppose that the bleak life of Harlem is "the danger he had almost died trying to escape." In part it is: Sonny says that he has to get out of Harlem, and he escapes first to the navy, then to Greenwich Village. The narrator realizes that Harlem is a place without a future; he sees his students' heads bump "against the low ceiling of their actual possibilities" and thinks that "all they really know were two darknesses, the darkness of their lives, which was now closing in on them, and the darkness of the movies, which had blinded them to that other darkness, and in which they now, vindictively, dreamed, at once more together than they were at any other time, and more alone." But if the danger were simply the grim facts of life in Harlem—the poverty, the lack of a future, the dope, the seemingly impenetrable wall of white racism—surely the narrator, and Sonny, could be more precise about them.

The fact that they are not is an indication that these things are simply aspects of the larger terror of existence in a universe devoid of meaning. The narrator imagines (and remembers) a child's first awareness of this terror, again employing the metaphor of darkness; ironically, the child's awareness comes after the reassurances of church and a Sunday dinner.

> And the living room would be full of church folks and relatives. There they sit, in chairs all around the living room, and the night is creeping up outside, but nobody knows it yet. You can see the darkness growing against the windowpanes and you hear the street noises every now and again, or maybe the jangling beat of a tambourine from one of the churches close by, but it's real quiet in the room. For a moment nobody's talking, but every face looks darkening, like the sky outside. . . . Everyone is looking at something a child can't see. For a minute they've forgotten the children. . . . Maybe there's a kid, quiet and big-eyed, curled up in a big chair in the corner. The silence, the darkness coming, and the darkness in the faces frighten the child obscurely. He hopes that the hand which strokes his forehead will never stop—will never die. He hopes that there will never come a time when the old folks won't be sitting around the living room, talking about where they've come from, and what they've seen, and what's happened to them and their kinfolk.

> But something deep and watchful in the child knows that this is bound to end, is already ending.

This first sense of the world's darkness—its menace—is soon borne out by experience. The narrator's mother tells him about his uncle's death and its effect on his father: "Your Daddy was like a crazy man that night and for many a night thereafter. He says he never in his life seen anything as dark as that road after the lights of that car had gone away." The "hole" that Sonny is in, then, is a metaphysical one, the result of his sense that the world is a place of meaningless pain. He writes from prison, "I wish I could be like Mama and say the Lord's will be done, but I don't know it seems to me that trouble is the one thing that never does get stopped and I don't know what good it does to blame it on the Lord. But maybe it does some good if you believe it."

There is, of course, no escape from this darkness. The only things that can make it tolerable are human companionship and perhaps some kind of awareness of the truth of our situation. The latter is traditionally associated with light, and it seems natural that light in this story should be the means of saving the characters from the menace of darkness. We know from Sonny's prison letter that he has seen "the sun up there, outside"; but most of the references to light suggest that it is even worse than the darkness. The headlights of the car that kills the narrator's uncle, for example, simply intensify the blackness they leave behind, and the children in the darkening living room are made more apprehensive when the light is turned on.

> In a moment someone will get up and turn on the light. Then the old folks will remember the children and they won't talk any more that day. And when light fills the room, the child is filled with darkness. He knows that every time this happens he's moved just a little closer to that darkness outside. The darkness outside is what the old folks have been talking about. It's what they've come from. It's what they endure. The child knows that they won't talk any more because if he knows too much about what's happened to *them,* he'll know too much too soon, about what's going to happen to *him.*

Sonny for one has learned too much too soon, and has fled to heroin as a result.

The dialectic of the story so far is uncompromisingly bleak. The only thing worse than the pain of existence is full consciousness of that pain; knowledge is presumably desirable but unquestionably dangerous, and there seems to be no way of acquiring it without being annihilated, mentally or physically, by its blinding white light. Even in the last scene of the story the musicians avoid the spotlight, knowing what it means. The narrator describes them as being "most careful not to step into that circle of light too suddenly: . . . if they moved into the light too suddenly, without thinking, they would perish in flame." The resolution of the difficulty is beautifully simple and thematically apt. The lights on the bandstand turn "to a kind of indigo" and in this muted light—a mixture of light and darkness—the musicians begin to play, at first hesitantly, then with growing confidence. "Without an instant's warning, Creole started into something else, it was almost sardonic, it was *Am I Blue.* And, as though he commanded, Sonny began to play. Something began to happen. And Creole let out the reins." Playing the blues in a blue light, they achieve an equipoise. The darkness of the human situation is there in the light and the music, as is the light of our awareness; but the annihilating power of each is controlled and shaped by art. "Creole began to tell us what the blues were all about. They were not about anything very new. He and his boys up there were keeping it new, at the risk of ruin, destruction, madness, and death, in order to find new ways to make us listen. For, while the tale of how we suffer, and how we are delighted, and how we may triumph is never new, it must always be heard. There isn't any other tale to tell, it's the only light we've got in all this darkness."

In that complex experience comes comfort—the knowledge that others have suffered and endured. The narrator remembers his uncle's death and his daughter's, but is gladdened: "It [Sonny's performance] was very beautiful because it wasn't hurried and it was no longer a lament. I seemed to hear with what burning he had made it his, with what burning we had yet to make it ours, how we could cease lamenting." What the narrator discovers is the paradox of the blues and of tragedy generally—that melancholy subject matter can be beautifully rendered, without essential distortion, and produce a kind of joy. The experience is not prettified, any more than the white light of knowledge is extinguished by the blue filter; but the *form* of the vision makes it tolerable and saves us from its destructive energy. Nothingness itself assumes a shape; "the man who creates the music is hearing something else, is dealing with the roar rising from the void and imposing order on it as it hits the air. What is evoked in him, then, is of another order, more terrible because it has no words, and triumphant, too, for that same reason. And his triumph, when he triumphs, is ours." In this scene, as Reilly rightly points out, the narrator comes to understand his brother and his own place in the community; the community he acknowledges, however, is not the black community alone but the whole human community of suffering.

The opposed images of darkness and light, and their paradoxical reconciliation in the blue spotlight, outline the essential thematic movement of **"Sonny's Blues,"** the very title of which can now be seen as a punning oxymoron. The theme is reinforced by another pair of images which deserve discussion—those of sound and silence.

Music is traditionally associated with order of one kind or another (the music of the spheres, etc.), and in the last scene of the story music communicates a tragic sense of life. Listening, then, is an attempt to understand the nature of things. Sonny says, "And other times—well, I needed a fix, I needed to find a place to lean, I needed to clear a space to *listen.*" The problem comes when one listens and hears nothing. Silence, like darkness, is a form of absence, a something *not* there, a quality of the void; and when Sonny listens he apparently hears only what Pascal called the terrifying silence of the interstellar spaces. Certainly the narrator has reason to associate silence and horror: the first sign of his daughter's polio is her silence after a fall. "When you have a lot of children you don't always start running when one of them falls, unless they start screaming or something. And, this time, Grace was quiet. Yet, Isabel says that when she heard that *thump* and then that silence, something happened in her to make her afraid. And she ran to the living room and there was little Grace on the floor, all twisted up, and the reason she hadn't screamed was that she couldn't get her breath." And, we recall, the children in the living room are frightened by the adults' silence as well as by the encroaching darkness. It is, then, no mere metaphor when the narrator says that Sonny in his teens "was at that piano playing for his life."

On the metaphysical level, silence is parallel to darkness; on the human level, it is indicative of a surrender to the coldness of the universe, a kind of moral death. Sonny expresses his rage by means of silence. When Isabel's family complains of the noise he makes at the piano, he stops playing, and his brother writes that "the silence of the next few days must have been louder than the sound of all the music ever played since time began." The narrator acknowledges his guilt about Sonny in similar terms:

". . . there stood between us, forever, beyond the power of time or forgiveness, the fact that I had held silence—so long!—when he had needed human speech to help him." After Sonny's release from prison the brothers do talk, but not with any real ease. "I wanted to say more, but I couldn't." It is only in the nightclub that any real communication occurs, and then in wordless ways. Sonny's music breaks the silence that has existed between the brothers, and breaks down the wall of reserve that has removed the narrator, for all practical purposes, from the human community. He teaches algebra—an abstract subject—and lives *above* Harlem in a housing project which "looks like a parody of the good, clean, faceless life." Himself almost faceless, he never reveals his name and says nothing about the effect his daughter's death had upon him: it is only as he listens to Sonny in the nightclub that he remembers the family's troubles and feels his tears begin to rise.

The moment of his redemption is no easy triumph of art, however. He remains aware "that this was only a moment, that the world waited outside, as hungry as a tiger, and that trouble stretched above us, longer than the sky." The music is, as poetry was for Robert Frost, a momentary stay against confusion, not an alternative to the real world. Lest the point be missed, Baldwin has included a guitar in the scene of the uncle's death: no Orphean lyre, it is destroyed along with its owner.

We have established, then, that Baldwin's ideas about the nature and function of art are conveyed more by the images of the story than by its narrative. Even in the last paragraph of **"Sonny's Blues,"** new images appear to deepen the argument. The narrator sends a round of drinks to the band: "There was a long pause, while they talked up there in the indigo light and after a while I saw the girl put a Scotch and milk on top of the piano for Sonny. He didn't seem to notice it, but just before they started playing again, he sipped from it and looked toward me, and nodded. Then he put it back on top of the piano. For me, then, as they began to play again, it glowed and shook above my brother's head like the very cup of trembling." Like many of Baldwin's images, this contains several levels of meaning. The drink is both a Damoclean sword and the cup of the brothers' communion of understanding; Donald Murray sees it [in *Studies in Short Fiction,* 1977] as "the Grail, the goal of the quest and the emblem of initiation." It is also "the cup of trembling" referred to in Isaiah. The passage alluded to suggests, in the context of the story, both despair ("There is none to guide her") and the universality of suffering—a suffering which is momentarily in abeyance, but which can return, like "the trouble stretched above us," at any moment.

Having said that, we have perhaps said enough; but a rereading of the story suggests other and deeper meanings in the image. There are repeated references in the story to trembling and shaking, usually as an appropriately fearful response to the silence and darkness of the world. At the beginning of the story, after reading of Sonny's arrest, the narrator encounters one of Sonny's old high school friends who is coming down from a "high," reentering the world, and "shaking as though he were going to fall apart." Later, when Sonny explains why some jazzmen use heroin, he says "It's not so much to *play*. It's to *stand* it, to be able to make it at all. On any level. . . . In order to keep from shaking to pieces." His own experience has shown him the necessity of facing the abyss: "I can never tell you. I was all by myself at the bottom of something, stinking and sweating and crying and shaking, and I smelled it, you know? *my* stink, and I thought I'd die if I couldn't get away from it and yet, all the same, I knew that everything I was doing was just locking me in with it. . . . I didn't know, I still *don't* know, something kept telling me that maybe it was good to smell your own stink, but I didn't think that *that* was what I'd been trying to do—and—who can stand it?" What Sonny has learned is part of the lesson all tragic heroes learn in their extremity: when Gloucester says to Lear "O, let me kiss that hand," Lear answers, "Let me wipe it first; it smells of mortality."

The wrong way of coping with the trembling is to retreat into illusion, as one does with heroin; the right way is to face the abyss in the manageable form that art gives it. The trembling of the drink is the authentic human trembling in the face of the empty immensity of the universe, but it is controlled by art—by the form of the glass and by the piano which causes the trembling. Once again, we are presented with an image of potentially destructive energy controlled and contained, as the white light is controlled and contained by the blue filter. It would not be going too far, I think, to see in the drink itself another emblem, the Scotch representing the harshness of reality and the milk the smoothness of art.

"Sonny's Blues" is so complete a treatment of the art-theme that it includes bad art as well as good, and suggests its effects. Bad art, like heroin, is merely a refuge from the real world. Early in the story, in a passage cited earlier, the narrator mentions the boys who spend their time in "the darkness of the movies, which had blinded them to that other darkness." Like the blue spotlight, the movie screen is a modulated light; unlike the spotlight, it illuminates nothing, providing only sterile fantasies which feed the boys' rage. The narrator says that they are "at once more together than they were at any other time, and more alone." Their fellowship is as delusory as the version of reality on the screen, for they are united only in frustration and anger; each of them dreams alone, "vindictively." The blues, on the other hand, provide a real sense of community, as does the music of the street revival: ". . . the music seemed to soothe a poison out of them; and time seemed, nearly, to fall away from the sullen, belligerent, battered faces, as though they were fleeing back to their first condition, while dreaming of their last." The singers address each other as "Sister," anticipating the narrator's recognition of brotherhood (literal and figurative) in the last scene.

The other form of false art in the story, though it is mentioned only once, is television, and here again an image is paired with its opposite. At various points in the story the narrator finds himself by a window, and his looking out is obviously analogous in meaning to the act of listening. Sonny, more of a seeker than his brother, is drawn to the window "as though it were the lodestone rock." Most of the

inhabitants of the housing project, on the other hand, "don't bother with the windows, they watch the TV screen instead."

Baldwin's ideas about the nature and function of art are conveyed more by the images of the story than by its narrative.

—Edward Lobb

Beyond the narrative events of "Sonny's Blues," then, is a level of symbolic discourse on the relation of art and life. Art is distinguished from fantasy by contrast with heroin and the cheap satisfactions of film and television; it is associated with light, sound, and form, and stands against darkness, silence, and "fear and trembling." But if it is to be good art and provide a true picture of experience, it must include the elements it fights against—hence the paradoxical nature of Baldwin's emblems of art: the union of darkness and light, of form and the trembling which shakes things apart, of the roar from the void and the order of music. These and the other pairs of opposites I have mentioned (sound and silence, window and television, tragic matter and joyous form) suggest that the whole story, including the characterization of the brothers, is based on the idea of contrast or paradox—a suspicion borne out by even the most casual details in the story. The narrator, for example, hears a boy whistling a tune which is, like the story itself, "at once very complicated and very simple."

But we should be loath to describe any story as though it were an essay, however fine. Critical paraphrase tends to reduce narrative to a structure of symbols and ideas, and what makes "Sonny's Blues" a compelling story is its rendering of life, not its comments on art. It is similar to Baldwin's other fiction in its insistence that people must understand their past if they are to have any future. The narrator must work through his and Sonny's past—as well as his father's and uncle's—if he is to move forward. In the nightclub, with his memories of hard times, he thinks that Sonny "could help us to be free if we would listen, that he would never be free until we did." This theme informs Baldwin's social criticism as well: America, too, must face the reality of its past and clear a space in which to listen. In "Sonny's Blues," the themes of art and life converge, for the chief obstacle to our obtaining a clear view of the past, individually or as a people, is simply our preference for bad art, for the pleasant lies which the media peddle and we in our sadness desire.

Keith E. Byerman (essay date 1982)

SOURCE: "Words and Music: Narrative Ambiguity in 'Sonny's Blues'," in *Studies in Short Fiction,* Vol. 19, No. 4, Fall, 1982, pp. 367-72.

[*In the following essay, Byerman considers Baldwin's story "a study of the nature and relationship of art and language."*]

"Sonny's Blues" has generally been accorded status as the best of James Baldwin's short stories. It tells of the developing relationship between Sonny, a musician and drug addict, and the narrator, his brother, who feels a conflict between the security of his middle-class life and the emotional risks of brotherhood with Sonny. The critics, who differ on whether the story is primarily Sonny's or the narrator's, generally agree that it resolves its central conflict. If, however, resolution is not assumed but taken as problematical, then new thematic and structural possibilities are revealed. The story becomes a study of the nature and relationship of art and language. The commentary on the story has centered on the moral issue; the purpose of this essay is to focus on the underlying aesthetic question.

"Sonny's Blues" moves within the tension between its openly stated message of order and a community of understanding and its covert questioning, through form, allusion, and ambiguity, of the relationship between life and art.

—Keith E. Byerman

According to Jonathan Culler [in *Structuralist Poetics: Structuralism, Linguistics, and the Study of Literature,* 1975], resolution can be accomplished in a story when a message is received or a code deciphered. In most cases the message is withheld in some manner—through deception, innocence, or ignorance—until a key moment in the narrative. In the case of **"Sonny's Blues,"** however, the message is apparent from the beginning and is repeatedly made available to the narrator. The story, in part, is about his misreadings; more importantly, it is about his inability to read properly. The source of this inability is his reliance on a language that is at once rationalistic and metaphoric. His sentences are always complete and balanced, and his figurative language puts on display his literary intelligence. Even in the description of his own emotional states, the verbal pattern overshadows the experience. Whenever the message is delivered, he evades it through language; he creates and then reads substitute texts, such as the messenger, or distorts the sense of the message by changing it to fit his preconceived ideas.

The message is first presented in the simplest, most straightforward manner, as a newspaper story: "I read about it in the paper, in the subway, on my way to work. I read it, and I couldn't believe it, and I read it again. Then perhaps I just stared at it, at the newsprint spelling out his name, spelling out the story." The information is clearly there,

"spelled out," a text that cannot be ignored. But the narrator's immediate action is to refract his emotions through metaphor: "I stared at it in the swinging lights of the subway car, and in the faces and bodies of the people, and in my own face, trapped in the darkness which roared outside." This oblique allusion to the underground man is followed in the next paragraph by a reference to the ice at the center of his emotional Inferno. What is noteworthy is that these images call attention to themselves as images and not simply as natural expressions of emotional intensity. His response has built into it a strong sense of the need for proper verbal expression. This deflection from emotion to art is accompanied by repeated statements on the impossibility of believing the message.

The second scene dramatizes and verifies the information presented by the newspaper story. The narrator encounters an addict who had been a friend of Sonny's. In fact, "I saw this boy standing in the shadow of a doorway, looking just like Sonny." Again there is a darkness and an explicit identification with Sonny. Again there is distancing through figurative language: "But now, abruptly, I hated him. I couldn't stand the way he looked at me, partly like a dog, partly like a cunning child." Such language prepares us for, while guaranteeing, the failed communication of this episode. The narrator is offered knowledge, but he chooses to interpret the messenger rather than the message. He expresses a desire to know, and remorse when he does not listen, but he also repeats his unwillingness to understand.

A further complication occurs when, in the midst of this encounter, the narrator turns his attention from the addict to the music being played in a bar. The mark of his refusal to know is in his act of interpreting those associated with the music. "The juke box was blasting away with something black and bouncy and I half watched the barmaid as she danced her way from the juke box to her place behind the bar. And I watched her face as she laughingly responded to something someone said to her, still keeping time to the music. When she smiled one saw the little girl, one sensed the doomed, still-struggling woman beneath the face of the semi-whore." Rather than listen to the conversation he is directly involved in, the narrator observes one he cannot possibly hear. In the process, he can distance himself by labeling the woman he sees. He is thereby at once protected from and superior to the situation. The music, a motif repeated in subsequent scenes, here is part of what the narrator refuses to know; he substitutes his words for the non-verbal communication that music offers. In telling the incident, he suggests that he is listening to the music to avoid the addict-messenger; in fact, their messages are identical, and he avoids both by imposing his verbal pattern.

A similar evasion occurs in the next major scene, which is a flashback within a flashback. The narrator's mother, after hearing her son reassure her that nothing will happen to Sonny, tells him the story of his father and uncle, a story that parallels the one occurring in the present time of the narration. Her story, of the uncle's death and the father's inability to prevent it, is a parable of proper brotherly relationships. After telling the tale, she indicates its relevance: "'I ain't telling you all this,' she said, 'to make you scared or bitter or to make you hate nobody. I'm telling you this because you got a brother. And the world ain't changed'." The narrator immediately offers his interpretation: "'Don't you worry, I won't forget. I won't let nothing happen to Sonny'." His mother corrects his impression: "'You may not be able to stop nothing from happening. But you got to let him know you's *there*'."

No ambiguity can be found here. The message is clearly delivered, in transparent, non-metaphoric language. What prevents it from being received can only be the substitutions in the pattern. The musically-talented uncle is Sonny's double and the helpless father is the narrator's. This parallel structure makes the point obvious to the reader, but the fact that it is *only* parallel justifies the continuation of the narrative. In his positivistic way, the narrator will not believe what does not occur to his immediate experience or what cannot be contained within his linguistic net. His mother's fatalistic message cannot be so contained. Thus, the story must continue until he has both evidence and the means of controlling it.

The final scene of the story, instead of validating the meaning, only deepens the ambiguity. The bar where Sonny plays and the people in it are presented as alien to the narrator's experience. The room is dark and narrow, suggestive not only of a birth passage, but also of the subway where the narrator first felt troubled by Sonny. The musicians tend to fit stereotypes of blacks: Creole, the band leader is "an enormous black man" and the drummer, "a coal-black, cheerful-looking man, built close to the ground . . . his teeth gleaming like a lighthouse and his laugh coming up out of him like the beginning of an earthquake." The language grows more serious when the music itself begins:

> All I know about music is that not many people ever really hear it. And even when on the rare occasion when something opens within, and the music enters, what we mainly hear, or hear corroborated, are personal, private, vanishing evocations. But the man who created the music is hearing something else, is dealing with the roar rising from the void and imposing order on it as it hits the air. What is evoked in him, then, is of another order, more terrible because it has no words, and triumphant, too, for that same reason.

Little preparation has been made for such a reaction to the music. The act of the musician seems a creative response to the impinging chaos described in the opening subway scene. But this perception springs full-bodied from the brow of a man who has repeatedly indicated his antagonism to such music. One resolution of this apparent contradiction might be found in his comment about the terrible wordlessness of what he is hearing. A man committed to language, he finds himself confronted with a form whose power seems precisely its ability to create order without language.

In this context, it is highly significant that he immediately undertakes to explain the music through the metaphor of conversation. "The dry, low, black man said something awful on the drums, Creole answered, and the drums talked back. Then the horn insisted, sweet and high, slightly detached perhaps, and Creole listened, commenting now and then, dry, and driving, beautiful and calm and old." If the terror of the music is its lack of words, then to explain it *as* language is to neutralize its power. By creating the metaphor, the narrator can control his experience and limit its effect. He can make the music fit the patterns that he chooses.

This is not readily apparent in what he calls the "tale" of Sonny's music. "For, while the tale of how we suffer, and how we are delighted, and how we may triumph is never new, it always must be heard. There isn't any other tale to tell, it's the only light we've got in all this darkness." While music is changed to language, with the attendant change in meaning, and while the obsession is still with bringing light and thus reason, the narrator is opening up the meaning with reference to "we" and to the emotional conditions of suffering and delight. His language seems less logical and self-consciously artistic than before.

The specifics of the tale strengthen its emotional impact. The music frees the narrator and perhaps Sonny: "Freedom lurked around us and I understood, at last, that he could help us to be free if we would listen, that he would never be free until we did." The narrator's freedom comes through his recapturing and acceptance of the past; the music conjures up his mother's face, his uncle's death, Grace's death accompanied by Isabel's tears "and I felt my own tears begin to rise." Yet for all the emotional content, the form remains very logically, artistically structured. Sentences are very carefully balanced and arranged, the emotion is carried on such verbs as "saw" and "felt," and finally "we," after a series of generalizations, quickly becomes "I" again. This scene only has to be compared to the prologue of *Invisible Man* to demonstrate the extent of control. Both scenes deal with the emotional impact of the blues, but whereas Ellison's is surrealistic and high paradoxical, with its narrator barely living through the history of the vision, Baldwin's narrator remains firmly planted in the bar and firmly in control of the emotion he describes.

The story's underlying ambiguity has its richest expression in the final metaphor, a cocktail that the narrator sends to Sonny. As a symbolic representation of the message of the narrative, the scotch and milk transformed into the cup of trembling suggests the relief from suffering that YHWH promised the children of Israel. Thus, Sonny's suffering will be made easier by the narrator's willingness to be involved in his life. But, as in earlier cases, this is not the only possible reading. First, the drink itself, scotch and milk, is an emblem of simultaneous destruction and nurture to the system; it cannot be reduced to one or the other. Sonny's acceptance of it indicates that his life will continue on the edge between the poison of his addiction and the nourishment of his music.

The narrator's reading of the drink as the cup of trembling offers a second ambiguity, which is not consistent with the first, for it implies clear alternatives. The cup of trembling was taken from Israel when YHWH chose to forgive the people for their transgressions. But it was YHWH who had given the cup of suffering to them in the first place. Thus, it becomes important to the meaning of the story which verse is being alluded to in the metaphor. If the cup is given, then Sonny will continue to suffer and feel guilt; if the cup is taken away, then Sonny returns to a state of grace. There is no Biblical reference to the cup merely remaining.

The choice of image indicates the continuation of the narrator's practice of reading events through the vehicle of his own language. But the very limits of language itself raise problems as to the meaning of the narrative. The need to turn an act into a metaphor and thereby "enrich" the meaning depends upon limitation in the use of language. The words, though, carry traces of meaning not intended. The result, as in this case, can be that the meaning can carry with is its very opposite. In such a situation, intended meaning is lost in the very richness of meaning.

"Sonny's Blues," then, is a story of a narrator caught in the "prisonhouse of language." Both in describing experiences and explaining them, he is locked into a linguistic pattern that restricts his understanding. With the presentation of such a character, Baldwin offers an insight into the limits of language and the narrative art. In the very act of telling his story, the narrator falsifies (as do all storytellers) because he must use words to express what is beyond words. The irony is that much of Baldwin's own writing—essays, novels, stories—is premised on the transparency and sufficiency of language rather than on its duplicity.

Clearly a dialectic is at work. **"Sonny's Blues"** moves within the tension between its openly stated message of order and a community of understanding and its covert questioning, through form, allusion, and ambiguity, of the relationship between life and art. With the latter, the story suggests that literary art contributes to deceit and perhaps anarchy rather than understanding and order. What makes this tension dialectical is that the artifice of narration is necessary for the existence of the story and its overt message. The measure of Baldwin's success is his ability to keep this tension so well hidden, not his ability to resolve the conflict. What finally makes **"Sonny's Blues"** such a good story is its author's skill at concealing the fact that he must lie in order to tell the truth.

Richard N. Albert (essay date 1984)

SOURCE: "The Jazz-Blues Motif in James Baldwin's 'Sonny's Blues'," in *College Literature,* Vol. XI, No. 2, 1984, pp. 178-85.

[*In the following essay, Albert examines the connotations of jazz and blues images and allusions in Baldwin's story in relation to the themes of individualism and alienation.*]

James Baldwin's **"Sonny's Blues,"** a popular selection among editors of anthologies used in introductory college literature courses, is one of his most enduring stories because it is less polemical than many of his later efforts and because it offers several common literary themes: individualism, alienation, and "Am I my brother's keeper?" The story has also generated some perceptive critical views, some of which emphasize Baldwin's metaphorical use of the blues. However, none of the criticism bothers to look more closely at the significance of the jazz and blues images and allusions in relation to the commonly-agreed-upon basic themes of individualism and alienation.

A closer examination of Baldwin's use of jazz and blues forms and of Louis Armstrong, Charlie Parker, the character Creole, and the song, "Am I Blue?" reveals some solid support for the basic themes, as well as some possible important thematic and structural flaws that might cause some readers to question whether Baldwin really understood the nature of the jazz/blues motif that he used. On the other hand, he may have intentionally injected "contraries" that imply an interpretation which emphasizes a coming together in harmony of *all* people—not just Sonny's brother and his people and culture.

The blues, both as a state of being and as music, are basic to the structure of the story. [In *Stomping the Blues,* 1976] Albert Murray says, "The blues as such are synonymous with low spirits," and both the narrator and his brother Sonny have had their share. The narrator's major source of discontent has been his selfish desire to assimilate and lead a "respectable," safe life as a high-school algebra teacher. When he learns of Sonny's troubles with drugs and the law, he feels threatened. Sonny, on the other hand, has a stormy relationship with his father. He is unhappy in Harlem and hates school. He becomes alienated from his brother because of his jazz-oriented life style and his continued attraction to Greenwich Village. Finally, Sonny's using and selling heroin leads to a jail sentence.

The blues as music, as opposed to "the blues as such," take into account both form and content. In this story, content (message) is all important. As music, the blues are considered by many blacks to be a reflection of and a release from the suffering they endured through and since the days of slavery. [In *The Jazz Book,* 1975] Joachim Berendt says, "Everything of importance in the life of the blues singer is contained in these [blues] lyrics: Love and racial discrimination; prison and the law; floods and railroad trains and the fortune told by the gypsy; the evening sun and the hospital . . . Life itself flows into the lyrics of the blues. . . ." When Sonny plays the blues at the end of the story, it is the black heritage reflected in the blues that impresses itself upon Sonny's brother and brings him back into the community of his black brothers and sisters.

Beyond this basic use of the blues motif as background for the unhappiness of the narrator and Sonny and their resultant alienation from one another, Baldwin uses the jazz motif to emphasize the theme of individualism. Sonny is clearly Thoreau's "different drummer." He is a piano player who plays jazz, a kind of music noted for individuality because it depends on each musician's ability to improvise his or her own ideas while keeping in harmony with the progression of chords of some tune (often well-known). It has often been described as being able to take one's instrument, maintain an awareness of one's fellow players in the group, and in this context spontaneously "compose a new tune" with perhaps only a hint of the original remaining, except at the beginning and end of the number. [In *Shadow and Act,* 1964] Ralph Ellison refers to this as the jazz musician's "achieving that subtle identification between his instrument and his deepest drives which will allow him to express his own unique ideas and his own unique voice. He must achieve, in short, his self-determined identity."

One of the greatest jazz improvisers of all time was Charlie Parker, Baldwin's choice as the jazz musician that Sonny idolizes. No better choice could have been made. Parker was one of a group of young musicians in the late 1940s and early 1950s who played what was called bebop, or bop. They developed new and difficult forms—faster tempos, altered chords, and harmonies that involved greater ranges of notes which were frequently played at blistering speeds. Parker was more inventive and proficient than any of the others. His records are widely collected today, especially by young, aspiring jazz musicians, and he remains an inspiration to many. An individualist beyond compare not only in his music, but also in his life style, he died in 1955 at the age of 34, the victim of over-indulgence in drink, drugs, and sex.

That Sonny should have Parker, whose well-known nickname was "Bird," as an idol is important. Parker flew freely and soared to the heights in all aspects of his life. He was one of a kind and he became a legend ("Bird Lives" is a popular slogan in jazz circles even today). Sonny's life begins to parallel Parker's early. Joachim Berendt says of Parker: "He lived a dreary, joyless life and became acquainted with narcotics almost simultaneously with music. It is believed that Parker had become a victim of 'the habit' by the time he was 15." So also, it seems, had Sonny. A further reference to Parker is made when the narrator thinks of Sonny when he hears a group of boys outside his classroom window: "One boy was whistling a tune, at once very complicated and very simple, it seemed to be pouring out of him as though he were a bird, and it sounded very cool and moving through all that harsh, bright air, only just holding its own through all those other sounds." The key words in this passage are "complicated," "bird," and "holding its own through all those other sounds," all of which evoke the image of Bird Parker blowing his cool and complicated improvisations over the accompaniment of the other members of a jazz combo.

When Sonny tells his brother that he is interested in playing *jazz,* the essential difference of the two brothers becomes evident. Sonny expresses his admiration for Charlie Parker, whom the older brother had never heard of. For the narrator, jazz means Louis Armstrong. Armstrong certainly was a highly-regarded, popular jazz musician—probably the best known in the world, having become

known as Ambassador Satch because of his frequent trips abroad—but among bop musicians he represented the older, more traditional form of jazz.

Baldwin's equating Sonny with Parker and his brother with Armstrong is important because it emphasizes the difference between the two brothers with reference to both individualism and knowing oneself. Sonny refers to Armstrong as "old-time" and "down home." There is a strong Uncle Tom implication in this and it is true that Armstrong was viewed this way by many of the young black musicians in the 1940s and 1950s. Had Armstrong become "the white man's nigger"? Had Sonny's brother? Probably so. He had tried, as best he could, to reject his black self through becoming a respectable math teacher and dissociating himself from black culture as much as possible. He was careful not to do those things that he felt whites expected blacks to do. Baldwin understood this attitude, acknowledging that only when he went to Europe could he feel comfortable listening to Bessie Smith, the well-known black blues singer of the 1920s and early 1930s. However, in fairness to Sonny's brother, it must be noted that after World War II bop musicians and their music were the subject of considerable controversy. [In *Jazz: A History of the New York Scene,* 1962] Samuel Charters and Leonard Kunstadt observe: "The pathetic attempts of Moslem identification, the open hostility, the use of narcotics—everything was blamed on bop. It was the subject of vicious attacks in the press, the worst since the days of 'Unspeakable Jazz Must Go,' and the musicians were openly ridiculed." It is in this context that we must consider the narrator's concern about Sonny and the life style that he seems to be adopting.

Up to the final section of the story, Baldwin uses jazz references well, but then some surprising "contraries" begin to appear. As Sonny begins to play his blues in the last scene, he struggles with the music, which is indicative of how he struggles with his life: "He and the piano stammered, started one way, got scared, stopped; started another way, panicked, marked time, started again; then seemed to have found a direction, panicked again, got stuck." As Sonny flounders about, Baldwin brings into play two key references that lead and inspire Sonny to finally find himself through his music: The character of Creole and the playing of the song "Am I Blue?" Baldwin's use of these two elements is, to say the least, unusual.

The use of Creole as the leader of the group Sonny plays with in this last and all-important section of the story is paradoxical. Baldwin seems to be emphasizing Sonny's bringing his brother back to a realization of the importance of his roots as epitomized in Sonny's playing of the blues. Why did Baldwin choose a leader who is not strictly representative of the black heritage that can be traced back through the years of slavery to West Africa with its concomitant blues tradition that includes work songs, field hollers, and "African-influenced spirituals"? Creoles were generally regarded as descendants of French and Spanish settlers in Louisiana. Over the years, many Creole men took as mistresses light-skinned girls and produced that class referred to as black Creoles, many of whom passed for white and set themselves above the Negroes. From the early 1800s they were generally well-educated and cultured, some even having gone to Europe to attend school. Music was also an important part of life among the Creoles. According to James Collier (and this is very important for the point I am making),

> . . . The black Creole was what was called a "legitimate" musician. He could read music; he did not improvise; and he was familiar with the standard repertory of arias, popular songs, and marches that would have been contained in any white musician's song bag. The point is important: The Creole musician was entirely European in tradition, generally scornful of the blacks from across the tracks who could not read music and who played those "low-down" blues [*The Making of Jazz: A Comprehensive History,* 1979].

After the Civil War, the advent of Jim Crow laws deeply affected the status of black Creoles. In particular, the passage of Louisiana Legislative Code III was devastating in that it declared that any person "with any black ancestry, however remote, would be considered black." Many Creoles with musical training were hard hit and sought work as musicians. The competition with Negroes was keen and unpleasant, but eventually, Leroy Ostransky notes [in *Jazz City: The Impact of Our Cities on the Development of Jazz,* 1978], both groups "discovered each other's strengths and the resulting synthesis helped bring about the first authentic jazz style, what came to be called the New Orleans style."

Though Creoles did contribute to the development of jazz as it is played in Baldwin's story, it must be remembered that the story seems to emphasize the importance of the strictly black experience and tradition, which for most people means the heritage that includes not only post-Emancipation Jim Crow laws, but also the indignities of slavery, the horrors of the middle-passage, and the cruelties of capture and separation from families in West Africa. The black Creoles were not distinctly a part of that culture.

The second confusing element in the last section of the story is Baldwin's use of the song "Am I Blue?" It is certainly not an example of the classic 12-bar, 3-lined blues form. However, it might be pointed out that in the context of this story it would not have to be, because Sonny is part of a jazz movement that is characterized by new ideas. Nevertheless, we must not forget the main thrust of the last scene: The narrator's rebirth and acceptance of *his* heritage. Certainly most musicologists would agree that blues music has a complexity that includes contributions from many sources, but the choice of song is questionable for other reasons.

It would have seemed appropriate for Baldwin to have chosen some song that had been done by one of his favorite blues singers, Bessie Smith. In *Nobody Knows My Name* he says: "It was Bessie Smith, through her tone and her cadence, who helped me dig back to the way I myself must have spoken when I was a pickaninny, and to re-member the things I had heard and seen and felt. I had buried them very deep." In relation to the idea of the narrator's rebirth through his experience of hearing Sonny play the blues, choosing a song made famous by Bessie Smith would have been fitting and would have reflected Baldwin's personal experiences. But this is not the case.

Why did Baldwin choose "Am I Blue?" a song far-removed from the black experience? It was written in 1929 by composer Harry Akst and lyricist Grant Clarke, who were both white, as far as I can determine. Akst was born on New York's East Side, the son of a classical musician who played violin in various symphony orchestras and wished Harry to become a classical pianist. However, Harry became a composer of popular music and eventually worked with well-known show business personalities like Irving Berlin and Fred Astaire. One of his best-known songs is "Baby Face." Grant Clarke was born in Akron, Ohio, and worked as an actor before going to work for a music publisher. In 1912, his "Ragtime Cowboy Joe" became a hit.

Akst and Clarke wrote "Am I Blue?" specifically for Ethel Waters, an extremely popular black singer who had paid her dues and sung her share of the blues through the years, but who had by 1929 achieved fame on the stage and in films. The song was written for the film musical "On With the Show." Ethel Waters received a four-week guarantee in the making of the film at $1,250 per week. Bessie Smith never achieved a comparable fame among general audiences. Ethel Waters seems to have been more in a class with Louis Armstrong in terms of general entertainment value and popularity. The bop musician's point of view was antithetical to the Uncle Tom image they had of Armstrong. Ralph Ellison observes: "The thrust toward respectability exhibited by the Negro jazzmen of Parker's generation drew much of its immediate fire from their understandable rejection of the traditional entertainer's role—a heritage from the minstral tradition—exemplified by such an outstanding creative musician as Louis Armstrong. Why would Baldwin choose a song made popular by Ethel Waters, rather than one by his favorite, Bessie Smith?

All of this is not to say that "Am I Blue?" is not in the blues tradition in terms of message. The lyric expresses the sadness of a lonely woman whose man has left her, not unusual content for all forms of blues songs through the years. But it is what Paul Oliver refers to [in *The Meaning of the Blues,* 1963] as one of those "synthetic 'blue' compositions of the Broadway show and the commercial confections of 52nd Street that purport to be blues by the inclusion of the word in the titles." Therefore, in view of the song's origin, Baldwin's fondness for Bessie Smith, and the possible intent of Sonny's playing the blues to bring the narrator back to an acknowledgment and affirmation of his roots, the choice of this particular song seems inappropriate.

And yet Baldwin may have known what he was doing. Is it possible that in **"Sonny's Blues"** he is indicating that tradition is very important, but that change is also important (and probably inevitable) and that it builds on tradition, which is never fully erased but continues to be an integral part of the whole? Ellison is again relevant here: "Perhaps in the swift change of American society in which the meaning of one's origins are so quickly lost, one of the chief values of living with music lies in its power to give us an orientation in time. In doing so, it gives significance to all those indefinable aspects of experience which nevertheless help to make us what we are." Both Ellison and Baldwin seem to be saying that we are an amalgam of many ingredients that have become fused over the centuries. We cannot separate ourselves, *all* people, from one another. Having Sonny, inspired by Creole, playing "Am I Blue?" for what we must assume is a racially mixed audience in a Greenwich Village club gives credence to these ideas and helps to explain what might otherwise appear to be some inexplicable incongruities.

Michael Clark (essay date 1985)

SOURCE: "James Baldwin's 'Sonny's Blues': Childhood, Light and Art," in *CLA Journal,* Vol. XXIX, No. 2, December, 1985, pp. 197-205.

[*In the following essay, Clark analyzes Baldwin's use of light and dark imagery and the role of art in "Sonny's Blues."*]

"Sonny's Blues" by James Baldwin is a sensitive story about the reconciliation of two brothers, but it is much more than that. It is, in addition, an examination of the importance of the black heritage and of the central importance of music in that heritage. Finally, the story probes the central role that art must play in human existence. To examine all of these facets of human existence is a rather formidable undertaking in a short story, even in a longish short story such as this one. Baldwin not only undertakes this task, but he does it superbly. One of the central ways that Baldwin fuses all of these complex elements is by using a metaphor of childhood, which is supported by ancillary images of light and darkness. He does the job so well that the story is a *tour de force,* a penetrating study of American culture.

One of the most important passages in this story is the description of Harlem's stultifying environment, a place where children are "smothered": "Some escaped the trap, most didn't. Those who got out always left something of themselves behind, as some animals amputate a leg and leave it in the trap." The implicit assumption here is that childhood is a holistic state, whereas the process of growing older maims the individual. Indeed, there is frequent evidence throughout the story that Baldwin sees childhood as a touchstone by which to judge the shortcomings of adulthood.

One of the more explicit statements of this same theme occurs in a flashback when the narrator remembers his own childhood home. There seems to be some autobiographical recollection here by Baldwin since he distances

this material even from the fictitious narrator: in the course of this passage the boy narrator is transmuted into an autonomous and anonymous "child":

> And the living room would be full of church folks and relatives. There they sit, in chairs all around the living room, and the night is creeping up outside, but nobody knows it yet. You can see the darkness growing against the windowpanes and you hear the street noises every now and again, or maybe the jangling beat of a tambourine from one of the churches close by, but it's real quiet in the room. For a moment nobody's talking, but every face looks darkening, like the sky outside. And my mother rocks a little from the waist, and my father's eyes are closed. Everyone is looking at something a child can't see. For a minute they've forgotten the children. Maybe a kid is lying on the rug, half asleep. Maybe somebody's got a kid in his lap and is absent-mindedly stroking the kid's head. Maybe there's a kid, quiet and big-eyed, curled up in a big chair in the corner. The silence, the darkness coming, and the darkness in the faces frightens the child obscurely. He hopes that the hand which strokes his forehead will never stop—will never die. He hopes that there will never come a time when the old folks won't be sitting around the living room, talking about where they've come from, and what they've seen, and what's happened to them and their kinfolk.

> But something deep and watchful in the child knows that this is bound to end, is already ending. In a moment someone will get up and turn on the light. Then the old folks will remember the children and they won't talk any more that day. And when the light fills the room, the child is filled with darkness. He knows that everytime this happens he is moved just a little closer to that darkness outside. The darkness outside is what the old folks have been talking about. It's what they've come from. It's what they endure. The child knows that they won't talk any more because if he knows too much about what's happened to *them,* he'll know too much too soon, about what's going to happen to *him.*

This passage has much of the same idea—and imagery—of Wordsworth's "Ode: Intimations of Immortality": growing up is an initiation into the trouble of this world. Wordsworth characterizes youth as a time of "light"; adulthood, on the other hand, embraces us like the doors of a prison closing around us, darkening our lives. The imagery that Baldwin uses replicates Wordsworth's, as does in part his theme. In childhood man is in a holistic state, closer to a heavenly condition.

If growing up in general entails the losing of an envied state, then growing up in the ghetto is even worse. The high school kids that the narrator must teach show every evidence—even in their youth—of having already "matured":

> I listened to the boys outside, downstairs, shouting and cursing and laughing. Their laughter struck me for perhaps the first time. It was not the joyous laughter which—God knows why—one associates with children. It was mocking and insular, its intent to denigrate. It was disenchanted, and in this, also, lay the authority of their curses.

These children are not children. Already, the seeds of their destruction are sown. These children are "growing up with a rush and their heads bumped abruptly against the low ceiling of their actual possibilities. They were filled with rage."

The implication of this story is that art—whether it be the music that Sonny plays or the fiction that Baldwin writes—can give us some temporary relief from brutal reality.

—Michael Clark

It is interesting to note that in the midst of this despair, the narrator's attention is grabbed by a solitary "voice" in the schoolyard: "One boy was whistling a tune, at once very complicated and very simple, it seemed to be pouring out of him as though he were a bird, and it sounded very cool and moving through all that harsh, bright air, only just holding its own through all those other sounds." As Suzy Goldman has astutely observed [in *Negro American Literature Forum*, 1974], this passage foreshadows the concern of the story, for Sonny will be the "one" child who stands out in the otherwise bleak landscape; he is the "singer" in the midst of all the other sounds. And he is the one person through all his hardships who has managed to maintain an unalloyed vision—as vital as a child's—in the midst of complication. For in this story, childhood is the measure of the man.

Baldwin makes good use of the childhood imagery throughout the story. When Sonny's junkie friend comes to tell the narrator of the fate of Sonny, the reader is confronted with a picture of a grotesque child, a person who "though he was a grown-up man, he still hung around that block, still spent hours on the street corners." When he grins, "it made him repulsive and it also brought to mind what he'd looked like as a kid." Here, then, is the adult who has never accepted adult responsibility, a mature man whose "childlike" qualities emphasize his adult deformity. Childhood here serves as the measure of adult shortcomings. And it is not the last time that the image is used in this story.

When the junkie and the narrator are walking towards the subway station, they pass a bar and the narrator spies a barmaid inside: "When she smiled one saw the little girl, one sensed the doomed, still-struggling woman beneath the battered face of the semi-whore." She is just one more example of the trapped animal who has become deformed in order to survive. The "little girl" deserves much better.

It is in the context of such examples as this that the core of this story achieves meaning. This is, after all, a story about a "baby brother." But in order to understand Sonny's position in the world, we might first look at the illustrative example of his father. This story is told by the mother to the narrator. It is meant to be a parallel to the main action.

When the father and his brother (the narrator's uncle) were youths, they were happy-go-lucky spirits. The uncle loved music, as is evidenced by his guitar. One bright, moonlit night, the father and uncle were walking down a hill and the uncle was struck by a car driven by some white men, who did not stop. The "accident" is a blatant example of racism; the people in the vehicle are drunk and "aim the car straight at him." This anecdote, or symbolic tableau, is meant to provide a thematic backdrop to the narrator's own situation. He, too, has a brother that is musically oriented. The mother tells the story so that the narrator might be more diligent in looking after Sonny. The design of this anecdote, however, is further illuminating. This incident in the father's life is parallel to the narrator's description of what took place in the living room of his youth: it is a maturing experience, after which the father's life is never the same. It marks the critical moment when youth gives way to adulthood and responsibility. And this scene partakes of the same imagery that controls the living-room scene, as well as the rest of the story. Before the accident, it was "bright like day," while after the terrible accident, the father "says he never in his life seen anything as dark as that road after the lights of that car had gone away. This accident marks the transmutation of the father's life from youth to adulthood. In addition, the hand of the author is manifest in the controlling imagery, in the change from light to darkness.

So far this essay has shown that the light and dark imagery is pervasive in **"Sonny's Blues"** and that this imagery can be roughly equated with the respective conditions of childhood and adulthood. The question still remains as to how exactly this information can lead us to a better appreciation of Sonny's character. To begin, it might be useful to contrast the narrator and Sonny. There is some evidence for seeing Sonny as a *doppelganger* for the narrator. At least, such lines as the following are susceptible to this interpretation: when the narrator discovers that Sonny has been arrested for heroin possession and use, he notes that "I couldn't believe it: but what I mean by that is that I couldn't find any room for it anywhere inside me. I had kept it outside me for a long time. I hadn't wanted to know." The *lawlessness* of Sonny is something that is excluded from the highly controlled rationality of the narrator, the very kind of split that we find in such classic stories of the "double" as Poe's "William Wilson." Let it suffice for our argument, however, to note only that the narrator possesses qualities that are ambiguous. He is certainly a "success"—he has a college degree and a conventional job teaching high school. He represents middle-class values. But more can be said. He teaches algebra, which suggests his devotion to the scientific and formulaic. When Sonny talks to him about music, he shows no empathy for jazz, especially not for the avant-garde music of players like Charlie "Bird" Parker.

Though the narrator has escaped the most terrible consequences of growing up in the ghetto, then, he still is maimed in some way—and he knows it. When he and Sonny are in a cab on the way to the narrator's apartment, he notes that "it came to me that what we both were seeking through our separate cab windows was that part of ourselves which had been left behind." Both of these characters have been damaged by life. It is significant, then, that the story opens with the narrator looking at a newspaper, reading about Sonny's arrest and then staring at the story "in the faces and bodies of the people, and in my own face, trapped in the darkness which roared outside." The narrator, indeed, is trapped in the darkness. Only the events of the story will show him how to escape.

Sonny's quest is best described by himself when he writes to the narrator: "I feel like a man who's been trying to climb up out of some deep, real deep and funky hole and just saw the sun up there, outside. I got to get outside." Sonny is a person who finds his life a living hell, but he knows enough to strive for the "light." As it is chronicled in this story, his quest is for regaining something from the past—from his own childhood and from the pasts of all who have come before him. The means for doing this is his music, which is consistently portrayed in terms of light imagery. When Sonny has a discussion with the narrator about the future, the narrator describes Sonny's face as a mixture of concern and hope: "[T]he worry, the thoughtfulness, played on it still, the way shadows play on a face which is staring into the fire." This fire image is reinforced shortly afterward when the narrator describes Sonny's aspirations once more in terms of light: "[I]t was as though he were all wrapped up in some cloud, some fire, some vision all his own." To the narrator and to Isabel's family, the music that Sonny plays is simply "wierd and disordered." but to Sonny, the music is seen in starkly positive terms: his failure to master the music will mean "death," while success will mean "life."

The light and dark imagery culminates in the final scene, where the narrator, apparently for the first time, listens to Sonny play the piano. The location is a Greenwich Village club. Appropriately enough, the narrator is seated "in a dark corner." In contrast, the stage is dominated by light, which Baldwin reiterates with a succession of images: "light . . . circle of light . . . light . . . flame . . . light." Although Sonny has a false start, he gradually settles into his playing and ends the first set with some intensity: "Everything had been burned out of [Sonny's face], and at the same time, things usually hidden were being burned in, by the fire and fury of the battle which was occurring in him up there."

The culmination of the set occurs when Creole, the leader of the players, begins to play *Am I Blue*. At this point, "something began to happen." Apparently, the narrator at this time realizes that this music *is* important. The music is central to the experience of the black experience, and it is described in terms of light imagery:

> Creole began to tell us what the blues were all about. They were not about anything very new. He and his boys up there were keeping it new, at the risk of ruin, destruction, madness, and death, in order to find new ways to make us listen. For, while the tale of how we suffer, and how we are delighted, and how we may triumph is never new, it always must be heard. There

isn't any other tale to tell, it's the only light we've got in all this darkness.

James Baldwin has written that "[h]istory is the present . . . You and I are history. We carry our history. We act our history." Sonny's "blues" becomes an apt symbol in this story because Sonny has managed to look back at and *use* his own personal life of grief. But from the narrator's perspective, Sonny has looked back even further than that. Undoubtedly, he has looked back to his childhood, to that time before the "amputations" that formed his adult consciousness. This explains what the narrator means when he says that he "seemed to hear with what burning he had made it his." In the context of much of the other light imagery of the story (i.e., the time associated with the light of childhood), this image signifies in practical terms that music taps the very roots of existence, that it puts the artist in touch with the fluid emotions that he has known in perfection only as a child. But Sonny looks back not only to his own past, but also back to *all* the experience that makes up his history—which is the history of his race. Contained in the music that Sonny is playing is the culmination of all the suffering that Sonny and his race have suffered. Consequently, sorrow is transformed into a pure emotion that is not solitary but communal. The music becomes an expression of history: "He had made it his: that long line, of which we knew only Mama and Daddy. And he was giving it back, as everything must be given back, so that, passing through death, it can live forever."

The implication of this story is that art—whether it be the music that Sonny plays or the fiction that Baldwin writes—can give us some temporary relief from brutal reality. The narrator sees Sonny's music as giving him a "moment" though "the world waited outside, as hungry as a tiger, and . . . trouble stretched above us, longer than the sky." Clearly, the moment is worth the effort.

Sonny has succeeded in making his life whole once again. Though he is an adult who has suffered much, who has suffered metaphoric "amputations," he has also through his music managed to recapture the holism that we usually associate with childhood. Baldwin emphasizes this when he has the narrator buy Sonny a drink at the close of the story: "a Scotch and milk." As Sonny began to play again, this drink sat atop the piano and "glowed." It is an apt symbol for the value of Sonny's success: milk, childhood, and light all suggest that this manchild has achieved a reconciliation with reality that is far superior to the narrator's conventional lifestyle.

Ronald Bieganowski (essay date 1988)

SOURCE: "James Baldwin's Vision of Otherness in 'Sonny's Blues' and *Giovanni's Room*," in *CLA Journal*, Vol. XXXII, No. 1, September, 1988, pp. 69-80.

[*In the following essay, Bieganowski compares the treatment of the theme of alienation in "Sonny's Blues" and Baldwin's novel.*]

For several decades now, James Baldwin has maintained his position of importance among black writers through his novels, stories, essays, and interviews, generating continued scholarly interest. In her recent book on Baldwin [*James Baldwin,* 1980], Carolyn Sylvander points to the "nuclear ideas and beliefs" around which Baldwin's works have developed and grown over the years. For many readers, Baldwin establishes as the basis of his fiction "the quest for identity," for "true, fundamental being" and the dislocations of the modern world. For instance, Shirley Ann Williams summarizes the core of Baldwin's fiction [in *James Baldwin: A Collection of Critical Essays,* edited by Keneth Kinnamon, 1974]: "Most of his characters have at the center of their portrayal an isolation from the society, the culture, even each other." While Baldwin's characters do show deep alienation from the world about them and certainly from other people, most significantly Baldwin's major characters show a profound alienation from themselves. That tension directs the energies of his stories.

One of the most recurrent but least defined of Baldwin's nuclear ideas in his equation: "To encounter oneself is to encounter the other." For several of his important characters, reconciliation with society and with each other can occur only after they have made peace with themselves. Two focal works, **"Sonny's Blues"** and *Giovanni's Room,* together define the full range of this equation between the *self* and *other* as well as reveal a recurrent process in his writings. As John Reilly suggests [in *Negro American Literature Forum,* July 1970], Baldwin's "leading theme—the discovery of identity—is nowhere presented more successfully than in the short story 'Sonny's Blues.'" *Giovanni's Room,* often overlooked because it appears to be Baldwin's weakest novel, represents, in Robert Bone's judgment [in *Tri Quarterly,* 1965], "a key position in Baldwin's spiritual development." Brother in **"Sonny's Blues"** and David in *Giovanni's Room* clearly focus Baldwin's vision of otherness requiring a profound sense of one's *self.*

For Baldwin, a fully human understanding of another person depends upon truthful self-knowledge: "One can only face in others what one can face in oneself." This interdependence between a vision of otherness and one's sense of self operates vividly in Baldwin's fiction. Such mutual knowledge operates at significant levels in *Go Tell It on the Mountain, Another Country, Tell Me How Long the Train's Been Gone, If Beale Street Could Talk,* and *Just Above My Head.* Specifically, Baldwin's masterfully fashioned **"Sonny's Blues"** can alert us to some brilliant facets of the larger, more roughly drawn, *Giovanni's Room*: Brother's understanding of himself allows him to recognize Sonny's pain as well as Sonny's own self-understanding; because David never comes fully to accept himself, he never truly loves Giovanni. Among Baldwin's writings, the two stories share a common narrative structure; they echo with comparable imagery, reflecting windows and mirror; most importantly, they address, with their central energies, this human truth based on the reciprocal knowledge of *self* and *other.* And finally, together these stories reveal Baldwin's larger devotion as artist to the freedom and fulfillment of the human person.

In each story, the narrator confronts his own self-image as he struggles with understanding, with love of the important other person in his life. Though Sonny's brother's preoccupation with himself makes him intolerant of Sonny's troubles, the pain and mystery of his daughter's death waken him to his wife's wound and to Sonny's need. Brother (Baldwin gives him no proper name) achieves his identity as Brother in his listening to Sonny. David, in *Giovanni's Room,* cannot turn his gaze fully away from himself toward Giovanni. David remains isolated in the egotism of his sympathies. As Robert Bone has pointed out, both Sonny and Giovanni share priestly roles as journeymen in suffering. More significantly, however, the narrators—Brother and David—contain the dynamic tension in each story. **"Sonny's Blues"** begins with Brother staring at his own reflection in a subway window and closes with his watching Sonny play; *Giovanni's Room* begins with David watching his reflection in the "darkening gleam of the window pane" and ends with his image trapped in the bedroom's mirror. Each story gains its vitality from the intimacy each narrator gains with himself through feeling compassion for Sonny and Giovanni.

II

"Sonny's Blues" shows the narrator's (Brother's) growth from apparent self-reflection, really self-absorption, to authentic self-knowledge gained through honestly listening to Sonny himself. The story opens with Brother's shock at the news of Sonny's arrest for using and selling heroin. The first paragraph records Brother's astonishment at this news: "I read about it in the paper, in the subway, on my way to work. . . . I stared at it in the swinging lights of the subway car, and in the faces and bodies of the people, and in my own face, trapped in the darkness which roared outside." Transfixed by Sonny's arrest, Brother identifies the dread reflected back to him in the subway window as finally dread not for Sonny but for himself: "I couldn't believe it: but what I mean by that is that I couldn't find any room for it anywhere inside me." Through Brother's further self-reflections, the story probes his feeling of being "trapped in the darkness which roared outside." Darkness outside reveals his own inner darkness.

Brother's reflection in the subway's window occurs simply because the train tunnel is darker than the lighted subway car. The outer darkness provides the background against which he can see himself. In an important reminiscence of his childhood, Brother describes the role outer darkness played at his family's Sunday night dinners. He remembers his mother along with older church folks and relatives on Sunday afternoon, talking after the big dinner:

> There they sit, in chairs all around the living room and the night is creeping up outside, but nobody knows it yet. You can see the darkness growing against the windowpanes and you hear the street noises every now and again, or maybe the jangling beat of a tambourine from one of the churches close by, but it's real quiet in the room. For a moment nobody's talking, but every face looks darkening, like the sky outside.

Brother's memory is from a child's perspective as he recalls that "everyone's looking at something a child can't see." An adult's stroking the child's forehead eases the fear caused by the coming night's blackness.

When the lights are turned on, the children are filled with inner darkness, confusion, insecurity. The children do not understand because they have not yet lived through outer darkness. In reminiscence, Brother recognizes what the adults then were seeing and talking about because now, as an adult, he understands that there exists outside a good deal of darkness. Brother's memory of those Sunday dinners ends with this recognition.

> The darkness outside is what the old folks have been talking about. It's what they've come from. It's what they endure. The child knows that they won't talk anymore because if he knows too much about what's happened to *them*, he'll know too much too soon, about what's going to happen to him.

Pain or suffering or death constitutes the bleak substance of experience from which these people fashion themselves. The adults, telling their stories, achieve a moment of authority over their experience and testify to the success, though perhaps minimal, with which, for the present, they have met the outer darkness. Because of the outer night, they have had to find inner light to live. In their talking, they bear witness as individuals and as a religious family to the presence of that inner light. After a painful argument, Brother leaves Sonny's room in the Village. With tears in his eyes, Brother whistles to himself, *"You going to need me, baby, one of these cold, rainy days."* At that moment, Brother believes that he is addressing Sonny. Later, in the midst of his own outer darkness, Brother realizes that he needs Sonny. Only when Brother admits that he lives in the nightmare of his child's death can he then understand what the adults were talking about after dinner and what Sonny plays in his music. The day of his daughter's funeral, Brother can write Sonny in jail, recognizing, "My trouble made his real."

Sonny, of course, knows dim streets as well as heroin's blankness. For him music, the blues, instead of talking, helps tame the terror of the roaring night. Sonny, in telling his own blues, gains some sense of who he is. Talking, telling, and playing the blues require a reciprocal understanding that starts with one's own sense of self. Trying to explain to Brother why he must play, Sonny describes the self-knowledge, the self-possession, necessary for authentic blues, for meaningful talk.

> You walk these streets, black and funky and cold, and there's not really a living ass to talk to, and there's nothing shaking, and there's no way of getting it out—that storm inside. You can't talk it and you can't make love with it, and when you finally try to get with it and play it, you realize *nobody's* listening. So *you've* got to listen. You got to find a way to listen.

The loneliness of Sonny's own storm tempers his spirit so that he gains some momentary hold on himself. Though

precarious, incomplete, and temporary, that sense of himself allows him to speak through his music. (Ida Scott, in *Another Country,* sings movingly not because of her vocal power but because she sings out of a profound sense of self.) As Sonny achieves a sense of identity through suffering his private pain, so analogously does Brother deepen his sense of self when he finds room inside for Sonny and his trouble.

While listening to a gospel singer in the street, Sonny recognizes in her song a parallel to his own trial: "Listening to that woman sing, it struck me all of a sudden how much she must have had to go through—to sing like that. It's *repulsive* to think you have to suffer that much." When Sonny tells through music his tale of suffering, Brother hears corroborated his own pain: his daughter's death and his temporary rejection of Sonny. In that moment of reciprocal understanding, Brother knows that "the man who creates the music is hearing something else, is dealing with the roar rising from the void and imposing order on it as it hits the air." For Brother, the musician, the artist addresses the darkness outside:

> For, while the tale of how we suffer, and how we are delighted, and how we may triumph is never new, it always must be heard. There isn't any other tale to tell, it's the only light we've got in all this darkness.

For Brother, Sonny's blues replaces the family's talk after Sunday dinner. Sonny, in the night club's center light, offers hope to those in the circles of darkness outside. As John Reilly concludes, Sonny, with his insight into suffering, can lead Brother to a discovery of self in community. Brother recognizes Sonny with his own "cup of trembling." He finally listens to Sonny telling how he suffers; in that listening Brother hears his own storm inside. Now he can fully acknowledge Sonny as "my brother." In affirming that relationship, Brother takes possession of his own identity. He who had no proper name throughout the story has learned who he is from Sonny. Brother, in saying "my brother" of Sonny, necessarily says "brother" of himself.

III

Brother begins his escape from the dark outside when the death of his daughter makes him think of Sonny and his trouble. Brother's route to freedom goes from self-image trapped in the subway window to recognizing Sonny as his own brother in the nightclub's spotlight. At the opening of *Giovanni's Room,* David looks at his reflection in the darkening window as night falls only to see his image eventually fade before the dawn. The reciprocal knowledge of self and other of which Brother is capable eludes David. David's self-images in the window and mirror frame this novel, revealing David's fatal blindness to Giovanni.

David's reminiscences during the last night of Giovanni's life and where they begin: with narcissistic fascination, shutting out all others. David's willfulness, along with his contempt for others, underlines this preoccupation with self.

David admits early pride in his will power, in his ability to make a decision and carry it through. He recognizes that he has been following through a choice he made many years before this darkening night: "I had decided to allow no room in the universe for something which shamed and frightened me. . . . This is certainly what my decision, made so long ago in Joey's bed, came to." Uncertain of his motives, David runs from Joey, confused by his feelings and by sex. Haunted by nightmares of his mother, disappointed in his father, David flees from his family. Panic, suffering, terror in others drive David to flight from them and from himself. A later incident when he was in the Army confirmed his fear. With the court-martial of his lover, David saw part of what he was fleeing. David says, "The panic his punishment caused in me was as close as I ever came to facing in myself the terrors I sometimes saw clouding another man's eyes." Such willfulness born out of fear isolates David in self-pity and self-deception. Because David fears to see his own confused interior, Giovanni's ill-kept room ultimately shames and frightens him.

David's willfulness matches Hella's own. Both say they believe that their true freedom can come through commitment, attachment, dedication. But both also define commitment in terms primarily of their own *self* rather than the *other*. David recognizes that people cannot "invent their mooring posts," though he continues to try to do so. And Hella describes her desire for commitment: "It isn't what I've *got*. It isn't even what I *want*. It's that *you've* got me." Their strong need for another person in their lives grows desperate with their insistent egoism.

Giovanni, of course, most clearly recognizes the pride in David's willfulness. Giovanni, chiding David for an American's notion of time, senses the arrogant determination that David shows:

> "Time always sounds like a parade *chez vous*—a *triumphant* parade, like armies with banners entering a town. . . . as though with enough time and all that fearful energy and virtue you people have, everything will be settled, solved, put in its place. And when I say everything," he added, grimly, "I mean all the serious, dreadful things, like pain and death and love, in which you Americans do not believe."

Though Giovanni may offer as a contrast his notion of time as commonplace as water in which everyone must live, nevertheless he finds David's self-confidence attractive because it complements his own attitude. But Giovanni's description of David's persistent deliberateness contains his most painful recognition of David's self-serving love.

> "You are not leaving me for a *woman*. If you were really in love with this little girl, you would not have had to be so cruel to me . . . You do not . . . love anyone! You never have loved anyone, I am sure you never will! You love your purity, you love your mirror. . . ."

Giovanni accurately describes David's attempts at love. David's resolve to avoid shame and fear so tyrannizes him that he can only retreat to self-esteem before others' needs for his care. Jacques directly challenges David for the aloof isolation that he appears to find most secure. At the first meeting of David and Giovanni, Jacques warns and criticizes David:

> "You play it safe long enough . . . and you'll end up trapped in your own dirty body, forever and forever— like me. . . . the way to be really despicable is to be contemptuous of other people's pain."

Jacques' anxiety proves true. David does not allow Giovanni's pain into his life because David will not take possession of his own pain and love. Contempt allows him to justify his willfulness as well as somewhat righteously embrace his lonely isolation. His self-pity feeds on his pride; his preoccupation with himself grows so that by the novel's end, David feels trapped with his self-image.

Unlike Brother in **"Sonny's Blues,"** who turns from making himself his primary object of concern, David becomes more and more fascinated with himself as his primary object. His feelings of being doubleminded, of being torn by "another me" from the "I" who reads, walks, or writes, of deep ambivalence in his affections, reveal his awful self-centeredness. At the end of the story on the morning of Giovanni's execution, David's actions show how thoroughly imprisoned he is with himself.

Night's darkness brings David to this "most terrible morning" of his life. The dawn does not bring a new light for David; Giovanni's death does not offer life for David. Instead, David sees confirmed the life that he has been living. Though he has packed his bags and cleaned the house, he still feels unable to move: "I pour myself a very little drink, watching, in the window pane, my reflection, which steadily becomes more faint. I seem to be fading away before my eyes—this fancy amuses me, and I laugh to myself." The self reflected in the darkness dissolves; this day could begin David's looking through that old self of willfulness toward the world outside. Thoughts of Giovanni approaching his death almost fill David's mind as he walks into the bedroom. There David becomes "terribly aware of the mirror." Out of the corner of his eye, he sees his naked body in the mirror: "The body in the mirror forces me to turn and face it. . . . It is trapped in my mirror as it is trapped in time and it hurries toward revelation." For David, his body remains a mystery; his sex troubles him. He remains preoccupied with his own uncertainty. But his painful questioning does not make Giovanni's or Hella's or anyone else's real for him. Here David represents, according to Charlotte Alexander [in *James Baldwin: A Collection of Critical Essays,* 1974], one of Baldwin's characters who seldom can confront in a reassuring way "the stink of reality." Unlike Brother, whose suffering makes Sonny's real for him, David stands transfixed by his own pain and death and love. David's pride keeps him from understanding that the "tale of how we suffer, and how we are delighted, and how we may triumph is never new," is never one's private tale. He continues to be contemptuous of others' pain because he despises his own anxiety, fear, and death.

IV

In these stories, honest understanding of others depends upon truthful acceptance of one's self. In both stories, the ability to see someone else requires looking selflessly beyond one's own immediate needs. In **"Sonny's Blues,"** this reciprocal vision of otherness is also described in the imagery of music. At the nightclub where Sonny plays his blues, Brother says:

> All I know about music is that not many people ever really hear it. And even then, on the rare occasions when something opens within, and the music enters, what we mainly hear, or hear corroborated, are personal, private, vanishing evocations.

Brother, of course, finally has that something open within and he can really hear Sonny's blues. David appears never to really hear Giovanni, fearing corroboration from Giovanni of the needs deep within David himself. Other Baldwin characters also struggle to gain their own self-understanding as they come to know another more deeply; certainly Leo Proudhammer of *Tell Me How Long* and Hall Montana of *Just Above My Head* do so.

Brother goes on with his consideration of music as he describes the musician. The artist hears something other than person, private, vanishing evocations. The musician addresses the roar rising from the void and imposes order on it. Sonny's playing provides a moment of revelation for Brother and for the reader. Sonny leads Brother to understanding himself and others through listening to the blues. In his vision of otherness, James Baldwin, through Brother's and David's telling their tales, leads his reader to human truth.

Some years before publishing these stories, Baldwin offered a description of the truth he believes fiction must approach. He writes in "Everybody's Protest Novel"

> Let us say, then, that truth, as used here, is meant to imply a devotion to the human being, his freedom and fulfillment.

Baldwin distinguishes this devotion to the human being from devotion to humanity, wanting to avoid devotion to a cause or to a cultural invention. He specifies this truth necessary to fiction by identifying what a human being is. The human person is

> . . . something resolutely indefinable, unpredictable. In overlooking, denying, evading his complexity—which is nothing more than the disquieting complexity of ourselves—we are diminished and we perish; only within this web of ambiguity, paradox, this hunger, danger, darkness, can we find at once ourselves and the power that will free us from ourselves. It is this power of revelation which is the business of the novelist, this journey toward a more vast reality which must take precedence over all other claims.

The reciprocal understanding necessary for Brother and Sonny and for David and Giovanni defines the reciprocal vision necessary to seeing the truth in Baldwin's fiction. One can only face in Baldwin's writing what one can face in oneself. For Baldwin, "our humanity is our burden, our life; we need not battle for it; we need only to do what is infinitely more difficult—that is accept it."

Patricia R. Robertson (essay date 1991)

SOURCE: "Baldwin's 'Sonny's Blues': The Scapegoat Metaphor," in *The University of Mississippi Studies in English,* Vol. IX, 1991, pp. 189-98.

[*In the following essay, Robertson traces the development of the scapegoat metaphor in Baldwin's "Sonny's Blues."*]

In James Baldwin's only book of short stories, ***Going to Meet the Man, "Sonny's Blues"*** stands out as the best, most memorable. This story is both realistic and symbolic, part autobiography and part fiction. So memorable is **"Sonny's Blues"** that a student once put it at the top of a list of thirty stories read for a course in fiction. She commented, "The story haunts you; its beauty continues in your mind long after the original reading and discussion." The story's haunting beauty comes from our participation in the scapegoat metaphor that creates the intricate tracery which holds the story together, forming a graceful spiral, a pattern of correspondences which informs and entices as it helps us to be free.

The scapegoat metaphor is developed through several images, the most important of which is music, with its links to suffering and brotherhood. But we are only dimly aware of this scapegoat pattern until we see the final, startling biblical image of the scotch and milk drink, "the very cup of trembling," which follows Sonny's playing of the blues and which clarifies the story's meaning. This "cup of trembling", then, is at once the Old Testament cup of justice and the New Testament cup of Gethsemane, or mercy. The Old Testament allusion to the "cup of trembling" leads directly to the scapegoat metaphor and the idea of pain and suffering of a people. The New Testament story of hope is carried in Sonny's name which suggests Christ symbolism and leads to the New Testament message of the 'cup of trembling' as the cup of Gethsemane which Christ drank, symbolizing the removal of sins for all who believe and hope for eternal life through belief in him. Sonny's name echoes this special relationship. Sonny, the scapegoat, is the hope of his particular world.

The power of guilt and suffering is revealed in Sonny's tenuous relationship with his own brother and in his immediate empathy with the revivalists; it has been foreshadowed in the anguish of the young friend who still feels a connection with Sonny. Through these people's responses we come to understand that brothers—literal or metaphorical—rescue, redeem, bring righteous anger, and act as scapegoats to open up the world of suffering; the friend begins this for Sonny's brother, the revivalists for Sonny, and Sonny for his brother and for us.

Further, the scapegoat metaphor is strengthened and enriched by the metaphor of shared suffering carried through music—either by a young boy's whistle, by the revivalist's hymns, or finally and most significantly by Sonny's hot piano on which he plays the blues. The blues metaphor also involves suffering and the sharing of suffering that supercedes race and time and cements us all together within our shared humanity. Sonny's music—the blues—has power to transform both his and our pain; through his sharing, Sonny becomes the ultimate scapegoat.

The term 'scapegoat' means 'sharing of pain'; it implies a true understanding of another's suffering. According to *Webster's New World Dictionary,* the scapegoat, the *caper emissarius,* or azazel, was originally "a goat over the heads of which the high priest of the ancient Jews confessed the sins of the people on the Day of Atonement, after which it was allowed to escape." More secularly and popularly, the scapegoat is "a person, group, or thing upon whom the blame for the mistakes or crimes of others is thrust."

Baldwin, himself, defines for us the scapegoat metaphor when he asserts "That all mankind is united by virtue of their humanity." He writes elsewhere, "'It is a terrible, an inexorable, law that one cannot deny the humanity of another without diminishing one's own: in the face of one's victim, one sees oneself.'" In another context, Jack Matthews, in *Archetypal Themes in the Modern Story,* asks "When is a person not himself?" He answers, "When he reminds you of someone else and you can't see the living presence because of the remembered image. Or when, through accident or muddled design, he begins to embody our own secret fears. In psychology, this is termed projection; in a story or folktale, it is a celebration of the Scapegoat theme." Thus the literary scapegoat, through his own personal suffering or by his metaphorical sharing of his own sorrow, may allow us to see into life and into ourselves and thus vicariously transfer our guilt and pain through him and his suffering.

In this story music is the thread that accompanies and develops the brotherhood/scapegoat metaphor. For in his music Sonny reveals both his suffering and his understanding of others' pain. His music becomes a mystical, spiritual medium, an open-ended metaphor simultaneously comforting the player and the listener and releasing their guilt and pain. No words *could* have expressed so well what Sonny's music conveyed effortlessly. For, according to Cirlot, [in *A Dictionary of Symbols,* 1962] "Music represents an intermediate zone between the differentiated or material world and the undifferentiated realm of the 'pure will' of Schopenhauer." The power of this emotional transfer is seen in the brother's response. For through Sonny's music his brother comes to understand his own life, his parents' experience, his daughter's death, and his wife's grief. The brother recapitulates his own, Sonny's, and the family's suffering here at the end of the story. But as Kirkegaard says, in *Repetition,* "repetition" replaces "the more traditional Platonic term anamnesis or recollection." This is "not the simple repeating of an experience, but the recreating of it which redeems or awakens it to life, the end of the process . . . being the apocalyptic promise: 'Behold, I make all things new.'" Sonny's awakening is done through his blues, and its effect is revealed through the brother's sudden understanding, conveyed in the final image of the Scotch and milk drink, "the very cup of trembling." This central biblical image reverberates with life and reinforces the scapegoat metaphor. This recreation of life is also what the blues are all about. We come full circle.

The scapegoat metaphor is first presented very quietly when Sonny's childhood friend offers to become a scapegoat, insisting upon his symbolic action when he tells Sonny's brother, "Funny thing, . . . when I saw the papers this morning, the first thing I asked myself was if I had anything to do with [Sonny's arrest for using and selling heroin]. I felt sort of responsible." The young man offers to take the blame for Sonny's fall, but his hesitant plea is offensive to the brother who, like us, does not understand the symbolic significance of the act. For, instead of accepting and sharing the man's guilt, the brother becomes angry at the friend's panhandling. He feels superior to him and rejects his offer and his sympathy.

Just prior to this meeting with the old friend a boy's whistle echoes through the school yard. The whistle is "at once very complicated and very simple; it seemed to be pouring out of him as though he were a bird, and it sounded very cool and moving through all that harsh, bright air, only just holding its own through all those other sounds." But this music creates a central abstract image, a tone poem carrying the sadness and guilt of the brother, a simple yet complicated sounding of pain.

This first subtle pairing of music with guilt and pain sets the tone for the story. This young man, this emotional 'brother,' cannot comfort Sonny's brother, but paradoxically his sincere concern increases the brother's understanding of Sonny's problems. Further, this sad young man illustrates the community's desperate need for a savior as well as setting up the scapegoat metaphor. For the brother sees in the friend as in a mirror the great sadness and courage of Sonny. He says "All at once something inside gave and threatened to come pouring out of me. I didn't hate him [the friend] any more. I felt that in another moment I'd start crying like a child." This emotional release is the first step toward understanding and the first presentation of the Old Testament scapegoat motif so delicately interwoven in this story.

The scapegoat metaphor is next presented and perfectly symbolized by the street revival. The street people are a paradigm of life, a kind of representative cross-section of humanity. All sorts of people watch and listen to the street revivalists—working people, children, older folks, street women, Sonny, and Sonny's brother who watches from above at the window. At this "old fashioned revival meeting" there are "three sisters in black, and a brother. All they [have are] their voices and their Bibles and a tambourine." These people sing "'Tis the old ship of Zion'. . . . it has rescued many a thousand!"

The listeners hear nothing new, only the old pain and suffering and the offer of relief from three sisters and a brother, mortals like themselves; yet these four make suffering real. Their music acts as a mirror for the watchers whose response illustrates the scapegoat metaphor in action: "As the singing filled the air the watching, listening faces underwent a change, the eyes focusing on something within; the music seemed to soothe a poison out of them; and time seemed, nearly, to fall away from the sullen, belligerent, battered faces, as though they were fleeing back to their first condition, while dreaming of their last." These spirituals are an amalgam of joy and the blues, touching everyone who listens and helping them share the guilt and pain of the human condition.

The revival, central to the brother's awareness since it incorporates music, religion, and suffering, helps Sonny to articulate the relationship between suffering and human understanding. Also, for Sonny, the woman revivalist serves as a scapegoat; she helps him to understand his own suffering just as she had helped those who listened and contributed to her cause. For Sonny, this insight into the woman's suffering makes his own pain bearable, makes it possible to reach out to his brother. For Sonny understands this scene. Touched by their pain, he alone articulates its universal meaning—suffering. New Testament echoes of brother and savior are palpable in his response: "It's *repulsive* to think you have to suffer that much." But ironically, the biblical scapegoat metaphor suggests group suffering as well as individual suffering.

Sonny's own pain has been personal and private. He had tried to tell his brother about his suffering in the letter from prison, but he was almost inarticulate. His suffering went beyond words. Now, after the brothers have experienced the revival, Sonny tries again to communicate with his brother by explaining his relationship with music: "you finally try to get with it and play it, [and] you realize *nobody's* listening. So *you've* got to listen. You got to find a way to listen," to distance the pain, to look at despair and deal with guilt in order to live. To play this way requires brutal honesty and empathy with the suffering of others. Sonny says, I "can't forget—where I've been. I don't mean just the physical place I've been, I mean where I've *been*. And *what* I've been. . . . I've been something I didn't recognize, didn't know I could be. Didn't know anybody could be." But the painful rendition of the revivalists shows him musically that others have been there too.

Significantly, Sonny invites his brother to hear him play right after the street revival when they talk for almost the first time. Sonny understands his own need and his brother's suffering because someone else's suffering mirrors his own, effectively causing his confession and his sharing of his own pain through his music, mirror of man's soul. Music is able to heal wounds, for when Sonny is in perfect harmony with himself and with his environment, when he understands, he plays the piano effortlessly. Now Sonny's confession of failure also prepares for the final scene where Sonny plays the blues, an appropriate musical form based on folk music and characterized by minor harmonies, slow tempo, and melancholy words. The blues, like the tuneless whistle and the melancholy spirituals sung by the revivalists, reinforce the idea of human suffering carried by the scapegoat metaphor. For the blues, sad and melancholy jazz, are a mood, a feeling, a means of escape and entertainment; the blues, especially, are a way of sharing suffering, a way of strengthening the idea of community. The blues, the tune without the words in this instance, help the inarticulate young pianist to communicate with his brother and with the world. Thus he enriches the central metaphor for the story. For according to C. W. Sylvander [in *James Baldwin,* 1980] "Art can be a means for release from the 'previous condition' when it is heard, listened to, understood."

The linkage between the scapegoat motif and the music is clearly revealed when Creole has the group play the blues and signifies that this particular rendition is 'Sonny's blues.' L. H. Pratt notes [in *James Baldwin,* 1978] that "Once the narrator draws near to listen, the blues becomes the means by which Sonny is able to lead his brother, through a confrontation with the meaning of life, into a discovery of self." Through the blues the brothers can communicate. The blues become the last and greatest reinforcer of the scapegoat metaphor. For through the music something magical happens.

The narrator comes to understand that "not many people ever hear [music]. [But] . . . When something opens within, and the music enters, what we mainly hear, or hear corroborated, are personal, private, vanishing evocations." The same thing is true of our suffering and our alienation from others. Until we understand another's pain, we cannot understand our own. We must be transformed as the musician is. The musician, a kind of scapegoat, removes the pain of existence and helps us understand our suffering.

Sonny—the name echoes his strong New Testament scapegoat position—takes the pain away for all those who listen when he plays the blues. But as Baldwin says, Sonny cannot be free unless we listen and we will not be free either until he removes our pain—or until we believe on his ability to remove that suffering; Sonny thus serves to free those who listen as the cup of Gethsemane serves to free those who believe. Sonny's name echoes this special relationship and speaks of his as the ultimate scapegoat.

The brother, then, represents us also as he vividly illustrates our human response to the scapegoat offer. We accept, as understanding and insight come through the music; we change, for the function of the scapegoat is vicarious death. The ancient scapegoat was presented *alive* and allowed to escape; but metaphorically he represented the death of sin and pain for those covered by his action. Metaphysically what happens when we hear, as Sonny knows, is a death of our old understanding or the old ways and a recreation of a new way of being. So finally, at the end, in the image of the Scotch and milk drink, an image so unprepared for as to be startling, we see Sonny's symbolic value as the scapegoat. The transformation occurs as the music plays, because for the musician "What is evoked . . . is of another order, more terrible because it has no words, and triumphant, too, for that same reason. And his triumph, when he triumphs, is ours."

Only in music can Sonny truly tell all and fulfill his function as a scapegoat. Only in music can he reach our hearts and minds. Thus the last and clearest presentation of the scapegoat metaphor comes at the end of the story. Here "Sonny's fingers filled the air with life, his life. But that life contained so many others. . . . It was no longer a lament." This is a clear expression of the scapegoat metaphor. For Sonny's sharing through music transforms the pain. As the narrator says, "Freedom lurked around us and I understood at last that he could help us be free if we would listen, that he would never be free until we did." This freedom is the Black's escape, the reader's escape, Sonny's escape. It is the scapegoat metaphor in action, a release for Sonny's brother and for us too. For Sonny "was giving it back, as everything must be given back, so that, passing through death, it can live forever."

The reversal of the situation at the end is important. The blues which Creole guides Sonny to play are central. For to play the blues one must first have suffered; then one creates the form to hold the pain, a fluid changing style where, according to John Reilly [in *BALF,* 1970], "One uses the skill one has achieved by practice and experience in order to reach toward others." The narrator expresses it best: "For, while the tale of how we suffer, and how we are delighted, and how we may triumph is never new, it always must be heard. There isn't any other tale to tell, it's the only light we've got in all this darkness."

Sonny's brother indicates that he both understands and symbolically shares Sonny's pain and guilt by sending the Scotch and milk drink. He affirms the religious connection with his comment, "For me, then, as they began to play again [the cup of Scotch and milk] glowed and shook above my brother's head like the very cup of trembling." The drink of Scotch and milk develops the image of Sonny as sinner and savior, the God/man, the scapegoat, the unlikely mixture which saves. This image conveys Sonny's complex purpose and suggests, on an earthly level, that Sonny's pain will continue, but his pain is shared and understood by his brother. On the second level it suggests that as God took away the pain for Israel, and as Christ takes away the pain and sin of the world for the believer, so does Sonny, the scapegoat, take away pain and guilt for his brother, for the listeners, and for us. As Keith Byerman said [in *SSF,* 1982], "The drink itself, Scotch and milk, is an emblem of simultaneous destruction and nurture to the system; it cannot be reduced to one or the other. Sonny's acceptance of it indicates that his life will continue on the edge between the poison of his addiction and the nourishment of his music." But Sonny *has* drunk the cup of pain before; now the brother joins in, empathizes, understands. Sonny drinks the Scotch and milk and continues to suffer, but part of his suffering is removed by his brother's understanding. For the brother, the action itself suggests increased understanding and a sharing of Sonny's pain.

The brother's final comment about the 'cup of trembling' emphasizes the narrator's understanding and reinterprets the image, making Sonny a true scapegoat for the reader and enlarging our vision as well. Only with the last image do we reflect on the biblical imagery, seeing Sonny's linkage to Aaron and to Christ. Then we concentrate on Sonny's name; he is transformed before our very eyes and we see in his ceremonial acceptance of the drink his function as a scapegoat, a substitute for all.

Pancho Savery (essay date 1992)

SOURCE: "Baldwin, Bebop, and 'Sonny's Blues'," in *Understanding Others: Cultural and Cross-Cultural Studies and the Teaching of Literature,* edited by Joseph Trimmer and Tilly Warnock, National Council of Teachers of English, 1992, pp. 165-76.

[*In the following essay, Savery places Baldwin's treatment of music within its historical and cultural context.*]

Well before James Baldwin died in 1987, the literary critical establishment had made up its mind about him. Thus, there was hardly any surprise when Lee A. Daniels's front page *New York Times* obituary lauded, "James Baldwin, Eloquent Essayist In Behalf of Civil Rights, Is Dead." Equally unsurprising was Mark Feeney's *Boston Globe* "Appreciation" entitled "A Forceful Voice on the Issue of Race." What James Baldwin had become was, to a large extent, black America's interpreter of black America to and for white America. As such, Baldwin was essentially mummified into the "Voice of the Civil Rights Movement," a historical relic of the 1950s through the 1970s. But even in this position, Baldwin was not always on solid ground. In 1963, the same year Baldwin published *The Fire Next Time,* considered by many his quintessential work, Amiri Baraka called Baldwin, in "Brief Reflections on Two Hot Shots," the "Joan of Arc of the cocktail party" and characterized his work as "the *cry,* the spavined whine and plea" (later published in 1966). Three years later [in *Visions of a Liberated Future: Black Arts Movement Writings,* edited by Michael Schwartz, 1989], Larry Neal would declare that "Baldwin has missed the point by a wide margin," because his "uncertainty over identity and his failure to utilize, to its fullest extent, traditional aspects of Afro-American culture has tended to dull the intensity of his work." And although Baraka would change by the time of Baldwin's death, calling him in "Jimmy!" "this glorious, elegant griot of our oppressed African-American nation" who "made us feel . . . that we could defend ourselves and define ourselves," it still seems that Baldwin will go down in literary history primarily as the witness to and conscience of America's years of racial confrontation. But is this accurate? What of the eight books of fiction Baldwin published? Not only do I want to suggest that we need to reevaluate the fiction, but I want to do so by looking at Baldwin's most celebrated short story and suggest that, even here, there is more to be seen than has been previously, and that **"Sonny's Blues"** demonstrates a full use of "traditional aspects of Afro-American culture."

In his 1937 Emersonial manifesto "Blueprint for Negro Writing," Richard Wright asserted the existence of "a culture of the Negro" whose main sources were "(1) the Negro church; and (2) the folklore of the Negro people." For Wright, this folklore expressed itself in "Blues, spirituals, and folk tales recounted from mouth to mouth." Wright criticized writers for not making more use of the folk tradition in their work, because in folklore "the Negro achieved his most indigenous and complete expression." Two years later, Saunders Redding published the first in-depth, full-length work of African American literary criticism, *To Make a Poet Black* (1987 [1939]). There, Redding, following up on Wright, read African American literature from the beginning to the end of the Harlem Renaissance, and found that only two writers had escaped the two traps he found continually lurking. These were the traps of writing from a "very practical desire to adjust himself to the American environment," and the trap of having to simultaneously write for two audiences in order to succeed. The two writers Redding found to be most successful, Sterling Brown and Zora Neale Hurston, were successful because of their works' immersion in "folk material."

The most successful African American writers have continued to mine this vein, but the critics have often been behind. I would like to suggest that Baldwin is a case in point. Although there have been interesting analyses of **"Sonny's Blues,"** none of them has gotten to the specificities of the music and the wider cultural implications. Music is not simply the bridge the narrator crosses to get closer to Sonny, nor is it sufficient to point out that the music in the climactic scene is labeled as blues. What kind and form of these particular blues make all the difference.

An interesting way to begin thinking about **"Sonny's Blues"** is to think about when the story is supposed to be taking place. We know from the acknowledgments that it was first published in the summer of 1957, but can we be more precise? Part of the story takes place during "the war," but which one is it, Korea or World War II, and does it matter?

Baldwin tells us that Sonny's father "died suddenly, during a drunken weekend in the middle of the war, when Sonny was fifteen." "[J]ust after Daddy died," Sonny's brother, whom we know is seven years older, is "home on leave from the army" and has his final conversation with his mother. In the passage, which begins with that wonderful evocation of the coming of the darkness on Sunday afternoon with the old and young together in the living room, "Mama" admonishes her older son to watch out for Sonny "and don't let him fall, no matter what it looks like is happening to him and no matter how evil you gets with him." But the narrator tells us that he did not listen, got married, and went back to war. The next time he comes home is "on a special furlough" for his mother's funeral. The war is still going on. The narrator reminds Sonny that Sonny must "finish school," "And you only got another year." The school that Sonny must finish is obviously high school. Thus, no more than a year or so has passed since the death of the father, who died "in the middle of the war." The United States was in World War II from December of 1941 until August of 1945. "The middle of the

war" would have been approximately 1943, or 1942 if you start from the beginning of the war in Europe. Thus, the crucial conversation between Sonny and his brother, in which Sonny first says he wants to be a jazz musician, takes place about 1944. If, on the other hand, the war being fought is the Korean War (June 1950 to July 1953), the conversation takes place about 1952.

When Sonny reveals to his brother that first he wants to be a musician, and then a jazz musician, and then not a jazz musician like Louis Armstrong but one like Charlie Parker, the brother, after asking "Who's this Parker character," says, "I'll go out and buy all the cat's records right away, all right?" From 1942 to 1944, there was a ban on recordings, at least in part due to a scarcity of materials because of the war. In 1944, Sonny's brother would not have been able to go out and buy new material by Bird (Parker) because there wasn't any. Bird's seminal recordings were made between 1945 and 1948. It is, thus, reasonable to conclude that the war is the Korean.

By 1952, Bird had already revolutionized music. And so when Sonny's brother asks Sonny to name a musician he admires and Sonny says "Bird" and his brother says "Who?," Sonny is justified with his, "Bird! Charlie Parker! Don't they teach you nothing in the goddamn army?" Sonny's brother, at age twenty-four in 1952, can certainly be expected to have heard of Bird. After all, he has heard of Louis Armstrong.

But it is in Sonny's response to Armstrong that one of the keys to the story lies. Sonny's brother admits that, to him, the term "jazz musician" is synonymous with "hanging around nightclubs, clowning around on bandstands," and is, thus, "beneath him, somehow." When, from this perspective, jazz musicians are "in a class with . . . 'good-time people'," his mentioning of Louis Armstrong needs to be looked at.

From one perspective, Louis Armstrong is one of the true titans of jazz. On the other hand, to many of the Bebop era, Armstrong was considered part of the old guard who needed to be swept out with the new musical revolution, and Armstrong himself was not positively disposed towards Bop. One turning point came in February of 1949 when Armstrong was chosen King of the Zulus for the Mardi Gras parade in New Orleans. To many, he seemed to be donning the minstrel mask of acceptability to the larger white world, and this seemed confirmed when, the same week, he appeared on the cover of *Time* (February 21, 1949). It would be "natural" that Sonny's brother, the future algebra teacher, would have heard of Armstrong, here the symbol of the old conservative, but not of Parker, not only the new and the revolutionary, but the "had been a revolutionary" for seven years. Sonny's response to Armstrong makes this clear:

> I suggested, helpfully: "You mean—like Louis Armstrong?"

> His face closed as though I'd struck him. "No. I'm not talking about none of that old-time, down home crap."

But the differences between Armstrong and Parker represent something much larger. Throughout history, African Americans have been engaged in intramural debate about the nature of identity. Du Bois, of course, put it best when he defined "double-consciousness" in *The Souls of Black Folk* and concluded:

> One ever feels his twoness,—an American, a Negro; two souls, two thoughts, two unreconciled strivings; two warring ideals in one dark body, whose dogged strength alone keeps it from being torn asunder.

Du Bois's battles with Booker T. Washington and later with Marcus Garvey are one of the major moments in African American history when this debate was articulated. But there have also been many others; for example, Frederick Douglass and Martin Delany debating whether Africa or America was the place for blacks, and King and Malcolm on the issue of integration. But in order to look at African American culture fully, we cannot limit ourselves to the study of politics and history. As numerous commentators have pointed out, music is the key to much of the African American dispute over this issue of culture; and, therefore, knowledge of it is essential. For example:

> The complexities of the collective Black experience have always had their most valid and moving expression in Black music; music is the chief artifact created out of that experience.
>
> (Williams, *Give Birth to Brightness: A Thematic Study in Neo-Black Literature,* 1972)

> To reiterate, the key to where the black people have to go is in the music. Our music has always been the most dominant manifestation of what we are and feel. . . . The best of it has always operated at the core of our lives, forcing itself upon us as in a ritual. It has always, somehow, represented the collective psyche.
>
> (Neal, *Visions of a Liberated Future,* edited by Michael Schwartz,1989)

> I think it is not fantastic to say that only in music has there been any significant Negro contribution to a *formal* American culture.
>
> (Baraka, *Blues People: Negro Music in White America,* 1963)

> The tenor is a rhythm instrument, and the best statements Negroes have made, of what their soul is, have been on tenor saxophone.
>
> (Ornette Coleman, quoted in Spellman, *Black Music: Four Lives,* 1970)

> There has never been an equivalent to Duke Ellington or Louis Armstrong in Negro writing, and even the best of contemporary literature written by Negroes cannot yet be compared to the fantastic beauty of the music of Charlie Parker.
>
> (Baraka, "Myth," 1966, *Home: Social Essays,* 1966)

[In *Blues, Ideology, and Afro-American Literature: A Vernacular Theory,* 1984] Houston Baker has gone as far as suggesting that there is a "blues matrix" at the center of African American culture and that "a vernacular theory" of African American literature can be developed from this idea.

What I am arguing in general is that music is the cornerstone of African American culture; and that, further, Bebop was an absolute key moment. In African American culture, Bebop is as significant as the Harlem Renaissance, and Armstrong and Parker's roles somewhat resemble those of Washington and Du Bois, and Du Bois and Garvey. Armstrong, Washington, and Du Bois (to Garvey) represented the known, the old, and the traditional whose accomplishments were noted but who were considered somewhat passé by the younger, more radical Parker, Du Bois (to Washington), and Garvey.

Musically, Bebop was to a large extent a revolt against swing and the way African American music had been taken over, and diluted, by whites. Perhaps no more emblematic of this is that the aptly named Paul Whiteman and Benny Goodman were dubbed respectively "The King of Jazz" and "The King of Swing." As Gary Giddins succinctly puts it [in *Celebrating Bird: The Triumph of Charlie Parker,* 1987]:

> Jazz in the Swing Era was so frequently compromised by chuckle-headed bandleaders, most of them white, who diluted and undermined the triumphs of serious musicians that a new virtuosity was essential. The modernists brandished it like a weapon. They confronted social and musical complacency in a spirit of arrogant romanticism.

[In *Music: Black, White & Blue,* 1972] Ortiz Walton describes the musical revolution as "a major challenge to European standards of musical excellence and the beginning of a conscious black aesthetic in music" because of Bebop's challenge to the European aesthetic emphasis on vibrato. This emphasis produced music that was easily imitable, and thus open to commercialization and co-optation. By revolting against this direction the music had taken and reclaiming it, "Afro-American musicians gained a measure of control over their product, a situation that had not existed since the expansion of the music industry in the Twenties."

Another aspect of this Bop reclamation was a renewed emphasis on the blues. Although some people seem to think there is a dispute over this issue, it is clear from listening to Parker's first session as a leader that "Billie's Bounce" and "Now's the Time" are blues pieces. In his autobiography, Dizzy Gillespie asserts:

> Beboppers couldn't destroy the blues without seriously injuring themselves. The modern jazz musicians always remained very close to the blues musician. That was a characteristic of the bopper.

To this we could add the following from Baraka:

> Bebop also re-established blues as the most important Afro-American form in Negro music by its

astonishingly comtemporary restatement of the basic blues impulse. The boppers returned to this basic form, reacting against the all but stifling advance artificial melody had made into jazz during the swing era.

We could also look at Bebop in terms of the movement from the diatonic to the chromatic, from a more closed to an open form, a movement in the direction of a greater concern with structure, the beginning of jazz postmodernism that would reach its zenith in the work of Ornette Coleman. In "The Poetics of Jazz," Ajay Heble concludes, "Whereas diatonic jazz attempts to posit musical language as a way of thinking about things in the real world, chromaticism begins to foreground *form* rather than *substance*" [*Textual Practice*, 1988].

What becomes clear in most of the above is that Bebop must be viewed from two perspectives, the sociopolitical as well as the musical. In Gary Giddins's words, "The Second World War severely altered the texture and tempo of American life, and jazz reflected those changes with greater acuteness by far than the other arts." When Bebop began in the 1940s, America was in a similar position to what it had been in the 1920s. A war had been fought to free the world (again) for democracy; and once again, African Americans had participated and had assumed that this "loyal" participation would result in new rights and new levels of respect. When, once again, this did not appear to be happening, a new militancy developed in the African American community. Bebop was part of this new attitude. The militancy in the African American community that manifested itself in the 1941 strike of black Ford workers and the 1943 Harlem riot also manifested itself in Bebop. As Eric Lott notes [in *Callaloo,* 1988]:

> Brilliantly outside, bebop was intimately if indirectly related to the militancy of its moment. Militancy and music were undergirded by the same social facts; the music attempted to resolve at the level of style what the militancy combatted in the streets.

Of course, this made Bebop dangerous and threatening to some, who saw it as (or potentially as) "too militant," and perhaps even un-American. And in response to this, Dizzy Gillespie retorts:

> Damn right! We refused to accept racism, poverty, or economic exploitation, nor would we live out uncreative humdrum lives merely for the sake of survival. But there was nothing unpatriotic about it. If America wouldn't honor its Constitution and respect us as men, we couldn't give a shit about the American way. And they made it damn near un-American to appreciate our music.

The threat represented by Bebop was not only felt by the white world, but by the assimilationist black middle class as well. Baraka offers these perspectives:

> When the moderns, the beboppers, showed up to restore jazz, in some sense, to its original separateness, to drag it outside the mainstream of American culture

again, most middle-class Negroes (as most Americans) were stuck; they had passed, for the most part, completely into the Platonic citizenship. The willfully harsh, *anti-assimilationist* sound of bebop fell on deaf or horrified ears, just as it did in white America.

[*Blues People,* 1963]

> Bebop rebelled against the absorption into garbage, monopoly music; it also signified a rebellion by the people who played the music, because it was not just the music that rebelled, as if the music had fallen out of the sky! But even more, dig it, it signified a rebellion rising out of the masses themselves, since that is the source of social movement—the people themselves!

[*Selected Plays and Prose of Amiri Barakal Le Roi Jones,* 1979]

> What made bop strong is that no matter its pretensions, it was hooked up solidly and directly to the Afro-American blues tradition, and therefore was largely based in the experience and struggle of the black sector of the working class.

[*Selected Plays and Prose of Amiri Barakal Le Roi Jones,* 1979]

In light of this historical context, Sonny's brother's never having heard of Bird is not just a rejection of the music of Bebop; it is also a rejection of the new political direction Bebop was representative of in the African American community.

When the story picks up several years later, some things have changed. Sonny has dropped out of high school, illegally enlisted in the navy and been shipped to Greece, returned to America, and moved to Greenwich Village. Other things have not changed: his brother has become an algebra teacher and a respected member of the black bourgeoisie. After Sonny has been released from prison, he invites his brother to watch him sit in "in a joint in the Village."

What is usually discussed concerning this final scene is that the brother enters Sonny's world, recognizes that he is only a visitor to that world tolerated because of Sonny, that here Sonny is respected and taken care of, and that here is Sonny's true family:

> I was introduced to all of them and they were all very polite to me. Yet, it was clear that, for them, I was only Sonny's brother. Here, I was in Sonny's world. Or, rather: his kingdom. Here, it was not even a question that his veins bore royal blood.

When the music Sonny plays is discussed, it is usually done either abstractly, music as the bridge that allows Sonny and his brother to become reunited and Sonny to find his identity, or simply in terms of the blues. It is, of course, totally legitimate to discuss the music in either of these ways. After all, music does function as a bridge between Sonny and his brother; and twice we are reminded in the same page that "what they were playing was the blues," and "Now these are Sonny's blues."

At the climactic moment of the story, when Sonny finally feels so comfortable that his "fingers filled the air with life," he is playing "Am I Blue." It is the first song of the second set, after a tentative performance by Sonny in the first set. Baldwin presents the moment of transition between sets by simply noting, "Then they finished, there was scattered applause, and then, without an instant's warning, Creole started into something else, it was almost sardonic, it was *Am I Blue*." The word "sardonic," it seems to me, is key here. One of the characteristics of Bebop is taking an old standard and making it new. As Leonard Feather explains [in *Inside Jazz (Inside Be-Bop)*]:

> In recent years it has been an increasingly common practice to take some definite chord sequence of a well-known song (usually a standard old favorite) and build a new melody around it. Since there is no copyright on a chord sequence, the musician is entitled to use this method to create an original composition and copyright it in his own name, regardless of who wrote the first composition that used the same chord pattern.

This practice results in a song with a completely different title. Thus, "Back Home Again in Indiana" becomes Parker's "Donna Lee"; "Honeysuckle Rose" becomes "Scrapple from the Apple"; "I Got Rhythm" becomes "Dexterity," "Confirmation," and "Thriving on a Riff"; "How High the Moon" becomes "Bird Lore"; "Lover Come Back to Me" becomes "Bird Gets the Worm"; and "Cherokee" becomes "Warming Up a Riff" and "Ko-Ko." But it is also characteristic of Bebop to take the entire song, not simply a chord sequence, and play it in an entirely different way. Thus, for example, Bird's catalogue is filled with versions of tunes like "White Christmas," "Slow Boat to China," "East of the Sun and West of the Moon," "April in Paris," and "Embraceable You."[6] As Baraka notes:

> Bebop was a much more open rebellion in the sense that the musicians openly talked of the square, hopeless, corny rubbish put forth by the bourgeoisie. They made fun of it, refused to play it except in a mocking fashion.

Baldwin's use of the word "sardonic," therefore, is clearly intended to tell us that something more is going on than simply playing a standard tune or playing the blues. "Am I Blue" is exactly the type of song that by itself wouldn't do much for anyone, but which could become rich and meaningful after being heated in the crucible of Bebop.

The point of all this is that, through his playing, Sonny becomes "part of the family again," his family with the other musicians; likewise, Sonny's brother also becomes part of the family again, his family with Sonny. But in both cases, Baldwin wants us to view the idea of family through the musical and social revolution of Bebop. Note the brother's language as Sonny plays:

> Then he began to make it his. It was very beautiful because it wasn't hurried and it was no longer a lament. I seemed to hear with what burning we had yet to make it ours, how we could cease lamenting. Freedom lurked around us and I understood, at last, that he

could help us to be free if we would listen, that he would never be free until we did.

In the mid to late 1950s, the word "freedom" is obviously a highly charged one. Not only does it speak to the politics of the Civil Rights Movement, but it also points forward to the "Free Jazz" movement of the late 1950s and 1960s, the music of Ornette Coleman, Cecil Taylor, Albert Ayler, and Eric Dolphy. Baldwin's concept of family is, therefore, a highly political one, and one that has cultural implications.

In *Black Talk,* Ben Sidran concludes about Bebop:

> The importance of the bop musician was that he had achieved this confrontation—in terms of aesthetics and value structures as well as social action—well before organized legal or political action. Further, unlike the arguments of the NAACP, his music and his hip ethic were not subject to the kind of rationalization and verbal qualification that had all too often compromised out of existence all middle-class Negro gains.

In **"Sonny's Blues,"** Baldwin makes clear that, contrary to many opinions, he is in fact a major fiction writer; and that, Larry Neal notwithstanding, he *has* used to its fullest extent "traditional aspects of Afro-American culture." The implications are clear. Not only does Baldwin's fiction need to be looked at again, but when we are looking at it, writing about it, and teaching it, we need to be conversant with the specific cultural context he is writing in and from. And when we are, new things are there to be seen and heard.

Thorell Tsomondo (essay date 1995)

SOURCE: "No Other Tale to Tell: 'Sonny's Blues' and *Waiting for the Rain*," in *Critique*, Vol. XXXVI, No. 3, Spring, 1995, pp. 195-209.

[*In the following essay, Tsomondo compares Baldwin's and Charles Mungoshi's view of history as evinced in "Sonny's Blues" and* Waiting for the Rain.]

In *Tropics of Discourse* Haydn White, identifies a marked hostility to historical consciousness in twentieth-century literature. The modern writer, he observes, "uses the historian to represent the extreme example of repressed sensibility in the novel and theatre." White cites Gide, Ibsen, Malraux, Camus, Huxley, and Sartre among others. He traces the hostility to history back to Nietzsche, who maintained that history cheats man by leading him to believe that whatever is worth doing has been done, thus robbing him of "that impulse to heroic exertion" that humanizes, if only temporarily, his absurd world. Man's memory, according to Nietzsche is the source of a false morality that encourages indulgence in debilitating voyeurism.

White's twentieth-century writer is Eurocentrically defined; and Nietzsche's history assumes an uninterrupted vista down the corridors of time, aided by the supposition that whatever has been done is deemed "good" in some universal sense. George Eliot's Casaubon, whom White sets forth as the English exemplification of the "perils of antiquarianism" may serve also to illustrate the limitation of assumptions such as these. A man with a "mind like the ghost of an ancient," Casaubon sets for himself the goal of discovering and recording for posterity the key to all mythologies. Casaubon's "key" would reduce all mythological experience, spatial and temporal, to a single ethnocentric code and, by dispensing with difference, close the door to critical discourse. Not surprisingly, this nightmarish indicant remains buried in, as it is simultaneously represented by, the gross and deadening materiality of Casaubon's dusty mass of records. Meanwhile, Ladislaw, signaling the repudiation of tradition by his dubious birth and means and by his bohemian lifestyle, is the figure of the artist who liberates Dorothea from Casaubon's damning legacy. The opposition that *Middlemarch* depicts privileges art, making it, in contradistinction to history, a quickening, emancipating force.

Two twentieth-century writers, the African American James Baldwin and the Zimbabwean Charles Mungoshi, share a view of history that is opposed to that which White's artists represent. In addition, these writers challenge, though in a paradoxical way, Nietzsche's claim that history frustrates heroic exertion. They also contradict, what, according to White, is Eliot's essential point: that "artistic insight and historical learning are opposed, and the qualities of the responses to life which they respectively evoke are mutually exclusive."

In Baldwin's **"Sonny's Blues"** and Mungoshi's *Waiting for the Rain,* not only is there no hostility between artistic insight and historical learning, but the artist is by necessity also a historian. "History" according to Harold Perkins, "is the summarized experience of society, as experience is the condensed history of the individual." The artist-historian, in **"Sonny's Blues"** as well as in *Waiting for the Rain,* is reminiscent of the African griot, master of the spoken word, "memory of mankind," who teaches "the history of the . . . ancestors so that the lives of the ancients might serve . . . as an example." For Baldwin and Mungoshi, therefore, the artist's credibility and appeal hinge on his historical knowledge; and his success as historian is dependent on his artistic skill. Further, for both writers, historical "correctness" coupled with creative expertise is indispensable to heroic action. In both works the artist-historian is a kind of poet-prophet committed simultaneously to solitary and communal experience, bound at once to tradition and to change.

Why, in an age when artistic insight and historical erudition are viewed as polarized are there twentieth-century writers, continents apart, making bedfellows of art and history and doing so, moreover, in strikingly similar ways? Baldwin's **"Sonny's Blues,"** set in the black ghetto of cosmopolitan New York City, tells the story of a young pianist dogged by heroin addiction and alienated from his family, who, nevertheless, in a heroic, bardic performance captures and relates a people's historical existence, there-

by leading his audience to a heightened, shared awareness of their cultural identity. Mungoshi's *Waiting for the Rain,* set in drought-stricken Manyene Tribal Trust Land of colonial Rhodesia, tells of a young drummer who, plagued by alcohol addiction and living on the fringe of his community, also recapitulates a people's tribal history in a musical performance. As "he tells their life to the drum" and relates the "story of the Founder of the Tribe," he leads his audience to an energetic reaffirmation of a "proud tradition." In both instances, memory, the return to the past, is motivated and accompanied not by a sense of amassment, "the burden of history," but by a sense of necessity.

> In Baldwin's "Sonny's Blues" . . . not only is there no hostility between artistic insight and historical learning, but the artist is by necessity also a historian.
>
> —*Thorell Tsomondo*

Herein lies the major difference between the view of history of White's twentieth-century writers and that of other artists whom the established canon ignores. The African, as well as the African American, retains a sense of the past that is acutely unstable. On the one hand, he must reject Western history, at least insofar as it has falsified and marginalized him; on the other, he is plagued by the awareness that his own history has been violently misshaped. Rather than feeling hostility to the past, the African and the African American quest for the continuity that it can provide. To a great degree, the African and the African American writer are concerned with the reconstruction of an invalidated tradition, and the quickening emancipating force that is art is the means by which they transform need into fullness.

For the black writer, art provides what Houston Baker [in *The Journey Back,* 1980], quoting Kenneth Burke, calls "terms for order," "the search for coherent arrangements of objects and events . . ." This search, according to Baker, has dual implications:

> At one level, the disruption of a prior unity, no matter how strained or tenuous. On a more abstract plane, it suggests a process existing on the far side of chaos. To understand our origins, we must journey through difficult straits. . . . Most of us take refuge in the safe harbor of dreams, envisioning glorious years of the distant past . . . Perhaps only poets, or writers confined to a situation that offers no alternatives, can and do make the effort at return. The black writer, having attempted the journey, preserves details of his voyage in that most manifest and coherent of all cultural systems—language. Through his work we are allowed to witness, if not the trip itself, at least a representation of the voyage that provides some view of our emergence.

If we extend Baker's "language" to include cultural signi-fying systems like music and art, then in highly complex terms, **"Sonny's Blues"** and *Waiting for the Rain* are more than representations of "the voyage," or "view[s] of our emergence." In these works, the text is an invitation to embark upon the journey ourselves; the text is an invita-tion to emerge.

Emergence, however, is not without its difficulties. It is not, like some simple expedition, a thing to be executed once and for all. The chaos in which "transplanted black life" evolves, the disorder resulting from the intrusion into, and near expunction of, traditional culture on the African continent cannot be simply "got beyond." For whether it be viewed from "this side of a prior unity" or from "the far side of chaos," this disorder is ineradicably part of the black experience. To put it another way, the chaos is the indelible mark of the peculiar estate of a non-past—"pe-culiar" because "non-past" here does not mean "vacancy." Rather, the terms conjures at once the notion of the ab-sence of a past as well as the inescapable presence of this (not)past. This shifting and problematic historical con-sciousness is the source of the Nietzschean "'impulse to that heroic exertion' which humanizes if only temporarily [the black's] absurd world." And the temporariness and the heroism are bound up together in the especial condi-tion that the black must embark again and again on the "journey through difficult straits" toward an understand-ing of his origin, like the Ancient Mariner perpetually rehearsing his interminable tale, ceaselessly resubmitting himself to the experience he tells. According to Baldwin's narrator, "while the tale of how we suffer, and how we are delighted, and how we may triumph is never new, it al-ways must be heard. There isn't any other tale to tell."

"Sonny's Blues" is Baldwin's rendering of "the tale." His text articulates its terms for order in an art form that en-capsulates the story of black life, namely, the blues and the related figure, jazz. The blues-jazz motif and its sig-nificance for black life and art in **"Sonny's Blues"** pro-vide the paradigm against which the narrative in retailing and weaving its various threads create a sense of passage. This designing of the story serves a double function: it furnishes a concentrated image of an historical experience that must be preserved and acclimated; at the same time, it presents this same experience as something to be (sur)passed.

The blues has the necessary ingredient for this purpose; it is grounded in tradition. In a "lyric encounter with histo-ry," it blends the personal and the social, past and present, to produce a prototypal discourse of essential cultural import. In the words of Jean Cocteau, black "life itself flows into the lyrics of the blues".

It is with just such a representative discourse that Sonny makes his musical debut. "He really began with the *spare flat statement* of the opening phrase of the song," there in "the *only* night-club on a *short, dark street, downtown*" (emphasis added). In this description, the language of boundaries carries a suggestion of restriction: The lyric engagement with history has its limits; "the blues were not

about anything very new." The artist's primary purpose is to find ways of keeping the blues fresh and vibrant. Their strength and value are contingent upon their performance and the response they elicit. Sonny, Creole, and the mem-bers of the band understand the condition of their charge: They

> were keeping it new, at the risk of ruin, destruction, madness, and death, in order to find new ways to make us listen. For, while the tale of how we suffer, and how we are delighted, and how we may triumph is never new, it must always be heard. There isn't any other tale to tell. . . .

As this passage suggests, however, "keeping it new" de-mands more than mere repetition; "new ways" must be found to revivify this single, time-worn, and familiar but indispensable tale. Harry Berger suggests that in art, reca-pitulation may be a sign of retrogression. He distinguishes *vision,* the grasp and repetition of inherited forms, from *revision,* the retrospective examination of the past from the artist's fresh point of view. If the writer as well as his audience is not to be absorbed into and negated by histo-ry, he must recast the given, imbuing it with new perspec-tive from his own standpoint. Baldwin's story and Son-ny's Blues are instances of this re-visionary process at work.

Sonny's climactic performance takes the blues poem, "Am I Blue" as its starting point. The critical moment in his recital comes when he moves center-stage, "into deep water" as the narrator puts it, to speak for himself. The atmosphere changes: something profoundly inspired takes place: "Sonny's fingers filled the air with life, his life. But that life contained so many others." From the bare first phrase of the song, "Sonny went all the way back. . . . he began to make *it* his" (emphasis added). The narrator accents Sonny's particularizing of the song: "I seemed to hear with what burning he had made it his, with what burning we had yet to make it ours. . . . He had made it his: that long line, of which we knew only Mama and Daddy."

Although it is not so stipulated, what Sonny plays in those final moments of the story is undoubtedly jazz.

> [Jazz is] . . . noted for individuality because it depends on each musician's ability to improvise his or her own ideas while keeping in harmony with the progression of chords of some tune (often well-known). It has often been described as being able to take one's instrument, maintain an awareness of one's fellow players in the group, and in the context spontaneously "compose a new tune" with perhaps only a hint of the original remaining. . . .
> [Richard N. Albert, *College Literature,* 1984]

The narrator's account of Sonny's treatment of the blues coincides beautifully with this definition of jazz.

Sonny triumphs then through improvisation. Improvisa-tion is an act of critical interpretation; criticism to quote

Oscar Wilde, "enables us to put our most recent phase at a distance and so go on to another. It disengages us so we may re-engage ourselves in a new way." Improvisation is an act of re-creation; the artist "perceives" potential in the given; he taps "the store of contrivances" inherently his own, and he produces a work that while acknowledging its indebtedness to its source, simultaneously proclaims its independence of it. In **"Sonny's Blues,"** subjective experience merges with the communal to produce text, context, and thereby, meaning. Thus, as his brother applauds Sonny's masterfully inventive composition, he is also able to *reconstruct* or interpret as well as *remember* in the music he hears, the narrative of his own life, of his family, even of his unknown ancestors; he has come to grips with history.

In **"Sonny's Blues"** then, improvisation is the alternative to (drug) addiction, the imprisoning store of experiences that is the "hidden menace" of the old neighborhood where "the same things happen," where there are only "the same things to remember"—the repetitive chords of a well-known tune. Earlier in the story, a well-known tune provides the stage of an "old-fashioned revival meeting." The song, "'Tis the old ship of Zion, it has rescued many a thousand," the "steady" beat of the tambourine, the three sisters all dressed in black create for the audience a familiar scene. Everyone within earshot had heard the song before; no one had ever been rescued. Instead, while they listen, time seems to evaporate "as though they were fleeing back to their first condition, while dreaming of their last." In this context, "revival" can be understood only ironically. The play on the term "meeting" suggests the collapse of conditions, first and last, into one, and thereby eclipses experience and life itself.

In contrast, the "life" with which Sonny fills the piano and his audience is generated by the power of the music. The source of this power is the creative act itself: something "terrible" and "triumphant" is evoked in the artist "dealing with the roar rising from the void and imposing order on it as it hits the air." Evidence of this power is its wordlessness; it has no name because it signifies *potential.* True, jazz developed from blues and is, therefore, interlined with the story of "how we suffer," but it is also interwoven with the story of "how we may triumph." At the high point of Sonny's recital, the narrator senses the change in atmosphere; and, as he struggles to describe what he cannot name, he launches euphorically into vague and abstract accounting: Something, which he can refer to only as *it,* "was very beautiful because it was no longer hurried and it was no longer a lament . . . Freedom lurked around us . . ." he concludes. Interestingly, this very vagueness makes a cogent point: more potent than the story that the music tells is the aesthetic intensification of feeling that it evokes, that transcends language because it signifies pure possibility.

Blues-jazz is at once an inscribed text—it traces and validates "that long line"—and it is a blank page always in the process of being written, ever to be written. In other words, in **"Sonny's Blues,"** blues-jazz operates as other fictional constructs do: as, on the one hand, a determinate

social-historical artifact and on the other, as a discourse under constant erasure. This circumstance further highlights the fact that the search for order and coherence is never finally fulfilled. At the very moment that Baldwin's narrator is feeling the exhilaration of connecting with his past and experiencing the *fullness* of community, he becomes aware that "this was only a moment." Suggestions of loss impinge on his consciousness and on the reader's. The narrator's thoughts shift to contemplate the transience of the sense of wholeness that he feels and the harsh persistence of that which imperils this sense: a world "as hungry as a tiger, . . . trouble . . . longer than the sky."

Disruption and threat of destruction recall a subject introduced earlier: the problem of survival and the need perpetually to begin. Of course, the idea of beginning is an inherent feature of art, which, by necessity, locates itself always in *medias res.* Especially in narrative—and narrative, discrete or concealed, is endemic to all works of art—beginning is of great significance. Acclaimed works like *Paradise Lost, The Prelude, Bleak House, Wuthering Heights,* and *Invisible Man* self-consciously raise the question. Inasmuch as **"Sonny's Blues"** concerns itself with history, origin, kinship, survival, and art, the subject of beginning becomes doubly consequential. The story's achronological plot, the various intranarratives, and the theme of survival raise the issue; and the text explicitly pushes the problem to the foreground: Sonny literally has trouble beginning: "he and the piano stammered, started one way, got scared, stopped; started another way, panicked, marked time, started again; then seemed to have found a direction, panicked again, got stuck."

Commenting on the nature and significance of beginning in fiction, Said points out that for the artist or historian "beginning will emerge reflectively and perhaps unhappily, already engaging him in awareness of its difficulty." Beginning, the "first step" toward "production of meaning," is an individual, intentional, and purposeful act, the opposite of origin, which is the "purely circumstantial existence of conditions." However, Said cautions, beginning cannot be separated radically from "origin"; rather it demands acceptance of the "risks and rapture." God himself makes a new start by preserving Noah and the ark, thus initiating the new with a fragment of the old. In this regard, however, Sonny and Baldwin have to be more resourceful than God, because for them the "fragment" is not preserved by divine will with palingenetic assurances. Besides, the circumstances under which Afro-American life evolved expunged the value of and esteem for heritage by converting into liability what is a necessary, indeed indispensable, human resource.

As early as 1951, six years before the publication of **"Sonny's Blues,"** Baldwin, in *Notes of a Native Son,* brooded upon the problems that this anomaly creates for the black artist in general and for him in particular:

> Negroes are Americans . . . They have no other experience besides their experience on this continent and it is an experience which cannot be rejected, which yet remains to be embraced.

And yet,

> One writes out of one thing only—one's own experience. Everything depends on how relentlessly one forces from this experience the last drop, sweet or bitter, it can possibly give. This is the only real concern of the artist, to recreate out of the disorder of life that order which is art. The difficulty then, for me, of being the negro writer was the fact that I was, in effect, prohibited from examining my own experience too closely by the tremendous demands and the very real dangers of my social situation.

Thus,

> I know . . . that the most crucial time in my own development came when I was forced to recognize that I was a kind of bastard of the West. . . .

Echoing in these statements is the unavoidable question: Where, how, and with what do I begin? Recognition of the dilemma helped Baldwin to locate himself in "the general social fabric," to come to terms with his social situation. It also explains why the author designed Creole to provide Sonny with both cue and direction.

Richard Albert finds some inconsistencies in the critical role Creole plays. He contends that Creoles had never regarded themselves as part of the black experience. They were generally viewed as offspring of French and Spanish settlers in Louisiana and later as descendants of Creole males and light-skinned mistresses. Although Jim Crow laws forced Creoles and blacks to work together and the "resulting synthesis helped bring about the first authentic jazz style," the black Creoles are not distinctly part of African American culture. Albert voices similar objections to Baldwin's use of the song, "Am I Blue": it does not observe the twelve-bar, three-lined blues form; it was written by Harry Akst and Grant Grayle, a white composer and lyricist, respectively; they wrote the song for Ethel Waters, a widely acclaimed black singer. Albert suggests that Bessie Smith, a less-established performer, would have been more suitable, especially because Baldwin once credited her with helping him to remember experiences he had buried.

Albert does concede, however, that Baldwin may have used Creole and "Am I Blue" to specific purpose: He may have wanted to demonstrate that although tradition is of great importance, change is both inevitable and necessary. Baldwin's text takes the subject further than Albert allows. It suggests that Baldwin, the self-styled misbegotten son of the West, having looked into his dim past, is using his art through Creole and "Am I Blue" to transform bastardy into legitimacy, into self and ethnic empowerment.

In Creole, the text creates a complex metaphor. On one level Creole signifies bastardy, the African American's social condition, issue of the intersection of conflicting cultural forces that tend to place identity in question. And yet the narrator describes Creole as an "enormous black man" who "erupted out of all that atmospheric lighting" in the "very dim" room; "we couldn't see." Although notions of indistinctness and vague derivations dominate the pas-

sage, this enormous black man is clearly drawn. Creole is big, confident, creative. And he takes charge: he "installed me, by myself at a table," he "took Sonny by the arm and led him to a piano," he "looked about him . . . as though he were making certain that all his chickens were in the coop." Creole "had them on a short rein"; he "let out the reins," and he "stepped forward to remind them that what they were playing was the blues." Creole "hit something in all of them, he hit something in me, myself." He "began to tell us what the blues were all about.

Creole "hit[s] something" in his colleagues and his audience because he shares with them a common experience: he is a kind of black Everyman. He also typifies the blues. Like them, he embodies the story of African American life, and, as his background suggests, he exemplifies the origin of that life. On still another level, Creole is the figure of the historian-artist; he knows and he tells what the blues are all about. To this end, he is invested with the authority, creative skill, and energy that marks *beginning*.

Through Creole, **"Sonny's Blues"** suggests that the artist must start with his own experience—which, ultimately, is inseparable from the experience of his race—and he must find in this experience, however "impure" and fragmented it may be, both the material and inspiration that he needs. Perhaps this is partly what Baldwin means when he says "we carry our history. We act in our history" (*A Rap on Race*). Thus, in Creole, Sonny, and blues-jazz, Baldwin's text figures anew the already-written text of African American history and, in the process, redefines the issue of that history within the construct of American civilization. In so doing, **"Sonny's Blues"** provides "orientation in time," making significant not only those "indefinable aspects of experience which . . . help to make us what we are," but those aspects that signal that we must yet become.

Accordingly, **"Sonny's Blues"** is a story about stories, a kind of narrative of possibilities; Baldwin's blues recreates **"Sonny's Blues,"** which in turn, "contain[s] [reconstructs] so many others." Aptly, the text lays great store in listening; perhaps the most important lesson that Sonny's brother, the narrator, learns is to listen. "You got to find a way to listen," Sonny tells him. Early in his narrative he dismisses Sonny's friend: "Look, don't tell *me* your sad story"; he had never thought that the "poor bastard" had one. By the end of his narration, he learns that everyone has a story: his mother, his father, his father's brother, Isabel, his daughter, Sonny, Sonny's friend—the list goes on and on—and that all these stories are inextricably part of his own. Indeed, his narrative of embedded tales constitutes an extended "family" chronicle. Told in retrospect, the narrator's blues—like Sonny's, like Baldwin's—exfoliate varied renderings that together rewrite yet another chapter in the history of "that long line."

In *Waiting for the Rain,* Mungoshi, too, renders the story of "that long line." Central to his novella is the Old Man's question: "Today we ask: Where are we? Who are we?" Like Baldwin, Mungoshi is interested in relocating a people's historical and cultural center. However, although the Zimbabwean artist writes a tale that in striking ways resembles **"Sonny's Blues"** and although the resemblances underscore the social-historical bond that the African and African American share, the divergences between the two stories identify the differences between the historical moments that the two writers confront and the artistic voice and strategies that the respective moment demands.

Thus, whereas Baldwin's bastardized characters must legitimize self through endless improvisation, Mungoshi's displaced ones must preserve the self by repeating or re-enacting the story of their origination. Baldwin's surrogate artist begins with memory, then bursts out into improvised song; Mungoshi's remains buried in the past for the entire performance. Baldwin portrays an ethnic group with a common experience and a common destiny. The artist is imbued, therefore, with heroic dimensions; he speaks of and for his community. Mungoshi presents a schizoid Shona people pulled simultaneously by opposing cultural forces. Baldwin's two surrogate artists, Creole and Sonny, belong to and work in the same tradition; the former musician serving as mentor to the latter. Garabha and Lucifer are antagonists pledged to conflicting forces, Shona and colonial European cultures respectively.

Published in 1975, *Waiting for the Rain* is set in colonial Rhodesia, where the Shona people have been living under the tyranny of white minority rule for decades. The text depicts problems that are the direct result of the sociopolitical dilemma. The people, dispossessed of the land that in Shona society is the source of religious as well as secular fortitude, suffer cultural disjunction. "In Shona cosmology" the land "is the abode of the ancestral spirits who exercise considerable control over the destiny of the living." To reject or betray the bond with the earth is to forfeit physical as well as spiritual well-being. To a great degree then, the endless drought and the Kafkaesque "waiting" are symptoms of cultural and spiritual bankruptcy.

The text illustrates this state of impoverishment by dramatizing schism as both the source and manifestation of the problem. Conflicting cultural forces lead to conflicting aesthetic sensibilities: Mungoshi splits his protagonist, the figure of the artist. He gives us Garabha and his counterpart, Lucifer. Garabha is a drummer, a vocation in which he has the unqualified support of his paternal grandfather who is, by trade, architect of the drum. This familial and generational endorsement establishes Garabha's position as the people's artist. Opposite him is Lucifer, also artist and poet. But Lucifer is alienated from his community as his sketch of his home or heritage shows: "[H]e draws a string of people in different postures of wailing, following a huge-wheeled cart drawn by emaciated oxen, and encompassing them all—but beyond them—the blood-red setting sun with a dark monster's-mouth centre." Above this Munch-like, nightmarish picture Lucifer pens a poetic description of a home constructed of dust and rubble on sweltering land, inhabited by vulture, carrion, and witch, circumscribed by despair and death. "I was born here against my will," he grieves (162).

The basis of Lucifer's estrangement is his European education at the boarding school in the city, run by his ac-quired "family," the Catholic priesthood. Eventually, one white priest bears Lucifer away from his village, sending him off to Europe to further his studies. At this point, Garabha returns to the bush from which he had come. Stratton describes these two paths as "the extreme polarities of contemporary Shona cultural division . . . providing an image of psychic split, the schizophrenia produced by the conflicting demands of two incompatible cultural formations."

However, the text does modify the antithesis. Although Lucifer rejects his heritage, he has found a direction that, laudable or not, he had the courage and conviction to take boldly. Garabha, on the other hand, is a wanderer and philanderer. Besides, he, too, harbors negative feelings of home and looks to "the horizon and the distant hills for sanctuary." The intersecting of opposing plot lines reorients the reader's attention to the larger issue: home or the community, the locus of the disorder. Tensions, suspicions, accusations, fear, and betrayals run rife among its members.

The single articulation of the possibility of communal cohesion takes place when Garabha, in a gesture that recalls Sonny's piano concert, leads his audience in a drum performance. Like Sonny, he has trouble beginning. Again, he gets the help he needs from a grandparent; his grandmother begins to chant a hunting song. The song charts a community in crisis against the backdrop of a river in flood. "Who will carry my arrow and spear for me—ho? / Who will fight for me—ho? / Fight the man eaters . . . ?" Couched in rhetorical terms, the hunting song recalls a prior time when communal interaction was possible, indeed indispensable, and when the forces challenging survival and success were natural and familiar.

Old Mandisa's song initiates an excursion into the past that lasts for the entire drum rehearsal. As Garabha plays the drum his "mind disappears"; he experiences a trance-like transport into the past, becoming lonelier and more distant the deeper he goes. He becomes absorbed into his subject; he is transformed literally into Samambwa, the great-great ancestor, founder of the tribe, whose story Garabha tells just as his grandfather had told it to him. This act of pure recapitulation suggests regression, and in the long run may be misleading because it buries the attention in the past. We will recall that Sonny remembers the story of "that long line" in order to transcend and recreate it.

The manner in which Samambwa's history is retold indicates its significance. In addition to Garabha's "replaying" it, the narrator simultaneously tells the story of the great-great ancestor's exploits. Interpolation of the story verbatim in the past tense, within and framed by the longer present tense narrative, sets forth the story as paradigm, the model against which present events are to be assessed. Further, the story spans a period stretching from prior to *Waiting for the Rain* to beyond it; it offers itself not only as a course but also as a means of restoration.

This elaborate rehearsal of "origin" imbues Garabha's performance and indeed the intranarrative itself with the quality of myth. In ritual concert the community remembers, celebrates, and participates in an original event that accounts for and gives meaning to their existence. As ritual, the commemoration suspends what Mircea Eliade calls "profane time," abolishing temporarily whatever threatens or would contaminate the memory of a sacred event. The act signifies an attempt at "pure" beginning free of the baggage of intervening experience.

But inasmuch as beginning cannot be radically separated from origin, it cannot be independent of circumstance either. Then there is the problem of "rupture," which, in *Waiting for the Rain,* remains an inescapable precondition. Thus, Garabha's sense of accomplishment is short-lived. He

> is aware that something is wrong: Lucifer. Lucifer is not here. And Garabha has been playing this today for Lucifer. Tears spring up in Garabha's eyes and he blindly walks out of the room. . . .
>
> A feeling of disaster—deep disaster—settles over Garabha. It has been shown beyond any doubt that he can never give anyone anything, try as he would. He has failed even to get through to his [psychic counterpart] brother, Lucifer.

Garabha's frustration is not without justification. The past may be invaluable as a place to begin, but not as a place to dwell. His frustration also calls into question the efficacy of the audience's sense of "this wonderful thing they have all shared in."

What the drum recital achieves is the construction of yet another set of oppositions: the past marked by wholeness and growth set against the present signifying division and loss. The seer, Mantandangoma, puts the problem thus:

> Of course they [Garabha's parents or the community as a whole] would rather go to church where they pray to someone of another tribe who doesn't know anything about them. And here is their own ancestor, Founder of the tribe, asking them to remember him and they turn their backs on him. Any wonder why this family is being slowly eaten away?

And the Old Man, acutely conscious of this problem, confesses that even he is bound to see double: two cultures, two periods, two drums.

As ironic counterpoint to this double vision, the text works the drum into a belabored symbol of cultural identification. The drum signifies individual integrity within the larger cultural constraints: "you have got *your* drum, at least"; "you stick to your drum"; avoid "playing the enemy's drum." The drum is an instrument of communion: Garabha plays "old tunes" for old friends, at whose behest he tells "their life to the drum," and he plays best when he is "absent," that is, free of self-conceit. The drum is a source of healing and stability: "as long as you play hard and listen to what it says and follow what it tells you— enough . . . You keep your heart . . . that's your drum. And that is my medicine to you"; also, "you won't be in

any trouble at all because you will be playing your own drum." The drum is a source of empowerment: "[W]hen he is playing the drum, Garabha feels that 'thing' he can't find words for"; "it is the sense of silent power. Power that doesn't make him arrogant or conceited. . . . It's a power that makes him feel very small and insignificant, yet at the same time making him feel that anything he turns his hand to, he will accomplish."

But just as insistently as these admonitions press home— and largely because of this insistence—the contending beat of "the enemy's drum" encroaches upon the reader's consciousness "making so much noise . . . that we can't even hear the beating of our own gullible little miserable hearts." In turn, this conflict and its effects throw into relief the need for and significance of "playing your own drum."

In its compass of contradictory signification, the figure of the drum enables the text to weight the side it would emphasize while simultaneously maintaining its dual perspective. Through this strategy, the drum symbol stresses the following points: (1) Shona cultural traditions must be preserved from total obscurity, and (2) in this endeavor, the individual is subordinate to community survival. These ideas, the gist of the Old Man's exhortations, bear the gravity of patriarchal authority and experience and, thus, in Shona society should be heeded. In effect, the Old Man answers the question that he posed earlier: "Today, we ask: Where are we? Who are we?" In the face of the present political situation, the Old Man suggests, it is of utmost importance that the Shona people hold on to that which defines and validates their identity; it is vital, he warns, that they discriminate between "bottled morality and our proud tradition." The Old Man, it would seem, places the society's hope for the future in an unadulterated, precolonial state of consciousness.

But almost imperceptibly the text shifts position. It posits at the edge of the narrative, so to speak, a position not entirely unlike that of **"Sonny's Blues."** As Garabha turns away from the village, disappointed and lonely, he begins to sing:

> The Old Man hears Garabha singing, fading away into the bush. This has taken him by surprise, the song . . . He begins to laugh. His mind is repeating the song on its own. He listens to his thoughts. . . . keeping the last image of the disappearing Garabha in his mind's eye and holding on to the song with his marrow. As song and image merge and mingle in his mind, the Old Man feels an elation he hasn't felt for a long time pervade him. It is only later that he realizes that the song and the tune *are not any of the old war chants.* It must be something that *the boy has made up himself,* he concludes. *Made up with the unerring ear of the old musicians.* With a heart that can make such poetry, the Old Man feels, the boy is home, *The House is in order.* But the boy doesn't know it yet. He is still searching. (emphasis added)

In Garabha's parting gesture, *Waiting for the Rain* projects a new improvised song, a "jazz age," so to speak, for the Shona future. Composed with the "unerring ear of the old musician," this "made up" tune would be, necessarily, the product of the individual and the communal, the familiar and the new, origin and beginning. The fact that the Old Man—custodian of Shona cultural heritage, scourge of European colonial legacy—hears, recognizes, and endorses the song as the harbinger of order goes a long way toward addressing and resolving the deep division that is the major concern of the novel.

Still, the work does not end on this note. Rather, it concludes with a wry reiteration of its theme of duality. The repetition, to a great extent, obscures Garabha's new song and accounts for the fact that its significance has gone unnoticed by many critics. In a ritual to mark Lucifer's departure, Raina throws on the fire the "medicine," "roots and leaves" that have been gathered by the young man's grandmother. And amid the "pungent odors," the smoke and sneezing, the Old Man calls upon the family's ancestors to protect his grandson:

> There is your child now. Out of our hands and into yours, my Fathers. . . . I speak to you my Father, Mandengu. Pass it on to your Father Nhema and all those who have gone before us, those in the hills of Manhize, and onto him who came alone from the north, Our Big Father, and ask him to pass it on to Him, who dwells in the Heavens . . .

At this strategic point in the Old Man's solicitation the other "Father," the Catholic mediator between "the Heavens" and earth, enters, and the traditional gives way to the Christian. The family repeat the Lord's Prayer and a prayer for travelers as the priest directs; then, with the sign of the cross, he petitions God's blessing on the household.

It is possible to read this ending as the reassertion of the text's thematic concern with the displacement of the traditional by the colonial and, consequently, as a tacit modification or negation of the Old Man's earlier optimistic response to Garabha's departing voice. Ironically, it is the Old Man himself who asks his ancestral "Big Father" to intercede with "Him, who dwells in the Heavens," as with comical dramatic precision the priest walks in and takes charge. However, it is also possible to interpret the scene as the symbolic enactment or composing of the new song, the envisioned reconciliation of past and present. But if the latter is the case, why is the scene presented with undisguised self-mockery? Why the ironic juxtaposition of the two competing tendencies? And why is Garabha already offstage at this point? Perhaps a combination of these two readings answers more nearly the questions that the episode raises.

The text's reiteration of duality, its parting declaration of ambivalence, is not surprising. The Shona artist is obviously discomforted with his subject and with the social inevitability he either will not or cannot dispel, not even fictionally. Garabha and Lucifer must go their separate ways. Mungoshi, the Shona artist writing in English, the "official" language, is caught somewhere in between; he cannot compose, like Baldwin or Sonny, a relatively confident and heroic tale, old yet new, variegated yet characteristic. At this historical juncture in pre-independent Zimbabwe, Mungoshi's text can only re-emphasize its story of division and defer the "new song" of healing and survival, of *beginning*.

FURTHER READING

Jones, Harry L. "Style, Form, and Content in the Short Fiction of James Baldwin." In *James Baldwin: A Critical Evaluation*, edited by Therman B. O'Daniel, pp. 143-50. Washington, D.C.: Howard University Press, 1977.
    Considers "Sonny's Blues" "the most perfectly realized story" in *Going to Meet the Man*.

Levensohn, Alan. "The Artist Must Outwit the Celebrity." *The Christian Science Monitor* 57, No. 301 (November 18, 1965): 15.
    Positive assessment of *Going to Meet the Man*, with particular emphasis on "Sonny's Blues."

Mosher, Marlene. "Baldwin's 'Sonny's Blues'." *Explicator* 40, No. 4 (Summer 1982): 59.
    Notes religious allusions in "Sonny's Blues."

———. "James Baldwin's Blues." *CLA Journal* XXVI, No. 1 (1982): 112-24.
    Explores Baldwin's use of the blues as a metaphor in "Sonny's Blues."

Ognibene, Elaine R. "Black Literature Revisited: 'Sonny's Blues'." *English Journal* 60, No. 1 (January 1971): 36-7.
    Examines the principal themes in "Sonny's Blues."

Pratt, Louis H. "The Fear and the Fury." In *James Baldwin*, pp. 31-49. Twayne Publishers, 1978.
    Discusses the ways in which Sonny is portrayed as the older and wiser of the brothers in "Sonny's Blues."

Ro, Sigmund. "The Black Musician as Literary Hero: Baldwin's 'Sonny's Blues' and Kelley's 'Cry for Me'." *American Studies in Scandinavia* 7, No. 1 (1975): 17-48.
    Considers the intellectual and philosophical influences on Baldwin at the time he wrote "Sonny's Blues," examining in particular the ways in which the story reflects the existential philosophies of Jean-Paul Sartre and Albert Camus.

Additional coverage of Baldwin's life and career is contained in the following sources published by The Gale Group: *Authors and Artists for Young Adults,* Vol. 4; *Black Literature Criticism; Black Writers,* Vol. 1; *Concise Dictionary of American Literary Biography, 1941-1968; Contemporary Authors,* Vols. 1-4 (rev. ed.), 124; *Contemporary Authors Bibliographical Series,* Vol. 1; *Contemporary Authors New Revision Series,* Vols. 3, 24; *Contemporary Literary Criticism,* Vols. 1, 2, 3, 4, 5, 8, 13, 15, 17, 42, 50, 67, 90; *Dictionary of Literary Biography,* Vols. 2, 7, 33; *Dictionary of Literary Biography Yearbook,* 1987; *DISCovering Authors; Drama Criticism,* Vol. 1; *Major 20th-Century Writers; Something about the Author,* Vols. 9, 54; *Short Story Criticism,* Vol. 10; **and** *World Literature Criticism.*

Notes from the Underground
Fyodor Dostoevsky

The following entry presents criticism of Dostoevsky's novella *Zapiski iz podpol'ya* (1864; *Notes from the Underground*). For a discussion of Dostoevsky's complete short fiction, see *Short Story Criticism,* Volume 2.

INTRODUCTION

Acclaimed as one of the classics of modern literature for its experimental form and style, thematic complexity, and innovative depiction of character psychology, *Notes from the Underground* is perhaps the most influential of Dostoevsky's works. The novella consists of "notes" on the philosophy and experiences of a retired, embittered recluse living in squalor in St. Petersburg. In creating the fictional author of the notes, who is commonly designated as the "underground man" by critics, Dostoevsky introduced the antihero into Russian fiction and firmly established the archetype of the outsider in world literature. The underground man has been cited as the figurative progenitor of various fictional characters of Franz Kafka, André Gide, Jean-Paul Sartre, and Albert Camus, among others, and *Notes* is typically considered the single greatest literary precursor of Existentialist thought. Yet the philosophical dimension of the novella is only one aspect of a work that also fuses sociology, psychology, and politics. Despite these complexities, *Notes from the Underground* is perceived as principally sounding a theme that reverberates throughout Dostoevsky's writings: that science and materialism, so emphasized in the modern age, are inadequate substitutes for religion, love, and human understanding.

Plot and Major Characters

The notes of the underground man consist of two sections, "The Underground," a theoretical creed setting forth the fictional author's personal philosophy, and "Apropos of the Wet Snow," in which he recollects several experiences of his twenty-fourth year that anticipate his present condition and philosophy. In the course of his diatribe, the fictional author reveals many traits: he is ineffectual, resentful, alienated, ambivalent, introspective, and self-contradictory. Although he claims that his first-person, monologic notes are not written for anyone else, he nevertheless addresses an imaginary audience and anticipates its responses, thus giving the work the tenor of dialogue. In "The Underground," the author attacks contemporary theories on the nature of humanity and refuses to submit to a life defined by laws of reason and science, which he equates with the incogitant passivity of a "piano-key." This denial has led him to acts of perversity and debauchery in the attempt to demonstrate free will and the intangible human qualities that he claims to cherish. The first incident described in "Apropos of the Wet Snow" is an ambiguous encounter with an army officer that the underground man interprets as a personal affront. For two years the narrator plots a revenge that produces equally ambiguous results. The author then relates another story in which he intrudes upon a dinner party held by former schoolmates and proceeds to embarrass himself by insulting the others and flaunting his averred superior intelligence. When the party subsides, the underground man follows his former schoolmates to a brothel, where he asserts his superiority over a prostitute, Liza (also transliterated as Lisa), whom he manipulates with a noble speech and a lofty offer of assistance. Three days later, Liza appears at the underground man's abode, only to realize his meanness and unhappiness. He is humiliated at having been exposed and is unable to accept her consoling love. Shortly thereafter the notes abruptly end, with the underground man purporting that he will write no more; a comment contradicted by the heretofore silent "editor" of the notes who closes the novella by adding that the underground man "could not help going on."

Major Themes

The overall complexity of *Notes from the Underground* has generated a wide variety of thematic interpretations. Many critics have contended that *Notes from the Underground* is in one sense a parody of, or response to, Nikolai Chernyshevsky's *What Is to Be Done?*, an 1863 utopian novel that propounds a radical socialist philosophy of enlightened self-interest, referred to as "rational egoism." This philosophy asserts the absolute hegemony of reason, insisting that all human behavior is dictated by rational laws of nature. In *What Is To be Done?*, Chernyshevsky evoked the image of the Crystal Palace, a structure originally constructed for London's 1851 World's Fair, as the ideal of human rationality. The underground man, however, attacks this triumph of science and engineering as a symbol of the absence of spontaneity and freedom. In *Notes,* critics have maintained, Dostoevsky showed the moral and psychological incompatibility of an autonomous personality and the purely deterministic world heralded by Chernyshevsky and other socialist radicals. The psychological aspects of the novella have also received close attention. Scholars have termed *Notes* the self-revelation of a pathological personality diversely diagnosed as narcissistic, borderline psychotic, paranoid, compulsive, or repressed. Some critics have found in Dostoevsky's own troubles a basis for the autobiographical, agitated tone of his *Notes.* Many have held that the novella disparages the narrow intellectualism and overrefined consciousness that Dostoevsky ascribed to Russians who were, in his estimation, contaminated by the corrupt rationalist trends of western European thought. Still others have focused on the underground man as a social type representative of individuals unable to establish a bond with humanity: an anonymous and isolated figure who experiences hostility toward the mechanized and bureaucratic aspects of society. *Notes* has also been considered an argument for existential choice, and, similarly a protest against utilitarianism, materialism, and positivism. Many of these diverse thematic strains tend to coalesce in the observations of critics who find at the heart of the underground man's desperation Dostoevsky's own distrust of scientific rationalism as a means of illuminating ethical problems and his deeply-felt Christian spirituality. Such critics construe *Notes* as a condemnation of the spiritual malaise of Dostoevsky's era and a theological cry of despair over modern moral disintegration personified in the unredeemed figure of the underground man.

Critical Reception

Notes from the Underground was a pivotal work for Dostoevsky for its inauguration of themes prominent in his later novels and its introduction of the acutely self-analytical, spiritually torn hero, who is a prototype for many other of his characters. However, the importance of *Notes* extends far beyond its significance in Dostoevsky's career, as evinced in George Steiner's estimation of the novella: ". . . when the traditional literary elements in

[*Notes from the Underground*] have been set aside, and when close affinities to Dostoevsky's other works have been noted, the profound originality of the thing continues to assert itself. Chords previously unheard had been struck with admirable precision. No other text by Dostoevsky has exerted more influence on twentieth-century thought or technique."

CRITICISM

Vasily Rozanov (essay date 1906)

SOURCE: *Dostoevsky and the Legend of the Grand Inquisitor,* translated by Spencer E. Roberts, Cornell University Press, 1972, 232 p.

[*A Russian journalist, philosopher, and critic, Rozanov married Apollinaria Suslova, the former mistress of Dostoevsky, when Rozanov was twenty-four and Suslova was forty. His* Legenda o velikom inkvizitore *(1891;* Legend of the Grand Inquisitor*), a study of Dostoevsky's* The Brothers Karamazov, *introduced a new critical approach to the author and aided revival of interest in Dostoevsky. In the following excerpt from a 1906 translation of the third edition of that work, Rozanov stresses the high value placed upon free will in* Notes from the Underground.]

In reading [***Notes from the Underground***], one is unexpectedly struck by our need for annotated editions—annotated not from the standpoint of the form and origin of literary works, as is already done, but from the standpoint of their contents and meaning—in order finally to decide the question of whether the idea contained in them is true, or whether it is false, and why, and to decide this by joint efforts, to decide it thoroughly and rigorously, in a way accessible only to science. For example, every line of ***Notes from the Underground*** is important; it is impossible to reduce the book to general formulas. Moreover, no thinking person can pass over the assertions made in it without considering them carefully.

There never was a writer in our literature whose ideals were so completely divorced from present-day reality. The thought never for a moment occurred to Dostoevsky to try to preserve this way of life and merely improve a thing or two in it. Because of the generalizing cast of his mind, he directed all his attention toward the evil concealed in the general system of a historically developed life; hence his hatred of and disdain for all hope of improving anything by means of individual changes; hence his animosity towards our parties of progressives and Westerners. Perceiving only the "general," he passed directly from reality to the extreme in the ideal, and the first thing he encountered there was the hope of raising, with the help of reason, an edifice of human life so perfect that it would give peace to man, crown history, and put an end to suffering. His criticism of this idea runs through all his works; it was expressed for the first time, and moreover in the greatest detail, in ***Notes from the Underground.***

The man from the underground is a person who has withdrawn deep within himself. He hates life and spitefully criticizes the ideal of the rational utopians on the basis of a precise knowledge of human nature, which he acquired through a long and lonely observation of himself and of history.

There never was a writer in our literature whose ideals were so completely divorced from present-day reality.

—*Vasily Rozanov*

The outline of his criticism is as follows: man carries within himself, in an undeveloped state, a complex world of inclinations that have not yet been discovered—and their discovery will determine his future history just as inevitably as the existence of these inclinations in him now is certain. Therefore, the predetermination of history and its crown by our reason alone will always be empty talk without any real importance.

Among those inclinations, in so far as they have already revealed themselves during the course of history, there is so much that is incomprehensibly strange and irrational that it is impossible to find any intelligent formula that would satisfy human nature. Is not happiness the principle on which this formula can be constructed? But does not man sometimes crave suffering? Are there really any pleasures for which Hamlet would give up the torments of his consciousness? Are not order and regularity the common features of every final system of human relations? And yet, do we not sometimes love chaos, destruction, and disorder even more passionately than we do regularity and creation? Is it possible to find a person who would do only what is necessary and good his whole life long? And would he not, by limiting himself to this for so long, experience a strange weariness; would he not shift, at least briefly, to the poetry of instinctive actions? Finally, will not all happiness disappear for man if there disappears for him the feeling of novelty, of everything unexpected, everything capriciously changeable—things to which he now adapts his way of life, and in so doing experiences much distress, but an equal joy? Does not uniformity for everyone contradict the fundamental principle of human nature—individuality—and does not the constancy of the future and of the "ideal" contradict his free will, his thirst for choosing something or other in his own way, sometimes contrary to an external, even a rational, decision? And can man really be happy without freedom, without individuality? Without all this, with the eternal absence of novelty, will not instincts be irresistibly aroused in him such as will shatter the adamantine nature of every formula: and man will wish for suffering, destruction, blood, for everything except that to which his formula has doomed

him for all eternity; in the same way that a person confined too long to a light, warm room will cut his hands on the glass of the windowpanes and run naked out into the cold, merely so as not to have to remain any longer in his former surroundings? Was it not this feeling of spiritual weariness that led Seneca into intrigue and crime? And was it not this that made Cleopatra stick gold pins into the breasts of her black slave girls, while eagerly looking them in the face, watching their trembling, smiling lips, and their frightened eyes? And finally, will the never-changing possession of the achieved ideal really satisfy a person for whom wishing, striving, and achieving is an irresistible need? And does rationality, on the whole, exhaust human nature? But obviously that is the only thing that its very creator—reason—can give to a final formula.

By nature, man is a completely irrational creature; therefore, reason can neither completely explain him nor completely satisfy him. No matter how persistent is the work of thought, it will never cover all of reality; it will answer the demands of the imaginary man, but not those of the real one. Hidden in man is the instinct for creation, and this was precisely what gave him life, what rewarded him with suffering and joy—things that reason can neither understand nor change.

The rational is one thing; the mystical is another thing again. And while it is inaccessible to the touch and power of science, it can be arrived at through religion. Hence the development of the mystical in Dostoevsky and the concentration of his interest on all that is religious, something we observe in the second and chief period of his work, which began with *Crime and Punishment.*

J. Middleton Murry (essay date 1916)

SOURCE: *Fyodor Dostoevsky: A Critical Study,* 1916. Reprint by Russell & Russell, 1966, 263 p.

[*In the following excerpt, Murry asserts that the narrator of* Notes *from the Underground,* who he considers the tortured victim of his own heightened consciousness, is Dostoevsky's rendering of himself.]

[In *The Insulted and Injured* Dostoevsky] sets down only what he saw and felt: What he thought he hid close within his heart, while he sought the way of unburdening his deeper soul, which was his passionate mind.

And within a year or two, after *The House of the Dead* had been written, he ventured to reveal something of that which was hidden. The imaginary writer of **Letters from the Underworld** is a man of thought, and not of action. He does not live at all, but thinks, and his thought has paralysed his being, until he can only sit down and contemplate the world that is, which he abhors yet can by no means escape. Evil and pain, they tell him, are the visible working of the iron laws of Nature: the things that are must be. "What have *I* to do with the laws of Nature, or with arithmetic," he answers, "when all the time those laws and the formula that twice two make four do not meet with my acceptance? Of course I am not going to beat my head against a wall if I have not strength enough to do so; yet I am not going to accept that wall merely because I have to run up against it and have no means to knock it down." This is at last open rebellion, even though it be confined within the ferment of his own soul. He will not accept life; he cannot refuse. To live demands a grosser soul than his; for in his acute sensibility the equilibrium which Dostoevsky the youth had sought between the inward life and the outward is lost beyond recovery. So clearly does he recognise the vanity of action, that the only actions left to him are those in which he has at least a faint hope of momentarily overwhelming his consciousness with the extremity of sensation. Therefore his existence passes in the underworld, from which he makes sudden and fantastic irruptions into the upper air of decent normal life, only because he knows that he will suffer there the torments of the damned.

These torments are all he has to hope for from life. If he folds his hands in contemplation, he suffers both from what he contemplates and yet more from the longing to break the bands of his inertia and to act, for his longing to act is infinitely greater than that of the man of action, not merely because the springs of action are weakened in him and he desires that which he has not, but because he is conscious of his own personality, and knows that he must assert his will simply for the sake of asserting his will. Even the existence of that will he has to prove to himself; therefore the actions of that will are bound to be senseless and evil and fantastical, precisely because they are crucial. Deliberately to do a senseless or an evil or a fantastical thing is to have asserted one's will in the highest, and to have convinced one's self of its reality, because no power on earth save the individual will could have accomplished it. That is his only reply to the life which he cannot accept. But to do good and to behave sensibly, they say, is in his interests. What does he care about his interests?

> I tell you that there is one occasion and one occasion only when man can wilfully, consciously desiderate for himself that which is foolish and harmful. This is the occasion when he yearns *to have the right* to desiderate for himself what is foolish and harmful and to be bound by no obligation whatever to desiderate anything that is sensible. It is his crowning folly; it is herein we see his ineradicable wayfulness. Yet such folly may also be the best thing in the world for him, even though it work him harm and contradict our soundest conclusions on the subject of his interests. This is because it is possible for his folly to preserve to him under all circumstances the chiefest and most valuable of all his possessions—his personality, his individuality.

This is a searching dialectic. Doubtless it underlay the evil Prince Valkovsky's "What's not nonsense is personality—myself" [in *The Insulted and Injured*], but Dostoevsky had not dared to lend it to him. Nevertheless, the obscure writer of the **Letters from the Underworld** confesses to a similar taste for ugly debauchery. Though his reasoning is ostensibly a protest against materialist and positivist philosophers, it strikes far beyond these obvious enemies. Not only the good of the positivist is impotent before it, but what other good can stand against it?

But Dostoevsky forbore to draw the last conclusion from his own logic. He left it so that it could be said that these confessions were no more than the ravings of a crazy, morbid mind. There is nothing crazy in the argument, however. Certainly it was only a skirmish before the battle, but it was fought with the skill of a master of strategy, and it was fought on a straight issue: Consciousness *contra mundum*. Of course the writer of those letters was a noxious insect which must be destroyed. But what if, given a certain datum, his noxiousness is inevitable? And further, what if that datum is nothing less than the possession of that which mankind has come to recognise as the proud differentia of man, of *homo sapiens*: the conscious reason? Is one who possesses this consciousness in the highest degree and has the courage to act upon it, to be destroyed as a noxious insect by the majority of other men who possess it in a lesser form or not at all? What if life has reached in the modern man a final form whose destruction by its own elements is inevitable? What if the good man, the normal man, the sound man, the living man, the social man are forms already superseded by something other which can find only in the underworld a possibility of continued existence, which desires to live, but cannot, because the conscious mind desires to accept life, but cannot?

The underworldling had thought these things. "True," he says,

> the normal man is gross—but then the normal man may have to be gross. How indeed do you know that his grossness is not one of his very best points? Anyway, I grow daily more confirmed in my suspicion that if one were to take the antithesis of the normal man—that is to say, the man of acute sensibility, the man who hails not from Nature's womb, but from a chemical retort—this comes rather too close to mysticism, a thing which I also suspect—the man born of the retort would sometimes feel so conscious that he was being outclassed by his antithesis, the man of action, that he would come to look upon himself despite his acute sensibility as a mouse rather than a human being. . . .

Yet wherein is he less than human? There is only one answer to this: because he feels and thinks more than his fellows. It is surely only a malignant mockery to suppose that a man who is more richly endowed with the essentially human faculties than other men, is less a man than they. Here is the beginning of an ugly and desperate paradox. It is true that he knows himself not a man, but a creature compounded in a chemical retort; but he also knows that the chemical process is that of life itself. He is one of the first of the new men who by the excess of their humanity are inhuman; and upon what power falls the responsibility of his creation? "Civilisation," he says, "develops nothing in man save an added capacity to receive impressions," and he might have added, "and to think upon the impressions he has received." In himself the last progress of the human consciousness has ended in a cul-de-sac.

So he lives in the underworld, his hands folded in contemplation, brooding upon the evil which life has wrought in himself. He has no desire, though he knows that he is a mouse in their comparison, to have the freedom of the company of the children of the day. He envies them, yet he would not accept life on their conditions, for he is, after all, more a man than they.

> That is to say, though I envy him, I find the underworld better—yet I am lying. I am lying because, even as I know that two and two make four, so do I know that it is not the underworld which is so much better, but something else, something else,—something for which I am hungry, but which I shall never find. Ah no! To the devil with the underworld! . . .

And this something else is a Way of life. The underworld is only living death. The tormented soul of this mouseman longs to *be,* to resign nothing of his humanity and yet to live. He longs for that which he knows to be impossible, for something within him whispers that it may yet be possible in defiance of his reason and his consciousness. But since upon these alone he must depend to show him the way to the future beatitude, he knows he will never slake his thirst at the fountain of life.

In the story of **"The Falling Sleet,"** he tells a ghastly history of one of his irruptions into the life that is, of how he desired and won the love of a simple heart, how he hated the woman who loved him and whom he loved, how he outraged her and drove her away in a final inspiration of devilish cruelty and was left alone once more. It was inevitable: and the secret of its inevitability is in the terrible words which Dostoevsky once used in *The Journal of an Author,* when, protesting against the panacea of love for humanity, he said that "love for suffering humanity in a soul which knows it can bring no alleviation to that suffering, will be changed into a hatred of humanity." That, he said, was profounder, even though they did not understand it, than all the gospels of all the preaching of universal love. And the outcast of the underworld, though he desired to love and to be loved, had within him a stronger desire, that he should not deceive himself or another by love. Love was no remedy for him who suffered from the contemplation of the whole life of which love was only a part; and truly it was better for the woman that she should have been driven away even as she was than that she should have remained with him or he with her. He was in rebellion against life, and since a man cannot live in rebellion, he did not live. There was no hope for him in life, nor any for one who should unite her life with his. He had deliberately and inevitably put himself outside life; he chose the underworld, because there was no other place for him, and if, when he yielded to the longing within him to be swallowed up in life, to act and to forget and to live, his action was cruel and revolting, that too was inevitable. His being was set in absolute negation to the life of which love is the noblest part.

But he was a sick soul, a mind diseased, a man corrupted by his own thought! Sickness is a two-edged conception. He was abnormal, it is true, and he and Dostoevsky in him was clearly conscious of the abyss that lay between his nature and that of normal men. But abnormality is not the same as sickness. What is sick cannot be sound, but the abnormal may well be true. What reason is there to suppose that the way of health and the way of truth are the same? We may argue endlessly that we dare not suppose that life should itself contain the principle of its own destruction, but why should it not? What evidence can a man derive from the contemplation of life which could make such a conception absurd? The conception is irrational; but life itself is irrational. Life seems to have evolved the human reason for the singularly irrational purpose of making known its own irrationality. The conception is terrible; life itself is not less terrible.

Mais autres temps, autres mœurs. There is another philosophy descended upon the earth in recent times. It may be thought that Dostoevsky's underworldling would find a stouter opponent in M. Bergson than in the positivists and social reformers of his day. If he had miraculously anticipated the doctrine of the bankruptcy of the reason, he had not known that the way of intuition and instinct was open to him. Perhaps he was not quite so simple. If the reason is bankrupt, man is not the less condemned to use it and to put faith in it. If he would resign its privilege, he cannot for all his desire. He is born to the purple. For better or worse it is his so long as mankind shall continue. And if by reason he has decided that reason is unprofitable, it is not likely to be atrophied by the destructive force of its own logic. Nor can man, still possessed of and possessed by reason, fling himself into the nirvana of instinct and intuition. The underworldling was not so simple-minded though he made the same attempt. Instinct and intuition are not detachable parts of the human soul. They are permeated now by the conscious reason and are changed. The underworldling made the attempt to lose his consciousness in them, with tragedy inevitable for a conclusion. Perhaps there is more real philosophy in his proud and final challenge to the normal, living men, that he, for all his sordidness and unchanging despair, had yet *lived* more than they.

> Well, gentlemen, heaven forbid that I should justify myself by seeking to include all my fellowmen with myself; yet, so far as I am concerned, I have but carried to a finish in my life, what you have never even dared to carry half-way, although you have constantly mistaken your cowardice for prudence, and have constantly cheated yourselves with comforting reflections. The truth is that I have been more *alive* than you. That is all. But look a little closer. We do not even know where present-day reality is to be found, nor what it is called. Whenever we are left to our own devices, and deprived of our bookish rules, we at once grow confused—we do not know what to do, nor what to observe, nor what to love, nor what to hate, nor what to respect, nor what to despise. We grow weary of being human beings at all—of possessing real, individual flesh and blood. We are *ashamed* of being human—we count it beneath our dignity. . . .

He is grown weary of his humanity. He must possess his soul in patience until out of his bankruptcy and impotence a new thing is created: but in the age-long waiting for the miracle what shall he do?

Dostoevsky, who was the man, had his one cure and his one refuge in creating him after his own image. Doubtless he knew that the solace of this activity might be denied to other men. They might even be stronger men and bolder. Had not even the villain Valkovsky let fall a dangerous word, one dangerous in itself, but altogether too dangerously near the exacter reasoning of the underworld? "What a man most needs is an *independent* will—no matter what the cost of such independence of volition, nor what it lead to. Yet the devil only knows what man's will—" The rest of that broken sentence is not the next chapter in the *Letters from the Underworld,* but in the rest of Dostoevsky's work. Suppose the anodyne of literary creation denied, suppose a man too strong to remain in the underworld, even though it is not a place but a state of soul, then there might be strange things to chronicle. "The devil only knows. . . ." It is true; but there have been those—Mihailovsky was one—who were convinced that they had seen the light of the Evil One in Dostoevsky's eyes.

D. S. Mirsky (essay date 1926)

SOURCE: "The Age of Realism: The Novelists (II)," in his *A History of Russian Literature Comprising "A History of Russian Literature" and "Contemporary Russian Literature,"* edited by Francis J. Whitfield, Alfred A. Knopf, 1949, pp. 245-90.

[*Mirsky was a Russian prince who fled his country after the Bolshevik Revolution and settled in London. While in England, he wrote two important histories of Russian literature,* Contemporary Russian Literature *(1926) and* A History of Russian Literature *(1926). In the following excerpt from the 1949 condensed edition of* A History of Russian Literature, *Mirsky extols* Notes from the Underground *as a work that transcends classification as mere art or literature due to the philosophic depths it plumbs.*]

Memoirs from Underground, the work that introduces us, chronologically, to the "mature" Dostoyévsky, contains at once the essence of his essential self. It cannot be regarded as imaginative literature pure and simple. There is in it quite as much philosophy as literature. It would have to be connected with his journalistic writings were it not that it proceeded from a deeper and more significant spiritual level of his personality. The work occupies a central place in the creation of Dostoyevsky. Here his essential tragical intuition is expressed in the most unadulterated and ruthless form. It transcends art and literature, and its place is among the great mystical revelations of mankind. The faith in the supreme value of the human personality and its freedom, and in the irrational religious and tragic foundation of the spiritual universe, which is above reason, above the distinction of good and evil (the faith, ultimately, of all mystical religion), is expressed in a paradoxical, unexpected, and entirely spontaneous form. The central posi-

tion of *Memoirs from Underground* in the work of Dostoyévsky was first discerned by Nietzsche and Rózanov. It stands in the center of the writings of Shestóv, the greatest of Dostoyévsky's commentators. Viewed as literature, it is also the most original of Dostoyévsky's works, although also the most unpleasant and the most "cruel." It cannot be recommended to those who are not either sufficiently strong to overcome it or sufficiently innocent to remain unpoisoned. It is a strong poison, which is most safely left untouched.

Vladimir Nabokov (essay date 1940)

SOURCE: "Fyodor Dostoevski: 'Memoirs from a Mousehole'," in his *Lectures on Russian Literature,* edited by Fredson Bowers, Harcourt Brace Jovanovich, 1981, pp. 115-25.

[*A Russian-born American man of letters, Nabokov was a prolific contributor to many literary fields. In the following excerpt from his lecture on* Notes from the Underground, *composed in about 1940, Nabokov derisively summarizes the plot of the novella, noting with displeasure Dostoevsky's use of generalities and his diffuse literary style, but applauding the humor, particularly in Chapter Four of the book's second section.*]

The story whose title should be "Memoirs from Under the Floor," or "Memoirs from a Mousehole" bears in translation the stupidly incorrect title of *Notes from the Underground.* The story may be deemed by some a case history, a streak of persecution mania, with variations. My interest in it is limited to a study in style. It is the best picture we have of Dostoevski's themes and formulas and intonations. It is a concentration of Dostoevskiana. Moreover it is very well rendered in English by Guerney.

Its first part consists of eleven small chapters or sections. Its second part, which is twice the length, consists of ten slightly longer chapters containing events and conversations. The first part is a soliloquy but a soliloquy that presupposes the presence of a phantom audience. Throughout this part the mouseman, the narrator, keeps turning to an audience of persons who seem to be amateur philosophers, newspaper readers, and what he calls normal people. These ghostly gentlemen are supposed to be jeering at him, while he is supposed to thwart their mockery and denunciations by the shifts, the doubling back, and various other tricks of his supposedly remarkable intellect. This imaginary audience helps to keep the ball of his hysterical inquiry rolling, an inquiry into the state of his own crumbling soul. It will be noticed that references are made to topical events of the day in the middle of the 1860s. The topicality, however, is vague and has no structural power. Tolstoy uses newspapers too—but he does this with marvelous art when, for example, in the beginning of *Anna Karenin* he not only characterizes Oblonski by the kind of information Oblonski likes to follow in the morning paper but also fixes with delightful historical or pseudo-historical precision a certain point in space and time. In Dostoevski we have generalties substituted for specific traits.

The narrator starts by depicting himself as a rude, waspish man, a spiteful official who snarls at the petitioners who come to the obscure bureau where he works. After making his statement, "I am a spiteful official," he retracts it and says that he is not even that: "It was not only that I could not become spiteful; I did not know how to become anything: either spiteful or kind, either a rascal or an honest man, either a hero or an insect." He consoles himself with the thought that an intelligent man does not become anything, and that only rascals and fools become something. He is forty years old, lives in a wretched room, had a very low rank in the civil service, has retired by now after getting a small legacy, and is anxious to talk about himself.

I should warn you at this point that the first part of the story, eleven little chapters, are significant not in what is expressed or related, but in the manner it is expressed and related. The manner reflects the man. This reflection Dostoevski wishes to fix in a cesspool of confessions through the manners and mannerisms of a neurotic, exasperated, frustrated, and horribly unhappy person.

The next theme is human-consciousness (not conscience but consciousness), the awareness of one's emotions. The more aware this mouseman was of goodness, of beauty—of moral beauty—the more he sinned, the deeper he sank in filth. Dostoevski, as so often happens with authors of his type, authors who have a general message to deliver to all men, to all sinners, Dostoevski does not specify the depravity of his hero. We are left guessing.

After every loathsome act the narrator commits, he says he crawls back into his mousehole and proceeds to enjoy the accursed sweetness of shame, of remorse, the pleasure of his own nastiness, the pleasure of degradation. Delighting in degradation is one of Dostoevski's favorite themes. Here, as elsewhere in his writing, the writer's art lags behind the writer's purpose, since the sin committed is seldom specified, and art is always specific. The act, the sin, is taken for granted. Sin here is a literary convention similar to the devices in the sentimental and Gothic novels Dostoevski had imbibed. In this particular story the very abstractness of the theme, the abstract notion of loathsome action and consequent degradation is presented with a not negligible bizarre force in a manner that reflects the man in the mousehole. (I repeat, it is the manner which counts.) By the end of chapter 2 we know that the mouseman has started writing his memoirs in order to explain the joys of degradation.

He is, he says, an acutely conscious mousey man. He is being insulted by a kind of collective normal man—stupid but normal. His audience is mocking him. The gentlemen are jeering. Unsatisfied desires, the burning thirst of parching revenge, hesitations—half-despair, half-faith—all this combines to form a strange morbid bliss for the humiliated subject. Mouseman's rebellion is based not upon a creative impulse but upon his being merely a moral misfit,

a moral dwarf, who sees in the laws of nature a stone wall which he cannot break down. But here again we flounder in a generalization, in an allegory, since no specific purpose, no specific stone wall is evoked. Bazarov (*Fathers and Sons*) knew that what a nihilist wishes to break is the old order that among other things sanctioned slavery. The mouse here is merely listing his grudges against a despicable world that he has invented himself, a world of cardboard instead of stone.

Chapter 4 contains a comparison: his pleasure, he says, is the pleasure of a person with a toothache realizing that he is keeping his family awake with his moans—moans that perhaps are those of an imposter. A complicated pleasure. But the point is that the mouseman suggests he is cheating.

So by chapter 5 we have the following situation. The mouseman is filling his life with bogus emotions because he lacks real ones. Moreover, he has no foundation, no starting point from which to proceed to an acceptance of life. He looks for a definition of himself, for a label to stick upon himself, for instance a "lazy-bones," or a "connoisseur of wines," any kind of peg, any kind of nail. But what exactly compels him to look for a label is not divulged by Dostoevski. The man he depicts lives only as a maniac, as a tangle of mannerisms. Dostoevski's mediocre imitators such as Sartre, a French journalist, have continued the trend to-day.

At the beginning of chapter 7 we find a good example of Dostoevski's style, very well rendered by Guerney revising Garnett:

> But these are all golden dreams. Oh, tell me, who was it first announced, who was it first proclaimed, that man only does nasty things because he does not know his own interests; and that if he were enlightened, if his eyes were opened to his real normal interests, man would at once cease to do nasty things, would at once become good and noble because, being enlightened and understanding his real advantage, he would see his own advantage in the good and nothing else, and we all know that not one man can, consciously, act against his own interests, consequently, so to say, through necessity, he would begin doing good? Oh, the babe! Oh, the pure, innocent child! Why, in the first place, when in all these thousands of years has there been a time when man has acted only from his own interest? What is to be done with the millions of facts that bear witness that men, *consciously,* that is, fully understanding their real interests, have left them in the background and have rushed headlong on another path, to meet peril and danger, and compelled to this course by nobody and by nothing, but, as it were, simply disliking the beaten track, and have obstinately, willfully, beaten another difficult, absurd path, seeking it almost in the darkness? So, I suppose, this obstinacy and perversity were pleasanter to them than any advantage.

The repetition of words and phrases, the intonation of obsession, the hundred percent banality of every word, the vulgar soapbox eloquence mark these elements of Dostoevski's style.

In this chapter 7 the mouseman, or his creator, hits upon a new series of ideas revolving around the term "advantage." There are, he says, cases when a man's advantage must consist in his desiring certain things that are actually harmful to him. This is all double talk, of course; and just as the enjoyment of degradation and pain have not been easily explained by the mouseman, so the advantage of disadvantage will not be explained by him either. But a set of new mannerisms will be arrayed in the tantalizing approximations that occupy the next pages.

What exactly is this mysterious "advantage"? A journalistic excursion, in Dostoevski's best manner, first takes care of "civilization [which] has made mankind, if not more blood-thirsty, at least more vilely, more loathsomely blood-thirsty." This is an old idea going back to Rousseau. The mouseman evokes a picture of universal prosperity in the future, a palace of crystal for all, and finally there it comes—the mysterious advantage: One's own free unfettered choice, one's own whim no matter how wild. The world has been beautifully rearranged, but here comes a man, a natural man, who says: it is merely my whim to destroy this beautiful world—and he destroys it. In other words, man wants not any rational advantage, but merely the fact of independent choice—no matter what it is—even though breaking the pattern of logic, of statistics, of harmony and order. Philosophically this is all bunkum since harmony, happiness, presupposes and includes also the presence of whim.

But the Dostoevskian man may choose something insane or stupid or harmful—destruction and death—because it is at least his own choice. This, incidentally, is one of the reasons for Raskolnikov's killing the old woman in *Crime and Punishment.*

In chapter 9 the mouseman goes on ranting in self-defence. The theme of destruction is taken up again. Perhaps, says he, man prefers destroying to creating. Perhaps it is not the achievement of any goal that attracts him but the process of attaining this goal. Perhaps, says Mouseman, man dreads to succeed. Perhaps he is fond of suffering. Perhaps suffering is the only origin of consciousness. Perhaps man, so to speak, becomes a human being with the first awareness of his awareness of pain.

The palace of crystal as an ideal, as a journalistic symbol of perfect universal life in aftertime, is again projected on the screen and discussed. The narrator has worked himself into a state of utter exasperation, and the audience of mockers, of jeering journalists he confronts, seems to be closing in upon him. We return to one of the points made in the very beginning: it is better to be nothing, it is better to remain in one's mousehole—or rat hole. In the last chapter of part one he sums up the situation by suggesting that the audience he has been evoking, the phantom gentlemen he has been addressing, is an attempt to create readers. And it is to this phantom audience that he will now present a series of disjointed recollections which will, perhaps, illustrate and explain his mentality. Wet snow is falling. Why he sees it as yellow is more emblematic than optical. He means, I suppose, yellow as implying unclean white, "dingy," as he also says. A point to be noticed is that he hopes to obtain relief from writing. This closes the first part, which, I repeat, is important in its manner, not matter.

Why part two is entitled "Concerning Wet Snow" is a question that can be settled only in the light of journalistic innuendoes of the 1860s by writers who liked symbols, allusions to allusions, that kind of thing. The symbol perhaps is of purity becoming damp and dingy. The motto—also a vague gesture—is a lyrical poem by Dostoevski's contemporary Nekrasov.

The events our mouseman is going to describe in the second part go twenty years back to the 1840s. He was as gloomy then as he is now, and hated his fellow men as he does now. He also hated his own self. Experiments in humiliation are mentioned. Whether he hated a fellow or not, he could not look into a person's eyes. He experimented—could he outstare anybody?—and failed. This worried him to distraction. He is a coward, he says, but for some reason or other every decent man of our age, he says, must be a coward. What age? The 1840s or the 1860s? Historically, politically, sociologically, the two eras differed tremendously. In 1844 we are in the age of reaction, of despotism; 1864 when these notes are set down is the age of change, of enlightenment, of great reforms as compared to the forties. But Dostoevski's world despite topical allusions is the gray world of mental illness, where nothing can change except perhaps the cut of a military uniform, an unexpectedly specific detail to meet at one point.

A few pages are devoted to what our mouseman calls "romantics," or more correctly in English "romanticists." The modern reader cannot understand the argument unless he wades through Russian periodicals of the fifties and sixties. Dostoevski and the mouseman really mean "sham idealists," people who can somehow combine what they call the good and the beautiful with material things such as a bureaucratic career, etc. (Slavophiles attack Westerners for setting up idols rather than Ideals.) All this is very vaguely and tritely expressed by our mouseman, and we need not bother about it. We learn that our mouseman, furtively, in solitude at night, indulged in what he calls filthy vice, and apparently for this purpose he visited various obscure haunts. (We recall St. Preux, the gentleman in Rousseau's *Julie* who also visited a remote room in a house of sin where he kept drinking white wine under the impression it was water, and next thing found himself in the arms of what he calls *une créature.*) This is vice as depicted in sentimental novels.

After the great chapter 4 the mouseman's irritation, humiliation, etc., become repetitious, and soon a false note is introduced with the appearance of that favorite figure of sentimental fiction, the noble prostitute, the fallen girl with the lofty heart. Liza, the young lady from Riga, is a literary dummy. Our mouseman, to get some relief, starts the process of hurting and frightening a fellow creature, poor Liza (Sonya's sister). The conversations are very garrulous and very poor, but please go on to the bitter end.

Perhaps some of you may like it more than I do. The story ends with our mouseman emitting the idea that humiliation and insult will purify and elevate Liza through hatred, and that perhaps exalted sufferings are better than cheap happiness. That's about all.

Eugene Goodheart (essay date 1968)

SOURCE: "Dostoevsky and the Hubris of the Immoralist," in *The Cult of the Ego: The Self in Modern Literature,* University of Chicago Press, 1968, pp. 90-113.

[*In the following excerpt, Goodheart examines the sources of the narrator's paradoxical vitality in* Notes from the Underground.]

Notes from the Underground (1864) inaugurates Dostoevsky's great creative period. There are anticipations of the underground man in earlier work, but he emerges full blown as a type for the first time in *Notes.* He haunts Dostoevsky's major novels in a way that makes it impossible to come to grips with them without first settling with him and with the tale that he inhabits as hero—or antihero. (He is present in the characters of Raskolnikov, Stavrogin, and Ivan Karamazov.)

Apart from the abrupt interruption at the end of the tale and a "footnote" at the beginning, Dostoevsky never appears in the traditional novelist's role of narrator and commentator. The story is completely occupied by the confessions of the underground man. This in itself is not extraordinary: many tales and novels of the eighteenth and nineteenth centuries are narrated by the hero or another character. In those cases, however, there is a coincidence between the moral vision of the novelist and the moral vision of the character—or if not coincidence, at least a sympathy which makes it possible without too much difficulty to identify the "point of view" of the tale or novel. The underground man, on the other hand, does not express the views of Dostoevsky.

Some of Dostoevsky's best critics have precipitously translated the underground man's powerful presence and intelligence into evidence of Dostoevsky's approval of him. Edward Wasiolek, in a recent study, admits the underground man's obnoxious qualities, but claims (with Berdayaev and Ivanov) that Dostoevsky "approves" of him because "in the very marrow of that cold and malignant spite [of the underground man] is a principle that is precious for him and for Dostoevsky: freedom."[1] Philip Rahv, in an earlier influential essay, states outright: "When it came to writing *The Brothers Karamazov,* Dostoevsky had wholly surmounted the standpoint of defiant and obdurate individualism exhibited in *Notes from the Underground.* . . . This type of individualism, with its stress on the unfettered human will and the inexhaustible intransigence of self-pride, is not really consonant with the religious valuation of life."[2] The identification between Dostoevsky and the underground man at the time that he wrote *Notes* certainly cannot be derived from external evidence. The

simple fact that Dostoevsky valued freedom is too tenuous as evidence for such an identification. Freedom itself is a battleground of conflicting views.

The underground man's most powerful weapon is his suffering. The suffering man proves his individuality and freedom by refuting through his very being the "scientific" (utilitarian) law that the enlightened man pursues pleasure and avoids pain.

—Eugene Goodheart

It is, however, evident at the outset that the immediate effect of *Notes* is to upset the kind of moral and intellectual equilibrium that the reader enjoys when his assumptions are not being attacked or undermined. Dostoevsky, it would seem, wants to preempt the moral authority of the reader for the underground man and use him as an "instrument" for judging the reader—without necessarily endorsing his views. The reader may loathe the underground man throughout the tale, but he will find it hard, if not impossible, to resist the underground man's final judgment of him.

> For my part, I have merely carried to extremes in my life what you have not dared to carry even half-way, and, in addition, you have mistaken your cowardice for common sense and have found comfort in that, deceiving yourselves. So that, as a matter of fact, I seem to be much more alive than you. Come, look into it more closely! Why, we do not even know where we are to find real life, or what it is, or what it is called. Leave us alone without any books, and we shall at once get confused, lose ourselves in a maze, we shall not know what to cling to, what to hold on to, what to love and what to hate, what to respect and what to despise. We even find it hard to be men, men of *real* flesh and blood, *our own* flesh and blood. We are ashamed of it. We think it a disgrace. And we do our best to be some theoretical "average" men. We are stillborn, and for a long time we have been begotten not by living fathers, and that's just what we seem to like more and more. We are getting a taste for it. Soon we shall invent some way of being somehow or other begotten by an idea. . . .[3]

The judgment is persuasive, mainly because it develops out of the experience and "wisdom" of the underground man.

There is, to be sure, the reader who is untouched by the tale, who sees in it little more than the peevish outburst of a sick and spiteful man. (This is a view—false, I think—that the underground man himself perversely provokes.) The tale may have failed of its effect. But the failure may be that of the reader, who for various reasons (personal or ideological) exhibits a moral and spiritual obstinacy which prevents him from responding to the strange vitality of the underground man. The question of why Dostoevsky should want us to respond—though he himself cannot be taken as an exponent of the character or polemical position of the underground man—remains to be answered. Whatever the reasons, the sense of disequilibrium is immediately experienced by the sensitive reader.

The "confessions" begin with our hero's admission that he is a "sick man . . . a spiteful man." He goes on to speak of his nastiness as a civil servant, and though he soon qualifies this by saying that he is exaggerating his spitefulness, the inconsistency only bewilders the reader and intensifies the unpleasantness that the underground man has deliberately (it would seem) created at the outset. But the reader is not allowed the rather comfortable feeling of revulsion to which he is constantly tempted, for the "confessions" modulate almost at once to paradoxical statements that arrest the reader's attention, statements to which the reader may not be able to give his immediate assent, but which have at least the resonance of profundity:

> And now I've been spending the last four years of my life in my funk-hole, consoling myself with the rather spiteful, though entirely useless, reflection that an intelligent man cannot possibly become anything in particular and that only a fool succeeds in becoming anything. Yes, a man of the nineteenth century must be, above all, a characterless person; a man of character, on the other hand, a man of action, is mostly a fellow with a very circumscribed imagination.[4]

The paradoxical character of such a statement inhibits any impulse to reject the statement peremptorily. We hesitate if only to understand, and the hesitation is fatal, for we find ourselves drawn into the logic and feeling of the underground man.

In this case, the paradox is in the identification of stupidity and character, on the one hand, and of intelligence and characterlessness, on the other. By intelligence, the underground man means acute consciousness, an activity that he characterizes as a "disease, a real honest-to-goodness disease."[5] He distinguishes acute consciousness from ordinary consciousness, "which is quite sufficient for the business of everyday life." He speaks of an acute consciousness of "the sublime and the beautiful" which virtually caused him to commit contemptible and degrading actions. "The more conscious I became of goodness and all that was 'sublime and beautiful,' the more deeply did I sink into the mire and the more ready I was to sink into it altogether."[6] Added to this is the strange feeling of delight *in the intense awareness* of his degradation. From this the underground man deduces the dubious proposition that "whatever happened, happened in accordance with the normal and fundamental laws of intensified consciousness and by a sort of inertia which is a direct consequence of those laws."[7] He implicitly identifies paralysis of the will and self-degrading actions, that is, actions which are not willed. Acute consciousness, paralysis of the will (hence characterlessness), self-degrading actions, feelings of de-

light: this is the puzzling dialectic of the underground man's psyche.

The dialectic is illuminated by the contrast the underground man makes between the man of acute consciousness and the man of action.

> You see, people who know how to avenge themselves and, generally, how to stand up for themselves—how do they, do you think, do it? They are, let us assume, so seized by the feeling of revenge that while that feeling lasts there is nothing but that feeling left in them. Such a man goes straight to his goal, like a mad bull, with lowered horns, and only a stone wall perhaps will stop him. (Incidentally, before such a stone wall such people, that is to say, plain men and men of action, as a rule capitulate at once. To them a stone wall is not a challenge as it is, for instance, to us thinking men, who, because we are thinking men, do nothing; it is not an excuse for turning aside, an excuse in which one of our sort does not believe himself, but of which he is always very glad. No, they capitulate in all sincerity. A stone wall exerts a sort of calming influence, and perhaps even a mystic one . . .).[8]

Though the underground man can do nothing, he refuses to reconcile himself to the stone wall paradoxically because "I have to deal with it and haven't the strength to knock it down." The inability to cope with the stone wall and the refusal to reconcile himself to it become the source of self-contempt and pride. In his imagination, where his courage mainly resides, he can conceive grandiose defiant gestures and refuse to submit to the inevitable. At moments the underground man wants us to regard this refusal as an act of will, but it is clear that the refusal grows out of his impotence, not his will. Indeed, he asserts at one point the fact that "the direct, the inevitable and the legitimate result of consciousness is to make all action impossible."[9]

The image of the stone wall is an analogue for scientific consciousness: "the laws of nature . . . the conclusions of natural science, mathematics." The stone wall that science rears is its denial of individuality and freedom. Laws of nature, determinism, abstractions (Petersburg, we should remember, is the most "abstract" and most "premeditated" of cities) deny the individual life by rationalizing it as an instance or an effect of these laws. The underground man's inertia *seems* like an effective refusal to participate in this abstracting process, but he himself knows that this inertia is part of the process of abstraction. Thus he regards himself as "the antithesis of the normal man . . . who of course has sprung not out of the lap of nature, but out of a test tube . . . then this test-tube begotten man sometimes capitulates to his antithesis to such an extent that for all his intense sensibility he frankly considers himself a mouse and not a man."[10]

The underground man's most powerful weapon is his suffering. The suffering man proves his individuality and freedom by refuting through his very being the "scientific" (utilitarian) law that the enlightened man pursues pleasure and avoids pain. The underground man tells us that he will suffer and with full consciousness if only to prove that he has freed himself from the tyranny of "a law of nature." "One's own free and unfettered choice, one's own whims, however wild, one's own fancy, overwrought though it sometimes may be to the point of madness—that is that same most desirable good which we overlooked and which does not fit into any classification, and against which all theories and systems are continually wrecked."[11] But is this really freedom? Though the underground man's fancy is often overwrought to the point of madness and his actions are whimsical and wild, we are never under any illusion that he is free—unless freedom is understood to be simply another word for perversity. In his relations with his friends and with the prostitute Lisa, the underground man behaves as if he has no will—as if his actions proceed from diabolical energies over which he has no control. The underground man himself is aware of his own *compulsive* nature: one might say that in "defying" the pleasure-pain calculus and taking delight in suffering, the underground man is being victimized by the laws of his own nature.

The underground man's suffering is a *necessity* of his nature. For this reason, Joseph Frank's view that the underground man's "masochism" is an indication not of pathology, but of his "paradoxical spiritual health," is dubious. Mr. Frank's reading simply masks the compulsive-pathological nature of the underground man's reaction under the opaque phrase: "moral-emotive response of his *human nature* to the blank nullity of the laws of nature."[12] The delight which the underground man experiences from his self-degrading acts is a compulsive response (or so *we* experience it in reading the story). Though we might want to claim for it a certain value, normative language like "spiritual health" will not do. Indeed, at the end of his confessions, the underground man stresses his typicality in a manner which makes the claim for "spiritual health" impossible. His distinction, we may recall, consists in his having dared to carry "to extremes in my life what you have not dared to carry even half-way." But he is like everyone else in his confusion, abstractness, and lack of flesh-and-blood reality. The underground man enacts the laws of nature, but he has discovered "laws" that are truer than those of the pleasure-pain calculus. The underground man has anticipated Freud.

If we admit to the compulsive-masochistic character of the underground man, then we should hesitate about viewing the story as a dramatic embodiment of the conflict between the competing principles of freedom and determinism—because the protagonist of "freedom" is himself unfree. Dostoevsky has perceived the enslaving nature of capricious or unlimited "freedom," but he has not as yet presented us with an image of true freedom. He makes us aware of the compulsive motives behind every action: all moral and religious attitudes undergo a psychological inspection. Thus whatever moral judgment we make must be informed by sensitivity to the psychic energy that creates the moral disposition of a character. (In general, to speak of freedom, good and evil—i.e., moral categories—in isolation from the psychic energy that informs moral behavior is to miss the essential in the Dostoevskian ethos.)

The condition from which the underground man suffers has been analyzed by Nietzsche in masterly fashion. Max Scheler considers the discovery of *resentment* to be one of Nietzsche's great achievements, perhaps his greatest, and he has devoted a book to the subject.[13] Scheler is right in crediting Nietzsche with the discovery in the sense that Nietzsche was the first to formulate the phenomenon in a conscious philosophical manner. But Dostoevsky had a profound novelist's grasp of resentment before Nietzsche. In his early novel *The Insulted and the Injured,* Dostoevsky gives us a very incisive portrait of the resentful man in the character of Natasha's father, Nikolay Sergeyvitch. The narrator of the novel describes him:

> I am convinced that everything was topsy-turvy and aching in his heart at that moment, as he looked at his poor wife's tears and alarm. I am sure that he was suffering far more than she was, but he could not control himself. So it is sometimes with the most good-natured people of weak nerves, who in spite of their kindliness are carried away till they find enjoyment in their own grief and anger, and try to express themselves at any cost, even that of wounding some other innocent creature, always by preference the one nearest and dearest. A woman sometimes has a craving to feel unhappy and aggrieved, though one has no misfortune or grievance. There are many men like women in this respect, and men, indeed, by no means feeble, and who have very little that is feminine about them. The old man had a compelling impulse to quarrel, though he was made miserable by it himself.[14]

This is a condition to which Dostoevsky was to return again and again. The man of resentment suffers from a physiological malaise—weak nerves. He is a man constitutionally incapable of expressing or controlling a strong emotion. When he does give vent to his feelings, he is often wild and chaotic, hurtful both to the object of the feeling and to himself. He tries to relieve himself of his misery, and in the process wounds an innocent creature and is made even more miserable. When he does not give vent to his feeling, his resentment is, in the memorable phrase of Scheler, "an evil secretion in a sealed vessel, like prolonged impotence."[15] This characterization fits the underground man, who differs from Natasha'a father in that he has turned his resentment into an ideological program and is therefore without the good intentions of Natasha's father, who merely suffers from weak nerves.

In Nietzsche's view, the man of resentment is the product of the habit of repression that was trained into Western man, principally by Christianity. The expression of strong feeling has been regarded in the Christian world as a form of pride, and so it has been taken as a mark of spiritual power to be able to repress strong feeling. This habit, which has had an inevitably deleterious effect on the physical constitution, has resulted, paradoxically, in the weakening of the power of repression and consequently in wild, uncontrolled emotional displays. To the man of resentment Nietzsche contrasts the aristocrat, the man of strong feeling who has cultivated the power of expressing it. He acts immediately on every impulse of revenge or anger or love without fear of the social consequences. In doing so, he is merely honoring the laws of life, which consists of "injuring, annihilating, oppressing."[16] We respond to this image of the aristocrat to the extent that we accept the concept of resentment: for if we harbor Christian and democratic sympathies for the victims of injury, annihilation, and oppression, we must nevertheless cope with the fact that the repression of the impulse to injure is often a losing battle. Not only does it poison the life of the man who has the impulse, but the rebellious impulse (refusing to brook repression any longer) may express itself with a destructiveness surpassing the violence of aristocratic anger. In this view, the man of resentment lives in an atmosphere of negation: he defines himself through envy, jealousy, and repressed anger. He exists solely in relation to his antithesis. The aristocrat, on the other hand, lives in an atmosphere of affirmation. He affirms himself: his negations simply enforce the distinction he makes between what is valuable (i.e., what he values) and what is not.

The underground man makes an equivalent distinction between the man of action and the man of thought, but since he is a resentful man, the contrast that emerges is not favorable to the man of action. What Nietzsche might have called the innocence of the aristocratic hero is, from the point of view of the underground man, a species of stupidity. The man of action is a kind of archaism, in the idiom of the tale, at once impossible and undesirable in the modern world. By permitting the underground man to expose the stupidity of the man of action (he has no more than animal intelligence about the stone wall) and to affirm by contrast his own moral penetration (in spite of the fact that he is also cowardly), Dostoevsky disequilibrates the reader, making the underground man fascinating and persuasive at the same time that the reader finds him repulsive. However deformed and corrupt he may be, the underground man seems near to some truth about human life, a nearness that both parodies and reveals the truth.

To be true to the moral intention of the story, we should preserve Dostoevsky's own conception of the underground man's activity—he *suffers*—without suppressing the idea of masochism altogether. If we simply convert the suffering into masochism, we conceal the affinities between the career of the underground man and the Christian drama. That those affinities were in Dostoevsky's mind is revealed by a letter he wrote in which he spoke of his intention in the *Notes* to present Christ as an alternative idea both to the doctrine of reason and self-interest and to the underground man's "freedom."[17] He never realized this intention, and indeed it is hard to see how he could have accomplished this within the orbit of the underground man's confessions. Nevertheless, the underground man does choose to dramatize his "freedom" through suffering, an activity in which he at least resembles the Christian penitent.

But with a difference! For the Christian, suffering is a mode of purification. By suffering, the Christian (ideally) exercises his freedom (with the grace of God) in order to win the greater freedom of communion with God. He suffers in order to purge himself of all the worldly things that *enslave* and *paralyze* the human will. For the under-

ground man, on the other hand, suffering is mainly a mode of negation. As the antithesis to the laws of nature, it is the source of chaos and disorder. For the underground man, suffering is an end in itself: nothing new in the moral or spiritual order emerges from it. It does not purify or re-create, and what the underground man needs and desires is to be re-created into authentic being. All his gestures in that direction are doomed to failure (his encounters with the officer who denies his very existence, his absurd and pathetic attempts at self-dramatization in the presence of his "friends," and the series of fiascos with Lisa), because they pretend to a selfhood that the underground man simply does not possess. In his need to to demonstrate his reality, to refuse the anonymity which seems to be his fate, he behaves aggressively to his friends, he exalts himself. Yet every moment of self-exaltation is followed by humiliation and self-abasement, because the self-exaltation cannot be sustained. Thus in a characteristic moment the underground man consoles himself with the sentiment that as a hero he is too "exalted a person to be entirely covered with dirt, and hence I could wallow in dirt with an easy conscience."[18] But he knows not only that the self-exaltation is untenable, but also that it proceeds perversely from an experience of his own degradation: he speaks of it as an attack of the "sublime and beautiful," a form of self-romanticizing, which comes upon him "when [he] was touching bottom."

It should be noted that the form of self-exaltation is antinomian: that to justify contemptible feelings and actions, the underground man imagines himself to be in a state of grace, which no action of his could possibly compromise. The claim is absurd, because the underground man's deepest conviction is that he is utterly without grace. The strongest emotion of his egocentricity is self-hatred; yet by that paradoxical logic which is peculiarly his own, he is able to contrive, if only sporadically, a kind of antinomianism without grace.

From the Christian point of view, the underground man is the archsinner, obsessed with his self-esteem, parodying the Christian idea of suffering, because his "martyrdom," after all, is in behalf of his self-esteem. As Joseph Frank points out in refuting the vulgar view of Dostoevsky as an exponent of "the religion of suffering," the underground man's suffering is a species of egoism. The underground man utterly lacks Lisa's capacity for sacrificing herself to alleviate the suffering of others. Thus after she has been insulted and humiliated by our hero, she shows an understanding of "what a woman who loves sincerely always understands first of all, namely that I was unhappy," and she "flung her arms around my neck."[19] In contrast, the underground man, who has the capacity to imagine the suffering of the others, sophistically justifies his cruelty to Lisa (for the humiliation of being the object of her compassion, a mark of her superiority to him) by viewing the insult as "a sort of purification. . . . I should have wearied her heart by thrusting myself upon her while now the memory of the insult will never die in her, and however horrible the filth that lies in store for her, the memory of that humiliation will raise her and purify her—by hatred, and, well, perhaps also by forgiveness."[20] This is the sophistry of the devil, for what evil cannot be justified in this manner? It is the angel, not the devil, who should speak of the good that comes out of evil.

But again we must equivocate, for the underground man's identification of freedom and negation has its basis in a genuine nihilistic vision of false law and order. The cardinal sin of scientific consciousness—according to the *Notes*—is that it is a false consciousness, that its laws do not truly explain human consciousness. The very fact of the underground man's suffering consciousness is proof of this. We respond unequivocally to this aspect of the underground man's claim. We are at a difficult juncture in Dostoevsky's "thought." Though our knowledge of Dostoevsky's Christian orthodoxy as well as our own moral sentiments would seem to suggest a repudiation of what the underground man stands for, such a reading of the *Notes* does not account for the reader's fascination with, even admiration for, the vitality of the underground man. As the underground man himself says at the end of the tale:

> For my part, I have merely carried to extremes in my life what you have not dared to carry even half-way, and, in addition, you have mistaken your cowardice for common sense and have found comfort in that, deceiving yourselves. So that, as a matter of fact, I seem to be much more alive than you.

The final lament is not that man has become immoral or evil, it is a lament over lost vitality: "We even find it hard to be men of *real* flesh and blood, *our own* flesh and blood." The underground man has value, one is tempted to say, *because* of the absence of the normal compromised qualities of men. He is a brilliant negation of these qualities (as he says, he has gone the whole way), and the fascination that he holds for us is in his capacity to create an intense life from this negation. "Suffering means doubt, negation . . . a man will never renounce real suffering, destruction and chaos."[21] He is, paradoxically, the most vital of men.

Notes

[1] Edward Wasiolek, *Dostoevsky: The Major Fiction*, p. 39.

[2] Philip Rahv, "The Legend of the Grand Inquisitor," *Partisan Review*, May-June, 1954, p. 268.

[3] Fyodor Dostoevsky, *The Best Short Stories of Dostoevsky*, p. 240.

[4] *Ibid.*, pp. 109-10.

[5] *Ibid.*, p. 111.

[6] *Ibid.*, p. 112.

[7] *Ibid.*, p. 113.

[8] *Ibid.*, pp. 114-15.

[9] *Ibid.*, p. 122.

[10] *Ibid.*, p. 115.

[11] *Ibid.*, p. 131.

[12] Joseph Frank, "Nihilism and *Notes from the Underground*," *Sewanee Review*, Winter, 1961, p. 10.

[13] Max Scheler, *Ressentiment*.

[14] Dostoevsky, *The Insulted and the Injured*, p. 64.

[15] Quoted in Albert Camus, *The Rebel*, p. 15.

[16] Friedrich Nietzsche, *The Genealogy of Morals*, p. 88.

[17] Alluded to in Frank, "Nihilism and *Notes*," p. 20.

[18] Dostoevsky, *Notes from the Underground*, p. 162.

[19] *Ibid.*, p. 231.

[20] *Ibid.*, p. 238.

[21] *Ibid.*, p. 152.

Edward F. Abood   (essay date 1973)

SOURCE: "Fyodor Dostoevsky: *Notes from Underground*," in *Underground Man*, Chandler & Sharp Publishers, 1973, pp. 13-29.

[*In the following essay, Abood analyzes* Notes from the Underground *as Dostoevsky's critique of nihilism and portrayal of the irrational psyche of the neurotic man.*]

Notes from Underground is a philosophic polemic in the form of a personal journal. Dostoevsky portrays the author of the "notes," the unforgettable Underground Man, in the actual process of writing his journal; Underground Man, in turn, is directing his notes to imaginary interlocutors, with whom he carries on a simulated philosophical debate. Although they do not actually say or do anything, he addresses them as "you" and "gentlemen"; and by means of the ideas and sentiments that he attributes to them, they soon take on a definite personality.

In Part I of his notes, Underground Man challenges his opponents by means of direct arguments, which together constitute a rambling essay. In Part II, he ridicules these people indirectly by recounting three incidents from his life, occuring approximately fifteen years before the actual writing of the notes. Only Part II contains the ingredients of the traditional novel (plot, character, setting and so forth), but it would be a mistake to read Part I solely as a philosophic tract. Although the full revelation of Underground Man's personality is deferred to Part II, we feel dramatic tension in almost every line of his monologue in Part I. Though still little more than a voice there, he succeeds nonetheless in creating the illusion of a trial, with his unseen adversaries acting as judge and himself as defendant. For his notes are not merely a journal, like *Steppenwolf* and *Nausea*; they are also a confession, functioning, like much of *Our Lady of the Flowers* and *The Fall,* as "corrective punishment" for the narrator. We are not told the actual cause of Underground Man's guilt until Part II; yet from his first nervous, querulous remarks in Part I, he reveals himself as a haunted man lashing out at the critics who stand in judgement of him.

These "gentlemen" are, in fact, the Nihilists of the Sixties, whom Dostoevsky unceasingly attacked in his later works. Nihilism, a radical development of the rationalism and liberalism of the Enlightenment, was rapidly spreading throughout the Russia of Dostoevsky's day. Rejecting faith for reason and tradition for reform, Nihilism inspired young Russian intellectuals (including Dostoevsky before his imprisonment) who were self-consciously measuring the backwardness of their native Russia against the "progress" in Western Europe. One of the most outstanding spokesmen for this doctrine was N. G. Chernyshevsky, whose *What Is To Be Done?* enjoyed widespread popularity both in czarist and Soviet Russia. But it is possibly even more significant because it was the occasion for the writing of **Notes from Underground.** The immediate target of Dostoevsky's satire is *What Is To Be Done?,* and the imaginary interlocutors whom Underground Man addresses may be taken as a collective embodiment of Chernyshevsky.

Chernyshevsky, who was a visionary Romantic, portrays in *What Is To Be Done?* a modern utopia. The author envisions a radical technology, which would convert the Russian steppes into arable land, produce "palaces" out of glass, and unravel the mysteries of electricity (the time is 1864). Chernyshevsky's social objectives, which would later be expounded by Lenin, include full employment and material abundance, cultivation of the arts, equality of the sexes, and the brotherhood of man. In short, it would be the perfect society, consisting of cheerful, rational men and women who see in their own well-being a pattern of the universal good.

Chernyshevsky constructs his theory out of two basic concepts: the "laws of nature" (as codified by science) and the particular nature of man, which ideally reflects these laws. According to the first assumption, the universe is analogous to a machine, the parts of which are connected in a single chain of cause and effect and function in accordance with a necessary principle, or "law," with predictable regularity. Science has offered man the means of discovering these laws and putting them to practical use, which would require a complete revamping of culture and society. The variable in this equation is man: Will he meet the challenge posed by science, and thus ameliorate his condition? Or will he backslide into the superstition and decadence of the prescientific era?

To answer these questions, Chernyshevsky makes another assumption, borrowed, in vulgarized form, from the English Utilitarians. Man is essentially an animal who, like all natural creatures, is motivated solely by pleasure and pain. What is desirable, and therefore "good," gives pleasure; what is repugnant, and therefore "evil," causes pain.

It is in man's nature to seek pleasure, not pain; he suffers only out of ignorance. Once he is able to distinguish what is good from what is harmful, he will automatically choose the good. That he is capable of recognizing his true self-interest is also axiomatic, because man is by nature rational. Man, then, is assured of happiness as long as he uses his reason. "Weigh everything," we are urged. "Choose whatever is useful for you."

What is true of the individual also applies to society as a whole. Society is simply an aggregate of individuals; thus if each man pursues his real self-interest, there results the "greatest good for the greatest number," that is, a happy society. The Utilitarians reject the notion that one man's good requires another man's suffering. It is only the pursuit of our mistaken, as distinguished from our enlightened, self-interest that causes us to inflict pain on others. In the long run, opposition to the common good, like the violation of nature, can only bring us greater suffering than the immediate pleasure it gives us. The proof of this dictum, argues the Utilitarian, lies in the fact that while the pleasure-bent average man covets his neighbor's possessions, his healthy respect for the law keeps him from appropriating them.

Underground Man begins his refutation of Chernyshevsky by comparing the *natural* man (in harmony with the laws of nature) with a bull, whose bellow is always followed by direct action. Such a man need never seek justification, or a "primary" cause, for his action, since he does not see beyond its immediate, or "secondary," cause.[1] For the same reason, he can just as easily abstain from action, just as a charging bull is stopped short by a stone wall. And what is the stone wall? "Why, of course, the laws of nature, the conclusions of natural science, of mathematics." According to the laws of mechanics, one gets a bump on the head if he butts a stone wall, and so the natural man withdraws in proper respect for the absolute, the unchallengeable wall. It is all as simple as two times two equals four.

The complicated Underground Man, on the other hand, cannot act or abstain from action according to so neat a formula. For he is driven by a different set of laws, the "laws of hyperconsciousness." He demands a basic reason for action, a primary as well as a secondary cause. He cannot satisfy himself, for example, that revenge is sufficient cause for slapping someone in the face. He would demand to know why the offender insulted him and what purpose would be served by his retaliation. And immediately he is caught up in an infinite regress of cause and effect: if A, then B; if B, then C, ad infinitum, until all impetus for action has been corroded away by thought and he sinks into his usual state of "acute inertia":

> Again, in consequence of those accursed laws of consciousness, my spite is subject to chemical disintegration. You look into it, the object flies off into air, your reasons evaporate, the criminal is not to be found, the insult becomes fate rather than an insult. . . .

Conversely, in those rare moments when he is spurred into action but is suddenly confronted by the wall, he is not so willing to come to a stop as natural man is. On the contrary, he bangs his head against it, out of pure spite. Again, he tortures himself with questions. Why should he be limited by the laws of nature? If they were intended as natural limits to his freedom, then why was he so built that he desires to rebel against them?—"Of course I cannot break through a wall by battering my head against it, but I am not going to resign myself to it simply because it is a stone wall and I am not strong."

This reply to Chernyshevsky is one of the earliest attacks against the whole tradition of rationalism and will be echoed by subsequent underground men in the twentieth century. Underground Man's principal contention is that Chernyshevsky and the Utilitarians commit their greatest error by basing their systems on man's reason. The mainsprings of action, Underground Man insists, are not rooted in reason, but in desire and will, in blind impulse, in those chaotic forces which lie beyond the fringe of consciousness. The intellectuals—including Underground Man, who reasons himself out of acting—are no less vulnerable to the force of passion than the unthinking peasant who drinks away his paycheck on Saturday night and sobers up in jail on Sunday. Reason may point out the folly of a man's actions. It may offer salutary suggestions for future behavior. It may even approve his present mode of living. But as a causal agent of action, argues the skeptical Underground Man, it is insignificant.

The corollary of this conclusion is also obvious, and Underground Man drives it home with malicious relish: If the individual knowingly acts against his own interest, will he not be even more likely to thwart the common good?

> Oh, tell me, who first declared, who first proclaimed, that man only does nasty things because he does not know his own real interests; and that if he were enlightened, if his eyes were opened to his real normal interests, man would at once cease to do nasty things, would at once become good and noble because, being enlightened and understanding his real advantage, he would see his own advantage in the good and nothing else. . . . Oh, the babe! Oh, the pure, innocent child!

In anticipation of Hesse and Camus, Underground Man maintains that history is the record of cruelty and inhumanity, notwithstanding the facile assurances of the Evolutionists, who proclaim that while mankind was morally barbarous in its infancy, it has become progressively more civilized. Underground Man, on the contrary, sees in the millenia only a refinement of man's methods of annihilation, while the essential Adam has remained unchanged.

We are thus incapable of sustained rational behavior, whether for our own good or anybody else's. But even if we could consistently abide by the dictates of reason, Underground Man declares that we "positively ought" to act irrationally, that is, according to impulse, desire and will:

> You see, gentlemen, reason, gentlemen, is an excellent thing, there is no disputing that, but reason is only

reason and can only satisfy man's rational faculty, while will is a manifestation of all life, that is, of all human life including reason as well as all impulses. . . .

To live by the rule and measure of the Utilitarians, without tension or conflict, is to renounce our humanity and assume the inert condition of objects. We would have to relinquish "what is most precious and most important— that is, our personality, our individuality"—and become "piano keys" or "organ stops," mechanically responding to the great forces of nature and society. In exchange for a rational existence, we would have to deny our freedom and passion, dull our sense of our own identity, and resign ourselves to the loss of what the modern-day Existentialists have called *authentic* being. Doubtless, the evangelistic fervor of Underground Man's irrationalism is personally motivated—the Utilitarians, after all, are his natural enemy. Nonetheless, it is a timely, if impotent, resistance to powerful currents which began in the eighteenth century, swelled to the breaking point in Dostoevsky's day, and have virtually transformed society since. With the extinction of the individual, Underground Man foresees the grim spectacle of computerized man, which Camus and Koestler will confront three-quarters of a century later.

In their tabulation of what is good for man, the Utilitarians rely on statistics and formulae derived from economics, biology, physics and sociology. They are concerned with collective man, man as a model or an abstraction, and see the individual man as no more than a microcosm of the generalized man. Therefore, they discount "random" deviations from the norm. Possibly, Underground Man does not go as far as Sartre, who maintains that freedom is man's essence. Yet Underground Man, always oriented to the personal, considers individual caprice to be man's "most advantageous advantage," and he insists on "one's own unfettered choice, one's own fancy, however wild it may be, one's fancy worked up at times to frenzy." Chernyshevsky, of course, says a man is free either to reject or conform to the laws of nature. But Underground Man cuts right through this simplistic synthesis of determinism and freedom: if man, constructed in the image of nature, *necessarily* obeys her laws once he recognizes them, then he is not free:

> Bah, gentlemen, what sort of free will is left when we come to tables and arithmetic, when it will all be a case of two times two makes four? Two times two makes four even without my will. As if free will meant that!

Underground Man insists on the freedom to say no, to "put out one's tongue" at the whole new order which Chernyshevsky and the Nihilists attempted to impose on society—the bulging shopping bags, the shining new cottages, the medical and pension funds, the organized leisure, the marvels of the assembly line—all epitomized for Underground Man in the Crystal Palace (an all-glass-and-aluminum structure on exhibit in London in 1851). While Chernyshevsky hails it as the crowning expression of man's genius and inventiveness, Underground Man sees it as nothing more than a building, which merely protects man from the elements, as the anthill does the ant. Progress, then, is an illusion. Science can go on transforming the world indefinitely, yet there will always remain the gaping hole beneath the skin, which even our prehistoric ancestors had to deal with. For unlike the ant, man is a spiritual creature who yearns for something—something beyond the Crystal Palace—which will satisfy the deepest longings of his soul.

But while Underground Man can actually see and touch the things that he despises, he can tell us nothing about his spiritual cravings. In the original text of *Notes from Underground,* he acknowledges the "necessity of faith and Christ." But when for some inexplicable reason the censors deleted this passage, Dostoevsky made no attempt to restore it, perhaps because on second reading of his manuscript he saw that his anti-hero cannot really argue for faith in Christ and at the same time remain an underground man. Indeed, this is the very crux of his problem: he cannot believe in anything. It now becomes clear why Underground Man's reasoning from effect to cause always leads him into the infinite regress—he can never arrive at a limit to the vicious logical process, that is, at the first cause, because God is the first cause and he cannot really believe in God (despite the token allusions he makes to Him). In the rationalistic, utilitarian, nihilistic world portrayed in *Notes from Underground,* he finds little inducement to faith, either in Christ or in anything else; and even when such an inspiration does appear, in the person of Liza the prostitute, it comes too late to have any effect on him. Thus, for all practical purposes, God is dead, although Dostoevsky will resurrect Him in subsequent novels. God is dead not only for Underground Man, who thinks too much, but also for his philistine opponents, who attempt to substitute reason and the laws of nature for Him.

Underground Man is left, then, with two choices: either join Chernyshevsky's contented Utilitarians in the Crystal Palace, or go underground. But if he has chosen underground, it is only as the lesser of two evils:

> Though I have said that I envy the normal man to the point of exasperation, yet I would not care to be in his place as he is now (though I will not stop envying him. No, no; anyway the underground life is more advantageous!) There, at any rate, one can—Bah! But after all, even now I am lying! I am lying because I know myself as surely as two times two makes four, that it is not at all underground that is better, but something different, quite different, for which I long but which I cannot find! Damn underground!

Thus Underground Man concludes at least his formal rebuttal of Chernyshevsky. As the above lines indicate, he does hint at the limitations of the life he has chosen, but they are left to the reader's imagination. What really comes through in Part I is the strength of his position, because the only other practical alternative is Chernyshevsky's deceptive utopia. Underground Man himself emerges as a spirited rebel refusing to follow the herd, instead of the lost and desperate man that he really is. Therefore, to comprehend the whole man we must look behind the philosopher's mask and consider such personal details as his physical appearance, his living quarters, his intimate feelings and experiences, and above all, his interaction with other people. While we do get flashes of the real man in Part I, it is only in Part II that he bodies forth as a distinct and complete literary character. Part II also gives us our first glimpse into the specific miseries of an underground existence.

Dostoevsky's hero is appropriate, almost to the point of caricature, to his mode of living. He is a forty-year-old man living in a squalid apartment (his mousehole) in one of the ghettos of St. Petersburg. Short and homely, generally wearing shabby clothes, he is about as prepossessing as a fly, or a mouse, with which he likes to compare himself. He is hypersensitive and neurasthenic and is given to chronic "sickly irritability." He suffers from innumerable ailments, usually psychogenic in origin: migraine headaches, insomnia and a disturbance which he has diagnosed as a liver disease, although he has never seen a doctor. More characteristic of subsequent underground men is his extreme withdrawal and isolation. By the time he writes his journal, he has inherited a small sum of money which allows him to quit a very dull job as a civil servant and assume a life of idleness. He is unmarried and has no immediate family, having been brought up by relatives of whom he makes the briefest mention. He is completely friendless. He belongs to no organizations or institutions, nor does he feel the slightest identification with the Church, the Czar, or the Russian soil. He is, in short, a self-declared exile from human society, with which he maintains only so much contact as is necessary for bare survival.

But if he has rejected the world outside, his apartment is hardly a retreat in which to hoard a few icons in safe seclusion from the vulgar world. It is more like a jail, turning him in upon himself. There he spends long hours daydreaming, imagining himself in "sublime and beautiful" roles that are impossible in "real" life; or he reads Romantic literature and philosophy which, with their emphasis on man's perfectability, he knows to be simply another form of dreaming. Even the "real" situations that take place outside of his room are only a game, though he is always deadly serious in his playacting. For as we have seen, Underground Man ultimately believes in nothing; and the more frenzied his participation in anything, the more hollow his satisfaction. Much of his physical activity—frequenting brothels and other "vile" places—serves no other purpose than to enable him to feel external sensations that might "stifle all that was continually seething" inside of him.

The three main episodes of Part II demonstrate what happens to him when he tries to escape his almost savage solitude and venture out of his room. The first episode begins, appropriately, with a crowd of people, including Underground Man, observing a tavern brawl. Lost in thought and oblivious of the fact that he is blocking the way, he suddenly feels himself lifted up by the shoulders and deposited to one side. The gentleman whose way he had blocked—a tall, muscular, sharply attired army officer—

walks on, unaware of Underground Man as anything but an object that had gotten in his way. A moment later, after he manages to shake off his confusion, Underground Man also leaves the scene, and the incident seems to be closed.

But for Underground Man, it has only begun. That night, and all the nights and days for the next two years, he broods about it. He learns all he can about the officer; writes a letter challenging him to a duel (but never sends it); writes a satirical sketch of him (but cannot get it published); stalks him through the streets (but never speaks to him). The closest he comes to any actual contact with the officer is on the narrow sidewalks of the fashionable Nevsky Boulevard; yet even here he steps aside for him, just as the officer on his part makes way for generals and other personages of high rank. Finally, after two years of obsession with the officer, he decides upon his "revenge": the next time he encounters the officer on the sidewalk, he will not give way to him, even if he has to bump into him. To carry out his plan, he borrows money and purchases a wardrobe, which he feels will give him courage; he carefully works out the details of his scheme, repeatedly visiting the spot where he will carry it off. But when the crucial moment comes, predictably he makes way for the officer again. After several such unsuccessful attempts, he decides to give up his plan. But immediately afterwards, he encounters the officer again, and instantly—without a moment's thought—he closes his eyes and runs head-on into him. And this time, the officer affair is definitely closed.

What this incident most dramatically exemplifies is the cleavage in Underground Man between action and thought. The natural man, in his place, would have responded instantly to the insult. Underground Man's reaction, on the other hand, is delayed. He takes the insult home to brood on, and we can imagine from his many sleepless nights the agony he goes through: the tortured self-recriminations and rationalizations, the compulsive recollections of the incident, the endless analysis of motives, the speculations as to what might have been done. Clearly he feels insulted; but from prolonged inertia he has lost the habit, if indeed he ever had it, of responding in the right manner and at the right moment. He repeatedly demonstrates that while he is capable of both reason and action, for him the two are not necessarily connected. His ultimate revenge does not easily and naturally follow from his rational preparations; it happens in spite of them, that is, by pure accident, since he actually gives up his plan moments before he executes it.

He acts; but his actions, like those of the Existentialist and Absurdist, do not derive their justification from their apparent purpose. What precipitates him into motion is not his commitment to a code of honor, for deep down inside of him honor, like all absolutes, has no meaning. Rather, it is his elemental, almost organic, need for action *for its own sake.* To be human is to be active, and the officer's provocation serves as a kind of catalyst to momentarily rouse the sedentary Underground Man from his dreams and his books. Revenge becomes an end in itself, long after the original insult has been forgotten. In effect, it is

a game, a surrogate reality of Underground Man's own creation, a ritual in which he can go through the motions of "real" living while remaining underground. But as for what happens afterwards, he tells us, ". . . if you read my first chapter, 'Underground,' you can guess for yourself." What we can guess is that he really derives little satisfaction from his sham triumph over the officer. For the hyperconscious Underground Man . . . knows all the while that he is only playing the buffoon in a theatrical farce. Though he continues to "thumb his nose" at Chernyshevsky's Crystal Palace, his actions remain those of a frustrated man.

The second major episode of Part II concerns itself with another of his sorties into the world of men. His solitude having become unendurable, he resolves to make one of his rare social calls. But since he has no current friends, he must fall back on the company of a group of his former school chums, between himself and whom there exists only a mutual dislike. In spite of this fact, he invites himself to a going-away party they are planning for another schoolfellow, one Zverkov, whom Underground Man also hates. On the following evening, they all meet in a hotel room. There is an initial exchange of insults between Underground Man and the others; then they simply ignore him for the rest of the evening. For three hours they sit at one end of the room while he paces the floor at the other, literally getting drunker by the minute. Finally, after a parting exchange of insults between him and them, they go off, presumably to a brothel. In a drunken rage, he starts off after them, determined to slap Zverkov in the face. But when he arrives at the brothel, he discovers they have gone elsewhere, and he is left to console himself with one of the inmates of the house.

We naturally wonder why Underground Man thrusts himself upon a group of people with whom he knows he cannot get along, and why he insists on remaining with them despite the suffering they subject him to. Clearly, he is held to them in spite of himself, just as he felt compelled to address himself to their counterparts, the interlocutors, in Part I. He is agonizingly aware of how absurd it is for him to associate himself with Zverkov and his friends, yet that knowledge itself only impels him more inevitably toward them:

> But what made me furious was that I knew for certain that I would go, that I would purposely go; and the more tactless, the more ill-mannered my going would be, the more certainly I would go.

As usual, his motivations here are so complicated as almost to defy analysis. Certainly, loneliness and boredom are factors: reunion with his schoolmates, if only to give them battle, is at least a change. Contact with other human beings is a necessary mode of realizing himself; like looking into a mirror or rereading something he has written, it is a kind of feedback that confronts him with himself. Finally, it enables him to burst out of the cocoon that he has woven around himself; he experiences with his companions a galvanization, the more so as they incite him to combat. The questions they put to him, the repartee they draw him into, the occasion itself—all demand that he assume some definite identity, some specific form, which his many years underground have blurred beyond recognition. He, of course, leaps to the challenge, for it offers him another role to play. And, as usual, the identity he assumes is perversely adapted to his audience.

Zverkov and the others are exemplifications of Chernyshevsky's Utilitarianism as viewed through the prism of Dostoevsky's satire. Ambitious, calculating and crude, they are all motivated by the one passion, success in the world. Even as children they had begun laying plans for securing a comfortable berth in the civil service or the army. Already they were attaching themselves to what would be useful to them and ruthlessly rejecting anything and anybody that did not further their advantage. Thus Underground Man, even had he himself been less obnoxious, would always have been an object of their disdain; for it was quite plain to everybody that, despite his excellence at his studies, he would never distinguish himself in the "real" world—the service, the professions or high society. Zverkov, on the other hand, was always the shining idol of the group because of the money behind him. All but Underground Man vied with one another for his notice, not because of any tangible favors he might confer on them, but because attachment to him was an honor in itself. Since his schooldays, time has only added to Zverkov's luster. He has come into his estate and is richer and more arrogant than ever; he has advanced in the army, partially through his own efforts, but mostly through his family's influence; and, according to his boasts, he is a perfect wonder with the women, though he will soon be ready to make the proper match and settle down to his country estate. He has not reached the age of thirty; yet he is already callous, jaded and cynical toward everything except his easy success in the world.

What must be emphasized, however, is that Zverkov and his immediate admirers are not isolated cases. Dostoevsky believed that their utilitarian outlook was rapidly becoming characteristic of that whole frantic society which found inspiration in a book like *What Is To Be Done?* But if they are representative, then his satirical portrait of them can only strengthen our sympathy for Underground Man. What choice does he, or any young middleclass Russian of the day, have? Unless he becomes a monk or chooses to become a peasant (like the visionary Tolstoy), he ordinarily goes into business, the civil service, the army, or the professions—all of which encourage ambition, competitiveness and self-interest. Underground Man, however, is not religious; and, like subsequent underground men, he belongs not to the soil but to the cold and friendless city, which is characterized in the novel by the "wet, yellow, dingy snow." Therefore, as dismal as it is, he chooses underground.

Yet we should not conclude from this that his ultimate choice is determined by moral scruples. To be sure, he expresses a loathing for Zverkov's values with the drunken toast: ". . . I hate phrases, phrasemongers and corseted waists . . . I love truth, sincerity and honesty . . . thought . . . true comradeship. . . ." But, ironically, Underground

Man too is a phrasemonger, and his phrases are certainly not to be taken as an accurate description of himself. As we have seen in the incident with the officer, he may take up a principle momentarily and even act in accordance with it. But he has no enduring belief in it. He has only taken it up because it is consistent with the role he is playing at the moment; and when in the next moment he drops the role, he also discards the principle. Since the only way he can interact with people is to antagonize them, the role he assumes here is that of the man of sentiment, the Romantic exponent of the sublime and the beautiful, because that figure is the antithesis of utilitarian Zverkov.

But if Underground Man is not genuinely committed to any expressed absolute, he does have real desires, however fluctuating they may be. Certainly another of his motives for clinging to his schoolfellows is his fundamental insistence that they take notice of him; and the more vile and outrageous his behavior, the more urgent his demand for attention. One of his innumerable, contradictory desires is that he and Zverkov establish a friendship, though he knows that he could not abide such a friendship even if it were possible. He harbors an elementary fear that he will be forgotten in his mousehole; and though he has chosen his own exile, he finds society's indifference to him intolerable. He plays on the conscience of Zverkov and his friends and, by implication, society—like the man who suffers from a toothache and who, through his incessant moans, deliberately inflicts that suffering on everyone else around him. Like the heroes of *Nausea, The Fall* and *Our Lady of the Flowers,* he will not be ignored. The merrymakers try to ignore him at the party and thus drive him away. He vows instead to

> . . . sit on to the end . . . you would be pleased, my friends, if I left. Nothing will induce me to go. I'll go on sitting here, and drinking to the end, on purpose, as a sign that I don't attach the slightest importance to you. I will go on sitting and drinking, because this is a public-house and I paid my entrance money. I'll sit here and drink. . . .

On the morning after, however, Underground Man's vow goes the way of all his resolutions. He writes a short note of apology to his erstwhile companions, taking full blame for the disastrous evening while generously exonerating his tormentors. Then he simply forgets about them. The apology, of course, hardly expresses his true feelings. Again, he is affecting the sublime and beautiful pose, for it would certainly be more natural for him to brood a few years over this affront as he did in the preceding episode. But a new threat has intervened, plunging him into such a profound anxiety that Zverkov and his companions lose all significance beside it. His new concern is the prostitute Liza, and so begins the third episode of Part II.

Arriving at the brothel and not finding Zverkov, he consoles himself by taking Liza to bed. Afterwards, still smarting from the humilization that Zverkov caused him, he resolves to avenge himself on her by making her feel guilty for being a prostitute. He describes to her the grim end she must come to while painting a pretty picture of family life, which she must forgo as a whore. Beginning to believe his own fabrications, he waxes so eloquent in his descriptions of marital bliss that he finally succeeds in making Liza feel remorse for her present life and disgust for herself. He assures her, however, that she can count on him for help should she choose to renounce that life, and before he leaves he gives her his address.

A few days later she does leave the brothel and, full of gratitude and love, goes straight to Underground Man, whom she considers her savior. He becomes hysterical: he proceeds to insult her, sadistically pointing out to her that he did not mean a word of what he said and that he had only wanted to make her suffer because of the suffering Zverkov had caused him. But when he breaks down and tearfully begins to confess his self-loathing and almost genuine sorrow—again, playacting becomes reality—he manages only to generate greater love and sympathy in her. She embraces him; but this arouses in him a new feeling of "mastery and possession," and so he takes her to bed again. We do not know the particulars of their lovemaking, except that he now "insulted her once and for all." Yet he attempts one more insult: he hands her a five-ruble note as she is leaving. When he discovers, moments later, that she has tossed it to the floor, he runs out after her, prepared to fall at her feet. But she is nowhere in sight, and Part II closes with Underground Man staring into the dark night, contemplating the wet and dingy snow.

This incident is both the ostensible and the most significant link between Parts I and II. Liza is the cause of that guilt which was hinted at in the first part. Her memory haunts him, even now, fifteen years later; it was to shake it off that he decided to write his notes, that is, his confession. If the incident does not actually seal Underground Man's doom, it at least defines it, once and for all, leaving no doubt either in his mind or the reader's as to how he will spend the rest of his days. In this episode, his confusion between make-believe and reality, his compulsion to seek out people and then strike out at them when they get too close, his arbitrary assumption of a position one moment and his equally arbitrary rejection of it the next, the constant tension between reason and impulse, his desperate self-assertion followed by his total self-debasement—all the skeins of his tangled personality—are brought together into a single, horrifying image.

Like the other episodes, this one throws into stark relief Underground Man's inability to establish meaningful human relations. But there is a difference. We can hardly blame him for despising Zverkov and the first officer, and his experience with them does not exclude the possibility that some rare soul may yet come along and break through his isolation. But when he rejects the gentle and profoundly sympathetic Liza, we know all hope is gone, especially as his savagery and cruelty increase with the intensity of her love: ". . . I was a despicable man, and what is more, incapable of loving her." Like the prostitute Sonia's love for Raskolnikov in *Crime and Punishment,* Liza's could conceivably redeem the lost soul of Underground Man. But whereas that great sinner, Raskolnikov, eventually asks for Sonia's cross, Underground Man is beyond redemption.

Fully aware that Liza is his last hope, he nonetheless cannot, or will not, accept her offer of love, thus grimly refuting once more the Utilitarian assumption that when we once see our true self-interest, we can, and will, pursue it.

His characters often appear grotesque through the lens of the realist; yet they are actually composites of attitudes and traits which are common, not only to underground men, but to all of us.

—Edward F. Abood

Dostoevsky offers various psychological reasons for his protagonist's incapacity to love or be loved: he never knew true love as a child; ordinarily frustrated in his attempts at self-assertion by sturdy fellows like Zverkov and the officer, he invariably attempts to dominate and tyrannize over the occasional friend that comes his way; enclosed within his self-contained universe, he is incapable of making the accommodation that love for another person demands. But Dostoevsky, despite his prodigious understanding of psychological motives, is always interested in the metaphysical basis for his characters' actions. Love is predicated on faith: the willingness to give total assent to what is only partially comprehended. But this is precisely what Underground Man is incapable of doing.

A child of his times, he insists on a rational justification for action, even though he devotes pages of argument in Part I to deny that such justification is possible and, in Part II, goes on to demonstrate the truth of his argument. To be sure, he has the impulse to love Liza. When, in the brothel, he sings the praises of love and marriage to her in order to torment her, he actually ends up by believing what he is saying—what begins as parody ends as a literal expression of a heartfelt need. Likewise, when he runs into the snow after the departed Liza, his one passion is to overtake her and beg her forgiveness. But like all of his impulses, the impulse to love Liza is short-lived, quickly checked by reason or supplanted by another impulse. Instead of pursuing her, he rationalizes himself into a state of immobility:

> To fall down before her, to sob with remorse, to kiss her feet, to beg her forgiveness! I longed for that. My whole heart was being rent to pieces, and never, never will I recall that moment with indifference. But—what for? I thought. Would I not begin to hate her, perhaps, even tomorrow, just because I had kissed her feet today? Would I give her happiness? Had I not again recognized that day, for the hundredth time, what I was worth? Would I not torment her?

It matters not whether he reasons first that life with Liza is impossible, and then rejects her, or whether deep down inside of him he denies her first and then finds the rational justification for that denial. Reason, in any event, is a melancholy ally. As with later underground men, it is easier for him to deny than to affirm, even when he has nothing to lose and everything to gain. He cannot simply let himself go with Liza; he cannot freely love. And primarily for that reason he, like other loveless protagonists, remains captive to underground.

Underground Man may be the neurotic par excellence, as so many of Dostoevsky's characters are. But it would be a mistake to see in Dostoevsky's writings nothing more than a pre-Freudian survey of abnormal psychology. His characters often appear grotesque through the lens of the realist; yet they are actually composites of attitudes and traits which are common, not only to underground men, but to all of us. As Dostoevsky's footnote to the novel shows, Underground Man is not an isolated case, but one of the inevitable "representatives of the current generation," and by extension, our own. At the conclusion of the novel, Underground Man anticipates his interlocutors' attempt to shrug off his notes as a personal record without general significance. But Underground Man—and here he is clearly speaking for Dostoevsky—does not let them off that easily:

> As for what concerns me in particular I have only, after all, in my life carried to an extreme what you have not dared to carry halfway, and what's more, you have taken your cowardice for good sense, and have found comfort in deceiving yourselves. So that perhaps, after all, there is more "life" in me than in you. Look into it more carefully! After all, we don't even know where living exists now, what it is, and what it is called! Leave us alone without books and we will be lost and in a confusion at once—we will not know what to join, what to cling to, what to love and what to despise. We are even oppressed by being men—men with real individual body and blood. We are ashamed of it, we think it a disgrace and try to contrive to be some sort of impossible generalized man.

Thus, by a curious twist, Underground Man and his imaginary opponents of Part I end up in the same camp. Like them, he is first and foremost an intellectual, who attempts to confine experience within a theoretical framework devoid of passion and impulse. He expresses loathing for cold, calculating reason while his interlocutors hold it up as man's chief asset; yet the roles he plays, particularly with Liza, are often just as artificial and inhuman as Chernyshevsky's robot. Though he is irrational in his behavior, in his thinking at least he pushes reason even beyond the safe and practical limits which the Utilitarians set to it. It is perhaps this stubborn lucidity and the anguish that accompanies it which most sharply set him off from the others. By contrast to the fatuous interlocutors, he sees his terrible position for what it is and has pronounced irrevocable judgement upon himself.

Notes

[1] Fyodor Dostoevsky, *Notes from Underground,* tr. Ralph E. Matlaw, New York, 1960. Subsequent quotations from *Notes from Underground* are from this edition.

A. Boyce Gibson　(essay date 1973)

SOURCE: "The Cellar and the Garret," in *The Religion of Dostoevsky,* SCM Press Ltd., 1973, pp. 78-103.

[*In the following excerpt, Gibson observes the Christian component of* Notes from the Underground.]

There are few documents in literature which look less Christian than **Notes from Underground.** The sick self-consciousness of the writer, his exasperated cynicism, his withdrawal from the world of action (for which he has nothing but contempt), even his exquisitely nasty brand of humour, put him in the category of repudiators and unbelievers. Yet as an introduction to the developed world-view of one who confessed and called himself Christian, they are indispensable. They are precisely the muck in which his Christian flowering has its roots.

Notes from Underground (literally 'from beneath the floor': the analogy of the futile scurrying mouse is repeatedly called upon) is the confession (or the boastings, or both) of a retired civil servant of forty, living alone on a small private income, hating the world and all that is in it, and alienated from its obviousness by what he calls a typically nineteenth-century intellect and sensitivity. He does not consider himself peculiar; on the contrary he is the real man of his time: the others just strut around on the surface. Listen to his peroration: 'I have only in my life carried to an extreme what you have not dared to carry half-way, and what is more, you have taken your cowardice for good sense, and have found comfort in deceiving yourselves. So that perhaps, after all, there is more life in me than in you . . . we are oppressed at being men—men with a real individual body and blood—we are ashamed of it, we think it a disgrace and try to contrive to be some sort of impossible generalized man . . . Soon we shall contrive to be born somehow from an idea.'[1] *We,* that is, all of us, as long as we face our age and generation. We *have* to be like that, unless we are to be cogs in a machine: the great machine of nature and reason. And this makes the utterances of Underground Man something half-way between self-congratulation and a general confession of original sin: the sin which makes him futile and the protest which makes him human are indistinguishable. To this we shall return.

In the meantime, what is he protesting about? First, the belief in the goodness of the natural man, *l'homme de la nature et de la vérité,* a phrase repeated in the text to the point of satire. What is wrong with this paragon is his 'innate stupidity': it is convenient, for it enables him, for example, to represent revenge as justice; whereas the 'mouse' with his 'acute consciousness' knows better.[2] He triumphs merely because he lacks sensibility; not because of any excellence, innate or acquired. The innately superior person (the mouse) is not good, but the bull is no better, only less aware. Second, the belief in action as a way of life; action inevitably contracts consciousness, the expansion of which is the great nineteenth-century achievement.[3] When it meets a stone wall it accepts it: the man of consciousness, not troubled by having to act, does not accept it, even if he knows it is there; and he keeps his emotional range at the proper level of universality. Third and consequentially, the belief in the finality of science, especially mathematics.[4] Why should two plus two make four, if I do not like it? Why should we be reconciled to impossibilities?[5] They are impossible all right, but why should I add my approval or withhold my disaffection? Fourth, the appeal to self-respect. Nobody with any subtlety of consciousness can have any. The 'mouse' will be ashamed, but will forget nothing, and even take pleasure in contemplating what he is ashamed of.

> But it is just in that cold, abominable half despair, half belief, in that conscious burying oneself alive for grief in the underworld for forty years; in that acutely recognized and yet partly doubtful hopelessness of one's position, in that hell of unsatisfied desires turned inwards, in that fever of oscillations, of resolutions determined for ever and repented of a minute later—that the savour of that sharp enjoyment of which I have spoken lies (pp. 57-8).

All these protests are significant of more to come: positive as well as negative. But the two main intellectual preoccupations are, fifth, Utilitarian morality, and sixth, psychological determinism. It is accepted that the *Notes* are primarily directed against Chernyshevsky's *What's to be Done?*[6] The rumblings in the cellar are intended to shake 'the palace of crystal'. Chernyshevsky believed that an ideal society could be created out of the rational adjustment of self-interest: as Bentham had put it, less lyrically but more concisely, 'golden conduct out of leaden motives'. Dostoevsky, knowing all about irrational perversity in himself and in his Siberian fellow-convicts, speaks with the Underground Man when he writes: 'Oh, the babe! Oh, the pure innocent child! . . . When in all these thousands of years has . . . man acted only from his own interest?' (pp. 64f.) He knows that men are neither as rational nor as selfish as they appear in the Utilitarian calculus. It is on this point of psychology that Dostoevsky first embarks on an open confrontation with the Western liberals; that it is put into the mouth of an angry mouse is neither here nor there; the mouse is recording an universal, and particularly a contemporary experience, and no amount of Utopian theorizing can be allowed to silence it. That people always follow their own interest is simply not true; and if society were scientifically planned so that everybody's interest coincided, the mouse would still scuttle for his hole and squeak his defiance.

This, it will be observed, is put forward as a statement about the facts of the case, and so far it carries no connotation of value. Nevertheless, one can discern a value judgment in the making. 'What man wants is simply *independent* choice, whatever that independence may cost and wherever it may lead' (p. 69). If a man's choice is tied inevitably to his interests, it is not a choice at all; so it might even be a duty to choose stupidly, by way of thumbing one's nose at the 'palace of crystal'. Various analogies are introduced to drive the point home; the ant-hill, the piano-key for theorists to play on, the stop of an organ to be pulled out as they choose. 'All human actions will be

tabulated . . . , mathematically, like tables of logarithms up to 108,000, and entered in an index; or, better still, there would be published certain edifying works of the nature of encyclopaedic lexicons, in which everything will be so clearly calculated and explained that there will be no more incidents or adventures in the world' (p. 68). And that is the end of human freedom. The mouse speaks for the dignity of the whole human species.

His anti-rationalism, his antipathy to scientific and particularly to mathematical paradigms, his sense of freedom as unlimited opportunity for good and for evil, his emphasis on the evil which in the absence of some antidote to humiliation is certain to prevail—all this is pure Dostoevsky and helps to explain his tensions and improvisations.

—A. Boyce Gibson

As so often, Dostoevsky accepts the view of reason propounded by his opponents, and attacking them, attacks reason with them. 'You see, gentlemen, reason is an excellent thing, but reason is nothing but reason and satisfies only the rational side of man's nature, while will is a manifestation of the whole life, that is, of the whole human life including reason and all the impulses. And although our life, in this manifestation of it, is often worthless, yet it is life and not simply extracting square roots.' He thus prepares the way for the reinstatement of religion on anti-rationalist terms. But, for the moment, the 'will' is paramount; and here the successors of Underground Man are the total voluntarists, Svidrigaylov and Stavrogin. The mere refutation of rationalism, even if successful, does not settle how will is to operate. Indeed, the translation of *volya* by *will,* though not positively incorrect, is too specific; *volya* also means freedom, not in the democratic sense of self-determination but in the anarchical sense of the absence of limits.[7] But Underground Man has a point; he knows all about perversity; he has tasted the bitter pleasures of biting off his nose to spite his face, and he sees that no account can be given under the Utilitarian formula of a phenomenon more common than superficial good sense is prepared to admit.

The sheer writing of *Notes from Underground,* especially Part One, is a masterpiece: the undertone of spite, irritability, helplessness and self-congratulation is brilliantly conveyed in the harshly turned sentences, the copious disconcerting parentheses, the blending of colloquialism and abstraction, the broken and persistent dialogue of the writer with himself, mainly in the form of mocking exchange with an imaginary interlocutor. But our concern with it is: how much of what Underground Man spits out through his chattering teeth is seriously to be ascribed to Dostoevsky? And what light does it throw on the nature of his religious pilgrimage?

1. The first question, which has its analogue throughout his great fiction, is here more than usually difficult to answer. At times Underground Man turns round and calls himself a liar. But his recognition of himself as a liar enters into his final expression of triumph. What, then, is Dostoevsky's own attitude towards him? The ironical tone of the writing suggests that it is clinical: whether autobiographical or not, the material is distanced and even judged. Dostoevsky certainly does not identify with his anti-hero. When he forces himself on a party of school-friends, is insulted, and walks up and down in front of them from eight o'clock to eleven between the table and the stove, extracting with satisfaction the last bitter drop from his humiliation; when, much more abominably, he raises the hopes of a recently recruited prostitute, and, when she comes to him in pure love, humiliates her and offers her payment 'from spite', because anything like love threatens his mutinous underground posture, the whole tone of the writing is hostile—even the Underground Man himself shows his abhorrence—the point of the episode is to show that this kind of thing can happen, and that the cycle of insult and humiliation is not in the same universe with the palace of crystal. The whole exercise is directed against the simple-minded one-track analysis of human nature issuing from the French Revolution and the English bourgeoisie. Yet something of the Underground enters into the world-view of Dostoevsky himself. His anti-rationalism, his antipathy to scientific and particularly to mathematical paradigms, his sense of freedom as unlimited opportunity for good and for evil, his emphasis on the evil which in the absence of some antidote to humiliation is certain to prevail—all this is pure Dostoevsky and helps to explain his tensions and improvisations. Underground Man is not only affirmed as a fact against the psychologist; he has hold of something which in any possible synthesis must remain intact. That is why he exclaims at the end to his 'audience': 'There is more life in me than in you.'

2. To explain fully the religious implications of his mutterings from the cellar, we should have to follow the theory of humiliation through the whole of his major fiction. But there are right from the start some indications which we must make the most of—both in the text and in contemporary writings outside it.

(*a*) In the reflections introductory to Part Two (p. 85) Dostoevsky returns to his theme of 'broad natures', 'who never lose their ideal even in the depths of degradation; and though they never stir a finger for their ideal, though they are arrant thieves and knaves, yet tearfully cherish their first ideal and are extraordinarily honest at heart'. Here is one of Dostoevsky's most persistent themes: there is for Russians no cut-off point for good and evil, as, it would seem, there is for the more legally minded Catholics and Protestants. There is, however, another side to it. The possibility of their co-existence depends on the duality of the nature concerned. Duality is a disease consequent on 'consciousness'.[8] 'Tell me this: why does it hap-

pen that at the very, yes, at the very moments when I am most capable of feeling every refinement of all that is "good and beautiful", as they used to say at one time, it would, as though by design, happen to me not only to feel but to do such ugly things, such that . . . Well, in short, actions that all, perhaps, commit but which as though purposely occurred to me at the very time when I was conscious that they ought not to be committed. The more conscious I was of goodness and all that was "good and beautiful", the more deeply I sank into my mire and the more I was ready to sink in it altogether. But the chief point was that all this was, as it were, not accidental in me, but as though it were bound to be so.'[9] The 'good and beautiful' are conceived as *ideals*; they are *entertained*; and they have no power.

We have noticed in Part One of this work the affinity of 'doubles' and 'ideals'; here we have it again. In the letter to Fonvizina, Christ is an 'ideal'. It is interesting to note just how Dostoevsky's Siberian experience had affected his attitude to ideals. In his 'Schiller' period he had actually thought 'ideals' could be realized. In *The House of the Dead* he learnt how little this intellectual prattle amounted to. Salvation, if available at all, would be a long and difficult business. He now does not think ideals can be realized; the most they can do is to light up the darkness and make it more evident. Properly speaking, this should mean that Christ can illuminate but cannot save. The change effected by Siberia was that this world is not the place to expect ideals to flourish in. The document in which the position is most clearly set out is to be found in Dostoevsky's notebooks for 1864; in an entry amounting to a funeral meditation immediately after the death of his first wife. It is also important as containing material far more explicitly Christian than anything he had written for more than twenty years.

(*b*) **Notes from Underground** was written in Moscow while his wife was dying, and Dostoevsky, who had not been conspicuously loyal or attentive to her, was at her side with the utmost consideration and devotion. The meditation, therefore, belongs to the same period of development as the **Notes.** It is spontaneous and confused, as one might expect under the circumstances. It starts from the assumption that no one here and now can love another as oneself—Christ commands the impossible. The 'law of personality' ties us down to earth. Only Christ could achieve it. Now Christ is the 'ideal' to which, according to the law of his nature, man tends. (So far he is simply ideal.) But then, he is also 'the incarnate ideal of man', and this means that man's full development is in following him. That he can only do by using the whole force of his 'I' to annihilate this 'I', 'and to make himself over to all and to each, individually and unconditionally. So that way the dialectic is achieved'. The law of the 'I' blends with the law of humanism, and in the fusion both (the 'I' and the all) are mutually annihilated to the advantage of both, and the highest end of each man's individual development is attained. 'That', he adds, 'is Christ's paradise'. But if that is the final end of man, to achieve it would put an end to man as an earthly being. It makes no sense to suppose that he must expire at the moment of achievement. Therefore, there is another life. We know little about it, but it has been predicted and foreshadowed by Christ, 'the final and ultimate ideal of man's whole development' who has 'presented himself to us in flesh and blood according to the law of our history'. Then follows a passage about the world in which there is no marrying or giving in marriage, poignantly relevant to the occasion, but we need not follow it. Then comes a parenthesis marked N.B., in which it is explained that Christianity cannot prevail here and now, because it is the ideal for our future development, and on this earth man is in a state of transition; as Christ himself said, to the end of this world there will be struggle and development ('doctrine of the sword'). Another N.B.: 'the nature of God is directly opposed to the nature of man'. This bears on the status of 'love everything as oneself'. It is in contradiction with the law of human development. And—a very important sentence—'that' (i.e. the law of human development) 'is not an ideal law, as the anti-Christs say, but the law of our ideal'. This (super-worldly) ideal is mainly shown on earth by the impact of its negation. 'When a man does not offer his "I" in sacrifice and *in love* for man or for some other being (Masha and I) he experiences suffering and calls it by the name of "sin": and the terrestrial condition is one of balance between that suffering and the paradise of joy procured by the fulfilment of the law, i.e. by sacrifice.' Without that it makes no sense.

It will be seen, even from this *précis*,[10] that Dostoevsky, at the time he wrote the *Notes,* was engaging in theological speculation in a definitely Christian sense; and this is enough to show that Underground Man is brought on the stage not as a mouthpiece for the author, but as an alarming indisputable fact. But the content bears examination. (1) In describing Christ as an 'ideal', Dostoevsky keeps his options open; he might very well not be Lord of the World. (2) In describing him as an ideal incarnate, he does something to dissipate the suspicion of dualism. (3) In emphasizing, for the first but not for the last time, the importance of personal immortality (the only official dogma of the church which he embraces unequivocally), he seems to edge away again from the world; it is because what has to be accomplished cannot be accomplished in the world that he so cherishes it; (4) thus slightly moderating, but not retracting, the appeal to eliminate the special 'I' here and now. This remains when all the 'Idealism' is pared off, and it is the basis of Dostoevsky's later Christian anthropology. There is already an oscillation between Christ the impossible and Christ as presence.

How far this should be read back into the *Notes* we should know better but for the imperial censor. That insensitive official took out a large portion of Part One, Chapter 10. Dostoevsky comments to his brother in a letter dated 5 April (26 March) 1864: 'It would have been better not to print the last chapter but one at all (it is the most important, where the essential idea is expressed), than to print it as it is, i.e. with cobbled-up sentences and full of self-contradictions . . . Those brutes of censors,—where I made a mock of everything and sometimes blasphemed *for form's sake,*[11] that is passed, but where I deduced from all this the necessity of faith and of Christ—that is suppressed.[12]

Dostoevsky never restored the excised passages, nor, as far as we know, were they preserved, to be published after his death, like 'Stavrogin's Confession'. So we can only guess at their contents.[13] But in this context Christ could only have been a projection of an ideal out of the depths.

If, then, it is asked, how is *Notes from Underground* a preparation for the struggle for God in Dostoevsky's inner experience, it may be said: (1) that it excludes the tacit compromise with Utilitarianism which was the fashionable religion of nineteenth-century England; (2) that it sets a sharp line between 'reason' which is *ex hypothesi* irreligious, and religion which, if permissible, will be unreasonable; (3) that the way of nature is not in the least godlike, and the average man's secular virtues lead him nowhere; (4) that the first and last enemy of religion is the experience of humiliation; (5) that 'ideals', being both the cause and the consequence of human doubleness, cannot save—even if they are presented as incarnate, for they are still not presences but presentations. A good deal of rubbish has been cleared away. But there is one issue on which Dostoevsky's clinical sympathy is at odds with his reflective judgment. Underground Man commends a life of consciousness as the only life possible for a man of modern sensibility: he has no use for the vulgarities of action. At times Dostoevsky will be found accepting this dichotomy, with the plus and minus signs reversed.[14] At other times he proffers a Russian version of 'practical reason'. In view of his increasing emphasis on 'active love', culminating in *The Brothers Karamazov,* this issue, unresolved in *Notes from Underground,* is one for which we must watch carefully in his later work.

That is as may be. What is certain is that *Notes from Underground* contains the basic psychological introduction to Dostoevsky's whole study of man, including his Christian study of Christian man.[15]

Notes

[1] Tr. Garnett. *White Nights and Other Stories,* pp. 154-5.

[2] *Notes from Underground,* ibid., p. 57.

[3] 'The legitimate fruit of consciousness is inertia', p. 62.

[4] Dostoevsky had always hated mathematics: see a letter to his father quoted by A. Steinberg, *Dostoevsky,* p. 23.

[5] P. 75: a theme which haunted Dostoevsky's imagination all through.

[6] Textual affinities are adduced by K. V. Mochulsky, *Dostoevsky: his Life and Work,* p. 251.

[7] It is one of the cases in which no translator could do any better.

[8] *Sozdaniye:* the elements of the word are exactly those of the Latin; and both are slanted towards 'self-consciousness', i.e. a conscious being sees himself in everything else. It could be argued that insofar as it casts one's own personal, or even one's own human, shadow over the world, it is self-destructive; and an enforced acquaintance with the Underground has at least the merit of showing up the doubleness (not to say duplicity) of the various German Idealisms. The remedy, of course,

is to go on and not back: to show that there is a consciousness which is not self-consciousness, because it is others-consciousness.

9 This sentence is not only revealing, it is, in its scapegrace scattered parenthetical intensity, a stylistic *chef-d'oeuvre*.

10 Part of the entry is translated into English in Magarshack, *Dostoevsky's Occasional Writings*, pp. 305-6, and the whole of it appears in French in *Dostoievski*, by Pierre Pascal, Text V, pp. 114-18.

11 That is, verisimilitude.

12 Letter 74 in J. Coulson, *Dostoevsky: a Self-portrait*, p. 124.

13 The only place in the existing Ch. 10 for the excised section is nearly at the end. 'Can I have been constructed simply in order to come to the conclusion that all my construction is a cheat? Can this be my whole purpose? I do not believe it.'

14 Especially in *Crime and Punishment*, which is the story of an intellectual who takes his ideas over-seriously. Cf. the advice of Porfiry Petrovich: 'fling yourself straight into life . . . and the flood will bear you to the bank and set you safe on your feet again' (p.412).

15 It is underplayed by post-revolutionary Russian critics. In that admirable collection, *Tvorchestvo Dosteovskogo*, Moscow 1959, which deals with other works at great length, it is mentioned only in passing. . . .

Isadore Traschen (essay date 1974)

SOURCE: "Existential Ambiguities in *Notes from Underground*," in *South Atlantic Quarterly*, Vol. 73, No. 3, Summer, 1974, pp. 363-76.

[*In the following essay, Traschen questions the notion of the underground man as an existential figure.*]

I

Like the work of Kierkegaard, Dostoyevsky's *Notes from Underground* anticipates many of the ideas which we nowadays call existential. I believe, though, that there has been some confusion in getting at the existential qualities of the central figure, the man from underground. I think a case can be made for a pretty strong modification of the usual assessment.

Before we get to the ideas, it is worth pointing out that the existential tenor is reflected in the conception of character, plot, and meaning. We have a characterless character in a plotless plot with a meaningless meaning. A "man of character, an active man, is preeminently a limited creature"; for the man from underground there is no "primary cause" from which to act. Consistent with the critique of rationalism, the traditional linear plot is abandoned in the first half, as is, at the end of the work, a resolution; for both a linear plot and a resolution imply a coherent scheme of things, with secure values. And if there is no such scheme, then whatever meanings we may draw from the work exist in a context of meaninglessness.

The central theme of the *Notes* is freedom, and the principal argument of the first part is that the prevailing positivism, rationalism, and scientism are fatal to it. Anticipating Skinner, the underground man charges that "science will teach man . . . that he never has really had any caprice or will of his own, and that he himself is something of the nature of a piano-key or the stop of an organ, and that there are, besides, things called the laws of nature; so that everything he does is not done by his willing it, but is done of itself, by the laws of nature." Thus we would not be responsible for our actions. Further, if everything is predictable, if everything is planned, "there will be no more incidents or adventures in the world." Those who would rationalize our lives, always in our interests, would not—in fact, could not—leave room for change, uncertainty, mystery, contingency. In the old conflict between essence and existence, the essentialists were finally, definitively taking over. The model was all; and the flesh—sweaty and sensuous—was in the way, the old temptation overcome at last. Modern civilization aspires to a total rationalization; it is, in effect, a benign conspiracy to eliminate actual living. Ernst Mach once said that the aim of science was to replace experience. Similarly, the underground man declares that "positiveness is not life, gentlemen, but is the beginning of death."

The attrition of our existential freedom is thus clearly seen in this central paradox of modern life, that the concern for our security and certainty is a cruelty, a benign enslavement. Of course, the gentlemen of the *Notes,* the healthy men of action who know that a wall is a wall, that a law of nature is a law of nature, will not only submit to the law, but will do so with the pleasurable feeling that they are sensible, modern, enlightened. The underground man was old-fashioned enough to believe that a man would want it otherwise. He argues that you may shower upon a man "every earthly blessing, drown him in a sea of happiness, so that nothing but bubbles of bliss can be seen on the surface; give him economic prosperity, such that he should have nothing else to do but sleep, eat cakes and busy himself with the continuation of his species, and even then out of sheer ingratitude, sheer spite, a man would play you some nasty trick. He would even risk his cakes and would deliberately desire the most fatal rubbish, the most uneconomical absurdity, simply to introduce into all this positive good sense his fatal fantastic element. It is just his fantastic dreams, his vulgar folly, that he will desire to retain, simply in order to prove to himself—as though that were so necessary—that men still are men and not the keys of a piano, which the laws of nature threaten to control so completely that soon one will be able to desire nothing but by the calendar." And so, to prove that man is free the underground man argues for his irrationality, that a man will not always act in his own interests, that he is the ungrateful animal, that twice two makes five if he wants it to, that "perhaps suffering is just as great a benefit to him as well-being." For "what man wants is simply independent choice, whatever that independence may cost." Consciousness, however disturbing, is freedom, and it has been abandoned in the idolatry of science . . . as if the scientific was the only way to know things.

The threat to our freedom was subtle; nothing crude or totalitarian, simply an incredible overestimation of logic and reason. In his letter to Benjamin Bailey, Keats says, "I have never yet been able to perceive how any thing can be known for truth by consequitive reasoning. . . . Can it be that even the greatest Philosopher ever arrived at his goal without putting aside numerous objections?" So the man from underground argues:

"You see, gentlemen, reason is an excellent thing, there's no disputing that, but reason is nothing but reason and satisfies only the rational side of man's nature, while will is a manifestation of the whole life, that is, of the whole human life including reason and all the impulses. And although our life, in this manifestation of it, is often worthless, yet it is life and not simply extracting square roots. Here I, for instance, quite naturally want to live, in order to satisfy all my capacities for life, and not simply my capacity for reasoning, that is, not simply one-twentieth of my capacity for life. What does reason know? Reason only knows what it has succeeded in learning (some things, perhaps, it will never learn; this is a poor comfort, but why not say so frankly?) and human nature acts as a whole, with everything that is in it, consciously or unconsciously, and, even if it goes wrong, it lives."

The underground man saw that every system constructed by lovers of mankind for the benefit of mankind was a "mere logical exercise"; that such systems were contradicted by the evidence of one's senses. For example, the humane intentions of our abstract civilization turn into blood "spilt in streams, and in the merriest way, as though it were champagne."

This abstract character of our life stimulates, by way of compensation, our "capacity for variety of sensations." It is precisely the "most civilized gentlemen," like the abstract, logical Ivy League and Wall Street gentlemen in Washington, "who have been the subtlest slaughterers." If civilization has not made mankind more bloodthirsty, it has made us "more vilely, more loathsomely bloodthirsty. In the old days he [man] saw justice in bloodshed and with his conscience at peace exterminated those he thought proper. Now we think bloodshed abominable and yet we engage in this abomination, and with more energy than ever."

II

From all this it would seem to follow that the underground man is a model of existential freedom. But if he is, it is with a savagely comic turn, and first of all in the conception of an abstract intellectual irredeemably paranoid, fuming in his underground hole, itself a comic paranoid inversion of that archetype of abstraction, the Ivory Tower. He is a parody of Hamlet, with his excessively refined sensibility, his awareness of all too many sides to a question. But his indecision is modern; there are no "primary causes" now on which to build, so our actions are problematic. His recourse is babbling—comic figures "talk and talk and talk." What we have is a comedy of consciousness, Hamlet burlesqued. In his proud unsociability he is also

like a Malvolio or an Alceste and is punished comically for it. In the tradition of comedy he is cast out, snubbed by his friends, who represent the going social order.

The romanticism of the underground man is also comic, adding to the ambiguity of this hero of freedom. His heroic, lonely protest against nineteenth-century rationalism and positivism is a prime romantic posture, as honorable as pouring blood on draft files. In both cases we have assertions of the value of the single person over the state. But the extremes he goes to! To prove a man is not predictable, he will not consult a doctor about his liver. It's bad, "well, let it get worse" . . . a heroic thumbing of the nose at science, but absurd, comic.

A primary ambiguity in the *Notes,* then, is that the romantic hero of freedom is fatally comic in his confrontations with the forces that make for our rationalization. So we must modify the soberness with which we might take his existential qualities. Now he is romantic not only in his adversary role, but also as a lover of the "sublime and the beautiful" in the manner of the Russian romantics of the 1840's with whom Dostoyevsky was once identified—a fact which may help to account for the violence and self-hatred. But here too—perhaps most of all here—his lofty positions are suspect, for both are varieties of idealism, and as such suffer its built-in ambiguity. Dostoyevsky was not the first to see the ambiguity in idealism, in the contradiction of flesh and spirit, but no one, I suppose, has so brilliantly and comically analyzed the sordid content of its contradictions. This motif is lightly sounded in the first part of the *Notes,* but receives its full development in the second. Here the ultimate analysis of the romantic idealist is the observation that he thinks and does ugly things at the very moment he is "feeling every refinement of all that is 'sublime and beautiful.'" Romantics are versatile; they are anti-utilitarian, yet "never lose sight of a useful practical object . . . through all the enthusiasms and volumes of lyrical poems." They have large, ideal conceptions; but these "broad natures . . . never lose their ideal even in the depths of degradation." Perhaps Dostoyevsky's most stunning insight is that eventually depravity becomes the romantic's normal condition, "*merely punctuated by attacks of idealism.*" These attacks, though, lend a "certain depth of meaning" to the depravity. Beyond this no analysis of idealism can go. Idealism is simply inverted debauchery—true of the state as well as the individual.

But this critique of romantic idealism which opens Part II of the *Notes* is abstract, like just about all of Part I. The bulk of the second part is otherwise, a sequence of concrete events. The existential is nothing if not concrete, and so these events become existential tests of the underground man, of his capacity for a lived life. And since he is an intellectual, therefore abstract, he fails all the way. That Part II is much longer is thus significant. The existential short-comings of the underground man as an intellectual are developed here first in repeated exposures of his bookishness. There was a hint of this theme earlier in the comic passage where the underground man says, "Listen sometimes to the moans of an educated man of the nineteenth century suffering from toothache, on the second or third day of the attack, when he is beginning to moan, not as he moaned on the first day, that is, not simply because he has a toothache, not just as any coarse peasant, but as a man affected by progress and European civilization, a man who is 'divorced from the soil and the natural elements,' as they express it nowadays." But the theme of his bookishness virtually explodes in Part II, almost in excess, as though Dostoyevsky could not contain himself. The underground man observes that he has "no resources except reading"; that he longs for a "more decent, a more '*literary*' quarrel with the officer who does not even notice him; that he is filled not only with ready-made phrases, but also ready-made, romantic fantasies, as when he imagines himself sent to Siberia after assaulting Zverkov:

> "'Never mind! In fifteen years when they let me out of prison I will trudge off to him, a beggar, in rags. I shall find him in some provincial town. He will be married and happy. He will have a grown-up daughter. . . . I shall say to him: Look monster, at my hollow cheeks and my rags! I've lost everything—my career, my happiness, art, science, *the woman I loved,* and all through you. Here are pistols. I have come to discharge my pistol and . . . I . . . forgive you. Then I shall fire into the air and he will hear nothing more of me.'"

"I was actually on the point of tears, though I knew perfectly well at that moment that all this was out of Pushkin's *Silvio* and Lermontov's *Masquerade*."

Now after another such fantasy, this time romanticizing family happiness to the prostitute Liza, she responds with an observation that shakes him to the core: "Why, you . . . speak somehow like a book." This remark, he says, "sent a pain to my heart." His heart, yes, because what his bookishness means is this: *in actual, concrete instances this exemplar of freedom is enslaved by conventional language and emotions.* As with Emma Bovary, his responses derive from the romantic literature of the time. The emotions of this spokesman for free will are not his own, not authentic. He is alienated from himself. There is a corollary here in his social conduct. "I had a sickly dread, too, of being ridiculous, and so had a slavish passion for the conventional in everything external. I loved to fall in the common rut, and had a whole-hearted terror of any kind of eccentricity in myself." He is so conventional, in fact, that we must ask if he is even as free in his theoretical stand against rationalism as he makes himself out to be? Can we say that just as his external behavior is conventional, that just as his internal behavior—his emotions and the language expressing them—is also conventional, so too his stand against rationalism is insufficient not only because it was only theoretical but also because it was, in the last analysis, just another romantic convention? The underground man with his 2 times 2 equaling 5, his refusal to have his liver treated, his spiteless spite, his undignified head-on collision with the officer in the interests of his dignity—in all this isn't Dostoyevsky satirizing the extreme yet conventional heroics of the romantics? And since the nonlinear form of Part I is the exception in his work, isn't there a critique of romanticism here too?

As a consequence of the underground man's bookishness, he fears real life, and this is his second existential failure, a further alienation. As he puts it in the scene with Liza, "I was so accustomed to think and imagine everything from books, and to picture everything in the world to myself just as I had made it up in my dreams beforehand, that I could not all at once take in this strange, that is real, circumstance." Bookish, therefore abstract, he cries, "Real life oppressed me with its novelty." The intellectual would rather theorize about life than live it. Literature may be a form of virtual life, as Suzanne Langer says; it may be an experiential mode; but in the light of the underground man aren't we, readers all, playing with words, indulging in some kind of word game? I would say that art is a passive experience rather than virtual life; and is only an aesthetic experience, that is, experience of an aesthetic form—not, certainly, of life. Though made up of images and events, verbal art is finally only words, and so abstract. Who would not say "Amen!" to what the underground man declares at the end? "We are all divorced from life, we are all cripples, everyone of us, more or less. We are so divorced from it that we feel at once a sort of loathing for real life, and so cannot bear to be reminded of it. Why, we have come almost to look upon real life as an effort, almost as hard work, and we are all privately agreed that it is better in books." As he says a few lines further on: "Why, we don't even know what living means now, what it is, and what it is called! Leave us alone without books and we shall be lost and in confusion at once."

Conventionalized emotions deriving from books can lead to an incapacity for and fear of life. We saw earlier that the man from underground had repudiated positivism as "not life" but the "beginning of death." But that, we can now see, was an abstract encounter; concretely, there is little desire for life in him either. No philosophy is worth anything, so the *Notes* implies, that is not lived; in this sense the *Notes* is an attack on the tradition of pure thought in Western philosophy, Platonist even when anti-Platonist.

His conventionalized emotions, bookish abstractness, and fear of actual life all lead to another existential failure in Part II; he cannot love. Martin Buber says that "all real living is meeting." To meet with another you must be locked together, locked in for keeps, like Othello with Desdemona, so that you feel pain or joy. (The agony of teaching, I venture to say parenthetically, is that you have only the trappings of meeting—you are rarely if ever locked in a relationship.) One kind of meeting is love. The underground man does not meet, hence he neither lives nor loves. He is infuriated with Liza for sensing that he is "incapable of loving her," that his "outbursts of passions had been simply revenge." He is at best capable of an erotic debauch which is the concrete reality underlying his abstract, romantic love. But this debauchery is another kind of alienation, for what it means is that he exploits women as sex objects, in the current vernacular. This non-relation is poisonous. The form it takes is his famous spite, a mean, superficial emotion expressing the envy of the inauthentic person. And his spite is spiteless; it has no "primary cause."

With only a spiteless spite, unable to love, impotent, he compensates through power, which only intensifies his alienation. "Save you!" he cries to Liza. "Power, power was what I wanted." As he says earlier, "It was the exercise of my power that attracted me most." His alienation through power is refined and sublimated through his moral impulse: "Even in my underground dreams I did not imagine love except as a struggle. I began it always with hatred and ended it with moral subjugation, and afterwards I never knew what to do with the subjugated object." If he cannot "live," he compensates with his ostensible moral as well as intellectual superiority as a means of subjugating others. It is nothing else but that sick, sterile missionary impulse exercised by every abstract power, church or state. Unfortunately, unlike the underground man, church and state think they know what to do with the subjugated object. His uncertainty is clear in the marvelous fantasy which follows. Fused here are all the unexistential qualities of the man from underground I have been talking about, his conventional romantic idealism, his bookishness, conventional emotions, incapacity for love, moral tyranny, and erotic debauchery: "What loving-kindness, oh Lord, what loving-kindness I felt at times in those dreams of mine! in those 'flights into the sublime and the beautiful'; though it was fantastic love, though it never was applied to anything human in reality, yet there was so much of this love that one did not feel afterwards even the impulse to apply it in reality; that would have been superfluous. Everything, however, passed satisfactorily by a lazy and fascinating transition into the sphere of art, that is, into the beautiful forms of life, lying ready, largely stolen from the poets and novelists and adapted to all sorts of needs and uses. I, for instance, was triumphant over every one; every one, of course, was in dust and ashes, and was forced spontaneously to recognize my superiority and I forgave them all. I was a poet and a grand gentleman, I fell in love; I came in for countless millions and immediately devoted them to humanity, and at the same time I confessed before all the people my shameful deeds, which, of course, were not merely shameful, but had in them much that was 'sublime and beautiful,' something in the Manfred style. Every one would kiss me and weep (what idiots they would be if they did not!), while I should go barefoot and hungry preaching new ideas and fighting a victorious Austerlitz against the obscurantists. Then the band would play a march, an amnesty would be declared, the Pope would agree to retire from Rome to Brazil; then there would be a ball for the whole of Italy at the Villa Borghese on the shores of Lake Como, Lake Como being for that purpose transferred to the neighborhood of Rome; then would come a scene in the bushes, and so on, and so on—as though you did not know all about it!"

III

The *Notes* is a Dostoyevskyan puzzle, and always has been if for no other reason than the fact that the intellectual, the kind of person Dostoyevsky valued least, even despised, was nonetheless the central and apparently heroic figure, even though conceived as an antihero. Drawing upon what I have been saying, I would like to make a try at putting the pieces together. First of all, though Do-

stoyevsky saw that the intellectual—liberal or radical—benignly conspired in our rationalization, he also conceded that the *romantic* intellectual, whatever his drawbacks, was an ally against the forces for rationalization. He even identifies somewhat with the type, especially with those avatars of the underground man, Raskolnikov and Ivan Karamazov. But having conceded the intellectual's value as a critic, he cuts it down by suggesting that this stand for freedom is conceived in conventionally romantic terms, and that further, because the underground man is an intellectual, he is abstract and thus inadequate to the task of offering *lived* alternatives. The tragedy of the underground man is that he aspires to freedom but is trapped in his bookish, conventional emotions. This is the fate of those who substitute abstractions, words, for a lived life. Consciousness is transcendence, says Sartre. But if you are not free to live what you are conscious of, transcendence of this sort isn't much. All it does is invite a debauchery of abstractions, book after book after book. We ought to be skeptical as well of the Socratic doctrine that the unexamined life is not worth living. Examine it all you want to, but again, if you can't break through to live it, it too is not much. There is one passage at the end which seems to point to some life in the underground man. Addressing his imaginary gentlemen, he declares, "I have only in my life carried to an extreme what you have not dared to carry halfway, and what's more, you have taken your cowardice for good sense, and have found comfort in deceiving yourselves. So that, perhaps, after all, there is more life in me than in you." More life, yes, than those who think it is only common sense to submit without question to our rationalization and the laws of nature. Compared to such he *has* thrown himself into an extreme situation; he seems to live. But he lives only theoretically. What we can say is that at best he is *alive* to the issues, but unable to *live* his thought. André Gide has pointed out that in Dostoyevsky's hierarchy of values the man of religion is highest, the man of passion next, and the man of intellect at the bottom. He goes on to say that for Dostoyevsky, "The antithesis of love is less hate than the steady activity of the mind. In his eyes it is intellect which individualizes, which is the enemy of the Kingdom of Heaven, life eternal, and that bliss where time is not, reached only by renouncing the individual self and sinking deep in a solidarity that knows no distinctions." This is like the underground man's own self-analysis: "though your mind works, yet your heart is darkened and corrupt, and you cannot have a full, genuine consciousness without a pure heart." Dostoyevsky may be antiromantic in one sense in the *Notes,* but he is equally in the tradition of the romantic movement's hostility towards the analytic intellect.

What can we say, then, about the accepted critical notion of the man from underground as an existential figure? Philip Rahv believed the *Notes* propels Dostoyevsky "towards a standpoint nowadays called existentialist," and he further says that the underground man has an "existential reality." Walter Kaufman says he sees "no reason for calling Dostoyevsky an existentialist," but he goes on to say "that part one of *Notes from Underground* is the best overture for existentialism ever written." And certainly he places the *Notes* in the context of existentialism in his anthology, *Existentialism from Dostoyevsky to Sartre.* William Barrett, to whom we owe a great deal for popularizing existentialism, says that perhaps the underground man "is not demanding a new truth at all, but only that truth should take some notice of his own concrete existence, with its aching liver, its humiliations and resentments." The underground man does confront the abstractions of science and progress with concretions like bad livers and toothaches, but these are more hypothetical than actual, no more realized than his freedom, which we have seen is only theoretical, only the rhetoric of the intellectual. There is no question that when he finds himself in a really concrete situation, he is not up to it. In response to Barrett and the others I would say that by ignoring Part II of the *Notes,* its deflation of the underground man's abstract pretensions, they misrepresent him. More generally, they take his existentialism too straight, too soberly; they do not see that it is presented comically.

In the final analysis, though ambivalent towards the underground man, the Raskolnikovs, and the Ivan Karamazovs, Dostoyevsky is unequivocal about the fallacy or "sin" of merely intellectualizing. But the *Notes* is the masterpiece it is because, among other reasons, it realizes the virtues of the intellect at the same time that it exposes its radical limits, its incompleteness when the sole human enterprise. This balancing of virtues and limitations dramatizes the division of the intellectual; Dostoyevsky's genius lies in treating the division comically.

The *Notes* is a devastating exposition of the unexistential character of the underground man; he is the totally alienated man. But this means that Dostoyevsky was after what we now call an existential, that is, a lived idea. For him this would have been a lived Christian life. What was missing in the *Notes,* and what would have made its puzzle easier, was the inclusion of the familiar Dostoyevskian figure of the saint, someone like Sonya Marmeladov, Alyosha Karamazov, or Father Zossima, those with that "pure heart" which could make for "a full, genuine consciousness." For just as the man from underground was divorced from life in the ways I have indicated, these overcame that divorce through love. Apparently Dostoyevsky at one time meant to attach such a quality to the underground man. In a letter to his brother he complains that for some reason the censors deleted those passages where he "deduced the necessity of faith and of Christ." And yet, as Rahv argued, this would have been unsatisfactory, aesthetically disturbing. If the passages had been included they would have been gratuitous, unconvincing, a kind of *deus ex machina,* if you will, not at all in keeping with the broken, fragmented, disintegrated character of the underground man. The work is more effective as it is, with him stewing forever in his own hell. But the involuntary omissions are important in confirming the hostility towards the man from underground as the intellectual, the incomplete man.

Dostoyevsky could see no secular, humanistic alternatives to the belief in Christ as a way of transcending our alienation. I would like to close with a word on two writers, Lawrence and Camus, who show us this alternative in their own Christ figures, transcendent on natural rather than

supernatural grounds. In *The Man Who Died* the Christ of the abstract Word is transformed into a Christ of the flesh; in *The Stranger,* which I will look at more closely, Meursault is identified in various ways with the crucified Christ. That the naturalistic Christ theme was intended is made clear by Camus in his 1957 preface: "I happen to say, and always paradoxically, that I had tried to portray in my character the only Christ that we deserved." The identification is suggested in many ways: for example, in Meursault's association with simple people, with outcasts like the pimp Raymond, with the "loose" Marie, analogous to Mary Magdalen; in his preference for the sensuous over the spiritual, as in his choice of Marie's "sun-gold face lit up with desire" rather than Christ's "divine face." This identification is climaxed in Camus' grasp of a paradox implied in the Crucifixion, that Christ, who loved man, was nonetheless alienated from the mob. So, too, with Meursault. His "absurd" ways also estrange him from the conventionalized crowd: "For all to be accomplished, for me to feel less lonely, all that remained to hope was that on the day of my execution there should be a huge crowd of spectators and that they should greet me with howls of execration." The paradox in this estrangement is that rather than alienation, he has a sense of universal belonging, the equivalent of Christ's love: "I laid my heart open to the benign indifference of the universe. To feel it so like myself, indeed so brotherly, made me realize that I'd been happy, and that I was happy still." Meursault was a stranger only to conventional society. He is at one with the universe, like Christ. But his universe is without Divine design; it is indifferent, "unsponsored," as Wallace Stevens put it.

"One does not discover the absurd without being tempted to write a manual of happiness"—so Camus in that exhilarating line from *The Myth of Sisyphus.* The absurd is the ground of Meursault's happiness; it "emptied me of hope," that is, from "the ideas that people tried to foist" on him. These ideas or hopes are so many illusions generated by abstractions like success, friendship, marriage, motherhood, and, finally, the Christian—and so Dostoyevskyan—hope of salvation through God's grace. The absurd thus leads to the ultimate difference with the traditional Christ, Meursault's rejection of the illusions of faith, hope, and love. He lives directly, without the mediation of these abstractions. Faith and hope are instances of what Camus calls "humiliated reason"; and love is a lie, as he indicates in his preface. "To lie is not only to say what is not. It is also, it is above all to say more than what is; and, as far as the human heart is concerned, to say more than one feels." Without faith, without hope, without love—here is a very different Christ from Dostoyevsky's. And yet Meursault is happy. Thus this affirmation of life is also Camus' reply to the Dostoyevskyan argument advanced through Kirilov that suicide is the logical consequence of atheism, a life without faith.

In Lawrence and Camus our alienation is overcome through a naturalistic rather than a supernatural Christ. The choice is like that of the heroine of Wallace Stevens' "Sunday Morning." I close with a stanza for the drama and the beauty with which the point is made:[1]

Why should she give her bounty to the dead
  [Christ]?
What is divinity if it can come
Only in silent shadows and in dreams?
Shall she not find in comforts of the sun,
In pungent fruit and bright, green wings, or else
In any balm or beauty of the earth,
Things to be cherished like the thought of heaven?
Divinity must live within herself:
Passions of rain, or moods in falling snow;
Grievings in loneliness, or unsubdued
Elations when the forest blooms; gusty
Emotions on wet roads on autumn nights;
All pleasures and all pains, remembering
The bough of summer and the winter branch.
These are the measures destined for her soul.

Notes

[1] By permission, from *The Collected Poems of Wallace Stevens,* 1967.
Copyright by Alfred A. Knopf, Inc.

Julia Annas (essay date 1977)

SOURCE: "Action and Character in Dostoyevsky's *Notes from Underground,*" in *Philosophy and Literature,* Vol. 1, No. 3, Fall, 1977, pp. 257-75.

[*In the following essay, Annas interprets* Notes from the Underground *in light of analytic philosophy, as a work that probes the subject of irrational action.*]

Notes from Underground was written with a specific purpose in mind: to answer Chernyshevsky's novel *What Is to Be Done?*[1] And many features of Dostoyevsky's work can only be understood when we bear in mind its specifically Russian setting. The narrator is a romantic idealist of the forties transformed into something rather different by 1864, and no doubt we lose much if we do not bear in mind that Dostoyevsky is looking back across the gulf of imprisonment and suffering at his own idealistic youth.[2] But the intense and radically peculiar nature of Dostoyevsky's writing takes us to a level of the work which is accessible to those without knowledge of the local conditions of the work's production. As Mochulsky says, "the author steadily emerges beyond the confines of the Russian intellectual . . . the underground man's paradoxes are not the whims of some half-mad eccentric, but a new revelation of *man about man.*" The book is "the philosophical preface to the cycle of the great novels" (p. 245). Even though Dostoyevsky's passionate and extreme temperament made him quite incapable of constructing a piece of precise philosophical argument, there is much of genuine philosophical interest in part I. It is not just a particular moral and political theory, like Chernyshevsky's, which is to be discredited, but something deeper, the presuppositions of a whole type of moral theory.

In this article I shall examine the implications of what Dostoyevsky says for the philosophy of action and thence for ethics. I shall argue that he challenges a very basic model of human action, which is both intuitively plausible and basic to many moral theories. I shall also argue that as the work stands, there is a lack of continuity between parts I and II on the philosophical as well as on the literary level. In concentrating on the consequences for moral theory, I shall be ignoring the social and political aspects of the work. It may well be urged that such a division of the moral from the political is unrealistic in treating a Russian writer. In defense I can only say that this narrowing of focus brings out in a sharper and more tractable way the philosophical issue which is my main concern.

I

Tell me, who was it who first declared, proclaiming it to the whole world, that a man does evil only because he does not know his real interests, and if he is enlightened and has his eyes opened to his own best and normal interests, man will cease to do evil and at once become virtuous and noble, because when he is enlightened and understands what will really benefit him he will see his own best interest in virtue, and since it is well known that no man can knowingly act against his best interests, consequently he will inevitably, so to speak, begin to do good. Oh, what a baby! Oh, what a pure innocent child! (Part I section 7; all quotations are from the translation by Jessie Coulson [London: Penguin, 1972].)

What exactly is the target here of the Underground Man?[3]

Every moral theory presupposes some theory of human action, although this may not be explicit; since moral philosophy is concerned with human actions, it must presuppose some account of what it is for a human action to be performed. One very influential tradition thinks of the paradigm of action as essentially aimed at some good: "Every art and every inquiry, and similarly every action and pursuit, is thought to aim at some good" is the opening sentence of Aristotle's *Ethics.*[4] What is it for every action to aim at some good? We have the assumption here that every action is purposive and rational; purposive in that there is some goal which the agent sees as a good and rational in that performing the action is believed by the agent to be an appropriate means or way of bringing about the desired goal. This model of action is developed very fully in Aristotle, but it is not conceptually linked to Aristotelianism alone; it appears, for example, in recent very influential articles on action by Donald Davidson.[5] According to Davidson, to give a reason for an action is to explain it by a combination of belief and "pro-attitude," a term introduced to cover all sorts of long- and short-term wanting and desire. Davidson notes that it follows that we can always work out some reasoning which gives the characteristic of the action that the agent found desirable: "from the agent's point of view there was, when he acted, something to be said for the action" ("Actions, Reasons and Causes," p. 691). Davidson sums up this line of thought neatly:

When a person acts with an intention, the following seems to be a true, if rough and incomplete, description of what goes on: he sets a positive value on some state of affairs (an end, or the performance by himself of an action satisfying certain conditions); he believes (or knows or perceives) that an action, of a kind open to him to perform, will promote or produce or realize the valued state of affairs; and so he acts (that is, he acts *because* of his value or desire and his belief). Generalized and refined, this description has seemed to many philosophers, from Aristotle on, to promise to give an analysis of what it is to act with an intention; to illuminate how we explain an action by giving the reasons the agent had in acting; and to provide the beginning of an account of practical reasoning, i.e. reasoning about what to do, reasoning that leads to action ("How is Weakness of the Will Possible?," p. 102).

We should note that accepting this model of action does not on its own have any implications about the kind of motivation that is necessary; it is quite possible to accept the model and reject any form of egoism. The fact that an agent seeks some good in any action does not imply that it is *his own* good that he seeks. This is why an attack on the rational model of action cuts much deeper than an attack on egoism (which is in turn why what is formally an attack on the egoistic theories of Chernyshevsky becomes something of much deeper interest). What is at stake is whether an agent must have in mind *some* good, his own or not, in order to act in the full sense.

All the same, the model will suggest an agent-centered picture of practical reasoning. For the agent's goal must be a good for him, if his action is to be in fact rational. And it may well make egoism seem a more plausible theory of motivation than any alternative, for initially at any rate it is hard to see how an agent could be motivated by something he sees as a good without some appeal being made to a desire of his own. This line of thought is wrong,[6] but it is not obvious why it is wrong, and it is understandable that Dostoyevsky should run together the two issues.

The rational model of action is intuitively plausible, but it runs up against another powerful intuition, namely that there *are* actions which are the agent's actions, initiated by him, but which are nonetheless pointless and irrational. The problem is sometimes called "weakness of will" or *akrasia,* following Aristotle's discussion of it. The difficulty is that an akratic or irrational act is one done by the agent even though he recognizes that there is an alternative (perhaps merely not acting) which it would be better to perform. In acting as he does, he recognizes the greater good, but is not moved to action by it. But is this not paradoxical? How can he be motivated to action when according to the model he can have no motive for what he does? There is no good which he seeks to obtain by doing what he does, or at any rate no good which is not outweighed by the recognized bad consequences of performing the action. But in that case, how can he be performing an action at all? He seems to be an agent in what he does, but if he acts he is going against his conception of the greater good, and how can this be?

The most obvious philosophical remedy is to say, as Plato does in the *Protagoras,* that irrational actions simply do not occur, because they cannot. Since action must be understood as purposive and rational, it is simply incoherent to describe someone as acting in defiance of the good he recognizes. So cases where this *seems* to happen must be explained away as really being cases of a *mistaken* conception of the good to be attained. Irrationality is really intellectual error; knowledge is virtue. We have already seen the Underground Man's opinion of this thesis.

Irrational actions present a paradox to any theory of action that wants to take the plausible view that the paradigmatic action is purposive and rational (in the sense explained). There are, of course, numerous ways of dealing with the problem. Probably the most common is to proceed in the hope that the paradox will turn out to be harmless or at least amenable to resolution in terms of the theory. This is Davidson's approach to the problem in "How is Weakness of the Will Possible?" But another reaction is clearly possible: to insist on the reality of irrational action and hold that if it creates problems for our theory of action then so much the worse for the latter.

Much of what the Underground Man says in part I consists of an attack (not a linear, cumulative attack, but a series of disconnected jabs) on the idea that action in the proper sense must be understood as rational and purposive. Section 7 in particular revolves around irrational action and holds that it not only exists but by its existence discredits any theory that ignores it or has to explain it away. There is a long description of the man who expounds clearly and at length what he ought to do and must do, aware of all the circumstances, and then a quarter of an hour later goes and does the exact opposite. Now of course a description of a case of irrational action cannot prove very much on its own. It does make the point that there is nothing obviously incoherent in the idea of such an event. But the rationalist opponent will be unimpressed; he will say that the case is actually incoherent, that difficulties will surface when one extends the description to the agent and his relation to the action, and that to claim that a description of irrational action shakes the analysis simply begs the question.

So more is needed than a mere assertion that irrational action occurs. And in section 7 the Underground Man does more; he turns to the whole notion of *advantage* employed by the opponent in his claim that a man can only act with some good or advantage in view. "Can you undertake to define exactly where a man's advantage lies? What if it sometimes happens that a man's advantage not only may but must consist in desiring in certain cases not what is good but what is bad for him? And if so, if such cases are even possible, the whole rule is utterly destroyed." He claims, that is, that the mere possibility of such a case proves his point. But is he still not begging the question? In fact he is not, because Dostoyevsky is quite subtle here. The Underground Man conducts the whole argument in his opponents' terms, so that they are forced to recognize a counterexample to the position they hold. He allows them to insist that action can only occur when there is some good in view, and that otherwise described it is incoherent—*still,* he claims, they lose their case because they omit the good or advantage that consists in acting all one's *other* goods and advantages. "Doesn't there, in fact, exist something that is dearer to almost every man than his own very best interests, or—not to violate logic—some best good (the one that is always omitted from the lists . . .) which is more important and higher than any other good . . . ?" Perhaps, that is, irrational action has to be described in terms of seeking some good so as not to "violate logic," that is, produce an inconsistent description of what is going on. But even if the opponent claims that when the action is properly described, i.e., as aiming at some good, it can be seen not to be irrational at all, this move gets him nowhere. For this "good" is no more than verbally similar to any recognized good. "'Well, but then it is still a good,' you interrupt. By your leave, we will explain further, and the point is not in a play on words, but in the fact that this good is distinguished precisely by upsetting all classifications. . . . In short, it interferes with everything." The opponent ought to worry about the case of a man acting knowingly but not so as to achieve any recognized good, for even if what happens has to be described formally in terms of seeking good of some kind, the opponent still cannot account for it, because the "good" here is one he has not considered and which comes into conflict with all the goods he *has* considered. He can draw no comfort from the fact that the perverse insistence on flouting all one's conceptions of good can itself be *called* "good"; he can win only a verbal victory. So the Underground Man feels free to describe as good the aim of acting against all one's notions of what is good and worthwhile. "One's own free and unfettered volition, one's own caprice, however wild, one's own fancy, inflamed sometimes to the point of madness—that is the one best and greatest good, which is never taken into consideration because it will not fit into any classification, and the omission of which always sends all systems and theories to the devil."

It is worth noticing that the emphasis on volition, *khoten'ye*, brings out the point that the agent is still to be considered the *author* of his acts, however irrational. They are caused by his desire or wanting, and so brought about in the normal way, even if he does not aim at any good in doing them. The English word "volition" is an artificial philosopher's term, and indeed suggests if anything an act of will that is opposed to the agent's desires, whereas *khoten'ye* at once brings to mind the very common verb *khotet'*, to want or like. The Underground Man is not suggesting that an irrational action can be motivated by an act of pure will, a volition unconnected to desire. On the contrary, he is insisting that it can be produced by some kind of desire, and be an expression of agency, in the face of the recognition that it is no good. In section 8 he insists that reason is only a part of human life, whereas *khoten'ye* is a "manifestation of the whole of life (*proyavlenie usei zhizni*), I mean of the whole of human life *including* both reason and speculation." It is hardly natural to say this of "volition" in English, although this is the translation Coulson uses.

This vindication of acting in the full sense against what one recognizes as good is developed in two main directions. First, the Underground Man is clear that such actions are nevertheless not motivated, and hence not explained, in any ordinary sense. In section 5 he contemplates the straightforward man who acts from a motive without questioning it. By contrast, the Underground Man is always questioning his motives until they lose their force for him. So if he acts it is purely out of *zlost'*. No one word can translate *zlost'* adequately; translators vary between "anger," "spite," "resentment," "malevolence," thus disguising Dostoyevsky's obsessive concentration on the one word. (It occurs 13 times in section 1 alone.) But while there is no adequate translation, it can probably be safely seen as whatever it is that actually gets a man to act against his conception of the good. The point here is that *zlost'*, while it may bring about an action, is not a motive for it, and does nothing to explain it. This is recognized quite explicitly: it might "serve quite successfully instead of a primary cause, precisely because it isn't a cause (*prichina*)." This is a paradoxical way of putting the point that an action produced by wanting of some kind but still against all the agent's conceptions of good is not motivated in any recognizable way. So we might want to say, "He had no motive; he just did it out of spite." This is not to deny that spite was what actually brought about the action, only that the action is not motivated in the usual way and not accessible to the usual kind of comprehension.

Second, the Underground Man feels it necessary to argue that the existence of the volition that brings about an irrational action is not threatened by determinism. He worries about determinism spasmodically throughout part I, but it is hard to find a clear point of view in what he says. He talks a lot about the laws of nature, but without any clear idea of what they actually are. In section 3, he throws together as examples of necessity the theory of evolution, psychological egoism and twice two equalling four; and this shows great ignorance, and perhaps lack of interest, in what a determinist might actually be trying to say. But this confusion does not matter after all, since in section 8, the most sustained discussion, neither the Underground Man nor his opponents are arguing about the *truth* of determinism; what they are disputing is whether or not it *matters* if determinism is true. The opponent is presented as thinking that it does not, even though he recognizes that if all our desires are predictable, they become controllable. He accepts this, holding that if our desires run on the rational lines laid down, this will remove freedom only in the sense that there will no longer be desires which are opposed to reason. But, he maintains, freedom to act against reason is not what we really mean by "freedom"; freedom is just the ability to do what it is rational to do, and so we are not deprived of anything by losing a will which goes against reason. It is obvious that this is a kind of compatibilism, though in Dostoyevsky's hostile presentation it is not clear or well-thought out, and much more work would have to be done to make it sound plausible. What the Underground Man insists on, by contrast, is quite clear: the possibility does make a difference, for if a man's desires can be predicted then they can be manipulated, and if they can be manipulated then he really is no more than a piano key, part of a mechanism constructed independently of him.

Occasionally he does maintain that determinism is actually false; it cannot be true because man does possess desires of such a type as to frustrate any attempt to manipulate them. (This is a thesis which is not necessarily tied to irrational actions, except insofar as he sometimes suggests that the desires in question are those which bring about irrational actions.) Sometimes, however, he seems to be less sure of this, recognizing that the desires on which he lays so much weight are, after all, merely desires which could in principle be just as predictable and manipulable as any others. But the main point is sustained: it does matter whether or not determinism is true, for, if so, it is no longer a man's own desires that bring about his actions, and he loses responsibility for them.[7]

A great deal of the discussion of part I, then, and not just the most obvious section 7, maintains that there do exist actions in the full sense of the word, which are freely produced by the agent's desires and thus genuinely originate from him, but which are nevertheless done in the knowledge that the agent believes them to produce no good, or less good then an alternative. The effect of this claim is of course to discredit the rational purposive paradigm of action, and with it the agent-centered picture of practical reasoning. It is incidentally interesting, in view of the fact that Dostoyevsky conflates this notion with that of motivation as egoistic, that the Underground Man never tries to discredit this picture of action by claiming that purely non-egoistic actions are possible. Moral philosophers have sometimes claimed that the agent-centered model of practical reasoning is wrong because an action can be performed purely out of duty, for example. But it never occurs to Dostoyevsky to appeal either to deontological notions or to altruism.

We would expect the rejection of the rational paradigm to have important consequences for the way we can regard character and action. And we find this, not only in what the Underground Man says, but in how he says it.

II

Philosophers who take action to be in the last analysis purposive and rational have trouble describing an agent's relation to an irrational action, even if they accept the latter as a coherent possibility. Aristotle is reduced to saying that the agent does not "choose" to do his akratic act, because for Aristotle (more so than for us) choice is linked to one's character and expresses it, and the akratic act is out of character. An irrational act does not reflect the agent's valuations, and so it cannot be seen as a product of his dispositions—his generosity or meanness, greed or thrift, courage or cowardice. It lacks understandable connection with his character. Most of our character-describing words applied to agents (not just the traditional virtues and vices) have implications about what the agent values and what choices he has made and will make.[8]

The Underground Man is like Aristotle's weak-willed man in whom weakness of will has become a chronic condition. And one result at any rate is inevitable: most char-

acter-describing words fail to get a grip on him, and his moral character collapses in fragments—or perhaps we should rather say that no attempt to apply to him notions involved in morally judging someone's character can begin to succeed. This is not because he is morally revolutionary; indeed, morally he is extremely conservative, holding without question, for example, the most conventional views about duels, slaps in the face, and so on. Rather, his moral character fails to form a whole because his actions frequently, indeed usually, cannot be described in terms of the rational paradigm; and because we thus cannot ascertain his values at the time of action, we cannot go on to characterize him in ways which carry implications about his past and future actions and choices. His single most striking feature is his inconsistency, which he describes (in the person of his interlocutor) in section 11. But this inconsistency does more than make him difficult to pin down by a third party. The book is written in the first person, and what is striking is the way that the writer displays his lack of grip on his own character. Because he does not regard his actions as reflecting and confirming considered value judgments, he cannot see them in the light of any lasting disposition or trait of character, and so he is left without any way of making connections between his own actions. If two of his actions or utterances do not cohere, he can regard one as tending to undermine the attitude expressed by the other; but he can also think of himself as just having changed his mind, and as being committed to both at different times. And a great deal of the time either this is what he does, or both possibilities are left open.

Part I is full of ways in which we are shown the Underground Man's disconnected state. He is always backtracking; each remark he makes tends at once to provoke a contradiction. "Who can be vain of his disease, still less swagger with it? Why do I say that, though? Everybody does it—we all show off with our diseases." He develops arguments and then breaks them off with dissatisfaction or a change of direction. He is incapable of keeping up a sustained argument or discussion—the relatively short part I is made up of eleven short sections, none very long and some not very homogeneous internally. Most important of all, he can sustain no confidence in what he says. He is always turning aside to ask questions or to invent objections from himself or from imaginary interlocutors. He knows that the interlocutors' parts are written by himself too, and that there is no genuinely distinct point of view, but he needs the fiction of an opponent of some kind, to dramatize his own lack of internal continuity. As well as providing constant questions and interpolated objections, the imaginary interlocutor enables the Underground Man to distance himself even from what he puts down in an apparently straightforward way. He frequently and obsessively insists that when we think he is serious he is in fact joking, or that when we think he is joking he is serious. He constantly offers advice, invites sympathy, wheedles and bullies. All this has the effect of reducing his commitment to any particular utterance. Several times he takes back something he has just said, on the grounds that he was lying, but the admission that he lied does not produce remorse; he has just changed his mind, and he does not regard what he said as a lapse from a generally truthful policy. The constant to and fro between the Underground Man and his imaginary opponents has been labeled "dialectical." Peace, for example, talks of the "counterpoint" of *Notes from Underground* and says, "In it can be seen the beginnings of that dialectical method of presenting ideas which is the hallmark of Dostoyevsky the mature artist" (p. 17). This is most misleading if it is thought to imply a conscious, anti-dogmatic methodology in argument, or some progression by means of confronting and transcending oppositions. There is no *development* in the argument; positions are confronted with other positions and then sometimes change, but there is no coming to grips with rival views or any attempt to use the interlocutor to clarify the narrator's own position. Rather, the interlocutor serves as a defense *against* maintaining and clarifying what the narrator has to say. The various dramatic devices serve to dissociate the Underground Man from what he says, and make it impossible to predict from the present passage what will be said next, or to judge what has been said in terms of what is being said now. We are never allowed to feel that we know where we are in the argument. This is both a philosophically interesting point and a dramatically effective device on Dostoyevsky's part. Since the Underground Man lacks a character that could group his actions in intelligible ways, it would be dramatically inept to have him deliver a consistent and well-constructed argument about his own lack of continuous character. It is precisely characteristic of him that we can understand what he says only in short momentary bursts, and that these do not add up to anything coherent.

Section 6 reveals the Underground Man's lack of character most strikingly. "Oh, if only it was only out of laziness that I do nothing! Lord, how much I should respect myself then! I should respect myself because I had something inside me, even if it was only laziness; I should have at any rate one positive quality of which I could be sure. Question: what is he? Answer: a lazy man; and it really would be very pleasant to hear that said of me. It would mean being positively defined, it would mean that there was something that *could* be said of me. 'A lazy man!'— that is a name, a calling, it's positively a career!" The point here is underlined by using for "quality" not the more neutral word *kachestvo,* but *svoistvo,* which literally means "something of one's own." The Underground Man does not regret lacking certain characteristics as opposed to certain others; he regrets lacking the ability to categorize himself in *any* way that makes long-term sense. When he describes himself, it is usually in terms of abuse, but he cannot even accuse himself of having a bad character. (The one good quality he thinks of himself as having is cleverness, but this is not a quality of *character*.) Hence, perhaps, the shrill tone of his abuse of himself and others, and the reason why *Notes from Underground* contains such an amazing number of variants on "disgusting," "revolting," "filth," "muck," and so on: his adverse comments are all based on disgust, which is a strong feeling but a momentary one. It is called forth by the appearances of things, the way they happen to strike one, as much as by the way they really are. Correspondingly, the feeling of disgust requires no reference to a trait or disposition of

character; it is more like a reaction which does not characterize the person in any lasting way.

The very first section presents us with the dilemma of the Underground Man. All the salient features are already there in its first five paragraphs. The strangeness of the narrator strikes us from his very first words, and it lies as much in the way he tells us about himself as in what he tells us about what he does.

The first paragraph introduces the writer as sick and nasty ("Ya chelovek bolnoi . . . ya zloi chelovek."). Again, there is no adequate English translation of the crucial word *zloi,* the adjective corresponding to *zlost'.* "Angry," Coulson's word here, is too feeble in not suggesting the note of nastiness and perversity. The nearest equivalent is perhaps "mean" in the American sense, suggesting both force and malevolence. We begin to see the perverse nature of the writer's beliefs. He thinks that his liver is bad, though he knows he has no ground for this belief. He is not having treatment although he thinks that he ought to. He is superstitiously respectful of doctors, although he is well-educated enough not to be. He refuses treatment out of spite (*zlost'*). So far we find a man who acts even aggressively against his own interests out of pure perversity. We may find it hard to see the point of acting like this, but there is no indication yet that this is not a coherent policy.

The second paragraph partly continues in this way. He makes a joke, decides that it is no good and leaves it in for that reason. But a new element is also introduced. Although his behavior was consistently that of someone utterly *zloi,* we are told, it did not really answer to the way he felt. He did not in fact care at all about the petitioners he got so angry with. Then why behave so badly to them? That turns out to have been the heart of his perversity ("glavniy punkt moei zlosti"). *Zlost',* which has been introduced as the mainspring of his behavior, makes a man act in ways in which he has no desire to act. It turns out that there is something permanently self-frustrating about *zlost'.* But there is still no indication that it is not something which could be a permanent state. Indeed, in describing the way in which he would turn on himself for occasionally letting good will determine his behavior, and act the way he felt instead of fighting it, he says that that was always his way—*obychai,* what is usual or customary, suggesting that there was some degree of dispositional reliability.

In the third paragraph, however, the picture splits apart. "I was lying when I said just now that I was a *zloi* civil servant. I was lying out of *zlost'.*" Translators who use, as Coulson does, unrelated words for these two occurrences surely destroy the sense of the sentence, which brings out precisely the problem of characterizing oneself as *zloi.* To be *zloi,* to act only or predominantly from *zlost',* is precisely to lack character, so to *characterize* oneself as *zloi* will at once lead to paradox. The *zloi* man is the man who acts out of perversity and breaks all links between action and character. Thus he is unable even to judge his own state coherently. Since he has no moral dispositions, he cannot consistently *judge* himself or even his own lack of moral dispositions. He has no ground on which to stand, as it were, either to approve or disapprove of his own *zloi* actions. When he denies, out of *zlost'*, that he acted out of *zlost'*, the denial has as much validity as the affirmation. The actions of the *zloi* man do not support—they even undermine—what he values; his actions are inconsistent with his valued objectives, and so cannot stand in coherent relations with any traits of character.[9]

This may seem to be overworking one particular sentence. But it is hard to ignore Dostoyevsky's words here, for now the fragmentation of the Underground Man's character is *shown* for the first time. He becomes obsessive and loses control, bursting out to the imaginary interlocutor, "You think that now I'm making some sort of confession to you, asking your forgiveness, don't you? . . . I'm sure you do . . . But I assure you it's all the same to me if you do think so."

In the fourth paragraph we find explicit recognition of the way the writer cannot characterize himself, and the paradoxes which result. Precisely because *zlost'* is the predominant force that moves him to action, he cannot make himself into a *zloi character,* any more than into any other sort of character—the nature of *zlost'* precludes this. One result is that no possible reflection on his own character can be found satisfying. He consoles himself with the thought that to act otherwise than as he does would be foolish, but this is merely a spiteful (*zlobniy*) thought, and only irritates him. There is no point in his even trying to have a consistent character. He is condemned to the state of permanent dissatisfaction and irritation that we find him displaying all the time. The paradoxes developed in the rest of this paragraph bring this out by their pointlessness: he thinks it desirable to lack character, and has thought so for forty years . . . he has the right to say that old age is disgusting because he is going to be old himself. . . .

Pointless paradox occurs in the final paragraph too. St. Petersburg is too expensive and unhealthy for him, but he won't leave. He starts to give a reason, but then breaks off—"It's all the same"; for the characterless man considerations like expense and climate cannot be weighed up objectively, for to do so would involve comparing his past and future states. These considerations have force only according to how he feels at the time. The section concludes with a final pointless paradox: the respectable man wants most to talk about himself, so he will too. The respectable (*poryadochniy*) man is the man whose life displays *poryadok,* order and organization; exactly the opposite of the Underground Man. The writer cannot even talk about himself without doing it *because* it is the exact opposite of what would be expected.

In this brief, peculiar and apparently unattractive section, Dostoyevsky has achieved something remarkable. He has shown us what happens to a man's character when his actions cease to be understandable in terms of reason and purpose and he becomes an irrational agent. We see the narrator's perversity, his *zlost'*, and while we understand how he can commit irrational actions we also see how action becomes dissociated from character, and the way in

which character dissolves and disappears. To lack character is not, of course, the same as to lack a sense of one's identity as a person; this characterless man has a very strong sense of himself as an individual, but he cannot judge himself by more than momentary reactions, and so his opinions and beliefs become fragmentary and unintegrated. Further, he is incapable of a whole range of attitudes and opinions that can only be developed in someone with character dispositions; he is incapable, for example, of love, trust and hate (as opposed to resentment). His moral world is composed of momentary attractions and repulsions, with the repulsions predominating, since his insistence on acting against his conception of the good weakens for him the practical and attractive force of good.

In so presenting breakdown of character as a "consequence" of a rejection of purposive, rational action as the norm, I may have made it sound as though it is or could be a distinct causal product. In fact the relation between character and action is complex, and it would be ill-advised to claim priority for either; they stand or fall together. The paradigm of rational action has its problems, but one reason why it remains entrenched at the basis of so much in philosophy is its tight, though not altogether obvious, links with the notion of moral character. If we cease to interpret what someone does in the light of the rational paradigm, we lose all comprehension of his character. Part I of *Notes from Underground* shows the horror of knowing that this has happened when the person is oneself.

III

In part I we have had displayed to us the fragmentation of the persistently irrational agent; we have seen his inability to continue in any line of thought, his insecurity, his inability to comprehend himself as a continuous whole, his tendency to judge and act by the moment rather than in terms of policy and character. All this has been shown in and by the fragmentation of the form, the broken paragraphs, inconsistencies, the need to question, argue, distance himself from what he says. This effect has of course been noticed before, for example by Mochulsky: "We perceive almost physiologically [*sic*] the underground man's division through the unsightliness of his style, the disharmony of syntax, the irritating brokenness of his speech. All Dostoyevsky's heroes are characterized by their language, but the verbal portrait of the man from underground is the most expressive" (p. 246). But what has not been sufficiently noticed is that there is a contrast here with part II.[10]

In part II we are given a narrative, which proceeds chronologically and with no peculiarities of form (except perhaps the excessively discursive and rambling opening section in which the writer's situation is established). It is true that the protagonist of the narrative, the "I" that the writer is writing about, persistently acts in an irrational way and has a fragmentary and elusive character. But *the "I" who is writing* shows none of this. He is the normal narrator, distanced from his protagonist but maintaining a single view of him throughout. There is no feeling of a man whose sense of continuity is precarious. There is the feeling rather of a man of forty looking back on past events and regarding himself with a morally established character. There is the sentimental touch of his having recalled Liza's face for fifteen years; there are even passages where he judges his earlier self in a morally rather stringent manner: "What I can say for myself with certainty is that although I committed this cruelty deliberately, it came from my wicked head, not from my heart."

There are a few points in the second part where the narrator turns to an interlocutor or breaks off with, "Gentlemen . . . ," in a way superficially like the outbursts of part I. But the function of these is rather different. In part II, section 1, for example, the narrator first says that he is not trying to justify his "debauched" behavior, then—"But no! that was a lie! To justify myself was exactly what I wanted to do. That observation is made for my own benefit, gentlemen. I won't lie. I have given my word. . . ." He is catching himself out in a lapse of from a general policy of truthfulness—precisely what does not happen in part I, where his self-accusations of lying are more like a mere swing between two opinions. Compare this passage from part I, section 11: "It would be better if I believed even a small part of everything I have written here. I swear, gentlemen, I don't believe a word, not one single little word, of all I have scribbled down! That is, I do perhaps believe it, but at the same time, I don't know why, I feel, or suspect, that I'm lying like a trooper." This is someone who really does have difficulty in distinguishing between telling a lie and being uncertain between two opinions because he is uncertain of his commitment to either. By contrast, the narrator of part II is in no such muddle, and is even fanatically truthful. When he comes to relate his ugliest action, in section 11, he says, "I wish I could lie now and write that I had done it without premeditation." But he does not in fact lie; it matters to him to face the truth. His asides do not express real shifts and are more like rhetorical flourishes. (The only exception is perhaps the long excursus on Russian romantics in section 1, but this is clearly signalled as a digression, separate from the narration.)

Part I, then, is written by a man who embodies the condition he is talking about; part II is not. At the literary level one may conclude that Dostoyevsky has made his point, and there would be nothing more to be gained by upsetting the narrative conventions in order to go on and on, showing that the narrator is a fragmented personality. If part II had continued in the style of part I, we would never be able to identify the relevant events very firmly; they would be seen in flashes and impressionistically, from different and perhaps contradictory points of view. Doing this could make a point, of course, but not one that Dostoyevsky wants to make.

From the philosophical point of view, however, the transition is somewhat problematic. The difficulties in fact begin at the very end of part I, where the transition to part II is made. The Underground Man begins to talk about the need to be honest with oneself and the terrible difficulty of facing one's own discreditable or ludicrous actions and owning up to them. It is his proposal to be completely honest with himself that formally leads him to write down

the story "A Propos of the Sleet." Further, he puts great energy and effort into this attempt to be honest. And he also sees it as helpful to himself, in that it may "write out" and so release him from, a painful memory that troubles him. But where does this mysterious determination to complete a project come from, still more the energy to carry it through? The Underground Man as we have seen him lacks the motivation to complete any project. He veers, as he himself recognizes, between *zlost'* and inertia. To carry out such a project one needs to believe that it is worth carrying out; but precisely this kind of belief cannot motivate him to action in any sustained way. Further, why should he be troubled by the painful memory? This presupposes a self with enough solidity to be troubled by owning one particular action. Even before getting on to part II, the reader is worried by the strange definiteness with which the writer begins to shape up and tell the story. It is not that we are surprised that he is interested in himself; but we *are* surprised that he proposes to be interested in a sustained, purposive and even creative way.

If part II is to follow part I coherently, there has to be some indication of a change in the transitional passage. And there is, though a cryptic and brief one. In part I, section 11, the Underground Man, after extolling his own point of view, becomes ambivalent; he would not choose to be the normal man, but he envies him. Then in a dramatic turn-around, he accuses himself of lying: "I'm lying, because I know, as sure as two and two make four, that it isn't the underground which I am eager for, but which I shall never find. Devil take the underground!" He at once undermines this forceful statement by disclaiming what he has just written; but on the other hand it has been supported by the curious section 10, in which some ambivalence appears about the idealizing systems of thought about human nature which have been so belabored up to now. The Palace of Crystal now appears not as a distorted monstrosity, but as a possibly attractive ideal, disconcerting only by its unattainability. And the Underground Man unexpectedly not only turns on himself for hating it, but expresses *regret* for being so constituted as to want to stick out his tongue at it. "I would let my tongue be cut right out in mere gratitude if only things were so arranged that I never wanted to put it out again . . . Why was I made with such desires? Can I have been made for only one thing, to come at last to the conclusion that my whole make-up is nothing but a cheat? Is that the whole aim? I don't believe it."

These passages presuppose that the writer recognizes some standard of ideal human behavior. Clearly, it must be very different from the theories derided so far, but all the same some ideal is in question. He has spent most of part I discrediting the rational model of action on the grounds that it falsifies human nature; in this sense he is a realist. Yet now we find cryptic intimations of some kind of idealism, and then we move on to the narrator of part II, who has the honesty, consistency and strength of character to face unflinchingly the darkest parts of himself.

The difficulty here is increased by the fact that we know from a letter of Dostoyevsky's that the censor excised a passage in section 10 in which the alternative to the underground was specified in religious terms. "It would have been better not to print the next to last chapter at all, than to print it as it is, i.e., with sentences torn out and full of self-contradictions. But what can be done? Those swines of censors—where I mocked at everything and sometimes *blasphemed for form's sake*—that's let pass, but where from all this I deduced the *need of faith and Christ*—that is suppressed." (Quoted by Mochulsky, p. 256.)

The passages have been lost, and critics differ as to the importance they might have had. Peace, although he talks of "positive religious ideas," (p. 12) says that "the Underground Man's cult of his own will is as yet chaotic and lacking in direction" (p. 5). Boyce Gibson on the other hand says that Dostoyevsky "prepares the way for the reinstatement of religion on anti-rationalist terms."[11] Mochulsky goes much further: "The dream of a genuine earthly paradise is the central idea of the *Notes*," and, ". . . the fundamental lie of humanism is refuted: that it is possible to reeducate man through reason and advantage. Dostoyevsky objects: 'No, evil is not overcome by education, but by a miracle. What is impossible to man, is possible to God. Not reeducation, but *resurrection*. Here is the reason for the "need of faith and Christ.'"[12]

Clearly, these are very different interpretations of the work, and it remains an open question how positive an ideal the Underground Man was to have recognized at the end of part I. The present problem is affected by it insofar as it emphasizes the difference in coherence between the narrator of part I and that of part II. The narrator of part II is of course far from being a Christian, although he does sometimes take on a rather pious tone in commenting on his earlier self's "debaucheries" and "crimes." But he has at least developed to a point from which he can and does moralize about his earlier self. The story presents the way in which his present self faces and comes to terms with his past action. He accepts that he is capable of the meanest and most unforgivable actions. For Dostoyevsky this puts him in a state where he might possibly turn to Christ. Any morality or religion based on any appeal to the agent's self-interest, however refined, has been ruled out; a religious appeal of an a-rational kind which operates through abnegation of the self is the only appeal possible for him. Such an appeal, moreover, would make sense for him.

But turning to Christ could make little sense for the writer of part I; there is no self to turn, or rather no *moral* self; he can recognize justice and right on an intellectual level, but they leave him cold. The writer of part I is not in a state to recognize and be motivated by any kind of ideal, however remote from an agent-centered ideal. The writer of part II is, although he may not yet do so. The confusion and raggedness left by the censor's pencil in part I, section 10 point up the problematic way in which the writer of part I becomes the writer of part II.

The extent of the censor's damage here can of course be exaggerated. *Notes from Underground* is meant to be a strange and disturbing book. All the same, if one interprets part I as illustrating, in the way it is written, a

philosophical point basic to Dostoyevsky's design, then it is hard to see the whole book as a unity.

IV

Insofar as Dostoyevsky's work, and *Notes from Underground* in particular, has been considered philosophically interesting, it has generally been in connection with existentialism. This is certainly true of the article on Dostoyevsky by Edward Wasiolek in *The Encyclopedia of Philosophy,* for example. Dostoyevsky is "considered a forerunner of existentialist thought." "The underground man is Dostoyevsky's totally free man. He carries revolt against limitation to its extreme and raises it to a philosophical principle. Like the existentialists who were to follow three-quarters of a century later, he is *en marge*; he is in revolt not only against society, but also against himself, not once, not only today or tomorrow, but eternally." It may seem unusual to look to Dostoyevsky for illumination of philosophical problems of "practical reason" and "action" that have occupied philosophers in a more analytic tradition. But the richness of a work can sometimes be best appreciated by seeing how it allows fruitful readings within quite different traditions. I am not suggesting that my interpretation of *Notes from Underground* is more justified or privileged than the more customary ones. Arguably, it is much further from any explicit thoughts that Dostoyevsky himself may have had about the book as he wrote it by his wife's deathbed. But I do think that it is legitimate to see the work as in fact illustrating a deep and troubling problem at the heart of what is at present the most prominent and plausible philosophical theory of action.

Notes

[1] For the relations of the books, see: Leonid Grossman, *Dostoyevsky: A biography,* translated by Mary Mackley (London: Allen Lane, 1971), pp. 310-311; Richard Peace, *Dostoyevsky: An Examination of the Major Novels* (Cambridge: Cambridge University Press, 1971), p. 7, 10-11, n. 3; Konstantin Mochulsky, *Dostoyevsky: his life and work,* translated by Michael A. Minihan (Princeton: Princeton University Press, 1967), p. 251.

[2] Cf. Mochulsky: "The dreamer-romantic of the forties has in the sixties been transformed into a cynic-paradoxalist. . . . The underground man's social and historical condition is defined by the same marks which earlier characterized the dreamer's state. This is 'one of the representatives of a generation still living,' i.e., an intellectual of the 'Petersburg period' of Russian history, poisoned by European culture, divorced from the soil and the people, an historical type who 'not only can, but also must exist in our society'" (pp. 244-5). Grossman: "It is as if he was trying to pay back the spiritual leaders of his youth for the terrible ordeals of his years as a convict" (p. 310). Some of the characteristics of the ineffectual dreamer-idealist foreshadow the hostile portrait of Stepan Verkhovensky in *The Devils*.

[3] More accurately we should call him the Underfloor Man. *Podpol'ye* means "under the floor," and *iz podpol'ya* has suggestions of something nasty creeping out from under the floorboards, rather then the more heroic overtones acquired by the English "underground."

[4] To simplify rather crudely: I am thinking of moral theories of a roughly "Aristotelian" kind, which, while not egoistic, nonetheless assume

that morality is an agent-centered affair, that it is part and parcel of the practical reasoning the agent carries on in his situation in the world. Nothing said here touches moral theories of a radically different type, e.g. Kantian theories.

[5] The most important here are: "Actions, Reasons and Causes," *Journal of Philosophy* 1963, pp. 685-700; "How is Weakness of the Will Possible?", in Joel Feinberg, ed., *Moral Concepts* (Oxford: Oxford University Press, 1969), pp. 93-113; "Freedom to Act" in Ted Honderich, ed., *Essays on Freedom of Action* (London: Routledge and Kegan Paul, 1973), pp. 139-156; "Agency" in Robert Binkley, Richard Bronaugh, and Antonio Marras, eds., *Agent, Action and Reason* (Oxford: Blackwell, 1971), pp. 3-25.

[6] The matter is complex; for a sharp discussion of the issues involved see Thomas Nagel, *The Possibility of Altruism* (Oxford: Clarendon Press, 1970).

[7] In what Dostoyevsky says about will we do find incoherent exaggeration, as that the individual's will is opposed not merely to philosophical and scientific theories but to mathematical necessity; it is an exercise of the individual's will to want two and two to equal five. This confusion is a consequence of Dostoyevsky's hasty and uncritical lumping-together of very different things under the heading "laws of nature."

[8] This is a very sketchy and vague gesture towards the problems of character and action. See Myles Burnyeat, "Virtues in Action," in Gregory Vlastos, ed., *The Philosophy of Socrates* (New York: Doubleday, 1971), pp. 209-234; N. Dent, "Virtues and Actions," *Philosophical Quarterly* 1975, pp. 318-335.

[9] There is a problem here of "self-ascription" analogous to that of ascribing evil traits of character to oneself; see Margaret Gilbert, "Vices and Self-Knowledge," *Journal of Philosophy* 1971, pp. 443-453. But the problem is more salient in the case of *zlost'*.

[10] Mochulsky says that the second part "is joined to the first stylistically" (p. 257). But his grounds for this refer in fact not to style at all but to continuity of themes: "the inner dialogue becomes external, the fight is transferred from the sphere of ideas into the plane of life, the imaginary enemies are embodied in real ones."

[11] Alexander Boyce Gibson, *The Religion of Dostoyevsky* (London, 1973), p. 81.

[12] Mochulsky, pp. 256 and 257. Mochulsky significantly finds it hard to explain why Dostoyevsky "never reestablished the original text in subsequent editions. Dostoyevsky's 'philosophy of tragedy' has remained without its mystical consummation" (p. 257). This fact remains "strange"—surely an inadequate account if the censored ideas were in fact the whole point of the work.

Tzvetan Todorov (essay date 1978)

SOURCE: "*Notes from the Underground*," in *Genres in Discourse*, translated by Catherine Porter, Cambridge University Press, 1990, pp. 72-92.

[*In the following essay, originally published in French in 1978, Todorov explores* Notes from the Underground *as a semiotically complex text that, in addition to being polemical and parodic, critiques master-slave and self-other ideologies.*]

> In a bookshop my hand just happened to come to rest on *L'Esprit souterrain,* [*Notes from the Underground*] a recent French translation. . . . The instinct of affinity (or what shall I call it?) spoke to me instantaneously—my joy was beyond bounds.
>
> Friedrich Nietzsche[1]

> I believe that with *Notes from the Underground* we reach the peak of Dostoevsky's career. I consider this book (and I am not alone) the capstone of his entire work.
>
> André Gide[2]

> *Notes from the Underground* . . . : no other text by Dostoevsky has exerted more influence on twentieth-century thought or technique.
>
> George Steiner[3]

Many more such testimonies could be cited, but there is hardly any need. The centurality of this text for Dostoevsky's work is a commonplace today, paralleling its centrality in the Dostoevsky myth that characterizes our era.

Dostoevsky's reputation may be assured, but the same cannot be said for the exegesis of his work. Countless critical texts have been devoted to him, as one might expect; the problem is that they deal only rarely with Dostoevsky's texts. The man had the misfortune of living an eventful life. What erudite biographer could resist the attraction of the prison years, the passion for gambling, the epilepsy, the tumultuous love affairs? Biographers who get beyond this level face a second obstacle. Dostoevsky was passionately interested in the philosophical and religious problems of his time; he transmitted his passion to his characters so that his books are infused with it. Thus his critics rarely speak of "Dostoevsky-the-writer," as people used to say. They all focus enthusiastically on his "ideas," forgetting that these ideas come embedded in novels. Furthermore, even if the biographers had adopted a different perspective, they could not have avoided the danger in its inverse form: one can hardly study Dostoevsky's "technique" without regard to the great ideological debates that animate his novels (Shklovsky claimed that *Crime and Punishment* was simply a detective novel with just one odd feature, namely that its suspense was induced by its interminable philosophical debates). To propose a reading of Dostoevsky today is in a sense to take up a challenge: one must manage to see Dostoevsky's "ideas" and his "technique" simultaneously, without unduly privileging one or the other.

Interpretive criticism (as distinguished from erudite criticism) habitually makes the mistake of declaring (1) that Dostoevsky is a *philosopher,* "literary form" notwithstanding, and (2) that Dostoevsky is *a* philosopher, whereas even the observer with the fewest possible preconceptions is struck at once by the diversity of the philosophical, moral, and psychological concepts that are juxtaposed in his work. As Bakhtin writes, at the beginning of a study to which we shall have occasion to return: "Any acquaintance with the voluminous literature on Dostoevsky leaves the impression that one is dealing not with a *single* author-artist who wrote novels and stories but with a number of philosophical statements by *several* author-thinkers. Raskolnikov, Myshkin, Stavrogin, Ivan Karamazov, the Grand Inquisitor, and others."[4]

More than any other of Dostoevsky's works except perhaps the "Legend of the Grand Inquisitor," *Notes from the Underground* is the text most responsible for the situation I have just described. This text has tended to give readers the impression of possessing direct testimony by Dostoevsky-the-ideologue. Thus we shall have to begin with this text if we wish to read Dostoevsky today, or, more generally, if we wish to understand his role in that endlessly changing whole we call *literature.*

Notes from the Underground is divided into two parts, called "Underground" and "A Propos of the Wet Snow."[5] Dostoevsky himself describes them as follows: "In this extract, entitled 'Underground,' the person introduces himself and his views and, as it were, tries to explain those causes which have not only led, but also were bound to lead, to his appearance in our midst. In the subsequent extract 'A Propos of the Wet Snow' we shall reproduce this person's *Notes* proper, dealing with certain events of his life" (107, note). It is in Part One, the narrator's plea for the defense, that readers have always found Dostoevsky's most "remarkable" ideas exposed. We too shall enter into the labyrinth of this text through Part One—without yet knowing where or how we shall be able to get out.

The Narrator's Ideology

The first theme taken up by the narrator is consciousness (*soznanie*). In this context, the term is opposed not to the unconscious but to lack of self-consciousness. The narrator depicts two types of men: one is simple and direct (*neposredstvennyu*), "*l'homme de la nature et de la vérité*" ["the man of nature and truth"] in French in the text who, when he acts, possesses no image of his own action; the other is conscious man. For the latter, every action is accompanied by its image, arising in his consciousness. What is worse, the image appears before the action has taken place and thereby renders the action impossible. The man of consciousness cannot be the man of action. "For the direct, the inevitable, and the legitimate result of consciousness is to make all action impossible, or—to put it differently—consciousness leads to thumb-twiddling. . . . Let me repeat, and repeat most earnestly: all plain men and men of action are active only because they are dull-witted and mentally underdeveloped" (122).

As an example let us take the case of an insult that would "normally" lead to revenge. This is indeed how men of action behave. "They are, let us assume, so seized by the feeling of revenge that while that feeling lasts there is nothing but that feeling left in them. Such a man goes straight to his goal, like a mad bull, with lowered horns, and only a stone wall perhaps will stop him" (115). The same cannot be said of the man of consciousness. "I argued that a man revenges himself because he finds justice in it. This of course means that he has found a primary cause, a basis, namely, justice. . . . But I can't for the life of me see any justice here, and therefore if I should start revenging myself, it would merely be out of spite. Now spite, of course, could get the better of anything, of all my doubts, and so could very well take the place of any primary cause just because it is not a cause. But what can I do if I have not even spite . . . Besides, my feeling of bitterness, too, is subject to the process of disintegration as a result of those damned laws of consciousness. One look and the object disappears into thin air, your reasons evaporate, there is no guilty man, the injury is no longer an injury but just fate, something in the nature of toothache for which no one can be blamed, and consequently there is only one solution left, namely, knocking your head against the wall as hard as you can" (123).

The narrator begins by deploring this excess of consciousness ("I assure you, gentlemen, that to be too acutely conscious is a disease, a real, honest-to-goodness disease. It would have been quite sufficient for the business of everyday life to possess the ordinary human consciousness, that is to say, half or even a quarter of the share which falls to the lot of an intelligent man of our unhappy nineteenth century" [111]); but at the end of his argument he observes that excessive consciousness is nevertheless the lesser of evils: "And though at the beginning I did argue that consciousness was the greatest misfortune to man, yet I know that man loves it and will not exchange it for any satisfaction" (140). "And, finally, gentlemen, it is much better to do nothing at all! Better passive awareness!" (142).

The corollary to this assertion is the solidarity between consciousness and suffering. Consciousness provokes suffering, condemning man to inaction, but at the same time it results from suffering. "Suffering! Why, it's the sole cause of consciousness!" (140). Here a third term, *pleasure,* intervenes and we find ourselves confronting a very "Dostoevskyan" statement; for the time being, I shall simply present it without attempting an explanation. On several occasions, the narrator declares that at the heart of the greatest suffering, provided he becomes fully conscious of it, he will find a source of enjoyment, "pleasure that sometimes reaches the highest degree of voluptuousness" (120). Here is an example: "It got so far that I felt a sort of secret, abnormal, contemptible delight when, on coming home on one of the foulest nights in Petersburg, I used to realise intensely that again I had been guilty of some particularly dastardly action that day, and that once more it was no earthly use crying over spilt milk; and inwardly, secretly, I used to go on nagging myself, worrying myself, accusing myself, till at last the bitterness I felt turned into a sort of shameful, damnable sweetness, and finally, into real, positive delight! Yes, into delight! . . . Let me explain it to you. The feeling of delight was there just because I was so intensely aware of my own degradation; because I felt myself that I had come up against a blank wall; that no doubt, it was bad, but that it couldn't be helped . . ."

(112-13). And in another passage: "And it is just in that cold and loathsome half-despair and half-belief—in that conscious burying oneself alive for grief for forty years—in that intensely perceived, but to some extent uncertain, helplessness of one's position—in all that poison of unsatisfied desires that have turned inwards—in that fever of hesitations, firmly taken decisions, and regrets that follow almost instantaneously upon them—that the essence of that delight I have spoken of lies" (116-17).

This suffering that conscious reckoning transforms into delight may also be purely physical, as for example with toothache. Here is the description of an "educated man" on the third day of his suffering: "His groans become nasty and offensively ill-tempered groans, and go on for days and nights. And yet he knows perfectly well that he is doing no good with his groaning; he knows better than anyone that he is merely irritating and worrying himself and others for nothing; he knows that the audience before whom he is performing with such zeal and all his family are listening to him with disgust, that they don't believe him in the least, and that in their hearts they know that, if he wished, he could have groaned differently and more naturally, without such trills and flourishes, and that he is only amusing himself out of spite and malice. Well, all those apprehensions and infamies are merely the expression of sensual pleasure" (120). This is what is called the *masochism* of the underground man.

Apparently without transition, the narrator moves on to his second major theme, reason, its role in man, and the value of behavior that attempts to conform exclusively to reason. The argument goes roughly as follows. (1) Reason can never know anything but the "reasonable," that is, only a "twentieth part" of the human being. (2) The essential part of the human being is constituted by desire, by the will, which is not reasonable. "What does reason know? Reason only knows what it has succeeded in getting to know (certain things, I suppose, it will never know; this may be poor comfort, but why not admit it frankly?), whereas human nature acts as a whole, with everything that is in it, consciously, and unconsciously, and though it may commit all sorts of absurdities, it persists" (133). "Reason is an excellent thing. There is no doubt about it. But reason is only reason, and it can only satisfy the reasoning ability of man, whereas volition is a manifestation of the whole of life, I mean, of the whole of human life, including reason with all its concomitant head-scratchings" (ibid.). (3) It is thus absurd to seek to establish a way of life—and impose it on others—on the basis of reason alone. "For instance, you want to cure man of his old habits and reform his will in accordance with the demands of science and common sense. But how do you know that man not only could but *should* be remade like that? And what leads you to conclude that human desires must *necessarily* be reformed? In short, how do you know that such a reformation will be a gain to man?" (140). Dostoevsky thus denounces the totalitarian determinism that underlies attempts to explain all human actions by referring to the laws of reason.

His own reasoning is based on arguments, and entails in turn certain conclusions. The arguments are of two sorts.

Some are drawn from collective experience, from the history of humanity: the evolution of civilization has not brought about the reign of reason, there is as much absurdity in the modern world as in ancient society. "Well, just take a good look round you: rivers of blood are being spilt, and in the jolliest imaginable way, like champagne" (128). The other arguments derive from the narrator's personal experience: not all desires can be explained by reason; if they could be, man would have acted differently—deliberately, in defiance of reason; the theory of absolute determinism is therefore false; against that theory the narrator defends the right to act on impulse (this is what Gide takes from Dostoevsky). Moreover, the love of suffering is contrary to reason, yet it exists (as we saw earlier and as the narrator reminds us here: "And man does love suffering very much sometimes. He loves it passionately. That is an undeniable fact" [139-40]). There is finally one other argument, intended to ward off a potential objection. Is it not the case that the majority of human actions are directed, at all events, toward reasonable goals? Here the answer is yes, but only superficially. In fact, even in carrying out an apparently reasonable action, man obeys a different principle: he accomplishes the action for its own sake, and not to achieve a result. "The important point is not where [the path] leads but that it should lead somewhere" (138). "But man is a frivolous and unaccountable creature, and perhaps, like a chess-player, he is only fond of the process of achieving his aim, but not of the aim itself. And who knows (it is impossible to be absolutely sure about it), perhaps the whole aim mankind is striving to achieve on earth merely lies in this incessant process of achievement, or (to put it differently) in life itself, and not really in the attainment of any goal" (138-9).

The conclusions drawn from this assertion apply to all social reformers (including revolutionaries), for such people imagine that they know man inside out, and from what is in fact partial knowledge they have derived the image of an ideal society, a "crystal palace." Since their knowledge of man is inadequate, their conclusions are mistaken; consequently, what they offer him is not a palace but a tenement, even a hencoop, or an anthill. "You see, if it were not a palace but a hencoop, and if it should rain, I might crawl into it to avoid getting wet, but I would never pretend that the hencoop was a palace out of gratitude to it for sheltering me from the rain. You laugh and you tell me that in such circumstances even a hencoop is as good as a palace. Yes, I reply, it certainly is if the only purpose in life is not to get wet. . . . For the time being, however, I refuse to accept a hencoop for a palace" (141). Totalitarian determinism is not only erroneous, it is dangerous: by dint of viewing men as cogs in the machinery, or as "domestic animals," one risks leading them into such a condition. This is what is called Dostoevsky's *antisocialism* (his conservatism).

The Drama of Speech

If *Notes from the Underground* were limited to Part One, and if this part were limited to the ideas we have just been discussing, the book's reputation would be hard to account for. Not that the narrator's assertions are inconsistent; nor should they be viewed from the distorted perspective of today and denied any originality. More than one hundred years have gone by since the publication of the *Notes* (1864), and we have become too accustomed since then, perhaps, to think in terms approaching Dostoevsky's. Even so, the philosophical, ideological, and scientific value of the author's declarations alone certainly does not suffice to distinguish this book from countless others.

But authorial pronouncements are not what we read, when we open *Notes from the Underground.* What we encounter is not a collection of thoughts but a narrative, a work of fiction. Dostoevsky's first real innovation consists in the miracle of this metamorphosis. The issue here is not a simple opposition of form to content. The notion of overcoming the incompatibility between fiction and nonfiction, between the "mimetic" and the "discursive," is also an "idea," and one to be reckoned with. We have to resist the temptation to reduce the work to isolated statements taken out of context and attributed directly to Dostoevsky the thinker. Now that we are familiar with the substance of the arguments that are to be presented, we need to see how these arguments are conveyed. For instead of observing the straightforward presentation of an idea, we are going to witness its *enactment.* And as befits a dramatic situation, several *roles* will be available to us.

A first role is attributed to the texts invoked or cited. From the time of its first publication onward, *Notes from the Underground* has been perceived by the public as a polemical text. In the 1920s, V. Komarovich explicated most of the references he found dispersed or dissimulated in the work. The text refers to a set of ideological propositions that dominated Russian radical and liberal thinking between 1840 and 1870. The expression "the sublime and beautiful," always put in quotes, refers to Kant, Schiller, and German idealism; "*l'homme de la nature et l'homme de la vérité*" refers to Rousseau (whose role is somewhat more complex, as we shall see); the positivist historian Buckle is cited by name. But the most direct adversary is a Russian contemporary: Nikolaï Chernyshevsky, guru of the radical youth of the 1860s, author of a utopian and didactic novel entitled *What Is To Be Done?* as well as several theoretical articles, one of which is called "On the Anthropological Principle in Philosophy." It is Chernyshevsky who defends totalitarian determinism, in the article cited as well as through the intermediary of the characters in his novel (Lopoukhov in particular). It is he, too, who sets another character (Vera Pavlovna) to dreaming in the crystal palace, in a scene that refers indirectly to Fourier's phalanstery and to the writings of Fourier's Russian followers. At no point, then, is the text of *Notes from the Underground* simply the impartial exposition of an idea; we are given a polemical dialogue in which the other interlocutor was quite present in the minds of contemporary readers.

Alongside this first role, which we might call "they" (referring to earlier discourses by others), there appears a second, that of "you," or the represented interlocutor. This "you" appears in the very first sentence, more precisely in the suspension points that separate "I am a sick man" from "I am a spiteful man" (107): the tone changes between the first clause and the second because the narrator hears or anticipates a pitying reaction to his first statement and goes on to reject it in the second. Shortly afterward, "you" appears in the text: "I don't suppose you will understand that" (108). "But doesn't it seem to you, gentlemen, that I might possibly be apologising to you for something? Asking you to forgive me for something? Yes, I'm sure it does . . ." (109). "If, irritated with all this idle talk (and I feel that you are irritated), you were to ask me . . ." (110), and so forth.

This direct address to the imaginary listener and the formulation of his presumed responses is pursued throughout the book. However, the image of "you" does not remain stable. In the first six chapters of Part One, "you" simply denotes an average reaction, that of Everyman, who is listening to this fevered confession, is suspicious, irritated, and so forth. In the seventh chapter, however, and through chapter ten, the role is modified: "you" is no longer satisfied with a passive reaction, he takes a position and his interventions become as lengthy as the narrator's. We are familiar with this position: it belongs to "they" (let us say, to simplify things, that it is Chernyshevsky's). It is to "they" that the narrator now speaks when he declares: "You gentlemen have, so far as I know, drawn up your entire list of positive human values by taking the averages of statistical figures and relying on scientific and economic formulae" (126). It is to this second "you-they" that the narrator says: "You believe in the Crystal Palace, forever indestructible . . ." (140). Finally, in the last (eleventh) chapter, we return to the initial "you," and this "you" becomes at the same time thematized in the narrator's discourse: "Now, of course, I've made up all this speech of yours myself. It, too, comes from the dark cellar. I've been listening to your words for forty years through a crack in the ceiling. I have invented them myself. It is the only thing I did invent" (144).

Finally, the last role in this drama belongs to "I," to an "I" that is of course doubled, for as we know, every appearance of "I," every naming of a speaker, posits a new enunciatory context in which it is another "I," not yet named, that is speaking. Here is at once the most powerful and the most original feature of this discourse: its aptitude to mix the linguistic freely with the metalinguistic, to contradict the one with the other, to pursue an infinite regression in the metalinguistic domain. Indeed, the explicit representation of the speaker allows for a series of figures. Here is the contradiction: "I was a spiteful civil servant" (108). On the next page: "Incidentally, I was rather exaggerating just now when I said that I was a spiteful civil servant" (109). The metalinguistic commentary: "I was rude and took pleasure in being rude. Mind you, I never accepted any bribes, so that I had at least to find something to compensate myself for that. (A silly joke, but I shan't cross it out. I wrote it thinking it would sound very witty, but now that I have seen myself that I merely wanted to indulge in a bit of contemptible bragging. I shall let it stand on purpose!)" (108). Or in another passage: "Let me continue calmly about the people with strong nerves . . ." (117). Self-refutation: "I assure you most solemnly, gentlemen, that there is not a word I've just written I believe in!" (143). Infinite regression (an example from Part Two): "Of course, on the other hand, you are quite right. As a matter of fact, it is mean and contemptible. And what is even meaner is that now I should be trying to justify myself to you. Enough of this, though, or I should never finish: things are quite sure to get meaner and meaner anyway" (164). And the entire eleventh chapter of Part One is devoted to the problem of writing: Why write? For whom? The explanation the narrator proposes (he writes for himself, to get rid of his painful memories) is in fact only one among several that are suggested at other levels of rereading.

The drama that Dostoevsky staged in **Notes** is the drama of speech, with its perennial protagonists: the present discourse, "this"; the absent discourses of others, "they"; the "you" of the addressee, always ready to turn itself into a speaker; and finally the "I" of the subject of the enunciation—which appears only when an enunciation enunciates it. The utterance, caught up in this play, loses all stability, all objectivity, all impersonality. Absolute ideas, the intangible crystallizations of a forever-forgotten process, have ceased to exist; ideas have become as fragile as the world around them.

The new status of ideas is one of the very points clarified in Bakhtin's study of Dostoevsky's poetics (a study that picks up on remarks by several earlier Russian critics: Ivanov, Grossman, Askoldov, Engelgardt). In the non-Dostoevskyan novelistic world, which Bakhtin calls monologic, ideas can have two functions. They may express the opinion of the author (and be attributed to a character only for convenience); or, if they are ideas to which the author no longer adheres, they may serve as psychic or social characteristics of a character (by metonymy). But as soon as an idea is taken seriously, it no longer belongs to anyone. "Everything [in a plurality of consciousnesses] that is essential and true is incorporated into the unique context of 'consciousness in general' and deprived of its individuality. That which is individual, that which distinguishes one consciousness from another and from others, is cognitively not essential and belongs to the realm of an individual human being's psychical organization and limitation. From the point of view of truth, there are no individual consciousnesses. Idealism recognizes only one principle of cognitive individualization: *error*. True judgments are not attached to a personality, but correspond to some unified, systematically monologic context. Only error individualizes."[6]

According to Bakhtin. Dostoevsky's "Copernican revolution" consists precisely in his annihilation of the impersonality and solidity of ideas. Here ideas are always "interindividual and intersubjective." "His form-shaping worldview does not know an *impersonal truth* and in his works there are no detached, impersonal verities" (96). In other words, ideas lose their singular, privileged status; they cease to be immutable essences and instead are integrated in a broader circuit of signification, in an immense symbolic game. For earlier literature (obviously such a

generalization is unfair), ideas are pure signifieds; they *are signified* (by words or acts) but do not *signify* themselves (except as psychological characteristics). For Dostoevsky and to varying degrees some of his contemporaries (like the Nerval of *Aurélia*), ideas are not the *result* of a process of symbolic representation, they are an integral *part* of it. Dostoevsky removes the discursive/mimetic opposition by giving ideas the role not only of *symbolized* but also of *symbolizer,* he transforms the idea of representation not by rejecting or limiting it but, quite to the contrary (although the results may look the same), by extending it into areas that had previously been foreign to it. In Pascal's *Pensées,* as in **Notes from the Underground,** one can find observations about a heart that reason does not know; but one cannot imagine the *Pensées* transformed into an "internal dialogue" in which the voice that is making pronouncements at the same time denounces itself, contradicts itself, accuses itself of lying, judges itself ironically, makes fun of itself—and of us.

When Nietzsche says of Dostoevsky that "I prize his work . . . as the most valuable psychological material known to me,"[7] he is taking part in a secular tradition that reads the psychological, the philosophical, and the social in the literary realm—but not literature itself, or discourse; a tradition that fails to see that Dostoevsky's innovation is far greater on the symbolic than on the psychological level, which here is only one element among others. Dostoevsky alters our ideas of ideas and our representation of representation.

But is there a relation between this theme *of* dialogue and the themes evoked *in* the dialogue? . . . Perhaps the labyrinth has not yet disclosed all its secrets. Let us try another path, by plunging into a still unexplored zone: the second oart of the book. Who knows, perhaps the indirect path will turn out to be the faster.

Part Two is more traditionally narrative; still, it does not exclude the elements of the drama of speech that we have observed in Part One. "I" and "you" behave as before, but "they" changes and takes on greater importance. Rather than entering into a dialogue or polemic—thus into a syntagmatic relation—like the earlier texts, the narrative takes the form of *parody* (a paradigmatic relation), by imitating and overturning the situations of earlier narratives. In a sense, **Notes from the Underground** has the same goal as *Don Quixote*: to make fun of a certain contemporary literature, attacking it as much through parody as through open polemics. The role played by chivalry novels in Cervantes's text is played in Dostoevsky's by Russian and Western Romantic literature in two different ways. On the one hand, the hero participates in situations that parody the peripeties of Chernyshevsky's *What Is To Be Done,* for example, in the meetings with the officer or with Lisa. Lopoukhov, in Chernyshevsky's novel has the habit of never giving way in the street except to women and old men; when on one occasion a rude character fails to stand aside, Lopoukhov, a man of great physical strength, simply shoves him into the ditch. Another character, Kirsanov, meets a prostitute and rescues her from her condition with his love (he is a medical student, just like Lisa's admirer).

The parodic intention is never acknowledged as such in the text. On the other hand, the underground man himself is always aware that he is behaving (or wants to behave) like the Romantic characters from the early part of the century. Various works and protagonists are mentioned in this context: Gogol (*Dead Souls, Diary of a Madman,* and, by allusion, *The Overcoat*), Goncharov (*A Common Story*), Nekrasov, Byron (*Manfred*), Pushkin (*The Shot*), Lermontov (*Masquerade*), George Sand, even Dostoevsky himself indirectly (*The Insulted and the Injured*). In other words, the liberal literature of the thirties and forties is mocked within situations borrowed from the more radical writers of the sixties, in such a way as to constitute an indirect indictment of both groups.

In contradistinction to Part One, the main role is played in Part Two by liberal and Romantic literature. The narrator-hero is an admirer of Romantic literature and would like to model his behavior on it. However—and here is where parody comes in—this behavior is in reality dictated by a totally different logic, which ensures the failure of the Romantic projects one after another. The contrast is quite striking, for the narrator is not content with vague and nebulous dreams; he imagines each scene to come in detail, sometimes several times in succession, and his predictions are always wrong. Let us take the case of the officer, first of all: he dreams (and we shall see in what respect the dream is Romantic) of a quarrel at the end of which he himself will be thrown out the window ("I would have given anything at that moment for a real, a more regular, a more decent, and a more, so to speak, *literary* quarrel!" [*Notes from the Underground,* 154]); in fact he is treated like someone who is unworthy of a quarrel, someone who does not even exist. Then, in connection with the same officer, he dreams of a reconciliation in love; but he only manages to bump into him—literally—"on the same social footing as he" (161). In the episode with Zverkov, he dreams of a party where everyone admires and loves him; the actual experience is intensely humiliating. With Lisa, finally, he cloaks himself in the most traditionally Romantic dream: "For instance, 'I'm saving Lisa just because she's coming regularly to see me and I'm talking to her. . . . I'm educating her, enlarging her mind. At last I notice that she is in love with me. I pretend not to understand,'" and so on (220). However, when Lisa arrives at his place, he treats her like a prostitute.

His dreams are even more Romantic when they are not followed by any specific action, as in the atemporal dream found in chapter 2: "For instance, I triumphed over everything; all of course lay in the dust at my feet, compelled of their own free will to acknowledge all my perfections, and I forgave them all. I was a famous poet and court chamberlain, and I fell in love; I became a multi-millionaire and at once devoted all my wealth to the improvement of the human race, and there and then confessed all my hideous and shameful crimes before all the people; needless to say, my crimes were, of course, not really hideous or shameful, but had much in them that was 'sublime and beautiful.' something in the style of Manfred" (163), and so forth. Or, in the Zverkov episode, when he anticipates three successive versions of a scene that will

never take place. In the first, Zverkov kisses his feet; in the second, they fight a duel; in the third, the narrator bitex Zverkov's hand, is sent to prison, and comes back fifteen years later to see his enemy: "'Look, monster, look at my hollow cheeks and my rags! I've lost everything—my career, my happiness, art, science, *the woman I loved,* and all through you. Here are the pistols. I've come to discharge my pistol and—and I forgive you!' And then I shall fire into the air, and he won't hear of me again. . . . I almost broke into tears, though I knew very well at that moment that the whole thing was *Silvio* and from Lermontov's *Masquarade*" (191-2).

All these dreams occur thus explicitly in the name of literature, a particular form of literature. When events threaten to turn out otherwise, the narrator calls them unliterary ("how paltry, *unliterary,* and commonplace the whole affair would be" [176]). Thus two logics, two conceptions of life take shape: literary or bookish life, and reality, or real life. "We have all lost touch with life, we are all cripples, every one of us—more or less. We have lost touch so much that occasionally we cannot help feeling a sort of disgust with 'real life,' and that is why we are so angry when people remind us of it. Why, we have gone so far that we look upon 'real life' almost as a sort of burden, and we are all agreed that 'life' as we find it in books is much better. . . . Leave us alone without any books, and we shall at once get confused, lose ourselves . . ." (239-40). Thus speaks the disillusioned narrator at the end of *Notes from the Underground.*

Master and Slave

What we have here is not just a rejection of daydreams. The events represented are not organized solely so as to refute the Romantic conception of man, but in terms of their own internal logic. This logic, never formulated but endlessly represented, explains all the apparently aberrant actions of the narrator and the people around him: it is the logic of master and slave, or, as Dostoevsky says, of "scorn" and "humiliation." Far from being the illustration of capriciousness, irrationality, and spontaneity, the behavior of the underground man obeys a very precise schema, as René Girard has already pointed out.

The underground man lives in a world with three levels: inferior, equal, superior. However, these values form a homogeneous series only on the surface. In the first place, the term "equal" can only exist when it is negated: the distinguishing feature of the master-slave relation is its exclusivity, its rejection of any third term. He who aspires to equality proves by that very fact that he does not possess it; he thus finds himself cast in the role of slave. As soon as one person occupies one pole of the relationship, his partner is automatically relegated to the other.

But being a master is no easier than being a slave. In fact, as soon as one finds one's own superiority confirmed, the superiority disappears by that very token: for superiority exists, paradoxically, only on condition that it be exercised with respect to equals. If one truly believes that the slave is inferior, superiority has no meaning. More precisely, superiority loses its meaning when the master perceives not only his relation to the slave but also the image of that relation; or, to put it another way, when he becomes *conscious* of it. This is precisely where we find the difference between the narrator and the other characters in *Notes from the Underground.* This difference may appear illusory at first glance. The narrator himself believes in it at the age of twenty-four: "Another thing that used to worry me very much at that time was the quite incontestable fact that I was unlike anyone and that there was no one like me. 'I am one, and they are *all,*' I thought—and fell into a melancholy muse" (149). But the narrator adds, sixteen years later: "From all that it can be seen that I was still a very young man" (ibid.). In fact, the difference exists solely in his own eyes; but that is enough. What makes him different from the others is the desire not to be different from them; in other words, his own consciousness, that very consciousness that he had exalted in Part One. As soon as one becomes conscious of the problem of equality, as soon as one declares that one wishes to become equal, one is declaring—in this world where only masters and slaves exist—that one is not equal, and thus—since only masters are "equal"—that one is inferior. Failure stalks the underground man at every turn: equality is impossible; superiority is devoid of meaning; inferiority is painful.

Let us take the first episode, the meeting with the officer. The narrator's desire to see himself thrown out the window might be thought odd, or it might be explained away by the "masochism" the narrator mentioned in Part One. The explanation, however, lies elsewhere, and if we judge his desire absurd, it is because we are taking into account only the explicitly posited acts, and not those they presuppose. Now a regulation quarrel *implies* the equality of the participants: only equals fight. (Nietzsche wrote—no doubt this was the psychology lesson he learned from Dostoevsky: "One does not hate as long as one still despises, but only those whom one esteems equal or higher."[8]) Obeying the same master-slave logic, the officer has to accept this proposition: to demand equality implies that one is inferior; the officer will thus behave like a superior. "He took me by the shoulders and, without a word of warning or explanation, silently carried me bodily from where I was standing to another place and passed me by as though he had not even noticed me" (*Notes from the Underground,* 154). And so our hero finds himself in the place of the slave.

Walled up in his bitterness, the underground man begins to dream—not exactly of revenge, but again of the state of equality. He writes the officer a letter (which he will not send) that is intended to get its recipient either to agree to a duel—implying the equality of the adversaries—or else bring him to the point where he would have "come running to me, fallen on my neck, and offered me his friendship. And how wonderful that would have been! Oh, how wonderfully we should have got on together!" (156)—in other words, to the equality of friendship.

Then the narrator discovers the path of vengeance. It consists in not giving way on Nevsky Avenue where both

men often walk. Once again, what he is dreaming of is equality. "'Why do you always have to step aside first?' I asked myself over and over again in a sort of hysterical rage, sometimes waking up at three o'clock in the morning. 'Why always you and not he? There's no law about it, is there? Why can't you arrange it so that each of you should make way for the other, as usually happens when two well-bred men meet in the street. He yields you half of his pavement and you half of yours, and you pass one another with mutual respect'" (158). And when the encounter takes place, the narrator notes: "I had put myself publicly on the same social footing as he" (161). This moreover is what explains the nostalgia he feels now for that unattractive creature ("I wonder how the dear fellow is getting on now" [161]).

The Zverkov incident obeys precisely the same logic. The underground man enters a room where old school friends are reunited. They too behave as if they do not notice him, which awakens in him the obsessive desire to prove he is their equal. Thus, learning that they are preparing to go out drinking in honor of another old comrade (who does not interest him in the slightest otherwise), he asks to participate in their festivities: to be like the others. Countless obstacles arise in his path; nevertheless, he is determined to surmount them and attend the dinner offered in Zverkov's honor. In his dreams, however, the narrator has no illusions: he sees himself either humiliated by Zverkov, or else, in turn, humiliating him. There is only the choice between self-abasement and contempt for others.

Zverkov arrives and behaves affably. But here again, the underground man reacts to what is implied, not what is explicit, and this very affability puts him on guard: "So he already considered himself infinitely superior to me in every respect, did he? . . . But what if, without the least desire to offend me, the fool had really got the preposterous idea into his head that he was immeasurably superior to me and could not look at me but with a patronizing air?" (178).

They are all seated at a round table; but the equality stops there. Zverkov and his friends make allusions to poverty, to the narrator's misfortunes, in short, to his inferiority—for they too obey the master-slave logic, and as soon as someone demands equality, they understand that he is in fact inferior. They cease to take notice of him, despite all his efforts. "It was quite impossible for anyone to abase himself more disgracefully and do it more willingly" (186). Then, on the first possible occasion, he again demands equality (to go to the whorehouse with them); he meets with rejection; new dreams of superiority follow, and so on.

The other role is not wholly denied him, however: he finds creatures weaker than himself in relation to whom he is master. But that brings him no satisfaction, for he cannot be master in the manner of the "man of action." He needs the process of becoming-a-master, not the state of superiority. This mechanism is evoked in abbreviated form in a school memory: "I did have a sort of friend once, but by that time I was already a tyrant at heart: I wanted to exercise complete authority over him, I wanted to implant a contempt for his surroundings in his heart. I demanded that he should break away from these surroundings, scornfully and finally. I frightened him with my passionate friendship. I reduced him to tears, to hysterics. He was a simple and devoted soul, but the moment I felt that he was completely in my power I grew to hate him and drove him from me, as though I only wanted him for the sake of gaining a victory over him, for the sake of exacting his complete submission to me" (174-5). For a conscious master, the slave offers no further interest once he has been reduced to submission.

But it is especially in the Lisa episode that the underground man finds himself at the other pole of the relationship. Lisa is a prostitute, at the bottom of the social scale: that is what allows the underground man for once to follow the dictates of the Romantic logic he cherishes, to be magnanimous and generous. But his victory is of so little moment that he can forget it: the very next day he is wholly preoccupied with his relationship with his masters. "But *obviously* that was not the chief and most important thing. What I had to do now, and that quickly too, was to save my reputation in the eyes of Zverkov and Simonov. That was the chief thing. And so preoccupied was I with the other affair that I forgot all about Lisa that morning" (215-16). He remembers her later only because he fears that when they next meet he will be unable to hang onto the superiority he had achieved. "Last night I seemed—er—a hero to her and—er—now—him!" (218). He fears that Lisa too may become *contemptuous* and that he will be once again *humiliated.* That is why the first question he asks her is "'Do you despise me, Lisa?'" (229). After a hysterical crisis, he begins to feel that "our parts were now completely changed, that she was the heroine now, while I was exactly the same crushed and humiliated creature as she had appeared to me that night—four days before . . ." (234). This triggers his desire to be master again; he possesses her, then hands her money as if she were a mere prostitute. But the state of mastery does not bring him pleasure, and all he wants is for Lisa to leave. Once she has gone, however, he discovers that she has not taken the money. Thus she is not inferior! She regains her full value in his eyes, and he rushes out after her. "Why? To fall on my knees before her, to sob with remorse, to kiss her feet, to beseech her to forgive me!" (238). Lisa was useless to him as a slave; she becomes necessary again as a potential master.

It is now clearer that the underground man's reveries are not external to the master-slave logic: they are the positive version of what the master's behavior represents negatively. The Romantic relation of equality or generosity presupposes superiority, just as the quarrel presupposes equality. Talking to Lisa about their first meeting, the narrator recognizes this fully: "'I had been humiliated, so I too wanted to show my power. That's what happened, and you thought I'd come there specially to save you, did you?'" (p. 231). "'Power was what I wanted then. I wanted sport. I wanted to see you cry. I wanted to humiliate you. To make you hysterical. That's what I wanted'" (ibid.). Not only is Romantic logic defeated at every turn by the

master-slave logic, it does not differ from master-slave logic; moreover, that is why "positive" dreams can alternate freely with "negative" ones.

The plot of Part Two of *Notes from the Underground,* taken as a whole, is merely an exploitation of these two basic figures in the master-slave game: the vain attempt to achieve equality, ending in humiliation; and the equally vain effort—for its results are ephemeral—to avenge oneself, which is only, in the best of cases, a compensatory device: one humiliates and despises, in order to have humiliated and despised. The first episode (involving the officer) presents a condensed version of both possibilities. Then the two modes appear in alternation, according to a principle of contrast: the underground man is humiliated by Zverkov and his comrades; he humiliates Lisa; he is again humiliated by his servant Apollon; he takes it out on Lisa. The parallelism of the situations is marked either by the identity of the character or by some resemblance in the details: thus Apollon "always lisped and minced his words" (222), while Zverkov speaks by "mouthing and lisping, which he never used to do before" (p. 178). The episode with Apollon, which dramatizes a concrete relation between master and servant, is emblematic of this set of hardly random incidents.

Being and Otherness

The underground man is continually driven to assume the role of slave. He suffers cruelly from this role, yet he seems to seek it out. Why? Because the logic of the master-slave relation itself is not an ultimate truth, it is a posited appearance concealing an essential presupposition that we now have to uncover. This center, this essence we are approaching holds a surprise in reserve for us, however: it consists in affirming the primordial nature of the relation with the other, in locating the essence of being in the other, in telling us that what is simple is double, and that the ultimate, undivided atom is made up of two. The underground man does not exist apart from his relation with the other, without the other's gaze. And not being is an even more distressing state than being nothing, than being a slave.

Man does not exist without the gaze of the other. The meaning of the gaze in *Notes from the Underground* may be misunderstood, however. In fact, references to it, which are numerous, seem at first glance to be inscribed within the master-slave logic. The narrator does not want to look at the others, for in doing so he would be recognizing their existence and by that very token granting them a privilege that he is not sure he has for himself; in other words, the gaze risks making him a slave. "When at work in the office I tried not to look at anyone . . ." (147). When he meets his old school friends, he insistently avoids their glances, he keeps his eyes fixed on his plate (180); "I just did my best not to look at them . . ." (185). When he looks at someone, he tries to put all his dignity—and thus his defiance—into his gaze. "I stared at him with hatred and malice" (155), he says about the officer; and regarding his school friends, "I looked at them impudently with leaden eyes" (182). Let us recall that the Russian words *prezirat'* and *nenavidt'*, to despise and to hate—terms used quite frequently in the text to describe just this feeling—both contain a root verb meaning to see or to look.

The others behave just the same way, with more success, most of the time. The officer passes by as though he has not seen him (154). Simonov tries not to look at him (170); his friends, once they are drunk, pay no attention to him (182). And when they do look at him, they do so just as aggressively, just as defiantly. Ferfichkin glares furiously at him (181). Trudolyubov throws "a disdainful glance in [his] direction" (183), and Apollon, his servant, specializes in scornful looks: "He started by fixing me with a stern glare which he kept up for several minutes at a time, particularly when he used to meet me or when I went out of the house. . . . He would suddenly and without any excuse whatsoever enter my room quietly and smoothly when I was either reading or pacing my room, and remain standing at the door, with one hand behind his back and one foot thrust forward, and stare fixedly at me. This time his stare was not only stern but witheringly contemptuous. If I suddenly asked him what he wanted, he would not reply, but continue to stare straight at me for a few more seconds, then he would purse his lips with a specially significant expression, turn round slowly, and slowly go back to his room" (223-4).

The rare occasions when the underground man manages to carry out his Romantic fantasies have to be analyzed from the same point of view. Success requires the total absence of any gaze. Not by coincidence, this is the scenario in the underground man's victorious encounter with the officer: "Suddenly, only three paces from my enemy, I quite unexpectedly made up my mind, shut my eyes, and—we knocked violently against each other, shoulder to shoulder" (160). The same scenario is played out, even more predictably, during the first encounter with Lisa. Very early in the conversation, the narrator tells us: "The candle went out. I could no longer make out her face" (196). Only at the very end, after his speechmaking is over, does he find "a box of matches and a candle-stick with a new unused candle" (213). Now it is precisely between these two moments of light that the underground man can make his romantic statements, can show the positive side of the master's face.

But this is merely the logic of the "literal," concrete gaze. In fact, in all these incidents, the underground man accepts the condition of inferiority, even seeks it out, because it allows the gaze of others to be fixed on himself, if only with scorn. The underground man is always mindful of the suffering that the humiliating gaze causes him; he goes after it nonetheless. To go to the home of his boss Anton Antonovich brings him no pleasure; the conversations he hears there are banal. "The usual topic of conversation was excise duties, the hard bargaining in the Senate, salaries, promotions, His Excellency, the best way to please him, etc., etc. I had the patience to sit like a damn fool beside these people for hours, listening to them, neither daring to speak to them, nor knowing what to say. I got more and more bored, broke out into a sweat, and was

in danger of getting an apoplectic stroke. But all this was good and useful to me" (165). Why? Because he had previously felt "an irresistible urge to plunge into social life" (164). He knows that Simonov despises him: "I suspected that he really loathed the sight of me . . . I could not help thinking that this particular gentleman must be sick and tired of me and that I was wasting my time going to see him" (166). But he goes on to explain that "such reflections merely spurred me on to put myself into an equivocal position" (ibid.). A gaze, even a master's gaze, is better than the absence of any gaze.

The entire scene with Zverkov and the schoolmates can be explained in the same way. The underground man needs their gaze; if he puts on distant airs, it is because he is waiting patiently "for them to speak to [him] first" (185). Subsequently, "I did my best to show them that I could do without them, at the same time deliberately stamping on the floor, raising myself up and down on my heels" (186). It is the same story with Apollon: he gets no use out of this crude and lazy servant, but he cannot let go of him either. "I could not get rid of him, as though he formed one chemical substance with me. . . . For some confounded reason Apollon seemed to be an integral part of my flat, and for seven years I could not get rid of him" (222-3). Here is the explanation of the irrational "masochism" reported by the narrator in Part One and relished by the critics. The underground man accepts suffering because the condition of a slave is finally the only one that assures him of the gaze of others; without that gaze, the human being does not exist.

In fact, Part One already explicitly contained that assertion, made on the basis of a postulate of failure: the underground man is precisely nothing, not even a slave, or, as he says, not even an insect. "Not only did I not become spiteful, I did not even know how to become anything, either spiteful or good, either a blackguard or an honest man, either a hero or an insect" (109). He dreams of being able to assert himself, if only through negative traits such as laziness, the absence of actions and good points. "I should have respected myself just because I should at least have been able to be lazy; I should at least have possessed one quality which might be mistaken for a positive one and in which I could have believed myself. Question—who is he? Answer—a loafer. I must say it would have been a real pleasure to have heard that said about myself, for it would have meant that a positive definition had been found for me and that there was something one could say about me" (124). For now he cannot even say that he is nothing (and get around the negation in the attribute); he *is not*, and the very verb of existence itself turns out to be denied. To be alone is no longer to be.

A great quasi-scientific debate occupies almost all the pages of ***Notes from the Underground,*** having to do with the very conception of man and his psychic structure. The underground man is seeking to prove that the conception opposed to his is not only amoral (it is amoral in a secondary, derivative way) but also inexact, false. The man of nature and truth, the simple and immediate man, imagined by Rousseau, is not only inferior to the conscious underground man; he does not even exist. Unified, simple, and indivisible man is a fiction. The very simplest is already dual; the human being has no existence prior to the other or independent of him. That indeed is why the dreams of "rational egoism" cherished by Chernyshevsky and his friends are condemned to failure, as is every theory that is not based upon the auality of being. This universality of the conclusions is asserted in the closing pages of *Notes*: "I have merely carried to extremes in my life what you have not dared to carry even halfway, and, in addition, you have mistaken your cowardice for common sense and have found comfort in that, deceiving yourselves" (240).

Thus in one and the same stroke the narrator rejects an essentialist conception of man and an objective vision of ideas; it is no accident that allusions to Rousseau are scattered throughout the text. Rousseau's confession was written *for others* but by an *autonomous* being; that of the underground man is written *for himself,* but he himself is already *double,* the others are in him, the outside is inside. Just as it is impossible to conceive of man as simple and autonomous, we have to transcend the idea of the autonomous text seen as an authentic expression of a subject, rather than as a reflection of other texts, as play among interlocutors. These are not two different problems, the one having to do with the nature of man, the other with language, one located among "ideas," the other in "form." We are talking about one and the same thing.

The Symbolic Game

Thus the apparently chaotic and contradictory aspects of *Notes from the Underground* turn out to be coherent. The moral masochism, the master-slave logic, the new status of the idea are all part of a single underlying structure, which is semiotic rather than psychic: the structure of alterity. Of all the essential elements singled out during our analysis, there remains just one whose place in the whole has not become apparent: the denunciations of the powers of reason, in Part One. Might these be a gratuitous attack on Dostoevsky's part against his enemy-friends the Socialists? But as we finish reading the text, we shall discover their place too, and their meaning.

In fact, I have left aside one of the most important characters in Part Two: Lisa. I have done so deliberately, for her behavior does not obey any of the mechanisms described up to now. For example, let us observe her gaze: it resembles neither the master's nor the slave's. "I caught sight of a fresh, young, somewhat pale face, with straight dark eyebrows, and with a serious, as it were, surprised look in her eyes" (193). "Suddenly, close beside me, I saw two wide-open eyes observing me intently and curiously. The look in those eyes was coldly indifferent and sullen, as though it were utterly detached, and it made me feel terribly depressed" (194-5). At the end of their meeting: "It was altogether a different face, altogether a different look from a few hours ago—sullen, mistrustful, and obstinate. Now her eyes were soft and beseeching, and at the same time trustful, tender, and shy. So do children look at people they are very fond of and from whom they expect some favour. She had light-brown eyes, beautiful

and full of life, eyes which could express love as well as sullen hatred" (213-14). At his place, after having witnessed a painful scene, her gaze retains its uniqueness: "she regarded me uneasily" (228); "she glanced at me a few times in mournful perplexity" (230); and so on.

The crucial moment in the story recounted in *Notes from the Underground* comes when Lisa, insulted by the narrator, reacts abruptly and in an unexpected manner, a manner that does not belong to the master-slave logic. The surprise is such that the narrator himself has to emphasize it: "But here a very odd thing happened. I was so used to imagining everything and to thinking of everything as it happened in books, and to picturing to myself everything in the world as I had previously made it up in my dreams, that at first I could not all at once grasp the meaning of this occurrence. What occurred was this: Lisa, humiliated and crushed by me, understood much more than I imagined" (233).

How does she react? "She suddenly jumped up from her chair with a kind of irresistible impulse and, all drawn towards me but still feeling very shy and not daring to move from her place, held out her hands to me. . . . It was here that my heart failed me. Then she rushed to me flung her arms round my neck, and burst into tears" (233). Lisa rejects both the master's role and the slave's; she does not wish to dominate or to take pleasure in her own suffering; she loves the other *for himself.* It is this outburst of light that makes *Notes* a much clearer work than it is usually considered to be; it is this very scene that allows the narrative to come to a close. While on the surface the narrative is presented as a fragment chopped off through the whim of fate, in fact the book could not have ended earlier, and there is no reason for it to go further; as "Dostoevsky" says in the closing line, "we may stop here" (240). Now we understand, too, something that has often troubled Dostoevsky's commentators. We know from one of the author's letters, contemporary with the book, that the original manuscript introduced a positive principle at the end of Part One: the narrator indicated that the answer lay in Christ. The censors suppressed this passage in the first edition of the book; curiously, Dostoevsky never reinserted it in later editions. The reason for this now becomes clear. The book would have had two endings instead of one, and Dostoevsky's point would have lost much of its force had it been placed in the narrator's mouth rather than in Lisa's action.

Several critics (Skaftymov, Frank) have already remarked that, contrary to popular opinion, Dostoevsky does not defend the underground man's views but rather contests them. The misunderstanding may arise because we are dealing with two simultaneous dialogues. First, there is the dialogue between the underground man and the defender of rational egoism (it hardly matters whether we attach to it Chernyshevsky's name, or Rousseau's, or someone else's). This debate bears upon the nature of man, and it contrasts two images, the one autonomous, the other dual; it is obvious that Dostoevsky accepts the second one as true. But this first dialogue only serves to sweep away the misunderstanding that obscured the real debate; here is where the second dialogue comes in, this time between the underground man on the one hand and Lisa, or, alternatively, "Dostoevsky," on the other. The major difficulty in interpreting *Notes from the Underground* lies in the impossibility of reconciling the arguments of the underground man, presented as true, with Dostoevsky's position as we know it from other sources. But this difficulty arises from the telescoping of the two debates into one. The underground man is not the representative of the moral position, inscribed by Dostoevsky into the text in his own name; he simply carries to its extreme consequences the position of Dostoevsky's adversaries, the radicals of the 1860s. But once these positions have been logically presented, the essential debate unfolds, even though it occupies only a part of the text. In this debate Dostoevsky, while placing himself in the framework of alterity, contrasts the master-slave logic with that of the love of others for their own sake, as this logic is embodied in Lisa's behavior. If in the first debate we find two descriptions of man that are opposed on the level of *truth,* in the second, where the solution to this problem is taken for granted, the author opposes two conceptions of proper behavior on the *moral* plane.

In *Notes from the Underground,* the second solution appears only for a brief moment, when Lisa abruptly holds out her arms to embrace the man who is insulting her. But starting with this book, the solution is asserted more and more forcefully in Dostoevsky's work, even though it remains as the mark of a limit rather than becoming the central theme of a narrative. In *Crime and Punishment,* the prostitute Sonia listens to Raskolnikov's confessions with the same love as Lisa. Prince Myshkin in *The Idiot* behaves the same way; so does Tikhon, who hears Stavrogin's confession in *The Demons.* And in *The Brothers Karamazov,* the same gesture is repeated, symbolically, three times: at the very beginning of the book, the *starets* Zossima approaches the great sinner Mitia and bows silently before him to the ground. Christ, who hears the speech of the Grand Inquisitor threatening him with burning at the stake, approaches the old man and silently kisses his bloodless lips. And Aliosha, after hearing Ivan's "revolt," finds in himself the same response: he approaches Ivan and kisses him on the mouth without saying a word. This gesture, varied and repeated throughout Dostoevsky's work, takes on a specific value. The wordless embrace, the silent kiss transcend language without renouncing meaning. Verbal language, self-consciousness, the master-slave logic, all three turn out to be on the same side; they remain the hallmarks of the underground man. For language, as we were told in the first part of *Notes from the Underground,* knows only the linguistic, just as reason knows only the reasonable—that is, a twentieth part of what constitutes a human being. The mouth that no longer *speaks* but *embraces* introduces the gesture and the body (according to the narrator of *Notes from the Underground* we have all lost our "proper body"); it interrupts language but inaugurates the symbolic circuit all the more forcefully. Language will be surpassed not by the haughty silence incarnated by "the man of nature and of truth," the man of action, but by this higher symbolic game that governs Lisa's pure act.

The day after the death of his first wife, during precisely the period when he was working on *Notes from the Underground,* Dostoevsky wrote in his notebook: "To love a person *as one's own self* according to the commandment of Christ is impossible. The law of individuality is the constraint, 'I' is the stumbling block . . . Meanwhile, after the appearance of Christ as *the idea of man incarnate,* it became as clear as day that the highest, final development of the individual should attain precisely the point (at the very end of his development, at the very point of reaching the goal), where man might find, recognize, and with all the strength of his nature be convinced that the highest use which he can make of his individuality, of the full development of his *I,* is to seemingly annihilate that *I* to give it wholly to each and everyone wholeheartedly and selflessly. And this is the greatest happiness."[9]

This time, I think, we may let the author have the last word.

Notes

[1] *Selected Letters of Friedrich Nietzsche,* ed. and trans. Christopher Middleton (Chicago and London: The University of Chicago Press, 1969) letter 149, to Franz Overbeck, February 23, 1887.

[2] *Dostoïevski: Articles et causeries* (Paris: Gallimard, 1923) 164-5.

[3] *Tolstoy or Dostoevsky: An Essay in the Old Criticism* (New York: Knopf., 1971).

[4] Mikhaïl Bakhtin, *Problems of Dostoevsky's Poetics,* trans. Caryl Emerson (Minneapolis: University of Minnesota Press, 1984) 5.

[5] Cited from *The Best Short Stories of Dostoevsky,* trans. David Magarshack (New York: Random House, 1964).

[6] Bakhtin, *Problems of Dostoevsky's Poetics,* 81.

[7] *Selected Letters,* letter 187, to Georg Brande, November 20, 1888.

[8] *Beyond Good and Evil: Prelude to a Philosophy of the Future,* trans. Walter Kaufmann (New York: Random House, 1966) chapter 4, "Epigrams and Interludes," no. 173, 92.

[9] *The Unpublished Dostoevsky, Diaries and Notebooks (1860-81),* ed. Carl R. Proffer (Ann Arbor: Ardis, 1973) vol. 1, 39 (April 16, 1864).

William J. Leatherbarrow (essay date 1981)

SOURCE: "Enlightened Malevolence: Notes from Underground," in *Fedor Dostoevsky,* Twayne Publishers, 1981, pp. 63-8.

[*In the following essay, Leatherbarrow discusses the underground man as Dostoevsky's unredeemed personification of human perversity and absurdity.*]

Dostoevsky's two-pronged attack on the ethics of reason and the insubstantial "solutions" of romantic idealism reaches its polemical climax in *Notes from Underground,* published in 1864 and written under appalling personal circumstances. Dostoevsky's first wife, Maria Dmitrievna, was dying, yet the author was obliged to continue work in order to provide material for the journal *Epoch,* which he ran with his brother as a successor to *Time,* but which was equally ill-starred. In *Notes from Underground* we stand on the threshold of Dostoevsky's maturity. The work crowns the achievements of his earlier period by synthesizing and deepening many former themes; it marks "an abrupt change in Dostoevsky's approach to characterization"[9] through its introduction of an acutely self-analytical hero, and stands as a prelude to the later novels. It is also remarkable for its new philosophical tenacity and toughness. The first of Dostoevsky's great novels of ideas, it gives philosophical respectability to many of its author's earlier preoccupations by its sharply analytical manner. In form it is highly experimental, for although ostensibly a monologue, the narrator's restless peregrination between different narrative voices and personae gives the work paradoxically greater polyphony and philosophical conflict than Dostoevsky's earlier works possessed.

In Part I of *Notes from Underground* the hero engages an imaginary interlocutor in a discussion of the nature of man which stresses the role of caprice and free will in human nature. This part, which has occasionally been published separately, is a bitter attack on scientific determinism and all philosophies which assert the primacy of necessity in human behavior. In stressing the importance of conscious free choice and diminishing the role of reason, self-interest, and contingency in human motivation, it is truly "the best overture for existentialism ever written."[10] Part II is a fictional pendant to Part I, both in its illustration of the hero's philosophical and psychological credo and in its subtle undercutting of his assumptions about himself. He relates an event which occurred many years earlier, when he indulged his love of capricious self-laceration by attending a dinner for a colleague whom he despised. The incident brings anguish to both the hero and his colleagues, but he perversely prolongs his offense against seemliness and at the same time he secretly smolders with the desire for reconciliation with those he despises. He follows them to a bordello, where he channels all his accumulated spite into the ruthless emotional blackmail of a naive young prostitute, Liza. When he has won Liza's trust and unsettled her with dreams of reform and idyllic family life, he reasserts his emotional and moral independence by paying for her services and thus confirming her inferiority to him.

By all standards *Notes from Underground* is one of the strangest and most urgent works of modern fiction. "Easily assimilated only by a profoundly diseased spiritual organism,"[11] it has found in modern urban man the ideally sympathetic reader, and in twentieth-century Existentialism a fuller discussion of its speculation about the nature of man. It is perhaps the greatest critique of narrow intellectualism and overrefined consciousness ever written, as well as a disturbing rejection of the ideals of the Enlightenment. Yet, as was always the case with Dostoevsky's mature work, the universal philosophical significance of *Notes from Underground* required the impetus of immediate polemic to give it form. It was intended as a refutation of the ideas of Nikolay Chernyshevsky (1828-89), a leading materialist philosopher, whose works—including the essay *The Anthropological Principle in Philosophy* (1860) and the novel *What Is to Be Done?* (1863)—had generated considerable interest by their assertion that the apparent complexity of human behavior could be explained on the basis of scientifically determinable principles. A disciple of Bentham and Mill, Chernyshevsky held that self-interest was a primary impulse in human nature, but that through the exercise of reason it could be made to coincide with the interests of society as a whole. He used the image of the Crystal Palace, built in London to house the 1851 World Exhibition, as a symbol of the future rational, technological utopia. Chernyshevsky's faith in rational self-interest, so clearly derived from Enlightenment ideals, offended Dostoevsky by stripping man of his mystery, by defining his behavior as the inevitable outcome of scientific law, and by depriving him of a soul and moral freedom, the two aspects of his being which, according to Christianity, could alone bring him to salvation.[12] The hero of *Notes from Underground* was conceived as the rotten apple in Chernyshevsky's barrel, an exaggerated incarnation of the perversity which is in all men, and which dissolves the foundations of all rational utopianism. He shrieks his revolt against determinism with hysterical insistence, but his voice is not Dostoevsky's. In this work, as elsewhere, we must acknowledge the primary law of Dostoevsky's artistic world: his characters speak for themselves and not necessarily for their author. Dostoevsky's dislike of scientific determinism was as keen as the Underground Man's, but that does not imply that he sympathized with the alternatives offered by his hero.

The Underground Man considers his condition representative, albeit extreme: "I have merely taken to its limits that which you are afraid to take half-way" (V, 178), he rebukes his reader. Moreover, he emphasizes that he and his behavior are very symptomatic of the nineteenth century, which he describes as "the age of negation" (V, 110), in clear contrast to the affirmative spirit of the Enlightenment. Negation is the essence of his revolt, as he zealously defends his freedom from the encroachment of anything that would limit it. A finely tuned consciousness is his key tactical weapon in this struggle: he constantly analyzes his behavior, ever alert—*en marge,* in the currency of Existentialism—to the dangers of consequentiality, contingency, and necessity, which in ordinary life prevent man from acting freely, consciously, and capriciously. He argues that man, in order to live authentically as a self-creating being, must resist all self-definition and refuse to submit to anything which would impair his freedom, even if this means acting against his own self-interest, flying in the face of reason, and rebelling against the very laws of nature. Here we see him for what he is: the antithesis spawned by the theses of the Enlightenment pushed to their logical limits, where they yield to absurdity. The Underground Man tries to get himself thrown from a billiard-room window, for he knows that such an act, although against his immediate self-interest, serves "a more advantageous advantage" (V, 111): the right to assert "his own willful, free volition, his own caprice, however wild, his own fantasy, inflamed sometimes to the point of madness" (V, 113). He acknowledges the logic of mathematics, but reserves for himself the right to make two and two add up to five if he wishes, for "twice two is four is no longer life, gentlemen, but the beginning of death" (V, 118-19). He submits to no scientific or natural law, for although he might accept its validity, he will not be imprisoned by that acceptance: "What are all these laws of nature and arithmetic to me if I don't happen to like them?" (V, 105). Suffering and pain are the usual outcome of such revolt, but even here the Underground Man derives an advantage, for suffering further refines consciousness and closes the circle of revolt.

The normal man of limited consciousness, bred in the lap of nature and not in the retort of self-analysis, lacks the Underground Man's existential freedom, but he does retain the ability to act. The conscious man acts when he has found grounds for action, but the heightened consciousness of the Underground Man dissolves every impulse to action in a sea of analysis, doubt, and contradiction. Like Hamlet, the Underground Man discovers that "the direct, immediate and legitimate fruit of consciousness is inertia" (V, 108):

> And thus the native hue of resolution
> Is sicklied o'er with the pale cast of thought.
> (*Hamlet*, Act III, Scene 1)

Here is the paradox in the Underground Man's stance: "all consciousness is an illness" (V, 102), and he envies the natural man's capacity for action, but at the same time he despises him for his stupidity. His own "freedom" is constraining, for he cannot move without compromising it. His self-denial at the end of Part I, when he insists that he has been lying "like a cobbler" (V, 121), shows us how demanding his freedom is: he must reject all he has said in order to avoid self-definition as a man who avoids self-definition! Such freedom is a denial of freedom; it is entirely negative, and saps the will it is supposed to liberate. As A. D. Nuttall observes,[13] the Underground Man is on the run, forever obliged to confirm his frail and sterile freedom in ever more outrageous outbursts of irrationality. In the words of Michael Holquist, "he is constantly making experiments in ontology, a mad scientist in the cluttered laboratory of his own identity."[14]

In his flight from the constraints of reason and necessity the hero of **Notes from Underground** incarnates the spirit of Romantic Man, and his Romanticism is particularly evident in his love of paradox and the exotic, as well as—equally importantly—in his literariness and responsiveness to the "noble and the beautiful" (V, 132). He is a romantic dreamer like Ordynov. Dreams provide an alternative retreat from the trials of reality and create an evanescent illusion of freedom. Throughout his confession the hero's constant rationalization of circumstances is matched by an equally constant tendency to refashion the reality of his existence into "beautiful forms of being" (V, 133). He dreams of reconciliation he cannot attain, of love, friendship, and acceptance, and his dreams ennoble his

squalid existence. He is, as Holquist carefully demonstrates, engaged in the Existential task of writing his own libretto of life, but he has "no rules to guide him except those which derive from his reading."[15] He is acutely aware of his own bookishness, in both the episode with his colleagues and his attempts to "save" Liza. Tragically, however, his razor-sharp consciousness also penetrates the illusions of romantic idealism. He cannot believe in his dreams, but the contrast between the impossible freedom and beauty of his fiction and the unseemly constraints of the real world inflames his spite still further. "They won't let me. . . . I can't . . . be good!" he sobs to Liza (V, 175), but this is because his concept of good is impossibly romantic, and he will not accept second best. He will be "either a hero or filth" (V, 133), and retreats to the Underground, his personal limbo located between fact and fiction, to feed on his wounded pride and take perverse pleasure in the piquant contrast of ideal and reality.

But the Underground affords no real retreat, and in the two concluding chapters of Part I the hero sees through its sham. "To hell with the Underground!" he cries, and goes on to put into the mouth of his imaginary interlocutor his most telling reservations. He recognizes that he is trying to escape the prison of reason through *rationalization* of his fears. He uses reason to expose both its own inadequacy and the insubstantiality of dreaming, but he never transcends it. His unreason is always reasoned, bred in the retort of his intellect. He complains that reason suppresses life, yet he knows nothing of life outside his Underground, which is itself a trap sprung by consciousness. His revolt is intellectual only—he lives vicariously within the confines of his own consciousness, effectively defusing his enthusiasm for "living life" (*zhivaia zhizn'*, V, 176). The affair with Liza confirms the life-denying qualities of the Underground Man. This deformed product of reason's retort, this captive of consciousness, defiles the simple, innocent life of the young prostitute. Life, in the guise of Liza, becomes the sacrificial victim of his rational spite. He might assert his independence and intellectual courage, but he is afraid of life. "You thirst for life, but resolve life's questions with logical confusion . . . and how afraid you are!" he reasons with himself. "There is some justice in your stance, but no moral purity" (V, 121). He prides himself on his consciousness, but this leads him only to sophistry. His heart remains uneducated, and "without a pure heart, full, correct consciousness is impossible" (V, 122). This idea that rational consciousness deforms "living life" will become an important motif in Dostoevsky's great novels, particularly in *Crime and Punishment* and *The Brothers Karamazov*.

Dostoevsky intended at the end of Part I to advocate Christian faith as a means of attaining moral freedom without falling into the trap of consciousness, but his design was frustrated by the intervention of the censor, who balked at the thought of Gospel passages emanating from this hero's profaned lips. His cuts outraged Dostoevsky: "That swine of a censor. The passages where I jeered at everything and sometimes blasphemed *for form's sake* he let through, but he suppressed the place where from all this I deduced the need for faith and Christ."[16]

So the Underground Man remains unredeemed, all his rhetorical flourish merely an attempt to dignify the fact that he is a squalid, pathetic, and impotent egoist. His unreconciled contradictions, which always threaten to disperse his being in a chain reaction of denial, are conveyed in the chorus of dissonant "voices" which constantly strain against the "monologic" form of the confession.[17] On the unstable interface where two worlds touch—the real, with its intractable and inhibiting laws of nature, and the ideal, with its deceptive liberation through the fiction of "the noble and beautiful"—the Underground Man carves out a third, the Underground itself. But his world is founded only upon perversity and denial, as he confronts the rational world with its absurdities and rebukes the romantic, ideal world for its groundless utopianism. He never really escapes the currency of either reason or romanticism, as his flair for intellectual paradox and romantic literariness confirms, and in rejecting the ethics of reason and romance he fails to generate an alternative. In his Underground he prides himself on his privileged vantage point, lacerates himself with his own estrangement, and delights in the intoxicating vertigo, which he believes derives from his being above morality, but which his ignorance of life suggests is the consequence of his being beneath it.

The test-tube man, infected with the very reason he despises, must discover other perceptual avenues into the world of "living life," must learn how to love life without necessarily understanding its rationale, and thereby regain the harmony with life which reason itself destroyed at the time of the Fall, and which reason tried unsuccessfully to rebuild in the aspirations of the Enlightenment. Partly through his own spiritual poverty, and partly through the monumental stupidity of Dostoevsky's censor, the hero of *Notes from Underground* fails to achieve all this. Raskolnikov, his successor in *Crime and Punishment,* is much more successful in his step toward salvation.

Notes

[9] E. J. Simmons, *Dostoevsky* (London, 1950), p. 106.

[10] W. Kaufmann, *Existentialism from Dostoevsky to Sartre* (Cleveland: World Publishing Co., 1956), p. 14.

[11] D. S. Mirsky, *A History of Russian Literature* (London: Routledge & Kegan Paul, 1964), p. 278.

[12] See D. Offord, "Dostoyevsky and Chernyshevsky," *Slavonic and East European Review* 57 (1979): 509-30.

[13] A. D. Nuttall, *Dostoevsky's Crime and Punishment* (Sussex: Sussex University Press, 1978), p. 22.

[14] M. Holquist, *Dostoevsky and the Novel* (Princeton, 1977), p. 64.

[15] Ibid.

[16] *Pis'ma,* I, 353.

[17] See Bakhtin, pp. 190-99.

Malcolm V. Jones (essay date 1985)

SOURCE: "Dostoevsky: *Notes from Underground* (1864)," in *The Voice of a Giant: Essays on Seven Russian Prose Classics,* edited by Roger Cockrell and David Richards, University of Exeter, 1985, pp. 55-65.

[*In the following essay, Jones investigates the nature of the underground man and examines the relation of Dostoevsky's* Notes from the Underground *to the philosophical currents of the modern period.*]

Dostoevsky's *Notes from Underground,* published in 1864, is well-established among the classics of modern European literature. Nearly 100 years after its publication the American scholar Joseph Frank wrote:

> Few works in modern literature are more widely read or more often cited than Dostoevsky's *Notes from Underground.* The designation 'underground man' has entered into the vocabulary of the modern educated consciousness, and this character has now begun—like Hamlet, Don Quixote, Don Juan and Faust—to take on the symbolic stature of one of the great archetypal literary creations. No book or essay on the situation of modern culture would be complete without some allusion to Dostoevsky's figure. Every important cultural development of the last half-century—Nietzscheanism, Freudianism, Expressionism, Surrealism, Crisis Theology, Existentialism—has claimed the underground man as its own; and when he has not been adopted as a prophetic anticipation, he has been held up to exhibition as a luridly repulsive warning.[1]

Writing in 1961, Frank naturally did not include more recent intellectual developments such as Structuralism and Post-structuralism, but might well wish to add them in revising his text today. A Deconstructive analysis of *Notes from Underground* might prove the most fruitful of all, though the aim of this article is much more modest and is based upon common-sense notions of reading and writing.

However, if such diverse and widespread interest establishes *Notes from Underground*'s place in the modern European consciousness, it also illustrates how many ways there are of understanding and interpreting it. Many a reader senses intuitively that here is a statement of great importance for anyone who wants to come to terms with modern man's spiritual problems, but unless he is familiar with some or all of those movements mentioned by Frank, he may be at a loss to know exactly what to make of it. After all, in Part I of the work there is no story to fall back on. This first part strikes one rather as a sort of emotional and philosophical outpouring, the confession of a man who is sick in mind, unable to integrate with society, and obsessed with certain profound philosophical problems with which he cannot cope.

The forty-year-old narrator is psychologically sick, and has been so since childhood. He is spiteful and petty, confused and self-contradictory. He has always felt an outsider (alienated from society as modern jargon has it); and because he has always found it so difficult to find his bearings in life, he has always been easy prey to fashionable intellectual attitudes. He cannot find a secure mooring in life on any level of his experience. He has no sense of the Holy (as Dostoevsky was to write some years later);[2] he is, as some critics have put it, a hollow man. Almost at the end of his notes, the Underground Man observes:

> We do not even know where living reality is now, what it is, or what it is called. Leave us alone without our wretched little books and we immediately grow confused and lose our way. We don't know what to adhere to, what to follow, what to love, what to hate, what to respect or what to despise. We even become weary of being human beings—human beings with their *own,* real flesh and blood . . .[3]

'Leave us alone without our books and we immediately grow confused and lose our way'. In Part II, where the narrator recalls his life at the age of twenty-four, it is Gogol, Nekrasov, Schiller, George Sand and composite fantasies from the Romantics, the Natural School and recent human history—particularly the age of Napoleon— that swarm in the Underground Man's mind. The motif of the wet snow is taken from the Natural School in whose works it often appeared; the epigraph is taken from Nekrasov; the ideal of *the sublime and the beautiful* is a late eighteenth-century concept to be found in the philosophy of Burke, of Kant, and most significant of all for Russia in the period of the 1840s, of the German poet, philosopher and dramatist, Schiller. The idea of the pure prostitute and the concept of acute sensibility as simultaneously a sign of superiority and a curse are both also well-known and widespread Romantic images.

Part I, when the narrator has reached the age of forty, is set in the 1860s, years marked first by the Great Reforms in Russia and then by the American Civil War and the Prussian seizure of Schleswig-Holstein, both of which leave a mark on the Underground Man's thought. Most important of all, however, a new set of ideas has taken possession of the Underground Man's mind. As one can see in retrospect, they have not altogether banished the old ideas, but it is these new ones, the creed of the progressives of the sixties, which have him in their thrall. The central figure in propagating this creed was Nikolai Chernyshevsky who at this time was incarcerated in the Peter and Paul fortress, but nonetheless had managed to publish an inflammatory novel, *What is to be done?* in 1863. Chernyshevsky was not merely a novelist; he was a philosopher and leader of progressive youth as well, and it is his ideas against which the Underground Man is rebelling even though he finds them irrefutable. They are utilitarian, rationalist and determinist ideas, which, in the tradition of the Enlightenment, present man as an ultimately rational creature, who only has to be shown his true interests to act in accordance with them and who lives in a world, moreover, where rational laws prevail in the moral as well as the natural sphere, so that his individual freedom is severely restricted, if not altogether illusory. Among the complex of ideas which have taken the Underground Man's mind captive and which can be identified in the text are

those of the French eighteenth-century philosopher Diderot, the French socialist Fourier, and more recently, those of Darwin, as published in his *On the Origin of Species* in 1859 and glossed by Huxley's *Man's Place in Nature* which had appeared in English in 1863 and in Russian translation in 1864. Similarly, there is a reference to the English writer H. T. Buckle, who for a time enjoyed a vogue among European intellectuals and the first volume of whose *History of Civilisation in England* was published in Russian translation in 1863.[4] In this work, Buckle had expressed the idea, from which the Underground Man dissents, that with the development of civilisation wars will cease.

Thus, the Man from Underground is up-to-date in his reading, but unfortunately he takes it all too personally. The first section of the narrator's notes probably does not strike the modern English reader as having very much to do with philosophy at all. Essentially it appears as the self-revelation of someone who is emotionally confused. But, in the second section, these introspective meanderings and complaints move in the direction of something recognisable as philosophy, with the narrator's ascription of his emotional problems to what he calls *the laws of consciousness.* He wants to understand and to explain why he feels pleasure in the knowledge that he is a scoundrel and in making other people uncomfortable; why he feels so many conflicting emotions doing battle within him; why he is spiteful and yet at the same time knows he is not really spiteful; why it is just at the moment when he is most sensitive to 'the sublime and the beautiful' that he does the most immoral things; why he feels such pleasure at his own degradation. The conclusion he comes to is that he is suffering from an excess of what he calls consciousness, of what we might perhaps call morbid, introspective reflection, and that this consciousness is subject to laws which deprive him of his free will. Whatever illusions he may have about acting in accordance with his ideal, or improving himself morally, these laws debar him from changing in any way. The man with an over-sensitive consciousness is tormented by ideals of goodness and beauty; yet he is lured into vice as well, and, finally, he knows that all this is completely beyond his control. Things will be as they will be. No-one is to blame for anything. None of this stops him from feeling his degradation, from smarting at insults or from dreaming of revenge; but he can never make up his mind to do anything because he knows that everything is subject to laws over which he has no control. This, at least, is the explanation he offers. He feels impotent, and he suffers all the humiliation and rancour of impotence.

The Underground Man develops this theme in his third section of Part I: he describes how he sweats and stews and plots revenge, but in the end achieves nothing and has no alternative but to withdraw into his underground and seethe, until eventually he is forced to accept the inevitable. A stupid man, the man of action or the man of Nature as he has been called, understands none of this and so charges on regardless. If the man of action encounters an obstacle, a stone wall, he does not understand what stands in his way, but just steps aside, and consequently he is not subject to unhealthy brooding. He is representative of normality. But the man who reflects on the philosophical implications is rendered immobile. He knows he is impotent and he suffers from the feeling of impotence, and is resentful. Resentment is an important idea in the thought of some of the existentialists, notably Nietzsche.[5] Camus, for instance, quotes Scheler's definition that resentment is the evil secretion of prolonged impotence in a sealed vessel;[6] and this seems to be exactly what the Underground Man is talking about.

The only thing to do is to take it out on other people. In section IV, the narrator introduces his famous metaphor of the educated man with toothache, which expresses perfectly his situation. The educated man knows that he can do nothing about his toothache, that whether it goes or gets worse is subject to natural laws over which he has no control. In a sense he enjoys the consciousness that he is the plaything of such laws. But he makes other people suffer too by his groans and thereby obtains some relief from his suffering.

In the following sections of Part I the Underground Man takes some of these ideas further. He affirms that the result of excess consciousness is inertia and ennui. Stupid people jump easily to conclusions; intelligent people get lost in their own analyses and can never find a sufficient cause for any course of action. He has never been able to become anything positive.

It is clear that in his heart of hearts the Underground Man does not know whether he is a free agent or not. He cannot refute the modern deterministic concept of scientific law, but the fact that he is obsessed with his own freedom or lack of freedom indicates that many of his attitudes tacitly assume that what he is suffering from is not so much a law of nature as an emotionally based feeling of impotence and/or moral cowardice. This is his fundamental problem, around which the whole fiction is built.

Consequently he comes to question the validity of these so-called laws. He asks whether it is after all so obvious that if man were shown his own interests in accordance with some mathematical table, he would in fact act in accordance with them. Has man, he asks, in the whole of recorded history, ever behaved rationally, even when he understands the correct rational course? Man is irrational and perverse. At times it may even be of benefit to man to do something contrary to his interests as seen from the rational standpoint, and if this is true then it undermines all rational schemes for regulating man's activities.

The narrator runs through a series of well-known historical events; he glances at Buckle's questionable view of civilisation; he alludes to the martial activities of the two Napoleons; he mentions Schleswig-Holstein and the still-raging American Civil War, and finds little to support the view of man's rationality. Diderot may have believed that man is like an organ stop or a piano key, and science may teach that the laws of nature determine man's actions; logarithm tables may be worked out for every conceivable eventuality; the Crystal Palace may be built. But, if for no

other reason than that he was bored, man would be certain to knock it down. The symbol of the Crystal Palace to represent an ideal, rationally ordered society derives in part from Dostoevsky's own visit in 1862 to the Crystal Palace at Sydenham, the centrepiece of Prince Albert's Great Exhibition, but even more from an episode in Chernyshevsky's novel *What is to be done?* where the image of the Crystal Palace represents the ideal of a technological utopia.[7]

No, the Underground Man concludes, the rationalists are wrong. Man is not ultimately rational. In all times and places men prefer to act as they choose rather than in accord with reason if the latter means sacrificing their individuality. Man prefers independent choice to a rational, comfortable existence.

But what if there is no such thing as independent choice? Here the Underground Man is brought back to the crux of his problem, and he replies that whereas reason may bring man to this conclusion, reason is only one of man's faculties. The faculty which represents the whole man is not reason, but will, and will says differently. This is the high point of his argument. The trouble is that he does not wholly believe this either, and he now resorts to arguments built not so much on confidence in his will or its freedom, as on a frenzied rebellion against the tyranny of reason. Man would rather do something perverse, or even go mad, than accept this tyranny. Man may be attracted by reason and creativity, but he is also attracted by chaos and destruction, perhaps because what he fears most of all is to bring his task to completion. Ants may behave in accordance with a mathematical model, but men are not ants. Twice-two-is-four may be very appealing to the reason, but twice-two-is-five has its fascination too. The Underground Man ultimately rejects the Crystal Palace, as he says memorably, because man cannot put out his tongue at it. But the narrator is exhausted by all this philosophising and the emotional toll which it takes, and sinks back into his Underground. Is this the best place after all, or is there something better for which he years?

The possibility that there might be something better than what the Underground Man calls the Underground relates to a passage which the censor refused to have in the text and which is now lost, but in which Dostoevsky intended to suggest the possibility of a Christian utopia, founded on love.

The Underground Man is certainly very unattractive, and no sane reader would choose the Underground as he does, but this is not really the point. Dostoevsky (as opposed to his narrator) is trying to convey something rather different. If it were true that man has no free will and this were to be appreciated by intelligent and sensitive beings, the kind of psychological predicament which would result would be the following: people with high ideals who were convinced that to realise such ideals was an impossibility and that they were the victims of inescapable laws would be reduced to an emotionally exhausting sense of impotence, against which they could protest only by caprice and perversity. . . . In his foreword Dostoevsky even claimed that people like this already existed. The fundamental problem was by no means a new one, nor is it outdated, since it is easy to find parallels today. No solution is offered in *Notes from Underground,* but Dostoevsky was to try to formulate an answer in terms of Christianity in his later works.

Many commentators on Dostoevsky have argued that it is its ideological aspect which is the most important, but others have said that the Underground Man's philosophising seems to require some external explanation, since his own commentary is clearly unreliable. The most appropriate position to adopt, it has been argued, is the psychological one. 'Its every aspect,' one commentator has written of *Notes from Underground,* 'including the philosophical speculations of Part I and the way in which the material is ordered, is an expression of the Underground Man's psyche.'[8] This is undoubtedly true, though the two approaches to the work are far from incompatible. One of the central and most significant features of Dostoevsky's work is his intuitive understanding of the way that ideas and personalities interact.

It is therefore important to look more closely at the Underground Man's emotional problems and the way in which they dispose him to certain philosophical attitudes. His is, of course, a very complex personality. One can discern in him tendencies towards aggression and the assertion of intellectual and moral superiority. Yet there are also tendencies towards self-effacement, a sense of moral culpability and a conviction of his own inferiority. The Underground is above all a symbol of withdrawal. One notes a tendency in the hero to withdraw altogether from other people, from moral problems and from intellectual turmoil, opposed by a periodic desire to integrate himself with the common run of humanity and even to achieve a genuinely warm human relationship with another person.

This extremely complex emotional problem can be analysed in accordance with various psychological theories, but here only its main features can be indicated.[9]

The Underground Man's problems begin with an unloved childhood. Not only is he an orphan, but he arrives at school full of suspicion of everyone and is greeted by taunts and jibes because he is different from everyone else. His basic response is to withdraw into himself and to find some compensation for his failure to establish positive relationships with others in a consciousness of his own intellectual and aesthetic superiority. (Later, in his address to Liza, he comes to romanticise what he has missed).

Although he stands apart from his fellows, however, he still years for human fellowship; though he tries to ignore their taunts, they still wound him and make him yearn for revenge; though he scorns their vulgarity, he envies their social ease; though he wants to dominate others, he is discontented when he succeeds; though he cherishes high ideals, he senses their other-worldliness; though he scorns the values of the world, he is humiliated by his poverty and by the derision of others. He knows that social integration and acceptance is beyond him and at times he withdraws, in consciousness of the superiority of his own

values. At other times he so desperately needs company that he is prepared to undergo humiliation, and even enjoys it up to a point. Or else, in an attempt to escape from inertia he takes refuge in a bout of debauchery.

The first few pages of Part II describe in some detail the young narrator's emotions and thoughts about his unhealthy withdrawal from others and about the extremes of self-deprecation and feelings of superiority which he experiences.

The first anecdote which he tells concerns the officer who brushes him aside like an insect as he leaves the billiard hall, and the torments which he undergoes as a consequence. His plans and fantasies reveal his many-sidedness to the full. He harbours a grudge for several years. Firstly, he writes a scurrilous tale which he intends to be published, then he composes a letter full of fine feelings but with the veiled threat of a duel in it. The article is not published, and the letter is not sent. Finally he wreaks his revenge after months and months of obsessive scheming by barging into the officer in the street in such a way that he is not even sure that the man has noticed. But what this episode shows most clearly of all is the state of mind suggested in Part I: the consequence of a feeling of impotence with regard to participation in the normal patterns of life. The whole affair is so completely out of proportion to its cause, so ludicrous in the hold it has taken on the narrator's imagination and the strain it imposes on his emotional resources, that it would be laughable if it were not so pathetic.

Then he tells of his withdrawal into Romantic dreams, and finally, he embarks on his recollections of the central episode in the second part, the story of Zverkov and Liza. This episode too displays all the Underground Man's problems: his desire to participate; his wish to impose himself as a superior spirit; his consciousness that he looks ridiculous; and his perverse pleasure in being humiliated. It displays too his delight in tormenting others, the basic hostility of his relationship with his so-called friends, his dreams of moral and aesthetic grandeur, and his readiness to take offence. We are taken through every detail of his confused and complex feelings, and of his interaction with Zverkov and his friends.

The Underground Man is just as repulsive and foolish at the meal to which he has invited himself as an unwelcome guest as he imagines he will be, and the result is predictable. He emerges in a state of turmoil, determined to restore his dignity in some fashion, and makes off for the brothel in pursuit of the rest of the party who have thankfully left him behind.

It is there that he meets Liza, and lectures her on the fate which awaits her if she pursues her profession much longer. All this he says as though reciting from a book, and this is more or less the truth, for he has indeed picked it up from books.

The psychological importance of his preaching is that, through it, he temporarily restores the sense of self-esteem which he had lost so disastrously at the dinner; and yet he is sowing the seeds of further disaster, for he does not really believe what he is saying. Although he draws on his own fantasy in what he says to Liza, he is on dangerous emotional ground, for he preaches love, a commodity which he cannot offer, but which he knows he desperately needs and lacks. This might, he senses, have been his salvation, but it is not, because when Liza later turns up at his house, catching him by surprise, he is humiliated by her finding him in his degraded and impoverished circumstances, and this brings out all his old impulses of vindictiveness and spite. . . . He takes his revenge on her for momentarily reversing their positions, by making love to her and then offering her money as she leaves, as though that was what she had come for.

When she leaves and he cannot catch her he is filled with remorse and self-hatred, but there is nothing he can do. He is once again impotent, not only in regard to the world, but in his attempt to order his own personality. Nor is this feeling in any way alleviated in his relations with his surly and recalcitrant manservant, who, though limited in outlook, has learnt to tyrannise the Underground Man just as the latter tries to tyrannise others. The hero is aware of the nature of his problem, and he is aware that there is something much better which is inaccessible to him, but since it is inaccessible there is nothing but the Underground after all.

Once we have looked at the Underground Man as he remembers himself, certain aspects of his philosophy become clearer. It is obvious that he makes use of his reading of the Romantics in his fantasies and also in his sermon to Liza, which derives in part from such fantasy.

But it is no less clear that it is his sense of impotence, displayed most clearly in the adventure with the officer, which lays the emotional basis for his acceptance of 'scientific determinism' and the constraints which that places upon free will. Such a doctrine confirms his own intuition that nothing he does or resolves to do can alter his position of emotional confusion and alienation from society. That position seems to receive support from his own discovery that the more he ponders and reflects, the more complex life seems, the more his resolution is eroded, and the less capable he is of doing anything at all except nurse his bitterness and resentment.

Furthermore, if scientific determinism in this crude sense were true, it would remove from him all moral responsibility, for if free will is illusory, no-one can be blamed for his actions, and talk of good and evil becomes meaningless. Yet the idea of the sublime and the beautiful lingers on in his consciousness and he cannot remain completely satisfied with such a view of life.

If the Underground Man's proneness to accept 'scientific determinism' and all its implications can be understood in terms of emotional problems which already existed before he had read a word of Chernyshevsky, so too can his reaction in affirming his right to be perverse. This has, after all, always been his way of dealing with intractable problems. When in a tight corner, he has never managed to do what rationally might be in his best interests. The rational has never been completely dominant in his life. On the contrary, it would seem that his every waking moment (and perhaps his sleep too) has been filled with the irrational, or at least the non-rational: with dreams and fantasies, with plans of revenge, vindictiveness and spite, with sadistic and masochistic yearnings of one kind or another. When he is already making himself ridiculous with Zverkov, he persists in plunging ever deeper into an inextricable morass of embarrassment and unnecessary discomfort. When he has an opportunity to establish a rapport with someone who understands and pities him, he reacts by destroying the burgeoning relationship. There is little that can be called rational here.

So the Underground Man's philosophical attitudes are rooted not only in contemporary cultural and philosophical views, but also in his own personality disorder. In trying to resolve the philosophical question he is also trying to resolve his spiritual problems, and in both he fails.

Of course, this identity of personal and philosophical is characteristic of much modern existentialist thought. For the existentialists, the primary problems are the problems of the individual brought face to face with the reality of living, that is of acting rather than observing. The existentialist philosopher is not one to stand on the touchline and assume a position of objectivity and impassivity. He is involved, or *engagé* as Sartre has it. Walter Kaufmann is surely right when he says that although there is no reason for calling Dostoevsky an existentialist, Part I of **Notes from Underground** is the best overture for existentialism ever written.[10]

Notes

[1] Joseph Frank. 'Nihilism and *Notes from Underground*', *Sewanee Review,* LXIX, 1961, p. 1.

[2] F. M. Dostoevskii, *Polnoe sobranie sochinenii v tridtsati tomakh,* Leningrad, 1972-, XVI, p. 330.

[3] *P.S.S.,* V, pp. 178-179.

[4] For further details see, *inter alia,* Joseph Frank.

[5] Friedrich Nietzsche, *The Genealogy of Morals.*

[6] Albert Camus, *The Rebel,* Penguin, Harmondsworth, 1975, p. 23.

[7] N. G. Chernyshevskii, *Polnoe sobranie sochinenii v pyatnadtsati tomakh,* Moscow, 1939-1950, XI, p. 277.

[8] Bernard J. Paris, 'Notes from Underground; a Horneyan Analysis', PMLA, LXXXVIII, 1973, p. 511.

[9] For example, Bernard J. Paris.

[10] Walter Kaufmann, *Existentialism from Dostoevsky to Sartre,* Meridian Books, Cleveland, 1956, p. 14.

Donald Gutierrez (essay date 1987)

SOURCE: "Dostoyevsky's *Notes from Underground:* Self-Degradation as Revelation of Self," in *The Dark and Light Gods: Essays on the Self in Modern Literature,* The Whitston Publishing Company, 1987, pp. 2-26.

[*In the following essay, Gutierrez studies the implications of Dostoevsky's underground man as the prototypical literary depiction of modern self-degradation.*]

I

In a passage from Section VI of *A Treatise of Human Nature* entitled "Of Personal Identity," Hume begins his famous attack on the conception of the self: "If any impression give rise to the idea of self, that impression must continue invariably the same thro' the whole course of our lives; since self is suppos'd to exist after that manner. But there is no impression constant and invariable. Pain and pleasure, grief and joy, passions and sensations succeed each other, and never all exist at the same time. It cannot, therefore, be from any of these impressions, or from any other, that the idea of self is derived; and consequently there is no such idea."[1] Hume, as I understand him, is saying that there is no such idea as the self because there is no element ("impression") that is sufficiently permanent to allow one to orient his being upon it, and thus stabilize his sense of self. Dostoyevsky's famous-infamous character, the Underground Man, in the Modernist classic *Notes From Underground,* comes impressively close for such a scoundrel to refuting this area of Humean scepticism. Indeed, Dostoyevsky's anti-hero in a complex way challenges Hume's implicit nihilism by—ironically—the very force of his own nihilistic being. Joseph Frank in a splendid essay on *Notes* has written about the moral implications of the Underground Man's character: "Far from wishing to portray the underground man as the embodiment of *evil,* the whole of *Notes* is quite the opposite. Only in a world where human choice can make a difference, only where there is no absolute determinism, is any morality possible at all; and Dostoyevsky adroitly defends the Underground Man's 'capriciousness' as the necessary precondition for any morality whatsoever."[2] Quoting from *Notes,* Frank buttresses this key point a little later in his essay in stating that man, to assure himself of freedom and moral autonomy, will "deliberately and consciously desire something that is injurious, stupid, . . . just because he wants to have the right to desire for himself even what is very stupid and not be bound by an obligation to desire only what is very sensible," for this right "preserves what is most precious and most important to us, namely, our personality and our individuality" (Frank, p. 14).

These insights seem significantly true. Frank's essay is also valuable for its rich sense of the literary and ideological culture nurturing (if by the spark of antithesis) Dostoyevsky's extraordinary novella. Yet, even Frank and other commentators strike me as failing to take a close look at the real horror of this story. This is understandable, for *Notes,* in its unrelenting depiction of a degraded human being analyzing and dramatizing his own degradation, is

not pleasant to behold. Yet it should be beheld, because whether or not the Underground Man is our double, he is too close to us to ignore with impunity—or with a clear conscience.

Frank claims that the Underground Man is continually jousting with the basic values of a Utopian novel published in 1863 named *What Is To Be Done?* by the Utopist radical Nicolai C. Chernyshevsky. Chernyshevsky appears to embody some of the ideals of the European Enlightenment in his belief in the innate virtue and reasonableness of humanity. Though Dostoyevsky and his main character are not one and the same, Dostoyevsky too is hostile to these beliefs. Although, furthermore, the basis of his resistance is ultimately religious, Christian, his artistry in *Notes* resides in his capacity to create and motivate a virtually semi-diabolic character who both in his thinking, and, later (in the second section), in his actions towards people, embodies "precepts" and practices that are despicable and that refute ready acceptance of innate human nobility. This in fact is one of the "discussions" going on in the story.

Another discussion is comprised of the narrator with himself in the sense that the narrator is irrevocably self-divided, and acutely aware of his division; he is continually doing things that he does and does not want to do. Indeed, anyone so deeply motivated as he is by spite and perversity (key words in the story), and who has his intelligence, is bound to possess a strong sense of his own dividedness. And if the Underground Man (or, more accurately, *The Man Who Lives in a Mousehole,* as Andrew A. MacAndrew translates the title) is also literary and intellectual, he comes disturbingly close to being like many bookish people. I suggest then that *Notes* is a deeply disturbing work because it graphs with close, if sometimes feverish, attentiveness the dissolution of a soul, the symbolic killing of a self, which in important respects is not so different from "ourselves." And If I find Frank's points about the narrator's moral significance inadequate, it is not because they are untrue but because his commentary and most commentaries on this still shocking work do not give us a sufficiently concrete sense of the horror of degradation and disintegration of being that Dostoyevsky somewhat sadistically exhibits for us. If I attempt to look into this dark pit at some length, it is not to extend Dostoyevsky's sadism. Rather, I wish to examine and assess the character of the degradation of *Notes* as an example of the extraordinary resiliency of the self, and to witness how far a self can go in its willed decomposition and still retain an identity.

II

Part of what makes this disagreeable fiction curiously readable and even appealing is its comic aspect as well as the distance it projects between author and narrator. The work has been called comic and tragic,[3] and in fact those two designations fairly accurately describe the two main sections and the modal progression of the work. At the start of Section One there is a disclaimer by "Dostoyevsky" of any biographical connection with the narrator in his statement that the work is fictitious, though "people like the author of these notes may, and indeed must, exist in our society. . . ."[4] The idea that the author of the "Notes" and Dostoyevsky are one and the same is essentially a naive tribute to Dostoyevsky's skill with confession as a fictional subgenre (whatever private springs of frustration and rage *Notes* might have welled from).[5] The whole trajectory of the work by its very nature would exclude "Dostoyevsky" as its author and victim, for that would be rather like Iago writing *Othello*.

Some of the complexity of *Notes* resides in its change of modes from comic to tragic, though the latter is implicit from the beginning, and is qualified by the irony of the Underground Man's self-deception and the profound sordidness of his existence.[6] Further, the comic dimension in Section One (which includes such attributes as farce, ridicule, and irony) helps to "objectify" the work distancing Dostoyevsky from its particularly dangerous authorial self-incriminativeness. . . . And the comedy helps to make the "tragic" impact greater by preceding it, which disorients our expectations.

One of the first actions in the story of our "mouse-man" concerns the officer in a tavern whose way he gets into as the latter is playing billiards. Being moved by the officer as if he were an object constitutes one of our anti-hero's first-mentioned degradations, which he examines, probes, tastes and re-tastes with a masochistic assiduity and torment typical of a strain in literature from the Romantics on to the present. His complaint that he had "'been treated as one treats a fly,'" (p. 30), embodies a descriptive motif of the narrator recurring throughout the story. The Officer (Man of Action) is large and burly, and our narrator (the Intellectual, the Man of Thought) is "small and thin," but he still thinks he could make trouble. Duelling is out because the officer looks like a man who could break our protagonist in two with one hand. This gives occasion for the narrator's proclivity to paradox and self-delusion, which in this instance is that though he acts like a coward "when the chips are down", (p. 130) he is not a coward at heart. Besides exemplifying the subgenre of the degradational confession, this revelation is true in the highly qualified sense that although our narrator would never confront the Officer, he nevertheless exhibits a certain audacious candor in the extreme soul-stripping revealed by his notes.

But our anti-hero does confront the Officer, if in his own ridiculously comic way. First, he responds to the first insult in a literary mode, by caricature in a short story, then in a "beautiful" letter to the Officer that he never mails. Considering that the letter is written two years after the event in the tavern, the narrator is clearly obsessed with the incident, and with his psychological opposite. But he finally has his satisfaction. He discovers that the Officer often goes for a walk on Nevsky Avenue. Accentuating the motif of his degradation, the narrator admits that he "'scurried along like a mouse in a most undignified way, skipping out of the path of important gentlemen, guards, officers, and ladies'" (p. 132). He notices that the Officer always walks straight ahead, over or through anyone. His plan is to show his mettle—and make up for his past humiliation by the Officer—by bumping into him. He realiz-

es that he'll get the worst of the encounter, but at least he will not have backed down. But he does back down, for, in his first attempt he skips aside. The same night, however, he accidentally encounters the Officer again: "'I closed my eyes and we banged hard against each other, shoulder against shoulder. I didn't yield an inch and walked past him as equal! He never even turned around, *pretending* [italics added—D. G.] not to have noticed a thing . . . Of course I got the worse of the collision, for he was much heavier.'" (p. 135).

But that such an event is a symbolic victory for our narrator is a dramatic indication of how degraded he feels he is. And though the event is comically ridiculous, the comedy also serves, as observed earlier, to distance both Dostoyevsky and reader from this dangerously insidious individual. The episode also provides the first substantially dramatized accounts of the depth of the narrator's sense of his own degradation. On the one hand he aspires to be the equal of a military officer, an official man of action, while, on the other hand, knowing, or feeling, that all the respectable people on Nevsky Avenue regard him as a "pestiferous fly." Thus the incident harbors a vertical gamut of the narrator's vivid realization of his own capacity for humiliation, and, as he contains (as we all do) a force in him resenting and resisting his being degraded, one becomes aware that this man could be dangerous not only to himself, but to others. In line with this possibility, the narrative modes of the first section (called "The Mousehole" or "The Underground"), which are confessional, unpleasantly comic, theoretical, private in character, will change in the second or "action section" of the novella.

To get a graphic idea of how the narrator's profound nastiness and introspection confirm an idea of self, it is well to start near the beginning of the story so as to take a closer look at the narrator's inner life and thought. Forty years old the Underground Man presents a picture of himself as being hopelessly useless:

> I couldn't manage to make myself nasty or, for that matter, friendly, crooked or honest, a hero or an insect. Now I'm living out life in a corner, trying to console myself with the stupid, useless excuse that an intelligent man cannot turn himself into anythig, that only a fool can make anything he wants out of himself. It's true that an intelligent man of the nineteenth century is bound to be a spineless creature, while the man of character, the man of action, is, in most cases, of limited intelligence. (p. 92)

Although the Underground Man often retracts his claims that he is telling the truth, the truth in this passage possesses some validity and general significance, for it intimates a sense of fatality and powerlessness often felt by the intellectual in modern society—and possibly a resultant if seldom overt self—contempt as well. Yet the essential point is less whether the Underground Man is really as useless as he thinks than that he feels he is useless. Indeed, as he says later, he has felt that way much of his life, from awkward, lonely days as a student to an alienated condition as an office worker during his twenties.

Yet he is also candid enough to admit his nastiness. The one student friend he has for a while he tries to dominate ruthlessly, and in his office phase as a young man his relations with other people are basically hostile; though he looks down on them, he also feels that they despise him, and thus lives amidst social conditions scarcely conducive to a stable or comforting sense of self.

The narrator's candor in fact goes so far as to reveal what has become a conventional theme of Modernist literature, that consciousness (he calls it "lucidity") is a disease. His consciousness is "diseased" partly because he is a man violently at odds with himself. The Underground Man indeed is, unless one counts Diderot's Rameau's Nephew, the archetypal alienated man in modern Western literature. His confessions are not cathartic; they don't make him feel or be any better. If anything, they make him worse. His self-conflict is too crudely put as Ego versus Id. For one reason, the Id in this fiction would have too much rationalistic and rationalizing intelligence on its side, or the ego too much idinal savagery and violence. In the *Ego and the Id,* Freud himself states that "The ego is not sharply separated from the Id; its lower portion merges into it."[7] The Underground Man's willingness to admit what a scum he is cannot be understood in terms of a mechanistic conception of the conflicts of Ego and Id in the Freudian schema. This could be an important point, if true, because it suggests how harrowingly penetrative and therapeutically irreducible Dostoyevsky's acrid vision of the lost soul really is. In fact, one of the quiet yet basic implications of *Notes* is the existence not only of the self but of the "soul" as well in view of how degraded, how damned, this man really is. But the evidence of damnation does not emerge climactically until late in the story.

Nevertheless, we are prepared for it early in *Notes,* and time after time: "'The more conscious I was of 'the good and the beautiful,' the deeper I sank into the mud [excrement], and the more likely I was to remain mired in it'" (p. 94), a condition, he goes on to say, that he comes to feel is not accidental, but constitutes his "normal state," for, as he says in frightening words, "'. . . finally I lost all desire to fight my depravity'" (p. 94). This disintegration of his essential being is described in a famous passage shortly afterwards:

> I reached a point where I felt a secret, unhealthy, base little pleasure in creeping back into my hole after some disgusting night in Petersburg and forcing myself to think that I had again done something filthy, that what was done couldn't be undone. And I inwardly gnawed at myself for it, tore at myself and ate myself away, until the bitterness turned into some shameful, accursed sweetishness and, finally into a great, unquestionable pleasure. Yes, yes, definitely a pleasure! I mean it! And that's why I started out on this subject: I want to find out whether others experience this sort of pleasure too. . . . I derived pleasure precisely from the blinding realization of my degradation; because I felt I was already up against the wall; that it was horrible but couldn't be otherwise; that there was no way out and was no longer possible to make myself into a different person; that even if there were still enough time and faith left to become different, I wouldn't want to change

myself; and that, even if I wanted to, I still wouldn't have done anything about it because, actually, there wasn't anything to change into. (p. 94).

Frank offers an insight into this key passage worth considering: "The ambiguous 'delight' of the Underground Man arises from the moral-emotive response of his *human nature* to the blank nullity of the *laws of nature.* It signifies his refusal to abdicate his conscience and submit silently to determinism, even though his reason assures him that there is nothing he can really do to change for the better. The 'masochism' of the Underground Man thus has a *reverse* significance from that usually attributed to it. Instead of being a sign of pathological abnormality, it is in reality an indication of the Underground Man's paradoxical spiritual health—his preservation of his moral sense.'"[8]

This is a powerful insight into *Notes,* but Frank fails to confront the literal reality of the text sufficiently. Deriving pleasure from the "blinding realization" of one's degradation in a gesture opposed to determinism may really be a sign of spiritual health or of a preserved moral sense. Moreover, it may indeed be more than a clinically-disposed-of case of masochism. But *Notes* is first and "blindingly" a realization of degradation so intense, so acrid, that the reader is meant to taste it, to feel it in his bones.

Being degraded is a common experience (if more common to some than to others), and can be experienced without the *via negativa* of Frank's exaltation of the exit. The Underground Man is cunning enough to know that he is not untypical, but his claiming more normality than he should is really typical of his proclivity to rationalize, as is his claim that he could not change, assuming he wanted to, because there is nothing to change into, no other kind of person to be. But the real reason he doesn't change is because he doesn't want to change. The Underground Man *wills* himself into a corner, denies and destroys any capacity for change or growth by a perverse "act" of will. His action is a willed non-action, a kind of moral sloth that any sentient person is bound to have experienced. So, though his masochism does harbor, as Frank says, a kind of moral energy, it is qualified by a deadly level of acedia in his nature. At the end of the episode with the prostitute Liza, the Underground Man asserts that "'all I did was carry to the limit what you haven't dared to push even half way—taking your cowardice for reasonableness, thus making yourselves feel better.'" (p. 203). This, again, is an ugly, self-serving rationalization—but it is sufficiently true to give us pause, and to suggest that the Underground Man is not merely, as Sacvan Bercovitch claims, the victim of Dostoyevsky's irony. For, if he were, he would not be the compelling, fascinating (if obnoxious) figure that he is. Conscience does make cowards of us all, said another self-divided individual, and to be called coward by as loathsome a person as the Undergroundling, if not a pungent insult, is certainly an involvement of the reader in the narrative that (as I shall consider later) bears significance. Dostoyevsky's basic if oblique point may be that the realization through "conscience" (which includes consciousness, and even Lawrentian "unconsciousness") about our "cowardice" and deep self-delusion may help us to struggle toward some measure of worth or integrity, but it would be very hard.

The narrator shortly after the "secret . . . pleasure" passage admits that there are moments when he "'liked to have his face slapped'" (p. 95). Though he claims that this pleasure would be the "pleasure and despair" (p. 95), though, further, it could be said that this last qualification represents the moral motif that Frank observes, one has also to face the full force here of both "pleasure" and of "despair." What our Underground Man is implying is that the humiliation of a face-slapping would give him *sexual* satisfaction; he might experience an ejaculation, perhaps even an orgasm, at this physical humiliation (and there is a real sense in which the whole narrative is one long sadomasochistic ejaculation).

The other term in this oxymoronic combination, despair, lends the needed ontological depth to this symbolic sexual degradation. Indeed, this is the term of potential salvation, despite the status of despair as a cardinal sin in Catholicism. For it would be worse if degradation were not responded to in *any* way, with no affect at all. This *would* be damnation, and though it is a state found in 20th century literature (as in William Burroughs' *Naked Lunch*), affectless despair represents nihilism, and is perhaps further than Dostoyevsky, with his religious affiliation, wanted to go. Indeed, the moral sense glittering dimly at the bottom of this abyss of confession is, as Frank points out, what gives *Notes* part of its considerable if oblique moral energy. Yet whatever moral character this novella harbors must also absorb the moral extremity embodied in the real possibility that our anti-hero is a sex-soiled soul; his despair itself could mean damnation.

Dostoyevsky's sense of degradation is more than excoriating; it is deeply piercing, penetrating all our egoistic defenses, threatening to blight our very core of being. In the quotation following, we continue to hear about the Underground Man's sense of resentment of the tavern Officer, but it is presented in broad enough terms to qualify strongly as one of the most overwhelming passages of metaphysical degradation in literature:

> In addition to being disgraced in the first place, the poor mouse manages to mire itself in more mud as a result of its questions and doubts. And each question brings us so many more unanswered questions that a fatal pool of sticky muck is formed, consisting of the mouse's doubts and torments as well as of the gobs of spit aimed at it by the practical men of action, who stand around like judges and dictators and laugh lustily at it till their throats are sore. Of course, the only thing left for it to do is to shrug its puny shoulders, and, affecting a scornful smile, scurry off ignominiously to its mousehole. And there, in its repulsive, evilsmelling nest, the downtrodden, ridiculed mouse plunges immediately into a cold, poisonous, and—most important—never-ending hatred. For forty years, it will remember the humiliation in all its ignominious details, each time adding some new point, more abject still, endlessly taunting and tormenting itself. Although ashamed of its own thoughts, the mouse will

remember everything, go over it again, and again, then think up possible additional humiliations. (p. 97).

III

I am suggesting that the core of the narrator's degradation is sexual, literally, a claim I will elaborate later in the [essay]. But it is also necessary to suggest in this last torturous confession, that something resides within or beneath the sexual element here, and that it is central to the meaning of the story itself. "'Desire,'" says our man "'. . . is the manifestation of life itself—of all life—and encompasses everything from reason down to scratching oneself'" (p. 112). When he goes on to assert that "'I . . . instinctively want to live, to exercise all the aspects of life in me and not only reason . . . ,'" (p. 112), we also realize that a major thematic tension girding the work is that of objectivity versus subjectivity. Implied more specifically above as reason versus desire, this tension amounts within the elusive contexts of *Notes* to an opposition between ideology and *libido,* basic life energy.

Students of Dostoyevsky have observed that he is making an attack in *Notes* on reason because 19th century ideologists like Chernyshevsky, influenced by 18th century European optimistic rationalism, asserted that rationality will solve or resolve all human problems, the consummation of which is imagized in the glittering metaphor of the Crystal Palace. An ideal of realized objectivism, this gaudy architectural symbol of the 19th century European ideologue represents a world free of whim, impulse, perversity, will, desire. But Dostoyevsky implies throughout *Notes* that these elements are not only essential to human experience, significance, and value; human life lacks ultimate moral possibility without them. In this light, Dostoyevsky, through his "untermënsch," is not a social reactionary resisting 19th century Western radical rationalism; he is also, and significantly, an early Modernist artist claiming like Thomas Hardy in "In Tenebris, II," that "If way there be to a better, it demand a full look at the worst." This credal battle-cry, so familiar to us now through the heritage of Modernist and vanguard writers and artists, makes an early and disguised appearance in the narrator of *Notes,* who more than once is described, if in self-deprecatory terms, as being a literary intellectual. Ultimately, of course, it is his literary "father," Dostoyevsky himself, who is the Modernist Ur-father here, but the role is shared with his unheroic "son," and there is a subtle sense in which one can regard the Underground Man as both a "poét maudit" and a travesty of one.

Through this travesty Dostoyevsky conveys a number of Modernist attitudes and values now taken for granted as part of our modern art culture. That that "culture" should appear in such despicable and bristling form lends force to Kingsley Widmer's reminder in the title of his monograph on literary modernism, *Edges of Extremity,* that modernism as a cultural heritage remains explosive and subversive if properly understood. For all the iconoclastic posturings and symbolic pretentiousness of Hermann Hesse and Harry Haller in *Steppenwolf,* Dostoyevsky's mouse-man is, except in one significant respect that I will broach later, a far more impressive literary realization of primal rebellion than Hesse's romanticized rebel-intellectual. Dostoyevsky and his narrator not only want to throw rocks at the crystal palace; they really want to strip all of us naked, and exhibit ourselves in the "glass" of satire. Thus Dostoyevsky's partial defense of libido, instinct, and caprice, even in their most revulsive embodiments, becomes the most radical gesture conceivable, and antedates Freud's idea of a biological libertarianism that resists cultural or societal control. This instinctual subjectivism goes beyond political revolution to render a basically ontological gesture of liberation through self-liberation. Before we build the Good Society, *Notes* graphically implies, we must first recognize and confront the totality of human nature. Dostoyevsky is suggesting that we will never have a good society, let alone a "Crystal Palace," until we have confronted the Underground Man in ourselves.

But how bad, how perverse, is the Underground Man? To find out, to see how much suffering he can masochistically absorb and sadistically impose, we must look into the climactic episodes of this novella, the Zverkov dinner-party and the subsequent episode involving the young prostitute Liza.

IV

A basic condition of alienation is loneliness. Solitary, the Underground Man yearns for human contact. Yet his human contacts invariably result in disastrous personal experiences that re-enforce his misanthropy and his self-loathing. Thus, the narrator is trapped in a vicious circle. One day, feeling desperately lonely, he is driven to visit a former school acquaintance named Simonov who with two other school acquaintances of the narrator is planning a going-away party for an army officer named Zverkov, a friend of theirs. This Zverkov is elegant, handsome, debonair, and, by his own estimation, a woman's man. He is also a large man (although almost everyone in this novella is bigger, apparently, than the narrator, a factor partly defining his plight). Thus, Zverkov harbors a doubles relationship (in the narrator's mind) with the Officer who had treated him like an object in the tavern. Zverkov is again the Man of Action, further glamorized by the adulation of Simonov and the other former school mates, and by his own boasting about amorous conquests. He is, in other words, the complete opposite of our anti-hero, the type the latter most loathes and feels threatened by. This temperamental and physical contrast is important, because it helps organize the novella in several ways. First, it not only focuses on the Man of Exploits: it also suggests in a fundamental way the real resolution of the narrator's on-going conflict with the Nevsky-Prospect Officer and the type he represents. We recall that the narrator, in an understandable self-delusion, had felt that he had taken the last round by having the impulsive audacity to bump into the Officer on the Prospect. The outcome of his engagement with the Man of Action in the form of Officer Zverkov is not only that he loses the next round—he loses a great deal more.

When the Underground Man arrives at Simonov's place, Simonov and his cronies, who represent "society" for the rest of the narrative, are surprised and displeased to see him: "'Apparently I was something like a housefly in their eyes . . . I had not expected that much contempt'" (p. 140). He hears (or overhears) the plans for the party for Zverkov. The narrator impulsively decides to invite himself to the party, partly out of spite to himself and to the others (who had hated him in school). The sensible, self-respecting thing to have done under the circumstances would have been to withdraw, but it is necessary with the Underground Man to keep the "principle" of perversity in mind continually. He invites himself to the dinner party precisely because it is made clear by the others that he is not wanted: "'. . . you never got along with Zverkov,'" he is pointedly informed (p. 143).

Indeed, he shouldn't invite himself, he shouldn't go, for he will get involved in a train of disastrous events. Yet by not being sensible or "rational" here he will certainly undergo suffering, the one state, he and Dostoyevsky think, that the Crystal Palace will banish. But even more deeply, there is perhaps something psychologically healthy beneath this perversity. The narrator invites himself to a social event whose planners frankly don't want him to attend. In inviting himself he is giving himself the opportunity or chance to be *accepted,* to have social judgement reversed. He wants in a way to be accepted. Acceptance is hardly what happens, yet to an extent it is a wholesome social impulse, and part of the same urge that drives him out of his lonely dwelling to have refreshening contact with other human beings. Alongside the narrator's perversity, spite, and sado-masochism is a desire for the inspiriting life of a social concourse and social approval.

After leaving Simonov's, he asks himself why he forced himself into the party, and realizes it is "spite": "'I'd go just to spite them, and the more wrong, the more tactless it was for me to go, the more certainly I'd go'" (p. 145). Another reason for going, perhaps partly rationalization, is given a little later: "'Had I not gone, I'd have taunted myself for the rest of my life: "so you didn't have the guts to face *reality,* eh?"'" (p. 148). When the narrator says right after this that "'I wanted to show the lot of them that I wasn't the coward I myself thought I was,'" we realize how profoundly divided he is between his inner and social being, and what a hopeless task he is undertaking. Though he is respected neither by others nor by himself, the fact remains that some spark of survival as self-respect persists in him. It is that spark, as well as the consequences of his perversity, that turns *Notes* from confessional comedy and satire into a sordid ontological tragedy transcending its polemical role in the context of 19th century Russian and European cultural politics.

Matters get off to a bad start by the narrator not being informed that the dinner-party time has been changed to an hour later. Thus he is the first to arrive, and must endure the peculiar ignominy of the guest who arrives too early for an event because he is not considered important enough to be informed of a time change. The rest of the party finally arrives, and after some superficial and patronizing sociability towards the narrator from Zverkov, the latent animosities re-emerge, which result in the narrator being ignored and thus savagely isolated. He thinks of leaving but doesn't. He also *doesn't* enjoy the pain this whole incident is giving him, and instead of being masochistic (or only masochistic), he becomes aggressive and hostile, even attacking Zverkov himself, the life and light of the party.

His attacking Zverkov while the latter is in the middle of relating an amorous conquest is significant. Our anti-hero, whose courage here derives from a rage of frustration and humiliation, even refuses to toast the Hero Zverkov, to everyone's amazed disgust. He proposes his own toast in which he declares his hatred of "'smut and those who talk smut. Especially the latter'" (p. 155). Zverkov is deeply offended, and the others rain insults on the narrator, who responds with a challenge of a duel that is laughed down. The others move from the table to a sofa, leaving the narrator alone and totally ignoring him, as he sits drenched in vindictiveness, self-pity, and simulated scorn.

Again he feels he should leave, but remains, out of "spite." He is suffering badly, and the suffering continues for three hours, as he paces back and forth by the table, pretending to ignore the carousing Zverkov party nearby:

'Now and then, with a stabbing, sickening pain, it occured to me that ten, twenty, perhaps forty years might pass and I'd still remember these, the most ridiculous and painful minutes of my life, with horror and disgust. One could not have gone further out of one's way than I had to inflict upon myself the cruelest of humiliations.' (p. 157).

Finally breaking down, the Underground Man asks for forgiveness, but is scorned by the whole dinner group, including Zverkov (who says "'*You* couldn't offend *me* under any circumstances!'") (p. 157). Finding out that the group is on its way to a brothel, the narrator allows this last degradation to lead to a worse one by asking Simonov to lend him money so that he too can join the gang. Simonov first turns him down brutally, then after our narrator pleads with him ("'I clutched at his coat. It was a nightmare'") (p. 158), almost throws the money at the narrator. Left alone, in a state of "horrible anguish," the narrator decides to go to the same brothel, where he thinks he will make atonement to his self-debasement by demanding forgiveness from Zverkov, or slapping his face.

V

Fortunately yet unfortunately, the Underground Man gets to the brothel too late to make contact with the Zverkov group. At desperately loose ends with himself, and in a very nasty mood, he selects a young woman named Liza to go to bed with. After intercourse, still feeling degraded and vicious, he launches a formidably insidious attack on the young prostitute. He describes her bleak future as a prostitute, and contrasts it with various images of happy family life with a sadistic, malignant imaginativeness that is "literary" in its cogency and articulateness, if pathological in motivation. First, he stresses her enslaved condition in the brothel: "'You'll never buy yourself out. It's as

though you'd sold your soul to the devil'" (p. 189). When at one point in his discourse Liza says that the narrator sounds like a book, he takes this remark in the worst sense, and thus begins to describe her condition with a penetrative viciousness:

'I tell you, when I came to just now and found myself here with you, I felt sick. As a matter of fact, people only come here when they're drunk. But if I'd met you somewhere else, and you'd led a decent life, I'd have trailed after you and probably fallen in love with you too . . . now I know that all I have to do is whistle and, whether you want to or not, you have to come with me . . . Just ask yourself what you're . . . selling into bondage. It's your soul you're selling, your soul, over which you have no power. You're selling it along with your body. You offer your love to the first drunkard who comes along, to tramp upon' (p. 175).

The narrator continues pouring it on, virtually annihilating any fantasies Liza may have woven to protect herself from her sordid present life. He says that her "house lover" doesn't, couldn't, really love her, that if she asked him to marry her, he'd probably beat her, that she will age quickly and before long the brothel-owner will make her feel very unwanted, insulting her as she sinks lower and lower ("'You'll lose everything; everything will go without return—youth, hopes, looks—and at 22 you'll look 35.'") He also mentions possible diseases she well could catch. Like another prostitute who ends up beaten and bleeding, weeping in front of a particularly brutal whorehouse called the Haymarket (as women do, claims the narrator, who have finally reached the bottom), Liza is shown the most harrowing degradation as her sure future in the mirror of the narrator's diabolical art. Moreover, as this woman, Liza's projected double, sits weeping and bleeding and swearing, "'drunken soldiers and cabbies gathered around her and taunted her'" (p. 177); this nightmare would be Liza's fate as well.

Nor does the Underground Man stop here. He describes Liza in the future, aging and despised, told openly by the brothelkeeper that she should die, and that "'they'll stow you somewhere in the dirtiest corner of the basement. And as you lie dying in the dank darkness, what will you think about in your loneliness?'" (p. 178). As if this were not enough, he describes what people will feel towards her after she is dead: "'no one will come to your grave, there'll not be a tear, not a sigh, not a prayer over you . . . it'll be as if you'd never even existed'" (p. 179).

There is art in this interminable exercise of psychological skin-stripping, as well as enormous spite, the venom stored up until the whole personality of the narrator resembles a tautened scorpion's tail. If he wants to break Liza's heart, turn her inside out, he has succeeded, but he has gone too far, and no longer enjoys this slow, thorough destruction of another human being ("'the fact is, I'd never, never witnessed such despair'") (p. 179). Yet somehow, as the narrator tries to leave, Liza, undergoing an extraordinary rebirth of spirit, all but embraces him. He in turn unwisely gives her his address, thus setting the scene for the final and worst degradation of the entire narrative.

The experience with Liza bothers him far more than the Zverkov-party events preceding it. He doesn't seem to know why this is so, though he is worried that she will come to his mousehole and see him in all his squalor. But it is possible that the deeper reason for his disturbance and worry about Liza is that he realizes he has aroused a soul in her. This he cannot stand, because he cannot summon the soul-lifting "sincerity" he was taken by Liza as having the night before in the brothel when he actually was trying to destroy her.

One problem about Liza appearing at the narrator's dwelling is the exposure of his bizarrely masochistic relationship with his servant Apollon. Their relationship exhibits the social and psychological irony of a servant who is master of his master. Apollon, who lisps, and is haughty and imperturbable, is dependent on the narrator only for his wages, and it is money alone that provides the latter with any power over the impudently imperious servant. Otherwise, Apollon embodies another dimension of humiliation of the narrator, intensified by the atmosphere of oblique homosexuality in this domestic situation, the cold tension and slightly nightmarish invasion of territorial space and proprieties of two men living together in hostile emotional intimacy. The relationship is basically frustrating to the Underground Man because, except for Liza, Apollon is the one person he is in a social position to dominate or even crush. Unfortunately for the narrator and Liza, Apollon is indomitable.

Thus what sets up the climactic scene of the narrator's damnation is Liza's entering his place at the very moment he is bashing himself hysterically on the rock of Apollon's imperturbability. She accidentally and blamelessly sees her hero disgracing himself with his own servant. Profoundly humiliated, the narrator is determined to make Liza "'pay dearly for *everything*'" (p. 192). "Everything" is italicized in the text to give it weight, and it should have weight, for in effect Liza is sacrificed for the narrator's lifetime of degradation. She indeed is to pay for *everything*, though this penalty harbors the deeper horror and disgrace for the narrator that she is innocent, and one of life's victims. Sold, as she informs the narrator, by her parents (p. 171), she is now subjected to the worst viciousness conceivable by the Underground Man.

Not realizing what the narrator really feels, Liza admits that she wants to leave the brothel for good. But the narrator who is in an agony (or ecstasy) of hypersensitivity and resentment, takes offense at her mild resentment at his five-minute lapses of angry, selfish silence. His vindictive fury pours over her like lava:

> 'Why did you come? Answer me!' I shouted in a rage. 'All right, my girl, I'll tell you why: you came because of all the 'touching' things I said the other night. But, for your information, I was laughing at you then, just as I'm laughing at you now. Why are you trembling? Yes, I say I was laughing. I had been insulted at a dinner party just before I came by the fellows who preceded me. I came to your place to take a punch at one of them, the officer, but I was too late. I had to vent my spite on someone else, and you happened to

> be around, so I poured my resentment out on you and had a good laugh. I'd been insulted, so I wanted to insult back' (p. 195).

The narrator is kicking someone who is down, in this case, a woman. Although he claims that "'My cynicism had crushed her,'" she will rebound even from this fiendish cruelty. The narrator, if nothing else, is honest with her about why he hates her. He also says, "'I can only play with words or dream inside my head; in real life, all I want is for you to vanish into the ground!'" (p. 196). And in an ecstasy of self-abasement, the narrator exposes himself totally:

> . . . you alone are responsible for everything because you happened to be at hand, because I'm a louse, because I'm the most disgusting, most laughable, pettiest, most stupid, and most envious of all the worms of the earth— which are in no way better than me, but which, hell knows why, never feel embarrassed. But me—all my life I've let all sorts of scum push me around—that's just like me! And do you think I care if you don't understand all this? What concern of mine are you? What concern is it of mine whether or not you rot in that house? Don't you realize that when I've finished telling you all this, I'll hate you just because you were here and listened to me? Why, a man only bares his soul like this once in a lifetime . . . (pp. 196-97)

Liza's response to all of this "existential" venom and masochistic exhibitionism is saintly, if disastrous for her; she embraces him in the one great and only act of self-sacrificing empathy in the entire work. At this point, the narrator feels that a role-reversal from the previous night has taken place: "'. . . she now had the heroic role, and I was the beaten-down, crushed creature she had been . . .'" (p. 189). His abjectness at this moment stimulates (the word is carefully chosen) the narrator to "'dominate and possess. Passion burned in my eyes as I fiercely clasped her hands. Ah, how I hated her, and how furiously I was drawn to her at the moment . . . she threw herself at me in rapture'" (p. 198).

Aside from Liza's dreadful misinterpretation of the narrator's cast of mind here, his ambivalence, which he will convey towards Liza a minute later as lust and vindictive degrading hatred, damns him. This ambivalence is the effect of all his pent-up misery and social despicableness, and he gets rid of it in the worst way he can—by literally pouring it, transformed into irrational hate, into another, vulnerable, innocent human being who, further, is deluded about the true nature of his passion until it is too late: "'A quarter of an hour later . . . she knew everything, for I had subjected her to the ultimate insult, but . . . no need to go into detail. She had guessed that my outburst of passion had actually been an act of revenge, a new effort to humiliate her, and that now, to my almost impersonal hatred, there was added a *personal* hatred for her'" (p. 199).

Now he personally hates Liza because he has been vindictive towards her, making him feel guilt that he converts self-protectively into hatred of the prostitute. What is the "ultimate insult" to Liza that our narrator doesn't want to go into? To convey vindictive or spiteful anger, the occasionally savage Mellors in D. H. Lawrence's *Lady Chatterley's Lover* sodomizes his beloved Connie on one dark "night of sensual passion." Lawrence further complicates and obscures this scene by implying doctrinal, heuristic values in Mellors's act. The analogous scene in *Notes* is briefer, and without having to spell things out (he couldn't have, anyway, given the literary censorship of the time), Dostoyevsky, I think, is suggesting that the narrator sodomizes Liza in a way that makes his true attitude towards her quite clear.

The damnation of the Underground Man is his entrapment by a habitual orientation towards hatred and self-hatred born of his incapacity to meet life and society in self-respecting terms.

—Donald Gutierrez

In thus demeaning the girl, the narrator also demeans himself. At least, he must think he does, for what follows indicates some guilty self-examination and semi-justification. He says that for him, love is only "bullying and dominating" (p. 199); love is a struggle "'starting with hatred and ending in the subjection of the loved object...'" (p. 199). Thus the Underground Man in effect justifies the maltreatment he has received from those stronger or more successful than himself by his willingness to behave or feel even more vindictiveness towards those weaker than or defenseless towards him.

Although the narrator is frequently described by critics and scholars as the ultimate sensibility in early modern alienation, the forerunner of the despised or dispossessed characters of Beckett, Céline, Henry Miller, B. Traven, it can also be said that by virtue of the narrator's sadomasochistic character structure and conduct, he affirms the repressive social and power structure of his day and society by acting like a person (low) in the pecking order. He thus loses the final, residual, desperate integrity that might have been sustained in surmounting a brutal social order by refusing to trample on or mistreat the one vulnerable human being lower on the pole than himself. In this extreme, intentional degrading of Liza, he condemns himself socially by justifying the very power and social hierarchy that makes him feel not only like a mouse, but like a worm.

But buggery, if it occurs, is not the last viciousness imposed by the narrator upon the young prostitute. A worse and final one remains, though it proceeds from the former, as the former proceeds from the narrator's humiliation by the Officer in the tavern. As Liza starts to leave, the narrator rushes after her, and puts some money in her hand. Yet he has an immediate revulsion to his brutal gesture:

"'The cruelty was so contrived and such *bad literature* that I couldn't bear it myself and leaped away to a far corner of the room; after that, full of shame and despair, I rushed after Liza" (p. 200). He can't find her, and, on returning to the room, finds the money he gave her on the table. Although the narrator has devastated the young prostitute, she maintains her integrity in a final, decisive gesture that makes his deliberate viciousness towards her impotent. Not unlike Hardy's Tess D'Urberville, Liza rises to the occasion, and whatever degradation or deprivation she is likely to encounter in a future probably made darker by the Underground Man's complex sadism, she can remember her dignified rejection of the narrator's "whore-money" with just pride.

On finding the money, the narrator runs out again looking for Liza. He realizes, though, that even if he found her, it would only lead to the compulsive cycle of repentance followed (the next day) by hatred "'because I kissed her feet today.... As though I hadn't found out today for the *hundredth time* [italics added] what I'm really worth? As though I could prevent myself from torturing her!'" (p. 201). This passage is followed by the hideous self-deception that his grave insult to Liza would actually do her good, even redeem and "purify" her, through hatred or even forgiveness. This is certainly, as Frank has observed,[9] a gross rationalization, and is part of the narrator's continuing self-debasement. But the preceding passage, indicating the Underground Man's habitual oscillation between penitence and viciousness, constitutes a broad way of describing his alternate masochism and sadism, an activity which also functions as part of the internal organization of *Notes.* Kissing her feet one day, verbally tearing her apart the next, the Underground Man occupies a circle of compulsively, irrevocably vicious and self-degrading impulses from which he will never escape. Such, again, is his damnation.

That his damnation is significantly sexual in character is important. The sexual motif, though not omnipresent in *Notes,* serves both as one of its major elements, and as its primary "plot" determinant. It is not accidental that the narrator's attack on Zverkov is made as the latter is making sexual boasts. This attack in turn leads to his drastic rupture with the Zverkov party, resulting in his three hours of deeply rankling isolation that finally degrades him into offering rejected apologies. All these dovetailed rejections and humiliations, interwoven by their relation to sexual topics and values, so dehumanize the narrator and desensitize his self-respect and even his sense of self, that he finally abases himself definitively by asking money of a man who has just scorned him—in order to have sex at a brothel, as part of a party of men who have treated him with the utmost contempt. In this psychological context, sex becomes a means through which the humiliation becomes ontological, a shaft driven through the narrator's selfhood. So transfixed, the narrator's still musters a little "*libido*"—he wants to insult Zverkov, provoke a duel, and save or at least partially redeem his honor (although as he has no honor, this is not easily accomplished). But as he well knows, this revenge of honor is an absurd fantasy, born of reading too much Russian romantic literature (Lermontov, Saltikov-Schredin, Pushkin). The ironic contrast effected here by Dostoyevsky with the heroes of the 19th century romance fictions, while satirizing that tradition, also makes Dostoyevsky's anti-hero look all the worse. Even had the Zverkov party still been at the brothel when the narrator arrived, he would either have lacked the courage to attack Zverkov physically, or if he had challenged him in any way, would again have been mocked, or perhaps, in one of his typical and extreme emotional reversals, have found himself kissing Zverkov's boots. And, in any event, what kind of a threat is a mouse or a fly to anyone?

Nevertheless, a literary or intellectual fly with a dangerous flair for words and a deep need to vindicate his soiled soul at *someone's* expense, *is* dangerous to anyone vulnerable to him. Liza thus becomes his victim, and it is through sex that the narrator virtually attempts to destroy her. Ironically, he first inadvertently gives her a kind of spiritual rebirth in the brothel. At his lodging the next day, he demolishes Liza's resurrectionary mood again, out of vindictive spite, though he is not able to destroy her selfhood. But he does devastate her, and does so by sexual and verbal means. Whatever the nature of his second (and last) sexual encounter with Liza, sodomy or otherwise, it embodies an attitude that would shove her towards the Haymarket.

VI

The damnation of the Underground Man is his entrapment by a habitual orientation towards hatred and self-hatred born of his incapacity to meet life and society in self-respecting terms. This evaluation of course means taking Dostoyevsky's protagonist literally. Yet a literal interpretation does not detract from the numerous symbolic readings of Dostoyevsky's Underground Man. Some of these interpretations are both impressive and true. Dostoyevsky's underling *is* the unreconstructed individualist, the man or person that no ameliorative, let alone utopian, society can tolerate or assimilate, because his very existence undermines its rationale for or claims to excellence. He exemplifies human nature inaccessible to rational social planning. He will always suffer or cause suffering, irregardless of any societal or theoretical assumption that suffering and perversity can be legislated out of existence. His very spitefulness is, ultimately, part of the essence of his (and our) humanity, if humanity is regarded as what is left in the viscera of rebellious subjectivity against any totalitarian polity of repressive control. And, as Dostoyevsky's creature satirizing the rationalist ideologues of the 19th century (Owen, Fourier, Chernyshevsky, Marx), the Underground Man reverberates with further significance. He is the anti-Romanticist retort to swashbuckling heroicism and to Organizational Man; he is as well the prototype of the protagonist as fascinating scum or bum prominent in Modernist literature. Unheroic, anti-humane, he is the Residual Man of the modern era.

But the Underground Man is first and basically his literal self, without which all the formidable symbolic meanings would not exist. He is first and foremost, and for whatever reason, an intelligent human being of disturbingly fascinating nastiness. He has his primary significance on that level, in that sphere. And it is on that level of literalness that his selfhood is most vividly projected and shown in the process of damning itself. The narrator's damnation of self is part of the literal reality of the story, and derives from this position more of its considerable force than critics have allowed. It does so because people don't like looking steadily into a cesspool, yet it is only by so doing that one can fully realize the nature or cause of the power of this characterization.

But if *Notes* is a story of damnation, partly registered through sex, if it is as well an extremely reflexive confessional, it goes well beyond being an isolated instance readily dismissed as being pathologically unique. Indeed, in an electrifying tactic effective in its being placed at the end of the narrative, Dostoyevsky has the Underground Man indicate (to cite a key passage again) that he holds a higher opinion of himself than of the reader: "'. . . All I did was carry to the limit what you haven't dared to push even halfway—taking your cowardice for reasonableness, thus making yourself feel better. So I may still turn out to be more *alive* than you in the end'" (p. 203). This passage is preceded by an overt attack on literature that romanticizes reality, for, and it is a central, pre-Eliotic attitude in *Notes,* human beings don't want to face reality—"'we're all cripples to some degree'" (p. 202). Although Bercovitch has argued convincingly that we cannot take the Underground Man at his own word because he is at times deeply self-deluded, it reduces the depth and thrust of the story *not* to take the narrator seriously here. He may be self-deluded, like many people; yet, again, like other deeply-divided protagonists of Modern literature, he reveals alarming perceptivity into human nature in the very act of discrediting himself.

Without transforming the narrator into a T. S. Eliot, one can still claim that Dostoyevsky's partial affirmation of him, without substantially enhancing the narrator's status, is made at the reader's expense. The narrator may be a swine, but at least he knows and accepts that he is, wallowing in the mire of his own degradation. He actually exhibits a kind of perverse metaphysical courage (though he also displays masochism, extreme compulsiveness, and self-deception) in his obsession to examine and reveal the abysses of his own being. Most of the rest of us would *not* do this—out of "reasonableness." The Underground Man calls our bluff; we lack his confessional gutsiness and pleasure in self-exposure, his fortitude and masochism in confronting extremely upsetting "material" in our experience, and *thus* we are less alive than he. To make matters even softer for ourselves, we (some of us) embrace a literary vision of life—"romanticism"—that lies about reality. Indeed, the narrator accuses us of being generally confused and disoriented: "'Left alone without literature, we immediately become entangled and lost—we don't know what to join, what to keep up with; what to love, what to hate; what to respect, what to despise! We even find it painful to be men. . . . We're stillborn. . . .'" (p. 203).

"Stillborn"—again the accusation of the reader being dead, or unrealized, because he is unchallenged, disoriented, indecisive. The Underground Man is, among other things, a travesty of Hamlet. He is a man who can never satisfactorily resolve "the whips and scorns of time," and who will let almost anyone tweak him by the nose, because of his radical self- and social-alienation. This little man, this agony of convoluted self, disturbs us both because he is in his very self a mockery of the likelihood of a Good Society, and because he is the Shadow or idinal side to our "real me," threatening too in the acuity and frenzied vitality of his intelligence. He also is perturbing because he reaches out of the text and holds us responsible for our worst self or selves. Rather than being merely a disintegrated self, the Underground Man is a person feverishly alive at his core of nihilistic individuality. By existing so intensely at this terrible center of negatively bared being, he suggests that some substance of self is at the bottom of human nature, and leaves little room for the reader to decide how deeply his self-scrutiny sounds our being as well. One of the most devastating accounts in fiction of self-damnation, *Notes* harbors the profound obverse implication that if there is a self to damn, there is also a self to cherish.

Notes

[1] David Hume, *A Treatise of Human Nature* (Oxford, England: Clarendon Press, 1967) 251-252.

[2] Joseph Frank, "Nihilism and *Notes from Underground*," *Sewanee Review,* v. 30, 1961, 12.

[3] Frank, ibid, (pp. 26, 27). George Steiner relates the tragic character of *Notes* to the *narrator's* inadequate manhood: "The tragedy of the Underground Man is, literally, his retreat from manhood. This retreat is made explicit through the cruel impotence of his assault on Liza." *Tolstoy or Dostoyevsky: An Essay in the Old Criticism.* (New York: Knopf, 1959), 225.

[4] Fyodor Dostoyevsky, *Notes from Underground* . . . (New York: NAL, 1961), 90. All further references to this text in this chapter are to this edition.

[5] Some Dostoyevsky scholars feel that there are areas of similarity between Dostoyevsky and his protagonist in *Notes.* Avraham Yarmolinsky claims that ". . . Dostoyevsky makes him [the Underground Man], to some extent, his own spokesman. Indeed, the wretch took more from his creator than his ideas—he embodied a potentiality of the author's nature." (*Dostoyevsky: A Life*) (New York: Harcourt, Brace, 1934), 192. According to Boyce Gibson, "Dostoyevsky certainly does not identify with his anti-hero . . . [yet] something of the Underground enters into the world view of Dostoyevsky himself. His anti-rationalism, his antipathy to scientific paradigms, his sense of freedom as unlimited opportunity for good and for evil . . . —all this is pure Dostoyevsky." *The Religion of Dostoyevsky* (London: SCM Press Ltd., 1973), 82-83. Walter Kaufman goes to the extreme of regarding Dostoyevsky and his narrator as virtually having as much in common as the author and protagonist in the autobiographical works of Augustine, Pascal, and Rousseau. *Existentialism from Dostoyevsky to Sartre* (New York: Meridian, 1956), 12-13.

[6] For a treatment of irony in *Notes* see Sacvan Bercovitch, "Dramatic Irony in *Notes from Underground*," *Slavic and East European Journal,* v. VIII, no. 3 (1964).

[7] Sigmund Freud, *The Ego and the Id* (London: Hogarth Press, 1959), 28.

[8] Frank, op. cit., 9-10.

[9] Frank, op. cit., 31.

J. Brooks Bouson   (essay date 1989)

SOURCE: "Narcissistic Vulnerability and Rage in Dostoevsky's *Notes from Underground*," in *The Empathic Reader: A Study of the Narcissistic Character and the Drama of the Self,* University of Massachusetts Press, 1989, pp. 33-50.

[*In the following excerpt, Bouson offers a psychoanalytic reading of Dostoevsky's "paradoxalist, narcissistic" underground man.*]

A narrative suffused with rage, Fyodor Dostoevsky's ***Notes From Underground*** depicts a character who provides a strategic point of entry into the troubled selfhood of Tragic Man. Suffering from shaky self-esteem, "neither a hero nor an insect" (130), the Underground Man is a spiteful individual who harbors a deep sense of injury and attempts to injure others. What will be partially disguised in most of our subsequent encounters with Tragic Man—his urgent need for attention and his enraged or depressed response to what he perceives as rejection—is openly dramatized in this text. That a number of commentators have all but avoided the anti-hero's perverse, angry personality, focusing instead on the philosophic discourse of ***Notes,*** is telling. In this critical tendency toward textual avoidances and abstractions, we find suggestive evidence of the ability of Dostoevsky's narrative to disturb and implicate its readers.

While ***Notes From Underground*** is "an abnormally unnerving story to read" and while there is something unsettling about the reader's "experience of proximity" to Dostoevsky's unstable anti-hero (Norman 289), many critics who have responded to this work have centered attention not on the anti-hero's disruptive presence or his shameful autobiographical account in Part 2 but, instead, on the ideological implications of his paradoxical discourse in Part I. Walter Kaufmann, for example, describes Part I of ***Notes From Underground*** as "the best overture for existentialism ever written" (14). Edward Wasiolek holds that the anti-hero perpetually "redefines himself by contradiction and denial" as a "pledge of his freedom" (43). According to Reed Merrill, "[t]he determined objective of the Underground Man is to prove conclusively that he is free to choose and to act" (515). In Merrill's view, the anti-hero is a "developed thinker" (506) who "*knows* that there are no truths except those temporarily created by his own caprice . . ." (512). Such apologists for the anti-hero, remarks Richard Weisberg, have used Part I of the novel "selectively" and have all but ignored Part 2 (554) in their defense of the Underground Man's claim that he acts irrationally and capriciously to assert his free will. We find a dramatic example of these critical omissions in the decision by some editors to publish only Part I of ***Notes.*** Through their textual avoidances and their selective representations of the text, such critics, as they repeat the anti-hero's denials of his utter lack of free choice, use philosophic formulas to shield themselves from his agonistic, destabilizing presence. For "[i]nsult," observes Liane Norman, "is a mode more or less constant" throughout *Notes* and is designed to "provoke defensive responses" from the reader (289).[1] And the fact that the anti-hero's "need for an audience's recognition and confirmation," as Terrence Doody comments, "is constant, desperate, and essential" (27) is also meant to elicit a response from the reader. That a number of critics have played the role of confirming audience for the anti-hero's capricious behavior, reading it as an indicator of his adherence to the principle of freedom, attests to the power of *Notes* to involve the reader in the narcissistic script which it dramatizes.

Casting the "notes" of his anti-hero as a confession, Dostoevsky invites our active listening. Despite the Underground Man's seductive free-will rhetoric, he compulsively performs and reperforms a predetermined plot, as the psychocritics have observed.[2] Now forty, the Underground Man recalls in Part 2 a series of shameful incidents which occurred sixteen years before, when he was twenty-four. Ostensibly, he records his past to obtain "relief" from and to "get rid of" his oppressive memories (156). But it becomes apparent, as he repeats with his "gentlemen" audience the same psychodrama he describes in his reminiscences, that he is condemned to reenact his past in the present. The Underground Man is, as he claims from the outset, a sick man. Literally every word of his paradoxalist's account points to his underlying sense of defectiveness, and his seething anger, floating anxieties, and atavistic urges are forcibly brought to the forefront of the reader's awareness. Despite his noisy declarations that he acts irrationally and capriciously to assert his free will, he is, as he suspects, "impelled," "bound" to act as he does (170, 132). Driven by his archaic grandiose needs, he wants to exert power over others and be the center of attention and when these demands are thwarted, as happens in the separate but interlocking incidents first with the officer, then with Zverkov, and finally with Liza, he reacts with defensive arrogance, grandiose fantasies, depression, and rage. Needing a self-object totally under his control, he creates his fictive gentlemen audience, acting out with them his desire to tyrannize over and compel the attention of others.

The device of the gentlemen narratees provides the actual reader confronting *Notes* with only a minimal protection from the text's punitive plot against its readers. The use of "you" in the anti-hero's addresses to the gentlemen serves to draw in readers, who are encouraged to identify both against and with the inscribed "you" in the text. Because the gentlemen are characterized as limited and as easily subdued by the anti-hero's superior intelligence, we are partially discouraged from identifying with the narratees in Part I and, instead, are urged to take the anti-hero's side in his argument against the rationalists and thus applaud his arrogant intellectualism. The imaginary gentlemen are inscribed as "bad readers." The implied "good readers"—those who accept the anti-hero's philosophy— are invited to temporarily share the anti-hero's illusion of

power as he demolishes the rationalist metaphysic, a maneuver apparently attractive to many twentieth-century critic/readers. But while we may be captivated by the prepotent intellectual displays found in Part 1 of *Notes,* the anti-hero's spiteful, sadistic fantasies and behavior, evident throughout the narrative, are designed to assault our sensibilities and thus align us with the gentlemen, who stand in the text as representatives of the normal codes of civilized behavior which the anti-hero so outrageously offends. If we feel unsettled by our close proximity to Dostoevsky's character, it is because we become implicated in the pathological drama enacted in the text, caught up in the same sick narcissistic script the anti-hero stages with the imaginary gentlemen.

Bound and not free, the Underground Man is compelled to remember his shameful past and to act out, again and again, his pathetic, absurd drama.

—J. Brooks Bouson

The Underground Man's telescoped memory of his relationship with his rejecting caretakers—they "crushed" him with "reproaches" and then, in effect, abandoned him (175)—reveals both the genesis and recurring pattern of his disordered personality. "If I had had a home from childhood," he tells Liza, "I shouldn't be what I am now. . . . I grew up without a home; and perhaps that's why I've turned so . . . unfeeling" (195). In his radical shifts in self-perception from arrogant superiority to deep self-contempt; in his intense mood swings from elated grandiosity to acute depression; in his hypersensitivity to slights, shame-propensity, and obsessive ruminations over shameful incidents; in his lack of impulse-control and his need to control or tyrannize others; in his feeling that he lacks a solid identity, that he cannot *be* anything—the anti-hero manifests some of the classic symptoms of the narcissistic disorder. Because he has never developed the inner resources of healthy narcissism, he is condemned to spend his life in a series of fruitless attempts to extract from others what he permanently lacks: an inner sense of worth and strength. He is also condemned to reexperience with others his early narcissistic injuries. "There in its nasty, stinking, underground home our insulted, crushed and ridiculed mouse promptly becomes absorbed in cold, malignant and, above all, everlasting spite," says the anti-hero in a parodic self-description. "For forty years together it will remember its injury down to the smallest, most ignominious details. . . . It will be ashamed of its imaginings, but yet it will recall it all, it will go over and over every detail . . . and will forgive nothing" (135). Bound and not free, the Underground Man is compelled to remember his shameful past and to act out, again and again, his pathetic, absurd drama. Similarly, the reader, temporarily bound in a relationship with the anti-hero, is compelled, like the imaginary gentlemen, to listen to his obsessive ruminations, detail by sordid detail. "It is nasty for you to hear my despicable moans," says the anti-hero at one point, indirectly expressing his malice toward his gentlemen audience as he describes the attitude of an educated man suffering from a toothache. "[W]ell, let it be nasty; here I will let you have a nastier flourish in a minute . . ." (138). Dostoevsky's *Notes* reads like an extended exercise in spite directed against those readers who, like some of the gentlemen narratees, might prefer to hear a story with something of the heroic or "the good and the beautiful" in it.

At the age of twenty-four the anti-hero's life, as he explains in his retrospective account, is "gloomy, ill-regulated, and as solitary as that of a savage" (157). Torn between his craving for the approval of others and his fear of rejection, he is "morbidly sensitive" (158). A lower-level government official, he both thinks his fellow clerks superior to himself and despises them as he defensively rejects his potential rejectors. To protect his vulnerable self, he emotionally distances himself from others: he assumes a posture of arrogant hostility in front of his coworkers and so inevitably comes to "loggerheads" with them (161). The fact that he both desires and shuns eye contact with them reveals his need for a confirming response from others and also his underlying anxiety about this need. Consciously experiencing wide vacillations in his self-esteem, he imagines himself as a hero and cultivated intellectual and he perceives himself as a "scoundrel," a "coward," an "impostor" (133, 158, 138), and as subhuman: a spiteful mouse, an eel, "a nasty, disgusting fly" (135, 164). Hating his face and finding it "stupid-looking," he assumes a "lofty expression" so he "might not be suspected of being abject" (158). Just as he hides from others behind a wall of defensive superiority, so he hides from himself behind a wall of fantasied superiority, imagining himself to be a Russian "romantic," one who attempts to "preserve" himself "like some precious jewel wrapped in cotton wool" (160). The jewel image is a signifier of what he lacks and most desires: an inner sense of preciousness and cohesiveness.

Because he lacks the sustaining self-esteem supplied by an inner feeling of worth, the Underground Man is caught up in a redundant narcissistic drama. "[O]ut of touch with 'real life,'" a "terrible dreamer" (218, 167), he retreats to a bookish fantasy world where he, for a time, can overcome his feelings of worthlessness by imagining himself a hero in the world's eyes. In his grandiose daydreams, whose plots are largely plagiarized from books, he fantasies himself triumphant over others: "every one, of course, was in dust and ashes, and was forced spontaneously to recognize my superiority. . . . I was a poet and a grand gentleman, I fell in love; I came in for countless millions and immediately devoted them to humanity, and at the same time I confessed before all the people my shameful deeds, which, of course, were not merely shameful, but had in them much that was 'good and beautiful,' something in the Manfred style" (168). Anticipating that his gentlemen narratees will condemn him for taking pleasure in such preposterous daydreams, he lashes out at them: "You will say that it is vulgar and contemptible to drag all this into

public after all the tears and transports which I have myself confessed. But why is it contemptible? Can you imagine that I am ashamed of it all, and that it was stupider than anything in your life, gentlemen?" (168-69). Because on this—and many similar—occasions the inscribed "you" in the text is accused of attitudes and responses the actual reader is likely to share, the anti-hero's condemnation of his narratees is experienced as an indirect attack on the reader. Like the gentlemen audience, the reader of *Notes* is persistently positioned as an antagonist and a coparticipant in the anti-hero's self-drama.

After three months of indulging in escapist fantasies, the anti-hero develops an "irresistible desire to plunge into society" (169). There he uses others as selfobjects by dominating over them or attempting to extract from them the approval he needs to temporarily replenish his enfeebled self. While he craves contact with "society," he also fears, in his encounters with others, both a loss of control and traumatic rejection, for he can become overstimulated and disorganized when he receives the acceptance he desires, and he reacts with angry grandiosity when his demands for confirming attention are frustrated. And thus he is forced, once again, to retreat to his bookish fantasy world where he uses reading to "stifle" all that is "continually seething" inside him: his "wretched passions," "sickly irritability," "hysterical impulses, with tears and convulsions," and bouts of overwhelming depression (161). Taking "refuge" in his daydreams of "the good and the beautiful" (167), he makes up heroic adventures based on literary plots so he can "live in some way" (139). But he remains aware that he, in a fundamental way, does not feel quite real. In his sardonic description of his "golden" dream of becoming "a sluggard and a glutton" with a "good round belly," he inadvertently acknowledges what the men of action have and what he lacks. "[R]eal and solid" (141), they have cohesive selves; a "spindly little fellow" (162), he, in contrast, is narcissistically infirm. A "characterless creature," devoid of "positive" qualities, unable to "become anything" (131, 140, 131), he suffers from an impoverished sense of self.

Attempting to gain a foothold on real life, he writes his confessions and as he writes he deliberately imagines an audience before him—a hostile audience that is totally under his control and that rivets its attention on him. Telling stories so he may "live in some way," the forty-year-old narrator describes in vivid detail, but without deep comprehension, the shame-provoking misadventures of his earlier years. While we are clearly meant to recognize what many critics have avoided—the compulsive aspects of the anti-hero's capricious behavior—and while we may gain some minimal distance from the anti-hero as we observe, in Part 2, how others react to him, his confessions are also designed to bind us in a narrative transaction. The "act of narration," as Peter Brooks comments, can be "far from innocent." "It is not simply, and not so much," writes Brooks, "that confessing excuses but that properly managed it taints." By the time the listener wants to ask "Why are you telling me this?" it is "already too late" for "like the Ancient Mariner's Wedding Guest, he has been made to hear" (261).

"You laugh? Delighted," the anti-hero taunts his gentlemen audience at one point. "My jests, gentlemen, are of course in bad taste, jerky, involved, lacking self-confidence" (138). In the black comedy of his bumping duel with the officer, which reads like an extended joke, the anti-hero purposefully flaunts his perversity as he exposes his self-pathology. Finding himself, after a prolonged period of reading, in desperate need of human contact, he enters a tavern where there has just been a brawl, determined to get into a fight and be thrown out a window. Instead, he is "put" in his "place" and "treated like a fly" by an officer who, finding the anti-hero blocking his path, moves him aside. "I could have forgiven blows," the Underground Man comments, "but I could not forgive his having moved me without noticing me" (162). As he nurses his grudge for *several years* and his resentment grows, he determines to pay back the officer. His self wounded, he responds with narcissistic rage which Kohut characterizes as the "need for revenge, for righting a wrong, for undoing a hurt by whatever means, and a deeply anchored, unrelenting compulsion in the pursuit of all these aims, which gives no rest to those who have suffered a narcissistic injury . . ." ("Thoughts on Narcissism" 637-38).

Finally, the anti-hero decides to retaliate by bumping into the officer during a stroll along the fashionable Nevsky Avenue where the wealthy and distinguished walk. To the anti-hero these strolls are particularly humiliating. He feels he is obliged to "wriggle along" eel-like as he moves aside for those of higher rank. Profoundly ashamed of the "wretchedness and abjectness" of his "little scurrying figure," he imagines himself "a mere fly in the eyes of all this world" (164). His revenge, then, expresses his desire to turn passive suffering into active mastery: he wants to assert his self-worth and to transform the unempathic gaze of the public into an approving one. Determined to be well dressed for his encounter, he chooses, with great care, a new hat, a beaver coat collar, and new gloves. In remodeling his external appearance, he acts out his desire to repair his defective self. Predictably, when he finally does bump into the officer, he gets "the worst of it" for the officer is "stronger" (166). Nevertheless, he feels avenged, elated, triumphant. "The point was," he explains, "that I had attained my object, I had kept up my dignity, I had not yielded a step, and had put myself publicly on an equal social footing with him" (166). Despite his so-called victory, within a few days his ingrained feelings of worthlessness resurface. Again he is driven back to his private underground world where he takes solace in his daydreams and imagines a "*ready-made*" heroic life miraculously opening out before him (167).

In the incident of Zverkov's farewell dinner party, the Underground Man reenacts, with a few minor variations, the narcissistic script rehearsed with the officer. Like the officer, Zverkov is a man of action. In the person of Zverkov—who has wealth, power, and status, is handsome, self-confident and a great womanizer—the anti-hero finds all the "heroic" qualities he secretly admires. After ungraciously inviting himself to the dinner party, he fantasies the role he hopes to play. He dreams of crushing his hated rival, Zverkov, and of "getting the upper hand, of domi-

nating" his friends, "carrying them away, making them like" him. "I knew . . . I did not really want to crush, to subdue, to attract them" (177), he says, consciously denying the wishes that compel him and that he enacts with his gentlemen audience.

At the dinner party, these narcissistic needs are frustrated. The Underground Man feels slighted by Zverkov's condescending attitude, humiliated when his friends seemingly cross-examine him about his lowly job and meager salary, upset about his shabby clothing, and rebuffed when he is mocked for his desire to show off his intelligence. Even worse, his "friends" abandon him to listen to Zverkov's stories. "No one paid any attention to me, and I sat crushed and humiliated" (181), the anti-hero recalls. Attempting to command their attention, he noisily paces before them for some three hours. "But it was all in vain. They paid no attention." While his "enemies" behave as though he is "not in the room" (184), the reader of *Notes* is compelled to act out the scripted role of listening audience to the anti-hero's increasingly pathological account.

Narcissistically injured when his "friends" ignore him, he defends himself by assuming himself superior. "Oh," he thinks to himself, "if you only knew what thoughts and feelings I am capable of, how cultured I am!" (184). Becoming enraged, he wants to flagrantly insult them as they have insulted him. Imagining them to be "pawns . . . inanimate pawns" (183), he experiences them as selfobjects that he wants to have completely in his power, a response in keeping with Kohut's description of narcissistic rage. The "enemy" who provokes a rage reaction, Kohut explains, is not perceived as "autonomous" but rather as "a recalcitrant part of an expanded self over which the narcissistically vulnerable person had expected to exercise full control" ("Thoughts on Narcissism" 644).

Despite his deep anger, the Underground Man also recognizes how shameful his behavior is and how this incident will haunt him for years to come. "[W]ith an intense, acute pang," he recalls, "I was stabbed to the heart by the thought that ten years, twenty years, forty years would pass, and that even in forty years I would remember with loathing and humiliation those filthiest, most ludicrous, and most awful moments of my life" (184). Like the narcissistically defective individual described by Kohut, the anti-hero responds to "the memory of a *faux pas* with excessive shame and self-rejection," his mind returning "again and again to the painful moment, in the attempt to eradicate" its reality (*Analysis* 231). The Underground Man reacts to his humiliating situation with extreme self-rejection. "I was so harassed, so exhausted," as he puts it, "that I would have cut my throat to put an end to it" (184).

In an ugly mood when he confronts Liza at the brothel, the Underground Man looks in a mirror and sees there a reflection of his jeopardized self. "My harassed face struck me as revolting in the extreme, pale, angry, abject, with dishevelled hair." Consciously, he disavows his need for a confirming response. "I am glad," he thinks to himself, "that I shall seem repulsive to her . . ." (189). But his obsessive fascination with Liza's gaze reveals his unacknowledged need to be looked at. Initially, her "wondering" eyes attract him. Later, her "coldly detached" and "utterly remote" look weighs on him, and when she does finally look at him, he finds "something unnatural" in her gaze (189, 190). Attempting to capture her attention, he describes, in his stilted, affected manner, the burial of a prostitute. Soon, however, he warms to the task and longs to "expound" his "cherished ideas" and "turn" Liza's "soul." "It was the exercise of my power," he recalls, "that attracted me most" (193, 194). Through storytelling, he both acts out his angry grandiosity and reveals his narcissistic wants and fears. Cast in the role of confidant, made an eyewitness to the anti-hero's cruelty toward Liza, which culminates in his sadistic assault on her, the reader of Dostoevsky's narrative becomes subjected to the corrosive anger that permeates the text.

Trying to get at Liza through "pictures, pictures" (197), the Underground Man describes, in sentimental detail, first a father's self-sacrificing love for his daughter and then an idealized vision of love, marriage, and the family. These romantic stories—the same kind of stories he tells himself in his corner—both defend against childhood experiences of abandonment and rejection and reveal the anti-hero's deep-seated need for a sense of connection with others. He speaks with "real feeling" and then becomes furious at the thought that Liza might laugh at him (197-98). When she responds that he speaks "like a book" (198), he feels not only rebuffed but also thwarted in his desire to dominate.

Telling another story, one designed to injure her, he describes her probable fate as a prostitute. As he expresses his angry death wish toward Liza, he also confesses his own deepest fears about his imperiled self. Despite Liza's pride, he begins, her decline is inevitable. Within a few short years she will become used up and diseased and when she is dying others will abandon her. She will be buried in a cold, wet grave, her name "will vanish from the face of the earth" as though she "had never existed, never been born at all," and she will be forced to knock on her coffin lid, begging to be let out to "live in the world again" (201). In this melodramatic and self-referential story, the Underground Man reveals the experiential core of his defective selfhood: his feelings of abandonment, loneliness, worthlessness, depletion, and self-unreality. Because he, in this instance and in his subsequent confrontation with Liza, must protect himself from his overwhelming needs, he feels at once emotionally engaged as he tells his story—"I worked myself up to such a pitch that I began to have a lump in my throat," as he describes it—and yet sees it as a game, an "exercise" of skill (202).

For the Underground Man, the real crisis occurs when Liza visits him just as he flies into a rage with his servant, Apollon. Mortified by Liza's untimely arrival and anticipating her rejection of him, he rejects her; feeling humiliated, he tries to humiliate her. He tells her he had been laughing at her before when he "talked sentimental stuff" to her. "I had been insulted . . . [and] I had to avenge the insult. . . . I had been humiliated, so I wanted to humiliate; I had been treated like a rag, so I wanted to show my power. . . ." (215). When the anti-hero tells Liza that he

shall hate her for having listened to his confessions, he indirectly informs the gentlemen of his deep resentment toward them. Confessing to Liza his feelings of utter worthlessness and shame, he reveals the agonizing sense of injury behind his defensive arrogance and hostility: "I am as vain as though I had been skinned and the very air blowing on me hurt" (216). When Liza responds by embracing him and thus giving him the warm, approving response he desires, he, unable to "restrain" himself, sobs in "genuine hysterics" (217). But this "genuine" response is short-lived. Subsequently, he withdraws emotionally, this defensive retreat feeding into his feelings of fraudulence and unreality. Acting out his need to tyrannize, to exact revenge and humiliate, he has intercourse with Liza and afterwards gives her money. After she leaves, the anti-hero feels remorseful, "horribly oppressed" and then depleted, "almost dead with . . . pain" (219, 221). Although he all but falls "ill from misery," he subsequently divorces himself from his feelings. Through bookish speech—"I remained for a long time afterwards pleased with the phrase about the benefit from resentment and hatred" (221)—he gains temporary mastery over his feelings. He retreats from an outer world that is unpredictable and threatening and takes refuge in his underground world where he maintains a tenuous grasp on his self-cohesion by insulating himself from real life and by reducing self-threatening experiences to bookish phrases.

A "paradoxalist" (222), the Underground Man noisily professes that he is "free." But he also admits that he feels impelled to act as he does, that he acts as "though of design" (139). When he is most aware of the "good and beautiful," he does ugly things, and this behavior seems "not accidental . . . but as though it were bound to be so" (132). Ironically, he avows that he wants to retain his "fantastic dreams" and "vulgar folly" to "prove" that he is not a piano key and that he preserves his "personality" and "individuality" through "caprice" (149, 148). "[W]hat *freedom* is left me," he asks, if "some day they calculate and prove to me that I made a long nose at some one because I could not help making a long nose at him . . ." (147). Through his intellectual displays, his logical exercises, his free-will philosophy, he attempts to defend against his underlying sense of powerlessness, his feeling that he cannot help acting as he does, that he is a piano key. Bound by the compulsion to repeat, he is driven to act out his so-called capricious behavior. And underneath it all— the arrogance, the rage, the demands for attention, the desire to control and hurt others—lies a gnawing sense of injury and pain, a deep "ache" (137). "[W]hy am I made with such desires?" he asks. "I would let my tongue be cut off out of gratitude if things could be so arranged that I should lose all desire to put it out" (153). Though he thirsts for something "quite different" (154), he is condemned to be the anti-hero, a nameless, "characterless creature" (131), and to feel not real and solid, but hollow, fraudulent, invalid—a babbling voice. He is trapped in the prison house of his self-pathology.

"I am a babbler, a harmless vexatious babbler . . ." (140), the anti-hero tells his gentlemen audience. His frantic babbling, his "talk and talk and talk" (153), enacts his instability as it defends against self-fragmentation. For as Kohut points out, the "shift of attention to verbalizable conflicts and anxieties" may be "defensively undertaken" to "stem the tide of disintegration" by focusing attention on "endlessly described conflicts and worries" and away from an "awareness" of the "potentially crumbling self" (*Restoration* 107, 108). The anti-hero writes not only to obtain relief from oppressive memories, as he claims, but also to counteract feelings of self-dissolution. And he writes not only to make up a life for himself, as he says, but also in a thwarted attempt to repair his broken self. He is correct in his speculation that there is something psychological in his need to write his confessions and address himself to imaginary readers. In his gentlemen audience he creates what he lacks in real life: a selfobject totally under his control.

Because the anti-hero is unable to satisfy his selfobject needs in the real world, he creates an imaginary audience that is both the image of his rejectors, the men of action, and a self-representation, a mirror reflection of his own arrogant, mocking attitude. His gentlemen readers laugh at him, find him insolent, contemptible, intrusive. "Isn't that shameful, isn't that humiliating?" he imagines his narratees saying to him as they perhaps wag their heads "contemptuously." "And how persistent, how insolent are your sallies, and at the same time what a scare you are in! You talk nonsense and are pleased with it; you say impudent things and are in a continual alarm and apologizing for them. . . . And how intrusive you are, how you insist and grimace!" (154). Imagining that they are taunting him, he taunts them: "Remember I spoke just now of vengeance. (I am sure you did not take it in)" (140). Rebuffed in the real world for his garish intellectual displays, he exhibits his cleverness and "bookish" intellect to a captive audience. He is perverse, attention seeking, demanding: "(A poor jest, but I will not scratch it out. I wrote it thinking it would sound very witty; but now that I have seen myself that I only wanted to show off in a despicable way, I will not scratch it out on purpose!)" (130); "I want now to tell you, gentlemen, whether you care to hear it or not, why I could not even become an insect" (131). Unable to tyrannize the men of action he encounters in the real world, he assumes complete power over his imaginary gentlemen: "Of course I have myself made up all the things you say. That, too, is from underground" (154). Aware of their probable responses, he makes hostile use of his insights: "Now, are you not fancying, gentlemen, that I am expressing remorse for something now, that I am asking your forgiveness for something? I am sure you are fancying that. . . . However, I assure you I do not care if you are. . . ." (130).

Denied in the real world when he sues for attention, the Underground Man acts out his need to procure the notice of others with his fictive gentlemen. He imagines them, variously, as "looking at" him with "compassion" (147) and as unable to understand him: "No, I refuse to consult a doctor from spite. That you probably will not understand. Well, I understand it, though" (129). Disavowing his need for audience approval, he claims that what they think is "a matter of indifference" to him (136). "[I]f you won't deign to give me your attention," he childishly threatens, "I will drop your acquaintance. I can retreat into my underground hole" (153). Ironically, in every word he writes—most particularly in his avowals of his independence from and indifference toward the gentlemen—he reveals just how dependent he is on them. The Underground Man, observes Mikhail Bakhtin, demonstrates his dependence on the other person through his anticipation of the other person's reply and his response to it (192). In "confessing and condemning himself," Bakhtin writes, the Underground Man "wants to provoke praise and acceptance." His self-condemnation is an implicit appeal that the "other person dispute his self-definition, but he leaves himself a loophole for the eventuality that the other person will indeed suddenly agree with him . . ." (195-96). Moreover, as J. R. Hall comments, the Underground Man attempts to assimilate his gentlemen readers and deny their "feared independence" by turning them "into a mere appendage" of his discourse, an "empty form" (136-37). Despite the anti-hero's claim that he writes as if he were addressing readers "simply because" he finds it "easier . . . to write in that form" (155), he is no more free to choose *not* to use this form of address than he is not to write his notes. He is compelled to create an imaginary audience, to dominate over it, and to attempt to both assimilate it and appropriate from it the narcissistic sustenance he craves so he can "live in some way."

In his interactive maneuvers with his gentlemen audience, we find an indirect disclosure of how storytelling and empathy are used in *Notes* as weapons to assault and trap the reader. The anti-hero recognizes that some of the gentlemen, like him, may use reading to effect a bookish retreat from real life or that they may read literature to temporarily build up the self or to seek refuge in the literary world of "the good and the beautiful." Aware of such needs, he actively mocks and subverts them. Through his confessions—"it's hardly literature so much as a corrective punishment" (221)—he exacts narcissistic revenge upon his narratees. When, as Rene Fortin observes, Dostoevsky's anti-hero, at one point, rejoices in the "nastiness he has inflicted" on the gentlemen and then mocks them by confessing the "pleasure" he takes in his own debasement, the reader who witnesses this behavior is transformed into "an accomplice in an act of psychological perversion" (242). Stories of "the good and the beautiful," the anti-hero implies, are nothing more than grandiose and idealizing fantasies. And stories, an illusory web of words, memorialize what is permanently lost and absent: the loving family relationship. The story he tells Liza of the loving father, mother, and child is covertly sadistic. "[W]hat husband's heart is not touched, seeing his wife nursing his child!" the anti-hero says to Liza as he tries to hurt her through his stories. "A plump little rosy baby, sprawling and snuggling. . . . When its father comes up, the child tears itself away from the bosom, flings itself back, looks at its father, laughs, as though it were fearfully funny, and falls again to sucking again. Or it will bite its mother's breast when its little teeth are coming, while it looks sideways at her with its little eyes as though to say, 'Look, I am biting!' Is not all that happiness when they are the three together, husband, wife and child?" (197). Embedded in this peripheral story of the loving family is another: that of the enraged, biting child. This unwritten story recalls a marginalized text found in Part 1 of the antihero's discourse—that of Cleopatra "sticking gold pins into her slave-girl's breasts" and deriving "gratification from their screams and writhings" (144). A self-styled "retort-made man" (135), the anti-hero aggressively encroaches upon and attacks his narratees with his biting, stinging narrative. In his story "all the traits for an anti-hero are *expressly* gathered together . . . and what matters most, it all produces an unpleasant impression, for we are all divorced from life, we are all cripples, every one of us, more or less" (221). Similarly, the narcissistic rage that suffuses *Notes* is acted out on the reader who, in becoming engrossed in the anti-hero's fictional world, becomes the victim of a verbal assault.

While the anti-hero's "word-address," as Mikhail Bakhtin writes, "is capable of agitating and touching one, almost like the personal appeal of a living person" (199), many critics have warded off the text's intended enmeshment of readers in the anti-hero's angry world by reducing his threatening presence to a bookish formula. Edward Wasiolek writes that the anti-hero's "metaphysic implies the psychology; the psychology—empirically observed—confirms the metaphysic" (44). While the anti-hero is a sick, spiteful person, he is, nevertheless, a "hero" according to Wasiolek because his overarching principle is "freedom"; moreover, he is a character Dostoevsky "approves of" (39) and thus, as Wasiolek implies, the reader is meant to approve of. Similarly, Reed Merrill, who describes the anti-hero as an "ethical dialectician" and as a character who has "tragic capability" (509, 507), claims that the Underground Man "can be excused" for being "neurotic, even characteristically paranoid" since he "knows his situation" and wants "to break out of it with a newly discovered dialectic of freedom" (516). In endorsing the anti-hero's aberrant, spiteful behavior by reading it as an expression of some higher philosophic principle, critics such as Wasiolek and Merrill unwittingly enact the inscribed role of confirming audience. And such critics also act out the Underground Man's self-aggrandizing hero fantasy when they laud him as an existential hero (e.g., Kaufmann, Wasiolek) or as a man who "[l]ike the classical hero . . . is willing to stand or fall by his own acts" (Merrill 507). Other critics, perhaps in a desire to diffuse the anger permeating the narrative, reperform Dostoevsky's intended rescue mission by arguing that the passages which were deleted by the censors—those which suggested a Christian solution to the anti-hero's problems—are a central interpretive key to the text and that Dostoevsky's "dominant message" in *Notes* is the necessity of "Christian love and self-sacrifice" for the attainment of "authentic freedom" (Jackson 172; see also Rosenshield).

Because a narrative aim of *Notes* is to make readers feel like passive victims of the anti-hero's affective storms, *Notes* may stimulate in some readers the same fear of passive surrender and helplessness experienced by the Underground Man. Manipulated, taunted, and trapped by the anti-hero's convoluted rhetoric and seductive game of assimilation, readers may be induced to replicate the anti-hero's defensive stratagems: i.e., to assert active mastery over passive suffering by attempting to assume critical dominion and authority over the text. Critics who focus almost solely on the anti-hero's paradoxalist "philosophy" and use intellectual formulas as a kind of shield or those who feel that one must "*see through*" Dostoevsky's character in order to get a "proper understanding" of the text (Frank, *Dostoevsky* 315) may be responding, at least in part, to such pressures. Because the gentlemen readers are "so easily mastered" and stand as the anti-hero's "rhetorical whipping boys" (Doody 31), some readers may form an identificatory bond with the anti-hero of Part 1 of *Notes* and thus partially defend against the text's intended subjugation of the reader. One critic, claiming that the anti-hero "becomes what he is because his life is the *reductio ad absurdum* of the metaphysics of the man of action," argues that the "more repulsive and hideous" the anti-hero portrays his life as being, "the more he underlines the incredible obtuseness of his self-confident judge" (Frank, "Nihilism" 12). In a reading of *Notes* informed by deconstruction that, in effect, rescues readers from the text's game of entrapment, another critic claims that the Underground Man wants his audience to "avoid being trapped by his own tropes or text" and to "recognize the power and limits of all texts, including his own . . ." (Consigny, "The Paradox" 351). Yet another critic, in an apparent desire to rescue the text from the "categories which various critical discourses have imposed upon it," describes how the "independence and self-sufficiency" of *Notes* "reassert themselves each time this work is subjected to an attempted critical domination" (Kavanagh 491). *Notes* may also engender feelings of contempt and anger in readers. One critic, for example, who focuses attention on the anti-hero's insulting behavior, does so in an essay that bristles with insults directed against the existentialist critics who have acted as apologists for Dostoevsky's character (see Weisberg). And yet another claims that "many people praise *Notes from the Underground* without any idea that they are unearthing a caricature of themselves written a century ago" (Girard 262).

A destabilizing story with its abrupt veering from philosophic abstractions to affective intensities, *Notes from Underground* creates in readers "an experienced need for order," as Liane Norman comments (289). It also creates a reactive need for closure, for aesthetic finality. These needs have been acted out again and again as critic/readers, replicating the text's split perceptions of the anti-hero as both a developed thinker and a chaotic personality, have attempted to make sense of his paradoxalist philosophy and/or his capricious behavior. That *Notes* is incomplete is indicated in the abrupt closure in which the authorial narrator, apparently having heard enough, arbitrarily determines to "stop" (222) his transcription of the anti-hero's confessions, this closure repeating a central scene in the text—the dinner party—in which the Underground Man's "friends" refuse to play the role of audience and ultimately abandon him. As Bakhtin states, *Notes from Underground* is an "internally endless speech which can be mechanically cut short, but cannot be organically completed" (197). In the words of Thomas Kavanagh, the anti-hero's endless writing becomes "the attempted yet never successful capture of the self by the self" (505). The narrative incompletion of *Notes* mirrors the anti-hero's incomplete self. When we, as critic/readers, endeavor to explain and interpret the anti-hero's notes, or, as other psychological critics and I have done, describe the psychological mechanisms governing his so-called capricious behavior, we perform a rescue mission. We attempt to capture, stabilize, and make whole through our theoretical constructs and structured critical art the broken self of the Underground Man. And in thinking about rather than with the character as interpreters, we also act out a self-rescue as we ward off the text's enmeshment of us in the anti-hero's perverse personality.

The "[m]an of our time," Kohut states, "is the man of the precariously cohesive self, the man who craves the presence, the interest, the availability of the self-cohesion-maintaining self-object" (*How?* 61). Fascinated with how artists anticipated the later findings of self psychology, Kohut explains this "anticipatory function of art" quite simply: "when dealing with the psychological world, understanding is of necessity the precursor of explaining" ("Reflections" 519). Dostoevsky is often said to have anticipated Freud. In the character of the Underground Man he anticipates Kohut's broken man, the narcissistically vulnerable individual whose self-cohesion is imperiled. A character we may respond to with intellectual fascination and a fascinated horror, the Underground Man, above all, compels our attention. As readers of *Notes from Underground,* we are maneuvered into providing Dostoevsky's anti-hero with the audience recognition he craves as we witness him carry to an extreme his paradoxalist, narcissistic impulses.

Notes

[1] It is speculated that *Notes,* which uses insult as a mode, had its origins in Dostoevsky's reaction to what he perceived as an insult. One of the impulses behind the novel may have been Dostoevsky's desire to pay back Nicoli Chernyshevsky—author of *What Is To Be Done?,* the utopian novel *Notes* actively mocks—after Chernyshevsky turned against him (see, e.g., Weisberg 559, n. 22).

[2] The psychological critics were among the first to focus particular attention on the Underground Man's character and to recognize the compulsive aspects of his behavior. For Barbara Smalley, the Underground Man acts out, "[t]o a marked degree," the "patterns of a paranoid personality" (390). Michael Sperber, using the theories of Otto Kernberg, labels the anti-hero as a borderline personality. Bernard Paris, in a Horneyan analysis, describes him as a "withdrawn man," a neurotic who protects himself through detachment. And for Richard Weisberg, the Underground Man acts out his deeply rooted sense of *ressentiment,* his sense of unresolved insult. "The *'ressentient'* man," writes Weisberg, "lives through, again and again, the event which has rendered him bitter and revealed his impotence, [and] re-senses and re-intellectualizes it to the point of creating a false ethic from it" (555).

Works Cited

Bakhtin, Mikhail. *Problems of Dostoevsky's Poetics.* Trans. R. W. Rotsel. Ann Arbor: Ardis, 1973.

Brooks, Peter. *Reading for the Plot: Design and Intention in Narrative.* New York: Random House, 1984; Vintage Books edition, 1985.

Consigny, Scott. "The Paradox of Textuality: Writing as Entrapment and Deliverance in *Notes From Underground. Canadian-American Slavic Studies* 12 (Fall 1978): 341-52.

Doody, Terrence. "The Underground Man's Confession and His Audience." *Rice University Studies* 61 (Winter 1975): 27-38.

Dostoevsky, Fyodor. *Notes From Underground.* Trans. Constance Garnett. *The Short Novels of Dostoevsky.* New York: Dial Press, 1945. 129-222.

Fortin, Rene. "Responsive Form: Dostoyevsky's *Notes From Underground* and the Confessional Tradition." *Essays in Literature* 7 (Fall 1980): 225-45.

Frank, Joseph. *Dostoevsky: The Stir of Liberation: 1860-1865.* Princeton: Princeton University Press, 1986.

———. "Nihilism and *Notes From Underground." Sewanee Review* 69 (1961): 1-33.

Girard, René. *Deceit, Desire, and the Novel: Self and Other in Literary Structure.* Trans. Yvonne Freccero. Baltimore: Johns Hopkins University Press, 1965.

Hall, J. R. "Abstraction in Dostoyevsky's 'Notes From the Underground.'" *Modern Language Review* 76 (1981): 129-37.

Jackson, Robert Louis. *The Art of Dostoevsky: Deliriums and Nocturnes.* Princeton: Princeton University Press, 1981.

Kaufmann, Walter, ed. *Existentialism from Dostoevsky to Sartre.* Cleveland: World, 1956.

Kavanagh, Thomas M. "Dostoyevsky's *Notes From Underground*: The Form of the Fiction." *Texas Studies in Literature and Language* 14 (Fall 1972): 491-507.

Kohut, Heinz. "Thoughts on Narcissism and Narcissistic Rage." *Search* 2: 615-58.

Merrill, Reed. "The Mistaken Endeavor: Dostoevsky's *Notes From Underground." Modern Fiction Studies* 18 (Winter 1972-73): 505-16.

Norman, Liane. "Risk and Redundancy." *PMLA* 90 (1975): 285-91.

Rosenshield, Gary. "The Fate of Dostoevskij's Underground Man: The Case for an Open Ending." *Slavic and East European Journal* 28 (Fall 1984): 324-39.

Wasiolek, Edward. *Dostoevsky: The Major Fiction.* Cambridge: MIT Press, 1964.

Weisberg, Richard. "An Example Not to Follow: *Ressentiment* and the Underground Man." *Modern Fiction Studies* 21 (Winter 1975-76): 553-63.

FURTHER READING

Amoia, Alba. "*Notes from Underground* (1864)." In *Feodor Dostoevsky,* pp. 167-74. New York: Continuum Publishing Co., 1993.

Offers background biographical information and a thematic analysis of *Notes from the Underground.*

Beatty, Joseph. "From Rebellion and Alienation to Salutary Freedom: A Study in *Notes from Underground.*" *Soundings* LXI, No. 2 (Summer 1978): 182-205.

Argues that *Notes* presents "a deeper, more satisfying account of freedom than that of rebellious, irrational caprice."

Behrendt, Patricia Flanagan. "The Russian Iconic Representation of the Christian Madonna: A Feminine Archetype in *Notes from Underground.*" In *Dostoevski and the Human Condition After a Century,* edited by Alexej Ugrinsky, Frank S. Lambasa, and Valija K. Ozolins, pp. 133-43. New York: Greenwood Press, 1986.

Probes the influence of Russian Orthodox representations of the Virgin Mary on Dostoevsky's depiction of Liza in *Notes from the Underground.*

Bercovitch, Sacvan. "Dramatic Irony in *Notes from the Underground.*" *The Slavic and East European Journal* VIII (1964): 284-91.

Observes the self-deception of the narrator of *Notes from the Underground,* maintaining that he attempts to justify his life by presenting it as the result of choice, though dramatic irony reveals that "his 'free choice' rests in every case upon a false alternative."

Bernstein, Michael André. "Lacerations: The Novels of Fyodor Dostoevsky." In *Bitter Carnival: 'Ressentiment' and the Abject Hero,* pp. 87-120. Princeton: Princeton University Press, 1992.

Describes Dostoevsky's underground man as a psychologically lacerated and abject individual whose psyche can be typified by its display of intellectualized suffering and *ressentiment.*

Cardaci, Paul F. "Dostoevsky's Underground as Allusion and Symbol." *Symposium* XXVIII, No. 3 (Fall 1974): 248-58.

Examines the idea of the underground in Dostoevsky's *Notes* as a symbol that "not only defines the conflict, the narrator, but also brings together structure, character, and theme to give the work its essential unity."

Carrier, Warren. "Artistic Form and Unity in *Notes from Underground.*" *Renascence* XVI, No. 3 (Spring 1964): 142-45.

Studies the structure of *Notes from the Underground,* which he calls "a compelling artistic whole."

Consigny, Scott. "The Paradox of Textuality: Writing as Entrapment and Deliverance in *Notes from Underground.*" *Canadian-American Slavic Studies* 12, No. 3 (Fall 1978): 341-52.

Contends that the underground man is trapped by "textuality" and his own "literariness" and, therefore, cannot directly perceive "reality."

Fagin, N. Bryllion. "Dostoevsky's Underground Man Takes Over." *The Antioch Review* XIII, No. 1 (March 1953): 23-32.

Acknowledges the warning offered by *Notes from the Underground* of the capriciousness of the "secret self"

and exposes the incompatibility of Soviet socialist doctrine and Dostoevsky's emphasis on the individual.

Flath, Carol A. "Fear of Faith: The Hidden Religious Messages of *Notes from Underground.*" *Slavic and East European Journal* 37, No. 4 (Winter 1993): 510-29.

Evaluates Dostoevsky's direct expressions of Christian faith in *Notes from the Underground.*

Gregg, Richard. "Apollo Underground: His Master's Still, Small Voice." *The Russian Review* 32, No. 1 (January 1973): 64-71.

Freudian analysis of Apollon's function in *Notes from the Underground* in which Gregg finds a "singular congruency" between the manservant's role and that of the superego.

Hall, J. R. "Abstraction in Dostoyevsky's *Notes from the Underground.*" *Modern Language Review* 76, No. 1 (January 1981): 129-37.

Perceives in the narrator of *Notes from the Underground* an abstract intellectualism that degenerates progressively into solipsism and allows his position to be undermined in the eyes of the reader.

Jackson, Robert Louis. "In the Darkness of Night: Tolstoy's *Kreutzer Sonata* and Dostoevsky's *Notes from the Underground.*" In *Dialogues with Dostoevsky: The Overwhelming Questions,* pp. 208-27. Stanford: Stanford University Press, 1993.

Traces affinities between *Notes from the Underground* and Leo Tolstoy's *Kreutzer Sonata* on the subject of sexuality.

Jones, Malcolm V. "*Notes from Underground:* The Cult of Perversity." In *Dostoyevsky: The Novel of Discord,* pp. 55-66. New York: Harper & Row, 1976.

Maintains that the narrator of *Notes from the Underground* views perversity as a rebuke to rationalism and scientific determinism.

Lethcoe, James. "Self-Deception in Dostoevskij's *Notes from the Underground.*" *The Slavic and East European Journal* X (1966): 9-21.

Concludes that self-deception is a major theme in *Notes from the Underground* and that "recognition of this theme provides a satisfactory explanation for the claims . . . of critics that the underground man's testimony is unreliable."

Murav, Harriet. "Dora and the Underground Man." In *Russian Literature and Psychoanalysis,* edited by Daniel Rancour-Laferriere, pp. 417-30. Amsterdam: John Benjamins Publishing Company, 1989.

Considers the narrator of *Notes from the Underground* in light of Freudian analysis of the melancholic individual.

Peace, Richard. "Early Writing and *Notes from Underground.*" In *Dostoyevsky: An Examination of the Major Novels,* pp. 1-18. Cambridge: Cambridge University Press, 1971.

Views Dostoevsky's *Notes from the Underground* as "an introduction to his major novels," which evinces "a strong polemical element" and rejects the romantic idealism of the 1840s as well as the rational egoism popularized by Nikolai Chernyshevsky in the 1860s.

Powys, John Cowper. "Memoirs from the Underground." In *Dostoievsky,* pp. 82-7. London: John Lane The Bodley Head, 1946.

> Discusses the psychology of the narrator of *Notes from the Underground,* declaring that the novella "is a revelation of the power of the lonely, self-existent, unpropitiated human mind."

Pribic, Rado. "*Notes from the Underground*: One Hundred Years After the Author's Death." In *Dostoevski and the Human Condition After a Century,* edited by Alexej Ugrinsky, Frank S. Lambasa, and Valija K. Ozolins, pp. 71-7. New York: Greenwood Press, 1986.

> Comments on the universality and enduring cogency of the underground man's philosophical, social, and psychological predicaments.

Rosenshield, Gary. "Artistic Consistency in *Notes from the Underground*—Part One." In *Studies in Honor of Xenia Gasiorowska,* edited by Lauren G. Leighton, pp. 11-21. Columbus, Ohio: Slavica Publishers, 1982.

> Argues for the aesthetic and thematic coherence of *Notes from the Underground* despite its shift from deterministic premises in Part I to an espousal of free will in Part II.

Sanborn, Pat. "Nasty Pleasures in *Notes from Underground.*" *North Dakota Quarterly* 54, No. 2 (Spring 1986): 200-11.

> Suggests that the underground man's identification of pain and despair as sources of satisfaction necessitates a reevaluation of traditional conceptions of pleasure.

Simmons, Ernest J. "*Notes from the Underground.*" In *Dostoevsky: The Making of a Novelist,* pp. 109-26. New York: Vintage Books, 1940.

Study of *Notes from the Underground* with a strong biographical influence, focusing especially on Dostoevsky's affair with Polina Suslova.

Smalley, Barbara. "The Compulsive Patterns of Dostoyevsky's Underground Man." *Studies in Short Fiction* X, No. 4 (Fall 1973): 389-96.

> Contends that the narrator's compulsive personality bars him from attainment of the freedom that he seeks.

Smith, Les W. "Confession from Underground: *The Double* and *Notes from Underground.*" In *Confession in the Novel: Bakhtin's Author Revisited,* pp. 43-66. Cranbury, N. J.: Associated University Presses, 1996.

> Investigates the relationship between the "author-creator" and the confessional narrator of *Notes from the Underground* in Dostoevsky's "polyphonic" novella.

Traschen, Isadore. "Dostoyevsky's *Notes from Underground.*" *Accent* XVI, No. 4 (Autumn 1956): 255-64.

> Characterizes Dostoevsky's attitude toward the narrator of *Notes from the Underground* as "ambiguous" and declares the narrator's romanticism and godless intellectualism sterile.

Weisberg, Richard. "An Example Not to Follow: *Ressentiment* and the Underground Man." *Modern Fiction Studies* 21, No. 4 (Winter 1975-76): 553-63.

> Declares that the "fundamental truth" of *Notes from the Underground* is: "a life defined by literary formulations and a total absence of social spontaneity cannot produce a 'free' or useful philosophy."

Yarmolinsky, Avrahm. "Ends and Beginnings." In *Dostoevsky: His Life and Art,* pp. 177-92. New Jersey: S. G. Phillips, 1957.

> Describes the events of Dostoevsky's life surrounding the writing of *Notes from the Underground* and the importance of Nikolai Chernyshevsky's philosophy of enlightened self-interest to the work.

Additional coverage of Dostoevsky's life and career is contained in the following sources published by The Gale Group: *DISCovering Authors*; *DISCovering Authors: British*; *DISCovering Authors: Canadian*; *DISCovering Authors: Most-Studied Authors Module*; *DISCovering Authors: Novelists Module*; *Nineteenth-Century Literature Criticism*, Vols. 2, 7, 21, 33, 43; *Short Story Criticism*, Vol 2; and *World Literature Criticism*.

John Fowles
1926-

British novelist, short story writer, nonfiction writer, poet, screenwriter, and essayist.

INTRODUCTION

Although he is known primarily as the author of the popular and critically acclaimed novels *The French Lieutenant's Woman* (1969) and *The Maggot* (1985), Fowles also wrote a novella and three short stories that comprise his single volume of short fiction, *The Ebony Tower* (1974), a best-seller in the United States. These works, which focus on failed attempts at self-discovery, represent variations on the themes and narrative methods explored in Fowles's novels. They also imitate and expand upon elements of Marie de France's twelfth-century romance *Eliduc,* a translation of which also is included in the book. Marked by strong narration and a richly allusive, descriptive style, Fowles's short fiction features resourceful characters confronted with complicated situations amid lavish backgrounds infused with legend, history, and art. However, since Fowles rejects the role of the omniscient narrator, and the stories lack satisfactory resolution—opting instead for ambiguous, open-ended conclusions—readers often have been annoyed. Fowles has defended this practice with his belief that an artist's responsibility demands that his characters have the freedom to choose and to act within their limitations. Critics frequently have emphasized the existential qualities manifested by Fowles's narrative technique, and many have admired his ability to actively engage his audience in the quest for answers.

Biographical Information

Born in Essex, England—a city on the outskirts of London—Fowles attended a suburban preparatory school until his family moved to rural Devonshire to escape the German air raids of World War II. There, he experienced the "mystery and beauty" of the natural world, the importance of which is evident in his fiction. He served two years as a lieutenant in the Royal Marines, but never saw combat, since the end of his training coincided with the end of the war. After receiving a B.A. with honors in French literature from Oxford University in 1950, Fowles taught at numerous schools in England and Europe, including two years in the early 1950s at Anargyrios College on the Greek island of Spetsai. These were crucial years to his artistic development for he first began to write there; the fictive island of Phraxos in *The Magus* (1965) is modeled on Spetsai. In 1963 Fowles published *The Collector* and the novel's success allowed him to

retire from teaching. Since 1958, Fowles has lived in Lyme Regis, a coastal town in southern England, which serves as the setting for *The French Lieutenant's Woman.* His other writings include a philosophical work, *The Aristos* (1964); the verse collection *Poems* (1973), written during his time in Greece; the novels *Daniel Martin* (1977) and *Mantissa* (1982); numerous nonfiction works; and an essay collection, *Wormholes* (1998). *The Collector, The Magus,* and *The French Lieutenant's Woman* were adapted for film and produced in 1965, 1968, and 1981, respectively.

Major Works of Short Fiction

Evincing a deep appreciation of nature, the Celtic-inspired stories of *The Ebony Tower* demonstrate the influence of French literary tradition and culture, as well as Fowles's nonconformist social consciousness. The collection opens with the novella *The Ebony Tower,* in which David Williams, a comfortably married, English art critic and abstractionist painter, is sent to Brittany, a rural district in

France, to interview William Breasley, a famous expatriate representational painter with a notorious personal reputation who openly despises abstract art. The conflict between the two painters, which prominently foregrounds the connection between art and life that informs the entire collection, develops not only out of their different approaches to art but also from Williams's unsuccessful attempt at infidelity with Diana, one of Breasley's art students and girlfriend. The novella is followed by Fowles's translation of *Eliduc,* a medieval quest romance in which the title character, a victorious and married knight from Brittany, seeks adventure in England. While there, he elopes with Guilliadun, an English king's daughter, who falls into a trance upon learning about his other wife, Guildeluec. Guilliadun revives only after Guildeluec intervenes with the aid of the magical red flower of the weasel. Acknowledging her husband's love for his new wife, Guildeluec leaves them and becomes a nun, reuniting with them by the romance's end in praise of Christianity. In the next story, "Poor Koko," an aged, diminutive scholar writing a biography about nineteenth-century novelist Thomas Love Peacock encounters a young thief who converses with the writer about diverse topics while stealing the household's goods. After failing to coerce the writer into making him the subject of his study, the thief destroys the professor's manuscript. Narrated some time after the robbery, "Poor Koko" interweaves Fowles's commentary on class conflict—the motivation for the crime—and the power of language to oppress. "The Enigma," the penultimate story, concerns the mysterious disappearance of John Marcus Fielding, a member of Parliament who strictly lived by routine and whose absence is never explained. Much speculation ensues, but an interview with Fielding's son's girlfriend, an aspiring novelist who suggests to the investigating detective that he imagine himself as a writer trying to conclude a book, shifts the focus of the story away from the missing M.P. to the ambiguities of male-female relationships, another persistent theme in Fowles's work. Finally, "The Cloud" recounts a vacation in central France taken by a group of English friends, including a recently widowed and depressed woman who tells a tale about a lost princess waiting for her prince. Subsequently, she disappears, too, which gestures once again toward the connection between life and art.

Critical Reception

Commentary about *The Ebony Tower* has centered mainly on two areas: whether or not the collected stories share continuity with each other and the significance of the collection in Fowles's body of writings. Many critics have read the collection as an integrated whole, citing Fowles's own statement in "A Personal Note," which precedes his translation of *Eliduc.* He wrote: "The working title of this collection of stories was *Variations,* by which I mean to suggest variations both on certain themes in previous books of mine and in methods of narrative presentation." Although some have stressed that the stories can adequately stand alone—as various studies of individual stories have attested—others have demonstrated the pervasive influ-

ence of Celtic romance in the stories, including the prominence of various quest motifs, the classical and medieval contexts of certain narrative elements, and the persistent emphasis on the relation between art and life. A number of critics have considered the collection's relation to Fowles's work as a novelist, investigating the thematic, artistic, narrative, and character parallels between the stories and Fowles's previous novels. In addition, several scholars have suggested that conventions of the short story form itself inform the themes and structure of the collection, pointing to Fowles's contributions to the postmodern development of the genre. Summarizing Fowles's achievement in the short story genre, David W. Endicott has concluded that "with *The Ebony Tower* he achieves a loosely thematic balance in stories that remain rich in the traditions that have greatly influenced his growth as an author."

PRINCIPAL WORKS

Short Fiction

The Ebony Tower (novella and short stories) 1974

Other Major Works

*The Collector (novel) 1963
The Aristos: A Self-Portrait in Ideas (nonfiction) 1964
†*The Collector* [with Stanley Mann and John Kohn] (screenplay) 1965
The Magus (novel) 1965
†*The French Lieutenant's Woman* (novel) 1969
†*The Magus* (screenplay) 1969
Poems (poetry) 1973
Shipwreck (nonfiction) 1974
Daniel Martin (novel) 1977
Islands (nonfiction) 1978
The Tree (nonfiction) 1979
The Enigma of Stonehenge (nonfiction) 1980
Mantissa (novel) 1982
A Short History of Lyme Regis (history) 1982
A Maggot (novel) 1985
Lyme Regis Camera (nonfiction) 1990
Wormholes: Essays and Occasional Writings (literary criticism and essays) 1998

---

*This work also was adapted for stage and produced in London at the King's Head Theatre in 1971.

†These works have been adapted for film.

CRITICISM

Christopher Lehmann-Haupt (review date 1974)

SOURCE: "More Magic from John Fowles," in *The New York Times Review of Books,* November 4, 1974, p. 35.

[*In the following assessment of* The Ebony Tower, *Lehmann-Haupt focuses on connections between the novella and stories in the collection, concluding that the work as a whole is "a thoroughly pleasing entertainment and a thoroughly mystifying conundrum."*]

"The working title of this collection of stories was *Variations*"—John Fowles interjects in "A Personal Note" about one-third of the way through his new book, *The Ebony Tower*—"by which I meant to suggest variations both on certain themes in previous books of mine and in methods of narrative presentation. . . ." But two considerations seemed to miltate against using *Variations* as a title, Mr. Fowles goes on to explain: first, his own fear that readers would "feel themselves at a disadvantage because they are unfamiliar with my work . . ." and, second, the fear of "the first professional readers" of the book that these "variations" were only visible in "a private mirage in the writer's mind." Well, after reading Mr. Fowles's new book, one realizes that neither he nor "the first professional readers" need really have worried. Except for the fifth and last story in the collection, **"The Cloud"** (which I'll come to by and by), the fictions in *The Ebony Tower* do work independently both of one another and of the author's earlier novels. *The Collector, The Magus* and *The French Lieutenant's Woman* (not to mention his collection of aphorisms, *The Aristos: A Self-Portrait in Ideas*). Yet one can understand why he wanted to call them *Variations,* for the book does call to mind certain themes from his earlier works; and the interrelationships among the stories make the fun of reading them all the greater.

Amusing Puzzles Persist

For instance, one comes away from the long title piece fully satisfied with the tale it tells of a young art critic named David Williams who visits an old, self-exiled English painter, Henry Breasley, in his rural French retreat and fails to act on his attraction to one of the old painter's two young female companions. Yet amusing puzzles persist after David has returned to his conventional marriage and the story of his temptation is done. What is the meaning, we wonder of the reference to Marie de France, and *Eliduc* (whatever that may be), and why all the talk about "the mystery of island Britain . . . filtering all over Europe *via* its French namesake?" What's the significance of the weasel that David runs over while driving away from Henry Breasley's estate? And what exactly did the old painter mean when he implied that the abstract artists he so abominates live in an "Ebony Tower" (as opposed to an "ivory tower")?

Sufficient unto itself, too, is the second story, a translation of a medieval tale called *Eliduc* by one Marie de France (aha!), about an honorable knight beholden to two ladies (aha!), one of whom is awakened from an endless sleep by a rose taken from the mouth of a weasel (aha!). *Eliduc* is a charming exercise in scholarship, to be sure, but we begin to see that Mr. Fowles is after more than charm: "One may smile condescendingly at the naivete's and primitive technique of stories such as *Eliduc*," he writes in "A Personal Note"; "but I do not think any writer of fic-

tion can do so with decency—and for a very simple reason. He is watching his own birth."

So it goes throughout **The Ebony Tower. "Poor Koko"** is an unusually provocative story about a man-of-letters awakened in the night by a young intruder, who proceeds to rob him more or less painlessly, to tie him up and gag him deferentially, and then—astonishingly—to throw his four years' worth of book-research into the fire. As a portrait of generational conflict, the story coheres completely. Yet when we ask just why the burglar destroyed the older man's work, we are forced to reconsider the title story (in which, after all, the young biographer is trying to expropriate the old artist's creative sources) and we are made to reflect further on the book's title (Is the burglar who destroys another enemy of the "Ebony Tower"?).

And **"The Enigma"** is a detective story about a happy, successful Member of Parliament who one day disappears without a trace. As a mystery, it absorbs completely. Yet one can't help noticing it's also Marie de France's *Eludic* updated and told from the viewpoint of one of the knight's ladies.

An Attempt at Escape?

Only the final story, **"The Cloud,"** does not stand independently. With its confusing cast of characters (I had to draw a chart to get everyone straight, and even so I was stuck with a leftover "David," who is either a misprint or an echo of the young biographer in the title story), its fragmented style, and its barely coherent plot-line, it forces the reader to look elsewhere for its meaning.

My own theory is that it represents Mr. Fowles himself trying to escape from "The Ebony Tower"—trying to paint with words as if he were Henry Breasley apprehending reality without escaping into abstraction. I'll even gamble to say **"The Cloud"** is a verbal rendering of a painting-in-progress that starts in Henry Breasley's studio—a painting that "put into words, [was] a pessimistic truism about the human condition." That's highly debatable, of course, but debate it many readers will. For, as he has done so often in the past, John Fowles has once again come through with a book that is at once a thoroughly pleasing entertainment and a thoroughly mystifying conundrum—a book that for my money at least is the most enjoyable piece of fiction to be published so far this season.

Isa Kapp (review date 1974)

SOURCE: "John Fowles Is Fair," in *The New Leader,* Vol. LVII, No. 24, December 9, 1974, pp. 6-8.

[*Below, Kapp offers a mixed appraisal of* The Ebony Tower.]

Though readers will never cease to long for great storytellers, the only ones around in America today—with the possible exceptions of Eudora Welty and John Cheever—

are Jewish authors like Isaac Bashevis Singer, Bernard Malamud and the Saul Bellow of *Henderson the Rain King.* They have somehow managed to nurture the gift, while the fiction writers who came after F. Scott Fitzgerald have in general either lost it or relegated it to shouldering heavy social burdens.

Norman Mailer, Kurt Vonnegut Jr. and Joseph Heller, for example, see themselves first and last as creatures of a society that disfigures us, and it is this disfigurement that they feel obliged to embody in their prose. Vonnegut has never risen from the rubble of bombed Dresden; Heller has moved from the lunacies of military life to the mundanities of an organization-man's existence; and the present Mailer is more the dazzled victim of moonshots, Marilyn Monroe and Women's Liberation than the master of his own imaginative fibres. Hardworking and responsible, these novelists are in much the same fix as wives who have given up their ambition to please and have taken on, in its place, a heavy regimen of household endeavor.

In fiction as in married life, however, high principle does not really compensate for the loss of pleasure and fascination. Perhaps this accounts in some measure for the not quite deserved popularity of a writer like John Fowles, who let it be known in *The French Lieutenant's Woman, The Magus* and even the slightly putrescent *The Collector* that he possessed both the leisure and the frivolity to amuse us. To his new book of five tales, **The Ebony Tower,** he again brings a regalia of storyteller's trappings: enigmas calculated to tantalize, impossible dreams, mysteries and revelations, and actual fragments of Celtic legends, such as the magical red forest flowers that arouse sleeping princesses. What may mesmerize American readers most of all, though, is that Fowles, being British, always begins not with society but with the solitary self, a withdrawn figure like the heroine of *The French Lieutenant's Woman,* staring out to sea, or into romantic infinity.

There is a kind of ancient vapor over this book, as if a witch with a light touch had laid a medieval spell upon us, yet three of the stories are based upon skillfully concocted situations in a very modern cultural ambience. The most engrossing is **The Ebony Tower,** in which an intelligent young art critic and abstract painter, David Williams, visits a famous old artist in the Brittany countryside. Vigorous, staccato in his speech, with two solicitous young mistresses who sometimes disport themselves naked on the grass and sometimes wait upon him in long Victorian skirts, Henry Breasley sounds (agreeably to a layman) like Picasso, but turns out to be very British and rambunctiously traditional, referring to the inventor of Cubism as "pick-arsehole."

David joins the trio in a picnic, swims with the girls, and argues about abstraction with Breasley—who calls it the "ebony tower," a cowardly escape from daylight, the human body and the facts of life. The visitor becomes enchanted with one of the mistresses, rejects her because he is a loyal husband, and broods as he drives away to meet his wife for a holiday in Paris, feeling he has passed up, both in life and art, the "real existential challenge."

We ought to have a lot more about art and artists in fiction. It is an attractive subject that has dwindled since James and Hawthorne—and Fowles does possess the requisite erudition and fluency (if a bit too much gloss). He also has the unusual knack of making an imperceptible elision between his fictional works of art and the real works that allegedly influenced them:

> There hung the huge *Moonhunt,* a painting David was going to discuss at some length and that he badly wanted to study at leisure again. . . . As with so much of Breasley's work there was an obvious previous iconography—in this case, Uccello's *Night Hunt,* which was in turn a challenged comparison, a deliberate risk. . . . Behind the mysteriousness and the ambiguity (no hounds, no horses, no prey . . . nocturnal figures among the trees, but the title was needed), behind the modernity of so many of the surface elements, there stood both a homage and a kind of thumbed nose to a very old tradition.

Yet it is not Fowles' handling of painting or the succinctly formulated clash over abstract art that is so effective in this story, or even such sensory amenities as the water pear eaten in the country garden, the long loaves of bread, the image of an urban Englishman in a French farmhouse kitchen. Fowles' rising stock in trade is simply Romance, the infectious notion—straight out of medieval legends like Tristan and Isolde, Launcelot and Guinevere (described by Denis de Rougement as the obsessive and destructive myth that dominates our ideas of love in the Western world)—that true passion is aroused only by what we cannot have. Thus David, lacking Breasley's force and "northern wildness" as a painter, and wanting to make love to a girl he cannot accommodate, is our typical romantic hero, and alter ego of the common reader.

Either Fowles is obsessed by the Arthurian myth or he knows we are (probably the latter, since he seems to me the least ingenuous of writers). Whatever the case, he follows the title story with a translation of a 12th-century Celtic tale by Marie de France called *Eliduc.* It is about a married knight who pledges eternal fidelity to his wife in Brittany, then goes off to fight for a King of England and to fall desperately in love with his daughter. Evidently people were less romantic in those days, for the knight's wife not only rescues his mistress from a death trance, but amicably offers to leave them together by retiring to a nunnery, an offer the knight promptly accepts. This outcome could easily be interpreted as an astringent comment on the self-effacement and dolor of the modern British husband in the preceding story, yet I don't think Fowles consciously intended it that way; he is merely, in his role of crafting a potential bestseller, a pushover for archetypes.

A rather arch type of romantic nostalgia apparently overtakes a Conservative Member of Parliament in **"The Enigma."** Fifty-seven, happily married, owner of a fine Elizabethan manor house, he disappears without a trace one afternoon after a brief, unprecedented visit to the British Museum. The police have not a clue to go on: Scandal and hanky panky seem out of the question, and even the Black September are unlikely suspects because his leanings have been slightly more pro-Arab than pro-Israel. Thirty pages of methodical sleuthing lead nowhere, until the bright young sergeant (with a public school education) falls for the girlfriend of the MP's son, and in the course of events they begin to hypothesize together over tea.

A remarkably empathetic young lady, she is both eager to help and has spotted, with Proustian subtlety, some unspoken yearning and sense of failure in the supposedly contented and conformist MP. Indeed, it may well have been the girl herself that he was trying to reach at the British Museum, not, she suggests, with any crude motive, but to gain through her a foothold in some less circumscribed life. Though the enigma is not completely tidied up, a somber solution is adumbrated. In the end, the sergeant and the young lady go to bed together for an appropriately Arthurian reason: Her fecund detective talents, unattainable to one of his methodical nature, have inspired him with a grand passion.

"Poor Koko" is Fowles' leap into the unrelievedly realistic Present, and no doubt for that very reason it is the most irritating story in the book. An elderly writer nearing the end of his lifelong ambition, a definitive biography of Thomas Love Peacock, is staying at the Dorset cottage of friends when it is broken into by a young burglar armed with the free-floating class antagonisms of the New Left. After some sparring, the writer begins to feel there is at least no danger of violence, and he allows himself a few supercilious ripostes. Just before departing, however, the burglar mercilessly burns all the manuscripts it has taken years of work to accumulate. We are invited to explain this gratuitous act of hatred, or at least to assent to the writer's theory that it was articulacy the burglar craved, that he wanted to borrow (or destroy) the magic power of the word and the writer had failed to offer it.

In an editorial aside, Fowles informs us that "Koko" is a Japanese word for the proper attitude of son to father—which is certainly dragging in a double decker of meaning and pathos by the tail. Unfortunately, the plot is remarkably reminiscent of Malamud's extraordinary story, "The Last Mohican"; the similarity only reminds us how brilliantly Malamud alternated the troubling theme of Fidelman's pursuit by the stateless beggar with the enlivening one of a timid American ex-painter's days in Rome, and how completely we participated in the underlying question of what one person owes another. In comparison, **"Poor Koko"** is a schematic and obligatory assessment of the older generation's delinquency toward the young.

It is obvious that Fowles is really at home with sentiment rather than morality, with those soft and blurry areas of response where one can mix something old and something new, something borrowed and something blue. He likes to spike a Victorian plot with a sprinkle of Freud and Marx, to mate television producers with personifications of fairytale princesses. His more natural short fiction, **"The Cloud,"** is not a proper story at all, but full of disparate elements held together, like a gorgeous Impressionist painting, by ripples of mood and reflections of light. We register some Jamesian prickles of disaffinity, noticing that one character is out of tune with all the others because she is more exact and more exacting—this is the romance, rarer than the others, of perfectionism.

In truth, we are not meant to suffer too keenly for her, merely to make out her form in the opulent shimmer of inky-blue dragon-flies, aquamarine parasols, hidden warblers, and a jade green river. For that matter, nothing in these deft, carefully composed stories, brimming like chocolate liqueurs with luscious images, need cause us any serious distress or alarm. Their author is more merchant than magus, dispensing innocuous adrenalin for the torpid mind. Could it be partial testimony to his success that, when we finish this book, we are ready for a writer who has the very elements of force and rashness which the narrator of **The Ebony Tower** envied in the old master, and look forward to reading fiction that is less artificial, less self-contained and even, if you can believe it, less diverting?

Irina Sofinskaya (essay date 1979)

SOURCE: "Myth and Reality: Points of Contact," in *Soviet Literature,* No. 1, 1979, pp. 160-66.

[*In the following essay, Sofinskaya considers the interaction among mysterious, symbolic aspects and ordinary, realistic events in Fowles's short fiction, assessing his contribution to the development of the short story genre.*]

The sixties and seventies saw a marked growth of interest by Soviet literary scholars in the "minor genres". Studies of classic examples of the Russian short story (Chekhov's stories) appeared, and monographs and joint studies of modern Russian and Western, particularly American, short stories were published. It was natural for analogies, coincidences and contrasts to emerge in any analysis of Russian, West European and American stories. A wealth of material for such juxtaposition is afforded by stories of John Fowles, which add up to only a small volume of writing (just one collection, **The Ebony Tower,** 1974) but constitute work of significance and substance. Its romantic aura is what primarily interests Soviet readers—an evident link with the tradition of early 19th-century English and German Romanticism. Such writing is not typical of the short forms of Russian prose, which saw virtually no development of Romantic narrative. From its very beginning (in the early 18th century) the "minor genre" in Russian prose inclined not so much to the Renaissance forms genetically linked with Romantic forms as to mediaeval legend, parable and biography. The bond with these forms may be clearly sensed even in Tolstoy's "folk tales".

Nor did Russian short stories adopt the individualistic spirit that is so much a feature of Western Romantic stories, a spirit alien to Russian social consciousness and to the democratic orientation of Russian literature as a whole. Thus the process of assimilating the various forms of the

Western short story, which was earlier in origin and more highly developed, came about in the Russian short story through surmounting "all that is alien, unnatural and non-existent in our morals" (V. F. Odoyevsky).

Sometimes [Fowles] resorts to the symbolism and imagery of Greek myths and Celtic legends, yet his attempt to make myths of reality is not an end in itself but a literary device enabling the author more strikingly to expose the contradictions of modern life and more deeply to probe the labyrinths of the human mind.

—Irina Sofinskaya

At the same time the Russian short story did also have points of contact with Romanticism. Such Russian authors as, for instance, Gogol, Saltykov-Shchedrin, Leskov, Garshin and Korolenko made frequent use of folk-lore themes in their writing, and interest in folk art was a feature of Romanticism too. It is a feature also of the prose of some present-day English authors—Iris Murdoch, Muriel Spark and John Fowles—who resurrect certain elements of Romantic narrative in their writing.

In his novel, *The Magus,* and also in his stories, Fowles portrays the contemporary scene and, principally, the state of mind of a Western intellectual (who in Fowles's view is modern man in general) full of doubts, contradictions and dissatisfaction with himself and with everything around him. Sometimes he resorts to the symbolism and imagery of Greek myths and Celtic legends, yet his attempt to make myths of reality is not an end in itself but a literary device enabling the author more strikingly to expose the contradictions of modern life and more deeply to probe the labyrinths of the human mind. In Fowles's work the legend or interpolated fairy-tale provides a stylistic and emotional key to grasping the real situation. Thus one of the five stories in the book—*Eliduc,* translated by the author from the Mediaeval French, sets the general mood of the book, its tone and, characteristically, there is hardly any noticeable change in tone when the narrative switches from tales of mediaeval knights to stories of modern life. The author is seeking not so much to convey the feeling of a particular period in history as to establish a particular system of aesthetic co-ordinates for the entire book of his stories.

As in all truly Romantic narratives a double reality exists in Fowles's works. Real happenings which the reader easily believes suddenly become mysterious and acquire an unexpected symbolic significance, while strange and mythical elements are written into a perfectly humdrum situation without any constraint or embarrassment. This Hoff-

manesque shifting of planes and these transitions from one literary plane to another create an atmosphere of ambiguity and imprecision and a dichotomy in his stories.

In *The Ebony Tower,* David Williams, a highly successful art connoisseur and painter visits the country home of a famous English artist, Henry Breasley, about whom he is writing a book. He finds himself in a totally unexpected situation that both intrigues and repels him. The wonderful landscape, the forest surrounding the castle and the presence of a beautiful and mysterious woman create an atmosphere recalling the tale of the Sleeping Princess, a theme to which the characters in the story themselves refer on numerous occasions. This atmosphere is enhanced by the splendid works of art which Breasley has in his collection.

Breasley is a very real person (at the beginning of the story we are given precise details of his life, his views on art, his predilections and plans), but like a kindred character in *The Magus,* he is the expounder of some sort of lofty wisdom, an all-powerful man of genius, yet at the same time a pitiful figure.

So there is a double element not only in the structure of the narrative but also in the characters themselves. This ambiguity and incompleteness in the portrayal of the characters is a legitimate artistic feature of the short story. Like the Romantic authors, John Fowles strives not so much to create fully-moulded, "set" characters as to convey the entire contradictory potential that lies within a particular person. Instead of strict character delineation Fowles prefers a continual switching of masks which conveys a man's innermost thoughts and feelings in the process of evolution, in the multiformity of their hues and accents.

An air of elusiveness and incompleteness in Fowles's works springs also from his "open" endings with their multiple meanings. Of the four stories in the volume which deal with the present day, only the first story (*The Ebony Tower*) has a straightforward ending. As for the other three—**"Poor Koko," "The Enigma"** and **"The Cloud"**—there is a mystery (or something inexplicable, as in **"Poor Koko"**) at the very start. Moreover, this mystery remains a mystery to the end, all that happens is that at the end of the story it acquires a more all-embracing and universal significance. With his open endings Fowles is asserting that the irrational element in life is so strong that most real situations flow over into mystery or paradox. Just as in real life something always remains unresolved and unexplored, so in a work of literature there must be no absolute ending but only an ending that gives rise to a new beginning or to something qualitatively new.

The two-level composition of Fowles's stories lends an element of play to his very style of writing: he gives us convincing proof of what he knows is a false notion and he casts doubt upon what appear to be thoroughly objective judgements. He thus creates an impression of the illusory nature of the real and of the significance of the imaginary. This is the very effect he seeks to produce: it enables the author to show the soullessness of present-day life, its extreme rationality and earthliness. Placing a typical modern man (Fowles regards Williams as just such a person) in an unusual and fantastic situation, in a world of mystery, unfettered impulses and desires, in a magic world of art, the author then sharply turns the situation "full circle": Williams returns to his ordinary and undistinguished way of life. The harmony and charm of the situation vanish; along with the multiplicity of meanings and the mysteriousness, something very important vanishes and one begins to sense a gaping void. An element of mystery and of the sublime must be brought into our lives, Breasley seems to say, and Fowles along with him, as he compares the landscapes unfolding before Williams's eyes with the canvases of Matisse, the Impressionists and of Hieronymus Bosch. Reality is shown transformed, it is made artistic and in this way the element which Fowles thinks reality lacks is introduced into it.

Depicting mystery as a very important component of reality, Fowles thereby opposes the ever increasing "disenchantment" of the world in which all objects and relationships are gradually being drawn into a process of all-round rationalist use and "demystification". He seeks to restore to objects and relationships their moral and aesthetic significance, thereby revealing the very close and profound bond between the moral and the aesthetic. Fowles counterposes the poetic element to the tendency of total relativism, which is linked with the total loss of one's bearings in the matter of values. Aesthetic consciousness (through creating works of art) *must strengthen* the shaky system of ethical standards. Hence the enormous importance which Fowles attaches to art, which is called upon to inspire reality and to bring poetry, illusion and mystery into it.

By posing the matter in this way Fowles sets himself the grandiose task of restructuring the consciousness of modern man. Modern man, he thinks, is not free, he is the prisoner of a great variety of laws: economic, moral and so on. He is living "in a world dominated by a desperate struggle for economic survival" (*The Magus*). But modern man is also a prisoner of his own prejudices, of scepticism, he is rationalistic in the extreme, his spiritual needs are confined to the desire to succeed. Man has lost the capacity of free self-expression—Fowles likens Williams's generation to animals put in a cage: "David and his generation, and all those to come, could only look back, like caged animals born in captivity, at the old green freedom" (*The Ebony Tower*).

Fowles rebels against the levelling down and the stereotyping that are a feature of our day, he affirms the uniqueness and singularity of each human personality. That is why the first and most evident plane of the story is the author's striving to bring into the consciousness of modern man the element of imagination, fantasy and spirituality, the highest manifestation of which he sees in art, moreover, in the genuine art which is devoted to man, and not to an abstract form or idea. The dream, the illusion and mystery which have deserted modern life are not exhausted by the sphere of art—it is something immeasurably bigger, but the "Godgame" of thought and imagina-

tion find concrete expression precisely in a splendid work of art. Thus one of Fowles's principal themes in the book emerges—the theme of art and its role in the life of man today.

The theme of art is most fully developed in the argument Henry Breasley and David Williams have about art. Fowles confronts two points of view—that of a realist artist and that of an admirer of modern abstract art. Their argument embraces mainly the field of painting but it clearly goes beyond the framework of that particular form of art and has a wider significance. David Williams, whose abstract canvases are as attractive, rational and lifeless as he is himself, is a complete contrast to Henry Breasley, who has never painted anything for sale, but has spent all his life in creative quests and has never compromised. He thinks that innumerable compromises have altered the very nature of art. Commercial art of whatever hue, whether brash or reticent, is called upon to embellish drawing rooms and is not a means of fostering people's appreciation of art. Man has vanished from the canvases of contemporary artists to be replaced by chill geometrical patterns. "The flow of abstract thought" has come to be regarded as the principal subject-matter of art.

Fowles gives a straightforward answer to the question as to what real art should be: should it be the abstract art which is the repository of abstract thoughts and forms and which Williams champions, or the humanist art that is preoccupied with man and his place in the world. In this instance the author's viewpoint is expressed by Mouse, the "enchanted princess" of *The Ebony Tower*. Art is the language of imagery. And like any language it exists not in order to be a repository of the rules of grammar, but as a means of talking with people and about people. The avantgarde artists, who have replaced man by a heap of geometrical patterns, and the living language of imagery by the arid language of mathematics, retreat from problems that are alive and vibrant into the "ebony tower" that has replaced the traditional ivory tower.

The Ebony Tower is what Fowles calls the standpoint of those artists who are indifferent to man and in whom people prompt only feelings of disillusionment and disgust. Expressing the author's view here, Breasley says that such artists are afraid of clarity, and hide behind "pure form". All the superficial freedoms of modernist (Fowles uses the term "avantgarde") art are a fiction, the result of complete impotence. Abstractions are the resort of an artist who either does not wish real life to be portrayed in his work or who finds this life of ours so pointless that he wishes to replace it with sheer professionalism or good taste. Breasley describes such creative work as geometry in art, as histrionics. "Abstract expressionism, neo-primitivism, op art and pop art, conceptualism, photorealism. . . . They were like lemmings, at the mercy of a suicidal drive seeking *Lebensraum* in an arctic sea, in a bottomless night, blind to everything but their own illusion" (*The Ebony Tower*).

Turning their backs on nature and reality, the modernists have severed the artist's links with his public. In Fowles's view this is the natural consequence of producing art for ratiocination and theorising and not for people. The very notion of an "artist" has altered. Artists like Breasley have become almost a rarity, they are being succeeded by the Williamses, mediocre and well-behaved fellow-travellers in art. Williams undoubtedly loses the argument about aesthetics, but he also loses the argument on the moral plane (Fowles thus establishes that link between the aesthetic and moral elements which is an important part of his philosophy). Williams is well-behaved not because the standards of behaviour instilled in him from childhood strike him as necessary and natural, but because of that shackling of the spirit, that "caged animal" mentality of his which restricts his creative possibilities and prevents him from giving himself up to genuine feeling. In essence it is he who proves to be the amoral person, and not Breasley.

The two-level composition which is an intrinsic feature of Fowles's stories derives not only from a Romantic counterposing of the real and the imaginary, but also from a counterposing of a scientific cognition of reality and the poetic (artistic) reflection of that reality. This theme may be traced with particular clarity in **"The Enigma,"** a story about the mysterious disappearance of a fairly well-known Conservative politician.

The ending of the story introduces an element of play and improvisation into a logical narrative which in this instance is composed with minute attention to detail. The author proposes solving "the enigma" (Fielding's disappearance) according to the laws of art. Various theories of suicide, of running away to hide with a beautiful girl and so on are put forward. Thus the pattern of "a story within a story" emerges from which it becomes clear that any logical explanation of Fielding's action solves nothing and therefore how the story ends is of no importance. Fowles counterposes story lines based exclusively on invention and fantasy to the young detective's scientific and logical approach to solving the "mystery". By this contrast the author is saying that there exists a kind of wisdom which cannot be grasped through logic. It lies in the very process of creative art which, by rousing intuition, imagination and the intellect, makes people ask questions about the meaning of life and of their own destinies. In the event, the reader returns to where he began: the main character in the story tries to introduce an element of the miraculous into his own life: he runs away from his own life in the hope of finding his real self.

Fowles fills the structure and imagery of the Romantic narrative to which he resorts with thoroughly modern substance. In a preface to the story *Eliduc* he refers to the general crisis of culture as manifested in Watergate, for instance. According to him, it is "far more a cultural than a political tragedy." He sees the principal consequence of the crisis to be a depersonalisation of the individual, a stereotyping that embraces every aspect of life. "Our stereotyping societies force us to feel more alone. They stamp masks on us and isolate our real selves," he writes in his treatise, *The Aristos*. In this sense he sees the writer's main task as preserving the individuality of man, keeping his innermost being intact. The way to achieve this and so to escape from the current cultural and mental crisis lies in an active combination of morality and of art.

The serious philosophical problems raised in Fowles's stories make them rather like an "intellectual novel" in a short literary form. His book illustrates the way in which philosophy is increasingly influencing modern literature, including the short story. Moreover, the attraction of literature and the arts to philosophy is accompanied by a reverse process too: philosophy today sometimes borrows devices from fiction, preferring to grasp reality by means of creative art rather than through logic and contemplation. This "meeting" of the two has led to an increasingly philosophical quality of creative art on the one hand, and to an increasingly artistic quality of philosophy on the other. At the intersection of these tendencies emerges the writing of many contemporary English prose-writers, among them John Fowles.

Raymond J. Wilson III (essay date 1982)

SOURCE: "John Fowles's *The Ebony Tower:* Unity and Celtic Myth," in *Twentieth Century Literature,* Vol. 28, No. 3, Fall, 1982, pp. 302-18.

[*In the essay below, Wilson argues that a "Grail Quest theme" links the stories of* The Ebony Tower, *citing literary precedents and structural and technical similarities to* The Magus.]

In the opening and title story of John Fowles's **The Ebony Tower,** David Williams meets a girl named Diana, finds himself falling in love with her, and at the crucial moment hesitates to consummate that love sexually, remembering his loyalty to his wife, Beth. There may well be an implication that David has failed himself and failed Diana because fear had prevented him from accepting the challenge of the quest.[1] While there is reason for adopting this view, other factors suggest the possibility that David's hesitation should be judged in light of the sexual ambivalence of the Celtic Quest myth that underlies the story, a point of view that leads to further speculation: that the Grail Quest theme, as modified by T. S. Eliot, connects the stories of **The Ebony Tower** and hints at its relation to the circular narrative structure and allusive technique of *The Magus.*

Eliduc, which Fowles translates and includes in **The Ebony Tower,** provides the specific Celtic inspiration for the initial story, but there is a more pervasive emotional connection to a broader Celtic theme. In **The Ebony Tower,** Fowles suggests that "modern criticism is blind to relationships that are far more emotional than structural."[2] In this statement, Fowles perhaps guides us to seek a point of reference to his collection in the emotional sources of Celtic literature, specifically in the Celtic theme with perhaps the greatest effect on modern literature, the Quest to restore fertility to the waste land. Jessie L. Weston traced this theme in *From Ritual to Romance* to a source in

India's ancient *Rig-Veda.* There she found the story of a young man named Rishyacringa, who is raised in the forest apart from women. When the land falls into unfruitfulness, a temptress in a luxurious barge lures the boy to the city, where the king gives him his daughter in marriage, "and so soon as the marriage is consummated the spell is broken, and rain falls in abundance."[3] The story apparently illustrates what Sir James Frazer called magic thinking, "actions that induced fertility in the animal world were held to be equally efficacious in stimulating the reproductive energies of the vegetable."[4]

Ancient Indian and Medieval Romance readers had a religious context for deciding whether or not the man should yield to temptation, but without such a sure footing, the modern reader of John Fowles has more trouble deciding, despite Fowles's casting *The Ebony Tower* in the mold of Medieval Romance.

—*Raymond J. Wilson III*

Weston then finds a parallel to the *Veda* story in the Grail legends of Celtic Romance in which a knight goes on a quest for the Grail, Christ's cup of the last supper. The quester, called Perceval, Gawain, or occasionally some other name, depending on the version of the legend, enters a waste land, the troubles of which stem from the fact that its ruler, the Fisher King, is dead or excessively aged or suffering from a sexual wound; and to cure the Fisher King, restoring fertility to the land, the knight must pass a series of tests.[5] In the Perceval version, the knight, who, like Rishyacringa of the *Rig-Veda,* was raised in the forest apart from women, encounters, like the Indian quester, a "temptation by a fiend, in the form of a fair maiden," on a luxurious barge (Weston, *From Ritual to Romance,* p. 32). Weston emphasizes the similarities but does not comment on a curious reversal: the Indian hermit-youth must succumb to the temptation in order to restore fertility to the land while, to attain the same end, Perceval must resist the temptation. The change possibly reflects the difference in values between ancient India and Medieval Europe, but even more, it may reflect the quest myth's evolution into a mystery religion "held to be the most appropriate vehicle for imparting the highest religious teaching" (*ibid.,* p. 158), where candidates for initiation into the mystery had to remain celibate for a period of time to purify themselves. The cumulative emotional source for Fowles's story thus contains both sides of David's dilemma.

Ancient Indian and Medieval Romance readers had a religious context for deciding whether or not the man should yield to temptation, but without such a sure footing, the modern reader of John Fowles has more trouble deciding,

despite Fowles's casting *The Ebony Tower* in the mold of Medieval Romance. David and Diana think of Diana as a "sleeping princess" (*ET,* p. 98, p. 91) in need of a "knight errant" (*ET,* p. 96, p. 90). Denied a moment of intimacy, Diana finds it frustratingly "ironic" that David's morality has made "Those dotty old medieval people" less quaint. The two now are like Tristan and Isolde, "Lying in the forest with a sword between them" (*ET,* p. 99, p. 92), and "All that nonsense about chastity" suddenly expresses her own emotional situation.[6] David's "quest" expands the medieval context, for, amid the old Celtic forests of Brittany, David, the young abstract artist and critic, has gone in search of Breasley, an old master of nonabstract art. The ebony tower of the title can be connected with the dark tower of Browning's poem, "Childe Roland to the Dark Tower Came."[7] Browning had drawn the image from an earlier literary work, a scene of the mad Lear expressing something akin to despair. Both Shakespeare and Browning make the dark tower an unquestionably negative image: for Lear the pathetically ironic refuge where the defeated, anguished former monarch washes up like a piece of flotsam; for Childe Roland, the object of his dangerous quest, the place toward which he must steel himself to approach despite his knowledge that many knights have died approaching it.

In Fowles's story, however, the ebony tower is not the object of David's quest; the tower symbolizes not Breasley toward whom David moves, but anything Breasley "doesn't like about modern art," that Breasley "thinks is obscure because the artist is scared to be clear" (*ET,* p. 50, p. 47). As such, the ebony tower would most likely be less unambiguously negative in its implications than the dark towers of Shakespeare and Browning. Just as the medieval quest had an underlying fertility theme, the old man puts his conflict with David into specific terms of sexual fertility, calling abstraction the "Triumph of the bloody eunuch" and impugning Williams' own potency, by saying "God help your bloody wife then" (*ET,* pp. 41-42, p. 39). Later David thinks of the conflict with Breasley "in the medieval context" as "a kind of ordeal" (*ET,* p. 58, p. 55). Then, like the Celtic quester, David undergoes the sexual temptation with Diana. He hesitates and Diana decides against the affair. Fowles's somewhat negative description of David's reunion with his wife as a "surrender" to "abstraction" is modified by David's more ambiguous claim to his wife that he "survived" (*ET,* p. 114, p. 106).[8] The reader emerges wondering if David has done the best thing. In trying to judge David's response to his sexual temptation, one must seek to discover the Celtic links between the various tales of *The Ebony Tower.* Initial critics of the book did not find a connection.

Early reviewers praised individual stories, but failed to see the links between stories that John Fowles claims for *The Ebony Tower.* "Whether others would recognize a common base and see a web of intricate relationships among these five stories, without the prompting proffered in 'a personal note' inserted in the middle of the book, is debatable," says Rene Kuhn Bryant for the *National Review* in a typical response.[9] The note she refers to carries Fowles's statement that he abandoned the title *Variations* since "professional readers, who do know my books, could see no justification for Variations whatever" (*ET,* p. 117, p. 109). By saying that "Fowles enjoys the enigmatic and plainly prefers puzzles to proofs, questions to answers," Bryant implies that we need not trouble with the thematic unity of this book or Fowles's claim to be working "variations both on certain themes in previous books of mine and in methods of narrative presentation" (*ibid.*). There are so many other "levels" on which we can read Fowles profitably, she says. But this neglects the fact that unsolved puzzles fail in their function. And critics' frustration soon turns to irritation. "There is invariably a contrived incompleteness," says Jan B. Gordon of *Commonweal,*[10] and Foster Hirsch complains in *America* that Fowles's short-story technique "probably could not be sustained over the length of a novel."[11] Such quick irritation occurs when the reader misses the allusive and thematic connection between stories. Specifically, Bryant claims that "'**The Cloud**,' which ends the book, has to be accounted a failure," and, while Hirsch senses "a symbolically charged mood" in "**The Cloud**," he does not connect this mood to its source in the Celtic theme of the early stories, finding the story less artful than the other narratives. Thus, the reviewers do not perceive that Fowles uses the myth of the quest for rebirth in "**The Cloud**," the final story of the volume, to supply a thematic conclusion, providing an implicit context for David Williams' actions.

While the Celtic connection of the first story and of the translated Celtic Romance is obvious and direct, the Celtic links of "**The Cloud**" come only through the medium of Eliot and *The Waste Land.* One might perhaps be tempted to claim that the dark mood introduced in the first story continues in the last, the negative motif of the ebony tower being now expressed by the black cloud of the title.[12] The story's surface certainly presents a nearly overwhelming dark mood, but the context of allusion introduces possibilities which lighten this darkness. The story's reliance on the Eliot allusions places the reader in a position somewhat analogous to the questing knight in the original Celtic Grail Romance, who had to ask the right questions about the symbols shown him; everything would be explained to him, his personal salvation assured, the King cured, and the land saved if only he would have the wits to ask the proper question. The reverse would occur if he does not ask (Weston, *From Ritual to Romance,* pp. 14-15). Similarly, in "**The Cloud**," asking the right questions, we suspect that the author is not playing a game of willful obscurity. Fowles's early attempts to alert us to *The Waste Land* allusions in "**The Cloud**," such as having "a kingfisher" fly across the path of the characters, are so forced that he apparently feels obliged to apologize for their blatancy. In a passage ostensibly referring to one of the children, Fowles calls the Eliot reference "unnecessary italics, always underlining the obvious" (*ET,* p. 260, p. 244).

Despite his veiled apology, Fowles proceeds with further direct clues: "A figure appears, from the trees, from the way they came: a fisherman, a peasant come fishing . . ." (*ET,* p. 263, p. 246). This Fisher-King figure plays no plot role, but Fowles gives him a mysterious aura to en-

hance his allusive function. Catherine, the story's grieving heroine, "leaves the water, as if he draws her after him" (*ET,* p. 264, p. 247). Then Fowles has Catherine quote directly from *The Waste Land* even to the eccentric deletion of the "d" in "goodnight": "Hurry up please it's time. Goodnight Bill. Goonight Lou. Goonight. Goonight" (*ET,* p. 264, p. 247).[13] In this passage, Eliot parodied Ophelia's mad scene, from which Fowles quotes at the head of the story. Fowles's use of it takes on added poignancy when we remember that he has just referred to Catherine with the words Shakespeare used to describe Ophelia's drowning, "Which time she chanted snatches of old tunes" (*ET,* p. 263, p. 246), from *Hamlet* IV. viii. 176.

Fowles further signals the "right questions" by his other allusions to Shakespearean works that Eliot quotes in *The Waste Land.* As the story begins, Catherine lies by the water's edge grieving, we soon discover, for a suicide-dead man, husband, or lover.[14] She hears a "rich, erratic, un-English song" (*ET,* p. 251, p. 235), which possibly echoes Eliot's allusion to *The Tempest,* where Ferdinand grieved on the shore "Musing upon the king my brother's wreck / And on the king my father's death before him" (III, 191-92). Ferdinand heard Prospero's soothing music in a passage quoted by Eliot: "This music crept by me upon the waters" (III, 257).

Catherine's friends do not have Prospero's magic music to soothe her grief. Instead, Annabel and Paul, her sister and brother-in-law, ask her to vacation with them in central France, where they are staying with their two children. A television executive named Peter, father of a four-year-old boy, and Peter's girlfriend Sally have joined them. When, despite the lush vegetation, Catherine emphasizes *The Waste Land* topography of "silent cliffs above, scorched lifeless planet, windless sun" (*ET,* p. 276, p. 258), we begin to suspect that Fowles, in his usual illusive, indirect manner, uses Eliot to provide a literary context for Catherine's emotional barrenness.

Catherine reacts like Eliot's hyacinth girl, who said, "You gave me hyacinths first a year ago" (I, 35). Similarly, when Annabel rushes to "her" butterfly-orchids "and kneels, oblivious to all but them," and is asked "Why are they yours?" she says, "Because I found them last year" (*ET,* p. 258, p. 242). Though Annabel provides this verbal echo, Catherine supplies the emotional connection; when the *Waste Land* lovers return we hear these words:

> . . . I could not
> Speak, and my eyes failed, I was neither
> Living nor dead, and I knew nothing,
> Looking into the heart of light, the silence.
>
> (I, 38-41)

Moments earlier Catherine had said, "I've got nothing to say. I can't think of anything" (*ET,* p. 256, p. 239). Stimulated into thought by Annabel's action toward the butterfly-orchids, Catherine now thinks like Eliot's hyacinth girl, "The most frightening is not wanting love from anyone, or ever again. . . . To forgive nothing and give nothing and want nothing was what it all really meant" (*ET,* p. 261, p.

244). Yet Catherine's need for sexually expressed love quickly surfaces in her overtures to Paul.

Paul, the good but ineffectual comforter, reminds us of Eliot's Prufrock, who said, "I shall wear the bottoms of my trousers rolled. / . . . I shall wear white flannel trousers, and walk upon the beach."[15] Just before the arrival of Fowles's fisherman, "Paul takes off his shoes and stockings, rolls up his trousers, methodical and comical, like an elderly tripper at the seaside" (*ET,* p. 262, p. 245). In this resonance we recognize Paul's Prufrock characteristics: "Paul with his prematurely aging hair and beard streaked black and white, almost cropped, obscurely nautical rather than literary, a dense shade too would-be intellectual and *distingué*" (*ET,* p. 262, p. 245). The group hunts crayfish, lobsterlike little beings that direct our thoughts to the "pair of ragged claws" which Prufrock says he should have been in Eliot's poem. Fowles works these allusions smoothly into the stream of his prose, and one must not make the mistake of feeling that they explain all the ambiguities away. In fact, by introducing added matter for thought, the allusions add ambiguities to the surface text at the same time that they provide a wider, more literary context for the action of the story.

Lured away by Fowles's magnetic fisherman, Catherine, like "Belladonna, the Lady of the Rocks" (I, 49), sits on a rock by a quiet pool and begins to cry, echoing not only the grieving Ferdinand of Eliot's *Tempest* allusion, mentioned above, but Eliot's line "By the waters of Leman I sat down and wept . . ." (III, 182). Finding Catherine crying by the waters, Paul tries to comfort her. She throws herself in his arms; and here we see the value of Fowles's careful Prufrocking of Paul. Paul, flinching, hesitating to become sexually involved with his wife's sister, will not "force the moment to its crisis." Thus, like J. Alfred and like David Williams in *The Ebony Tower,* Paul cannot change the course of the woman's life. Catherine slips off again to be alone and ultimately to have a sexual encounter with Peter, who is also defined by *Waste Land* references.

Coming to the waterside spot "where Catherine wandered earlier" (*ET,* p. 296, p. 276), Peter thinks about swimming but decides against it, fearing that the stream is "Definitely too fast." He thus follows the *Waste Land* advice of Eliot's Madame Sosostris, who warned her customer to "Fear death by water" (I, 55). Eliot places this water in the context of Spenser's departed, white-bodied water nymphs from "Prothalamion," who, in Eliot's parody, had played at picnics with the "loitering heirs of city directors" (III, 175-81). At Fowles's picnic, white-bodied Sally takes the role of the water nymph and Peter is the ironic parody of the city directors. He is literally a director in Eliot's sense of a business executive; and, perhaps in a bit of wry Fowles humor, Peter is a television director.

Peter climbs in the hot sun away from the water, toward the shadow of the red cliff, which elicits a memory of a *Waste Land* passage "where the sun beats":

> . . . Only
> There is shadow under this red rock,

(Come in under the shadow of this red rock),
And I will show you something different from either
Your shadow at morning striding behind you
Or your shadow at evening rising to meet you;
I will show you fear in a handful of dust.

> (I, 24-30)

The red rock in *The Waste Land* promises shade and thus presumably relief from the sun's blasting. It is entirely different from any previous experience but is something feared. In the end, the episode amounts to a mere handful of dust, paralleling the hyacinth-girl motif it immediately precedes in *The Waste Land.* The virgin feared the new action, sought it as relief from the waste land, and found it disappointing—as inconsequential as a handful of dust. The mocking, apparently male voice, beckoning "I will show you . . . ," subsequently reveals insight into the female disappointment that puzzles us until we discover that the voice resounds in the mind of Tiresias, a man who had been a woman.[16]

Fowles possibly provides his character with overtones of rock by calling him Peter, *petrus* being Latin for rock, and Peter's climb to the base of the cliff associates him more specifically with the red rock: "The heat. He turns and stares up at the cliff that towers above, gray and reddish ochre, one or two overhangs already casting shadow in the westering sun. Angles. Death" (*ET,* p. 297, p. 277). The passage reveals Fowles's careful juggling of fictional and symbolic elements, for the rock is gray as well as red in a concession to realism, Fowles adding, for purely emblematic purposes, the waste land concept "Death."

Peter may also have an indirect spiritual affinity with the clerk who seduced Eliot's typist in *The Waste Land.* The situation of the people on holiday, just released from oppressive work, parallels *The Waste Land*'s "At the violet hour, when the eyes and back / Turn upward from the desk . . ." (III, 215-16). Peter says: "Just the rat race. Set us dumb helots free, we collapse into total inertia." Then: "You need training for this." Then: "You've forgotten how us poor working sods live" (*ET,* p. 252, p. 236). Later thoughts reinforce the theme, evoking images of Eliot's Unreal City. "When all one sees, somehow, is a tired rush of evening people, work-drained automata . . . fragments, illusions, fantasies, egos . . . unreal enough, oh, quite unreal enough without the added unreality . . ." (*ET,* p. 275, p. 257) of television ideas. These are apparently Catherine's thoughts, but Fowles leaves their attribution intentionally ambiguous so that they come at us prophetically out of the blue, indirectly reminding us of the pain suffered by Tiresias who had "foresuffered all," helpless to make things better in *The Waste Land* (III, 243): "one can be only profoundly lucky, above, chosen, helpless," she says (*ET,* p. 275, p. 257).

Eliot's "young man carbuncular" was "One of the low on whom assurance sits / As a silk hat on a Bradford millionaire" (III, 233-34). In some of its aspects, the Eliot line resembles the way Catherine reacts to Peter. They talk of Barthes, whose views of our culture in *Mythologies* could aptly be summed up by Eliot's "heap of broken images" (I, 22). Peter suggests she work up a script for television based on Barthes. In the next moment he insults her by adding, "Scriptwriters are ten a penny" (*ET,* p. 281, p. 263). She refuses the script-writing job, and as Peter debates with her she suddenly realizes:

> . . . it is very simple, she hates him; although he is fortuitous, ignorable as such, he begins to earn his right to be an emblem, a hideous sign. For he is not testing—or teasing—Barthes and semiotics, but her. He means childish little male things like: why don't you smile at me, what have I done, please show respect when I watch my language because I know you don't like my language. (*ET,* p. 280, p. 262)

Besides depicting Catherine's contempt for Peter, the passage suggests a possible relationship between *The Waste Land* and **The Ebony Tower.** Eliot's waste-land characters resemble what Catherine calls Peter—they may be seen as "emblems," "hideous signs" that represent all the life-in-death automatons who inhabit the waste land of the modern world. On the other hand, the conventions of fiction require Fowles's characters to be believable; they must "earn" their "right to be an emblem," earning it by echoing words and actions of *The Waste Land* while maintaining complete fictional verisimilitude.

Similar to *The Waste Land,* the central "hideous sign" of **"The Cloud"** is an act of loveless sex. As the moment of sexual encounter approaches in **"The Cloud,"** the *Waste Land* allusions thicken without detracting from fictional realism and excitement. We see Catherine waiting, again like "Belladonna," in the rocks below the red cliff. Her thoughts trace the theme of Eliot's *The Waste Land*:

> We hate, Barren. Had clutched at anything but this: the cowardice, waiting, wanting-not-daring.
>
> Death. . . . which left today like a fragile grain between two implacable and immense millstones. Nothing. All was past before it happened; was words, shards, lies, oblivion. (*ET,* p. 298, p. 278)

Although these lines express profound, personal emotions, the culmination of Catherine as a fictional character, they also have wider significance, revealing Catherine's literary function as an emblem of all the waste landers, a possibility reinforced by her further thoughts:

> The dying cultures, dying lands.
> Europe ends.
> The death of fiction; and high time too.
> (*ET,* p. 298, p. 278)

Just as Peter appears on the scene, Fowles sums Catherine up with a phrase that rings in our minds: "Young dark-haired corpse with a bitter mouth" (*ET,* p. 299, p. 279). Peter's seduction of Catherine closely follows Eliot's episode of the typist and the carbuncular agent's clerk, as suggested by this set of intriguing but not definitive quotations, alternating aspects of the two seductions:

Eliot: On the divan are piled (at night her bed) Stockings, slippers, camisoles, and stays (III, 226-27).

Fowles: [Catherine too lies on her clothes:] He sees the folded Levi's and pink shirt she has been using as a pillow (*ET,* p. 300, p. 280).

Eliot: The time is now propitious, as he guesses, . . . she is bored and tired (III, 235-36).

Fowles: It is a change of attitude so sudden, so unexpected, so banal, so implicitly friendly despite the expressionlessness of her face, that he grins (*ET,* p. 301, p. 281).

Eliot: Endeavors to engage her in caresses Which still are unreproved, if undesired (III, 237-38).

Fowles: She shows not the least response to his circling palm, though he rubs more firmly, more slowly, down each side, down the center to the small of the back (*ET,* p. 302, p. 282).

Eliot: Flushed and decided, he assaults at once (III, 239).

Fowles: . . . all is erect, cocked, wild, in all senses wild; the bloody nerve, the savage tamed; the knowing one will . . . (*ET,* p. 302, p. 282).

Eliot: Exploring hands encounter no defense; His vanity requires no response, And makes a welcome of indifference (III, 240-42).

Fowles: She makes no response at all. . . . (*ET,* p. 303, p. 282)
She lies inert. . . . [He thinks:] She is excited, whatever she pretends (*ET,* p. 303, p. 283).

The two works have something more in common than the mere fact of a "seduction." Both have sequences of five actions and their similar emotional concomitants: lying upon clothing, one-sided male assessments, passive acceptance, the male "decided" and "knowing one will," and male vanity. Two parallel seduction sequences could perhaps occur coincidentally in a case where two authors both seek to apply the same myth to modern life, but direct conscious or unconscious evocation of Eliot by Fowles might perhaps seem a more likely explanation.

Further details add evidence that Ellot served as a model for the emblematic dimension of Fowles's story, a dimension that is only one of many levels of meaning. When Peter finds the spot where Catherine had earlier cried, "He unzips his shorts and urinates in the water" (*ET,* p. 296, p. 276). On the surface one wonders if Fowles's including such a scene in the story has any function or whether it is a completely gratuitous detail, yet one can see even this in the context of Eliot. In an earlier version of *The Waste Land,* Eliot's young man carbuncular "Delays only to urinate, and spit," after the sexual affair, emphasizing his callous casual approach.[17] Peter has a similar attitude. For him the sex scene is "just the sick game of a screwed-up little neurotic in heat" (*ET,* p. 304, pp. 283-84). Later, Peter tries to allay Sally's suspicions by saying, "I'm saving necrophilia for my old age" (*ET,* p. 308, p. 288). Physical death emphasizes the emotional death of sex without love.

Jessie Weston said about the parallels she saw between the Grail legends and the rebirth motif, that any one or two allusions "taken separately, might be regarded as accidental, [but] in their *ensemble* can hardly be thus considered" (Weston, *From Ritual to Romance,* p. 33). Cautiously applying the analogous argument to Eliot and Fowles, we turn to the dark cloud, which at first may seem only to reinforce the extremely dark surface mood of the story. Immediately after the sexual episode, the picnickers pack up and leave the suicidal woman behind even though a dangerous thunderstorm threatens. If accepted, the Eliot allusions would be important here because they alleviate this otherwise desperately pessimistic ending, for Eliot's thunderstorm had positive as well as negative elements. The thunder words from Hindu myth, *Datta, Dayadhvam, Damyata* (give, sympathize, control), offer encouragement to the hope for regeneration on both physical and emotional planes—"The awful daring of a moment's surrender . . . I have heard the key / Turn . . . your heart would have responded / Gaily, when invited . . ." (IV, 404, 412, 421). Allusion to *The Waste Land*'s ending provides a plausible motive for Fowles to call major attention to Eliot's positive thundercloud by naming the entire story **"The Cloud,"** hinting perhaps of a similar hopeful possibility in **"The Cloud,"** and spurring the reader to search for other allusive hints. Two points discovered in such a hunt introduce ambivalence into **"The Cloud,"** throwing at least a modicum of doubt on the story's pessimism: Catherine's princess story and Fowles's allusive method such as one suspects he uses in *The Magus.*

Catherine told her little niece a story about a sleeping princess raised by animals in the woods. At the "emblem level" the princess is the female counterpart of Rishyacringa of the *Rig-Veda* and Perceval of the Grail Romance, who were also raised in the forest apart from people and were thus sexually innocent. The little princess loses her prince and still waits naked in the woods for the prince to return. Thus love fails to achieve sexual consummation, reversing the *Rig-Veda* outcome and presumably depriving the waste land of renewed fertility. The last sentence of **"The Cloud"** reads, "The princess calls, but there is no one, now, to hear her" (*ET,* p. 312, p. 291). This is the pessimistic ending which one may feel awaits Catherine herself; but, because her little niece resisted the unfruitful ending, Catherine amended it, saying that the knight will come soon, they will be happy, and have "Lots of babies" (*ET,* p. 293, p. 274). In the waste land, prospective birth and new life are optimistic.

Another "story" also adds ambiguity to **"The Cloud"** and possibly mitigates its pessimism. Fowles claims that *The Ebony Tower* works variations on the themes and methods of his earlier works. One such work originally had an ambiguous ending that relied on an allusive narrative technique to introduce the possibility, not the certainty, of optimism. This work, *The Magus* as originally written, provides a pattern, a variation of which may be employed in the ending of **"The Cloud."** In *The Magus* Fowles carefully parallels the experience of his young hero Nicholas to that of Orpheus.[18] Nicholas, who has been cruel to his girlfriend Alison, meets a magician-teacher, "The Magus," who makes Nicholas believe that Alison has committed suicide for love of the young man. Then, in a drug-aided underworld experience, The Magus puts Nicholas through Orpheus-like tests and restores him to the possibility of fruitful love with Alison, the novel ending in apparent ambiguity. Nicholas has ordered Alison to meet him in the waiting room of a train station, a significant possible selection because a sign near the villa of The Magus read *SALLE D'ATTENTE,* the waiting room. Fowles does not tell us whether she meets him or not, the last paragraph of the novel merely containing these lines: "I gave her bowed head one last stare, then I was walking. Firmer than Orpheus, as firm as Alison herself, that other day of parting, not once looking back."[19]

Anyone knowing the myth of Orpheus and Eurydice will recognize the somewhat optimistic hint of these lines, because Orpheus won for Eurydice the right to follow him back to the land of the living. All that was necessary was that he not turn around until he got all the way out of the underworld. Orpheus turned too soon; Nicholas did not turn. That he walked away "firmer than Orpheus . . . not once looking back" provides an optimistic option for interpretation which depends on allusion. This is true even though the allusion introduces ambiguity to the novel's otherwise pessimistic ending, and does not resolve it. In the revised version of *The Magus,* Fowles removed the overt reference to Orpheus's not looking back, assuring, whether or not it was his intention to, that no one would reduce his ambiguous ending to an arbitrary certainty. In **"The Cloud,"** Eliot's myth may operate much like the Orpheus myth in *The Magus* to introduce the ambiguity of optimistic possibilities for the ending of the story, thus working a "variation" on the earlier technique.

The Ebony Tower's allusion to *The Waste Land,* with its Tarot-deck characters, further validates Fowles's claim that *The Ebony Tower* works "variations both on certain themes in previous books of mine and in methods of narrative presentation" (*ET,* p. 117, p. 109). For "The Magus" is also a Tarot-deck character like the Man with Three Staves who is Eliot's Fisher King.[20] Fowles emphasizes the Tarot origin by quoting Arthur Edward Waite's *The Key to the Tarot* before the title page of *The Magus.* Furthermore, Fowles used four lines from Eliot's "Little Gidding" as the theme for Nicholas' quest and as the method of narrative presentation of *The Magus,* Fowles quoting Eliot:

> We shall not cease from exploration
> And the end of all our exploring
> Will be to arrive where we started
> And know the place for the first time.
>   (quoted from *The Magus,* p. 65)

That this circling narrative structure also unifies *The Ebony Tower* becomes evident when we trace the purported circle through the stories and follow it back to its starting point. After the obvious Celtic influences in the first story and of the translation of *Eliduc,* the circle arcs toward **"Poor Koko,"** which opens with an Old Cornish epigraph and dramatizes the waste-land themes of emotional barrenness and the failure of communication. When a young burglar burns the narrator's book manuscript, the victim explains that the very "poverty" of the youth's verbal expression acts to "castrate the wish it implied!" (*ET,* p. 185, p. 174). The narrator continues his metaphor of sexual sterility, claiming that the burglar wanted to overcome his emotional impotence through "the loan of some of this magic power" of the written word. The vandal wanted, says the narrator, initiation into the "secret society" (*ET,* p. 186, p. 175) of language power. The story thus evokes a cluster of ideas with close emotional ties to Weston's analysis of mystery religions with power to overcome spiritual sterility for their initiates.

"The Enigma," with its mystery theme, continues the metaphoric circle's arc. Before his baffling disappearance, John Marcus Fielding was a "zombie" (*ET,* p. 242, p. 226), a word that evokes both Eliot's references to the walking dead of Baudelaire and Dante and Fowles's later depiction of Catherine as a living corpse. Isobel, the girlfriend of Fielding's son, tells police that they have not asked the right questions in their quest for the missing Fielding. In this she resembles those who told Perceval the same thing. Isobel suspects that Fielding sought "immortality of a kind" (*ET,* p. 242, p. 226) through death by water, a major theme of Eliot's poem. Michael Jennings, the policeman who falls in love with Isobel, thinks of her as "someone alive, where everyone else had been dead" (*ET,* p. 224, p. 209). In a metaphor that could easily be drawn from the Frazer-Weston theme of Eliot's poem, Michael thinks that she stimulates in him "a potential that lay like unsown ground, waiting for just this unlikely corngoddess . . ." (*ET,* p. 236, p. 220). Her fertility, like the "magic" of the preceding story, flows from the written word: Isobel works for a publisher and writes books herself. Even on the physical plane, she spends most of the story in France, helping her pregnant sister bring new life into the world. The story ends optimistically in a "tender" and apparently fruitful love affair which has "poetries no enigma . . . can diminish or demean" (*ET,* p. 247, p. 231).[21]

The Celtic connections of **"Poor Koko"** and **"The Enigma"** fit Fowles's description as "far more emotional than structural" (*ET,* p. 118, p. 110). But in the Celtic connection, through Eliot, to **"The Cloud,"** the structural and emotional parallels reinforce each other. The Eliot allusions of **"The Cloud"** carry the thematic circle through the final story; and the pattern does not stop there. A circle returns to its starting point; and Catherine's princess story establishes a solid connection between Catherine of **"The Cloud"** and Diana of *The Ebony Tower.* Since Catherine invents the story, her little princess presumably reflects Catherine's emotional state on the realistic character level. Naked and innocent, the little princess

is timid like a "mouse" (*ET,* p. 287, p. 268). Diana, in the novel's opening story, is nicknamed "The Mouse," and we see her naked in the woods twice. Like Catherine's heroine, Diana is described as a sleeping princess in need of a knight errant. The potential knights are similar. David is kindly, loyal to his wife, and weak like Paul of **"The Cloud,"** and both resemble Prufrock. Neither David nor Paul accepts the role of knight errant in which the situation and the respective women casts them. In each case there is an apparently negative impact on the women, yet the positive moral implications of their refraining from sexual involvement become evident when their behavior is compared to Peter's despicable cruelty.

The question posed by the opening story was whether David, while having no intention of remaining in Diana's life, should have consummated a sexual affair with her. The implications of the last story suggest that David's abandoning Diana the next day might have been nearly as cruel as Peter's abandoning Catherine at the end of **"The Cloud."** Would Diana have become another of Eliot's hyacinth girls, a sexual encounter, turned to in desperation, becoming a mere handful of dust?

The ambivalence of ancient Indian affirmation of sexuality, and Medieval European prohibition of it, is mediated in *The Ebony Tower* by Eliot's two-sided image. On one side we see the loveless sex of the typist; on the other, the joyous renewing experience of sex akin to a boat under sail expressed ambiguously by the thundercloud at the end of *The Waste Land.* Have we, as Fowles predicted, "arrived where we started / And know the place for the first time"?

"The unexplained mystery," says Fowles, "as every agnostic and novelist knows, is black proof of an ultimate shirking of creative responsibility. I have a dead weasel on my conscience; and deeper still, a dead woman" (*ET,* p. 117, p. 109). By the "weasel," he refers to an incident imported from *Eliduc* into *The Ebony Tower.* By the "woman," Fowles clearly refers to Catherine. Whether she literally kills herself or not, Fowles has left her for dead. Without the redeeming possibility of optimism from *The Waste Land*'s thundercloud, with its hope for spiritual, emotional, and physical rebirth, Fowles might indeed have Catherine on his conscience.[22] It may be that Fowles avoids such a pitfall by his allusive technique and circular structure, and that he thereby fulfills his "creative responsibility."

Notes

[1] Carol M. Barnum, "The Quest Motif in John Fowles's *The Ebony Tower*: Theme and Variations," *Texas Studies in Literature and Language,* 23 (Spring 1982), pp. 138-57, holds this view.

[2] John Fowles, "The Ebony Tower," *The Ebony Tower* (Boston: Little, Brown, 1974), p. 118, paperback edition Signet (1975), p. 110. All references to *The Ebony Tower* (cited as *ET* in parenthesis) are to these two editions.

[3] Jessie L. Weston, *From Ritual to Romance* (Cambridge: Cambridge Univ. Press, 1920), paperback edition Anchor (1957), p. 31.

[4] Weston (*ibid.*, p. 34) cites Sir James Frazer, *The Golden Bough, Adonis, Attis, Osiris,* p. 5. Theodor H. Gaster, *The New Golden Bough,* abridged (New York: Criterion Books, 1959), paperback edition Mentor (1964), pp. 339-41, summarizes the section from which Weston quotes.

[5] The source of the Grail Romances has been lost. Weston reconstructs it by compiling this version from the stories that have survived. No extant version has all of these elements.

[6] Kerry McSweeney, "John Fowles's Variations in *The Ebony Tower,*" *Journal of Modern Literature,* 8, ii (1980-81), says, "These specific romance allusions, however, are much less important in 'The Ebony Tower' than the palpable aura of mystery, strangeness, and ordeal imparted by romance motifs" (pp. 321-22).

[7] Barnum, "The Quest Motif in John Fowles's *The Ebony Tower,*" p. 139. Significantly, however, the parallels pointed out by Barnum occur only as David departs from Breasley's property, not as he approaches as in the Browning poem.

[8] Barnum sees the ending as less ambiguous than this analysis suggests and more clearly pessimistic, saying that if David had succeeded he would have done more than survive; he would have lied (Barnum, *ibid.,* p. 147). Interestingly, Robert Browning once agreed with a friend that the meaning of the "Childe Roland" poem may be "He that endureth to the end shall be saved," a sentence that parallels David's notion, *Norton Anthology of English Literature,* 4th ed., ed. M. H. Abrams, *et al* (New York: Norton, 1979) f.p. 1254.

[9] Rene Kuhn Bryant, "Skillful Angler," *National Review,* Jan. 17, 1975, pp. 51-53.

[10] Jan B. Gordon, "The Ebony Tower," *Commonweal,* June 20, 1975, pp. 220-21.

[11] Foster Hirsch, "The Ebony Tower," *America,* Jan. 11, 1975, pp. 18-19.

[12] Barnum, "The Quest Motif in John Fowles's *The Ebony Tower,*" p. 156.

[13] Eliot's own notes emphasize *The Waste Land*'s connection to Frazer and to Weston's analysis of Celtic Romance and the Fisher King. (See Eliot's notes to I, 46 and title of Part V.) He thus established an imaginative sequence that is independent of whether Weston's thesis is historically accurate. In *The Waste Land* Eliot adds the need for emotional rebirth to the theme, just as the mystery religions had added spiritual rebirth to the notion of vegetative rebirth. Eliot makes loveless sex the central image of emotional death.

[14] Barnum, in "The Quest Motif in John Fowles's *The Ebony Tower,*" only says that the man Catherine loved "went away" (p. 155). However, Catherine at one point asks Paul, "Are you and Bel frightened I shall try to kill myself as well?" By the "as well," I take it she implies that the man she loved had killed himself.

[15] T. S. Eliot, "The Love Song of J. Alfred Prufrock," line 121, 123. References to this poem in parentheses are to line numbers. Barnum pointed out a parallel between David Williams of "The Ebony Tower" and Eliot's Prufrock.

[16] As a close comparison to *Isaiah,* xxxii, 2, shows, Eliot's red rock has overtones of the Old Testament, but Eliot adds the color; Isaiah calls it a "great" rock. By coloring it red (with possible phallic implications), juxtaposing it with the hyacinth girl episode, and placing it in the mind of Tiresias, Eliot makes the image resonate in harmony with his theme of the emotional and spiritual failure of sexuality in the waste land.

[17] T. S. Eliot, *The Waste Land: A Facsimile and Transcript of the Original Drafts Including the Annotations of Ezra Pound* (New York: Harcourt, 1971), ed. Valerie Eliot, p. 47. Eliot deleted the reference to urination upon Pound's marginal comment that it was, "Probaly (*sic*) over the mark." Fowles either reacted to Eliot's character on parallel lines with Eliot or alluded to the earlier manuscript.

[18] Avrom Fleishman, "*The Magus* of the Wizard of the West," *Journal of Modern Literature,* V, 2 (Apr. 1976), explicates the Orpheus allusions of *The Magus* and draws attention to Fowles's quotation from "Little Gidding" and to Fowles's use of the Tarot in *The Magus.*

[19] John Fowles, *The Magus* (Boston, Little, Brown, 1965), p. 606, Dell paperback edition (New York: 1973), p. 604.

[20] See Eliot's note to *The Waste Land* (I, 46): "The Man with Three Staves (an authentic member of the Tarot pack) I associate, quite arbitrarily with the Fisher King himself."

[21] Barnum claims that Isobel's corn-goddess aspects are potentials that she never fulfills, and that the sexual consummation is a secular parallel to the archetypal encounter, just as Fielding's disappearance is a secular mystery, the best the characters can do in the absence of openness to archetypal mystery. Such an interpretation would not alter the structural point being made here.

[22] Having explicated the stories as depicting mostly failed characters existing in a primarily dark mood, Barnum, "The Quest Motif in John Fowles's *The Ebony Tower,*" p. 156, admits that "Fowles's view of life is not one of Despair." I believe that the structural and allusive hints of *The Ebony Tower* support this view.

James W. Sollisch (essay date 1983)

SOURCE: "The Passion of Existence: John Fowles's *The Ebony Tower,*" in *Critique: Studies in Modern Fiction,* Vol. XXV, No. 1, Fall, 1983, pp. 1-10.

[*In the following essay, Sollisch relates the principal themes of* The Ebony Tower *to Fowles's version of humanity's Fall: "not from innocence to knowledge but from knowledge to mystery."*]

The fiction of John Fowles is concerned primarily with the search for mystery and self-knowledge. Without mystery, there is no real life, no passion to exist. To Fowles, "Mystery, or unknowing is energy."[1] Most of his characters begin without mystery, secure in their conventions and eventually are forced to see beyond the stale metaphors of their lives into the world of mystery. Some characters, like Nicholas Urfe in *The Magus,* eventually accept the existential responsibility of being—they are forced to see into the mystery, and they embrace it; others catch a glimpse of this passion and push it back beneath the conventions of their lives like David Williams in *The*

Ebony Tower. Whichever way, almost every major character in Fowles's fiction is allowed—forced—to see the mystery of reality, and all are changed by it whether they accept the mystery or suppress it.

The Ebony Tower, which Fowles called *Variations* as a working title, further explores many of the fictional and philosophical situations put forth in *The Magus.* Variations on the quest for self-knowledge, variations on the godgame and absconding god themes, and variations on his use of mystery all occur in the novella, three short stories, and the translation of Marie de France's twelfth-century romance which make up the collection entitled **The Ebony Tower.** In this collection Fowles often sets up a timeless garden of Eden into which he places a character repressed by certain conventions. What ensues is Fowles's version of the Fall: man falls not from innocence to knowledge but from knowledge to mystery. We see this pattern first in *The Magus,* and it occurs here in the novella **The Ebony Tower,** in **"Poor Koko,"** and in **"The Cloud."**

Another key variation is this collection is Fowles's use of the absconding god pattern that we see at the end of *The Magus* when Nicholas realizes: "It was logical, the perfect climax to the godgame. They had absconded, we were alone. . . . How could they be so incurious? So load the dice and yet leave the game."[2] This pattern is varied in every story in **The Ebony Tower.**

The fictional themes and variations explored in **The Ebony Tower** and *The Magus* have roots in a system of philosophical thought put forth by Fowles in *The Aristos,* a book of aphorisms which Fowles has described as "my own self-portrait in ideas . . . a self-description of a writer who is determined to remain free from all parties, classes, churches, cliques, and movements."[3] Fowles believes that one of the greatest heresies and tyrannies of our time is the commonly held belief that only the specialist has a right to hold opinions—and then only in his field.[4] In *The Aristos* Fowles presents his naked opinions and philosophies on a multitude of subjects ranging from the nature of mystery to religion to games. He presents his case in as dogmatic and unrhetorical a manner as possible. The result is a very clear roadmap to his system of thought, and since Fowles is a fiction writer of ideas, *The Aristos* is an invaluable informant to his fictional themes and variations. Here *The Aristos* will be used to inform three major patterns and variations that occur in the original works of Fowles's collection **The Ebony Tower**: his concept and use of mystery, his concept and use of the Fall, and his concept and use of the absconding god.

Fowles defines and redefines mystery for us in *The Aristos.* Every philosophical belief he holds can be reduced to its lowest common terms: the need for man to generate mystery in every aspect of his life. He writes in *The Aristos*: "Mystery or unknowing is energy. As soon as a mystery is explained it ceases to be a source of energy. . . . We are intended to solve much of the mystery; it is harmful to us. We have to invent protections against the sun in many situations; but to wish to destroy the sun? The easier

mysteries, how at a superficial level things work mechanically, how things are 'caused,' have been largely solved. Many take these mysteries for the whole mystery. The price of tapping water into every home is that no one values water any more" (28). The protagonists in this collection of stories: David Williams, the narrator in **"Poor Koko,"** Michael Jennings, and all the characters in **"The Cloud"** with the exception of Catherine need to learn the value of mystery: they need to learn to value water again.

David Williams is defined for us as a "fully abstract artist" who has been a studio teacher and lecturer and who is now a reviewer. We learn that he is well liked, has always been successful, and has a happy marriage. Fowles tells us in summation that "David was a young man who was above all tolerant, fair-minded and inquisitive."[5] At our first view, we tend to see David as a sort of ideal, but he is soon starkly contrasted with the famous artist Henry Breasley, whose work David has come to review. Breasley is a fierce individualist, a representational painter who calls abstraction the "greatest betrayal in the history of art. . . . Triumph of the bloody eunuch" (36). Breasley is inarticulate, rude, and above all intolerant. We learn from Diana, one of Breasley's young live-in assistants, that "Henry thinks one shouldn't show toleration for things one believes are bad" (39). In every way Breasley is a contrast to Williams: the contrast becomes a conflict between reality and abstraction. Reality and Breasley stand for life, passion, and mystery; abstraction and Williams stand for convention, security, and death. Breasley tells Williams: "Don't hate, can't love. Can't love, can't paint" (40). Diana translates for him: "Making is speaking. . . . Art is a form of speech. Speech must be based on human need, not abstract theories of grammar" (40). The challenge has been made to David: throw off your conventions, your abstractions, and embrace reality and all its mystery. Conchis offers Nicholas the same challenge in *The Magus* when he forces Nicholas to see life as reality and to stop viewing it as art, as if he were a character in a novel. Conchis finally teaches Nicholas that man "needs the existence of mysteries. Not their solutions" (223). David never fully grasps this truth, but he is plunged into self-knowledge, and the test comes in the form of Eden and the Fall.

David goes to meet Breasley at Breasley's home which is located in the forest of Brittany. It is called *Manoir de Coëtminais.* Coët means "wood" or "forest." When David enters Coët, he sees two young women sunbathing naked in the garden. The women turn out to be Breasley's live-in assistants who help him with everything from sex to painting. They are Diana and Anne, nicknamed "Mouse" and "Freak," and are often naked. A feeling of timelessness and innocence pervades the setting of this novella. At one point while David is watching the two women sunbathe, he reflects: "Another echo, this time of Gauguin; brown breasts and the garden of Eden. Strange, how Coët and its way of life seemed to compose itself so naturally into such moments, into the faintly mythic and timeless" (51). This setting is a variation of Bourani, the Edenic-like setting of *The Magus.* The effect of these settings are to lull the protagonist (and the reader as well) into a state of openness. He becomes more susceptible to things that would ordinarily be shocking to him and is prepared for the temptation in the garden. In *The Magus* the temptation is the beautiful ideal of womanhood: Lily/Julie. Because ideal, she is unreal, an illusion, and therefore something to transcend. In **The Ebony Tower** the temptation is another beautiful woman, yet a very real one: the Mouse. In the sunbathing scene mentioned above, the Mouse even offers an apple to David, making obvious the many suggestions of the Fall.

Fowles's variation of the Fall can be traced to *The Aristos:* "The enormous price of knowledge is the power to imagine and the consequent power to compare. The 'golden' age was the age before comparison; and if there had been a Garden of Eden and a Fall, they would have been when man could not compare and when he could" (60). Fowles expands this definition later: "I interpret the myth of the temptation of Adam in this way. Adam is hatred of change. . . . The Serpent is imagination, the power to compare, self-consciousness. Eve is the assumption of human responsibility, of the need for progress and the need to control progress. The Garden of Eden is an impossible dream. The Fall is the essential *processus* of evolution. . . . Adam is stasis, or conservatism; Eve is kinesis, or progress" (165). Seen in these terms, David Williams falls from the security of his life and conventions to mystery, change. The temptress is Eve (the Mouse, nicknamed by Breasley to combine "Muse" with the "O" shaped vulva) who offers him kinesis through comparison. Breasley is a god figure (like Conchis in *The Magus,* which Fowles wanted to title *The Godgame*), standing for a counterpole of existence for David to compare himself with. David at the end of the novella feels like "the laboratory monkey allowed a glimpse of his true lost self. . . . Underlying all this there stood the knowledge that he would not change" (96). David remains Adam; he falls only briefly: "a moment's illusion; her reality just one more unpursued idea kept among old sketchbooks at the back of a studio cupboard" (98).

We see this re-enactment of the garden and the Fall again and again in Fowles's canon. One should note that it is always men who fall in Fowles's work, and almost always women who tempt and educate the men (an exception occurs in **"Poor Koko"**). A critic has asserted that without equality one cannot gain entrance into mystery and points to the master-slave relationship set up in *The Magus* (which recalls *The Collector*) as representing a struggle for equality.[6] Women always control the relationship no matter how subservient they appear. The argument rings true for Alison and Nicholas in *The Magus,* for the Mouse and David in **The Ebony Tower,** and for Catherine and Peter in **"The Cloud"** (although Peter does not gain any knowledge of mystery), and for Isobel and Jennings in **"The Enigma."** Fowles tells us in *The Aristos* that women "know more about human nature, more about mystery, and more about keeping passion alive" than men (95). In **"The Enigma,"** a parody of the detective story, Michael Jennings, a detective attempting to solve the mystery of the missing Parliament member Marcus Fielding, learns that some more important mysteries should remain un-

solved. Isobel Dodgson, the Eve of the story, is described by Jennings as "someone alive, where everyone else had been dead, or playing dead; someone who lived in the present, not the past" (199). She takes Jennings from the rational world of solving mysteries, of finding and establishing facts, to a final understanding that "the tender pragmatisms of flesh have poetries no enigma, human or divine, can diminish or demean—" (218).

An exception to women tempting men with the understanding of mystery occurs in the second original work of the collection, **"Poor Koko."** In this story we have another example of the unlived life. Like David Williams and Nicholas Urfe, the anonymous narrator of **"Poor Koko"** has spent his whole life behind conventions, always warding off reality. He says, "Nor can I deny that books— writing them, reading, reviewing, helping to get them into print—have been my life rather more than life itself" (131). The narrator, an elderly man of words, is quite conventional and trite in his use of language, and his use of stale metaphors and dated expressions of speech have already been pointed out.[7] The narrator, like David Williams, is plunged into an Edenic setting; this time it is a small quaint cottage in North Dorset lent to him by friends. He has gone there from his home in London to finish writing a biography of Thomas Love Peacock. Again the pattern of the Fall is re-enacted: the narrator is forced to fall from security to mystery by a young man who comes to rob the cottage. During the robbery, the young man treats the narrator very considerately. He gently ties him up before he leaves and appears to intend no harm. Then, for no explainable reason, he burns the narrator's only manuscript and all his notes. The effect of this act violently jars the narrator from his conventional world into a state of passion and unknowing. The next year of his life is spent trying to solve the mystery, and the writing of the story is his conscious attempt to understand it.

The narrator makes the mistake (from Fowles's perspective) of trying to solve the mystery; however, the attempt provides him with a source of energy he has apparently never harnessed before. He attempts to rewrite the book and tells us: "I found that my memory was a good deal better than I had previously suspected. Some kind of challenge was involved" (158). Since Fowles is the author, the narrator's book should be far superior from memory, without the security and staleness of his notes, than it would have been otherwise. Clearly, the narrator has grown from his encounter with the unknown. Although he insists on formulating theories as to why the robber committed his gratuitous act, he closes the story with what he calls "my incomprehensible epigraph." He says that this shall have the last word—a fitting ending to Fowles's story and one that the narrator could not have thought of without Fowles's help.

Fowles often uses the technique of the absconding god in his fiction: we see it in *The Magus* and with variation in every story of **The Ebony Tower.** The technique is central to his art and to his thinking. He writes in *The Aristos:* "If there had been a creator, his second act would have been to disappear" (19). The mystery and hazard so vital to

Fowles's view of life is impossible with a conventional, intrusive, and omniscient god. "A god who revealed his will, who 'heard' us, who answered our prayers, who was propitiable, the kind of god simple people like to imagine would be desirable: such a god would destroy all our hazard, all our purpose and all our happiness" (18). Fowles, in playing the godgame of being an author, tries to give his characters as much free choice as possible, which the end of so much of his work illustrates. At the end of *The Magus* we are unsure whether Nicholas ends up with Alison or not. That Catherine kills herself is implied in **"The Cloud,"** but we can never be perfectly sure. Fowles discusses such ambiguity in an interview: "I must confess I like endings where the reader has a certain element of choice, and can feel: 'Well it might have gone this way or it might have gone the other way.'"[8] In order to educate his protagonists to a level where they can make their own decisions, Fowles often employs a god figure such as Conchis. In order to keep the character's options open, to maintain a high element of hazard and mystery, the god figure must disappear and leave the character with pure freedom of choice.

The most literal example of the absconding god figure in Fowles's fiction is Conchis in *The Magus*. In naked terms Nicholas realizes "it was logical, the perfect climax to the godgame. They had absconded" (666). In ***The Ebony Tower*** the variations on this theme are more subtle and require a looser definition of the "absconding god." In the novella, Henry Breasley is a god figure—he literally owns the forest surrounding Coët and tells David, "Rather proud of my forest. Worth a dekko" (45). Since the garden of Eden is recreated within that forest and the Fall occurs there, the suggestion of Breasley as god is a logical one. Another suggestion of Breasley as god occurs when Anne is angry over Diana's falling out with David. She refers in anger to Breasley as "that sadistic old shit up there" (91). Breasley, so central to the dramatic and philosophical conflict of the novella, disappears (71), well before the actual Fall scene takes place. In a sense, Breasley has created the conditions for the Fall and then absconded. He never enters the novella again, and thus David is existentially free to choose and compare for himself.

In the next story, **"Poor Koko,"** the technique is varied even further. We might refer to the robber as the "absconding satan." Fowles's belief in counterpoles is so strong that we can assume god and the serpent to be interdependent. In *The Aristos* he writes: "The obvious counterpole of an idea is the contrary idea. *The world is round; the world is not round. . . .* Now the contrary idea (*the world is not round*) is at first sight the most dangerous enemy of the pole idea; but all those subsidiary counterpoles (other concerns, other events, other exigencies, other ideas) that distract the mind from the pole idea endanger it far more; in fact to the extent that they do not signal it, but submerge it, they reduce it to nothingness. There is thus a paradoxical sense in which the contrary idea signals and supports the idea to which it is superficially opposed" (83). The robber creates the mystery, as god figures do in Fowles, and he also acts as tempter, as serpent or satan figures do. The difference is not that important; what is

essential from Fowles's perspective is that mystery has been created.

Absolutely necessary to the existential lesson behind this story is that the robber absconds and is never apprehended. His gratuitous act and his subsequent disappearance force the narrator into the unknowing, the vital energy of existence. The robber teaches the narrator that the "nightmare is the reality" (156)—the existential lesson Fowles imparts to us. To hide behind stale metaphors is to abstract reality, to commit the sin that David Williams commits. Because the robber disappears without a trace, the narrator learns or begins to learn that the nightmare is the reality; stale metaphors will not hide it.

In the next story of the collection, **"The Enigma,"** we see a missing member of Parliament in the role of the absconding god. In an interview Fowles provides us with a neat piece of evidence for Marcus Fielding as a god figure: "I've always felt that if God existed he'd probably be very much like a conservative member of Parliament, and therefore a man to be avoided."[9] The parallels between Fielding and God go further: Fielding never appears in the pages of the story, as God never appears in the world He created; the second act of Fowles's god would be to disappear. Fielding has created a perfect mystery (as God has done) and left purely without a trace.

The story begins in much the way a conventional detective story would begin, in a scientific manner, quoting statistics on the types of missing persons, but the story soon proves to be quite a switch from the conventional (Fowles wrote in *The Aristos*: "Yet man is starved of mystery: so starved that even the most futile enigmas have their power still. If no one will write new detective stories, then people will still read the old ones"—108). The people of the story with the exception of Isobel are all conventional, conservative, and in Fowles's view livers of the unlived life. The search for Fielding is foreshadowed by the story's beginning: it will be purely rational and based on facts. The message here is clearly that this approach will be futile, as it proves to be. Man cannot solve the mystery of God or of existence with rational means. This lesson Isobel finally teaches to Jennings, the detective. She accepts Fowles's theory of the absconding god and tells Jennings: "Theologians talk about the *Deus absconditus*—the god who went missing? Without explaining why. That's why we've never forgotten him" (214).

The final message of the story is that the search for the absconding god is irrelevant besides being impossible. Reality, the human relationship, is what is important, Fowles ends the story with a poetic flourish in stark contrast to the way he began: "The tender pragmatisms of flesh have poetries no enigma, human or divine, can diminish or demean—indeed, it can only cause them, and then walk out" (218).

"The Cloud" shares many thematic similarities with the other stories in ***The Ebony Tower,*** but it is a very elusive work. Most commentators on Fowles shy away from this story, one calling it "Fowles's most difficult work to penetrate, certainly the most opaque in *The Ebony Tower.*"[10] The story is very impressionistic, and the focus is constantly shifting, reflected in the verb tense which changes from past to present at least twice, remaining mostly in the present. Note the impressionistic use of color, light, and shadow in the opening paragraph: "Already a noble day, young summer soaring, vivid with promise, drenched in blue and green, had divided them, on the terrace beside the mill, into sun and shadow. . . . Inky blue dragonflies fluttered past; then a butterfly of pale sulphur-yellow. From across the river, one saw a quietly opulent bourgeois glade of light, bright figures, red and aquamarine parasol blazoned on top . . . with the word *Martini*; the white cast-iron furniture, sun on stone, the jade green river, the dense and towering lighter green walls of willows and poplars. Downstream, the dim rush of the weir, and a hidden warbler; a rich, erratic, unEnglish song" (221). This passage is really a word-painting. The scattered details, the use of shadow, light, and color, the blurred and then suddenly poignant details all produce the effect of an impressionistic painting. The entire story follows in this vein. Conversations are given only in part. Details and important exposition is withheld. The whole story flutters on the page, moving in and out of focus. In Fowles's work, language and metaphor are always once removed from reality, and this work seems to be an attempt to capture reality as wholly as possible. One gets the sense that Fowles is sorry he had to do it with words.

The story shares an Edenic setting and a variation of the absconding god/satan with the other stories in the collection. It is set in a timeless forest setting in France, and references to snakes, lizards, and serpents abound. The first sighting of a snake provokes a response from Paul: "Oh well. Proves it's paradise, I suppose" (223). Catherine, the temptress/god figure in this story is very early identified with snakes. "Catherine lies silent behind her dark glasses, like a lizard; sun-ridden, storing, self-absorbed; much more like the day than its people" (224).

The Fall that is recreated here is much less obvious than in the other stories. Part of the difficulty involved with fitting the story into the pattern of varied themes is the total lack of didacticism in **"The Cloud."** No character learns anything. Catherine is the only character who seems to possess any knowledge of mystery and existence, but she enters the story already equipped with such knowledge. The Fall is only implied. Catherine, who literally tempts Peter in the climactic seduction scene, metaphorically tempts everyone with her withdrawn, enigmatic behavior. At the end of the story, Catherine disappears. A cloud appears, "a mysterious cloud, the kind of cloud one will always remember because it is so anomalous" (271), and we assume that Catherine has committed suicide. The last lines of the story recall the fairy tale that Catherine has told to Emma: "They disappear among the poplars. The meadow is empty. The river, the meadow, the cliff and the cloud. The princess calls, but there is no one, now, to hear her" (274). The sense of emptiness suggests Catherine's suicide. The Fall, the plunge from knowing into unknowing, is implied: Catherine, who has brought enigma and mystery to the other characters, has disap-

peared, and we assume the other characters will be plunged into mystery by the discovery of her death.

Appropriately, Fowles placed **"The Cloud"** at the end of *The Ebony Tower.* Its elusiveness, its sense of immediate reality reflected in its present tense, force the reader into the unknowing. Even the literary critic, that analyzing, rational animal, is plunged into mystery. The story remains an enigma; we are left wanting more. It is a fitting end to a collection of stories by a man who wrote in *The Aristos* that "Our universe is the best possible because it can contain no Promised Land; no point where we could have all we imagine. We are designed to want: with nothing to want, we are like windmills in a world without wind" (19).

Notes

[1] John Fowles, *The Aristos* (Boston: Little, Brown, 1970), p. 28. Subsequent references are to this edition.

[2] John Fowles, *The Magus* (New York: Dell, 1978), p. 666. Subsequent references are to this edition.

[3] John Fowles, on the dust jacket of *The Aristos.*

[4] Fowles, *The Aristos,* p. 8.

[5] John Fowles, *The Ebony Tower* (Boston: Little, Brown, 1974), p. 15. Subsequent references are to this edition.

[6] Lucien Le Bouille, "John Fowles: Looking for Guidelines," *Journal of Modern Literature,* 8, No. 2 (1980-81), 203-10.

[7] Kerry McSweeney, "John Fowles's Variations in *The Ebony Tower,*" *Journal of Modern Literature,* 8, No. 2 (1980-81), 303-24.

[8] Robert Robinson, "Giving the Reader a Choice—A Conversation with John Fowles," *The Listener,* 31 October 1974, pp. 584-85.

[9] John F. Baker, "John Fowles," *Publisher's Weekly,* 25 November 1974, pp. 6-7.

[10] Barry Olshen, *John Fowles* (New York: Frederick Ungar, 1978), p. 103.

Rimgaila Salys (essay date 1983)

SOURCE: "The Medieval Context of John Fowles's *The Ebony Tower,*" in *Critique: Studies in Modern Fiction,* Vol. XXV, No. 1, Fall, 1983, pp. 11-24.

[*In the essay below, Salys explains the allusions to medieval fiction and painting in* The Ebony Tower, *making connections between the modern and medieval contexts of the novella.*]

Allusions to medieval fiction and painting pervade John Fowles's novella *The Ebony Tower.* His heroes and heroines see themselves and others as Tristan and Yseult,

Guildelüec and Guilliadun of Marie de France's *Eliduc,* and St. George, the princess, and even the dragon in Pisanello's famous fresco. Fowles as narrator introduces his story with an epigraph from Chrétien de Troyes's *Yvain* and himself suggests further relationships to medieval art and fiction—such as his hero's resemblance to Eliduc—which his characters do not remark. The setting of *The Ebony Tower* is also elaborately medieval. The story takes place in Henry Breasley's fifteenth-century farmhouse in the forest of Paimpont, a remnant of the Brocéliande of Arthurian legend. Breasley himself is fascinated by the International Gothic, a fifteenth-century style characterized by obsession with chivalric motifs. The various medieval elements of the novella seem to create a romantic mood or background (the ambiance of what Fowles calls "the Camelot syndrome") for a modern quest tale: a young painter-critic tilts in ideological combat with an older artist, falls adulterously in love with the latter's mistress, but then fails to win her and departs, convinced of the wisdom of the older man's convictions, though he himself is unable to live them.[1]

Fowles's uses of the medieval in *The Ebony Tower* are, however, by no means limited to providing settings for a modern story. In his juxtaposing of medieval and modern, he postulates a complex analogy—first, between medieval and modern art and, finally, between medieval and modern life. The medieval paintings of *The Ebony Tower* (Uccello's *Night Hunt,* Pisanello's *The Vision of St. Eustace* and *St. George and the Princess*) in both their style and subject reveal the heart of Fowles's thinking on nature and the depiction of nature in art and, as the story unfolds, express his view of modern man and the existential dilemma. Allusions to medieval fiction (*Eliduc, Yvain,* the Tristan stories) similarly elaborate and extend the meaning of the modern story by suggesting the archetypal basis of its major characters and conflicts. The progressive unfolding of this complex analogy of medieval art and life is the subject of this discussion.

The question of man's relationship to nature is a leitmotif of Fowles's fiction. A primary metaphor through which he expresses his aesthetic theory and explores human relationships is the forest—nature untamed and undefined. Fowles's recently published essay, *The Tree,* presents the concept of nature that best explains the meaning of the forest in *The Ebony Tower.* He points out that during the Middle Ages, "good" or "virtuous" nature existed only within the "*hortus conclusus, or emblematic walled garden of civilization.*" Medieval fiction and art consistently depicted the forest chaos outside the formal garden as a menacing unknown.[2] The inspiration for Breasley's *Moonhunt,* the major work in the Coëtminais series, which Williams is planning to discuss at length in his essay on Breasley and studies closely upon arriving at the *manoir,* is Paolo Uccello's famous *Night Hunt.* The medieval fear of untamed nature is made explicit in the Uccello picture to which Breasley's masterpiece is a "challenged comparison":[3] Crimson-clad courtiers and servants pursue stags into the depths of the forest, yet the figures in the foreground seem to hesitate in trepidation before the mysterious dark green wall. They are afraid to enter.

In the same way, the fragmentary passage of Chrétien de Troyes's *Yvain* chosen as the epigraph to *The Ebony Tower* is calculated to bring the hero to a full stop before entering the magical forest of Brocéliande:

> . . . Et par forez longues et lees
> Par leus estranges et sauvages
> Et passa mainz felons passages
> Et maint peril et maint destroit
> Tant qu'il vint au santier tot droit . . . (1)

The original continues without interruption:

> Plain de ronces et d'oscurté,
> Et lors fu il a seürté;
> Qu'il ne pooit mes esgarer.[4]

The epigraph obviously refers to David Williams, the latter day knight-errant, setting off in quest of the real Henry Breasley (or so he thinks). As a modern man he no longer fears the forest and is almost indifferent to it. The old man's deep feeling for his Paimpont calls forth only a "Blackheath" response in Williams—a desire for a summer retreat in Wales or the West Country (80).

In *The Tree* Fowles makes explicit what is suggested in William's alienation from nature: we are hostile to the woodlands because they are a form of disorder which we cannot master (the urge to label and categorize having been inherited from Linnaeus). Furthermore, we are addicted to looking for purpose in everything we do and are indifferent to nature because "its only purpose appears to be being and surviving."[5]

Henry Breasley is one of Fowles's "green" heroes (others are Sarah Woodruff and Daniel Martin) for whom the forest means the freedom to be oneself. In *The Ebony Tower* and the novels, this forest is as much metaphorical as literal. Because the old English greenwood "where the squirrel could jump from the Severn to the Wash and never once touch ground" has steadily been disappearing since 1600, Fowles claims that we have transferred "the England of the trees to our minds."[6] To his heroes this forest has two related functions. First, as a screen, it corresponds to a kind of protective coloration or behavior: "the wild old outlaw, hiding behind the flamboyant screen of his outrageous behavior and his cosmopolitan influences, was perhaps as simply and inalienably native as Robin Hood" (81). Second, behind the screen, at the forest's center, exists the necessary isolation and freedom to live and create as one chooses: "The grotesque faces the old fellow displayed were simply to allow his real self to run free. He did not really live at the *manoir*; but in the forest outside. All his life he must have had this craving for a place to hide" (80).

Just as in the *Night Hunt* Uccello draws the observer's eye even deeper into the forest as it follows the stags and dogs at the center of the picture, the painter of the *Moon-hunt* leads the young people into the heart of *his* forest, even keeping them on the right path. When they try to leave the path before reaching the marker oak, he recalls them to it and leads them on to their destination, which is deeper in the forest than they had realized. The idyllic picnic by the lake at the heart of the forest is the manifestation of the old man's freedom, the revelation of his true self: "Soon, during the eating, the girls' bare bodies seemed natural. They seemed to still something in the old man as well. There were no more obscenities, but a kind of quiet pagan contentment" (59). For Fowles, then, the forest is the sanctuary for the private, "wild" self.

Although Williams does not fear the forest in a physical sense, he panics when his sustaining "civilized" assumptions about life and art are challenged by Breasley. He finds himself at the heart of the forest and is forced to face *himself*, what he is, what he could be. In Paimpont he begins to discover potential freedom in his growing attraction to the Mouse. The evening after the picnic, when their love is imminently possible, the noctural silence around David and Diana as they talk in her studio makes it seem "as if they were quite literally in the forest" (91). Later, as their love fails to develop, they symbolically draw back, like Uccello's hunters, before a gate at the end of the orchard, beyond which a path enters the "black wall of the forest" (96). Williams stares into the trees and sees himself there as he could have been, "someone else, in another life" (98). When he leaves Coët the next day, he imagines Diana, the hunter goddess, "out there somewhere in the trees, waiting for him" (106). For Williams, finally, the retreat from self-discovery is epitomized in his turning his back on the forest.

The medieval fear of untamed nature evident in Uccello's *Night Hunt* is also apparent in the works of Pisanello, two of whose paintings Fowles uses to characterize Breasley and Williams. At the beginning of his visit, Williams remembers that Breasley had once named Pisanello as a central influence and confessed that *The Vision of St. Eustace* "had haunted him all his life" (13).[7] Here (as he generally does throughout *The Ebony Tower*) Breasley speaks for Fowles. The painting shows Eustace out hunting in a forest full of birds, animals, and flowers, where he is confronted by a stag bearing the image of the crucified Christ between its antlers. In *The Tree* Fowles is more explicit about Pisanello's treatment of nature: *Eustace* is a long-time favorite because of Pisanello's characteristically medieval artifice in his representation of nature. Most twelfth-century artists lacked the techniques to paint realistically, but this was not true of Pisanello, whose preliminary sketches of animals for *Eustace* are almost photographically true to life. The cultural blindness of medieval convention prevented the naturalistic representation of wild nature, so when wilderness and wild creatures had to be shown, they were stylized, as in *The Vision of St. Eustace.* Fowles concludes that "what is truly being hounded, harried and crucified in this ambiguous little masterpiece is not Christ, but nature itself."[8]

The medieval fear of nature leading to the fear of reproducing it faithfully in art is analogous to Breasley's reasoning about the failure of abstract art, a crucial point in the "modern" plot of *The Ebony Tower.* The old man is able to paint only when he is in the forest, in touch with

life through nature and women, who are more in harmony—"Bleeding and all that" (24)—with the natural order. The obverse of Breasley's love of nature is his hatred of abstract theories which "deny human facts" (46) and abstract painting which depicts this denial. He himself is comically inarticulate because painting rather than language is his real form of self-expression. For him language is an abstract medium which interferes with the expression of his reality; to Breasley, the articulate Williams is no more than a "gutless bloody word-twister" (44), whose abstraction distances him from both nature and women.

Ebony tower, the retreat from human reality in modern art, is built upon the artist's fear of representing his own experience of life in his art. In the end, Williams comes to agree with Breasley that turning away from reality had lead to a lemming-like drive (111) to artistic suicide: "Perhaps abstraction, the very word, gave the game away. You did not want how you lived to be reflected in your painting; or because it was so compromised, so settled-for-the-safe, you could only try to camouflage its hollow reality under craftsmanship and good taste. Geometry. Safety hid nothingness" (109-10). While the medieval fear of depicting reality naturalistically corresponds to the cowardice inherent in abstract art, it nonetheless differs crucially as a response to nature. Medieval art, because it is representational, at least *reveals* the fear, both expresses and evokes the emotions generated by the artist's response to nature. Uccello's horsemen are afraid to enter the forest. Thus, Breasley's *Moon-hunt* specifically recalls the Uccello masterpiece, and there is no contradiction in Breasley's deriding Williams' fear of representing nature, while at the same time making that emotion a theme of his own work. In the same way, Breasley's nod to Uccello is analogous to Fowles's fascination with Pisanello's distortion of nature in *The Vision of St. Eustace.* In the works of both Breasley and Fowles one sees "both a homage and a kind of thumbed nose to a very old tradition" (18).

Fowles also makes use of Pisanello to suggest the nature of the world beyond Breasley's forest—the cultural milieu of David Williams and the ebony tower of abstraction he inhabits. Breasley knows (and presumably admires) Pisanello's masterpiece in the International Gothic style, *St. George and the Princess,* but Fowles has the old man attribute the hanged men in one of his Coët paintings to Foxe's *The Book of Martyrs* and not the Verona fresco. The disclaiming of influence is significant because the *St. George* is meant to be Williams' picture, not Breasley's, and it is Williams who makes the analogy between himself and the saint. At the crucial moment when Williams must choose between Beth and Diana, Fowles introduces the painting as an emblem of his complex state of mind:

> There rose a confrontation he had once analyzed, the focus of that same Pisanello masterpiece, not the greatest, but perhaps the most haunting and mysterious in all European art, that had come casually up with the old man earlier that evening: the extraordinarily averted and lost eyes of the patron saint of chivalry, the implacably resentful stare of the sacrificial and to-be-saved princess

of Trebizond. She had Beth's face now. He read meanings he had never seen before. (99)[9]

The historical circumstances of Pisanello's *St. George* deepen our understanding of Williams' predicament and illuminate the values at stake in his choices. Critics have commented on the anxious, melancholy qualities of the painting, tracing them to developments in Italian cultural and social history. At the beginning of the fifteenth century the feudal aristocracy still ruled Italy, but its primacy was being challenged by a prosperous merchant class. Pisanello's aristocratic patrons, the Gonzaga and Este families, had French and Italian versions of the Breton legends (among which the Arthurian cycle was the most popular) in their libraries. "Illustrated texts were eagerly read by the noblemen and the ladies and knights of the court, who liked to see reflected in the literary and visual fantasies of those unreal adventures of chivalry a comforting ideal image of their world in crisis."[10] The *St. George* has been interpreted as a nostalgic farewell to the Middle Ages, its hero's anguish as that of someone caught in a period of decline.[11]

Like Pisanello, Fowles catches the spirit of an age in crisis, and the message is the same. Breasley represents an ideal which Williams acknowledges but ultimately cannot emulate. Toward the end of the stay at Coët, he realizes that he is living in a period of decline even more "decadently" concerned with taste and style than the International Gothic: "Art had always gone in waves. Who knew if the late twentieth century might not be one of its most cavernous troughs? He knew the old man's answer: it was" (109).

In recalling the *St. George* painting, Williams personally identifies with the hero (he has already been called "knight-errant"). Most readers, following the topos of the legend, plug in the rest: Diana as the princess (reinforced by her self-identification with the sleeping princesses of fairy tales), Breasley as the dragon from whom David must rescue her. Williams, however, interprets the painting to suit the circumstances of his personal crisis and sees the picture as a metaphor for the eternal triangle (Fowles's frequent man with two women). Williams contemplates the slaying not of Breasley but Diana, "the girl cast as dragon" (99); Beth, the princess-wife, although David chooses to save her, implacably resents the idea of his having a choice, as well as his reluctance. Like the figures in the painting, Williams and Beth seem separate, preoccupied with self.

The choice of lover is, of course, a metonym for the greater existential choice facing Williams. During her stay at Coët Diana has adopted the old man's way of life and, under his tutelage, has begun afresh in her own work. As a Breasley convert, she offers Williams the possibility of an entirely different, free, and creative life at a moment when his own work is beginning to turn toward nature for its subjects (15). Like St. George, Williams too is "lost"; his anguish, like that of the saint, stems from the loss "of a freedom whose true nature he had only just seen" (102). In choosing Beth, Williams opts for the safety of a civilized (and perhaps frigid) princess, rather than the risk of loving the delicate but earthy Diana. Fowles suggests that in turning away from Diana and the free life of the forest Williams chooses a life devoid of both true love and genuine art.

In the same way that Fowles's juxtaposing of medieval and modern art reveals the similar challenges and contrasting responses of the two ages, his extensive allusions to medieval fiction illuminate the differing responses of medieval and modern heroes to the timeless, archetypal challenges of the quest.

—Rimgaila Salys

In the same way that Fowles's juxtaposing of medieval and modern art reveals the similar challenges and contrasting responses of the two ages, his extensive allusions to medieval fiction illuminate the differing responses of medieval and modern heroes to the timeless, archetypal challenges of the quest. The significance of medieval fiction in **The Ebony Tower** is epitomized in Fowles's symbolic use of the medieval staircase of the Coëtminais manor house, which is spotlighted twice in the course of the story—at Williams' arrival and again just before the first dinner. When David first enters the house unannounced, he notices an "ancient wooden staircase with worn and warped medieval-looking banisters that led upward" (5). Soon afterward, as the Mouse leads him up the same staircase, his ascent assumes the deeper meaning implied in her double-entendre:

"Your wife?"

He explained about Sandy's chicken pox, the last-minute crisis. . . .

The level eyes appraised him again.

"Then I'll show you where you are?"

"If you're sure. . . ."

"No problems."

She made a vague gesture for him to follow her, and turned to the stairs. . . .

She touched the age-blackened handrail that mounted beside them.

"This is fifteenth century. They say." (7-8)

In the course of the story Williams ascends this emblematic staircase to self-discovery through the tests and trials of the quest. This association is reinforced when Fowles highlights the "diagonal of the medieval staircase" a second time, just before dinner, which proves to be an "ordeal" of the reluctant champion of abstract art.

In "A Personal Note" Fowles explicitly identifies the Celtic romance as the source of the mood and partly of the theme and settings of *The Ebony Tower* (117).[12] This explanation, however, is intentionally displaced from its apparently logical role as the introduction to the collection. Fowles places the preface after rather than before *The Ebony Tower* so that the reader is obliged to see the title story first as a tale of modern love and art and then, equipped with the *Eliduc* perspective and Fowles's suggestions in "A Personal Note," to reconsider it as a much more complex "variation" upon medieval archetypes. In addition to Marie de France's *Eliduc,* Fowles also draws upon Chrétien de Troyes's *Yvain,* the Tristan legends, and traditional settings of Celtic romance as sources of analogues to the characters and themes of the novella. Each of these sources serves to underscore a different feature of the modern story.

Breasley's Paimpont is a remnant of Brocéliande, the magical forest and site of countless adventures in the Arthurian legends. Time stands still in the seemingly changeless forest, making possible the juxtaposition of eras felt so strongly by Williams and the Mouse. To David, the picnic by the lake is "time-escaped." The magical forest casts its spell, both good and evil. Diana feels cut off from the outside world in her forest womb: "My parents, I've simply got to go home and see them. I keep putting it off. It's absurd. As if I'm under a spell" (89). Within the ambiance of this enchantment both Williams and Diana see themselves as prince, knight-errant, and sleeping fairytale-princess respectively (98, 100). At the same time, a sense of "melted time" and the "spell-like and legendary" (97) allows Williams the freedom to imagine life as it would be with Diana. Beyond the confines of Brocéliande, the spell under which they can be lovers ceases. Time returns to normal. At Orly, Williams' wife comes toward him "with the relentless face of the present tense," as he himself slowly emerges from the Coët enchantment with "a sense of retarded waking" (114).

The casual self-identification of David and Diana as knight and princess is reinforced by Fowles's systematic allusions to medieval romances. *The Ebony Tower* bears an epigraph from *Yvain* (quoted earlier), which invites the reader to interpret the details of Williams' experience as analogues to a medieval quest. The traditional journey is initially pleasant: the landscapes of the South of France delight his artist's eye, and he enjoys the "bachelor freedom" of travelling without family. However, like any other knight, he is faced with numerous obstacles as he nears his goal.

The entrance to Coët is impeded by a series of symbolic barriers; first, he is barred by a gate, which he stops to open and shut before driving through. Half a mile further he comes upon a second, apparently more formidable gate with a padlock and a sign discouraging visitors and warn-

ing against the dog. His initially euphoric mood is by now dispelled. Williams is "momentarily discomfited" by the absence of a welcome and begins to feel the uneasiness of a stranger in a foreign land: "Somewhere close in the trees behind him a bird gave a curious trisyllabic call, like a badly played tin flute. He glanced around, but could not see it. It wasn't English; and in some obscure way this reminded David that he was" (4). Forced to leave his "steed" at the second barrier, he climbs over and sets off on foot.

In the magic forest of Paimpont physical barriers are replaced by obstacles to perception: Williams soon learns that things are never what they appear to be. The padlocked gate at the entrance to Coët is never locked, he later learns from Diana. After clambering over the false barrier, he next confronts the obverse of the same test: the door to the *manoir* is unexpectedly unlocked and open, and just within, two women sunbathers are surprisingly unclothed. Here again the appearance is deceptive. The naked girls lead him wrongly to assume a harem arrangement. Diana, who seems at first totally accessible, proves— at another threshold—to be ultimately unattainable when she closes the door to David's advances. Anne is a "preposterous" creature, a "neurotic golliwog" (20), who reads *The Magus,* which Williams (a reader of thrillers, the literary equivalent of abstract painting in the formulaic emptiness) decides must be a book on astrology. He supposes the girls must be exploiting the old man in some way (the opposite proves true). His initial estimate of the old man is equally erroneous. The young critic is at first sure that he already knows all about Henry Breasley: "In many ways his journey was not strictly necessary. He had already drafted the introduction, he knew pretty well what he was going to say" (10). Of course, he knows nothing. Even the servants are not what they appear to be. Before dinner, Breasley takes Williams to the kitchen to introduce him to Jean-Pierre and Mathilde who run the house and garden. The reassuringly "tranquil couple" turn out to be a parricide ex-convict and Breasley's model and ex-mistress (66-67).

Breasley himself misleads the visitor by his comments about the two girls. Of Diana: "Thinks she's Lizzie Siddal" (19), although Anne, the redhaired ex-groupie better fits the description. However, as the story progresses, David notices that Anne, "alias the Freak" (20), is in fact the most sensible of the group. She sheds her outrageous dress and behavior and emerges as both perspicacious and warmhearted. After the first dinner, she covers her low-cut black evening dress with a white jumper, as if preparing to nurse the thoroughly soused old man (48). She dresses even more conventionally for the second: "a black Kate Greenaway dress sprigged with little pink and green flowers. Its cottage simplicity somehow suited her better; or better what David had begun to like in her" (81-82). Anne, too, makes David aware of the darker sides of the Breasley-Diana relationship: "it's like she's got a father fixation or something" (83); "Just she needs a nice bloke. Just one. To tell her she's okay, she's normal, she turns men on" (104). Seen from Anne's down-to-earth perspective, Diana, in her abnormal sex life with Breasley, may be the real "Freak."

The adventures of *Yvain or the Knight with the Lion* are broadly analogous to David's. Like him, Yvain travels to a foreign land and, in the same forest of Brocéliande where David confronts Breasley and Diana, faces the double challenge of combat with the Knight of the Fountain and the love of the knight's lady. Yvain successfully slays the knight and, with the help of a maidservant, Lunette (the prototype of Anne, the Freak), marries the beautiful widow. Yvain then sets off again, promising his wife to return within one year. His numerous tournament successes cause him to forget his promise; when he returns, he is spurned by his wife. The grief-stricken knight then loses his sanity and wanders in the woods until rescued and cured by a kindly hermit. He then devotes himself to the service of women in need, and in time learns humility, becomes the perfect knight, and is reconciled with his wife.[13]

Both Williams and Yvain undergo two ordeals: the first—combat with another male—obvious and easily passed with the help of a female companion; the second—turning upon the love of a woman—unexpected and ending in failure. Yvain defeats the knight and wins his widow but then fails to return to his wife within the promised year and loses her. The first obstacle Williams faces is Breasley's crusty "fie-foh-fum" exterior and militant hatred of abstract art. With Diana's help he survives the dinner ordeal, during which he is under personal and professional attack, and gains access to the "real" Breasley at the picnic by the forest pool: "The ordeal had indeed been like a reef; and now David was through, after the buffeting, to the calm inner lagoon" (59). The second test requires him to choose between freedom (Diana and the way of life represented by Breasley) and the safety of Beth and the old life. He fails through indecision and is rejected by Diana. His failure impels him to re-examine his art and his love and leads him to a painful sense of the emptiness of his life and world. Yvain's painfully acquired self-knowledge moves him to become the perfect knight; Williams also learns the truth but is unable to change.

Just as the *St. George and the Princess* provides an analogue for Williams' rejection of Diana in favor of Beth, the medieval love triangle of Tristan-Yseult-King Mark bears on the competition of Breasley and Williams for the love of Diana. The Tristan tale is mentioned specifically only twice in *The Ebony Tower*: Breasley cites it in his humorous disquisition on the Celtic romance (55), and during the night walk in the orchard, Diana alludes to the circumstances of King Mark's discovery of the lovers in the forest (99). Another, more subtle, reference hints at the medieval-modern analogy much earlier in the story. At the beginning of his stay at Coët, Williams tells Breasley about the recently discovered Pisanello frescoes in the Gonzaga Palace at Mantua. Discovered during the late sixties, the large mural in the Sala del Pisanello depicts various episodes and characters from the Arthurian tradition. A battle scene covers one wall; the adjoining wall shows a group of knights moving away from the battleground toward several ladies looking out from a high balcony. In his book on the discovery of the frescoes, Giovanni Paccagnini identifies the battle scene as the Tourney of Louverzep, during which Tristan distinguishes

himself by fighting successfully for and against King Arthur and defeating even Lancelot. Tristan presents the standard of victory first to Yseult and then to Guinevere. Paccagnini identifies the two women on the balcony as Yseult and her companion, Brangwain.[14] This Yseult (reproduced from Paccagnini) appears on the dustjacket of the first edition of *The Ebony Tower.*

For Fowles, the human situation is immutable; individual responses to the ordeals of the quest will change in different ages, but the tests themselves are archetypal.

—Rimgaila Salys

Diana is clearly Yseult's double, both in the circumstances of her relationship to Breasley (King Mark) and Williams (Tristan) and in her physical resemblance to the Yseult of the Mantua fresco. In describing Diana's "Quattrocento delicacy" and "wheaty hair" (61), arranged carelessly but in a classical style, Fowles clearly refers the reader to his model—the dustjacket portrait of Yseult, whose stray locks of wispy golden hair are appropriately acknowledged in Fowles's description of Diana's "managing to seem both classically elegant and faintly disheveled" (72). This resemblance between Diana and Yseult is first stressed only after David has begun to fall in love with her. As if he were gazing at the portrait of Yseult, he becomes conscious of her head and hair, first when (while King Mark sleeps) he swims after her "distant head" in the lake, and that same evening when "the same head faced him across the dinner table and he was beginning to find it difficult to think of anything else" (72).

The archetype in the Tristan story is the older man with a young wife who takes a young lover. As an analogue to the modern story of *The Ebony Tower* the Tristan legend has special relevance to the relationship of Williams and Diana to Breasley. Breasley wants to marry Diana; both Williams and Diana hesitate to betray him. When Williams tries to convince Diana to leave Coët, he feels a traitor, "but in a good cause" (94). After the walk in the orchard, Williams pauses guiltily to look down the corridor toward Henry's room before walking to Diana's at the other end (103). The following morning Anne guesses correctly that Diana has refused to sleep with Williams, at least partly from a sense of obligation toward the old man.

Diana's devotion to Breasley is also expressed in her misinterpretation of the forest episode in the Tristan and Yseult story: "It's so ironic. You read about Tristan and Yseult. Lying in the forest with a sword between them. Those dotty old medieval people. All that nonsense about chastity. And then . . ." (99). The Béroul version of the legend makes clear that the sword separating the sleeping couple, when they are discovered by King Mark, has been placed there accidentally by Tristan, exhausted after a day's hunting.[15] The two years the lovers spend hiding in the greenwood are the happiest of their lives and far from chaste. Tristan and Yseult live in the freedom of the forest as their modern counterparts were meant to. In her desire to be faithful to Breasley, Diana chooses to ignore or forget the message of the legend.

Of all the medieval tales Fowles employs in **The Ebony Tower,** Marie de France's *Eliduc* presents the most complete analogue in character and plot, for Eliduc (unlike Tristan or Yvain) is, like David Williams, already married when his quest begins. Both *Eliduc* and **The Ebony Tower** are about a happily married man who falls in love with a beautiful young woman in a foreign land,[16] and in both stories the hero breaks faith with a wife and a liege lord. Eliduc has sworn fealty to the King of Exeter for one year and is aware of the consequences of his love for Guilliadun: "he could never show her this longing, which could disgrace him—on the one hand for breaking his promise to his wife, on the other because of his relationship with the king."[17] He leaves Exeter to aid the King of Brittany before the year of service is completed and then returns to spirit away Guilliadun. Williams feels exactly the same constraints. He hesitates to sleep with Diana (for whom Breasley is something of a father figure, according to the Freak), not only because of his loyalty to his wife, but also because of a sense of obligation toward the old man, whom he cannot help admiring.

Unlike Yvain, Eliduc is a static character who shows no psychological development. Marie tells us that the story is really about two women, and it is Guildelüec, not her husband, who makes choices, first by reviving Guilliadun and then by offering to enter a convent,[18] thereby freeing Eliduc to marry his beloved. In contrast, Fowles obliges his hero, who is the center of the story (and not the two girls), to act;[19] he must make an existential choice. As it turns out, Williams chooses by not choosing: "His crime had been realized too late; at the orchard gate, when she had broken away; and he had let her, fatal indecision" (107).

Eliduc ends happily because Guildelüec is able to bring Guilliadun back to life by placing the weasel's red flower in the girl's mouth.[20] Because there are no modern miracles, Williams "kills" the Mouse by abandoning her; he runs over her animal namesake on the road leaving Coët:

> Something orange-brown, a mouse, but too big for a mouse, and oddly sinuous, almost like a snake, but too small for a snake, ran across the road just in front of his car. . . . It was a weasel. One of his wheels must have run straight over it. . . . A tiny malevolent eye still stared up, and a trickle of blood, like a red flower, had split from the gaping mouth. (107)

The lifegiving red flower of medieval romance has become in its modern analogue the blood of the victim.

What does Fowles accomplish through the medieval-modern parallels in **The Ebony Tower**? The contrast of the two worlds, implicit in his allusions to *Yvain, Eliduc,* and the Tristan legend, serves primarily to reflect the evasions, hollowness, and surrender of his modern lovers, David and Diana. Yvain finally overcomes the obstacle in his marriage; Williams is separated from his lover and distanced from his wife. In spite of King Mark, Tristan and Yseult are true and complete lovers; David and Diana are perversely chaste. The lovers of *Eliduc* are miraculously reunited; in total contrast to his wonderworking counterpart in *Eliduc,* the squashed weasel of **The Ebony Tower** brutally confirms the end of the affair.

In spite of the obvious contrast between the medieval and modern contexts of the novella, the parallels between them suggest the special importance Fowles sees in their analogous circumstances. Breasley speaks for Fowles when he comically explains his own penchant for medieval allusions in his paintings:

> "Just here and there, don't you know, David. What one needs. Suggestive. Stimulating, that's the word." Then he went off on Marie de France and *Eliduc.* "Damn good tale. Read it several times. What's that old Swiss bamboozler's name. Jung, yes? His sort of stuff. Archetypal and all that." (55)

For Fowles, the human situation is immutable; individual responses to the ordeals of the quest will change in different ages, but the tests themselves are archetypal. His characteristic technique of juxtaposing historical periods in his novels—most often the Victorian and the modern, as in *The Magus, The French Lieutenant's Woman,* and *Daniel Martin*—expresses this belief in the structure of his fiction. By means of his allusions to literature and art—the medieval context—Fowles counterbalances the markedly sixties flavor of **The Ebony Tower,** making us see Williams and the others as representative of all time, as well as our time.

Notes

[1] The quest motif has been commented on by many critics, especially Barry N. Olshen, *John Fowles* (New York: Ungar, 1978), pp. 93, 96-98, and Robert Huffaker, *John Fowles* (Boston: Twayne, 1980), pp. 117-21.

[2] John Fowles and Frank Horvat, *The Tree* (Boston: Little, Brown, 1979), n. pag.

[3] John Fowles, "The Ebony Tower," *The Ebony Tower* (Boston: Little, Brown, 1974), p. 18. Subsequent references are to this edition.

[4] Chréstien de Troyes, *Yvain (Le Chevalier au Lion),* ed. Wendelin Foerster and T. B. W. Reid (Manchester: Manchester Univ. Press, 1948), p. 22. In translation by Ruth Harwood Cline, *Yvain or the Knight with the Lion* (Athens: Univ. of Georgia Press, 1975), p. 22, the entire passage reads: "on into forests deep and wide. / He went through many wicked passes, / through many treacherous, wild morasses / and eerie places, and rode all day / until he saw the narrow way. / The thorns and briars made it obscure. / At that point Sir Yvain felt sure / there was no chance he'd lose his way."

[5] Fowles, *The Tree,* n. pag.

[6] John Fowles, "On Being English but Not British," *Texas Quarterly,* 7 (Autumn 1964), 158.

[7] Huffaker, pp. 121-22, briefly discusses Uccello and Pisanello in relation to "The Ebony Tower" but reaches different conclusions.

[8] Fowles, *The Tree,* n. pag.

[9] The traditional title of the painting, according to Vasari, is *St. George Freeing the Princess of Trebizond.* Pisanello made a medal for the Byzantine emperor, John Paleologos VIII, who visited Italy in 1438. His beautiful wife, Maria Komnena, Princess of Trebizond, is thought to be the inspiration for the heroine in the painting. See Anthony Bryer, "Pisanello and the Princess of Trebizond," *Apollo,* 76, No. 8 (October 1962), 601-03.

[10] Giovanni Paccagnini, *Pisanello,* trans. Jane Carroll (New York: Phaidon, 1973), p. 46.

[11] The background material for this paragraph is drawn from Paccignini, pp. 45-54, as well as Liana Castelfranchi Vegas, *International Gothic Art in Italy,* trans. B. D. Phillips (London: Thames and Hudson, 1968), pp. 8-10, and Enio Sindona, *Pisanello,* trans. John Ross (New York: Harry Abrams, 1961), pp. 7-14.

[12] Fowles's references to Marie's "Lanval" is an example of the "mood" of the Celtic romance operating in "The Ebony Tower." In a footnote to the "Eliduc" translation, while commenting on the erotic value of the female hand throughout the Middle Ages, he unexpectedly brings in a passage from an entirely different story, "Lanval," apparently because he wishes the reader to make the connection between Guilliadun and Diana, her modern counterpart: "I may mention here that the seductive use of see-through fabrics is well attested from other (shocked masculine) sources of the period. It helps to visualize Guilliadun—Guilli-means golden—to borrow another of Marie's stories (*Lanval*): 'She was dressed like this: in a white linen shift, loosely laced at the sides so that one could see the bare skin from top to bottom. She had an attractive slim-waisted figure. Her neck was as white as snow on a branch; bright eyes in a pale face, a lovely mouth, a perfect nose, dark eyebrows; but her hair was wavy and corn-colored. In the sun it had a light finer than gold thread'" (128). The Mouse's hair is "brown and gold" (7); at dinner Williams notices that she is wearing a high-necked, but loosely woven Edwardian blouse "that allowed minute interstices of bare flesh . . . rather prim and demure except, as he soon realized, that nothing was worn underneath it" (32).

[13] Cline, pp. xii-xiii.

[14] Paccagnini, pp. 71-72.

[15] See Béroul, *The Romance of Tristan and The Tale of Tristan's Madness,* trans. Alan S. Fedrick (New York: Penguin, 1970), p. 88.

[16] The two heroes travel in opposite directions across the English Channel because a knight must, of course, quest in unfamiliar territory. The most extensive discussion of the relationship of "Eliduc" to "The Ebony Tower" is Constance Hieatt, "Eliduc Revisited: John Fowles and Marie de France," *English Studies in Canada,* 3 (Fall 1977), 351-58.

[17] John Fowles, "Eliduc," *The Ebony Tower,* p. 131.

[18] Williams learns that Coëtminais means "forest of the monks" and that Breasley's estate was once abbatial land (39).

[19] Hieatt, p. 357.

[20] According to *The Book of Beasts,* trans. and ed. T. H. White (London: Jonathan Cape, 1964), pp. 91-92, the animal "is called a *weasel* (mustela) as if she were an elongated mouse. . . . Weasels are said to be so skilled in medicine that if by any chance their babies are killed, they can make them come alive again if they can get at them."

Timothy C. Alderman (essay date 1985)

SOURCE: "The Enigma of *The Ebony Tower*: A Genre Study," in *Modern Fiction Studies,* Vol. 31, No. 1, Spring, 1985, pp. 135-47.

[*Below, Alderman shows how a fundamental convention of the short story genre informs the themes and structure of* The Ebony Tower.]

The stories collected in John Fowles's **The Ebony Tower** constitute two books. One book is a grouping of stories written and translated by one author, apparently associated with but not fastened to each other very firmly, to be read in any order, with or without reflection on the whole. The second book, however, is an integrated collection of short stories, a contemporary example of the genre that includes *1001 Nights, Merrie Tales of Skelton,* and *Dubliners,* to name some others spanning the centuries and cultures. This genre has developed through a long history predating and then coexisting with the novel and, more recently, with the unintegrated collection of stories. Briefly, this often unrecognized genre consists of separate stories (sometimes novellas, sketches, or parables, sometimes interspersed with poetry or even essays) that form a dynamic relationship with each other and with the reader. For the integrated collection is known above all for its tension between cohering, centripetal forces and separating, centrifugal forces. My purpose here is to show how this generic classification informs the thematic and structural bases of **The Ebony Tower.**

A commonplace of genre criticism holds that the category in which we place a work of art affects an audience's perception of the art; knowing that one is reading a detective story, for example, sets up expectations for its language, structure, and characters. Moreover, one appreciates a work differently by apprehending how the author uses genre conventions. Thus, to read Fowles's stories as an integrated collection is to perceive a different book, one that uses the conventions of the genre in a particular way for particular results.

Quickly listed, those genre conventions involve the two basic dynamic centripetal and centrifugal forces. The centripetal are explicit and implicit framing devices readers encounter at the beginning of the collection, between, at the end, and/or among the stories. Explicit frames exist in prologues or "frame stories" (as in *The Canterbury Tales* or *The Pastures of Heaven*), interchapter pieces (discussion after the tales in the *Decameron,* Hemingway's news report chapters between the stories in *In Our Time*), and/

or epilogues (*The Canturbury Tales, The Pastures of Heaven*). These frames function as organization, explanation, and justification for the stories they enfold. Yet they are not only pretexts for gathering the stories, however different they seem to be, but also contexts for the effects of the stories, offering thematic clues through tone, setting, and image patterns. In addition, the explicit frames may provide a fixed time period, a set of characters or narrators, a basic theme—sometimes in a stripped-down or abstract form—that the stories echo, develop, or oppose. Therefore, the explicit frames contribute organizing and unifying elements to stories that otherwise may seem arbitrarily grouped. The overt frame invites and encourages its readers to perceive the stories in a meaningful association.

Many integrated collections substitute for or reinforce the explicit frames with implicit ones. Instead of or in addition to prologues and epilogues, these examples use a continuous or related setting or chronology, a single or limited set of characters or narrators, and repeated themes or motifs. *The Merrie Tales of Skelton,* for instance, uses the fictionalized English poet as the implicit linking device, whereas Faulkner's *The Unvanquished* or *Go Down, Moses* uses a multitude of such techniques to create association and unified reference. The implicit frame also invites and encourages its readers to perceive the separate stories as a meaningful grouping, sometimes so effectively that critics misclassify integrated collections as novels.

In contrast to the centripetal, the centrifugal forces pull the stories apart. Should the explicit and implicit frames fail to convince a reader, or if the reader fails to perceive the frames, these separating elements disrupt the process of integration. Such elements include the discontinuities of the stories, with or without interchapters; the reader's sense of closure in each story; the variety in types or genres of stories (parable, fable, *Lai,* sketch, detective story, fantasy, and so on); and sometimes the sheer numbers of stories. The collection may seem too complicated or chaotic to be apprehended as a meaningful association.

As one perceives both centripetal and centrifugal forces, a tension is created between two books or two reactions to the book: between the tendency to read the book as a mostly arbitrary collection and to read it as a process of opposing forces that together determine the book's formal identity and its inclusion in the genre. Examples of the genre of integrated collections of short stories consist of works that balance unity and diversity, the explicit and the implicit, and the synthesized and the dissociated.

II

We see the dissociating forces in *The Ebony Tower* in several stages. No prologue opens the book; the narrators and characters do not reappear; and the stories are of noticeably different categories, including a detective story and a medieval romance. They also display different kinds of narrative technique. The first story, or novella, for instance, offers a somewhat centralized plot and self-interpretation, whereas the last story focuses on a group and

offers only enigmatic clues. In addition, Fowles's publishers rejected his proposed title, *Variations,* saying that the idea of variations on themes in his other books and on methods of narrative presentation was unjustified (Fowles 109).

However, as Fowles explains in his "Personal Note," the book uses variations on his earlier work because, for one thing, there are correspondences to his novels. Literally speaking, a character in **The Ebony Tower** reads *The Magus,* and the general situation in the story superficially resembles that of the novel. Moreover, **The Ebony Tower** is an integrated collection because its explicit and implicit framing connections balance those centrifugal forces to create a tension, one that forms an analogy between the existential ordeals of the stories and the generic options the reader confronts as the book unfolds.

In his "Personal Note," which serves as the explicit frame for the collection, Fowles sets out several devices that integrate the book. He cites the Celtic tale's importance by claiming the others are variations on the mood, theme, and setting of *Eliduc.* That basic clue can be extended. In an immediate, transitional sense, Fowles uses a motif in one story to connect it with the next. The weasel Williams kills in the first story sets the tone of his day, his journey away from the green world of crisis to his conventional, "bloodless" life and relationships. In the "Personal Note" that follows Fowles writes that the weasel is on his conscience, and then another weasel is killed in *Eliduc.* The prosaic blood from Williams' weasel reminds him of a red flower, but the red flower carried by the dead weasel's mate in *Eliduc* magically restores life. The weasel connection, therefore, is not merely a repetition but a contrasting motif reflecting the opposed worlds and outcomes for the protagonists in the first two stories. Fowles also uses the detective story motif overtly in two contiguous stories. In **"Poor Koko,"** the narrator's manuscript is literally a victim, his own complacency the metaphorical victim. To the detective Jennings in **"The Enigma,"** the mystery he investigates grows comparable to a fictional mystery in Isobel's hands, thus making the detection both literal and literary. Both stories revolve around inexplicable acts—a character's disappearance and the manuscript's destruction—which we can term enigmas. Beyond this kind of transitional device, Fowles extends the clues by erecting implicit frames: the recurring narrative patterns and the recurring themes, roles, and setting.

III

Although the stories of this collection are of different types or styles, as Barry Olshen implies in his study of Fowles, these different stories are linked by a general narrative pattern of shifting directions (93). Expectations aroused at the onset of each story are subsequently removed, qualified, or reversed. The shifts may involve not only the reader's sympathies for the character and anticipations for the plot but also the expectations of the characters themselves. Fowles has crafted a fictional environment where the characters struggle to understand life's twists; the readers then try to understand these stories and characters (and then how the stories relate—by chance or by design). The patterns the reader perceives mirror the patterns of life: surprises, tests, false conclusions, and, sometimes, understanding.

In the first story, *The Ebony Tower,* David Williams visits the estate of an old artist, Breasley, to find the "legend," the old faun and his nymphs. In stages he re-views the artist as a tiger ripping at the world, then as a paper tiger, and finally as a poseur manipulating Williams' reactions. The female attendants progress from being harem girls to individual women. Soon the focus of the story itself shifts because the younger critic who came to analyze the older artist finds himself in need of analysis. *The Ebony Tower,* which began with an assured Williams, ends with his complete self-disillusionment.

The shifting patterns in *Eliduc,* Fowles's translation of a Breton *Lai* by Marie de France, concern how the knight Eliduc tests and is tested by the three contexts Fowles cites in the "Personal Note": the feudal, Christian, and courtly love systems. Although the bonds of these systems create potentially tragic conflicts—between two kings and two women—they are resolved unexpectedly and happily.

The contrast between the unhappy and happy shifts in the first two stories becomes mixed in "Poor Koko," the third. The seclusion and peace of the narrator/critic is broken by an intruder, but the robber surprises his host with his manner and uncertain motives. The critic expects initially to dine out on this story for months, but the seemingly humorous event becomes horrific when the thief destroys his study of Peacock. The twist comes again as the narrator realizes that this victimizer is also his victim, because by his superior class and education—his articulateness symbolized by the manuscript—he has suppressed the lowerclass robber. He concludes: "I presented a closed shop, a select club, an introverted secret society, and that is what he [the robber] felt he had to destroy" (175).

With the mysterious disappearance of Fielding, a member of Parliament, the fourth story begins. "The Enigma" takes a surprising turn with the detective Jennings, however, because his and our attention focuses less on the facts of the disappearance than on his relationship to Isobel, a tangential figure in the case. Hardly a likely source of information, she and her insights into Fielding twist the story around. The detective case is not solved, for Fielding is never found, but Jennings begins to find an authentic self in his contact with Isobel.

In the final story, "The Cloud," the shifting narrative pattern involves the darkening setting, from simple and idyllic to complex and threatening. Characters move from "islands" or tableaux, rearranging their familial, sexual, and business relationships. For instance, Peter Hamilton, a television producer, uses Sally as a mistress, desires Annabel, his writer's wife, but ends up raping her sister Catherine. The story moves from a gentle introduction, with characters lolling in the sun, to an unsettled close with children squabbling, Catherine missing, and a cloud replacing the sun.

Although the narrative shifts emphasis and direction in each story, each has relatively static proceedings. Olshen describes the action as minimal, with internal rather than external change predominating (93). *The Ebony Tower* focuses attention on a series of encounters among the four characters, consisting mostly of talk, and then on Williams' continuing efforts to understand this puzzling relationship. His job is to "learn" the characters of Breasley, Diana, and Anne. The second story, *Eliduc,* is the apparent exception that proves the static nature of the rest, for in the medieval story Eliduc fights battles and travels back and forth to Brittany and England; relationships are broken, made, and remade in a narrative covering many years. In contrast, *The Ebony Tower* presents the artist, his women, and Williams as already established; the process of understanding the characters and relationships is the "action" of the story. This static nature appears in the narrator's story in "Poor Koko," which takes place long after the robbery itself, and his analysis of the theft emphasizes primarily the conversation rather than the action. Gathering and analyzing information are also the actions of "The Enigma," where most of the story consists of Jennings' interviews with other characters, culminating in the long conversation with Isobel. In "The Cloud," characters' movements highlight relationships, and the people wander about the countryside mostly to sit and talk. Even Catherine's possible suicide remains an implication, not a dramatized scene. Indeed, the last story, as well as the first, is dominated by a series of tableaux rather than by dramatic action.

To describe the four original stories as static, however, is to overemphasize one aspect of their development, because in each story one highly charged action takes place toward the end. In the first this action occurs during the night scene where Williams and Diana almost make love. The failed opportunity haunts Williams as he leaves to rejoin his wife. In "Poor Koko" the night scene depicts the thief's burning of the narrator's notes as the latter sits tied in a chair. Jennings' arrival at Isobel's apartment is the crucial action of "The Enigma," for what he says, how he appears, and where they are make the chance meeting provide opportunities for developing more than a policemen/witness relation. Finally, in "The Cloud" the crisis scene occurs when Hamilton accidently encounters the solitary Catherine. Little is said at this point: they proceed by nuance and gesture. Numbed to his presence, Catherine allows (?) the man to use her body rather brutally.

The recurrence of narrative patterns in *The Ebony Tower* also involves the manner in which Fowles adjusts the verb tenses in each story. In describing "The Cloud," which moves in and out of present tense, Huffaker believes the effect of this shifting is to destroy the reader's distinction "between what has happened, what is happening, and what continually happens; in this story they are all the same" (129). The source of this timeless quality must be *Eliduc,* for Fowles was conscious of the verb tenses in his translation of the medieval story: "The shifts to the narrative present (like those into dialogue) are all in the original" (116n). Thus in *Eliduc* certain parts are summarized in the past tense, usually the circumstances leading up to a change or up to a conversation; then the dialogue and much of the action takes place in the "eternal" present tense.

In *The Ebony Tower* the present tense appears at the very end of the story after Williams has left the estate. As he meets his wife at the Paris airport, the past tense associated with this trip and his self-discovery drops away. Now he is back in his own world, his marriage, and his failures. The shifted verb tense signifies, as he describes his wife, the "relentless face of the present tense" (106), "relentless" because, whatever occurred before, he must live in the present and either change his view of life or remain hopelessly stagnant. Similarly, the present tense in "**Poor Koko**" appears at the beginning and ending of the story, for the narrator sequesters the past in the middle. In the present he is trying to introduce and to understand his enigmatic visitor; in the past, and in the past tense, he simply acted instinctively and vengefully. The present tense in "**The Enigma**" also appears at the beginning of the story, here used primarily to describe ongoing conditions, that is, what kind of people disappear. In general, then, Fowles uses the shifting verb tense to signal different literary time, of course, but sometimes to suggest timelessness, and sometimes to emphasize the eternal existential present in which vital characters choose to live. When Jennings meets Isobel, his immediate reaction suggests such an interpretation: "He had an immediate impression of someone alive, where everyone else had been dead, or playing dead; of someone who lived in the present, not the past . . ." (209). The past tense is, in some sense, the tense of dead fictions.

IV

The second set of implicit frames Fowles invokes concerns themes, roles, and setting. Through repetition and variation, one encounters the ordeal motif associated with existential choice, sexual and class conflict, a recurring pattern of roles, and the escape to or exile in the green world.

The ordeal as a motif is most closely associated with medieval literature, and in *Eliduc* the characters face a number of tests. Eliduc must confront two kings and his attraction to Guilliadun; his wife must face his infidelity; and the lovers must face nature's test in the channel storm. By surviving these ordeals, and through the manipulation of Fowles/Marie de France, Eliduc and his wives earn their happy lives, and the systems remain intact. Eliduc's choices in his ordeals reflect existential dilemmas, deciding what freedom or responsibility comprise, keeping faith, or choosing one's values. Thus the ordeal most often is not only a physical test of stamina but a crisis in which characters must determine what to do, who to be, and how to live with their choices. Although Eliduc makes a stand against two of the three systems by romancing Guilliadun, his crisis dissolves when his wife "magically" decides to enter a convent. The authors' manipulation that allows this to occur apparently represents the random forces of existence; an author playing the godgame can imitate the operation of chance.

The existential ordeals in the medieval story serve as the abstract structure the other stories may echo or oppose. The ordeal in *The Ebony Tower* relates to the one in *Eliduc*, as Fowles implied in an interview (Robinson 584), because Williams' fidelity to his wife is also tested by his attraction to Diana. The initial ordeal, however, is Breasley's first night attack on the modern art Williams paints and writes about. The two ordeals Williams undergoes are really one because his self-assurance and complacency govern his work and his marriage. Regarding marital fidelity, for instance, he reflects on the untested nature of his marriage: "Fidelity was a matter of taste and theirs just happened to conform to it" (191). Faced with the dual challenge, he fails his ordeals, paradoxically, by remaining faithful, whereas Eliduc succeeds by becoming an adulterer. The solution is that one must accept chance and the responsibility for the choices it provokes. Williams recognizes that he never does make the serious conscious choices; instead he floats to the popular, instinctive, or safe option in life, in his work, and in his marriage. Eliduc makes his choice, and ironically this antifeudal and unChristian act validates the three-fold system, for the characters involved happen to end up true to themselves and the systems. Williams, in contrast, sees that he "had never really had, or even attempted to give himself, the far greater existential chance" (101).

The explicit ordeal in "**Poor Koko**" takes place on the night the helpless narrator watches his attacker move about his cottage. In effect, this ordeal represents the failure of his past life, for aside from one adulterous affair long ago, he had also been a complacent drifter in life. The random nature of life—represented by the intruder's burning his manuscript notes—stuns him: why me? Why now? Why this? Why here? he asks himself. By recognizing how he is also the victimizer, he develops the courage to go and rewrite the study of Peacock, accepting that it and he will not be the same as before.

The recurring motif of adultery—here the central crisis, there a minor element—figures again into "**The Enigma.**" As a passing note, Mrs. Fielding, complacent and semiaristocratic, worries that her husband's disappearance signifies his infidelity to her and their caste, for she imagines the MP has a lower-class lover. The more important ordeal, semiadulterous this time, concerns Jennings' encounter with Isobel, another man's fiancée. Initially he imagines she has only a slight chance to help him solve the riddle, but that slight chance is enough, and the opportunity that follows becomes the ordeal of existential choice. Isobel refuses to maintain what he perceives is the proper interviewer/subject stance. Then the association of one's feelings toward job and sex again occurs, only here with more positive results than in *The Ebony Tower*. Jennings used to be remarkably unconscious of his job as a policeman:

> He had a notion of due process of justice, even if it had never really been put to the test. . . . Essentially he saw life as a game, which one played principally for oneself and only incidentally out of some sense of duty. Being on the law's side was a part of the rules, not a moral imperative. (199)

His untested complacency shattered by Isobel, Jennings begins to recognize life's potential with her as a model: "Something about her possessed something he lacked: a potential that lay like unsown ground, waiting for just this unlikely corn-goddess, a direction he could follow, if she would only show it. An honesty, in one word" (219).

"The Cloud" offers an ordeal primarily to Catherine, trying to overcome the death of her husband, her sister's bland husband, and his crass friend Hamilton. Hamilton is one of the complacent males in this story, and his credo—self-interest—overcomes any self-doubts (unlike Williams or Jennings or the narrator of **"Poor Koko"**) and overcomes the perplexed Catherine. Her implied suicide, or the fact of her disappearance after he rapes her, reflects her inability to surmount the ordeal. When Hamilton encounters her alone, the narration describes this as his "unexpected fork in the road" (281); but he takes his usual route. Afterward, the Rogers similarly run from the coming storm, refusing to face the implications of Catherine's disappearance.

In short, Fowles emphasizes the significance of the existential choice, associated with ordeals, by designing variations on it in every story. A series of male characters have their complacency tested, sometimes shattered, by a turn of fortune and by the choices and recognitions that turn causes. Moreover, in four out of the five stories the choice crystalizes in a woman and a romantic, sexual, or extramarital relationship. By using two males in **"Poor Koko,"** Fowles removes the sexual feature, but this variation confirms the point about integrated collections and implicit frames. The stories do not simply repeat the same pattern; rather, they offer the author the opportunity to explore an idea in several manners, contradicting one result or motif with another, creating a tension about the "real" meaning that defines this genre.

Reinforcing the implicit frame provided by narrative patterns and the ordeals and existential choices, Fowles adds another layer to his design with recurring references to class conflict, sometimes associated with the previously discussed sexual element. In *The Ebony Tower* Breasley the self-educated bohemian confronts Williams the conventionally educated bourgeois. This opposition, repeated in the two women (Diana from the middle class and Anne from the lower), reflects yet again the differing existential response to life, for here the lower-class woman has learned honesty the hard way, by living in less than cushioned circumstances. Later Williams chooses Diana for an affair because she appeals to his bourgeois conventionality. Yet women make up the ultimate lower class for him because in Williams' obsession with testing his marital vows he makes Diana into an object without equal freedom in the decision.

The class conflict in *Eliduc* is woven into the feudal order and the courtly love tradition, a privilege of the aristocrats. Here the three main characters freely choose or withdraw from each other and never treat each other as objects. The objectified ones are the servants, such as the page Guilliadun uses as her emissary. The one temptation

to use an equal as an object, Guildeluec's threat to her husband's lover, dissolves in a magical transformation, which in this story takes the place of the more prosaic recognitions of chance in the others.

The tension among [Fowles's] short stories serves as an analogy to the existential dilemma that is Fowles's central thesis.

—Timothy C. Alderman

The class conflict in **"Poor Koko"** constitutes one of its central themes, in contrast to its subsidiary position in the first two tales where sexual conflict or testing comes to the fore. Because education and democracy have failed to remove the rigid distinctions between the lower classes and the middle and upper groups, the thief and the critic face each other across a gulf—represented by their varying skills with language—almost as wide as in the medieval story.

In **"The Enigma"** Fowles recombines the class/sexual axis, for Jennings with his middle-class education can maneuver both the lofty Mrs. Fielding and the "petty bourgeois mentality" of the police. Although he can "pass very well as a rich, trendy young man about town" (190), his poses collapse before Isobel, a more direct person than the other upper-class types but also a very attractive woman. The class and sexual conflict abates because these two can take the chance offered them to be authentic.

Although class conflict subsides in importance in **"The Cloud,"** Fowles continues to play variations on his theme. Here I would note the privileged position of the British vacationers in France as well as a resentment of their inferiors, voiced by Hamilton when Annabel suggests France is too expensive for the lower classes: "'You're joking. You don't realize what some of them earn these days'" (255). Of more importance here is the vicious sexual conflict embodied most in Hamilton, who sees women as objects. His rape of Catherine represents a male victory in the battle between "the brutalizing male ego and the civilizing female intelligence" (Huffaker 128-129). Yet it also represents the most complacent male refusing or ignoring the opportunity that a woman can be as a person.

The penultimate implicit framing device prominent in *The Ebony Tower* is related to the others, for the repetition of basic roles in the stories and of a basic relationship within the plot echoes the recurrences in motifs and narrative patterns. These roles are the master/magician/parent figure in relation to the servant/initiate/son figure.

Clearly Breasley operates like a magus, as the "master of antique mysteries," playing an enigmatic role to Williams, his initiate, surrogate son, and servant. Because Williams has come to Coëtminais to gather material for the book on Breasley, he is both serving the artist's reputation and learning from him. In contrast, the relationship is internalized in *Eliduc,* with Marie de France and Fowles, her translater, working out mistress-to-servant, magician-to-initiate, and mother-to-son roles. She taught him as long ago as his undergraduate days, and he serves her now by presenting her work to the modern public.

The narrator makes a special point of explaining that his title **"Poor Koko"** refers to the Japanese notion of correct filial behavior. The thief is surrogate son, in Oedipal rage, burning his father's book to destroy him. The father/master role reverses in the relationship, however, because the older man bows to his tormentor by writing this story of their encounter, a promise he made that night. The narrator has been a poor magician, for he had not allowed the initiate into the "secret society"; but he atones by revealing honestly his doubts and his new understanding.

The master/magician/father figure in **"The Enigma"** is played partly by a character not present in the story, namely the missing MP, Fielding. He functions as a father, not a very good one, to his rebellious son Peter. He failed to initiate Peter probably because the "magician" lost faith in his powers as a politician. As a master/magician he operates on Jennings, the detective, showing by example how to effect a disappearing act and how to shake off the conventional forms of life Jennings confronts as well. Isobel assumes the other part of these guiding roles for Jennings, initiating him into the vital, free, living-in-the-present existence she embodies.

In **"The Cloud"** these roles are less important, and the depressing tone of the story is the result. One parent sees his role as a temporary duty: "Peter [Hamilton] wanders on a little way with his son, free it seems to play father for a minute or two now that he has had his say, his business, his morning's justification for existing" (245). The other father, Paul Rogers, leaves much of the parenting to his wife Annabel. Moreover, the allusions to *Hamlet* throughout this last story provide a less than positive image of the father's role. At the end, the family group—Annabel, Paul, and the younger daughter Emma—make a unit, but an ominous one: "The three walk on, less quickly, yet not idly; as if there is something to be caught up or, perhaps, to escape from" (291). To want to escape from the green world, however, is a reversal of the other stories' values, as will be seen below. The initiation Catherine provides Emma, in the fairy tale, is likewise unhappy. Fowles has thus effectively qualified the more positive views contained in the previous stories.

The last frame to be offered represents one of the most important links between the stories, for the escape to or exile in the Celtic green world evokes Fowles's explicit frame in the "Personal Note" as well as an implicit design that associates the stories and their meanings. In the first story of the collection the tension arises in Williams' mind over Breasley's position away from England, recognized both as an escape from a world the older artist abhors and

an exile from a society that has only recently begun to admire his work. Significantly, the escape/exile is set in the green Celtic forest of Coëtminais, first mentioned in the story as a theme in Breasley's recent paintings. Later Williams fuses the artistic and real-life values expressed in this vision of Breasley's achievement: "Perhaps it constituted the old man's real stroke of genius, to take an old need to escape from the city, for a mysterious remoteness, and to see its ancient solution, the Celtic green source, was still viable" (69). The evidence of this story, and of the others, shows the green world as perhaps one of the only "viable" restoratives for people caught in the vice of contemporary existence.

Along with the beauty of nature, the birds and the trees, the peace and the restfulness, the Celtic-inspired green world also brings with it an atmosphere of magic, foreboding, and enigma. The magic in **The Ebony Tower** is the spell the women and Breasley cast over Williams. This painter and critic adds the literary note to the group's discussion of *Eliduc* (which Breasley has read) and the green world's magic by calling it a Jungian archetype (51). Diana further amplifies this by referring to the area as her "little forest womb" (84). For her and Anne this green world is a place of exile until they are sufficiently morally toughened and psychologically and artistically educated by the experience with Breasley.

The magic of course is more literal in *Eliduc,* when the knight's wife uses the weasel's red flower to restore her rival. Yet her pragmatic (and convenient) attitude to Guilliadun must also reflect the magical effects of the forest. Anxious and scheming at the castle, she becomes clearheaded and resolute in the deserted abbey with her rival. The green world is also the haven for the unconscious princess, and it becomes in the end the secluded retreat/exile for all three characters in their abbeys.

The narrator of **"Poor Koko"** comes to the green source only for the seclusion and quiet, admitting he was no lover of country living. In fact, one can judge any character in the collection by his/her feeling for the woods. This narrator has to recognize that he can think more clearly since he arrived and, further, that the Sabine farm has its charms: it provokes a "genuine sense of joy" (140). Ironically, reality intrudes in the form of the thief, but it is a reality magical in effect. The isolation of the cottage enables the thief to act so unusually and thereby to cause the minor transformation in his victim.

"The Enigma" presents a clear escape/exile to the green world if we conclude that Fielding did value his Tetbury House as much as the farm manager and Isobel say he did. If he did commit suicide there, he becomes an eternal mystery, she suggests, famous forever in his disappearance, whereas his regular life would have condemned him to a conventional extinction. When Jennings cannot get permission to search the pond, the green world closes up around its mysteries, unviolated.

"The Cloud," however, demonstrates the violation by barbarians of the green world. Hamilton, for example, urinates in the clear fishing stream, polluting it as the rest are despoiling their pretty little vacation hideaway. Also, within the outward green world Catherine creates another, inner one in her fairy tale to Emma. This world within a world is as ambiguous as the one in the rest of the story because her forlorn princess searches and waits for the prince to come back to her in vain. The aura of a magical spell is reinforced by the peculiar narrative structure that Catherine refers to as "islands." The islands, essentially the scenes and tableaux enacted by the characters, seem to be floating in time and space, a sensation enhanced by the adjustment of the verb tenses.

Because this story is set entirely in France with English characters, as **The Ebony Tower** is, the temptation would be to see a framing picture· identifying the green world as France. But Celts lived on both sides of the channel, as *Eliduc* makes clear; the green world is possible in either nation. It is no panacea, but it is the last chance for the characters in **The Ebony Tower.**

V

To catalogue the explicit and implicit frames Fowles develops as I have done is not to cancel the effects of the centrifugal forces at work in the collection. For all their coherent strength, these unifying elements simultaneously set off or reflect back the differences and variations. The tension among them—this tension that defines an integrated collection of short stories—serves as an analogy to the existential dilemma that is Fowles's central thesis. By placing these stories together, he offers readers the chance to make something of their recognition of the relationships between and among the stories. Their coherence cannot be absolute, just as the interpersonal association will not be absolute. After all, Eliduc and his wives end up separate from each other in their two respective abbeys yet together in the forest, each happy in this the latest association.

Works Cited

Fowles, John. *The Ebony Tower*. New York: NAL, 1974.

Huffaker, Robert. *John Fowles*. Twayne's English Authors Series 292. Boston: Twayne, 1980.

Olshen, Barry N. *John Fowles*. New York: Ungar, 1978.

Robinson, Robert. "Giving the Reader a Choice—A Conversation with John Fowles." *The Listener* 31 Oct. 1974: 584.

Ellen McDaniel (essay date 1987)

SOURCE: "Fowles as Collector: The Failed Artists of *The Ebony Tower*," in *Papers on Language and Literature*, Vol. 23, No. 1, Winter, 1987, pp. 70-83.

[*In the following essay, McDaniel traces the character development of the protagonists of* The Ebony Tower *in terms of a paralysis-action dichotomy that she identifies as a major feature of Fowles's fiction, emphasizing their relationship to the protagonists of his novels.*]

The world of John Fowles's fiction is polarized by a powerful pair of contrary forces, described by the author in *The Aristos* as *stasis* and *kinesis* (165).[1] For Fowles, these forces of inertia and motion, usually thought of as laws of the physical world only, also govern the moral and emotional development of human beings. *Stasis* is a life-denying force characterized by passivity, conservatism, the absence of change, and sterile lifelessness. *Kinesis* governs all that moves, matures, and improves; it is a life-affirming force that drives the evolution and amelioration of the human condition. The main characters in Fowles's fiction always are compelled to choose between these two alternatives. To live by the laws of *stasis* is, metaphorically, to become a Prufrock "pinned and wriggling" or a stuffed and dried hollow man. The alternative is preferable but hardly easy. To evolve, Fowles's protagonists must demonstrate exceptional courage and responsibility.

Fowles characteristically represents the kinetic force of evolution as female and its static counterpart, fossilization, as male. The females in Fowles's fiction are pragmatic people, who as life-givers and preservers know the need for change and variation. Males, however, are Fowles's dreamers, who hesitate and only "think of doing" (**Ebony Tower** 299). In *The Aristos,* Fowles points to the Edenic myth as the first dramatization of this sexual schism. According to Fowles, Adam and his male successors have all regretted the Fall into responsibility and work. The preservation and evolution of life have become, principally, the work of Eve and her descendants (165). However, not all of his males are like Ferdinand Clegg, nor are all his women like Sarah Woodruff. He grants that "there are, of course, Adam-women and Eve-men"; in fact, "few, among the world's great, progressive artists and thinkers, have not belonged to the [Eve] category." Fowles's male protagonists often undergo a metamorphosis that changes them from Adam-men to Eve-men. Nicholas Urfe, Charles Smithson, and Daniel Martin—well-taught by the cast of Eves and Eve-men they encounter—come to recognize the need to create "Eve societies," which Fowles describes as those cultures or communities "in which the woman and the mother, female gods, encourage innovation and experiment, and fresh definitions, aims, modes of feeling" (*Aristos* 166).

All the female principals in Fowles's novels display the courage of the original Eve in their fearless revolt against the rules of a dull paradise. Each offers to the Adam of her world fruit plucked from the trees of knowledge and life; she tempts him with her knowledge of a new life and challenges him to risk the Fall. In the Undercliff, an "English Garden of Eden," in a scene D. H. Lawrence might have written, Sarah offers Charles a pair of tests. "Will you not take them?" she asks Charles as he stares at the objects, hesitating (138). In accepting the tests—unmistakably meant as testicles, symbols of fertility and courage—Charles receives his manhood and a physical and emotional knowledge of this Eve. He takes Sarah's lead in redefining himself so that he "should never be the same again" (174).

Parnassus, in Greece, is the setting for another Eden and another Fall in *The Magus*. In a spontaneous pastiche of the Edenic drama, Alison offers herself to Nicholas who, like Adam, tries to resist her seduction:

> "Let's have a swim."
>
> "It'll be like ice."
>
> "Yah."
>
> She pulled her shirt over her head, and unhooked her bra, grinning at me in the flecked shadow of the arbour.
>
> "The place is probably alive with snakes."
>
> "Like Eden."
>
> She stepped out of her jeans and her white pants. Then she reached up and snapped a dead cone off one of the arbour branches and held it out to me. [268]

Nicholas takes the cone and yields to Alison's temptation, believing that he glimpses Eve "through ten thousand generations." The tenderness he feels for Alison at that moment seems a fragment of the same tenderness that had inspired their mythic ancestors's first physical passion. Nicholas soon lapses into his boorish Adam-self again, but during his brief reunion with Alison, he "made love, not sex" (269). Love poses a difficult challenge for the protagonists of Fowles's novels, but each man's Eve proves to be a patient persuader who is ultimately successful in her aim.

Because creation can begin only after Adam has fallen from his false paradise, Fowles banishes his major protagonists from their comfortable, indolent worlds. They land on the stony ground of their underdeveloped feelings, which they must fertilize and nurture. They are postlapsarian Adams who find themselves, in Gully Jimson's words, in "the real world . . . hard as rocks and sharp as thorns" where they have to build their own gardens, "make the bloody things and pile up the rocks and keep the roses in beds."[2] However, Fowles is not only concerned with the development of his characters after their falls. He also fully characterizes the lazy, prelapsarian Adam, content with innocence and afraid of letting his Eden go. This hesitating male who scolds his Eve and recoils from her temptation is the character who opens each of Fowles's novels and who peoples all of his short stories in *The Ebony Tower*. David Williams in *The Ebony Tower,* for example, will not take the apple. In a scene that resembles the Parnassus episode in *The Magus*, with characters lunching naked beside a clear pool in a place David calls the Garden of Eden, Mouse offers David an apple. Although the offering disturbs David, it does not move him. Hence, the apple winds up in an "old-fashioned English blackberry-and-apple pie" (75), a symbol for the domesticity into which David retreats to hide from forbidden knowledge. Conformity and conservatism are this Adam's loadstones,

exerting their force against independence and change. The power of stasis has a magnetism that insists on its negative autonomy, and it pulls with Charybdian strength at the best intentions of Fowles's protagonists. The protagonists of the novels ultimately overcome this inertia; the protagonists of the short stories do not.

An understanding of protagonism in Fowles's work begins with an examination of this deadening and irresponsible human stasis that he meticulously characterizes. In the novels, Fowles's protagonists eventually leave this condition behind to pursue a quest initiative, usually defined by a woman. However, Fowles also draws character portraits of people who are hopelessly grafted to stasis and unable to evolve. These portraits he has collected in *The Ebony Tower*: David Williams in the title story, Marcus Fielding in **"The Enigma,"** the scholar in **"Poor Koko,"** and Catherine, the Adam-woman of **"The Cloud."** These characters, like James Joyce's Dubliners, have removed themselves from life's evolutionary current and withdrawn into shadows, corners, and "ebony towers" where life can be waited out.

Fowles blackens the familiar ivory tower because he perceives an individual's withdrawal from the lifestream as anything but an ascension into lofty white heights. Such a retreat is a black death-like removal that cuts the individual off from the life-source of human community. The tower as metaphor is explicitly defined in *The Ebony Tower*'s title story. Mouse tells David Williams, the young art critic who has come to interview the famous painter with whom she lives, that the ebony tower is what Breasley believes has taken the place of the ivory tower. For Breasley, the expression stands for anything that is "obscure because the artist is scared to be clear" (50). Later, after his rejection of Mouse in the garden, David learns that in addition to obscurity and fear, the symbol stands for weak indecision, complacency, and selfishness.

Fowles's "Personal Note" to the reader of *The Ebony Tower* contributes some additional observations that help to explain this important symbol. Fowles claims to have inserted the medieval tale *Eliduc* into the collection to remind the reader of three "real-life systems": feudalism, Christianity and *amour courtois*. All were supported by codes of trust that insisted that humans keep their promises to each other. In fostering greater honesty and trust among people, these institutions helped to civilize human relations. Feudalism "laid a vital importance on promises sworn between vassal and lord"; all civilized life depended on "a man being as good as his word." Christianity placed responsibility for the immortal soul on the human heart and human actions. And courtly love stressed keeping faith in love and was an attempt "to bring more civilization (more female intelligence) into a brutal society." *Eliduc* is "anachronistically told" in *The Ebony Tower* to remind the reader of the defilement or loss of trust in most aspects of contemporary human intercourse—from love and sex to language and art (122).

Although none of the protagonists in *The Ebony Tower* successfully evolves into what Fowles calls the *aristoi*, the plot of each story turns upon the small progress they do make. However, their advances are made only within the province of knowledge, not action. In the Fowles world, to see and to know are not enough; the individual must also act and change. "Cleggness" reappears in *The Ebony Tower* as a veneer hiding an Arnoldian buried life. For the scholar in **"Poor Koko"** and Marcus Fielding in **"The Enigma,"** the veneer has become highly polished over the years. They have lived hollow and complacent lives well into middle age. Their sudden acknowledgement of failure comes too late to reanimate fossil-hard possibilities that might have made them other than what they became. Catherine in **"The Cloud"** still has the youth these men have lost but is victimized instead by a deep-seated despair over her husband's death, which mires her in the past. However, in *The Ebony Tower,* Fowles most straightforwardly characterizes the failed artist-protagonist in the slick and glib David Williams.

David Williams is a painter-turned-art critic visiting Coetminais to learn Henry Breasley's "sources" and the "secrets" of his originality. Because David is himself a highly derivative painter, influenced by many sources and formal training, he has trouble understanding Breasley's almost instinctual approach to art. Breasley tells David that he "Painted to paint . . . Like shitting," asserting that he has severed himself from his roots in other artists' work (77-78). David mistrusts Breasley's claim and presses him to come clean. However, David is met by challenges from this master, which make him and not Breasley the object of the novella's investigation.

The tables are turned on David at dinner, where Breasley issues him his first challenge. With an obvious contempt for abstract painting, the kind of painting David does, Breasley opens the attack:

> "Footsteps of Pythagoras, that right?"
>
> The old man stayed intent on his soup. David glanced for help at the girl opposite.
>
> "Henry's asking if you paint abstracts."
>
> Eyes on his laden spoon, the old man muttered quickly, "Obstructs."
>
> "Well, yes. I'm afraid I do."
>
> He knew it was a mistake before the Mouse's quick glance. The old man smiled up.
>
> "And why are we afraid, dear boy?"
>
> David smiled lightly, "Just a figure of speech." [37]

Afraid, rooted and "static" (113), David makes a poor showing at dinner. This young artist who paints without honesty or feeling is scorned by Breasley for his betrayal of art, a betrayal which the old painter calls the "triumph of the eunuch." So-called artists like David place commercial value, good taste, and critical approval above

human content in their work. They have extracted the human "fundaments" from art, warm flesh and "spunk" (41-42), and replaced them with formal logic and geometry.

Once a painter of abstracts like David but newly influenced by Breasley, Mouse has learned to take artistic risks, painting trellises of flowers in "pinks and grays and creams, a palette of dangers." David "would have been afraid of it himself, the inherent sentiment, the lack of accent" and chooses "autumn and winter" colors, the colors of death (86). "You did not want how you lived to be reflected in your painting" (109), David believes. Abstraction also governs David's use of language, encumbering the verbal as well as the pictorial expression of human truths. In another scene between Breasley and David, as David studies the new "Kermesse" painting in Breasley's studio, the young art critic becomes aware that the final *imago* had been accomplished through a "constant recomposition and refinement away from the verbal." All of the literalness had progressively disappeared through the working sketches until it had been eliminated completely. Ironically, David's job will be to put Breasley's art back into words. The mysterious "inwardness" (26) of the painting, which remains after the exorcism of the verbal, will be translated back into "tawdry words," obscuring the unsaid human mysteries (112).

Language becomes an insurmountable barrier between Breasley and Williams. Although Mouse serves as translator, she is unable to translate what needs to be communicated. Breasley finally throws up his hands and yells, "What the hell's he talking about?" after one of David's dissertations on technique, but David is too busy counting obscenities and grammatical mistakes to hear the attempt at contact in Breasley's frustration. Breasley appeals— "Trying to tell you something"—to which David replies, "I know." But David doesn't know. He does not understand that "making is speaking," that "speech must be based on human needs" (45-46), that "bodies means more than words" (100).

Thus, David fails with Breasley; but the second challenge from Mouse in the garden shows David failing even more miserably. Again, in language as abstract and obscure as his painting, David demonstrates that he is bound to conventions of morality as well as to conventions of art. Mouse is Eve offering herself and a "new existence" (112) to this Adam who is too afraid to accept. "It was here, the unsaid. He knew it in every nerve and premonitory fiber. His move: he withdrew back into speech" (99). So David speaks, and the delay, the choosing not to act, damns him. Possession and security are the authorities in his life. Sex with Mouse would have to be a quick "sinking, knowing, possessing, release" (102) so that the "crypto-husband" (51) could get back home and make certain that his wife had no other man in bed with her: "His real fear was of losing that certainty" (97).

Human facts and feeling must be in art, in speech, and in sexual relations. "We're not brutes," Mouse tells David (101). But David does not understand until Mouse turns away from him and he is expelled from Coet that his brutality lies in his violation of love, not law. The Middle Ages fathered the belief that mutual trust should underpin all male-female relationships. But the same period also spawned a bastard in believing that chastity could insure this trust. David's practice of fidelity is a spurious destroyer of real love. It metaphorically castrates him and makes him unable to respond when love is offered. David is the "eunuch" in the garden at Coet, forsaking human needs for conventional morality.

Still, David is able to glimpse beneath the "phony shine" of his conventional armor (100) the man inside him who would not renounce the knowledge that Mouse offers. He is also left, at the end of the story, in a waiting room, reminiscent of Nicholas Urfe's SALLE D'ATTENTE in *The Magus*. The airport waiting room is an ambiguous symbol that can represent David's arrival at a terminus, consistent with Fowles's characterization of him in the story, or his point of departure, still possible because David is young, intelligent, and sensitive enough to change. Youth and change are inextricably joined in Fowles's fiction, and as long as David possesses qualities of the *aristoi*—and he does, generally—with time enough to mature them, there is hope for him. Not so with Fowles's Peacock scholar in **"Poor Koko"** and the conservative MP of **"The Enigma."** In the second and third stories of *The Ebony Tower,* Fowles makes untypical use of old men, who appear to be offering us a backward glance over lives already lived as David Williams is likely to live his. Although each man musters courage enough to perform a single important action, neither can correct a life already lived so poorly. Illustrating this best, and most ironically, is yet another waiting room, the cloakroom of the British Museum in **"The Enigma."** There Marcus Fielding leaves his briefcase, full of the papers and schedules that have defined his life, before abandoning that life altogether.

By contrast, the scholar in **"Poor Koko"** only temporarily puts aside his life's work. Before returning to the dreary reconstruction of his book on Thomas Love Peacock, he grants the young burglar his wish to be written about. **"Poor Koko"** is an examination of the boy who presents himself to the scholar as a living and therefore preferable subject for study. However, the story is also the scholar's fairly honest examination of himself. The self-probing lies in the older man's consideration of the linguistic craft and wit he has at his disposal. He may use them as he chooses in "serious" studies of dead authors like Peacock or in amusing stories like **"Poor Koko"**; but his writing of the latter ironically reveals that Peacock was more deserving of his wit and the boy of his seriousness.[3]

Wit is the villain of this tale. In the scholar's life, wit has protected him from criticism and disapproval. When he was hated for his puny size and bookworm ways, he could turn his weapon of wit on his critics and disarm them with humor. Over the years, his layers of self-protective wit thickened into an armor of cynical condescension, which made him impervious to any human contact, either critical or friendly. Appropriately, the scholar's greatest work is *The Dwarf in Literature,* a title reflecting his own dimin-

utive size and character. Early in the story, he admits that books have been his whole existence: "writing them, reading, reviewing, helping to get them into print—have been my life rather more than life itself" (147).

Like the "word-twister" (44) critic David Williams, the scholar has used language as an exclusionary medium, sharing it with few and denying it to many. As a result, he is both ill-equipped and unwilling to respond seriously to questions and challenges from his assailant. Deaf to the burglar's appeals, the scholar bates and belittles the young man with words, both spoken and written. The ironic result is that the burglar feels more victimized than his victim. Thus, he retaliates by gagging the scholar and, in silence, incinerating his weapon of words. The scholar is left with only a myopic remembrance of the burglar's victorious upturned thumb and the echo of his grievance, which the scholar later perceives covered a "cry for help": "Man, your trouble is you don't listen hard enough" (184).

It is intentional that the title **"Poor Koko"** and its epigraph in Old Cornish are "incomprehensible" so that we can see how willingly the scholar now comes to our linguistic aid. He translates their meaning for us, explaining that *Koko* is a Japanese word meaning "correct filial behavior, the proper attitude of son to father." This ironic appellation reminds him that although he is childless and an old man, he could have shown a father's love and responsibility to the deprived young man. The epigraph translated reads: "Too long a tongue, too short a hand; / But tongueless man has lost his land." With this couplet, he reminds himself that language is a gift to be shared, not hoarded. The gift-giving opportunity missed, the scholar is left a "poor clown"—another definition he offers for "poor Koko"—his wit and humor of little comfort to him in his barren old age (186-87).

Marcus Fielding of **"The Enigma"** also approaches the end of his career a foolish old man in his own estimation. Certainly, he has not been a political, financial, or social fool, but humanly and emotionally, he has been foolish indeed. The narrator tells us that it was against all "social and statistical probability" that a man like Fielding would have disappeared (191). And Fielding's life was probable. His life was carefully planned and predictable, as the testimonies of his family, employees, and colleagues confirm. The expanse of reportage that opens this short story is somewhat reminiscent of Tolstoy's biography of Ivan Illych. Both men, moving always through "proper channels" (208) and controlled entirely by their duties, lead lives that read like catalogues or inventories, with no highs or lows, no passion or change, no defeat or exultation.

If we can believe Isobel—another of Fowles's fictionalizing *magi*—Fielding's death or disappearance has the *harakiri* quality of face-saving. A Clegg-like collector of mementoes, pictures, and press clippings of himself, Fielding has had to have evidence that he lived because he felt no other sense of it. Finally, she suggests, a better buried life percolates up through his pretentious "lifestyle" and sets off a battle between self and soul. Unable to admire the man whose career decorated the pages of his carefully assembled scrapbooks, Fielding chooses to save the face the scrapbooks never revealed. Therefore, he walks out of his life. He also walks out of Isobel's story of him as well, for although much of Isobel's fiction rings true, there is no evidence that her speculations *are* true. Still, neither the unrevised fact of Fielding's past nor the revisable fiction of his present and future have any power over him. He is pure mystery, unique and provocative for the first time in his life.

In fact, however, Marcus Fielding becomes a protagonist in this story only because Isobel's fiction-within-a-fiction has made him one. The protagonist of the frame fiction is, of course, Michael Jennings, the detective, who, unexpectedly, must respond to her fiction by becoming something of a literary sleuth or critic. The real world, not surprisingly, wants nothing of his "what-if" speculations about Fielding's disappearance and will not let him act on his and Isobel's intuitive conjecturing. Jennings is another sketch of the Ebony Tower protagonist, whose initial complacency as a detective is developed with some irony. As one reader comments, "the challenge Isobel presents to him with her fictions and her female kinetic force and Jennings' awakening to a more difficult and engaged life" is central to this story.[4] Though his interest to this story is paler than Fielding's, who is the "enigma," Jennings is more important as a character because of his *living* and even jaunty potential as an *aristoi*, which is restored and enlivened by a love affair, a mystery, and his own valuable self-searching and discovery. Jennings is the one hopeful portrait of a protagonist that Fowles gives us in this collection.

However, the most interesting portrait in *The Ebony Tower* is that of Catherine in **"The Cloud,"** the story that Fowles believes is the best in the collection.[5] Stylistically unique from anything Fowles has done, and more difficult than the other stories, **"The Cloud"** presents a characterization of a sensitive and potent writer who is "without will" (299). This artist is also especially unlucky since she does not meet a magus who can help her. The only magus in **"The Cloud"** is a make-believe wise owl, which Catherine invents for a fairy tale she tells her niece.

In **"The Cloud,"** Catherine is with her sister's family and their friends on a day's outing in France. However, because of the recent death of her husband, she is tearful and distraught. As she tells her sister Bel, her husband's death has shattered her "continuity" and left her afraid of "being left behind and of going on" (260-61). This uncertain present threatens Catherine with a terrifying and lonely freedom. Jean-Paul Sartre recognized such freedom as the necessary *angst* that precedes responsible creation. Certainly Nicholas Urfe, Charles Smithson, and Daniel Martin all lost or gave up safe relationships before they found freedom; and only after much frustration and loneliness did they discover opportunities for self-creation in the freedom they acquired. Catherine, however, will not accept the freedom to define herself once she loses the relationship that had defined her in the past. She tries to protect herself from her past loss and future uncertainty by preserving that definition. She tells her brother-in-law

that the time before her husband's death keeps crowding into her present: "Nothing has happened yet. Now is still before it happened." When past reality is allowed to move in and take over the present, past reality becomes present "fantasy," as Catherine clearly understands. But although Catherine realizes that her present reality is counterfeit, she is too weak to "do anything about it" (268).

Like Fowles's other protagonists, Catherine is weakened by the flaws of pride, insecurity, and arrogance. She is a talented and intelligent woman but is consumed by a despairing pessimism that fights against her few attempts to break with the past. To Catherine, the world seems a hopeless wasteland. Its mediocrity and ugliness make her unwilling to build anything new in it. Even the most "acceptable atom" she sees in it, the family, is not a safe and harmonious construct. Just as she begins to feel some security in her family, the atom shatters. Its composition has a transient unity, adhering one moment and disintegrating the next. A scrupulous observer, Catherine watches the atom compose and then decompose itself:

> The sparkling water, the splashing feet; the dragonflies and butterflies; the buttercups and oxeyes and little blue flowers like splashes of sky. The voices, movements; kaleidescope, one shake and all will disappear. Bel's freckled-milky skin as she smiles, her vacant Juno smile, beneath the wide brim of her rush hat. . . . Nuclei, electrons. Seurat, the atom is all. The first truly acceptable island of the day. *En famille*; where children reign. For bonny sweet Robin is all my joy. . . .
>
> 'It's lovely,' bawls Candida back at them, with her usual ineffably judicious authority. 'Come on. We don't want to eat yet.'
>
> 'I wish I believed in hitting children,' murmurs Bel.
> [262-63]

Catherine despairs at reality's imperfection and is alienated by it. Candida's bawling and Bel's muttered threat shake the kaleidescope of Catherine's aesthetic vision. So much clashes that Catherine turns away from her companions and retreats, leaving the wasteland behind her:

> Catherine . . . begins to wander away, pretending to look at flowers, her back to the voices, the shouts, the damns and buggers. Oh, that's a beauty. Bags him tonight. Hurry up please it's time. Goodnight Bill. Goodnight Lou. Goodnight. Goodnight. [264]

The shallow activities of her companions offend Catherine. But although she despises the silly flirtations, exploitive business interests, and "husks of talk" (275), she is guilty of similar wrongdoing. Bel correctly points out that Catherine "undervalues" everything (257). She snubs reality because it can be unpleasant and painful, and she dislikes people because they are not what she thinks they should be. However, the specific crime of which she is guilty is her dishonest use of language. She is like Peter, the glib TV producer who uses language as commercial camouflage to hide truths that are too difficult or real to be marketable. Unconcerned that she represents accurately the significance of Barthes and semiotics in a script he wants her to write, Peter asks Catherine only for a consumable distillation that can be "got across on telly" (280). Although Catherine does not share Peter's shallow commercial interests, she does share his impulse to hide truth beneath a fabric of fantasy and manipulation. Almost before she knows what she is doing, her thoughts follow an irrevocable sequence of "words, shards, lies, oblivion" (298).

The "sort of true" (285) story Catherine tells her niece Emma is an example of the kind of fantasy that Catherine has erected between herself and the ugly but true tragedy of her husband's death. Catherine's fable is about a princess who gets lost in the forest after wandering too far from where her family is picnicking. Her family looks for but cannot find her, so she is left behind. The princess, of course, is Catherine. Both women are brown and naked, and they wait in the forest for their lost lovers to return. The owl in Catherine's story magically freezes the princess in time so that she will still be young and beautiful when the prince returns. Catherine also believes herself unchanged as she strains her imaginings to peer into the "black hole" of death, where her own prince now resides.

Emma insists on a "happily-ever-after" conclusion to the tale and then leaves to join her family. For Catherine, however, the story is what she is living and therefore has no ending. She remains behind, stretching herself out on a rock like a "corpse," and tries to imagine a reunion with her dead lover:

> One lies in one's underclothes, behind dark glasses and fast-closed lids, aware of process . . . hidden and waiting. It must be close. One thought of it even with Emma, since he is there, also waiting, every moment now. That is why one can't stand other people, they obscure him, they don't understand how beautiful he is, now he has taken on the mask; so far from skeleton. But smiling, alive, almost fleshed; just as intelligent, beckoning. The other side. [297-99]

Now that her husband is there, the "other side" seems a far more congenial place to her than the life she presently lives in and hates. Catherine thinks of suicide, but nothing in the story suggests that her suicide is likely. She is described only as passive and inert, dreaming futile dreams of a restored past or afterlife reunions.

"With tears of self-pity, hand hidden in furtive hair," Catherine masturbates in a pitiful attempt to make love to the dead (298). She surrenders completely to a necrophilic dream vision but soon pays dearly for her capitulation. Vulnerable and half-naked, she is discovered by the "hunting man" (288), an incarnation of the hunter who terrifies the princess and the forest animals in Catherine's story. Peter, who is life's inevitable exploiter of the weakwilled, stalks and overpowers the self-pitying dreamer. His real flesh comes between Catherine and her ephemeral vision, obscuring her smiling, beckoning dead lover. When he uncovers Catherine's "black-shuttered" eyes and presses down on her, her vision shatters like another view in the kaleidoscope. With no strength or courage to resist reality's rape, she lies "self-defiled" under Peter, an accessory to this crime against herself (298-99).

When Peter leaves, Catherine turns "quietly and submissively" onto her stomach, buries her face in the ground, and "waits" (304). Catherine will continue to wait, hoping for some change but never changing herself. She lies in her forest of illusion afraid to admit so many painful truths: the prince will not return, she cannot kill herself, and she does not believe that she can create a new life alone. Fowles might say of Catherine what he said of Miranda Grey in *The Aristos*: "If she had not died she might have become something better, the kind of being humanity so desperately needs" (10). However, Catherine's death is spiritual and moral, not physical. She has Miranda's talent, intelligence, and feeling but not her courage and will. She is more like Virginia Woolf's character, Clarissa Dalloway, who perceives life as "dangerous." Thus, Catherine lies pressed and mounted on the last page of *The Ebony Tower* like one of Clegg's beautiful but lifeless butterflies. An artist fearful of truth and scornful of life, only able to create death-in-life with her fertile imagination, Catherine is an unredeemed artist of the ebony tower. Fowles therefore abandons her in a forest of false fiction: . . . composing and decomposed, writing and written. Young dark-haired corpse with a bitter mouth; her hands at her sides, she does by thinking of doing (299).

The Ebony Tower is a collection of working sketches of characters who reappear in Fowles's novels. The major characters in the four short stories, David Williams, poor Koko, Marcus Fielding, and Catherine, resemble respectively Nicholas Urfe, Daniel Martin, Charles Smithson, and Miranda Grey. However, the similarities all these characters share make them variations on a theme—the reason, perhaps, that Fowles first planned to call this collection *Variations* (121). The rubric for protagonism in all of Fowles's fiction is the main character's struggle against emotional, moral, or artistic paralysis, the Fowlesian "fatal flaw" which can undermine the other *aristos* qualities in the individual. The broader canvas of the novel allows Fowles time to correct this flaw in his novels's protagonists. However, in *The Ebony Tower,* mainly negative portraits are collected of characters who become aware of their paralysis as a condition they cannot change or cure. They will not risk a venture into the fast-running evolutionary stream but retreat into black "ivory towers" to escape the world they should be serving. Fowles's battalion of magi characters is charged with toppling this tower of fears, vanities, and deception, but the magi of *The Ebony Tower* are not as successful as their counterparts in the novels. Although they are able to make the protagonists of the stories aware of their deficiencies, they cannot make them change. The protagonists are only able to see themselves in double exposure with their failed selves overlying dim images of better buried lives. Sharing the twin faults of deficient will and meager courage, these characters make up Fowles's collection of human fossils who are unable to evolve even to rescue themselves from extinction.

Notes

[1] References to works by Fowles, cited in the text by page number, are to these editions: *The Aristos* (Boston: Little, 1970); *The Ebony Tower* (Boston: Little, 1974); *The French Lieutenant's Woman* (Boston: Little, 1969); *The Magus: A Revised Version* (Boston: Little, 1977); *Mantissa* (Boston: Little, 1982).

[2] Joyce Cary, *The Horse's Mouth* (London: Joseph, 1944) 173.

[3] In his introduction to the *Modern Fiction Studies* 1985 special issue on Fowles, "John Fowles and the Crickets," William J. Palmer elaborates on Fowles's mistrust of critics, a profession or interest that all of his Ebony Tower protagonists pursue.

[4] I am grateful to Timothy C. Alderman for his helpful comments in evaluating this essay for publication.

[5] Fowles, personal interview, 20 August 1977. My interview with Fowles at his home in Lyme Regis was arranged by William J. Palmer, Professor of English at Purdue University, and was supported by a grant from the Purdue Research Foundation.

Carol M. Barnum   (essay date 1988)

SOURCE: "*The Ebony Tower*: Variations on the Mythic Theme," in her *The Fiction of John Fowles: A Myth for Our Time,* The Penkevill Publishing Company, 1988, pp. 77-99.

[*In the essay below, Barnum offers a comprehensive overview of Fowles's* The Ebony Tower, *noting similarities between the stories, particularly the recurring theme of missed opportunities, as well as similarities between Fowles's short fiction and his novels.*]

John Fowles's fourth work of fiction, **The Ebony Tower,** continues the theme of the novels in the more precise format of the short story. The working title for the collection was *Variations,* Fowles's intent being to show variations on the theme of his previous fiction. But since early readers found the title (and its connections) obscure, it was abandoned in favor of the present title. If, however, we consider Fowles's stated intent, we see a pattern emerging of the protagonist's struggles to take the journey toward self-discovery or individuation, the emphasis of the stories in this collection being on the bleaker aspects of failed attempts.

Also included in the collection is Fowles's translation of the medieval romance *Eliduc,* which, as he explains in "A Personal Note" preceding it, is connected to **The Ebony Tower** in the same way that medieval romance is connected to modern fiction—as a natural outgrowth. Thus, the stories of **The Ebony Tower** not only demonstrate variations on the ancient theme of the quest, but also variations on the theme of Fowles's fiction.

The title story describes a quester who inadvertently stumbles into the realm of myth, only to find that he cannot rise to the challenge of the quest and is therefore ejected from the mythic landscape. The other three stories in the collection are all centered on enigmas (one of the stories is titled **"The Enigma"**) or mysteries of modern life. These mysteries arise because "mystery" in the sacred sense no longer appears valid in modern man's existence. The movement of the stories is generally downward toward darkness, modern man depicted as being less and less able to take the mythic journey of self-discovery because he is trapped in a wasteland world that bewilders him.

David Williams of **The Ebony Tower** is the typical Fowlesian protagonist: well-born and bred, self-assured, and representative of his age and class. Driving through the forests of Brittany, the landscape of the Celtic romance, he is unsuspecting of the mythic encounter that awaits him. Since David's approach to life is one of "intelligent deduction," as opposed to "direct experience," he is ill prepared for the journey he is about to undertake. As a source of information, his journey will not be wasted; as a source of psychic growth, not the expressed purpose but the implied opportunity, his journey will be wasted because his rational response will prove insufficient to the challenge.

Turning off the main road into the forest lane, David comes to the "promised sign" announcing *Manoir de Coëtminais: coët* meaning "wood" or "forest" and *minais* meaning "of the monks,"[1] the sacred wood of the mythic quest. Fowles's description of David's experience within this mythic domain has similarities linking it to Robert Browning's poem "'Childe Roland to the Dark Tower Came,'" not the least of which is the association between the dark tower and the ebony tower. The differences are also interesting. While Roland fears his journey because he knows its dangers, David relishes his journey, being unsuspecting of danger. Roland is directed to the path off the main road by a "hoary cripple" who is "posted there" to point the way; David is directed by the posted "promised sign" (p. 4). The day is bleak on Roland's arrival, sunny on David's; but when David leaves Coëtminais, the day becomes as bleak as it is in Browning's poem. For David's departure the sky is "clouded over" and the landscape is of "dull, stubbled plains" (p. 111), a setting which corresponds with "the gray plain all round" and "stubbed ground" of Roland's landscape. In Roland's view "all hope of greenness" is gone, and when David leaves Coëtminais the same holds true: "an end now to all green growth" (p. 111). The essential difference, however, between the two journeys is that Roland has spent his life preparing for his journey and will rise to the challenge, while David has spent his life avoiding the challenge, living comfortably but superficially. When he finds himself faced with the dark tower of his existence, he cannot rise to meet it; therefore, his departure from the mythic landscape is as bleak as Roland's approach, or bleaker because Roland has at least the hope of success in the face of adversity, while David must live the rest of his life with the surety of his failure.

David comes to Breasley as an admirer of his art for its "mysterious" and "archetypal" qualities, which some critics called "'Celtic'" "with the recurrence of the forest motif, the enigmatic figures and confrontations" (p. 13). Breasley pretends to downplay the Celtic influence but tells David at the same time:

> 'Just here and there, don't you know, David. What one needs. Suggestive. Stimulating, that's the word.' Then he went off on Marie de France and *Eliduc.* 'Damn' good tale. Read it several times. What's the old Swiss bamboozler's name. Jung, yes? His sort of stuff. Archetypal and all that.' (p. 55)

In discussing the significant influences on his art, Breasley links the medieval quest with the Jungian archetypes, seeing the two as united in his work, just as Fowles unites the two strains in this story and in his fiction as a whole.

David knows that his art, as well as his lifestyle, is different from Breasley's; therefore he is not entirely surprised to meet the two girls who live with Breasley: Anne, dubbed "the Freak," and Diana, dubbed "the Mouse." Like the twins in *The Magus,* these two girls serve as mirror images, two halves that complement one another as two aspects of womankind. Diana, the Mouse, is described as ethereal, distant, feminine, and almost always dressed in white. Her counterpart, Anne, the Freak, is described as "aboriginal," sexual, coarse, and almost always dressed in black. Taken together, Diana and Anne, Anne's name contained within Diana's, form the archetype of the anima for David. David is attracted to the Mouse, finding the Freak somewhat offensive. His later failure to meet the challenge of the quest stems partly from the fact that he cannot accept the "freak," her sexuality, in the Mouse and respond positively to it. Breasley understands the dual nature of both girls, but his secret about the significance of the Mouse's name—"muse" with the feminine "o" drawn in the shape of a vulva—strengthens her role as an anima figure in the story, not only for David but for Breasley. Fowles ascribes to the power of the muses as well, telling an interviewer, "'I *do* believe in inspiration. I almost believe in muses. In fact, I wrote a short story last year that did bring the muses into modern life.'"[2]

Somewhat confused by his initial encounter, David feels like an outsider within the mythic domain, and he wishes his wife were with him to support his persona and protect him from the dangers of "so many ripening apples" (p. 29), an obvious reference to the temptation of the forbidden fruit in the Garden of Eden. At the same time, David thinks of his wife as "poor old Beth" (p. 10) and "predictable old Beth" (p. 29), revealing the nature of their relationship in its unfruitfulness. Thus to handle the confusing situation he faces, he provides himself with rational explanations for the things he sees in much the same way that Charles and Nicholas try to understand their own as well as others' behavior by ascribing rational explanations to them.

Related to David's need for a rational approach to life is his need to express everything verbally, to compartmentalize all experience within the boundaries of language. Language is certainly important, as any novelist will admit, but language cannot be a substitute for feeling. In an

interview after the publication of ***The Ebony Tower,*** Fowles discusses David's use of language, calling it "a kind of smooth language . . . which is losing meaning."[3] Breasley, on the other hand, is barely verbal, speaking for the most part in a kind of abbreviated language of fragments and phrases and communicating his important thoughts and feelings through his canvasses. Breasley can, however, use language effectively when necessary, as he demonstrates by means of a verbal attack upon David after dinner, drawing from him a symbolic "drop of blood" (p. 39). David mistakes the verbal wound for his initiation, thinking prematurely that he has passed the test. Unlike Gawain, the medieval quester who is similarly wounded by the Green Knight but who learns from the wound an important lesson, David has not learned anything yet except the art of carefully sidestepping an argument. In this case, however, he does not know how to respond to "the violently personal nature of the assault" (p. 42) Breasley mounts with such barbs as, "'You really a painter, Williams? Or just a gutless bloody word-twister?'" (p. 44), to which David replies, "'Hatred and anger are not luxuries we can afford anymore'" (p. 44). This elicits further insults from Breasley who, by now quite drunk, explains to David that he is trying to tell him something important, although he confesses to his inadequacy with words (David's presumed strength). In his abbreviated style he summarizes: "'Don't hate, can't love. Can't love, can't paint. . . . Bloody geometry. No good. Won't work. All tried it. Down the hole'" (p. 46). He concludes "with a strange lucidity": "'Ebony Tower. That's what I call it'" (p. 47). The meaning of the term is not explained until later by the Mouse, who tells David that it signifies anything Breasley does not like about modern art, in particular the obscurity of artists who are afraid to be clear. Fowles elaborates on the meaning of the term:

> I see the ebony tower as not so much an 'opposite' of the ivory one, as an inevitable consequence of it . . . if one stays too long in retreat in the sacred combe. Thus, a great deal of unnecessary 20th century 'obscurity' is a direct cultural result of 19th century ivory-towerism— art for art's sake, and so on. The trouble for me is not, so to speak, at the top—let us say, in the genius with which Mallarmé uses ambiguity and obscurity (and with undoubted sincerity in his greatest stuff); but the only-too-easy loophole it provides for the less gifted. Deliberately making your work incomprehensible is uncomfortably close to making it impossible to judge.[4]

David recognizes the creative powers in the old man, as evidenced in his canvasses, but fails to see their absence in his own art or life; he merely sees his existence as different from Breasley's, thinking the old man's self-imposed exile is based on the knowledge that "his persona would never wash in the Britain of the 1970s" (pp. 55-56). He does, however, envy Breasley's lifestyle and success: "To someone like David, always inclined to see his own life (like his painting) in terms of logical process, its future advances dependent on intelligent present choices, it seemed not quite fair" (p. 53).

Logical process begins to break down within the mythic landscape as David realizes that much of what he is learning about Breasley cannot be put in his introduction because "like the forest itself, the old man had his antique mysteries" (p. 56). In the same vein, at a picnic in the woods with Breasley and the girls, he likens Coët to the Garden of Eden, seeing the place and its lifestyle as "faintly mythic and timeless" (p. 59). The Mouse concurs, telling David how she came to Coët: "'Bump. You're in a different world'" (p. 63). He also is beginning to recognize more in the Freak's character than he previously realized, seeing in her look, which is "both questing and quizzing" (p. 70), a directness and gentleness that he previously missed, and thus recognizing an "identity and a complimentarity" (p. 70) between the two girls (as aspects of the anima archetype). Quickly, he feels drawn toward the three as a part of a living quaternity, which he completes, the result of which brings him an experience of the mandala archetype.

At the same time, David is feeling the influence of the Mouse in her role as the projection of the anima archetype:

> He knew it and concealed it . . . not only to her, partly also to himself: that is, he analyzed what he had so rapidly begun to find attractive about her—why that precise blend of the physical and the psychological, the reserved and the open . . . called so strongly to something in his own nature. Strange, how these things hit you out of the blue, were somehow inside you almost before you could see them approaching. He felt a little bewitched, possessed; and decided it must be mainly the effect of being without Beth. (pp. 72-73)

Several interesting points are revealed in this passage. One is that David recognizes the power of the Mouse as the anima archetype, even her power to bewitch or possess him, but he wants to *analyze* the situation so as to control it and to control the "something" it calls to in his nature: the anima within. In the midst of this analysis, a sentence intrudes in the second person where the sentences before and after are in the third person. Is this sentence, through the sudden use of "you," reflecting the voice of David's inner self, that which he seeks without knowing it? It speaks of the way "things hit you out of the blue" coming from "somewhere inside you," and it foreshadows the experience he will have with the Mouse in the garden. But the next sentence is safely back in the more distant third person as David attributes the strange things he is feeling to the absence of Beth, the projection of his persona.

Breasley, continuing in the archetypal role as David's guide, tells him that he does not provide answers to questions about his sources: "'Let it happen. That's all. Couldn't even tell you how it starts. What half it means. Don't want to know'" (p. 78). Like Conchis in *The Magus* who tells Nicholas that "every answer is a form of death," Breasley is interested in life, not answers. Speaking of "*trop de racine,*" he calls it "'too much root. Origin. Past. Not the flower. The now. Thing on the wall. *Faut couper la racine.* Cut the root off'" (p. 78). His message for David is that too much reliance on the past, the root, stifles growth in the present, the flower. Although the present is con-

nected to the root of the past, it cannot be chained to it; if this happens, one must cut the root off to save the flower.

The more David learns from Breasley in his capacity as teacher and guide and the Mouse in her capacity as anima, the more he feels drawn into the quest. There is, however, the danger of becoming too attached to the mythic realm, thus fearing to leave it. Such a fate has befallen the Mouse who sees Coët as the "'little forest womb . . . [where] everything remains possible'" (p. 90). On the contrary, her possibilities for full growth cannot be realized as long as she stays within the protection of the domain. Part of David's task as mythic quester is to rescue her from her "forest womb" and provide her with safe passage back to the real world. David senses the challenge he faces:

> He felt he had traveled much farther than expected, into the haunted and unpredicted; and yet in some strange way it seemed always imminent. It had had to come, it had had causes, too small, too manifold to have been detected in the past or to be analyzed now. (pp. 90-91)

For once he does not analyze, accepting that he has come to the central task of his journey. As he is awakened to the anima within, seen as Diana, she is awakened to the animus, which she projects on David, and the moment in which they must act in acknowledgment of each other is fast approaching.

The moment is "here, now, the unsaid" (p. 96) as they move to the Edenic garden with its "ghostly apple trees." And still, although it is "his move," David cannot make it, withdrawing instead, under the influence of the shadow archetype, "into speech" (p. 96). Knowing his inadequacy, he wishes for "two existences" (p. 97), finding himself unable to be united into one whole existence and yet not wanting to forsake this moment. Thoughts of Beth and the world he has left behind freeze him in inaction while one half of him nevertheless yearns to incorporate Breasley's teachings through his actions, as he thinks:

> Why deny experience, his artistic soul's sake, why ignore the burden of the old man's entire life? Take what you can. And so little: a warmth, a clinging, a brief entry into another body. One small releasing act. And the terror of it, the enormity of destroying what one had so carefully built. (pp. 97-98)

Again his inner self speaks to him through the voice of the second person. Momentarily, the inner voice wins out and he takes Diana in his arms, but she, sensing his hesitation, pulls away, and he does not take her to him again, resorting instead to a fatherly kiss on the top of her head and ineffectual back-patting. From this point on, the struggle to regain a sense of the moment when all was potential is futile.

David has failed not only himself, by refusing to accept the anima within even after acknowledging its presence, but also Diana, by falling short of what she has needed to break the spell of Coët and facilitate her return to the real world. Thinking of his impending expulsion from the mythic landscape, he contemplates the ramifications of his failure, knowing that he cannot return, being "banned for life now" (p. 106). And worse than Adam, also banned for life from the Garden of Eden, he has left his Eve behind, the manifestation of the anima archetype in the person of Diana.

Leaving Coët, he runs over an object in the road. At first he thinks he has hit a mouse (an oblique reference to Diana, the Mouse) or a snake (a reference to the serpent in the Garden of Eden); but, on turning back, he discovers that he has hit a weasel, the same animal wounded in the tale of *Eliduc,* whose forest he now rides through. Fowles uses the weasel as a symbol that links the motif of his story with that of *Eliduc.*[5] Unlike Eliduc, however, who successfully loved two women and whose tale demonstrates love as a connecting force, David cannot truly love either woman in his life. Thus, his tale demonstrates love as a dividing force since David is a divided man, caught between two worlds. Instead of being able to save the weasel that in *Eliduc* bears the life-restoring red flower, he kills it, and the blood that trickles from its mouth in the shape of the red flower now signifies his present psychic state of death without rebirth. The weasel's body is crushed but the head escapes, indicating the death of magic or creative powers with only the intellect or rational powers surviving.

The remainder of the story comprises David's analysis of his dilemma, not necessary for understanding the story's thesis, but in keeping with David's analytical character. He recognizes that fear, a manifestation of the shadow archetype, has prevented him from accepting the challenge of the quest, and he sees his art as reflecting his failure towards life: "You did not want how you lived to be reflected in your painting; or because it was compromised, so settled-for-the-safe, you could only try to camouflage its hollow reality under craftsmanship and good taste" (pp. 109-110). Broadening the scope of his failure, David sees it as representative of his age. While Breasley is still connected to the past through a life-giving "umbilical cord," David and his contemporaries are "encapsulated in book knowledge" (p. 110). The authorial voice intones:

> David and his generation, and all those to come, could only look back, through bars, like caged animals, born in captivity, at the old green freedom. That described exactly the experience of those last two days: the laboratory monkey allowed a glimpse of his lost true self. (p. 110)

As the mythic quester who quests for all, David is correct in seeing his failure as the failure of his age.

Yet, knowing that he has failed, he also knows that he will eventually forget his failure. The "wound" he has suffered will be covered by a scar, which in time will fade, leaving no trace; but until that moment comes, he will have to live with the realization that "he had refused (and even if he had never seen her again) a chance of a new existence,

and the ultimate quality and enduringness of his work had rested on acceptance" (p. 112). Now in Paris he thinks of Coët as "in another universe" and he feels the loss of his paradise as "the most intense pang of the most terrible of all human deprivations; which is not of possession, but of knowledge" (p. 113). Fowles elaborates on David's predicament in an interview: "I meant simply that David knows after Coëtminais that his life will never be the same, but restricted by his new knowledge of himself. His dreams of himself are shipwrecked; but because he is decent he must learn to live with what he knows, with his newly revealed lacks and faults."[6] A last urge in him toward salvation through knowledge is kept in check by "the tall shadow of him" (p. 113), his inability to break through the complacency and confinements, perhaps even decency, of his persona. David is not shadow-possessed, like Clegg in *The Collector,* but neither has he conquered the shadow.

In the last passage, which describes Beth's approach from the plane, Fowles switches from past to present tense in the same way he does in the last page of the revised version of *The Magus.* The major difference, however, is that in *The Magus* the present tense expresses the limitless possibility of the future awaiting Nicholas. For David, the present is an entrapping tense, keeping him frozen in failure because of his denial of the future. The passage reads: "She comes with the relentless face of the present tense. . . . He composes his face into an equal certainty" (p. 114); it continues: "He has a sense of retarded waking, as if in a postoperational state of consciousness some hours returned but not till now fully credited; a numbed sense of something beginning to slip inexorably away" (p. 114).

In Fowles's use of the "postoperational state" to describe David's condition, we hear an echo of T. S. Eliot's "The Love Song of J. Alfred Prufrock" in which the night is "spread out against the sky / Like a patient etherised upon a table." Other images reinforce the connection with Prufrock, another quester who dares not meet the challenge of life because, like David, he is a divided man, suffering from what Eliot calls "dissociation of sensibility." Like Prufrock who "prepare[s] a face to meet the faces that you meet," David wears a persona that allows him to meet the faces he meets, particularly the face of his wife who now approaches. Also like Prufrock, who has "heard the mermaids singing, each to each," David has caught a liberating glimpse of life's potential at Coët, only to suffer Prufrock's fate when "human voices wake us, and we drown." In similar terms, Fowles describes David as one who "knows one dreamed, yet cannot remember. The drowning cry, jackbooted day" (p. 114). He wakes to reality, the human voices of the present drowning out the dream of the anima (which for Prufrock is symbolized by the mermaids' cry); and "he surrenders to what is left: to abstraction" (p. 114). Eliot's "dissociated" man, Prufrock, becomes Fowles's abstract man, David Williams. In response to his wife's implied question about the weekend, David says, "'I survived'" (p. 114), a statement of hollow victory which concludes the novella and leaves us with the sinking sense of David's lost possibilities, his death-in-life in the eternal present, synonymous with Prufock's waking to drown. Had David succeeded in his quest, he would have done far more than survive: he would have lived.

The remaining stories in the collection are connected to the title story by the theme of lost opportunities. The sense of gloom that the ebony tower signifies becomes more pervasive, ending with the image of the dark cloud which overtakes the sun in the last story. In the first of these, **"Poor Koko,"** the narrator's "ordeal," as he calls his encounter with the young thief who burns his writing, brings him the closest of the protagonists of the remaining stories to an understanding of his personal failure, but it leaves him helpless to do anything more than explain it. His quest for self-knowledge is not voluntarily sought but forced upon him by the unusual circumstance of the robbery and his desire to understand it.

The details of the experience that begin the writer's journey are these: having gone to the country to work on his manuscript, he is awakened by a young thief. They engage in an encounter that crosses generational as well as attitudinal lines and that culminates in the thief's burning the writer's manuscript, a seemingly incomprehensible act. Following the act comes an equally incomprehensible gesture: the thief's cocked thumb in the writer's face. His departure leaves the writer the task of understanding the incomprehensible while subjected to "the acrid smell, surely the most distressing of all after burnt human flesh, of cremated human knowledge" (p. 175). What, in effect, has happened is that the heart of the writer, his life's work, has been put to death, and he must now construct a new one grounded in an understanding of his relationship and responsibility towards other people.

The writer begins by analyzing the robber's last "cocked thumb" gesture. At the time of its occurrence, he saw it puzzlingly as a sign of mercy when there was no mercy shown. Later he establishes other meanings for the gesture—all inappropriate to the situation. Finally, after seeing the gesture used by a football player to signal courage to the crowd before the game begins, the writer interprets the thief's gesture as a warning to him: "a grim match was about to start and the opposing team he represented was determined to win" (p. 183). Hidden also in the gesture, as the writer analyzes it, is the thief's feeling that the odds are stacked in the writer's favor. Burning the papers begins the match.

The writer continues his analysis of the evening based on the linguistic implications of the thief's use of two words: "man" and "right." In the thief's frequent use of "man," the writer sees an attempt to bring them together within the family of man, while at the same time showing the vast differences that separate them. Through his use of "right" (with a question implied) he expresses his "underlying mistrust . . . of language itself" (p. 184). The writer, in his analysis, is, of course, expressing Fowles's view of the deterioration of language, a view he reiterates in discussing the story: "The point I was trying to make is that though I should like to see life become more simple in many (social) ways, language was not one of them."[7] Thus, in the story, the young thief's frustration at the old man

comes from his inability to use language to express himself and his anger at the old man's refusal to share the power of language with him. Understanding this, the old man writes, "I must very soon have appeared to the boy as one who deprived him of a secret—and one he secretly wanted to possess" (p. 185).

On a larger scale, the clash between the boy and the writer is seen as the clash between generations, between a world in which language is meaningful and one in which it is empty, stripped of its "magic" and "mystery" in the profound sense. The writer, again probably speaking as Fowles's mouthpiece, raises the conflict to a universal plane, seeing the problem as extending beyond this particular encounter to include television, the arts, social and political institutions, and the educational system. To strengthen the universal nature of the conflict, Fowles refrains from assigning names to the two main characters; they maintain their generalized roles as the old man and the boy, the writer and the thief. Even while their clash takes on universal proportions, it does not absolve the writer of his responsibility in the matter, which he sees as stemming from his "deafness." The deafness, while not specifically elucidated, is linked to the title of the story, which the writer explains is deliberately obscure. In illuminating its various meanings, he sheds light on the problem existing between himself and the boy, between his view of life and the boy's, between a world in which language and symbol have meaning and the present state of the world in which they do not. For example, when he asked friends to analyze the meaning of the title of his story, the consensus was that it derived from an unusual spelling for Coco the clown. On one level, as the writer explains, this is an accurate interpretation if the title refers to both participants and if "poor" carries its several meanings. However, as the writer continues, he had in mind *koko,* the Japanese word meaning "correct filial behavior, the proper attitude of son to father" (p. 186); thus, the title means inadequate or inferior filial behavior, indicating the failure of the relationship between the "father" and "son" of the story. Further, the writer illuminates the meaning of the "incomprehensible epigraph" following the title, saying that it "shall have the last word, and serve as judgment on both father and son" (p. 187):

> Too long a tongue, too short a hand;
> But tongueless man has lost his land.

Inherent in the epigraph, now brought to light through the still viable powers of the old man, is the idea that language must serve to reach out from father to son but must at the same time be accompanied by human love, the "hand." For if man loses his language, the power of the word to communicate, he loses his heritage, his roots. The epigraph "comes with a sad prescience" (p. 187) from old Cornish, an extinct language without a land, since it may foreshadow the fate of English and other contemporary languages if the writer, as the representative "father," keeps his "tongue" to himself, refusing to communicate through his "hand" the love and spirit of the language as a reflection of heritage, "the land." The title of the story and its epigraph are obscure, as is the meaning of the boy's action toward the old man—each requires translation. But the question remains as to whether the writer's new-found understanding, forced on him through such unusual circumstances, can save his age from the fate of extinction. It certainly comes too late to save the boy or provide him with the foundation for a correct filial relationship based on love, understanding, and the old man's transference of the creative power of language.

In the succeeding story, **"The Enigma,"** a mystery of a different kind is presented: the disappearance of John Marcus Fielding, prominent businessman, family man, Member of Parliament. Since the disappearance has no apparent criminal motivation, the question is raised as to why a man who seemed to have everything would want to abscond from life. The answer, as it is pieced together by hypothesis and conjecture, is that a life that seemed to offer a man everything in actuality provided him with an incurable feeling of emptiness; therefore, he set out to create his own mystery through his disappearance.

Since Fielding has disappeared before the story begins, the focus is on Sergeant Michael Jennings, whose life is connected to Fielding's by more than just the investigation. One of their connections involves their concern with keeping up appearances. Peter Fielding, the M.P.'s son, tells Jennings, "Maybe you don't know the kind of world I was brought up in. But its leading principle is never, never, never show what you really feel" (p. 215). Jennings is not much different, being described as one who "took very good care indeed not to show his feelings" (p. 203) when dealing with his peers and superiors on the force. He can just as easily "put on his public school manner" when addressing Mrs. Fielding. This ability to change face, that is, to assume the persona appropriate to the situation without revealing his true feelings, has served him well (as it has Fielding).

Another connection between Fielding and Jennings involves his attraction toward Isobel Dodgson, Peter's girl friend. At first sight of her, Jennings has "an immediate impression of someone alive, where everyone else has been dead, or playing dead; of someone who lived in the present, not the past" (p. 224). In her vitality, she serves as a potential anima figure for Jennings; and their meeting shifts the story's focus away from Fielding's disappearance to the developing relationship between Jennings and Isobel, such that the enigma now includes the young couple and the question of their future relationship. The conflict that caused Fielding to disappear soon manifests itself, however, in Jenning's relationship toward Isobel, whom he sees at first as fresh, independent, and not taken in by "the Sunday color-supplement view of values" (p. 226) which Fielding and his world represent, until she brings him abruptly down to earth with her crude statement about policy brutality. His expectations dashed, Jennings feels "shocked more than he showed, like someone angling for a pawn who finds himself placed in check by one simple move" (p. 226). Disappointed unconsciously by her failure to live up to her potential as an anima figure for him, Jennings nevertheless feels himself consciously relieved to be returned to more familiar ground, now seeing Isobel

as a sex object who appeals to him through the more familiar world of the senses.

Isobel is not easily categorized, however. When she tells Jennings her intuitions about Fielding, her ability to see "'someone else, behind it all'" (p. 230), she demonstrates again her potential as anima, her ability to see a man whole (Sarah's and Alison's gift), but her potential remains undeveloped since she is as much a product of the contemporary wasteland as is Fielding or Jennings, and, like Jennings, is not on the mythic journey.

From a small detail that she has not divulged to previous investigators, Isobel weaves a story for Jennings that "explains" Fielding's disappearance. Jennings listens while at the same time trying to "calculate how far he could go with personal curiosity under the cover of official duty" (p. 233). As they talk, they discover, despite their different backgrounds, "a certain kind of unspoken identity of situation" (p. 235). In the pragmatic world in which they exist, "identity of situation" rather than identity of feeling forms the basis for a relationship. Still, he sees in her something different that speaks to something inside him, but he does not know how to attain it because he has lost the means of communication; he therefore falls back on sexual communication as the only avenue he knows, despite the fact that

> something about her possessed something that he lacked: a potential that lay like unsown ground, waiting for just this unlikely corn-goddess; a direction he could follow, if she would only show it. An honesty, in one word. He had not wanted a girl so fast and so intensely for a long time. Nevertheless, he made a wise decision. (p. 236)

The allusion to Isobel as a corn-goddess relates her to the vegetative myths and the regeneration cycle. What Jennings seeks without knowing it is rebirth through the experience of the archetypes, here expressed as union with the anima, but he does not know how to journey toward such an experience and seeks direction from her. If she were serving in her potential capacity as anima, she might provide the direction he seeks, leading him to experience the archetypes and to approach wholeness. But she is not the anima; she only possesses the unrealized potential, as deeply locked inside her as it is in Jennings. His "wise decision" in its very nature reveals his inherent problem: decision does not produce archetypal encounter.

Isobel's "fiction" concludes open-endedly with Fielding's walking out. When prompted for a better ending, she says that the real author of the story is not she or anyone else, but the system: "'Something that had written him. Had really made him just a character in a book'" (p. 240). Using an analogy that figures prominently in *The French Lieutenant's Woman,* Isobel describes Fielding as being "'like a fossil—while he's still alive'" (p. 240). Trapped by the system that "limited" and "prevented" him from changing or evolving, he left it behind, thereby creating a sense of mystery his own life lacked. Of course, as Isobel tells her story about Fielding, she and Jennings, one cannot forget, are also characters in the story, just as much written by the system that defines them as is Fielding. Equally, they are products of Fowles's fiction, with Fowles using them and the various stories within the story to make a point about the condition of modern existence that "writes us" and denies us the freedom we need to take the mythic journey.

Through the stories in *The Ebony Tower,* Fowles sounds a warning by showing us the despair inherent in contemporary life if we cannot take the journey out of the darkness toward wholeness and individuation.

—Carol M. Barnum

While Isobel tells her story, she is unconsciously tracing "invisible patterns" on the table top with her finger: "a square, a circle with a dot in it" (p. 242). What she traces is the archetype of the mandala, the circle-in-the-square pattern that indicates wholeness.[8] Significantly, Isobel's patterns are invisible, unrecognized by the pair as they discuss a man who, lacking wholeness and the creative powers of archetypal encounter, has killed himself. Jennings, now only referred to as "the sergeant," takes no notice of Isobel's patterns, wondering instead if she is naked beneath her dress. Meanwhile, Isobel raises "the pattern-making finger" and concludes, "'Nothing lasts like a mystery'" (p. 242). The finger which draws the pattern of the mandala but does not contain its power is the finger that points to the crux of Fielding's dilemma: life without mystery cannot be endured. Since Fielding, along with Isobel and the sergeant, lacks mystery in his life in the sacred sense, provided through an attachment to meaningful rituals and symbols, he can only attain mystery in the profane sense, created by his own disappearance and described in Isobel's story.

In similar fashion, Isobel and the sergeant create their own mystery in their budding relationship. What they are now faced with is not the solution to Fielding's mystery but the solution to the mystery between them, which the sergeant sees as still another "test," both "test" and "mystery" being used in the limited, non-mythic sense. Fowles writes, "The point was a living face with brown eyes, half challenging and half teasing; not committing a crime against that" (p. 245). The "crime" is not committed in that they plan to continue the relationship, but the language Fowles employs to describe their "first tomorrow" has a distinctly criminal cast when the sergeant "deprive[s]" her of her clothes, finding her "*defenseless* underneath, though hardly an innocent *victim* in what followed" (p. 247; italics mine). Since they are both consenting adults desirous of the anticipated sexual encounter, the criminal language Fowles employs is humorously ironic. Isobel and the ser-

geant create their own mystery on the sensual level, and while it does not lead to archetypal encounter since they are not on the mythic journey, it is not unpleasurable and provides some respite from the sterility of the wasteland. As the concluding sentence of the story attests: "The tender pragmatisms of flesh have poetries no enigma, human or divine, can diminish or demean—indeed it can only cause them, and then walk out" (p. 247). Although the two characters that remain do not take the mythic journey, whose potential has been hinted at but never realized, they do achieve a union of sorts which is "tender" even while being pragmatic. The flesh provides a poetry of its own, and it will have to suffice since it appears to be all that remains. Instead of clearing up the enigma of Fielding's disappearance, Fowles provides us with a new enigma, inherent in the last sentence with its deliberately ambiguous pronouns. Fowles, himself, may shed meaning on the story if we consider his words in *The Magus*: "To view life as a detective story, as something that could be deduced, hunted and arrested, was no more realistic (let alone poetic) than to view the detective story as the most important literary genre, instead of what it really was, one of the least" (p. 502). Perhaps Fowles is telling us that the detective story part of **"The Enigma"** is of less importance than the more "poetic" story between Jennings and Isobel. If that is the case, the conclusion to the story, which is no conclusion but a new beginning, will have to suffice since in the age of anti-myth—the setting for this story and others in the volume—mystery in the sense of enigma is all that remains. Or, as John B. Humma writes, "The Spillanesque winding-up (detective beds heroine) may seem to trivialize a serious story otherwise, but it is in keeping with the genre. Moreover, 'the tender pragmatisms of flesh' which Jennings achieves with Isobel counterpoint all that is lost by David Williams, who had hung back at his portal."[9]

"The Cloud," the last story in the collection, continues the motif of the collection in its descent toward darkness. It begins by painting a picture of a summer day, "vivid with promise" (p. 251), but the participants are divided into sun and shadow, hinting from the start the breakdown in communication that is part of the story's thesis. Further, the two women described in the opening paragraph are lying "stretched as if biered" (p. 251), a description which introduces the image of death that dominates by the end of the story. The two men, Peter and Paul, have no connection to the wisdom of the apostles (although Peter is called "Apostle Peter"); their actions are futile and pointless for the most part. The scene even includes a snake which frightens the children, but of which Peter says philosophically, "'Proves it's paradise, I suppose'" (p. 254). All is not Edenic, however much the aura of a "different world" is suggested; the participants are divided from each other and themselves and find themselves strangers in paradise. The crux of the problem is stated by one of the voices (possibly Catherine's):

> What one lost, afterward, was what one had never had strongly at the best of times: a sense of continuity. . . . So now everything became little islands, without communication, without farther islands to which this

that one was on was a stepping-stone, a point with point, a necessary stage. Little islands set in their own limitless sea, one crossed them in a minute, in five at most, then it was a different island but the same: the same voices, the same masks, the same emptiness behind the words. Only the moods and settings changed a little; but nothing else. And the fear was both of being left behind and of going on: of the islands past and the islands ahead. (pp. 260-261)

We are again in the land where no one ever goes beneath the level of the persona, where people meet only in masks. In this existence, actions have no meaning because man is going nowhere, having lost his sense of a past and finding himself without hope for the future. It is the age of anti-myth, the world of the wasteland. Yet the voice continues, asking to be proven wrong, to be surprised, to be provided with something or someone to "string the islands together again" (p. 261). But the narrative structure, islands of thought breaking from present into past tense and back again, moving from person to person without continuity, echoes the thesis of the story. Fowles strengthens that thesis through his inclusion of a section from *The Waste Land*: "Hurry up please it's time. Goonight Bill. Goonight Lou. Goonight. Goonight" (p. 264), by means of which he connects Eliot's theme of the breakdown of communication in the wasteland world to his own.[10]

Within this wasteland world, Catherine, the tragic figure of the piece, can relate least well to the others in the group and is incapable of maintaining the persona of happiness they wear, having succumbed to the archetype of the shadow in its manifestation as despair. Her view of life is contrasted with the others. Paul, for instance, exemplifies "decency, mediocrity, muddling through" (p. 268); he copes with the future by continually "trying." Annabel, his wife, is the "presiding mother-goddess," although "slightly blowsy," indicating her connection with an ancient tradition but one that is greatly reduced in the contemporary world. While there is talk among them, the failure of language is as evident here as it is in Eliot's poem. Life in this wasteland full of the "tired rush of evening people, work drained automata" (p. 275) is life after "the harvest is in. All that's left are the gleanings and leasings: fragments, allusions, fantasies, egos. Only the husks of talk, the meaningless aftermath" (p. 275). The image of the harvest, traditionally associated with the vegetative myth of regeneration, now offers no hope for a new harvest to follow: only the "husks of talk" remain, language without the living symbol.

There remains, however, the power of the story, the repository of myth. Catherine is coaxed by her niece Emma into telling her a story about a princess. As Catherine creates her story of the lonely, sad princess, she also creates her own future (in much the same way that Fielding does in **"The Enigma"**), finding a myth she can become a part of. The story ends with the princess waiting for the return of the prince who has abandoned her, but with whom she will be reunited soon. As Emma returns to the picnickers, Catherine contemplates death, the future she had created for herself in the fairy tale. Like the princess in

the tale, she fears men and can find no one to trust and love, since the man she loved committed suicide. Thus, like Prince Florio, he has gone away, but he returns as Smiling Death, "alive, almost fleshed; just as intelligent, beckoning" (p. 298). In a last, meaningless act and under the influence of the shadow archetype, she dryly seduces Peter who has come upon her on his walk away from the others.[11]

Afterwards, Peter descends from the hills and, like the apostle for whom he is named, denies Catherine, claiming not to have seen her, as the Apostle Peter descended from the Mount of Olives and claimed not to have known Christ. Because he does not tell the others that he has been with Catherine, they leave her to her fate, assuming she has gone ahead. As they emerge into the clearing, they see "a mysterious cloud," which seems "feral and ominous, a great white-edged gray billow beginning to tower over the rocky wall, unmistakable bearer of heavy storm" (p. 309). The picnickers depart, "the princess calls [through the cry of the bird of Catherine's story], but there is no one, now, to hear her" (p. 312), as Catherine has apparently given in to her despair and committed suicide.[12] Only the black cloud remains to roll over the deserted meadow.

The dark mood introduced in the first story by the symbol of the ebony tower is now transformed into the symbol of the dark cloud. The characters in this collection of stories have failed, for the most part, in their lives because they have not reached out and communicated to their fellow man the love that is needed to turn the wasteland into the garden. David Williams sees what life lacks but is incapable of changing it; the old writer in **"Poor Koko"** learns through his failure to communicate with the young thief what the failure of language means for the future; the M.P. of **"The Enigma"** disappears in an attempt to create a mystery that is lacking in his meaningless existence, and we are left with "the tender pragmatisms of flesh" that form the basis for the relationship between the sergeant and the girl; and Catherine in **"The Cloud,"** having lost love and despairing of ever finding it again, commits suicide.

Although the general tone of these stories is dark, Fowles's view of life is not one of despair, as his novels *The Magus, The French Lieutenant's Woman,* and *Daniel Martin* attest, each treating protagonists who break out of wasteland existences into self-awareness and understanding because of their ability to take the mythic journey. As Robert K. Morris writes:

> Fowles's intent as a novelist, and as a writer of these fictions, is to strike the sane balance between art and life at a time when both seem vulnerable to excess, and neither seems susceptible to control. Perhaps only when art descends from the ebony tower will it be able to light up Fowles's cheerless 'bottomless night' and once more tell us, as it has in the past, something about life.[13]

Through the stories in **The Ebony Tower,** Fowles sounds a warning by showing us the despair inherent in contemporary life if we cannot take the journey out of the darkness toward wholeness and individuation.

Notes

1 John Fowles, *The Ebony Tower* (Boston: Little, Brown, 1974), p. 39. All further references to the title story and any other story in the collection appear in the text.

2 Daniel Halpern and John Fowles, "A Sort of Exile in Lyme Regis," *London Magazine,* March 1971, p. 39.

3 Interview on *The Today Show,* NBC, 11 November, 1974.

4 Letter received from John Fowles, 5 August, 1981.

5 For a fascinating examination of the subtle ways in which Fowles's translation of *Eliduc* possibly changes the meaning of the story, see Ruth Morse, "John Fowles, Marie de France, and the Man with Two Wives," *Philological Quarterly,* 63, no. 1 (Winter, 1984), 17-30.

6 Unpublished interview with the author, 16 March, 1984.

7 Letter received from John Fowles, 9 April, 1980.

8 In a letter of 9 April, 1980, Fowles says that the circle with the dot "was meant to be the universal printer's symbol for full stop, or period. The square, a space or paragraph symbol. But I will now claim your interpretation as conscious!"

9 John B. Humma, "John Fowles' *The Ebony Tower:* In the Celtic Mood," *Southern Humanities Review,* 17, No. 1 (1983), 42. For an even more positive view of the ending, see David Brownell, "John Fowles' Experiments with the Form of the Mystery Story," *Armchair Detective,* 10 (1977), 184-186.

10 Fowles has admitted the obvious influence of Eliot, particularly in "The Cloud." See also Raymond J. Wilson, III, "Allusion and Implication in John Fowles's 'The Cloud,'" *Studies in Short Fiction,* 20, No. 1 (1983), 17-22, for his discussion of the connection between *The Waste Land* and "The Cloud."

11 Fowles gives his view of the act as "not necessarily a final act of despair—at least possibly one of exorcizing self-disgust. It came to me first as that." Letter from Fowles, 5 August, 1981.

12 Curiously, Fowles says that he did not necessarily mean that Catherine commits suicide, remarking, "If she dies, who tells the story?" Letter from Fowles, 5 August, 1981.

13 Robert K. Morris, "A Forest of Fictions," Rev. of *The Ebony Tower, The Nation,* 13 September 1975, p. 215.

Frederick M. Holmes (essay date 1989)

SOURCE: "John Fowles's Variation on Angus Wilson's Variation on E. M. Forster: 'The Cloud,' 'Et Dona Ferentes,' and 'The Story of a Panic'," in *Ariel: A Review of International English Literature,* Vol. 20, No. 3, July, 1989, pp. 39-52.

[*In the following essay, Holmes compares and contrasts similarities and differences among the three stories, asserting that the stylistic devices, thematic development, and narrative mode of "The Cloud" surpass the originality of the other two.*]

The working title of John Fowles's **The Ebony Tower** was *Variations,* and Kerry McSweeney has shown that the short fictions which make up the volume do present variations on the techniques and themes of Fowles's own novels and on the works of other writers (101-50). One of those writers is Angus Wilson. McSweeney remarks that in its methods of characterization and narrative presentation Fowles's story **"The Cloud,"** in particular, is reminiscent of Wilson's fiction. McSweeney goes on to say that "the social and professional background of the characters, their fatuities, banalities, and self-deceptions, and the skilful use of children as reflectors of adult behaviour all recall Wilson's short fiction, as does the way in which the narrator of **'The Cloud'** slips in and out of the minds of several of the characters" (112). I would argue further that one particular story of Wilson's, "Et Dona Ferentes," bears such a close resemblance to **"The Cloud"** that Fowles might have been consciously influenced by it when writing his more expansive story, which was published twenty-five years after Wilson's.

It is interesting that Wilson's story also reveals the possible influence of an earlier fiction (in addition to Virgil's famous poem, from which Wilson's title is taken): E. M. Forster's "The Story of a Panic," which was written in 1904.[1] The basic likeness is that both stories depict the incarnation of Pan in an adolescent boy who disrupts an outdoor gathering of family and friends. As a consequence, a dramatic conflict develops in both stories between the primitive and the civilized, between anarchic sexual energies and the restraining influence of a refined culture. However, Forster and Wilson employ disparate narrative modes to develop this conflict along very different thematic lines. In fact, the parallels between Fowles's and Wilson's stories are closer and more numerous than those between Wilson's and Forster's. What is perhaps surprising, though, is that **"The Cloud"** seems no less distinctive and fresh for being so seemingly derivative than do the other two stories. Indeed, Fowles has built on Wilson's techniques to create a fiction which is not only original but also more rewarding artistically than "Et Dona Ferentes."

That all three stories bear the idiosyncratic stamps of their authors challenges the currently fashionable axiom of semiology that literature is the creation, not of authors who make deliberate choices, but, in the words of Jonathan Culler, "of writing itself" (38). Of course, it is true that every text is necessarily composed and read within a preexisting and partially determining linguistic and cultural matrix or "discursive space" (Culler 38). Every text is a potentially infinite intertext of codes and conventions whose presence is discernible in previous texts but "whose origin can scarcely ever be located" (Barthes 39). However, one need not demonstrate that authors create the linguistic codes they use or the contexts within which their works acquire meaning in order to argue that they can exercise deliberate control over how their works are situated within the intertext. Authors have the power to ignore some pre-existing conventions and select others more congenial to their purposes. Because those formulae can be deployed in an infinite variety of configurations, writers can achieve a degree of originality. Indeed, as Frank Kermode notes (102), the only meaningful novelty in literature is that attained by texts which make use of shared conventions, since communication is impossible without them. Such originality can be manifested even when authors focus narrowly on a small segment of the intertext, on one or more identifiable, precursor texts which can be singled out as influences. As I hope to show in this paper, even in such cases, intertextuality can facilitate the creativity of individual writers rather than negate it.

I

The similarity between the dramatic situations created by Forster and Wilson in "The Story of a Panic" and "Et Dona Ferentes" is readily apparent. Both stories show the effects of a primitive force of nature on a group of educated people who have planned a decorous outing in a picturesque rural location. Set in Italy, "The Story of a Panic" depicts the contagion of uncontrollable anxiety amongst a genteel set of English tourists: the narrator, his wife, and daughter; Mr. Leyland, an artist; Mr. Sandbach, a clergyman; and the two Miss Robinsons and their four-teen-year-old nephew, Eustace, in whom the god Pan is incarnated. Wilson's characters are Edwin and Monica Newman; their adolescent children, Richard and Elizabeth; Monica's mother, Mrs. Rackham; and one outsider, Richard's Swedish chum, Sven. The latter, Eustace's counter-part as an avatar of Pan, is the source of the emotional turbulence which disrupts the family picnic occurring in the Dorset countryside.

The ways in which Forster and Wilson depict the manifes-tation of an ancient god in a modern setting underscore the differences between the fictional modes in which the stories are cast. Whereas the identification of Sven with Pan is only figurative, a passing fancy in the mind of the sexually stirred Edwin Newman (188), the visitation of the god in Forster's story is presented as a literal event. Although never visibly present, Pan leaves footprints be-hind in the appropriate shape of a goat's (11). As do a number of Forster's short fictions, "The Story of a Panic" takes the form of what Lionel Trilling calls "mythical fantasy" (35) and exhibits the spirit, not of a mystical reversion to pagan beliefs, but of "natural and naturalistic piety" (45). That is to say, the supernatural element serves the creation of a parable illustrating the alienation of an effete, over-refined social class from natural sources of vitality and freedom (Summers 237-38; Cavaliero 43). Wilson is also interested in his characters' separation from nature, but he employs social and psychological realism rather than fantasy. Their methods contrast interestingly. While Forster generates dramatic irony by presenting a marvellous occurrence from the limited perspective of an uncomprehending narrator with an ordinary, mundane world view, Wilson creates an undramatized narrator ca-

pable of godlike feats of omniscience who nevertheless restricts himself to everyday experiences, who is content to record the thoughts and social gestures of characters leading unexceptional lives.

These differences in fictional mode and point of view aside, there is a basic similarity between the ways in which the two writers conceive of the elemental natural forces asso-ciated with Pan. In both stories the primitive energies manifest themselves as a peremptory homoeroticism which plunges all of the characters into emotional turmoil by threatening to overturn socially accepted relationships and codes of behaviour. The homosexual desire is overt in Wilson's story and latent in Forster's, in which the narra-tor condemns the friendship of Eustace and the Italian waiter Gennaro only as a transgression of social barriers, not sexual ones (16). However, as Judith Herz points out (57), Forster acknowledged retrospectively that in the sto-ry he had unconsciously implied the existence of an erotic attraction between the youths. Eustace's greeting of Genna-ro after the picnic is especially suggestive in this regard:

> Eustace sprang to meet him, and leapt right up into his arms, and put his own arms round his neck. And this in the presence, not only of us, but also of the landlady, the chambermaid, the facchino, and of two American ladies. . . . Gennaro, instead of attending to the wants of the two new ladies, carried Eustace into the house, as if it was the most natural thing in the world. (16)

The most significant difference between the two stories is that Forster's is more affirmative than Wilson's concern-ing the value of atavistic, Dionysian urges. As Claude Summers indicates (240), "The Story of a Panic" cele-brates, although not unambiguously, the transforming, lib-erating power of elemental nature. Eustace's possession by Pan is an ecstatic revelation of the unity and primal vigour that connects him to the universe at large. The vision, though, is achieved at a cost which the story does not gloss over: an inability to function socially. Eustace tells Gennaro, "'I understand almost everything. . . . The trees, hills, stars, water, I can see all. But isn't it odd! I can't make out men a bit'" (25). Nevertheless, a reading of the story leaves no doubt that the civilized adults who remain oblivious to the wonder of Eustace's experience and who try to suppress his new potency represent an insensible culture cut off from the natural sources of its own life. The sacrificial death of Gennaro is meant to underscore the essential destructiveness of this society. Fundamentally, the story equates the primal instincts with freedom and vitality. P. N. Furbank supports this conten-tion in avowing that the story communicated Forster's own "feeling of standing in the sunlight at last and possessing his own soul" (1:92).

In "Et Dona Ferentes," on the other hand, the emphasis is on the destructive rather than the redemptive potential of primitive desires. The story associates Edwin's lust for Sven, not with freedom and enhanced awareness, but with shame, selfish motives, and the suffering of others. There is no sense, as there is in Forster's story, that the panic and discomfort which the characters undergo is a deserved retribution for their denial of their own natures. In Wilson's story it is human nature itself, not the puritanical mores of polite society, which is dangerous. While "Et Dona Ferentes" never implies that Edwin's homosexuality is in and of itself base or immoral, its eruption has devastating consequences for his wife and children which are not compensated for by any growth on the part of Edwin or Sven. The latter's resemblance to Pan amounts only to physical grace and attractiveness, not to any nobility of character or largeness of vision. The response to that beauty in Edwin is not accompanied by Eustace's rapturous insight into the nature of things; it only reacquaints him with a shameful weakness. Whereas Forster imbues the relationship of Eustace and Gennaro with dignity and tenderness, Wilson makes Edwin's infatuation with the shallow and calculating Sven seem pathetic. One might summarize the essential difference between the two stories by saying that in Wilson's middle-age is reined in and chastened by the very force of nature which sets youth triumphantly free in Forster's.

II

It is obvious from the foregoing analysis that, despite a core likeness which suggests the possibility of direct influence, "Et Dona Ferentes" is markedly different from "The Story of a Panic" in many important respects. However, the case is quite otherwise with the very close relationship between **"The Cloud"** and "Et Dona Ferentes." The numerous parallels between these two stories give rise to evaluative considerations which do not emerge in a treatment of the first pair. In other words, because the stories are so similar, the characteristics which make one work artistically superior to the other come to the fore. I want now to demonstrate qualitative differences by showing how Fowles builds on Wilson's techniques to create a fiction which is in every way more subtle, complex, and rich than "Et Dona Ferentes," a fine piece of work though it is.

The basic narrative situations, settings, and themes of the two stories are clearly alike. Each dramatizes the interactions of a group of family and friends who are having a picnic in the country on a hot summer day. Set in France rather than England, **"The Cloud"** features a slightly larger and less homogeneous group of characters: Bel and Paul; their two small daughters, Candida and Emma; Bel's sister, Catherine; and Paul's friend Peter, his girlfriend, Sally, and his son, Tom. In each story, the harmony and beauty of the vividly evoked pastoral setting is intended to contrast ironically to the discord lying just beneath the surface of the human festivity. To highlight this disjunction, both stories mention that the colours of garments which characters wear clash with those in nature (Wilson 190; Fowles 221). Forces which break the ties of family and community and isolate the individual in the prison of the self are important themes in both stories.[2] These destructive forces precipitate crises which are punctuated in both stories by violent changes in the weather. In "Et Dona Ferentes," the thunderstorm signals the threat posed to the Newman marriage by the resumption of Edwin's homosexual desires. And in **"The Cloud,"** the storm which

looms at the conclusion symbolizes the dissolution of Catherine's identity and her possible suicide.

The two stories are also similar in associating the conflicts presented, not only with the common misunderstandings which arise on account of the imperfections of well-meaning people, but also with the destructive behaviour of extremely egocentric and shallow characters: Sven and Peter. Sven does not quite belong in Wilson's gallery of such characters as *Hemlock and After*'s Hubert Rose, who seems motivated by a transcendent power of evil, but, dominated entirely by vanity and greed, he is the only character in the story whose inner life is intended to be repugnant to the reader (193-95). Peter's selfishness *is* associated with evil by Fowles, through the symbolism of the adder about which he warns Catherine prior to sodomizing her (293), an act which she invites in her despair in order to defile herself. Of the two destructive male characters, Peter is more fully and interestingly developed than Sven, who is, despite the authentically stilted cadences of his English speech, a rather superficially drawn character defined entirely by callowness and narcissism. Peter, on the other hand, the energetic, professionally charming BBC producer with his eye on the main chance, is a fascinating variation on a familiar type in Fowles's fiction: the inauthentic male who is afflicted with what William Palmer calls "collector consciousness" (45), the tendency to categorize and control rather than to experience living reality. Catherine, the character whose views most closely approximate Fowles's, identifies Peter as one to "whom the real, the living, the unexplained is the outlaw; only safe when in the can" (242). Although he seems very different in personality and circumstances from Clegg in *The Collector*, Peter also exemplifies the banal evil which can result from an outlook on things which is essentially life-denying.

In neither story, however, are the dissonant human relationships attributed primarily to what could broadly be defined as evil. Sven turns Edwin's homosexual desires to his own venal purposes, but he does not create those longings; nor is he responsible for the inability of the family members to empathize with one another, although his disruptive effect on Edwin and Monica's marriage does occasion those problems. And in Fowles's story, Peter is even less to blame for all of the crossed purposes and unhappiness. It is not Peter but the death of Catherine's husband which causes her breakdown, although her morbid sensitivity to Peter's shallowness does increase her despair. But the sibling rivalry of Emma and Candida, the inability of Sally to minister successfuly to Tom's needs, the wrangling of Bel and Paul, and their failure to assuage Catherine's grief have nothing to do with Peter.

Both Wilson and Fowles stress commonplace difficulties which hinder their characters from bridging the gaps of age, gender, and differing values in order to make connections of sympathy and love with one another. "Fond as I am of Monica," her mother thinks, "I wouldn't be able to help, whatever may be wrong" (189), and, after Monica's hysterical outburst following Edwin's departure with Sven, her son chastises himself as follows: "I've failed again," thought Richard. "When I was reading about Stefan Tro-fimovich's death, I wanted to be there so that I could make him happy, to tell him that for all his faults I knew he was a good man. But when my own mother is in trouble I can't say anything" (198). In **"The Cloud,"** which is a deeper exploration of human estrangement, Catherine is not only cut off from others by her own individuality and the mortality of someone she had loved, but also, owing to the extremity of her condition, from the very continuity of her own experience:

> So now everything became little islands, without communication, without farther islands to which this that one was on was a stepping stone, a point with point, a necessary stage. Little islands set in their own limitless sea, one crossed them in a minute, in five at most, then it was a different island but the same: the same voices, the same masks, the same emptiness behind the words. (229)

One reason why Fowles's fictional investigation of what isolates people is more penetrating than Wilson's is that, in addition to doing what Wilson does, creating memorable representations of people failing to communicate, he shows what is problematic about the processes of communication themselves, including those of his own story.[3] This comes explicitly to the fore in Catherine's synopsis of Roland Barthes's *Mythologies* (244-47). Her discussion of the deviousness of sign systems and the corruptions to which they are susceptible attunes the reader to what is poisoning the interpersonal relations of the story's characters. The connection between the story itself and the types of communication employed by its characters is that all, Fowles would hold, are fictions. For him all human reality is metaphorical and, in some sense, humanly created, and hence fictions such as those which he writes are not really distinct from other, supposedly more empirical, interpretations which people communicate to one another ("Notes on an Unfinished Novel" 139). McSweeney expresses Fowles's position succinctly: "one's perception of reality, one's phenomenological world, is the work of the imagination" (110).

The problem with which Fowles's story grapples, though, is that the conditions of modern life have interfered with our capacity to be nourished and linked to one another through fictions, whether they be the images of the self which individuals project or, in this age of the *crise de roman,* stories such as "Et Dona Ferentes" and **"The Cloud."** Such fictions are of vital importance, but we have learned to think of them as decentred, inconclusive structures of words cut loose from any legitimating origin or transcendent authority. "We tell ourselves stories in order to live," says Joan Didion in *The White Album,* and her essay describes a difficult time "when I began to doubt the premises of all the stories I had ever told myself" (11-12). This is exactly the plight of Catherine, who is pathologically aware of the baselessness of all of the fictions which structure life. "One is given to theories of language," she broods, "of fiction, of illusion; and also to silly fancies. Like dreaming one is a book without its last chapters, suddenly: one is left forever on that last incomplete

page" (230). Her words foreshadow a convergence of the plot of her life with the plot of the story she inhabits, which is also suspended without resolution or closure. At the finish, with the storm impending and the others ready to leave, Catherine has still not returned from the forest. Her fate never is disclosed.

Unlike "Et Dona Ferentes," then, **"The Cloud"** turns its interest in the relationship between literature and life reflexively back upon itself. Wilson does raise this theme through the references of some of the characters to the books which they are reading, and he relates the issue to the difficulties which his characters have in relating to one another. But his treatment of this theme is less rich than Fowles's, and it does not extend to his own attempt to affect the lives of his readers through his story. It amounts to little more than the recognition that some people, such as Richard and his grandmother, Mrs. Rackham, live too much in literature to be effective in dealing with real people, while others, such as Sven, live too little in books and have under-developed imaginations as a consequence. Fowles, however, goes one step further and interrogates the capacity of his own story to enrich the lives of his readers. He makes **"The Cloud"** self-conscious in this fashion by creating within it a story-telling surrogate for himself, Catherine. The charming fairy tale which she creates for Emma is an idealized, ironic version of the story which she inhabits. Catherine would love to believe that the tale of the lovely princess waiting to be rescued by the heroic prince represents her own condition, which is also one of suffering and loss. But her fate is a cruel reversal of the princess's expectations, for shortly after Catherine tells the story Peter, the ironic counterpart of the prince, arrives to deepen her despair and, perhaps, to precipitate her suicide.

The implications of this conclusion with regard to the ameliorative or redemptive power of the story itself are obviously bleak, and consequently it would seem that Fowles's treatment of this theme is not only more extensive but also more pessimistic than Wilson's. The conclusion of "Et Dona Ferentes" offers at least the possibility that the forces of isolation need not prevail. At the story's finish, Edwin and Monica agree to take a vacation together in an attempt to overcome what is driving them apart. While less hopeful on the level of plot, however, **"The Cloud"** is more optimistic than its ending suggests inasmuch as Catherine's inability to sustain herself by means of fictions is itself embodied in a fiction of considerable potency. By casting her harrowing experience into the form of a moving, imaginative fiction, Fowles paradoxically surmounts the barriers to communication by affirming their reality.

Narrative technique is another area in which **"The Cloud"** is more complex and artistically refined than "Et Dona Ferentes." To a greater degree than Wilson's, Fowles's method of telling the story reflects and helps to develop the themes. It also bears witness to his desire to make his form an aspect of his content and to explore the relationship between those themes and the story which incarnates them. In this respect, the differences between the two men's methods of narrative presentation are even more significant than the similarity which McSweeney mentions: the extensive use of several characters as centres of consciousness for an undramatized voice. The technique by which Fowles's narrator provides access to the thoughts and feelings of his characters is more arch and elusive than that of Wilson's narrator. The reader has no trouble discerning the points at which Wilson's omniscient narrator enters and leaves the minds of the characters, and, despite his intimacy with them, it is always clear that his voice is distinct from theirs. But Fowles's narrator employs free indirect discourse more frequently than does Wilson's. Consequently, one finds it difficult to tell just when he is recording the perceptions of one of his characters and when he is speaking in his own voice. It is also hard to tell at certain points which character the narrator is inhabiting. Throughout the story the focus of narrative consciousness jumps without warning or transition from one character to another. The effect of such free indirect discourse, as Shlomith Rimmon-Kenan says, is to enhance the "polyvocality of the text by bringing into play a plurality of speakers and attitudes" and ultimately to dramatize "the problematic relationship between any utterance and its origin" (113). And the reader is unsettled even more because, as Barry Olshen shows (103), Fowles withholds crucial expository information about the sources of the tensions amongst the characters. Unlike Wilson, Fowles thus builds into his narrative method the jarring nature of the social intercourse which the story dramatizes, and he buffets the reader to make him feel the effects of the conflicts which set the characters at odds.

The means by which Wilson and Fowles tell their stories affect the way in which they develop their characters, and, again, as McSweeney observes, there is a basic similarity. Both expose and to some extent satirize the limitations of their characters, who are drawn from the same social class. But here, too, there is an important difference which, to my mind, testifies to the superior richness of **"The Cloud."** The relation of Wilson's narrator to his characters is one of omniscient superiority. He understands their foibles perfectly and can plumb their depths to expose the inner workings of their psyches. But one feels that this is possible in part because the characters are too easily known, too little more than the sum of their weaknesses. In fact, all of the characters, with the exception of Monica and Edwin, seem to be rather flat caricatures who are defined almost totally by their predictable blind spots and flaws. Although Fowles's narrator is also psychologically omniscient, his relation to the characters of **"The Cloud,"** like his method of exhibiting the workings of their minds, is, at first, more enigmatic. He is less evenhanded with his characters than is Wilson's narrator, whose point of view is noncommittal. Against this position it could be argued that Wilson sympathizes most with Monica, since, as Averil Gardner rightly notes, the story's Virgilian title represents her perspective (25). It is she who has a motive to fear the significance of the gift over which Sven maliciously gloats near the story's conclusion. The ring identifies him as the object of Edwin's passion. Despite the title, though, Monica no more embodies the story's point of view than do any of the other characters. Given her situation, her wasp-

ish shrillness is understandable, but it seems intended by Wilson to repel the reader. In any case, she elicits no more sympathy than does Edwin. Their marriage perfectly exemplifies Wilson's dictum that "apprehensions of moral ambiguity in relationships should be the stuff of short stories; at any rate, they are of mine" (*The Wild Garden* 98).

Fowles's narrator exhibits a less ambiguous attitude to his characters. It gradually becomes apparent that he identifies most with Catherine, who, as McSweeney notices (112), has an imaginative quickness and openness to mystery which accord with Fowles's existentialist values. And through her consciousness Fowles's narrator aims more venom at Peter than Wilson's narrator does at any of his characters, Sven included. And yet, despite a seemingly more restricted point of view, **"The Cloud"** has more respect for the complexity and otherness of its characters as representations of people who do not exist merely to serve the author's thematic purposes. Even the under-developed Sally, for whom Fowles manages to generate a surprising amount of sympathy, bursts the stereotype of the empty-headed, sexy starlet. She proves to be a rather ordinary, conventional woman who suffers because she is unable to interest Peter in any but a sexual way or to establish a real bond with his son. Out of her cultural and intellectual depth with Catherine, Bel, and Paul, Sally is also a victim of the isolation which destroys Catherine's emotional balance. In contrast, Wilson's Richard, for example, never seems more than the too-predictable stereotype of the bookworm who is ineffectual with real people.

It has not been my intention in this essay to denigrate the artistry of Angus Wilson, whose excellence as a novelist is well established. Wilson's canon contains works such as *No Laughing Matter* which are every bit as distinguished and artistically sophisticated as Fowles's best fiction. And one should note in fairness that "Et Dona Ferentes" was an early piece published before structuralism was developed and self-conscious fiction became popular, whereas **"The Cloud"** was written long after Fowles's apprenticeship as a writer. What I have tried to show is not that Fowles is a better writer than Wilson but that Wilson's apparent influence on Fowles no more resulted in mere imitation than did Forster's apparent influence on Wilson. Rather Fowles turned his countryman's methods and concerns to his own distinct purposes in order to create a subtler and more compelling story.

Notes

[1] I am indebted to Dr. John Stape of the University of Western Ontario, who first directed my attention to the similarities between "Et Dona Ferentes" and "The Story of a Panic."

[2] Peter Faulkner observes that the title of *The Wrong Set* is particularly apt because in all of its stories Wilson's "central concern is with characters who find themselves with wrong sets of relationships; can there be relationships, the volume asks, which allow and help all concerned to grow and develop, or are they necessarily props for some and prisons for others? The somberness which underlies the wit comes from the fact that the answer suggested is negative" (4).

[3] For a discussion of this issue in relation to the collection as a whole, see Holmes.

Works Cited

Barthes, Roland. "Theory of the Text." Trans. Ian McLeod. In *Untying the Text: A Post-Structuralist Reader.* Ed. Robert Young. Boston: Routledge, 1981. 31-47.

Cavaliero, Glen. *A Reading of E. M. Forster.* Totowa, N.J.: Rowman and Littlefield, 1979.

Culler, Jonathan. *The Pursuit of Signs: Semiotics, Literature, Deconstruction.* Ithaca, N.Y.: Cornell UP, 1981.

Didion, Joan. *The White Album.* New York: Simon and Schuster, 1979.

Faulkner, Peter. *Angus Wilson: Mimic and Moralist.* London: Secker and Warburg, 1980.

Forster, E. M. *The Collected Short Stories of E. M. Forster.* 1947. London: Sidgwick and Jackson, 1965.

Fowles, John. "Notes on an Unfinished Novel." 1969. In *The Novel Today: Contemporary Writers on Modern Fiction.* Ed. Malcolm Bradbury. London: Fontana, 1977. 136-150.

———. *The Ebony Tower.* Boston and Toronto: Little, Brown and Co., 1974.

Furbank, P. N. *E. M. Forster: A Life.* 2 vols. New York and London: Harcourt, Brace, Jovanovich, 1978.

Gardner, Averil. *Angus Wilson.* Boston: Twayne, 1985.

Herz, Judith Scherer. *The Short Narratives of E. M. Forster.* London: Macmillan, 1988.

Holmes, Frederick M. "Fictional Self-Consciousness in *The Ebony Tower.*" *Ariel* 16:3 (1985): 21-38.

Kermode, Frank. *The Sense of an Ending: Studies in the Theory of Fiction.* Oxford: Oxford UP, 1967.

McSweeney, Kerry. *Four Contemporary Novelists: Angus Wilson, Brian Moore, John Fowles, V. S. Naipaul.* Kingston and Montreal: McGill-Queen's UP, 1983.

Olshen, Barry. *John Fowles.* New York: Frederick Ungar, 1978.

Palmer, William J. *The Fiction of John Fowles: Tradition, Art, and the Loneliness of Selfhood.* Columbia: U of Missouri P, 1974.

Rimmon-Kenan, Shlomith. *Narrative Fiction: Contemporary Poetics.* London and New York: Methuen, 1983.

Summers, Claude J. *E. M. Forster.* New York: Frederick Ungar, 1983.

Trilling, Lionel. *E. M. Forster: A Study.* London: The Hogarth Press, 1944.

Wilson, Angus. *The Wild Garden: Or Speaking of Writing.* London: Secker and Warburg, 1963.

———. *The Wrong Set and Other Stories.* 1949. London, Toronto, Sydney, and New York: Panther-Granada, 1982.

Ulrich Broich (essay date 1990)

SOURCE: "John Fowles, 'The Enigma' and the Contemporary British Short Story," in *Modes of Narrative, Approaches to American, Canadian and British Fiction,* edited by Reingard M. Nischik and Barbara Korte, Königshausen & Neumann, 1990, pp. 179-89.

[*Below, Broich analyzes "The Enigma" in the context of the mimetic and aesthetic traditions of British short fiction, acknowledging the story's seminal influence on the postmodern, experimental short story form.*]

I

If you were to ask professors of English literature to name a few contemporary British short stories which are of comparable interest and importance to those by Jorge Luis Borges or Robert Coover, James Joyce or Katherine Mansfield, you would very often receive no reply. A look at recent research confirms the impression that either no outstanding British short stories have been published during the last two or three decades or that, if these works exist, they have so far not been duly recognized.

There are many excellent studies of the contemporary American short story and *Die amerikanische short story der gegenwart* (1976), a collection of essays edited by Peter Freese, contains about a dozen interpretations of American short stories published after 1960; but hardly any corresponding studies of the contemporary British short story have been published. Thus, Karl Heinz Göller and Gerhard Hoffmann finish their collection *Die englische Kurzgeschichte* (1973) with interpretations of short fiction by John Wain, Alan Sillitoe and John Brunner, none of which was published later than 1960. When Walter Allen published his survey *The Short Story in English* in 1981 the situation had not changed, the most recent British author of short fiction covered in Allen's book being Alan Sillitoe. Even the eight-volume compendium *Critical Survey of Short Fiction* published in the same year does not go beyond Angus Wilson in its chapter on "British Short Fiction in the Nineteenth and Twentieth Centuries."[1]

A similar lack of recognition for the recent British short story may be inferred from the most widely distributed collections of short fiction. Thus the popular *Penguin Book of English Short Stories,* edited by Christopher Dolley, which was first published in 1967 and last reprinted in 1987, ends with a story by Angus Wilson published in 1949.[2] There was a major change, however, when, in 1987, Malcolm Bradbury edited *The Penguin Book of Modern British Short Stories,* in which British short fiction of the last twenty years is well represented.

As far as I know, there are only two recent studies which devote more than a few pages to the British short story after 1960: an article by Walter Evans and a chapter in a book by Clare Hanson, both of which were published in 1985.[3] It is symptomatic, however, that these authors have, on the whole, selected completely different authors for their analysis. Clare Hanson restricts her chapter on "Post-modernist and Other Fictions," apart from Beckett and Borges, to Ian McEwan, Adam Mars-Jones and Clive Sinclair, whereas Walter Evans regards Angela Carter, Christine Brooke-Rose, John Fowles, Giles Gordon, Wilson Harris, Gabriel Josipovici, and Ian McEwan as the most interesting and innovative contemporary writers of short fiction in Britain. The fact that only one writer is represented in both studies suggests that either hardly any contemporary British writer of short stories has so far won general recognition or that no outstanding British short stories have been published after 1960.

This preliminary impression is supported by the apparent neglect of the short story by some of the leading contemporary British novelists. Some of them, like Iris Murdoch, appear not to have published any short stories at all, while others like Anthony Burgess or William Golding, for example, have written only very few stories which are neither well-known nor representative of their achievement as writers of outstanding fiction. Again, one gets the impression that the situation of the contemporary British short story is quite different from that of short fiction in the United States, in Ireland, or in other English-speaking countries of the world.

All this reminds one of the situation of English short fiction in the nineteenth century. The American short story of that period soon gained international recognition, and some American writers like Edgar Allan Poe even specialized in the short story rather than the novel. The leading writers of fiction in Victorian England either chose not to write short stories at all or, like Dickens and Hardy, contributed only marginally to the production of short fiction. A change took place, of course, around the turn of the century when Kipling and Conrad and, soon afterwards, James Joyce and Katherine Mansfield produced short fiction which was not only able to compete with the best American works in this genre, but also to innovate the short story and adapt it to the poetics of modernism. But even so, most of these authors cannot simply be classified as British, as they were born or lived in other parts of the world—Anglo-India, Poland, Ireland, and New Zealand. When, in the thirties and forties of this century, the United States again took over the lead in the production of short stories, the British contributions to this genre still remained worthy of attention, but were certainly less innovative and exciting than the short fiction published in the United States.

This applies even more strongly to the short stories published in Britain during the fifties by authors like Graham Greene, Alan Sillitoe, John Wain or even Angus Wilson. One might, therefore, tend towards the conclusion that there has been a decline of the British short story during the last few decades. This impression would be confirmed by H. E. Bates, who, when he published the first edition of *The Modern Short Story* in 1941, was still quite optimistic as far as the future of the British short story was concerned, but who in the preface to the second edition published in 1972 stated that the innovative impulse in British short fiction had declined.[4]

Of course it is difficult—and perhaps too early—to answer the question why this is so. Possible answers, however, may be sought in various directions.

First of all one may point out that there has been a general decline of British fiction during the last few decades, which the short story shares with the novel. The main reason for this development, in its turn, may be seen in an aversion to innovative fiction, which is often said to be characteristic of the average English reader as well as the writer of today. Thus David Lodge writes:

> There is a good deal of evidence that the English literary mind is peculiarly committed to realism, and resistant to non-realistic literary modes to an extent that might be described as prejudice. It is something of a commonplace of recent literary history, for instance, that the 'modern' experimental novel, represented diversely by Joyce, Virginia Woolf and D. H. Lawrence, which threatened to break up the stable synthesis of the realistic novel, was repudiated by two subsequent generations of English novelists.[5]

Malcolm Bradbury gives a similar diagnosis:

> where the novel in other countries changed and advanced, in England it retreated: there was, to quote from the title of another of the books, a 'reaction against experiment' which separated English fiction from other developments. In particular, there was a reversion to provincialism and little Englandism, an 'I Like It Here' philosophy that asserted, in effect, that Joyce and Woolf, Proust and James, hadn't or shouldn't have happened, [. . .] the serious contemporary novel was therefore being written somewhere else: in France, or Germany, or the States. The serious young reader therefore held in his hands Butor or Barth or Barthelme or Beckett or Borges, and the homebrew was largely offered either as light relief or as evidence that we could survive locally in the event of a holocaust.[6]

Both Lodge and Bradbury do not mention short fiction—which may be symptomatic—and moreover they have in common an assumption which might be questioned: that good fiction today has to be innovative, non-realistic, experimental. However true that may be or not, they offer one explanation to our problem. One might of course object that experimental fiction has partly come into fashion again in Britain in recent years; Annegret Maack in her book *Der experimentelle englische Roman der Gegenwart* (1984) has assembled an overwhelming amount of material to prove this point. Even so, few experimental English novels of the last two decades have won international recognition comparable to that of North or South American novels, and British short fiction seems to share the fate of the British contemporary novel.

Nevertheless this explanation is not sufficient. It does not explain why so many contemporary British writers do not write short fiction at all or do so only marginally. One reason is certainly that the media for the publication of fiction in Britain are far less interested in short stories than they are, for example, in the United States. Though there are some periodicals in Britain which do publish short stories, none is comparable to *The Kenyon Review* or *The New Yorker,* which in the United States have become institutions by having printed a great amount of more or less innovative short fiction for various decades. This would also explain why some innovative British authors of short fiction published their first stories in American magazines.[7] At the same time British publishers do not seem very interested in publishing collections of short stories. Edward Hyams undertook an experiment to prove this point by approaching, under the mask of a promising, but yet unknown young writer, some leading English publishers and literary agents and offering them a collection of short stories. In most cases, he found no interest at all, and in some cases he was even advised to write novels instead.[8]

A more thorough investigation into the reasons for this apparent neglect of the short story in Britain remains yet to be written. The same applies to a critical assessment of the British short stories written after 1960, a field in which the chapters by Clare Hanson and Walter Evans mentioned above mark only a very first step.

Neither of these tasks will be attempted in the present paper. Instead, a different approach will be taken. Against the background of these introductory remarks, I shall give an analysis of John Fowles' **"The Enigma"** (1974), which deserves to be ranked among the most interesting and best English short stories of the last twenty years and, what is more important, may be shown to be representative of the present situation of the contemporary British short story or at least of one of its most characteristic forms.

So far, Fowles has published only one collection of short stories, a volume entitled **The Ebony Tower,** which came out in 1974 and which contains, among other stories, **"The Enigma."** Thus, short fiction has remained a marginal genre in Fowles' oeuvre—a fact which is just as representative of the situation of short fiction in Britain today as **"The Enigma"** itself.

II

The beginning of **"The Enigma"** is deceptively familiar:

> The commonest kind of missing person is the adolescent girl, closely followed by the teenage boy. The majority in this category come from working-class homes, and almost invariably from those where there is serious parental disturbance. There is another minor peak in the third decade of life, less markedly working-class, and constituted by husbands and wives trying to run out on marriages or domestic situations they have got bored with. The figures dwindle sharply after the age of forty; older cases of genuine and lasting disappearance are extremely rare, and again are confined to the very poor—and even there to those, near vagabond, without close family.

When John Marcus Fielding disappeared, he therefore contravened all social and statistical probability.[9]

The reader thus learns at the very outset that the sudden disappearance of John Marcus Fielding, 57-year-old Tory M.P., is the central enigma of the story. Apart from the fact that in conventional detective fiction the central enigma is nearly always supplied by a mysterious murder, the following narration seems to follow closely the conventions of the genre, which demand that the major part of the story should be taken up by the investigation carried out by the police or by a private investigator and that all story elements should be strictly functional and lead towards the solution of the central enigma. In Fowles' story the investigation is first conducted by a special squad from New Scotland Yard and later on, when they have proved to be completely unsuccessful and no one really wants the mystery solved any more, by a police detective called Michael Jennings.

Short fiction has remained a marginal genre in Fowles' oeuvre—a fact which is just as representative of the situation of short fiction in Britain today as "The Enigma" itself.

—Ulrich Broich

Also, the methods of investigation are meant to seem familiar to the reader of detective fiction: the action mainly consists of a series of interviews and interrogations of the missing man's family, his secretary, and his colleagues. Moreover, Fowles keeps emphasizing the kinship of his story to conventional detective fiction by using terms usually employed in this genre (like "evidence," "red herring," pp. 204, 215), by lists of clues and possible solutions (pp. 198-200), or by intertextual allusions to other authors of detective fiction (references to Agatha Christie, pp. 236, 237 and to the "rules" of the detective story, p. 232). Also by locating the story partly in London and partly in an upper-middle-class country house Fowles is following a convention established by English writers of detective fiction as early as in the so-called Golden Age of the genre.

At the same time, the story creates the impression that it is also following another code: that of realist fiction—i. e. of fiction that does not draw the reader's attention to its own fictionality but to the social reality of a specific time and place. This impression is clearly established by the opening paragraph quoted above, which is a general statement on the statistics of missing persons in what resembles nonfictional prose. In the further course of the story the sociopolitical background to its action is more strongly elaborated than in detective fiction of the usual kind. The beginning of the story is set at a precise time: at 2:30

p.m. on Friday, July 13th, 1973; that is, one year before its first publication. The political background of this period, in which Marcus Fielding was active as a prominent Tory backbencher, is evoked by references to Edward Heath, Harold Wilson and Enoch Powell, to political scandals, affairs and other events of this time like the Lambton-Jellicoe case,[10] Watergate,[11] the Lonrho affair,[12] and the London letter-bomb epidemic of August 1973.[13] The political tensions between Marcus Fielding and his son Peter, who is characterized as "vaguely NL (New Left)" and "temporary pink" (p. 206), also help to place the story firmly in the period right after 1968.

Thus the story gives the reader the impression that it is following a familiar pattern and that it will end, as a true detective story ought to, in the discovery of a surprising solution to the enigma of Marcus Fielding's disappearance, and, probably, in a solution with a political point. But after Fleet Street has declared the Fielding case dead, after Michael Jennings' superiors are no longer interested in a solution, and after Jennings has interviewed all the likely informants, the story imperceptibly takes a different turn when Jennings sets out to interview Isobel Dodgson, the girl friend of the missing man's son.

Michael Jennings has ruled out kidnapping, political abduction or a fit of amnesia as possible causes for Marcus Fielding's disappearance. After realizing, therefore, that the only explanation may be a voluntary act of the missing man, Jennings has been trying in vain to find a motive for such a sudden decision. Apparently, Fielding played to perfection all the roles demanded of him—that of the reliable Tory politician, of a committed country squire, of a faithful husband, and of a good father—making it thereby improbable that he could have become a dropout of his own free will. By not allowing anyone to see behind the "facade" (p. 222) of his roles, however, Fielding also made it just as impossible to say anything about his true identity as if he were an actor seen only on the stage (p. 210). All the people whom Jennings has interviewed have confirmed how perfectly Fielding played his various roles, and none of these people is able to give any indication of that crack in the facade of this wealthy, successful man which Jennings is so desperately looking for. But in any case, Fielding seems to have been a man who was permanently keeping "reality at bay" (p. 208), who was not very much "alive" or "real" himself.

Isobel Dodgson appears to Jennings to be quite different, not only from Marcus Fielding, but also from his whole family and social class: "He had an immediate impression of someone alive, where everyone else had been dead, or playing dead" (p. 217), of someone who was able to be herself (p. 227). Although Isobel had met Fielding only a few times, Jennings expects her to help him to understand the missing man's psyche because being so "alive" herself, she may have recognized whether and how Fielding was "alive" behind his conventional façade and thus may give a psychological clue to the solution of the enigma.

Nevertheless, as far as evidence is concerned, Isobel can give Jennings only the tiniest clue; Fielding was last seen in the British Library before he disappeared, apparently a completely unplanned visit. On the evening before his disappearance, Isobel had told Fielding that she would be working in the reading room of the British Library the following day. Thus, the possibility arises that Fielding might have wanted to see the girl, perhaps in order to ask her to help him to disappear. But as Isobel did not work in the British Library on that day after all, they did not meet, which means that another chain of reasoning has landed in yet another dead end.

Isobel's next move in trying to provide an explanation is of a completely different kind and seems to subvert the realistic texture of the story which Fowles has so carefully been building up. She confronts Jennings with the following statement: "'Nothing is real. All is fiction'" (*ibid.*).

The policeman of course does not understand this sweeping, apparently postmodernist statement, and so Isobel explains:

> Lateral thinking. Let's pretend everything to do with the Fieldings, even you and me sitting here now, is in a novel. A detective story. Yes? Somewhere there's someone writing us, we're not real. (*ibid.*)

Freed from the restrictions of reality, Isobel then goes on to develop various endings a novelist might give to a story in which she, Jennings and Marcus Fielding figure as fictional characters, which she then evaluates according to aesthetic criteria. First of all she dismisses "'the *deus ex machina* possibility'" because it is "'not good art'" (*ibid.*). She then develops a scenario in which Fielding meets her in the British Library and she helps him to go into hiding, but she rejects this ending as well, because it is not imaginative enough. Finally she develops a scenario which "'disobeys the unreal literary rules'" of the detective story and does not end, as conventional detective stories do, "'with everything explained'" (p. 232). This breaking of the rules may take place when the central character takes on a life of his own when he walks out on the writer who has created him. In this particular scenario this may mean, according to Isobel:

> There was an author in his [Fielding's] life. In a way. Not a man. A system, a view of things? Something that had written him. Had really made him just a character in a book. [. . .] So in the end there's no freedom left. Nothing he can choose. Only what the system says. [. . .] He's like something written by someone else, a character in fiction. Everything is planned. Mapped out. He's like a fossil—while he's still alive. (pp. 232f.)

If the Marcus Fielding of this scenario realizes all this and wants to get out of "the book," he must logically want to disappear without leaving any traces, without the mystery being solved. "'If he's traced, found, then it all crumbles again. He's back in the book, being written. A nervous breakdown. A nutcase'" (pp. 234f.). This version of the story would, therfore, have to end with Fielding killing himself and nobody ever finding out.

The ending of the story, into which Isobel's version of how things may have happened is put in the form of a *mise en abyme,* is just as open. The Fielding case is never solved, and there is only an ending to the story of Isobel and Jennings: at the end, they have dinner and make love.

It must have become clear by now that towards the end, **"The Enigma"** takes on typical characteristics of what has been called the postmodernist way of writing:

—the dividing line between fiction and reality seems to be deconstructed,

—fiction turns into metafiction (and here it is of course symptomatic that Isobel is a would-be novelist; perhaps her surname Dodgson is even an allusion to Lewis Carroll, who anticipated postmodernist techniques and views in the nineteenth century),

—the *mise en abyme,* by which fictions are interpolated into the fictional 'reality' of the story,

—the open ending or rather the alternative endings if one takes the scenarios developed by Isobel into account,

—the deconstruction of the pattern of the detective story so frequent in postmodern writing.

But the impression that the realistic texture of the story is insidiously subverted by the use of these postmodernist techniques is misleading. Marcus Fielding is for Isobel by no means a fictional character who walked out on his author (like the characters in Flann O'Brien's *At Swim-two Birds*).[14] Rather Isobel is using a postmodernist convention from the realm of fiction in order to explain why the "real" Marcus Fielding may have walked out on the sociopolitical system which he had faithfully served for such a long time. It is therefore significant that she is using the convention of the character walking out on its author only as a fiction or as a comparison to make her point:

—"'Let's *pretend* everything to do with the Fieldings [. . .] is in a novel'" (p. 229),

—"'There was an author in his life. *In a way.* Not a man. A system, a view of things?'" (p. 232),

—"'He's *like* something written by someone else, a character in fiction'" (p. 233),

—"'He feels more and more *like* this minor character in a bad book'" (p. 234).[15]

Thus it becomes clear that the statement "'Nothing is real. All is fiction'" is itself a fiction—a fiction which helps Isobel to make two points: first she implies that fiction may very well be true to life and help us to understand reality, perhaps even more so than other forms of discourse, by its capacity for "lateral thinking"; and second, she suggests a psychological interpretation for Marcus

Fielding's disappearance. This explanation leads us to the philosophical assumptions behind Fowles' fiction. In *The French Lieutenant's Woman* (1969) Fowles compared the well-adapted Victorians to fossils, because they have lost their freedom and have ceased to be "alive." Sarah is the only character who succeeds in committing the "leap" into freedom, whereas Charles does not have the courage to "leap" and to become "alive." **"The Enigma"** is based on the same existentialist position. Marcus Fielding may have felt that he, too, may have become "like a fossil" (p. 233) by being "just a high-class cog in a phony machine" (p. 234). Paradoxically, however, his "leap" into becoming "alive" may have meant suicide for him, whereas Isobel and Jennings become "alive" by their mutual love across the boundaries of class, political views, and education.

There is even a third point behind Isobel's statements. Literature may become "fossilized" as well as life by following dead conventions, and it is by breaking the conventions that literature may become alive and at the same time true to life.

All this distinguishes **"The Enigma"** sharply from works of experimental, postmodernist fiction in which the conventions of detective fiction are radically deconstructed. As has repeatedly been observed, authors like Michel Butor, Alain Robbe-Grillet, Peter Handke, Thomas Pynchon or Vladimir Nabokov have frequently used the pattern of detective fiction in order to subvert the basic premises on which it is based. They have repeatedly tried to demonstrate that human reason is not compatible with the enigma of reality and, at the same time, that literature is not able to represent reality.[16] **"The Enigma,"** however, begins as a story in the realist tradition, then for a moment seems to topple over into experimental, self-reflexive and anti-illusionist fiction, only in order to return, admittedly on a different level, to the context of social realism with which it began.

Though Fowles "quotes" various postmodernist conventions, **"The Enigma"** resembles much more closely a story-within-the-story told by the detective Sam Spade in Dashiell Hammett's *The Maltese Falcon* (1930). Here, seemingly quite out of context, Sam Spade narrates how a man called Flitcraft walked out on his family and on his job quite out of the blue without leaving any traces, exactly like Marcus Fielding in **"The Enigma."** The point Sam Spade wants to make by this story is that human behaviour is very often not rational and that therefore the rationalist assumptions behind the conventional detective story cannot adequately cope with it. But there is another point to Sam Spade's story: years after his "leap" into the unknown, Flitcraft is discovered by accident in a town far away from his previous domicile; he has settled down to a similar job and to a family exactly like the one he left years ago. This seems to imply that, though the assumptions behind conventional detective fiction are too simplistic to help us to understand human motivation, there is a rational pattern behind human actions after all, and this pattern can also be represented in literature. Even though the missing man in **"The Enigma"** is *not* found and the enigma of his disappearance is *not* solved, there seems to be a similar assumption behind Fowles' story, thus connecting it more strongly with the earlier experiments in detective fiction by Hammett, Dürrenmatt and others, than with the more radical deconstructions of the genre in, for example, *Pale Fire* or *The Crying of Lot 49*.

III

For all these reasons, **"The Enigma"** can be called representative of contemporary British fiction and of the British short story in particular. There have been two traditions of British short fiction: a tradition characterized by social realism and a tradition characterized by experimentation and an emphasis on aesthetic, rather than mimetic qualities. The short story in Britain first acquired an international reputation during the period of High Modernism, when it broke with the tradition of social realism and conventional storytelling. But on the whole, in short fiction perhaps more strongly than in the novel, the strong point of British authors was not the experimental, the phantastic or the metafictional story but the story firmly rooted within the tradition of realism.

Even after 1960, in British short fiction works of both kinds have stood side by side. **"The Enigma,"** as we have seen, tries to amalgamate, though perhaps not quite successfully, these two traditions.[17] Nevertheless, the disquieting assumptions of postmodernism subvert the realistic texture of the story only temporarily, and in the end, as we have also seen, the realistic texture is established again. In this manner, the disturbing implications of statements like "'Nothing is real. All is fiction'" are "domesticated" again.

This "domestication" of postmodernism is to be found in many other contemporary British short stories, and in novels as well.[18] Readers may prefer this kind of fiction for its avoidance of radical experimentation, or they may find it unexciting in comparison to the more daring fiction by foreign authors. But one might agree at least on this: that these texts in their avoidance of radical positions are very English. This applies to **"The Enigma"** as well.

Notes

[1] *Critical Survey of Short Fiction,* ed. Frank N. Magill, 8 vols. (Englewood Cliffs, N.J.: Salem Press, 1981ff.), vol. 2, pp. 513-27. This statement also applies to the article "Short Fiction Since 1950," vol. 1, pp. 278-322 in this handbook. Even the dictionary of authors in this compendium fails to mention some of the leading contemporary writers of short fiction in Britain.

[2] *The Second Book of English Short Stories,* ed. Christopher Dolley (Harmondsworth: Penguin, 1987 [1972]) also does not go beyond Angus Wilson, Muriel Spark and Kingsley Amis. Since the end of the 1970s Penguin has also published a paperback magazine of contemporary short stories under the title *Granta*.

[3] "The English Short Story in the Seventies," in Dennis Vannatta (ed.), *The English Short Story 1945-1980: A Critical History* (Boston: Twayne, 1985), pp. 120-72; "Postmodernist and Other Fictions," in Clare Hanson, *Short Stories and Short Fictions, 1880-1980* (London: Macmillan, 1985), pp. 140-72. Another exception is Birgit Moosmüller's M.A. thesis

"Postmodern Aspekte in der englischen Short Story der Gegenwart" (typescript, München 1988), to which the present article is indebted for some valuable information.

[4] H. E. Bates, *The Modern Short Story: A Critical Survey* (Boston, Mass.: The Writer, 1972 [1941]), p. 9.

[5] "The Novelist at the Crossroads," in *The Novel Today: Contemporary Writers on Modern Fiction,* ed. Malcolm Bradbury (Manchester: Manchester Univ. Press, 1977), pp. 84-110, here p. 88.

[6] "The State of Fiction: A Symposium," contribution by Malcolm Bradbury, *The New Review,* 5, No. 1 (Summer 1978), 24-27, here 25.

[7] This applies, for example, to some of the stories by Ian McEwan (cf. Evans, "The English Short Story in the Seventies," p. 121).

[8] "The International Symposium on the Short Story: Part Four," contribution by Edward Hyams on England, *The Kenyon Review,* 32 (1970), 89-95, here 94f.

[9] All quotations are taken from John Fowles, *The Ebony Tower* (London: Pan Books, 1986 [1974]), pp. 185-239, here p. 187.

[10] Pages 189, 195; in 1973, Anthony Lord Lambton, junior minister in charge of Royal Air Force affairs, and Earl Jellicoe, Conservative Leader in the House of Lords, had to resign after *The News of the World* had reported about their connections with prostitutes (see "Pressing Hard," *Newsweek,* June 18, 1973, pp. 15f.).

[11] Page 208; the Watergate affair began in 1972 and led to Nixon's resignation in August, 1974.

[12] Page 201; for details on this affair, in which the Lonrho (London and Rhodesian Mining and Land) Company and the "adventurer capitalist" "Tiny" Rowland figured prominently, see Anthony Sampson, *The Changing Anatomy of Britain* (London etc.: Hodder and Stoughton, 1982), pp. 331-35.

[13] Page 239; at the end of August, 1973, more than 30 explosive devices, some of them contained in letters, were discovered in London. Though IRA spokesmen refused to claim responsibility for these bombs, the IRA was held to be responsible for them (see "The IRA Blitz," *Newsweek,* September 3, 1973, pp. 26ff.).

[14] Fowles used the same motif in *The French Lieutenant's Woman.*

[15] Words not bold in the original text.

[16] For postmodernist deconstructions of the detective story see Stefano Tani, *The Doomed Detective: The Contribution of the Detective Novel to Postmodern American and Italian Fiction* (Carbondale/Edwardsville: Southern Illinois Univ. Press, 1984).

[17] See also Malcolm Bradbury, "Introduction," in *Modern British Short Stories,* ed. Malcolm Bradbury (Harmondsworth: Penguin, 1988 [1987]), p. 13.

[18] See also my article on Fowles' novel *Mantissa,* "Kritik am postmodernen Roman im postmodernen Roman? Einige Bemerkungen zu John Fowles' *Mantissa* (1982)," in Hans Holländer/Christian W. Thomsen (eds.), *Besichtigung der Moderne: Bildende Kunst, Architektur, Musik, Literatur, Religion: Aspekte und Perspektiven* (Köln: Dumont, 1987), pp. 109-20.

Thomas C. Foster (essay date 1994)

SOURCE: *"The Ebony Tower* and *Mantissa,"* in his *Understanding John Fowles,* University of South Carolina Press, 1994, pp. 91-118.

[In the following excerpt, Foster provides a thematic analysis of the collection The Ebony Tower.*]*

The novella **The Ebony Tower** will be quite familiar in structure and substance to readers of *The Magus*. A young Englishman travels to a foreign, isolated locale, where he meets an obstreperous-yet-wise old man, who is accompanied by two young women, one of whom becomes a love interest for the young man. Through a series of encounters that are as symbolic as realistic, the young man receives the opportunity for growth and development, which nevertheless he fails to achieve. The surface details differ, as does the element of crisis and resolution, yet the basic stories are closely related. David Williams, an artist and writer, has gone to Brittany to interview Henry Breasley, an expatriate British artist, for a book on Breasley's work. There is a built-in antipathy between the two, since Williams is an abstract expressionist and Breasley is an abstraction-hating traditionalist whose main sources are distinctly medieval and Renaissance. Breasley, the very model of the artist-as-old-rake, has with him two young women, whom he calls the Mouse (real name Diana) and the Freak (Anne). The Mouse acts as amanuensis, drafter, and muse; indeed, the old man explains to David that her nickname is a corruption of muse, with the *o* a symbolic representation of the vulva. For Breasley inspiration is inseparable from sex, whereas for David Williams art is entirely cerebral and sexless. The Freak plays out the role of post-1960s libertine, providing the openly sexual element in the artistic masque as well as companionship for Diana.

At the same time the three residents play these roles, however, they act out another set. Diana is not only the muse but the imprisoned princess as well. She is an aspiring artist, a former student at the prestigious Royal College of Art, but she will not become an artist in her own right until she escapes from the isolation of Breasley's world. In this context Breasley's gruffness and impossible behavior cast him as the ogre, yet he has less to do with Diana's "imprisonment" than does the outside world, which has given her little reason to join it. This scenario casts David as the knight-errant who has come to rescue the princess; yet, while the role holds great attraction for him, he may be miscast. That such an interpretation is put on the situation and events by the characters is made clear throughout the novella: there are references to Chrétien de Troyes and Marie de France, to Robin Hood and the myth of the "old green England," and to unspecified princes and knights-errant.

From the outset the text announces that David Williams has stumbled into another world. The estate is called Coëtminais—literally, "the wood of the monks," the sacred wood—and stands as a self-contained refuge from modernity, complete with sham fortification in the form of a rickety gate with a rusty, nonfunctional lock. The rituals of Coët are essentially manorial, the rhythms traditional rather than modern. Breasley's longtime muse is Mathilde (yet another Fowlesian *M* name for books and muses), the subject of his postwar nudes and now his cook. Her husband, who spent those postwar years in prison for murder, acts as groundskeeper and handyman, and the couple appears exactly as elderly retainers of the manor. Mathilde is the only person with whom Breasley never loses his temper; Diana describes his attitude toward her as that of a vicar with his favorite parishioner.

The comparison points up the tendency of the atmosphere to veer into the overtly religious, the sacred wood being monastic as well as magical. The girls, Diana especially, use the estate as a cloistered, "safe" environment; Diana has come after a disastrous love affair in the outside world and now fanatically guards her privacy. Even Rennes, the nearby town, has become too much for her with its traffic, its population, and, particularly, its men. She recounts a tale of meeting two young men in town, then panicking that they would wish to come out to Coët, even as she realizes that she is being silly—"As if I was a virgin or something. A nun."[1] She has become a nun, after her own fashion, a nun of art rather than of the church. Denying herself the conventional pleasures of sexuality and companionship, she has instead become wedded to the institution that is Henry Breasley. Indeed, she has considered, is still considering, his literal offer of marriage. Such an eventuality would prove calamitous to her own art and even her life, the narrative makes clear: the artist cannot retreat into another's fantasy but, instead, must engage the world on one's own terms. It is this possibility from which David Williams must save her. Retreat into the cloister is one of the perils facing the heroine of romance, the other being destruction by villainy; here they amount to largely the same thing.

Of course, this being Fowlesian territory, the cloistered atmosphere carries with it a distinctly sexual element. The Mouse shows up at dinner in a high-necked Edwardian dress but without a stitch on underneath. Breasley's talk about the girls is shot through with sex, as is their own talk, especially the Freak's. When they all stroll off for a picnic by the lake, Anne and Diana make a considerable show of stripping down to swim nude and, with the old man's assistance, entice David to join them. Traditionally, of course, the questing knight is confronted with distractions and temptations, with sex or false romance featuring as prominently as self-doubt or indecisiveness. The two come together in David's case. On the last night of his visit he and Diana are alone (through the Freak's rather obvious stage management), and the means by which he can help save her, clearly, is through sex. David finds himself in the position of either being unfaithful to his wife, Beth, or being false to himself and thereby failing Diana's need. If this dilemma resembles that in Marie de France's medieval romance *Eliduc,* on which it is based, the resolution looks much more like Fowles: David contrives to fail in both directions. He pulls back from Diana's need when she expresses it, not out of marital loyalty but, rather, out of fear of censure (Fowles's antipathy toward the "suburban" dimensions of David's psyche is typical) and a fear of risking any part of himself. David, readers have already come to understand, must always play safe. Then, after Diana has had to accept his rejection, so that the act would be nothing more than sex, he proposes that they could still go to bed, thereby sacrificing any claim to fidelity. She refuses him, and so he remains faithful to Beth despite himself. There can be no sense of triumph or virtue on any level for David Williams.

Clearly, the moral universe Williams faces is murkier than the one confronting Eliduc. Whereas Marie's hero could perform his act of contrition by building an abbey to which both women in his life could retire, that outcome is precisely the one Diana needs to avoid. Eliduc wins the heart of the princess while serving her father; David can win the princess, but that outcome will prove devastating to Breasley, while leaving her behind will destroy her. In no sense can he have both Diana and Beth; the role of modern women (and they both have talents and career aspirations of their own to prove the point) will not lead to such a tidy resolution. Yet he also lacks the boldness, the courage in its original sense, the heart, to bring about a positive outcome. Modern through and through, David seeks acceptance rather than honor, is driven by approval rather than passion. The medieval quester embodied the aspirations of his society; the Fowlesian postmodern quester embodies the shortcomings of his. *The Ebony Tower,* then, stands as an ironic reworking of *Eliduc,* as Carol M. Barnum has pointed out, with the images and situations presented but reversed or undercut.[2] David thinks, "Would any decent prince have refused [Diana]?" yet refuse her he does. The ultimate, usually unstated, goal of the quest is self-knowledge and growth, and this is true of the ironic quest as well. Yet David's self-knowledge will not help him, for he finds himself unable to grow; he comes up against his limitations and cannot break through.

All of the romance elements, of course, have artistic implications, since all the principals are themselves artists. Breasley is a throwback to the past; he claims not to know the names of modern artists or to know them disparagingly. Picasso becomes "Pick-arsehole" and then "Pick-bum." The art of Coët is similarly old-fashioned: the chief piece is Breasley's immense *Moon-Hunt,* recalling Paolo Uccello's painting *Night Hunt* (1465). Breasley derides the abstract expressionism practiced by David and his contemporaries as overly cerebral and bloodless. He calls it unsexed art, which the Mouse translates as meaning that "abstraction represents a flight from human and social responsibility" (39), although Breasley's own version is more colorful, involving blunt references to bodily parts and functions. He has no use for artists who play safe, and he suspects David is such a one. David, as if to prove the point, has thought of his own work as "going well on walls," as being domestically acceptable. Breasley is the novella's version of Conchis from *The Magus,* the wise old man who acts as mentor, if cryptically, to nonplussed youth. Yet neither his teachings or Diana's peril can save David Williams from himself. The implications are clear: he is destined to be a second-rater, incapable of the ferocity, the passion, and the depth of feeling required of the

great artist. These qualities, so manifest in Breasley (whatever his deficiencies as a social animal), elude David.

Breasley is, in his idiosyncratic way, a seeker of truth. Whereas David desires chiefly not to offend—he is forever looking for the diplomatic way to make a statement, for answers that will gain approval, for the consensus view— Breasley says exactly what he thinks, without consideration for the views of the feelings of others. David constantly feels tested in his exchanges with the old artist, yet he never considers the possibility of Breasley's statements being taken at face value. If one is at odds with the artistic standards of one's time, the novella asks, must one accommodate one's opinions, or one's art, to those standards? Robertson Davies asks a very similar question in *What's Bred in the Bone,* in which his protagonist paints two anonymous masterpieces in the style of the sixteenth century then gives up original artwork. Significantly, both Fowles and Davies are masters of the big novel, throwbacks to fiction of the Victorian greats, yet both are also steeped in contemporary fictional theory and practice. In *The Aristos* Fowles calls the Renaissance "the last period in which content was at least conceded equal importance" to style.[3] Breasley's art, then, like that of Davies's Francis Cornish, recalls the Renaissance's insistence on content, on communal rather than private meaning, on shared iconography. In being so radically *individual,* Breasley ironically insists on an art that is less private, less a product of romanticism. He embraces truth, what the Mouse calls "human fact" (43), with the ferocity and certainty of Dante consigning enemies to Hell.

The problems of truth and knowledge are addressed in the following stories of the volume. In **"Poor Koko"** Fowles presents a narrator who is largely consumed by solipsism and who discovers the dangers of encountering the world. The protagonist-narrator, a writer, has taken up residence in a cottage owned by friends in order to work in solitude on his biography of the nineteenth-century novelist and essayist Thomas Love Peacock—a decidedly minor literary figure. Physically puny and myopic, he uses his intellect and his vocabulary as weapons of intimidation. On his first night in the cottage he is awakened by a burglar, who imprisons him, first in bed without his glasses and then in a chair restrained by sticky tape. After collecting his take, the burglar unaccountably destroys the writer's manuscript, notes, working text of Peacock, and typewriter. He follows this act by incongruously giving the writer the "thumbs-up" gesture the writer associates with mercy. As most readers note, **"Poor Koko"** is the only Fowles work in which the conflict does not involve gender as a major issue. Because these two characters are male, the terms of their antagonism are necessarily placed elsewhere, chiefly on age and class. Indeed, the older man calls attention to this fact by his choice of title: *Koko,* he tells his readers, is a Japanese word for "correct filial behavior, for the proper attitude of son to father" (176).

The battleground for this conflict is language: throughout their encounter the two engage in a war of words, with communication and books figuring prominently in their conversation. While the burglar engages in a lengthy monologue on his craft, on social inequality, on Marx, the narrator critiques his use of language. Certain linguistic tics catch his attention: the use of *right* at the end of sentences, calling the older man "dad" and the omnipresent "man." The narrator is most comfortable dealing with the world through the filter of criticism, whereas the burglar believes in language as praxis. For example, the narrator chooses to understand the other's use of *man* as a desperate attempt to speak frankly as "a kind of recognition, perhaps even a kind of terror of all that did separate us. It may not be too farfetched to say that what I failed to hear . . . was a tacit cry for help" (173). Of course, it is too farfetched to say such a thing. He has just acknowledged the near universal usage of *man* among the young, yet he goes on to assert that it must have special resonance in his own case.

Most hilarious, however, is his analysis of the use of *right.* The burglar appends the word to the end of a great many phrases in the way an American might use "you know" or a Canadian "eh." This does not, however, stop the narrator from deconstructing the usage as a special instance: "It means in effect, *I am not at all sure that I am right.* It can, of course, be said aggressively: 'Don't you dare say I am wrong!' But the thing it cannot mean is self-certainty. It is fundamentally expressive of doubt and fear, of so to speak hopeless *parole* in search of lost *langue.* The underlying mistrust is of language itself" (173-74). He goes on to see this supposed linguistic deprivation as "the true underprivilege." In so doing, he reveals anew his prejudices, almost all of which grow out of class and privilege: the young man's "working-class" language is not the narrator's "middle-class," educated language, so it must perforce be inferior. The narrator's language is meant to be elitist and exclusive; his books are for the literary few. That he can refer to his work *The Dwarf in Literature* as a potboiler suggests the degree of his removal from common readers, much less nonreaders. He suspects the young man of having a better mind than his language suggests, that the young man may even be playing him for a fool, yet he largely dismisses such possibilities. The narrator, in other words, can see everything except his own privileged position, and that exception blinds him completely.

The young man, on the other hand, approaches language as being within the realm of practical action. His accusations against the older man take the form of failing to communicate on a meaningful plane: "You're just saying words, man" (151), and "Man, your trouble is you don't listen hard enough" (162). That is to say, the writer fails at both ends of the speech transaction. His disdain prevents him from treating the younger man as a genuine audience, and he spouts a good deal of high-flown but ultimately irrelevant or useless rhetoric. Similarly, the narrator is indeed guilty of only hearing the younger man through his own highly subjective filter—of not taking the burglar's words as statements of his position. The young man uses his language to explain why he steals from houses, why he attacks property, why he would never "do" a museum. His reasons are sufficiently clear, if inelegantly phrased by the narrator's standards. There is even a sort

of poetic compression to his speech. When he binds the writer to the chair he also gags him, which is both part of the villain's ritual and a withholding of speech. It is only after the writer is bound that the burglar performs his ultimate speech act, burning the manuscript. This final act represents the young man's assertion of power—physical power taking on an aspect of linguistic power. He has entered into writing the Peacock book by causing it to be written again; the writer can bring no word of the restored book into being without finding himself reminded of this destruction.

The conflict between their attitudes toward language and the immolation of the Peacock study remind readers of the metafictional dimension of the story. This is a tale in which the basic material of fiction, language, is called into question. Before the writer is gagged the two discuss the possibility of his writing the young man's story or of the young man writing it himself. The narrator likes to believe his fate was sealed when he refused to write about the burglar, but in fact he was already being tied up at that point. Moreover, although they each say they will not write about the young man, he is being written about. He's a stickler for telling it "how it really is" (160), while the older man goes in for analysis, for imposing his view on his material. The young man may, as the writer maintains, want the word *magic* used on himself, but he wants a certain level of mimesis as well as a certain fluency; it is unlikely that the story at hand would meet with his approval.

There is a tendency among critics to see the narrator as one who has been brought from blindness to whole sight through his encounter with the burglar.[4] The evidence, however, is not encouraging. He has certainly gained some measure of understanding over his previous state, and he does acknowledge that he was guilty of not hearing at the time. Yet his hearing in the present is little better. He understands the young man only in terms of his own prejudices and presuppositions, and he attempts to shape the narrative according to his own elitist impulses, as his choice of title suggests (even his own friends fail to understand it). His failure to grasp completely the opportunity for change fits into the larger pattern of Fowlesian problematic. Nicholas Urfe has the chance but fails in *The Magus,* David Williams certainly fails in the title novella of this collection, as do the characters in **"The Cloud."** Even Charles Smithson's growth is open to debate, depending on which ending of *The French Lieutenant's Woman* one inclines toward. To leap too quickly at positive resolutions simply because they are available constitutes a danger for the reader of Fowles.

Resolutions become even more elusive in the final two stories of the collection, **"The Enigma"** and **"The Cloud."** The former plays off readerly expectations concerning the mystery genre. Yet just as **"Poor Koko"** undermines the thriller form it employs, so **"The Enigma"** simultaneously exploits and subverts the conventions of the detective story. And, like *The French Lieutenant's Woman,* the story emphasizes its fictionality, its made-up quality. When John Marcus Fielding suddenly disappears without a trace,

Detective Mike Jennings is called upon to solve the case. The story has all the elements of a conventional mystery: the important person who vanishes and leaves political and social as well as familial questions unanswered, the detective who needs to solve the case for personal as well as professional reasons, the upper-class family that resists investigation and must be handled with great sensitivity and tact, the loyal-to-the-death secretary of the great man, the beautiful young woman who may or may not know something significant. Fielding is the generic upper-class modern man: conservative M.P., board member for City companies, country squire, lawyer, honorary master of foxhounds; indeed, it may be just this generic quality that he wishes to escape, if disappearance or suicide was his intent. In the hands of Agatha Christie or P. D. James the story would proceed according to plan: the detective, Hercule Poirot or Adam Dalgliesh, would pursue facts in the face of resistance and mystification, and in the end, through either brilliant insight (Poirot) or dogged determination (Dalgliesh), he would unmask the villain. As a member of the official force, a special branch sergeant, Jennings follows more closely in the procedural detective model of James, with a major exception: while he can run down leads and eliminate some possibilities, he ultimately cannot solve the case. Characters—the rebellious son, the loyal secretary, the publicity-shy wife, colleagues and rivals—are forthcoming or not (in line with their own interests) to varying degrees with facts and opinions.

Jennings's efforts, however, lead nowhere until he interviews the son's girlfriend, Isobel Dodgson. Like the others, Isobel can (or will) provide no substantial evidence to help solve the case. The difference is that she enters into a discussion of the imaginative possibilities of the case, tracing out possible scenarios for what happened to Fielding after he left his briefcase in the British museum reading room. Isobel offers Jennings a course in lateral thinking, in treating the mystery not like a real case but like a literary text, which, as readers know, it is: "Let's pretend everything to do with the Fieldings, even you and me sitting here now, is in a novel. A detective story. Yes? Somewhere there's someone writing us, we're not real" (221). She then comes up with several solutions and explanations as bookish possibilities. The most intriguing part of her discussion is that Fielding, dissatisfied with the character part he was saddled with, decided to take up authorship and write himself into a new story, which necessarily entailed writing himself out of the old one.

As the metafictional dimension of the story expands, readers are reminded of her literary connections. Isobel works for a publisher and has recently been involved with bringing out illustrated Victorian volumes. More significantly, she shares her surname with Lewis Carroll, the man who dropped Alice into Wonderland. And Fielding also carries the surname of a famous novelist; indeed, one of the themes of *Tom Jones* is the question of identity and finding out who one really is—it too is part detective story. Until she raises her literary possibilities, his name is mere happenstance, but once she makes Jennings explore the imaginative possibilities, the way humans must each be responsible for writing their own stories, then "Fielding" begins to

take on added meaning. The story, in Isobel's hands, becomes the flip side of *Alice in Wonderland*: once the "main character," as she calls him, falls through the hole in the road, the ordinary world becomes a wonderland, a looking-glass world in which nothing is quite as it seems, in which one can no longer be certain about matters of identity and knowledge. When she suggests, for instance, that, "if our story disobeys the unreal literary rules, that might mean that it's truer to life" (223), Fowles uses her to develop the characters in his story and to critique the conventions that lead readers to expect, for instance, the tidy ending. He implies, through her analysis of Fielding, that characters do have a life of their own and that, like the lives of the readers, that life may be messy, untidy, without closure. She suggests, finally, that "nothing lasts like a mystery" (226), that Fielding has left his mark on the world by leaving it, which she compares to the absconding of the Supreme Author. From Fowles's existentialist position (which Isobel seems to share) the departure of God requires each of us to compose our own stories, our own lives.

The detective story, like any genre story, cannot stand much deconstructing before it begins to disintegrate. As Isobel weaves her fantastic explanations, the mystery (and Jennings's interest in solving it) evaporates, replaced by a love story between storyteller and audience. Jennings begins by seeing her as a sex object, noticing her breasts and wanting her in a way he hasn't wanted anyone recently. Yet, as she talks, she begins to come alive for him as a person, as an intellect and a spirit to reckon with. If he wants her sexually, she seduces him narratively. When at last, the mystery abandoned, they wind up in bed, the language refers humorously to his trade: she is "deprived" of her clothing "and proven, as suspected, quite defenseless underneath, though hardly a victim in what followed" (230-31). The narrative closes by suggesting that this surely unforeseen eventuality is the only concrete result of Fielding's disappearance, and yet it is quite enough. The relationship of Jennings and Isobel stands as the only genuinely human contact in the story, the only meeting in which the characters are really alive. Fielding has revealed a wasteland of intellect and feeling through his absconding, and Jennings has been appointed by New Scotland Yard to be the questing knight. It may be, as Carol Barnum has suggested, that the quest ultimately fails because Jennings and Isobel are too much of their own time, or that they "are not on the mythic journey,"[5] however much he may see her as a corn goddess. Yet the quester's true object is not the Grail but, rather, self-knowledge. In achieving a relationship beyond that seen among other characters, the two may have done what they can—all anyone can—to bring renewal to the wasteland.

If Jennings and Isobel represent the possibility of renewal, the characters in the succeeding story, **"The Cloud,"** demonstrate the wasteland world without renewal. Fowlesian irony dominates the story, locating sterile and vapid people in a little Eden; he upends T. S. Eliot's version by placing his hollow characters in a lush and fertile setting, thereby heightening the discrepancies. Paul and Annabel Rogers; their young daughters, Candida and Emma; their television producer friend, Peter Hamilton, and his current starlet girlfriend, Sally; Peter's young son, Tom; and Bel's sister, Catherine, on holiday together in central France, have gone picnicking to a secluded spot near a river—another of Fowles's famous "green enclosures." Yet this is a spoiled paradise. It holds not one but two snakes, the first a grass snake the children find early in the story. Later Peter comes across a poisonous adder then sees Catherine, who enigmatically allows him to make love to her (who seduces whom, and why, is unclear). The conjunction of the serpent, knowledge (clearly sexual), and death—Catherine has probably followed her husband in committing suicide immediately after the meaningless sex with Peter—completes this tale of the Fall from the ideals of romance. Within this framework of tawdry behavior and genuine pain, Fowles sketches out several familiar themes: the inability to communicate, intertextuality, the presence of death as both a driving force and a possible outcome, the unknowability of the Other, and the failure of the quester vis-à-vis the damsel in distress.

The conversations are, for the most part, shallow and misleading, as characters hide or misrepresent their true selves, speaking of trivialities. They also speak in a sort of shorthand, so that, when they discuss what has happened to make Catherine so unhappy, the reader is left largely ignorant and is forced to surmise her history from their fragmentary rendering. Even the narrative possesses an incomplete quality, drawing heavily on the characters' thoughts without attributing them as such. This technique, Fowles's version of free indirect speech, bears considerable resemblance to Virginia Woolf's use of it in *Mrs. Dalloway,* especially in its use of the indeterminant *one*:

> One liked old Paul, for all his going on. One envied old Paul; very nicely, as what in essence one would like one day for oneself, did Bel. She was so unobvious. The dryness, the mock simplicity that took no one in; fifty Sallys in her little finger; and a smashing pair of tits, that dress last night. (277)

> It must be close. One thought of it even with Emma, since he is there, also waiting, every moment now. That is why one can't stand other people, they obscure him, they don't understand how beautiful he is, now he has taken on the mask; so far from skeleton. But smiling, alive, almost fleshed; just as intelligent, beckoning. The other side. Peace, black peace. (278)

The first of these passages is from Peter—crass, self-interested, sex obsessed. The second is from Catherine—fraught with pain, also egocentric, unable to get beyond the Self, death obsessed. These two passages occur shortly before they encounter each other and suggest the mixed motives behind their sex as well as the more general inability of the two to communicate: since neither can get outside the Self, neither is capable of empathy or even of comprehension of the Other.

The two passages also reveal another of the narrative devices that Fowles employs in the story, the mix of verb tenses. He has already pointed out, in a footnote to *Eliduc,* Marie de France's free hand with verb tenses as a normal device of the medieval romance. And he has himself dabbled with mixed tenses at the end of *The Magus* and in **The Ebony Tower.** Yet he jumbles them more sytematically in this story than in any previous effort. In part such a strategy emphasizes Catherine's time confusion, in which the present is less alluring than either the past, in which her husband is still alive, or the deathly future from which he beckons. The present-past mixture also points up Fowles's more general sense of timelessness, which has been present throughout his work. His metafictional interest makes him aware that a text is always being written for the first time with each new reader, even as it already exists for those who have previously encountered it. This story, then, anticipates the unstable verb tenses and narrative viewpoints of his novel-in-process, *Daniel Martin.*

The story's time shifting underscores its use of intertextual strategies. The characters, members of the Fowlesian smart set, chart their lives with references from the Bible to *Hamlet* to *The Waste Land* to television programs. They understand Sally, for example, in terms of her standard acting role, the trendy, shallow girlfriend. When they spot the snake Peter remarks that it "proves it's paradise, I suppose." As Catherine watches some fishermen at the river, she recalls T. S. Eliot's "Hurry up please it's time. Goonight Bill. Goonight Lou. Goonight. Goonight" (247) from, significantly, *The Waste Land.* Like the speaker of Eliot's poem, she connects nothing with nothing. Her mind flits between the void of her life and the void of death. As she explains the theories of Roland Barthes to Peter, who is drawing her out for information for a possible television documentary, she explains that semiology studies the various sign systems by which humans communicate. Yet her tragedy is that she cannot communicate by any signs: the others are unwilling to hear her main story, about her husband's death, and they fail to grasp the signs she sends out. Only little Emma is willing to listen, and Catherine tells her a fairy tale.

That fairy tale reverses the intertextual strategies of the rest of the story, as Catherine charts her fiction with references to her own life as well as to fairy-tale conventions. Her story involves a princess who is lost and frightened of men. When she meets her prince she has no clothes nor a palace, so he cannot marry her. An old owl, who is a magician, permits her to have clothing or a palace, but not both, and, in trying to have one and then the other, she loses Prince Florio once again. They live in the forest in a kind of eternal present, in which they are both seventeen and in which she perpetually calls his name, the song of the oriole. Catherine tells Emma that she talked to the princess out in the woods before lunch. The story allows Catherine to dramatize her situation within a traditional narrative structure. She borrows elements from Ovid and the Brothers Grimm, yet the central features are her own: nakedness, homelessness, alienation, loss of the loved one, and the attempt at reunion with the lover. Emma notes that the story violates the genre by lacking a happy ending, but Catherine is incapable of providing one, since she sees no such possibility in the personal situation she is fictionalizing. Her final disappearance into mystery is couched in terms of the princess, the oriole, calling but no one being there now to hear her.

Throughout the story Catherine has been aware of her dead husband summoning her to join him, yet the final image arises from her story rather than from the larger fiction. While her fate goes unstated, the dark cloud—this story's manifestation of the ebony tower—suggests that she has joined her husband through suicide. Still, her fate remains forever suspended, in a now of indeterminacy, like the closing frieze of *The Magus*.

Like Isobel in the previous story, Catherine has the sense that she is in a novel, although she feels that the art form is no longer viable, that it sullies her. She is, then, both "writing and written" (279), both creating her situation and already created, contemplating the death readers do not see and having already achieved it. Like Sarah Woodruff, she exercises will in the midst of powerlessness, rejecting the text of her experience which society would write for her in favor of writing her own text, yet of course existing only in a text of Fowles's creation, in which her actions are not real but are, rather, metaphors for the real. That metaphorical level at which these stories operate may help explain the sense of thinness of which some reviewers complained when the book appeared or the general lack of attention the book has received.[6] Still, the stories in *The Ebony Tower* remain some of Fowles's most interesting and most thematically revealing work.

Notes

[1] John Fowles, *The Ebony Tower* (Boston: Little, Brown, 1974) 86. Subsequent references will be noted parenthetically.

[2] Carol Barnum, *The Fiction of John Fowles: A Myth for Our Time* (Greenwood, Fla.: Penkeville, 1988) 85.

[3] Fowles, *The Aristos* (Boston: Little, Brown, 1970) 192. Subsequent references will be noted parenthetically.

[4] See, for instance, Robert Huffaker, *John Fowles* (Boston: Twayne, 1980) 125.

[5] Barnum 94.

[6] The collection is excluded, for instance, from discussion by both Katherine Tarbox, *The Art of John Fowles* (Athens: U of Georgia P, 1988); and the revised edition of Peter Wolfe, *John Fowles: Magus and Moralist* (Lewisburg, Pa.: Bucknell UP, 1979).

Richard Bevis (essay date 1996)

SOURCE: "Actaeon's Sin: The 'Previous Iconography' of Fowles's 'The Ebony Tower'," in *Twentieth Century Literature*, Vol. 42, No. 1, Spring, 1996, pp. 114-23.

[*In the following essay, Bevis explicates the function and purpose of Fowles's allusions to the Greek myth of Artemis and Actaeon in* The Ebony Tower.]

The Ebony Tower (1974) has not exactly bowled over commentators on John Fowles. Katherine Tarbox found the book "so similar to *The Magus*" that she did not give it a chapter in *The Art of John Fowles* (2). Linda Hutcheon views the volume as Fowles's failed chance to break through the limitations of his treatment of women (Cooper viii). However, I find the title story more interesting than most critiques have, not because Fowles said that it demystified *The Magus* (Salami 136), but because he did not say how it mystifies the reader.

In *The Ebony Tower,* David Williams, a young English painter, art teacher, and critic, goes to hunt down Henry Breasley, an aging expatriate artist living at Coëtminais in Brittany, on behalf of a London publisher doing a book on his work. In the end, however, it is Williams who is brought to bay, shocked from his habitual complacency by the encounter with Breasley and two young Englishwomen attending him; the assignment turns into an appalling revelation of his shortcomings as an artist and a man.

> Coët had been a mirror, and the existence he was returning to sat mercilessly reflected and dissected in its surface. . . . Coët had remorselessly demonstrated what he was born, still was, and always would be: a decent man and [an] eternal also-ran. (101, 105)

Fowles's ruthlessness with his protagonist, perhaps the most striking feature of the story, rises to a crescendo here at the end. Williams, a fundamentally good, if rather tentative, human being, must no longer pose as an artist. He is forced to see himself as a fake, a mere functionary of "the ebony tower"—the whole pseudo-modern-art establishment of critics, educators, and abstractionists—made to self-destruct, to accept and even extend Breasley's drunken denunciation of his fair-mindedness as "sheet yellowbelly" (40). Qualities such as tolerance and honesty, turned inside out, are revealed as cloaks for his terror of vanity, of selfishness, of the Id; "safety hid nothingness" (102). Somehow, until these scarifying moments, he has missed the essential point that "art is fundamentally amoral" (105). Worst of all, Williams believes that he will in time rationalize even this experience, reinterpreting his cowardice as common sense and forgetting the truths he learned at Coët.

In a paper read at the 1978 MLA Special Session on Fowles, Ina Ferris argued that much of Fowles's fiction was a working out of the myth of Orpheus and Eurydice, and of an image from Eliot's "Burnt Norton": "Down the passage which we did not take / Toward the door we never opened / Into the rose garden." "Fowles's novels," she wrote, "typically centre on a rejected passage which may once again be found. They are second-chance stories" in which "a woman is central, for woman holds the key to the rose-garden" (5). But what is remarkable about *The Ebony Tower* is precisely the exclusion of this second chance, both within the narrative present and, the author decrees, for all time; the myth and the modern poem apply, not with the twist Ferris gives them, but with all the pessimistic force of their original forms. A woman still holds the key to the rose garden, but will not open the door for David Williams. Fowles gives us not only "the Jamesian theme of the unlived life" (Hirsch 18), but an assertion that his thirty-one-year-old protagonist is not *going* to live, that he has not the capacity for the artist's life.

On its surface, Fowles's story is an ingenious modernization of themes and characters from French medieval literature. The epigraph comes from the section of Chrétien de Troyes' *Ywain* that recounts the hero's journey toward his adventure. Coëtminais is situated in the forest of Paimpont or Brocéliande, where several of Chrétien's romances are set, and Breasley at one point discourses "on Marie de France and *Eliduc*" (51). At the conclusion of *The Ebony Tower* the author steps forward, in what he calls "A Personal Note," to emphasize the seminal importance of *Eliduc,* which he then translates in its entirety as the second story of the volume. David Williams—a would-be knight-errant on a quest to rescue a maiden from the forest (Cooper 150)—perceives his sojourn at Coët as a test, the "ordeal" of Celtic lore, but only half understands the nature of the challenge. The shape of his education is that of Chrétien's Arthurian poems, in that the protagonist must survive *two* tests of his mettle; one measure of Williams's inadequacy is that he is caught off guard by the second. Somewhat bruised his first night on the reefs of Breasley's strong convictions, he seems the next day to float into the calm waters of acceptance. Too late he realizes that "It had been like a trap. . . . The real rock of truth had lain well past the blue lagoon" (100-01).

This is all very well in a general way, though neither of the romances cited by Fowles is a particularly close or helpful parallel. Ywain, like Williams, is tested, and upon occasion found wanting, in the Bois de Brocéliande, but at the end he is "in contentment" (Chrétien de Troyes 64), whereas Williams is in hell, tearing at his own vitals. *Eliduc* is likewise tangential to *The Ebony Tower*: although they share a forest setting, a dead weasel, and the theme of infidelity, the characters and endings do not dovetail, and any attempt to take Fowles literally and make them do so will bind somewhere. Breasley associates the Mouse and the Freak with the "two gels in *Eliduc*" (51), for example, but although Diana *could* be Guilliadun, Eliduc's "other woman," it is Beth Williams, not Anne, who would approximate Guildelüec. As for the hero, Eliduc is too lovetorn to be Breasley, too successful to be Williams, and more mendacious and devious than either. The tales' conclusions are diametrically opposite; the actual outcome of the *lai* is demoted by Fowles to an adolescent fantasy, a cruel joke, in *The Ebony Tower* (100). The relationship of these romances to the modern story is almost entirely negative: it inverts them.

It may seem a futile enterprise to differ with an author about his sources, especially one who has already, in the "Personal Note" appended to the story, rejected critical acumen in this regard: "perhaps modern academic criticism is blind to relationships that are far more emotional than structural" (110). But there are other forces at work here than academic blindness; we have grounds for distrusting the author's candor on this point. The early realization

that Fowles was an artful writer soon became a suspicion that he played tricks on his readers. Foster Hirsch called him "a master of dissimulation" (19), and Peter Prince detected in *The Ebony Tower* "a hint of artfulness . . . beneath the art. . . . at times a faintly suspect note," though he did not elaborate (513).

The 1978 MLA papers heard this "faintly suspect note" more broadly in Fowles's work. Steven Cohan called *The Magus* "an implied attack on [his] reader . . . who is made to feel foolish and even a bit cheap for having believed in the fiction. . . . Conchis's smile of dramatic irony is actually that of Fowles the storyteller. . . ." (5). Patrick Scott found the references to Alain Robbe-Grillet in chapter 13 of *The French Lieutenant's Woman* "teasing and ironic in tone . . . the sign of playful dispute between two educated equals, author and reader, rather than . . . critical signposts to direct the hapless pedagogue" (3). More significantly for the point at issue, Scott pointed out that Fowles, for all his citations of Victorian literature in the novel, never gets around to mentioning J. A. Froude's story "The Lieutenant's Daughter" (1847), which, if it is not the source of, certainly has remarkable parallels in plot and structure to *The French Lieutenant's Woman* (5-6). Pamela Cooper has more recently noted an anti-academic theme in Fowles's work (9, 146).

It is important to understand the significance of the distrust of professors of literature and professional critics that Fowles shares with many artists. In *Daniel Martin* (1977), he treated this distrust as an archetypal antipathy:

> No creator can like critics. There is too much difference between the two activities. One is begetting, the other is surgery. However justified the criticism, it is always inflicted by someone who hasn't, a eunuch, on someone who has, a generator; by someone who takes no real risks on someone who stakes most of his being, economic as well as immortal. (104)

While the speaker here is Daniel Martin, it could equally well be Fowles explaining his relationship with the critical establishment, or Breasley's with Williams. On this question the personal and the fictive coincide. In a subsequent interview Fowles remarked that English critics especially tend to act like schoolmasters dealing with backward pupils: "And there's this weird feeling . . . that the true basis of authority must lie in the analyzing academic. Now that I hate; that I hate" (Tarbox 180).

Of course Fowles has every right to hold this view, but we have an equal right to trace its consequences in his work. Hence, presumably, springs that sympathetic identification of the author with Breasley that is the obverse of the undermining of Williams. The old painter seems a grotesque and pitiable figure at times, yet the plot relentlessly bears him out, even as Williams is being hoist on the petard of his own smugness. Breasley, like Fowles and Daniel Martin, does not care for critics in general: Williams has been warned to expect "baiting," since the old man has often "on past record" been known "to be hopelessly cryptic, maliciously misleading or just downright rude" (9-10). One manifestation of his malice has evidently been a kind of contemptuous playfulness with influence-hunting critics; the questioner who was given two artistic sources, one correct, one a joke, "for once received a partly honest answer" (12).

Such a deception—the logical outgrowth of attitudes shared by Breasley and Fowles—has particularly interesting implications for **The Ebony Tower.** In apparent contrast to Breasley, Fowles seems open and helpful about his sources, yet they prove less satisfactory on closer examination, and in view of the two men's deep-seated affinities in those areas both care most about, common prudence demands a second, more sceptical look. What we see then, I think, lying just beneath the surface of the story, is a substructure of Greek myth, not mentioned by Fowles in his "Personal Note," though more functional and more relevant than the Breton literature he cites. Since recognition of this myth opens up another level of comprehension, it may seem odd that Fowles would not point out that the story of Artemis and Actaeon underlies and supports his tale at every turn. Let me present the evidence for that statement before dealing with the question of motive.

The myth of Actaeon is best known from the third book of Ovid's *Metamorphoses,* where Artemis is called by her Roman name: Diana. In Greek mythology Diana-Artemis is primarily goddess of the hunt, of the moon (as Cynthia), and of night or the underworld (as Hecate). She is also Robert Graves's "White Goddess," the one original deity, not only a muse but the great mother of all muses. The huntress Artemis is militantly virginal, but "chaste Cynthia" is said to have slipped with Endymion, and the more broadly Diana is considered the more earthy she becomes—at Ephesus she was the fertility goddess—and the less essential her virginity seems (Rose 112-14). In *The Magus,* one of Lily's roles at Conchis's estate is that of Artemis, protectress of maidens, but her final appearance in the novel is of quite a different character. In *The Ebony Tower* Anne is reading *The Magus* beside the lake, and poor David Williams thinks it is a book on astrology.

Fowles links his plot and characters to Diana and Actaeon in ways too numerous to be coincidental. The Mouse's real name is Diana, and Breasley explains her nickname as "Muse" plus an 0-shaped vulva between the 'M' and the 'u'—a "crude and outlandish pun" that nevertheless recurs to Williams near the bitter end, when his artistic and erotic selves are disintegrating: "if one wanted signs as to the nature of the rejection" (101). Diana has her namesake's sexual ambiguity: she is "a rather attractive bit of seventies bird" (30) with a sexual past, whom Williams finds "bizarrely modest and handmaidenly" (7). "There was something preternaturally grave about her, almost Victorian . . ." (8). Diana tells Williams that she has become reticent with strange men, "As if I was a virgin or something" (86). Her devotion to the forest at Coëtminais, her belief in its mysteries and legends, her moonlit rambles in the garden recall the essential Attribute of Artemis-Diana in all accounts, summed up by the label *Agrotera*: "Lady of the Wild" (Rose 113).

The parallels between Williams and Actaeon—hunters who become prey after intruding upon a privileged domain and violating its laws—are more detailed. Actaeon ceases hunting at midday because the morning has been so productive, but wanders on through the woods and stumbles upon the sacred grove of Diana ("*errans / pervenit in lucum*": *Meta.* 3:175-76). Thus he unluckily sees the goddess naked in a pool. Diana splashes water that turns him into a stag, and he is torn to pieces by his own hounds. When Williams arrives at Coëtminais for a working break, he sounds rather complacent about his budding career: "things in general were shaping up well" (15). Though an invited guest, Williams cannot help feeling like an intruder as he drives down the *chemin privé* and lets himself through one gate only to find his way barred by another, which appears padlocked and warns him of a *chien méchant.* Reaching the house on foot, he can see no one about ("he had arrived sooner than suggested"), but, the door being open, walks in. Out back he glimpses "two naked girls" lying on the lawn "in a close pool of heat." Only after his eyes have "registered the warm tones of the two indolent female figures" for a "few seconds" does he return to the front entrance "Where he had first intruded" and discover the handbell, whose ringing Diana answers (5-6). Later he learns that "Coëtminais" means "the monks' forest"—i.e., another sacred grove or *lucus*—and sees the two women naked a second time, swimming in a woodland pool.

It is not idleness or voyeurism that is Williams's unforgivable sin against the place, however, but rather his retreat from the opportunities for knowledge that present themselves there. Coëtminais and Breasley stand for the pursuit of complete artistic self-fulfillment, whatever the consequences to anyone, ruthless egoism, an absolute freedom to know and re-create and develop, openness to all experiences and disregard of conventional values. Williams is too decent and careful for such abandon; he cannot follow where Coët beckons. His romance with Diana ends as quickly as it began, in the deep pain of reluctant mutual rejection, and he returns to his wife devastated by this blinding vision of personal shortcomings. This new self-loathing, released by the offended muse to gnaw at his spiritual being, is his counterpart of the hounds of Actaeon.

The latter stages of the story and of the myth as told by Ovid correspond closely. In *The Metamorphoses* the last of Diana's changes is to introduce fear into the hunter's heart ("*additus et pavor est,*" 3:198). One of the reasons Williams "bungl[es] the adventure of the body" is his sudden fright, as it begins, over the prospect of losing his sexual security with Beth if he sleeps with Diana: "And the terror of it, the enormity of destroying what one had so carefully built" (101, 91). The theme of his plunge into the abysm of self is timorousness; during the nightmare drive to Paris he becomes convinced that his "decency" has simply been fear of sin, his "tolerance" a "terror of vanity," his artistic and critical conservatism "a fear of challenge" (100).

Actaeon flees from Diana until he finds a still pool that reflects his new identity. There he groans and bursts into tears, for among his losses is that of speech; he cannot express his grief, nor, later, can he identify himself to his hounds (*"verba animo desunt"*: *Meta.* 3:231). Only now does the full meaning of Diana's taunt become clear: "Tell people you have seen me naked—if you can!" As Williams departs for Paris, he realizes that Coët has been a judgment on his whole being and mode of life. And language—the articulateness that has been a source of pride and a meal ticket—language fails him now. "Look, the crossed wires are mainly words," he tells Diana in their last agonized moments (94), and by the time he reaches Paris the draft introduction of his book on Breasley looks "hopeless" and "tawdry": "The banality, the jargon, the pretense of authority" (104; cf. Tarbox's interview with Fowles, 180). He feels "the sting of imminent tears" for "the first time in many years." Despite his earlier resolve to tell Beth everything, he cannot render Coët truthfully without destroying himself; full disclosure would be suicidal. Faced with her questions at the airport, he "surrenders to . . . abstraction. 'I survived,'" he replies (106). Breasley had attacked abstractionists (including Williams) as cowards.

As one might expect in a story about a meeting between two artists, the author alludes to a number of paintings—some real, some fictitious—several of which provide additional evidence that Williams and Diana are acting out mythic roles. The only work by Breasley hanging in the long room at Coët is the one Williams is most anxious to see, as he plans to discuss it at some length in his book: *Moon-hunt.* A neater summary of the goddess Diana's attributes could hardly be desired. The title deliberately obscures whether the hunt is by the moon, for the moon, or simply by moonlight, and the painting itself extends this ambiguity. To Williams it has "an obvious previous iconography": "Uccello's *Night Hunt* and its spawn down through the centuries" (17). In Uccello's diptych, the lines formed by horses and hunters, pursuing hounds and fleeing stags all converge upon an invisible point in the forest. But Breasley's *Moon-hunt* has "no hounds, no horses, no prey": only "nocturnal figures among trees," foreshadowing, perhaps, David's walk with Diana in the orchard under "a rising moon" on his last night at Coët (17, 89).

Night Hunt (also alluded to in *The Collector*) supplies the hitherto missing elements of the Actaeon myth: stags and hounds. These also occur in Pisanello's *The Vision of St. Eustace,* which Breasley cites as his "central source." The title of that painting is conjectural; except for the crucified figure in the distance, it looks like a hunting scene, with a horseback rider among dogs and game. And lurking on the fringes of the story is MacMillan, the "*chien méchant*" charged with protecting Coët from interlopers, a vaguely menacing beast who barks wildly as Williams and Diana return from their *éclaircissement.*

Such is the case for the foundation of Graeco-Roman myth beneath the modern story and the Celtic lore to which the author points as his source. We must now deal with the postponed question of motive: why does Fowles include the myth? And why conceal it, while pretending to be so frank about his literary influences? For readers of Fowles's other fiction, the second question is not difficult. The tactic extends the author's rhetoric from his characters to his relationship with his readers, of whom he has previously shown himself highly conscious and manipulative. It is a concealment such as Breasley might practice on Williams, or Maurice Conchis on Nicholas Urfe; it makes each of us the *ingenu* whose leg is being pulled by a slightly contemptuous creator. Beginning with *The Magus* (1965), Fowles's fiction has occasionally overflowed its borders, like a baroque painting, into the world beyond the artistic frame. Conchis's concept of "meta-theatre" provides the aesthetics both for his own "godgame" and for Fowles's handling of his audience. Conchis describes meta-theatre as "a new kind of drama"

> . . . in which the conventional relations between audience and actors were forgotten. In which the conventional scenic geography, the notions of proscenium, stage, auditorium, were completely discarded. . . . Artaud and Pirandello and Brecht were all thinking . . . along similar lines. . . . But the element that they could never bring themselves to discard was the audience. Here we are all actors. . . . I am an actor too. . . . That is why I say things both of us know cannot be true. Why I am permitted to lie. (366-67)

Like Conchis and other meta-dramatists, Fowles plays with theatrical illusion, questioning it, breaking it, brilliantly re-establishing it; he pulls his armchair up to the proscenium to assure us that the arch is only a figment of our imaginations and that we are not merely spectators but collaborators and backstage visitors. In both *The Magus* and *The French Lieutenant's Woman* he stops the narrative to expatiate on the problems of the novel as a genre, or to replay the last chapter with a different ending or two. In **The Ebony Tower,** some other implications of the meta-theater are brought into play: we are drawn into the action, used in the author's own godgame, and educated in the vulnerability and limitations of the bourgeois mentality. The apparent reader-surrogate, David Williams, is actually the prey. And in "A Personal Note"—when we might assume that the curtain is down, that the author is being forthright with us—we are, I think, deceived, or more precisely told a half-truth, about what we have just seen. And why should we believe Fowles, anymore than the young men in his stories should have believed Conchis or Breasley? The drama and the lesson of Coët thus meta-theatrically leap the boundaries of the story and land at (or on) our feet.

To return to my first question: Fowles's reason for including the myth is comparatively straightforward, its function obvious. The desire to expose and destroy Williams—not just the individual but the type—made the choice of Actaeon as mythic analogue a natural and effective one. Each is torn asunder by something of his own that he thought he controlled, but that turns upon him in response to a *force majeure.* His hounds do not recognize Actaeon in the stag and so devour him; Williams's mind, seeing him for the first time as "an eternal also-ran" and a "yellowbelly," is equally pitiless. His spirit is torn by a civil war pitting past against present, critic against artist, head against heart.

He has been living a lie—has not really been living—and no epithet is too harsh to be deployed against him: coward, slave, monkey, eunuch, impostor, cripple. The Muse, as Robert Graves puts it, "demands either whole-time service or none at all"; both Actaeon and Williams find that casual devotion is sooner or later disastrous. The frenzy of a pack of bloodthirsty dogs falling on their victim is an apt metaphor for the psychic savaging of David Williams.

Amid the fury of his self-denunciation, one almost forgets the ventriloquist-author making the sounds to prove that a man such as Williams has lost his soul to the Ebony tower. There is a wish-fulfilling zest in Fowles's demolition of Williams that Daniel Martin would appreciate; the critic-teacher-dilletante artist is annihilated by two days in the presence of the real thing. Again, comparison with the story as told in the *Metamorphoses* is enlightening, this time for what it shows about tone: the bland irony of the Roman, the terrible, almost crusading earnestness of the Englishman. "*Quod enim scelus error habebat?*" asks Ovid, introducing his version (3:142). Rolfe Humphries translates this as "What crime is there in error?" and Frank Justus Miller as "What crime had mere mischance?" But neither does justice to the subtlety of the line. "*Error*" in classical Latin meant primarily "wandering," secondarily, "straying from the right path." Rarely did it have the modern sense of "mistake"; that was "*erratum.*" A more accurate rendering, then, might be "What crime is there in wayward wandering?"

Fowles's handling of the tale provides a precise and shattering answer along the lines of Graves's warning. "Crime" in the legal sense is shown to be an inadequate concept, neither as profound nor as subtle as art requires. David Williams sins not only against himself, against his gifts, but against the Muse, who requires more than the part-time service of off-duty hunters and academicians. And of a sin against this deity there is, for an artist, no expiation.

Works Cited

Chrétien de Troyes. Trans. R. W. Ackerman and F. W. Locke. New York: Ungar, 1957.

Cohan, Steven M. "The Lovelace Figure in *The Magus.*" John Fowles and the Tradition of the Novel. Special Session. MLA Convention. Hilton Hotel, New York. 30 Dec. 1978.

Cooper, Pamela. *The Fictions of John Fowles.* Foreword by Linda Huthceon. Ottawa and Paris: U of Ottawa P, 1991.

Eliot, T. S. *Four Quartets.* San Diego: Harcourt Brace Jovanovich, 1971.

Ferris, Ina. John Fowles and the Tradition of the Novel. Special Session. MLA Convention. Hilton Hotel, New York. 30 Dec. 1978.

Fowles, John. *Daniel Martin.* Toronto: Totem-Collins, 1978.

———. *The Ebony Tower.* New York: Signet, 1975.

———. *The Magus.* New York: Dell, 1973.

Froude, James Anthony. "The Lieutenant's Daughter." *Shadows of the Clouds.* London: Oliver, 1847.

Hirsch, Foster. "The Ebony Tower." *America* 132 (1975): 18-19.

Prince, Peter. "Real Life." *The New Statesman* 11 (Oct. 1974): 513.

Rose, H. J. *A Handbook of Greek Mythology.* New York: Dutton, 1959.

Salami, Mahmoud. *John Fowles's Fiction and the Poetics of Postmodernism.* London and Toronto: Associated University P, 1992.

Scott, Patrick. "John Fowles, James Anthony Froude, and the Sociology of Innovation and Traditionalism in the British Novel." John Fowles and the Tradition of the Novel. Special Session. New York. 30 Dec. 1978.

Tarbox, Katherine. *The Art of John Fowles.* Athens: U of Georgia P, 1988.

FURTHER READING

Aubrey, James R. "The Fiction of John Fowles." In his *John Fowles: A Reference Companion,* pp. 109-17. New York: Greenwood Press, 1991.

    Summarizes and interprets *The Ebony Tower,* including commentary on the composition and critical reception of the individual stories.

Davidson, Arnold E. "*Eliduc* and 'The Ebony Tower': John Fowles's Variation on a Medieval Lay." *The International Fiction Review* 11, No. 1 (Winter 1984): 31-6.

    Compares the novella *The Ebony Tower* with *Eliduc.*

Holloway, Watson L. "The Killing of the Weasel: Hermetism in the Fiction of John Fowles." *English Language Notes* XXII, No. 3 (March 1985): 69-71.

    Sketches the influence of medieval occult lore in Fowles's fiction, centering on an image from *The Ebony Tower.*

Holmes, Frederick M. "Fictional Self-Consciousness in John Fowles's 'The Ebony Tower'." *Ariel* 16, No. 3 (July 1985): 21-38.

    Examines "the fictional reflexiveness" of the stories in *The Ebony Tower,* showing how "the artificiality of the stories as fabricated structures composed of words" elucidates Fowles's fictional themes.

Huffaker, Robert. "*The Ebony Tower.*" In his *John Fowles,* pp. 116-30. Boston: Twayne Publishers, 1980.

    Offers a psychological analysis of *The Ebony Tower.*

Humma, John B. "John Fowles' *The Ebony Tower*: In the Celtic Mood." *Southern Humanities Review* XVII, No. 1 (Winter 1983): 33-47.

    Discusses the Celtic romance themes of testing and of the green man or woman in *The Ebony Tower.*

Jesús Martinez, María. "Astarte's Game: Variations in John Fowles's 'The Enigma'." *Twentieth Century Literature* 42, No. 1 (Spring 1996): 124-44.

Elucidates the means by which "The Enigma" subverts conventions and readers's expectations of the detective-story genre.

McSweeney, Kerry. "John Fowles's Variations in *The Ebony Tower.*" *Journal of Modern Language* 8, No. 2 (1980/1981): 303-24.

Investigates thematic, artistic, and narrative parallels between *The Ebony Tower* and Fowles's preceding novels.

Morse, Ruth. "John Fowles, Marie de France, and the Man with Two Wives." *Philological Quarterly* 63, No. 1 (Winter 1984): 17-30.

Explores "emotional" connections among *Eliduc,* Fowles's "accurate" translation of it, and his version of it in *The Ebony Tower.*

Wilson, Raymond J., III. "Allusion and Implication in John Fowles's 'The Cloud'." *Studies in Short Fiction* 20, No. 1 (Winter 1983): 17-22.

Details the significance of allusions to T. S. Eliot's *The Wasteland* in "The Cloud" with respect to lightening the story's dark mood.

Additional coverage of Fowles's life and career is contained in the following sources published by The Gale Group: *Concise Dictionary of British Literary Biography, 1960 to Present*; *Contemporary Authors,* **Vols. 5-8;** *Contemporary Authors New Revision Series,* **Vols. 25, 71;** *Contemporary Literary Criticism,* **Vols. 1, 2, 3, 4, 6, 9, 10, 15, 33, 87;** *Dictionary of Literary Biography,* **Vols. 14, 139;** *DISCovering Authors: British*; *DISCovering Authors: Canadian*; *DISCovering Authors: Most-Studied Authors Module*; *Major 20th-Century Writers,* **Vol. 1;** **and** *Something about the Author,* **Vol. 22.**

Vernon Lee
1856–1935

(Pseudonym of Violet Paget) English short story writer, novelist, essayist, biographer, dramatist, and critic.

INTRODUCTION

Best known for her perceptive essays on intellectual and cultural trends in the early twentieth century, Lee also wrote short stories that employ historical milieus and supernatural themes. Some critics have compared her work to that of Henry James; others have noted the influence of E. T. A. Hoffmann on her fantastic stories. Although she has not gained a substantial readership in modern times, Lee is recalled in memoirs and biographies as one of the best minds of her day. According to Irene Cooper Willis, "Vernon Lee was a remarkable personality, deeply learned and eloquent, with far reaching historical sympathies."

Biographical Information

Lee was born in France to British parents. During her childhood, her family traveled extensively throughout Europe; as a consequence of this upbringing, she became intimate with various languages and cultures. Eventually her family settled in Florence, and Lee began applying the precocious learning of her adolescence to the study of Italian art. In 1881 Lee visited London where she began to establish herself in English literary society. She became acquainted with many of the prominent literary figures of the time, including Dante Gabriel Rosetti, Oscar Wilde, Walter Pater, and Henry James, and her writing often satirized the aesthetic movement of which they were a part. Lee continued writing essays and stories well into the twentieth century, using her work to examine the changing intellectual trends of her era.

Major Works of Short Fiction

Lee published a limited number of short stories, most of which are characterized by the use of supernatural themes and historical backgrounds. *Hauntings,* her first and most popular collection of short fiction, was published in 1890. In these transcendent tales, Lee examines the intrusion of the past upon the present. The detailed historical background displayed in these stories lends them that sense of distance from contemporary life that Lee believed essential to works of supernatural fantasy. For example, in the story "Oke of Okehurst," a young painter is commissioned to paint the portrait of Mrs. Oke, the troubled wife of a country squire. He discovers that both the wife and her

husband are obsessed by a family tragedy of several centuries earlier, when the husband's ancestor had murdered the lover of his wife. Insisting that she is romantically involved with the ghost of the dead lover, Mrs. Oke drives her husband into a homicidal rage in which he kills both her and himself. Likewise, in "Amour dure" a Polish scholar visiting Italy falls in love with an historical seductress, an attraction that later proves fatal for the scholar.

Critical Reception

Scholars have provided mixed critical reactions to Lee's short fiction. Most critics praise her aesthetic and intellectual approach to the time and subjects of her work. John Clute found Lee's short fiction more appealing than her work in other genres, noting that her stories contain "hints of something like greatness." Others, however, have derided her stories for a lack of originality and imagination. Nonetheless, while critical assessment of her short fiction has been slight, Lee's stature as an important Victorian intellectual continues to attract the attention of scholars.

PRINCIPAL WORKS

Short Fiction

Hauntings 1890
Ottilie (short novel) 1893
Pope Jacynth and Other Fantastic Tales 1904
The Snake Lady, and Other Stories 1954

Other Major Works

Studies of the Eighteenth Century in Italy (essays) 1880
Belcaro (essays) 1881
The Countess of Albany (biography) 1884
Euphorion (essays) 1884
Miss Brown (novel) 1884
Baldwin (prose dialogues) 1886
Juvenilia (essays) 1887
Renaissance Fancies and Studies (essays) 1895
Limbo, and Other Essays (essays) 1897
Genius Loci (travel essays) 1899
Ariadne in Mantua (drama) 1903
Penelope Brandling (novel) 1903
The Enchanted Woods (travel essays) 1905
Gospels of Anarchy (essays) 1908
The Sentimental Traveller (travel essays) 1908
Vital Lies (essays) 1912
Louis Norbert (novel) 1914
The Tower of Mirrors (travel essays) 1914
Satan the Waster (prose dialogue) 1920
The Handling of Words (essays) 1923
The Golden Keys (travel essays) 1925
Music and Lovers (essays) 1932

CRITICISM

Anthenaeum (review date 1904)

SOURCE: A review of *Pope Jacynth and Other Fantastic Tales,* in *Anthenaeum,* Vol. 2, No. 4027, December 31, 1904, p. 903.

[*In the following essay, the critic offers a negative assessment of the stories in* Pope Jacynth and Other Fantastic Tales.]

The lady who writes under the pen-name of Vernon Lee has a well-defined literary personality; and these tales are much what those familiar with her work might have expected from her. They belong to that order of tale which has affinities with the literary hybrid called prose-poetry—a form which betrays its hybrid nature by its sterility, its inability to beget vital literary offspring. The poetic affinities of that order of tale are specially evident in this—that instead of the treatment being a vehicle for the tale, the tale is a vehicle for the treatment. We are all familiar with such poems as the 'Isabella,' where Boccaccio's tale is retold merely to afford a theme for Keats's luxuriant imagery and imagination. Any love-tale would have sufficed as well, but Keats happened to choose this. Precisely the same is the function which the story subserves in such tales as these; just such its relative importance. It is an excuse for workmanship. The writer (it would seem) is not specially interested in the story as a story; he sees in it an opportunity for his sense of arrangement and symmetry, his grace of narration—above all, for the display of his style. It is, of course, a legitimate branch of art—but about its value one may fairly debate. In its nature it is very self-conscious; its simplicity (when it is simple) is an elaborate simplicity; and even its perfection is a frozen or carven perfection. One may admire, but one is not moved. One may have a certain tepid pleasure, but one is scarcely interested. It seems to belong to the region of conscientious dilettantism, of refined trifling, and one views it as one views an object of *virtù*. Such eclipse of matter by manner in a tale appears to require nothing less than the splendid compensations of poetry.

Vernon Lee's tales are a typical specimen of their class. She is too trained an artist for them to be less than artistic. Though they are called "fantastic," only two of them have the special quality which readers of stories usually associate with the adjective. The others would perhaps be better described by the term "fanciful." Those two have the element of the supernatural. But in Vernon Lee's style the supernatural loses all trace of weirdness. It remains simply exotic. "Exotic" is, indeed, the very word to describe all these tales. The themes are chosen, with one exception, from those mediæval legends which are the favoured treasure-house for all lovers of the exotic, and are handled in the style of cultured strangeness which we have learnt to expect in such *réchauffés* of mediæval imaginings. It is as different as possible from the spirit of the legends themselves; but that contrast is part of the exotic effect at which the writers aim.

It is on style, indeed, that we must chiefly dwell—for style is the most prominent fact in the book. It has the contrasts which we note between the spirit of the legends and their handling. An artful and conscious simplicity in manner and structure is combined with an ostentatious richness and research of diction. It is a style like enamels and mosaic in its sensuous and studious selection—a union of flamboyance and restraint, which would be flamboyant were the taste less sensitive, and would be restrained were the taste less sensuous. It is a style which the example of Mr. Pater (to whose school it may be said to belong) has linked in memory with the spirit and suggestions of the Italian Renascence—an eclectic style which does not escape the peril of eclecticism—the lack of central flame, of the living spirit. It perfectly harmonizes with the treatment; and the first two tales in particular and successful in their kind—curiously and artificially wrought productions of the decadent spirit at sedulous play. The last tale has another note—the satirical and ironic; very slight, it suggests that the writer might do well in this manner. But, as a whole, the book leaves the impression of cultivated trifling. It is without the imaginative magic which might have lifted it into a higher region.

Horace Gregory (essay date 1954)

SOURCE: "The Romantic Inventions of Vernon Lee," in *The Snake Lady and Other Stories,* by Vernon Lee, Grove Press, 1954, pp. 6-24.

[*In the following excerpt from the introduction to Lee's short story collection, Gregory examines thematic and stylistic aspects of Lee's fiction.*]

It was a clever, bookish, studious child who in 1880 had written *Studies of the Eighteenth Century in Italy,* and she was a child born of a mother who outlived, victoriously it seemed, two less spirited, less vigorous husbands; Violet Paget was the daughter of the second union and was born in Boulogne, France in 1856. The household soon moved to Italy and a son by the first marriage, Eugene Lee-Hamilton shared it.

Lee-Hamilton was both the light and shadow of the family. Like the sons of some few other old families of England's northern boundaries, he had been trained to enter the diplomatic services. From the time of the ambitiously successful Tudor kings sons of these families stood at variance from the policies of Court and Parliament; their conservatism held claims to an ancient heritage; it was their privilege, so they felt, to be first critics of whoever became Prime Minister and to accept lesser posts in the foreign service as a duty to an elder disestablished order. Wilfred Blunt was one of these and so was Eugene Lee-Hamilton; like Blunt he was a junior member of the British legation in Paris when the city fell to the Germans in 1870. The generals of the German occupation drove members of the British Embassy out of Paris into refuge and starvation; in this sense the War of 1870 was a preview of what happened during World War II, and Lee-Hamilton, as he escaped to Portugal and later to his mother and half-sister in Florence, was among those who were not equal to the occasion. He took to a wheeled bed from which he refused to move for twenty years; he was the invalided Phoenix of the family, its poet, its commentator on world and literary affairs; when he chose to speak, and his physicians permitted him to speak only at far-spaced and briefest intervals, his words were of first and of final authority. His half-sister was both his guardian and his servant.

Lee-Hamilton was not fated to die in his wheeled bed; when his twenty-year reign over it had been completed, he rose from his rest, visited the United States and married a young English woman; they had one child, a daughter, who died in infancy and shortly after her death, Lee-Hamilton languished into the grave. Edith Wharton, inaccurate as she was in reporting the bald facts and dates concerning her acquaintance with Lee-Hamilton, was correct when she wrote of the extremes of his invalidism and his vigor. When he visited her on his journey to the United States, he talked and rode a bicycle in and around her Long Island estate as though he were possessed by the spirit of an eighteen year old boy; he was supremely gay. The professional psychiatrist may find ready answers to the peculiarities of his behavior.

His half-sister was in a position to know the extremes of his temperament well. In his passion for literary distinction he published two books of verse and was among the first of Violet Paget's serious critics; an invalid has time for careful reading and critical meditation. There can be no doubt that the relationship between half brother and sister was of daily, almost hourly intimacy; there is no need to think that their interviews were always those of painful anxiety or of sickroom boredom; moments of lassitude and speculations on guilt and love were reserved for Lee-Hamilton's pallid sonnets. After reading his thoroughly literary exercises in verse, done in the approved manner of Walter Pater's young men recently arrived from Oxford, after summing up a few facts of his curious career, Eugene Lee-Hamilton seems to have been a latter-day version of Bramwell Bronte, and as such, demon and all, was an invaluable asset to a gifted younger half-sister.

He may or may not have contributed to Violet Paget's odd and sometimes profound storeroom of knowledge which she called a "lumber room filled with cobwebs" that is so evident in her *Studies of Eighteenth Century Italy.* But there can be no doubt that he upheld for her, by demanding that she read to him aloud, the standards of Walter Pater's aesthetics, an admiration for Pater's essays on the Renaissance, that he transfused to her a hatred of war, a distrust of many things which were German and yet reserved for her an appreciation of Winckelmann and Goethe. Did she become possessed by him? Or he by her? Neither can be proved—except that as a writer she was the stronger of the two; she visibly outgrew him and lived to write fiction in which the forces of divine good and satanic evil act out their drama, in which the themes of dual personality and demonic possession are the mainsprings of action.

Thus by a roundabout route we come to the shorter fiction of the young woman who adopted in conservative nineteenth century fashion the semi-masculine pen name of Vernon Lee. "Vernon" recalled from a short distance Violet, and the latter part of the pseudonym was a literal transcription of the hyphenated prelude to her elder half-brother's surname. One can read into this choice of a pen name some hint of family solidarity and intimacy—how much or how little it is impossible to say. No reviewers of Vernon Lee's early books were deceived into thinking their author was a man; the disguise was transparent and it was probably intended to be so; it was enough, however, to ward off intimate questions that touched upon Violet Paget's private life; that was not the world's business; her books provided all the answers she cared to give.

Within the twenty-five years after 1881, the publication date of her *Studies in Eighteenth Century Italy,* a number of short novels and stories appeared under the pen name of Vernon Lee. The first was a by-product of her *Studies,* **"The Prince of a 100 Soups,"** a narrative inspired by her readings in Carlo Gozzi, the tales of E. T. A. Hoffmann, the great German Romanticist, and the Italian comedy of masks. She offered the narrative as a tribute to her love of the Italian puppet show and of the Commedia dell'Arte. Today this little extravaganza reveals no more than a glittering flow of narration and girlish, high-spirited facility; Vernon Lee had no gift for the writing of fantastic comedy; her wit, her gifts were of another kind; nor could she present a piece of what was then the modern "problem novel," her *Miss Brown* in enduring terms. These early books were fluttering demonstrations or a talent for writing; they are of interest only to the biographer who may wish to pierce the veil of Vernon Lee's personality by way of reading her early ventures into fiction. Yet among these first attempts in 1883 and in 1884 she did succeed in drawing upon the true sources of her genius. Genius may seem a large word to describe the quality of imagination she had and displayed so lucidly—she never claimed it. But if genius can find a definition within writing of less than monumental scope, genius was hers, and something more than the flicker of its presence came into being in a short novel, *Ottilie* and a biography, *The Countess of Albany.*

Ottilie has for its subtitle "An Eighteenth Century Idyl." There was probably a slight hint of irony in Vernon Lee's choice of "Idyl" to describe the nature of her provincial romance set within an imaginary Franconia a hundred years before *Ottilie* was written. It would be easy to say that its young author was all too obviously an enthusiastic reader of the *Tales of Hoffmann,* the *Sorrows of Werther,* the *Adolphe* of Benjamin Constant—that she was and her romance does not disguise its literary heritage. But it was also written as though its author had never read an English novel; the romance could have been presented as a rarely felicitous translation from French, Italian or German and few critics would have suspected a hoax. In her preface of 1883 Vernon Lee laid claim only to being an essayist, not a writer of romantic tales or novels; she confessed to being haunted by the spirits of men and women whose names she had not read in historical researches and could not dispel their presence in her imagination; this she insisted was the raison d'etre of *Ottilie.*

So much for the prudence and candor with which Vernon Lee submitted her romance of *Ottilie* to the public. As to why it can be reread today with pleasure, interest and a sense of rediscovery is another matter. Up to the moment that she wrote her idyl no writer in English of the nineteenth century with the exceptions of two Americans, Edgar Allan Poe and Fitz-James O'Brien and one Anglo-Irishman, Sheridan Le Fanu, had entered so deeply into the psychology of unspoken human relationships as Vernon Lee. *Ottilie,* in its external calmness of confessing a brotherly-sisterly relationship of guilt and love is scarcely a Gothic novel; her manner of presenting the theme of possession, of one psyche haunted by another, is too serene to reflect the fires of hell which burn so violently in the pages of Hoffmann and of Poe. Behind the three figures of Ottilie, her lover and her brother stands the unnamed figure of Johann Joachim Winckelmann whose studies in Greek and Latin and whose journey to Italy inspired Goethe and whose writing brought a belated awareness of the Renaissance and neo-Classicism into Germany. The heady results of Renaissance passion in conflict with cool drafts of neo-Classic attitudes both imported from Italy worked curious magic in the *Sturm und Drang* of Germanic literature of which Ottilie's brother was the catalyst and Ottilie the

victim. The three figures in the romance are possessed by forces greater than themselves; none escapes the working of destiny. Within its genre we have had few examples in twentieth century fiction to equal *Ottilie*: to find them we must turn to "The Blood of the Walsungs" of Thomas Mann, to "Les Enfants Terribles" of Jean Cocteau, and in respect to an external serenity in reciting the romance, *Ottilie* remains superior.

No less accomplished in its telling of complex emotions in a steady voice is Vernon Lee's biography of Louise, Princess of Stolberg, who at eighteen had married the middle aged, dissolute, exiled Bonnie Prince Charlie and became the Countess of Albany residing in Florence. The book appeared in a series, long since forgotten, of "famous women" which contained commissioned biographies of such notables as Margaret Fuller, George Sand and Mary Wollstonecraft; the series was one of those noble ventures, like "men of letters" series, which publishers every quarter century or so are led into sponsoring and which for the most part show how dull gifted writers can be in fulfilling the terms of a contract to write on the subject of their great predecessors. The majority of such brief lives and studies cram the dusty corners of second hand bookshops mercifully hidden from the opinions of posterity.

Vernon Lee's *Countess of Albany* has none of the atmosphere which usually surrounds a commissioned duty to write a brief study of an heroine in arts, politics or letters; in 1885 it puzzled one reviewer who protested that Louise of Stolberg was not famous enough, that she was no more or less than an unfortunate princess whom historians of England, as well as of Italy, slighted or ignored. In 1885 Vernon Lee's *Countess* was as unlike books of its kind as it is today; the book was and still is freshly written as though its author had been haunted by a little princess who became under the alcoholic guardianship of Charles Edward the platonic mistress of the Italian poet, Alfieri. Alfieri as Vernon Lee portrayed him was one who had the passions of another Henri Beyle, who might well have stepped out of an autobiographical passage of "La Chartreuse de Parme." Famous or not Louise d'Albany, as she was known, was in an utterly fantastic situation between two men, one, an aging heir to a lost throne and a ruined cause and the other a poet at war with himself, consumed by the ironic passions of intellectual and all too fleshly loves. Neither eighteenth century Rome nor Florence had witnessed a more complex, ghost-ridden, potentially violent love affair. Louise d'Albany was a heroine made for Vernon Lee; she survived her Prince and her fiery haired poet, as well as the hero of her age, Napoleon, and grew to look at seventy like a squat, fat, unwieldy housekeeper, who waddled through the streets of Florence draped in a red shawl.

With few exceptions the best of Vernon Lee's stories are set within the landscapes of Italy, the suburbs of Rome, Venice or Florence or in the streets lining the canals and rivers of those cities. These scenes are less of tourist Italy than of an Italy that exists in the imagination of the intimate traveler who is haunted by places and sees behind fretted ironwork and discolored facades an entrance to romantic passion, mystery, drama, hopes and despairs. Not the least of her stories is **"Prince Alberic and the Snake Lady,"** a story within a story and which has at its center a legend that echoes the tales brought from the East into southern Europe by the Crusaders to the Holy Land. I leave the story for the readers of [*The Snake Lady, and Other Stories*] to discover—except to remind them that the snake in the legend is of an origin which is of the East and is not to be confused unwittingly with the serpent of Eden's garden. This snake descends from the benevolent dragons of the East and is the heiress of Good, now transformed in the Christian world to Evil. It is this mutation of the snake lady and her magic qualities, compounded of both Good and Evil which endows Vernon Lee's version of the legend with its undercurrents of inherited fears and ecstasies. Beneath the charms of what seem to be no more than a Gothic fairy tale, deeper realities exist, and behind their psychological revelations, lies the conflict of Western taboos against the religions of the East. No one has told the story of the snake-dragon with more persuasion than Vernon Lee.

A foil to the legend of Prince Alberic is a fifteenth century story, **"A Wedding Chest"** which tells of the romance behind the painted panel of the chest, described in the Catalogue of the Smith Museum, Leeds, England, as "the Triumph of Love." This entirely sanguinary little romance is filled with the blood-stained shadows of fifteenth century Italian courtship and revenge; and lively ghosts they are, breathing the passions of holy and profane love with the violence of John Webster's tragedies. Scarcely less memorable is Vernon Lee's version of a legend concerning Domenico Neroni, a painter whose name is scarcely mentioned by Vasari, and who was, as she described him in her *Renaissance Fancies and Studies,* a fifteenth century seeker of pagan perfection. His journey into the ancient world, invoking pagan spirits and unmentionable rituals and ecstasies, is the story I have selected from her essay on Neroni. As in the story of Prince Alberic the soul of its protagonist is possessed by forces of a world that exist behind the world of every day reality.

Hauntings was an appropriate title for a collection of four tales by Vernon Lee, three of which, **"Amour dure,"** **"Dionea"** and **"A Wicked Voice"** I have selected for inclusion in the present book. I omit **"Oke of Okehurst"** for several reasons. The setting of that story is in England, and though English was its author's language in which she wrote so well, geographical England, its countryside, its mores, its civilization as well as its pre-civilized antiquity were not hers. Literally as well as imaginatively England to Vernon Lee was foreign land; it was not her Europe. She could not penetrate with ease its island mists, its intimations of a life that stirred behind appearances. The figures who move through **"Oke of Okehurst"** are story tellers' Englishmen and women; their conversation is of the good craftsman's art, their fancies, their imaginings are of a kind to be found in the stories of any expert teller of supernatural tales in which the stage properties of early Stuart castles and estates prevail.

"Amour dure," **"Dionea"** and **"A Wicked Voice"** are all within the charmed circle of Vernon Lee's Italy; each has

the singular marks of her authority. The particular spell cast by Dionea the Genoese, the spell of the Uranian Venus, is of Mediterranean probability and not of the Irish Sea nor the English Channel; her province in Vernon Lee's "world Atlas" is of Southern Europe; and the haunting echoes of the voice heard in **"A Wicked Voice"** are of a kind that is appropriate only to Venetian gardens, the canals and night-shadowed, narrowly turning streets of Venice. In Vernon Lee's *Hauntings* the spirit of place haunts the reader, and in reading her stories I am at times reminded of a little English woman I once knew, who after securing a hard-won Master's degree at Oxford was for many years a governess-tutor of well-to-do American girls in Germany. She guided her charges up and down the Rhine, an eager, round-eyed Lorelei who spoke faultless Oxford German. Of people she could remember almost nothing; names and faces quickly vanished beyond the reaches of her memory. "I am haunted by places," she would say half wistfully, "Stuttgart and Ulm, Nurmberg and Frankfort, the stones of their streets, the roofs of their houses are in my dreams; I am possessed by them, they own me." In the same fashion Vernon Lee's tales and romances are possessed by genii of time and place as well as the personality of their author. It is through her eyes that a present generation of readers at home or abroad may set their blue guide books aside to rediscover Europe. And if the Italy they find is unlike any other Italy in English fiction, it is because no English writer since Vernon Lee (and I am aware of the Italys of Henry James, E. M. Forster, Norman Douglas, and D. H. Lawrence, all excellent of their various kinds) has peopled Italy with such enduring ghosts and shades. One sees them glimmering in Rome's fountains, one sees them pace the waters of the Arno, and hears echoes of their voices across the Grand Canal; they are moonlit visitors.

Perhaps no Mediterranean cycle of romances and legends is complete without an image, however ironic and fantastic, of Don Juan. In her **"Virgin of Seven Daggers"** both Don Juan and Spain arrive and with them a brimming lake of Hell's fires. Her Don Juan is not perhaps the greatest of the heroes who answered to his name, but he is vivid enough, and his presence is enriched by the grace of the **"Virgin of the Seven Daggers."** And with Don Juan the reader of the present volume has a last and memorable look into the resources of Vernon Lee's baroque imagination.

The Canadian Forum (review date 1956)

SOURCE: A review of *Pope Jacynth and More Supernatural Tales,* in *The Canadian Forum,* Vol. 36, 1956, p. 118.

[*In the following essay, the critic provides a mixed assessment of Lee's stories in* Pope Jacynth and More Supernatural Tales.]

Vernon Lee (Viola Paget, 1856-1935, a distinguished student of Italian art and literature), has no particular gift for the supernatural as such. Almost without exception, the most impressive literary ghost-stories deal with perversions of the power of the imagination to create life in the place of death—"Oh, who sits weeping upon my grave And will not let me sleep?" complains a typical victim of the living, and Cathy weeps at the window to which Heathcliff has dragged her. [In Lee's *Pope Jacynth and More Supernatural Tales*] the compulsive interplay between the quick and the dead is the theme of one of these stories, but it is crudely handled and the climax falls flat. Three others, uncertainly balanced between charm and whimsy, are concocted saints' legends, another is a conventionally constructed ghost-story, in a sixth a reborn pagan goddess erupts into the life of a German artist with catastrophic results (enacted on a conveniently-placed sacrificial altar). The remaining piece, probably the strongest in the book, is not a story at all, but an essay on "Ravenna and her ghosts." Here the spectres as it were float up out of the landscape, whose evocation—indeed, materialization before the reader—is her particular gift, applied especially to the landscape of Italy where most of the stories are set. In rendering that she shows an extraordinary power and great versatility—the places she observes pass through different lights and seasons, are at one moment full of people and at another quite desolate, but at all times overpower the reader with their own quality. As a story-teller she exploits this gift, so that her people and spirits are partly embodiments of their settings; but as soon as her attention shifts to them as personalities, her hold slackens. She is not really interested in personality except as an aura surrounding a figure of legendary dimensions: the ghost of Theodoric she marches briefly through Ravenna is far more compelling than any of her "real" people.

The most genuinely macabre passage in the book is the description, too long to quote, of the church in the Ravenna marshes where once the harbour was. To Vernon Lee the landscape here and everywhere is a human presence that includes both the dead and the living: hence the effort to bring back the dead has no meaning for her, as they exist in the continuing life of the scene, and the old myths as a part of "nature" are bound continually to be re-enacted. The past has its place in the present scene, partly as a secret life within it that can be sensed but hardly described, but partly also as having gone to make up its material body. She says of the ancient churches of Ravenna: "Those pillared basilicas, which look like modern village churches from the street, affect one with their almost Moorish arches, their enamelled splendor of ultra-marine, russet, sea-green and gold mosaics, their lily fields and peacocks' tails in mosque-like domes, as great stranded hulks, come floating across Eastern seas and drifted ashore among the marsh and rice-field." In Vernon Lee's prose as in the life of the city, such things share with us in a common present: this she achieves not by supernatural means but by a humanizing view of the material and "natural."

Julia Briggs (essay date 1977)

SOURCE: "A Sense of the Past: Henry James and Vernon Lee," in *Night Visitors: The Rise and Fall of the English Ghost Story,* Faber, 1977, pp. 111-23.

[*In the following excerpt, Briggs examines similarities between the fiction of Vernon Lee and Henry James.*]

When T. S. Eliot's Gerontion declared that he had no ghosts, he rejected his past, both personal and cultural, and his deliberate deracination was seen as one source of his barrenness. Although only too often ghosts may act as unpleasant reminders of actions preferably forgotten, by digging up long-buried corpses or reawakening tender consciences, total repression of the past or deliberate evasion of its consequences carry even greater penalties. One of these was dramatized by Dickens in his story *The Haunted Man and the Ghost's Bargain* (1848): here Redlaw, in consigning his unhappy memories to oblivion, forfeited his capacity for human compassion. In an era increasingly characterized by social upheaval, it becomes correspondingly important to retain tradition and older ways of thinking, to remember our ghosts, if we are to maintain a sense of stability. The natural tendency to overestimate the past at the expense of the present may be further exaggerated by the very rapidity with which that past is disappearing, and nostalgia, in various forms, may result. The Catholic revival and the interest in folklore and primitive belief discussed in the previous chapter included strong retrospective elements. Ghosts were a traditional medium of communication between the past and the present, the dead and the living, and thus the ghost story might be used to assert continuity at a time when it seemed threatened on many fronts.

For writers with a special interest in the past, the ghost story offered certain advantages over other forms such as the historical novel since it could present a direct, rather than a vicarious, encounter, occurring within a contemporary setting which increased its immediacy. It could legitimately treat past events while viewing them through modern eyes, and retaining them within a modern framework. It might even give covert expression to an author's desire to discover and confront the past, in whatever fearful form it might adopt.

The ghost as a link with a past from which we are afraid of being disinherited or disconnected had a particular appeal for a number of American writers. T. S. Eliot's work constantly alludes to such a fear, but it was more directly voiced in certain ghost stories by Henry James and Vernon Lee. These two American ex-patriates used the form to express, among other things, their desire for integration into a European society whose links with the past had remained comparatively unimpaired. They hoped to find their bearings within this newly-adopted culture, even, perhaps, to embrace the very forces which had originally driven their grandparents abroad. The ambiguity of the ghost, skeleton in the cupboard or welcome messenger of a bygone world, provided an exact counterpart to the complexity of their feelings towards their new surroundings.

For Henry James, tradition was a crucial aspect of the European culture which he cared for so deeply, and within which he hoped eventually to create his own niche as a writer. His initial attitude to the European past was thus one of ardent enthusiasm. When his passionate pilgrim encounters a ghost, a warning of his approaching death, he can only feel an exultation that, under the circumstances, is ironic: 'I'm—O, EXCITED! This is life! This is living!' Vernon Lee's heroes, falling in love with some fascinating monster long since dead, reflect a cruder, but still deeply felt response to history, and to the music, literature and painting through which it lived for her, and on which she wrote with knowledge and eloquence.

The European *genius loci,* that spirit of place which Vernon Lee used as the title of a book of essays, worked its spell most powerfully on well-informed visitors from the New World to whom every mouldering stone whispered its history. Nathaniel Hawthorne was the first to search for a myth that gave adequate expression to his sense of the vital Italian past. It is conveyed in *The Marble Faun* (1860) through the mystic identification of the modern sculptor, Donatello, with the classical statue of a faun. For the romantic poets, especially Byron, the grandeur and awe of a particular landscape or architectural feature derived chiefly from its historic associations. As he meditated on the great works of man or nature, the past seemed to be on the point of materializing before his eyes. A number of ghost stories arose from similar feelings of awe or delight occurring in a particular setting. Others dramatized historical perceptions of a more general order, such as inspired Browning's monologues, vignettes exemplifying the character of a society through one individual.

In their different ways, both Henry James and Vernon Lee were strongly influenced by Hawthorne. Like him, they explored the implications of their European heritage not only in travel essays but also through the use of the supernatural. In fact a closer connection exists between James's travel sketches and his ghost stories than has generally been recognized. An enchanted observer, James peopled the sights he saw with fictional or historic spirits: at Ludlow he could readily imagine the heroines of Jane Austen or Fanny Burney having their first love affair (these essays are collected in *English Hours,* 1905). At Haddon Hall, in Derby, he felt that 'by listening with the proper credulity, [he] might surely hear on the flags of the castle court ghostly footfalls' belonging to Dorothy Vernon, as she eloped with Lord John Manners. It was at Haddon Hall that James felt most deeply moved by 'the spirit of the scene', and his account of the experience vividly anticipates one of the greatest moments in ghostly fiction: when the governess in *The Turn of the Screw* (1898), wandering through the gardens of Bly in the evening twilight and dreaming of coming suddenly upon the master, instead glimpses the appalling figure of Peter Quint upon the tower. The essay begins with a walk along the Wye ('whose parsimonious three letters suggest and rhyme with Bly', as Leon Edel has observed). Like the governess, James seems to expect some kind of revelation—'To walk in quest of an object that one has more or less tenderly dreamed of, to find your way, to steal upon it softly. . . .' It takes the following form:

> The twilight deepened, the ragged battlements and the low, broad oriels glanced duskily from the foliage, the

rooks wheeled and clamoured in the glowing sky; and if there had been a ghost on the premises I certainly ought to have seen it. In fact I did see it, as we see ghosts nowadays. I felt the incommunicable spirit of the scene, with the last, the right intensity.

Elsewhere in James's travel writings it is evident that 'this interminable English twilight which I am never weary of admiring' held a particular appeal for him. The slow summer dusk is celebrated in several of his accounts of English cathedrals: both Wells and Exeter were best seen 'when the long June twilight turns at last to a deeper grey and the quiet of the close to a deeper stillness'. Of Rochester he wrote, 'English ruins always come out peculiarly when the day begins to fail. Weather-bleached . . . they turn even paler in the twilight and grow consciously solemn and spectral.' For James, the witching hour is dusk, not midnight. The quick-fading American sunsets of James's childhood made him relish the lingering evening light, yet coming to it as an adult, he perceived something potentially chilling in the stillness, the sudden silence, when 'the rooks stopped cawing in the golden sky and the friendly hour lost, for the minute, all its voice' (*The Turn of the Screw*). . . .

Vernon Lee (born Violet Paget, in 1856) fell under the spell of *The Marble Faun* when in Rome with her parents during the winter of '68-9, especially as the American artistic colony described by Hawthorne ten years earlier, the 'white marmorean flock' of lady sculptors, was still much in evidence. As an adult, Vernon Lee settled in Florence and became a prominent member of the English community there. Henry James knew her well, and at first admired her talents, though he was later hurt by her tasteless caricature of his mannerisms in a short story entitled **'Lady Tal'**. All her life she remained fascinated by Italy, enthralled by its colour and passion and a romantic vision of its past which owed much to Browning, for she peopled it with Renaissance artists, dukes and monks, eighteenth-century musicians and ladies in dominoes.

Vernon Lee's fame as a writer of ghost stories rests on a single volume, **Hauntings,** published in 1890. The first tale, **'Amour dure'**, gives characteristic expression to her romantic passion for the high Renaissance. It is almost 'My Last Duchess' in reverse. Begun as a historical novel entitled *Medea da Carpi*, the story concerns a coldly ambitious woman whom men found irresistible, a version of Lucrezia Borgia or Vittoria Corambona. When Vernon Lee failed to place the novel with a publisher, she ingeniously rewrote it in the form of a diary of one Spiridion Trepka, a Polish historian who takes his place as the last lover over whom the duchess, now three hundred years dead, exerts her fatal fascination. The story is neatly constructed, and the device of the diary works well, allowing the reader to remain one step ahead of the narrator. The weakest moment is the melodramatic climax in which the Pole is warned of his danger by Medea's earlier betrayed lovers. Although the experience is inevitably romanticized, the sensation of being deeply attracted to a portrait or piece of writing of another age is common enough to endow a certain conviction.

Trepka was not initially drawn to his Medea by the discovery of her portrait, however. Her history had caught his attention first, and the finding of her portrait in the archives of 'Urbania' occurs at a later stage and provides a further portent of his fate. **'A Wicked Voice'** effectively begins with the examination of an engraving of an eighteenth-century singer, Zaffirino. If **'Amour dure'** belongs to the world of Browning's 'My Last Duchess' or *The Ring and the Book,* this tale portrays the society of 'A Toccata of Galuppi's'. It was inspired by a visit to the Philharmonic Academy of Bologna in the company of the young painter, John Sargent, where he and Vernon Lee saw a portrait of the great eighteenth-century singer, Carlo Broschi. Nicknamed Farinelli, his marvellous voice had, according to legend, soothed the mad Philip of Spain, and she had passionately longed to hear it. But the power of the singer in **'A Wicked Voice'** is of diabolic origin. He was nicknamed 'Zaffirino' on account of 'a sapphire engraved with cabalistic signs presented to him one evening by a stranger'—none other than the Devil himself.

The tale of a musician's pact with the Devil is traditionally told of violinists rather than singers and, as if to meet this objection, the second paragraph of **'A Wicked Voice'** begins 'O cursed human voice, violin of flesh and blood'. In conception this story may owe something to E. T. A. Hoffmann's elaborate 'Rath Krespel', where the heroine's uniquely beautiful voice is mystically linked with the tones of a wonderful violin. The musical gifts of Paganini and Tartini had at different times been attributed to satanic inspiration, and several stories of the nineties take up this theme. John Meade Falkner's *The Lost Stradivarius* (1895) concerns a diabolic compact, and Thomas Hardy's great short story 'The Fiddler of the Reels', drops more than a hint that Mop Ollamoor's powers are not altogether natural.

Zaffirino's sapphire confers on him supernatural powers, of a sexual, as well as a musical nature, so that 'the first song could make any woman turn pale . . . the second make her madly in love, while the third song could kill her off on the spot, kill her for love, there under his eyes, if he only felt so inclined'. Zaffirino is in fact a male version of Medea, possessing the same cruel and sadistic attitude to the opposite sex. The scene in which he watches the Procuratessa die during the course of his last song (described twice, since it is seen first in a dream, and later re-enacted in a haunted house) is similar in its self-indulgent lingering to the scene where Medea watches the Prinzivalle tortured to death. Further points of comparison with **'Amour dure'** become apparent when it is remembered that the male narrator's passion for a voice in **'A Wicked Voice'** would more logically attach itself to a woman's. If Zaffirino is regarded as an essentially female rôle, it becomes clear that three of the four stories in *Hauntings* are narrated in the first person by a creative male attracted to a cold and sadistic female who is unobtainable, either because she is dead, or in love with the dead. The fascination exerted by the seductive beauty of the dead is one of the obsessive elements in Vernon Lee's fantasies. The figure of the cruel and fatal woman, however, is also highly characteristic of the period, as Professor Praz has amply illustrated in *The Romantic Agony.*

Medea and Alice Oke have several forebears in d'Aurevilly's *Les Diaboliques,* or in de l'Isle Adam's merciless Queen Ysabeau in *Contes Cruels.*

If the compulsive elements in her writing are in some ways a weakness, they are in other respects a source of strength. The cruel lady may represent a fascinating if forbidden ideal, but the imaginative narrator usually shares his creator's vitality. In **'A Wicked Voice'**, the story is told by a Wagnerian composer who had been working on an opera of 'Ogier the Dane', but is now doomed to compose trite eighteenth-century melodies—a genuinely comic invention in an otherwise melodramatic story. In **'Oke of Okehurst'** (originally entitled 'A Phantom Lover') the narrator is an artist whose personality is partly based on that of the portrait painter, John Sargent, her life-long friend. What remains in the memory even after the cold heroine and her murdered cavalier poet, Lovelock, have been forgotten, are the fine evocations of the Jacobean house in its rainswept Kentish setting, a scene that might well have appealed to a landscape painter. The tale has an extra twist in that the narrator refuses to accept a supernatural explanation. He himself has seen nothing, and is doubtful whether anyone else has, though his account does ample justice to the sinister atmosphere of Okehurst. Technically speaking, therefore, the story conforms to the 'psychological' prototype, that is, the reader is left uncertain whether to accept a rational explanation or to believe that the events had a supernatural origin. The narrative unfolds at a leisurely pace, with a wealth of small incidents that emphasize the similarities between the present-day Alice Oke, and her seventeenth-century ancestress whose portrait, a treasured heirloom, somehow challenges the painter-narrator to surpass it. Vernon Lee treats the concept of the 'phantom lover' with delicacy, and the implausible denouement with sufficient speed to make this the best of her ghost stories.

Running through *Hauntings* is the theme of the fascination that the dead exert over the living, the power that past beauty, whether of face or voice, can command, even after its own decay. Henry James's early story, 'The Last of the Valerii', enacts a similar infatuation with the antique world, but his conception of the ghost story was in general much less narrow than Vernon Lee's. A small group of his stories represent his sense of self-discovery as a European in terms of a not unwelcome confrontation with a ghostly past, but these are only aspects of a much wider-ranging achievement in the genre. Frequently he used contemporary settings and themes, focusing on social or moral dangers, as he does preeminently in *The Turn of the Screw.* His versatility enabled him to use the supernatural for a variety of purposes, some of which are discussed in chapter 7. Vernon Lee, on the other hand, used this medium primarily as an expression of her response to the past, where she found release from the behavioural constraints that her own times imposed upon women who, like herself, were over-endowed with masculine traits, longed for emancipation and preferred their own sex to men. Once through the magic doors, she could imagine herself as a man, or at least a woman as coldly and dangerously beautiful as Medea or Alice Oke.

In the preface to *Hauntings* she admitted that she had little interest in the ghost story when it was set in the drearily familiar world, 'for what use has it got if it land us in Islington or Shepherd's Bush?' She rejected modern urban life in favour of a mode closer to romantic historical fiction. According to her prescription, a ghost story should consist of

> . . . the past, the more or less remote Past, of which the prose is clean obliterated by distance—that is the place to get our ghosts from. Indeed we live ourselves, we educated folk of modern times, on the borderland of the Past, in houses looking down on its troubadours' orchards and Greek folks' pillared courtyards; and a legion of ghosts, very vague and changeful, are perpetually to and fro, fetching and carrying for us between it and the present.

Her ghost stories reflect the attractions of such a past, washed clean of its trivializing prosiness. If much of her work was escapist in tendency, its strength lay in her recognition of the power of the escapist impulse, and with it, the power of history to obsess, even to possess the writer, so that confrontation with the dead becomes the desired, the logical outcome of his research. For such a dedicated historian the ghost story might express not only a sense of the continuing vitality of the past, but his profound desire to experience it personally, at first hand. Thus normal caution is overcome and, as in James's nightmare, the haunted pursues the haunter. This subconscious longing pervades the work of another historian, M. R. James, whose heroes, in spite of sensible warnings, deliberately expose themselves to ghosts, symbols of the longed-for and unattainably 'other' world of the past.

Peter Gunn's response to *Ottilie*:

[In *Ottilie*] Vernon Lee has conveyed a vivid sense of the restless stirrings of the time, when the brittle surface of French culture among the upper classes in Germany was broken into fragments by impulses loosed with the discoveries of Winckelmann and the writings of Lessing, Herder, Schiller, and Goethe. The characters of the brother and sister are drawn with great economy and psychological subtlety. By the choice of such undistinguished persons, set in this little Franconian backwater, Vernon Lee succeeds in revealing immediately and intimately to the reader the reactions of specific men and women to great historical events. Not that Ottilie was conscious of the intellectual and spiritual ferment of the *Sturm-und-Drang* period; her life was too simple and remote for that; and if her brother was indeed aware of it, his character was so formed that some such *dénouement* as befell him was inevitable, irrespective of the events of the time. Yet, in and through the domestic tragedy of this humdrum couple there is borne in on us what it meant to be German living in that revolutionary but ambiguous age, which we see reflected in such literary works as *Laocoon, Werther*, and *Hermann and Dorothea*. *Ottilie* is one of the most subtle and successful of Vernon Lee's stories.

Peter Gunn, in his Vernon Lee: Violet Paget,
1856-1935, *Oxford University
Press, 1964, pp. 83-84*

John Clute (essay date 1985)

SOURCE: "Vernon Lee," in *Supernatural Fiction Writers: Fantasy and Horror, Volume 1,* edited by E. F. Bleiler, Charles Scribner's Sons, 1985, pp. 329-35.

[*In the following essay, Clute offers a thematic overview of Lee's supernatural tales.*]

Under the cover of "Vernon Lee"—the pseudonym of an expatriate—Violet Paget is a forgotten woman, a figure of the nineteenth century who lived much of her life in the twentieth, weaving for herself, over her later years, a legend of impenetrable eccentricity. Traces of that deaf, spinsterish, rude, interminable monologist survive in literary chronicles, and undoubtedly in some living memories. Far less easy to encounter is the young Miss Paget, born in France, childhood friend of the painter John Singer Sargent, precocious author (already as Lee) of *Studies of the Eighteenth Century in Italy* (1880), formidable advocate of Walter Pater's austere aestheticism, uneasy associate of Henry James (whom she eventually alienated), and author of some of the finest tales of the supernatural in English.

The recent explosion of studies of women writers has left her anonymity intact. She does not appear, for instance, in Ellen Moers's magisterial *Literary Women* (1976), a book whose focus is on the nineteenth century. It is certainly the case that she is hard to characterize and even to locate, for she was an inveterate traveler, rarely resident in England, where she felt increasingly ill at ease as the years passed. Of her considerable literary production, about a quarter is fiction. Justly or unjustly, none of her five novels has been in print for many years, though *The Prince of the Hundred Soups* (1883), a harlequinade of some ambition, modeling its characters on the commedia dell'arte, may warrant revival; and *Miss Brown* (1884), however rough-hewn, comprises a mordantly comprehensive anatomy of English culture at a time when pre-Raphaelitism had arguably decayed into sham-medieval posturing. *Louis Norbert: A Two-Fold Romance* (1914) has perhaps suffered through misidentification as a novel of the supernatural, being in truth a subtle study in temperaments with a this-worldly resolution. Only her shorter fiction remains available to contemporary readers, and that in scattered form.

Of Lee's total production of more than forty volumes, at least thirty are nonfiction studies of Italian culture, belles lettres, travel books, polemical incursions into moral philosophy and aesthetics, pacifist denunciations of all parties involved in the destructive tragedy of World War I, and singletons like *The Handling of Words* (1923), a collection of close readings of literary texts that has had some influence on twentieth-century criticism. None of this output—much of it combining intense erudition with a mesmeric sense of place—is readily available today. Uneven, diffuse, recondite, her corpus is now occasionally referred to in footnotes.

From the beginning, Lee's life was one of estrangement, in both a geographical and a psychological sense. She was born at Château St. Léonard, near Boulogne, France, on 4 October 1856, the child of her domineering mother's second marriage. Matilda Adams' first marriage, to a Captain Lee-Hamilton (died 1849), produced a child, Eugene Lee-Hamilton, an invalid for psychosomatic reasons for much of his life, the demanding confidant of his younger sister, and eventually the author of a moderately successful novel of the supernatural, *The Lord of the Dark Red Star* (1903); like much of his far more capable sister's best work, this tale is set in medieval Italy and evidences much research. Eugene's tutor, Henry Ferguson Paget, from an émigré family, was Vernon Lee's father. He was of an erratic disposition, with an obscure past, though he had taught for a time in Poland, like the protagonist of at least one Lee story. He seems to have been the cause for much of the Paget family's incessant shifting back and forth across the Continent, a circumstance that, though surely unsettling, did enable his young daughter to experience at first hand the stable, glittering, rooted Europe that existed prior to the trauma of the Franco-Prussian War (1870-1871). Lee's distaste for World War I can be linked to her perceptions of this earlier cataclysm.

Complexly and powerfully, Lee's Italian tales of the supernatural expose their protagonists to the intolerable suasion of the dream of a past . . . where it is possible to engage in a world of ambient meaning, to love, to machinate, and above all to experience unmodulated aesthetic joy.

—*John Clute*

By 1868, the family had reached Italy; as a country of the imagination, as a field of study, and as a place to dwell, it became home for Vernon Lee, though several years passed before she was able to settle there permanently. Her first two books illustrate this clearly enough. *Studies of the Eighteenth Century in Italy,* which with considerable daring virtually invents that century as a subject of serious study for scholars of Italy, made her name overnight and remains of value today; and in *Tuscan Fairy Tales (Taken Down from the Mouths of the People)* (1880), it is possible to discern some of the forces that shape her later and more significant fiction. There is the antiquarian passion, the lust for the past; there is the scholarly indirection of approach (the tales are told as to an anonymous note-taker, and it is impossible to work out to what degree they are authentic dictations from the "people" of Tuscany); and there is of course the obsession with the Italy that had won her heart—an Italy haunted by the largesse of earlier centuries, a past constantly visible in artifacts, the immemorial gestures of live people, the odors and shapes of the land itself. Her Italy is animate or, rather, possessed.

The stories in *Tuscan Fairy Tales,* like much of Lee's later work, though far more simply, reflect that possession. "The Three Golden Apples," for instance, applies an Italianate glamour to the traditional tale of the youngest son who undergoes all the experiences befitting the early life of a hero, eventually returns to the open air from an underground kingdom with an enchanted princess whom he marries, and becomes king. But there is no complexity to the story, no hauntedness; there is no narrator. In her mature fiction, Lee almost always mediates the glamour of the beckoning past through the complex consciousness of a contemporary narrator, who does not, of course, necessarily escape scot-free, repressions intact, from the implications of the tale.

As an adult, Vernon Lee was short, frail, the victim of several nervous breakdowns, and displayed, as Irene Cooper Willis states in the privately printed *Vernon Lee's Letters* (1937), "a kind of fundamental helplessness which the violence of [her] nature tended to precipitate into impatience and rage." She traveled much, with increasingly long sojourns in Italy; eventually she made something of a permanent home for herself in Florence, though she was often elsewhere. She befriended the famous and harangued them on every subject under the sun. As the years passed, rumors that she was a lesbian with whom young girls were not safe narrowed her range of acquaintances. Her mind was acquisitive, ardent, quarrelsome, omnivorous, increasingly melancholy, and haunted by the past. She became deaf, deeply truculent, isolated, and often, as Willis states, "described herself as an alien, having no ties, of nation, blood, class or profession." Most of her best fiction was written before the turn of the century, though some of it waited many years for publication. The legendary harridan—whom some remember today—was decades past the difficult passions of her supernatural tales when she died on 13 February 1935.

Excluding the contents of *Tuscan Fairy Tales,* there are, more or less, seventeen tales of the supernatural in her oeuvre, plus one allegory, *The Ballet of the Nations* (1915), which she later expanded into a full-length cosmic drama, *Satan the Waster* (1920), not remarkably dissimilar to Thomas Hardy's *The Dynasts* (1903-1908). About the total number it is impossible to be exact. Some stories, like "A Wedding Chest," while not specifically supernatural, do evoke the same intense, supernal Italy of the best of the supernatural tales. It is also possible that some fiction remains uncollected—though one magazine publication that has been added to the supernatural canon ("The House with the Loop-Holes," from the August 1930 *Life and Letters*) on examination turns out to be an essay containing a perfectly worldly anecdote about marriage. Given the state of her reputation fifty years after her death, it is perhaps not surprising that no proper checklist of Lee's works exists. We must rest content with the seventeen identified tales.

Most of them can be found in three collections: *Hauntings* (1890), *Pope Jacynth, and Other Fantastic Tales* (1904), and *For Maurice: Five Unlikely Stories* (1927); one tale, *Sister Benvenuta and the Christ Child* (1906), has appeared only in booklet form; and a few can be found in scattered volumes of Lee's other works. Most, but not all, of the supernatural tales can also be found in two posthumous collections assembled in the 1950's.

There is little point in attempting to sort Lee's fiction into chronological order. Publication dates in her case often had little to do with dates of composition, and in any case the two decades after 1885 can be treated as the high plateau of both her life and her creative output. At the beginning of this period she was something of a prodigy; at its close her readership was dwindling, she was seen as a figure of the past, and the exile of her later years had begun. She had not reached greatness by 1905; the chance of creating a masterpiece had passed.

Of Lee's best fiction, only two stories are set outside of Italy. In its quiet way, the earlier of these—first published in booklet form as **"A Phantom Lover"** (1886) and subsequently in *Hauntings* as **"Oke of Okehurst"**—is as much a tour de force as her flamboyant Don Juan fantasy, **"The Virgin of the Seven Daggers"** (written 1889; published in *For Maurice*). Perhaps somewhat undervalued because of its drenched, tepid English setting, and because its protagonists are at least superficially routine creations, **"Oke of Okehurst"** nevertheless demonstrates that its author, in 1886, breathed the same literary atmosphere as Henry James and was capable of anticipating some of his explorations into the relationship between the narrator and what he narrates.

The story seems simple enough and hardly worth the thousands of words spent on it. Young Mr. Oke, a country squire from Kent, engages a popular portrait painter (probably based on Sargent) to do his wife. The painter, who tells the tale, comes to rain-soaked Okehurst to find Mr. Oke's wife a figure of aesthetic allure but elusive to his brush. It slowly becomes clear that both Mr. and Mrs. Oke are obsessed—indeed haunted—by a family tragedy of several centuries earlier, when an ancestral Mr. Oke had murdered the lover of an earlier Mrs. Oke. The contemporary Mrs. Oke is obsessed by her likeness to the earlier and sadistically intent on displaying to her husband her amorous involvement with the ghost of the dead lover. Eventually she drives Mr. Oke into a murderous frenzy in which he kills both her and himself. The narrator is given Mrs. Oke's locket. The lock of hair inside it, he is convinced, is the ghost's.

From the very first sentences of the story, however, the reader may notice hints that **"Oke of Okehurst"** is not at all straightforward. Here, as throughout, the narrative voice is that of the painter, and from the first it signals his will to aesthetic control over his material:

> That sketch up there with the boy's cap? Yes; that's the same woman. I wonder whether you could guess who she was. A singular being, is she not? The most marvellous creature, quite, that I have ever met: a wonderful elegance, exotic, far-fetched, poignant; an artificial perverse sort of grace and research in every outline and movement. . . .

And so on, for several hundred words. If, at this point, the reader notices the close (indeed parodic) resemblance of these opening phrases to those that inaugurate any of several dramatic monologues by Robert Browning, he may well realize that Lee is depicting an unreliable narrator, and be prepared to see the painter take a far from passive role in the events to follow. In poems like "Fra Lippo Lippi" and "Andrea del Sarto," Lee's friend Browning allowed his narrators to betray their intimate involvement in stories that are ostensibly objective. This is precisely what happens in **"Oke of Okehurst."**

Becoming obsessed with the elegant tale of ghosts and murder and sexual obsession, the narrator of the tale is soon manipulating both Okes into full belief in the haunting:

> I had met in Mrs. Oke an almost unique subject for a portrait-painter of my particular sort, and a most singular, *bizarre* personality. I could not posibly do my subject justice so long as I was kept at a distance, prevented from studying the real character of the woman. I required to put her into play.

And later:

> Mrs. Oke herself, I feel quite persuaded, believed or half believed [in the haunting]; indeed she very seriously admitted the possibility thereof, one day that I made the suggestion half in jest.

Before the story ends, he has also convinced Mr. Oke that the wife who is tormenting him (she mocks him, refuses to sleep with him) is a reincarnation and that she is having an affair with the ghost of her murdered lover. The ensuing tragedy comes as a direct consequence of the narrator's creation of the story that he needs for his art.

If the contemporary reader detects an adumbration here of Henry James's *The Turn of the Screw* (1898), he is unlikely to be misguided. **"Oke of Okehurst"** depicts a folie à trois, and the reader is left as ambivalent about what truly happened as he is clearly meant to be in the later tale. Lee's novella can only gain by being read as an early tour de force in the presentation of an unreliable narrator. In this light, a quiet, overextended anecdote can be seen as a tale of genuine horror.

The Okes have no real power to ensnare the narrator of their tale; in the Italian stories, on the other hand, the Okes are replaced by the bright, implacable erotic complexity of Italy itself, from which no narrator is safe in his contemporary selfhood. Complexly and powerfully, Lee's Italian tales of the supernatural expose their protagonists to the intolerable suasion of the dream of a past whose allure is similar to that of a secondary universe as J. R. R. Tolkien defined it, where it is possible to engage in a world of ambient meaning, to love, to machinate, and above all to experience unmodulated aesthetic joy. But in Lee's world there is no final surcease from punishment; the dream of the secondary universe—at times expressed in passages redolent of an almost oceanic bliss—bears the retribution of death within it. The ghosts that convey its siren song—

more or less literally in stories like **"Dionea"**—are finally poisonous. The reason for this is clear and deeply melancholy. In contrast to the work of a modern writer of stature like Robert Aickman, whose ghosts signalize the failure to achieve a full life, Lee's hauntings almost invariably punish the attempt to do so.

Of course, much of the supernatural fiction of the nineteenth century treats self-fulfillment in terms of the grotesque. Rarely, however, is the issue drawn so clearly or by a writer so skilled in evoking that which it is death to inhabit. Lee's biography offers a pat but telling explanation for this circumstance. Within the formidable dragon she made of herself in old age is discernible a very young person indeed, an adolescent Violet Paget, begetter of this bellicose Vernon Lee. The fiction, almost all of which was written well before Lee turned fifty, refuses the liberties of the world with a renunciatory passion that could indeed be called adolescent. The reasons for this lifelong act of refusal are speculative, though contributing factors might well include frustrated homosexuality, exile, physical unattractiveness, and being a woman in the nineteenth century. The result is a body of work that reaches significant stature only at rare moments of what seems to be self-forgiveness.

The stories contained in *Hauntings* certainly leave no doubt about their punitive effect. In **"Amour dure,"** which is subtitled "Passages from the Diary of Spiridion Trepka," a Germanized Polish scholar briefly resident in Urbania finds contemporary Italy as estranging as the rest of his dour life and slowly becomes obsessed with a figure from the city's Renaissance past, the seductive Medea da Carpi, an ambitious machinator in the internecine politics of the time and a woman whose sexual favors no man survives for long. (Females whom it is death to love appear not infrequently in nineteenth-century fiction, certainly in that written by men.) Finally, gaining control of Urbania from her, the brother of her murdered second husband has her strangled by women. But she has sworn revenge and, in spirit form, promises herself to Trepka if he will violate the statue of her executioner, whose spirit will then be exposed to her. Trepka obeys and receives his promised reward—he is found stabbed to the heart.

"Dionea" is more complexly told than **"Amour dure,"** in that it represents the letters of an Italian doctor to the benefactress who has provided funds for the upbringing of an apparent orphan, Dionea, who turns out to be an avatar of the pagan gods. She returns to the sea at story's close, after creating unendurable conflicts for an expatriate artist, who attempts to paint Dionea but finds her amoral pagan brightness fatally seductive. His attempts at aesthetic objectivity soon crumble in the face of Dionea's impersonal but haunting sexual allure, for she is reality unclothed; and for any of Lee's protagonists transfixed by the sight of that for which they long, reality is death. In a parody of religious ritual excess, he soon manages to sacrifice both himself and his wife to the unrelenting, indifferent goddess.

Art is also a frail buckler in **"A Wicked Voice."** Though the composer-narrator's aesthetic involvement in late-nineteenth-century music is presented with considerable and

sophisticated acuity, he soon becomes inextricably entwined in a search for a ghost castrato from the eighteenth century who taunts him with fragments of what might be called—in the terms of this intricately argued fiction—pure melody. That reality unclothed can be embodied in the voice of a castrato suggests—it is never fully explicit in Lee's fiction—an extraordinary association between the amorality of art and unforgivable perversion. The narrator's anguished peroration to **"A Wicked Voice"** can stand for the mutilating savagery of Lee's own refusal of the haunting licentiousness of art:

> O wicked, wicked voice, violin of flesh and blood made by the Evil One's hand, may I not even execrate thee in peace; but is it necessary that, at the moment when I curse, the longing to hear thee again should parch my soul like hell-thirst? And since I have satiated thy lust for revenge, since thou has withered my life and withered my genius, is it not time for pity? May I not hear one note, only one note of thine, O singer, O wicked and contemptible wretch?

As this quotation amply demonstrates, Lee is a writer of acute self-consciousness, and it would be presumptuous to suggest that any analysis of the relationship between her life and the strictures of her fiction would reveal material of which she was unaware. This knowingness is sufficiently clear in the stories contained in *Hauntings* but is nowhere more eloquently rendered than in the finest tale in *Pope Jacynth, and Other Fantastic Tales.* **"Prince Alberic and the Snake Lady"** suffuses, through its complexly circuitous rendering of the love-death epiphany of young Alberic and his benign lamia, a sense of wise, relaxed forgiveness. As a result, the tale is told with a liquid gravity not found elsewhere in Lee's fiction; the seeming impassiveness of the narration (for in this case no narrator as such serves as a center of guilt-ridden consciousness) does not ultimately conceal the author's empathy with Alberic and his transcendent fate. The note of chastened irony that permeates the telling of **"Prince Alberic and the Snake Lady"** seems somehow shared with its protagonist; though we never actually enter Alberic's mind and though his most heightened moments are only hinted at, we seem to judge through his eyes the decaying world he is so soon to escape.

Alberic's parents are dead, and so he is raised in solitude at the court of his grandfather, Duke Balthasar Maria, the ruler of Luna, a small Italian principality at the close of the seventeenth century. His main solace as a child from the sophisticated perversity of the duke and his courtiers is a faded tapestry at the heart of which is depicted a scene from the story of his namesake and ancestor, the first Alberic. Returned from the Crusades, the first duke is rendered with his arm protectively about a beautiful lamia—a figure half woman, half snake. He is eventually (we learn much later) to betray her.

The duke soon destroys the tapestry, because it is no longer fashionable, and rusticates young Alberic to a ruined castle. And it is here, lambently and in passages of sustained responsiveness to the genius loci, that Alberic finds himself, for this castle is like the tapestry. He climbs toward the heart of the ruins, "from discovery to discovery, with the growing sense that he was in the tapestry, but that the tapestry had become the whole world." It is, once again, like entering a secondary universe, but this time it is redemptive, knowing, sweet. Finally he reaches the well at the center of things:

> The well was very, very deep. Its inner sides were covered, as far as you could see, with long delicate weeds like pale green hair, but this faded away in the darkness. At the bottom was a bright space, reflecting the sky, but looking like some subterranean country. Alberic, as he bent over, was startled by suddenly seeing what seemed a face filling up part of that shining circle; but he remembered it must be his own reflection, and felt ashamed. So, to give himself courage, he bent over again, and sang his own name to the image. But instead of his own boyish voice he was answered by wonderful tones, high and deep alternately, running through the notes of a long, long cadence. . . .

There is an echo here not only of **"The Three Golden Apples"** (from *Tuscan Fairy Tales*) insofar as the quotation represents a passage of self-discovery for the hero, but also of the legend of Narcissus, because his discovery of the lamia in his own reflection—for it is her voice that answers him—hints at the immortality, or stasis, of love-death.

The woman Alberic finds (it is a sharp, subtle touch) identifies herself as his godmother. We do not see their sexual embrace. We see Alberic grow to magnificent, princely adulthood. We see him imprisoned by his perverse grandfather. We see him remain faithful to the small snake he carries into his cell. When the duke has the snake mangled to death, Alberic also dies, so as to remain with her. But we do not really know what Alberic thinks. We remember mainly the scene already quoted, and one later, at night:

> A spiral dance of fireflies, rising and falling like a thin gold fountain, beckoned him upwards through the dewy grass. The circuit of castle walls, jagged and battlemented, and with tufts of trees profiled here and there against the resplendent blue pallor of the moonlight, seemed twined and knotted like huge snakes around the world.

This is not the language of a writer unconscious of the resplendence of the allure that is elsewhere refused. It is a language redolent with achieved meaning.

On a smaller scale, much of Lee's remaining fiction reiterates the concerns of her best work, though we have omitted to this point making reference to those tales, always ironic, that deal with the Christian church. Of most interest in this category are **"Pope Jacynth," "The Legend of Madame Krasinska"**—in which an innocent American in Europe is submitted to a far more grotesque fate than ever Henry James cared to depict—*Sister Benvenuta and the Christ Child,* and **"The Virgin of the Seven Daggers."** All have something of the mock-antiquarian tone of writers like Richard Garnett, though the last is a far more intensely realized jeu d'esprit than anything Gar-

nett ever wrote. Don Juan swears eternal loyalty to his favorite version of the Virgin Mary, the statue called the Virgin of the Seven Daggers, before attempting by necromantic means to woo a Moorish princess entombed for four hundred years by her father's magic. After a bravura transit through the land of the dead, the don is forced to remain faithful to the Virgin when the princess asks who is the more beautiful. He is then beheaded. He awakens in Granada, only slowly to discover that he is genuinely dead. A miracle then occurs: regardless of the murders he has committed, and of other sins, the Virgin redeems him, and he is borne upward through her church, in the direction of heaven.

A fair assessment of Vernon Lee can only attend full examination of her formidable, eccentric oeuvre. Her novels may (or may not) be salvageable for a new generation. In the shorter fictions of her youth it is possible to discern hints of something like greatness. It seems that she herself could not allow these hints to flourish. This is our misfortune. Our good luck rests in the passages of wisdom that remain, which haunt us.

Irene Cooper Willis (essay date 1987)

SOURCE: An introduction to *Supernatural Tales: Excursions into Fantasy,* by Vernon Lee, Peter Owen Limited, 1987, pp. 7-18.

[*In the following essay, Willis explores the defining characteristics of Lee's short fiction.*]

Robert Browning's tribute to Vernon Lee which is quoted on the jacket of [*Supernatural Tales: Excursions into Fantasy*] was written in the last year of his life, 1889, before these stories of hers were published. Browning knew her only as the author of her first books on Italian music, painting and sculpture, which made her name in London literary circles in the '80s. When *Studies of the Eighteenth Century in Italy* was published in 1880 the youth of the author astonished its readers. It seemed an amazing book for a girl of twenty-four to have written. Few, if any, were in a position to criticise the learning displayed in it, for it was a pioneer work, a piece of literary archæology, the study of a period not distant in time but forgotten, if ever recognised, as the *mise en scène* that it was of a remarkable efflorescence of national art. Italian music, Italian drama of the eighteenth century, the world of fine ladies, *cavalieri serventi,* pedants, Arcadian rhymesters and poetasters in which the composers and singers, playwrights and actors, the music of Pergolesi, Cimarosa, Jommelli and Marcello arose, were united in this book in a romantically transfigured way. Vernon Lee had discovered that vanished world accidentally, she always insisted, wandering in and around the deserted gardens of the Villa Doria Pamfili in Rome when she was a girl of fourteen and for the next ten years she was absorbed in all the records that she could find of that, to her, fascinating period. She described her impassioned study in the Preface to a new edition of her book in 1907.

Belcaro, Euphorion and other essays followed the publication of *Studies of the Eighteenth Century* in quick succession and received unstinted praise not only from critics but from contemporary writers on art. Walter Pater, to whom *Euphorion* was dedicated, wrote to her:

> It (the essay on The Portrait Art, in *Euphorion*) is a typical example of the excellence of your work. What especially impresses me is the very remarkable learning by which I mean far more than an extensive knowledge of books and direct personal acquaintance with Italy, learning in the sense in which it is above all characteristic of Browning. I mean that these essays of yours are evidence of a very great variety and richness of intellectual stock, apprehensions, sympathies and personal observations of all kinds such as make the criticism of art and poetry a real part of the criticism of life.

John Addington Symonds wrote to her:

> You have the great gift denied to so many wielders of the pen of what George Meredith calls "writing", i.e., of presenting the object with absolute evidence through words to the naked eye.

The learning and the power of description which impressed Walter Pater and J. A. Symonds are very marked in these stories. Most of them were the fruit of her youthful research. In the above mentioned Preface she wrote:

> My eighteenth century lore was acquired at an age (more precisely between fifteen and twenty) when some of us are still the creatures of an unconscious play instinct. And the Italy of the 18th century, accidentally opened to me, became so to speak . . . the remote lumber room of discarded mysteries and of lurking ghosts where a half-grown young prig might satisfy, in unsuspicious gravity, mere childlike instincts of make believe and romance. Save for a few funny little pedants, gnawing a bit of memoir or making those singular little heaps of historical detritus (special to Italy) called *publicazioni per nozze,* no one ever seemed to enter my lumber room of an Italian eighteenth century and I was left to transform it into a place of wonders, an Aladdin's or Monte-Cristo's cave; every rickety table or chair a throne or a fervid scaffold; every yellow roll of paper a Nostradamus's Manual of Necromancy; every rag of tinsel hanging from a nail a robe embroidered with pearl and sequin—nay, a garment like *Peau d'Ane's,* woven of sun and moonbeams. These essays are the log-book of my explorations through that wonder-world of things moth eaten and dust engrained, but sometimes beautiful and pathetic in themselves, and always transfigured by my youthful fancy; they are the inventory of my enchanted garret.

She was writing here of her first book on eighteenth century music but this passage, I think, holds the clue to her power of feeling herself into—the German language calls it "einfühlung", 'empathy', a mental activity deeper than mere sympathy—scenes and dramas which stirred her imagination. The enchanted garret was the source of these 'fantastic tales' and the utterly sincere, compellingly creative, make-believe instincts of youth account for their almost stark objectivity.

Vernon Lee (whose real name was Violet Paget) was born in 1856 and died in 1935. I was privileged to be a friend and her executor and can at least give the bare facts of her life. Her father was the son of an *emigré* French nobleman named De Fragnier; he married a Miss Paget, whose name he took; founded a college at Warsaw for the education of the nobility and brought up his son there. Her mother was the daughter of a Welsh landowner, Edward Hamlin Adams, of Middleton Hall, Carmarthenshire, who after making a fortune in Jamaica returned to England and was M.P. for Carmarthenshire in the Reform Parliament. Matilda Adams was a woman of culture and character; she left England in youth to escape from the English Sunday, had great charm and, notwithstanding ceremonious manners, a choice vocabulary of eighteenth century oaths.

She married twice: first, a Mr. Lee Hamilton, by whom she had a son, Eugene; secondly, the father of Vernon Lee. Eugene entered the Foreign Office but in 1873 collapsed into twenty years of prostrate invalidism during which he composed and published poetry. Eventually, under psychological treatment, he recovered but not before he had exhausted his mother's health and his half-sister's patience. Owing to his illness the Pagets, after moving about in France, Germany and Italy, settled in Florence and lived at first in the city but afterwards in a villa outside it. From 1881 onwards, Vernon Lee came yearly to England to make literary contacts and knew most people of note in the literary and artistic world and the fringes of society around it. Watts, Herkomer, Sargent, Whistler, Rossetti, Oscar Wilde, Browning, Pater, Henry James, Gosse, Alfred Austin, Thomas Hardy, Mrs. Humphry Ward, Mrs. Clifford, H. G. Wells, the Ponsonbys, Ethel Smyth, Maurice Baring and many others were among her friends and acquaintances. That she did not add to the wide reputation that she won with her first books was due to a switching of her interest to a direction where the majority of general readers could not or were not disposed to follow her. She became absorbed in psychological æsthetics and her two books, *Beauty and Ugliness* (1912), and *Music and its Lovers* (1932), were for the above reason doomed to failure.

Some details of the origins of two of these stories, **"The Virgin of the Seven Daggers"** and **"A Wicked Voice"**, are given by Vernon Lee in her Introduction to the "five unlikely tales" included in **For Maurice,** dedicated to Maurice Baring.

"The Virgin of the Seven Daggers" was sketched during a short visit to Granada in 1889, where she was bored and in low spirits.

> I dare say I may have cultivated animosity against that great Spanish art of the Catholic Revival, have lacked appreciation of its technical innovations and psychological depth. Anyhow there it is: I detest the melancholy lymphatic Hapsburgs of Velasquez, the lousy, greedy beggars of Murillo, the black and white penitents of Ribera and Zurbaran, above all the elongated ecstatics and fervent dullards of Greco. I disliked it no doubt

because of having grown up among Antique and Renaissance art. I disliked it from a temperamental intuition that there is cruelty in such mournfulness and and that cruelty is obscene. All of which aversion came to a head . . . and just in proportion to that natural devotion of mine to the Beloved Lady and Mother, Italian or High Dutch, who opens her scanty drapery to suckle a baby divinity, did that aversion concentrate on those doll-madonnas in Spanish churches, all pomp and whalebone and sorrow and tears wept into Mechlin lace. Feeling like this it seemed natural that the typical Spanish hero (for dear Don Quixote was at once made European by translators like Skelton), the offspring of ruthless Conquistadores, should be the conquering super-rake and super-ruffian, decoying women, murdering fathers, insulting even dead men and glorying in wickedness: Don Juan in one of his (not at all Mozartian or Byronian) legendary impersonations, like Don Miguel de Manara or Calderon's Ludovic Enio. And natural, furthermore, that he and that knife-riddled Spanish Madonna should be united by common ancestry in the wickedness of man's imagination, but also by a solemn compact: that Don Juan's one and only act of faith in his career of faithlessness should be towards her, and be what deprived Hell of his distinguished presence. So, in those icy winter afternoons when sunset put sinister crimson on the snowy mountains and on the turbid torrent beneath the Alhambra, there shaped itself in my mind what Baudelaire called an *Ex-Voto dans le Gout Espagnol,* the imagined story coagulating round one of the legends told me many years before by that strange friend who used to boast, in his queer Andalusian French, that: "Yé suis Arave." Meaning Moorish. Moorish! For there had been other folks, as terrible maybe, but far more brilliant and amiable, before the coming of Don Juan and his farthingaled madonna of the many poignards. What brought home to me this alleviating circumstance was what I chanced to witness one unforgettable winter morning. A snowstorm from the Sierra had raged all night; but now the towers of the Alhambra stood out like rose-carnations against the washed and sunny blue. And behold a miracle! the snow melting on the imbricated roofs and dripping into the tanks and channels, broke their long-dormant waters into wide ripples, till the whole imaged palace swayed gently, as if awakening to life. There was an Infanta, so my friend had told me, buried with all her treasure and court somewhere beneath the deserted Moorish palace. . . . And with the vision in those jade green waters, there wavered into my mind the suspicion that there might well have been an almost successful rival of Don Juan's gloomy Madonna, a temptation worthy of his final damnation, along with a supreme renunciation worthy of his being, at last saved.

I helped out the notion, in returning from Spain, by re-reading a book much thumbed in childhood, Lane's Arabian Nights with enchanting (why aren't they republished?) illustrations by William Harvey. There was also a brief glimpse of real Moors at Tangier, especially of a little Moorish bride, with blue and red triangles painted on her cheeks like my Infanta's.

An earlier version of **"The Wicked Voice"** is included in *For Maurice* and in the Introduction Vernon Lee tells how this version, **"Winthrop's Adventure"**, first published in *Fraser's Magazine,* January, 1881, came to be transmogrified into the later story.

It was her interest in the 18th century singer Farinelli, or Farinello, that started the story. She and young John Sargent, afterwards the well-known painter, "a couple of romantic hobbledehoys" as she said, used to stand spellbound before the portrait of Farinelli in the music school at Bologna and, in evening rambles through the moonlit porticoes of that mediæval city, indulge in ghostly fancies about his famous voice which had cured the melancholia of Philip V of Spain and had been equally indispensable to his somewhat feeble-minded successor, Ferdinand VI.

Farinelli, however, was only the focus of Vernon Lee's interest. The true leitmotiv was:

> a feeling of love and wonder at the miracle of the human voice, which seemed the more miraculous in that I had never heard great singers save in fancy. That was one half. The other was the attraction and terror, the mysteriousness of bygone times. Between these two, as between its tonic and dominant, moved my leitmotiv, you might have labelled it 'a silly, secret longing to hear a great singer of the past' which, in the absence of gramophones, was a longing for the unattainable, with the passion only unattainable objects can inspire.

The particular singer didn't really matter, and varied according to the old music, the memoirs also I happened to be reading; also, occasionally, with the old, old people (my master, Romani, for instance) on whose words about Malibran or Velluti, I used to hang. For a long time the singer was a certain Pacchierotti of the 1780's; and even nowadays and after the experience of Caruso's posthumous 'Celeste Aïda', I can still be (ever so faintly) thrilled on reading about him in Fanny Burney and her Father, in Beckford and Stendhal, and experience a tiny little sadness when I realise that though my grandparents may have done so I never can hear him. Be this as it may, about 1874, the leitmotiv was of course connected with Farinelli whom, at the bottom of my present heart, I don't think I would much go out of my way to hear. Anyhow the something I then wrote, the first draft, at least as regards framework and scenery, of *Winthrop's Adventure* was about how 'I', who was also of course John, spent a thunderstormy night in a derelict villa and there encountered, *hear* (and I fear had some conversation with!) a vocal ghost who was Farinelli's. Why Farinelli should have, or be, a ghost, seeing that he died of old age in his bed, surrounded by attached heirs and 'furnished with the consolations of religion' with probably (as befits an ex-royal favourite) a special benediction from His Holiness Pius VI conveyed by His Eminence the Cardinal Archbishop come on purpose in his gala coach—why Farinelli should trouble to haunt a dismantled villa was not apparent. But sufficiently 'motivated' or not, *a ghost is a ghost* when one has written oneself into the small hours, sitting quite alone in an Italian country house with all the servants long gone to bed, the lamp guttering and owls hooting. So that night over the first version of *Winthrop's Adventure* was a *bonâ fide,* indeed my only, ghostly experience, complete with cold hands, dank hair, a thumping heart and eyes one didn't dare to raise from the writing table for fear of dark corners; and as regards the final wrench, the opening of doors, echoing along corridors, the (at last!) refuge in bed, all that was so terrible as to have left no more memory behind than if I had fainted before my manuscript till the next morning.

However, there is a shocking prosaic practicality in the vocation of a writer, something (as is shown by the example of Goethe) warranted to kill off any emotion, no matter how genuine, in the attempt to communicate it to readers. So, after a little time that eerie midnight was forgotten, I began to revise what I had then written; and became aware that since nothing had happened to Farinelli in that villa of his, you couldn't decently set him up as a ghost. Whereupon, with the ruthlessness of a true artist, I bundled him out of my story. And substituted another singer, one who never existed, who could therefore be conveniently murdered in a convenient love affair with a lady of quality. . . . I recast it some fifteen years afterwards with a full-fledged technique and self-criticism. The Singer, whom I had prepared for ghostly functions by a violent death, had now to be assassinated for something better than a vague intrigue with somebody's great-grand-aunt. Or rather: had he not better do the murdering himself? haunt not in pointless solitude merely to sing a posthumous song; but haunt in company with an appropriate victim, be doomed to ghostly repetition of that murderous song of his? (For he had obviously to do the murdering with a song.) He had to become a vocal villain, deliberately revenging himself for virtuous disdain by inspiring a shameful passion in the proud lady whom his singing stabbed to death. His voice—how far had I got from poor excellent Farinelli and his cure of Philip V with the three songs by Hasse sung every evening for ten years?—his voice, I mean the voice of my new version, was a wicked voice, and the story called after it. As wicked (in the original French it was even wickeder, a *Voix Maudite*) as ever you could make it: a voice seeking fresh victims even in its posthumous existence. And of course that quite genuine, childish desire to hear, or rather to have heard, one of those eighteenth century singers was camouflaged as an unholy suicidal longing wherewithal to torment, sap the true inspiration of an unfortunate modern composer, who, being a Wagnerian, held vocalists in abhorrence and expressed himself disrespectfully about the eighteenth century music they had sung, and on one fatal evening went so far as to caricature them before the portrait of the wicked voice's owner: whence his vengeance. All of which was not only most ingeniously invented but most solidly executed: not an ounce of irrelevance or of author's self expression about it all. Naturally the background, the accessory characters, were brought up to date, the date of Tourgéneff's *Chant de l'Amour Triomphant* and Wilde's *Salome*. No more Bologna either, and Bologna music-school and dull Bologna country-lanes: Venice with a Venetian full moon, vanishing gondolas, unaccountable songs on the lagoon; and a mainland villa with a genuine Tiepolo ballroom and the haughty wife of a Procurator of St. Mark killed off in gala dress and all her diamonds. None of which had a grain of reality; whereas that prosy music-school, those evening talks (interspersed with ices

at the café in the Piazza), those soaking drives in search of Farinelli's villa, all that *had* been reality, with such reality of feeling as belongs perhaps only to the self-complacent imagination and to adolescence. . . .

Those genuine feelings of those youthful days of mine I can sometimes almost recapture, catch the swish of them vanishing in the distance of years. I mean the ineffable sense of the picturesqueness and wonderfulness of everything one came across: the market-place with the stage coach of the dentist, the puppet show against the Gothic palace, the white owl whom my friend John and I wanted to buy and to take home to the hotel, the ices we ate in the mediæval piazza, the skewered caramelles and the gardenias and musky, canary gaggias hawked about for buttonholes; the vines festooned over corn and hemp, the crumbling villas among them, the peasants talking like W. W. Story's Roba di Roma . . . 'Kennst dudas Land?' . . . a land where the Past haunted on . . . a land where on full-mooned terraces, and in company with countesses—in those Roderick Hudson days a countess was herself an exotic—you might listen to not the intermezzo of Cavalleria but mysterious eighteenth century songs, might almost hear the voice (not wicked, oh no, ever so virtuous) of Farinelli himself.

But the Stories must speak for themselves. Vernon Lee was a remarkable personality, deeply learned and eloquent, with far reaching historical sympathies.

No tribute to her would be complete without reference to her political opinions. It was rare, in the pre-1914-18 war period, to find a writer and an æsthete as in touch with European liberal opinion as she was and so alive to the various national policies which led to the war. She was an acknowledged pacifist and in speech, writing and money supported propaganda for a just and reasonable peace. Her book, *Satan the Waster* (John Lane, 1920), a treasury of pacifist doctrine, was reviewed in *The Nation* by Bernard Shaw, who wrote: "Vernon Lee has the whole European situation in the hollow of her hand . . . knows history philosophically . . . is a political psychologist".

FURTHER READING

Fremantle, Anne. "Vernon Lee, a Lonely Lady." *Commonweal* LX, No. 12 (June 25, 1954): 297-99.
    Biographical sketch and brief review of *The Snake Lady*.

Wharton, Edith. "Life and Letters." In her *A Backward Glance*, pp. 112-42. New York: D. Appleton-Century Co., 1934.
    Reminiscence calling Vernon Lee a "highly cultivated and brilliant woman."

Additional coverage of Lee's life and career is contained in the following sources published by The Gale Group: *Contemporary Authors*, Vol. 104; *Dictionary of Literary Biography*, Vols. 57, 153, 156, 174, 178; and *Twentieth-Century Literary Criticism*, Vol. 5.

Siegfried Lenz
1926-

German short story writer, novelist, playwright, and essayist.

INTRODUCTION

Along with Günter Grass, Heinrich Böll, and Martin Walser, Siegfried Lenz is a leading figure in post-World War II German literature. Best known for his novels, Lenz has also garnered popular and critical acclaim for his stories, which are noted for their realism and traditional narrative style. His writing often probes themes of duty, authority, and responsibility, though the political resonance of his fiction is more often understated than overt. According to William P. Hanson, Lenz's "ultimate interest is in people and their relationships, and the multiple possibilities inherent in human character. Not the black and white strokes, but the grey shaded areas of human experience are what he can reproduce with a fine sensitivity. Responsibility and aspiration, indifference and weakness are his chief concerns."

Biographical Information

Lenz was born in Lyck, a small town in Masuria, East Prussia, which is now part of Poland. He entered the navy in 1943, still a teenager, and served on a cruiser in the Baltic. Lenz deserted in Denmark during the last months of the war and handed himself over to British authorities. After the war he studied literature at the University of Hamburg, and eventually became an editor of the newspaper *Die Welt.* Lenz published his own short stories in *Die Welt,* as well as his first novel, *Es waren Habichte in der Luft* (*Hawks Were in the Air*), in 1951. An original member of the Gruppe 47, an influential cadre of post-war writers in the 1950s, his first real literary success was a book of stories about his native Masuria, *So zärtlich war Suleyken* (*So Tender Was Suleyken*). These stories he ostensibly wrote to give his wife an idea of his homeland. Lenz's next major work was his novel *Deutschstunde* (*The German Lesson*), published in 1968. This book about the conflict between duty and responsibility in a small town during the war was a critically acclaimed best-seller, and considered by many to be Lenz's best work. Lenz was active politically in the 1960s as a campaign speaker for the Social Democratic party. In 1970 he accompanied Chancellor Willy Brandt to Poland to witness the signing of a German-Polish treaty. Lenz has received numerous awards for his novels and short stories, including many of the highest honors in German literature. He is esteemed for the seriousness of his work, and the way he raises difficult issues without dogmatically providing answers.

Though he is a popular author in Germany, with many of his novels and short stories adapted for film and television, he is not as well known outside of Germany as some of his contemporaries.

Major Works of Short Fiction

So Tender Was Suleyken was Lenz's first collection of short stories to reach a wide audience. This collection, which is considered among the most sentimental of Lenz's works, is atypical of Lenz's oeuvre. The issues most associated with Lenz—responsibility and moral choice, especially during wartime—are fully present in his later collections, *Jäger des Spotts* (*Hunter of Ridicule*) and *Das Feuerschiff* (*The Lightship*). Many of the stories in these works, which are clearly influenced by Ernest Hemingway, involve heroism and failure in battles against the elements. The title story of *The Lightship* concerns a captain's struggle against criminals who try to hijack his ship. The captain is unwilling to resist the criminals until they move the lightship, which marks the channel, and thus endanger other ships in the area. The point at which resistance is warranted is a theme that occurs again and again in Lenz's fiction. This is an important aspect of his best-selling novel *The German Lesson,* as well as in the novella *Ein Kriegsende (An End of the War)*. This story, which Lenz helped adapt for German television, tells of a cruiser sent on an impossible rescue mission just as the surrender has been announced. The captain is set on continuing with the mission, but the crew mutinies and the quartermaster takes control of the ship. The quartermaster sails the ship into a Danish harbor where, after a quick court-martial, he is condemned to death and shot. This masterful tale exhibits Lenz's great skill at telling a story from the inside. The perspective of the captain, who is willing to rescue wounded soldiers despite the risks, as well as the viewpoint of the frightened crew and the resourceful, responsible quartermaster, are all fully developed, so that there is no clear or right solution in the story. Thus, the quick and brutal decision of the military court comes as a particular shock. Aside from the more experimental stories collected in *Einstein überquert die Elbe bei Hamburg (Einstein Crosses the Elbe near Hamburg)*, Lenz's work is highly traditional. Many of his works, such as *So Tender was Suleyken, Der Geist der Mirabelle (Spirit of the Yellow Plum)* and the novel *Heimatmuseum (The Heritage)*, deal with village or small town life in provincial Germany, and thus are more endearing and accessible to Germans than to Lenz's audience abroad. However, critics agree that his best works, though concerned with specifically German problems—such as responsibility for actions under the Nazis—are deeply philosophical and reach a level of universal human understanding.

Critical Reception

Lenz has been considered one of the three or four leading authors in Germany since the 1950s. His novel *The German Lesson* was acclaimed internationally, and several of his later novels have been widely translated. His short stories have a devoted following in Germany, and many critics consider him more skilled in short fiction than in the novel. Lenz has received high literary honors in Germany, and has been invited to lecture abroad many times. Despite his popularity and renown at home, Lenz has not achieved the international stature of his contemporaries, Grass and Böll. This may be because his style is more restrained. Even so, Lenz is clearly one of Germany's most valued authors, deeply respected for the depth and seriousness of his work.

PRINCIPAL WORKS

Short Fiction

So zärtlich war Suleyken [So Tender was Suleyken] 1955
Jäger des Spotts [Hunter of Ridicule] 1958
Das Feuerschiff [The Lightship] 1960

Das Wunder von Striegeldorf: Geschichten 1961
Stimmungen der See: Erzählungen 1962
Lehmanns Erzählungen; oder, So schön war mein Markt: Aus den Bekenntnissen eines Schwarzhändlers 1964
Der Spielverderber: Erzählungen 1965
Das Wrack, and Other Stories 1967
Die Festung und andere Novellen 1968
Gesammelte Erzählungen 1970
Lukas, sanftmütiger Knecht 1970
Erzählungen 1972
Meistererzählungen 1972
Einstein überquert die Elbe bei Hamburg 1975
Der Geist der Mirabelle: Geschichten aus Bollerup 1975
Die Kunstradfahrer und andere Geschichten 1976
Der Anfang von etwas 1981
Ein Kriegsende 1984
Die Erzählungen: 1949-1984. 3 vols. 1986
Das serbische Mädchen 1987
The Selected Stories of Siegfried Lenz 1989

Other Major Works

Es waren Habichte in der Luft: Roman [*Hawks Were in the Air*] (novel) 1951
Das schönste Fest der Welt: Hörspiel (radio play) 1956
Der Mann im Strom: Roman (novel) 1957
Zeit der Schuldlosen: Drama (radio play) 1961
Deutschstunde [*The German Lesson*] (novel) 1968
Das Vorbild [*Exemplary Life*] (novel) 1973
Heimatmuseum [*The Heritage*] (novel) 1978
Drei Stücke (play) 1980
Der Verlust: Roman (novel) 1981
Exerzierplatz: Roman [*Training Ground*] (novel) 1985

CRITICISM

C. A. H. Russ (essay date 1966)

SOURCE: "The Short Stories of Siegfried Lenz," in *German Life and Letters,* Vol. 19, 1966, pp. 241-51.

[*In this essay, Russ surveys many themes and stylistic devices used by Lenz in the stories collected in* Jäger des Spotts, Das Feuerschiff, *and* Der Spielverderber.]

Siegfried Lenz belongs to that talented echelon of writers born in the later 1920s, and currently reaching the height of their powers. In our own country, translations of his work have been both published and broadcast. Yet he has not so far attracted the attention of 'Germanisten' here to the extent that one might have expected. It is in the hope of rectifying this situation, in some measure, that I would like to offer an interim survey of one department of his work.

Most of us gained our first knowledge of Lenz from *So zärtlich war Suleyken,* published in 1955. Now such an introduction is misleading. It seems not to be generally known that the 'Suleyken' collection was composed with the special aim of picturing the world of Lenz's boyhood for the benefit of his wife. The comedy with which the East Prussian background is affectionately infused sharply distinguishes these stories from those evoking grimmer memories of the region and of its recent history. For reasons of this kind, the present paper concentrates on Lenz's other collections, *Jäger des Spotts* (1958), *Das Feuerschiff* (1960) and *Der Spielverderber* (1965).

The timeless figure of the loser, the man who fails to survive the moment of truth, the fallen idol, dominates Lenz's fiction.

—*C. A. H. Russ*

At the end of his illuminating *Autobiographische Skizze,* Lenz declares that he demands of the writer 'ein gewisses Mitleid, Gerechtigkeit und einen nötigen Protest'. A protest against what? Is it voiced in his own stories? We should remind ourselves here that Lenz belongs to the *Gruppe 47.* As this suggests, those of his tales set in his own country regard it with critical detachment. His attack on, his 'protest' against, the commercialized values of contemporary West Germany is, if tempered by charity and humour, nevertheless real. He shows us a society where public relations are more important than the quality of private lives, and where only poverty may not be advertised, a society at which a story like '**Mein verdrossenes Gesicht**' pokes fun. The hero of this tale is an ex-serviceman who acquires a social niche of Böll-like futility, posing for advertisements which exploit his habitually gloomy expression. Similarly parasitic jobs are performed by the hired Father Christmases in '**Risiko für Weihnachtsmänner**', and by 'Der Amüsierdoktor', in the story of that name, whose doctorate has secured him an occupation that begins when the real work of his firm has stopped:

> seit drei Jahren beziehe ich mein Gehalt dafür, dass ich die auswärtigen Kunden unseres Unternehmens menschlich betreue: wenn die zehrenden Verhandlungen des Tages aufhören, werden die erschöpften Herren mir überstellt, und meinen Fähigkeiten bleibt es überlassen, ihnen zu belebendem Frohsinn zu verhelfen, zu einer Heiterkeit, die sie für weitere Verhandlungen innerlich lösen soll.

Yet, although so many of Lenz's stories are 'Geschichten aus dieser Zeit' (as he sub-titles the collection *Jäger des Spotts*), firmly set against the background of modern Germany, he is not just a chronicler of his country's recent history and present society, important as this function of the contemporary German writer continues to be. He sees himself as a reformer, but he insists that his protest is subordinated to, and conveyed by, his art: 'Ich schätze nun einmal die Kunst herauszufordern nicht so hoch wie die Kunst, einen wirkungsvollen Pakt mit dem Leser her-

zustellen, um die bestehenden Übel zu verringern'. Lenz, we may add, although delineating German scenes and situations so vividly, tries to look beyond them to more universal issues. This may be illustrated by his tale '**Stimmungen der See**', which depicts the clandestine attempt of three men to cross the Baltic. On internal evidence alone, it is hard to decide whether the action occurs during the war or afterwards, whether, in other words, the fugitives are trying to escape from the Nazi police State or from communist East Germany. Now what Lenz is doing in '**Stimmungen der See**' is to concentrate on psychological tensions set against the background of the sea that he knows and describes better than any other German writer of our time. The 'Stimmungen' are human as well as natural. The story's historical point of departure is, in the final analysis, irrelevant to its timeless themes: tension between the generations, the interplay of hope and fear, and man's cruelty to man.

Lenz has explained how a limited historical phenomenon—the collapse of Nazism—led him to the central issue of his stories:

> Dann wurden die Mächtigen machtlos, die Meister der Gewalt büssten ihre Herrschaft ein, und seit damals hat mich dieser Augenblick immer wieder beschäftigt: um selber verstehen zu lernen, was mit einem Menschen geschieht, der 'fällt', abstürzt, verliert, habe ich einige Geschichten geschrieben, in denen der Augenblick des 'Falls' dargestellt wird. Schreiben ist eine gute Möglichkeit, um Personen, Handlungen und Konflikte verstehen zu lernen (*Autobiographische Skizze*).

Lenz's concern, then, is with generally valid, universal themes which, as in '**Stimmungen der See**', transcend any purely historical context. Indeed, the timeless figure of the loser, the man who fails to survive the moment of truth, the fallen idol, dominates Lenz's fiction. Sometimes the character is trapped by external forces, or by the action of others, but sometimes, too, his own failings are unmasked. Whether he be tycoon, farmer, athlete, journalist, or teacher, his status—his security—will be demolished. The techniques with which Lenz handles this simple theme in his tales repay closer study.

We may first consider five of the 'Ich-Erzählungen' which form a substantial proportion of Lenz's short stories. Each of the five employs a narrator-observer who records the 'fall', or defeat, that he has witnessed. In '**Die Festung**', a son recalls how his father, a dispossessed East Prussian farmer, finding his tenure of new land cancelled, in turn, by an army requisition, ensconced himself in an improvised fortress as futile as the son's sandcastle. In '**Risiko für Weihnachtsmänner**' and '**Ein Haus aus lauter Liebe**', a hired outsider stumbles on a travesty of family life. The narrator of the former story, wearing his 'Uniform der Freude' as Father Christmas, finds himself enacting the grotesque charade of handing presents to a childless couple: his former commanding officer, now unbalanced, and his wife. The babysitter hired for the 'Haus aus lauter Liebe' discovers that a 'family-loving' tycoon has, if not a skeleton in the cupboard, an embarrassing father kept under lock and key. Two other stories in this group probe the world of organization men, to arrive at similarly disillusioned findings. Thus, in 'Der grosse Wildenberg', the narrator is confronted in the great man's sanctum with a lonely figure-head who is delighted to receive a visitor; and in 'Der seelische Ratgeber', which deserves to be read in conjunction with Nathanael West's *Miss Lonelyhearts,* the assistant to the editor of an advice column gradually realizes, as do we with him, that the editor's own private life is a catalogue of mismanaged relationships.

The narrator-observer of 'Der seelische Ratgeber' is also a narrator-victim. The idol falls, but so, in a sense, does his admirer: the effect is all the sharper in that his disillusionment, although constantly implicit, is not articulated until the final sentence. Narrator-victims appear in other tales. Lenz again shows us characters who, through their own fault or not, emerge as vulnerable or unable to fulfil expectations. In the narratives to which we now turn, however, the 'ich' himself is exposed. Thus, in 'Lukas, sanftmütiger Knecht', a white farmer recounts his desperate journey terminating in the discovery that the Mau Mau had reached his home before him. The narrator of the lighter 'Mein verdrossenes Gesicht' cannot sustain the gloomy expression on which his career as a photographer's model depends. The 'Amüsierdoktor' suffers even greater discomfiture, and nearly goes the way of all fish. Once more, then, the commercial world comes under Lenz's scrutiny, as in the first group of 'Ich-Erzählungen'. However, whereas the great Wildenberg's powerlessness is seen through the eyes of his visitor, the model and the 'Amüsierdoktor' themselves retail their misadventures. Narrator-victims have replaced narrator-observers. In 'Lieblingsspeise der Hyänen', on the other hand, we find both devices. They are not here combined, as we have seen them to be in the figure of the editorial assistant of 'Der seelische Ratgeber'. Instead, the narrative structure, one 'Ich-Erzählung' inside another, entails a situation in which the first narrator—the observer—listens to the second, American narrator—the victim—lamenting that his womenfolk's obsessive visits to shoe-shops throughout the family's European tour have prevented his re-visiting the scenes of his wartime experiences.

'Schwierige Trauer' requires separate attention. It is an 'Ich-Erzählung' in the form of an apostrophe to a dead member of the narrator's family: the mayor of an Eastern border town preoccupied, on the flight to the West, with saving trivial documents, whatever the human cost. Here the 'ich' is not so much the observer, or victim, but rather the agent of the denunciation directed against the mayor, who is, of course, in the terms of our discussion, the idol with feet of clay. Personal anger may explain the, for Lenz, unusual technical choice of a dynamic fictive narrator, for the writer was an eye-witness of the flight from the East.

We turn to stories outside the 'Ich-Erzählung' category. As we have seen, the latter includes tales dealing with inadequacy or defeat, observed by the narrator in others or himself. Now, in further works, characters observe *each other's* failure to meet a challenge. We might term this the

device of the character-observer. The observed challenge arises, in each case, on the physical plane, but its implications transcend that level. Like 'Stimmungen der See', these stories marry physical action and psychological reaction in a manner typical of Lenz's work. In 'Drüben auf den Inseln', a young man drowns as his sweetheart looks on helplessly—the intruder into a closed world has succumbed to the elemental forces within it; and in 'Das Wrack' a son observes his father's frustrated exhaustion as he dives repeatedly, and fruitlessly, to search a submerged wreck. 'Silvester-Unfall', another of Lenz's many explorations of close relationships, shows a family watching its head, who is doomed by disease, during the forced festivities of his last New Year's Eve. Here, as in 'Das Wrack', the act of observation is underlined by repeated allusion to it. In such other tales as 'Der Läufer', 'Ball der Wohltäter' and 'Jäger des Spotts', the witnesses of defeat are multiple, although Lenz's victim-figure in the latter story may (almost literally) snatch some measure of victory from its jaws.

In these narratives, employing character-observers, the agent of man's failure is nature itself, represented by the sea, by animals, and by the vulnerability of the human body to exhaustion, age and disease. Even the deed which leads to the athlete's disqualification, in 'Der Läufer', seems more a reflex action, or bodily accident, than wilful. Elsewhere, however, Lenz portrays the victims of *other characters.* The latter engage in more than observation, are less passive than most of the narrators of the 'Ich-Erzählungen' (recalling, rather, the opponents confronting some of the narrator-victims), and may therefore be termed character-agents. Thus, 'Der längere Arm' and 'Nur auf Sardinien' each portrays a wife's undermining of her husband's self-respect. 'Die Flut ist pünktlich' heightens the theme of marital tension: a wife alters her husband's watch, ensuring that he will be cut off by the tide, freeing her for a new life with another man. This second man, however, is also presented as a kind of victim, watching the husband walk out from terra firma and remaining unaware of the woman's capacity for evil until it is too late. 'Stimmungen der See', as already indicated, also hinges on antagonism between characters. One of them—the Professor—is divested of his precarious authority. Lorenz, his young companion, brings this home to him, and to us, by alluding to the Professor's classroom humiliation of years before, and by openly abusing his old teacher. The idol has not merely fallen, it has been pushed over!

We may claim that Lenz treats his central theme with considerable versatility, observing his figures of defeat from varying angles, and sometimes actually identifying them with his fictive narrators. In emphasizing his resourcefulness, we are moving from description to evaluation. Let us, to the same end, and however tentatively, now review some other aspects of his work as a short-story writer, beginning with some observations concerning literary influences.

Lenz readily admits his indebtedness to other, notably foreign, writers. Among those named in the *Autobiogra-*

phische Skizze are Camus and Hemingway. As he points out in the same essay, his university studies included 'Anglistik' and 'Literaturgeschichte', and these have undoubtedly influenced his development. His treatment of leit-motifs, transposing and modifying the constituents of a motif, creating diversity within unity, is somewhat reminiscent of Thomas Mann's technique, although neither as elaborate nor, frankly, as subtle. The English-speaking reader, however, will probably be most sensitive to general resemblances between Lenz's work and Hemingway's (the use of anaphora, the recurrent theme of the test, or moment of truth), and to such parallels as those between the beginnings of *For Whom the Bell Tolls* and '**Stimmungen der See**', or the endings of *The Old Man and the Sea* and the title-story of the collection *Jäger des Spotts,* or the sub-title of that collection—'Geschichten aus dieser Zeit—and *In our Time.* Like Hemingway, too, Lenz works into his fiction various kinds of specialized knowledge, entering, for instance, the esoteric world of the athlete in '**Der Läufer**' (and in the thematically related novel *Brot und Spiele*).

We must not, however, ascribe to direct influence what may result from affinity and from similarities of background. Like Hemingway, Lenz knows and loves the sea, and enjoys fishing, which, as he tells us, has influenced his approach to his art. Again, the economy evinced in Lenz's descriptive passages and in his dialogue partly derives, as in Hemingway's case, from the practice of journalism.

Another familiar literary effect employed in Lenz's stories is that of the 'Pointe'. The closing sentences of, for example, '**Der seelische Ratgeber**' and '**Nur auf Sardinien**' round off the works in question decisively and illuminatingly. The same device operates in '**Risiko für Weihnachtsmänner**' and '**Mein verdrossenes Gesicht**', the endings of which closely resemble each other, and in '**Der Verzicht**'. In the latter tale, which is set, unusually for Lenz, directly in the period of the war, the last Jew left in an East Prussian community has almost reached the place of his execution, and a new captor takes charge of him. The Jew's unresisting acceptance of his fate, and Lenz's avoidance of 'die Kunst herauszufordern', are, in the closing sentences, crowningly and paradoxically exemplified:

> Ein junger, breitgesichtiger Mann kam ihnen entgegen, sein Gewehr schräg vor der Brust. Er trat zwischen sie. Er befahl Heinrich Bielek [the first captor] zurückzugehen. Als er sich umdrehte, bemerkte er, dass der Mann in der erdbraunen Joppe, den er weiterzuführen hatte, ihm bereits mehrere Schritte stillschweigend vorausgegangen war.

If Lenz is a practitioner of conventional techniques rather than an experimental writer, this brings compensations. There are few German storytellers of our time who so grip the reader as Lenz does in '**Nur auf Sardinien**' or, particularly, in '**Lukas, sanftmütiger Knecht**'. He is, quite simply, adept in the traditional art of seizing and retaining the reader's attention. This bears both on his liking for a 'Pointe', towards which the story drives, and on the enig-

matic titles designed to whet the reader's curiosity: '**Jäger des Spotts**', '**Risiko für Weihnachtsmänner**', '**Die Glücksfamilie des Monats**', etc. The opening sentences of his tales are often equally intriguing. Lenz likes to plunge *in medias res,* referring to characters or events as if we were familiar with them already, and thus stimulating our desire to *acquire* that familiarity. Equally conventional, and equally enjoyable, is Lenz's use of surprise. To take other titles, consider how he arouses false expectations by such ironic headings as '**Ein Freund der Regierung**' and '**Ein Haus aus lauter Liebe**'.

Lenz also turns convention to his own advantage by reinvigorating outmoded or debased forms. If *So zärtlich war Suleyken* is a collection of latter-day 'Dorfgeschichten', and a story like '**Silvester-Unfall**' a modern 'Familiengemälde', as it were, such tales as '**Der seelische Ratgeber**' and '**Mein verdrossenes Gesicht**' represent a kind of twentieth-century 'Dümmlingsmärchen', recording the impressions of an innocent abroad in the jungle of advertising and the mass media. Most important, Lenz takes the narrative of action, the adventure story, for example, and shapes it so that it illuminates the human qualities and relationships that fascinate him. In '**Stimmungen der See**', we have noticed, the sea forms the setting of an exciting tale of action with psychological undertones (in the context of such works, it is tempting to recall that other exile from Eastern Europe, Joseph Conrad). In '**Der Läufer**', memories passing through the athlete's mind during his last race comprise over half the narrative. These recollections are themselves a retrospect of his career, so that physical action and psychological exploration are wedded.

As a practised writer of 'Hörspiele', Lenz is, of course, a master of dialogue. Thus, '**Der längere Arm**' is devoted to a conversation between husband and contemptuous wife; and '**Die Nacht im Hotel**', largely given up to a nocturnal dialogue in a dark room, is, as it were, a radio-play transposed to the sphere of prose fiction.

The sheer range of Lenz's short stories is impressive. We have already studied both his versatility in handling his central theme of the moment of truth, and the interplay of physical and psychological interest characterizing his work. The same resourcefulness enriches his treatment of background, be it the north German winter scene of '**Der Anfang von etwas**', the meridional landscape of '**Nur auf Sardinien**', or the lush Kenyan setting of '**Lukas, sanftmütiger Knecht**'. A different kind of versatility embraces the tragedy of '**Schwierige Trauer**' and the comedy of '**Der Amüsierdoktor**'. Again, the raw material of Lenz's tales, his vocabulary as such, is remarkably wide, ranging from nautical words ('wriggen', 'krängen', 'achteraus') to precise allusions to the bric-à-brac of modern civilization ('Kunststofflöffel', 'Bauchladen', 'Einkaufsnetz'). To characterize his style, however, we must look more deeply, to the realistic and the figurative elements of his narrative prose, and we may now review each of these in turn.

Lenz the realist reveals a keen eye for visual detail, from the momentary flash of the sun on an aircraft cockpit high above the fugitives' boat in **'Stimmungen der See'**—an elusive symbol of liberty (or danger?)—to the effects of heat on lead, conveying both the suspense generally inherent in the context of 'Bleigiessen' and the menace latent in the particular setting of **'Silvester-Unfall'**.

Lenz's description of nature also testifies to his accuracy as an observer: even the negative phenomenon of darkness is exploited, in **'Stimmungen der See'**:

> Als der erste Vorläufer des Sturms sie erreichte, war es finster über dem Wasser, eine fahle Dunkelheit herrschte, es war nicht die entschiedene, tröstliche, ruhende Dunkelheit der Nacht, sondern die gewaltsame, drohende Dunkelheit, die der Sturm vorausschickt.

And the variety of settings referred to previously is, of course, articulated in specific local colour.

In the field of human sensation, we find a series of realistic effects with, again, the familiar psychological undertones. Thus, in **'Jäger des Spotts'**, 'das dumpfe Glücksgefühl der Erschöpfung' resembles the 'weiche, wohlige Müdigkeit' provoked by the simple meal described so mouth-wateringly in **'Die Festung'**. The fusion of physical sensation and psychological process becomes, in **'Der Anfang von etwas'**, an aspect of human communication: 'Hoppe spürte, wie sich Paulas Finger um seinen Unterarm schlossen, ihr Erschrecken sich im wachsenden Druck der Finger fortsetzte'. The proferred hand conveys false feeling in **'Ein Haus aus lauter Liebe'** and genuine distress in **'Die Festung'**. Everyday gestures are endowed with meaning.

To return to **'Der Anfang von etwas'**, this story also exemplifies Lenz's realistic treatment of *sound*. As Hoppe prepares to cast his belongings into the river, the privacy and secrecy of his intended action are conveyed by the distance and impersonality of the sound that he hears: 'Er . . . spähte die Pier hinab, musterte die Luken der Speicher, stand und lauschte auf das schleifende Geräusch einer fernen Strassenbahn'. The enormous care devoted to realistic detail in Lenz's stories may be finally illustrated from this same tale by the accumulation of visual and acoustic elements relating to the fruit-machine.

For his descriptive material, then, Lenz draws heavily on the sights, sensations, gestures and sounds of everyday life. Yet, as we have noticed, the descriptive elements in question often carry some deeper implication. Even in that highly documentary account of the operation of a fruit-machine, unexpected abstract nouns link the mechanical process and the feelings of the players: 'wenn die Stille schon Verlust zu bedeuten schien, Aufforderung und neuen Einsatz, dann erfolgte mit herausfordernder Verzögerung ein Rasseln'. Lenz is not, therefore, a mere chronicler of surface reality. What we have seen to be true of his themes is true also of his style. He is neither merely polemical in his approach nor merely naturalistic in his technique. Among the means by which his prose acquires extra dimensions are metaphor, as in the passage just cited, and simile. Their conjunction with the 'documentary' elements

further typifies Lenz's versatility. Let us now review the role of figurative usage in his stories.

'Drüben auf den Inseln' includes a good example of the meaningful location of images in the structure of Lenz's work. The loss of young life which forms the climax of the story is prefigured, in the second paragraph, by the comparison of a motionless windmill to a dead, black flower. Similarly, at the start of **'Der Anfang von etwas'**, the hero's chance of a new life is anticipated not only by the story's title, and by its being set on 'Silvestermorgen', but perhaps also by the reference to his shadow: 'Unter dem Schneetreiben kam Hoppe hervor, nur ein Schatten zuerst, eine mühsame Ankündigung seiner selbst'.

The maritime world, which he knows so well, furnishes Lenz with crisp and appropriate images. In **'Drüben auf den Inseln'**, for example, the hermit-like existence of the islanders is perfectly caught in an image drawn by one of them from her own environment: 'Jeder lebt abgeschlossen für sich wie eine Muschel'.

Images with an ornithological reference are also recurrent. However, it is in the treatment of nature itself, and of concomitant elements, that Lenz gives full rein to his figurative talent, particularly, as we would expect, in the context of the sea. Thus, in **'Die Flut ist pünktlich'**, we again find, as in **'Drüben auf den Inseln'**, an early image prefiguring the tragic dénouement. To the dead, black flower in the image previously discussed we may compare the motionless, black strip of water, 'der wie zur Erinnerung für die Flut dalag, nach sechs Stunden wieder zurückzukehren und ihn aufzunehmen mit steigender Strömung'. In **'Die Flut ist pünktlich'**, as in **'Stimmungen der See'**, the sea appears endowed with a life of its own, and able to claim its puny victims at will. This is implied both by the titles of the two stories and by an image which they share: that of the *breathing sea*. **'Stimmungen der See'** contains, as well, images like that of the 'Muschel', above, in which the figurative reference is itself rooted in the narrative milieu, thus: 'Die Ruderblätter fächelten leicht im Wasser wie die Brustflossen eines lauernden Fischs (*sic*)'. Complementally, the coast-line on the horizon is compared to the blade of an oar. The effect of these echoes, or correspondences, within one image, and between two images, is actively to sustain the narrative unity. Lenz does not use the sea as an avenue to 'poetic', lyrical effect. On the contrary, figurative language here brings the scene more sharply before us. Further figures in the natural description convey the 'Stimmungen' imbuing both the setting and the fugitives: clouds seem hampered in their progress; the sun rises, only to vanish again—'so als hätte sie sich nur überzeugen wollen, dass das Boot noch trieb und die Männer noch in ihm waren'. This sombre transformation of a traditional symbol of hope, the rising sun, may be counterbalanced by the shadow-motif in **'Der Anfang von etwas'**, which, it was tentatively suggested, may have an (unexpectedly) optimistic implication. What is certain is that a figure describing the falling snow in **'Der Anfang von etwas'** reflects the hero's imprisoned existence and, then, his escape from it: 'Aus dem Windschatten sah Hoppe den Weg zurück . . . schräg ging der

Schnee nieder, wie hinter gespannten Schnüren eines weissen Gitters verbarg er das andere Ufer'. The story ends with Hoppe gazing at his possessions, symbols of the past, vanishing 'hinter dem weissen Gitter des Schneetreibens', then going on his way to a new freedom.

A particularly prominent kind of figurative language in Lenz's tales articulates his almost obsessive preoccupation with the human head, and especially the human face. Many of the images falling under this rubric represent caricature. This is best exemplified by the range of facial description in 'Der Anfang von etwas'. Such figurative elements often help, of course, to establish personality and atmosphere. The 'eichelförmige Augen' of the man sent to fetch the last of the Jews in 'Der Verzicht' convey menace and cunning; the 'knolliges, kartoffelartiges Gesicht' of the wife in 'Silvester-Unfall' conspires with her husband's forced smile and his face's resemblance to a mask composed of dissimilar halves to heighten the strained, unnatural atmosphere of the macabre festival.

In the treatment of *sound,* too, the element of documentary transcription, already reviewed, is counterbalanced by arresting figurative usage. Thus, in 'Der Läufer', the hero's awareness of his surroundings as his last race begins is expressed largely by aural elements of this kind:

> und er hörte das Brausen der Stimmen, hörte die murmelnde Bewunderung und die Sprechchöre, die . . . wie ein skandiertes Echo durch das Stadion klangen ... die Sprechchöre sprangen wie Fontänen auf, hinter ihm und vor ihm.

In 'Der Anfang von etwas', Hoppe's unexpected opportunity is 'echoed' in sound. Early in the tale, noises are 'verstümmelt' and 'erstickt' in the falling snow. At the end, the change of reference in the imagery to one of physical well-being underlines, like the modulation of the 'Gitter' motif previously discussed, the transformation of his life:

> dann trat er zurück, hob ohne Zögern den Karton an und liess ihn knapp neben der Pier zwischen die Eisschollen fallen: ein tiefes 'Wumm' drang zu ihm herauf, ein Laut wie ein tiefes zufriedenes Aufseufzen.

Perhaps Lenz's favourite figure is an adjective qualifying an abstract noun in a surprising juxtaposition. In 'Mein verdrossenes Gesicht', the heartiness generated between reunited wartime comrades is epitomized in a phrase of this kind: 'schulterklopfende Fröhlichkeit'. Sometimes the juxtaposition is so startling as to amount to oxymoron: 'vorschriftsmässige Begeisterung'; 'biedermännische Tücke', 'Schwierige Trauer'.

A writer who financed his university studies by combining the roles of black marketeer and blood donor is, perhaps, likely to have a sharpened sense of the incongruous. Be that as it may, the element of paradox revealed in the phrases just quoted forms the stylistic counterpart of the desire to question accepted truths, to explore established reputations, and to test performance, which, as we have

seen, furnishes Lenz with a wealth of interrelated characters and situations. Language, too, is scrutinized in new and unexpected guises. Yet Lenz is no more a revolutionary in the realm of narrative tone than in that of social criticism. The judicious desire to 'conclude a pact' with the reader, rather than overtly to challenge him, informs the style as well as the content of his short stories. He has, indeed, been termed the most conventional writer of his generation in his use of language. On the other hand, there are signs that Lenz's inquiries may now be leading him to a greater degree of technical experiment. His latest novel, *Stadtgespräch,* represents an attempt to practise on the grand scale the form of the narrative apostrophe, or harangue, already adumbrated in 'Schwierige Trauer'. A recent short story, 'Der sechste Geburtstag', essays the—for the male writer—difficult task of employing a female fictive narrator. We may hope that other experiments will follow in the years to come. For, if Lenz succeeds in fusing experiment with the traditional narrative virtues which are his already, he may emerge as a major artist.

Colin Russ (essay date 1973)

SOURCE: "The Macabre Festival: A Consideration of Six Stories by Siegfried Lenz," in *Deutung und Bedeutung: Studies in German and Comparative Literature,* Mouton, 1973, pp. 275-93.

[*In the following essay, Russ discusses thematic similarities between six stories that are set during festivals or holidays.*]

Siegfried Lenz's fiction discloses a continual preoccupation with a limited number of central, interrelated themes, which are yet varied in very interesting ways. In particular, the complex of motifs embracing the sudden reversal of fortune, the loss of authority or status, and the revelation of vulnerability, has proved a rewarding field for this writer's searching and prolific imagination. In his *Autobiographische Skizze* he explains how he was led to this area by a fact of contemporary history, the fall of the National Socialists:

> Dann wurden die Mächtigen machtlos, die Meister der Gewalt büßten ihre Herrschaft ein, und seit damals hat mich dieser Augenblick immer wieder beschäftigt: um selber verstehen zu lernen, was mit einem Menschen geschieht, der "fällt", abstürzt, verliert, habe ich einige Geschichten geschrieben, in denen der Augenblick des "Falls" dargestellt wird. Schreiben ist eine gute Möglichkeit, um Personen, Handlungen und Konflikte verstehen zu lernen.

Now this particular thematic concern of Lenz's ultimately turns on a discrepancy between appearance and reality: what seems secure is insecure, what is taken for granted rests on sand. The clash of *Sein* and *Schein* in this writer's interpretation sometimes involves a 'moment of truth', in which their divergence becomes evident. Yet beside a story like "Die Festung", in which a sudden catastrophe, refuting the security in which the characters have seemed ensconced, forms the nub of the action, we find a tale like "Silvester-Unfall", for example, which deals with a static crisis in that it explores the knowledge of the inevitability of disaster, and the situation that such knowledge conditions. Again, "Vorgeschichte", as the title implies, looks beyond the catastrophic events at its centre. In his essay "Warum ich nicht wie Hemingway schreibe", Lenz describes how he came to find the American master's theme of the limited 'moment of truth' too restrictive, and how he then turned to wider perspectives:

> Ich erfuhr, wie wichtig es ist, die Hypotheken der Vergangenheit anzuerkennen, überhaupt einen Gaumen für die Bedeutung von Vergangenheit zu zeigen— etwas, was mein literarisches Vorbild nicht tat, nicht tun konnte. Ich lernte einzusehen, daß Leben nicht nur aus Momenten gewaltsamer Erprobung besteht. Ich kam zu der Überzeugung, daß auch andere Augenblicke Würde beanspruchen oder verleihen als nur die Nähe des Todes. Und schließlich machte ich die Erfahrung, daß in dieser Welt eine verändernde Intelligenz wirksam ist, die bei Hemingway nicht vorkam. Was mich interessierte, und was ich bei meinem Vorbild vermißte, das ist die Zeit zwischen und nach den Niederlagen, das sind die Jahre der Entscheidungslosigkeit, das sind die Vorspiele und Nachspiele zu den Sekunden der Prüfung.

Among the results of Lenz's explorations, as adumbrated above, we encounter a number of paradoxical stories in which his characteristic preoccupations are articulated in the context of various social occasions, ranging from such family events as a birthday or a wedding to more general festivities, certain of which, like Christmas, may equally, of course, be celebrated in the domestic circle. In each of these festivals, as we shall call them, what should be an occasion for relaxation becomes a source of strain, discord replaces sociability, or sadness and tragedy overlie or efface the atmosphere of the "Fest". The latter may occupy the whole or just part of a story. It may proceed as expected and then take a disastrous turn, or it may be characterized throughout by a latent, incongruous tension, a distinction similar to that between, on the one hand, the 'moment of truth' and, on the other, a more broadly evident discrepancy between appearance and reality. In five of the six stories to be considered, the occasions in question are darkened by such motifs as illness, accident and suicide, so that we may define the focus of our investigation as the *macabre* festival. Our enquiry may conveniently be pursued in three stages. Let us first outline the contents of the tales, then proceed to study various motifs and devices which recur in them before observing, finally, some of the ways in which Lenz nevertheless succeeds in varying his treatment of the central *donnée*.

I

In offering, to begin with, brief summaries of the six stories under review, we must bear in mind that such abridgments are necessarily simplified and do scant justice to the narrative skill for which Siegfried Lenz is noted, but we may hope that at least the main contours of the plots emerge. Aspects of particular relevance to the subsequent discussion will be emphasized where possible.

"Silvester-Unfall" (1958) depicts a New Year's Eve meal, and its aftermath, in the family circle of Rudolf Mummer. A veteran waiter, Mummer wears the garb of his profession for the occasion. He has been given only a few months to live, but is as determined to survive until the maturity of his insurance policy on his sixty-fifth birthday, in October, as he is anxious to inject his own forced geniality into the present proceedings. After the meal, the family starts to read the future by means of "Bleigießen". As the doomed father holds the spoon in the flame, his son pulls at his wrist in order to stop matters going any further. The hot lead spills onto the son's hand. The last seconds of the old year tick away, and the new one begins.

The narrator of **"Risiko für Weihnachtsmänner"** (1958) presents himself at an agency for the hiring of Father Christmases. By coincidence, he is, as "Weihnachtsmann", driven out to the home of his former colonel. The latter is now mentally unbalanced. The visit of Father Christmas, distributing presents to him and his childless wife, who abets his fantasy, is linked in his mind to the killing of a "Weihnachtsmann" in the war. The narrator, wounded on the same occasion, shares the memories but not the fantasy, and returns to the agency in its *Kleinbus* with diminished enthusiasm.

"Ball der Wohltäter" (1959) is written in the form of a harangue, addressed by Fred Puchta to Barbara Bredow, a singer whose career has waned. They have returned from a charity ball which Puchta has persuaded the latter to attend in order to re-establish valuable contacts. Drinking too much, she has forced her singing on an unreceptive audience at the ball, and been dragged away by Puchta. Back at her lodgings, he is demanding an IOU for the price of her ticket to the ball.

In **"Vorgeschichte"** (1961), a banker's daughter tells a listener of the hold which Bard, now the speaker's husband, had exerted on the banker and which had secured him a post in the bank, accommodation with the family, and ultimately the daughter herself. After an abortive journey undertaken by the speaker in order to clarify her father's dependence on him, Bard had himself told her of a bank-robbery, an 'inside job', in which he, Bard, had been involved when still a lad. In the course of the wedding festivities, now nearly nine years ago, the father had hanged himself.

The narrator of **"Der sechste Geburtstag"** (1964) is a mother, a compulsive drinker, who tells of the bringing forward from September to April of the sixth birthday of her son, stricken with leukaemia. She recalls seeing her husband off to work, journeying in a stuffy tram-car, buying presents in the toy department of a store, failing to enjoy refreshments in the store's restaurant, and returning home to the celebration which culminates in the son's being informed by his sister that it is *not* his birthday, and in his taking no notice of her. The parents' wordless encounter in the hall forms the end of the account.

The central character of **"Die Glücksfamilie des Monats"** (1964), the narrator's father, is a school caretaker with a speech impediment. A woman reporter, accompanied by a photographer, brings the family the tidings that a newspaper has selected them as the "Glücksfamilie" of the month, and will sponsor their visits to events of their choice. At the first of these, the "Ostafrika-Tag", the handicapped father's attempt at a speech ends in a fiasco. At the second event, a launching, the father is struck by a hawser. At the hospital, the mother tells the narrator that the father has now lost the faculty of speech completely. She settles back in calm silence.

II

Various motifs and technical devices recur in these stories and underline their interrelationship. Most of our examples of the aspects under review will be drawn directly from the context of the given festivals. In some cases, however, the motifs and devices in question serve, so to speak, as advance warnings that the coming festive events will go awry, or that they are not to be taken at face-value. Now and then, on the other hand, their effect is retrospective, as they underline disasters that have occurred.

The 'authenticity' of the various festivals is often undermined by the motifs of *pretence* and *the acting of a role,* creating an impression of superficiality, while a more problematic state of affairs lurks behind the given façades. Thus, in **"Silvester-Unfall"**, the appropriately named Mummer's first appearance implicitly suggests a performer's entrance, with the kitchen-door serving as curtain which is "aufgezogen", as it were, in two senses. He behaves as if he and his wife were partners at a dance, or a banquet:

> Dann, als sie es nicht vermutete, öffnete er die Tür, zog sie ganz auf und trat mit leicht vorgestreckten Händen in den Türrahmen.

> Eine warme Essenswolke strömte an Mummer vorbei in die Stube, und er stand da in seinem alten, schäbigen Kellnerfrack: ausgezehrt, schwärzlich im Gesicht, gewaltsam grinsend, ein leichter Mann mit einer Jockey-Figur, alt und doch von unschätzbarem Alter; seine Stirn war schweissbedeckt. Triumphierend sah er die Frau an, rieb die Handrücken am Frack ab; dann ging er tänzelnd auf sie zu, zog sie vom Hocker und bot ihr seinen Arm.

> "Ich lasse bitten", sagte er.

Dressed for the part, Mummer is also acting the role of waiter, but adopts yet a further, complementary identity as he toasts his wife in imitation of those whom he has served: "Er trank ihr zu, steif, wortlos, mit vorgeneigtem Oberkörper, wie sie sich auf dem Schnelldampfer *Patria* zugetrunken hatten." The narrator of **"Risiko für Weihnachtsmänner"** also dresses up, as Father Christmas. Ultimately, the 'act' breaks down: after the macabre encounter with the deranged colonel the narrator fears the vicissitudes in which his role might again entangle him. This collapse of the

festive charade is mirrored in **"Der sechste Geburtstag"**, with the sister's progression from an initial willingness to abet the pretence—"sie war bereit, zu schweigen und mitzuspielen"—to her reluctance to maintain the deception—"Ich musste sie bitten, musste sie sogar verwarnen, in unserem Sinne mitzuspielen"—and finally to her betrayal of the truth, ironically abortive though it be. In **"Die Glücksfamilie des Monats"**, the mother is "keineswegs versucht, mitzuspielen" when she is offered the role invented for her by the newspaper, but the insincere reporter is quick to produce "gespielte Bewunderung" in order to encourage the father to play *his* role, which will be accompanied by ridicule and terminated by tragedy. Both parents must, in due course, pose for the photographer as directed, however absurdly. In the description of the "Ostafrika-Tag", the motif of the assumed image is developed to a satirically confusing extreme:

> Man wartete auf das Staatsoberhaupt, doch das Staatsoberhaupt erschien nicht, sondern ein Mann, der ihm sehr ähnlich war, den gleichen Gang, den gleichen Blick, die gleiche Kopfhaltung hatte und vorbereitet schien, die gleiche Rede wie das Staatsoberhaupt zu halten.

The motif of the *mask* often accompanies or anticipates the false or historionic elements in Lenz's festivals. It may be explicit, or implicit, as in the reference to the reporter's feigned admiration, cited above, and the mother's reluctance, in the same scene, to adopt "ein anderes Gesicht". In **"Silvester-Unfall"** Mummer's attempt to counterfeit gaiety is underlined by a grotesquerie centred on this motif:

> Verstohlen seinem Blick ausweichend, beobachtete Ruth ihren Vater, wie er dasass und sich zu schaurigem Triumph zwang, ihnen zuzuwinkerte, wobei sein Gesicht sich einseitig verzerrte gleich einer Maske, die auf jeder Hälfte anders geschnitzt ist. . . .

In **"Risiko für Weihnachtsmänner"**, the narrator is literally masked, but his own false nose, the reminder of his war wounds, cannot be concealed by the seasonable disguise:

> Alles passte, die Stiefel passten, die Mütze, nur die Maske passte nicht: zu scharf drückten die Pappkanten gegen meine künstliche Nase; schliesslich nahmen wir eine offene Maske, die meine Nase nicht verbarg.

The **"Ball der Wohltäter"** is a masked ball in all senses but the literal one. Puchta urges Barbara Bredow to feign, or rather don, a festive spirit ("Heiterkeit anzulegen"), and everybody puts on an appropriately dutiful expression for an unwanted speech concerning the charity. In **"Vorgeschichte"**, the father receives the news of the projected wedding (where he will commit suicide) with masked reactions:

> Mein Vater, . . . der kein Fest ausliess, der überall gesucht war wegen seiner behäbigen Würde—er gehörte zu jeder Feier wie die Lorbeerbäume in den Kübeln—,

schien sich vor dem Fest zu fürchten, das mir galt und doch auch ihm.

. . . ich weiss heute nur, dass seine Angst ihn davor zurückhielt, sich gegen etwas aufzulehnen, was er nicht nur missbilligte, sondern sogar hasste. Frag mich nicht, wieviele Masken er trug: als er mich zur Tür brachte, nahm sein Lächeln schon wieder zu, und als er sich übers Geländer beugte und mir nachwinkte, musste ich annehmen, dass seine erste Reaktion nur ein Irrtum gewesen war.

Pretence and the wish to deceive, and the discrepancy between appearance and reality that they involve, also underlie a complex of references to *constrained and forced attitudes,* which may represent a hollow 'triumph'. Mummer's "erzwungene Fröhlichkeit" and "gewaltsame Vergnügtheit", together with his triumphant gaze, are all mentioned very early and anticipate his daughter's view of him quoted above. The "Glücksmutter" gradually assumes an "erzwungene, unwirsche Heiterkeit" in keeping with the festive image forced upon her. The "Dauerlächeln" worn by her husband at the "Ostafrika-Tag"—another mask—is a more benevolent variation of Mummer's forced smile, which provides a leitmotif in **"Silvester-Unfall"**. The latter's triumphant grin is grotesquely mirrored in the visual appearance of the festive carp:

. . . das Maul war offen wie in grinsender Gier, die Haut des Fisches hatte eine blassblaue Färbung. Die Frau starrte auf ihr Kopfstück, an dem Gewürznelken klebten, Pfefferkörner, sie glaubte durch den Dampf das Kopfstück grinsen zu sehen, und sie hob die Hände auf den Tisch und schob den Teller behutsam von sich fort. Mummer merkte es nicht, er entkorkte eine Weinflasche, füllte die Gläser und lächelte triumphierend und hob sein Glas: "Auf unser Silvester, Lucie."

Indeed, we often find in these stories that "Feste" are undermined by the motifs of *smiling* and *laughter,* whether in advance or, as here, during the enactment of the events in question. Far from pointing to happiness, such references signpost the problematic or cruel realities lurking beneath, and refuting, surface appearances. The colonel smiles as the perplexed "Weihnachtsmann" hesitantly opens his sack. At the **"Ball der Wohltäter"**, the "Bereitschaft zu schnellem Lächeln" is obligatory. The (more explicit) leitmotif of Bard's "kleines, infames Lächeln" helps to generate foreboding in **"Vorgeschichte"**; when the narrator tries to uncover his past, she elicits only his friends' meaningful but uninformative "Grinsen". In **"Der sechste Geburtstag"**, a workman gives the mother a smile that is "schnell und gemein", and from the saleswoman she gets one that is "zurechtweisend". The reporter, bringing to the "Glücksfamilie des Monats" the glad tidings of their selection, "legte ein Vertrauen in ihr Lächeln, das . . . durch nichts gerechtfertigt schien". Beside her stands the photographer, "etwas zerstreut, doch gleichfalls lächelnd". The "Glücksvater" attracts the contemptuous grin of schoolboys, and both at the "Ostafrika-Tag" and at the launching ceremony people laugh at him. He is liberated from mockery only by his disaster:

"Seine Sprache", sagte Mutter, "jetzt wird ihn keiner mehr hochnehmen. Keiner wird mehr lachen über ihn. Vielleicht ist das sein Glück."

"Er wird sie wiederfinden, seine Sprache. Bestimmt", sagte ich.

"Wenn er nichts mehr sagen kann, werden sie ihn in Frieden lassen", sagte Mutter; sie hob den Kopf und sah mich an, und in ihrem Blick lag keine Verzweiflung.

The lack of spontaneity and of unambiguous festive exuberance conveyed by the motifs so far discussed is equally underlined by references to various kinds of *silence,* found in all the stories under review. We have already alluded to Mummer's formal, wordless toast. The unforeseen sterility of the domestic "Fest" in **"Risiko für Weihnachtsmänner"** seems carried over into its immediate, mute aftermath:

Unten wartete der Kleinbus auf mich; sechs frierende Weihnachtsmänner sassen im Laderaum, schweigsam und frierend, erschöpft vom Dienst an der Freude; während der Fahrt zum Hauptquartier sprach keiner ein Wort.

In **"Vorgeschichte"**, Bard's "Lautlosigkeit" seems full of menace; silence greets the announcement of his bank appointment, and the breakfast before the wedding is marked by the father's cutting remarks to him and the silence with which he receives them. The start of the **"Ball der Wohltäter"** is a calculated "stummes Befragen, stummes Messen und Handeln"; its festive atmosphere is further diminished by the need for silence for the speaker, and Barbara Bredow's performance elicits no applause (just as her letters and telephone calls have been ignored). Silent interrogation also takes place in **"Der sechste Geburtstag"**, when the mother arrives home for the party and is met by her daughter's "stumm befragende Skepsis", different in kind from the latter's earlier willingness to 'keep quiet'. For his part, the son undoes his presents without a word, and the story ends with the total breakdown of verbal communication between husband and wife—the rest is silence:

Ich wischte mir die Lippen ab, zündete eine Zigarette an, als Alfred lächelnd aus der Küche kam, auf Zehenspitzen zu mir, dann etwas flüstern wollte und es nicht tat, sondern einfach an mir vorbeiging, als hätte er mich gar nicht dort stehen sehn.

An extended use of the motif characterizes **"Die Glücksfamilie des Monats"**, where the father's constant battle to retain the faculty of speech reaches a climax at the "Ostafrika-Tag":

Er blieb einfach stehn im Zentrum des Schweigens, lange, viel zu lange, liess so die Erwartung wachsen und setzte sich immer noch nicht, obwohl sein Dastehen jetzt schon ein Versprechen bedeutete, das er einlösen musste durch ein Wort. Vielleicht kam ihm das Schweigen auch wie eine drängende Aufforderung vor:

er setzte sich nicht. Er schloss die Augen, warf den Kopf hin und her, machte zunächst langsame, schnappende Bewegungen und liess dann seine Lippen zittern, seine Lippen verfärbten sich und wurden schmal und scharf vor Begehren nach dem ersten Wort.

After the fiasco that ensues, the father is unable to speak and his wife, too, remains silent. The story culminates, of course, in the permanent silencing of the "Glücksvater", when he is literally struck dumb in the accident at the launching ceremony, a development prefigured in miniature by the **"Silvester-Unfall"**, which renders Mummer's son "stumm vor überwältigendem Schmerz". The "Glücksmutter" was clearly right to receive the news of the family's honour with an unmoved silence.

The *act of observation,* a favourite motif of Lenz's, is yet another factor militating against a spontaneous festive atmosphere; a spectator stands back in order to watch, or a character feels himself under scrutiny. Thus, in **"Silvester-Unfall"**, the son and daughter repeatedly observe their doomed father. At the **"Ball der Wohltäter"**, Puchta enjoins Barbara Bredow to treat it as a military operation where one must keep one's eyes open, only to find her becoming the object of the contemptuous stares of others. In **"Der sechste Geburtstag"**, the mother is scrutinized by the saleswoman and then, it nightmarishly seems, by all the other customers in the restaurant:

> . . . ich . . . las [die Getränkekarte] bis zu dem Augenblick, in dem ich mich dringend beobachtet fühlte. Was war denn geschehen, was wollten sie alle von mir? Wodurch erregte ich ihr Interesse? Alle an den Nebentischen, kleine untersetzte Frauen, alte Männer, selbst Kinder musterten mich, nicht lächelnd oder beiläufig, sondern befremdet fast, mit interessiertem Befremden.

Back at home, her daughter's observant gaze is a symptom of an incipient dissociation from the party preparations:

> Jutta stand viel herum und beobachtete mich bei den Vorbereitungen, und auf einmal sagte sie: "Vielleicht freut er sich gar nicht." "Warum", sagte ich, "warum soll er sich nicht freuen?" "Wenn er merkt, dass heute gar kein Geburtstag ist." . . .

> Ich merkte, dass Jutta . . . sich am liebsten geweigert hätte mitzufeiern . . .

The festivals in these tales are frequently devalued by *seedy, unappetizing* or *inefficient features* in the settings or in the characters themselves. Mummer's New Year celebration is punctuated by the sound of a water-closet above and tawdry music from below. His kitchen overlooks the "schwarze Schlucht des Hofes" and a "Ruinenplatz". The tram-car carrying the narrator of **"Der sechste Geburtstag"** on her journey to buy presents is crowded and stuffy. Barbara Bredow, living in a "schäbige Pension" has used a dress as pledge for the rent; and she is confronted at the ball by a lethargic band (then replaced by better, but sulky musicians). The reporter bringing the "Glücksfamilie des Monats" the glad tidings of their selection has a defective handbag, lacks a pencil and is as physically unappetizing as the secretary in the (makeshift) office where the "Weihnachtsmann" receives his briefing before he goes out into the "kalte[n] Regen".

"Risiko für Weihnachtsmänner" illustrates most clearly the *commercialization* which cheapens certain of the festive occasions in these tales: the Father Christmases are *hired.* As the narrator ironically recalls: "Ich schwang den Sack auf die Schulter, stapfte fest, mit schwerem freudebringendem Schritt die Treppe hinauf—der Schritt war im Preis einbegriffen." In her quest for gifts, the narrator of **"Der sechste Geburtstag"** encounters representatives of the commercial world, a festively attired individual ushering her into the store, a condescending saleswoman and an uninterested waiter. The whole artificially festive action of **"Die Glücksfamilie des Monats"** arises from the intrusion of the commercialized mass media into private life.

When the mother of the stricken child in **"Der sechste Geburtstag"**, having left him in bed, is confronted, in the tram-car, by an advertisement eulogizing "die Vorzüge einer Matratze", we see not only, once more, Lenz's sceptical interest in the commercial world but also an *irony* equally characteristic of these tales, and equally directed to diminishing the atmosphere of festival. The doomed boy himself, whose sixth birthday has been brought forward, is described as "seinem Alter voraus". His place at the celebration is marked by a "Halbbogen aus Blumenköpfen", which conspires with the lighted candles to create an unintended but ironically appropriate funereal impression, and his last words in the story are: "Weg, laß mich." **"Silvester-Unfall"**, too, includes phrases with concealed macabre implications; an unintentional, ominous reminder of the father's "eleventh hour" situation sounds in his daughter's words: "Wir können doch nicht so sitzen und warten, bis es zwölf ist. Silvester ist doch nicht zum Warten da, oder?" In **"Risiko für Weihnachtsmänner"**, the narrator is congratulated on his metaphorical "gute Nase", enabling him to seek out the officer's house, but takes the remark, here with conscious irony, as applying to the nose with which plastic surgery has equipped him.

Within individual stories, *leitmotifs* and *other internal correspondences* provide equally vivid oblique comments on the action, as we have already noticed, and this, like the use of irony, represents a recurrent technical resource in these tales. **"Ball der Wohltäter"** is both introduced and rounded off by the familiar motif of commercialization, with references to the "Preis für die Eintrittskarte". On the figurative level, Puchta buys the tickets for the ball as an investment ("wie eine sichere Aktie"). The evening itself gets under way as a "festliche Börse", at which everybody's "Kurswert" is calculated. The "einladende Traurigkeit" in which Barbara Bredow has specialized is referred to three times; its meretricious quality is emphasized by another familiar motif, the smile, especially as she sets out for the ball:

Immerhin sah ich dich lächeln mit deiner einladenden Traurigkeit (vielleicht war es auch nur eine vorsichtige Imitation deines einstigen Lächelns), und ich war plötzlich zuversichtlich, so fuhren wir nach Bellkamp hinaus.

In **"Vorgeschichte"**, the leitmotif of Bard's "kleines, infames Lächeln" is reinforced by several allusions to his polite, condescending manner. In **"Der sechste Geburtstag"**, both saleswoman and waiter are "gleichgültig". The photographer in the **"Glücksfamilie des Monats"** is characterized by the vacuous phrase "und so weiter", with which he lards his conversation.

Certain of these tales include one or more subsidiary social occasions in which, as it were, the problematic aspects of the focal "Feste" are reflected in miniature. In this sense, the social event becomes itself a repeated motif. Thus, a Sunday lunch scene in **"Vorgeschichte"**, coloured by the familiar motifs of the forced smile and of observation, is deprived of all sociability and becomes a harbinger of the discordant breakfast before the wedding and of its grim sequel:

> Während Bard von diesem Freund erzählte, beobachtete ich nur Vater, und ich sah, daß er grinste und sich amüsierte—oder vorgab, sich zu amüsieren—, so beflissen, weißt du, qualvoll bemüht; denn er konnte nie etwas anderes sein als er selbst, ein gravitätischer Sparkassen- und Bankdirektor, der nie lachte, auf keinen Witz einging und dafür eine Überzeugung hatte: in seinen Augen rechtfertigte das Leben kein Gelächter . . .

As we have seen, the mother's break for refreshments in **"Der sechste Geburtstag"** turns into a claustrophobic fantasy. In **"Die Glücksfamilie des Monats"**, the initial visit of the reporter and the photographer is compared to that of a Father Christmas and represents the "Auftakt' to the central events; its bonhomie is described, as we have noticed, in sceptical terms. Again—and here one moves beyond a technique of "reflection in miniature" to a fuller duplication—we must observe that **"Risiko für Weihnachtsmänner"** turns on *two* macabre Christmas festivals, the memory of the first haunting the second. Another doubling of the festival motif, but now relating to present and *future*, lies in the fact that Mummer expresses at "Silvester" the determination to survive until his next birthday. On a more satirical level, an official speech at the launching in **"Die Glücksfamilie des Monats"** is kept short, as the speaker has to perform his task for another ship on the same day.

Having established how various narrative features recur in this set of stories, echoing and underlining their thematic affinities, let us now turn to the complementary question of their diversity. How is repetition avoided, how is the author's versatility revealed? Such questions may be approached by visualizing five of the six tales as forming an interconnected, but varied series: **"Silvester-Unfall"** plays exclusively in the domestic circle; **"Der sechste Geburtstag"** also centres on a closed family unit, but yet widens the perspective in that a member of it, the mother, goes

out into an environment that is indifferent, indeed (in her eyes) inimical, before she returns to the private horror at home; **"Risiko für Weihnachtsmänner"**, a third domestic portrait, reverses the situation in the sense that it is narrated by a visitor to the macabre festival. In **"Vorgeschichte"**, the visitor is more calculating, and the menace is now no mere hallucination. The disaster strikes publicly, as the guests are celebrating the wedding; **"Die Glücksfamilie des Monats"** also represents a catastrophic 'invasion' of the family by outside forces, but now the disaster is accidental, albeit even less private. From the claustrophobic sphere of **"Silvester-Unfall"**, at one end of the series, we have moved to the equally ambiguous world of public events at the other end.

The treatment of *locale* in these stories is a source of narrative diversity, and related to the progression just described. Again, **"Silvester-Unfall"**, **"Risiko für Weihnachtsmänner"** and **"Der sechste Geburtstag"** exhibit similarities: in each of them the action ends where it has begun. Thus, in **"Silvester-Unfall"**, we move from the Mummers' living-room to the kitchen, and back again to the living-room. The settings in **"Risiko für Weihnachtsmänner"** are equally symmetrical: office—bus—domestic *milieu*—bus—office. **"Der sechste Geburtstag"** opens with the narrator's husband leaving her at the front door of the flat, as she promises not to drink during the day ahead, after which there is almost at once a reference to her taking a shower, and then she goes to the children in their room. After the description of the shopping expedition, we return to the flat for the critical episode in the children's room (the sister's betrayal of the truth), then the mother snatches a drink in the bathroom, and, finally, the husband walks silently past her in the hall. Here, then, we may speak not only of symmetry, but of an elaborated mirror image relationship, in which the sequence of references to place at the start of the story is, with the detail of nightmare, reversed at its end. The interconnection is further strengthened by the positioning of characters, by the motif of drink, and by references, of a familiar kind, to the husband's smile, both in the opening sequence—as he plays the role of a man with plenty of money—and in the final sentence. There are even balancing allusions to his "Fingerkuppen", at the start, and "Zehenspitzen", at the end! **"Vorgeschichte"** plays in several rooms of the family house, as well as beyond it. A mirror image different in kind from that just discussed is visible here when we compare the start and finish of the story. At the beginning, Bard in effect blackmails his way into the father's study; at the end, the father commits suicide in Bard's room. As in **"Vorgeschichte"**, a wider, public setting is employed in **"Die Glücksfamilie des Monats"**, for the enactment of the disaster. In the latter story, changes of scene are, of course, inherent in the 'honour' for which the family has been singled out. The tragedy of the tale is epitomized in the progression from home to hospital which it encompasses.

The treatment of *time* differentiates the six tales in a generally similar fashion. Once again, **"Silvester-Unfall"**, **"Risiko für Weihnachtsmänner"** and **"Der sechste Geburtstag"** may be grouped. In each of them, the action is of short duration. In all three tales, however, the present is overshadowed by another period of time, the past on the Eastern Front in **"Risiko für Weihnachtsmänner"**, and the ineluctable future in **"Silvester-Unfall"** and **"Der sechste Geburtstag"**. We might visualize the participants in this trio of domestic festivals as characters standing in a spotlight, clearly exposed to us at this moment, yet only a step from the menacing darkness. In **"Ball der Wohltäter"**, the focal events are again of short duration, and they are again coloured by the 'intrusion' of another time—the singer's success and decline. However, the emphasis is somewhat different. Whereas in **"Risiko für Weihnachtsmänner"** the past, as it were, lives on, to be embellished in a macabre ritual, it is irremediably lost in **"Ball der Wohltäter"**, and the attempt to recapture it leads to the fiasco. The latter story is further characterized by the device of the framework conversation, so that there are, in fact, three dimensions of time in play: the singer's former career (followed by two years' isolation), the phase centred on the ball, and Puchta's harangue in the early hours of the following day. Similarly, in the even more widely ranging **"Vorgeschichte"**, we have, first, the time of the bank-robbery, secondly, the events culminating in the wedding and suicide, and, finally, the framework conversation nearly nine years after the disaster. Here, in a further variation, the remoter past is at first irrecoverable; the narrator's journey in order to clarify it is abortive. Then it is revealed by Bard's own account of the bank-robbery. The past, 'coming alive' in an Ibsenian fashion worthy of the Scandinavian setting, operates as remorselessly as in **"Risiko für Weihnachtsmänner"**. The 'duplication' of macabre festivals noted in the latter story appears in more ramified form in **"Vorgeschichte"**: the father's suicide becomes part of the grim legacy, the wedding-day will never end for the speaker, who will always hear her father's grudging toast at the reception, and year after year the anniversary passes uncelebrated. In brief, the "Gaumen für die Bedeutung von Vergangenheit", which Lenz found missing in Hemingway's work, proves well-cultivated in these stories of his own.

The diverse treatment of *speech* further exemplifies Lenz's versatility in these tales. **"Silvester-Unfall"** and **"Risiko für Weihnachtsmänner"** both make free use of direct speech and both, indeed, end with a pungent utterance. **"Der sechste Geburtstag"**, on the other hand, uses dialogue sparingly; the tale is centred on the *inner* voice of the narrator, and even when speech is employed it may appear remote, and this character may remain dissociated from it: "Ich . . . hörte Richard fragen: Wann geht der Geburtstag los?, und ich hörte mich antworten: Am Nachmittag. . . ." **"Ball der Wohltäter"** presents one side of a verbal passage of arms—Puchta's harangue—and leaves the reader to supply Barbara Bredow's interjections. Their substance may be deduced from Puchta's responses to them. In other words, *we* are placed in the former's shoes. The related experiment in **"Vorgeschichte"** also turns on the use of a speaking voice, but without such clear evidence that the listener, addressed as Christina, makes verbal response. The story is thus, in effect, a monologue, a kind of spoken *Ich-Erzählung*. In **"Die Glücksfamilie des Monats"**, the father's impeded speech is integral to the

plot, and the photographer is characterized, as we have seen, by means of a spoken cliché, but the story ends, as we found **"Der sechste Geburtstag"** to end, in eloquent silence.

We have already pointed to indirect 'advance warnings' in these tales. The paradoxes and discrepancies on which the narratives turn make it equally interesting, and particularly necessary, to examine in a final illustration of their diversity, the ways in which the discordant elements of the festivals in them become explicit. The awareness of both the characters *and* the reader must be considered. Now in **"Silvester-Unfall"**, we may assume, only the reader remains to be initiated into the "Henkersmahlzeit" situation. As early as the second sentence, we learn that it is Mummer's "letztes Silvester", and the fuller details are revealed after approximately a quarter of the story. In **"Der sechste Geburtstag"**, in which fatal illness again overshadows a "Fest", and in which again the victim is not expected to reach his next birthday, a clue is given, once more, on the first page:

> . . . ich versprach, nichts zu trinken an diesem achtzehnten April, den wir uns auserwählt hatten, um Richards sechsten Geburtstag zu feiern. Zuerst hatten wir den Geburtstag Anfang Mai feiern wollen, wenn Alfred sein Gehalt bekommen hätte, doch der Arzt meinte, je früher desto besser . . .

After a third of the story, the fact of the son's leukaemia is introduced. However, neither the stricken child nor his sister understands the situation, hence the latter's reluctance to 'perform', so that there prevails even more tension than in **"Silvester-Unfall"**, tension which is shared by the parents in the tale and the reader of it. In each of the stories apart from these two, the speakers have been shocked by an unexpected development which now also shocks the reader. This is presented 'neat' in the middle of **"Risiko für Weihnachtsmänner"**:

> . . . nach heftigem Klopfen und nach ungestümem "Herein!", das die Frau mir aus dem Zimmer zurief, trat ich ein.

> Es waren keine Kinder da; der Baum brannte, zischend versprühten zwei Wunderkerzen, und vor dem Baum, unter den feuerspritzenden Kerzen, stand ein schwerer Mann in schwarzem Anzug, stand ruhig da mit ineinandergelegten Händen und blickte mich erleichtert und erwartungsvoll an: es war Köhnke, mein Oberst in Demjansk. Ich stellte den Sack auf den Boden, zögerte, sah mich ratlos um zu der schmalen Frau, und als sie näher kam, flüsterte ich: "Die Kinder? Wo sind die Kinder?"

> "Wir haben keine Kinder", antwortete sie leise, und unwillig: "Fangen Sie doch an."

Before this passage, the only relatively obvious warning that the festival will turn sour lies in the paradoxical title of the story. Similarly, the catastrophe near the end of the other *Ich-Erzählung* in this quartet, **"Die Glücksfamilie** des Monats", even if preceded by earlier mishap, comes as a bolt from the blue for the reader. In **"Ball der Wohltäter"** and **"Vorgeschichte"**, we do not have a relationship of *Ich-Erzähler* and reader, but instead, a *Rahmen* which contains, in each case, two partners who both already know of the catastrophe. The oblique references made by the one are immediately intelligible to the other, but not to the eavesdropping reader, whose curiosity is aroused by this special kind of 'advance warning'. This is well exemplified in the first paragraph of **"Ball der Wohltäter"**, when Puchta can allude, in general terms, to facts not fully revealed to the reader until the *last* paragraph:

> . . . du erinnerst dich doch wohl, wo, und fast möchte ich auch sagen: wem du in der letzten Nacht erschienst, und zwar so wirkungsvoll, dass man schon viel für dich empfinden muss, um dein Erscheinen vergessen zu können.

Similarly, the description of the wedding-day in **"Vorgeschichte"** is introduced by an ominous, confidential remark concerning the father, addressed to the narrator's listener: "schliesslich ist dir ja bekannt, was auf meiner Hochzeit geschah, wofür er sorgte". And a further oblique reference preludes the catastrophe: "Aber das Schlimmste stand uns noch bevor, und du weisst, was ich meine . . ."; but the reader learns what is 'meant' only in the closing lines of the story.

III

Although we have concentrated our attention on six tales, the theme of the macabre festival and related motifs also appear elsewhere in Lenz's work. Thus, in his radio-play *Das schönste Fest der Welt,* the host sets off the bombs planted at his monster party when his adversaries fail to do so, only to find that the guests receive this as entertainment. Again, the novel *Deutschstunde* includes descriptions of a birthday celebration (chapter 4) and of a gathering of a "Heimatverein" (chapter 6) both of which take an unpleasantly serious turn. In **"Der Anfang von etwas"**, a story with a "Silvester" setting, the hero misses his boat, which is then sunk in an accident. Reading the report of his own death, he leaves it unchallenged and sets off on the new life made possible by this "Silvester-Unfall" and, indeed, symbolized by the "Silvester" motif. In four of Lenz's other stories, we look, as it were, for the "Fest" that never materializes: **"Jäger des Spotts"**, a pendant to *The Old Man and the Sea,* depicts a hunter whose magnificent booty is devoured by bears before he can get it home; **"Der Amüsierdoktor"** describes the narrator's failure to divert a client of his firm with sundry entertainments; a brief birthday episode in **"Der Spielverderber"** is, in effect, shorn of festive elements as is the "Rekordfeier" in the novel *Brot und Spiele*; and, in **"Das Examen"**, a husband's academic success cannot be celebrated as planned, because his wife feels too unwell.

The variations on, and echoes of, the macabre festival seem infinite. Indeed, Lenz is exploring a theme of great antiquity. Belshazzar's Feast is an archetypal example of it, and the evocative power of such timeworn motifs as the Dance of Death and the Witches' Sabbath owes much to it. Situations related to it, in one way or another, occur in a multiplicity of literary works, as is clear even from such an arbitrarily selective view as one confined—*pace* Banquo's ghost—to drama and fiction of the nineteenth and twentieth centuries. Lenz's tales, like Pinter's plays and like the film *Black Orpheus,* testify to the continuing fascination exerted by the macabre festival. Still arresting and relevant in our own time, the theme bears on a perennial experience: the awareness that happiness may be illusory and that our celebrations and festivals may prove hollow and ephemeral. The stories of Siegfried Lenz that we have considered articulate and give form to this feeling, as they point to the darkness beyond the light, the skeleton at the feast.

William P. Hanson   (essay date 1974)

SOURCE: "Siegfried Lenz's Short Story 'Die Festung'," in *Modern Languages,* Vol. 55, No. 1, March, 1974, pp. 26-32.

[In the following essay, Hanson uncovers the techniques that make Lenz's story "Die Festung" one of his best.]

Siegfried Lenz is one of the most highly respected and gifted writers in present-day Germany. He has not achieved the same notoriety, nor the same exposure as Günter Grass, his friend, and fellow-campaigner on behalf of the S.P.D., but at the age of 47 he has a body of work behind him which must put him, not only in Germany but probably in Europe also, in the forefront as a writer, particularly in the field of the short story. Where Grass is baroque imagination, poetic wordplay and Black Comedy, Lenz is a skilled, more subdued craftsman, with a keen eye for detail, an impressive and careful control of language and a fine sense of the architecture of his stories. Stylistically he is the absolute antithesis of Grass who exploits German vocabulary and syntax ruthlessly and often bewilderingly, whereas Lenz's style is fundamentally simple; he breaks down sentences, lingers on particular words and phrases, often repeating them 'leitmotivartig'. He is less spectacular than Grass in every respect, but he possesses all the qualities of the born story-teller, has already treated in his stories a wide range of themes and subjects from his Baltic origins (the mood he can evoke here is in some ways reminiscent of Storm), his present Hamburg domicile and from contemporary Germany in general. He has written vividly too of southern regions that he has visited, most notably Sardinia and Kenya. What is perhaps more important, he has already indicated a stylistic and technical versatility which, whilst in no way putting him with the 'avant garde' as an innovator, suggests that he is a writer at work within the most respectable traditions of fiction. Little wonder that his name is now often mentioned in the same breath as Hemingway, who, Lenz maintains, has been an important influence on his work, Conrad and Thomas Mann. Lenz belonged, like Grass, to the Gruppe 47, but this does not mean that he emerges from his stories and novels as a politically committed writer nor that he 'speaks for a generation' in the sense that Böll did in the late 'forties and early 'fifties in stories like, 'Der Zug war pünktlich', 'Und sagte kein einziges Wort' or 'Das Brot der frühen fahre'. Indeed, the political significance of the Gruppe 47 has in the past been much exaggerated. It always functioned primarily as a forum for ideas about 'Work in Progress'. Lenz is first and foremost a creative writer, his medium, prose and the tradition on which he has drawn has been that which E. M. Forster defines as the 'and then tradition'. Action is his starting point in many of the stories that he has written so far. His narratives have been predominantly linear—his novel *Deutschstunde* is a significant exception—and he has shown himself to be eminently capable of arousing tension. To hold the reader to the line of a story until its very last word is no mean achievement, but Lenz has achieved much more than this. Lenz is a realist whose ultimate interest is in people and their relationships, and the multiple possibilities inherent in human character. Not the black and white strokes, but the grey shaded areas of human experience are what he can reproduce with a fine sensitivity. Responsibility and aspiration, indifference and weakness are his chief concerns.

Lenz was born in 1926 in East Prussia at Lyck, 'die Perle Masurens' as he nostalgically remembers it, and lives today in Hamburg and Denmark. Since 1951, when his first novel *Es waren Habichte in der Luft* earned him a literary prize, he has been a full-time writer, regularly publishing novels, short stories and a number of radio plays. His five volumes of short stories indicate a clear predilection for the shorter prose form and he is of course by no means alone here. The 'Kurzgeschichte' has been the dominant form in Germany since the war and this perhaps can be accounted for, as Professor Hinton Thomas has suggested, by the fact that 'the short story offers the writer valuable liberties in a time of uncertainty and flux'. It is true to say that what Lenz refuses to give us in his stories is certainty. His *method,* however, is *assured* and the short story **'Die Festung'** is an impressive illustration of this.

'Die Festung' appeared in 1958 in the collection of short stories *Jäger des Spotts*—stories which defy a neat collective paraphrase but which all reveal Lenz's ability to grip the reader, to use a wide range of fictional devices, to create a wide range of settings in which to develop themes concerning the hunt and the hunted, the scornful and the scorned. It is tempting to see his work in mythical terms but his landscapes do not take on the nightmare or fairy-tale quality of Kafka's. His work does not have the strangeness of Kafka's fictional world. Lenz is a concrete writer in another, older tradition. **'Die Festung'** is among the most subtle, and the most moving, of all the stories in the volume. It is a tight and compact piece of prose writing, has tension which makes us read it through rapidly because we are made to feel that its outcome is important and it has an intensely human quality—the people in it we recognize as real. Its realism is totally satisfying—even, as the two men and the boy are described sitting down to bacon, eggs, coffee and bread, physically satisfying! It is a masterpiece of verbal economy, where much is suggested and little is said. Lenz is aware, as were the great 19th

century writers of *Novellen,* of the value of the omission. The story is set in a region of windswept reeds and sea and river-washed peat near the Baltic coast. This is an area where there are squalls and storms even in high summer. The narrator relives an incident in his boyhood as if for the first time; he observes his father working his land, scything the grass by a river bank, totally absorbed in his task, aided by his massive, half-idiot labourer Noah Tisch. The boy builds a castle in the sand by a shed. A stranger arrives and talks with the boy's father, out of sight of the boy down the slope by the river bank. The man goes off through the wind and is soon lost on the dark horizon of a gathering storm. The father comes up from the river bank, makes a hole with his foot in the wall of the boy's castle and goes on to destroy it. The three of them have breakfast. We learn that the stranger has come to inform the boy's father that the army is going to re-claim their land for military manoeuvres. The father had been given this land on a 99-year lease after he had lost his own land in Masuria in Poland at the end of the war. The two men go out again from the cottage. When the boy joins them he sees that Noah has built a sturdier castle for him and is now helping his father to put barbed wire around their remote croft. They are going to make their gesture when the soldiers come. As Lenz has written in another, yet here very relevant context:—'Die Welt erprobt, zeichnet und zerbricht den Menschen; sein Problem heißt: Ausdauer gewinnen; wer keine Ausdauer aufbringt, wird die Feuerprobe nicht bestehen'.

What are the various elements in this extremely simple tale that when put together transform it into such an effective 'Kurzgeschichte', a model of the form? The tone of the story is influenced by the fact that the 'point of view' of the narrative is almost wholly that of the young boy describing the events as they actually happened. This accounts for the basic tension in the story—like the boy we have to wait until we learn the significance of the visitation—and it accounts too for the child-like quality of much of the narrative, its total simplicity. There is a complete lack of analysis. The atmosphere that the boy conveys is clearly part of the effectiveness of the story—the darkening sky with the approaching storm, the black crows rising up from the poplars (they recur and function as a leitmotiv), the wind, the salty air. This is a 'flaches trauriges Land', but it is a desolate region that has become a home, a farm, security. 'Hier, unter dem weiten Himmel, in all der Weglosigkeit und Verlorenheit, bekam er das neue Land . . .'. The Wilderness has had to serve as the Promised Land and Lenz is showing again that nearness of opposites, a nearness that is accentuated at a moment of crisis, that is a recurrent feature of many of his stories. The atmosphere too is made more real as a result of Lenz's verbal precision, most clearly illustrated perhaps in the impressively observed breakfast scene. 'Ich spürte ihre wunderbare Gier, ich spürte die Wärme des Essens, und die weiche, wohlige Müdigkeit, die es hervorrief, und ich empfand zum ersten Male die räuberische Schönheit des Essens: die geöffneten Lippen, das Brechen, das Mahlen'. Lenz's keen eye for detail—the way, for example, the father drags his feet through the grass to clean his boots of mud, the sand that momentarily rests on his instep as he breaks down his son's vulnerable castle walls, the 'wippendes Brett' over which Noah pushes his barrow—creates a clear and full set of visual images with the maximum of economy.

Where Grass is baroque imagination, poetic wordplay and Black Comedy, Lenz is a skilled, more subdued craftsman, with a keen eye for detail, an impressive and careful control of language and a fine sense of the architecture of his stories.

—William P. Hanson

It is not, however, just the tension, the atmosphere and the linguistic control that makes the story successful, but also, and possibly primarily, the people in it. To talk of characterisation here is perhaps to use the wrong word. Lenz does not try to apply the methods of the novel to those of the short story. What he gives is not a broad and detailed insight into characters, but indications, clues which set off chain reactions in the mind of the reader who feels consequently that he is actually experiencing the story he is reading. The boy through whose eyes we see everything, gives his simple factual account, reveals his simple childmind. We feel that he is the one who has to learn some kind of lesson from the experiences narrated in the story. (A similar father/son relationship can be found in the story **'Das Wrack'** which is also part of *Jäger des Spotts*.) There is in the boy a sense of total trust, an understanding that is beyond words and is only made clear in the story through gesture. Thus as his father destroys his castle: ' . . . und während er zuschlug und zerstörte, was ich begraben hatte, suchte ich seinen Blick. Er wich mir nichts aus, ich sah in seine tiefliegenden Augen, ich tat es schweigend und fassungslos . . .' Then, 'gab er mir die Hand . . . und da ergriff ich sie mit beiden Händen'. This is a tense moment; the boy, like us, does not know what it all means, but a gesture—a look, a clasping of hands—indicates not only that this is a critical situation but also indicates strength, communion. (Lenz in many of his stories likes to establish a situation where an action can just as easily go one of two ways, ways which represent the difference between success and failure. The story **'Der Läufer'** plays agonisingly on this device.) The man who comes to talk to the boy's father has a vital role in the story, since he is the means by which we are made aware that the story is dealing with a crucial situation, but here, particularly, Lenz does not achieve the effect he is seeking by giving us a study of the man in depth. The boy describes his arrival: 'den Mann . . . , der in jenem Juni vor dem Gewitter den kleinen Weg heraufkam . . . Diesen Weg kam der Mann herauf, er war klein und mager und steckte in einem schwarzen Tuchanzug, ich hatte ihn nie vorher gesehen'. Momentarily he stands over the father,

higher up the bank and then disappears out of the boy's sight to deliver his information. Then the boy sees him again: '. . . da kam der schwarze, magere Man schon wieder herauf, blickte nach dem Gewitter, und ging, von einem Windstoß getroffen, den Weg zur Holzbrücke eilig jetzt und sich vom Wind treiben lassend'. And this is all we have of him in the story—'der Mann', 'das Gewitter', 'klein', 'mager', 'schwarz',—and of course this is all we need. He hangs darkly over the whole story like one of the storm clouds that we know are overhead. We sense something almost devilish. Finally, of the two main characters in the story, the father and his faithful labourer, it is hard to decide which is evoked the more successfully. Noah Tisch is a brilliantly observed sketch. He is deficient mentally, but physically he is massive ('er [reichte] bis zum Teerdach des Schuppens'), powerful and yet gentle in a way that perhaps only the mentally deficient can be. The picture of Noah is made more effective through contrasts, both within Noah himself and in the way he contrasts with the father, and also in the boy's simple—and very real—response to him. Noah with his 'sanftes, irres Lachen' grunts and groans as he works 'als ob er unter Dampf stünde'. The boy touches on the essential contrast in the man: '. . . er lachte ständig sein sanftes, irres Lachen, *doch* (my italics) er besaß eine so fürchterliche Kraft, daß es einen schaudern konnte'. He is an elemental man—we remember the way his whole face is alight, as he dips his way through his breakfast—and the elemental is both attractive *and* frightening. (Lenz is again touching on opposing impulses.) Noah emerges as real because he is a simple man, a manual worker who expresses himself physically rather than mentally and this in most cases is all we would have to go on in real life. Lenz gives us here what we get in day-to-day encounters with other people. The central feature of Noah's life is his affection for and fidelity towards the boy's father, with whom he has been since they worked the dry fields together in Sunowo in Masuria: ' . . . sie hatten gesät zusammen und gerodet und geerntet, und Noah liebt meinen Alten mehr als alles auf der Welt . . .' and now with that instinct that is clearly the man, he senses that the father is threatened. This is turn is sensed by the boy: '. . . ich spürte, dass auch er gespannt war'. (It is important to notice how this idea of 'gespannt sein' which is articulated here for the first time fits easily and naturally into the story at this point. That the reader is quite ready for it is a further indication that Lenz has established a tense atmosphere with the arrival of the 'schwarze magere Mann'.) Noah's instinctive reaction when he senses that his much-loved master is threatened brings out the contrasts in the man—and the boy is frightened:

> Ich ängstigte mich vor ihm, wie ich mich seit je geängstigt hatte vor diesem Mann, wenn sein Lachen breiter und starrer wurde, wenn der Ausdruck seines milden Irrsinns verschwand und sein Kopf zu nicken begann, dieser mächtige, schwere, tragische Kopf. Niemand wußte, was dies breite Lachen und das Nicken des Kopfes ankündigte: eine tumultuarische Wut oder eine ebenso tumultuarische Zärtlichkeit.

A power at the very core of humanity, and yet a power that can destroy is what we are made to sense in Noah, 'dieser mächtige, schwere, tragische Kopf'. Lenz evokes a character in depth here without seeming to probe deeply at all. This is a measure of his skill as a short story writer. The father, the man from Sunowo (note how frequently the idea recurs), is the key figure in the story. He has had to leave his homeland, to begin again and now finds that after all his dogged, single-minded efforts he is probably going to have to move on again. Work is his task which he has pursued relentlessly: 'Wenn mein Vater arbeitete, dann arbeitete er, und es gab nichts in der Welt, das ihn abhalten oder unterbrechen konnte'. There is total application, total concentration as he scythes the grass by the river's edge. We have a vivid and precise picture of the man: '. . . sein Gang war schleppend, der Kopf immer schräg gelegt, ein runder, kurzgeschorener Kopf, und sein Rücken war schon ein wenig gekrümmt'. A timeless figure is evoked here (surely the fact that he is wielding a scythe is not a mere chance), a man who has been condemned to wander, like the mayor in **'Schwierige Trauer'**, and who looks as though he is going to be forced to wander Europe again. But he refuses to let this happen. This is the decision that results from the crisis that is depicted in the story. His work has been a 'Verzweiflungsarbeit'; he has desperately stuck to his difficult task right up to the appearance of the dark stranger: 'er hatte das Land für neunundneunzig Jahre übernommen: daran hielt er sich, mein Alter, der Neusiedler'. Despite the new crisis he is going to keep to his task. This is what he finally decides after he had duly pondered the implications of the visitation that day. The reader of course is kept in suspense whilst he ponders: '. . . wir wussten, dass etwas gesagt werden musste, und dass das, was zu sagen war, nur von meinem Alten kommen konnte. Aber mein Alter sagte nie etwas, das halb und unbedacht war und das er nicht zu Ende gekaut hatte'.

What now of the ending of the story? Does it have a meaning? Indeed, need it have a 'meaning'? Does Archibald Macleish's idea that 'a poem must not mean but be' not apply equally well to a short story of this kind? The breakfast over, Noah 'lachte sein mildes, irres Lachen' and accompanies the father out into the courtyard. When the boy joins them he finds that the two men are at work on the barbed wire, 'und während sie das alles taten, hörte ich sie murmeln und leise lachen, und mein Alter lachte wie Noah Tisch'. There is a wholly convincing ambiguity about this. Are we to assume that the gesture that the father is now making is futile, that he must inevitably fail and is now, like Noah, virtually out of his mind? Or are we to assume that this gesture, though small, signifies hope and the possibility that they will not be moved on again after all? (A further question one might ask is whether in fact the reader is right to ask questions that look for an answer *outside* the narrative in some hypothetical continuation of the story. The story stops with the common laugh of Noah and the father and the trio waiting inside their newly established compound. Is it fruitful to try to take the analysis further once the story itself has finished?) Even if we try to surmise an action outside the action of the story we do not, however, get very far. Madness or hope? It certainly seems unlikely that Noah's rabbit gun which he is holding at the ready as the story ends, will have much effect on the soldiers when they come, but on the other hand we know too from the story that there is a strength in Noah and the father, the man from Sunowo, that is stronger than that of guns. But the ambiguity remains and that perhaps is what short stories are for! Certainly Lenz fulfils in his short stories that fantasy he had as a student in Hamburg concerning a future career as a teacher calling for his students to accept paradox and contradiction: '. . . sie sollten die Chancen des Widerspruchs, des Widerrufs bekenntnishaft kennenlernen'.

The attempt has been made here to try to give some indication of how this particular short story of Lenz's 'works'. One can of course go only so far with this. One can isolate and look at the various elements that make up the story and suggest how these elements are treated and what the author indicates through them. But when these elements are seen together again, when the story is re-read and re-experienced as a unit one can only feel like Gerhart Hauptmann when faced with Holz's compendium of rules for Naturalistic art: 'Mit diesen Regeln kann man Schuhmacher ausbilden; das Geheimnis aber bleibt'. Analysis will take us so far into a story like **'Die Festung'** and then we must *sense* that everything fits, that the author has had us in his grip during the course of his story, has suggested to us something of human character and human relationships, has given us the 'feel' of real life, has mirrored a world in a grain of sand. The 'truth' of this story—as Lenz puts it himself in an essay specifically concerned with fictional truth—'. . . fügt sich keinem Plan, sie überzeugt und betrifft uns, indem sie uns einer Erfahrung innewerden läßt, die über die bloße Tatsache weit hinausgeht'.

At the end of his valuable article on Lenz written in 1965, C. A. H. Russ suggests, that if Lenz succeeds 'in fusing experiment with the traditional narrative virtues which are his already, he may emerge as a major artist'. Suffice it to add here that since this suggestion was made Lenz has produced a novel of considerable proportions, *Deutschstunde* (1968), which has been widely acclaimed as a bold technical achievement. When asked recently in an interview with Marcel Reich Ranicki what had pleased him most about the enthusiastic reception of the novel he replied: 'Die kritische Rechtfertigung, den Roman als eine dem Helden auferlegte Strafarbeit zu erzählen'. In short, he felt that his experiment had been a success. More recently still, Lenz has published a short story, **'Einstein überquert die Elbe bei Hamburg—Geschichte in drei Sätzen'** which is 'eine Photographie zum Lesen' of the packed harbour at Hamburg and a 'tour de force' of experimental writing. We may well now be dealing with a major artist. But Lenz consciously shuns the more extreme devices of the current avant-garde. He is clearly unimpressed by the collage-technique of a Handke or the documentations of a Peter Weiß or Heinar Kipphardt. For his part he will continue to work 'an Geschichten— Geschichten, mit denen gewiß nichts entschieden wird, die vielleicht aber ein bißchen von der Identität der Wirklichkeit lüften können'. Thus what is most impressive in this most recent story is not the experiment in itself but what we were able to observe already in **'Die Festung'**, namely his artistic control, the precision of his language, the structuring of his story, his control over the leitmotiv-like phrase or gesture, which gives a total cohesion to his stories and his ability through a character sketch to *suggest* a depth of character without actually describing it in depth. Lenz is clearly a master of the small gesture; his technique is that of cumulative suggestion. It was the technique of the great Realists of the 19th century, of Storm, Raabe and Fontane, and it was Thomas Mann's way. Lenz is in very good company already.

Brian Murdoch (essay date 1974)

SOURCE: "Ironic Reversal in the Short Stories of Siegfried Lenz," in *Neophilologus,* Vol. LVIII, No. 4, October, 1974, pp. 406-10.

[*In this essay, Murdoch analyzes Lenz's use of irony in the stories "Der Amüsierdoktor" and "Mein verdrossenes Gesicht."*]

Studies of the prose fiction of Siegfried Lenz have offered in the main an overall view of the writer's work, concentrating primarily upon recurrent thematic motifs, with some comment on language and style. Such studies have praised Lenz in general terms for the originality of his wit, and for the restrained nature of his social satire: Lenz's social criticism—and it is visible most clearly, perhaps, in the short stories—takes the form not of "angriffslustige Satire", but rather of "leise Komik". The precise nature—and originality—of Lenz's achievement in the field of the satirical short story must be evaluated, however, through detailed analysis of narrative technique based upon concrete examples from his work: generality is in any case dangerous with a writer such as Lenz, whose short stories are varied in initial intent, and indeed not uniformly effective.

There is, of course, a well-established tradition in recent German literature of the short story as a vehicle of social criticism through satire. One thinks of writers as diverse as Tucholsky, Kästner, and somewhat later Böll, Gaiser, Risse and so on. Lenz's debt to Böll is well-known as is his acknowledgement of the influence of Borchert with regard both to style and to content. Elements of style and individual themes in the short stories of Lenz may frequently be traced to these two writers in particular, and Lenz's actual originality lies in structure and handling, rather than theme as such.

The notion of a sudden ironic reversal at the end of a narrative (or drama) may be found in a wide range of contexts and literary modes. Its best-known form is possibly the tragic form implied in the Aristotelean anagnorisis and peripeteia, although it might equally well be comic—as in, for example, *Le mariage de Figaro.* In his short stories Lenz makes frequent use of the final irony in a serious sense to underline one of his favorite themes, that of the "loser". **"Das Wrack"**, **"Lukas, sanftmütiger Knecht"** (both in *Jäger des Spotts*) and **"Stimmungen der See"** (in *Das Feuerschiff*) might be cited as examples

of this. These stories all deal, however, with the universal theme of man against fate. In the stories whose aim is the satirizing of aspects of contemporary (German) society, the ironic reversal is also frequent, although it is at once less tragic, less predictable, one might even say less hackneyed—although Lenz is open to this criticism both in his "universal" and his social-satirical short stories. At its best, however, the ironic reversal in the latter type of story, while still sudden, remains closely connected with what has gone before. The irony of the whole story prepares the reader for the final irony and lends a structural unity to the whole piece while underlining the final point. The present note seeks to illustrate this aspect of Lenz's narrative technique with reference to two particularly effective examples, short stories which do not contain the tragic implications of **"Lukas"**, but which are nevertheless comic only in the ambiguous sense of much of Dürrenmatt's drama. The stories in question are **"Mein verdrossenes Gesicht"** (from *Jäger des Spotts*) and **"Der Amüsierdoktor"** (from *Das Feuerschiff*).

"Mein verdrossenes Gesicht" may be linked on a superficial level with a story with a similar title by Böll: "Mein trauriges Gesicht" (1950). Intentional or not, Lenz's title provides an interesting intensification in the adjective which might betray a difference of attitude on the part of the two writers to the society that each describes. There is, however, no sustained parallelism between the two works, although the starting-point is similar, and both stories exploit in logical terms an absurd initial situation. The overall symbolism of both stories is, of course, the same: the face standing for the whole person. This *pars pro toto* is familar too, incidentally, from Borchert's "Draussen vor der Tür", in the scene between Beckmann and the theater director, and Beckmann's spectacles are, of course, a recurrent symbolic motif in that play.

The face of Böll's narrator (both stories are told in the first person) leads him into trouble. Lenz's narrator, on the other hand, finds that his equally disturbed face is, initially at least, his fortune. We are not told why his face is so *verdrossen*: but we assume in the course of the narrative that the dissatisfaction is a general reaction to the times, specifically to the postwar materialist society in which the narrator does not fit. He has tried various jobs, and has when we meet him "Verschiedenes in Aussicht". The war itself had been forgotten, and even such positive effects as the war could have had—the closeness of comradeship—have been lost. Bunsen, a war-time associate of the narrator, cannot even remember the narrator's name, in spite of his "schulterklopfende Fröhlichkeit". The opening words of the story are significant, and imply a universal acceptance of the brave new world:

> Auch er ist hier hängengeblieben, auch Bunsen, mein
> Bootsmannsmaat aus dem Krieg . . .

The repeated *auch* is both striking and effective.

The narrator, incidentally, remains nameless (as does Böll's), and this lends a certain universality to the narrative (although not in the same sense as with **"Lukas"** or even **"Das Wrack"**). The figure of the narrator combines, in fact, the same elements of individual interest and quasi-expressionist anonymity as Borchert's anti-hero in "Draussen vor der Tür".

Although the narrator's *Verdrossenheit* arises from a dissatisfaction with the materialist world, the basic irony of the story is that he obtains, on the strength of his looks, a job as a photographer's model for advertisements in which he directs his displeasure at people who do *not* participate to the fullest extent in the materialism. "Die Verdrossenheit in deinem Gesicht", he is told, "ist Kritik und Anklage". It is, but not in the sense that the photographer means when he says so. The idea of *klagen,* ambiguous as it has become, recurs in the story. The face becomes "ein stiller, anklagender Mond" rising over the materialist society—and here the nature of the condemnation is especially ambiguous. The general irony is compounded, incidentally, through the idea of the camera as such: the camera does not lie, but these photographs are as much a lie as the motivation behind them. The practices of advertising are secondary targets of the satire in the story, however.

The materialist nature of the advertisements are carefully chosen, and comic in their own right:

> Ich durfte meinen natürlichen Kummer einsetzen, um den Zeitgenossen zu minimaler Pflicht anzuhalten, dem Haarausfall überlegen zu begegnen, Sekt ständig bereit zu halten . . .

The term *Zeitgenosse* recurs frequently, and underlines the aim of the story in that respect.

The narrator seems to take a pride in his job, futile as it is. The cause of the original *Verdrossenheit* is forgotten. The ironic reversal comes about, however, when the narrator has to turn his opprobious look towards a fellow-model, "ein kleiner, vergrämter Mann" who is to represent the man without humor, refusing to buy "das Goldene Hausbuch des Humors". But the narrator involuntarily feels sympathy for the man, and his face loses its lucrative quality. The ending of the piece is ironic in that the cause for *Verdrossenheit* has returned, the material exploitation of the little man—the partner is several times referred to as *klein*. As an additional irony, of course, the entire situation that has provoked the sympathy on the narrator's part is as unreal as the rest of the advertizing sessions.

For the narrator, however, the reversal is a recognition, and his reaction is simple: "jetzt kann ich nicht mehr". The general tone of the statement—the last words of the story—is perhaps deliberately ambiguous. The ending of the story may be positive: the man, for all that he has lost his livelihood, has gained in humanity. On the other hand, however, he has perhaps only *confirmed* his original discontent, losing in the process even the outward expression of it. He ends as a more complete loser than he began, the final reversal confirming the original situation rather than taking it to a logical conclusion.

"Der Amüsierdoktor" calls to mind even more clearly the comment by Schwarz on Böll's departing from an absurd premise. It also recalls Böll's own equally futilely occupied doctor, Dr. Murke. If Dr. Murke's Ph.D. qualifies him to spend time cutting *Gott* from a pretentious speech, this is at least a slightly more intellectual pastime than that of Lenz's (again anonymous) doctor. His job is not in a radio-station, but in a factory whose concern is with machines for the processing of fish. The situation recalls not only that of many of Böll's characters, but also that of Dürrenmatt's Archilochos in *Grieche sucht Griechin*, although where Dürenmatt's tale is deliberately ludicrous, Lenz's combines—as does Böll—exaggerated seriousness with quasi-*reportage*. Thus we are introduced to the products of the factory in some detail, particularly the magnificent "Robespierre", "ein Modell, das einen zwei Meter langen Thunfish in vier Sekunden zu Fischkarbonade machte . . .".

But the narrator's job has, in fact, nothing to do with the machinery. His task is to entertain the customers after the completion of their transactions. The nature of the customers that one might expect to be interested in fish-processing machinery forms a basis for a number of incidental witticisms (as in the case of the "seelisch vermummter Mensch aus Spitzbergen"), and the incidental humor persists throughout the work. One example may serve to illustrate this: Wanda, a showgirl whose forte is appearing in a "glass of champagne" act, is known to the narrator because "ihre Kinder und meine Kinder gehen zusammen zur Schule". In her act Wanda makes provocative gestures, "was man ihr als Flüchtling nicht zugetraut hätte".

The story centers on one incident, however: the attempts to divert one Pachulka-Sbirr, a giant *Naturmensch* from the Aleutian Islands. The job itself is sufficiently ridiculous, and the character of Pachulka-Sbirr underlines this. The reactions of the Aleutian islander to the various entertainments offered him are in themselves comical, but they are at the same time an expression of social criticism. Thus Pachulka-Sbirr is taken to a "Lokal, in dem sich, von Zeit zu Zeit, drei Damen künstlerisch entkleideten". In fact, the three strippers perform a parody on the familiar classical "Judgement of Paris", and invite a member of the audience to play Paris. Pachulka-Sbirr, placed into this role, responds by eating the apple.

There are various implications. Apart from the intrinsic humor, the scene is an implied criticism aimed at the devaluation of potentially serious, religious or intellectual matters that is encountered so often in Böll—in *Nicht nur zur Weihnachtszeit,* for example. But as far as Pachulka-Sbirr goes, the scene can only be painful. The *Naturmensch* is being placed into an artificial and ridiculous situation for his own amusement. It is to the distress of the *Amüsierdoktor* that he does not show pleasure, neither here, nor when faced with similar scenes. Pachulka-Sbirr is forced by the idea of pleasure to make a fool of himself.

The ironic reversal in **"Der Amüsierdoktor"** forms a nice play on the title, for the narrator comes close to requiring a medical doctor. The aim has been to take Pachulka-

Sbirr's mind off the world of fish-processing machinery: but the only thing that amuses him is, ironically connected precisely with it. The narrator, showing the customer the machine "Robespierre" climbs into it and is almost chopped up—we recall the fate of Robespierre himself on his own guillotine. The tables are turned—the *Amüsierdoktor* is placed in a ludicrous situation just as has happened to Pachulka-Sbirr. We laugh with the Aleutian fish-dealer *at* the man whose job it is to produce laughter, and the social criticism is underlined at the same time. It is the petty-vulgar and futile society that produces a job for an *Amüsierdoktor* that is the butt of the satire, and it is even significant that the narrator is *not* chopped up: there is certainly no room here for the importance of death. The satirist does not seek to annihilate, rather to ridicule, and we are not in Kafka's *Strafkolonie*, either.

The narrator learns something here too. The knives of "Robespierre" stay in his mind:

> ". . . wenn ich heutzutage an Heiterkeit denke, sehe ich über mir lustig blinkende Messer schweben, extra gehärtet . . ."

The choice of the term *lustig* is a nice one. Thus here and in the earlier short story, the point is brought home by the realisation of the reversal on the part of the first-person narrator.

Böll, and indeed Dürrenmatt, take the absurd premise to its conclusion, and it is that logical development that is offered to the reader or audience so that a decision may be made. Lenz's starting point here can be equally absurd. But instead of developing the situation fully, he gives it a sudden twist, a secondary irony which threws into relief the irony that is there throughout the entire story. It is the showing of the two sides if an ironical situation—one, that is, in which things are other than what they seem—with which Lenz achieves his satire, his underlining of human foibles in general terms.

Esther N. Elstun (essay date 1974)

SOURCE: "How It Seems and How It Is: Marriage in Three Stories by Siegfried Lenz," in *Orbis Litterarum*, Vol. XXIX, No. 2, 1974, pp. 170-79.

[*In this essay, Elstun analyzes the discrepancy between appearance and reality in three Lenz stories: "Ein Haus aus lauter Liebe," "Der längere Arm," and "Der sechste Geburtstag."*]

In the afterword to Siegfried Lenz's *Gesammelte Erzählungen* Colin Russ speaks of a "moment of truth" in these stories, "den Augenblick, in dem ein Mensch preis-gegeben und auf die Probe gestellt wird." A reading of the *Erzählungen* confirms his observation and reveals this additional fact: in a striking number of the stories the "moment of truth" concerns the deterioration of a male-female relationship, and the woman's role is a decisive

one. My purpose here is to analyze three of these "moments of truth"—in **"Ein Haus aus lauter Liebe"** (1952), **"Der längere Arm"** (1959) and **"Der sechste Geburtstag"** (1964)—giving particular attention to the female characters and the roles they play.

The external action of **"Ein Haus aus lauter Liebe"** consists of the observations and experiences of a student during a baby-sitting assignment in the home of a wealthy industrialist. At the same time, and much more important-ly, the external action serves as a means of treating the real subject, which is a household whose members give the lie to the story's title: everything the student/narrator observes and experiences in the brief course of the evening reveals devastating discrepancies between appearance and reality, between the industrialist's protestation of his own and his wife's familial love and the actual state of affairs (the alcoholic old father—an obvious embarrassment to the couple—is locked away in an upstairs room and the wife has a lover).

The exposure of these discrepancies begins in the opening sentences of the story, where the description of the house is at striking odds with the title: "Es war ein neues, stroh-gedecktes Haus, die kleinen Fenster zur Strassenseite hin waren vergittert, sie sahen feindselig aus wie Schieß-scharten, und keins der Fenster war erleuchtet."

Lenz uses the same effective juxtaposition of appearance and reality in his masterful characterization of the indus-trialist's wife. Before she herself appears, her husband remarks to the student: "Es fällt uns so schwer, dass ich schon absagen wollte. Wir bringen es nicht übers Herz, die Kinder abends allein zu lassen . . . Wir leben nur für unsere Kinder, wir kennen nichts anderes, meiner Frau geht es genauso." Just as the description of the house belies the title, these remarks create a deliberately false impression of the wife that is contradicted by her actual character, as subsequently revealed.

Milly is a superb example of Lenz's skill at characteriza-tion; with remarkable economy of language and style he has achieved a character sketch of her that is both vivid and complete. Through his sure but minimal strokes of the pen, Milly emerges as a hard, sensual, dishonest young woman who accepts the status and material security of marriage to a wealthy industrialist while holding him in contempt. Lenz conveys none of this through detailed description or exposition. Milly's character is instead re-vealed by brief but telling allusions to her walk, features, gestures and dress. Her vocation is itself a symbol of the hollowness and falsity of her marriage: she is an actress. Her hardness is suggested by repeated references to her footsteps, each time described as "hart und schurfend" her physical appearance ("blond und schmalstirnig und sehr jung") and especially her mouth ("breit" and "überge-schminkt") suggest her sensuality. The only jewelry she wears is a cross, but it is thin and black. A single gesture symbolizes her silent contempt for her husband: "Die sehr junge Frau drehte ihm den kräftigen Rücken zu . . ." These are the student/narrator's and the reader's impressions of Milly; her lover's subsequent telephone call does not greatly surprise us, but merely confirms already existing impressions.

Can one properly speak of a "moment of truth" in **"Ein Haus aus lauter Liebe"**? Russ contends: "Es zieht sich aber durch alle Variationen hindurch—und mit oder ohne Ich-Erzähler—der rote Faden des 'Falls', der unvermittelt eintretenden, verhängnisvollen—aber möglicherweise auch komischen—Entwicklung, die einen Menschen um sein Ansehen, sein Glück, sein Selbstgefühl, ja sogar um sein Leben bringen kann. Diese Entwicklung kann die dargestellte Handlung krönen . . . oder aber sie lauert in einer unabwendbaren Zukunft, welcher die Charaktere hilflos entgegensehen . . ." If this applies to **"Ein Haus aus lauter Liebe,"** then only in a limited sense. The story does not present an overt crisis that disrupts the lives of the characters; instead, it shows the effects of a hollow relationship whose disintegration obviously began long before, if indeed a true relationship ever existed at all. Neither does the story indicate a future development that will force the industrialist and his wife to confront the truth of their lives. If anything, the story's ending suggests that the future will be the same as the present, a continuation of the role-playing and self-delusion that have been revealed as the reality of life in this household. To the factory owner's question, "Sie waren doch alle brav, meine Lieben?" the student/narrator, now fully aware of the realities of the situation, replies: "Ja, sie waren alle brav." Like Lenz himself, the narrator remains "der gelassene Mitwisser," presenting the characters and their situation without comment, let alone intervention.

In this story, then, there is a "moment of truth" only for the student/narrator and the reader. The characters are exposed and unmasked, but not to each other. Within the framework of the story they continue to preserve appearance and illusion, albeit for different reasons: the industrialist, one suspects, because he is too weak to face the truth, his wife for selfish reasons of her own.

In **"Der längere Arm,"** by contrast, the characters are unmasked to each other as well as to the reader. This tightly-compressed story relates in little more than eight pages a fateful "moment of truth" between a husband and wife. Their argument, which exposes the husband as a shabby and ineffectual blackmailer, represents the final step in the disintegration of their relationship. The argument has just begun as the story opens: "'Immer, wenn du Pech hast,' sagte Ruth Eisler gereizt, 'denkst du gleich an diesen alten Godepiel. Du glaubst wohl, er habe nichts anderes zu tun, als für dein Pech zu sorgen.' 'Er hat nichts anderes zu tun,' sagte Eisler, 'oder doch nichts Besseres.'" This preliminary "exchange of shots" lays the groundwork for the verbal duel that ensues, mounting in intensity and in the awfulness of its disclosures until it shatters their lives.

The expository passage that follows serves several functions simultaneously. It first sets the scene, an "Alltagsszene" of a husband and wife at the breakfast table. This deliberately deceptive use of the familiar and commonplace is a very effective means of heightening the reader's sense of shock at the revelations which follow;

the crisis, or more exactly, its impact upon the reader, is all the more profound because of the ordinariness of the setting. On the symbolic level this descriptive passage provides a kind of "Vorausdeutung" of the Eislers' confrontation, beginning as it does with the words, "Sie sass ihm gegenüber . . ." Finally, this passage gives us Lenz's initial characterization of the wife, and though other details are added later, the character sketch is essentially complete at this early point in the story.

Like Milly, Ruth Eisler is young and blond, but the similarity ends there. Ruth is a tired housewife, and her husband is clearly the source of her weariness and dissatisfaction. Again, Lenz conveys almost none of this by direct and detailed description of Ruth herself; the impressions are instead evoked by references to her reactions as she watches her husband eat. She looks at him with an expression of "müder Missbilligung." Her hands lie folded on the table, a gesture that suggests her effort at restraint and self-control. She glances at the crumbs and eggshells around her husband's plate "mit unhörbarem Seufzen . . . als kalkulierte sie bereits das Mass an Arbeit, das er ihr heute hinterlassen würde." A later passage tells us that "in den letzten beiden Jahren ihrer Ehe hatte sie damit angefangen, ihn bei seinem Nachnamen zu nennen"—a clear sign of Ruth's contempt for her husband, but also an indication of how long she has lived with the situation in a posture of weary resignation. It is likewise clear that she no longer exerts the effort to hide her feelings from Eisler: "Unsicher blickte er auf sie hinab; er hasste es, sie vorwurfsvoll zurückzulassen, wenn er fortging, aber diesmal wusste er, dass er lange brauchen würde, um ihre müde Missbilligung, diese träge Verachtung, die sie für ihn zu empfinden schien, aus der Welt zu schaffen."

Though the Eisler's marriage had begun to deteriorate before the affair with the insurance executive, Godepiel, it is Eisler's obsession to get even with him that brings Ruth to the point of no return. For months she has listened to Eisler's threats and promises ("Ich werde es schon machen, Ruth . . . Und eines Tages werde ich Godepiel alles zurückzahlen"); by now his cliché-ridden litany has become intolerable: "Sie blickte sich schnell um, als ob sie etwas suchte, womit sie sich beschäftigen könnte, nur um ihm nicht zuhören zu müssen; doch ehe sie sich erhob, begann es wieder, setzte ein wie eine Grammophonnadel, die mehrere Rillen der Platte übersprungen hat, so dass sie, einem stärkeren Zwang nachgebend, sitzen blieb." Hearing it all again, Ruth is driven to abandon her posture of resigned endurance; she precipitates the final crisis in their relationship by baring the facts and confronting Eisler with the truth and her awareness of it. By the time she has finished, he is stripped of whatever "Selbstgefühl" he possessed, and the damage to their relationship is clearly irreparable: "[er] sah sie hasserfüllt an, mit dem verblüfften Hass eines Mannes, der sich von seiner Frau durchschaut fühlt." These lines confirm the accuracy of Ruth's assessment of her husband and their present situation, and at the same time suggest that their relationship will never be the same again. If the reader has any doubts about this, they are dispelled by the closing passage of the story: "Er hockte unbeweglich da, schob dann tastend seine Hand zu ihr hinüber und fragte, indem er in die Tasse blickte: 'Was soll denn werden, Ruth?'" Her rejection of his proffered hand symbolizes her final rejection of him.

Having been exposed as a shabby profiteer and would-be blackmailer, Eisler obviously does not command the reader's respect at this point. The closing lines of the story raise the question of whether Ruth is any more deserving of the reader's esteem than her husband. Eisler says: "O Gott, was soll ich denn tun, Ruth?" Having reduced him to this state of shame, helplessness and defeat, she replies, "Trink deinen Kaffee aus, ich kann ihn nicht wegschütten." Her words betray a complete lack of compassion, a terrible indifference to the devastating effect her disclosures have had upon him. Eisler has unquestionably caused her to suffer, but her face now bears an expression of triumph. She has (literally and otherwise) had the last word, and in this sense the title of the story refers even more to her than to Godepiel. Ruth's answer also re-focuses attention upon the everyday setting of the story; in this sense her words are a final confirmation of the fact that there is nothing left between her and Eisler except the routine motions and superficial activities of everyday life.

Like the other two stories discussed here, **"Der sechste Geburtstag"** begins with a disarmingly familiar "Alltagsszene": a husband saying goodbye to his wife as he leaves for the office. The reader quickly learns, however, that the life of this family is far from ordinary, despite the parents' efforts to preserve the appearance of normalcy.

The external action of the story consists of the preparations for and the celebration of the sixth birthday of the couple's son—on an arbitrarily selected date, because he is dying of leukemia and will not live to see his real birthday. Again, however, the external action serves as a framework for the author's treatment of a deeper subject: the effects of this personal tragedy upon the family, and especially upon the relationship of the parents.

Lenz's characterization of the wife in **"Der sechste Geburtstag"** is both less and more than his sketches of Milly (**"Ein Haus aus lauter Liebe"**) and Ruth Eisler (**"Der längere Arm"**). We do not know what this woman looks like; Lenz does not even tell us her name. In this instance, instead of using outward appearance or other external elements to create impressions of character, Lenz has the wife "characterize" herself, by making her the first-person narrator of the story. This use of the first person is familiar to the modern reader as a highly effective means of transmitting the inner state of a character in the most direct and immediate way. It also establishes the point of view that prevails throughout the story: we accompany the wife as she shops for the birthday party, we suffer with her as she struggles to keep her promise to her husband, Alfred, not to drink on this day, we observe the artificial birthday celebration through her anxious eyes, and we experience her ultimate failure, the breaking of her promise, from her point of view.

For this woman, the sixth birthday is one long day of trial, a "moment of truth" expanded to excruciating proportions.

Her suffering becomes apparent very early in the story, when she boards a crowded streetcar to go shopping: "Meine Knöchel schwollen, meine Lippen brannten . . . Ich sah auf meine Hand hinab, sah, dass sie zitterte, und wusste, warum ich dieser Fahrt so wenig gewachsen war; mit einem einzigen Schluck hätte ich sie leichter ertragen."

In the department store the enormity of her task—selecting birthday gifts for a boy who will soon be dead—overwhelms the reader as it does her. Her mental images of the birthday toys several months hence, standing ownerless in Richard's room or stored in the attic, render her incapable of making a selection and her need for a drink becomes acute: "Ich wusste, unter welchen Umständen mir ein Kauf leichter gefallen wäre. Die Schwäche kehrte wieder, eine kleine unbestimmte Übelkeit. Meine Haut sträubte sich gegen etwas oder verlangte etwas. Ich spürte ein wohlvertrautes Schwindelgefühl."

Every other preparation for the birthday party, to say nothing of the celebration itself, constitutes a similar trial for this woman, but she keeps her promise until Richard's sister, in a fit of childish anger and disappointment, reveals to him that today is not his birthday at all: "Ich ging nicht zu ihnen [den Kindern] hinein, wartete auch nicht auf Richards Antwort, die Übelkeit wurde so gross, dass ich ins Badezimmer ging, nicht einmal abschloss, sondern einfach nur einen Schluck nahm und die Flasche sofort wieder wegstellte und auf den Korridor trat . . ." Here again Lenz has fostered a false impression in the reader, in order to heighten the impact of the woman's ultimate failure: as the story progresses and she manages to pass each test despite intense mental and physical suffering, we begin to think that she will have the strength to survive this day after all. Her failure is then all the more crushing for the fact that it comes when the day is nearly over.

Having accompanied this woman throughout the day, the reader feels only compassion for her as she fails the final test. Her husband feels no such compassion; the last sentence of the story leaves no doubt that her failure signals the end of any genuine relationship between them: "Ich wischte mir die Lippen ab, zündete eine Zigarette an, als Alfred lächelnd aus der Küche kam, auf Zehenspitzen zu mir, dann etwas flüstern wollte und es nicht tat, sondern einfach an mir vorbeiging, als hätte er mich gar nicht dort stehen sehen." Thus, as in **"Der längere Arm,"** the closing passage of the story presents the final breakdown of the relationship between husband and wife. It is precipitated by the wife's failure to keep her promise, but the encounter presented in the closing passage suddenly becomes a "moment of truth" for the husband as well. It is now he who is put to the test, and he does not pass it. Instead, his lack of compassion and understanding constitutes a failure that parallels his wife's.

It is apparent that the three stories discussed here share some important similarities. Indeed in many respects they are variations on a single theme. Stated in general terms, the underlying theme of all three stories is the glaring discrepancy between appearance and reality: in **"Ein Haus aus lauter Liebe"** we find the appearance of familial love and the reality of marital infidelity and cruel treatment of an aging father; in **"Der längere Arm"** the husband appears to be a successful, self-assured architect and turns out to be a shabby (and unsuccessful) blackmailer; in **"Der sechste Geburtstag"** there is an overwhelming discrepancy between the appearance of festivity and the cruel reality of the son's impending death.

Stated more specifically, all three stories treat the theme of appearance and reality in terms of eroded marital relationships and domestic and marital crisis in an everyday setting. Each of the stories begins with an "Alltagssituation": a couple going out for the evening (**"Ein Haus aus lauter Liebe"**); a husband and wife at the breakfast table (**"Der längere Arm"**); a husband and wife saying goodbye as he leaves for work (**"Der sechste Geburtstag"**); and each story ends in the same familiar household setting. In **"Ein Haus aus lauter Liebe"** there is no crisis in the overt sense, no occurrence or confrontation that leads to a final breakdown of the marital relationship. In a sense, however, the situation is one of on-going crisis: the relationship is revealed as an empty edifice, a house of cards that might tumble at any moment, or (as the ending suggests) that may remain precariously intact as long as the industrialist and his wife go through the necessary motions, outwardly preserving the fictions of love and contented family life. In the other two stories, of course, the crisis is painfully apparent to the characters as well as to the reader, and leads to the overt breakdown of the relationship.

Another element the three stories have in common is the motif of failure, a variation of the theme of guilt. One is reminded in this connection of Günther Busch's observation that "Lenz schildert den Werdegang von Opfern, nicht die Karriere von Siegern" ["Eine Rechtfertigung?" *Frankfurter Hefte*, Vol. XVIII, No. 7, 1963]. In two of the stories there is first of all the patent failure of one partner (the husband in **"Der längere Arm"** and the wife in **"Der sechste Geburtstag"**), which leads to a critical confrontation that signals the end of the relationship. For the purposes of this discussion, however, the important point is that in all three stories the failure of one partner is matched by the failure of the other: in **"Der sechste Geburtstag"** the wife breaks her promise and the husband refuses to forgive her; in **"Der längere Arm"** the husband is revealed as a contemptible blackmailer and his wife, in the final analysis, as a pitiless and unforgiving woman; and in **"Ein Haus aus lauter Liebe"** the faithlessness of the wife is paralleled by the hypocrisy and self-delusion of the husband. In all three stories both partners in the marital relationship carry a burden of guilt, both appear as "Versager." They are also "Opfer"—victims of themselves and of each other.

In addition to the thematic elements discussed above, the three stories reveal certain similarities of technique and structural development. First of all, the structure of each story comprises an integral part of Lenz's treatment of his central theme. In fact in this respect the "what" and the "how" of the stories are so skillfully meshed that it would be difficult to draw a clear dividing line between them. In each case the external action serves two purposes: it depicts the realm of appearances and at the same time functions as a frame for the author's portrayal of the inner reality. This places the two realms in sharp and immediate juxtaposition and intensifies the reader's recognition of the discrepancy between them.

Finally, each story confines itself to a single episode in the life of the family the author has chosen to scrutinize. That of itself is not unusual, given the limitations of the short-story genre. What is unusual is that despite their episodic nature, these stories are open-ended. That point has already been made with respect to **"Ein Haus aus lauter Liebe,"** but it applies equally to **"Der längere Arm"** and **"Der sechste Geburtstag"**: Lenz does not resolve the crisis he presents, he makes no moral pronouncements, offers no solutions and gives no indication of whether the crisis will be followed by a literal parting of the ways. (On the thematic level that question is immaterial, of course; it is clear that, whatever happens, these are relationships that have ceased to exist in any meaningful sense of the word.) In terms of craftsmanship, however, Lenz achieves a triple effect by giving the episodic story an open ending. In severing the story-line at the chosen point he (1) re-focuses our attention upon each story's underlying theme, the discrepancy between everyday appearance and the inner reality; (2) strengthens the impact of the crisis, forcing the reader to reflect upon its unnerving implications (thus making a "co-creator" of the reader); and (3) heightens the sense of realism, i.e. the reader's awareness that each of these fictitious episodes, like life itself, is fraught with unresolved problems. Structurally and technically, then, these stories corroborate the narrative stance we have come to associate with Lenz, aptly summed up by Reich-Ranicki's phrase, "der gelassene Mitwisser."

Peter Demetz (review date 1989)

SOURCE: "More German Lessons," in *The New York Times Book Review*, November 26, 1989, p. 14.

[*In the following assessment of* The Selected Stories of Siegfried Lenz, *Demetz names Lenz "the last gentleman of German writing" in view of the deft understatement of Lenz's political themes.*]

Among the few postwar German writers who have reached an international audience, 63-year-old Siegfried Lenz has been least tempted to be an educator of the entire nation or a front-page prophet of dire events. In matters of language he is less innovative than Günter Grass, who has never been particularly coy in his public appearances, and far less eager to push his somewhat left-of-center political views than Heinrich Böll, who, in his recurrent fits of rage, wrote with a hammer, not with a pen. In his inclinations and habits, Mr. Lenz is a quiet north German who believes that perhaps his writing will do more to enlighten his fellow citizens than speeches from grandstands; and being a skeptic who in the last year of World War II deserted from the navy (handing over his gun to a Danish student), he supports the Social Democrats without wanting to be a member of the party organization.

In 40 years of writing, he has produced a wide range of stories and novels (his famous *German Lesson* was translated into 19 languages), plays for the theater and other media and at least three collections of critical essays, including his conversations with the psychoanalyst Manes Sperber and the philosopher Leszek Kolakowski. His voice has remained as sober, steady and *sympathisch* as ever—so much so that many of his critics have long asked whether it is really possible to say anything about the brutalities of recent German history as calmly as he prefers to do.

The Selected Stories of Siegfried Lenz, edited and ably translated by Breon Mitchell, offers an ambitious panorama of his slowly changing narratives. Unfortunately, at least one-third of the pieces by now belong to literary history rather than to contemporary writing, and their translation comes at least 15 years too late. It was not the best of ideas to include so many of his village stories—nostalgic, easy and rarely impressive. Readers who do not happen to come from distant East Prussian Masuria (now part of Poland) or from the provinces of Schleswig-Holstein probably can do without them—in spite of their sturdy peasants and fishermen, always shrewd and lovable, and the boards groaning with a Gogolian abundance of "bacon, eggs, smoked ham, cabbage soup, honey, onion cake, and canned pears."

Mr. Lenz's early political parables, written in the 1950's, are all of the most welcome persuasion, unmasking the lies of the dictators and the cynical manipulation of public opinion in totalitarian regimes; but they are also curiously abstract, without precise color or singular characters, inevitably lacking edge and analytical force. One story, "Heilmann," is an instructive example of how a good German honestly wants to confront the realities of the Holocaust and fails to offer more than pious sentimentalities. The merchant Heilmann, the "last man of the Hebrew faith" in a distant corner of Masuria, had long waited for the moment "when it was his turn as well." He sleeps fully dressed to be ready, and when the local policeman whom he has known since he was a boy takes him away, they stomp together through the forest. When the aging policeman has a stomach cramp and rests in a hut, Heilmann carefully undoes the man's belt buckle, laying his rifle across his lap, until they are again ready to march to a border village where captive Jews dig trenches and shots are heard. Mr. Lenz has constructed a rather Teutonic character haplessly in awe of authority and inevitable fate; Heilmann has decided "to forgo any action which might alter what he had so often expected, experienced, and lived through in nights of listening and dreaming." He does not want to give in "to the weakness of hope" and, in his Wagnerian loyalty to destiny, even walks ahead of the police.

Yet Mr. Lenz is far too sensitive to be content forever to imitate existential epiphanies à la Hemingway, as did many younger writers returning from the war, or to create plaster cast dictators and paper Jews. In the 1970's he threw away his literary blinkers, looked more directly at the vicissitudes of West German society after the "economic miracle" and began to experiment with combinations of narrative styles and ingenious syntactic games. (It is a pity that the selection does not include the exhilarating story **"Einstein Crosses the Elbe Near Hamburg,"** which illuminates the relativity of "facts" in three incredibly long sentences that form the text.) There are foolish scholars in highly subsidized research institutes (**"Eskimo Lamps"**), German physicians burdened by their memories of how they behaved 40 years ago (**"The Punishment"**), a once-powerful corporation manager who has been shunted aside and now listens even to lowly job applicants (**"The Great Wildenberg"**) and a young woman who, having given up her own studies to enable her refugee friend to finish his, suddenly collapses when she hears that he has completed all his courses successfully (**"The Exam"**).

In his best stories Mr. Lenz continues to rely on suggestive understatement but fastidiously avoids the allegorical. In **"The Waves of Lake Balaton,"** a West German couple eagerly wait to see relatives from the German Democratic Republic for a brief Hungarian vacation, but the East Germans immediately go to see the last wild horses of the plains rather than stay a few hours with the Westerners, who do not even know how condescending they themselves are. In **"The End of a War,"** the most powerful story in this volume, a minesweeper is sent by the high command in 1945 to rescue wounded German soldiers from Baltic shores controlled by Soviet ships and planes. The crew refuses to follow orders and, a few hours after the official capitulation of Nazi Germany, returns to a base only to run up against unchanged navy ideas of order and honor and a hastily summoned court martial. (When the sailors address their commander, they say "Mr. Kaleu" in this version. But "Kaleu" is not, as the translator seems to believe, a family name; it is an abbreviated navy term of rank, *Kapitän-Leutnant,* and what they are saying is "Captain-Lieutenant, Sir!") **"The End of a War"** is a compassionate and corrosive story of large implications, and it shows what Mr. Lenz, the last gentleman of German writing, can really do.

Amy Kepple Strawser (review date 1993)

SOURCE: A review of *The Selected Stories of Siegfried Lenz,* in *Southern Humanities Review,* Vol. XXVII, No. 2, Spring, 1993, pp. 186-87.

[*In this brief review of* The Selected Stories of Siegfried Lenz, *Strawser raises some interesting points about Lenz's popularity in Germany and in the United States, and about the quality of Lenz's acclaimed story "Ein Kriegsende."*]

In the United States, Great Britain, and Canada, the three most widely known and read German authors of novels and short fiction from the postwar period are certainly Heinrich Böll, Günter Grass, and Christa Wolf. Most of the works of these writers were promptly rendered in

English and appeared in translation within several years of their original publication. Such has also been the case for the novels of Siegfried Lenz, who is best known in both German and English literary circles for his novel *Deutschstunde* (1968; *The German Lesson,* 1971). The publication of **The Selected Stories of Siegfried Lenz** now makes the short stories and folk tales of this veteran author accessible to North American and other English-speaking audiences.

Although Lenz is a respected writer in his native land, his work may simply be too well-liked by the general reading public abroad to often be the object of study among critics in the United States. Similar to the fate of Hermann Hesse, whose work fell out of grace with literary scholars in the academy after the enormous resurgence of popular interest in his novels during the sixties, the writings of Siegfried Lenz by and large remain outside the canon, graduate reading lists, and undergraduate anthologies. In spite of, or perhaps due to his popularity as a fiction writer in Germany, his books are not often taught at the university level in this country. And despite this academic snubbing of Lenz by professors and scholars of German literature in the States, much of his short fiction is exemplary of the German narrative prose written since the end of World War II.

Breon Mitchell has chosen a broad selection of Lenz's stories from those collected in **Die Erzählungen 1949-1984.** Under the headings "Tales of Our Times," "Tales from the Village," and "German Lessons," he presents the translated pieces chronologically within each section. That is, while the narratives are arranged under each heading according to when they were written, Mitchell gives no explanation in his brief afterword as to the reasoning behind these groupings—which are apparently thematic or stylistic—except to say that the editorial decisions have been approved by the author. Thus the tales from both of Lenz's imaginary villages, Suleyken and Bollerup, appear in the book's middle section, although the tales of Suleyken stem from the mid-fifties and those of Bollerup from twenty years later. It is possible that the translations adhere to an ordering similar to that of the German edition (which unfortunately was unavailable), yet it would have been helpful if the logic behind this somewhat arbitrary arrangement of the contents had been clarified. The translator, whose most recent effort is an English version of Lou Andreas-Salomé's memoirs (*Looking Back,* 1991), here provides highly readable texts throughout.

There is a great range in the type of short fiction in this collection, from the endearing invented folk narratives about village life, each no longer than half a dozen pages in length, to several brief selections from the book's first part which spoof the practices of such contemporary institutions as the research academy (**"Eskimo Lamps, or The Trials and Tribulations of a Specialist"**) and the military (**"An Acceptable Level of Pain"**) with caustic irony and wit. Two longer stories which close the "Tales of Our

Times" section are memorable on account of both content and narrative style. **"The Exam"** relates a day in the life of a young housewife who, having sacrificed her own studies for her marriage, awaits the outcome of her husband's academic day of reckoning. The author paints a quite convincing portrait of this woman's as-yet-unacknowledged compromised existence through descriptions of her anxieties, inner monologues, and deadening daily routine, which reveal deep-seated ambivalences about her social and familial roles. **"Fantasy,"** an interesting experiment as a "complex triple-narrative . . . in which the author offers the reader a metatextual tour de force on truth and fiction" ("Translator's Afterword"), displays Lenz's skill at shifting gears in his narrative prose by fleshing out a scene of everyday life from the perspectives of several different characters, all aspiring fiction writers.

The final selection in this collection has garnered sharp criticism as well as critical acclaim among literary scholars in Germany. **"The End of a War"** (1984) has created controversy surrounding the author's (sympathetic?) portrayal of the fate of the crew from a German minesweeper during the final days of the Second World War, who are court-martialed for mutiny after not having followed orders to rescue wounded fellow soldiers of the nearly defeated German army. Indeed, one can see how Lenz's narrative perspective here is at best on shaky ground ideologically; this story from the mid-1980s fails to approach the subject of Third Reich history with the critical reflection afforded by forty years of historical distance. Thus it is difficult to understand why this piece seemed to some of the author's contemporaries such a stunning achievement, as outlined in Wolfgang Beutin's "*Ein Kriegsende von Siegfried Lenz: Eine Kritik*" (in *Siegfried Lenz: Werk und Wirkung,* 1985). While the issues aroused by the last entry remain problematic, the majority of the stories collected here remain worth reading.

FURTHER READING

Geldrich-Leffman, Hanna. "The Eye of the Witness: Photography in Siegfried Lenz's Short Stories." *MLN* 104, No. 3 (April 1989): 696-712.

Analyzes the meaning of the visual in Lenz's short stories, with particular attention to his portrayal of cameras and photography.

Murdoch, Brian, and Malcolm Read. *Siegfried Lenz.* London: Oswald Wolff, 1978, 150 p.

Covers all Lenz's fiction up to 1978, with detailed summaries and analysis.

Woods, Roy. "Siegfried Lenz's 'Ein Kriegsende': Text and Film." *New German Studies* 15, No. 3 (1988-1989): 207-24.

Discusses the short story "Ein Kriegsende" in tandem with the film derived from it.

Additional coverage of Lenz's life and career is contained in the following sources published by The Gale Group: *Contemporary Authors,* Vol. 89-92; *Contemporary Literary Criticism,* Vol. 27; and *Dictionary of Literary Biography,* Vol. 75.

Thomas Wolfe
1900-1938

(Full name Thomas Clayton Wolfe) American novelist, short story and novella writer, essayist, dramatist, and poet.

INTRODUCTION

Wolfe is considered one of the foremost American writers of the twentieth century. He is generally recognized for his four major novels—*Look Homeward, Angel* (1929); *Of Time and the River* (1935); *The Web and the Rock* (1939); and *You Can't Go Home Again* (1940)—in which he took the facts of his own life and wove them into an epic celebration of the struggle of the lonely, sensitive, and artistic individual to find spiritual fulfillment in America. More recently, critical attention has also been focused on Wolfe's shorter fiction, a series of short stories and novellas, many of which are fragments or portions of his longer novels. These works, including the stories of *From Death to Morning* (1935), *The Hills Beyond* (1941), and two later collections, represent to many critics some of Wolfe's most refined literary expressions of urban and rural life in America in the early twentieth century.

Biographical Information

Wolfe was born in Asheville, North Carolina in 1900. The city and its inhabitants, as many he encountered in his life, would later serve as models for his intensely autobiographical fiction. At the age of sixteen, Wolfe entered the University of North Carolina, where he developed an interest in drama and prepared for a career as a playwright. Upon graduation he continued his education at Harvard, studying English under John Livingston Lowes, whose theories concerning the importance of a subconscious fusion of literary influence, personal experience, and imagination had a significant effect on Wolfe's writing. Wolfe received his master's degree in 1922, and accepted a teaching post at New York University with the hope of having his plays accepted for production on Broadway. Unsuccessful in this endeavor and wearied by teaching, Wolfe resigned his position in 1925, and determined to live entirely by his writing. Shortly after reaching this decision Wolfe met Aline Bernstein. Their five-year relationship offered Wolfe the emotional and financial support that enabled him to write his first and what many critics consider his best novel, *Look Homeward, Angel.* In the ensuing years, Wolfe produced many pieces of short fiction and prepared to write his next "big book." Facing financial problems in the early thirties, he received a break when he was awarded a $5000 prize from *Scribner's Magazine* for his novella *A Portrait of Bascom Hawke* in 1932. Encouraged to continue in the genre, he produced *The Web of Earth*—drawn from discussions with his mother about her life—later that same year. Again running low on

funds, Wolfe next completed his novella *No Door* in 1933, a work that was published in two installments in *Scribner's Magazine* in 1933 and 1934, and which later become part of his full-length *Of Time and the River.* The year 1935 saw the publication of his first collection of short fiction *From Death to Morning,* which failed to make the same impression as his first two novels. Following several more years of intense creative activity, Wolfe left New York in 1938 for a tour of the western United States, leaving his editor Edward C. Aswell with a mass of manuscript consisting of all of his recent writings. While in the West, Wolfe contracted pneumonia and soon after died. After Wolfe's death, Aswell honed his manuscripts to produce two more full novels, *The Web and the Rock* and *You Can't Go Home Again,* as well as the novel fragment and stories contained in *The Hills Beyond.*

Major Works of Short Fiction

Although Wolfe's short stories and novellas reflect the same thematic patterns as his full-length works, featuring studies of loneliness and estrangement and an almost obsessive regard for time and the past, they are generally thought to demonstrate an attitude of technical experimentation and artistic control otherwise lacking in the novels. In all, Wolfe produced seven novellas and fifty-eight short stories, most of which appeared in periodicals in the 1930s and were not published in book collections until decades after Wolfe's death. Among his most highly esteemed shorter works, the novella *A Portrait of Bascom Hawke* demonstrates Wolfe's exploration of the disparities of youth and age as an old man, weakened by time, looks back upon his childhood. "The Lost Boy," which appeared in Wolfe's collection *The Hills Beyond,* begins with the loss of innocence experienced by Grover Gant at the 1904 St. Louis World's Fair, and ends with the return of his brother, Eugene, to the same place decades later, where he experiences an intense loneliness and nostalgia for what has been lost. Late in his career, Wolfe frequently used his short fiction for the purpose of social commentary. Prompted by several visits to Hitler's Germany in the 1920s and 1930s—particularly his last in 1936, during which Wolfe was welcomed with immense respect and adoration—*I Have a Thing to Tell You* is nevertheless a scathing commentary on the atmosphere of suspicion, racial hatred, and distrust created by the Nazi dictator. Set in New York City, *The Party at Jack's* (written in 1937 and first published in 1939) critiques the indifferent rich whose sterile lives of luxury contrast sharply with the stark poverty—but enduring hopefulness—of Brooklyn's lower classes.

Critical Reception

Criticism of Wolfe's fiction has in many ways been dominated by the pronouncements of Bernard DeVoto in his 1936 essay "Genius is Not Enough." In the article, DeVoto decried Wolfe's extensive reliance on editors, his heavy use of autobiographical material, and—citing the aesthetic failings of *Look Homeward, Angel*—his inability to form a tightly-structured novel. While these ideas have become commonplace in regard to Wolfe's novels, many scholars have since dismissed charges of prolixity and formlessness in Wolfe's writing when focusing on his shorter fiction. Critical consensus in the latter half of the twentieth century has identified many of Wolfe's short stories and novellas as among his most brilliant and artistically controlled work. Scholars have noted, in particular, his more economical style in many of his shorter works, as well as a tendency toward experimentalism in narrative form. In addition, many commentators, led by C. Hugh Holman in his 1961 introduction to *The Short Novels of Thomas Wolfe,* have perceived in these writings a tight aesthetic unity, brought about not only by Wolfe's overarching theme of the individual's loneliness in time, but also by the extraordinary narrative craftsmanship of his fictional works written on a smaller scale.

PRINCIPAL WORKS

Short Fiction

From Death to Morning 1935

The Hills Beyond (short stories, sketches, and unfinished novel) 1941
The Short Novels of Thomas Wolfe 1961
The Complete Short Stories of Thomas Wolfe 1987

Other Major Works

The Return of Buck Gavin (drama) 1919
The Mountains (drama) 1921
Welcome to Our City (drama) 1923
Look Homeward, Angel: A Story of the Buried Life (novel) 1929
Of Time and the River: A Legend of a Man's Hunger in His Youth (novel) 1935
The Story of a Novel (essay) 1936
The Face of a Nation (poetry) 1939
The Web and the Rock (novel) 1939
You Can't Go Home Again (novel) 1940
A Stone, a Leaf, a Door (poetry) 1945
Mannerhouse (drama) 1948
The Letters of Thomas Wolfe (letters) 1956
The Autobiography of an American Novelist (essays) 1983
Beyond Love and Loyalty: The Letters of Thomas Wolfe and Elizabeth Nowell (letters) 1983
My Other Loneliness: Letters of Thomas Wolfe and Aline Bernstein (letters) 1983

CRITICISM

Wallace Stegner (essay date 1950)

SOURCE: "Analysis of 'The Lost Boy'," in *Thomas Wolfe: Three Decades of Criticism,* edited by Leslie A. Field, New York University Press, 1968, pp. 255-60.

[*In the following essay, originally published in 1950, Stegner characterizes "The Lost Boy" as an adept and magical incantation to time and the power of the past.*]

The writings of Thomas Wolfe, whatever their other virtues, are not usually notable for the strictness of their form. At any length Wolfe was large and loose; his talents were antipathetic to the concentration and control by which the short story has always been marked. But **"The Lost Boy"** is something of an exception. It is large enough and loose enough, but it does have an unmistakable form, which arises immediately and inevitably out of the intention and is inseparable from it.

"The Lost Boy" has within it most of what Thomas Wolfe made his total message. It has the haunting evocation of the past, the preoccupation with Time, the irreparable loneliness of the individual, the constant solipsistic attempt to convert the remembered into the real. The characteristic search for the father is apparently not here, but the search for the brother which is the subject of this story is so closely related as to seem a part of Wolfe's extraordinary longing to project himself backward toward someone loved and respected and envied and lost. And the style and manner are Wolfe's typical manner; the form the story takes does not hinder his incantatory flow of words.

Wolfe was a magician, a witch doctor, drawing upon the same profundities of awe and ecstasy and fear which primitive religions and magic and superstition draw upon. His writing impulse was very often directed toward the laying of ghosts, the evoking of spirits, the making of medicine to confound restricting Time, the exorcism of evil, the ritual expiation of sin. It is entirely appropriate that the form of this story should be very close to that of a primitive or superstitious ritual. The story is as surely an act of healing as a Navajo Yehbetzai, as much a superstitious rite as the calling up of a spirit at a séance. It has the same compulsive, ritualistic, gradual accretion of excitement toward the point of the ghost's appearance. It observes rules older than literary criticism and taboos embedded in the subconscious of the race. This is a very subsurface story; it comes close to being pure necromancy. Story and ritual are one; the form is utterly compulsive, though perhaps largely unconscious.

It does not begin like an exercise in voodoo, but like one of Wolfe's hymns to Time. In the beginning Wolfe evokes the Square in all its concreteness, from the dry whisking of the tails of the fire-horses to the catalogue of implements in the hardware store window. Here is Grover, the lost boy, before he was lost; here is Grover "caught upon a point of Time." Grover is real in a real place, but the Square is more than a square, Grover is a child who is more than a child. There is a quality of trance: the returning plume of the fountain, the returning winds of April, the streetcars that go and come, the chanting of the strong repetitious rhetoric and the sonority of recurrent sounds put a magic on this Square even at its most real. Grover's birthmark is a mark of difference and perhaps of doom. And we cannot miss the heightening of everything, from Grover's gravity to old Gant's Old-Testament potency as the Father. Gant is all but God. It is not accidental that he works at an altarlike bench among half-formed shapes of angels and that he strikes awe into Grover. Neither is it accident that Grover prays to him and that Gant in a godlike rage seizes him by the hand and goes to enforce justice upon old twisted Crocker. The father leaves an absence in the story because after the first section he is not mentioned again. His absence is like the absence of Grover. He duplicates and parallels that tantalizing ghost.

There are magic words in this story with magic powers to evoke. "St. Louis" and "the Fair" are two of them. It will be observed that the story follows a course from the Square where Grover's real life was, through Indiana to St. Louis, to the street called King's Highway, to the house where the family lived during the summer of the Fair, and finally to the room where Grover died. There is a progression from the more general to the more particular, a constant working closer to the point of mystery. But at the same time there is progression of another kind. This story fades and sharpens, comes and goes, like the fountain plume and the streetcars, and like the memory that recreates the past and sees it fade again, but it always works closer and

closer toward the mystery of Grover, the mystery of Time, the thing which is being summoned and the thing which has been lost. As it comes closer it grows in tension; its climax, surely, will be the dramatic appearance of this ghost, the dramatic revelation of mystery.

But the spell moves slowly. The lost boy must be built up bit by bit. First his mother and then his sister bear testimony about him, recreating him in quality and feature. Their testimony is like that of mourners at a funeral of one much loved: they have fixed the dead in their minds so that he cannot entirely disappear or be entirely lost. Through the mother, as the family travels down through Indiana to St. Louis and the Fair, we see Grover from one side. Through the sister, less sentimental, more touched with questionings, more moved by irrecoverable loss, we see him from another, and we follow him through the St. Louis summer to his death.

For the sister the Past is dead, the things they were and dreamed as children are dead, there is a kind of horror in thinking of how sad and lonely is the gap between Then and Now, and a sharper compulsion to cling to it and linger over it and understand it. Through the sister's part of the story we have come closer to the place of magic, and we have come much closer to Grover, for at the heart of her recollection is the photograph. There is his veritable face; there are the faces of all of them as they were— caught and petrified unchanged, but strange, almost unbelievable. Wolfe makes the same use of the photograph that a medicine man might make of nail parings or hair cuttings or gathered-up footprints in the mud: the possession of this picture gives us a power, by associative magic, over Grover's spirit.

And in both these witnesses note the hypnotic mumbling of the spell—the words and images that will roll Time back and restore the lost, or seem to for a moment:

> . . . you remember how it was, and see again those two funny, frightened, skinny little kids with their noses pressed against the dirty window of that lunchroom thirty years ago. You remember the way it felt, the way it smelled, even the strange smell in the old pantry in that house we lived in then. And the steps before the house, the way the rooms looked. And those two little boys in sailor suits who used to ride up and down before the house on tricycles . . . And the birthmark on Grover's neck . . . The Inside Inn . . . St. Louis, and the Fair.

Over and over the images are recalled, the words of magic repeated. In section four the story begins to tighten toward its climactic moment. It has here the same trancelike repetitions, the same bewitched enslavement to memory, and it insists more upon the supernatural. In Eugene's childhood King's Highway had been "a kind of road that wound from magic out of some dim and haunted land," but he finds it now a common street, and his compulsive return toward the core of the mystery is delayed and made irritable by the contrasts between what he remembers and what really is. Finding the street, the house, the steps, he pauses and looks back "as if the street were Time," and waits "for a word, for a door to open, for the child to come."

But neither the dead nor the child that he himself once was can be recalled so easily. He knows he is close to them. He feels how it is all the same "except for absence, the stained light of absence in the afternoon, and the child who had once sat there, waiting on the stairs." It is as tantalizing as a séance where the ghost is coy. Eugene is near to making contact, but the thing fades and weakens, and he strengthens and deepens the incantation, running over and over the images that come from the past, trying by their repetition to enforce them upon the present. He is at a threshold, and he gives us the contrasted images of the hot backyard and the cool cellar which is the Past, the lost place in Time that he wants now to return to. Now, as then, the thought of the dark cellar fills him "with a kind of numb excitement, a kind of visceral expectancy."

It sharpens and fades for him. He feels that if he could only sit on the stairs as he had long ago "he would be able to get it back again. Then he would be able to remember all that he had seen and been, the brief sum of himself."

He moves closer, inside the house, up to the very door of the room where Grover has died. Now comes Mrs. Bell's occult knowledge that Grover died in that room. Without being told, she knows. The presence is between them, somehow. They feel him.

And suddenly he is evoked and present and palpable. The witch doctor has made the Past real by naming its every particle, chanting and cataloging the memories it is made of. Now he brings up the ghost by the same "name" magic. "Say *Grover!*" the ghost is saying. "No—not Gova— Grover! Say it!"

Among many primitive tribes the name is a secret revealed to none, for fear strength and life will be exposed with it. Among organizations as various as street gangs and Catholic sisterhoods the spiritual or special self has its special name. Among the ancient Irish it was a capital crime to put a man by name into a poem, for both poem and name were potent with magic and power could be got over anyone so be-spelled. It is the name that reveals Grover briefly and brings him up from the dark cellar of Time. It is as if, if only the child Eugene could say the name right, Grover might now literally appear. But this attempt to cross between Forever and Now is never more than half successful. The closest we get to Grover's quiet ghost is his little brother's lisping "Gova."

But this is enough. Wolfe's magic, like Eugene's, invokes the ghost briefly and holds him a moment before he fades. The ghost that troubled Eugene, the rival that he loved and half envied, is laid and quieted. The man sick with Time is healed, the voodoo spell is finished, the spirit has spoken its cryptic word and departed. "And out of the enchanted wood, that thicket of man's memory . . . the dark eye and the quiet face of his friend and brother— poor child, life's stranger and life's exile, lost like all of us, a cipher in blind mazes, long ago—the lost boy was gone forever and would not return."

When the ghost has been summoned and held briefly and allowed to fade, the story is over. Ritual and story are one, with one shape. What suspense the story has is the suspense of the growing, circling, nearing incantation. Its climax is the moment of confrontation. Its peculiar emotional power comes from the chanting, the repetition, the ceremonial performances, the magical tampering with Time, the sure touching of symbols that lie deep among the sources of all superstition and all religion, above all by the anguished invocation of the dead. No one who has lived at all with his dead can be left entirely unmoved by this.

Not a line of this story, not a trick in it, could have been learned from any generalization about the shaping of fiction. The shape this story takes it takes by a process of transplantation, associated images and ideas being moved from one category of thought to another. A formal ritual becomes a formal fiction by what William James calls "similar association." Material and form are so nearly one that they can never be effectively separated.

Lois Hartley (essay date 1961)

SOURCE: "Theme in Thomas Wolfe's 'The Lost Boy' and 'God's Lonely Man'," in *Thomas Wolfe: Three Decades of Criticism,* edited by Leslie A. Field, New York University Press, 1968, pp. 261-67.

[*In the following essay, originally published in 1961, Hartley examines the theme of loneliness in Wolfe's story "The Lost Boy."*]

In Thomas Wolfe's story **"The Lost Boy"** three related themes are eventually absorbed into what became perhaps the major theme of Wolfe's writing and of his life. The first of these is the theme of change, of the loss of illusions through change, and it is so closely related to the second, the loss of innocence through experience, that the two can only be examined together. The third is the theme of loneliness, and it is with the implications of this theme that I wish ultimately to deal.

One is aware of time, of change, from the first paragraphs of the story when the boy Grover is conscious of the light that "came and went and came again" in the square of Altamont, of the strokes of the town clock booming across the town, of the streetcars on their quarter-hourly schedule. Yet to Grover this is a sort of change without significance, and he is unaware of any more significant kind of change, for he is not yet "the lost boy": "It seemed to him that the Square, itself the accidental masonry of many years, the chance agglomeration of time and of disrupted strivings, was the center of the universe. It was for him, in his soul's picture, the earth's pivot, the granite core of changelessness, the eternal place where all things came and passed, and yet abode forever and would never change."

In the central episode of part one of **"The Lost Boy,"** Grover goes into the candy store of the Crockers to buy candy with stamps given him for running errands. He buys fifteen-cents' worth of candy, but accidentally pays with eighteen-cents' worth of stamps. Crocker refuses to return the three cents in stamps. He and his wife imply that Grover stole the stamps, and put Grover out of the shop. Now "something had gone out of day. He felt the overwhelming, soul-sickening guilt that all the children, all the good men of the earth, have felt since Time began. And even anger had died down, had been drowned out, in this swelling tide of guilt, and 'This is the Square'—thought Grover as before—'This is Now. There is my father's shop. And all of it is as it has always been—save I.'" Through time and experience Grover has changed. He is now the lost boy. He has learned something about separateness, about isolation, about inhumanity; and perhaps Grover's feeling of guilt is a symptom of this failure in fellowship.

The lost boy moves across the square to his father's stone-cutter's shop; it may be significant that he passes the "angel with strong marble hands of love." Grover intends to maintain deliberately a sort of separation from his father, for he fears that his father will hear of the Crockers' accusation. Then suddenly he finds himself blurting, "Papa, I never stole the stamps." Gant's nearly immediate action is to take Grover to Crocker's shop and to demand repayment. Then Grover is alone again in the square: "And light came and went and came again—but now not quite the same as it had done before. The boy saw the pattern of familiar shapes and knew that they were just the same as they had always been. But something had gone out of day, and something had come in again. Out of the vision of those quiet eyes some brightness had gone, and into their vision had come some deeper color. He could not say, he did not know through what transforming shadows life had passed within that quarter hour. He only knew that something had been lost—something forever gained." Grover has lost something of innocence; he has gained in experience and knowledge.

If this first episode of the story says something tentatively about time and change, it says something more about isolation, about loneliness. In the autobiographical essay "God's Lonely Man," which appeared with **"The Lost Boy"** in the volume *The Hills Beyond* (1941) but which was begun perhaps seven years previously, Wolfe said:

> The whole conviction of my life now rests upon the belief that loneliness, far from being a rare and curious phenomenon, peculiar to myself and to a few other solitary men, is the central and inevitable fact of human existence. When we examine the moments, acts, and statements of all kinds of people—not only the grief and ecstasy of the greatest poets, but also the huge unhappiness of the average soul, as evidenced by the innumerable strident words of abuse, hatred, contempt, mistrust, and scorn that forever grate upon our ears as the manswarm passes us in the streets—we find, I think, that they are all suffering from the same thing. The final cause of their complaint is loneliness.

Grover, the "dark-eyed and grave," the "too quiet and too listening" boy, is like Wolfe himself in that "there are times when anything, everything, all or nothing, the most trivial incidents, the most casual words" can strip him of defenses, can plunge him into despair, can take from him hope and joy and truth. They can show him his separateness and yet send him searchingly to his father, who also has lonely eyes and who is immediately responsive to his son, but whose indignation surely has an element of failure in it as he lashes at Crocker: "You never knew the feelings of a father, or understood the feelings of a child; and that is why you acted as you did. But a judgment is upon you. God has cursed you. He has afflicted you. He has made you lame and childless as you are—and lame and childless, miserable as you are, you will go to your grave and be forgotten!" There is a loneliness too in the light that came and went, in the strokes of the town clock, even in the "His Master's Voice" dog, in the music-store window, listening to the silent horn, listening for the unspeaking voice.

In parts two and three of **"The Lost Boy,"** the mother, Eliza Gant, and the sister remember Grover, but they reveal also their nostalgia regarding time and change and disillusionment. The tone for these sections is partially set by the poetic refrain playing variations on the final line of part one: "Just then a buggy curved out through the Square, and fastened to the rear end was a poster, and it said 'St. Louis' and 'Excursion' and 'The Fair.'"

Years after the family went to the St. Louis Fair, the Exposition of 1904, the mother remembers "all of you the way you looked that morning, when we went down down through Indiana, going to the Fair." Her children have all grown up and gone away, and she says she is proud of them all, but she adores in memory grave and earnest, curious and intelligent Grover. He is for her, paradoxically, the symbol of all that has changed, of all who have either died or gone away, and yet of the changeless, because he is fixed forever in memory as he was "that morning when we went down through Indiana, by the river, to the Fair." The mother has known change and loss, and even in the words of her refrain there is a loneliness.

In part three Wolfe emphasizes the sister's disillusionment and her bewilderment in the face of time and change. She too remembers Grover and the summer of the Fair, the summer when Grover died of typhoid; she remembers also her lost ambitions—to be a famous pianist, to be an opera star:

> All my hopes and dreams and big ambitions have come to nothing, and it's all so long ago, as if it happened in another world. . . . Sometimes I lie awake at night and think of all the people who have come and gone, and how everything is different from the way we thought that it would be. Then I go out on the street next day and see the faces of the people that I pass. . . . Don't you see something funny in people's eyes, as if all of them were puzzled about something? As if they were wondering what had happened to them since they were kids? Wondering what it is that they have lost?

She feels the separateness and yet the likeness of people, who all lose something, who all reach points other than those of their dreams. And again there is a loss of innocence, a nostalgia regarding time and change, and a loneliness comprehending them both.

Wolfe's treatment of the theme of loneliness is detailed and thoughtful. And since this theme appears to be highly characteristic of modern American literature and thought, Wolfe's statement is meaningful for us all.

—Lois Hartley

The fourth and final section of the story describes the brother Eugene's return to St. Louis, many years later, in search of the magic of the past and particularly in search of the "lost boy." Here change through time and loss of innocence are strongly dramatized. Eugene finds the house of that summer of the Fair very much the same, but the feeling is different and he himself is different, and different too is the magic street, the King's Highway, which "had not been a street in those days but a kind of road that wound from magic out of some dim and haunted land, and that along the way . . . got mixed in with Tom the Piper's son, with hot cross buns, with all the light that came and went, and with coming down through Indiana in the morning, and the smell of engine smoke, the Union Station, and most of all with voices lost and far and long ago that said 'King's Highway.'" In the change in the King's Highway, which is now just a street, in the absence of Grover, in the absence of the child he himself used to be, in the fact that "as a child he had sat there feeling things were *Somewhere*—and now he *knew*," Eugene is aware of time and change and the effect of experience.

And above all there is the mood of loneliness, of remembered loneliness and present loneliness. He remembers how, as a boy, he felt "a kind of absence in the afternoon" after the streetcar had passed, "a sense of absence and vague sadness" in the afternoons when he sat alone in the house, on the hall steps, and listened to the silence; he remembers how he waited in loneliness for the return of Grover and the family from the Fair. But his present loneliness is more inclusive and more sophisticated. He knows the summer desolation of the great American cities; he knows the desolation, the separateness

> that one feels at the end of a hot day in a great city in America—when one's home is far away, across the continent, and he thinks of all that distance, all that heat, and feels, "Oh God! but it's a big country!" And he feels nothing but absence, absence, and the desolation of America, the loneliness and sadness of the high, hot skies, and evening coming on across the Middle West, across the sweltering and heat-sunken land, across all the lonely little towns, the farms, the fields.

He feels that he should not have come and must not come again, that lost magic is forever lost, that his brother was "life's stranger, and life's exile, lost like all of us, a cipher in blind mazes." And he himself seems "drowned in desolation and in no belief."

If the prevailing mood of **"The Lost Boy"** is loneliness, then the story should be examined in the light of "God's Lonely Man," Wolfe's tragic and definitive statement on his own loneliness. First, we should be aware that he sees loneliness as "the central and inevitable fact of human existence" and that he knows that it is sometimes evidenced in such ways as the mistrust and meanness of Crocker and the shrill words of scorn of Gant. He knows that men are both cursed and blessed by separateness, for he has learned that upon the doubt and despair of loneliness may be built the triumph and joy of creativity.

In "God's Lonely Man" Wolfe has much to say about the Old Testament as the chronicle of loneliness and the New Testament as an answer to loneliness through love, but although he says that "the way and meaning of Christ's life is a far, far better way and meaning than my own," he repudiates it as his own way: "For I have found the constant everlasting weather of man's life to be, not love, but loneliness. Love itself is not the weather of our lives. It is the rare, the precious flower. Sometimes it is the flower that gives us life. . . . But sometimes love is the flower that brings us death." In **"The Lost Boy"** love is present— the love of Eugene, particularly, for life; the love of all the family for Grover, although this feeling sometimes appears to be better described as pride than love. But love is not presented as a solution and is not pervasive. It must not be emphasized as a theme in the story nor inferred as a solution to the loneliness, the separateness. No solution is given.

In **"The Lost Boy"** Eugene seems "drowned in desolation and in no belief," and in "God's Lonely Man" Wolfe, himself a lonely man, "is united to no image save that which he creates himself, . . . is bolstered by no other knowledge save that which he can gather for himself with the vision of his own eyes and brain. He is sustained and cheered and aided by no party, he is given comfort by no creed, he has no faith in him except his own." It is in this sense that "God's Lonely Man" is a tragic statement, for although such independence may be heroic and Promethean, such denial of dependence implies a tragedy of misunderstanding. And even when Wolfe asserts that "suddenly, one day, for no apparent reason, his faith and his belief in life will come back to [the lonely man] in a tidal flood," we wish that it would come back for an apparent reason, that it might be the result of the re-ascendancy of reason and judgment, or of the healthful wedding of judgment and feeling.

Yet his faith in life does come back, and he is compelled to speak whatever truth he knows, in his renewed confidence; and among the truths which Wolfe speaks, out of his loneliness, is that "the lonely man, who is also the tragic man, is invariably the man who loves life dearly— which is to say, the joyful man." Like Eugene in **"The**

Lost Boy," he knows loneliness, death, time, change: "Out of this pain of loss, this bitter ecstasy of brief having, this fatal glory of the single moment, the tragic writer will therefore make a song for joy. . . . And his song is full of grief, because he knows that joy is fleeting, gone the instant that we have it, and that is why it is so precious, gaining its full glory from the very things that limit and destroy it." These lines from "God's Lonely Man" may be taken as a description of **"The Lost Boy,"** for surely this story describes the pain of loss, the bitter ecstasy of brief having, and it is a song for joy at the same time that it is a cry of grief.

Wolfe's treatment of the theme of loneliness is detailed and thoughtful. And since this theme appears to be highly characteristic of modern American literature and thought, Wolfe's statement is meaningful for us all.

C. Hugh Holman (essay date 1961)

SOURCE: Introduction to *The Short Novels of Thomas Wolfe*, in *Thomas Wolfe: A Collection of Critical Essays,* edited by Louis D. Rubin, Jr., Prentice-Hall Inc., 1973, pp. 165-77.

[*In the following essay, originally published in 1961, Holman studies Wolfe's seven short novels, which he argues represent some of the author's best work, and which "helped to sustain his reputation, demonstrated his artistry and control of his materials, and perhaps instructed his sense of form."*]

To present a collection of the short novels of Thomas Wolfe will seem to many of his readers a quixotic or even a perverse act, for Wolfe exists in the popular fancy and even in the opinion of many of his most devoted admirers as the fury-driven author of a vast but incomplete saga of one man's pilgrimage on earth, a saga so formless that the term *novel* can be applied to its parts only with extreme caution and so monumental that it exploded the covers of four vast books in which its portions were imprisoned. Of the book upon which he embarked after *Look Homeward, Angel,* Wolfe wrote: "What I had to deal with was material which covered almost 150 years in history, demanded the action of more than 2000 characters, and would in its final design include almost every racial type and social class of American life." In a letter in 1932 he said, "The book on which I have been working for the last two or three years is not a volume but a library."

Much of the criticism of Wolfe's work has centered on its seemingly uncontrolled and formless exuberance, and it has become almost a critical truism that he possessed great talent but little control, a magnificent sense of language but a limited awareness of the demands of plot, a sensuous recall that was nearly total but an almost shocking unwillingness to subject his material to critical elision.

Yet, paradoxically, Thomas Wolfe produced some of his best work in the middle length of the short novel, the length between 15,000 and 40,000 words. Indeed, during the grueling years between the publication of his first novel in 1929 and *Of Time and the River* in 1935, his reputation was sustained and enriched by his short novels as much as it was by Sinclair Lewis's brief but telling praise for him as a "Gargantuan creature with great gusto for life" in his Nobel Prize address in 1930.

Wolfe's whole career was an endless search for a language and a form in which to communicate his vision of reality. "I believe with all my heart," he declared in *The Story of a Novel,* ". . . that each man for himself and in his own way . . . must find that way, that language, and that door—must find it for himself." This passion to find a mode of expression was coupled in Wolfe with a thoroughly organic view of art, one in which the thing to be said dictates the form in which it is uttered. He once wrote Hamilton Basso: "There is no accepted way: there are as many art forms as there are forms of art, and the artist will continue to create new ones and to enrich life with new creations as long as there is either life or art. So many of these forms that so many academic people consider as masterly and final definitions derived from the primeval source of all things beautiful or handed Apollo-wise from Mount Olympus, are really worn out already, will work no more, are already dead and stale as hell."

Look Homeward, Angel had almost automatically assumed a simple but effective narrative form. The record of childhood and youth, cast at least semi-consciously in the *bildungsroman* pattern of James Joyce's *A Portrait of the Artist as a Young Man,* had found its theme and taken its shape from the sequential flow of lyric feeling which it expressed. After its publication, Wolfe began a desperate search for another form into which to pour his materials. His letters between 1930 and 1934 are crowded with ambitious plans, nebulous projections of structure, plot, and myth, all pointed toward forming his next book. Increasingly its matter grew and the problems of the control of that matter enlarged.

By the fall of 1931 Wolfe found himself immersed in a struggle for form whose magnitude and difficulty, as well as spiritual and emotional anguish, he recorded touchingly in *The Story of a Novel.* In November, badly in need of money and in black despair over "the book," he turned to a body of materials in which he had earlier worked and began shaping them into a short novel. These materials dealt with his experiences in Cambridge and with his uncle, Henry Westall. In its finished form the short novel, *A Portrait of Bascom Hawke,* pictured an old man resigned to the death of dreams as he is seen through the eyes of a youth still half blinded by the visions of glory which the old man has given up. The two points of view, the youth's and the old man's, together gave a sense of the flow and corrosion of time. The result was a portrait in depth, done with irony, poignance, and tolerant laughter, of an eccentric who might have stepped from the pages of Dickens.

Fortunately, Wolfe had connections at this time with a publishing house which had a magazine, *Scribner's,* that was interested in the short novel as a literary form. Ludwig Lewisohn was generally correct when he asserted in 1932 that the short novel "is a form with which, in the English-speaking world, neither editors nor publishers seem ever to know what to do, trying to palm it off now as a short story and now as a novel." But in 1931 and 1932 *Scribner's Magazine* was publishing a novella in each issue, as a result of its second $5,000 Prize Short Novel contest, the announced aim of which was "to open up a field of fiction—the long-story field—which had been almost wholly neglected." In these contests, the best entries were published as they were received, and the prize was awarded to the best novel from both the published and unpublished entries. The characteristics of the short novels *Scribner's* was seeking were declared to be "adequate space for the development of character and setting, combined with precision and solidity of structure." The magazine had begun publishing short novels with James Gould Cozzen's *S. S. San Pedro* in August, 1930, the first of twelve long stories published as part of the first Prize Contest. Among the others were long tales by W. R. Burnett, André Maurois, and Marjorie Kinnan Rawlings. The contest was won by John Peale Bishop's *Many Thousands Gone.*

When Wolfe submitted *A Portrait of Bascom Hawke* to Maxwell Perkins in January, 1932, the second Prize Contest was nearing its February 1 closing date. Among the nine short novels published as a part of the second contest, in addition to *A Portrait of Bascom Hawke,* were long tales by Sherwood Anderson, Edith Wharton, and Katherine Anne Porter. The judges—Burton Rascoe, William Soskin, and Edmund Wilson—declared the contest to be a tie between John Herrmann's *The Big Short Trip* and Wolfe's short novel, which was published in the April, 1932, issue of the magazine. Wolfe and Herrmann divided the $5,000 Prize between them.

A Portrait of Bascom Hawke gained considerable critical praise, such as that which Laurence Stallings gave it in *The New York Sun,* where he wrote: "Has anyone failed to admire a story in the *Scribner's Magazine* (for April) by Thomas Wolfe? There's an eddy of energy for you; and a lyrical paean to life. . . . It seems to me that Thomas Wolfe has shown in this story that his *October Fair,* announced for next fall, will be even finer than . . . *Look Homeward, Angel.* . . . He seems to have all the gifts, all the talents . . . *A Portrait of Bascom Hawke* is the book of the month."

Apparently Wolfe had been ignorant of the existence of the Short Novel Contest until he submitted *A Portrait* to Perkins in January. Learning of the contest he resolved to write another novel to enter in it, despite the fact that less than a month remained before the contest ended. It was actually Perkins who entered *A Portrait of Bascom Hawke* in the contest which it won.

As his intended entry Wolfe set to work on a short novel fashioned on his mother's endless stories of the past. During the month of January she visited him in Brooklyn, and the immediate source of *The Web of Earth* was almost certainly her conversations. The Short Novel Contest had

been over more than a month before the story was finished, but *Scribner's* promptly purchased it and published it in the July, 1932, issue.

This novella, the longest of Wolfe's short novels, comes to the reader entirely through the voice of its narrator, Delia Hawke (later changed to Eliza Gant when the novel was reprinted in *From Death to Morning*). Wolfe insisted, "It is different from anything I have ever done," and added, "that story about the old woman has got everything in it, murder and cruelty, and hate and love, and greed and enormous unconscious courage, yet the whole thing is told with the stark innocence of a child." The seemingly disparate elements of the story—disjointed in temporal and logical sequence—are effectively knit together by the powerful personality of the narrator and by her obsessive search in the events of her life for the meaning of the spectral voices that spoke "Two . . . Two" and "Twenty . . . Twenty" in "the year that the locusts came."

In writing *The Web of Earth* Wolfe followed James Joyce again, as he had done in *Look Homeward, Angel.* He compared his "old woman" with Molly Bloom and seemingly felt that his short novel had a structure like that of the interior monologue at the conclusion of *Ulysses.* In her resilience, her undefeatable energy, and her vitality Eliza (or Delia) approaches "the earth goddess" and is, as Louis D. Rubin, Jr. has pointed out, reminiscent of the end of the "Anna Livia Plurabelle" sequence of *Finnegans Wake,* a sequence which was published in the little magazine *transition* about the same time. In this short novel one understands what Wolfe meant when he referred to Eliza Gant's people as "time-devouring." Thus, *The Web of Earth* becomes a fascinating counterpiece to *A Portrait of Bascom Hawke*; for each is a character sketch of an elderly person, but where Bascom Hawke is defeated and despairingly resigned, Eliza Gant is triumphant and dominant; where Bascom is the male victim of time, Eliza is the female devourer of time; where Bascom's is the vain grasp of intellect and reason in a mad and fury-driven world, Eliza's is the groping of mystery, passion, and fear in a world where reason always falls victim to the decay of time. Never did Wolfe articulate more effectively than in these two short novels the fundamental polarities of his childhood and youth.

With these two short novels successfully behind him, Wolfe next turned to organizing into short novel form blocks of the material which he had written for the still formless "big book." In the period between March, 1933, and March, 1934, he put together four long stories or short novels from these materials, finding in the limits of the novella a means of focusing matter whose organization in larger blocks still defied him.

Scribner's Magazine bought three of these long tales and published them in successive issues in the summer of 1934. **"The Train and the City,"** a long short-story of 12,000 words, appeared in the May issue. Percy MacKaye praised this story highly, still, it lacks the unity which Wolfe had achieved in his first two short novels. *Death the Proud Brother* appeared in the June issue, and was later republished as a short novel in *From Death to Morning.* This story of 22,000 words was a skillfull attempt to unify a group of seemingly disparate incidents in the city through their common themes of loneliness and death, "the proud brother of loneliness." Wolfe regarded this story very highly, saying, "It represents *important* work to me," and his novelist friend Robert Raynolds praised it highly. Although it is a successful effort to impose thematic unity upon disconnected instances of death in the city, it is less effective than Wolfe's other novellas.

The third long story was *No Door,* in its original form a short novel of 31,000 words, although it was published by *Scribner's* as two long stories, *No Door* in July, 1933, and **"The House of the Far and the Lost"** in August, 1934. In arranging the materials of this novel, Wolfe selected a group of intensely autobiographical incidents all centering on his sense of incommunicable loneliness and insularity, dislocated them in time, and bound them together by a group of recurring symbols arranged in *leitmotif* patterns, extending and enriching a method he had used in **Death the Proud Brother.** Through the recurring images and the repeated phrases of a prose poem used as a prologue, he knit together one portion of his life. In its concluding episode are united the themes of youth's exuberance and age's sad wisdom, which had been central to *A Portrait of Bascom Hawke,* and the enduring earth, which had been central to *The Web of Earth.*

It was in the early months of 1933 that *No Door* was completed, and by March it had been accepted by *Scribner's.* Its completion coincided with Wolfe's discovery of a plan which made work on the "big book" feasible for him again. He wrote to George Wallace: ". . . just after you left in January . . . I plunged into work and . . . I seemed suddenly to get what I had been trying to get for two years, the way to begin the book, and make it flow, and now it is all coming with a rush." Since the structure of *No Door* is essentially that of *Of Time and the River,* since the prologue to *No Door* reappears with only minor changes as the prologue to the long novel, and since the writing of *No Door* coincides with the finding of a "way to begin the book," it is probable that the short novel was the door through which Wolfe entered *Of Time and the River.* John Hall Wheelock praised *No Door* highly, and Maxwell Perkins agreed to bring out a limited edition of the short novel in its original form. However, its absorption into *Of Time and the River* was almost complete, and it seemingly has survived as a unit only in the form of its brief first incident, published as a short story in *From Death to Morning,* where it achieved notoriety as the basis for a libel suit brought against Wolfe and Scribner's by Marjorie Dorman and her family in 1936.

Yet *No Door* represents as sure a mastery as Wolfe ever demonstrated of the subjective, autobiographical materials for which he is best known. Of the section published as "The House of the Far and the Lost," Robert Penn Warren wrote in a review almost brutally unsympathetic to *Of Time and the River*: "Only in the section dealing with the Coulson episode does Mr. Wolfe seem to have all his resources for character presentation under control. The

men who room in the house . . . with the Coulsons themselves are very precise to the imagination, and are sketched in with an economy usually foreign to Mr. Wolfe. . . . Here Mr. Wolfe has managed to convey an atmosphere and to convince the reader of the reality of his characters without any of his habitual exaggerations of method and style. This section . . . possesses what is rare enough in *Of Time and the River,* a constant focus." The Coulson episode is clearly the most striking one in *No Door.* It is also an integral part of that work, and the entire short novel possesses the strong virtues that Mr. Warren here assigns to the only portion of it which survived as a unified part of the long novel.

One other short novel resulted from Wolfe's arranging of materials from the "big book" during this period. It was *Boom Town,* a story of approximately 20,000 words, portraying the real estate craze in Asheville in the satiric manner of Sinclair Lewis. This short novel was published in the *American Mercury* in May, 1934, but it had been written before *No Door.*

The discovery of an organizing principle for the "big book" brought a temporary end to Wolfe's work in the short novel form; for the next two years he devoted himself single-mindedly to *Of Time and the River.* Thus during his first period—the one of which he said, "I began to write with an intense and passionate concern with the designs and purposes of my own youth"—Thomas Wolfe produced, in addition to his two long novels, five short ones: *A Portrait of Bascom Hawke, The Web of Earth, Death the Proud Brother, Boom Town,* and *No Door.* These short novels helped to sustain his reputation, demonstrated his artistry and control of his materials, and perhaps instructed his sense of form.

When he entered the second period of his career—that of which he said, "[My] preoccupation [with my own youth] has now changed to an intense and passionate concern with the designs and purposes of life"—he found himself once more facing the problem of finding a new and adequate form in which to express his vision of experience. This search for an organic structure was complicated by his growing difficulties with his publishers and his increasing unwillingness to follow the advice of his editor, Maxwell E. Perkins. In this situation, in some respects like that of 1931, Wolfe turned his attention again to elements of his experience that lent themselves to expression in the short novel form.

In the summer of 1936 he made his last visit to Germany, a nation that he loved and that had heaped adulation upon him. On this trip he was forced to face the frightening substratum of Nazism, what he called "a picture of the Dark Ages come again—shocking beyond belief, but true as the hell that man forever creates for himself." And he said, "I recognized at last, in all its frightful aspects, the spiritual disease which was poisoning unto death a noble and mighty people." That fall he used the short novel form to dramatize this perception of the truth about Hitler's Germany, and he elected to give his account, which he entitled *I Have a Thing to Tell You,* the sharp intensity and the almost stark directness of the action story. At this time Wolfe had great admiration for the directness and simplicity of Ernest Hemingway's style, and in this short novel of Germany he came closest to adopting some of its characteristics. Nothing Wolfe ever wrote has greater narrative drive or more straightforward action than this novella. The simplicity and objectivity of *I Have a Thing to Tell You* were seldom sustained for any length of time in Wolfe's work before 1936.

Since Wolfe's success in achieving the larger unity for which he strove in the last three long novels is considerably less than total, the materials which he had organized into short novels have an integrity and a consummate craftsmanship which they seem to lack in the long books.

—*C. Hugh Holman*

This short novel also displays clearly the growing concern with the issues of the outer world which had begun to shape Wolfe's thinking. Its publication in the *New Republic* as a serial in March, 1937, despite his disclaimers of propaganda intent, indicates a marked advance in the expression of political and social concerns for Wolfe.

During much of 1937, Wolfe's energies were expended in his long and tortuous break with his publishers, Charles Scribner's Sons, certainly one of the two major emotional cataclysms of his life (the other was his earlier break with his mistress, Aline Bernstein). He was also deeply discouraged about his projected book, feeling that his long-planned and talked-of *October Fair,* often announced, was somehow being dissipated in fragments. In this despairing state, he was led by his growing sense of social injustice to attempt another experiment with a short novel as a vehicle of social criticism. He worked on this new novella, *The Party at Jack's,* during the early months of the year and spent the summer in revising and rewriting it.

Wolfe felt that he was attempting in *The Party at Jack's* "one of the most curious and difficult problems that I have been faced with in a long time," the presentation of a cross-section of society through a representation of many people, ranging from policemen, servants, and entertainers to the leaders in the literary world and the rich in the events of a single evening during which they were brought together through a party and a fire in the apartment house in which the party occurred. He used several devices, including the recurring quivering of the apartment house as the trains run in tunnels through its seemingly solid rock foundations and the conversations of the doormen and elevator operators, to underscore the contrast among the characters and to comment on society. Wolfe feared

that readers would think this short novel to be Marxist, a charge against which he defended it, saying: ". . . there is not a word of propaganda in it. It is certainly not at all Marxian, but it is representative of the way my life has come—after deep feeling, deep thinking, and deep living and all this experience—to take its way. . . . It is in concept, at any rate, the most densely woven piece of writing that I have ever attempted."

The Party at Jack's is, as Wolfe asserted, free of autobiography, except in the most incidental ways. It is also in Wolfe's late, more economical style. Its taut prose and its rapid movement, together with its effective but implicit statement of social doctrine, make it one of Wolfe's most impressive accomplishments.

Almost immediately after completing *The Party at Jack's,* Wolfe plunged into the organizing of his materials into another "big book" for his new publishers, Harper and Brothers, a task which he was prevented from completing by his death in September, 1938. He had written—in addition to a mass of manuscript out of which three later books were assembled—two novels, a number of short stories, and seven short novels.

Upon these seven short novels Wolfe had expended great effort, and in them he had given the clearest demonstrations he ever made of his craftsmanship and his artistic control. Each of these seven novellas is marked in its unique way by a sharp focus and a controlling unity, and each represents a serious experiment with form. Yet they have virtually been lost from the corpus of Wolfe's work, lost even to most of those who know that work well.

There were two reasons for these losses. In the first place Wolfe's publishers, and particularly his editor, Maxwell E. Perkins, were anxious that the long, introspective *Look Homeward, Angel* be followed by an equally impressive work. Perkins urged Wolfe to continue the Eugene Gant story and discouraged his coming before the public in a different form or manner. Wolfe at one time wanted *Look Homeward, Angel* to be followed by *No Door,* a work of less than 40,000 words, and that small book might have been followed by a volume which Wolfe described to his mother that would contain *A Portrait of Bascom Hawke, The Web of Earth,* and "another story which [he had] written," probably **"The Train and the City."** At this time, however, Wolfe was happy to rely on his editor's judgment, and did not trust his own.

A second reason for the loss of these short novels is the nature of Wolfe's work and his attitude toward it. All the separate parts of his writing formed for him portions of a great and eternally fragmentary whole. It was all the outgrowth of the same basic desire, the Whitmanesque attempt to put a person on record and through that person to represent America in its paradox of unity and variety, at the same time employing as his essential theme the eternal and intolerable loneliness of the individual lost in the complex currents of time. As a result, Wolfe was forever reshuffling the parts of his work and assembling them in different patterns, in a way not unlike the shifting elements of the Snopes material in Faulkner's continuing legend of Yoknapatawpha County. Thus Wolfe took the materials he had presented first as short novels and interwove them into the larger frames and subject matters of his "big books," fragmenting, expanding, and modifying them, and often destroying their separate integrity. Only two of his short novels escaped this process; and these two—**Death the Proud Brother** and **The Web of Earth**—were published in a collection of his shorter works, **From Death to Morning,** which has never received the critical attention that it deserves.

In his short novels Wolfe was dealing with limited aspects of experience, aspects that could be adequately developed in the limits of 15,000 to 40,000 words and that could be organized into what he proudly called **The Party at Jack's,** "a single thing." When later he fragmented these short novels and distributed the fragments within the larger design of the "big books," he robbed them of their own unity in order to make them a portion of a larger and more complex unity—"a single thing" of complex and multifarious parts. Indeed, Wolfe's treatment of his short novels when he incorporated them later into his long books (and there is no reason to doubt that he would have approved the use made by his editor of the longer versions of **I Have a Thing to Tell You** and **The Party at Jack's** in **You Can't Go Home Again**) is a key to one of Wolfe's central problems, the finding of a large form sufficient to unify his massive imaginative picture of experience. This large form that he sought would give, apparently, not the representation of a series of sharply realized dramatic moments in the life of his protagonist (and through him of America) but an actual and significant interweaving of these moments into a complex fabric of event, time, and feeling. That he struggled unceasingly for the mastery of this vast structure is obvious from his letters, from *The Story of a Novel,* and from the long books themselves. Whether he was moving toward its realization is a matter of critical debate today, as it was at the time of his death. However much one may feel that he was (and I share that belief), the fact remains that none of the published novels after *Look Homeward, Angel* succeeded in finding a clearly demonstrable unity, in being "a single thing."

The intrinsic qualities of the short novel were remarkably well adapted to Wolfe's special talents and creative methods. Although he was skilled at the revelatory vignette, in which he imprisoned a character in an instance in time, those characters and actions which were central to his effort and experience he saw in relation to the expanding pattern of life. Experience and life itself were for him, as Herbert Muller has noted, remarkably "in process." One of the distinctive aspects of Wolfe's imagination is its tendency to see life as a thing of "becoming." He saw time—"dark time," he called it—as being at the center of the mystery of experience, and its representation on three complex levels was a major concern of his work. The individual scene or person had little value to him; it had to be put back in time to assume meaning. Wolfe was very explicit about this element of his work. In *The Story of a Novel* he says: "All of this time I was being baffled by a certain time element in the book, by a time relation which

could not be escaped, and for which I was now desperately seeking some structural channel. There were three time elements inherent in the material. The first and most obvious was an element of actual present time, an element which carried the narrative forward, which represented characters and events as living in the present and moving forward into an immediate future. The second time element was of past time, one which represented these same characters as acting and as being acted upon by all the accumulated impact of man's experience so that each moment of their lives was conditioned not only by what they experienced in that moment, but by all that they had experienced up to that moment. In addition to these two time elements, there was a third which I conceived as being time immutable, the time of rivers, mountains, oceans, and the earth; a kind of eternal and unchanging universe of time against which would be projected the transience of man's life, the bitter briefness of his day. It was the tremendous problem of these three time elements that almost defeated me and that cost me countless hours of anguish in the years that were to follow."

Ultimately in the portrayal of an incident or an individual against this complex pattern of time, that incident or individual must be seen through a perceiving and remembering self, such as David Hawke, the youth who can read the corrosion of time in the contrast between his exuberance and his uncle's resignation, in **A Portrait of Bascom Hawke.** Eliza Gant's fabric of memories in **The Web of Earth** is a record of the impact of time on her. The individual incidents of **No Door** assume their importance as portions of a personal history as they are reflected in the narrator's memory. To be fully understood, such events and people must be set against the innumerable other events and people which the perceiving self has known; it is this larger context in time which Wolfe attempts to give these short novels when he incorporates them in his longer works. We can think of an event as being an objective experience which is perceived and recalled later by the self that first knew it directly; then it, as fact and as memory, becomes a part of the totality of experience that makes the web of meaning for that self. Wolfe's short novels represent that portion of the process in which the incident is remembered, isolated, organized, and understood as incident by the self. Their later fragmentation and inclusion in the long novels represent his attempt to absorb them into his total experience and to use them in all the complexity of life as elements in his search for ultimate meaning. Hence he breaks up the sequence of actions, introduces new incidents, and frequently expands the wordage of the short novels when they are incorporated into the larger structures. These incidents thereby lose some of their artistic and inherent right to achieve unity by exclusion, and they tend to become diffuse.

Since Wolfe's success in achieving the larger unity for which he strove in the last three long novels is considerably less than total, the materials which he had organized into short novels have an integrity and a consummate craftsmanship which they seem to lack in the long books. It is for this reason that we are justified in reprinting here the five best short novels of Thomas Wolfe in the form in which he prepared them for magazine publication. In the short novel form Wolfe was a master of his craft, and these successful products of his efforts should not be forgotten.

Edward A. Bloom (essay date 1964)

SOURCE: "Critical Commentary on 'Only the Dead Know Brooklyn'," in *Thomas Wolfe: Three Decades of Criticism,* edited by Leslie A. Field, New York University Press, 1968, pp. 269-72.

[*In the following essay, originally published in 1964, Bloom focuses on mood, tone, and theme in "Only the Dead Know Brooklyn," contending that the story tells us that "to cease striving, to endure the atrophy of the sense of wonder and inquiry . . . is to perish."*]

Until the concluding paragraphs, the story ["**Only the Dead Know Brooklyn**"] has what might be taken for a clear enough literal meaning. That is, we read a rather amusing account of an experience in Brooklyn, a well-tried subject. But the literal, we discover, does not carry us very far. What does simple paraphrase reveal? A stranger in Brooklyn looking for a location asks some natives for directions. None can agree on the location or a way of getting there, and they quarrel among themselves. Ironically, although they have lived in Brooklyn all their lives and pride themselves on their familiarity with the city, they do not have this particular information.

It is then that the truculent first-person narrator takes over, tries to guide the stranger and fails. But at the same time he has the irrepressible curiosity of the legendary Brooklynite, and pumps the stranger to discover his motives. The narrator learns—to his intense surprise—that the unnamed stranger habitually wanders around Brooklyn with a map, looking for places that have pleasant-sounding names. Suddenly, without forewarning, the stranger asks the narrator (also unnamed) whether he can swim, and whether he has ever seen a drowning. The story ends on this puzzling note and the narrator, with justification, considers the incident one of some lunacy. For such peculiar things simply do not happen in Brooklyn.

Before we consider the actual meaning, point, or significance of the story, let us look at the fundamental details of technique.

MOOD. Although we may choose to identify Wolfe with the stranger, the author at no time exposes his private personality. Rather, he permits two unidentified characters to carry the entire emotional and intellectual burden. The feeling of the story thus becomes fairly complex, even ambivalent. The stranger evokes a mood of wistfulness and sympathy. We can appreciate the esthetic hunger which drives him. Simultaneously, though we respect his yearning, we wonder whether the discovery is ever as rich as the anticipation. These are emotional details implied in the dialogue between protagonist and antagonist. The antithesis of the stranger is the narrator—commonplace, literal, irascible, and yet kindly. He intensifies a feeling of futility because of his banal repudiation of the search for beauty. The mood, then, combines sadness and frustration with provincial humor and unresolved optimism for the stranger's success.

TONE. By subtle means the author is able to assert his attitude toward the reader. First he warns us in the title that only the dead know Brooklyn. Then he draws attention to normal impatience with idealistic, impractical quests such as the stranger's. Consequently, Wolfe implies the confusion and crudity of the vast area in which the search takes place. Toward this end he relies upon the aimless arguments of the anonymous speakers, who are like disembodied voices representative of ordinary mankind. Contrasting with this disorder is the map to which the stranger refers throughout the story. Presumably a symbol of order and stability, this manmade device is hopelessly misleading. Wolfe appears to say that the individual really has nothing material to guide him in his groping for values; only innate desire can direct him toward knowledge and beauty, which cannot be charted on a map: note the random (if esthetically motivated) manner in which the stranger selects the places he will visit.

Looking for an ultimate truth which he cannot readily isolate, he nevertheless persists. Each new place that he visits may provide him with the insight he seeks, so he must continue to roam about. Indeed, to cease striving, to endure the atrophy of the sense of wonder and inquiry— as the narrator has done—is to perish. Once the stranger hits upon the notion of drowning, it becomes a disturbing metaphor to connote human failure. The word "drowning" offers a significant clue to the tone of the story, because as a form of suffocation, drowning can be incorporeal as well as physical. The literal-minded narrator responds to the stranger as though he were talking about physical death. But the latter is not concerned here with physical death, only with that other death, the wasting away of the spirit. Although the stranger's attitude must be inferred, the inference follows logically from his consistent inattention to mundane matters. While the narrator returns to his world of actuality, the stranger pursues his ineffable search. In Brooklyn, where physical drowning is an impractical feat, the stranger consults his map and contemplates another kind of smothering. From his depiction of these men at cross-purposes, Wolfe has established tone in a twofold way: 1) to show us the aimlessness and inner bankruptcy of ordinary life; 2) to admonish and warn us against surrendering to spiritual and esthetic indifference.

Tone and mood are closely bound in with theme. The search for order, beauty, and individuality, it is suggested, may indeed be fruitless but must never be abandoned. Striving for positive values, one must also contend with ugliness and ignorance, for the good and the bad coexist. Yet that there can be no guarantee of success is implied in the ironical title. The dead are those who, like the narrator, have physically survived the material confusion and stifling effects of existence. Their survival, however, has depended upon an unquestioning attitude, one that is antithetical to the ultimate truth sought by the stranger. If people like the narrator are alive physically, the stranger's questions appear to disclose, they are dead spiritually. They know Brooklyn—which is life—only on the confused surface, and fragmentarily at that. The stranger, therefore, is left with a riddle of the disparity between material appearance and its hidden meaning. His own resolution of the riddle is left unstated, but we may assume that he will continue his search for answers.

Against the very real backdrop of Brooklyn, the atmosphere is paradoxically hazy and unrealistic. It emerges as a pervasive feeling of futility and impersonality—possibly an overwhelming challenge to individualism. Wolfe withholds names from his characters, who—as in allegory—are representative of society, of everyman. The conflict is not between flesh-and-blood people but between concepts: the restless individual search for the bluebird and the passivity of acceptance. The struggle is one between a broad idea of absorptive materialism and threatened ideals. The surface humor of the dialect turns to bitter realization through our awareness of the complete absence of humor in the situation. There is, indeed, a sense of tragedy, enlarged by the blindness of the narrator to his own loss of individuality.

Except for superficial details, everything in this story is implicit. Wolfe does not tell us through any direct means the exact nature of the problem with which he is concerned. Nor does he develop his characters explicitly. Everything must come out through dialogue or through the rational process of the narrator's puzzlement. Only by inference do we discover Wolfe's allegorical intention of representing Brooklyn as modern confused society which suffocates individuality. By inference also we recognize that for most people this state of suffocation is acceptable, while those who resist are stigmatized as outsiders and eccentrics.

Clayton L. Eichelberger (essay date 1967)

SOURCE: "Wolfe's 'No Door' and the Brink of Discovery," in *The Georgia Review,* Vol. XXI, No. 3, Fall, 1967, pp. 319-27.

[*In the following essay, Eichelberger analyzes Wolfe's short novel* No Door, *calling it "his most effectively controlled presentation of the dominant theme of loneliness and aloneness which stands central to his life and work."*]

Initial contact with the immensity of the novels of Thomas Wolfe sometimes so overwhelms the reader that he has difficulty from that moment on thinking of Wolfe as the author of anything other than his four major works. Yet to reduce the contribution of Wolfe to these major novels is to disregard some of his best and most disciplined work such as *The Web of Earth* and *No Door. No Door,* especially, is a case in point, for critics have almost entirely ignored it. In her biography of Wolfe, Elizabeth Nowell

mentions it in passing, and that primarily in relation to the $125,000 libel suit which it triggered. Chronologically, it was one of the short pieces which grew out of the writing of *Of Time and the River* in 1933; a two-installment portion of it was published in *Scribner's* that year. But for the most part it went unnoticed until it was resurrected by C. Hugh Holman in 1961 and printed for the first time as it was originally written.[1] By then all Wolfe readers had certainly encountered *No Door,* but they had come across it fragmented and scattered in so many places and rewritten in so many forms for specific occasions that the thematic integrity and artistic discipline of the original piece were entirely lost.[2] This is indeed unfortunate, and most unfair to Wolfe, for *No Door* is perhaps his most effectively controlled presentation of the dominant theme of loneliness and aloneness which stands central to his life and work.

No Door is structurally divided into four sections, each one headed by a month and a year as title. Section I, "October: 1931," was published independently under the title *No Door* as the first item in *From Death to Morning.*[3] Appearing separately, it does exhibit a certain integrity in that it establishes social separation and personal alienation. The protagonist, a young writer who remains nameless throughout the composition but who is obviously the Wolfe-Gant amalgam of *Of Time and the River,* begins by observing, "It is wonderful with what warm enthusiasm well-kept people who have never been alone in all their life can congratulate you on the joys of solitude." This observation is made specific in an extended illustrative narrative. The young writer has been invited to dine with one of his admirers, "a most aesthetic-looking millionaire." In a pent-house apartment surrounded by luxuries which bespeak "a quiet but distinguished taste," the writer feels suddenly far removed from the desolation and poverty, the hunger and loneliness of his Brooklyn apartment. He takes on the role of an outsider who for a moment indulges in the type of life for which he yearns, and for that moment it seems to him that the great vision of the city which for years has burned in his heart is about to come true, that "some glorious happiness of fortune, fame, and triumph" will be his at any minute. Yet in the same moment he knows this cannot be.

The social disparity between the writer's painful existence and the "most aesthetic-looking millionaire's" manner of living is starkly underscored when conversation reveals that the wealthy, middle-aged admirer envies the freedom, the youth, the insularity of the writer and at the same time fails to fully appreciate the position of wealth and power which attracts the young man. And just as no door opens to admit the writer to the glorious life of his dream, so abysmal lack of perception and understanding prevents the wealthy host from seeing the anguish and pain which is the lot of the writer, the "loneliness, black, bitter, aching loneliness" for which there are no words. The writer tries to communicate his knowledge to his host but concludes, ". . . when you try to tell the man about it you cannot, for what is there to say?" The magnetic attraction which solitude holds for man, the painful experience of what Wolfe elsewhere calls "the habit of loneliness," the reality of social separation fuse to form a poignant moment of awareness.

Paradoxically, while "October: 1931" thus has an inherent integrity of its own, its function as Section I of *No Door* is expository in nature: it introduces character, establishes conflict, and provides an avenue to the development of theme. In this expository capacity it was conceived. Chronologically it is the last of the four sections, and as such it establishes the frame for the series of three backflashes which make up the remainder of the short novel. The protagonist, inspired by the pent-house experience and his need "to break out of the prison of his own loneliness," searches back through his life for crucial moments of estrangement and recalls his search for doors opening out from himself. In doing so, he encounters a three-pronged dilemma which holds him, which indeed holds all men, in thrall; and while a resolution is suggested in the final section of the novel, the moment is still too early in the life of this young man to permit him to accept what he has just begun to understand.

The first horn of the dilemma is a purely mechanical one. It is also a general one in that it pervades all sections of *No Door* and all of Wolfe's creative work. Simply put, it is concerned with the limitation of language and the inability of man to put into words the total truth of which he is most urgently aware. Repeatedly the narrator bemoans the fact that what he has to say, what he so desperately feels he must say if he is to have life, if he is to be released from his aloneness, is just one word away. But he cannot find that word. It is the "no door" that stands between him and the fulfillment of his creative genius. So he fails always to define the exact relationship or degree of estrangement which exists between him and others and falteringly focuses on the moment of confrontation as "one of those simple and profound experiences of life which people seem always to have known when it happens to them, but for which there is no language" (p. 197). Speaking of English faces and aspects of English life which remind him of home, again he falters:

> It was a life that seemed so near to me that I could lay my hand on it and make it mine at any moment. I seemed to have returned to a room I had always known, and to have paused for a moment without any doubt or perturbation of the soul outside the door.

> But I never found the door, or turned the knob, or stepped into the room. When I got there I couldn't find it. It was as near as my hand if I could only touch it, only as high as my heart and yet I could not reach it, only a hand's breadth off if I would span it, a word away if I would speak it. (p. 190)

The failure was an agonizing one for a sensitive writer who felt he had to more than touch, who had to grasp, to devour, if he was to be.

The failure of direct expression, however, does not constitute an unsurmountable barrier to communication. One can still express himself through illustration and suggestion.

This accounts in part for the multitudinous vignettes and catalogues which fill the pages of the Wolfe novels. It also explains in part his heavy reliance on symbol. Repeatedly he tries by a desperate rather than a calculated combination of details and concretions to elevate the reader into an awareness of what he is trying to say. And when he is successful, a transcendent light breaks forth between the lines, and an epiphany burns to life.[4] But the single word, the door to precise and consummate expression, remains unfound. In that sense, the language barrier, the first of the barriers, remains unbreached. It becomes "no door."

The second horn of the dilemma, the specific theme of Section II, "October: 1923," is the protagonist's futile resistance to the passage of time and to the changes which that passage brings with it. This barrier of no return establishes temporal alienation and, in a real sense, is the sharpest of the three horns in that it evokes, bound up as it is with personal grief, the most intense and passionate outpouring in the novel. The inability to communicate which is so apparent in the pent-house episode turns the writer back into himself, and he retreats in memory to what was perhaps the most crucial moment in his life: October, 1923, the October in which he returned home for the first time after the death of his father. In image, rhythm, and depth of emotion, this second section of *No Door* is undoubtedly one of the most highly lyrical stream-of-consciousness passages Wolfe produced. It was incorporated with only minor changes in *Of Time and the River* as the transition between Books II and III. Thus it stands introductory to the search-for-a-father motif which gives continuity to the well-known Telemachus section of that novel.

"October: 1923" actually begins with a return to the writer's fifteenth year and a selective four-page summary of the years of "solitude and wandering" which intervened between then and October, 1923. This autobiographical survey fixes the foundation for one vividly remembered night in the life of the young man when sense of loss and recognition of inevitable change strip him of even minimal security, fill him with grief-laden helplessness and fear, and goad him into flight. A concrete narrative frame is constructed. The protagonist has returned home in October. Lying alone in a bed in his mother's house, immediately beneath the room where his brother had died in another October, he listens to the storm wind sweeping the night, he feels the "moving darkness" pressing upon him, he hears the distant howling of the dogs and the silence of early frost. This narrative situation anchors the half-conscious nighttime reverie; and fictive fact, memory, and subconscious symbolic interpretation of fact and memory are intricately interwoven to produce two and three levels of meaning at the same time. So the howl of the dogs and the silent frost mingled with memories of similar experiences in other Octobers become reminders of the inevitability and presence of death; and the mysterious but ceaseless movement of the wind and darkness strikes pain to the young man's heart as they remind him that his father is dead, that time sweeps relentlessly and endlessly forward, and there can be no return.

Desperately he tries to cling to what was, to deny what is. October, he reflects, is the month of return; so surely his father will return now and things will be as they were. October, he remembers, is the month of harvest and abundance. But then he recalls the consuming flames of autumn, and they strike a thorn of memory into his heart. The frost, the voices of dogs, the ceaseless wind, the pressing dark, the fire, and later the trains that roar *like wind* in the trees, the flooded river which sweeps *like a wind* to the sea, and an imagined death knell which *may* sound in the night—all combine to lead him to the plaintive question he has asked before: What is there to say? He will call again for the return of his father; but the voices of passing time and death will drown out his words, and he will turn in flight. The door he sought which would reverse time and permit him to sustain life as he had known it remains unfound. His insularity in terms of time past is established, so he can only turn toward morning.

In the suddenly remembered dream of "new lands, morning, and a shining city" which thus ends Section II, the quest for yet another door, self-discovery through identification with others, is begun. Flight from that October night in his mother's house leads the protagonist back to England and his work. But Section III, "October: 1926," presents another problem: the young writer finds himself alone, and there is no door to lead him from this aloneness. "October: 1926," the longest section in *No Door,* is a mixture of cases which are constant reminders of man's alienated state mixed with frequent observations relative to the inadequacy of language and the missing word which stands between experience and communication. Portions of it are included in *Of Time and the River,* and a major part of it was published in *Scribner's* under the title **"The House of the Far and Lost."**[5]

Flight does not afford escape. Removal to far places does not alter the constancy of truth. Instead it intensifies the young writer's awareness that he is alone; and more and more he begins to discover that what is true of him is true also of others. He looks into the faces on the street and in the shops. Repeatedly he seems to be on the verge of recognition, on the very brink of identification. But always the moment is lost even before it is found. The Coulsons, in whose house he has a room, have been cruelly separated from the society which has been their heritage, and one instinctively knows that the separation was not of their choosing. The cruelty of the severance is intimated by the disturbing and undefinable reaction to the Coulson name and address, the suddenly alerted awareness and frozen response, the secretive and sinister laughter behind closed doors. The fact that the reason for the social banishment is never disclosed only serves to intensify the reality and unreasonableness of man's alienated state. Furthermore, the individual members of the family are separated from each other. The house in which the young writer lives with them consists of walls and closed doors. An impenetrable secret fills the air that moves through the house. A brooding sorrow lurks behind the masked faces of the Coulson family. For them all doors are closed, and there is no escape. The Coulson sorrow is the sorrow of man.

Three mechanics who also room in the Coulson house provide a second example. One is fortyish and maimed; the other two are youthful and seemingly strong. Like the Coulsons they are ruined people. They "had lost their lives because they loved the earth too well, and somehow had been slain by their hunger" (p. 199). All three exhibit a perverse desire to forget their lostness and the meaninglessness of their lives. They give themselves to frenzied movement across the earth in pursuit of pleasure and to an unrealistically staged devotion to jazz. They are moved by "the madness of desperation, the deliberate intent of men to cover up or seek oblivion at any cost of effort from some hideous emptiness of the soul" (p. 200). Their roots have been severed. Dialogue with them cannot be established, even by others who are alone. The door between them and life is closed. So, in Section III, no door opens from the aloneness of the young writer. He too is lost, irretrievably separated from others, slain by his hunger.

The final section of *No Door* is the only one set in April, and significantly so. April is the month of beginnings, but not without the bitter awareness that what is born must die. "Late April: 1928" constitutes a return to New York, the setting of the first section, in a mechanical way thus unifying the short novel. In this concluding section, the protagonist seems to face up to the dilemma of man's existence, and the narrative moves toward resolutions as he comes to recognize that the door for which he has been seeking does not exist and that man's only solution to the dilemma must be acceptance.

Such acceptance is demonstrated by the truck drivers observed at the beginning of Sction IV. The vantage point from which the protagonist looks out on New York is an apartment window facing a dingy storage warehouse. The world he sees is masculine and physical. The men who work on the docks and drive the trucks are men of blood and muscle, men of oath and gesture, tough men with seamed faces, men born into and accepting the reality of the iron and asphalt city. These men are without memory. They are without dream. They live in the present, unaware of the past and unmolested by the future. They accept their aloneness, for while they work furiously, they also work *unamiably.* They give themselves to the "narrow frontier of their duty"; they cut their lives "sparsely into its furious and special groove." They have no hesitation, confess neither ignorance nor error, and know no doubt. They accept themselves without question, and they are not agonized by what they are not. So they stand in sharp juxtaposition to the protagonist who is haunted by the passage of time and searches for a door into understanding. His life, "by a cruel comparison with the lives of these men who had learned to use their strength and talents perfectly in a life demanding manual skill, and the mastery of sensuous materials, seemed blind, faltering, baffled, still lost in clouds of chaos and confusion" (p. 222).

Eventually one man stands out from all the others. Day after day he can be seen, always seated at a desk and always doing nothing, his face fixed with an "abstracted stare" as he looks out on the fury and desperation of life which surrounds him. In that face the young writer sees "a timeless image of fixity and judgment," and the indolent man becomes to him "the impartial, immutable censor of all the blind confusion and oblivion of a thousand city days, and of the tortured madness and unrest" of his own life. Goaded by the secrecy of the judgment and by his agonizing sense of inadequacy, he throws himself into the demented streets of night until day comes "incredibly like birth, like hope, like joy again." One could add, like April, because it is in this April that understanding begins to dawn and that the novel moves toward resolution as the protagonist comes to the very brink of discovery.

The face in the warehouse window serves as a catalyst which precipitates a vision of an unknown man sitting in the window of an old house at the end of the day. Looking out quietly, his calm and sorrowful face reflects "the immutable exile of an imprisoned spirit." His voice is soundless; but it carries the knowledge of a million tongues, for it is no less than the voice of all men and all experience. In toneless syllables it assures the young man that the madness, the hunger, the fury of youth will pass away; that the despair that comes with the cognizance that the earth is too large for one life will pass away; but that some things will never change. Above all, the voice suggests, man comes eventually to accept his limitations. He comes finally to recognize that he cannot master all knowledge, that "we know what we know, we have what we have, we are what we are." Transmuted to a fixed position in time, leaning on the sill of the window of evening, man comes to know that most things are vanity, most things are ephemeral as far as the individual is concerned; but the perennial desperation of young men *en masse* as they become conscious of their insignificance in the universe will not change, the miracle of life will not change, the blade and leaf will endure while the proud edifices created by men crumble. The bitterness of life will always endure, and all that belongs to the earth, "all things proceeding from the earth to seasons, all things that lapse and change and come again upon the earth" will always be the same. For "only the earth endures, but it endures forever" (pp. 229-231).

The vision is not new to the world, but it is new to each youth as he comes to the discovery of himself. Man is imprisoned by the very nature of his existence, and there is no door to lead him out of the prison of himself. He is destined to live alone, and he destined to die alone. The world he seeks to devour is too large for him to contain. He must come to know what he is, to recognize and to accept his limitations, and with the preacher to cast all idle dreams and pretense aside. He must understand that the miracle of life is eternal, and he must come to believe that it will prevail. "Child, child," counsels the tongueless image, "Have patience and belief. . . ." In this new understanding lies April, *cruel* April in that the knowledge is not without its portion of bitterness. It marks the beginning of life and hope which will be driven to their roots by the frost of October, but which will be sustained by the earth like a pulse, like a cry, "like a flower, forever bursting from the earth, forever deathless, faithful, coming into life again like April." The climactic vision in *No Door*

parallels that of Ben's ghost at the end of *Look Homeward, Angel*, and the message is essentially the same. One must come to know himself in his time, and he must come to believe that the spirit of man is deathless. Only thus will he find meaning in his existence.

The fact that understanding goes before acceptance is clearly reflected in the reverse structure of *No Door*. Understanding comes in "Late April: 1928"; but in "October: 1931," the section with which the novel begins, the writer protagonist still dreams of and hungers for an existence other than his own. He has not yet come to accept the essential and enduring truth of his insularity. He still yearns for a life other than the one he knows. It is this instinctive and stubborn and frustrating search for meaning beyond the limitations of self, this obsessive unwillingness to accept life and live it, the inability to bridge the precipitous gorge between understanding and acceptance that sustain the search motif in the novel; and it is the protagonist's failure to find fulfillment in resigning himself to the only life he has, thus escaping aloneness by identifying his state with the mortal state of all men, that gives meaning to *No Door*.

Notes

[1] *The Short Novels of Thomas Wolfe,* ed. C. Hugh Holman (New York, 1961), pp. 155-231. Citations in my text are to this volume.

[2] For a brief record of the publication history of "No Door," see *The Short Novels,* pp. 157-158.

[3] New York, 1935.

[4] See Maurice Natanson, "The Privileged Moment: A Study in the Rhetoric of Thomas Wolfe," *QJS,* XLIII (1957), 143-150.

[5] *Scribner's Magazine,* XCVI (August, 1934), 71-81.

Leo Gurko (essay date 1975)

SOURCE: "Two Stories," in *Thomas Wolfe: Beyond the Romantic Ego,* Thomas Y. Crowell, 1975, pp. 159-67.

[*In the following excerpt, Gurko examines Wolfe's short stories "In the Park" and "The Lost Boy," both of which present the theme of life appreciated through the contemplation of death.*]

Wolfe had a flair for short fiction as well as long: he turned out to be a very good and very skillful writer of short stories. He composed his own special brand of stories which depended less on plot than mood, less on action and incident than on perception and the feel of things. A fair number made their way into the novels. Two collections—one published while Wolfe was alive, the other posthumously—stand by themselves, and are reasonably representative of his efforts along these lines. They include some particularly well-known stories, like **"Chickamauga"** and *The Web of Earth,* the one narrated by a returning veteran of the Confederate Army, the other by Eliza Gant in an extended recollection of her mountain ancestors. Both display Wolfe's underrated capacity to get out of himself and into the minds of others.

Instead of surveying everything in the two volumes, let us concentrate on two especially splendid tales, one from each book. If Wolfe had written nothing else, these would have been enough to establish his genius and justify his standing among the formidable writers of his day.

The first of these, **"In The Park,"** appeared in the earlier collection which came out in 1935, *From Death To Morning.* It is a reminiscence, apparently by Mrs. Jack, of her life as a young girl in New York at the turn of the century, and of one evening in particular at the beginning of May. She was eighteen, the year before her father died, and the coming of a radiant spring that year seemed to coincide with her own age, with the sense of New York bursting with opulence and energy, and her feeling for her father, an actor with a highly developed appetite for living.

After the evening performance of the play in which he is performing, he takes her to a Broadway restaurant where they eat, drink, and chatter amiably with a pair of stage-struck priests. Then they go for a ride in a horseless carriage to Central Park. They are stopped by a mounted policeman who scolds them for frightening his horse. The car breaks down. It mysteriously starts up again, and carries them triumphantly into the park where, under the glistening stars, they ride about all night. At dawn they hear the birds breaking into song, an eloquent finale to an ecstatic occasion. And on that note the story ends.

In terms of plot it could scarcely be lighter or thinner. It consists of some engaging chatter in a restaurant and a ride in the park. Neither the conversation nor the ride leads anywhere in particular; they have no visible aim aside from registering their own existence. Yet the story is a delicate masterpiece, revealing Wolfe's ability to work in a small frame—which was quite as much within his power as his better-known, more widely publicized ability to operate in a large expanse. What he is after is the sense of joy, of life at high tide, not because anything special is happening but as a thing in itself, generating its own radiance, a radiance to which the high-spirited young girl narrating the tale in the first person is responding with uncommon depth of feeling.

This response is aroused by any number of objects: the fine spring night; the "velvety lilac texture" of the sky, "glittering with great stars"; the streets outside the theatre crowded with hansoms; New York in an intoxicating earlier era; DeWolfe Hopper, the actor, running around "pretending to be a horse and neighing, and trying to climb up a lamppost"; the old car itself with "its rich wine color, its great polished lamps of brass . . . and all its wonderful and exciting smells." These make up a rich compost of external detail, strategically drawn from both society and nature. No wonder the narrator exclaims: "Everyone seemed to be as happy and elated as we were, it seemed as if a new world and new people had burst out of the earth with

the coming of spring. . . . I saw all of it, I felt myself a part of it all, I wanted to possess it all."

But the story is something more than a simple exercise in romantic enthusiasm. It is kept from soaring off into the blue by the somber presence of death. Death in two forms: as a premonition and as an actuality. On two occasions, near the beginning and just before the end, the girl mentions the fact that it all took place the year before her father died. And on a third occasion, as they enter the park and feel the first rush of ecstatic pleasure in their new surroundings, she looks at her father and suddenly knows that he is going to die. This so heightens her feelings and so sharpens her perceptions that the lengthy final paragraph of the story records in great detail and with scientific precision the exact cries of the numerous birds at dawn.

Her premonition of her father's approaching death escalates her appreciation of life and her sensory response to it. The intrusion of death jolts us but at the same time intensifies our awareness of life's familiar attractions. The birds break into their chorus every morning, though we usually pay little attention to them. By compelling our attention, death becomes an agent of life and is thus absorbed into the story's inner flow.

The naturalness and skill with which the tale is put together are revealed in the opening lines. The narrator gropes in her mind and memory to get back to that magic evening long years ago. For a few sentences she slides about uncertainly: "That year I think we were living with Bella; no, we weren't, I guess we were living with Auntie Kate—well, maybe we were staying with Bella: I don't know, we moved around so much, and it's so long ago. It gets all confused in my mind now." Then the fog of time miraculously lifts and suddenly everything is in the clear. The evening in question detaches itself from its murky background and glistens into focus. In this way, proceeding from confusion to clarity, one enters the story.

One exits from it along the same path, only in the reverse direction, from the spellbinding clarity of the bird songs to confusion and uncertainty again as memory begins to lapse. "That was the year before he died and I think we were staying at Bella's then, but maybe we were staying at the old hotel, or perhaps we had already moved to Auntie Kate's: we moved around so much, we lived in so many places, it seems so long ago, that when I try to think about it now it gets confused and I cannot remember."

This refrain at the end illustrates the familiar operation of memory. It also supplies **"In The Park"** with a band or circle of cottony haze inside which lies preserved and intact, like some magically propertied jewel, the briefly caught but blazingly lucid glimpse of an earlier time and place.

The same process on a larger, more complex scale is seen at work in **"The Lost Boy,"** the second of Wolfe's superb short stories. This appeared in *The Hills Beyond,* the last of the books Edward Aswell assembled after the author's death. It deals with the death in boyhood of Grover, Ben Gant's twin, during the St. Louis World's Fair of 1904.

Divided into four parts, each told from a different point of view, the story is an intricate attempt to make tragedy coherent. Grover's death from typhoid fever is cruel, unexpected, and sudden. It has a shattering effect on everyone there: on his sister Helen who had gone about town with him on that last day; on his mother, whose passion for profit had brought them to St. Louis in the first place; on Eugene, only four at the time but already conscious of the tragedy which aroused in him feelings and vibrations he would be unable to explain until many years later. The story conveys the shock of death but equally the effort to absorb the shock, recover from it, and eventually conquer it.

Part One begins with Grover back home in Altamont, standing in front of Mr. Crocker's shop in the town square, greedily contemplating the freshly made candy in the window. The temptation is too strong. He enters, buys the candy, pays Mr. Crocker—a mean, spiteful figure out of Dickens—in stamps, is cheated on the change. Burning with injustice, he rushes across the street to his father, who invades the Crocker premises, gets Grover's money back, and helps his son through a small painful crisis in his young life. In the deliberate chronology of the four parts, the first starts with the father, the source and the beginning in the biological scheme of things.

Part Two shifts to the mother. With her narration, Grover passes into the minds of others. In Part One he had appeared directly and in his own person before us, the one occasion that he was wholly alive and himself. Then, as a foreshadowing of his approaching death, he loses his status as an independent, self-contained being and begins his existence in the consciousness of those around him. Beginning with his mother, whose thoughts contain everything of Grover's life and death.

She remembers the trip to St. Louis, with the train bowling along the Indiana countryside. She remembers Grover, now twelve, working at the Fair, how good he was at shopping and bargaining, what a grave, serious, disciplined, intelligent boy he had already become. She remembers the lacerating impact of his dying, a wound that continued to bleed within her for an endless time.

She never forgets Grover. Years later, after Eugene has become a celebrated writer, a scholar came South in quest of information about him. She remembers how surprised he was when she told him that Grover had been smarter than Eugene, and in saying that and thinking it, she finds Grover becoming more vividly fixed in her memory than ever. Thus Grover's life appears in two sections, before and after death. The section before death is the shorter one, and is exceeded in both length and power by the lucidity and vibrancy of his psychological continuation in the thoughts of his survivors. The story is of course about life and death, but it is also about immortality. Grover's posthumous existence outlives his mortal one.

The speaker of Part Three is Helen, sister and next in the biological progression of **"The Lost Boy."** She brings us the voice of someone much closer to Grover in age than his father and mother. But she is still older than he, old enough to feel the full brunt of his death, to feel it as something ghastly and inexplicable. Now deep into her adult life, she still cannot accommodate herself to it. How could it have happened? she asks Eugene. Why is the world filled with stupid empty people who go on living while someone as fine as Grover is cut down so young? To these familiar, conventional questions she has no answer.

Helen remembers how on that last afternoon Grover had decided to spend his pay on a treat instead of dutifully bringing it home. The two of them had gone into a cheap eatery and gorged themselves on pork and beans. After all this time, she remembers the sense of liberation the "treat" had given them. And not a moment too soon, for no sooner had they gotten home, even before Grover had a chance to be properly scolded, he came down with his sudden fatal fever, and by the next day was gone. For the rest of her life Helen was distraught and baffled by the tragedy. Grover's legacy to her was a deep groove of angry bewilderment from which she was destined never to recover.

Finally, in Part Four, we come to Eugene, the youngest of the narrators. He was present when Grover died but was too young at the time to understand fully what was going on. His response, necessarily delayed, comes later, more than thirty years later in fact, and Part Four is an account of Eugene's return to St. Louis in the 1930s in search of his lost brother. He goes back to the street where they lived during the Fair, searches out the house they occupied, which miraculously is still standing, and makes his way to the very bedroom where Grover fell ill and died. None of this is easy. The city has changed, the street is not as it was, and the present owner of the house is a stranger who proves accommodating only after Eugene explains to her, not without awkwardness, what he is after.

What he is after is not wholly clear to himself. It somehow seems terrifically important that he recapture and reoccupy the original scene. By reliving Grover's death, perhaps he can exorcise it, lay it to rest, quiet and settle the spirit of his brother so prematurely lost. But he is also moved by the opposite impulse. In getting Grover to die again, this time in his mind's eye, he will absorb the event into himself in a way that he was too young to do the first time. The quest for Grover is a quest for emotional understanding.

Grover's passing must not only be witnessed, it must also be felt. It is the emotion that triumphs over death, so that Eugene's search for the emotion aroused by the original catastrophe is in some obscure way a search for life. The story reaches its final intention at this point. Man does conquer death: by feeling it in all its horror, awfulness, and pain he absorbs it into himself, and thus survives. As Grover survives, in the clarity and strength of the feelings engendered by his terrifying departure in those around him.

The climactic nature of Part Four begins to emerge. Because he was so young when Grover died, Eugene is the only figure who must voluntarily, and with an immense effort of the will, engage himself in the reenactment of the tragedy. The others—Eliza, Helen—involuntarily caught up in it as captive and compelled witnesses, were able to experience it at the time.

In going back to the place of Grover's departure, Eugene relives not only Grover's death but Grover himself. The lost boy is never so real as when he is on the abrupt verge of being snatched away. If that moment can be fixed, preserved, sealed off from time, memorialized, kept intact, then Grover cannot be reduced and is ours forever.

So Eugene obscurely reasons, or perhaps only obscurely feels. The story is a supreme episode in Wolfe's relentless quest for immortality. The search for Grover is also a search for the secret process by which the human can be saved from the dissolution of time and the laxness of memory. Wolfe was a fervent, lifelong pursuer of these matters, and **"The Lost Boy"** is one of his great demonstrations in the art of robbing death to shore up life.

William Domnarski (essay date 1980)

SOURCE: "Thomas Wolfe's Success as Short Novelist: Structure and Theme in *A Portrait of Bascom Hawke,*" in *The Southern Literary Journal,* Vol. XIII, No. 1, Fall, 1980, pp. 32-41.

[*In the following essay, Domnarski describes* A Portrait of Bascom Hawke *as a "tightly structured work" and investigates its themes of the cycles of life, youth, age, and time.*]

Maxwell Perkins said that Thomas Wolfe was a born writer if there ever was one.[1] Few critics have disagreed with that assessment of Wolfe's natural talent. Even Bernard DeVoto, who turned his heavy artillery on Wolfe in 1936, conceded that Wolfe had genius. But genius was not enough for DeVoto.[2] Others have felt the same way, thus making the vital issue in Wolfe's critical reputation not whether he had talent, but what he did with it.

The most frequent charges levelled against Wolfe have stressed his prolixity, structural formlessness, and excessive interest in autobiography.[3] These weaknesses can be seen in each of Wolfe's long novels. In contrast, however, they are not present in his short novels, which have received little attention despite their excellence.[4] In many ways these short novels present the best of Wolfe. Here he is under control, with the defined length of the short novel form imposing necessary restrictions on him.

An examination of structure and theme in *A Portrait of Bascom Hawke,* which Wolfe completed in 1932, illustrates his achievement as a short novelist. The novel is a brilliant portrait of the eccentric Bascom Hawke, who is modelled after Wolfe's uncle Henry Westall, but it is also a book about the narrator, David Hawke, who is Wolfe himself. The contrast between the elderly, despairing uncle and his young, hopeful nephew stands at the heart of

the novel, with the ideas of life and death and growth and decay dominating. Wolfe summarized his hopes for **Bascom Hawke** in a note to Perkins. He wrote, "I've simply tried to give you a man—as for plot, there's not any, but there's this idea which I believe is pretty plain—I've always wanted to say something about *old men* and *young men,* and that's what I've tried to do here. I hope the man seems real and living to you and that it has the unity of this feeling I spoke about."[5]

Wolfe overstates **Bascom Hawke's** lack of plot. Scenes from Bascom's past, as well as what might pass as part of a day in his life, make up most of the novel. The only present tense narrative action centers on a conversation between Bascom and his nephew David late in the book. Wolfe's novel is not rooted in the present. Rather, the present is used as a complementary means of illuminating the past—both Bascom's past and the inexorable force of time—and the future. The concept of eternal time holds the novel and its two major characters together. This continuum helps Wolfe achieve "the unity of this feeling" that he mentions to Perkins.

The plot of **Bascom Hawke** might be spare, but the novel is tightly structured. It opens with Bascom emerging from a Boston subway exit on his way to work as a real estate conveyancer. At this point we are part of the crowd reacting to the cadaverous, grimacing man as others on the street would. We cannot fail to notice this elderly man, whose "grimaces were made by squinting his small sharp eyes together, widening his mouth in a ghastly travesty of a grin, and convolving his chin and cheek in a rapid series of pursed lips and horrible squints as he swiftly pressed his rubbery underlip against a few enormous horse teeth that decorated his upper jaw."[6] More important, we see Bascom as he verbally assaults motorists who have nearly run him over because he has ignored the rules of safe pedestrian traffic. Bascom baits these unsuspecting motorists into arguments to show, in his distinctively imperious manner, his knowledge and their ignorance of automobile law.

Wolfe seems to pause following this opening scene. A clear transition sentence announces the physical description of Bascom that will follow. The description begins with his tall, tough, and angular body and proceeds to his worn and ill-fitting clothes that make him appear more like a beggar than the prosperous businessman he is. This discrepancy leads into an account of Bascom's history. All that our narrator tells us not only helps shade in Bascom's portrait, but also heightens the tension between youth and age and furthers our understanding of Bascom's bitter despair at the novel's conclusion. In a passage that takes on increased importance as we move through the novel, our narrator tells us that "Bascom's youth, following the war between the States, had been scared by a bitter poverty: at once enriched and warped by a life that clung to the earth with a root-like tenacity, that was manual, painful, spare and stricken, and rebuilt itself—fiercely, cruelly, and richly—from the earth" (13).

Poverty constricted Bascom's physical world and turned him to literature, where he found the joys of life otherwise denied him. He read voraciously and ended up at Harvard. There he lived monkishly and established a brilliant record as an undergraduate and graduate theology student. We read that "at thirty [Bascom] was a lean fanatic, a true Yankee madman, high-boned, with gray thirsty eyes and a thick flaring sheaf of oaken hair—six feet three inches of gangling and ludicrous height, gesticulating madly and obliviously before a grinning world. But he had a grand lean head: he looked somewhat like the great Ralph Waldo Emerson—with the brakes off" (14).

Like Emerson, Bascom first entered and then left the ministry. For twenty years he moved from town to town and from church to church hoping to find spiritual satisfaction. But it never came. After much soul-searching, and after investigating the Episcopal, Presbyterian, and Unitarian churches, all with the hope of finding one that quelled his growing religious skepticism, Bascom turned his back on God and became an agnostic. Freed in a way, Bascom next sought to make as much money as possible as a real estate conveyancer in Boston, perhaps to avenge his youthful poverty. But he had lost more than just his faith during those twenty years. Beginning with his marriage to Louise, Bascom had also gained and lost a family. He and Louise are still together when we meet them in the novel, but Bascom sees his marriage as dead and his wife lost to him as a result of her insanity. His children, in a different way, are also lost because once they came of age they fled from home and never returned.

Having brought us up to date, Wolfe then continues the novel with scenes from a typical day at the office for Bascom. The description is again organized and meticulous. We are shown the outside and inside of the office building before meeting Bascom's office-mates. Their characters reflect the dullness of the office. There is the banal Miss Brill, the meager-looking Samuel Friedman, and the self-satisfied Stanley Ward. They do not understand Bascom and therefore make fun of his eccentricities. John T. Brill, the loud and dominating figure in the office, on the other hand, understands and respects Bascom, so much so that he brags of Bascom's intellect to visitors as though Bascom were his son. Bascom and Brill come from different backgrounds and have different sensibilities, yet there is much common ground between them; nephew David writes:

> Brill was a lewd and innocent man. Like my uncle, by comparison with these other people, he seemed to belong to some earlier, richer, and grander period of the earth, and perhaps this was why there was more actual kinship between them than between any of the other members of the office. These other people . . . belonged to the myriads of the earth, to the numberless swarms that with ceaseless pullulation fill the streets of life with their gray immemorable tides. But Brill and my uncle Bascom were men in a thousand, a million: if one had seen them in a crowd he would have looked after them, if one had talked with them, he could never have forgotten them. (30-31)

One reason we cannot forget Brill's conversation is that it is earthy and vulgar. We sense that Brill naturally incor-

porates obscenities into his language, but we also sense that he uses as many vulgarities as possible when Bascom is around. This is consistent with Brill's character and his relationship with Bascom, for Brill takes great delight in jokingly trying to offend him. The lengthy section discussing their relationship details many examples of Brill teasing Bascom. He teases Bascom, for instance, about his eccentric aversion to eating in restaurants. Bascom tries to explain that he finds the preparation of restaurant food unhealthy and that he will eat only raw health foods, but we know, as does Brill, that Bascom is simply reluctant to spend money. The same can be said about Bascom and overcoats. He claims that he never wears them because they carry cold-inducing germs; the truth is that Bascom is too cheap to part with the money needed for a warm overcoat.

But even though Bascom cringes at Brill's coarse language, and even though he finds himself the butt of many jokes, he admires and respects Brill. Brill is a man of character—of forceful and aggressive character. Brill lusts after life, and this is reflected in his language, his "invective" as Bascom terms it. In different ways, Bascom and Brill are remarkable men in that they understand life's possibilities and have been willing, in their different ways, to go after what they want. Bascom might bristle at his coarse language, but he also wishes that he had the peculiar kind of strength to use it. Brill's scathing invective thus links the section about the two men with the following section, a digression that focuses on an extramarital affair Bascom was once tempted to have while he vacationed in Florida.

The woman, a plump, sensuous widow, appears an odd match for Bascom. She is so dull-witted, for example, that she misunderstands his long and very obvious poem about his agnosticism. Ordinarily, Bascom would be offended by such stupidity in anyone. The widow may be stupid, but she is shrewd. She recognizes that he is the man she wants and she knows how to get him: by appealing to his vanity and by appearing willing to listen to his harangues. Bascom, who feels underloved and underappreciated by his wife, falls prey to the widow. Their relationship builds and moves to a climax when the widow offers herself sexually to Bascom, who has ambivalent feelings about the offer. On the one hand, he wants to fill the void created by his marriage to Louise. At the same time he cannot break free from social and marital conventions, nor can he overcome his repressed religious beliefs defining the appropriate expressions of love and sex. He wants to defy convention in the way that Brill defies convention when he unleashes his invective, but he does not have the necessary kind of daring. He feels frustrated by his inadequacy. Hence, Bascom declines the widow's offer and the romance ends.

With the conclusion of the aborted romance, the focus of the novel shifts to David, whom we hardly know, even though fifty pages of this short novel have passed. David is ostensibly detailing a conversation he had with Bascom, but their conversation fades into the background as David tells us about himself and his life in Boston. We soon realize that David's life has certain parallels to Bascom's. Both came to Harvard from North Carolina, and both possessed a nearly insatiable appetite for books and life. The following quotations reveal much about David. In addition, the quotations illustrate the sense of vitality that Wolfe infused into *Bascom Hawke.* In the first quotation, David demonstrates his love for life and learning when he discusses his burning ambition to know everything, an ambition Bascom had fifty years earlier. David says:

> My hunger and thirst had been immense: I was caught up for the first time in the midst of the Faustian web— there was no food that could feed me, no drink that could quench my thirst—like an insatiate and maddened animal I roamed the streets, trying to draw up mercy from the cobblestones, solace and wisdom from a million sights and faces, or prowled through the endless shelves of high-piled books tortured by everything I could not see and could not know, and growing blind, weary, and desperate from what I read and saw. I wanted to know all, have all, be all—to be one and many, to have the whole riddle of this vast and swarming earth as legible, as tangible in my hand as a coin of minted gold (50).

The second quotation reflects David's sensitivity to life, to the earth, and to the products of the earth. He says:

> The air will have in it the wonderful odors of the market . . . the delicate and subtle air of spring touches all these odors with a new and delicate vitality; it draws the tar out of the pavements also, and it draws slowly, subtly, from ancient warehouses, the compacted perfumes of eighty years: the sweet thin piney scents of packing boxes, the glutinous composts of half a century, that have thickly stained old warehouse plankings, the smells of twine, tar, turpentine and hemp, and of thick molasses, ginseng, pungent vines and roots and old piled sacking; the clean ground strength of fresh coffee, brown, sultry, pungent, and exultantly fresh and clean; the smell of oats, baled hay and bran, of crated eggs and cheese and butter; and particularly the smell of meat, of frozen beeves, of slick porks and veals, of brains and livers and kidneys, of haunch, paunch, and jowl; of meat that is raw and of meat that is cooked . . . (53).

This section outlining David's exuberant view of life sets the stage for the climactic concluding section. David is in Bascom's office to visit; but what transpires is not really a conversation between the two, as Bascom does almost all the talking. Through his monologue, as well as through the further glimpses into Bascom's past that David gives us, we begin to understand the idea about *young men* and *old men* that Wolfe told Perkins he had.

Bascom's denegration of women occupies much of his harangue. The reason for this denegration stems from his unhappy marriage to Louise. Bascom had wanted to possess her totally when they married, and when he realized after they were wed that he could not do so because Louise's beauty invariably brought complimentary looks from other men, a kind of madness overcame him. He raged with a black jealousy and felt that marriage and love had betrayed him. Because his life was self-centered and self-contained, Bascom could not cope with the idea that he

shared his wife, even if sharing amounted only to having other men look at her. Unable to cope, and determined to maintain his fierce individuality and integrity, Bascom did what only he could: he forgot about Louise and treated her with indifference.

The results of this indifference were profound. The gap between Bascom and Louise widened to an unbreachable abyss. Because she could not understand the cause of Bascom's indifference, Louise slowly but inexorably lost her mind. Their children were also affected by his behavior. Bascom also treated them with indifference because he saw them as his wife's children, not his own. Moreover, he imposed his miserly ways on his children and denied them many of the pleasures he too had been denied as a child. As soon as they could, the children escaped from home, bearing bitter grudges that remained with them.

Bascom, then, sees his life as a series of frustrations and betrayals. His life at thirty, which had so much promise because he had been able to overcome the handicaps of youthful poverty with intelligence and perseverance, was attacked by the betrayals of his wife, his children, and his faith. These betrayals relate directly to the theme of the earth that Wolfe develops in *Bascom Hawke.* Wolfe describes Brill as a product of the earth, for example, because he possesses a challenging spirit and a lust for life. Similarly, Wolfe describes Bascom as a product of the earth because his tenacious desire to survive and prosper helped him escape from his bleak childhood. But at the same time, the theme of the earth also carries implications of organic unity, the sense that the individual is integrally bound with society, which represents the fruits of the earth. It is not surprising, therefore, that when Wolfe wants to show David as a product of the earth, he uses the above quotations that focus on David's relationship with the earth and its bounty. The sense of organic unity also extends to the concept of family, both in the particular terms of spouse and children and in the broader concept of the family of man. Believing he has been betrayed by a wife who is not really a wife to him, and by children who despise him, Bascom experiences frustration and bitter loneliness, a loneliness that is compounded by his loss of religious faith. Bascom communicates this genuine despair to David, who in turn tells us that by understanding Bascom we can understand the history of man's loneliness, his dignity, his grandeur, and his despair (39).

Bascom has lost and suffered much. Though some strength remains (his scolding of Boston motorists shows this), he is only a shell of the man he once was. David understands the life Bascom has lived and wants to graft Bascom's experiences onto his own to enrich the life he is to continue living. Sitting with Bascom in his office, David says:

> And now, as I looked at the old man, I had a sense of union with the past. It seemed if he would only speak, the living past, the voices of lost men, the pain, the pride, the madness and despair, the million scenes of the buried life—all that an old man ever knew—would be revealed to me, would be delivered to me like a priceless treasure, as an inheritance which old men owed to young, and which should be the end and effort

of all living. My savage hunger was a kind of memory: I thought if he could speak it would be fed (67).

But Bascom does not tell David what he wants to hear. Bascom only says, "It was so long ago . . . so long ago. I have lived so long. I have seen so much. I could tell you so many things" (67).

As the novel draws to its conclusion, David imagines a scene in which a group of old men and women are sitting at a dinner table. Like Bascom, they have suffered and lived on. David discovers in his vision, as he did with Bascom, that these people cannot speak of their pasts. He learns that the past cannot be transmitted. It must be lived again.

The enduring human condition is *Bascom Hawke*'s major theme. Bascom and David epitomize the continual cycle of hope, frustration, and despair, which is followed by renewed hope for the future. Wolfe's short novel is really about the birth and death of dreams. But the acknowledgement we see in old Bascom that dreams die does not stamp *Bascom Hawke* with pessimism. Rather, the novel affirms life. The affirmation of life at the novel's conclusion is to seek, to live. David says this with great beauty and force after he realizes that he cannot rekindle the flame of life in Bascom. He says:

> Then I got up and left him and went out into the streets where the singing and lyrical air, the man-swarm passing in its million-footed weft, the glorious women and the girls compacted into a single music of belly and breasts and thighs, the sea, the proud, potent, and clamorous city, all of the voices of time fused to a unity that was like a song, a token and a cry. Victoriously, I trod the neck of doubt as if it were a serpent: I was joined to the earth, a part of it, and I possessed it; I would be wasted and consumed, filled and renewed eternally; I would be emptied without weariness, replenished forever with strong joy. I had a tongue for agony, a food for hunger, a door for exile and a surfeit for insatiate desire: exultant certainty welled up in me, I thought I could possess it all, and I cried: 'Yes! It will be mine!' (71)

The juxtaposition between David and Bascom highlights what might be called the human cycle, which reflects nature's cycle of birth, growth, decay, and rebirth. Not surprisingly, the earth and what it represents play vital roles in *Bascom Hawke.* Wolfe structures his novel around the development of this theme. He begins with Bascom's youth and then amplifies this idea of the earth with comparisons and contrasts with John T. Brill, another product of the earth. David, the new Bascom, is next identified with the earth, thus providing the final contrast between youth and age. David's triumph stems from his willingness to risk life's disappointments, the disappointments of lost love and frustrated emotions that wearied the once hearty Bascom.

Wolfe knew what he was doing when he wrote *Bascom Hawke.* He carefully draws us into Bascom's world and then proceeds to make Bascom and his plight come alive for us in the subsequent sections. Every section has a purpose, and every character has a function. *Bascom Hawke* contains the great language, the great themes, and the great characterizations that Wolfe erratically achieved in novels such as *Look Homeward Angel* and *Of Time and the River.* Significantly, *Bascom Hawke* is a tightly structured work—something his long novels are not—that contains all of these elements. It is a novel that should be read and remembered.

Notes

[1] Maxwell Perkins, *Editor to Author: The Letters of Maxwell Perkins* (New York: Charles Scribner's Sons, 1950), p. 68.

[2] See Bernard DeVoto, "Genius Is Not Enough," *Saturday Review* XIII (April 25, 1936), pp. 3-4, 14-15.

[3] See Robert Penn Warren, "A Note on the Hamlet of Thomas Wolfe," reprinted in *Selected Essays of Robert Penn Warren* (New York: Random House, 1958), p. 183.

[4] Professor Hugh Holman was the first to point to Wolfe's talent as a short novelist. In his introduction to *The Short Novels of Thomas Wolfe* (New York: Charles Scribner's Sons, 1961), Holman writes, "In the short novel form Wolfe was a master of his craft . . . these successful products of his efforts should not be forgotten."

[5] Quoted in Holman's introduction to *The Short Novels of Thomas Wolfe,* p. xx.

[6] Thomas Wolfe, *A Portrait of Bascom Hawke,* collected in *The Short Novels of Thomas Wolfe,* pp. 4-5. All future references are in the text and are to this edition.

Timothy Dow Adams (essay date 1980)

SOURCE: "The Ebb and Flow of Time and Place in 'The Lost Boy'," in *Southern Studies,* Vol. XIX, No. 4, Winter, 1980, pp. 400-08.

[*In the following essay, Adams evaluates the coming and going pattern of memory, time, and location in Wolfe's story "The Lost Boy."*]

Thomas Wolfe's famous phrase, "You can't go home again," was often repeated at his seventy-fifth birthday celebration in Asheville in October of 1975. Although this phrase was usually associated with Wolfe's difficulties with his home town after he published *Look Homeward, Angel,* it could have also applied to his other childhood home in St. Louis, Missouri, where he lived for six months in 1904 and where he returned in September 1935 to visit the actual house where he had lived during the World's Fair of 1904. Wolfe's return to St. Louis, like his first visit to Asheville following *Look Homeward, Angel*'s publication, became a literary work, **"The Lost Boy,"** which used a strong and particular sense of time and place to show that "you can't go home again" applies to all childhood homes.

The use of the past, coupled with a pervasive fascination with time, has been characteristic of Southern writing almost since its beginning. As Allan W. Becker notes in an essay on Ellen Glasgow's place in the Southern literary tradition, "The sense of the past which we find in these writers (Roberts, Gordon, Tate, Warren, Faulkner, Wolfe, etc.) is almost a constant in Southern fiction. Kennedy, Simms, Cooke, Caruthers—all wrote of earlier times in the South: but their viewpoint differs from the new, in that regionalism contains an awareness of the presentness of the past."[1] The prevalence among Southern writers of this particular way of using the past—an awareness of its constant influence on the present—is discussed by Louis D. Rubin in an essay on Southern historical writing in which he says: "The present was focused into perspective by the image of the past lying behind it. Their own contemporary life was seen not only for its own sake but as formed and influenced by the life that had preceeded it."[2] Rubin suggests that the first post-World War I generation of Southern writers was especially concerned with the past's encroachment on their present, and influence on their future, because of the time and place of their existence, because they were of the new South, but were able to understand the older South into which they had been born. Georges Poulet, in an extensive essay on time and literature, makes the point that this inner drive to isolate a moment in the present, in order to look backward and forward, is characteristic of a change in century:

> Begotten by feeling, imbued more and more with feeling, the thought of the century which is ending becomes more and more apt to discover in the depths of its vibrant actuality the interflowing images of reminiscence and premonition. Always isolated in the moment which gave it form, it sees this moment incessantly invaded, disorganized. Transfigured by states of mind from beyond, there comes to be superimposed upon actual existence the awareness of another existence, an existence which overlaps the frame of each moment. It is as if to exist meant to live two lives as the same time: the life lived day by day; and the life lived before and beyond the day or the moment; a life which lengthens into duration.[3]

These comments on time are particularly applicable to the works of Wolfe, as Rubin has shown in his essay, "Thomas Wolfe: Time and the South,"[4] and as H. Blair Rouse writes in his study of time and place in Southern fiction: "In the writing of Thomas Wolfe, time is a potent factor in the presentation of all the meaning of the lives of the characters; the past merges with the present and projects into the future."[5]

Wolfe's long story, **"The Lost Boy,"** is a classic example of the Southern use of time which I have been discussing, because the story studies the past's interplay with the future and the present on so many levels. The story itself illustrates the effect of time on Wolfe, because he wrote it sometime in 1937 after having visited St. Louis.[6] The story reverts to an earlier time when Wolfe used Eugene Gant as his protagonist. Seeing the past come into the present by his visit to St. Louis, Wolfe wrote **"The Lost Boy"** which retells, from another point of view and with many embellishments, the same scene in *Look Homeward, Angel,* described by Rubin as illustrative of Wolfe's use of the past and time.

"The Lost Boy" is organized into four sections: Grover, his mother, his sister, and his brother. The story begins with a picture of Grover, who is the lost boy, in the town square of Altamont. The second section, the mother's is a monologue, addressed to Eugene—Grover's younger brother—in which the mother rambles about Grover and the trip to the World's Fair. In the third section, Helen—Grover's and Eugene's sister—recalls the events at St Louis surrounding Grover's death. The last section details Eugene's visit to the house where Grover died, thirty years later. These four sections of the story are held together by several patterns of time.

For example, as the sections unfold, time moves in a straight chronological fashion, from the time when Grover was actually alive, through subsequent attempts to remember him, until the last section, which takes place after Eugene has tried, and failed, to get at the past by talking with his mother and sister. Each section has a different narrator but each narrator picks up the story where the previous teller has left it.

The sections of **"The Lost Boy"** are also held together by the concept of Eugene's growing awareness of how he had felt at the age of four about Grover. In the first section, Eugene is not mentioned. In the second, he is addressed by his mother, but he is only a small part of her recollection. In the third section, Eugene is also addressed and even questioned, but he is still a passive character, secondary to Grover. Eugene becomes progressively more a part of each section until the last, in which his point of view is presented as he tries to recapture the past as it relates to him. Eugene is interested both in reconstructing Grover from the past and in reconstructing himself. To Eugene, both Grover and himself are the lost boy. Thus the story moves from the past toward the present in an attempt to regain the past. As the sections progress, the continuing story of Grover is also being presented, so that we find out more and more information about him, in a manner similar to the revelation of the past in *Absalom! Absalom!*. As in Faulkner's novel, each attempt to remember the real Grover is only an approximation, filtered through the memory of each speaker.

An important device which links all four parts and which appears in various forms throughout the story, is a repeated pattern of ebb and flow, coming and going and coming again. It is a pulsating pattern of stopping and starting which imparts a definite rhythm to the story. This pattern serves not only to bind the four parts to each other, but is also, in itself, a metaphor for the way memory works. The past comes and goes in the memories of each member of Grover's family. There is an elusive quality about the past that causes the memory of it to come and go, now becoming clear, now growing vague. This ebbing and flowing is seen in the universal phenomenon of a forgotten fact which is said to be on the tip of one's tongue, floating closer to conscious knowledge, and then retreating into the recesses of the mind, only to come back again, after it is no longer needed.

The pattern of coming and going is present from the first sentence of **"The Lost Boy"**: "Light came and went and came again, the booming strokes of three o'clock beat out across the town in thronging bronze from the courthouse bell, light winds of April blew the fountain out in rainbow sheets, until the plume returned and pulsed, as Grover turned into the square."[7] There is a feeling in that sentence of ebb and flow—of pulsation. It is there in the light, which comes and goes, and in the throbbing peals of the bell, which vibrate in beats across the square. The fountain reflects this sense of pulsation, both as the spray is blown by gusts of wind and as the water spurts up from its base. In the next paragraph of the story, these images, with a little variation, are repeated. The courthouse square is a study of coming and going. Street cars come into the square from each compass point, pause briefly, and then move back out on their runs. Grover, ruminating in the midst of this flowing scene, realizes that the square remains the same, despite the changing rhythm of everything in it. Caught in the flux of life all around him, Grover is pensive. He thinks of the square as a permanent fixture. He fixes the year, month, and hour; and for a moment, he is caught on a point in time, just as old Gant and Eugene are in similar scenes in *Look Homeward, Angel.* After this brief moment of calmness, the story again begins to flow; Grover passes the shops, enters the candy store and encounters the proprietor. Then he is back out on the square. Wagons roll past but he does not see them. He stands in the square, again feeling that it is the center of the universe and that it represents Now. Grover enters his father's shop where the scene is quiet and restful. The stones are waiting. A stone angel, to be used as a grave-marker, is languid; there is a layer of stone dust on the chisels. The scene has a Keatsian quality of suspended action, especially when compared with the previous scenes of constant alternation of movement and calmness. Then Grover blurts out the story of the incident with the candy store owner and the father jumps into action. He comes and goes among his gravestones. He begins sentences and stops in mid-thought. With a sudden burst, he grabs Grover "and they went out flying. Down the aisle they went by all the gravestones, past the fly-specked angels waiting there, and down the wooden steps and across the Square. The fountain pulsed, the plume blew out in sheeted iridescence, and it swept across them" (p. 13). W. O. Gant atones for Crocker, the candystore owner, and his treatment of Grover by demanding his son's money back and hurling bitter words at the crippled Crocker. Suddenly Grover is alone and back out on the square again, as the light comes and goes. The switching from violent action to reflective peace continues throughout the first section. Grover knows that "something had gone out of the day and something had come in again" (p. 14). The pattern of coming and going is present in Grover's thoughts as well as in the physical action of the first section. After his father's help, Grover realizes that he has lost a measure of innocence but gained an equal amount of experience. "Out of the vision of those quiet eyes some brightness had gone, and into their vision had come some deeper color. He

could not say, he did not know through what transforming shadows life had passed within that quarter hour. He only knew that something had been lost—something forever gained" (p. 14). As the first section ends, Grover sees a poster advertising the St. Louis World's Fair. The sense of ebb and flow in this section is pervasive. It can be felt in the square, in the boy's alternation between coming into others' lives, and going into the square for quiet thought before jumping back into the flow of life all around him. The pattern is seen in the movements of Crocker, who rocks as he walks, coming and going from the rear of his store, and in the boy's father, who alternates between the calmness of his work and the fury of his actions in defense of his son.

Section II is the mother's monologue. In describing Grover, she also holds to this pattern of coming and going, focusing and unfocusing. She talks about Grover and how he acted on the train to St. Louis, but she constantly interrupts her story to revert to the present. She says she can remember exactly how Grover looked on the trip, "with his black eyes, his black hair, and with the birthmark on his neck—so grave, so serious, so earnest-like—as he sat by the train window. . . . It was so long ago, but when I think of it, it all comes back, as if it happened yesterday" (p. 22). The pattern of coming and going is repeated in this section. Grover is calm in the midst of change, just as he was in the square. He quietly watches the changes in the countryside that he sees from the train window, while the other children are running up and down in the aisle, looking from side to side. As the mother talks, Grover comes and goes. She changes from the past to the present and then back to another time in the past.

Section III of **"The Lost Boy"** is Grover's sister Helen's monologue. At first Helen talks about the strangeness of looking at an old photograph and thinking of the present and "how everyone either dies or grows up and goes away" (p. 23). The past comes back to her while she thinks about the picture. She begins to talk about Grover and the time when the family lived in St. Louis. Helen reminds Eugene about his difficulty as a young child with the pronunciation of Grover's name. In her attempt to recall all of the events leading up to Grover's death, Helen repeats the pattern of ebb and flow that is so prevalent in the earlier sections. "My God, I wish I knew the answer to these things. I'd like to find out what is wrong—what has changed since then—and if we have the same queer look in our eyes, too. Does it happen to us all, to everyone? . . . Grover and Ben, Steve, Daisy, Luke and me— all standing there before that house on Woodson street in Altamont—there we are, and you see the way we were— and how it all gets lost. What is it, anyway, that people lost? . . . It seems that it must be something we heard somewhere—that it happened to someone else. And then it comes back again. . . . It all comes back as if it happened yesterday. And then it goes away again, and seems further off and stranger than if it happened in a dream" (p. 30).

Section IV, the last part of the story, is Eugene's portion. He is back in St. Louis looking for the house where Grover died, looking for the past, lost thirty years before. At first Eugene talks to a stranger to try to locate the house. He thinks of the street called King's Highway, which to himself as a four year old boy was "a kind of road that wound from magic out of some dim and haunted land, and that along the way it had got mixed in with Tom the Piper's son, with hot cross buns, with all the lights that came and went, and with coming down through Indiana in the morning, and the smell of engine smoke, the Union Station, and most of all with voices lost and far and long ago that said 'King's Highway'" (p. 31). Then Eugene is back in the present, still looking for the house. He sees that King's Highway is just a city street now. Eugene finds the house but feels "nothing but absence, absence, and the desolation of America" (p. 33). Again Eugene's thoughts slip back into the past. He is four years old sitting on the stairs feeling a vague sadness because everyone was gone, working at the Fair. He had waited until they would all return and spent the time wondering what the future would bring. Now in St. Louis thirty years later, knowing what the future brought, Eugene wants to return to the past by sitting on the actual stairs of his former house. He thinks that he could remember all that he had seen and been, recapture his own universe as a child.

> But as he thought it, he knew that even if he could sit here alone and get it back again, it would be gone as soon as seized, just as it had been then—first coming like the vast and drowsy rumor of the distant and enchanted Fair, then fading like cloud shadows on a hill, going like faces in a dream—coming, going, coming, possessed and held, but never captured, like lost voices in the mountains long ago—and like the dark eyes and quiet face of the dark, lost boy, his brother, who, in the mysterious rhythm of his life and work, used to come into this house, then go, and then return again (p. 38).

When Eugene sees the same room where Grover died, "The years dropped off like fallen leaves: the face came back again . . ." (p. 41), and he remembers the same episode about his trying to pronounce Grover's name that his sister had told him in section III of the story. When Helen told him the story, he could not remember, but now, in the very house where it took place, he does remember—"It all came back, and faded, and was lost again" (p. 41). As Eugene leaves the house, he looks back and sees that it is only a house again. His ability to relive the past is gone now and Grover, the lost boy, is also gone, never to return. Through the constant use of the pattern I have been tracing in each section of the story, Wolfe emphasizes Eugene's attempts to escape from the distortions and blurrings of thirty years of elapsed time. He comes nearer and nearer to controlling his memories of Grover and then his ability begins to fade as he leaves the room where Grover died.

In his essay on Wolfe and time, Rubin continues his comments by saying that Wolfe "was a thoroughgoing romantic; his writing has the intensity of fiction written by an artist who is seeking furiously, through his literary craft, to impose on his recalcitrant experience his own highly personal valuations."[8] This view of Wolfe as a romantic trying to evaluate his past, is described by Poulet as typical of the romantic's use of time:

> Incarcerated in the instant, the romantic escapes into thought all the rest of his life. Or rather he tries to envelop his thought in the consciousness of the present moment. It is no longer a question, as it was in the preceding century, of extracting from the moment all its sensuous substance; it is a question of giving the moment all the profundity, all the infinity of duration of which man feels capable. To possess his life in the moment is the pretension or the fundamental desire of the romantic.[9]

"The Lost Boy" also illustrates by its use of place the pattern of coming and going and the difficulty of focusing on the past. St. Louis and the World's Fair serve as further metaphors for a looking backward and forward simultaneously. The Louisiana Purchase Universal Exposition, as the St. Louis Fair of 1904 was officially called, was designed for the dual purpose of celebrating the centennial of the Louisiana Purchase and demonstrating America's progress since 1804. Some of the major events and displays commemorated the past, but the major emphasis of the fair was on the future.[10] Thomas Wolfe, returning to St. Louis after thirty-one years, must have been as surprised as the Eugene of "The Lost Boy" was to see how the entire fairgrounds had vanished. What had seemed magical to a four year old boy, seemed magical still because it had vanished completely. Part of the planning for the fair included plans for the restoration of the park where the fairgrounds were located. David R. Francis, the president of the Louisiana Purchase Exposition Company, explains in his mammoth book on the fair that the "Board of Public Improvements" required the "removal of all buildings except the palace of Art and removal of the Intramural railway,"[11] as well as the following ordinance, "Within twelve months after the close of such Fair or Exposition fully restore the park selected as a site, or, in the case of Forest Park, that portion thereof above described, by doing all necessary grading, the restoration and repair, or the formation of all walks or roads, the planting of trees, the placing of sod and the planting of shrubs and plants, all in accordance with plans to be approved by the Board. . . ."[12] One of the buildings became a city museum; a few others became part of Washington University, but the majority were torn down immediately.

Eugene's attempt at reconstructing the past by visiting St. Louis and looking for his house is complicated by the fact that by 1935 hardly any traces of the fair remain. Street names had been changed, vegetation had grown, and the site of the largest and most famous World's Fair ever, had been transformed into an ordinary city park. The fantastic, magical fair—"A fair so comprehensive, so perfectly planned, that had some disaster wiped out every culture on the face of the earth, all could have been reconstructed from the materials on hand . . ."[13]—had come into his life and gone out of it as though a dream.

St. Louis is itself an example of the difficulty of focusing the past because it is a city whose identity has changed with time. The St. Louis celebrated by W. C. Handy in "St. Louis Blues," is in the same traditional Southern state as Mark Twain's Hannibal, but Missouri was a compromise state and by 1904 the city is thought of as only partly Southern. Eugene says of St. Louis, "He feels the way one feels when one comes back, and knows that he should not have come, and when he sees that, after all, King's Highway is—a street; and St. Louis—the enchanted name—a big, hot, common town upon the river, sweltering in wet, dreary heat, and not quite South . . ." (p. 33). Eugene's impression that St. Louis was not quite a Southern city anymore by 1904 is echoed in Henry James' *The Bostonians,* published only eighteen years before the St. Louis Fair, when Mrs. Farrinder declares that she has been warned not to lecture in Southern cities on the history of feminism. She is answered by Verena Tarrant, who replies, "*I had a magnificent audience last spring in St. Louis.*"[14] She is answered by an anonymous voice, "Oh, well, St. Louis—that's scarcely the South."[15] St. Louis is partly Southern, partly Western and partly Mid-Western. Although the city calls itself "Gateway to the West," Wolfe thought of St. Louis as a Mid-Western city: "The loneliness and sadness of the high, hot skies, and evening coming on across the Middle West" (p. 33).

Wolfe's visit to St. Louis in 1935 and his subsequent literary use of that visit to describe the difficulty of recapturing the past by revisiting past locations, foreshadows his return to Asheville in 1937 and his well-known phrase, "you can't go home again," a phrase which Wolfe associated with "the old forms and systems of things which once seemed everlasting but which are changing all the time,"[16] and which he expressed in the pattern of ebb and flow in time and place that permeates **"The Lost Boy."**

Notes

[1] Allan W. Becker, "Ellen Glasgow and the Southern Literary Tradition," *Modern Fiction Studies,* 5 (1959-60), 301.

[2] Louis D. Rubin, Jr., "The Historical Image of Modern Southern Writing," *Journal of Southern History,* 22 (May 1956), 154.

[3] Georges Poulet, "The Course of Human Time," trans. by Eliot Coleman, *The Hopkins Review,* 6 (Spring-Summer, 1953), 27.

[4] Louis D. Rubin, Jr., "Thomas Wolfe: Time and the South," *Writers of the Modern South: The Faraway Country* (Seattle, 1963), 72-104.

[5] H. Blair Rouse, "Time and Place in Southern Fiction," in *Southern Renaissance,* ed. by Louis D. Rubin, and Robert D. Jacobs (Baltimore, 1966), 132.

[6] Elizabeth Nowell, *Thomas Wolfe: A Biography* (Garden City, 1960), 379.

[7] Thomas Wolfe, "The Lost Boy," in *The Hills Beyond* (New York, 1941), 1. Future citations are to this edition.

[8] Rubin, "Thomas Wolfe: Time and the South," p. 103.

[9] Poulet, p. 27.

[10] Edward J. Coff, "St. Louis Celebrates," *Missouri Historical Society Bulletin,* (October 1954), 54.

[11] David R. Francis, *The Universal Exposition of 1904* (St. Louis, 1913), 667.

[12] Francis, p. 668.

[13] Coff, "St. Louis Celebrates," p. 67.

[14] Henry James, *The Bostonians* (New York, 1956), 51.

[15] James, *The Bostonians,* p. 52.

[16] Thomas Wolfe, *You Can't Go Home Again* (New York, 1940), 706.

David K. Hall   (essay date 1983)

SOURCE: "Contrast as Device in Wolfe's 'The Child by Tiger'," in *The Thomas Wolfe Review,* Vol. 7, No. 1, Spring, 1983, pp. 8-11.

[*In the following essay, Hall probes Wolfe's use of the literary device of contrast to highlight his theme of "the dual nature of man" in "The Child by Tiger," a story later incorporated into his novel* The Web and the Rock.]

It has been suggested by more than a few critics that Wolfe lacked the disciplined control of literary devices needed to write a tight and effective story. The contention is made, in fact, by Wolfe fans and critics alike, that it is the power of his language more than anything else that carries the brilliance of Wolfe.

But Wolfe was not unaware of literary device. What is more, he used it extremely well. To point this out it is expedient to lift the segment **"The Child by Tiger"**[1] from his novel *The Web and the Rock* and examine in it Wolfe's use of literary device.

"The Child by Tiger" is a story about the dual nature of man; his evil and his goodness. Wolfe draws this duality in extreme forms in the single character of Dick Prosser and in the group character of the town crowd. Contrasts of imagery, character, action and point of view are the strongest literary devices in the story working to emphasize Wolfe's point about the two-sided nature of man.

Perhaps the least important of the contrasts are the changes in point of view. There are at least three of them, and all are minor variations of third-person limited narration. These point-of-view changes are most noticeable for how the story development alters with each section. Most of the story is told from a third-person "reporter" point-of-view. Yet interspersed throughout the story are lines indicating that Wolfe wants us to get a sense of some of the characters' thoughts and feelings, and the point of view is thus brought somewhat closer to a limited omniscience.

The story begins in a third-person "reporter" point-of-view, introducing George Webber, Randy Shepperton and Dick

Prosser. In this section we are shown Prosser's benevolent attributes, especially as they affect George and Randy. Prosser teaches them, for instance, how to throw and kick a football, and gives them kindly-superintended sparring lessons. This also gives us some clues to Prosser's dual nature for, although we are never admitted to his thoughts, the quality of the activities he provides instruction in is rather violent. A foreshadowing (another literary device) of his role in the story is developed.

In one incident Prosser is chauffeuring Randy's father when a drunken white drives into the Sheppertons' car. The drunk and Prosser get out of their cars, and when the drunk begins punching, Prosser does not retaliate. Wolfe has effectively depicted the side of Prosser devoted to good.

But Wolfe immediately sets up a contrast of character and action. Prosser does not move after being punched, but "the whites of his eyes were shot with red," and "his bleeding lips bared for a moment over the white ivory of his teeth." Prosser's apparent surface tranquility, his subjection to the punching, is broken by his sub-surface rage that gets expressed by his reddened eyes and bared teeth. The "pure" symbolism of the words "white ivory," and the "evil" symbolism of the words "shot with red" are manifestations of a contrast specific to Prosser.

This contrast is heightened a little later when Prosser's rifle is discovered on the table in his room next to his Bible. The image is a striking one: An instrument of violence side by side with an instrument of staid meekness. And when Prosser finds the boys staring at his rifle, his menacing side is underscored again by the use of the image of reddened eyes; "he was there above them, his thick lips bared over his gums, his eyes gone small and red as rodents'."

The point of view switches shortly after this part in the story, becoming more of an effaced third-person narration. During this part of the story the action ceases, except that George Webber falls asleep, and Wolfe takes occasion to set up a mood of isolation and menace through the use of the imagery of snow in the South.[2] There is a contrast between the active preceding section and this relatively actionless section. This section is not completely outside of the story,[3] because it is presented as the meditation of Webber, who "went to sleep upon [the] mystery" of the falling snow.

Wolfe writes, "the storm howled on," and "all life seemed to have withdrawn into thrilling isolation." The snow brings something "dark and jubilant," and also brings "the thrilling isolation of its own white mystery." And as the snow is falling Wolfe writes about the opposing sides of nature, dividing the world into opposite symbols: "In every man there are two hemispheres of light and dark, two worlds discrete, two countries of his soul's adventure. . . . Thus, at the head of those two poles of life will lie the real, the truthful image of its immortal opposite." A strong background of isolation and conflict is established, with the "white mystery" of the snow surrounding the black Pross-

er. We anticipate what might result from the "powers discrete that wage perpetual warfare in the lives of all men living."[4]

Action resumes as the point of view returns to a third-person "reporter" narrative. Webber is suddenly awakened in the night by the sound of the town firebell ringing "bronze with peril, clamorous through the snow-numbed silence of the air." Webber and Shepperton find out that Prosser has "gone crazy and is running wild." A crowd has gathered, incensed; Prosser has gone on a killing spree. The crowd grows more and more unruly and finally breaks out in an act of violence itself, forcing its way into the hardware store and looting it of rifles. There is a single, violent mob-will which, like Prosser's dark side, Wolfe likens to an animal. The boys could hear coming from the crowd "a low and growing mutter, an ugly and insistent growl." "There was no mistaking the blood note in that foggy growl." Earlier the townsfolk had rescued Prosser from the fist-swinging drunk, but now they are a bloodthirsty savage lynch crowd gathered to track and kill him.

The events of Prosser's killing spree and the posse's search are told from the "reporter" point-of-view, but this section contains much less of the type of effaced omniscience used in the preceding section. In fact, this section begins, "This was what had happened," and the tale of Prosser's murders and run from the law is unfolded very much as if it were being recounted in a newspaper article.

Prosser's earlier kind and loyal actions are contrasted with the savage killing unfolded in this section. He has become the opposite of his earlier self, killing seven men, and Wolfe's foreboding symbolism of opposing hemispheres looms up in the mind. It doesn't seem to be too drastic a measurement of the human condition.

Descriptions of Prosser on his killing spree involve cat-like imagery, suggested by phrases such as "his great black paw" implying the more brutal tiger rather than the domesticated cat. Shooting at anything in his way, Prosser "covered the ground with cat-like speed," and walked across the snow "straight as a string, right out of town." Black and white is contrasted as Prosser leaves footprints in the snow. After a day of searching the mob finds him and empties "all their ammunition on the riddled carcass." His body is brought to town and hung on display in the front window of the undertaker's where, in contrast to what they say about their abhorrence of it, the hypocrites flock to see it.

The final section of the story is two-part itself. The first part begins only "a day or two" after Prosser dies. The boys and Mr. Shepperton re-enter Prosser's room for the first time since his death and find the Bible that Prosser often read "open and face downward" on the table, apparently open to what Prosser last read from it—the twenty-third Psalm. Mr. Shepperton reads it aloud, then "closed the book and put it down upon the table, the place where Dick had left it. And they went out the door, he locked it, and they went back into that room no more, forever." It is done as though they are shutting the door on the knowledge of man's evil character, as though to help the boys keep some form of innocence, realize only the good side of man. At least George Webber can not, for in the second part of the final section Webber recalls the savage side of Prosser from an older point of view.

From this older, more mature point of view, Webber remembers Prosser before the killings, and events up through finding his Bible after the killings. From this older viewpoint he reflects on the appropriateness of the twenty-third Psalm, on the docility of the message of it. And he feels that Blake's poem about the world's unexplained savagery befits Prosser's nature better, and quotes "Tyger! Tyger!" Blake's poem effectively completes the animal images and actions of the story. Blake contrasts lamb with tiger, meek with savage, as does Wolfe. Wolfe concludes that Prosser was "a symbol of man's evil innocence, and the token of his mystery, a projection of his own unfathomed quality, a friend, a brother, and a mortal enemy, an unknown demon—our loving friend, our mortal enemy, two worlds together—tiger and a child."

The contrasting imagery, actions, characters and sections of point-of-view work well, as literary devices they help to strengthen and clarify Wolfe's point about the duality of human nature. It seems to me that Wolfe sought for these literary tools, intending to use them. Once he had found them, he used them like a true craftsman. His contrasts are well woven into the story, thus showing his mastery of the use of them. There may be something to the beauty and power of Wolfe's language which could obscure his use of literary device. But this story would certainly never have achieved its end so well had it not been crafted so well.

Notes

[1] Unless otherwise indicated, all quotations are taken from "The Child By Tiger" in *The Thomas Wolfe Reader,* edited by C. Hugh Holman (New York: Charles Scribner's Sons, 1962), pp. 500-526.

[2] This is suggested by Floyd C. Watkins in *Thomas Wolfe's Characters* (Norman: Univ. of Oklahoma Press, 1957), p. 106.

[3] Richard S. Kennedy interprets it this way in *The Window of Memory* (Chapel Hill: The Univ. of North Carolina Press, 1962), p. 317.

[4] Quoted from Wolfe by Richard Walser in *Thomas Wolfe: An Introduction and Interpretation* (New York: Barnes & Noble Inc., 1961), pp. 95-97.

James D. Boyer (essay date 1983)

SOURCE: "The City in the Short Fiction of Thomas Wolfe," in *The Thomas Wolfe Review,* Vol. 7, No. 2, Fall, 1983, pp. 36-40.

[*In the following essay, Boyer outlines developments in Wolfe's presentation of the city in his stories, noting his "growing compassion for and identification with city-dwellers" throughout his career.*]

In the summer of 1937 Thomas Wolfe returned to Asheville. He had not been back since the great outcry against him after the publication in 1929 of *Look Homeward, Angel,* that nakedly autobiographical novel that had exposed and enraged many people in his home town. The Asheville reception in 1937 was a warm one. Wolfe had become famous in the intervening years and people had forgiven him. Family and friends flocked around him, and for a while the attention was pleasant and flattering. But by fall the joys of the old home town had worn thin, and Wolfe went hurrying back to New York City. He had found that he couldn't go home again, or more accurately, that fourteen years of living in New York City had made it his real home.

When he had come to the city in 1925, Wolfe was, of course, as much the provincial as his fictional protagonists, Eugene Gant and George Webber. He had grown up in the mountain country of Asheville, had gone to a rural university in Chapel Hill, and had spent three years cloistered at Harvard. After that, from 1925 until his death in 1938, he made New York his home. He had brought to the city more than the usual number of fears and prejudices. Those fourteen years show a significant change in his feelings toward the city, a growth in understanding and sympathy for its people that is clearly reflected in his writing.

Wolfe's earliest fiction dealing with New York is **"The Train and the City,"** a story published in *Scribner's Magazine* in May 1933, but written in 1930 or earlier. That story reflects deep division in the feelings of his protagonist between what he had anticipated of the city and what he found it to be. In a passage early in the story he pictures the city as he experienced it on a glorious first day of spring when everything came to life:

> Over the immense and furious encampment of the city there trembled the mightly pulsations of a unity of hope and joy, a music of triumph and enchantment that suddenly wove all life into the fabric of its exultant harmonies. It quelled the blind and brutal stupefactions of the street, it pierced into a million cells, and fell upon ten thousand acts and moments of man's life and business, it hovered above him in the air, it gleamed and sparkled in the flashing tides that girdled round the city, and with a wizard's hand it drew forth from the tombs of winter the gray flesh of the living dead.

The wonders of that day rekindle in the speaker his childhood vision of the city:

> It was a vision simple, golden, unperplexed, carved from deep substances of light and shade, and exultant with its prophecy of glory, love and triumph.

> I heard, far-off, the deep and bee-like murmur of its million-footed life, and all the mystery of the earth and time was in that sound. I saw its thousand streets peopled with a flashing, beautiful, infinitely varied life. The city flashed before me like a glorious jewel, blazing with the thousand rich and brilliant facets of a life so good, so bountiful, so strangely and constantly beautiful and interesting that it seemed intolerable that I should

miss a moment of it. I saw the streets swarming with the figures of great men and glorious women, and I walked among them like a conqueror, winning fiercely and exultantly by my talent, courage, and merit, the greatest tributes that the city had to offer, the highest prize of power, wealth, and fame, and the great emolument of love.[1]

The feelings are, of course, those generalized anticipations of the rural-bred youth heading for the city, a vision more powerful perhaps in the 1920's than now, but still close enough to our own experience to rekindle strong feelings, if only nostalgia.

But a few phrases in those passages—"the blind and brutal stupefaction of the streets" and "the gray flesh of the living dead"—reveal a contrasting response that surfaces in the narrator even as he tries to recapture the childhood vision. This response, a feeling of mistrust and repulsion, deepens as he moves from description of place to description of people: "'I saw again,' he says, the million faces—the faces dark, dingy, driven, harried, and corrupt, the faces stamped with all the familiar markings of suspicion and mistrust, cunning, contriving, and a hard and stupid cynicism. There were the faces thin and febrile, of the taxi drivers, the faces cunning, sly and furtive, the hard twisted mouths and rasping voices, . . . the faces cruel and arrogant and knowing of the beak-nosed Jews, the brutal heavy figures of the Irish cops." The reader feels embarrassment for the antagonism and prejudice of the narrator as he goes on: "Hard mouthed, hard-eyed, and strident tongued, with their million hard gray faces, they streamed past upon the streets forever, like a single animal, with the sinuous and baleful convolutions of an enormous reptile." Though the narrator tries to tie these people in with his vision of wonder over the city, the reader remains unconvinced. Clearly the real city is, for the narrator, filled with strange, frightening, unfriendly people.

In another early story, *Death, the Proud Brother,* (*Scribner's Magazine,* June 1933) Wolfe gives us further insight into what was wrong with city life; here the city is impersonal, isolating, mechanical, violent. The story is a graphic account of four unrelated city deaths: a street vendor is crushed by a truck, a worker falls to his death from a steel beam high above a construction site, a skidrow bum crushes his head in a drunken fall, and an Irishman dies peacefully on a subway bench. What pervades each of these incidents is the impersonality of the city: the truck driver who has killed the street vendor continues on, unaware of the death his truck has caused; the death fall of the riviter causes a traffic jam that angers the inconvenienced people; the dead drunk is the butt of jokes by two callous sophisticates. And although the narrator describes the fourth death differently, telling how death came quietly and bestowed dignity and awe on the man in the subway, the reader is still made aware of a disturbing detachment on the part of those present—the crowd makes jokes and a young black prostitute lures away a vulpine-faced Italian. The city, judged by these four episodes, is uncaring. In it man appears to lose the capacity for compassion and brotherhood. The narrator's anger is so intense at one point that

the action of these city people made him "want to smash them in the face." The tone of the story changes dramatically in the long lyric apostrophe to death, loneliness and sleep that ends it, but that beautiful lyric fails to erase the narrator's angry feelings toward man alive.

This sense of city man as "man swarm"—abrasive, strident, reptilian, vulpine and uncaring—reflects Wolfe's early response to the city. Characteristic of his writing done before 1932, the response tells us more about his own isolation and defensiveness during that period than about the city, for as he lives in the city over a period of years, especially after his move from Manhattan to Brooklyn in 1931, his angry tone is softened considerably. *No Door,* written after that move, shows some beginning steps in that change of feelings. In its opening section, where the narrator is conversing with a pleasant, aesthetic-looking millionaire, it is clearly the wealthy host who is naive about city life and the narrator who understands the real richness of life there. And the city people, as the narrator describes them now, contribute to the richness. Of his landlady in Brooklyn, he explains "what a good and liberal-hearted woman she is; how rough and ready, full of life and energy, how she likes drinking and the fellowship of drinking men, and knows all the rough and seamy sides of life. . . ."[2] And other neighbors are favorably presented too. Even as he describes the neighbors who fight and brawl, or the prostitute in the street at 2:00 a.m. who screams at her escort, "Yah gotta pay me, yuh big bum," and the escort who counters, "I won't pay yuh until you start acting like a lady," he presents them with the pride and affection of an insider. And ironically, though the overall theme of *No Door* has to do with man's inescapable isolation, the narrator appears to be experiencing acceptance and feeling community with these people. *No Door* is clearly a turning point.

This changing attitude toward the city and its people is further illustrated in one of Wolfe's simplest and most impressive short stories, **"Only the Dead Know Brooklyn,"** published two years later in 1935.[3] Here one of the city people, a Brooklynite, narrates the story. Like earlier city people he is pugnacious, brash, and uneducated. But he is curious and kind, too. While waiting for a subway one evening, he encounters a tall, half-drunk, half-crazed stranger. (The reader at once recognizes this stranger as the familiar Wolfe protagonist.) The stranger is exploring Brooklyn with a map and wants to find "Benson-hoist," and the Brooklynite is anxious to help. But as the stranger talks of wandering through the Red Hook section at night, clearly not a sensible thing to do, and questions what the Brooklynite would do if he ever found someone drowning in Brooklyn, the native explains that people don't drown in Brooklyn, then begins to realize just how drunk or crazy the stranger is, and gets off the subway early to escape, repeating that it would take a whole lifetime to know Brooklyn,—that in fact, only the dead really know Brooklyn.

The reader, of course, has more understanding of the whole situation than does the narrator. The reader sees that the stranger with the map is trying to absorb the city, to experience everything; he understands that drowning, while not a literal but a metaphorical danger, is a serious danger nonetheless for the stranger. (It is Wolfe's greatest struggle with the protean city.) But the final wisdom in the story is given to the city man, even though he doesn't fully understand the implications of his own words: "It'd take a guy a lifetime to know Brooklyn t'roo and t'roo. An even den, yuh wouldn't know it all." Though the tall stranger in the story hasn't learned yet, Wolfe is clearly learning to curb the insatiable appetite for experience.

The extent to which Wolfe came to identify with the lower classes in the city—in his fiction and in his life—is spelled out in one of the final stories he worked on before his final trip west in 1938 and his death. *The Party at Jack's* concerns the other side of the society of the city, the very rich. Wolfe had, of course, come to know personally the ways of the rich through his relationship with Aline Bernstein. She worked as a designer in the theater, but her husband had amassed a fortune as a stockbroker, and through their parties Wolfe came to know a significant circle of the rich and powerful of the city. And for a time he had viewed that life as a glorious goal to reach out for. But through his years of living in Brooklyn, by observing first hand the poverty and deprivation of the poor, he had begun to recognize the injustice and evil of the system that supported Aline's family and others of that privileged class. Having moved from his romantic period to one of great social concern, Wolfe wrote *The Party at Jack's* to make clear where he stood.

The story covers a single day in 1929, just before the great stock market crash, and is set in the fashionable apartment of Esther Jack, mistress of Wolfe's final protagonist, George Webber. The central event of the story is a party George attends, at which the fashionable people gather. At the party, aspiring writer George meets other writers, critics, stage stars and aging dilettantes. Chief entertainment for the evening is Piggy Logan and his circus of wire dolls. The party is a rather dismal affair, at least for George. As it draws to a close, fire breaks out in the building, causing those still present to flee to the streets. Though the fire is soon extinguished and things returned to normal, the experiences of the evening, the luxury and pointlessness of the whole affair, convince George that he must break with Esther Jack and her world of sterile luxury.

Wolfe calls *The Party at Jack's* the most densely woven piece of writing that he had ever attempted. In the story, a sweeping attack on the capitalistic system, virtually everything is symbolic. Richard Kennedy, in *The Window of Memory,* has given a careful analysis of the social criticism.[4] The apartment building, complete with elevator operators and serving girls, represents a whole world of wealth and privilege. Beneath runs the subway, whose rumblings, scarcely felt above, suggest the shakiness of this system of privilege resting on the working classes who pass beneath. The fire in the building, suggestive, perhaps, of the depression itself, causes much concern but only temporary dislocation for these privileged souls. But the uncertainty remains. Characters in the story represent important types: old John Enborg is the willing servant who works for and defends the Jacks and their class; Amy Van Leer, the aging socialite whose inability to articulate ideas—and whose bored resignation represent the "lost generation," those who had experienced too much too soon; and the Jacks themselves, the liberals of the world, basically good people who are yet caught up in and responsible for the evils of the system. And images are used to reinforce narrative: Piggy Logan's grotesque mechanical circus serves as a striking image of the tastelessness of the cult and the reduction of art among the wealthy class. Characters, events, images—all function in the story to condemn the privileges of the wealthy, the greed and the essential sterility of the upper classes. Wolfe's final statement on the city, it aims its criticism not at the city as such, but at its privileged class. It demonstrates Wolfe's real allegiance to and love for the city people he had been living with.

Though he pictured city man as poor, often the victim, often alienated, he showed a growing compassion for and identification with these people throughout his career. As a result, he was able to write of Brooklyn in summer, "There are so many million doors tonight. There's a door for everyone tonight, all's open to the air, all's interfused tonight . . . and there is something over all tonight, something fused, remote and trembling . . . upon the huge and weaving ocean of the night in Brooklyn." And before that fatal Western trip, he had carefully reinstalled himself in a Manhattan apartment. After his reconciliation with the South, he did come home again, to New York City.

Notes

[1] "The Train and the City," *Scribner's Magazine,* 93 (May, 1933), 285-286.

[2] "No Door," *Scribner's Magazine,* 94 (July 1933), 47.

[3] "Only the Dead Know Brooklyn," *The New Yorker,* 11 (June 15, 1935), 13-14.

[4] *You Can't Go Home Again* (New York: Harper and Brothers, 1940), p. 430.

Elizabeth Evans (essay date 1984)

SOURCE: "*From Death to Morning, The Hills Beyond,* and the Short Novels," in *Thomas Wolfe,* Frederick Ungar Publishing Co., 1984, pp. 95-133.

[*In the following excerpt, Evans discusses and evaluates the writing of Wolfe's collections of short fiction* From Death to Morning, The Hills Beyond, *and* The Short Stories of Thomas Wolfe.]

Although Wolfe published many short stories, he admitted that he did not know what magazines wanted and declared he would "like nothing better than to write something that was both very good and very popular: I should be enchanted if the editors of *Cosmopolitan* began to wave large fat checks under my nose, but I know of no ways of going about this deliberately and I am sure I'd fail miserably if I tried" (*Letters,* p. 325). Most often his short stories were segments of the larger manuscript he was always working on at the time, and he felt uncertain about excising a portion and shaping it as a short story. Once when he sent Elizabeth Nowell approximately seven typed pages out of a manuscript (a piece about two boys going to the circus) he wrote, "The thing [**"Circus at Dawn"**] needs an introduction which I will try to write today, but otherwise it is complete enough, although, again, I am afraid it is not what most people consider a story" (*Letters,* p. 402). (**"Circus at Dawn"** was published in *Modern Monthly* in 1935; it was also included in *From Death to Morning.*) Wolfe generally left such decisions and selections up to Nowell.

All fourteen stories that *From Death to Morning* (1935) comprises appeared in magazines or academic journals between July 1932, when *The Web of Earth* was published, and October 1935, when **"The Bums at Sunset"** appeared. Seven of these stories were published by *Scribner's Magazine,* two by *Modern Monthly,* and one each by *The New Yorker, Vanity Fair, Cosmopolitan, Harper's Bazaar,* and the *Virginia Quarterly Review*—a wide variety of publications. Letters in 1933 indicate that Wolfe was hard pressed for money; selling stories was therefore essential. He was down to $7, he said, when the sale of *No Door* to *Scribner's Magazine* brought him $200. Although he welcomed this sum, Wolfe wrote George Wallace (a former member of Professor Baker's 47 Workshop at Harvard) that he was considering taking his stories to another agent, one who had indicated he could get higher prices than *Scribner's Magazine,* Wolfe's most frequent publisher, offered. Obviously Wolfe would indeed welcome "large fat checks" from *Cosmopolitan.* These stories earned him funds first as single sales and then in the collected volume *From Death to Morning.* This volume appeared eight months after *Of Time and the River* was published, making 1935 an important year of publication for Wolfe.

Wolfe attributed the unenthusiastic reviews of *From Death to Morning* to the criticism that continued to be made about *Of Time and the River*: excessive length. The favorable reviews stressed the lyrical prose, humor, realism, and engaging characters. Nevertheless, this neglected volume generally has been underrated, with just a few stories receiving serious attention; indeed, Richard Kennedy thinks that *From Death to Morning* is a book that discourages a second reading. While critics wisely avoid extravagant claims for this collection, they need not shy away from confidently praising Wolfe's variety of narrative forms, his range of subject matter, the large number of effectively drawn characters, the careful attention to place, and the emotional power. Indeed, emotional power is the significant feature, one that Wolfe conveys best through a pervasive feeling of loneliness in characters and through some extraordinarily violent scenes.

Narrative forms include the episodic, epistolary, stream-of-consciousness, as well as slice-of-life, the form that describes **"Only the Dead Know Brooklyn"** and **"The Bums at Sunset."** Each of these stories concerns a problem, for which no solution is reached. Like most of the stories in this collection, these two implicitly explore the theme of loneliness that is prevalent even in *The Web of Earth,* a piece of writing whose main character, Wolfe says, "is grander, richer and more tremendous" than Joyce's Molly Bloom at the end of *Ulysses* (*Letters,* p. 339). In both **"Only the Dead Know Brooklyn"** and **"The Bums at Sunset,"** the characters are flat, distinguished only by age and basic reactions. The bums are a chance collection of lonely men exiled for unknown reasons from families and productive work. Both stories center on the arrival of a stranger. In **"The Bums at Sunset,"** the appearance of the young, uninitiated bum threatens those who know the ropes and are suspicious of his lack of experience. "What is dis anyway?" one of them sneers, "a - - - - noic'ry [nursery], or sump'n." In **"Only the Dead Know Brooklyn,"** the big guy who presumes to learn all of Brooklyn by asking directions and studying his map baffles the narrator, who declares, "Dere's no guy livin' dat knows Brooklyn t'roo and t'roo." While the voice of the Brooklyn native narrates this story, an omniscient voice tells the story of **"The Bums at Sunset,"** and his diction contrasts with the bums' ungrammatical speech and limited vocabulary in its use of figurative language; for example, the fading light of sunset looks, he says, "like a delicate and ancient bronze." And in picturing these nondescript men, the narrator emphasizes that their inescapable loneliness tells "a legend of pounding wheel and thrumming rod, of bloody brawl and brutal shambles, of the savage wilderness, the wild, cruel and lonely distances of America."

"Gulliver," a brief character study of an excessively tall man, relates the discomfort of someone who never fits into chairs, beds, or Pullman car berths—of a giant in a world of normal-sized people. Furthermore, the central character is subjected to the same insults wherever he goes: "Hey-y, Mis-teh! . . . Is it rainin' up deh?" His physical size dominates the story and causes the pain and incommunicable loneliness that mark his life. In **"The Far and the Near,"** a very short piece originally entitled "The Cottage by the Tracks," Wolfe tells a sentimental story about a railroad engineer who finally discovers the reality of what he had thought to be an idyllic scene: a mother and a daughter who live in a country cottage near the tracks. For twenty years the engineer has waved to them as his train roared past, and now that he has retired, he comes to greet them in person. From the moment the older woman opens the door, he knows he should not have come. The idyllic scene he saw for years now fades before her suspicious attitude, her harsh voice, and her unsmiling face. The engineer is left disappointed and lonely, since the reality of the unfriendly cottage inhabitants precludes his hopes of friendship with them and indeed ruins his memory. If the engineer has any other life to go to, we are not told of it.

The subjects of loneliness and death coalesce in the story of the dying man in **"Dark in the Forest, Strange as Time."** Because he is ill, the man must go away alone for the winter to warmer climate; his wife promises that she will join him in the spring. Other people board the train, many of them talking and laughing as they leave. The dying man's wife settles him in the compartment, turns, and quickly leaves to join her young, robust lover who waits on the platform. This desertion is repeated in a lesser way with the American youth assigned to this same compartment. His good health and youth contrast sharply with the dying man's condition. And when the youth leaves the compartment for the conviviality of the dining car, the older man dies. He never fulfills his modest desire of knowing well just "vun field, vun hill, vun riffer."

As it appears in *From Death to Morning, No Door* is only the first segment of a much longer work of the same title, a short novel Max Perkins considered bringing out in a limited edition. He did not do so, however. In the original version, this first segment is subtitled "October 1931." Structurally, the brief version in *From Death to Morning* fails to develop a unified plot. The story begins in the luxurious apartment of the host, a rich man who has taken the requisite trip to Europe, collected a suitably impressive collection of sculpture and rare books, and lives among furnishings that are of "quiet but distinguished taste." His young mistress is at his side when his guest (a writer) relates painful glimpses of Brooklyn's low life. The host appears to listen, but he responds incongruously—"grand," "marvelous," "swell"—even though the young man tells of men who live in alleyways, beat their wives, and consider murder and robbery honest toil. In some detail the guest relates an episode about the loud demands of a lonely prostitute for her $3 payment. Her client refuses to pay her until, as he puts it, she will "staht actin' like a lady." Oblivious to the irony, the host continues to murmur "grand," and he envies the young man the rich experience of living among such people.

In the final pages Wolfe abandons the host, his mistress, the tinkling cocktail glasses, and the penthouse balcony to recount the haunting story of a priest's death. One of Wolfe's finest vignettes, this episode stays in the narrator's mind "like the haunting refrain of some old song—as it was heard and lost in Brooklyn." At evening, a man and a woman appear in their respective apartment windows to talk, their voices issuing banalities such as "Wat's t' noos sinct I been gone?" Although Father Grogan has died while this speaker was away, the priest's death is little more than a piece of news to be reported by one nameless character to another. It is not a grief to be shared, as one can see by the response to the news: "Gee, dat's too bad . . . I musta been away. Oddehwise I woulda hoid." Although the narrator is fully aware of the tragic implications of the priest's death, he makes no overt judgments about the insensitive speakers. The scene ends with a simple line: "A window closed, and there was silence." The casual announcement of Father Grogan's death and the equally casual reaction lead the narrator to consider time, in whose relentless power fame is lost, names are forgotten, and energy is wasted. Indeed, Father Grogan and all mankind die in darkness; they are remembered only superficially, if at all.

Related as it is to loneliness and violence, the theme of human dejection is present throughout these stories. The host may be wealthy, but he is a man who has never really lived. Indeed, Wolfe says this man measures time not by actual deeds but "in dimensions of fathomless and immovable sensations." His young guest lives in a run-down section of Brooklyn, an environment in stark contrast to his host's penthouse. When the young man describes the abject conditions of his neighborhood, the host considers such tales colorful and alive, unlike his own rich but dead world. The diverse reactions of these two men cannot be reconciled. The unrelieved loneliness, the failure of communication, and the narrator's search for certitude and meaning are problems introduced but left unresolved. Solutions are hinted at through brief passages whose imagery expresses a momentary harmony—"all of the colors of the sun and harbor, flashing, blazing, shifting in swarming motes, in an iridescent web of light and color for an instant on the blazing side of a proud white ship." The color flashes and then is gone, however; what remains for the narrator is unspeakable loneliness.

Like **"Only the Dead Know Brooklyn"** and **"Dark in the Forest, Strange as Time,"** this short version of *No Door* is a poignant examination of people who do not know how to express their deepest feelings, of people who do not or cannot share the burden or happiness of another, of people who are overwhelmed by loneliness.

In June 1935, *Modern Monthly* published Wolfe's story **"The Face of War."** Much of the plot stems from the summer of 1918, when Wolfe worked in the Norfolk shipyards. Like *Death the Proud Brother* (the story that follows **"The Face of War"** in *From Death to Morning*) this story focuses on four separate episodes, uses shocking violence, and emphasizes loneliness. In the first episode, Wolfe objectively relates the senseless beating of a black construction worker at Langley Field by the slouchy, shambling figure of a Southern white man who is egged on by his worthless office clerk. Wolfe's imagery suggests the bestial nature of these characters. The white boss wields a club "in his meaty hand," and his abnormal voice is described "as high thick throat-scream of blood-lust and murder." His office clerk creeps about "with rat's teeth bared" and "the coward's lust to kill." The clerk keeps a safe distance from the black man and urges his boss "to shoot the bastard if he tries to hit you." After the beating, the black man staggers about with a broken nose, buckling knees, and a ripped skull. He had seen the enemy coming and had half crouched, "ape-like" with arms like "great paws." His "white eyeballs" were now fixed, and he was ready to leap or run. The victim never utters a word and finally is left unconscious before his enemies. The "paunch-gut man" and his "white rat-face" clerk behind him beat the black man because the boss will be damned "if a Goddamn Nigger can talk back to a white man." This episode is particularly important since Wolfe does not include many black characters or often present racial issues and confrontations in his fiction. While he by no means attacks the subject with Faulkner's eye for its complexity, Wolfe was neither callous nor oblivious to the injustices that befell blacks.

Violence also erupts in the second episode of **"The Face of War"** when three young, friendly, blue-eyed, slow-talking Southern men appear. Having finished their construction job for the day, they are stopped abruptly by a foul-mouthed armed guard who accuses them of mischief. He pulls his gun, snarls, and stares at them with "eyes a-glitter, narrow as a snake." The guard's senseless verbal attack bewilders them. His crude words contrast sharply with the calm passage that had earlier described the boys as they walked near the water's edge, talking of home, college, and plans for the weekend.

Throughout the story the August sun beats mercilessly, and in the third episode it shines on the raw pine brothel set up hastily in wartime. Recruited from northern and midwestern cities, the prostitutes are neither alluring nor beautiful, and their aggressive behavior covers any display of tenderness. The men are nameless except for one called Georgia. Dressed in khaki uniforms, they stand in line, impatiently calling to the occupants of the tiny cubicles to "come on out an' give some of duh rest of us a chanct, f'r Chris' sake!" The prostitutes are rapacious, weary-eyed, and hard-visaged. Their obscene language contrasts ironically with another side of them, which Wolfe describes as a "fearful, almost timid desire to find friendship, gentleness, and even love among the rabble-rout of lost and ruined men to whom they minister." Georgia recognizes a prostitute named Margaret as a girl from home. As if they had met under proper social circumstances, she says, "How are all the folks down home? . . . Tell 'em that I sent my love." She prods the youth to promise that he will "ask for Margaret" next time, and then she is gone, "engulfed into the great vortex of the war." With this unseemly collection of men and women, Wolfe symbolizes the chaotic conditions of wartime, when virtue and life are easily destroyed.

The fourth episode concerns a paternalistic army lieutenant who curses at but also protects his black charges. The loading dock is suffocatingly hot as food and munitions of all sorts are put on the war-bound ship. Described by the lieutenant as "poor dumb suffering second cousins of an owl," the black troops are nearly left behind, since they have not been cleared of venereal disease. Because the lieutenant intervenes at the last minute, they are once again checked and this time declared clean by the ship's doctor and allowed to board. Clamoring their gratitude to the white man, they rush forward, bound for war and probable death.

"The Face of War" is filled with ironic juxtapositions. The tranquility of civilian life gives way to the harsh demands of wartime. Ships carry both food and weapons; the companionship of the troops contrasts with their eagerness to kill the enemy; and the raw, sensual, make-shift brothel is the opposite of the old life Margaret and Georgia knew back home in Hopewell. At the end of the story, the ship is loaded, shouting is replaced by silence, and the oppressive heat yields to "the breath of coolness." Death may await the ship's occupants, but for this night they remain in "the oncoming, undulant stride of all-enfolding and deep-breasted night."

One of the longest stories in *From Death to Morning, Death the Proud Brother,* tells of four deaths in New York City that the narrator witnesses. The first three are violent and occur in different locations at different times of the year. In a swift and horrifying accident, an Italian street vendor is killed by a truck on a spring day. For five pages, Wolfe presents details that characterize the nameless victim. His small pots and pans now are rubble, and his blood stains the sidewalk that a shop owner rushes out to clean. Business resumes and the street vendor drops from the memory of those who saw him daily. Related in six pages, the second death occurs in a new downtown building on an icy night in February when a drunken bum falls into a pile of iron beams and smashes his head. Wolfe then devotes twelve pages to the third death, that of a rivet catcher who misses the fiery steel tossed to his bucket and plunges to his death. The time is a May morning, ironically bright and sparkling. In contrast to the violence of these three is the fourth death, that of a nondescript man sitting on a subway bench; he collapses almost imperceptibly. Wolfe takes twenty-six pages to relate this final episode, which occurs at 1:00 A.M. in the Times Square station.

Each death involves the reactions of strangers. City people, the narrator thinks, accept death, "its violence, bloody mutilation, and horror calmly as one of the natural consequences of daily life." For example, a wealthy lady praises her chauffeur when he extricates her car quickly from the traffic snarl following the construction worker's death. To many onlookers, this dead man is a mere statistic: "Say—dat makes duh fourt' one on dat building—did yuh know dat?" Youthful onlookers are singularly unsympathetic, existing as testimony to "a new and desolate race of youth upon the earth that men had never known before—a race hard, fruitless, and unwholesome." They are simply curious and momentarily diverted; to them grief is "out of date and falsely sentimental." Older witnesses are equally insensitive and are interested only in repeating the news: "Sure! I seen it! I seen it! Dat's what I'm tellin' yuh!" Policemen, interns, and priests perform their respective functions because they must. In the end, the police tell the crowds, "Yuh gotta move. It's all oveh," more concerned with restoring the flow of traffic than with the fact of death. Such a sweeping judgment of city dwellers makes Wolfe's criticism somewhat stereotyped; nevertheless, although he was a city dweller all of his adult life, he did remain somewhat apart from the city and somewhat suspicious of its natives.

Regardless of their backgrounds, witnesses to violent, bloody, fatal accidents press forward to stare; however, people confronted with the quiet death of the man in the subway stand back timidly. "Stunned, awed, bewildered, and frightened," they see that a man's death can come so quietly that it is difficult to perceive. In a way, this death is the most frightening because it reminds us that we face death alone. The youthful narrator, moved by these tragedies, quotes the line from a Thomas Nashe poem on the plague year, "Brightness falls from the air." Nevertheless, the narrator's own youth and vigor make him hopeful about the future: "I knew I should see light once more and know new coasts and come into strange harbors, and see again, as I had once, new lands and morning." Such bursts of lyricism are poignantly juxtaposed to the realistic details of death and dying.

Stylistically, much of **Death the Proud Brother** is starkly realistic. For instance, when the callous young couple pass the corpse of the bum, they look at him and remark that perhaps he might join their late night excursion: "Who *else* can we get?" they remark. Further, as the policemen remove the dead man from the subway station, they grumble when the lifeless arms tumble off the stretcher, and they finally secure them with the man's own necktie. Once they reach the street, a taxi driver "lifted his cap obsequiously to the dead man. 'Taxi, sir! Taxi!'" The policemen laugh and swear. Concrete details enhance the powerful realism in many parts of the story. For example, we are told that the Italian vendor's cart held such things as cheap candies, a greasy-looking orange-juice bottle, cheap knives, and a small oil stove. Although similes, metaphors, apostrophes, hyperbole, and catalogues are used effectively in this story, the image of the clicking turnstiles in the subway emitting their dull wooden notes perhaps makes the most profound impression. Through those turnstiles scurry passengers who rush to meet their schedules, and their routine leaves little time even to observe that a man has died. The dead man in the subway will probably go to a pauper's grave, mourned and remembered by none. All four of these victims led commonplace lives, but each is given "for an instant the immortal dignities of death, proud death, even when it rested on the poorest cipher in the street."

By far the most significant selection in **From Death to Morning** is the long story (or novella) **The Web of Earth.** This piece, a complicated monologue delivered by Eliza Gant to her son during a visit to his Brooklyn Heights apartment, consists of tales linked weblike by the filament of association. A word or a sound in the tale she is telling sends Eliza to another story, but no matter how far the new directions takes her, she retraces her steps, finishing each tale in turn. She begins with her earliest recollections at age two and continues with events from childhood, marriage, motherhood, and old age. Her memories are almost all sad and painful, but her spirit is resilient. The first tale is of men she saw returning from the Civil War shoeless, hungry, aged; their joy in reunion is undercut by their lament for the dead. Her other childhood memories are of vicious tricks played by brothers, sisters, and cousins on each other; she does not relate any pleasant childhood adventures.

Recollections of W. O.'s imprudent behavior color her memories about married life. Once when Eliza was pregnant and W. O. had begun a drinking spree, she walked into Ambrose Radiker's saloon and demanded that he sell W. O. no more liquor. It was a request Radiker would gladly have granted if he could, since W. O. often attacked the saloon's light-skinned black worker. W. O. would swear the man was Chinese, a race of which he had an unexplained terror. The latter fact moves Eliza's attention to W. O.'s comic, but appalling, display in a Chinese laundry, where, accompanied by Eliza, Ben, and Luke, he retrieves his shirts after much arguing and many threats.

W. O. never does produce the much-called-for laundry ticket, to the frustration of the owner.

A lot of what Eliza tells concerns death: the Civil War victims; Bill Pentland, who announced the day and hour of his death, turned his head to the wall and fulfilled his prediction; W. O.'s first wife, Cynthia, who died of consumption; and the cold-blooded murders committed by Ed Mears and Lawrence Wayne. This latter episode includes details of the murderers' escape from prison, their separation and flight, and their later days out west. When Mears first escapes, he comes to the Gants' house, since he has no shoes and only W. O.'s will fit him. Throughout all these tales, Eliza's strength never wavers. She survives the births of children and drunken days of W. O.; she even lectures the murderer Ed Mears so effectively that he hands her his gun before he flees across the mountains.

The structure of the story defies analysis, so intricately are Eliza's tales interconnected. Rereading **The Web of Earth** impresses one with Wolfe's technical skill as well as with the stamina of the protagonist, an old woman who has survived much. The ending unifies the themes of suffering, endurance, and hope when after countless digressions, Eliza finally explains the mysterious words that opened the story: "Two . . . two . . . twenty . . . twenty." These words are a sign of the birth of the twins, Grover and Ben, twenty days after the evening Ed Mears came to beg shoes "at twenty minutes to ten o'clock on the seventeenth of October." (Yet both Grover and Ben, of course, died young.)

Eliza conveys present time by commenting on the sound of the ships in the Brooklyn harbor, and her son must keep pointing out to her the direction of those ships. This setting is new to her, and she has difficulty in getting her bearings. However, she is, in a sense, a compendium of human experience, and she admonishes her son, "My dear child, eat good food and watch and guard your health: it worries me to think of you alone with strangers." She herself has endured a life filled with sadness, loss, and disappointment. Yet when her contemporary, Miller Wright, weighed down with the burdens of the Depression, asks her, "Eliza, what are you going to do?" she says, "Do! . . . I'm going to pitch right in and work till I'm eighty and then . . . I'm goin' to cut loose and *just raise hell!*" Although her optimism is unfailing, the story is filled with tales and recollections that tell of death, despair, and loneliness.

While the pieces in **From Death to Morning** vary sharply in quality and while many are more accurately described as sketches than short stories, Wolfe emerges in this work as "a serious experimenter in fiction" (Holman, *Loneliness*, p. 14). *The Hills Beyond* (1941), the last book from Wolfe's posthumous papers edited and published by Edward Aswell, falls into three parts. First there are ten pieces ranging from two of Wolfe's best short stories ("**The Lost Boy**" and "**Chickamauga**") to short sketches such as "**No Cure for It**," which may have been written, Aswell contends, as early as 1929. The second part, entitled **The Hills Beyond,** is a ten-chapter fragment of a novel set in

Old Catawba (North Carolina). Although Wolfe goes back as far as September 1593 to relate the setting of the state of Old Catawba (a story similar to that of the Lost Colony in North Carolina), the fragment centers on the patriarch William "Bear" Joyner and his numerous offspring from two marriages. The final portion of the volume is a forty-page note that Edward Aswell wrote about his role as Wolfe's editor. Here Aswell comments on Wolfe's working habits during the last year of his life as well as on various pieces included in the volume. Unfortunately, except for the two excellent stories mentioned above, there is little in *The Hills Beyond* that enhances Wolfe's reputation. However, some critics have seen significance in Wolfe's returning to the North Carolina mountains for his setting and subject matter and others have praised his detached third-person narration in the novel fragment.

"The Lost Boy," by far the best piece in the volume, uses the Gant family again and focuses upon Grover's childhood in Part I, particularly his initiation experience in the Crockers' candy store. Paid in postage stamps for work he has done at Reed's drugstore, Grover, age eleven, cannot resist the smells of the candy and breaks his own resolve to stay away from the stingy Crockers. He goes into the store for 15 cents' worth of chocolate fudge. His stamps had been accepted as payment before, but now Crocker will not refund three one-cent stamps that represent an overpayment. The boy asks for their return, but he has an inherent respect for his elders. These old people who run the candy store are neither plump nor cheerful as such owners might be expected to be. Their hands are like bird talons; furthermore, they accuse Grover of misdealings and threaten to call the police about the postage stamps. Grover's embarrassment sends him to his father, who storms from his shop across the street into the Crockers' store. W. O. throws down the needed pennies, retrieves the boy's stamps, and delivers an invective against the Crockers worthy of the Old Testament prophets: "God has cursed you. He has made you lame and childless as you are—and lame and childless, miserable as you are, you will go to your grave and be forgotten!"

Through the images that begin the story, "light came and went and came again," Wolfe suggests the realization that Grover has come to. Adults, he had thought, are to be respected and depended upon. The Crockers, however, accuse him falsely and humiliate him. Although W. O. rescues him, afterwards he says only "Be a good boy" to a child who has never been anything but good. Grover struggles to regain his sense of reality and looks carefully at his physical surroundings: things are just as they have always been—the square, the fountain, the horse at the water trough, his father's shop. Irrevocable change, however, has come to Grover himself:

> But something had gone out of the day, and something had come in again. Out of the vision of those quiet eyes some brightness had gone, and into their vision had come some deeper color. He could not say, he did not know through what transforming shadows life had passed within that quarter hour. He only knew that something had been lost—something forever gained.

What Grover has lost is a great part of his childhood innocence; what he has gained is the inevitable experience of the world.

The remaining three parts of this story take place years after Grover's death at age twelve, as the mother, sister, and brother remember Grover and in so doing reveal much about themselves. Part II is Eliza's monologue as she talks to Eugene, telling him again about the trip to St. Louis long ago. In particular, she relates details about the Fair in St. Louis and remarks on Grover's maturity and manliness. She coyly recounts how she fooled the reporter from New Jersey who came to interview her about her famous son, Eugene the novelist. Eliza hinted to the reporter that Grover, not Eugene, was her brightest son. Her bragging memories mingle and reveal much of her past. At the end of this section, Wolfe returns to the pervasive idea of time and loss as Eliza says, "It was so long ago, but when I think of it, it all comes back, as if it happened yesterday. Now all of you have either died or grown up and gone away, and nothing is the same as it was then."

Part III, "The Sister," is Helen's monologue. Like the Ancient Mariner, Eugene's older sister is compelled to tell her story, and she tells Eugene about the time in St. Louis that led to Grover's illness and death. Now in middle age, Helen realizes that her ambitions are unfulfilled—she will never be a famous singer in an opera house. Since Eugene has been to college and reads books, he should have answers to her questions. What happens, she wants to know, to all of our expectations and dreams? Wolfe uses a photograph of the Gant family when they were young and full of plans to symbolize the dreams of youth. Helen ponders the photograph; turning to Eugene, she asks, "Does it happen to us all, to everyone? . . . Grover and Ben, Steve, Daisy, Luke and me—all standing there before the house on Woodson Street in Altamont—there we are, and you see the way we were—and now it all gets lost. What is it, anyway, that people lose?"

Part IV, "The Brother," shows Eugene's attempt to answer Helen's questions. As a grown man, Eugene goes to St. Louis. Working from fragments of childhood memories, he finds the house where the Gants lived during the summer of 1904, the summer of the World's Fair, the summer that Grover died. Inside the house, Eugene peers into a mirror at the bottom of the stairs and momentarily enters the past. He hears Grover's voice, but the recapturing of this childhood experience lasts only for an instant. The "lost boy" of the title is not just Grover, who was lost through death at an early age. It is also Eugene, who learns that one cannot recapture the past save for a fleeting moment. Helen must face the fact that the dreams of childhood often are unrealized; Eugene learns that none of the past can be recaptured, and Helen will learn this too. From all four points of view in this story, Wolfe explores the idea of time and loss and most effectively shows the regret adults have for the past and many of its associations.

"Chickamauga" is the first-person narrative of a Civil War veteran who will be 95 on his next birthday. Although the digressions are not as numerous as Eliza's in

The Web of Earth, several features in these two works are similar. Like Eliza, the old veteran has a remarkable memory. He recalls that, seventy-five years before, on August 7, 1861, "at seven-thirty in the morning . . . I started out from home and walked the whole way to Clingman." There he joined the Twenty-ninth Regiment and headed for battle. Wolfe effectively uses the Civil War as subject matter and renders experience other than his own. The narrator and his friend, Jim Weaver, march off to war; Jim resents every day that keeps him away from home and his love, Martha Patton. Now the old man, Jim's friend so many years ago, describes a day of battle: "The bloodiest fightin' that was ever knowed, until that cedar thicket was soaked red with blood, and than was hardly a place left in thar where a sparrer could have perched." The narrator describes in homely terms the difficulty of taking Missionary Ridge: it was "like tryin' to swim the Mississippi upstream on a boneyard mule." When Jim Weaver dies in battle, the narrator retrieves from Jim's pockets his watch, his pocket knife, and Martha Patton's letters. Like the sister in **"The Lost Boy,"** the narrator is bewildered at this turn of events: "Hit's funny how hit all turns out— how none of hit is like what we expect." His friend is dead; it is the narrator who lives, goes home, and marries Martha Patton.

In comparison to **"The Lost Boy"** and **"Chickamauga,"** the remaining stories and sketches in *The Hills Beyond* are slight indeed. **"No Cure for It"** is a brief sketch about the growing pains of a gangly boy. Here Wolfe revives names from *Look Homeward, Angel*—Eliza, Gant, Dr. McGuire—and the material in this sketch is similar in tone to that first novel. **"Gentlemen of the Press,"** a short piece that was probably written in 1930, uses the devices of a play script to designate speakers, time, and setting. The cub reporter, Red, spins an outlandish tale about Abraham Lincoln being a descendant of Napoleon, and the older men listen with amused tolerance. Red's earnestness is a part of his youth. His ridiculous tale, however, is juxtaposed with reports coming in over the wire services telling of new French casualties in World War I.

"A Kinsman of His Blood" is similar to the Bascom Pentland material in *Of Time and the River.* In this story, Wolfe changes Pentland's name to an earlier version— Bascom Hawke—and tells about one of Bascom's children, who changes his identity and loses touch with reality, talking of nonexistent love affairs. **"The Return of the Prodigal"** is in two parts: "The Thing Imagined," which is an imagined account by Eugene Gant of his coming home, and "The Real Thing," which is a realistic account of Eugene's return to Altamont. In the second part, Wolfe uses many details of his 1937 trip to Asheville, including a street shooting he witnessed in nearby Burnsville, North Carolina, while he was en route.

The brief sketch **"On Leprechauns"** belongs to the George Webber material, and **"Portrait of a Literary Critic"** is Wolfe's satirical picture of the inept type of critic that he loathed. **"The Lion at Morning,"** which belongs to the pre-Depression sections of *You Can't Go Home Again,* portrays James Wyman, Sr., a wealthy banker who begins his day amid routine luxury and unexpected scandal. **"God's Lonely Man"** is Wolfe's personal anatomy of loneliness. Aswell suggests that his version went through several drafts and at one point had the title "On Loneliness at Twenty-three."

Besides these stories and sketches, this collection contains the first six chapters of a novel that was to be called by the title Aswell used for the posthumous collection of fragments *The Hills Beyond.* These chapters tell the stories of George Webber's maternal ancestors, the Joyners, whose history begins with William "Bear" Joyner. Wolfe traces the founding of the state, Old Catawba, and particularly satirizes the desire among some of these residents to trace their ancestry:

> In the South, particularly, this preoccupation seems to absorb most of the spare energies of the female population for it is an axiom of Southern life that a woman without "family" is nothing. A woman may be poor; she may be abysmally ignorant (and usually is); she may have read nothing, seen nothing, gone nowhere; she may be lazy, nasty, vain, arrogant, venomous, and dishonest; her standards of morality, government, justice may not differ one whit from that of the lynching mob: but if she can assert, loudly and without challenge, that her "family" is older (and therefore better) than other families, then her position in the community is unquestioned, she is the delicate flower of "Southern culture," she must not be "talked back to"—she is, in short, "a lady."

Wolfe's satire includes The Society of the Sons and Daughters of the Aborigines, who would grasp dueling pistols if anyone hinted at a drop of black blood in their ancestry. Just as fervently, however, they claim kin with Indians, "their dusky ancestors of some two and a half centuries before."

William "Bear" Joyner is Wolfe's legendary character, a descendant of Mike Fink, Davy Crockett, and Paul Bunyan, and the Yankee peddler. Extraordinary in every way, Bear founded a large clan. His first wife, Martha Creasman, died in childbirth, and the fates of their surviving children (Zacharias, Hattie, Robert, Theodore, and Rufe) are the primary subject matter of the fragment. Even though Bear's second wife bore him "fourteen or sixteen children . . . there were so many of them, and their destinies were so diverse, that even their number has been disrupted," it is the first set of children who are considered in the narrative. A lawyer like his brother Robert, the colorful Zacharias becomes governor of Old Catawba and later a United States senator. In whatever office he holds, he is generally effective. He exposes social climbers by telling their true history: many have descended from escaped convicts and are themselves people "raised on hawg and hominy." Wolfe perhaps reflects his own distrust of lawyers when he describes them here as "that articulate tribe which was to breed and multiply with such astonishing proliferation during the next century." The assumption that lawyers will enter politics is borne out in Zacharias; however, his brother Robert has no desire to "get into politics." Robert is content to remain a lawyer; his refusing the gains that politics can bring leads people to say that "he was a fine man, of course, but a little queer."

Although Wolfe's accomplishments are considerable if one evaluates all of his work, most careful readers nevertheless judge him to be a failed artist.

—*Elizabeth Evans*

The most elaborate satire in the fragment concerns the brother Theodore. Unable to pass the bar, Theodore marries a "Drumgoole of the Virginia Drumgooles," produces several children, and operates a "military school," the Joyner Heights Military Academy. Zacharias calls Joyner Heights "Hogwart Heights" and derides his brother's every endeavor, especially the pretentious military training provided at the school when the Civil War is imminent. Zack declares that "they had a devil of a time getting those twenty-seven pimply boys straightened up as straight as they could get—which is to say, about as straight as a row of crooked radishes." But when the war comes, those same pimply boys march off and many die. Theodore becomes more foolish after the war. Although he has no legitimate military claim, he is now Colonel Joyner and bears himself, the narrator says, as if "a whole regiment of plumed knights [were] in his own person."

The final four chapters of the fragment center on Robert Joyner, who lost a leg in the Civil War—a fact, that his son Edward learns from a history book. Reading an account of the Battle of Spottsylvania, Edward comes upon the name Joyner in a passage that ends, "among others, I saw Joyner among his gallant mountaineers firing and loading until he was himself shot down and borne away by his own men, his right leg so shattered by a minie ball that amputation was imperative." Bewildered, the boy takes the book to his mother and asks, "What the book says— is that father?" Her answer comes quickly: "Your father is so proud, and in some ways a child himself. He wouldn't tell you. He could not bear to have his son think that his father was a cripple." Now a judge, Robert Joyner is impatient with the old veterans who hang around the courthouse hoping for sympathy. Robert befriends John Webber, a stranger to Libya Hill who arrives with the construction crew of the hotel. Webber's reputation as a fine workman earns him respect, and Wolfe seems to pair him with Robert Joyner, implying that these two men share many of the same good qualities.

The fragment ends with Edward Joyner, now fifty, recalling the day years ago when he discovered that his father had been a Civil War hero. That discovery in turn explains his father's impatience long ago with the hangers on from the war who haunted the courthouse for undeserved sympathy. With Edward's recollection, Wolfe abandons the objective narration that characterizes the fragment and concludes with a meditation on time that is, like so many of Wolfe's lyric passages, quite effective: "And time still passing . . . time passing like river flowing . . . knowing that this earth, this time, this life, are stranger than a dream."

The material in *The Hills Beyond* deserves attention primarily because it shows the variety of writing styles Wolfe tried. But the six chapters of the title fragment are not promising, and certainly the fragment provides no evidence, as some have claimed, that Wolfe's writing had taken a turn away from the autobiographical style of the earlier work. Much material here derives from the folklore tradition and also from Wolfe's own early work. Furthermore, although satire is prevalent throughout the fragment and in some of the stories, it lacks the power to chastise and reform. Except for making **"The Lost Boy"** and **"Chickamauga"** more readily available in this volume, Edward Aswell did little to advance Wolfe's reputation by publishing *The Hills Beyond,* a book that contains much mediocre writing.

In 1961, Scribner's published *The Short Novels of Thomas Wolfe,* a volume edited by C. Hugh Holman, whose introduction and headnotes, along with Wolfe's texts, constitute an indispensable part of the Wolfe canon. Wolfe had difficulty determining what a short story should be, and he agonized over the proper form of a novel. Only a handful of his short stories are first rate, and among his novels only *Look Homeward, Angel* achieves satisfactory form. However, he wrote some of his most successful work in the intermediate-length form of the novella (roughly 20,000 to 30,000 words). In addition to the five short novels in this edition, Holman mentions three others. **"The Train and the City,"** a 12,000-word story, appeared in *Scribner's Magazine* in May 1934. The longer and more successful work *Death the Proud Brother* appeared in the June 1934 issue of the same publication. *Boom Town,* which was published in the May 1934 issue of the *American Mercury,* satirizes the real estate craze that swept Asheville before the Depression. Like the previous two works, *Boom Town* was drawn from the large manuscript Wolfe was writing; furthermore, this long story was the first of Wolfe's work that Elizabeth Nowell placed after she became his agent. The five short novels that Holman edited represent Wolfe's best work except for *Look Homeward, Angel* (see additional discussions of these short novels earlier in this chapter). Each had been published in magazines in the 1930s, and except for *The Web of Earth* all were then placed in various sections of Wolfe's last three novels. At the time, these magazine publications provided a much-needed source of income for Wolfe; indeed, one of the short novels, *A Portrait of Bascom Hawke,* tied for the *Scribner's Magazine* short-novel contest. Wolfe split the $5,000 prize with John Herrmann. Based on Wolfe's uncle Henry Westall, Bascom Hawke is Wolfe's most eccentric character. After *A Portrait of Bascom Hawke* appeared in *Scribner's Magazine,* the material it contains was widely dispersed into various sections of *Of Time and the River.* Although the appearance of Bascom in the novel is most interesting, the full short novel presents him, his family, and his co-workers more colorfully and appealingly. The unity gained in the short novel form was almost totally lost when the work was broken apart.

The longest of the five novellas, *The Web of Earth,* appeared in *Scribner's Magazine* in July 1932. When he included this Joycean interior monologue in the collection *From Death to Morning,* Wolfe changed the protagonist's name from Delia Hawke to Eliza Gant and made a few minor additions. Thus, unlike the other titles in the Holman edition of the short novels, *The Web of Earth* has always been readily available in its original form.

Until the Holman edition appeared, however, *No Door* had never been published in its original four parts, which total some 31,000 words. Since this version was much too long for a single issue, *Scribner's Magazine* published it as two long stories, the first entitled *No Door,* and the second **"The House of the Far and Lost."** Later the first episode of the original version was used as a short story in *From Death to Morning* and **"The House of the Far and Lost"** was used virtually unchanged in *Of Time and the River.* The remainder of the total 31,000-word version was worked into five sections of *Of Time and the River* and one section of *You Can't Go Home Again.* Without question the discussion of the Coulsons, an English family, is the most interesting part of *No Door.* Wolfe presents the alcoholic husband, the wife who gazes out upon the foggy cold weather and declares that in her heart Italy is home, and the daughter, Edith, who in young womanhood resigns herself to a bleak family existence. When Eugene urges Edith to come away with him to America, he declares to her, "Failure and defeat won't last forever." To these words Edith responds, "Sometimes they do." Some secret in the past surrounds this family, but Eugene never learns what it is. Furthermore, he never comes to know his fellow boarders, the three men who squeeze into their small car each day, speed to their factory work, and spend every evening performing American jazz. These men seem compelled to play, yet they do not seem to enjoy the music. The leader, Captain Nicholl, has a mutilated arm; his disfigurement suggests the spiritual wound in the Coulson family. They may be a family that lives beneath a common roof, but each lives a separate life.

The last two short novels in the Holman edition are convincing evidence of Wolfe's growing social awareness and of his ability to write direct, simple, and objective prose. *I Have a Thing to Tell You* was Wolfe's awakening to the perils of Nazi Germany. He portrays Berlin no longer as a city of enchantment and friends but instead as a "world hived of four million lives, of hope and fear and hatred, anguish and despair, of love, of cruelty and devotion." Wolfe insisted that this work was not intended as propaganda, and to prevent such accusations he refused to allow a Yiddish translation.

As many critics have pointed out, Wolfe was fortunate that his first publisher had a monthly publication; indeed, *Scribner's Magazine* brought out much of Wolfe's work. His stories and short novels that appeared in this maga-

zine gave Wolfe needed income and kept his name before the reading public, thus enhancing his critical reputation. It was fitting that the May 1939 issue of *Scribner's Magazine* published one of the last pieces Wolfe wrote, *The Party at Jack's,* some nine months after Wolfe's death. The editor commented on Wolfe's career and included in the issue's preliminary pages a letter from Max Perkins, who had written, "The credit for Thomas Wolfe belongs to Scribner's if to anyone." Heeding Perkins's suggestion, the editor also included a photograph of the recently completed oil portrait of Wolfe painted by Perkins's son-in-law, Douglas Gorsline.

The Party at Jack's was the last piece of Wolfe's unpublished work that *Scribner's Magazine* brought out; in the same issue, however, "An Angel on the Porch" was reprinted with this editorial note:

> Thomas Wolfe's **"An Angel on the Porch"** was published in the August 1929 issue of *Scribner's Magazine* with these words . . . "The first work of a new writer about whom much will be heard this fall." That was almost exactly nine years before Wolfe's death. We are republishing **"An Angel on the Porch"** in this issue as an appropriate companion for *The Party at Jack's.* The first and we are sorry to say, the last Thomas Wolfe to appear in *Scribner's Magazine.*

Like *I Have a Thing to Tell You,* this final short novel is a statement of strong social concern written in taut, objective prose. The reader who assumes that Wolfe's writing was always lengthy, discursive, and laden with rhetorical devices probably would not guess these last two short novels to be his work. Wolfe spent much of the summer of 1937 finishing *The Party at Jack's;* much of this work was done while he stayed in a cabin near his Asheville home for several weeks. Holman considers it one of Wolfe's "most impressive accomplishments" (*Short Novels,* p. xvi).

As previously discussed, the social satire in *The Party at Jack's* focuses on the absurd performance of Piggy Logan and his circus as well as on the wealthy residents of a luxury Park Avenue apartment building. This short novel also includes Wolfe's invective against pompous literary critics, particularly in the character Seamus Malone. In addition, the action places George Webber in the home of his mistress, Esther Jack. Here he watches her fulfill the roles required of her without ever entirely ignoring him. For George, she is the ideal woman, as appealing in middle age as she is in the portrait painted of her when she was twenty-five. The portrait hangs in Jack's apartment and during the party several guests comment that both portrait and subject have lasting beauty and grace. Of this George Webber is certain.

Thomas Wolfe did not live to have a second act as a writer; critics continue to speculate whether or not his stylistic excesses might have been curtailed had he continued to write throughout a long life. Although the published corpus is fairly substantial, it is by no means of uniform worth. Wolfe's reputation in the 1980s suffers because his major works are severely flawed. He suffers too because many people, discouraged by the length and the obvious indulgences in style, do not read him, except perhaps for *Look Homeward, Angel.* The charges of egotism, of autobiographical dependence, of rhetorical excess, and of lack of narrative control are made again and again. And although Wolfe's accomplishments are considerable if one evaluates all of his work, most careful readers nevertheless judge him to be a failed artist.

Suzanne Stutman   (essay date 1985)

SOURCE: "Technique in 'The Child by Tiger': Portrait of a Mature Artist," in *The South Carolina Review,* Vol. 18, No. 1, Fall, 1985, pp. 83-8.

[*In the following essay, Stutman praises the artistic technique of "The Child by Tiger," in which she observes Wolfe "fashioned a notable artistic statement about one man's quest for selfhood and mankind's inescapable and tragic inhumanity."*]

Almost fifty years ago, Bernard DeVoto stated in his famous—or perhaps infamous—essay, that "Genius is Not Enough." DeVoto, in essence, was accusing Thomas Wolfe of using only the characters, settings, and events which occurred within his own life, thus limiting his work to mere autobiography instead of using these elements to create inspired fiction. The implication which persists to this day sustains the position that Wolfe's work at its best represents a kind of "happy accident" accomplished by some miraculous or haphazard circumstance. In addition, it is perceived that all of Wolfe's manuscripts required some outside editing, of which Wolfe himself was incapable: a Perkins, if you will, to cut and paste together the best of Thomas Wolfe, leaving the extraneous and purple passages forgotten on the cutting room floor. A close study of the short story **"Child by Tiger"** refutes such allegations. Indeed, in this story of a black man's rampage through a small Southern town and the ultimate complicity of evil he evokes in the white townspeople, Wolfe has fashioned a tale of great artistry and technical perfection. His careful treatment of character, point of view, imagery and theme come flawlessly together to present his own "meditation on history." In **"Child by Tiger"** Wolfe has fashioned a notable artistic statement about one man's quest for selfhood and mankind's inescapable and tragic inhumanity.

Wolfe's story about a black man who goes berserk and kills several people, black and white, before he is himself killed, took many years to evolve into its final form. As did Styron some thirty years later, in *Confessions of Nat Turner,* Wolfe used an actual occurrence as the backbone for his tale. In 1906, when Wolfe was six years old, Willie Harris, alias James Harvie, came to the town of Asheville. After buying a secondhand gun, Harris proceeded on a rampage through the town, killing five people. (Dick Prosser, even more dramatically, killed nine.) This event caused quite a stir in the quiet little town of Asheville. It was

recorded in *The Asheville Citizen* from November 14 to 16, 1906. It is possible that as a child Wolfe remembered viewing the riddled body of the Negro as it was displayed morbidly in a shopkeeper's window. In addition to using this information as part of his story about the black man, he also made reference to the incident at the end of *You Can't Go Home Again,* when recounting the capture of "Fuss and Fidget," the nervous little Jewish man who attempted to escape from Nazi Germany: "This is the tragedy of man's cruelty and his lust for pain—the tragic weakness which corrupts him, which he loathes, yet he cannot cure. As a child, George had seen it on the faces of men standing before a window of a shabby little undertaker's place, looking at the bloody, riddled carcass of a Negro which the mob had caught and killed" (692-693).

One thing is relatively certain. As Richard Kennedy states, the major fabric of the story came from Wolfe's imagination, for "Wolfe had only heard the story; he did no research" and had probably never even seen the newspaper articles describing the event (321, n. 13).

The complex character of Dick Prosser which evolved was, according to Floyd Watkins, a composite of three black men: first, Willie Harris; second, a beloved Negro janitor of the Bingham Academy in Asheville, admired for his "intelligence, good humor, devotion, meticulousness and humility"; and third, the Reverend Robert Parker Rumley, a fanatic black preacher who preached the same sermon, "De Dry Bones in De Valley," over and over again (108, 109). This sermon was transcribed and printed in Asheville in 1896, and is quoted in part by Dick when, in a moment of almost mystical transfixion, he prophesies to the awestruck boys the coming of the Day of Judgment.

It took a full seven years for the story of Dick Prosser to evolve into its final form. As early as 1930, Wolfe mentioned a black man in a letter to Perkins in regard to his then current work-in-progress: ". . . in the chapter called 'The Congo,' the wandering negro who goes crazy and kills people and is finally killed by the posse as he crosses the creek, is known to David, the boy . . ." (174-175). Originally, Wolfe had intended his black man to be a much less complex character than he later became, one who would primarily depict the savage nature akin to the character in Vachel Lindsay's "The Congo." In his Notebook in 1930 he mentions the black man in degrading animalistic terms as "Nigger Dick—the coon who is hunted by the posse" (Kennedy and Reeves, 518). By 1933, the story was mentioned in the *Notebooks,* in one of Wolfe's legendary lists, as "The Nigger Killer" (Kennedy and Reeves, 607).

Other circumstances occurred to influence Wolfe and to alter his method of composition before he once again took up the material concerning the rebel black man. In 1935, Wolfe had begun a new method of composition which allowed him greater technical control over his material. He would dictate to a secretary, then revise the triple spaced typewritten manuscripts by adding or deleting information, writing between the lines and in the margins. After the secretary once again retyped his new revisions, he would either refile them for later use, or, with the help of

Elizabeth Nowell, reword those which seemed to possess enough original integrity to be used as short stories. His trip to Nazi Germany in 1936 certainly served to enhance Wolfe's social awareness, as he became increasingly preoccupied with the theme of man's inhumanity to man—a theme which pervades much of his later literature. His empathy for Jesse Owens, whom he had cheered in the Olympic Games, also served to deepen his awareness of the suffering which man inflicts upon his fellow man. From January 1 until July 1, 1937, Wolfe worked upon his story of Dick Prosser. What had begun as "The Congo" seven years earlier had evolved into his greatest short story, and the one for which he was paid the highest amount: a staggering $1200.00 when it was published by *The Saturday Evening Post* on September 11, 1937. In addition, with other revisions, including a change from the first person to the third person point of view, this story later took its place in Part I of *The Web and the Rock* as one of the episodes in the early life of George Webber, the young seer who brings together in Whitmanesque fashion all of the events which happen in the life of a small Southern town.

As early as 1930, Wolfe had fixed on the general narrative method of his work-in-progress, which incorporated the earliest framework of his future tale as well:

> "Now the general movement of the book is
> from the universal to the individual:
> in Part I we have a symphony of many voices
> . . . through which a thread begins to
> run . . . we have a character which appears
> at first only as a window, an eye, a . . .
> seer . . ." (Nowell, 174).

The unravelling action, the complex and mysterious personality of Dick, the growing awareness of evil which subtly enters the lives of these innocent and uninitiated boys, is all filtered through the consciousness of the young narrator. As "seer" he is able to record events objectively, as a sensitive "eye" he sees and responds to all of the subtle contradictions involved in Dick's complex and provocative personality, while also recording his own sensitive perceptions and the reactions of the crowd around him. It is through the narrator's all-encompassing, ever-expanding awareness that we experience the story, a point of view so finely perceived and described that we are almost within the mind of the central character and the action of the tale.

Because of their innocence, the boys are able to accept Dick not only as the stereotyped "darkie" the adults assign him to be, but as their friend. Dick fills an important gap in their lives, becoming like a kindly, all-knowing, and all-powerful big brother. He plays football with them, and coaches them at boxing, seeing to it "with his quick wrathfulness, his gentle and persuasive tact," that they don't hurt one another. They are proud when the grownups as well realize that Dick is exceptional—no ordinary "darkie": "He could cook, he could tend the furnace, he could do odd jobs, he was handy at carpentry, he knew how to drive a car—in fact, it seemed to the boys that there was very little that Dick Prosser could not do." Mr. Shepper-

ton himself declared that Dick was "the smartest darkie that he'd ever known." In addition, he "knew his place," and had gone around to the Shepperton's back door to present his qualifications. He was willing, he modestly stated from the start, to do any job for any wage. Indeed, he delivered to his masters more than they bargained for.

In "Child by Tiger" Wolfe has fashioned a notable artistic statement about one man's quest for selfhood and mankind's inescapable and tragic inhumanity.

—Suzanne Stutman

Dick is a good man, a religious man, a meticulous and orderly former military man. He exhibits in all he does a sense of reason, a rage for order and discipline. When the boys, Dick's trusted friends, are granted entrance to his immaculate whitewashed room, his few possessions are neatly in place, and on the table George observes with reassurance that "there was always just one object—an old Bible with a limp cover, almost worn out with constant use, for Dick was a deeply religious man." And yet, there seems to be another side to this mysterious black man, a side which frightens the children without their knowing why: "He went too softly, at too swift a pace. He was there upon them sometimes like a cat," and at times he appears mysteriously, "like a shadow." Indeed, Dick begins to evolve throughout the tale as a kind of mysterious doppleganger, representing symbolically the shadowy other, lurking, ever ready to leap, within the dark hemisphere of man's unconscious. At times, after reading the Bible, he would enter into a trance-like state, translating their white man's familiar and comfortable religion into an alien form:

> There would be times when he would almost moan when he talked to them, a kind of hymnal chant, a religious ecstasy, some deep intoxication of the spirit, and that transported him. For the boys, it was a troubling and bewildering experience. . . . there was something in it so dark and strange and full of a feeling they could not fathom . . . and the trouble in their minds and in their hearts remained. . . .

Then he would speak mysteriously of the Day of Judgment:

> O young white fokes. . . . de day is comin' when He's comin' on dis earth again to sit in judgment. . . . O white fokes, white fokes—de Armageddon day's a-comin', white fokes—and de dry bones in de valley.

The boys would cast aside their shadowy apprehensions, however, as they listened to Dick singing "in his voice so full of Africa" their own, familiar hymns, just as they cast aside their misgivings when they enter into Dick's unlocked room and find the rifle. Next to the Bible on the table, in contrast to its reassuring image, they see the black box containing one hundred rounds of ammunition. Suddenly, Dick is upon them "like a cat . . . a shadow . . . his eyes . . . small and red as rodents." He reassures the boys that he has bought the rifle so that he can take them shooting on Christmas morning. Swearing to keep Dick's secret, they enter into the conspiracy, what becomes to their horror as the tale unravels, a guilty partnership of evil into which, ultimately, all of the characters, old and young, black and white, are united.

With careful use of imagery, characterization, and symbolism, Wolfe had laid the allegorical groundwork for his tale. Through his description of the actual insurrection and the reaction of the townspeople, he is free to develop even further his contrasting themes and images of good versus evil, black versus white, man versus beast, North versus South, and finally, known versus unknown. George Webber "went to sleep upon this mystery, lying in the darkness listening to that exultancy of storm, to that dumb wonder, that enormous and attentive quietness of snow, with something dark and jubilant in his soul that he could not utter." The snow, coming from the alien North, brings with it its own "white mystery." Through this oxymoron Wolfe establishes the polarity, the complex worlds of contradiction that exist not only within Dick, but within all mankind: "In every man there are two hemispheres of light and dark, two worlds discreet, two countries of his soul's adventure."

Imagery of sound is added to the imagery of light and dark when George awakens at two in the morning to the sound of the alarm. The town is "ablaze with light from top to bottom," as the bell speaks an alien tongue similar to that mysterious moaning jargon of Dick's religious chanting, "a savage, brazen tongue calling the town to action, warning mankind against the menace of some peril, secret, dark, unknown, greater than fire or flood could ever be." Perhaps, then, this is the judgment day which Dick had prophesied. "It's that nigger!" Nebraska Crane shouts. Randy, his face "white as a sheet," tells George "It's Dick! . . . They say he killed four people." Suddenly they become aware of their complicity in evil: ". . . two white-faced boys, aware now of the full and murderous significance of the secret they had kept, the confidence they had not violated, with a sudden sense of guilt and fear as if somehow the crime lay on their shoulders." Having established this pattern, or melody, or imagery, Wolfe can now with a few deft strokes establish his central theme: that of man's common propensity for both good and evil. As the boys "lit" out for town, they noticed that every house was "lighted up." Even the hospital was "ablaze" with light. Against the backdrop of artificial lights, the imagery reverses itself: the white men who form the mob are transformed into "the dark figures of running men across the white carpet of the square."

Animal imagery, as well as imagery of blood and sound and darkness, fuse together as the violence of the black man is answered by the reaction of the white mob: "From that crowd came a low and growing mutter, an ugly and insistent growl" and George hears ". . . the blood note in that foggy growl." As if in response to this sound from the mob, the boys hear behind them "one of the most savagely mournful and terrifying sounds that night could know. . . . the savagery of blood was in it and the savagery of man's guilty doom was in it too" as the hounds raced "across the snow-white darkness of the Square." Reaching a crescendo of violence the lynch mob "writhing angrily now, like a snake" lets out a "bloody roar" and breaks the window of Joyner's store to loot for guns. The storm from the North which brought the evil gust of snow is "answered" by the storm of violence with which the mob hurls itself upon the Square, until it "looked as if a hurricane had hit it." Black and white have been fused now, in a corresponding cacophony of violence.

It is only after this dramatic comingling of imagery has reached its climax that Wolfe allows the narrator and the reader to piece together the chronology of events. That Dick was having an affair with Pansy Harris, "the Negro wench," was unimportant, for "adultry among Negroes was assumed." As his first black victim fell upon the snowy ground "a huge dark stain of blood soaked-snow widened out around him." Dick proceeds on his mission of destruction methodically, like an angel of death, destroying anyone in his path, white or black. As more and more information is filtered through, the town intensifies its waking nightmare. George notes that "there was no more sleep for anyone that night. Black Dick had murdered sleep."

By the creek, when he knows he has been surrounded, Dick responds as mysteriously as before. Instead of running for freedom, as a caged animal would do, Dick reacts like a soldier preparing to sleep for the night: ". . . and, as quietly and methodically as if he were seated in his army barracks, he unlaced his shoes, took them off, placed them together neatly at his side, and then stood up like a soldier, erect, in his bare feet, and faced the mob." Dick restores to himself his sense of quiet and military order. He chooses to die not like a cornered beast, but with dignity, like a man. The mob, in an orgy of violence, riddles the body, again and again. "It was in this way," George notes, "bullet riddled, shot to pieces, open to the vengeful and the morbid gaze of all, that Dick came back to town." After the body has been placed in the undertaker's window, the boys, who had been Dick's closest friends, come to look at the body with the rest of the town. In so doing, by participating in the dark and morbid curiosity of the crowd, their initiation into evil, into man's archetypal heart of darkness, has been complete.

> And something had come into life—into their lives—
> that they had never known about before. It was a kind
> of shadow, a poisonous blackness filled with bewildered
> loathing. The snow would go, they knew . . . and all
> of this would be as if it had never been. . . . For they
> would still remember the old dark doubt and loathing
> of their kind, of something hateful and unspeakable in
> the souls of men. They knew that they would not forget.

Dick has transcended his blackness to become the unifying symbol of all mankind: man, mysterious, ineffable, containing within himself the paradoxical polarity of good and evil:

> . . . a symbol of man's evil innocence, and the token of his mystery. A projection of his own unfathomed quality, a friend, a brother, and a mortal enemy, an unknown demon—our loving friend, our mortal enemy, two worlds together—a tiger and a child.

Works Cited

Kennedy, Richard S. *The Window of Memory: The Literary Career of Thomas Wolfe.* Chapel Hill, NC: University of North Carolina Press, 1962.

Kennedy, Richard S. and Paschal Reeves. *The Notebooks of Thomas Wolfe,* Vol. II. Chapel Hill NC: University of North Carolina Press, 1970.

Nowell, Elizabeth. *Thomas Wolfe.* New York: Doubleday and Company, 1960.

Watkins, Floyd C. *Thomas Wolfe's Characters: Portraits from Life.* Norman, OK: University of Oklahoma Press, 1957.

Wolfe, Thomas. *You Can't Go Home Again.* New York: Harper and Brothers, 1940.

James D. Boyer (essay date 1987)

SOURCE: "A Reevaluation of Wolfe's 'Only the Dead Know Brooklyn'," in *The South Carolina Review,* Vol. 20, No. 1, Fall, 1987, pp. 45-9.

[*In the following essay, Boyer argues that "Only the Dead Know Brooklyn" effectively presents a message urging readers to experience life with intensity rather than to attempt to experience all things in life.*]

When Leslie Field assembled and edited *Thomas Wolfe: Three Decades of Criticism* in 1968, he noted in his introduction that little criticism had been written on Wolfe's short fiction. *Three Decades,* in fact, includes analyses of only three Wolfe stories. One of these analyses is Edward Bloom's short essay on **"Only the Dead Know Brooklyn."** That story, often anthologized, is a fine one, capable of illustrating through its structure and its theme much about Wolfe's growth as a short story writer. Unfortunately Bloom gets things jumbled in his analysis, obscuring what is an important theme for Wolfe and an important recognition for those who wish to assess his development. Bloom's analysis has stood unchallenged in the literature for eighteen years. I should like here to reexamine the story, to clarify Wolfe's theme, and to explain why this story is especially useful in understanding Wolfe's development.

"Only The Dead Know Brooklyn" was first published in *The New Yorker* in 1935, one of thirteen Wolfe stories placed in nine different magazines that year. Often these stories show the extent of his experimentation with form in ways that the novels don't. Here the most striking formal aspect is the point of view. The reader may recall that all of Wolfe's novels and the fragmentary **Hills Beyond** come to us through third-person narration, almost always through the angle of vision of the Eugene Gant-George Webber protagonist; only Esther Jack is given any substantial separate point of view, and her speculations and concerns center primarily on George, too. By contrast, already in earlier stories, **The Web of Earth** and **"One of the Girls in Our Party,"** Wolfe had successfully used different first-person narrative voices, both of them women. In **"Only the Dead Know Brooklyn"** we encounter still another voice, this time that of a Brooklyn tough guy.

This Brooklynite differs markedly from Wolfe's earlier fictional portraits of city people. If we look carefully at the city people in **"The Train and the City"** or **Death, the Proud Brother,** Wolfe's earliest fictional renderings of the city, we see a sneering, strident, insensitive, combative city dweller, one who produces revulsion in the young narrator of those stories: "Hard-mouthed, hard-eyed, and strident-tongued, with their million hard gray faces, they streamed past upon the streets forever, like a single animal with the sinuous and baleful convolutions of an enormous reptile" (TTatC, 293). But years of living in the city (he lived in Brooklyn itself from March, 1931, to February, 1935) were changing Wolfe's feelings toward these city dwellers, and we see the change clearly reflected in this narrator: more like Grogan in the companion Brooklyn story **"Gulliver"** than like those earlier voices, he is still pugnacious, brash, uneducated, assertive, but he is curious and kind, too, anxious to understand and help the stranger whose adventure in Brooklyn he gets tangled in, and willing to put himself out to do so, up to a point.

In a subway station the Brooklynite meets this tall stranger, who is asking directions to (as the narrator says it) "Eighteen Avenoo an' Sixty-seven' Street." After a near fist fight with another Brooklyn native who tries to give directions to the tall stranger and claims to know more of Brooklyn than he, the narrator boards the subway with the stranger to give him further directions unhindered. But as the stranger talks oddly of getting to know Brooklyn by wandering the streets, of visiting "Bensonhoist" at night just to see it, of the map that had guided him to Red Hook the night before, and finally of the peculiar fear of "drownin' in Brooklyn," the narrator decides to get off the subway at the next stop: "I could see by den he was some kind of nut," he says. "He had dat crazy expression in his eyes an' I didn't know what he might do." Looking back from some later, unspecified vantage point, the narrator speculates, "Maybe he's found out by now dat he'll neveh live long enough to know duh whole of Brooklyn."

The reader's understanding of the action of the story, at least if he has read the Wolfe novels, goes far beyond that of the bewildered narrator. We begin to recognize this big stranger from the start, when the Brooklynite tells us, "Well, he's lookin' wild, y'know, an' I can see dat he's had plenty, but still he's holdin' it; he talks good an' is walking straight enough." And his identity is absolutely confirmed when we find him determinedly exploring Brooklyn with a map of Red Hook and "Bensonhoist." He is indeed the familiar protagonist of *Of Time and the River,* though now, as we have said, viewed from the outside. We remember from that novel his incessant reading of books, followed by his incessant prowling of the city streets, his frantic trips out into the country followed by his frantic returns lest he miss any activity in the city. We perceive here in this story his all-too-real frantic state of mind, his endless searches for understanding through physical contact, his determination to "know" Brooklyn, to follow his map.

When the Brooklynite asks the stranger what specific address he's looking for, the tall man answers that he's not looking for any in particular: "Oh," dat guy says, "I'm just goin' out to see duh place . . . I just like duh sound of duh name—Bensonhoist, y'know—So I t'ought I'd go out an' have a look at it." The reader understands this explanation, but suspicion grows in the narrator that a joke is being played upon him. He is reassured that he is being told the truth when the tall man really does produce a well-marked map and describes some of his experiences in the late-night bars, but he feels increasing apprehension when the tall man talks of his fear of drowning. The stranger is talking of drowning in the kaleidoscope of city life, but the narrator, literal-minded, understands the metaphor not at all. Thus there is both good humor and pathos in their short exchange:

"What becomes of people after dey have drowned out heah?" [the tall stranger] says.

"Drowned out where?" I says.

"Out heah in Brooklyn."

"I don't know watcha mean," I says. "Neveh hoid of no one drowning heah in Brooklyn unless you mean a swimmin' pool. Yuh can't drown in Brooklyn," I says. "Yuh gotta drown somewhere else—in duh ocean where deie's wateh."

"Drownin'," duh guy says, lookin' at his map.

"Drownin'."

Which, as we have said, causes the alarmed narrator to get off at the next stop.

Much of the pleasure we experience in reading the story grows from the dramatic irony. We see this tough city character frightened by a man we know to be neither dangerous nor crazy. But though we know that the narrator doesn't understand the real plight of the stranger, we also come to see that in unconscious ways he is voicing a greater wisdom than the tall stranger's. When the stranger asks him, "How long would it take a guy to know duh place?" the narrator says, "You get dat idea outa yoeh head right now . . . you ain't neveh gonna get to know Brooklyn." And when the stranger protests that he has a map, the narrator insists, "You ain't gonna get to know

Brooklyn wit no map." We see that the narrator is right on both the literal and the metaphorical levels, even though he does not comprehend the real nature of the stranger's search.

We see that the tall man's sense of drowning comes not from the substance of his life but from a faulty perception of it. He is driven to try to see all, to experience all, to explore each street personally. He is suffering from what Wolfe elsewhere refers to as the "Faustian sickness." His prowling of the streets brings him not more knowledge or satisfaction but an increasing, franitc state of unrest. Wolfe gives the final word and the final wisdom to the Brooklynite who, without fully comprehending, says at the end of the story, "Maybe he's found out by now dat he'll neveh live long enough to know duh whole of Brooklyn." In fact, only the dead can know.

In his commentary in *Three Decades,* the only previous extended analysis of the story, Bloom sees the stranger's search in a very different way from that sketched above. "Looking for an ultimate truth which he cannot readily isolate," Bloom asserts, "he [the tall stranger] nevertheless persists. Indeed, to cease striving, to endure the atrophy of the sense of wonder and inquiry—as the narrator has done—is to perish. . . . The search for order, beauty and individuality, it is suggested, may indeed be fruitless but must never be abandoned" (270).

But the narrator has not suffered the "atrophy" of his "sense of wonder and inquiry"; it is in his mind, filled with wondering, that the story takes place. He keeps trying to figure this fellow out, and his genuine helpfulness and sympathy for this stranger tell us something about Wolfe's growing understanding of the city people among whom he lived during his Brooklyn years.

And the drowning that the tall stranger fears is a metaphor not, as Bloom describes it, for "the wasting away of the spirit," but for life's overabundance. Wolfe had, earlier in his career, seemed to defend this insatiable desire to see, say, think and feel all, in a highly romantic scene in *Of Time and the River,* when Eugene Gant takes final leave of Francis Starwick, who had been his closest friend but who had turned out to be a "mortal enemy" of art and of Eugene. He is, Eugene has come to believe, a sterile, decadent poseur, and in this melodramatic scene Eugene tells him so. And Starwick, accepting Eugene's picture of him, glorifies Eugene's excessive lust for experience: "Whatever anguish and suffering this mad hunger, this impossible desire, has caused you. . . . I would give my whole life. . . . [to] know for one hour an atom of your anguish and your hunger and your hope" (783).

But Wolfe had matured since he had written that scene, and in fact, in this story the tall man's search is not for "order" or "beauty" or "individuality" as Bloom suggests; it is for raw, undifferentiated experience, unending and unnecessary—what Wolfe calls in *The Story of a Novel,* which he also published in 1935, "an almost insane hunger to devour the entire body of human experience" (46). Wolfe has come to see, as he describes later in that same work, that "the unlimited extent of human experience is not so important for [the writer] as the depth and intensity with which he experiences things" (47). He has discovered, in fact, what the Brooklynite knows—"You'll neveh live long enough to know duh whole of Brooklyn." When Wolfe republishes this story in *From Death to Morning,* he follows it with **"Dark in the Forest, Strange as Time,"** a story in which an old, dying German delivers the same message to the young man: "You are very young. Yes. Now you want to see it all, to haf it all—but you haf nothing. Zat is right—yes? Fields, hills, mountains, riffers, cities, peoples—you wish to know about zem all. Vun field, vun hill, vun riffer . . . zat iss enough" (109).

What seems significant to me for this discussion is not only the interpretation of this story, but the clue it gives us to the direction of Wolfe's writing career. Not only does the writing from this time on move outward, away from its early concern with the exuberant young man, but the focus becomes simpler and surer—one little charwoman to illustrate the little people of Britain, one black killer on a rampage to illustrate the plight of the black man in the South, one timid little lawyer to illustrate the plight of man living in fascist Germany. This is not to suggest that Wolfe ever became a taker-outer rather than a putter-iner, as Fitzgerald had urged him to become, but it is to insist that there is dramatic, observable change in both the theme and structure of his later fiction, and that we see that change already taking place in 1935, when **"Only the Dead Know Brooklyn"** was first published.

This story is one of Wolfe's shortest and best of his middle period of production. Its effectiveness rests on its humorous and believable narrative voice, on the dramatic irony springing from that voice, and on a dramatic tension between the lightness of tone and the seriousness of the protagonist's concern. And its message, that the writer must not experience all, but must experience a few things intensely, shows important growth in Wolfe as a writer and as a man.

Works Cited

Bloom, Edward A. "Critical Commentary on 'Only the Dead Know Brooklyn,'" in *Thomas Wolfe: Three Decades of Literary Criticism.* Ed., Leslie Field. New York University Press, 1968.

Wolfe, Thomas. *From Death to Morning.* New York: Charles Scribner's Sons, 1935.

———. *Of Time and the River.* New York: Charles Scribner's Sons, 1935.

———. "Only the Dead Know Brooklyn," *The New Yorker.* II (June 15, 1935), 13-14.

———. *The Story of a Novel.* New York: Charles Scribner's Sons, 1936.

———. "The Train and the City," *Scribner's Magazine.* XCIII (May, 1933), 285-294.

Carol Johnston (essay date 1989)

SOURCE: "Thomas Wolfe's First Triumph: 'An Angel on the Porch'," in *The Thomas Wolfe Review,* Vol. 13, No. 2, Fall, 1989, pp. 53-62.

[*In the following essay, Johnston looks at the publication history and literary technique of "An Angel on the Porch," calling it "a far more complexly crafted and important piece . . . than it has been credited with being."*]

In Hendersonville, NC, stands not an angel, but THE ANGEL: THE ANGEL that stood on the front porch of the Wolfe marble shop on Pack Square and which now, in some kind of mad irony, adorns the grave of the *very* proper wife of a Methodist minister; THE ANGEL that served as the original for the titles of Thomas Wolfe's first nationally published story and his first novel; THE ANGEL that in its description mimics the one that W. O. Gant first spied in a Baltimore shop window and that made him want to become a stonecutter; THE ANGEL of white Carrara marble that he sold decades later to the proprietor of a house of ill-repute; THE ANGEL that walks to and fro like a huge wound doll of stone—at best a mute and mechanical representation of death—as Eugene confers with the reality of death, his brother's ghost, in the last chapter of *Look Homeward, Angel;* THE ANGEL whose inscrutable smile stands for the unverifiable promise of salvation—at once the marker of death and the covenant of life; THE ANGEL poised clumsily upon cold phthisic feet, holding a stone lily in one hand and wearing "a smile of soft stone idiocy" on its face that Gant both cursed and loved—the marble focus of his life's intensity and waste: the art never mastered, the ideal never achieved, the romanticized vision of life and death that misleads him, the wife—long dead—and cold, the harlot buried, the ambition thwarted, the lifeblood of sexuality—frozen, the spiritual design perverted into commodity, the artistic dream corrupted both by the warm temptation of women and the cold, parsimonious nature of wife; THE ANGEL that, more than any other symbol, has become identified with the work of Thomas Wolfe—not with the marbles of the father's failed art and life, but with the transformation of all the beauty and passion of that failure into art—into a novel that his son would call *Look Homeward, Angel.*

Yet, for at least one moment in January 1929, just returned from Europe, penniless, Thomas Wolfe would have scrapped the entire scene in chapter 19 in which THE ANGEL is sold—torn all but a few brief scattered mentions of THE ANGEL out of the novel, leaving in it and in our consciousness as "barren a crater" as was left in old Gant's heart when at 64 he too parted with it and, for one brief moment, saw himself move "deathward in a world of seemings." It would have indeed been a dark irony if Wolfe—whose vision of old Gant's artistic failure was so closely identified with his selling of THE ANGEL—had also, in a moment of desperation, abandoned it—in an attempt to find a publisher for his novel.

The moment took place during Wolfe's first meeting with Maxwell Perkins in the Scribner's office on 2 January

1929. Wolfe was trembling visibly *and* with good reason: of his fourteen publications, all—with the exception of a prize-winning undergraduate essay and an article published in his hometown newspaper—had appeared in University of North Carolina publications. If the term "writer" should be applied to someone who at least in part supports himself with his writing, Wolfe was—despite the prodigious number of pages he had produced—no writer. He had come to discuss the publication of his manuscript, *O Lost,* a loosely-structured novel that had already been rejected by several publishers. It was with some surprise, then, that he found the discussion between himself and the unknown young editor before him focused not on that novel, but on a single chapter—the section in which W. O. Gant sells the marble angel to "Queen" Elizabeth, a local madam, to be erected over the grave of a twenty-two year old prostitute, Lily Reed. Wolfe, sensitive to the coarse suggestiveness of the section, began to backpedal: "I know you can't print it," he broke in. "I'll take it out at once." Perkins was undoubtedly startled, as his response suggests: "Take it out. Why it's one of the greatest short stories I've ever read." Wolfe hung between hope and despair for several minutes, interpreting the response to mean that Perkins and Scribner's were interested in publishing a story taken from the novel—and not the novel itself. By the end of the session, however, the order of printing had been decided: Wolfe was to revise the "Queen" Elizabeth section, adding introductory material, and then submit it to *Scribner's Magazine,* which as Perkins assured him, would almost certainly accept it; he was in addition to rework sections of the novel that they had discussed and return with those sections within the week (See Nowell, *Letters,* pp. 168-169; Turnbull, pp. 138-139; and Berg, pp. 131-132).

Five days later, on 7 January, following a second meeting with Perkins, Wolfe emerged from that same office a professional writer: he had an unsigned contract for the publication of his first novel and an advance of $500 in his pocket, only 10% or $50 of which was ear-marked for his literary agent, Madeline Boyd (Nowell, *Letters,* p. 164). Within the week he would write his sister Mabel that *Scribner's Magazine* had accepted the story, offering him $150 for it (Nowell, *Letters,* p. 173). At first, he called it "Look Homeward, Angel," after the line in Milton's "Lycidas," but reconsidered and changed it to **"An Angel on the Porch."** Months later, as his first novel went to press, the Scribner's editors urged him to find a new title for the novel *O Lost.* He made a number of suggestions, none of which clicked, before one editor asked him what the original title of **"An Angel on the Porch"** had been. His response, "Look Homeward, Angel," became the title of the new novel (Magi and Walser, p. 117), and THE ANGEL, itself, assumed a position of emphasis and symbolic value in the novel that, had the novel remained titled *O Lost* or the nineteenth chapter been removed, it would never have assumed.

The circumstances surrounding the publication of **"An Angel on the Porch"** are intriguing. First, there is genuine disparity in critical response to it: Floyd Watkins, in his *Thomas Wolfe's Characters: Portraits From Life,*

describes the scene as "relatively minor" (p. 18); yet Maxwell Perkins thought it a "great" short story—and prior to his meeting with Wolfe about it, read the piece to Ernest Hemingway (Nowell, *Letters,* p. 168). Neither Perkins nor Hemingway nor any of the editors at Scribners could have known, as the late Charmian Green has only recently shown in her article "Wolfe's Stonecutter Once Again: An Unpublished Episode," that the seed of that scene had existed in Wolfe's imagination as early as 1920-1923, long before he began work on *Look Homeward, Angel.* Nor, in choosing the story as a means of introducing Wolfe to the American Public in *Scribner's Magazine* could Perkins have foreseen the circumstances that would result in the retitling of that novel after the central symbol in that story.

We have good reason, then, to ask at least four questions about **"An Angel on the Porch"**: (1) Why did Perkins choose to introduce Wolfe to the American public by publishing this particular selection from the novel in *Scribner's Magazine*? (2) Why was Wolfe so willing to see this material cut from the novel? (3) How does our reading of the selection as a short story differ from our reading of it as a chapter within the context of the novel? and (4) Is **"An Angel on the Porch"** as fine a short story as Perkins credited it with being?

The answer to questions one and two—why Perkins chose to publish the story and why Wolfe was willing to sacrifice it—may well be the same: the coarseness and unconventionality of the subject matter. Although today madams and prostitutes dot the TV set, in the late 1920's the introduction of the owner of a house of ill repute and the description of the death of a young prostitute from what appears to have been an abortion would have been considered sensitive. As Wolfe wrote in a 27 March 1928 letter to Dr. James B. Munn:

> I give you my book with a feeling of strong fear. When you read my play two or three years ago, you spoke about it in a way I shall not forget. The one criticism I remember concerned a page or two of dialogue which was tainted by coarseness. You spoke mildly and gently of that, but I felt you were sorry it had been written in. Now I give you a book on which I have wrought out my brain and my heart for twenty months. There are places in it which are foul, obscene, and repulsive. Most of those will come out on revision. But please, Dr. Munn, believe that this book was honestly and innocently written. Forgive me the bad parts, and remember me for the beauty and passion I have tried to put in it. It is not *immoral,* it is not *dirty*—it simply represents an enormous excavation in my spirit. (Nowell, *Letters,* pp. 131-132)

In 1928, Charles Scribner's Sons, with its long background of serious religious publishing, was particularly conservative. *Scribner's Magazine,* its house organ, was used as collateral reading by many schools in mixed classes, and its editors felt obliged to refrain from assailing the ears of vulnerable young schoolgirls with coarse or vulgar scenes (Berg, pp. 107-108). Wolfe had good reason, then, to expect that Scribner's would ask him to eliminate some of the coarser scenes from the novel—and this undoubtedly, led to the confusion about the "Queen" Elizabeth scene in Perkins's office at his first meeting with Wolfe. What Wolfe had no way of knowing was, as Roger Burlingame has noted, that 1928 was a turning point in the firm—and that the time was ripe for publication of just that kind of frank realistic material that Wolfe was most afraid would damage his chance for publication. As Burlingame comments, by 1928 "Some of the younger, restive folk in the house seemed to feel that *Scribner's Magazine* was 'in a rut'" (Berg, pp. 110-111). Perkins was one of these. The effect was to create a questioning of Scribners' conservatism at all levels, which resulted in a liberalizing of its publishing policies at almost the exact moment that *Look Homeward, Angel* was submitted to that publishing house.

Just three months before the publication of *Look Homeward, Angel,* the short story **"An Angel on the Porch"** appeared in the August 1929 issue of *Scribner's Magazine,* an issue that featured the fourth installment of *A Farewell to Arms.* The first installment of the Hemingway novel, published in the May issue, had resulted in the banning of the June issue in Boston and, as Scribner's noted, in a run on the remaining issues in other cities. Wolfe's story of an old man's movement toward death and the purchase of a "soft faced angel" to memorialize the grave of a young prostitute appears, with several other pieces, lodged between the beginning of the fourth installment of Hemingway's *A Farewell to Arms* and its conclusion. It was, thus, securely positioned at a point in the issue through which Hemingway's readers would have had to pass as they read the installment—between what many consider the coarsest scene in Hemingway's novel, Frederic Henry's return to his unit prior to the attack on Caporetto, his friend Rinaldi's discussion of syphilis, their suspicion that the unit priest is also a victim of that disease—and, several pages later, the implied seduction of two Italian schoolgirls. **"An Angel on the Porch"** and *A Farewell to Arms* stand alone in their realism in an issue filled with genteel reading that includes an article on bronco-busting by Will James and historical and romantic fiction by Conrad Aiken and others. Perkins had made his statement.

All this suggests why Perkins was open to publishing a particularly unconventional section of *Look Homeward, Angel* in the August issue of *Scribner's,* but it does not explain why he chose to publish this particular section. Possibly he felt it was a portion of the novel that could stand on its own while suggesting to *Scribner's* readers the nature of Wolfe's subject matter and the quality of his prose. Although "Queen" Elizabeth never appears at any other place in the novel and is only mentioned at one other point, references to the angel and to Gant's obsession with it are made throughout the novel. In addition, the quality of Wolfe's prose in this section is as good as it is anywhere else in the novel, with the possible exception of his description of his brother Ben's death. The novelty of the subject matter, the potential of the section to stand on its own, and the virtuosity of the prose style may well have prompted Perkins's decision. It remains to be seen, however, whether **"An Angel on the Porch"** is truly a "great" short story.

It is almost impossible, with Wolfe's epic work etched into our imaginations, to perceive how this section of the novel functions outside of the novel: to distinguish between the ironies of the prose text itself as opposed to the ironies that develop as a result of its context. The reader of the *Scribner's Magazine* story in August 1929 would have been unaware, however, of several things that deepen our sense of the irony of the story. (1) He would not have known that W. O. is in the process of selling the very monument that mimics in its description the angel of the first chapter that prompted him to become a stonecutter—and, because of that, unaware that the act symbolizes the selling-out of the dream of a failed artist; (2) that Gant had never himself been able to carve the face of an angel, but had been limited to carved lambs and hands; (3) that "Queen" Elizabeth shares, in at least the first five letters of her name, the name of Gant's wife Eliza; (4) as Gant praises the "Queen's" business skills—her wealth and her property—the reader of the short story would be unaware that these are the same traits he denounces in his wife; (5) that throughout the early chapters of the novel Eliza is likened several times to an angel (Eugene describes her on one occasion when she turns on him as a "dark angel" and Ben refers to her by the same name); (6) that W. O.'s attack on the angel at the end of the story: "Fiend out of hell . . . you have impoverished me, you have ruined me, you have cursed my declining years, and now you will crush me to death—fearful, awful, and unnatural monster that you are" (**"An Angel on the Porch,"** 209), echoes his invective toward Eliza in Chap. 11 of the novel:

> Woman, you have deserted my bed and board, you have made a laughing stock of me before the world, and left your children to perish. Fiend that you are, there is nothing that you would not do to torture, humiliate and degrade me. You have deserted me in my old age; you have left me to die alone. Ah, Lord! It was a bitter day for us all when your gloating eyes first fell upon this damnable, this awful, this murderous and bloody Barn. There is no ignominy to which you will not stoop if you think it will put a nickel in your pocket. You have fallen so low not even your own brothers will come near you. "Nor beast, nor man hath fallen so far." (*Look Homeward, Angel,* p. 132)

(7) he would have been unaware that Gant's wife Cynthia had died of a tubercular hemorrhage, but a hemorrhage nonetheless, as Lily Reed dies of a hemorrhage; (8) that as W. O. struggles with cancer and his body becomes waxy and translucent and, ultimately, paralyzed, he will take on the characteristics of the angel he curses and reviles, and that at the moment he learns of his cancer he is described as sitting "like a broken statue, among the marbles" (*Look Homeward, Angel,* p. 432); (9) that the $420 that Elizabeth pays for the statue echoes the $450 Horse Hines quotes Luke for Ben's casket—leading the narrator to comment that in death Ben had been given more money than he had ever been given living (*Look Homeward, Angel,* p. 569); (10) he would have been unaware of the manic struggle for life that would follow upon the heels of Gant's recognition of his own mortality or (11) of Eugene's sentimentalized recreation of Lily Reed's fate in

Chap. 20—in which the obviously pregnant girl is saved not only from "death" but from "a fate worse than death." (12) And, finally, he would have been unaware that Lily Reed's dance with the bashful cowboy ghost in that chapter would prefigure the counterpoint of the angel and ghost in the novel's last chapter—a careful contrast of romanticized and realistic views of life and death.

So what would that reader in August 1929 have seen in the story? Obviously he would have seen the humor and irony in a brothel owner's purchase of a marble angel to mark the grave of a prostitute of "great opportunity." He would have noted the irony of the maudlin verse that W. O. and Elizabeth choose to inscribe on the monument and seen in it an attack on Romantic literature:

> She went away in beauty's flower,
> Before her youth was spent;
> Ere life and love had lived their hour
> God called her, and she went.
>
> Yet whispers Faith upon the wind:
> No grief to her was given.
> She left *your* love and went to find
> A greater one in heaven.

Not only do the traditional rhyme scheme and meter reduce the moment of death to a romantic cliché, but the passage, like the angel monument, is inappropriate for this young girl. Lily Reed, a young prostitute, could hardly have been assumed to have died "Ere . . . love had lived its hour." Neither can it be assumed that in her death brought on by an abortion "No . . . grief to her was given." In addition the implication of the last two lines, "She left *your* love and went to find / A greater one in heaven" is that she has moved from one house of ill repute on earth to a big one in the sky.

Apart from the hints of complexity of character—the brothel madam whose genteel manners result in her being likened to royalty and who "loves" one of her girls enough to purchase an expensive and ornate monument for her grave—and the marbleman, marking his own movement toward death as he creates the markers for the death of others, abusing and reviling all that he loves in the angel, while treating the town prostitute with gallantry, there *is* much in this story that is extraordinary even when it is read outside of the context of the novel. Much of that has to do with Wolfe's complex prose style: his ability to create rhapsodic moments and his ability to lead his characters and his readers to epiphanies.

As printed in *Scribner's Magazine,* the story consists of 87 paragraphs, 54 of dialogue and 33 of exposition. The dialogue between Gant and Jannadeau, and Gant and Elizabeth moves the story along a simple sequential time line—from late afternoon to evening. Basically, the dialogue delineates a simple business transaction between a local madam and a stonecutter. The expository paragraphs, however, use repetitive structures—words and phrases, grammatical structures, and alliterated sounds—to create an echo effect in the narrative that signals W. O.'s in-creasing obsession with memory. These repetitive structures build to the epiphany of the story's final paragraphs in which the action appears to freeze, dialogue fades into the background, and time collapses in on itself. In these final paragraphs, life stops "like an arrested gesture, in photographic abeyance" and Gant feels himself move "deathward." The final epiphany is represented in a meeting of the man and the moment—in which the action, like the angel or any work of art—freezes in time—and the memories of youth and age collapse in upon each other. In this moment Gant, whose intense struggle to live will unleash almost manic energies, perceives the inevitability of his own death.

The story line begins and ends with a reference to time; progressing naturally from late afternoon to evening; yet both the initial and the final time references carry within themselves the seeds of the sense of simultaneity created by memory—the collapse of time in the face of death—on which the story focuses. It is no coincidence that the only important character in the story beside Gant and Elizabeth is Jannadeau, a man involved in maintaining timepieces. At the beginning of the story he courts Gant's conversation in a discussion of current events, but when at the end Gant drifts off into memory, Jannadeau draws "his great head turtlewise a little farther into the protective hunch of his burly shoulders" and ignores him. The first sentence of the story sets the action in the late afternoon; yet, the time reference is only apparently simple—it is a "late afternoon" in "young summer." The contrast of age and youth is obvious, what is less obvious is that this particular "late afternoon" in which Wolfe sets the story (and which corresponds with the late afternoon of Gant's maturity) functions within the context and not in opposition to the "young summer." So in the story, Gant's memories of his relationship with Elizabeth twelve years earlier form the context within which his actions on the day of the story have meaning. Similarly, at the end of the story, in paragraph 85, the moon is described as standing like a phantom of itself. Late afternoon has become evening. The moon—like Gant with his memories—carries within itself its own prefiguration. The sense of simultaneity—the confusion of past and present—is further complicated by the stonecutter's gallant greeting "Good evening" in the fourth paragraph of the story—only three paragraphs after the reader has been told that it is late afternoon—and long before the moon is pictured as a phantom of itself. Medial time references, appearing in paragraphs 26, 30, 48, and 54, are inevitably incremental. The first mentions 12 years (the passage of time since Elizabeth and Gant have known each other physically), the second 15 years (the time within which Elizabeth has not changed), the third 22 years (the age of Lily Reed at her death), and the last 64 (Gant's age at the time of the story).

Wolfe was the master of repetition. And this particular story is a study in the use of repetition as a unifying element as well as a rhapsodic element. The most emphatic repetitions revolve around the description of the angel and are clustered around paragraphs 5, 10, and 67. The "stones, the slabs, and the cold carved lambs of death" described in the second sentence of the first paragraph are repeated with variation in paragraphs 5, 10, and 11. The variation is at points minute, but enough to create an echo effect: the sense of something heard before—but somehow differently. In paragraph 5 the "stones, the slabs, and the cold carved lambs of death" becomes "smooth granite slabs of death, carved lambs and cherubim." In paragraph 10 the initial phrase is repeated exactly as it appears in the first paragraph. In paragraph 11 the variation is significant and the phrase mutates into "the dove, the lamb, and the cold joined hands of death." Other examples of this kind of repetition are the reference to the angel's inappropriate leer in paragraphs 10 and 84; the echo of the young prostitute's name, Lily, in the flower held in the angel's hand; the almost verbatim repetition of Elizabeth's professed love for Lily in paragraphs 46 and 55; the repetition of the word "pity" in paragraphs 49 and 54; the repetition of the word "gallantly" in reference to Gant in paragraphs 4 and 10 (reminiscent of Eliza's father's playful description of Gant not as W. O., but as L. E. Gant earlier in the novel); and the play between Gant's "furtive" and "fugitive" eyes appearing in paragraphs 10, 20, and 23.

All of this repetition creates a powerful sense of *déja vu* which, along with the redundancy in the rhythmic structure (over 1/4 of the paragraphs are three or four sentences in length: generally a short introductory sentence, a long medial sentence with periodic elements in it, and a short concluding sentence) creates a kind of incantation building to the transcendent vision of the next-to-the-last paragraph. This effect is even further magnified by Wolfe's careful use of consonance and assonance, as in the masterful interplay of "s," "o," "a," "c," "l," "m," and "n" sounds in the second sentence of the story:

> Surrounded by the stones, the slabs, the cold carved lambs of death, the stonecutter leaned upon the rail and talked with Jannadeau, the faithful burly Swiss who, fenced in a little rented place among Gant's marbles, was probing with delicate monocled intentness into the entrails of a watch.

The same sounds are repeated and emphasized in paragraphs 5, 11, and 67—in the reverberated sibilance of the three descriptions of the angel in the story: in paragraph 5 "an angel poised upon cold phthisic feet, with a smile of soft stone idiocy, stationed beside the door upon Gant's little porch" (in this 22-word passage "s" and "th" sounds are repeated 10 times); in paragraph 11 "the soft stone face of the angel" (in this 7-word passage "s" and "th" sounds are repeated 3 times); and in paragraph 67 "it held a stone lily delicately in one hand. The other hand was lifted in benediction, it was poised clumsily upon the ball of one phthisic foot, and its stupid white face wore a smile of soft stone idiocy" (in this passage of 39 words the "s" and "th" sounds are repeated 13 times). This repetition, then, builds to the resounding sibilance of the first sentence of the 86th paragraph, the final reverie:

> And in that second the slow pulse of the fountain was suspended, life was held, like an arrested gesture, in photographic abeyance, and Gant felt himself alone move deathward in a world of seemings . . .

(In this 34-word passage, the "s" and "th" sounds are repeated 14 times).

Thomas Wolfe when he put his mind to it—which was most of the time—could write. I want to establish the virtuosity of this particular short story—and to suggest, by doing so, that it has been undervalued and unappreciated. I was able to locate numerous anthologized printings of **"The Child by Tiger"** (6); **"The Far and the Near"** (4); **"House of the Far and Lost"** (4), **"The Lost Boy"** (6), and **"Only the Dead Know Brooklyn"** (8), but no anthologized printings of **"An Angel on the Porch."** Yet this is an ideal work for introducing students to Wolfe's characters and to his prose style—a microcosm of *Look Homeward, Angel*. I suspect this is why Perkins chose it as a means of introducing Wolfe to the American public. As to the quality of the story itself, it lacks the social tensions and conflicts of **"The Child by Tiger"** (which may still lay claim to being Wolfe's "finest" short story), but it is a far more complexly crafted and important piece, both within and without the novel, than it has been credited with being.

Works Cited

Berg, A. Scott. *Max Perkins: Editor of Genius.* New York: E.P. Dutton, 1978.

Green, Charmian. "Wolfe's Stonecutter Once Again: An Unpublished Episode." *Mississippi Quarterly,* 30 (Fall 1977), 611-623.

Magi, Aldo P., and Richard Walser. *Thomas Wolfe Interviewed: 1929-1938.* Baton Rouge and London: Louisiana State University Press, 1985.

Nowell, Elizabeth. *Thomas Wolfe: A Biography.* Garden City, New York: Doubleday, 1960.

————. *The Letters of Thomas Wolfe.* New York: Scribners, 1956.

Turnbull, Andrew. *Thomas Wolfe.* New York: Scribners, 1967.

Watkins, Floyd. *Thomas Wolfe's Characters: Portraits From Life.* Norman: University of Oklahoma Press, 1957.

Wolfe, Thomas. "An Angel on the Porch." *Scribner's Magazine,* 86 (August 1929), 205-210.

————. *Look Homeward, Angel.* New York: Scribner's, 1929.

Patricia Gantt (essay date 1993)

SOURCE: "Weaving Discourse in Thomas Wolfe's 'The Child by Tiger'," in *Southern Quarterly,* Vol. 31, No. 3, Spring, 1993, pp. 45-57.

[*In the following essay, Gantt analyzes the intermingling of narrative voices, racial ideology, and literary discourse in Wolfe's story "The Child by Tiger."*]

In the more than fifty years since Thomas Wolfe published **"The Child by Tiger,"** critics have examined the story from a multiplicity of stylistic and thematic view-points. Aware of the autobiographical elements in Wolfe's work, some have searched for indications of the artist's life inscribed in his fiction. Many have concentrated on this prolific writer's outpouring of words; others, knowing the story appears in chapter 8 of *The Web and the Rock* (1939), have regarded how it figures into the *Bildungsroman* or the Wolfe canon. More recent critics have historicized Wolfe's narrative as a document of class and race tensions of the time.

These disparate views have focused on several of the same questions, all centering on Dick Prosser, the compelling protagonist: How do we account for this man? Why does he turn "overnight" from a solicitous mentor into a mass murderer? Of what social forces is he an emblem? As readers we continue to be intrigued, like the citizens of the author's literary locale, Libya Hill: "It was a mystery and a wonder. . . . Men debated and discussed these things a thousand times—who and what he had been, what he had done, where he had come from—" (39-40).[1] Indeed, Wolfe does present a powerful enigma in Prosser, a man so strongly constituted of both innocence and experience.

Yet **"The Child by Tiger"** has dimensions beyond our enduring fascination with its protagonist. Wolfe's story is not only a matter of plot, character or theme (narrative product), but an example of the weaving of discourse (narrative process). It illustrates not only how one man changes a small mountain town, but how fiction comes to be, and invites us to posit the Bakhtinian questions: Who speaks? What is the speaker's dialogic imperative? Where do the heteroglot forces of language collide? And—since one cannot separate discourse from the ideology which both produces it and is shaped by it—whose speech is precluded, and by whom?

The narrating voice Wolfe has chosen is George ("Monk") Webber, a man relating a series of events he has played over and over in his mind since their occurrence twenty-five years before. Thus we encounter the first "mixture of social languages within the limits of a single utterance" (Bakhtin 358). There is not just one point of view, but a genuine hybridization of a whole triad of discourses: that of the artist, that of the narrator as an adult and that of the "somnambulist," memory, through which the story unfolds (Welty 223). Events appear to come not from an authorial presence, but from a second party who searches for "the answer" to acts of individual and community violence witnessed as a child (Wolfe 40). Webber seeks through telling the story to recover the past, which Peter Brooks perceives as "the aim of narrative" (311).

Further, Wolfe employs the narratological device of seeming to relate the tale to an outsider, someone who—like its teller—has an urge for closure which time has not provided: "that bloody chronicle of night," though remembered, is still unaccounted for (Wolfe 33). To multiply the hybridization, much of what is thought to have happened has been pieced together from a series of stories told by various people, who are themselves weavers of narratives rising from whatever ideologies they hold, and therefore

just as unreliable as he. There can be no "the truth," no closure, no "meaning," only a nexus of perspectives. Characters sometimes reflect, sometimes refract the ideology of the narrator—and all are manipulated by the author.

An early consideration in uncovering what M. M. Bakhtin calls "all the available orchestrating languages" in Wolfe's story is its editing history (416). The 1936 working title for his fictional account of the 1906 Asheville incident was "Nigger Dick" (Donald 409). Before the story could be published, Wolfe traveled to Berlin to spend royalties from the sale of his books in Germany, since Hitler would not permit such monies to be sent out of the Reich (Daniels 1). His trip coincided with the 1936 Olympics. Inspired by Jesse Owens's showing there, as well as by Hitler's display of intolerance and the ominous strengthening of the regime in which that intolerance thrived, Wolfe rewrote his early draft (Donald 410). His revision gives a more balanced, thoughtful picture than can be found in the earlier version, both of the man who commits the initial violence and of the even more brutal mob which pursues and mutilates him. The "new" story appeared as **"The Child by Tiger"** in the *Saturday Evening Post* for 11 September 1937 (409). After Wolfe's death a few months later, his editor, Edward Aswell, bypassed the revision and returned to the original "Nigger Dick" draft for inclusion in a text he was piecing together from various fragments of the writer's work. Although retaining the *Post* title, he made another major change in shifting from the original first-person point of view to third person (468). Thus one faces a multiple language even before considering the internal elements of the piece, since there are three textual variants with conflicting ideological subtexts.

The author's designation of a dual-voiced narrator is plain from the first line of the story. It begins with four words set in the past ("One day after school"), and counterbalances with an almost identical number of syllables reminding us of the present ("twenty-five years ago") (24). Though Wolfe gives an individual narrator ostensible control over the telling, the story is in no way single or linear. The author layers the narrating voice with rich textures of other voices, both from within the story and from a multiplicity of exterior sources. George Webber expresses

> an utterance that belongs, by its grammatical (syntactic) and compositional markers, to a single speaker, but that actually contains within it [multiple] utterances . . . speech manners . . . styles . . . "language" . . . semantic and axiological belief systems . . . there is no formal—compositional and syntactic—boundary between these utterances, styles, languages, belief systems (Bakhtin 304-05).

The interplay of these multiple languages and perspectives, their "hybrid construction," is one of the most intricate aspects of Wolfe's story, as well as a possibility of speech Bakhtin considers particular to fiction (304).

The past "I" is the voice of Monk Webber, an easily-impressed, hero-worshipping boy who takes most statements at their literal value. He is fascinated with "Shepperton's new Negro man" because Prosser incorporates all the macho virtues Monk's little neighborhood gang prizes: he can play football, shoot and box; to Monk's friends, "There [is] nothing that he [does] not know" (26). In addition, Prosser treats the boys with a dignity they are unused to, but welcome immensely, calling each one "Mister" except the son of his employer, for whom he reserves the title "Cap'n." Frozen in time by memory, Monk remains essentially the same throughout the story, acknowledging himself to be emotionally still a "boy" after the recalled violence has played out (38).

The present "I" is a grown-up Monk—now George—who reflects on these long-ago incidents from an adult's point of view. While remembering those times when Prosser instructs the boys in boxing, Wolfe merges both voices, past and present, in Webber. The narrator says, "He never boxed with us, of course," blending both the awe-stricken boy and the adult, and follows with a purely adult perspective: "There was something amazingly tender and watchful about him" (24-25). Presenting the passage as a stylistic unit, Wolfe interweaves two dialogues—that of a child who does not dare to hope for full status with an adult, and that of the adult who realizes the operative racism precluding their interaction as equals, a bias having nothing to do with the disparities in their ages and amounts of strength. He also mixes the freshness of recalled impressions from childhood with an adult's more sophisticated ability to articulate them, a technique we see practiced in fiction more contemporaneous to ourselves— say, by Frank O'Connor or Shirley Ann Grau—than to Wolfe's fellow modernists. The child grown up can better evaluate and possibly identify with Prosser's protectiveness, even as in retrospect he senses implicit social undercurrents in their relationship.

Frequently the narrator's child/man voice seems a vehicle for expressions of "the intentions and actions of the author," as in the selection of incidents designed to enhance the reader's esteem for Prosser (Bakhtin 314). At other times the narrator conveys incidents and ideologies the boy Monk would not have been privy to—exchanges he admits "no one ever saw" which must have taken place in the Sheppertons' kitchen, for example—to convey ideology elsewhere (28). The narrator is variously at one with and in opposition to the boys and the town, mixing discourses of adult and child, poor white and middle class, self-styled hero and legal authority, black women and white, male and female, the law-and-order advocate and the mob. In all these dialogues we see tensions between belief systems—apparent, too, in more directly-provided detail, such as the emblematic naming of the town merchant who capitalizes on the tragedy as Cash Eager.

An especially notable hybrid, ideologically-loaded construction occurs when Ben Pounders declaims his important role in the "accomplishments" of the posse that has tracked Prosser down (Wolfe 38). Ostensibly a monologue, the passage is actually an act of "authorial unmasking," exposing the speaker, as well as that segment of society which both absorbs his exaggerations and extols his be-

havior (Bakhtin 304). Pounders describes his "heroic accomplishments" to a "fascinated" crowd; he "boasts of another triumph," is said to be a "proud possessor of another scalp" and is even called a "hero" (Wolfe 38).

Yet it is clear that he is anything *but* heroic when one looks at the dialogic descriptions of the man and his audience. The animal imagery Wolfe employs in depicting Pounders invokes odium rather than approbation. Pounders has a "ferret face," a "mongrel mouth"—both indications of slyness and inferiority (38). He has a "furtive and uneasy eye" (38). His occupation, "collector of usurious lendings to the blacks," also indicts him, carrying the weight of Biblical injunction (38). The title "nigger hunter" is applied to Pounders only with an obvious sneer (38). The author further has the braggart spit tobacco juice into the slush of filthy snow and point grotesquely at a hole in Prosser's corpse "with a dirty finger" (38). Hardly descriptive of one worth emulating.

Note, too, the juxtaposition of the leader of the boys' gang, Nebraska Crane—"fearless, blunt, outspoken as he always was"—against the "little group of fascinated listeners" who "goggled with a drugged and feeding stare" (38). Set against "the leaden reek of day, the dreary vapor of the sky," the faces and bloodlust of "the poolroom loafers, the town toughs, the mongrel conquerers of the earth" invite disgust (38). Nebraska is the only one present strong enough to confront Pounders; though a boy, he is the only "man" there worthy of the name. When Pounders pauses for admiration, Nebraska

> put two fingers to his lips and spat between them, widely and contemptuously.
>
> "Yeah—*we!*" he grunted. "*We* killed a big one! We— we killed a b'ar, we did! . . . Come on, boys," he said gruffly. "Let's be on our way!"
>
> And, fearless and unshaken, untouched by any terror or any doubt, he moved away. And two white-faced, nauseated boys went with him. (38)

Nebraska's inherent assessment of Pounders and his cronies is clear: they do not even have the grace to feel shame for their vindictive bloodletting. Nor do they at any level acknowledge the irony in having creatures like themselves control the destiny of a man like Prosser, merely because they are white and he is black. Wolfe has unmasked their self-absorbed ideology of oppression through the guise of reportage, with double voicing that assures Pounders's pronouncements will not have the authority generally invested in monologue. Following that boasting with Nebraska's incisive undercuts, the author both demonstrates the mixture of language systems which constitutes narrative and privileges a more egalitarian ideology.

One of the most fundamental aspects of the novel as narrative is its spongelike quality, its ability to incorporate various genres, to re-accentuate "both artistic (inserted short stories, lyrical songs, poems, dramatic scenes, etc.) and extra-artistic (everyday, rhetorical, scholarly, religious genres and others)" (Bakhtin 320). Wolfe's **"The Child by Tiger"** is particularly rich in this regard, for it makes extensive use of both artistic and extra-artistic genres. Language sources range from weather reports and excerpts from Asheville newspapers to Shakespearean drama, romantic poetry and contemporary fiction. Wolfe also interweaves the language of hymns and the Bible, as well as both the style of delivery and the substance of a familiar black folk sermon. No component of the story is more illustrative of narrative's status as a heteroglot medium.

The title, as well as story itself, is dependent on William Blake's *Songs of Innocence* and *Songs of Experience,* especially the "Tiger," which is quoted within the narrative as a possible key to the puzzle of Dick Prosser. The headnote to the story is the first four lines of the poem: "Tiger, tiger, burning bright / In the forests of the night, / What immortal hand or eye / Could frame they fearful symmetry?" (24). Blake's lyric serves the Bakhtinian function of allowing the novel to "reprocess reality," as George Webber uses its central probes to speculate about his childhood hero: "'*What* the hammer? *What* the chain?' No one ever knew" (Bakhtin 321, Wolfe 39). The poem is also the indirect source for the many parallel cat images that dot the description of Prosser. The first sentence in which he appears mentions "his great black paw" (25). With his several admirable skills, he is described as being "crafty as a cat" (25). His movements, too, are catlike: Wolfe says, "He was there upon you sometimes like a cat"; "The Negro was out of the car like a cat"; "then he was on us like a cat" (26-28). To reinforce the feral image, Prosser's eyes go red when he is angered, as when a drunk who has sideswiped Shepperton's car smashes Dick in the face: "But suddenly the whites of his eyes were shot with red, his bleeding lips bared for a moment over the white ivory of his teeth. . . . there were those who saw it and remembered later how the eyes went red" (27). Only Prosser's *eyes* show resistance, for the code of that small southern town says he cannot defend himself against any white man. The narrator refers to this encounter with the drunk as an example of "a flying hint," recalled afterwards when the town attempts to comprehend Dick's behavior (27). Incidents like this one go far in explaining the man's sudden release of long-held frustrations into blind violence. Wolfe later drops the cat imagery for a time, returning to it only after Prosser's grisly death—his lifeless body riddled with bullets twice, then senselessly hanged and riddled again—to depict Ben Pounders with his "mongrel mouth" (38). Narratological closure includes two additional stanzas of Blake's poem and a last feline image—"He was . . . a tiger and a child" (40). Thus Wolfe leaves the reader with an expression of the dual sides of Prosser and, by obvious extension, of us all.

Then, too, the adversarial position of town whites plays off Prosser's feline qualities. While he is the independent cat, the townspeople are painted as dogs. More powerful than the author's "cat," they are also cruder, more brutal and more conforming than he. When Monk gets to the square shortly after the alarm goes out that "that nigger" has "gone crazy and is running wild," he learns that Dick has "killed six men" (30-31). The confusion at the square

reminds the boy of "a dog fight"; he mentions the "ugly and insistent growl" of the crowd, its "blood note in that foggy growl" more frightening than that of actual hounds which arrive "swiftly, fairly baying at our heels" (32). Dehumanizing the wild mob gathering in the square works well to reinforce their pack mentality, which does not seek the *why* of events, only someone to punish. Town society—except for the boys and to some extent the elder Shepperton—fails to show Prosser respect, fearing his skills and apparent self-possession.

Although he is the focus of the story, Dick Prosser actually is given very little to say, underscoring the voicelessness endemic to southern blacks in the early years of this century. His every word is mantled in borrowed language or masked in terms acceptable to the white society which pushes him aside and effectively robs him of power. Who speaks for him? Boys, a white adult narrator, other whites in the town, etc.—never the man directly for himself, unless we interpret his violence as a kind of discourse. A telling scene is when Dick stands, cap in hand, at the side door of a "white" church he is not allowed to attend, listening "during the course of the entire sermon" (27). There can be no doubt that he has much to articulate, for he carries the burden Toni Morrison describes as "adult pain that rest[s] somewhere under the eyelids" (2 October 1990). What he does give voice to consists mostly of a passion-filled amalgam of Bible verses, snatches of sermons and hymn lyrics, shared not with other adults, but with the boys only. It is comparatively safe for him to reveal his thoughts to children, who customarily have little social power. They are the only ones, for instance, to whom he shows his gun, left over from a mysterious—possibly military—past.

Central to Dick's less guarded speech is his call for racial equality, expressed in pleadings to "love each othah like a brothah" and implicit warnings that "judgment day" is coming:

> "Oh, young white fokes," he would begin, moaning gently, "de dry bones in de valley. I tell you, white fokes, de day is comin' when He's comin' on dis earth again to sit in judgment. He'll put de sheep upon de right hand and de goats upon de left. Oh white fokes, white fokes, de Armageddon day's a-comin,' white fokes, an' de dry bones in de valley." (26,27)

Although these nonsecular speeches *are* admittedly a form of social mask—especially since couched in dialect—they are the least inhibited ones given to any black in the piece, and the only ones made by a black character who is not at the time wearing the expected mask of subservience. Such passages invite the reader to view Dick's night of violence as a specie of Armageddon and the man himself as an avenging angel, destroying agents of oppression and those complicitous with it. Like Bigger Thomas, Prosser argues through his acts of violence for an acknowledged sense of self.

Wolfe's source for Prosser's sacred text is apparently a traveling African-American preacher, Robert Parker Rumley, who "won fame throughout Western North Carolina" delivering essentially the same sermon to crowds of blacks and whites (Watkins 138). Based on Ezekiel 37: 1-10, it is referred to as "De Dry Bones in de Valley." Wolfe was born four years after the publication of Rumley's sermon and "must have heard it or stories about it" (139). Certainly the words of the "deeply religious" Prosser echo Rumley's oration and provide increasingly complex texture to the narrative (Wolfe 25).

Direct incorporation of biblical language is a part of Wolfe's weave of discourse, as well. Prosser spends long hours reading the Bible in his monklike cell at the Sheppertons, emerging with his eyes red with weeping. Days after the terrible violence has taken place, Shepperton and the boys go into that room, only to find a Bible symbolically "open and face downward" in rejection, turned to the Twenty-third Psalm (39). Whether Prosser has rejected God and holy text, or simply been unable to find solace there when faced with daily exhibitions of men's *un*holiness, we cannot know. Certainly the instruction of the biblical voice in those spare surroundings serves as a vivid counterpoint to the violence and chaos that have come into their lives. Shepperton begins to read "The Lord is my shepherd," but stops when he reaches "the valley of the shadow of death" with its threat of evil (39). Wolfe's choice of this particular passage underscores Prosser's faith, since the Bible is the only personal object in his austere room. Our sympathy for the man, increases, too, as we recall his habit of emerging after hours spent with the Bible, eyes "red, as if he had been weeping" (26). In Wolfe's selection and Shepperton's reading, *we* read Prosser's struggle for ascendency of the lamb over the tiger within him.

In addition to borrowing actual words from extratextual sources and reinvesting them with meaning, Wolfe's narrative reaccentuates other genres merely by adopting the cadence of familiar lines. A pointed example is his use of a rhythm unmistakably derived from Shakespeare's *Macbeth*. When the ambitious Thane of Cawdor emerges from Duncan's chamber with his guilty, bloodstained hands, he says, "Methought I heard a voice cry 'Sleep no more! Macbeth does murder sleep'" (II, ii 35-36). Wolfe evokes that exact cadence when he describes the aftermath of the blood scene around the square: "But there was no more sleep, I think, for anyone that night. *Black Dick had murdered sleep*" (36, emphasis added). Those six syllables, accented just as the original ones were when written centuries ago, are to Albert E. Wilhelm an "obvious" framing gesture (179). They demonstrate the liveliness of narrative prose, which cannot be confined to "one linguistic timbre," but can embrace other works just by taking on their peculiar rhythms (Bakhtin 324).

Narratives at times weave in other narratives. Voices they subsume can contain declarations of authorial intention to call up themes embedded in works recast. Wolfe does so in concluding with a direct echoing of Joseph Conrad's *Heart of Darkness*. The struggle between good and evil— even between shades of evil—so manifest in Conrad's tale is an inherent part of Wolfe's. In fact, that struggle is the subtext of all the languages and genres he incorporates in **"The Child by Tiger."** The narrator says of Dick Prosser:

> He came from darkness. He came out of the heart of darkness, from the dark heart of the secret and undiscovered South. He came by night, just as he passed by night. He was night's child and partner, a token of the other side of man's dark soul, a symbol of those things that pass by darkness and that still remain, a symbol of man's evil innocence, and the token of his mystery, a projection of his own unfathomed quality, a friend, a brother and a mortal enemy, an unknown demon, two worlds together—a tiger and a child (40).

The evocation is multiple, drawing parallels between colonialist Africa and the modern South. Primarily it connotes Kurtz, Conrad's protagonist, who looks into his own heart, sees there man's potential for evil, and dies screaming, "The horror! The horror!" (147). The narrator uses this recasting of Conrad's title and theme to posit by inference his theory that each of us has within the dual sides of a Kurtz or a Dick Prosser—"a tiger and a child" (40). Wolfe borrows Conrad here to exemplify "the potential for violence that [lies] in the hearts of all men," rather than the violent outpourings of one aberrant human being (Donald 409). Weaving this story into his own allows Wolfe another *langue* for discourse, since Conrad's tale of imperialism carries an implicit political context.

The extra-artistic genres Wolfe incorporates in his narrative web provide some of the most interesting doublevoicedness. A child of six when the occurrences he drew from for his tale took place, Wolfe would assuredly have heard Asheville townspeople speak of them then and for many years to follow, their biases framing the tellings. Later, when the author could have direct access to newspaper accounts of 14-20 November 1906, he would find them to be also only "the story as we get it, pieced together," full of the ideologies of those who fabricated them (Wolfe 35). The *Asheville Citizen* for 14 November carries the headline: "Brave City Officers Fall Dead on Streets Acting in Line of Duty" (1). Under the guise of journalistic objectivity, this newspaper and those of the next week are in fact like all discourse—fraught with the prejudices of their creators, whose utterances are produced by a matrix of social forces.

The paper traces the story of Will Harris (Dick Prosser), naming him a "fiend" who so terrifies the "childlike" "negroes of that distict" that they could provide "absolutely no valuable information" (1). It also records the cries of townspeople for "another Ku Klux . . . And had a Ben Cameron (Ben Pounders?) arisen from the crowd and given the old war cry of the Klan, thousands would have followed" (1). Subsequent papers bear weighted reports such as this: "The negro was desperate, inspired by bravado at this time. Clearly he wished to defy all the world— he cared nothing for consequences" (15 November: 6). Harris is purported to have said, "I am from Hell and don't care who sends me back" (6). The *Citizen* from the day Harris's body was brought back into town depicts "a vast, seething, excited crowd" in danger of crushing one another in their eagerness to view the "mutilated desper-ado" on display; the same edition contains the story of an innocent black man, shot by mistake by an overly-enthu-siastic deputy (1). The next day's editorial is a congratu-latory message to the "southern manhood" of Asheville who "remained cool and acted with wisdom" (4). A vis-iting salesman, for some reason asked to comment, said he "expected to see a good deal of shooting and general disorder" (4). Such an ideological context must have in-fluenced Wolfe, causing him to speak of the episode of "the coon who is hunted by the posse" as a good source for fiction (Donald 409). The story as told in *The Web and the Rock* is a more direct descendant of racist ac-counts in the newspapers, but both narratives probably reflect the *Citizen*'s designation of Harris as a "wild beast" and its accounts of the rivalry over who fired "the fatal bullets" (16 November: 1). Headlines and columns, whether directly or indirectly incorporated by Wolfe, present an-other thread in the weaving of discourse.

History, too, enters into the meshing of Wolfe's narrative. It can be no coincidence that the one man who tries to maintain calm in the crowd is Hugh McNair, "taller by half a foot than anyone around him, his long gaunt figure, the gaunt passion of his face, even the attitude of his outstretched bony arms, strangely, movingly Lincolnesque" (32). Wolfe inserts this physical comparison to the Great Emancipator as an apparent commentary on the nobility of one who speaks up for reason and equity over passion and vengeance. In just this way, an author utilizes "every utterance as an ideologeme" (Bakhtin 429). Wolfe's anal-ogy to Lincoln is both an indicator of the spirit of the mob and the author's valorization of McNair's appeal to them to be rational: "Wait a minute!" he says. "You men wait a minute! . . . You'll gain nothing, you'll help nothing if you do this thing!" (32). But McNair is shouted down.

Wolfe's "polyphonic" discourse contains a variety of oth-er sources, most embedded in dialogue. He inserts folk sayings ("straight as string" and "We—we killed a b'ar, we did!"), idiomatic expressions ("tote" for carry), dialect ("When you gits a little oldah yo' handses gits biggah and you gits a bettah grip") and even a verbal palimpsest from a speech by another of white society's victims, Chief Jo-seph of the Nez Perce Indians (35, 38, 26). Telling of the visit the boys and Shepperton make to Prosser's room, the narrator says, "And we went out the door, he locked it, and we went back into that room no more forever" (39). That unusual phrase, "no more forever," surely recalls Chief Joseph's declaration that he "will fight no more forever" (Linton 216). Such a diversified chorus of artis-tic and extra-artistic voices ensures the richness of narra-tive discourse.

What do we do, then, after we have noted all this verbal luxuriance, this intricate dialogic weave Wolfe has creat-ed? Granted that it provides a useful—even fascinating—way into a clearer understanding of fiction, that it illus-trates the all-inclusive possibilities of the novel, that it guarantees the dynamism of that genre as an art form in a state of becoming. But there is more. Terry Eagleton has expressed the aim of our investigation this way:

> Any body of theory concerned with human meaning, value, language, feeling and experience will inevitably engage with broader, deeper beliefs about the nature of human individuals and societies, problems of power and sexuality, interpretations of past history, versions of the present and hopes for the future. (195)

"The Child by Tiger" is not a record of aseptic dis-course. There is no such thing, as both Bakhtin and Eagle-ton declare. The story is a record of power—or rather, of powerlessness—a testimony to the politics immanent in every discourse, every text. Thus comes the final inquiry: Who speaks for whom?

Wolfe's narrative, like the "bloody chronicle" which in-spired and the newspaper articles which influenced it, remains enmeshed in racist ideology. Consider the news-paper accounts of those appalling November days. They are a tissue of remarks by the white power structure of community and press—even a traveling salesman gets to speak. But where are the remarks from the actual black community? Even though several blacks are directly in-volved—eyewitnesses, victims of the violence, donators of money to aid families of policemen shot by Harris—they are given no chance to comment on what happens. Their donations are cited Jim Crow style, at the end of the published list, with the designation "colored" by each (15 November: 1). Common practice allowed the newspaper, ironically called the *Citizen,* to refer to a black man as "the little darkey" (17 November: 5). We need not ask which citizens the paper primarily wished to serve.

This same prejudicial ideology is what Wolfe tried to eradicate from his story when he changed its title from "Nigger Dick" and revised the content. He told Jonathan Daniels that his view of the "poisonous and constricted hatreds" he witnessed during his 1936 trip to Germany had made him "enormously interested in politics for the first time in my life," and that he wished to work for "social progress and social justice" (Daniels, 23 October 1936: 3-4). He started with his writing. We can only spec-ulate about the increasingly liberal course his fiction might have taken had he lived long enough to effect more of the changes he spoke to Daniels about. That he was partially successful is evident from the many racial and anti-Semitic slurs deleted from the version Aswell chose for *The Web and the Rock*. The public at the time of the story's first appearance thought it quite liberal. In fact, it nearly be-came a casualty to the dominant white ideology of 1937, when few wanted to read stories of black men's rage. Both *Collier's* and *Redbook* rejected it before the *Post* bought it, fully expecting to lose some of their usual read-ership by daring to print such a controversial piece (Kennedy 56-59). Wolfe's portrayal of Dick Prosser in the *Post* version is, however, far from being "the one full-scale Afro-American in his writing . . . neither patronizing nor prejudiced" that Donald claims it to be (409). Its saturation with racism, expressed mostly by the adult nar-rator, marks it as a document of disempowerment.

Even in revision, Wolfe first mentions Prosser as a gener-ic, owned thing: "Shepperton's new Negro man"; Shepperton himself declares Dick to be "the smartest darkey that he'd ever known" (24, 26). The dialect in which Wolfe cloaks Prosser's words makes him sound like Uncle Remus ("Ise tellin' you," etc.) (26). His voice is said to be "full of Africa," although other characters' voices are not full of the lands of their white origins (27). Prosser has been "in the service of former masters" (27). His Army days are spent as a member of "crack Negro troops" (25). He drives the Sheppertons to a church he cannot attend; hit by a drunken white, he cannot retaliate. His friend Pansy is described as "a comely Negro wench . . . black as the ace of spades," who nightly carries home scraps from the Shepperton kitchen where she cooks (27). When Prosser discovers the boys peeping into his room, his one sanctuary, he flashes into anger, then reassumes his mask, chuckling and cajoling them not to report what they have seen. When the narrator fixes on the Blake poem for the image which best suits Prosser, it is one, he remarks condescendingly, "Dick, I know, had never heard, and one perhaps he might not have understood" (39). While we can commend Wolfe for improvements that he did make, we can also draw a significant observation from the catalog of what he includes, even in the "purged" version. That observation impacts not only on Wolfe studies, but on our canonical choices or investigations of other authors, and certainly on our own speech acts.

Bakhtin reminds us of how politically-invested the threads we weave into our discourse are, both through accident and careful crafting. Our very medium is one where ideologies "battle it out in the arena of utterances" (Bakhtin 431). Do we not, then, have an obligation not only to examine texts, but to re-examine the languages in which we speak, as well as those we validate by their inclusion in the canon, to see if we are encouraging a diverse chorus of social voices? I say yes. My Eagletonian "hope for the future" is that in our search for more than "meaning" in a text, we be aware of how language is put together—and why. Bakhtin says the novel is "the encyclopedia of the life of the era . . . the maximally complete register of all social voices of the era" (430). When we examine texts, we must ask not only "What do they mean?" but treat them as the political documents they are. We can be especially alert to whether all the social voices of an era have had a chance to be heard, or if they speak only through their silences. We must ask: "Who speaks?" "In what way?" "Why does s/he speak?" "What is omitted in that speech?" "For whom does s/he speak?" and—most significantly—"Who never gets to speaks at all, and what shall we do about it?" In that way, we will use our considerable power as scholars for acts of reclaiming.

Notes

[1] For fidelity to authorial intentions, I have chosen to deal with Perrine's reprint of the story as Wolfe last saw it published in the *Saturday Evening Post* in 1937. For critical convenience, I borrow the name of the narrator, George ("Monk") Webber, from the Aswell fabrication; the narrator is nameless in "The Child by Tiger."

Works Cited

Asheville Citizen. 14 Nov.-20 Nov. 1906.

Bakhtin, M. M. *The Dialogic Imagination.* Trans. Michael Holquist. Austin: U of Texas P, 1981.

Brooks, Peter. *Reading for the Plot.* New York: Vintage, 1984.

Conrad, Joseph. *Into the Heart of Darkness.* New York: Harper, 1910.

Daniels, Josephus. Papers. Southern Historical Collection. Wilson Library, U of North Carolina, Chapel Hill.

Donald, David Herbert. *Look Homeward: A Life of Thomas Wolfe.* Boston: Little, 1987.

Eagleton, Terry. *Literary Theory.* Minneapolis: U of Minnesota P, 1983.

Kennedy, Richard S., ed. *Beyond Love and Loyalty: The Letters of Thomas Wolfe and Elizabeth Nowell.* Chapel Hill: U of North Carolina P, 1983.

Linton, Calvin D., ed. *The Bicentennial Almanac.* New York: Thomas Nelson, 1975.

Morrison, Toni. Address. U of North Carolina, Chapel Hill. 2 Oct. 1990.

Watkins, Floyd C. "De Dry Bones in de Valley." *Southern Folklore Quarterly* (June 1985): 136-40.

Welty, Eudora. *The Optimist's Daughter.* New York: Vintage, 1972.

Wilhelm, Albert E. "Borrowings from *Macbeth* in Wolfe's 'The Child by Tiger.'" *Studies in Short Fiction* 14 (Spring 1977): 179-80.

Wolfe, Thomas. "The Child by Tiger." *Literature: Structure, Sound, and Sense.* Ed. Laurence Perrine. Atlanta: Harcourt, 1978. 24-40.

———. *The Web and the Rock.* New York: Harper, 1939.

John L. Idol, Jr. (essay date 1993)

SOURCE: "The Narrative Discourse of Thomas Wolfe's 'I Have a Thing to Tell You'," in *Studies in Short Fiction,* Vol. 30, No. 1, Winter, 1993, pp. 45-52.

[*In the following essay, Idol explores Wolfe's discourse of "steadfast opposition to the suspicion, mistrust, hatred, betrayal and atrocities in German society under Hitler's crazed sway" in* I Have a Thing to Tell You.]

Writing to Dixon Wecter of the imminent publication of *I Have a Thing to Tell You,* Thomas Wolfe said:

> It cost me a good deal of time and worry to make up my mind whether I should allow publication of the story because I am well known in Germany, my books have a tremendous press there, I have many friends there, and I like the country and the people enormously. But the story wrote itself. It was the truth as I could see it, and I decided that a man's own self-respect and integrity is worth more than his comfort or material advantage. (*Letters* 614)

When Wolfe speaks of the story's having written itself, he is, of course, speaking as an experienced writer, as a practiced hand now turning out some of his best pieces of fiction. It is possible, too, that he means to suggest that the action of the piece occurred in real life pretty much as he presents it in the story. Thus, he could mean that the plot took care of itself, the real-life happenings providing a suitable beginning, middle, and end. Whether the plot easily came to him because of his experience as a storyteller or from his faithful recording of events as they unfolded as he left Germany by train in early September 1936, Wolfe wanted to engage his readers in a narrative discourse, to reveal the truth as he saw it, to ask his readers to make a metaphoric transference from this one example of Nazi oppression to whatever land or ruler tried to imprison people physically or spiritually. The thing he had to tell was both a protest against abridged or denied civil rights and a testimony of his commitment to expose man's inhumanity to man. What he had just witnessed in Hitler's Germany deeply concerned him, had revealed to him something dark, ugly, and vicious, had shown him that the country he revered next to his own was headed toward unspeakable atrocities.

The impulse driving Wolfe to tell his story, to engage his readers in narrative discourse, seems readily explainable as one of "the motors of desire" that Peter Brooks identified as forces impelling narratives in his *Reading for Plot*:

> Narratives portray the motors of desire that drive and consume their plots, and they also lay bare the nature of narration as a form of human desire: the need to tell as a primary human drive that seeks to seduce and to subjugate the listener, to implicate him in the thrust of a desire that can never quite speak its name—never can quite come to the point—but that insists on speaking over and over again its movement toward that name. (61)

What seems clear from a close reading of *I Have a Thing to Tell You* is that the "motors of desire" driving Wolfe were diametrically opposing forces, forces causing him personal anguish, forces convincing him, ultimately, that he must relate his story as persuasively as possible if humanity were to be warned about falling victim to dark, evil, malicious powers. One motor of his desire was his enjoyment of Germany's celebration of his work, an eager acceptance bringing with it fame, money and lavish hospitality, lionizing at its best. Another motor of desire, driven by his sense of his paternal ancestry, was his love of Germany, its people, its accomplishments, its romantic ambience. Tugging at him in a contrary direction was the desire to reveal how far Hitler's Germany had gone in breeding hatred, mistrust, and betrayal among its citizens and how far Hitler and his henchman were willing to go to crush citizens who still cherished freedom of thought, movement and association. To embody those desires in a plot, Wolfe traced the experiences of his protagonist as he bid farewell to German friends and took a train to Paris.

Of course, as a plot device, a trip is no doubt as old as the art of storytelling, as classical, biblical and Oriental ex-

amples remind us. In the version I am using (bMS Am 1883 [734] in the Wisdom Collection), a second draft changed slightly and added to by Wolfe and used by Edward Aswell as Book VI of *You Can't Go Home Again,* Wolfe divided the typescript into three uneven sections, marked "The Hotel," "The Station," and "The Train." I choose that version because it represents the story as Wolfe shaped it for publication before it was trimmed by him and Elizabeth Nowell for its appearance in *The New Republic* in three installments in March 1937. (The section entitled "The Dark Messiah" in Book VI of *You Can't Go Home Again* was not part of the original novella, most of it having been written in February of 1938 [Kennedy 333]). This second typescript version is told from the first-person point of view and narrates the experiences of Paul Spangler (later to be called George Webber).

Behind the novella lie some notebook entries of considerable interest, many of them tellingly political. On the topic of freedom of speech and thought Wolfe scribbled, "In Germany you are free to speak and write that you do not like Jews and that you think Jews are bad, corrupt and unpleasant people. In America you are not free to say this" (*Notebooks* 829). But the freedom to write ethnic slurs was being bought at a very high price:

> Nothing good can be said about the Italian or German dictatorships. If one suggests that benefits from these dictatorships have been considerable, the slot-machine answer, with a slight sneer is, "Oh, yes, we know—the streets are clean and the trains run on time, but do you think that these blessings compensate for the loss of human liberties, freedom of speech, etc., etc." (*Notebooks* 830)

Continuing his weighing of fascism as he had come to know it, he jotted down a list of pros and cons:

Fascism

For	Against
Physical Clean-ness	Repression of free speech
Healthy People	A Cult of Insular Superiority
Effective Relief	With This a Need for Insular
A Concentration of	Dominion
National Energy	

(*Notebooks* 831)

Still later he recorded a plan taking shape for a new story: "I am going to tell you a little story and it is a little story that may hurt me too. I am taking a chance when I tell it" (*Notebooks* 835). Musing further on a problem forced upon him by the ethnic background of one of the characters to appear in the story, Wolfe confessed: "I don't like Jews, and if most of the people that I know would tell the truth about their feelings, I wonder how many of them would be able to say that they liked Jews" (*Notebooks* 835). But his perception of what lay ahead for humanity if Hitler and his followers were not checked led him to proclaim: "I have a thing to tell you. . . . brothers, we must brothers be—or die" (*Notebooks* 835). In foreseeing that he would be hurt by publishing the projected story, Wolfe was right. Following its publication, Wolfe's works were banned in Nazi Germany.

He sensed that the narrative discourse generated by the story would proclaim his steadfast opposition to the suspicion, mistrust, hatred, betrayal and atrocities in German society under Hitler's crazed sway. His story would expose Nazism as he had come to know it and dramatize how the chain of humanity could be severed if mankind refused to acknowledge and defend brotherhood

How best to embody those ideas in his story was a question that Wolfe as a storyteller had to answer through plot. His opening scene, Paul Spangler's conversation with Franz Heilig, establishes the fact that Hitler's Germany has created suspicion, mistrust and hatred. In heavy irony, Franz, confiding his fear that he will be punished for having his girl share his one-room place with him, says, "I vill now tell you somesing. Under ze Dritte Reich ve are all so happy, everysing is so fine and healsy zat it is perfectly God damn dretful." Through Franz, Wolfe reveals how the Nazis have treated Jews:

> "All ze Chews have been taken from zeir work, zey have nozzing to do any more. Zese people come around—some stupid people in zeir uniforms," he said contemptuously. "And zey say zat everyone must be an Aryan man—zis wonderful plue-eyed person eight feet tall who has been Aryan in his family since 1820. If zere is a little Chew back zere—zen it is a pity." (bMS Am 1883 [734], 7, 14)

These passages prepare readers for actions taken later at Aachen against a Jewish lawyer trying to leave the country with more marks than permissible. Franz's statement about Paul's current fame in Germany and the risk he would run if he wrote a story criticizing Hitler's regime carry Wolfe further into the narrative discourse now being opened with his readers. German repression of anything unfavorable to the Nazi line touches not only living arrangements and harassment of Jews but the freedom of artistic expression as well. Wolfe here reminds readers that writers in America suffer repression, too, not as victims of official government action but as targets of leftist or rightist groups more concerned with political correctness than with artistic merit. Spewing acid for Wolfe on both esthetic and political groups, Franz spits out his loathing for Expressionists, Surrealists, Communists and anyone dedicated to spreading or promoting propaganda: "I hate them—zese bloody awful little men" (23). Franz tears into them because he considers these special interest groups enemies of free expression: "You must say ze sings zey want you to say or zey kill you" (25).

This opening scene with Franz thus opens the questions that Wolfe wishes to pursue, offers firsthand evidence of the troubling discoveries he is making about Nazi Germany, and prepares us to accept a developing thesis that Germany's crushing of political and artistic freedom could be setting a pattern for much of Europe and the United States.

The second scene, set on the platform of the Bahnhof Am Zoo, forces us to respond to the hints about suspicion and mistrust offered in the first scene. When Paul introduces Else von Kohler to Franz, the two Germans stare at each other coldly, hostilely, a response leading Paul to observe: "It had in it a quality that was different from anything I had ever seen at home, a quality that was at once shockingly cold and naked and disturbingly subtle. It was as hard as steel and flashing as a rapier" (31). The issue here seems to be less esthetic than sexual, though the former does arise in Else's critique of the drawing of Paul by Franz's friend. Franz appears to move in Berlin's homosexual circle, whereas Else seems to embody the essence of heterosexuality.

This scene continues its revelation of the German character when Paul's friend Lewald joins the farewell party on the platform. When Lewald speaks to Else, his manner seems bluff, boyish, and exuberant, indeed full of high spirits and "jolly good will" (38). Paul finally sees that Lewald's "boyish ingenuousness was just a mask" and that his "soul and character were sly, shrewd, subtle, devious, crafty, cunning, dexterous as hell" (38). This episode eventually underscores the feelings of hostility and alienation existing among Paul's German friends. Hoping that Paul won't be caught up in bitter rivalries for his allegiance or by some group's hope that his pen will be used in their behalf, Else says to him in reference to Franz: "You must not listen to zis bitter man! . . . You are religious man. You are artist. And ze artist *is* religious man" (33).

The third part of the story proves that statement to be true, for it is there that Paul and the people he encounters in his compartment on the train to Paris come to realize the need to become their brother's keeper if civilized society is to survive. The narrative thread holding this third section together is more tightly woven than the thread running through the first two parts. Whereas there has been a degree of acquaintance among the Germans of the first two parts, all but the Rubenesque mannequin manufacturer and her employee, a young sculptor, are utter strangers. At first glance it is difficult for Paul to understand why the German woman and the young man should be traveling together, so different seem their mien and breeding, she appearing theatrical, he, countrified. Puzzling as this unlikely couple is, Paul has trouble getting a fix on an elegantly dressed young man sitting by the window. "Certainly he did not look English or American. There was a kind of foppish, almost sugared elegance about this costume that one felt somehow was continental, even though one did not know from what place on the continent he came" (44). But what strikes Paul with a "sense of shock" is the fact that the young man is reading an American book, a popular work entitled *The Saga of Democracy.* For the time being, this passenger will remain another "isolato," to borrow one of Melville's most profound coinages.

Still to be introduced is the person whose arrest at Aachen will prove once again Melville's assertion that "every mortal that breathes . . . has [a] Siamese connexion with a plurality of other mortals" (320). That last person to enter the compartment is "a drab, stuffy, irascible-looking little fellow of the type that one sees a thousand times a day" . . . "the kind of fellow" . . . who is "always fidgeting and fuming about . . . always, in short, trying by every crusty, crotchety, sour, ill-tempered method in his equipment to make himself as unpleasant, and his traveling companions as uncomfortable, as possible" (48-49). His mannerisms will eventually lead Paul to call him "old Fuss-and-Fidget." His nervousness, looks of suspicion, and his pointing at the "Nicht Raucher" sign when Paul and the elegant young man take out cigarettes present serious obstacles if "a Siamese connexion" is ever to be formed with him. He will be, in short, the most isolated of the isolatoes as the train rushes across the German country-side from Berlin to Hanover. In his isolation, Paul tries to pass a wearisome time by dozing.

> Time after time I started out of this doze to find old Fuss-and-Fidget's eyes fixed on me in a look of such suspicion and ill-tempered sourness that the expression barely escaped malevolence. I woke up one time to find his gaze fixed on me in a stare that was so protracted, so unfriendly, that I felt anger boiling up in me. (51-52)

Not until Hanover is the ice broken among members of this group. The first bond to be formed is between Paul and the elegantly dressed young man with a continental look, the naturalized American now identified as Johnnie Adamowski, symbolically much more appropriate than the surname *Stefanowski* used in *The New Republic* version of the story. This naturalized American, this new Adam, enables Wolfe to give voice, even if it is a bit on the enthusiastic side, to American ideas. Unhappy about conditions in Europe during his return to Poland to visit relatives, Adamowski asserts, "I am sick of Europe. Every time I come I am fed up. I am tired of all this foolish business, these politics, this hate, these armies and this talk of war. . . . It will be good after all this to back [in America] where all is Peace—where all is Friendship—where all is Love" (54-55). In his role as narrator, Paul confides that he had "reservations on this score but did not utter them" (55). Despite Paul's reluctance to argue, Wolfe effectively highlights America's most cherished values by having Adamowski state his preference for the New World, where New Adam is free to try to achieve his highest dreams.

Once the ice is broken, Paul and Johnnie rapidly establish bonds: they have mutual friends in New York, enjoy eating and drinking together, and share the goal of spending all their German marks before the train reaches the border. When they return to their compartment, their eager and easy dialogue begins to draw the others into conversation as well. It becomes obvious that their companions have discussed them during their absence. Now curiosity begins to bind them. The mannequin maker and her youthful companion begin to open up, and even Fuss-and-Fidget relaxes somewhat and finally identifies himself as a lawyer on his way to a Parisian conference. Helping to break down any remaining reserve is Johnnie's sharing of the food his family had packed for him. The group is becoming, as Chapter 42 of *You Can't Go Home Again* would

have it, "The Family of Earth." A "Siamese connexion" has been formed; a monkey rope has been found.

Another bond cementing them, one that leads to a test of its strength and one that leads to the arrest of Fuss-and-Fidget, is money. Their grievance about German policy restricting the amount of money a person can take out of Germany prompts them to acts of friendship, acts of brother-keeping, that mere fellow companions on a train trip would never perform. Evidence of this appears in Johnnie's eagerness to befriend the German woman by taking into his keeping some of her excessive marks and Paul's acceptance of Fuss-and-Fidget's proffered ten marks. Through these actions, Wolfe involves his readers even more deeply in the narrative discourse he has been conducting as the action of his plot further unfolds itself. These passengers have discovered their common humanity and are acting to protect one another from oppressive political policy.

But instantly the discourse has a darker, terrifying, and fearful symbolic element added. That comes with the appearance of the customs official, "a burly-looking fellow . . . a Germanic type with high blunt cheekbones, a florid face and tawny mustaches, combed out sprouting, in the Kaiser Wilhelm way. His head was shaven, and there were thick creases at the base of his skull and across his fleshy neck" (80). He will symbolize all that is "loathsome, sinister, and repellent" (80) in Hitler's government. Paul's "trembling with a murderous and incomprehensible anger" and desire "to smash that fat neck" and "pound that inflamed and blunted face into a jelly" (80-81) catch us up in his revulsion. We feel that he indeed does have something vitally important to tell us about man's inhumanity and the need to stand together against it.

All these humane feelings in Paul now well up for Fuss-and-Fidget, now identified for the first time as a Jew. Paul's informant is the Rubenesque mannequin maker, who now rejects part of the bond she had formed because she shares many of her countrymen's biases against Jews: "These Jews!" she cried, "These things would never happen if it were not for them! They make all the trouble. Germany has had to protect herself. The Jews were taking all the money from the country" (89).

With the revelation of her feelings Wolfe asks us to make still another metaphoric transference, this one demanding that we acknowledge that seemingly decent German citizens, whom this culturally rich fading beauty symbolizes, share heavily in Germany's mistrust and mistreatment of Jews. That becomes part of what Paul feels he must tell us, too. Still, Wolfe leaves her some humanity, despite her energetic attempt at justifying Fuss-and-Fidget's arrest. As the regathered companions reflect on his fate, she finally "gravely, quietly" said, "He must have wanted very badly to escape" (89).

Before his discourse could end, Wolfe had one more drive to ponder, one more metaphoric transfer to request of his readers. This drive was how now to deal with his love of Germany, a land that seemed more than a mere second home to him. No doubt speaking through Paul, he wrote,

"I was the other half of my heart's home, a haunted part of dark desire. . . . It was the dark lost Helen I had found, it was the dark found Helen I had lost—and now I knew, as I had never known before, the priceless measure of my loss,—the priceless measure of my gain" (92). He came to realize that he had to give up Germany, to suffer the consequences of his desire to tell the truth. And he came, more profoundly still, to realize that he must one day give up the earth, for

> something has spoken in the night; and told me I shall die, I know not where. Saying, "To lose the earth you know for greater knowing, losing the life you have, for greater life; leaving friends you loved, for greater loving; to find a land more kind than home, more large than earth. (93)

Thus the final words of the narrative discourse conducted through this simple and much tested travel plot invite us to join Wolfe in his concluding metaphoric transfer. The sustaining metonymy of the train trip is that humanity rides together to eternity. The best hope that each passenger will arrive unscarred by atrocities is to travel together as brothers and sisters, to keep charged, in Hawthorne's phrase, "the magnetic chain of humanity" (1064).

Works Cited

Brooks, Peter. *Reading for the Plot: Design and Intention in Narrative.* New York: Knopf, 1984.

Hawthorne, Nathaniel. *Tales and Sketches.* Ed. Roy Harvey Pearce. New York: Library of America, 1982.

Kennedy, Richard S. *The Window of Memory: The Literary Career of Thomas Wolfe.* Chapel Hill: U of North Carolina P, 1962.

Melville, Herman. *Moby-Dick: or The Whale.* Ed. Harrison Hayford et al. Evanston, IL: Northwestern U—Newberry Library, 1988.

Wolfe, Thomas. "I Have a Thing to Tell You." William Wisdom Collection, Houghton Library, Harvard University (bMs Am 1883 [734]). Quoted by permission of Paul Gitlin, Administrator, C. T. A., Estate of Thomas Wolfe, 919 Third Avenue, New York, New York 10022 and the William Wisdom Collection, Harvard University, by permission of the Houghton Library. The periodical version of the story appears in three installments in *The New Republic,* 10 March 1937, pp. 132-36; 17 March, pp. 159-64; 24 March, pp. 202-207. As a section of *You Can't Go Home Again,* it runs from page 634 through page 704.

————. *The Letters of Thomas Wolfe.* Ed. Elizabeth Nowell. New York: Scribner's, 1956.

————. *The Notebooks of Thomas Wolfe.* Ed. Richard S. Kennedy and Paschal Reeves. Chapel Hill: U of North Carolina P, 1970.

Joseph Bentz (essay date 1994)

SOURCE: "The Influence of Modernist Structure in the Short Fiction of Thomas Wolfe," in *Studies in Short Fiction,* Vol. 31, No. 2, Spring, 1994, pp. 149-61.

[*In the following essay, Bentz characterizes Wolfe as an experimentalist in short fiction whose use of non-traditional plot structure and thematic epiphany align his short stories with those of his modern contemporaries.*]

The most famous attack on the fiction of Thomas Wolfe is Bernard DeVoto's 1936 essay "Genius is Not Enough." In it DeVoto identifies three points of weakness in Wolfe's fiction that critics have returned to repeatedly over the years. The first criticism is Wolfe's lack of artistic control and looseness of form. DeVoto blasts *Look Homeward, Angel* for "long whirling discharges of words, unabsorbed in the novel, unrelated to the proper business of fiction, badly if not altogether unacceptably written, raw gobs of emotion, aimless and quite meaningless jabber, claptrap, belches, grunts, and Tarzanlike screams" (132). The other two familiar criticisms in DeVoto's essay are that Wolfe's editors ("the assembly line at Scribner's") made too many of the artistic decisions that should have been made by the novelist, and that Wolfe misused and overused autobiographical material. Not all critics have been as hostile as DeVoto, and certainly Wolfe has had his defenders, but the issues DeVoto raised have set the agenda for much of the debate about Wolfe for the past 50 years.

Most of the critical focus over the years has centered on Wolfe's sprawling novels, but with the publication in 1987 of *The Complete Short Stories of Thomas Wolfe,* this other body of his work has begun to receive attention. Wolfe wrote 58 short stories, but until the complete collection was published, 35 of these stories had never been published in book form, and one had never been published anywhere (Skipp xvii). The overemphasis on Wolfe's seemingly loosely structured novels has obscured his experimentation in the short story. While the structure of his novels owes a greater debt to nineteenth-century fiction than to the modernist fiction of the 1920s and '30s, the structure of many of Wolfe's short stories was heavily influenced by modernism.

Modernist short-story writers rejected traditional attitudes toward form in the short story. Richard Kostelanetz, an historian of the American short story, describes some key features of modernist short-story structure:

> In the short story of the 1920's . . . the action is greatly pruned until the story appears rather plotless. Yet every detail serves an artistic function; nothing seems unconsidered or accidental. The short stories in the Twenties exhibit greater emotional complexity and ambiguity, as well as a more discriminating sense of emphasis and an increased brevity of representation (in short, a modified, more selective, realism). . . . Instead of concentrating on plot development, the authors resort to rhetorical strategies and parallelism and repetition; the narrator often speaks in the first person and may be a major participant in the action rather than just an observer of it; and the story's end comes as an anticlimax after the earlier epiphany. (220)

Modernists rejected traditional form in the short story because they believed that form presents a misleading picture of the nature of reality. As Clare Hanson explains,

"Modernist short fiction writers distrusted the well-wrought tale for a variety of reasons. Most importantly they argued that the pleasing shape and coherence of the traditional short story represented a falsification of the discrete and heterogeneous nature of experience" (55). She adds that the "rounded finality of the tale" was rejected, "for story in this sense seemed to convey the misleading notion of something finished, absolute, and wholly understood" (55).

Scholars have generally understood and accepted the modernist approach in the fiction of Wolfe's contemporaries, but Wolfe's experiments in modernism have often faced hostility. When Wolfe rejects a traditional plot story for a more experimental approach, his work is called "formless"; when his contemporaries such as Sherwood Anderson engage in similar experiments, it is called "modernism." A brief look at the critical response to Anderson will illuminate some of the points I wish to make about Wolfe.

Arthur Voss, in his history of the short story in America, credits Anderson with the "liberation" of the short story (183). Anderson, as he puts it, "revolted against the stereotyped and conventional fiction of his time" (183). Anderson's novel *Winesburg, Ohio,* like many of Wolfe's stories, does not have a plot in the traditional sense of the term. The "plot story," as A. L. Bader defines it, is any story

> (1) which derives its structure from plot based on a conflict and issuing in action; (2) whose action is sequential, progressive, that is, offers something for the reader to watch unfold and develop, usually by means of a series of complications, thus evoking suspense; and (3) whose action finally resolves the conflict, thus giving the story "point." (108)

Waldo Frank describes the form of Anderson's stories, in contrast, with a term that has often been applied to aspects of Wolfe's writing. He says, "The form is lyrical" (84). He compares the form, for instance, to the "lyrical art of the Old Testament psalmists and prophets in whom the literary medium was so allied to music that their texts have always been sung in synagogues" (Frank 85). He describes the design of individual stories as "a theme-statement of a character with his mood, followed by a recounting of actions that are merely variations on the theme" (85). The few stories in which Anderson attempts a straight narrative, Frank argues, are the least successful. Frank is not the only scholar to describe the structure of *Winesburg, Ohio* in terms of its lyrical nature. Irving Howe says the stories' impact depends "less on dramatic action than on a climactic lyrical insight" (103).

The point here is not to say that Anderson and Wolfe were trying to accomplish the same goals. They are very different writers. But their stories share an emphasis on a "climactic lyrical insight" rather than on traditional plot. Because some critics have insisted on foisting a traditional attitude toward structure on Wolfe's work, what passes for a "lyrical form" in Anderson might be called "long whirling discharges of words" in Wolfe.

As A. L. Bader points out, the critics' reaction to modernist short-story structure has often been one of puzzlement or outright hostility:

> Readers and critics accustomed to an older type of story are baffled by a newer type. They sense the underlying and unifying design of the one, but they find nothing equivalent to it in the other. Hence they maintain that the modern short story is plotless, static, fragmentary, amorphous—frequently a mere character sketch or vignette, or a mere reporting of a transient moment, or the capturing of a mood or nuance—everything, in fact, except a story. (107)

It is interesting to note how similar this reaction is to the reaction Wolfe's stories have received from some critics. When Wolfe's first collection of short stories, *From Death to Morning,* was published in 1935, for example, the reviewers had trouble categorizing the stories. Ferner Nuhn wrote that few of the pieces could be called short stories "in any strict sense; lyrical essays, themes with variations, moods of reminiscence, they might perhaps be called" (7). Harold Mumford Jones wrote,

> I think it is Chesterton who remarks there is no such thing as a Dickens novel, but only a series of segments cut off from that vast and flowing thing which is Dickens. *From Death to Morning* is a collection of fourteen segments cut off from that vast and flowing thing which is Thomas Wolfe. (13)

Jones said the collection could best be described as "a group of sketches, for none of them rises into a full-bodied short story" (13).

Later critics were even more hostile toward Wolfe's approach toward form. Martin Maloney, for instance, wrote in 1955,

> In Wolfe's Faustian world, "stories," (meaning the common conventions of modern fiction) did not and probably could not exist: 'life' alone mattered. Wolfe did not write 'stories,' but instead produced a single, long, complex narrative, imposing no formal structure on it. . . . (168)

This stereotype about the structure of Wolfe's stories remains to this day. In a review of *The Complete Short Stories of Thomas Wolfe,* in 1987, Monroe K. Spears praised many of the stories but also claimed that "Wolfe was afflicted by a kind of literary bulimia, devouring life insatiably and expelling it in his writing, which he was unable to restrain or control" (34).

How did Wolfe approach the structure of the short story? Wolfe had trouble fitting his work into established categories no matter what genre he experimented with. He gave up drama because his plays were too long and wordy, but when he switched to the novel, which better suited his talents, he still had difficulty keeping his work short enough to meet his publisher's expectations. For instance, Wolfe's first manuscript, "O Lost," which later was trimmed to become *Look Homeward, Angel,* was 1,113 typed pages long, or about 330,000 words, which was about three times the length of most novels in the 1920s (Donald 176). Wolfe also liked to save material discarded from one project to use it in a later one. As Leslie Field explains,

> Wolfe was not the sort of writer who creates a novel and then a second one with freshly composed material. . . . Thus some of his writing for *You Can't Go Home Again* could belong to the *Look Homeward, Angel* period of composition, or sections of *The Web and the Rock* could very well be discards from *Of Time and the River.* (Field, *TW and His Editors* 3-4)

Wolfe took an equally unconventional approach toward short-story writing. Most of the stories were adapted from the massive manuscripts that eventually became his novels. Some stories, because of their innovative approach toward point of view, narrative technique, or subject matter, could not be fit into the novels and stood alone as short stories. Often the stories were published to keep Wolfe's name before the public or to earn him badly needed money. Not surprisingly, Wolfe's unconventional approach toward short-story writing brought mixed results. As J. R. Morris describes Wolfe's achievement in a review of the 1987 collection, "Whether they are truly short stories or simply fragments of that one endless story Thomas Wolfe spent his life writing, the 58 pieces of short fiction in ***The Complete Short Stories*** include some of Wolfe's best writing, and, alas, some of his worst" (127).

Despite Wolfe's unusual writing methods, his stories share important characteristics with those of his contemporaries in the modernist era. Short-story historian Eileen Baldeshwiler identifies two types of stories that were prominent in the modernist period. The larger group of narratives, which she calls "epical," are "marked by external action developed 'syllogistically' through characters fabricated mainly to forward plot, culminating in a decisive ending that sometimes affords a universal insight, and expressed in the serviceably inconspicuous language of prose realism" (443). This kind of short story, which I earlier identified as the "plot story," is the kind critics say Wolfe had difficulty structuring. The second kind of story, which Baldeshwiler calls "lyrical," and which I call "modernist," "concentrates on internal changes, moods, and feelings, utilizing a variety of structural patterns depending on the shape of the emotion itself, relies for the most part on the open ending, and is expressed in the condensed, evocative, often figured language of the poem" (443).

Besides its open ending and heightened language, the modernist short story also emphasizes not a linear plot, but rather a single significant moment of insight. In Clare Hanson's words, "The emphasis of modernist short fiction was on a single moment of intense or significant experience" (55). Nadine Gordimer writes, "Short story writers see by the light of the flash; theirs is the art of the only thing one can be sure of—the present moment. Ideally, they have learned to do without explanation of what went before, and what happens beyond this point" (180). Various scholars have commented on James Joyce's influence

on Wolfe. Joyce's term for the "light of the flash" was "epiphany." It is appropriate to examine Wolfe's stories using that term. In *Stephen Hero* Joyce defined the term:

> By an epiphany he meant a sudden spiritual manifestation, whether in the vulgarity of speech or of gesture or in a memorable phase of the mind itself. He believed that it was for the man of letters to record these epiphanies with extreme care, seeing that they themselves are the most delicate and evanescent of moments. (Joyce 211)

Wolfe was aware that stories that abandon the traditional linear plot structure in favor of the more open-ended modernist structure were often misunderstood by readers and critics. In a letter to Hamilton Basso he wrote,

> We [Americans] have hunted always for the short cut, the practicable way, and I think the effect of this—it does not seem to me at all far fetched to think—has been to hunt for the short cut, the easy and practicable way, the neat definition, everywhere: hence the neat glib finish of the O. Henry type of short story, the "punch at the end," the "gag," and many other kinds of gimcrackery. (*Letters* 632-33)

Wolfe insisted on breaking free of such constraints in many stories. Not all of his stories fit the modernist mode; many of them are more traditionally structured, and some of them defy categories altogether. But measuring some of them against modernist rather than traditional criteria may reveal Wolfe's real artistic achievement.

A good example of a Wolfe story written in the modernist mode is **"No Cure for It,"** published in ***The Hills Beyond.*** An amusing story of about 2,000 words, it records an incident in which a worried mother, Eliza Gant, calls Doctor McGuire to her home to examine her seven-year-old son Eugene, because the ways in which his body is maturing "don't seem natural" (**"No Cure"** 534). His arms and legs seem too long and out of proportion to the rest of his body, she thinks. Doctor McGuire, who is more amused than concerned by Eugene's condition, asks the boy to wrap his leg around his neck, which the boy does with no problem, as Eliza puckers her face in worry and disapproval and says, "Get out of here! I don't like to look at anything like that!" Doctor McGuire declares that Eugene is all right, but calls him "a little monkey" (534). The doctor says, "He'll get all of his parts together some day and grow out of it!" At this point Eugene's father, who has a penchant for hyperbolic rhetoric, comes home and blames the boy's condition on Eliza: "Woman, this is your work! Unnatural female that you are, you have given birth to a monster who will not rest until he has ruined us all, eaten us out of house and home, and sent me to the poorhouse to perish in a pauper's grave!" (535). But later he tones down this rhetoric, reassuring Eugene by telling his son it was the same with him when he grew up, and that someday Eugene will be a big man.

The story at first glance is a comic anecdote about growing up, made funnier by Eliza's exaggerated worry, the father's outrageous hyperbole, and the doctor's amusement at the whole situation. The story gains further significance, however, by the references Wolfe includes about the flux of time and time's impingement upon the boy's life. The story begins with Eliza calling the boy, and the next sentence says, "He heard her call again, and listened plainly to her now, and knew she would break in upon his life, his spell of time, and wondered what it was she wanted of him" (533). He makes no move and does not answer her. He merely listens as she invites the doctor inside and has a conversation with him. When they reach the room where he is stretched out on the couch, he continues to lie there, "listening to the time-strange tocking of the clock" and regarding his brown bare legs and sun-browned toes "with a look of dreamy satisfaction" (533). It is as if time has transported him beyond the here and now, giving him a fascinating sense of detachment from himself. When Eliza scolds him for not answering her, he scrambles up sheepishly, "unable to deny that he had heard her, yet knowing, somehow, that he had not willingly disobeyed her" (533). He did not have the words to identify or describe the detachment this new awareness of time had given him, but it had made him unable to respond to her before.

Wolfe returns to the theme of time at the end of the story. Eugene's father has just comforted him by telling the boy he will grow up to be a big man someday. The last paragraph is a scene of suspended animation, with the mother, father, and doctor looking at the boy, as he considers them. The story ends, "He thought his father was the grandest, finest person in the world, and as the three of them looked at him he could hear, in the hush of brooding noon, the time-strange tocking of his father's clock" (536). This story does not follow a traditional plot. It is modernist in its emphasis on, in Hanson's words, the "single moment of intense or significant experience" (180). There is nothing inherent in the fairly ordinary incident that makes it a "significant moment" for the protagonist. It is only the boy's ability, even if he cannot verbalize it, to connect that moment with the past, future, and eternal time, that makes the experience so important.

What does the boy learn about time? It would be easy to answer too reductively, but a few discoveries are clear. At the beginning of the story he discovers he can lose himself in a "spell of time," a period of reflectiveness in which time seems suspended, until ordinary reality, in the form of Eliza, breaks him out of it. He gets a taste of being outside of time, but he cannot stay out of its flow for long. At the end of the story he discovers that even though at present his body is all out of proportion, time brings change. The sound of his father's clock represents the force of time that will make him a man. Therefore, as he gazes at his parents and the doctor at the end of the story, he grins proudly and is "worried about nothing" (536).

Wolfe uses time in an even more elaborate way in one of his best and most famous stories, **"The Lost Boy."** The story was published by *Redbook* in 1937 and appeared with some changes in *The Hills Beyond*. In 1992 Wolfe scholar James Clark edited a much longer version of the story, which was published as a novella by the University

of North Carolina Press. The version I refer to here is the *Redbook* version, which is the one included in *The Complete Stories.* This story, like **"No Cure for It,"** has no plot in the traditional sense. It is, however, carefully structured. The story is about the narrator's attempt to "find" his brother who died more than 30 years before at the 1904 World's Fair in St. Louis. The narrator searches for him by recreating the stories he has heard about him and by going to St. Louis to see the house where his brother Robert had died when the narrator was only four years old.

The story is in four parts. The first part is the narrative of an incident that happened to Robert in his hometown before the family went to the fair. The second section is from Robert's mother's point of view and includes her reminiscences of him. The third section contains memories of Robert from his sister's point of view. The last section is from the narrator's point of view, in which he describes his visit to the house where Robert died.

The story shares a number of structural and thematic characteristics with **"No Cure for It."** **"The Lost Boy,"** like the other story, contains an epiphanic moment in which the character comes to a realization about time and his own relationship to it. In fact, **"The Lost Boy"** contains two such moments, one for Robert, the "lost" brother whom the narrator is trying to search through time to "find" or recreate, and one for the narrator himself, as his search reaches its climax. In both stories the encounters with time are presented in the mystical or "lyrical" language that was such a hallmark of Wolfe's writing.

Wolfe's symbol for "time immutable" in **"The Lost Boy,"** as well as in other stories, such as **"An Angel on the Porch,"** **"The Bell Remembered,"** and the novel *Look Homeward, Angel,* is the town square. Robert begins the story in the square, where he senses "the union of Forever and Now":

> Light came and went and came again: the great plume of the fountain pulsed, and the winds of April sheeted it across the Square in rainbow gossamer of spray. The street cars ground into the Square from every portion of the town's small compass and halted briefly like wound toys in their old quarter-hourly formula of assembled Eight. The courthouse bell boomed out is solemn warning of immediate Three, and everything was just the same as it had always been. (Wolfe, **"Lost Boy"** 359)

Robert surveys every building and landmark on the square, listing them one by one, and concludes, "here is the Square that never changes; here is Robert almost twelve—and here is Time" (359). As Wallace Stegner describes this section of the story, "There is a quality of trance: the returning plume of the fountain, the returning winds of April, the streetcars going and coming, the chanting of the strong repetitious rhetoric and the sonority of recurrent sounds put a magic on this Square even at its most real" (256).

After the description of the Square at the beginning of the story, Robert has his confrontation with "old stingy Crockers," the candy shop owner. Robert does not have enough money to pay for the candy, so he uses postage stamps to pay for part of it, as he had done before in Crocker's store. Robert accidentally overpays Crocker by three one-cent stamps. Realizing his mistake, Robert asks Crocker to give him back the three stamps. Crocker ponders for a moment, and then answers, "I don't like this kind of business. I'm not a post office. The next time you come in here and want anything, you'll have to have the money for it" (362). He does not return the stamps. When Robert again demands that Crocker return the stamps, Crocker and his wife imply that Robert probably stole the stamps anyway. Crocker shouts at the boy, ordering him to leave the store and never come back.

Angry and humiliated, Robert leaves the store and steps onto the Square, which just moments before this humiliating incident had represented stability and time immutable to him. People walk by, but he doesn't notice them. He stands "blindly, in the watches of the sun, but something had gone out of the day" (363). His anger gives way to the "soul-sickening guilt that all the children, all the good men of the earth, have felt since time began. And even anger had been drowned out, in the swelling tide of guilt." His sense of stability had been shattered. In his own way he realizes that unlike the Square, he is subject to the sometimes violent flow of present time: "'There is the Square,' thought Robert as before. 'This is Now. There is my father's shop. And all of it is as it has always been—save I'" (364).

Robert immediately goes to his father's stonecutting shop nearby and tells him what has happened. His father takes Robert back to the store and humiliates Crocker into returning the stamps. Though Robert and his father are triumphant, Robert realizes the experience has changed him. He has become aware of two kinds of time: present time, in whose flow he finds himself caught, and time immutable, in whose stability he had always depended. His realization is presented this way:

> And light came and went and came again into the Square—but now not quite the same as it had done before. He saw that pattern of familiar shapes, and knew that they were just the same as they had always been. But something had gone out of the day, and something had come in again: out of the vision of those quiet eyes some brightness had been lost; into their vision some deeper color come. He could not say, he did not know through what transforming shadows life had passed within that quarter-hour. He only knew that something had been gained forever—something lost. (366)

The narrator, who is Robert's younger brother, has a very different but equally significant encounter with time in the last section of the story. In this section the narrator, now a man in his thirties, goes back to St. Louis, where his brother Robert had died 30 years before when part of the family lived there during the 1904 World's Fair. The narrator finds King's Highway, which was near the house where the family had lived. Memories of this place begin to flood his mind, and he searches some more until he finds the house. He is ready for some kind of encounter

with the lost brother, and with Time. He says, "And again, again, I turned into the street, finding the place where the two corners meet, the huddled block, the turret, and the steps, and paused a moment, as if the street was Time" (375). He has prepared the reader for this encounter too, because before this point the story has presented not only Robert's encounter with Crockers, but also reminiscences of Robert from his mother's voice and memories of Robert from his sister's voice. Before the reader arrives in St. Louis with the narrator, the reader knows the same family legends about Robert that the narrator remembers. When the narrator reaches the house where the family had lived, he, as well as the reader, expects to "find" Robert.

Someone is living in the house, but the narrator knocks on the door and explains to the current resident that he had lived there during the World's Fair. They discuss all the changes that have been made to the house, and finally she invites him in. As soon as he goes in he is almost able to cut through time and bring back the brother who was lost in it. But the past keeps fading away from him, and he cannot quite keep it in his grasp:

> All of it was just the same except the strained light of absence in the afternoon, and the child who sat there, waiting on the stairs, and something fading like a dream, something coming like a light, something going, passing fading like the shadows of a wood. And then it would be gone again, fading like cloud shadows in the hills . . . like the dark eyes and the quiet face, the dark lost boy, my brother, who himself like shadows, or like absence in the house, would come, would go, and would return again. (378)

The woman takes the narrator through the house, and he tells what the place used to be like. Finally they go into the room where Robert had died, and he tells her of his brother's death. After they discuss him for a while, she says, "I guess you don't remember him, do you? I shouldn't think you would." Though he answers, "No, not much," her question triggers the encounter with the past that he had been waiting for:

> The years dropped off like fallen leaves: the face came back again—the soft dark oval, the dark eyes, the soft brown berry on the neck, the raven hair, all bending down, approaching—the whole ghost-wise, intent and instant, like faces from a haunted wood. (379)

What follows is a flashback scene in which the older brother is trying to get the young narrator to say "Robert," but he can only manage to say "Wobbut." It is the climactic scene—the epiphany—of the story, and when it is over, so is the narrator's search for the lost boy: "I knew that I would never come again, and that lost magic would not come again . . ." (380). The narrator had been able to "find" the brother for a fleeting moment, but now he knows, as the last line of the story says, that the boy "was gone forever and would not return" (380). Robert's encounter in the story is with present time, and the narrator's is with the past, but both of them come to the understanding in the story that they are caught in time's flow and can do nothing to stop it.

Wolfe's achievement in **"The Lost Boy"** would have been impossible if he had used a traditional plot structure. The purpose of each section of the story is to recreate or "find" the lost boy in a new way. Each section looks at him from a different perspective until, in the final section, when the narrator has his mystical encounter with the boy in the house where Robert died, the reader has been so saturated with details about the boy that the reader is just as ready as the narrator is for the epiphanic encounter. Robert's life is not told in chronological order. Instead, he is re-created the way dead loved ones most often are—by the scattered anecdotes and memories of family legend. In the middle section the narrator allows Robert's mother and sister to relate their memories of the boy in their own voices. Like the narrator, the mother and sister are "searching" for Robert in their memories of him. Their stories are not concise little anecdotes, but instead are halting, full of ellipses, full of digressions. Their stories of Robert become entangled with stories of their own lives. We see clearly that they are not showing us *the* Robert, but only *a* Robert who is a product not only of their memory but partially of their imagination. Like the narrator, we must sift through the various versions of Robert to "find" the lost boy. Robert's sister, for instance, intertwines the story of her own life with her memories of Robert's life. Throughout her section of the story the sister refers to a family photograph that prompts her memories.

> I was thinking of it just the other day, and I wonder what Robert would say now if he could see that picture. For when you look at it, it all comes back—the boarding house, St. Louis and the Fair. . . . And all of it is just the same as it has always been, as if it happened yesterday. . . . And all of us have grown up and gone away. And nothing has turned out the way we thought it would. . . . And all my hopes and dreams and big ambitions have come to nothing. (374; original ellipses)

In a modernist way, **"The Lost Boy"** searches through time and memory in order to find the moment of significance. It meanders around the way memory does. Wallace Stegner's final comment on **"The Lost Boy"** is also true of **"No Cure for It"**:

> Not a line of this story, not a trick in it, could have been learned from any generalization about the shaping of fiction. The shape this story takes it takes by a process of transplantation, associated images and ideas being moved from one category of thought to another. (260)

"The Lost Boy" and **"No Cure for It"** are just two of Wolfe's stories influenced by modernist structure, but there are numerous others. Some of the best examples include **"The Train and the City," "The Four Lost Men,"** and **"A Prologue to America."** Other stories have modernist characteristics, even though they are not predominantly modernist. The end of **"An Angel on the Porch,"** for instance, deals with time in an epiphanic and mystical way that is similar to **"No Cure for It"** and **"The Lost Boy."**

"Circus at Dawn," "April, Late April," "The Promise of America," "The Newspaper," and **"No More Rivers"** also contain certain characteristics of modernist structure. Wolfe's work does not fit into generic categories very neatly. But analyzing the stories according to their modernist characteristics shows that contrary to what many critics have written, the unusual structure of many of his works was due not to a lack of concern for form or an inability to control his art; instead, Wolfe's works show that he was an experimentalist very much in tune with the bold new approach to fiction that characterizes the writers of his time.

Works Cited

Bader, A. L. "The Structure of the Modern Short Story." May 107-15.

Baldeshwiler, Eileen. "The Lyric Short Story: The Sketch of a History." *Studies in Short Fiction* 6 (1969): 443-53. Rpt. in May 202-13.

Clark, James W., Jr., ed. *The Lost Boy: A Novella.* By Thomas Wolfe. Chapel Hill: U of North Carolina P, 1992.

DeVoto, Bernard. "Genius is Not Enough." Field, *TW: Three Decades,* 85-104.

Donald, David Herbert. *Look Homeward: A Life of Thomas Wolfe.* New York: Fawcett, 1987.

Field, Leslie. *Thomas Wolfe and His Editors.* Norman: U of Oklahoma P, 1987.

———, ed. *Thomas Wolfe: Three Decades of Criticism.* New York: New York UP, 1968.

Frank, Waldo. "*Winesburg, Ohio* After Twenty Years." White 84-88.

Gordimer, Nadine. "South Africa." *Kenyon Review* 30 (1968): 457-61. Rpt. as "The Flash of Fireflies" in May 178-81.

Hanson, Clare. *Short Stories and Short Fictions, 1880-1980.* New York: St. Martin's Press, 1985.

Howe, Irving. "The Book of the Grotesque." White 101-13.

Jones, Howard Mumford. "Thomas Wolfe's Short Stories." Rev. of *From Death to Morning,* by Thomas Wolfe. *Saturday Review of Literature.* 30 Nov. 1935: 13. Rpt. in *Thomas Wolfe: The Critical Reception.* Ed. Paschal Reeves. New York: David Lewis, 1974. 80-82.

Joyce, James. *Stephen Hero.* Ed. John J. Slocum and Herbert Cahoon. New York: New Directions, 1944.

Kostelanetz, Richard. "The Short Story in Search of Status." *Twentieth Century* 174 (Autumn 1965): 65-69. Rpt. in May 214-25.

Maloney, Martin. "A Study of Semantic States: Thomas Wolfe and the Faustian Sickness." Field, *TW: Three Decades,* 153-76.

May, Charles E., ed. *Short Story Theories.* Athens: Ohio UP, 1976.

Nuhn, Ferner. "Thomas Wolfe, Six-Foot-Six." Rev. of *From Death to*

Morning, by Thomas Wolfe. *New York Herald Tribune Books.* 17 Nov. 1935: 7. Rpt. in *Thomas Wolfe: The Critical Reception.* Ed. Paschal Reeves. New York: David Lewis, 1974. 79-80.

Skipp, Francis E., ed. Preface. *The Complete Short Stories of Thomas Wolfe.* New York: Scribner's, 1987. xvii-xxvii.

Spears, Monroe K. "Big Bad Wolfe?" Rev. of *The Complete Short Stories of Thomas Wolfe,* ed. Francis E. Skipp. *New York Review of Books* 24 Sept. 1987: 34-37.

Stegner, Wallace. "Analysis of 'The Lost Boy.'" Field, *TW: Three Decades,* 255-60.

Voss, Arthur. *The American Short Story.* Norman: U of Oklahoma P, 1973.

White, Ray Lewis. *Studies in Winesburg, Ohio.* Columbus, OH: Merrill, 1971.

Wolfe, Thomas. *The Complete Short Stories of Thomas Wolfe.* Ed. Francis E. Skipp. New York: Scribner's, 1987.

———. "The Lost Boy." *Complete Stories* 359-80.

———. "No Cure for It." *Complete Stories* 533-36.

———. *The Letters of Thomas Wolfe.* Ed. Elizabeth Nowell. New York: Scribner's, 1956.

———. *The Story of a Novel. The Autobiography of an American Novelist.* Ed. Leslie Field. Cambridge, MA: Harvard UP, 1983. 3-89.

FURTHER READING

Boyer, James. "The Metaphorical Level in Wolfe's 'The Sun and the Rain'." *Studies in Short Fiction* 19, No. 4 (Fall 1982): 384-87.

Analyzes the literary technique of Wolfe's short story "The Sun and the Rain" and explores its pervasive symbolism of the earth as a source of strength.

Doten, Sharon. "Thomas Wolfe's 'No Door': Some Textual Questions." *The Papers of the Bibliographical Society of America* 68, No. 1 (January-March 1974): 45-52.

Examines textual evidence provided by manuscripts of Wolfe's short novel *No Door* in order to assess his method of composing short fiction, and the relation of such works to Wolfe's longer novels.

Forssberg, William. "Part Two of 'The Lost Boy': Theme and Intention." *Studies in Short Fiction* IV, No. 2 (Winter 1967): 167-69.

Focuses on the theme of discontinuity of identity in the second part of Wolfe's short story "The Lost Boy."

Idol, John L., Jr. "Thomas Wolfe's 'A Note on Experts'." *Studies in Short Fiction* XI, No. 4 (Fall 1974): 395-98.

Discusses a rare and uncompleted sketch of a sports writer published on a limited scale in 1939 as "A Note on Experts."

———. "Wolfe's 'The Lion at Morning' and 'Old Man Rivers'." *The Thomas Wolfe Newsletter* 1, No. 2 (Fall 1977): 21-4.

Studies two fictional sketches of editors Wolfe composed from his real-life acquaintances.

———. "Germany as Thomas Wolfe's Second Dark Helen: The Angst of 'I Have a Thing to Tell You'." *The Thomas Wolfe Review* 19, No. 1 (Spring 1995): 1-9.

Explores the anguish Wolfe felt and later captured in fiction following his visits to Hitler's Germany in the late 1920s and early 1930s.

Kennedy, Richard S. *The Window of Memory: The Literary Career of Thomas Wolfe.* Chapel Hill: The University of North Carolina Press, 1962, 461 p.

An important, well-documented, biographical and critical study of Wolfe, which includes sections on *From Death to Morning,* the short novel *I Have a Thing to Tell You,* and other significant pieces of Wolfe's shorter fiction.

Owen, Guy. "'An Angel on the Porch' and *Look Homeward, Angel.*" *The Thomas Wolfe Newsletter* 4, No. 2 (Fall 1980): 21-4.

Argues that "An Angel on the Porch" is "a meticulously revised and reshaped version of Chapter XIX" in *Look Homeward, Angel* that stands on its own as "a mature work of art."

Phillipson, John S. "Thomas Wolfe's 'Chickamauga': The Fact and the Fiction." *The Thomas Wolfe Review* 6, No. 2 (Fall 1982): 9-22.

Traces the real-life sources of Wolfe's short story "Chickamauga."

Pencak, William. "'Only the Dead Know Brooklyn'—Or Do 'The Bums at Sunset'?" *The Thomas Wolfe Review* 19, No. 2 (Fall 1995): 44-51.

Investigates the theme of transcendence from squalor and death in two of Wolfe's short stories set in Brooklyn.

Stutman, Suzanne. "Reconsideration: Mediation, Aline Bernstein, and Thomas Wolfe's 'The Good Child's River.'" *MELUS* 14, No. 2 (Summer 1987): 95-101.

Examines Wolfe's use of his former lover, Aline Bernstein, as a symbol of an "earth mother goddess" in his story "The Good Child's River."

Walser, Richard, ed. *The Enigma of Thomas Wolfe: Biographical and Critical Selections.* Cambridge: Harvard University Press, 1953, 313 p.

A collection of essays on Wolfe's life and work, containing important critical comments by his editors, Margaret Church, W. P. Albrecht, and others.

Watkins, Floyd C. *Thomas Wolfe's Characters: Portraits from Life.* Norman: University of Oklahoma Press, 1957, 194 p.

Identifies the actual persons, places, and events
fictionalized in Wolfe's works.

Additional coverage of Wolfe's life and career is contained in the following sources published by The Gale Group: *Concise Dictionary of American Literary Biography, 1929-1941*; *Contemporary Authors*, Vols. 104, 132; *Dictionary of Literary Biography*, Vols. 9, 102; *Dictionary of Literary Biography Documentary Series*, Vols. 2, 16; *Dictionary of Literary Biography Yearbook*, Vols. 85, 97; *DISCovering Authors*; *DISCovering Authors: British*; *DISCovering Authors: Canadian*; *DISCovering Authors: Most-Studied Authors Module*; *DISCovering Authors: Novelists Module*; *Major 20th-Century Writers*, Vol. 1; *Twentieth-Century Literary Criticism*, Vols. 4, 13, 29, 61; and *World Literature Criticism*.

Appendix:

Select Bibliography of General Sources on Short Fiction

BOOKS OF CRITICISM

Allen, Walter. *The Short Story in English*. New York: Oxford University Press, 1981, 413 p.

Aycock, Wendell M., ed. *The Teller and the Tale: Aspects of the Short Story* (Proceedings of the Comparative Literature Symposium, Texas Tech University, Volume XIII). Lubbock: Texas Tech Press, 1982, 156 p.

Averill, Deborah. *The Irish Short Story from George Moore to Frank O'Connor*. Washington, D.C.: University Press of America, 1982, 329 p.

Bates, H. E. *The Modern Short Story: A Critical Survey*. Boston: Writer, 1941, 231 p.

Bayley, John. *The Short Story: Henry James to Elizabeth Bowen*. Great Britain: The Harvester Press Limited, 1988, 197 p.

Bennett, E. K. *A History of the German Novelle: From Goethe to Thomas Mann*. Cambridge: At the University Press, 1934, 296 p.

Bone, Robert. *Down Home: A History of Afro-American Short Fiction from Its Beginning to the End of the Harlem Renaissance*. Rev. ed. New York: Columbia University Press, 1988, 350 p.

Bruck, Peter. *The Black American Short Story in the Twentieth Century: A Collection of Critical Essays*. Amsterdam: B. R. Grüner Publishing Co., 1977, 209 p.

Burnett, Whit, and Burnett, Hallie. *The Modern Short Story in the Making*. New York: Hawthorn Books, 1964, 405 p.

Canby, Henry Seidel. *The Short Story in English*. New York: Henry Holt and Co., 1909, 386 p.

Current-García, Eugene. *The American Short Story before 1850: A Critical History*. Twayne's Critical History of the Short Story, edited by William Peden. Boston: Twayne Publishers, 1985, 168 p.

Flora, Joseph M., ed. *The English Short Story, 1880-1945: A Critical History*. Twayne's Critical History of the Short Story, edited by William Peden. Boston: Twayne Publishers, 1985, 215 p.

Foster, David William. *Studies in the Contemporary Spanish-American Short Story*. Columbia, Mo.: University of Missouri Press, 1979, 126 p.

George, Albert J. *Short Fiction in France, 1800-1850*. Syracuse, N.Y.: Syracuse University Press, 1964, 245 p.

Gerlach, John. *Toward an End: Closure and Structure in the American Short Story*. University, Ala.: The University of Alabama Press, 1985, 193 p.

Hankin, Cherry, ed. *Critical Essays on the New Zealand Short Story*. Auckland: Heinemann Publishers, 1982, 186 p.

Hanson, Clare, ed. *Re-Reading the Short Story*. London: MacMillan Press, 1989, 137 p.

Harris, Wendell V. *British Short Fiction in the Nineteenth Century*. Detroit: Wayne State University Press, 1979, 209 p.

Huntington, John. *Rationalizing Genius: Ideological Strategies in the Classic American Science Fiction Short Story*. New Brunswick: Rutgers University Press, 1989, 216 p.

Kilroy, James F., ed. *The Irish Short Story: A Critical History*. Twayne's Critical History of the Short Story, edited by William Peden. Boston: Twayne Publishers, 1984, 251 p.

Lee, A. Robert. *The Nineteenth-Century American Short Story*. Totowa, N. J.: Vision / Barnes & Noble, 1986, 196 p.

Leibowitz, Judith. *Narrative Purpose in the Novella*. The Hague: Mouton, 1974, 137 p.

Lohafer, Susan. *Coming to Terms with the Short Story*. Baton Rouge: Louisiana State University Press, 1983, 171 p.

Lohafer, Susan, and Clarey, Jo Ellyn. *Short Story Theory at a Crossroads*. Baton Rouge: Louisiana State University Press, 1989, 352 p.

Mann, Susan Garland. *The Short Story Cycle: A Genre Companion and Reference Guide*. New York: Greenwood Press, 1989, 228 p.

Matthews, Brander. *The Philosophy of the Short Story*. New York, N.Y.: Longmans, Green and Co., 1901, 83 p.

May, Charles E., ed. *Short Story Theories*. Athens, Oh.: Ohio University Press, 1976, 251 p.

McClave, Heather, ed. *Women Writers of the Short Story: A Collection of Critical Essays*. Englewood Cliffs, N. J.: Prentice-Hall, 1980, 171 p.

Moser, Charles, ed. *The Russian Short Story: A Critical History*. Twayne's Critical History of the Short Story, edited by William Peden. Boston: Twayne Publishers, 1986, 232 p.

New, W. H. *Dreams of Speech and Violence: The Art of the Short Story in Canada and New Zealand*. Toronto: The University of Toronto Press, 1987, 302 p.

Newman, Frances. *The Short Story's Mutations: From Petronius to Paul Morand*. New York: B. W. Huebsch, 1925, 332 p.

O'Connor, Frank. *The Lonely Voice: A Study of the Short Story*. Cleveland: World Publishing Co., 1963, 220 p.

O'Faolain, Sean. *The Short Story*. New York: Devin-Adair Co., 1951, 370 p.

Orel, Harold. *The Victorian Short Story: Development and Triumph of a Literary Genre*. Cambridge: Cambridge University Press, 1986, 213 p.

O'Toole, L. Michael. *Structure, Style and Interpretation in the Russian Short Story*. New Haven: Yale University Press, 1982, 272 p.

Pattee, Fred Lewis. *The Development of the American Short Story: An Historical Survey*. New York: Harper and Brothers Publishers, 1923, 388 p.

Peden, Margaret Sayers, ed. *The Latin American Short Story: A Critical History*. Twayne's Critical History of the Short Story, edited by William Peden. Boston: Twayne Publishers, 1983, 160 p.

Peden, William. *The American Short Story: Continuity and Change, 1940-1975*. Rev. ed. Boston: Houghton Mifflin Co., 1975, 215 p.

Reid, Ian. *The Short Story*. The Critical Idiom, edited by John D. Jump. London: Methuen and Co., 1977, 76 p.

Rhode, Robert D. *Setting in the American Short Story of Local Color, 1865-1900*. The Hague: Mouton, 1975, 189 p.

Rohrberger, Mary. *Hawthorne and the Modern Short Story: A Study in Genre*. The Hague: Mouton and Co., 1966, 148 p.

Shaw, Valerie. *The Short Story: A Critical Introduction*. London: Longman, 1983, 294 p.

Stephens, Michael. *The Dramaturgy of Style: Voice in Short Fiction*. Carbondale, Ill.: Southern Illinois University Press, 1986, 281 p.

Stevick, Philip, ed. *The American Short Story, 1900-1945: A Critical History*. Twayne's Critical History of the Short Story, edited by William Peden. Boston: Twayne Publishers, 1984, 209 p.

Summers, Hollis, ed. *Discussion of the Short Story*. Boston: D. C. Heath and Co., 1963, 118 p.

Vannatta, Dennis, ed. *The English Short Story, 1945-1980: A Critical History*. Twayne's Critical History of the Short Story, edited by William Peden. Boston: Twayne Publishers, 1985, 206 p.

Voss, Arthur. *The American Short Story: A Critical Survey*. Norman, Okla.: University of Oklahoma Press, 1973, 399 p.

Walker, Warren S. *Twentieth-Century Short Story Explication: New Series, Vol. 1: 1989-1990*. Hamden, Conn.: Shoe String, 1993, 366 p.

Ward, Alfred C. *Aspects of the Modern Short Story: English and American*. London: University of London Press, 1924, 307 p.

Weaver, Gordon, ed. *The American Short Story, 1945-1980: A Critical History*. Twayne's Critical History of the Short Story, edited by William Peden. Boston: Twayne Publishers, 1983, 150 p.

West, Ray B., Jr. *The Short Story in America, 1900-1950*. Chicago: Henry Regnery Co., 1952, 147 p.

Williams, Blanche Colton. *Our Short Story Writers*. New York: Moffat, Yard and Co., 1920, 357 p.

Wright, Austin McGiffert. *The American Short Story in the Twenties*. Chicago: University of Chicago Press, 1961, 425 p.

CRITICAL ANTHOLOGIES

Atkinson, W. Patterson, ed. *The Short-Story*. Boston: Allyn and Bacon, 1923, 317 p.

Baldwin, Charles Sears, ed. *American Short Stories*. New York, N.Y.: Longmans, Green and Co., 1904, 333 p.

Charters, Ann, ed. *The Story and Its Writer: An Introduction to Short Fiction*. New York: St. Martin's Press, 1983, 1239 p.

Current-García, Eugene, and Patrick, Walton R., eds. *American Short Stories: 1820 to the Present*. Key Editions, edited by John C. Gerber. Chicago: Scott, Foresman and Co., 1952, 633 p.

Fagin, N. Bryllion, ed. *America through the Short Story*. Boston: Little, Brown, and Co., 1936, 508 p.

Frakes, James R., and Traschen, Isadore, eds. *Short Fiction: A Critical Collection*. Prentice-Hall English Literature Series, edited by Maynard Mack. Englewood Cliffs, N.J.: Prentice-Hall, 1959, 459 p.

Gifford, Douglas, ed. *Scottish Short Stories, 1800-1900*. The Scottish Library, edited by Alexander Scott. London: Calder and Boyars, 1971, 350 p.

Gordon, Caroline, and Tate, Allen, eds. *The House of Fiction: An Anthology of the Short Story with Commentary*. Rev. ed. New York: Charles Scribner's Sons, 1960, 469 p.

Greet, T. Y., et. al. *The Worlds of Fiction: Stories in Context*. Boston, Mass.: Houghton Mifflin Co., 1964, 429 p.

Gullason, Thomas A., and Caspar, Leonard, eds. *The World of Short Fiction: An International Collection.* New York: Harper and Row, 1962, 548 p.

Havighurst, Walter, ed. *Masters of the Modern Short Story.* New York: Harcourt, Brace and Co., 1945, 538 p.

Litz, A. Walton, ed. *Major American Short Stories.* New York: Oxford University Press, 1975, 823 p.

Matthews, Brander, ed. *The Short-Story: Specimens Illustrating Its Development.* New York: American Book Co., 1907, 399 p.

Menton, Seymour, ed. *The Spanish American Short Story: A Critical Anthology.* Berkeley and Los Angeles: University of California Press, 1980, 496 p.

Mzamane, Mbulelo Vizikhungo, ed. *Hungry Flames, and Other Black South African Short Stories.* Longman African Classics. Essex: Longman, 1986, 162 p.

Schorer, Mark, ed. *The Short Story: A Critical Anthology.* Rev. ed. Prentice-Hall English Literature Series, edited by Maynard Mack. Englewood Cliffs, N. J.: Prentice-Hall, 1967, 459 p.

Simpson, Claude M., ed. *The Local Colorists: American Short Stories, 1857-1900.* New York: Harper and Brothers Publishers, 1960, 340 p.

Stanton, Robert, ed. *The Short Story and the Reader.* New York: Henry Holt and Co., 1960, 557 p.

West, Ray B., Jr., ed. *American Short Stories.* New York: Thomas Y. Crowell Co., 1959, 267 p.

Short Story Criticism Indexes

Literary Criticism Series
Cumulative Author Index

SSC Cumulative Nationality Index
SSC Cumulative Title Index

How to Use This Index

The main references

> **Calvino, Italo**
> 1923–1985 .... CLC 5, 8, 11, 22, 33, 39,
> 73; SSC 3

list all author entries in the following Gale Literary Criticism series:

BLC = *Black Literature Criticism*
CLC = *Contemporary Literary Criticism*
CLR = *Children's Literature Review*
CMLC = *Classical and Medieval Literature Criticism*
DA = *DISCovering Authors*
DAB = *DISCovering Authors: British*
DAC = *DISCovering Authors: Canadian*
DAM = *DISCovering Authors: Modules*
    DRAM: *Dramatists Module*; *MST*: *Most-Studied Authors Module*;
    MULT: *Multicultural Authors Module*; *NOV*: *Novelists Module*;
    POET: *Poets Module*; *POP*: *Popular Fiction and Genre Authors Module*
DC = *Drama Criticism*
HLC = *Hispanic Literature Criticism*
LC = *Literature Criticism from 1400 to 1800*
NCLC = *Nineteenth-Century Literature Criticism*
PC = *Poetry Criticism*
SSC = *Short Story Criticism*
TCLC = *Twentieth-Century Literary Criticism*
WLC = *World Literature Criticism, 1500 to the Present*

The cross-references

> See also CANR 23; CA 85-88;
>   obituary CA116

list all author entries in the following Gale biographical and literary sources:

AAYA = *Authors & Artists for Young Adults*
AITN = *Authors in the News*
BEST = *Bestsellers*
BW = *Black Writers*
CA = *Contemporary Authors*
CAAS = *Contemporary Authors Autobiography Series*
CABS = *Contemporary Authors Bibliographical Series*
CANR = *Contemporary Authors New Revision Series*
CAP = *Contemporary Authors Permanent Series*
CDALB = *Concise Dictionary of American Literary Biography*
CDBLB = *Concise Dictionary of British Literary Biography*
DLB = *Dictionary of Literary Biography*
DLBD = *Dictionary of Literary Biography Documentary Series*
DLBY = *Dictionary of Literary Biography Yearbook*
HW = *Hispanic Writers*
JRDA = *Junior DISCovering Authors*
MAICYA = *Major Authors and Illustrators for Children and Young Adults*
MTCW = *Major 20th-Century Writers*
NNAL = *Native North American Literature*
SAAS = *Something about the Author Autobiography Series*
SATA = *Something about the Author*
YABC = *Yesterday's Authors of Books for Children*

Literary Criticism Series
Cumulative Author Index

Alcott, Louisa May 1832-1888...**NCLC 6, 58; DA; DAB; DAC; DAM MST, NOV; SSC 27; WLC**
See also AAYA 20; CDALB 1865-1917; CLR 1, 38; DLB 1, 42, 79; DLBD 14; JRDA; MAICYA; SATA 100; YABC 1

Aldanov, M. A.
See Aldanov, Mark (Alexandrovich)

Aldanov, Mark (Alexandrovich) 1886(?)-1957 **TCLC 23**
See also CA 118

Aldington, Richard 1892-1962 .... **CLC 49**
See als CA 85-88; CANR 45; DLB 20, 36, 100, 149

Aldiss, Brian W(ilson) 1925- . **CLC 5, 14, 40; DAM NOV**
See also CA 5-8R; CAAS 2; CANR 5, 28, 64; DLB 14; MTCW 1; SATA 34

Alegria, Claribel 1924- .... **CLC 75; DAM MULT**
See also CA 131; CAAS 15; CANR 66; DLB 145; HW

Alegria, Fernando 1918-.................. **CLC 57**
See also CA 9-12R; CANR 5, 32, 72; HW

Aleichem, Sholom .... **TCLC 1, 35; SSC 33**
See also Rabinovitch, Sholem

Aleixandre, Vicente 1898-1984 ... **CLC 9, 36; DAM POET; PC 15**
See also CA 85-88; 114; CANR 26; DLB 108; HW; MTCW 1

Alepoudelis, Odysseus
See Elytis, Odysseus

Aleshkovsky, Joseph 1929-
See Aleshkovsky, Yuz
See also CA 121; 128

Aleshkovsky, Yuz .... **CLC 44**
See also Aleshkovsky, Joseph

Alexander, Lloyd (Chudley) 1924- .. **CLC 35**
See also AAYA 1, 27; CA 1-4R; CANR 1, 24, 38, 55; CLR 1, 5, 48; DLB 52; JRDA; MAICYA; MTCW 1; SAAS 19; SATA 3, 49, 81

Alexander, Samuel 1859-1938 .... **TCLC 77**

Alexie, Sherman (Joseph, Jr.) 1966-...**CLC 96; DAM MULT**
See also CA 138; CANR 65; DLB 175, 206; NNAL

Alfau, Felipe 1902- .... **CLC 66**
See also CA 137

Alger, Horatio, Jr. 1832-1899 .... **NCLC 8**
See also DLB 42; SATA 16

Algren, Nelson 1909-1981 ... **CLC 4, 10, 33; SSC 33**
See also CA 13-16R; 103; CANR 20, 61; CDALB 1941-1968; DLB 9; DLBY 81, 82; MTCW 1

Ali, Ahmed 1910- .... **CLC 69**
See also CA 25-28R; CANR 15, 34

Alighieri, Dante
See Dante

Allan, John B.
See Westlake, Donald E(dwin)

Allan, Sidney
See Hartmann, Sadakichi

Allan, Sydney
See Hartmann, Sadakichi

Allen, Edward 1948- .... **CLC 59**

Allen, Fred 1894-1956 .... **TCLC 87**

Allen, Paula Gunn 1939- .... **CLC 84; DAM MULT**
See also CA 112; 143; CANR 63; DLB 175; NNAL

Allen, Roland
See Ayckbourn, Alan

Allen, Sarah A.
See Hopkins, Pauline Elizabeth

Allen, Sidney H.
See Hartmann, Sadakichi

Allen, Woody 1935-...**CLC 16, 52; DAM POP**
See also AAYA 10; CA 33-36R; CANR 27, 38, 63; DLB 44; MTCW 1

Allende, Isabel 1942-..... **CLC 39, 57, 97; DAM MULT, NOV; HLC; WLCS**
See also AAYA 18; CA 125; 130; CANR 51, 74; DLB 145; HW; INT 130; MTCW 1

Alleyn, Ellen
See Rossetti, Christina (Georgina)

Allingham, Margery (Louise) 1904-1966 **CLC 19**
See also CA 5-8R; 25-28R; CANR 4, 58; DLB 77; MTCW 1

Allingham, William 1824-1889 ......**NCLC 25**
See also DLB 35

Allison, Dorothy E. 1949- ....**CLC 78**
See also CA 140; CANR 66

Allston, Washington 1779-1843 ....**NCLC 2**
See also DLB 1

Almedingen, E. M. ....**CLC 12**
See also Almedingen, Martha Edith von
See also SATA 3

Almedingen, Martha Edith von 1898-1971
See Almedingen, E. M.
See also CA 1-4R; CANR 1

Almodovar, Pedro 1949(?)-..............**CLC 114**
See also CA 133; CANR 72

Almqvist, Carl Jonas Love 1793-1866 **NCLC 42**

Alonso, Damaso 1898-1990 ....**CLC 14**
See also CA 110; 131; 130; CANR 72; DLB 108; HW

Alov
See Gogol, Nikolai (Vasilyevich)

Alta 1942- ....**CLC 19**
See also CA 57-60

Alter, Robert B(ernard) 1935- ....**CLC 34**
See also CA 49-52; CANR 1, 47

Alther, Lisa 1944- ....**CLC 7, 41**
See also CA 65-68; CAAS 30; CANR 12, 30, 51; MTCW 1

Althusser, L.
See Althusser, Louis

Althusser, Louis 1918-1990 ....**CLC 106**
See also CA 131; 132

Altman, Robert 1925- ....**CLC 16, 116**
See also CA 73-76; CANR 43

Alvarez, A(lfred) 1929- ....**CLC 5, 13**
See also CA 1-4R; CANR 3, 33, 63; DLB 14, 40

Alvarez, Alejandro Rodriguez 1903-1965
See Casona, Alejandro
See also CA 131; 93-96; HW

Alvarez, Julia 1950- ....**CLC 93**
See also AAYA 25; CA 147; CANR 69

Alvaro, Corrado 1896-1956 ....**TCLC 60**
See also CA 163

Amado, Jorge 1912-.....**CLC 13, 40, 106; DAM MULT, NOV; HLC**
See also CA 77-80; CANR 35, 74; DLB 113; MTCW 1

Ambler, Eric 1909-1998 ....**CLC 4, 6, 9**
See also CA 9-12R; 171; CANR 7, 38, 74; DLB 77; MTCW 1

Amichai, Yehuda 1924- ... **CLC 9, 22, 57, 116**
See also CA 85-88; CANR 46, 60; MTCW 1

Amichai, Yehudah
See Amichai, Yehuda

Amiel, Henri Frederic 1821-1881 ....**NCLC 4**

Amis, Kingsley (William) 1922-1995 **CLC 1, 2, 3, 5, 8, 13, 40, 44; DA; DAB; DAC; DAM MST, NOV**
See also AITN 2; CA 9-12R; 150; CANR 8, 28, 54; CDBLB 1945-1960; DLB 15, 27, 100, 139; DLBY 96; INT CANR-8; MTCW 1

Amis, Martin (Louis) 1949-...**CLC 4, 9, 38, 62, 101**
See also BEST 90:3; CA 65-68; CANR 8, 27, 54, 73; DLB 14, 194; INT CANR-27

Ammons, A(rchie) R(andolph) 1926-...**CLC 2, 3, 5, 8, 9, 25, 57, 108; DAM POET; PC 16**
See also AITN 1; CA 9-12R; CANR 6, 36, 51, 73; DLB 5, 165; MTCW 1

Amo, Tauraatua i
See Adams, Henry (Brooks)

Amory, Thomas 1691(?)-1788 ....**LC 48**

Anand, Mulk Raj 1905- .. **CLC 23, 93; DAM NOV**
See also CA 65-68; CANR 32, 64; MTCW 1

Anatol
See Schnitzler, Arthur

Anaximander c. 610B.C.-c. 546B.C....**CMLC 22**

Anaya, Rudolfo A(lfonso) 1937- ..... **CLC 23; DAM MULT, NOV; HLC**
See also AAYA 20; CA 45-48; CAAS 4; CANR 1, 32, 51; DLB 82, 206; HW 1; MTCW 1

Andersen, Hans Christian 1805-1875 **NCLC 7; DA; DAB; DAC; DAM MST, POP; SSC 6; WLC**
See also CLR 6; MAICYA; SATA 100; YABC 1

Anderson, C. Farley
See Mencken, H(enry) L(ouis); Nathan, George Jean

Anderson, Jessica (Margaret) Queale 1916- **CLC 37**
See also CA 9-12R; CANR 4, 62

Anderson, Jon (Victor) 1940-..**CLC 9; DAM POET**
See also CA 25-28R; CANR 20

Anderson, Lindsay (Gordon) 1923-1994 **CLC 20**
See also CA 125; 128; 146

Anderson, Maxwell 1888-1959**TCLC 2; DAM DRAM**
See also CA 105; 152; DLB 7

Anderson, Poul (William) 1926- ...... **CLC 15**
See also AAYA 5; CA 1-4R; CAAS 2; CANR 2, 15, 34, 64; DLB 8; INT CANR-15; MTCW 1; SATA 90; SATA-Brief 39

Anderson, Robert (Woodruff) 1917- . **CLC 23; DAM DRAM**
See also AITN 1; CA 21-24R; CANR 32; DLB 7

Anderson, Sherwood 1876-1941...**TCLC 1, 10, 24; DA; DAB; DAC; DAM MST, NOV; SSC 1; WLC**
See also CA 104; 121; CANR 61; CDALB 1917-1929; DLB 4, 9, 86; DLBD 1; MTCW

Andier, Pierre
See Desnos, Robert

Andouard
See Giraudoux, (Hippolyte) Jean

Andrade, Carlos Drummond de .... **CLC 18**
See also Drummond de Andrade, Carlos

Andrade, Mario de 1893-1945 .... **TCLC 43**

Andreae, Johann V(alentin) 1586-1654 **LC 32**
See also DLB 164

Andreas-Salome, Lou 1861-1937 ... **TCLC 56**
See also DLB 66

Andress, Lesley
See Sanders, Lawrence

Andrewes, Lancelot 1555-1626 .... **LC 5**
See also DLB 151, 172

Andrews, Cicily Fairfield
See West, Rebecca

Andrews, Elton V.
See Pohl, Frederik

Andreyev, Leonid (Nikolaevich) 1871-1919
TCLC 3
See also CA 104

Andric, Ivo 1892-1975 .... **CLC 8**
See also CA 81-84; 57-60; CANR 43, 60; DLB
147; MTCW 1

Androvar
See Prado (Calvo), Pedro

Angelique, Pierre
See Bataille, Georges

Angell, Roger 1920- .... **CLC 26**
See also CA 57-60; CANR 13, 44, 70; DLB 171,
185

Angelou, Maya 1928-...**CLC 12, 35, 64, 77;**
BLC 1; DA; DAB; DAC; DAM MST,
MULT, POET, POP; WLCS
See also AAYA 7, 20; BW 2; CA 65-68; CANR
19, 42, 65; CLR 53; DLB 38; MTCW 1;
SATA 49

Anna Comnena 1083-1153 .... **CMLC 25**

Annensky, Innokenty (Fyodorovich) 1856-1909
TCLC 14
See also CA 110; 155

Annunzio, Gabriele d'
See D'Annunzio, Gabriele

Anodos
See Coleridge, Mary E(lizabeth)

Anon, Charles Robert
See Pessoa, Fernando (Antonio Nogueira)

Anouilh, Jean (Marie Lucien Pierre) 1910-1987
CLC 1, 3, 8, 13, 40, 50; DAM DRAM; DC
8
See also CA 17-20R; 123; CANR 32; MTCW
1

Anthony, Florence
See Ai

Anthony, John
See Ciardi, John (Anthony)

Anthony, Peter
See Shaffer, Anthony (Joshua); Shaffer, Peter
(Levin)

Anthony, Piers 1934- ..... **CLC 35; DAM POP**
See also AAYA 11; CA 21-24R; CANR 28,
56, 73; DLB 8; MTCW 1; SAAS 22; SATA
84

Anthony, Susan B(rownell) 1916-1991
TCLC 84
See also CA 89-92; 134

Antoine, Marc
See Proust, (Valentin-Louis-George-Eugene-)
Marcel

Antoninus, Brother
See Everson, William (Oliver)

Antonioni, Michelangelo 1912- .... **CLC 20**
See also CA 73-76; CANR 45

Antschel, Paul 1920-1970
See Celan, Paul
See also CA 85-88; CANR 33, 61; MTCW 1

Anwar, Chairil 1922-1949 .... **TCLC 22**
See also CA 121

Apess, William 1798-1839(?) ...... **NCLC 73;**
DAM MULT
See also DLB 175; NNAL

Apollinaire, Guillaume 1880-1918... **T C L C**
3, 8, 51; DAM POET; PC 7
See also Kostrowitzki, Wilhelm Apollinaris de
See also CA 152

Appelfeld, Aharon 1932- .... **CLC 23, 47**
See also CA 112; 133

Apple, Max (Isaac) 1941-.............. **CLC 9, 33**
See also CA 81-84; CANR 19, 54; DLB 130

Appleman, Philip (Dean) 1926- ....**CLC 51**
See also CA 13-16R; CAAS 18; CANR 6, 29,
56

Appleton, Lawrence
See Lovecraft, H(oward) P(hillips)

Apteryx
See Eliot, T(homas) S(tearns)

Apuleius, (Lucius Madaurensis) 125(?)-175(?)
CMLC 1

Aquin, Hubert 1929-1977 .... **CLC 15**
See also CA 105; DLB 53

Aragon, Louis 1897-1982... **CLC 3, 22; DAM**
NOV, POET
See also CA 69-72; 108; CANR 28, 71; DLB
72; MTCW 1

Arany, Janos 1817-1882 .... **NCLC 34**

Aranyos, Kakay
See Mikszath, Kalman

Arbuthnot, John 1667-1735 .... **LC 1**
See also DLB 101

Archer, Herbert Winslow
See Mencken, H(enry) L(ouis)

Archer, Jeffrey (Howard) 1940- ..... **CLC 28;**
DAM POP
See also AAYA 16; BEST 89:3; CA 77-80;
CANR 22, 52; INT CANR-22

Archer, Jules 1915-............................**CLC 12**
See also CA 9-12R; CANR 6, 69; SAAS 5;
SATA 4, 85

Archer, Lee
See Ellison, Harlan (Jay)

Arden, John 1930- ...... **CLC 6, 13, 15; DAM**
DRAM
See also CA 13-16R; CAAS 4; CANR 31, 65,
67; DLB 13; MTCW 1

Arenas, Reinaldo 1943-1990...**CLC 41; DAM**
MULT; HLC
See also CA 124; 128; 133; CANR 73; DLB
145; HW

Arendt, Hannah 1906-1975 .... **CLC 66, 98**
See also CA 17-20R; 61-64; CANR 26, 60;
MTCW 1

Aretino, Pietro 1492-1556 .... **LC 12**

Arghezi, Tudor 1880-1967 .... **CLC 80**
See also Theodorescu, Ion N.
See also CA 167

Arguedas, Jose Maria 1911-1969...**CLC 10,**
18
See also CA 89-92; CANR 73; DLB 113; HW

Argueta, Manlio 1936-........................**CLC 31**
See also CA 131; CANR 73; DLB 145; HW

Ariosto, Ludovico 1474-1533 .... **LC 6**

Aristides
See Epstein, Joseph

Aristophanes 450B.C.-385B.C. ... **CMLC 4;**
DA; DAB; DAC; DAM DRAM, MST; DC
2; WLCS
See also DLB 176

Aristotle 384B.C.-322B.C. ... **CMLC 31; DA;**
DAB; DAC; DAM MST; WLCS
See also DLB 176

Arlt, Roberto (Godofredo Christophersen)
1900-1942 .... **TCLC 29; DAM MULT;**
HLC
See also CA 123; 131; CANR 67; HW

Armah, Ayi Kwei 1939-...**CLC 5, 33; BLC 1;**
DAM MULT, POET
See also BW 1; CA 61-64; CANR 21, 64; DLB
117; MTCW 1

Armatrading, Joan 1950- .... **CLC 17**
See also CA 114

Arnette, Robert
See Silverberg, Robert

Arnim, Achim von (Ludwig Joachim von
Arnim) 1781-1831 ...... **NCLC 5; SSC 29**
See also DLB 90

Arnim, Bettina von 1785-1859 .... **NCLC 38**
See also DLB 90

Arnold, Matthew 1822-1888...**NCLC 6, 29;**
DA; DAB; DAC; DAM MST, POET; PC
5; WLC
See also CDBLB 1832-1890; DLB 32, 57

Arnold, Thomas 1795-1842 .... **NCLC 18**
See also DLB 55

Arnow, Harriette (Louisa) Simpson 1908-1986
CLC 2, 7, 18
See also CA 9-12R; 118; CANR 14; DLB 6;
MTCW 1; SATA 42; SATA-Obit 47

Arouet, Francois-Marie
See Voltaire

Arp, Hans
See Arp, Jean

Arp, Jean 1887-1966 ....**CLC 5**
See also CA 81-84; 25-28R; CANR 42

Arrabal
See Arrabal, Fernando

Arrabal, Fernando 1932-.... **CLC 2, 9, 18, 58**
See also CA 9-12R; CANR 15

Arrick, Fran ....**CLC 30**
See also Gaberman, Judie Angell

Artaud, Antonin (Marie Joseph) 1896-1948
TCLC 3, 36; DAM DRAM
See also CA 104; 149

Arthur, Ruth M(abel) 1905-1979 ...... **CLC 12**
See also CA 9-12R; 85-88; CANR 4; SATA 7,
26

Artsybashev, Mikhail (Petrovich) 1878-1927
TCLC 31
See also CA 170

Arundel, Honor (Morfydd) 1919-1973...**CLC**
17
See also CA 21-22; 41-44R; CAP 2; CLR 35;
SATA 4; SATA-Obit 24

Arzner, Dorothy 1897-1979 .... **CLC 98**

Asch, Sholem 1880-1957 .... **TCLC 3**
See also CA 105

Ash, Shalom
See Asch, Sholem

Ashbery, John (Lawrence) 1927-...**CLC 2, 3,**
4, 6, 9, 13, 15, 25, 41, 77; DAM POET
See also CA 5-8R; CANR 9, 37, 66; DLB 5,
165; DLBY 81; INT CANR-9; MTCW 1

Ashdown, Clifford
See Freeman, R(ichard) Austin

Ashe, Gordon
See Creasey, John

Ashton-Warner, Sylvia (Constance) 1908-1984
CLC 19
See also CA 69-72; 112; CANR 29; MTCW
1

Asimov, Isaac 1920-1992...**CLC 1, 3, 9, 19, 26,**
76, 92; DAM POP
See also AAYA 13; BEST 90:2; CA 1-4R; 137;
CANR 2, 19, 36, 60; CLR 12; DLB 8; DLBY
92; INT CANR-19; JRDA; MAICYA;
MTCW 1; SATA 1, 26, 74

Assis, Joaquim Maria Machado de
See Machado de Assis, Joaquim Maria

Banks, Iain
See Banks, Iain M(enzies)
Banks, Iain M(enzies) 1954- .... **CLC 34**
See also CA 123; 128; CANR 61; DLB 194;
INT 128
Banks, Lynne Reid .... **CLC 23**
See also Reid Banks, Lynne
See also AAYA 6
Banks, Russell 1940- .... **CLC 37, 72**
See also CA 65-68; CAAS 15; CANR 19, 52,
73; DLB 130
Banville, John 1945- .... **CLC 46**
See also CA 117; 128; DLB 14; INT 128
Banville, Theodore (Faullain) de 1832-1891
NCLC 9
Baraka, Amiri 1934-...**CLC 1, 2, 3, 5, 10, 14,
33, 115; BLC 1; DA; DAC; DAM MST,
MULT, POET, POP; DC 6; PC 4; WLCS**
See also Jones, LeRoi
See also BW 2; CA 21-24R; CABS 3; CANR
27, 38, 61; CDALB 1941-1968; DLB 5, 7,
16, 38; DLBD 8; MTCW 1
Barbauld, Anna Laetitia 1743-1825...**NCLC 50**
See also DLB 107, 109, 142, 158
Barbellion, W. N. P. .... **TCLC 24**
See also Cummings, Bruce F(rederick)
Barbera, Jack (Vincent) 1945- .... **CLC 44**
See also CA 110; CANR 45
Barbey d'Aurevilly, Jules Amedee 1808-1889
NCLC 1; SSC 17
See also DLB 119
Barbusse, Henri 1873-1935 .... **TCLC 5**
See also CA 105; 154; DLB 65
Barclay, Bill
See Moorcock, Michael (John)
Barclay, William Ewert
See Moorcock, Michael (John)
Barea, Arturo 1897-1957 .... **TCLC 14**
See also CA 111
Barfoot, Joan 1946- .... **CLC 18**
See also CA 105
Baring, Maurice 1874-1945 .... **TCLC 8**
See also CA 105; 168; DLB 34
Baring-Gould, Sabine 1834-1924 .. **TCLC 88**
See also DLB 156, 190
Barker, Clive 1952- .... **CLC 52; DAM POP**
See also AAYA 10; BEST 90:3; CA 121; 129;
CANR 71; INT 129; MTCW 1
Barker, George Granville 1913-1991...**CLC 8,
48; DAM POET**
See also CA 9-12R; 135; CANR 7, 38; DLB
20; MTCW 1
Barker, Harley Granville
See Granville-Barker, Harley
See also DLB 10
Barker, Howard 1946- .... **CLC 37**
See also CA 102; DLB 13
Barker, Jane 1652-1732 .... **LC 42**
Barker, Pat(ricia) 1943- .... **CLC 32, 94**
See also CA 117; 122; CANR 50; INT 122
Barlach, Ernst 1870-1938 .... **TCLC 84**
See also DLB 56, 118
Barlow, Joel 1754-1812 .... **NCLC 23**
See also DLB 37
Barnard, Mary (Ethel) 1909- .... **CLC 48**
See also CA 21-22; CAP 2
Barnes, Djuna 1892-1982...**CLC 3, 4, 8, 11,
29; SSC 3**
See also CA 9-12R; 107; CANR 16, 55; DLB
4, 9, 45; MTCW 1
Barnes, Julian (Patrick) 1946-**CLC 42; DAB**
See also CA 102; CANR 19, 54; DLB 194;
DLBY 93

Barnes, Peter 1931- .... **CLC 5, 56**
See also CA 65-68; CAAS 12; CANR 33, 34,
64; DLB 13; MTCW 1
Baroja (y Nessi), Pio 1872-1956 .... **TCLC 8;
HLC**
See also CA 104
Baron, David
See Pinter, Harold
Baron Corvo
See Rolfe, Frederick (William Serafino Austin
Lewis Mary)
Barondess, Sue K(aufman) 1926-1977... **C L C
8**
See also Kaufman, Sue
See also CA 1-4R; 69-72; CANR 1
Baron de Teive
See Pessoa, Fernando (Antonio Nogueira)
Baroness Von S.
See Zangwill, Israel
Barres, (Auguste-) Maurice 1862-1923
TCLC 47
See also CA 164; DLB 123
Barreto, Afonso Henrique de Lima
See Lima Barreto, Afonso Henrique de
Barrett, (Roger) Syd 1946- .... **CLC 35**
Barrett, William (Christopher) 1913-1992
CLC 27
See also CA 13-16R; 139; CANR 11, 67; INT
CANR-11
Barrie, J(ames) M(atthew) 1860-1937...**TCLC
2; DAB; DAM DRAM**
See also CA 104; 136; CDBLB 1890-1914;
CLR 16; DLB 10, 141, 156; MAICYA; SATA
100; YABC 1
Barrington, Michael
See Moorcock, Michael (John)
Barrol, Grady
See Bograd, Larry
Barry, Mike
See Malzberg, Barry N(athaniel)
Barry, Philip 1896-1949 .... **TCLC 11**
See also CA 109; DLB 7
Bart, Andre Schwarz
See Schwarz-Bart, Andre
Barth, John (Simmons) 1930-...**CLC 1, 2, 3, 5,
7, 9, 10, 14, 27, 51, 89; DAM NOV; SSC 10**
See also AITN 1, 2; CA 1-4R; CABS 1; CANR
5, 23, 49, 64; DLB 2; MTCW 1
Barthelme, Donald 1931-1989...**CLC 1, 2, 3,
5, 6, 8, 13, 23, 46, 59, 115; DAM NOV;
SSC 2**
See also CA 21-24R; 129; CANR 20, 58; DLB
2; DLBY 80, 89; MTCW 1; SATA 7; SATA-
Obit 62
Barthelme, Frederick 1943- ...... **CLC 36, 117**
See also CA 114; 122; DLBY 85; INT 122
Barthes, Roland (Gerard) 1915-1980... **C L C
24, 83**
See also CA 130; 97-100; CANR 66; MTCW 1
Barzun, Jacques (Martin) 1907- .... **CLC 51**
See also CA 61-64; CANR 22
Bashevis, Isaac
See Singer, Isaac Bashevis
Bashkirtseff, Marie 1859-1884 ...... **NCLC 27**
Basho
See Matsuo Basho
Bass, Kingsley B., Jr.
See Bullins, Ed
Bass, Rick 1958-................................. **CLC 79**
See also CA 126; CANR 53
Bassani, Giorgio 1916- .... **CLC 9**
See also CA 65-68; CANR 33; DLB 128, 177;
MTCW 1

Bastos, Augusto (Antonio) Roa
See Roa Bastos, Augusto (Antonio)
Bataille, Georges 1897-1962 .... **CLC 29**
See also CA 101; 89-92
Bates, H(erbert) E(rnest) 1905-1974..**CLC 46;
DAB; DAM POP; SSC 10**
See also CA 93-96; 45-48; CANR 34; DLB 162,
191; MTCW 1
Bauchart
See Camus, Albert
Baudelaire, Charles 1821-1867...**NCLC 6, 29,
55; DA; DAB; DAC; DAM MST, POET;
PC 1; SSC 18; WLC**
Baudrillard, Jean 1929- .... **CLC 60**
Baum, L(yman) Frank 1856-1919 ... **TCLC 7**
See also CA 108; 133; CLR 15; DLB 22; JRDA;
MAICYA; MTCW 1; SATA 18, 100
Baum, Louis F.
See Baum, L(yman) Frank
Baumbach, Jonathan 1933- .... **CLC 6, 23**
See also CA 13-16R; CAAS 5; CANR 12, 66;
DLBY 80; INT CANR-12; MTCW 1
Bausch, Richard (Carl) 1945- .... **CLC 51**
See also CA 101; CAAS 14; CANR 43, 61; DLB
130
Baxter, Charles (Morley) 1947-...**CLC 45, 78;
DAM POP**
See also CA 57-60; CANR 40, 64; DLB 130
Baxter, George Owen
See Faust, Frederick (Schiller)
Baxter, James K(eir) 1926-1972 .... **CLC 14**
See also CA 77-80
Baxter, John
See Hunt, E(verette) Howard, (Jr.)
Bayer, Sylvia
See Glassco, John
Baynton, Barbara 1857-1929 .... **TCLC 57**
Beagle, Peter S(oyer) 1939- .... **CLC 7, 104**
See also CA 9-12R; CANR 4, 51, 73; DLBY
80; INT CANR-4; SATA 60
Bean, Normal
See Burroughs, Edgar Rice
Beard, Charles A(ustin) 1874-1948...**TCLC
15**
See also CA 115; DLB 17; SATA 18
Beardsley, Aubrey 1872-1898 .... **NCLC 6**
Beattie, Ann 1947- .... **CLC 8, 13, 18, 40, 63;
DAM NOV, POP; SSC 11**
See also BEST 90:2; CA 81-84; CANR 53, 73;
DLBY 82; MTCW 1
Beattie, James 1735-1803 .... **NCLC 25**
See also DLB 109
Beauchamp, Kathleen Mansfield 1888-1923
See Mansfield, Katherine
See also CA 104; 134; DA; DAC; DAM MST
Beaumarchais, Pierre-Augustin Caron de 1732-
1799 .... **DC 4**
See also DAM DRAM
Beaumont, Francis 1584(?)-1616...**LC 33;
DC 6**
See also CDBLB Before 1660; DLB 58, 121
**Beauvoir, Simone (Lucie Ernestine Marie
Bertrand) de** 1908-1986...**CLC 1, 2, 4, 8,
14, 31, 44, 50, 71; DA; DAB; DAC; DAM
MST, NOV; WLC**
See also CA 9-12R; 118; CANR 28, 61; DLB
72; DLBY 86; MTCW 1
Becker, Carl (Lotus) 1873-1945 ..... **TCLC 63**
See also CA 157; DLB 17
Becker, Jurek 1937-1997 .... **CLC 7, 19**
See also CA 85-88; 157; CANR 60; DLB 75

Becker, Walter 1950- .... **CLC 26**
Beckett, Samuel (Barclay) 1906-1989...**CLC 1,**
2, 3, 4, 6, 9, 10, 11, 14, 18, 29, 57, 59, 83;
DA; DAB; DAC; DAM DRAM, MST,
NOV; SSC 16; WLC
See also CA 5-8R; 130; CANR 33, 61; CDBLB
1945-1960; DLB 13, 15; DLBY 90; MTCW
1
Beckford, William 1760-1844 .... **NCLC 16**
See also DLB 39
Beckman, Gunnel 1910- .... **CLC 26**
See also CA 33-36R; CANR 15; CLR 25;
MAICYA; SAAS 9; SATA 6
Becque, Henri 1837-1899 .... **NCLC 3**
See also DLB 192
Beddoes, Thomas Lovell 1803-1849 **NCLC 3**
See also DLB 96
Bede c. 673-735 .... **CMLC 20**
See also DLB 146
Bedford, Donald F.
See Fearing, Kenneth (Flexner)
Beecher, Catharine Esther 1800-1878...**NCLC**
30
See also DLB 1
Beecher, John 1904-1980 .... **CLC 6**
See also AITN 1; CA 5-8R; 105; CANR 8
Beer, Johann 1655-1700 .... **LC 5**
See also DLB 168
Beer, Patricia 1924- .... **CLC 58**
See also CA 61-64; CANR 13, 46; DLB 40
Beerbohm, Max
See Beerbohm, (Henry) Max(imilian)
Beerbohm, (Henry) Max(imilian) 1872-1956
TCLC 1, 24
See also CA 104; 154; DLB 34, 100
Beer-Hofmann, Richard 1866-1945... **T C L C**
60
See also CA 160; DLB 81
Begiebing, Robert J(ohn) 1946- .... **CLC 70**
See also CA 122; CANR 40
Behan, Brendan 1923-1964...**CLC 1, 8, 11, 15,**
79; DAM DRAM
See also CA 73-76; CANR 33; CDBLB 1945-
1960; DLB 13; MTCW 1
Behn, Aphra 1640(?)-1689 .. **LC 1, 30, 42;**
DA; DAB; DAC; DAM DRAM, MST,
NOV, POET; DC 4; PC 13; WLC
See also DLB 39, 80, 131
Behrman, S(amuel) N(athaniel) 1893-1973
CLC 40
See also CA 13-16; 45-48; CAP 1; DLB 7, 44
Belasco, David 1853-1931 .... **TCLC 3**
See also CA 104; 168; DLB 7
Belcheva, Elisaveta 1893- .... **CLC 10**
See also Bagryana, Elisaveta
Beldone, Phil "Cheech"
See Ellison, Harlan (Jay)
Beleno
See Azuela, Mariano
Belinski, Vissarion Grigoryevich 1811-1848
NCLC 5
See also DLB 198
Belitt, Ben 1911- .... **CLC 22**
See also CA 13-16R; CAAS 4; CANR 7; DLB
5
Bell, Gertrude (Margaret Lowthian) 1868-1926
TCLC 67
See also CA 167; DLB 174
Bell, J. Freeman
See Zangwill, Israel
Bell, James Madison 1826-1902 ... **TCLC 43;**
BLC 1; DAM MULT
See also BW 1; CA 122; 124; DLB 50

Bell, Madison Smartt 1957- ..... **CLC 41, 102**
See also CA 111; CANR 28, 54, 73
Bell, Marvin (Hartley) 1937- ..... **CLC 8, 31;**
DAM POET
See also CA 21-24R; CAAS 14; CANR 59; DLB
5; MTCW 1
Bell, W. L. D.
See Mencken, H(enry) L(ouis)
Bellamy, Atwood C.
See Mencken, H(enry) L(ouis)
Bellamy, Edward 1850-1898 .... **NCLC 4**
See also DLB 12
Bellin, Edward J.
See Kuttner, Henry
Belloc, (Joseph) Hilaire (Pierre Sebastien Rene
Swanton) 1870-1953...**TCLC 7, 18; DAM**
POET; PC 24
See also CA 106; 152; DLB 19, 100, 141, 174;
YABC 1

Belloc, Joseph Peter Rene Hilaire
See Belloc, (Joseph) Hilaire (Pierre Sebastien
Rene Swanton)

Belloc, Joseph Pierre Hilaire
See Belloc, (Joseph) Hilaire (Pierre Sebastien
Rene Swanton)
Belloc, M. A.
See Lowndes, Marie Adelaide (Belloc)
Bellow, Saul 1915-...**CLC 1, 2, 3, 6, 8, 10, 13,**
15, 25, 33, 34, 63, 79; DA; DAB; DAC;
DAM MST, NOV, POP; SSC 14; WLC
See also AITN 2; BEST 89:3; CA 5-8R; CABS
1; CANR 29, 53; CDALB 1941-1968; DLB
2, 28; DLBD 3; DLBY 82; MTCW 1
Belser, Reimond Karel Maria de 1929-
See Ruyslinck, Ward
See also CA 152
Bely, Andrey .... **TCLC 7; PC 11**
See also Bugayev, Boris Nikolayevich

Belyi, Andrei
See Bugayev, Boris Nikolayevich
Benary, Margot
See Benary-Isbert, Margot
Benary-Isbert, Margot 1889-1979 .... **CLC 12**
See also CA 5-8R; 89-92; CANR 4, 72; CLR
12; MAICYA; SATA 2; SATA-Obit 21
Benavente (y Martinez), Jacinto 1866-1954
TCLC 3; DAM DRAM, MULT
See also CA 106; 131; HW; MTCW 1
Benchley, Peter (Bradford) 1940-...**CLC 4, 8;**
DAM NOV, POP
See also AAYA 14; AITN 2; CA 17-20R; CANR
12, 35, 66; MTCW 1; SATA 3, 89
Benchley, Robert (Charles) 1889-1945
TCLC 1, 55
See also CA 105; 153; DLB 11
Benda, Julien 1867-1956 .... **TCLC 60**
See also CA 120; 154
Benedict, Ruth (Fulton) 1887-1948...**TCLC 60**
See also CA 158
Benedict, Saint c. 480-c. 547 .... **CMLC 29**
Benedikt, Michael 1935- .... **CLC 4, 14**
See also CA 13-16R; CANR 7; DLB 5
Benet, Juan 1927- ....**CLC 28**
See also CA 143
Benet, Stephen Vincent 1898-1943...**TCLC 7;**
DAM POET; SSC 10
See also CA 104; 152; DLB 4, 48, 102; DLBY
97; YABC 1
Benet, William Rose 1886-1950 ... **TCLC 28;**
DAM POET
See also CA 118; 152; DLB 45

Benford, Gregory (Albert) 1941- ..... **CLC 52**
See also CA 69-72; CAAS 27; CANR 12, 24,
49; DLBY 82
Bengtsson, Frans (Gunnar) 1894-1954
TCLC 48
See also CA 170
Benjamin, David
See Slavitt, David R(ytman)
Benjamin, Lois
See Gould, Lois
Benjamin, Walter 1892-1940 .... **TCLC 39**
See also CA 164
Benn, Gottfried 1886-1956 .... **TCLC 3**
See also CA 106; 153; DLB 56
Bennett, Alan 1934- .... **CLC 45, 77; DAB;**
DAM MST
See also CA 103; CANR 35, 55; MTCW 1
Bennett, (Enoch) Arnold 1867-1931... **T C L C**
5, 20
See also CA 106; 155; CDBLB 1890-1914;
DLB 10, 34, 98, 135
Bennett, Elizabeth
See Mitchell, Margaret (Munnerlyn)
Bennett, George Harold 1930-
See Bennett, Hal
See also BW 1; CA 97-100
Bennett, Hal ....**CLC 5**
See also Bennett, George Harold
See also DLB 33
Bennett, Jay 1912- .... **CLC 35**
See also AAYA 10; CA 69-72; CANR 11, 42;
JRDA; SAAS 4; SATA 41, 87; SATA-Brief 27
Bennett, Louise (Simone) 1919-....**CLC 28;**
BLC 1; DAM MULT
See also BW 2; CA 151; DLB 117
Benson, E(dward) F(rederic) 1867-1940
TCLC 27
See also CA 114; 157; DLB 135, 153
Benson, Jackson J. 1930- .... **CLC 34**
See also CA 25-28R; DLB 111
Benson, Sally 1900-1972 .... **CLC 17**
See also CA 19-20; 37-40R; CAP 1; SATA 1,
35; SATA-Obit 27
Benson, Stella 1892-1933 .... **TCLC 17**
See also CA 117; 155; DLB 36, 162
Bentham, Jeremy 1748-1832 .... **NCLC 38**
See also DLB 107, 158
Bentley, E(dmund) C(lerihew) 1875-1956
TCLC 12
See also CA 108; DLB 70
Bentley, Eric (Russell) 1916- .... **CLC 24**
See also CA 5-8R; CANR 6, 67; INT CANR-6
Beranger, Pierre Jean de 1780-1857
NCLC 34
Berdyaev, Nicolas
See Berdyaev, Nikolai (Aleksandrovich)
Berdyaev, Nikolai (Aleksandrovich) 1874-1948
TCLC 67
See also CA 120; 157
Berdyayev, Nikolai (Aleksandrovich)
See Berdyaev, Nikolai (Aleksandrovich)
Berendt, John (Lawrence) 1939- ..... **CLC 86**
See also CA 146; CANR 75
Beresford, J(ohn) D(avys) 1873-1947...**TCLC 81**
See also CA 112; 155; DLB 162, 178, 197
Bergelson, David 1884-1952 .... **TCLC 81**
Berger, Colonel
See Malraux, (Georges-)Andre
Berger, John (Peter) 1926- .... **CLC 2, 19**
See also CA 81-84; CANR 51; DLB 14
Berger, Melvin H. 1927- .... **CLC 12**
See also CA 5-8R; CANR 4; CLR 32; SAAS 2;
SATA 5, 88

Berger, Thomas (Louis) 1924-... **CLC 3, 5, 8, 11, 18, 38; DAM NOV**
See also CA 1-4R; CANR 5, 28, 51; DLB 2; DLBY 80; INT CANR-28; MTCW 1

Bergman, (Ernst) Ingmar 1918-...**CLC 16, 72**
See also CA 81-84; CANR 33, 70

Bergson, Henri(-Louis) 1859-1941...**TCLC 32**
See also CA 164

Bergstein, Eleanor 1938- ...**CLC 4**
See also CA 53-56; CANR 5

Berkoff, Steven 1937- ...**CLC 56**
See also CA 104; CANR 72

Bermant, Chaim (Icyk) 1929- ...**CLC 40**
See also CA 57-60; CANR 6, 31, 57

Bern, Victoria
See Fisher, M(ary) F(rances) K(ennedy)

Bernanos, (Paul Louis) Georges 1888-1948
TCLC 3
See also CA 104; 130; DLB 72

Bernard, April 1956- ...**CLC 59**
See also CA 131

Berne, Victoria
See Fisher, M(ary) F(rances) K(ennedy)

Bernhard, Thomas 1931-1989...**CLC 3, 32, 61**
See also CA 85-88; 127; CANR 32, 57; DLB 85, 124; MTCW 1

Bernhardt, Sarah (Henriette Rosine) 1844-1923
TCLC 75
See also CA 157

Berriault, Gina 1926-...**CLC 54, 109; SSC 30**
See also CA 116; 129; CANR 66; DLB 130

Berrigan, Daniel 1921- ...**CLC 4**
See also CA 33-36R; CAAS 1; CANR 11, 43; DLB 5

Berrigan, Edmund Joseph Michael, Jr. 1934-1983
See Berrigan, Ted
See also CA 61-64; 110; CANR 14

Berrigan, Ted ...**CLC 37**
See also Berrigan, Edmund Joseph Michael, Jr.
See also DLB 5, 169

Berry, Charles Edward Anderson 1931-
See Berry, Chuck
See also CA 115

Berry, Chuck ...**CLC 17**
See also Berry, Charles Edward Anderson

Berry, Jonas
See Ashbery, John (Lawrence)

Berry, Wendell (Erdman) 1934-...**CLC 4, 6, 8, 27, 46; DAM POET**
See also AITN 1; CA 73-76; CANR 50, 73; DLB 5, 6

Berryman, John 1914-1972...**CLC 1, 2, 3, 4, 6, 8, 10, 13, 25, 62; DAM POET**
See also CA 13-16; 33-36R; CABS 2; CANR 35; CAP 1; CDALB 1941-1968; DLB 48; MTCW 1

Bertolucci, Bernardo 1940- ...**CLC 16**
See also CA 106

Berton, Pierre (Francis Demarigny) 1920-
CLC 104
See also CA 1-4R; CANR 2, 56; DLB 68; SATA 99

Bertrand, Aloysius 1807-1841 ...**NCLC 31**

Bertran de Born c. 1140-1215 ...**CMLC 5**

Besant, Annie (Wood) 1847-1933 ...**TCLC 9**
See also CA 105

Bessie, Alvah 1904-1985 ...**CLC 23**
See also CA 5-8R; 116; CANR 2; DLB 26

Bethlen, T. D.
See Silverberg, Robert

Beti, Mongo ... **CLC 27; BLC 1; DAM MULT**
See also Biyidi, Alexandre

Betjeman, John 1906-1984...**CLC 2, 6, 10, 34, 43; DAB; DAM MST, POET**
See also CA 9-12R; 112; CANR 33, 56; CDBLB 1945-1960; DLB 20; DLBY 84; MTCW 1

Bettelheim, Bruno 1903-1990 ...**CLC 79**

Betti, Ugo 1892-1953 ...**TCLC 5**
See also CA 104; 155

Betts, Doris (Waugh) 1932- ...**CLC 3, 6, 28**
See also CA 13-16R; CANR 9, 66; DLBY 82; INT CANR-9

Bevan, Alistair
See Roberts, Keith (John Kingston)

Bey, Pilaff
See Douglas, (George) Norman

Bialik, Chaim Nachman 1873-1934...**TCLC 25**
See also CA 170

Bickerstaff, Isaac
See Swift, Jonathan

Bidart, Frank 1939- ...**CLC 33**
See also CA 140

Bienek, Horst 1930- ...**CLC 7, 11**
See also CA 73-76; DLB 75

Bierce, Ambrose (Gwinett) 1842-1914(?)
TCLC 1, 7, 44; DA; DAC; DAM MST; SSC 9; WLC
See also CA 104; 139; CDALB 1865-1917; DLB 11, 12, 23, 71, 74, 186

Biggers, Earl Derr 1884-1933 ...**TCLC 65**
See also CA 108; 153

Billings, Josh
See Shaw, Henry Wheeler

Billington, (Lady) Rachel (Mary) 1942-
CLC 43
See also AITN 2; CA 33-36R; CANR 44

Binyon, T(imothy) J(ohn) 1936- ...**CLC 34**
See also CA 111; CANR 28

Bioy Casares, Adolfo 1914-1984... **CLC 4, 8, 13, 88; DAM MULT; HLC; SSC 17**
See also CA 29-32R; CANR 19, 43, 66; DLB 113; HW; MTCW 1

Bird, Cordwainer
See Ellison, Harlan (Jay)

Bird, Robert Montgomery 1806-1854...**NCLC 1**
See also DLB 202

Birkerts, Sven 1951- ...**CLC 116**
See also CA 128; 133; CAAS 29; INT 133

Birney, (Alfred) Earle 1904-1995...**CLC 1, 4, 6, 11; DAC; DAM MST, POET**
See also CA 1-4R; CANR 5, 20; DLB 88; MTCW 1

Biruni, al 973-1048(?) ...**CMLC 28**

Bishop, Elizabeth 1911-1979...**CLC 1, 4, 9, 13, 15, 32; DA; DAC; DAM MST, POET; PC 3**
See also CA 5-8R; 89-92; CABS 2; CANR 26, 61; CDALB 1968-1988; DLB 5, 169; MTCW 1; SATA-Obit 24

Bishop, John 1935- ...**CLC 10**
See also CA 105

Bissett, Bill 1939- ...**CLC 18; PC 14**
See also CA 69-72; CAAS 19; CANR 15; DLB 53; MTCW 1

Bitov, Andrei (Georgievich) 1937- ...**CLC 57**
See also CA 142

Biyidi, Alexandre 1932-
See Beti, Mongo
See also BW 1; CA 114; 124; MTCW 1

Bjarme, Brynjolf
See Ibsen, Henrik (Johan)

Bjoernson, Bjoernstjerne (Martinius) 1832-1910 ...**TCLC 7, 37**
See also CA 104

Black, Robert
See Holdstock, Robert P.

Blackburn, Paul 1926-1971 ...**CLC 9, 43**
See also CA 81-84; 33-36R; CANR 34; DLB 16; DLBY 81

Black Elk 1863-1950...**TCLC 33; DAM MULT**
See also CA 144; NNAL

Black Hobart
See Sanders, (James) Ed(ward)

Blacklin, Malcolm
See Chambers, Aidan

Blackmore, R(ichard) D(oddridge) 1825-1900
TCLC 27
See also CA 120; DLB 18

Blackmur, R(ichard) P(almer) 1904-1965
CLC 2, 24
See also CA 11-12; 25-28R; CANR 71; CAP 1; DLB 63

Black Tarantula
See Acker, Kathy

Blackwood, Algernon (Henry) 1869-1951
TCLC 5
See also CA 105; 150; DLB 153, 156, 178

Blackwood, Caroline 1931-1996 ..**CLC 6, 9, 100**
See also CA 85-88; 151; CANR 32, 61, 65; DLB 14; MTCW 1

Blade, Alexander
See Hamilton, Edmond; Silverberg, Robert

Blaga, Lucian 1895-1961 ...**CLC 75**
See also CA 157

Blair, Eric (Arthur) 1903-1950
See Orwell, George
See also CA 104; 132; DA; DAB; DAC; DAM MST, NOV; MTCW 1; SATA 29

Blais, Marie-Claire 1939-...**CLC 2, 4, 6, 13, 22; DAC; DAM MST**
See also CA 21-24R; CAAS 4; CANR 38, 75; DLB 53; MTCW 1

Blaise, Clark 1940- ...**CLC 29**
See also AITN 2; CA 53-56; CAAS 3; CANR 5, 66; DLB 53

Blake, Fairley
See De Voto, Bernard (Augustine)

Blake, Nicholas
See Day Lewis, C(ecil)
See also DLB 77

Blake, William 1757-1827...**NCLC 13, 37, 57; DA; DAB; DAC; DAM MST, POET; PC 12; WLC**
See also CDBLB 1789-1832; CLR 52; DLB 93, 163; MAICYA; SATA 30

Blasco Ibanez, Vicente 1867-1928...**TCLC 12; DAM NOV**
See also CA 110; 131; HW; MTCW 1

Blatty, William Peter 1928-**CLC 2; DAM POP**
See also CA 5-8R; CANR 9

Bleeck, Oliver
See Thomas, Ross (Elmore)

Blessing, Lee 1949- ...**CLC 54**

Blish, James (Benjamin) 1921-1975...**CLC 14**
See also CA 1-4R; 57-60; CANR 3; DLB 8; MTCW 1; SATA 66

Bliss, Reginald
See Wells, H(erbert) G(eorge)

Blixen, Karen (Christentze Dinesen) 1885-1962
See Dinesen, Isak
See also CA 25-28; CANR 22, 50; CAP 2; MTCW 1; SATA 44

Bloch, Robert (Albert) 1917-1994 ...**CLC 33**
See also CA 5-8R; 146; CAAS 20; CANR 5; DLB 44; INT CANR-5; SATA 12; SATA-Obit 82

Busch, Frederick 1941-...**CLC 7, 10, 18, 47**
See also CA 33-36R; CAAS 1; CANR 45, 73;
DLB 6
Bush, Ronald 1946- .... **CLC 34**
See also CA 136
Bustos, F(rancisco)
See Borges, Jorge Luis
Bustos Domecq, H(onorio)
See Bioy Casares, Adolfo; Borges, Jorge Luis
Butler, Octavia E(stelle) 1947-...**CLC 38;**
BLCS; DAM MULT, POP
See also AAYA 18; BW 2; CA 73-76; CANR
12, 24, 38, 73; DLB 33; MTCW 1; SATA 84
Butler, Robert Olen (Jr.) 1945-...**C L C**
81; DAM POP
See also CA 112; CANR 66; DLB 173; INT 112
Butler, Samuel 1612-1680 .... **LC 16, 43**
See also DLB 101, 126
Butler, Samuel 1835-1902...**TCLC 1, 33;**
DA; DAB; DAC; DAM MST, NOV;
WLC
See also CA 143; CDBLB 1890-1914; DLB 18,
57, 174
Butler, Walter C.
See Faust, Frederick (Schiller)
Butor, Michel (Marie Francois) 1926-
CLC 1, 3, 8, 11, 15
See also CA 9-12R; CANR 33, 66; DLB 83;
MTCW 1
Butts, Mary 1892(?)-1937 .... **TCLC 77**
See also CA 148
Buzo, Alexander (John) 1944- .... **CLC 61**
See also CA 97-100; CANR 17, 39, 69
Buzzati, Dino 1906-1972 .... **CLC 36**
See also CA 160; 33-36R; DLB 177
Byars, Betsy (Cromer) 1928- .... **CLC 35**
See also AAYA 19; CA 33-36R; CANR 18, 36,
57; CLR 1, 16; DLB 52; INT CANR-18;
JRDA; MAICYA; MTCW 1; SAAS 1; SATA
4, 46, 80
Byatt, A(ntonia) S(usan Drabble) 1936-
CLC 19, 65; DAM NOV, POP
See also CA 13-16R; CANR 13, 33, 50, 75;
DLB 14, 194; MTCW 1
Byrne, David 1952- .... **CLC 26**
See also CA 127
Byrne, John Keyes 1926-
See Leonard, Hugh
See also CA 102; INT 102
Byron, George Gordon (Noel) 1788-1824
NCLC 2, 12; DA; DAB; DAC; DAM MST,
POET; PC 16; WLC
See also CDBLB 1789-1832; DLB 96, 110
Byron, Robert 1905-1941 .... **TCLC 67**
See also CA 160; DLB 195
C. 3. 3.
See Wilde, Oscar (Fingal O'Flahertie Wills)
Caballero, Fernan 1796-1877 .... **NCLC 10**
Cabell, Branch
See Cabell, James Branch
Cabell, James Branch 1879-1958 .... **TCLC 6**
See also CA 105; 152; DLB 9, 78
Cable, George Washington 1844-1925
TCLC 4; SSC 4
See also CA 104; 155; DLB 12, 74; DLBD
13
Cabral de Melo Neto, Joao 1920-...**C L C**
76; DAM MULT
See also CA 151
Cabrera Infante, G(uillermo) 1929-
CLC 5, 25, 45; DAM MULT; HLC
See also CA 85-88; CANR 29, 65; DLB 113;
HW; MTCW 1

Cade, Toni
See Bambara, Toni Cade
Cadmus and Harmonia
See Buchan, John
Caedmon fl. 658-680 .... **CMLC 7**
See also DLB 146
Caeiro, Alberto
See Pessoa, Fernando (Antonio Nogueira)
Cage, John (Milton, Jr.) 1912-1992
CLC 41
See also CA 13-16R; 169; CANR 9; DLB
193; INT CANR-9
Cahan, Abraham 1860-1951 .... **TCLC 71**
See also CA 108; 154; DLB 9, 25, 28
Cain, G.
See Cabrera Infante, G(uillermo)
Cain, Guillermo
See Cabrera Infante, G(uillermo)
Cain, James M(allahan) 1892-1977
CLC 3, 11, 28
See also AITN 1; CA 17-20R; 73-76; CANR
8, 34, 61; MTCW 1
Caine, Mark
See Raphael, Frederic (Michael)
Calasso, Roberto 1941- .... **CLC 81**
See also CA 143
Calderon de la Barca, Pedro 1600-1681
LC 23; DC 3
Caldwell, Erskine (Preston) 1903-1987
CLC 1, 8, 14, 50, 60; DAM NOV; SSC 19
See also AITN 1; CA 1-4R; 121; CAAS 1;
CANR 2, 33; DLB 9, 86; MTCW 1
Caldwell, (Janet Miriam) Taylor (Holland)
1900-1985 ...... **CLC 2, 28, 39; DAM**
NOV, POP
See also CA 5-8R; 116; CANR 5; DLBD 17
Calhoun, John Caldwell 1782-1850**NCLC 15**
See also DLB 3
Calisher, Hortense 1911-...**CLC 2, 4, 8,**
38; DAM NOV; SSC 15
See also CA 1-4R; CANR 1, 22, 67; DLB 2;
INT CANR-22; MTCW 1
Callaghan, Morley Edward 1903-1990
CLC 3, 14, 41, 65; DAC; DAM MST
See also CA 9-12R; 132; CANR 33, 73; DLB
68; MTCW 1
Callimachus c. 305B.C.-c. 240B.C.
CMLC 18
See also DLB 176
Calvin, John 1509-1564 .... **LC 37**
Calvino, Italo 1923-1985...**CLC 5, 8, 11,**
22, 33, 39, 73; DAM NOV; SSC 3
See also CA 85-88; 116; CANR 23, 61; DLB
196; MTCW 1
Cameron, Carey 1952- .... **CLC 59**
See also CA 135
Cameron, Peter 1959- .... **CLC 44**
See also CA 125; CANR 50
Campana, Dino 1885-1932 .... **TCLC 20**
See also CA 117; DLB 114
Campanella, Tommaso 1568-1639 ...... **LC 32**
Campbell, John W(ood, Jr.) 1910-1971
CLC 32
See also CA 21-22; 29-32R; CANR 34; CAP
2; DLB 8; MTCW 1
Campbell, Joseph 1904-1987 ....**CLC 69**
See also AAYA 3; BEST 89:2; CA 1-4R; 124;
CANR 3, 28, 61; MTCW 1
Campbell, Maria 1940- .... **CLC 85; DAC**
See also CA 102; CANR 54; NNAL
Campbell, (John) Ramsey 1946-...**C L C**
42; SSC 19
See also CA 57-60; CANR 7; INT CANR-7

Campbell, (Ignatius) Roy (Dunnachie)
1901-1957 .... **TCLC 5**
See also CA 104; 155; DLB 20
Campbell, Thomas 1777-1844 .... **NCLC 19**
See also DLB 93; 144
Campbell, Wilfred .... **TCLC 9**
See also Campbell, William
Campbell, William 1858(?)-1918
See Campbell, Wilfred
See also CA 106; DLB 92
Campion, Jane ....**CLC 95**
See also CA 138
Campos, Alvaro de
See Pessoa, Fernando (Antonio Nogueira)
Camus, Albert 1913-1960...**CLC 1, 2, 4,**
9, 11, 14, 32, 63, 69; DA; DAB; DAC;
DAM DRAM, MST, NOV; DC 2; SSC
9; WLC
See also CA 89-92; DLB 72; MTCW 1
Canby, Vincent 1924- .... **CLC 13**
See also CA 81-84
Cancale
See Desnos, Robert
Canetti, Elias 1905-1994...**CLC 3, 14, 25,**
75, 86
See also CA 21-24R; 146; CANR 23, 61;
DLB 85, 124; MTCW 1
Canfield, Dorothea F.
See Fisher, Dorothy (Frances) Canfield
Canfield, Dorothea Frances
See Fisher, Dorothy (Frances) Canfield
Canfield, Dorothy
See Fisher, Dorothy (Frances) Canfield
Canin, Ethan 1960- ....**CLC 55**
See also CA 131; 135
Cannon, Curt
See Hunter, Evan
Cao, Lan 1961- .... **CLC 109**
See also CA 165
Cape, Judith
See Page, P(atricia) K(athleen)
Capek, Karel 1890-1938 ... **TCLC 6, 37; DA;**
DAB; DAC; DAM DRAM, MST, NOV; DC
1; WLC
See also CA 104; 140
Capote, Truman 1924-1984...**CLC 1, 3, 8,**
13, 19, 34, 38, 58; DA; DAB; DAC;
DAM MST, NOV, POP; SSC 2; WLC
See also CA 5-8R; 113; CANR 18, 62; CDALB
1941-1968; DLB 2, 185; DLBY 80, 84;
MTCW 1; SATA 91
Capra, Frank 1897-1991 ....**CLC 16**
See also CA 61-64; 135
Caputo, Philip 1941- ....**CLC 32**
See also CA 73-76; CANR 40
Caragiale, Ion Luca 1852-1912 ...... **TCLC 76**
See also CA 157
Card, Orson Scott 1951-... **CLC 44, 47,**
50; DAM POP
See also AAYA 11; CA 102; CANR 27, 47, 73;
INT CANR-27; MTCW 1; SATA 83
Cardenal, Ernesto 1925-........**CLC 31; DAM**
MULT, POET; HLC; PC 22
See also CA 49-52; CANR 2, 32, 66; HW;
MTCW 1
Cardozo, Benjamin N(athan) 1870-1938
TCLC 65
See also CA 117; 164
Carducci, Giosue (Alessandro Giuseppe)
1835-1907 .... **TCLC 32**
See also CA 163
Carew, Thomas 1595(?)-1640 .... **LC 13**
See also DLB 126

Colum, Padraic 1881-1972 .... **CLC 28**
See also CA 73-76; 33-36R; CANR 35; CLR 36; MAICYA; MTCW 1; SATA 15
Colvin, James
See Moorcock, Michael (John)
Colwin, Laurie (E.) 1944-1992... **CLC 5, 13, 23, 84**
See also CA 89-92; 139; CANR 20, 46; DLBY 80; MTCW 1
Comfort, Alex(ander) 1920- .... **CLC 7; DAM POP**
See also CA 1-4R; CANR 1, 45
Comfort, Montgomery
See Campbell, (John) Ramsey
Compton-Burnett, I(vy) 1884(?)-1969 **CLC 1, 3, 10, 15, 34; DAM NOV**
See also CA 1-4R; 25-28R; CANR 4; DLB 36; MTCW 1
Comstock, Anthony 1844-1915 ...... **TCLC 13**
See also CA 110; 169
Comte, Auguste 1798-1857 ..... **NCLC 54**
Conan Doyle, Arthur
See Doyle, Arthur Conan
Conde, Maryse 1937- .... **CLC 52, 92; BLCS; DAM MULT**
See also Boucolon, Maryse
See also BW 2
Condillac, Etienne Bonnot de 1714-1780 **LC 26**
Condon, Richard (Thomas) 1915-1996 **CLC 4, 6, 8, 10, 45, 100; DAM NOV**
See also BEST 90:3; CA 1-4R; 151; CAAS 1; CANR 2, 23; INT CANR-23; MTCW 1
Confucius 551B.C.-479B.C....**CMLC 19; DA; DAB; DAC; DAM MST; WLCS**
Congreve, William 1670-1729...**LC 5, 21; DA; DAB; DAC; DAM DRAM, MST, POET; DC 2; WLC**
See also CDBLB 1660-1789; DLB 39, 84
Connell, Evan S(helby), Jr. 1924- **CLC 4, 6, 45; DAM NOV**
See also AAYA 7; CA 1-4R; CAAS 2; CANR 2, 39; DLB 2; DLBY 81; MTCW 1
Connelly, Marc(us Cook) 1890-1980 ..**CLC 7**
See also CA 85-88; 102; CANR 30; DLB 7; DLBY 80; SATA-Obit 25
Connor, Ralph .... **TCLC 31**
See also Gordon, Charles William
See also DLB 92
Conrad, Joseph 1857-1924...**TCLC 1, 6, 13, 25, 43, 57; DA; DAB; DAC; DAM MST, NOV; SSC 9; WLC**
See also AAYA 26; CA 104; 131; CANR 60; CDBLB 1890-1914; DLB 10, 34, 98, 156; MTCW 1; SATA 27
Conrad, Robert Arnold
See Hart, Moss
Conroy, Pat
See Conroy, (Donald) Pat(rick)
Conroy, (Donald) Pat(rick) 1945-...**C L C 30, 74; DAM NOV, POP**
See also AAYA 8; AITN 1; CA 85-88; CANR 24, 53; DLB 6; MTCW 1
Constant (de Rebecque), (Henri) Benjamin 1767-1830 .... **NCLC 6**
See also DLB 119
Conybeare, Charles Augustus
See Eliot, T(homas) S(tearns)
Cook, Michael 1933- .... **CLC 58**
See also CA 93-96; CANR 68; DLB 53
Cook, Robin 1940-...**CLC 14; DAM POP**
See also BEST 90:2; CA 108; 111; CANR 41; INT 111

Cook, Roy
See Silverberg, Robert
Cooke, Elizabeth 1948- .... **CLC 55**
See also CA 129
Cooke, John Esten 1830-1886 .. **NCLC 5**
See also DLB 3
Cooke, John Estes
See Baum, L(yman) Frank
Cooke, M. E.
See Creasey, John
Cooke, Margaret
See Creasey, John
Cook-Lynn, Elizabeth 1930- .... **CLC 93; DAM MULT**
See also CA 133; DLB 175; NNAL
Cooney, Ray .... **CLC 62**
Cooper, Douglas 1960- .... **CLC 86**
Cooper, Henry St. John
See Creasey, John
Cooper, J(oan) California ...... **CLC 56; DAM MULT**
See also AAYA 12; BW 1; CA 125; CANR 55
Cooper, James Fenimore 1789-1851 **NCLC 1, 27, 54**
See also AAYA 22; CDALB 1640-1865; DLB 3; SATA 19
Coover, Robert (Lowell) 1932-... **CLC 3, 7, 15, 32, 46, 87; DAM NOV; SSC 15**
See also CA 45-48; CANR 3, 37, 58; DLB 2; DLBY 81; MTCW 1
Copeland, Stewart (Armstrong) 1952- **CLC 26**
Copernicus, Nicolaus 1473-1543 .. **LC 45**
Coppard, A(lfred) E(dgar) 1878-1957 **TCLC 5; SSC 21**
See also CA 114; 167; DLB 162; YABC 1
Coppee, Francois 1842-1908 .... **TCLC 25**
See also CA 170
Coppola, Francis Ford 1939- .... **CLC 16**
See also CA 77-80; CANR 40; DLB 44
Corbiere, Tristan 1845-1875 .... **NCLC 43**
Corcoran, Barbara 1911- .... **CLC 17**
See also AAYA 14; CA 21-24R; CAAS 2; CANR 11, 28, 48; CLR 50; DLB 52; JRDA; SAAS 20; SATA 3, 77
Cordelier, Maurice
See Giraudoux, (Hippolyte) Jean
Corelli, Marie 1855-1924 .... **TCLC 51**
See also Mackay, Mary
See also DLB 34, 156
Corman, Cid 1924- .... **CLC 9**
See also Corman, Sidney
See also CAAS 2; DLB 5, 193
Corman, Sidney 1924-
See Corman, Cid
See also CA 85-88; CANR 44; DAM POET
Cormier, Robert (Edmund) 1925-..**C L C 12, 30; DA; DAB; DAC; DAM MST, NOV**
See also AAYA 3, 19; CA 1-4R; CANR 5, 23; CDALB 1968-1988; CLR 12, 55; DLB 52; INT CANR-23; JRDA; MAICYA; MTCW 1; SATA 10, 45, 83
Corn, Alfred (DeWitt III) 1943- ....**CLC 33**
See also CA 104; CAAS 25; CANR 44; DLB 120; DLBY 80
Corneille, Pierre 1606-1684 ...... **LC 28; DAB; DAM MST**
Cornwell, David (John Moore) 1931- **CLC 9, 15; DAM POP**
See also le Carre, John
See also CA 5-8R; CANR 13, 33, 59; MTCW 1

Corso, (Nunzio) Gregory 1930-...**CLC 1, 11**
See also CA 5-8R; CANR 41; DLB 5, 16; MTCW 1
Cortazar, Julio 1914-1984...**CLC 2, 3, 5, 10, 13, 15, 33, 34, 92; DAM MULT, NOV; HLC; SSC 7**
See also CA 21-24R; CANR 12, 32; DLB 113; HW; MTCW 1
CORTES, HERNAN 1484-1547 .... **LC 31**
Corvinus, Jakob
See Raabe, Wilhelm (Karl)
Corwin, Cecil
See Kornbluth, C(yril) M.
Cosic, Dobrica 1921- .... **CLC 14**
See also CA 122; 138; DLB 181
Costain, Thomas B(ertram) 1885-1965 **CLC 30**
See also CA 5-8R; 25-28R; DLB 9
Costantini, Humberto 1924(?)-1987 **CLC 49**
See also CA 131; 122; HW
Costello, Elvis 1955- .... **CLC 21**
Cotes, Cecil V.
See Duncan, Sara Jeannette
Cotter, Joseph Seamon Sr. 1861-1949 **TCLC 28; BLC 1; DAM MULT**
See also BW 1; CA 124; DLB 50
Couch, Arthur Thomas Quiller
See Quiller-Couch, SirArthur (Thomas)
Coulton, James
See Hansen, Joseph
Couperus, Louis (Marie Anne) 1863-1923 **TCLC 15**
See also CA 115
Coupland, Douglas 1961- .... **CLC 85; DAC; DAM POP**
See also CA 142; CANR 57
Court, Wesli
See Turco, Lewis (Putnam)
Courtenay, Bryce 1933- .... **CLC 59**
See also CA 138
Courtney, Robert
See Ellison, Harlan (Jay)
Cousteau, Jacques-Yves 1910-1997 ..**CLC 30**
See also CA 65-68; 159; CANR 15, 67; MTCW 1; SATA 38, 98
Coventry, Francis 1725-1754 .... **LC 46**
Cowan, Peter (Walkinshaw) 1914- ....**SSC 28**
See also CA 21-24R; CANR 9, 25, 50
Coward, Noel (Peirce) 1899-1973 **CLC 1, 9, 29, 51; DAM DRAM**
See also AITN 1; CA 17-18; 41-44R; CANR 35; CAP 2; CDBLB 1914-1945; DLB 10; MTCW 1
Cowley, Abraham 1618-1667 ....**LC 43**
See also DLB 131, 151
Cowley, Malcolm 1898-1989 .... **CLC 39**
See also CA 5-8R; 128; CANR 3, 55; DLB 4, 48; DLBY 81, 89; MTCW 1
Cowper, William 1731-1800 ...**NCLC 8; DAM POET**
See also DLB 104, 109
Cox, William Trevor 1928- .... **CLC 9, 14, 71; DAM NOV**
See also Trevor, William
See also CA 9-12R; CANR 4, 37, 55; DLB 14; INT CANR-37; MTCW 1
Coyne, P. J.
See Masters, Hilary
Cozzens, James Gould 1903-1978 **CLC 1, 4, 11, 92**
See also CA 9-12R; 81-84; CANR 19; CDALB 1941-1968; DLB 9; DLBD 2; DLBY 84, 97; MTCW 1

Danois, N. le
   See Gourmont, Remy (-Marie-Charles) de
Dante 1265-1321 .... **CMLC 3, 18; DA; DAB; DAC; DAM MST, POET; PC 21; WLCS**
d'Antibes, Germain
   See Simenon, Georges (Jacques Christian)
Danticat, Edwidge 1969- .... **CLC 94**
   See also CA 152; CANR 73
Danvers, Dennis 1947- .... **CLC 70**
Danziger, Paula 1944- .... **CLC 21**
   See also AAYA 4; CA 112; 115; CANR 37; CLR 20; JRDA; MAICYA; SATA 36, 63, 102; SATA-Brief 30
Da Ponte, Lorenzo 1749-1838 .... **NCLC 50**
Dario, Ruben 1867-1916 .... **TCLC 4; DAM MULT; HLC; PC 15**
   See also CA 131; HW; MTCW 1
Darley, George 1795-1846 .... **NCLC 2**
   See also DLB 96
Darrow, Clarence (Seward) 1857-1938 **TCLC 81**
   See also CA 164
Darwin, Charles 1809-1882 .... **NCLC 57**
   See also DLB 57, 166
Daryush, Elizabeth 1887-1977... **CLC 6, 19**
   See also CA 49-52; CANR 3; DLB 20
Dasgupta, Surendranath 1887-1952 **TCLC 81**
   See also CA 157
Dashwood, Edmee Elizabeth Monica de la Pasture 1890-1943
   See Delafield, E. M.
   See also CA 119; 154
Daudet, (Louis Marie) Alphonse 1840-1897 **NCLC 1**
   See also DLB 123
Daumal, Rene 1908-1944 .... **TCLC 14**
   See also CA 114
Davenant, William 1606-1668 .... **LC 13**
   See also DLB 58, 126
Davenport, Guy (Mattison, Jr.) 1927- **CLC 6, 14, 38; SSC 16**
   See also CA 33-36R; CANR 23, 73; DLB 130
Davidson, Avram 1923-1993
   See Queen, Ellery
   See also CA 101; 171; CANR 26; DLB 8
Davidson, Donald (Grady) 1893-1968 **CLC 2, 13, 19**
   See also CA 5-8R; 25-28R; CANR 4; DLB 45
Davidson, Hugh
   See Hamilton, Edmond
Davidson, John 1857-1909 .... **TCLC 24**
   See also CA 118; DLB 19
Davidson, Sara 1943- .... **CLC 9**
   See also CA 81-84; CANR 44, 68; DLB 185
Davie, Donald (Alfred) 1922-1995...**CLC 5, 8, 10, 31**
   See also CA 1-4R; 149, CAAS 3; CANR 1, 44; DLB 27; MTCW 1
Davies, Ray(mond Douglas) 1944- ... **CLC 21**
   See also CA 116; 146
Davies, Rhys 1901-1978 .... **CLC 23**
   See also CA 9-12R; 81-84; CANR 4; DLB 139, 191
Davies, (William) Robertson 1913-1995 **CLC 2, 7, 13, 25, 42, 75, 91; DA; DAB; DAC; DAM MST, NOV, POP; WLC**
   See also BEST 89:2; CA 33-36R; 150; CANR 17, 42; DLB 68; INT CANR-17; MTCW 1

Davies, W(illiam) H(enry) 1871-1940 **TCLC 5**
   See also CA 104; DLB 19, 174
Davies, Walter C.
   See Kornbluth, C(yril) M.
Davis, Angela (Yvonne) 1944- . **CLC 77; DAM MULT**
   See also BW 2; CA 57-60; CANR 10
Davis, B. Lynch
   See Bioy Casares, Adolfo; Borges, Jorge Luis
Davis, Harold Lenoir 1896-1960 ...... **CLC 49**
   See also CA 89-92; DLB 9
Davis, Rebecca (Blaine) Harding 1831-1910 .... **TCLC 6**
   See also CA 104; DLB 74
Davis, Richard Harding 1864-1916 **TCLC 24**
   See also CA 114; DLB 12, 23, 78, 79, 189; DLBD 13
Davison, Frank Dalby 1893-1970 ..... **CLC 15**
   See also CA 116
Davison, Lawrence H.
   See Lawrence, D(avid) H(erbert Richards)
Davison, Peter (Hubert) 1928-...**CLC 28**
   See also CA 9-12R; CAAS 4; CANR 3, 43; DLB 5
Davys, Mary 1674-1732 .... **LC 1, 46**
   See also DLB 39
Dawson, Fielding 1930- .... **CLC 6**
   See also CA 85-88; DLB 130
Dawson, Peter
   See Faust, Frederick (Schiller)
Day, Clarence (Shepard, Jr.) 1874-1935 **TCLC 25**
   See also CA 108; DLB 11
Day, Thomas 1748-1789 .... **LC 1**
   See also DLB 39; YABC 1
Day Lewis, C(ecil) 1904-1972...**CLC 1, 6, 10; DAM POET; PC 11**
   See also Blake, Nicholas
   See also CA 13-16; 33-36R; CANR 34; CAP 1; DLB 15, 20; MTCW 1
Dazai Osamu 1909-1948 .... **TCLC 11**
   See also Tsushima, Shuji
   See also CA 164; DLB 182
de Andrade, Carlos Drummond
   See Drummond de Andrade, Carlos
Deane, Norman
   See Creasey, John
de Beauvoir, Simone (Lucie Ernestine Marie Bertrand)
   See Beauvoir, Simone (Lucie Ernestine Marie Bertrand) de
de Beer, P.
   See Bosman, Herman Charles
de Brissac, Malcolm
   See Dickinson, Peter (Malcolm)
de Chardin, Pierre Teilhard
   See Teilhard de Chardin, (Marie Joseph) Pierre
Dee, John 1527-1608 .... **LC 20**
Deer, Sandra 1940- .... **CLC 45**
De Ferrari, Gabriella 1941- .... **CLC 65**
   See also CA 146
Defoe, Daniel 1660(?)-1731 ..... **LC 1, 42; DA; DAB; DAC; DAM MST, NOV; WLC**
   See also AAYA 27; CDBLB 1660-1789; DLB 39, 95, 101; JRDA; MAICYA; SATA 22
de Gourmont, Remy(-Marie-Charles)
   See Gourmont, Remy (-Marie-Charles) de
de Hartog, Jan 1914- ....**CLC 19**
   See also CA 1-4R; CANR 1
de Hostos, E. M.
   See Hostos (y Bonilla), Eugenio Maria de

de Hostos, Eugenio M.
   See Hostos (y Bonilla), Eugenio Maria de
Deighton, Len .... **CLC 4, 7, 22, 46**
   See also Deighton, Leonard Cyril
   See also AAYA 6; BEST 89:2; CDBLB 1960 to Present; DLB 87
Deighton, Leonard Cyril 1929-
   See Deighton, Len
   See also CA 9-12R; CANR 19, 33, 68; DAM NOV, POP; MTCW 1
Dekker, Thomas 1572(?)-1632 ..**LC 22; DAM DRAM**
   See also CDBLB Before 1660; DLB 62, 172
Delafield, E. M. 1890-1943 .... **TCLC 61**
   See also Dashwood, Edmee Elizabeth Monica de la Pasture
   See also DLB 34
de la Mare, Walter (John) 1873-1956 **TCLC 4, 53; DAB; DAC; DAM MST, POET; SSC 14; WLC**
   See also CA 163; CDBLB 1914-1945; CLR 23; DLB 162; SATA 16
Delaney, Franey
   See O'Hara, John (Henry)
Delaney, Shelagh 1939-...**CLC 29; DAM DRAM**
   See also CA 17-20R; CANR 30, 67; CDBLB 1960 to Present; DLB 13; MTCW 1
Delany, Mary (Granville Pendarves) 1700-1788 .... **LC 12**
Delany, Samuel R(ay, Jr.) 1942-...**CLC 8, 14, 38; BLC 1; DAM MULT**
   See also AAYA 24; BW 2; CA 81-84; CANR 27, 43; DLB 8, 33; MTCW 1
De La Ramee, (Marie) Louise 1839-1908
   See Ouida
   See also SATA 20
de la Roche, Mazo 1879-1961 .... **CLC 14**
   See also CA 85-88; CANR 30; DLB 68; SATA 64
De La Salle, Innocent
   See Hartmann, Sadakichi
Delbanco, Nicholas (Franklin) 1942- **CLC 6, 13**
   See also CA 17-20R; CAAS 2; CANR 29, 55; DLB 6
del Castillo, Michel 1933- .... **CLC 38**
   See also CA 109
Deledda, Grazia (Cosima) 1875(?)-1936 **TCLC 23**
   See also CA 123
Delibes, Miguel .... **CLC 8, 18**
   See also Delibes Setien, Miguel
Delibes Setien, Miguel 1920-
   See Delibes, Miguel
   See also CA 45-48; CANR 1, 32; HW; MTCW 1
DeLillo, Don 1936-...**CLC 8, 10, 13, 27, 39, 54, 76; DAM NOV, POP**
   See also BEST 89:1; CA 81-84; CANR 21; DLB 6, 173; MTCW 1
de Lisser, H. G.
   See De Lisser, H(erbert) G(eorge)
   See also DLB 117
De Lisser, H(erbert) G(eorge) 1878-1944 **TCLC 12**
   See also de Lisser, H. G.
   See also BW 2; CA 109; 152
Deloney, Thomas 1560(?)-1600 .... **LC 41**
   See also DLB 167
Deloria, Vine (Victor), Jr. 1933-...**CLC 21; DAM MULT**
   See also CA 53-56; CANR 5, 20, 48; DLB 175; MTCW 1; NNAL; SATA 21

Doeblin, Alfred 1878-1957 .... **TCLC 13**
  See also Doblin, Alfred
  See also CA 110; 141; DLB 66
Doerr, Harriet 1910- .... **CLC 34**
  See also CA 117; 122; CANR 47; INT 122
Domecq, H(onorio) Bustos
  See Bioy Casares, Adolfo; Borges, Jorge Luis
Domini, Rey
  See Lorde, Audre (Geraldine)
Dominique
  See Proust, (Valentin-Louis-George-Eugene-)
  Marcel
Don, A
  See Stephen, SirLeslie
Donaldson, Stephen R. 1947-...**CLC 46;
  DAM POP**
  See also CA 89-92; CANR 13, 55; INT CANR-
  13
Donleavy, J(ames) P(atrick) 1926-...**CLC
  1, 4, 6, 10, 45**
  See also AITN 2; CA 9-12R; CANR 24, 49, 62;
  DLB 6, 173; INT CANR-24; MTCW 1
Donne, John 1572-1631...**LC 10, 24; DA;
  DAB; DAC; DAM MST, POET; PC 1;
  WLC**
  See also CDBLB Before 1660; DLB 121, 151
Donnell, David 1939(?)- .... **CLC 34**
Donoghue, P. S.
  See Hunt, E(verette) Howard, (Jr.)
Donoso (Yanez), Jose 1924-1996...**CLC 4,
  8, 11, 32, 99; DAM MULT; HLC**
  See also CA 81-84; 155; CANR 32, 73; DLB
  113; HW; MTCW 1
Donovan, John 1928-1992 .... **CLC 35**
  See also AAYA 20; CA 97-100; 137; CLR 3;
  MAICYA; SATA 72; SATA-Brief 29
Don Roberto
  See Cunninghame Graham, R(obert) B(ontine)
Doolittle, Hilda 1886-1961...**CLC 3, 8, 14,
  31, 34, 73; DA; DAC; DAM MST, POET;
  PC 5; WLC**
  See also H. D.
  See also CA 97-100; CANR 35; DLB 4, 45;
  MTCW 1
Dorfman, Ariel 1942-...**CLC 48, 77; DAM
  MULT; HLC**
  See also CA 124; 130; CANR 67, 70; HW; INT
  130
Dorn, Edward (Merton) 1929- ... **CLC 10, 18**
  See also CA 93-96; CANR 42; DLB 5; INT 93-
  96
Dorris, Michael (Anthony) 1945-1997...**CLC
  109; DAM MULT, NOV**
  See also AAYA 20; BEST 90:1; CA 102; 157;
  CANR 19, 46, 75; DLB 175; NNAL; SATA
  75; SATA-Obit 94
Dorris, Michael A.
  See Dorris, Michael (Anthony)
Dorsan, Luc
  See Simenon, Georges (Jacques Christian)
Dorsange, Jean
  See Simenon, Georges (Jacques Christian)
Dos Passos, John (Roderigo) 1896-1970
  **CLC 1, 4, 8, 11, 15, 25, 34, 82; DA;
  DAB; DAC; DAM MST, NOV; WLC**
  See also CA 1-4R; 29-32R; CANR 3; CDALB
  1929-1941; DLB 4, 9; DLBD 1, 15; DLBY
  96; MTCW 1
Dossage, Jean
  See Simenon, Georges (Jacques Christian)
Dostoevsky, Fedor Mikhailovich 1821-1881
  **NCLC 2, 7, 21, 33, 43; DA; DAB; DAC;
  DAM MST, NOV; SSC 2, 33; WLC**

Doughty, Charles M(ontagu) 1843-1926
  TCLC 27
  See also CA 115; DLB 19, 57, 174
Douglas, Ellen .... **CLC 73**
  See also Haxton, Josephine Ayres;
  Williamson, Ellen Douglas
Douglas, Gavin 1475(?)-1522 .... **LC 20**
  See also DLB 132
Douglas, George
  See Brown, George Douglas
Douglas, Keith (Castellain) 1920-1944
  TCLC 40
  See also CA 160; DLB 27
Douglas, Leonard
  See Bradbury, Ray (Douglas)
Douglas, Michael
  See Crichton, (John) Michael
Douglas, (George) Norman 1868-1952
  TCLC 68
  See also CA 119; 157; DLB 34, 195
Douglas, William
  See Brown, George Douglas
Douglass, Frederick 1817(?)-1895
  **NCLC 7, 55; BLC 1; DA; DAC; DAM
  MST, MULT; WLC**
  See also CDALB 1640-1865; DLB 1, 43, 50,
  79; SATA 29
Dourado, (Waldomiro Freitas) Autran
  1926- .... **CLC 23, 60**
  See also CA 25-28R; CANR 34
Dourado, Waldomiro Autran
  See Dourado, (Waldomiro Freitas) Autran
Dove, Rita (Frances) 1952-...**CLC 50, 81;
  BLCS; DAM MULT, POET; PC 6**
  See also BW 2; CA 109; CAAS 19; CANR 27,
  42, 68; DLB 120
Doveglion
  See Villa, Jose Garcia
Dowell, Coleman 1925-1985 .... **CLC 60**
  See also CA 25-28R; 117; CANR 10; DLB
  130
Dowson, Ernest (Christopher) 1867-1900
  TCLC 4
  See also CA 105; 150; DLB 19, 135
Doyle, A. Conan
  See Doyle, Arthur Conan
Doyle, Arthur Conan 1859-1930...**TCLC
  7; DA; DAB; DAC; DAM MST, NOV;
  SSC 12; WLC**
  See also AAYA 14; CA 104; 122; CDBLB 1890-
  1914; DLB 18, 70, 156, 178; MTCW 1;
  SATA 24
Doyle, Conan
  See Doyle, Arthur Conan
Doyle, John
  See Graves, Robert (von Ranke)
Doyle, Roddy 1958(?)- ....**CLC 81**
  See also AAYA 14; CA 143; CANR 73; DLB
  194
Doyle, Sir A. Conan
  See Doyle, Arthur Conan
Doyle, Sir Arthur Conan
  See Doyle, Arthur Conan
Dr. A
  See Asimov, Isaac; Silverstein, Alvin
Drabble, Margaret 1939-...**CLC 2, 3, 5, 8,
  10, 22, 53; DAB; DAC; DAM MST,
  NOV, POP**
  See also CA 13-16R; CANR 18, 35, 63; CDBLB
  1960 to Present; DLB 14, 155; MTCW 1;
  SATA 48
Drapier, M. B.
  See Swift, Jonathan

Drayham, James
  See Mencken, H(enry) L(ouis)
Drayton, Michael 1563-1631.......**LC 8;
  DAM POET**
  See also DLB 121
Dreadstone, Carl
  See Campbell, (John) Ramsey
Dreiser, Theodore (Herman Albert) 1871-
  1945...**TCLC 10, 18, 35, 83; DA; DAC;
  DAM MST, NOV; SSC 30; WLC**
  See also CA 106; 132; CDALB 1865-1917;
  DLB 9, 12, 102, 137; DLBD 1; MTCW 1
Drexler, Rosalyn 1926- .... **CLC 2, 6**
  See also CA 81-84; CANR 68
Dreyer, Carl Theodor 1889-1968 ...... **CLC 16**
  See also CA 116
Drieu la Rochelle, Pierre(-Eugene) 1893-1945
  TCLC 21
  See also CA 117; DLB 72
Drinkwater, John 1882-1937 ... **TCLC 57**
  See also CA 109; 149; DLB 10, 19, 149
Drop Shot
  See Cable, George Washington
Droste-Hulshoff, Annette Freiin von 1797-1848
  NCLC 3
  See also DLB 133
Drummond, Walter
  See Silverberg, Robert
Drummond, William Henry 1854-1907
  TCLC 25
  See also CA 160; DLB 92
Drummond de Andrade, Carlos 1902-1987
  CLC 18
  See also Andrade, Carlos Drummond de
  See also CA 132; 123
Drury, Allen (Stuart) 1918-1998 .... **CLC 37**
  See also CA 57-60; 170; CANR 18, 52; INT
  CANR-18
Dryden, John 1631-1700 .. **LC 3, 21; DA;
  DAB; DAC; DAM DRAM, MST, POET;
  DC 3; PC 25; WLC**
  See also CDBLB 1660-1789; DLB 80, 101, 131
Duberman, Martin (Bauml) 1930-......**CLC 8**
  See also CA 1-4R; CANR 2, 63
Dubie, Norman (Evans) 1945-.... **CLC 36**
  See also CA 69-72; CANR 12; DLB 120
Du Bois, W(illiam) E(dward) B(urghardt)
  1868-1963 ... **CLC 1, 2, 13, 64, 96;
  BLC 1; DA; DAC; DAM MST, MULT,
  NOV; WLC**
  See also BW 1; CA 85-88; CANR 34; CDALB
  1865-1917; DLB 47, 50, 91; MTCW 1; SATA
  42
Dubus, Andre 1936-...**CLC 13, 36, 97; SSC
  15**
  See also CA 21-24R; CANR 17; DLB 130;
  INT CANR-17
Duca Minimo
  See D'Annunzio, Gabriele
Ducharme, Rejean 1941- ....**CLC 74**
  See also CA 165; DLB 60
Duclos, Charles Pinot 1704-1772 .... **LC 1**
Dudek, Louis 1918- ....**CLC 11, 19**
  See also CA 45-48; CAAS 14; CANR 1; DLB 88
Duerrenmatt, Friedrich 1921-1990
  **CLC 1, 4, 8, 11, 15, 43, 102; DAM
  DRAM**
  See also CA 17-20R; CANR 33; DLB 69,
  124; MTCW 1
Duffy, Bruce (?)- .... **CLC 50**
Duffy, Maureen 1933-................. **CLC 37**
  See also CA 25-28R; CANR 33, 68; DLB 14;
  MTCW 1

Gaines, Ernest J(ames) 1933-...**CLC 3, 11, 18, 86; BLC 2; DAM MULT**
See also AAYA 18; AITN 1; BW 2; CA 9-12R; CANR 6, 24, 42, 75; CDALB 1968-1988; DLB 2, 33, 152; DLBY 80; MTCW 1; SATA 86

Gaitskill, Mary 1954- .... **CLC 69**
See also CA 128; CANR 61

Galdos, Benito Perez
See Perez Galdos, Benito

Gale, Zona 1874-1938 ...... **TCLC 7; DAM DRAM**
See also CA 105; 153; DLB 9, 78

Galeano, Eduardo (Hughes) 1940-.. **CLC 72**
See also CA 29-32R; CANR 13, 32; HW

Galiano, Juan Valera y Alcala
See Valera y Alcala-Galiano, Juan

Galilei, Galileo 1546-1642 .... **LC 45**

Gallagher, Tess 1943- ...... **CLC 18, 63; DAM POET; PC 9**
See also CA 106; DLB 120

Gallant, Mavis 1922-...**CLC 7, 18, 38; DAC; DAM MST; SSC 5**
See also CA 69-72; CANR 29, 69; DLB 53; MTCW 1

Gallant, Roy A(rthur) 1924- .... **CLC 17**
See also CA 5-8R; CANR 4, 29, 54; CLR 30; MAICYA; SATA 4, 68

Gallico, Paul (William) 1897-1976 ..... **CLC 2**
See also AITN 1; CA 5-8R; 69-72; CANR 23; DLB 9, 171; MAICYA; SATA 13

Gallo, Max Louis 1932- .... **CLC 95**
See also CA 85-88

Gallois, Lucien
See Desnos, Robert

Gallup, Ralph
See Whitemore, Hugh (John)

Galsworthy, John 1867-1933...**TCLC 1, 45; DA; DAB; DAC; DAM DRAM, MST, NOV; SSC 22; WLC**
See also CA 104; 141; CANR 75; CDBLB 1890-1914; DLB 10, 34, 98, 162; DLBD 16

Galt, John 1779-1839 .... **NCLC 1**
See also DLB 99, 116, 159

Galvin, James 1951- .... **CLC 38**
See also CA 108; CANR 26

Gamboa, Federico 1864-1939 ..**TCLC 36**
See also CA 167

Gandhi, M. K.
See Gandhi, Mohandas Karamchand

Gandhi, Mahatma
See Gandhi, Mohandas Karamchand

Gandhi, Mohandas Karamchand 1869-1948
TCLC 59; DAM MULT
See also CA 121; 132; MTCW 1

Gann, Ernest Kellogg 1910-1991 ..... **CLC 23**
See also AITN 1; CA 1-4R; 136; CANR 1

Garcia, Cristina 1958- .... **CLC 76**
See also CA 141; CANR 73

Garcia Lorca, Federico 1898-1936
TCLC 1, 7, 49; DA; DAB; DAC; DAM DRAM, MST, MULT, POET; DC 2; HLC; PC 3; WLC
See also CA 104; 131; DLB 108; HW; MTCW 1

Garcia Marquez, Gabriel (Jose) 1928-
CLC 2, 3, 8, 10, 15, 27, 47, 55, 68; DA; DAB; DAC; DAM MST, MULT, NOV, POP; HLC; SSC 8; WLC
See also AAYA 3; BEST 89:1, 90:4; CA 33-36R; CANR 10, 28, 50, 75; DLB 113; HW; MTCW 1

Gard, Janice
See Latham, Jean Lee

Gard, Roger Martin du
See Martin du Gard, Roger

Gardam, Jane 1928- ....**CLC 43**
See also CA 49-52; CANR 2, 18, 33, 54; CLR 12; DLB 14, 161; MAICYA; MTCW 1; SAAS 9; SATA 39, 76; SATA-Brief 28

Gardner, Herb(ert) 1934- .... **CLC 44**
See also CA 149

Gardner, John (Champlin), Jr. 1933-1982
CLC 2, 3, 5, 7, 8, 10, 18, 28, 34; DAM NOV, POP; SSC 7
See also AITN 1; CA 65-68; 107; CANR 33, 73; DLB 2; DLBY 82; MTCW 1; SATA 40; SATA-Obit 31

Gardner, John (Edmund) 1926-...**CLC 30; DAM POP**
See also CA 103; CANR 15, 69; MTCW 1

Gardner, Miriam
See Bradley, Marion Zimmer

Gardner, Noel
See Kuttner, Henry

Gardons, S. S.
See Snodgrass, W(illiam) D(e Witt)

Garfield, Leon 1921-1996 .... **CLC 12**
See also AAYA 8; CA 17-20R; 152; CANR 38, 41; CLR 21; DLB 161; JRDA; MAICYA; SATA 1, 32, 76; SATA-Obit 90

Garland, (Hannibal) Hamlin 1860-1940
TCLC 3; SSC 18
See also CA 104; DLB 12, 71, 78, 186

Garneau, (Hector de) Saint-Denys 1912-1943 .... **TCLC 13**
See also CA 111; DLB 88

Garner, Alan 1934-...**CLC 17; DAB; DAM POP**
See also AAYA 18; CA 73-76; CANR 15, 64; CLR 20; DLB 161; MAICYA; MTCW 1; SATA 18, 69

Garner, Hugh 1913-1979 .... **CLC 13**
See also CA 69-72; CANR 31; DLB 68

Garnett, David 1892-1981 .... **CLC 3**
See also CA 5-8R; 103; CANR 17; DLB 34

Garos, Stephanie
See Katz, Steve

Garrett, George (Palmer) 1929-...**CLC 3, 11, 51; SSC 30**
See also CA 1-4R; CAAS 5; CANR 1, 42, 67; DLB 2, 5, 130, 152; DLBY 83

Garrick, David 1717-1779...**LC 15; DAM DRAM**
See also DLB 84

Garrigue, Jean 1914-1972 .... **CLC 2, 8**
See also CA 5-8R; 37-40R; CANR 20

Garrison, Frederick
See Sinclair, Upton (Beall)

Garth, Will
See Hamilton, Edmond; Kuttner, Henry

Garvey, Marcus (Moziah, Jr.) 1887-1940
TCLC 41; BLC 2; DAM MULT
See also BW 1; CA 120; 124

Gary, Romain ....**CLC 25**
See also Kacew, Romain
See also DLB 83

Gascar, Pierre .... **CLC 11**
See also Fournier, Pierre

Gascoyne, David (Emery) 1916- ....**CLC 45**
See also CA 65-68; CANR 10, 28, 54; DLB 20; MTCW 1

Gaskell, Elizabeth Cleghorn 1810-1865
NCLC 70; DAB; DAM MST; SSC 25
See also CDBLB 1832-1890; DLB 21, 144, 159

Gass, William H(oward) 1924-...**CLC 1, 2, 8, 11, 15, 39; SSC 12**
See also CA 17-20R; CANR 30, 71; DLB 2; MTCW 1

Gasset, Jose Ortega y
See Ortega y Gasset, Jose

Gates, Henry Louis, Jr. 1950-...**CLC 65; BLCS; DAM MULT**
See also BW 2; CA 109; CANR 25, 53, 75; DLB 67

Gautier, Theophile 1811-1872...**NCLC 1, 59; DAM POET; PC 18; SSC 20**
See also DLB 119

Gawsworth, John
See Bates, H(erbert) E(rnest)

Gay, Oliver
See Gogarty, Oliver St. John

Gaye, Marvin (Penze) 1939-1984...**CLC 26**
See also CA 112

Gebler, Carlo (Ernest) 1954- ....**CLC 39**
See also CA 119; 133

Gee, Maggie (Mary) 1948-..........**CLC 57**
See also CA 130

Gee, Maurice (Gough) 1931-.............**CLC 29**
See also CA 97-100; CANR 67; SATA 46, 101

Gelbart, Larry (Simon) 1923- .... **CLC 21, 61**
See also CA 73-76; CANR 45

Gelber, Jack 1932- ....**CLC 1, 6, 14, 79**
See also CA 1-4R; CANR 2; DLB 7

Gellhorn, Martha (Ellis) 1908-1998...**CLC 14, 60**
See also CA 77-80; 164; CANR 44; DLBY 82

Genet, Jean 1910-1986...**CLC 1, 2, 5, 10, 14, 44, 46; DAM DRAM**
See also CA 13-16R; CANR 18; DLB 72; DLBY 86; MTCW 1

Gent, Peter 1942-...............................**CLC 29**
See also AITN 1; CA 89-92; DLBY 82

Gentlewoman in New England, A
See Bradstreet, Anne

Gentlewoman in Those Parts, A
See Bradstreet, Anne

George, Jean Craighead 1919- ....**CLC 35**
See also AAYA 8; CA 5-8R; CANR 25; CLR 1; DLB 52; JRDA; MAICYA; SATA 2, 68

George, Stefan (Anton) 1868-1933
TCLC 2, 14
See also CA 104

Georges, Georges Martin
See Simenon, Georges (Jacques Christian)

Gerhardi, William Alexander
See Gerhardie, William Alexander

Gerhardie, William Alexander 1895-1977
CLC 5
See also CA 25-28R; 73-76; CANR 18; DLB 36

Gerstler, Amy 1956- ....**CLC 70**
See also CA 146

Gertler, T. ....**CLC 34**
See also CA 116; 121; INT 121

Ghalib .... **NCLC 39**
See also Ghalib, Hsadullah Khan

Ghalib, Hsadullah Khan 1797-1869
See Ghalib
See also DAM POET

Ghelderode, Michel de 1898-1962...**C L C 6, 11; DAM DRAM**
See also CA 85-88; CANR 40

Ghiselin, Brewster 1903- .... **CLC 23**
See also CA 13-16R; CAAS 10; CANR 13

Ghose, Aurabinda 1872-1950 .... **TCLC 63**
See also CA 163

Gombrowicz, Witold 1904-1969...**CLC 4, 7, 11, 49; DAM DRAM**
See also CA 19-20; 25-28R; CAP 2
Gomez de la Serna, Ramon 1888-1963
CLC 9
See also CA 153; 116; HW
Goncharov, Ivan Alexandrovich 1812-1891
NCLC 1, 63
Goncourt, Edmond (Louis Antoine Huot) de 1822-1896 .... **NCLC 7**
See also DLB 123
Goncourt, Jules (Alfred Huot) de 1830-1870 .... **NCLC 7**
See also DLB 123
Gontier, Fernande 19(?)- .... **CLC 50**
Gonzalez Martinez, Enrique 1871-1952
TCLC 72
See also CA 166; HW
Goodman, Paul 1911-1972 ..... **CLC 1, 2, 4, 7**
See also CA 19-20; 37-40R; CANR 34; CAP 2; DLB 130; MTCW 1
Gordimer, Nadine 1923-...**CLC 3, 5, 7, 10, 18, 33, 51, 70; DA; DAB; DAC; DAM MST, NOV; SSC 17; WLCS**
See also CA 5-8R; CANR 3, 28, 56; INT CANR-28; MTCW 1
Gordon, Adam Lindsay 1833-1870
NCLC 21
Gordon, Caroline 1895-1981...**CLC 6, 13, 29, 83; SSC 15**
See also CA 11-12; 103; CANR 36; CAP 1; DLB 4, 9, 102; DLBD 17; DLBY 81; MTCW 1
Gordon, Charles William 1860-1937
See Connor, Ralph
See also CA 109
Gordon, Mary (Catherine) 1949-...**CLC 13, 22**
See also CA 102; CANR 44; DLB 6; DLBY 81; INT 102; MTCW 1
Gordon, N. J.
See Bosman, Herman Charles
Gordon, Sol 1923- .... **CLC 26**
See also CA 53-56; CANR 4; SATA 11
Gordone, Charles 1925-1995...**CLC 1, 4; DAM DRAM; DC 8**
See also BW 1; CA 93-96; 150; CANR 55; DLB 7; INT 93-96; MTCW 1
Gore, Catherine 1800-1861 .... **NCLC 65**
See also DLB 116
Gorenko, Anna Andreevna
See Akhmatova, Anna
Gorky, Maxim 1868-1936 ...... **TCLC 8; DAB; SSC 28; WLC**
See also Peshkov, Alexei Maximovich
Goryan, Sirak
See Saroyan, William
Gosse, Edmund (William) 1849-1928
TCLC 28
See also CA 117; DLB 57, 144, 184
Gotlieb, Phyllis Fay (Bloom) 1926-
CLC 18
See also CA 13-16R; CANR 7; DLB 88
Gottesman, S. D.
See Kornbluth, C(yril) M.; Pohl, Frederik
Gottfried von Strassburg fl. c. 1210...**CMLC 10**
See also DLB 138
Gould, Lois .... **CLC 4, 10**
See also CA 77-80; CANR 29; MTCW 1
Gourmont, Remy (-Marie-Charles) de 1858-1915 .... **TCLC 17**
See also CA 109; 150

Govier, Katherine 1948- .... **CLC 51**
See also CA 101; CANR 18, 40
Goyen, (Charles) William 1915-1983
CLC 5, 8, 14, 40
See also AITN 2; CA 5-8R; 110; CANR 6, 71; DLB 2; DLBY 83; INT CANR-6
Goytisolo, Juan 1931-...**CLC 5, 10, 23; DAM MULT; HLC**
See also CA 85-88; CANR 32, 61; HW; MTCW 1
Gozzano, Guido 1883-1916 .... **PC 10**
See also CA 154; DLB 114
Gozzi, (Conte) Carlo 1720-1806
NCLC 23
Grabbe, Christian Dietrich 1801-1836
NCLC 2
See also DLB 133
Grace, Patricia 1937- .... **CLC 56**
Gracian y Morales, Baltasar 1601-1658
LC 15
Gracq, Julien .... **CLC 11, 48**
See also Poirier, Louis
See also DLB 83
Grade, Chaim 1910-1982 .... **CLC 10**
See also CA 93-96; 107
Graduate of Oxford, A
See Ruskin, John
Grafton, Garth
See Duncan, Sara Jeannette
Graham, John
See Phillips, David Graham
Graham, Jorie 1951- .... **CLC 48**
See also CA 111; CANR 63; DLB 120
Graham, R(obert) B(ontine) Cunninghame
See Cunninghame Graham, R(obert) B(ontine)
See also DLB 98, 135, 174
Graham, Robert
See Haldeman, Joe (William)
Graham, Tom
See Lewis, (Harry) Sinclair
Graham, W(illiam) S(ydney) 1918-1986
CLC 29
See also CA 73-76; 118; DLB 20
Graham, Winston (Mawdsley) 1910-
CLC 23
See also CA 49-52; CANR 2, 22, 45, 66; DLB 77
Grahame, Kenneth 1859-1932 .. **TCLC 64; DAB**
See also CA 108; 136; CLR 5; DLB 34, 141, 178; MAICYA; SATA 100; YABC 1
Grant, Skeeter
See Spiegelman, Art
Granville-Barker, Harley 1877-1946
TCLC 2; DAM DRAM
See also Barker, Harley Granville
See also CA 104
Grass, Guenter (Wilhelm) 1927-...**CLC 1, 2, 4, 6, 11, 15, 22, 32, 49, 88; DA; DAB; DAC; DAM MST, NOV; WLC**
See also CA 13-16R; CANR 20, 75; DLB 75, 124; MTCW 1
Gratton, Thomas
See Hulme, T(homas) E(rnest)
Grau, Shirley Ann 1929- ..**CLC 4, 9; SSC 15**
See also CA 89-92; CANR 22, 69; DLB 2; INT CANR-22; MTCW 1
Gravel, Fern
See Hall, James Norman
Graver, Elizabeth 1964- .... **CLC 70**
See also CA 135; CANR 71
Graves, Richard Perceval 1945- .... **CLC 44**
See also CA 65-68; CANR 9, 26, 51

Graves, Robert (von Ranke) 1895-1985
CLC 1, 2, 6, 11, 39, 44, 45; DAB; DAC; DAM MST, POET; PC 6
See also CA 5-8R; 117; CANR 5, 36; CDBLB 1914-1945; DLB 20, 100, 191; DLBD 18; DLBY 85; MTCW 1; SATA 45
Graves, Valerie
See Bradley, Marion Zimmer
Gray, Alasdair (James) 1934- .... **CLC 41**
See also CA 126; CANR 47, 69; DLB 194; INT 126; MTCW 1
Gray, Amlin 1946- .... **CLC 29**
See also CA 138
Gray, Francine du Plessix 1930-...**CLC 22; DAM NOV**
See also BEST 90:3; CA 61-64; CAAS 2; CANR 11, 33, 75; INT CANR-11; MTCW 1
Gray, John (Henry) 1866-1934 ...... **TCLC 19**
See also CA 119; 162
Gray, Simon (James Holliday) 1936-
CLC 9, 14, 36
See also AITN 1; CA 21-24R; CAAS 3; CANR 32, 69; DLB 13; MTCW 1
Gray, Spalding 1941- ......**CLC 49, 112; DAM POP; DC 7**
See also CA 128; CANR 74
Gray, Thomas 1716-1771...**LC 4, 40; DA; DAB; DAC; DAM MST; PC 2; WLC**
See also CDBLB 1660-1789; DLB 109
Grayson, David
See Baker, Ray Stannard
Grayson, Richard (A.) 1951- ...... **CLC 38**
See also CA 85-88; CANR 14, 31, 57
Greeley, Andrew M(oran) 1928- ...... **CLC 28; DAM POP**
See also CA 5-8R; CAAS 7; CANR 7, 43, 69; MTCW 1
Green, Anna Katharine 1846-1935...**TCLC 63**
See also CA 112; 159; DLB 202
Green, Brian
See Card, Orson Scott
Green, Hannah
See Greenberg, Joanne (Goldenberg)
Green, Hannah 1927(?)-1996 .... **CLC 3**
See also CA 73-76; CANR 59
Green, Henry 1905-1973 .... **CLC 2, 13, 97**
See also Yorke, Henry Vincent
See also DLB 15
Green, Julian (Hartridge) 1900-1998
See Green, Julien
See also CA 21-24R; 169; CANR 33; DLB 4, 72; MTCW 1
Green, Julien .... **CLC 3, 11, 77**
See also Green, Julian (Hartridge)
Green, Paul (Eliot) 1894-1981 .**CLC 25; DAM DRAM**
See also AITN 1; CA 5-8R; 103; CANR 3; DLB 7, 9; DLBY 81
Greenberg, Ivan 1908-1973
See Rahv, Philip
See also CA 85-88
Greenberg, Joanne (Goldenberg) 1932-
CLC 7, 30
See also AAYA 12; CA 5-8R; CANR 14, 32, 69; SATA 25
Greenberg, Richard 1959(?)- .... **CLC 57**
See also CA 138
Greene, Bette 1934- .... **CLC 30**
See also AAYA 7; CA 53-56; CANR 4; CLR 2; JRDA; MAICYA; SAAS 16; SATA 8, 102
Greene, Gael .... **CLC 8**
See also CA 13-16R; CANR 10

Habermas, Jurgen
See Habermas, Juergen
Hacker, Marilyn 1942-...CLC 5, 9, 23, 72,
91; DAM POET
See also CA 77-80; CANR 68; DLB 120
Haeckel, Ernst Heinrich (Philipp August)
1834-1919 .... TCLC 83
See also CA 157
Haggard, H(enry) Rider 1856-1925
TCLC 11
See also CA 108; 148; DLB 70, 156, 174,
178; SATA 16
Hagiosy, L.
See Larbaud, Valery (Nicolas)
Hagiwara Sakutaro 1886-1942...TCLC
60; PC 18
Haig, Fenil
See Ford, Ford Madox
Haig-Brown, Roderick (Langmere) 1908-
1976 .... CLC 21
See also CA 5-8R; 69-72; CANR 4, 38; CLR
31; DLB 88; MAICYA; SATA 12
Hailey, Arthur 1920- ...... CLC 5; DAM
NOV, POP
See also AITN 2; BEST 90:3; CA 1-4R;
CANR 2, 36, 75; DLB 88; DLBY 82;
MTCW 1
Hailey, Elizabeth Forsythe 1938- .... CLC 40
See also CA 93-96; CAAS 1; CANR 15, 48;
INT CANR-15
Haines, John (Meade) 1924-............. CLC 58
See also CA 17-20R; CANR 13, 34; DLB 5
Hakluyt, Richard 1552-1616 .... LC 31
Haldeman, Joe (William) 1943-...CLC 61
See also CA 53-56; CAAS 25; CANR 6, 70,
72; DLB 8; INT CANR-6
Haley, Alex(ander Murray Palmer) 1921-1992
CLC 8, 12, 76; BLC 2; DA; DAB; DAC;
DAM MST, MULT, POP
See also AAYA 26; BW 2; CA 77-80; 136;
CANR 61; DLB 38; MTCW 1
Haliburton, Thomas Chandler 1796-1865
NCLC 15
See also DLB 11, 99
Hall, Donald (Andrew, Jr.) 1928-...CLC 1,
13, 37, 59; DAM POET
See also CA 5-8R; CAAS 7; CANR 2, 44, 64;
DLB 5; SATA 23, 97
Hall, Frederic Sauser
See Sauser-Hall, Frederic
Hall, James
See Kuttner, Henry
Hall, James Norman 1887-1951 ..... TCLC 23
See also CA 123; SATA 21
Hall, Radclyffe
See Hall, (Marguerite) Radclyffe
Hall, (Marguerite) Radclyffe 1886-1943
TCLC 12
See also CA 110; 150; DLB 191
Hall, Rodney 1935-........................ CLC 51
See also CA 109; CANR 69
Halleck, Fitz-Greene 1790-1867 .... NCLC 47
See also DLB 3
Halliday, Michael
See Creasey, John
Halpern, Daniel 1945-................. CLC 14
See also CA 33-36R
Hamburger, Michael (Peter Leopold) 1924-
CLC 5, 14
See also CA 5-8R; CAAS 4; CANR 2, 47; DLB
27
Hamill, Pete 1935- .... CLC 10
See also CA 25-28R; CANR 18, 71

Hamilton, Alexander 1755(?)-1804
NCLC 49
See also DLB 37
Hamilton, Clive
See Lewis, C(live) S(taples)
Hamilton, Edmond 1904-1977 ...... CLC 1
See also CA 1-4R; CANR 3; DLB 8
Hamilton, Eugene (Jacob) Lee
See Lee-Hamilton, Eugene (Jacob)
Hamilton, Franklin
See Silverberg, Robert
Hamilton, Gail
See Corcoran, Barbara
Hamilton, Mollie
See Kaye, M(ary) M(argaret)
Hamilton, (Anthony Walter) Patrick
1904-1962 .... CLC 51
See also CA 113; DLB 10
Hamilton, Virginia 1936-...CLC 26; DAM
MULT
See also AAYA 2, 21; BW 2; CA 25-28R;
CANR 20, 37, 73; CLR 1, 11, 40; DLB 33,
52; INT CANR-20; JRDA; MAICYA;
MTCW 1; SATA 4, 56, 79
Hammett, (Samuel) Dashiell 1894-
1961...CLC 3, 5, 10, 19, 47; SSC 17
See also AITN 1; CA 81-84; CANR 42;
CDALB 1929-1941; DLBD 6; DLBY 96;
MTCW 1
Hammon, Jupiter 1711(?)-1800(?)...NCLC
5; BLC 2; DAM MULT, POET; PC 16
See also DLB 31, 50
Hammond, Keith
See Kuttner, Henry
Hamner, Earl (Henry), Jr. 1923-...CLC 12
See also AITN 2; CA 73-76; DLB 6
Hampton, Christopher (James) 1946-
CLC 4
See also CA 25-28R; DLB 13; MTCW 1
Hamsun, Knut ....TCLC 2, 14, 49
See also Pedersen, Knut
Handke, Peter 1942-...CLC 5, 8, 10, 15,
38; DAM DRAM, NOV
See also CA 77-80; CANR 33, 75; DLB 85, 124;
MTCW 1
Hanley, James 1901-1985 ..... CLC 3, 5, 8, 13
See also CA 73-76; 117; CANR 36; DLB 191;
MTCW 1
Hannah, Barry 1942- .... CLC 23, 38, 90
See also CA 108; 110; CANR 43, 68; DLB 6;
INT 110; MTCW 1
Hannon, Ezra
See Hunter, Evan
Hansberry, Lorraine (Vivian) 1930-1965
CLC 17, 62; BLC 2; DA; DAB; DAC;
DAM DRAM, MST, MULT; DC 2
See also AAYA 25; BW 1; CA 109; 25-28R;
CABS 3; CANR 58; CDALB 1941-1968;
DLB 7, 38; MTCW 1
Hansen, Joseph 1923- ....CLC 38
See also CA 29-32R; CAAS 17; CANR 16,
44, 66; INT CANR-16
Hansen, Martin A(lfred) 1909-1955
TCLC 32
See also CA 167
Hanson, Kenneth O(stlin) 1922- ....CLC 13
See also CA 53-56; CANR 7
Hardwick, Elizabeth (Bruce) 1916-
CLC 13; DAM NOV
See also CA 5-8R; CANR 3, 32, 70; DLB 6;
MTCW 1

Hardy, Thomas 1840-1928.....TCLC 4, 10,
18, 32, 48, 53, 72; DA; DAB; DAC;
DAM MST, NOV, POET; PC 8; SSC 2;
WLC
See also CA 104; 123; CDBLB 1890-1914;
DLB 18, 19, 135; MTCW 1
Hare, David 1947- .... CLC 29, 58
See also CA 97-100; CANR 39; DLB 13;
MTCW 1
Harewood, John
See Van Druten, John (William)
Harford, Henry
See Hudson, W(illiam) H(enry)
Hargrave, Leonie
See Disch, Thomas M(ichael)
Harjo, Joy 1951- .... CLC 83; DAM MULT
See also CA 114; CANR 35, 67; DLB 120, 175;
NNAL
Harlan, Louis R(udolph) 1922-.........CLC 34
See also CA 21-24R; CANR 25, 55
Harling, Robert 1951(?)- .... CLC 53
See also CA 147
Harmon, William (Ruth) 1938-...CLC 38
See also CA 33-36R; CANR 14, 32, 35; SATA
65
Harper, F. E. W.
See Harper, Frances Ellen Watkins
Harper, Frances E. W.
See Harper, Frances Ellen Watkins
Harper, Frances E. Watkins
See Harper, Frances Ellen Watkins
Harper, Frances Ellen
See Harper, Frances Ellen Watkins
Harper, Frances Ellen Watkins 1825-1911
TCLC 14; BLC 2; DAM MULT, POET;
PC 21
See also BW 1; CA 111; 125; DLB 50
Harper, Michael S(teven) 1938-...CLC 7,
22
See also BW 1; CA 33-36R; CANR 24; DLB
41
Harper, Mrs. F. E. W.
See Harper, Frances Ellen Watkins
Harris, Christie (Lucy) Irwin 1907-...CLC
12
See also CA 5-8R; CANR 6; CLR 47; DLB
88; JRDA; MAICYA; SAAS 10; SATA 6,
74
Harris, Frank 1856-1931 .... TCLC 24
See also CA 109; 150; DLB 156, 197
Harris, George Washington 1814-1869 NCLC
23
See also DLB 3, 11
Harris, Joel Chandler 1848-1908 ...TCLC 2;
SSC 19
See also CA 104; 137; CLR 49; DLB 11, 23,
42, 78, 91; MAICYA; SATA 100; YABC 1
Harris, John (Wyndham Parkes Lucas)
Beynon 1903-1969
See Wyndham, John
See also CA 102; 89-92
Harris, MacDonald ....CLC 9
See also Heiney, Donald (William)
Harris, Mark 1922- ....CLC 19
See also CA 5-8R; CAAS 3; CANR 2, 55; DLB
2; DLBY 80
Harris, (Theodore) Wilson 1921-
CLC 25
See also BW 2; CA 65-68; CAAS 16; CANR
11, 27, 69; DLB 117; MTCW 1
Harrison, Elizabeth Cavanna 1909-
See Cavanna, Betty
See also CA 9-12R; CANR 6, 27

Hempel, Amy 1951- .... CLC 39
See also CA 118; 137; CANR 70
Henderson, F. C.
See Mencken, H(enry) L(ouis)
Henderson, Sylvia
See Ashton-Warner, Sylvia (Constance)
Henderson, Zenna (Chlarson) 1917-1983
SSC 29
See also CA 1-4R; 133; CANR 1; DLB 8;
SATA 5
Henley, Beth .... CLC 23; DC 6
See also Henley, Elizabeth Becker
See also CABS 3; DLBY 86
Henley, Elizabeth Becker 1952-
See Henley, Beth
See also CA 107; CANR 32, 73; DAM
DRAM, MST; MTCW 1
Henley, William Ernest 1849-1903...TCLC
8
See also CA 105; DLB 19
Hennissart, Martha
See Lathen, Emma
See also CA 85-88; CANR 64
Henry, O. .... TCLC 1, 19; SSC 5; WLC
See also Porter, William Sydney
Henry, Patrick 1736-1799 .... LC 25
Henryson, Robert 1430(?)-1506(?)LC 20
See also DLB 146
Henry VIII 1491-1547 .... LC 10
Henschke, Alfred
See Klabund
Hentoff, Nat(han Irving) 1925- .... CLC 26
See also AAYA 4; CA 1-4R; CAAS 6; CANR
5, 25; CLR 1, 52; INT CANR-25; JRDA;
MAICYA; SATA 42, 69; SATA-Brief 27
Heppenstall, (John) Rayner 1911-1981
CLC 10
See also CA 1-4R; 103; CANR 29
Heraclitus c. 540B.C.-c. 450B.C...CMLC 22
See also DLB 176
Herbert, Frank (Patrick) 1920-1986
CLC 12, 23, 35, 44, 85; DAM POP
See also AAYA 21; CA 53-56; 118; CANR 5,
43; DLB 8; INT CANR-5; MTCW 1; SATA
9, 37; SATA-Obit 47
Herbert, George 1593-1633 ..... LC 24; DAB;
DAM POET; PC 4
See also CDBLB Before 1660; DLB 126
Herbert, Zbigniew 1924-1998 ..... CLC 9, 43;
DAM POET
See also CA 89-92; 169; CANR 36, 74; MTCW
1
Herbst, Josephine (Frey) 1897-1969
CLC 34
See also CA 5-8R; 25-28R; DLB 9
Hergesheimer, Joseph 1880-1954 .. TCLC 11
See also CA 109; DLB 102, 9
Herlihy, James Leo 1927-1993 .... CLC 6
See also CA 1-4R; 143; CANR 2
Hermogenes fl. c. 175- .... CMLC 6
Hernandez, Jose 1834-1886.... NCLC 17
Herodotus c. 484B.C.-429B.C....CMLC 17
See also DLB 176
Herrick, Robert 1591-1674 ...LC 13;
DA; DAB; DAC; DAM MST, POP; PC 9
See also DLB 126
Herring, Guilles
See Somerville, Edith
Herriot, James 1916-1995 .....CLC 12;
DAM POP
See also Wight, James Alfred
See also AAYA 1; CA 148; CANR 40; SATA
86

Herrmann, Dorothy 1941- .... CLC 44
See also CA 107
Herrmann, Taffy
See Herrmann, Dorothy
Hersey, John (Richard) 1914-1993...CLC
1, 2, 7, 9, 40, 81, 97; DAM POP
See also CA 17-20R; 140; CANR 33; DLB 6,
185; MTCW 1; SATA 25; SATA-Obit 76
Herzen, Aleksandr Ivanovich 1812-1870
NCLC 10, 61
Herzl, Theodor 1860-1904 .... TCLC 36
See also CA 168
Herzog, Werner 1942- ....CLC 16
See also CA 89-92
Hesiod c. 8th cent. B.C.- .... CMLC 5
See also DLB 176
Hesse, Hermann 1877-1962...CLC 1, 2,
3, 6, 11, 17, 25, 69; DA; DAB; DAC;
DAM MST, NOV; SSC 9; WLC
See also CA 17-18; CAP 2; DLB 66; MTCW 1;
SATA 50
Hewes, Cady
See De Voto, Bernard (Augustine)
Heyen, William 1940- .... CLC 13, 18
See also CA 33-36R; CAAS 9; DLB 5
Heyerdahl, Thor 1914- .... CLC 26
See also CA 5-8R; CANR 5, 22, 66, 73;
MTCW 1; SATA 2, 52
Heym, Georg (Theodor Franz Arthur)
1887-1912 .... TCLC 9
See also CA 106
Heym, Stefan 1913- ....CLC 41
See also CA 9-12R; CANR 4; DLB 69
Heyse, Paul (Johann Ludwig von) 1830-
1914 .... TCLC 8
See also CA 104; DLB 129
Heyward, (Edwin) DuBose 1885-1940
TCLC 59
See also CA 108; 157; DLB 7, 9, 45; SATA
21
Hibbert, Eleanor Alice Burford 1906-1993
CLC 7; DAM POP
See also BEST 90:4; CA 17-20R; 140; CANR
9, 28, 59; SATA 2; SATA-Obit 74
Hichens, Robert (Smythe) 1864-1950
TCLC 64
See also CA 162; DLB 153
Higgins, George V(incent) 1939-...CLC
4, 7, 10, 18
See also CA 77-80; CAAS 5; CANR 17, 51;
DLB 2; DLBY 81; INT CANR-17; MTCW 1
Higginson, Thomas Wentworth 1823-1911
TCLC 36
See also CA 162; DLB 1, 64
Highet, Helen
See MacInnes, Helen (Clark)
Highsmith, (Mary) Patricia 1921-1995
CLC 2, 4, 14, 42, 102; DAM NOV, POP
See also CA 1-4R; 147; CANR 1, 20, 48, 62;
MTCW 1
Highwater, Jamake (Mamake) 1942(?)-
CLC 12
See also AAYA 7; CA 65-68; CAAS 7; CANR
10, 34; CLR 17; DLB 52; DLBY 85; JRDA;
MAICYA; SATA 32, 69; SATA-Brief 30
Highway, Tomson 1951-...CLC 92; DAC;
DAM MULT
See also CA 151; CANR 75; NNAL
Higuchi, Ichiyo 1872-1896 ...... NCLC 49
Hijuelos, Oscar 1951- ..... CLC 65; DAM
MULT, POP; HLC
See also AAYA 25; BEST 90:1; CA 123;
CANR 50, 75; DLB 145; HW

Hikmet, Nazim 1902(?)-1963 ..... CLC 40
See also CA 141; 93-96
Hildegard von Bingen 1098-1179...CMLC
20
See also DLB 148
Hildesheimer, Wolfgang 1916-1991
CLC 49
See also CA 101; 135; DLB 69, 124
Hill, Geoffrey (William) 1932-...CLC 5,
8, 18, 45; DAM POET
See also CA 81-84; CANR 21; CDBLB 1960
to Present; DLB 40; MTCW 1
Hill, George Roy 1921- .... CLC 26
See also CA 110; 122
Hill, John
See Koontz, Dean R(ay)
Hill, Susan (Elizabeth) 1942-.... CLC 4,
113; DAB; DAM MST, NOV
See also CA 33-36R; CANR 29, 69; DLB 14,
139; MTCW 1
Hillerman, Tony 1925- ... CLC 62; DAM
POP
See also AAYA 6; BEST 89:1; CA 29-32R;
CANR 21, 42, 65; SATA 6
Hillesum, Etty 1914-1943 .... TCLC 49
See also CA 137
Hilliard, Noel (Harvey) 1929- ....CLC 15
See also CA 9-12R; CANR 7, 69
Hillis, Rick 1956- .... CLC 66
See also CA 134
Hilton, James 1900-1954 .... TCLC 21
See also CA 108; 169; DLB 34, 77; SATA
34
Himes, Chester (Bomar) 1909-1984
CLC 2, 4, 7, 18, 58, 108; BLC 2; DAM
MULT
See also BW 2; CA 25-28R; 114; CANR 22;
DLB 2, 76, 143; MTCW 1
Hinde, Thomas .... CLC 6, 11
See also Chitty, Thomas Willes
Hindin, Nathan
See Bloch, Robert (Albert)
Hine, (William) Daryl 1936- ..... CLC 15
See also CA 1-4R; CAAS 15; CANR 1, 20;
DLB 60
Hinkson, Katharine Tynan
See Tynan, Katharine
Hinton, S(usan) E(loise) 1950-...CLC 30,
111; DA; DAB; DAC; DAM MST, NOV
See also AAYA 2; CA 81-84; CANR 32, 62;
CLR 3, 23; JRDA; MAICYA; MTCW 1;
SATA 19, 58
Hippius, Zinaida .... TCLC 9
See also Gippius, Zinaida (Nikolayevna)
Hiraoka, Kimitake 1925-1970
See Mishima, Yukio
See also CA 97-100; 29-32R; DAM DRAM;
MTCW 1
Hirsch, E(ric) D(onald), Jr. 1928-..... CLC 79
See also CA 25-28R; CANR 27, 51; DLB 67;
INT CANR-27; MTCW 1
Hirsch, Edward 1950- .... CLC 31, 50
See also CA 104; CANR 20, 42; DLB 120
Hitchcock, Alfred (Joseph) 1899-1980
CLC 16
See also AAYA 22; CA 159; 97-100; SATA
27; SATA-Obit 24
Hitler, Adolf 1889-1945 .... TCLC 53
See also CA 117; 147
Hoagland, Edward 1932- .... CLC 28
See also CA 1-4R; CANR 2, 31, 57; DLB 6;
SATA 51

Jibran, Kahlil
　See Gibran, Kahlil
Jibran, Khalil
　See Gibran, Kahlil
Jiles, Paulette 1943- .... **CLC 13, 58**
　See also CA 101; CANR 70
Jimenez (Mantecon), Juan Ramon 1881-
　　1958 ....**TCLC 4; DAM MULT, POET;**
　　HLC; PC 7
　See also CA 104; 131; CANR 74; DLB 134;
　　HW; MTCW 1
Jimenez, Ramon
　See Jimenez (Mantecon), Juan Ramon
Jimenez Mantecon, Juan
　See Jimenez (Mantecon), Juan Ramon
Jin, Ha 1956- .... **CLC 109**
　See also CA 152
Joel, Billy .... **CLC 26**
　See also Joel, William Martin
Joel, William Martin 1949-
　See Joel, Billy
　See also CA 108
John, Saint 7th cent. - .... **CMLC 27**
John of the Cross, St. 1542-1591...**LC 18**
Johnson, B(ryan) S(tanley William) 1933-
　　1973 .... **CLC 6, 9**
　See also CA 9-12R; 53-56; CANR 9; DLB
　　14, 40
Johnson, Benj. F. of Boo
　See Riley, James Whitcomb
Johnson, Benjamin F. of Boo
　See Riley, James Whitcomb
Johnson, Charles (Richard) 1948-
　　CLC 7, 51, 65; BLC 2; DAM MULT
　See also BW 2; CA 116; CAAS 18; CANR
　　42, 66; DLB 33
Johnson, Denis 1949- .... **CLC 52**
　See also CA 117; 121; CANR 71; DLB 120
Johnson, Diane 1934- .... **CLC 5, 13, 48**
　See also CA 41-44R; CANR 17, 40, 62; DLBY
　　80; INT CANR-17; MTCW 1
Johnson, Eyvind (Olof Verner) 1900-1976
　　CLC 14
　See also CA 73-76; 69-72; CANR 34
Johnson, J. R.
　See James, C(yril) L(ionel) R(obert)
Johnson, James Weldon 1871-1938
　　TCLC 3, 19; BLC 2; DAM MULT, POET;
　　PC 24
　See also BW 1; CA 104; 125; CDALB 1917-
　　1929; CLR 32; DLB 51; MTCW 1; SATA
　　31
Johnson, Joyce 1935- .... **CLC 58**
　See also CA 125; 129
Johnson, Lionel (Pigot) 1867-1902
　　TCLC 19
　See also CA 117; DLB 19
Johnson, Marguerite (Annie)
　See Angelou, Maya
Johnson, Mel
　See Malzberg, Barry N(athaniel)
Johnson, Pamela Hansford 1912-1981
　　CLC 1, 7, 27
　See also CA 1-4R; 104; CANR 2, 28; DLB
　　15; MTCW 1
Johnson, Robert 1911(?)-1938 .... **TCLC 69**
Johnson, Samuel 1709-1784...**LC 15; DA; DAB;**
　　DAC; DAM MST; WLC
　See also CDBLB 1660-1789; DLB 39, 95, 104,
　　142
Johnson, Uwe 1934-1984 .. **CLC 5, 10, 15, 40**
　See also CA 1-4R; 112; CANR 1, 39; DLB 75;
　　MTCW 1

Johnston, George (Benson) 1913-
　　CLC 51
　See also CA 1-4R; CANR 5, 20; DLB 88
Johnston, Jennifer 1930- ....**CLC 7**
　See also CA 85-88; DLB 14
Jolley, (Monica) Elizabeth 1923-...**CLC 46;**
　　SSC 19
　See also CA 127; CAAS 13; CANR 59
Jones, Arthur Llewellyn 1863-1947
　See Machen, Arthur
　See also CA 104
Jones, D(ouglas) G(ordon) 1929- ......**CLC 10**
　See also CA 29-32R; CANR 13; DLB 53
Jones, David (Michael) 1895-1974...**C L C**
　　2, 4, 7, 13, 42
　See also CA 9-12R; 53-56; CANR 28; CDBLB
　　1945-1960; DLB 20, 100; MTCW 1
Jones, David Robert 1947-
　See Bowie, David
　See also CA 103
Jones, Diana Wynne 1934- .... **CLC 26**
　See also AAYA 12; CA 49-52; CANR 4, 26,
　　56; CLR 23; DLB 161; JRDA; MAICYA;
　　SAAS 7; SATA 9, 70
Jones, Edward P. 1950- .... **CLC 76**
　See also BW 2; CA 142
Jones, Gayl 1949- ..**CLC 6, 9; BLC 2; DAM**
　　MULT
　See also BW 2; CA 77-80; CANR 27, 66; DLB
　　33; MTCW 1
Jones, James 1921-1977...**CLC 1, 3, 10, 39**
　See also AITN 1, 2; CA 1-4R; 69-72; CANR
　　6; DLB 2, 143; DLBD 17; MTCW 1
Jones, John J.
　See Lovecraft, H(oward) P(hillips)
Jones, LeRoi .... **CLC 1, 2, 3, 5, 10, 14**
　See also Baraka, Amiri
Jones, Louis B. 1953- ....**CLC 65**
　See also CA 141; CANR 73
Jones, Madison (Percy, Jr.) 1925- ....**CLC 4**
　See also CA 13-16R; CAAS 11; CANR 7, 54;
　　DLB 152
Jones, Mervyn 1922- .... **CLC 10, 52**
　See also CA 45-48; CAAS 5; CANR 1;
　　MTCW 1
Jones, Mick 1956(?)- ....**CLC 30**
Jones, Nettie (Pearl) 1941- ....**CLC 34**
　See also BW 2; CA 137; CAAS 20
Jones, Preston 1936-1979 ....**CLC 10**
　See also CA 73-76; 89-92; DLB 7
Jones, Robert F(rancis) 1934- ....**CLC 7**
　See also CA 49-52; CANR 2, 61
Jones, Rod 1953- ....**CLC 50**
　See also CA 128
Jones, Terence Graham Parry 1942-
　　CLC 21
　See also Jones, Terry; Monty Python
　See also CA 112; 116; CANR 35; INT 116
Jones, Terry
　See Jones, Terence Graham Parry
　See also SATA 67; SATA-Brief 51
Jones, Thom 1945(?)- .... **CLC 81**
　See also CA 157
Jong, Erica 1942-...**CLC 4, 6, 8, 18, 83;**
　　DAM NOV, POP
　See also AITN 1; BEST 90:2; CA 73-76; CANR
　　26, 52, 75; DLB 2, 5, 28, 152; INT CANR-
　　26; MTCW 1
Jonson, Ben(jamin) 1572(?)-1637...**LC 6,**
　　33; DA; DAB; DAC; DAM DRAM, MST,
　　POET; DC 4; PC 17; WLC
　See also CDBLB Before 1660; DLB 62,
　　121

Jordan, June 1936-...**CLC 5, 11, 23, 114;**
　　BLCS; DAM MULT, POET
　See also AAYA 2; BW 2; CA 33-36R; CANR
　　25, 70; CLR 10; DLB 38; MAICYA; MTCW
　　1; SATA 4
Jordan, Neil (Patrick) 1950- .... **CLC 110**
　See also CA 124; 130; CANR 54; INT 130
Jordan, Pat(rick M.) 1941- .... **CLC 37**
　See also CA 33-36R
Jorgensen, Ivar
　See Ellison, Harlan (Jay)
Jorgenson, Ivar
　See Silverberg, Robert
Josephus, Flavius c. 37-100 .... **CMLC 13**
Josipovici, Gabriel 1940-.........**CLC 6, 43**
　See also CA 37-40R; CAAS 8; CANR 47;
　　DLB 14
Joubert, Joseph 1754-1824 .... **NCLC 9**
Jouve, Pierre Jean 1887-1976 .... **CLC 47**
　See also CA 65-68
Jovine, Francesco 1902-1950 .... **TCLC 79**
Joyce, James (Augustine Aloysius) 1882-
　　1941...**TCLC 3, 8, 16, 35, 52; DA; DAB;**
　　DAC; DAM MST, NOV, POET; PC 22;
　　SSC 3, 26; WLC
　See also CA 104; 126; CDBLB 1914-1945;
　　DLB 10, 19, 36, 162; MTCW 1
Jozsef, Attila 1905-1937 .... **TCLC 22**
　See also CA 116
Juana Ines de la Cruz 1651(?)-1695
　　LC 5; PC 24
Judd, Cyril
　See Kornbluth, C(yril) M.; Pohl, Frederik
Julian of Norwich 1342(?)-1416(?) .... **LC 6**
　See also DLB 146
Junger, Sebastian 1962- .... **CLC 109**
　See also CA 165
Juniper, Alex
　See Hospital, Janette Turner
Junius
　See Luxemburg, Rosa
Just, Ward (Swift) 1935-.........**CLC 4, 27**
　See also CA 25-28R; CANR 32; INT CANR-
　　32
Justice, Donald (Rodney) 1925- .. **CLC 6, 19,**
　　102; DAM POET
　See also CA 5-8R; CANR 26, 54, 74; DLBY
　　83; INT CANR-26
Juvenal .... **CMLC 8**
　See also Juvenalis, Decimus Junius
Juvenalis, Decimus Junius 55(?)-c. 127(?)
　See Juvenal
Juvenis
　See Bourne, Randolph S(illiman)

Kacew, Romain 1914-1980
　See Gary, Romain
　See also CA 108; 102
Kadare, Ismail 1936- .... **CLC 52**
　See also CA 161
Kadohata, Cynthia ....**CLC 59**
　See also CA 140
Kafka, Franz 1883-1924...**TCLC 2, 6, 13,**
　　29, 47, 53; DA; DAB; DAC; DAM MST,
　　NOV; SSC 5, 29; WLC
　See also CA 105; 126; DLB 81; MTCW 1
Kahanovitsch, Pinkhes
　See Der Nister
Kahn, Roger 1927- ....**CLC 30**
　See also CA 25-28R; CANR 44, 69; DLB 171;
　　SATA 37
Kain, Saul
　See Sassoon, Siegfried (Lorraine)

Key, Ellen 1849-1926 .... **TCLC 65**
Keyber, Conny
See Fielding, Henry
Keyes, Daniel 1927-...**CLC 80; DA; DAC;**
DAM MST, NOV
See also AAYA 23; CA 17-20R; CANR 10, 26,
54, 74; SATA 37
Keynes, John Maynard 1883-1946
TCLC 64
See also CA 114; 162, 163; DLBD 10
Khanshendel, Chiron
See Rose, Wendy
Khayyam, Omar 1048-1131...**CMLC 11;**
DAM POET; PC 8
Kherdian, David 1931- .... **CLC 6, 9**
See also CA 21-24R; CAAS 2; CANR 39; CLR
24; JRDA; MAICYA; SATA 16, 74
Khlebnikov, Velimir .... **TCLC 20**
See also Khlebnikov, Viktor Vladimirovich
Khlebnikov, Viktor Vladimirovich 1885-1922
See Khlebnikov, Velimir
See also CA 117
Khodasevich, Vladislav (Felitsianovich)
1886-1939 .... **TCLC 15**
See also CA 115
Kielland, Alexander Lange 1849-1906
TCLC 5
See also CA 104
Kiely, Benedict 1919- .... **CLC 23, 43**
See also CA 1-4R; CANR 2; DLB 15
Kienzle, William X(avier) 1928- .. **C L C**
25; DAM POP
See also CA 93-96; CAAS 1; CANR 9, 31, 59;
INT CANR-31; MTCW 1
Kierkegaard, Soren 1813-1855
NCLC 34
Killens, John Oliver 1916-1987...**CLC 10**
See also BW 2; CA 77-80; 123; CAAS 2;
CANR 26; DLB 33
Killigrew, Anne 1660-1685 .... **LC 4**
See also DLB 131
Kim
See Simenon, Georges (Jacques Christian)
Kincaid, Jamaica 1949-...**CLC 43, 68; BLC**
2; DAM MULT, NOV
See also AAYA 13; BW 2; CA 125; CANR 47,
59; DLB 157
King, Francis (Henry) 1923-...**CLC 8, 53;**
DAM NOV
See also CA 1-4R; CANR 1, 33; DLB 15, 139;
MTCW 1
King, Kennedy
See Brown, George Douglas
King, Martin Luther, Jr. 1929-1968
CLC 83; BLC 2; DA; DAB; DAC;
DAM MST, MULT; WLCS
See also BW 2; CA 25-28; CANR 27, 44;
CAP 2; MTCW 1; SATA 14
King, Stephen (Edwin) 1947-...**CLC 12, 26,**
37, 61, 113; DAM NOV, POP; SSC 17
See also AAYA 1, 17; BEST 90:1; CA 61-64;
CANR 1, 30, 52; DLB 143; DLBY 80;
JRDA; MICW 1; SATA 9, 55
King, Steve
See King, Stephen (Edwin)
King, Thomas 1943- .... **CLC 89; DAC; DAM**
MULT
See also CA 144; DLB 175; NNAL; SATA 96
Kingman, Lee .... **CLC 17**
See also Natti, (Mary) Lee
See also SAAS 3; SATA 1, 67
Kingsley, Charles 1819-1875 . **NCLC 35**
See also DLB 21, 32, 163, 190; YABC 2

Kingsley, Sidney 1906-1995 .... **CLC 44**
See also CA 85-88; 147; DLB 7
Kingsolver, Barbara 1955-...**CLC 55, 81;**
DAM POP
See also AAYA 15; CA 129; 134; CANR 60;
INT 134
Kingston, Maxine (Ting Ting) Hong 1940-
CLC 12, 19, 58; DAM MULT, NOV;
WLCS
See also AAYA 8; CA 69-72; CANR 13, 38,
74; DLB 173; DLBY 80; INT CANR-13;
MTCW 1; SATA 53
Kinnell, Galway 1927-...**CLC 1, 2, 3, 5,**
13, 29
See also CA 9-12R; CANR 10, 34, 66; DLB
5; DLBY 87; INT CANR-34; MTCW 1
Kinsella, Thomas 1928- .... **CLC 4, 19**
See also CA 17-20R; CANR 15; DLB 27;
MTCW 1
Kinsella, W(illiam) P(atrick) 1935-
CLC 27, 43; DAC; DAM NOV, POP
See also AAYA 7; CA 97-100; CAAS 7;
CANR 21, 35, 66, 75; INT CANR-21;
MTCW 1
Kipling, (Joseph) Rudyard 1865-1936
TCLC 8, 17; DA; DAB; DAC; DAM
MST, POET; PC 3; SSC 5; WLC
See also CA 105; 120; CANR 33; CDBLB
1890-1914; CLR 39; DLB 19, 34, 141, 156;
MAICYA; MTCW 1; SATA 100; YABC 2
Kirkup, James 1918- .... **CLC 1**
See also CA 1-4R; CAAS 4; CANR 2; DLB
27; SATA 12
Kirkwood, James 1930(?)-1989 ....**CLC 9**
See also AITN 2; CA 1-4R; 128; CANR 6, 40
Kirshner, Sidney
See Kingsley, Sidney
Kis, Danilo 1935-1989 .... **CLC 57**
See also CA 109; 118; 129; CANR 61; DLB
181; MTCW 1
Kivi, Aleksis 1834-1872 .... **NCLC 30**
Kizer, Carolyn (Ashley) 1925-...**CLC 15,**
39, 80; DAM POET
See also CA 65-68; CAAS 5; CANR 24, 70;
DLB 5, 169
Klabund 1890-1928 .... **TCLC 44**
See also CA 162; DLB 66
Klappert, Peter 1942- .... **CLC 57**
See also CA 33-36R; DLB 5
Klein, A(braham) M(oses) 1909-1972
CLC 19; DAB; DAC; DAM MST
See also CA 101; 37-40R; DLB 68
Klein, Norma 1938-1989 .... **CLC 30**
See also AAYA 2; CA 41-44R; 128; CANR 15,
37; CLR 2, 19; INT CANR-15; JRDA;
MAICYA; SAAS 1; SATA 7, 57
Klein, T(heodore) E(ibon) D(onald) 1947-
CLC 34
See also CA 119; CANR 44, 75
Kleist, Heinrich von 1777-1811
NCLC 2, 37; DAM DRAM; SSC 22
See also DLB 90
Klima, Ivan 1931- .... **CLC 56; DAM NOV**
See also CA 25-28R; CANR 17, 50
Klimentov, Andrei Platonovich 1899-1951
See Platonov, Andrei
See also CA 108
Klinger, Friedrich Maximilian von 1752-1831
NCLC 1
See also DLB 94
Klingsor the Magician
See Hartmann, Sadakichi

Klopstock, Friedrich Gottlieb 1724-1803
NCLC 11
See also DLB 97
Knapp, Caroline 1959- .... **CLC 99**
See also CA 154
Knebel, Fletcher 1911-1993 .... **CLC 14**
See also AITN 1; CA 1-4R; 140; CAAS 3;
CANR 1, 36; SATA 36; SATA-Obit 75
Knickerbocker, Diedrich
See Irving, Washington
Knight, Etheridge 1931-1991 .. **CLC 40;**
BLC 2; DAM POET; PC 14
See also BW 1; CA 21-24R; 133; CANR 23;
DLB 41
Knight, Sarah Kemble 1666-1727 .. **LC 7**
See also DLB 24, 200
Knister, Raymond 1899-1932 .... **TCLC 56**
See also DLB 68
Knowles, John 1926-...**CLC 1, 4, 10, 26;**
DA; DAC; DAM MST, NOV
See also AAYA 10; CA 17-20R; CANR 40, 74;
CDALB 1968-1988; DLB 6; MTCW 1;
SATA 8, 89
Knox, Calvin M.
See Silverberg, Robert
Knox, John c. 1505-1572 .... **LC 37**
See also DLB 132
Knye, Cassandra
See Disch, Thomas M(ichael)
Koch, C(hristopher) J(ohn) 1932- ....**CLC 42**
See also CA 127
Koch, Christopher
See Koch, C(hristopher) J(ohn)
Koch, Kenneth 1925- ...... **CLC 5, 8, 44;**
DAM POET
See also CA 1-4R; CANR 6, 36, 57; DLB 5;
INT CANR-36; SATA 65
Kochanowski, Jan 1530-1584 ....**LC 10**
Kock, Charles Paul de 1794-1871 **N C L C**
16
Koda Shigeyuki 1867-1947
See Rohan, Koda
See also CA 121
Koestler, Arthur 1905-1983... **CLC 1, 3,**
6, 8, 15, 33
See also CA 1-4R; 109; CANR 1, 33; CDBLB
1945-1960; DLBY 83; MTCW 1
Kogawa, Joy Nozomi 1935-.. **CLC 78; DAC;**
DAM MST, MULT
See also CA 101; CANR 19, 62; SATA 99
Kohout, Pavel 1928- .... **CLC 13**
See also CA 45-48; CANR 3
Koizumi, Yakumo
See Hearn, (Patricio) Lafcadio (Tessima Carlos)
Kolmar, Gertrud 1894-1943 .... **TCLC 40**
See also CA 167
Komunyakaa, Yusef 1947-...**CLC 86, 94;**
BLCS
See also CA 147; DLB 120
Konrad, George
See Konrad, Gyoergy
Konrad, Gyoergy 1933- .... **CLC 4, 10, 73**
See also CA 85-88
Konwicki, Tadeusz 1926-...**CLC 8, 28, 54,**
117
See also CA 101; CAAS 9; CANR 39, 59;
MTCW 1
Koontz, Dean R(ay) 1945- ..... **CLC 78; DAM**
NOV, POP
See also AAYA 9; BEST 89:3, 90:2; CA 108;
CANR 19, 36, 52; MTCW 1; SATA 92
Kopernik, Mikolaj
See Copernicus, Nicolaus

Landis, John 1950- .... **CLC 26**
See also CA 112; 122

Landolfi, Tommaso 1908-1979 .... **CLC 11, 49**
See also CA 127; 117; DLB 177

Landon, Letitia Elizabeth 1802-1838
NCLC 15
See also DLB 96

Landor, Walter Savage 1775-1864...**NCLC 14**
See also DLB 93, 107

Landwirth, Heinz 1927-
See Lind, Jakov
See also CA 9-12R; CANR 7

Lane, Patrick 1939- ...... **CLC 25; DAM POET**
See also CA 97-100; CANR 54; DLB 53; INT 97-100

Lang, Andrew 1844-1912 .... **TCLC 16**
See also CA 114; 137; DLB 98, 141, 184; MAICYA; SATA 16

Lang, Fritz 1890-1976 .... **CLC 20, 103**
See also CA 77-80; 69-72; CANR 30

Lange, John
See Crichton, (John) Michael

Langer, Elinor 1939- .... **CLC 34**
See also CA 121

Langland, William 1330(?)-1400(?) ... **LC 19; DA; DAB; DAC; DAM MST, POET**
See also DLB 146

Langstaff, Launcelot
See Irving, Washington

Lanier, Sidney 1842-1881 ..... **NCLC 6; DAM POET**
See also DLB 64; DLBD 13; MAICYA; SATA 18

Lanyer, Aemilia 1569-1645 .... **LC 10, 30**
See also DLB 121

Lao-Tzu
See Lao Tzu

Lao Tzu fl. 6th cent. B.C.- .... **CMLC 7**

Lapine, James (Elliot) 1949- ..... **CLC 39**
See also CA 123; 130; CANR 54; INT 130

Larbaud, Valery (Nicolas) 1881-1957
TCLC 9
See also CA 106; 152

Lardner, Ring
See Lardner, Ring(gold) W(ilmer)

Lardner, Ring W., Jr.
See Lardner, Ring(gold) W(ilmer)

Lardner, Ring(gold) W(ilmer) 1885-1933
TCLC 2, 14; SSC 32
See also CA 104; 131; CDALB 1917-1929; DLB 11, 25, 86; DLBD 16; MTCW 1

Laredo, Betty
See Codrescu, Andrei

Larkin, Maia
See Wojciechowska, Maia (Teresa)

Larkin, Philip (Arthur) 1922-1985
CLC 3, 5, 8, 9, 13, 18, 33, 39, 64; DAB; DAM MST, POET; PC 21
See also CA 5-8R; 117; CANR 24, 62; CDBLB 1960 to Present; DLB 27; MTCW 1

Larra (y Sanchez de Castro), Mariano Jose de 1809-1837 .... **NCLC 17**

Larsen, Eric 1941- .... **CLC 55**
See also CA 132

Larsen, Nella 1891-1964 .... **CLC 37; BLC 2; DAM MULT**
See also BW 1; CA 125; DLB 51

Larson, Charles R(aymond) 1938- .. **CLC 31**
See also CA 53-56; CANR 4

Larson, Jonathan 1961-1996 ..... **CLC 99**
See also CA 156

Las Casas, Bartolome de 1474-1566
LC 31

Lasch, Christopher 1932-1994...**CLC 102**
See also CA 73-76; 144; CANR 25; MTCW 1

Lasker-Schueler, Else 1869-1945...**TCLC 57**
See also DLB 66, 124

Laski, Harold 1893-1950 .... **TCLC 79**

Latham, Jean Lee 1902-1995 .... **CLC 12**
See also AITN 1; CA 5-8R; CANR 7; CLR 50; MAICYA; SATA 2, 68

Latham, Mavis
See Clark, Mavis Thorpe

Lathen, Emma .... **CLC 2**
See also Hennissart, Martha; Latsis, Mary J(ane)

Lathrop, Francis
See Leiber, Fritz (Reuter, Jr.)

Latsis, Mary J(ane) 1927(?)-1997
See Lathen, Emma
See also CA 85-88; 162

Lattimore, Richmond (Alexander) 1906-1984
CLC 3
See also CA 1-4R; 112; CANR 1

Laughlin, James 1914-1997 .... **CLC 49**
See also CA 21-24R; 162; CAAS 22; CANR 9, 47; DLB 48; DLBY 96, 97

Laurence, (Jean) Margaret (Wemyss) 1926-1987**CLC 3, 6, 13, 50, 62; DAC; DAM MST; SSC 7**
See also CA 5-8R; 121; CANR 33; DLB 53; MTCW 1; SATA-Obit 50

Laurent, Antoine 1952- .... **CLC 50**

Lauscher, Hermann
See Hesse, Hermann

Lautreamont, Comte de 1846-1870
NCLC 12; SSC 14

Laverty, Donald
See Blish, James (Benjamin)

Lavin, Mary 1912-1996 ..**CLC 4, 18, 99; SSC 4**
See also CA 9-12R; 151; CANR 33; DLB 15; MTCW 1

Lavond, Paul Dennis
See Kornbluth, C(yril) M.; Pohl, Frederik

Lawler, Raymond Evenor 1922- .... **CLC 58**
See also CA 103

Lawrence, D(avid) H(erbert Richards) 1885-1930...**TCLC 2, 9, 16, 33, 48, 61; DA; DAB; DAC; DAM MST, NOV, POET; SSC 4, 19; WLC**
See also CA 104; 121; CDBLB 1914-1945; DLB 10, 19, 36, 98, 162, 195; MTCW 1

Lawrence, T(homas) E(dward) 1888-1935
TCLC 18
See also Dale, Colin
See also CA 115; 167; DLB 195

Lawrence of Arabia
See Lawrence, T(homas) E(dward)

Lawson, Henry (Archibald Hertzberg) 1867-1922 .... **TCLC 27; SSC 18**
See also CA 120

Lawton, Dennis
See Faust, Frederick (Schiller)

Laxness, Halldor ....**CLC 25**
See also Gudjonsson, Halldor Kiljan

Layamon fl. c. 1200- .... **CMLC 10**
See also DLB 146

Laye, Camara 1928-1980...**CLC 4, 38; BLC 2; DAM MULT**
See also BW 1; CA 85-88; 97-100; CANR 25; MTCW 1

Layton, Irving (Peter) 1912-...**CLC 2, 15; DAC; DAM MST, POET**
See also CA 1-4R; CANR 2, 33, 43, 66; DLB 88; MTCW 1

Lazarus, Emma 1849-1887 .... **NCLC 8**

Lazarus, Felix
See Cable, George Washington

Lazarus, Henry
See Slavitt, David R(ytman)

Lea, Joan
See Neufeld, John (Arthur)

Leacock, Stephen (Butler) 1869-1944
TCLC 2; DAC; DAM MST
See also CA 104; 141; DLB 92

Lear, Edward 1812-1888 .... **NCLC 3**
See also CLR 1; DLB 32, 163, 166; MAICYA; SATA 18, 100

Lear, Norman (Milton) 1922- .... **CLC 12**
See also CA 73-76

Leautaud, Paul 1872-1956........ **TCLC 83**
See also DLB 65

Leavis, F(rank) R(aymond) 1895-1978
CLC 24
See also CA 21-24R; 77-80; CANR 44; MTCW 1

Leavitt, David 1961-...**CLC 34; DAM POP**
See also CA 116; 122; CANR 50, 62; DLB 130; INT 122

Leblanc, Maurice (Marie Emile) 1864-1941
TCLC 49
See also CA 110

Lebowitz, Fran(ces Ann) 1951(?)-...**CLC 11, 36**
See also CA 81-84; CANR 14, 60, 70; INT CANR-14; MTCW 1

Lebrecht, Peter
See Tieck, (Johann) Ludwig

le Carre, John .... **CLC 3, 5, 9, 15, 28**
See also Cornwell, David (John Moore)
See also BEST 89:4; CDBLB 1960 to Present; DLB 87

Le Clezio, J(ean) M(arie) G(ustave) 1940-
CLC 31
See also CA 116; 128; DLB 83

Leconte de Lisle, Charles-Marie-Rene 1818-1894 .... **NCLC 29**

Le Coq, Monsieur
See Simenon, Georges (Jacques Christian)

Leduc, Violette 1907-1972 .... **CLC 22**
See also CA 13-14; 33-36R; CANR 69; CAP 1

Ledwidge, Francis 1887(?)-1917 .... **TCLC 23**
See also CA 123; DLB 20

Lee, Andrea 1953- .... **CLC 36; BLC 2; DAM MULT**
See also BW 1; CA 125

Lee, Andrew
See Auchincloss, Louis (Stanton)

Lee, Chang-rae 1965-........................**CLC 91**
See also CA 148

Lee, Don L. ....**CLC 2**
See also Madhubuti, Haki R.

Lee, George W(ashington) 1894-1976
CLC 52; BLC 2; DAM MULT
See also BW 1; CA 125; DLB 51

Lee, (Nelle) Harper 1926-.. **CLC 12, 60; DA; DAB; DAC; DAM MST, NOV; WLC**
See also AAYA 13; CA 13-16R; CANR 51; CDALB 1941-1968; DLB 6; MTCW 1; SATA 11

Lee, Helen Elaine 1959(?)- .... **CLC 86**
See also CA 148

Lee, Julian
See Latham, Jean Lee

Lewis, (Harry) Sinclair 1885-1951
TCLC 4, 13, 23, 39; DA; DAB; DAC;
DAM MST, NOV; WLC
See also CA 104; 133; CDALB 1917-1929;
DLB 9, 102; DLBD 1; MTCW 1

Lewis, (Percy) Wyndham 1882(?)-1957
TCLC 2, 9
See also CA 104; 157; DLB 15

Lewisohn, Ludwig 1883-1955 .... **TCLC 19**
See also CA 107; DLB 4, 9, 28, 102

Lewton, Val 1904-1951 .... **TCLC 76**

Leyner, Mark 1956- .... **CLC 92**
See also CA 110; CANR 28, 53

Lezama Lima, Jose 1910-1976...**CLC 4,**
10, 101; DAM MULT
See also CA 77-80; CANR 71; DLB 113; HW

L'Heureux, John (Clarke) 1934-
CLC 52
See also CA 13-16R; CANR 23, 45

Liddell, C. H.
See Kuttner, Henry

Lie, Jonas (Lauritz Idemil) 1833-1908(?)
TCLC 5
See also CA 115

Lieber, Joel 1937-1971 .... **CLC 6**
See also CA 73-76; 29-32R

Lieber, Stanley Martin
See Lee, Stan

Lieberman, Laurence (James) 1935-...**CLC**
4, 36
See also CA 17-20R; CANR 8, 36

Lieh Tzu fl. 7th cent. B.C.-5th cent. B.C.
CMLC 27

Lieksman, Anders
See Haavikko, Paavo Juhani

Li Fei-kan 1904-
See Pa Chin
See also CA 105

Lifton, Robert Jay 1926- .... **CLC 67**
See also CA 17-20R; CANR 27; INT CANR-
27; SATA 66

Lightfoot, Gordon 1938- .... **CLC 26**
See also CA 109

Lightman, Alan P(aige) 1948- .... **CLC 81**
See also CA 141; CANR 63

Ligotti, Thomas (Robert) 1953-...**CLC 44;**
SSC 16
See also CA 123; CANR 49

Li Ho 791-817 .... **PC 13**

Liliencron, (Friedrich Adolf Axel) Detlev
von 1844-1909 .... **TCLC 18**
See also CA 117

Lilly, William 1602-1681 .... **LC 27**

Lima, Jose Lezama
See Lezama Lima, Jose

Lima Barreto, Afonso Henrique de 1881-1922
TCLC 23
See also CA 117

Limonov, Edward 1944- .... **CLC 67**
See also CA 137

Lin, Frank
See Atherton, Gertrude (Franklin Horn)

Lincoln, Abraham 1809-1865 .... **NCLC 18**

Lind, Jakov .... **CLC 1, 2, 4, 27, 82**
See also Landwirth, Heinz
See also CAAS 4

Lindbergh, Anne (Spencer) Morrow 1906-
CLC 82; DAM NOV
See also CA 17-20R; CANR 16, 73; MTCW 1;
SATA 33

Lindsay, David 1878-1945 .... **TCLC 15**
See also CA 113

Lindsay, (Nicholas) Vachel 1879-1931
TCLC 17; DA; DAC; DAM MST, POET;
PC 23; WLC
See also CA 114; 135; CDALB 1865-1917;
DLB 54; SATA 40

Linke-Poot
See Doeblin, Alfred

Linney, Romulus 1930- .... **CLC 51**
See also CA 1-4R; CANR 40, 44

Linton, Eliza Lynn 1822-1898 .... **NCLC 41**
See also DLB 18

Li Po 701-763 .... **CMLC 2**

Lipsius, Justus 1547-1606 .... **LC 16**

Lipsyte, Robert (Michael) 1938-...**CLC 21;**
DA; DAC; DAM MST, NOV
See also AAYA 7; CA 17-20R; CANR 8, 57;
CLR 23; JRDA; MAICYA; SATA 5, 68

Lish, Gordon (Jay) 1934-...**CLC 45; SSC**
18
See also CA 113; 117; DLB 130; INT 117

Lispector, Clarice 1925(?)-1977 .... **CLC 43**
See also CA 139; 116; CANR 71; DLB 113

Littell, Robert 1935(?)- .... **CLC 42**
See also CA 109; 112; CANR 64

Little, Malcolm 1925-1965
See Malcolm X
See also BW 1; CA 125; 111; DA; DAB;
DAC; DAM MST, MULT; MTCW 1

Littlewit, Humphrey Gent.
See Lovecraft, H(oward) P(hillips)

Litwos
See Sienkiewicz, Henryk (Adam Alexander
Pius)

Liu, E 1857-1909 .... **TCLC 15**
See also CA 115

Lively, Penelope (Margaret) 1933-...**CLC**
32, 50; DAM NOV
See also CA 41-44R; CANR 29, 67; CLR 7;
DLB 14, 161; JRDA; MAICYA; MTCW 1;
SATA 7, 60, 101

Livesay, Dorothy (Kathleen) 1909-
CLC 4, 15, 79; DAC; DAM MST, POET
See also AITN 2; CA 25-28R; CAAS 8;
CANR 36, 67; DLB 68; MTCW 1

Livy c. 59B.C.-c. 17 .... **CMLC 11**

Lizardi, Jose Joaquin Fernandez de 1776-
1827 .... **NCLC 30**

Llewellyn, Richard
See Llewellyn Lloyd, Richard Dafydd Vivian
See also DLB 15

Llewellyn Lloyd, Richard Dafydd Vivian
1906-1983 .... **CLC 7, 80**
See also Llewellyn, Richard
See also CA 53-56; 111; CANR 7, 71; SATA
11; SATA-Obit 37

Llosa, (Jorge) Mario (Pedro) Vargas
See Vargas Llosa, (Jorge) Mario (Pedro)

Lloyd, Manda
See Mander, (Mary) Jane

Lloyd Webber, Andrew 1948-
See Webber, Andrew Lloyd
See also AAYA 1; CA 116; 149; DAM DRAM;
SATA 56

Llull, Ramon c. 1235-c. 1316 .... **CMLC 12**

Lobb, Ebenezer
See Upward, Allen

Locke, Alain (Le Roy) 1886-1954...**TCLC**
43; BLCS
See also BW 1; CA 106; 124; DLB 51

Locke, John 1632-1704 .... **LC 7, 35**
See also DLB 101

Locke-Elliott, Sumner
See Elliott, Sumner Locke

Lockhart, John Gibson 1794-1854
NCLC 6
See also DLB 110, 116, 144

Lodge, David (John) 1935-...**CLC 36; DAM**
POP
See also BEST 90:1; CA 17-20R; CANR 19,
53; DLB 14, 194; INT CANR-19;
MTCW 1

Lodge, Thomas 1558-1625 .... **LC 41**

Lodge, Thomas 1558-1625 .... **LC 41**
See also DLB 172

Loennbohm, Armas Eino Leopold 1878-1926
See Leino, Eino
See also CA 123

Loewinsohn, Ron(ald William) 1937-
CLC 52
See also CA 25-28R; CANR 71

Logan, Jake
See Smith, Martin Cruz

Logan, John (Burton) 1923-1987...**CLC 5**
See also CA 77-80; 124; CANR 45; DLB 5

Lo Kuan-chung 1330(?)-1400(?) .... **LC 12**

Lombard, Nap
See Johnson, Pamela Hansford

London, Jack ...**TCLC 9, 15, 39; SSC 4;**
WLC
See also London, John Griffith
See also AAYA 13; AITN 2; CDALB 1865-
1917; DLB 8, 12, 78; SATA 18

London, John Griffith 1876-1916
See London, Jack
See also CA 110; 119; CANR 73; DA; DAB;
DAC; DAM MST, NOV; JRDA; MAICYA;
MTCW 1

Long, Emmett
See Leonard, Elmore (John, Jr.)

Longbaugh, Harry
See Goldman, William (W.)

Longfellow, Henry Wadsworth 1807-1882
NCLC 2, 45; DA; DAB; DAC; DAM MST,
POET; WLCS
See also CDALB 1640-1865; DLB 1, 59;
SATA 19

Longinus c. 1st cent. - .... **CMLC 27**
See also DLB 176

Longley, Michael 1939-..................... **CLC 29**
See also CA 102; DLB 40

Longus fl. c. 2nd cent. - .... **CMLC 7**

Longway, A. Hugh
See Lang, Andrew

Lonnrot, Elias 1802-1884 .... **NCLC 53**

Lopate, Phillip 1943-......................... **CLC 29**
See also CA 97-100; DLBY 80; INT 97-100

Lopez Portillo (y Pacheco), Jose 1920-
CLC 46
See also CA 129; HW

Lopez y Fuentes, Gregorio 1897(?)-1966
CLC 32
See also CA 131; HW

Lorca, Federico Garcia
See Garcia Lorca, Federico

Lord, Bette Bao 1938-........................ **CLC 23**
See also BEST 90:3; CA 107; CANR 41; INT
107; SATA 58

Lord Auch
See Bataille, Georges

Lord Byron
See Byron, George Gordon (Noel)

Lorde, Audre (Geraldine) 1934-1992
CLC 18, 71; BLC 2; DAM MULT,
POET; PC 12
See also BW 1; CA 25-28R; 142; CANR 16,
26, 46; DLB 41; MTCW 1

Maclean, Norman (Fitzroy) 1902-1990 **CLC 78; DAM POP; SSC 13**
See also CA 102; 132; CANR 49

MacLeish, Archibald 1892-1982...**CLC 3, 8, 14, 68; DAM POET**
See also CA 9-12R; 106; CANR 33, 63; DLB 4, 7, 45; DLBY 82; MTCW 1

MacLennan, (John) Hugh 1907-1990...**CLC 2, 14, 92; DAC; DAM MST**
See also CA 5-8R; 142; CANR 33; DLB 68; MTCW 1

MacLeod, Alistair 1936-...**CLC 56; DAC; DAM MST**
See also CA 123; DLB 60

Macleod, Fiona
See Sharp, William

MacNeice, (Frederick) Louis 1907-1963 **CLC 1, 4, 10, 53; DAB; DAM POET**
See also CA 85-88; CANR 61; DLB 10, 20; MTCW 1

MacNeill, Dand
See Fraser, George MacDonald

Macpherson, James 1736-1796 ..... **LC 29**
See also Ossian
See also DLB 109

Macpherson, (Jean) Jay 1931- .... **CLC 14**
See also CA 5-8R; DLB 53

MacShane, Frank 1927- .... **CLC 39**
See also CA 9-12R; CANR 3, 33; DLB 111

Macumber, Mari
See Sandoz, Mari(e Susette)

Madach, Imre 1823-1864 .... **NCLC 19**

Madden, (Jerry) David 1933-...**CLC 5, 15**
See also CA 1-4R; CAAS 3; CANR 4, 45; DLB 6; MTCW 1

Maddern, Al(an)
See Ellison, Harlan (Jay)

Madhubuti, Haki R. 1942-...**CLC 6, 73; BLC 2; DAM MULT, POET; PC 5**
See also Lee, Don L.
See also BW 2; CA 73-76; CANR 24, 51, 73; DLB 5, 41; DLBD 8

Maepenn, Hugh
See Kuttner, Henry

Maepenn, K. H.
See Kuttner, Henry

Maeterlinck, Maurice 1862-1949 .... **TCLC 3; DAM DRAM**
See also CA 104; 136; DLB 192; SATA 66

Maginn, William 1794-1842 .... **NCLC 8**
See also DLB 110, 159

Mahapatra, Jayanta 1928-...**CLC 33; DAM MULT**
See also CA 73-76; CAAS 9; CANR 15, 33, 66

Mahfouz, Naguib (Abdel Aziz Al-Sabilgi) 1911(?)-
See Mahfuz, Najib
See also BEST 89:2; CA 128; CANR 55; DAM NOV; MTCW 1

Mahfuz, Najib .... **CLC 52, 55**
See also Mahfouz, Naguib (Abdel Aziz Al-Sabilgi)
See also DLBY 88

Mahon, Derek 1941- .... **CLC 27**
See also CA 113; 128; DLB 40

Mailer, Norman 1923-...**CLC 1, 2, 3, 4, 5, 8, 11, 14, 28, 39, 74, 111; DA; DAB; DAC; DAM MST, NOV, POP**
See also AITN 2; CA 9-12R; CABS 1; CANR 28, 74; CDALB 1968-1988; DLB 2, 16, 28, 185; DLBD 3; DLBY 80, 83; MTCW 1

Maillet, Antonine 1929- . **CLC 54; DAC**
See also CA 115; 120; CANR 46, 74; DLB 60; INT 120

Mais, Roger 1905-1955 .... **TCLC 8**
See also BW 1; CA 105; 124; DLB 125; MTCW 1

Maistre, Joseph de 1753-1821 .... **NCLC 37**

Maitland, Frederic 1850-1906 .... **TCLC 65**

Maitland, Sara (Louise) 1950- .... **CLC 49**
See also CA 69-72; CANR 13, 59

Major, Clarence 1936-...**CLC 3, 19, 48; BLC 2; DAM MULT**
See also BW 2; CA 21-24R; CAAS 6; CANR 13, 25, 53; DLB 33

Major, Kevin (Gerald) 1949- .... **CLC 26; DAC**
See also AAYA 16; CA 97-100; CANR 21, 38; CLR 11; DLB 60; INT CANR-21; JRDA; MAICYA; SATA 32, 82

Maki, James
See Ozu, Yasujiro

Malabaila, Damiano
See Levi, Primo

Malamud, Bernard 1914-1986...**CLC 1, 2, 3, 5, 8, 9, 11, 18, 27, 44, 78, 85; DA; DAB; DAC; DAM MST, NOV, POP; SSC 15; WLC**
See also AAYA 16; CA 5-8R; 118; CABS 1; CANR 28, 62; CDALB 1941-1968; DLB 2, 28, 152; DLBY 80, 86; MTCW 1

Malan, Herman
See Bosman, Herman Charles; Bosman, Herman Charles

Malaparte, Curzio 1898-1957...**TCLC 52**

Malcolm, Dan
See Silverberg, Robert

Malcolm X .... **CLC 82, 117; BLC 2; WLCS**
See also Little, Malcolm

Malherbe, Francois de 1555-1628 .... **LC 5**

Mallarme, Stephane 1842-1898... **NCLC 4, 41; DAM POET; PC 4**

Mallet-Joris, Francoise 1930- .... **CLC 11**
See also CA 65-68; CANR 17; DLB 83

Malley, Ern
See McAuley, James Phillip

Mallowan, Agatha Christie
See Christie, Agatha (Mary Clarissa)

Maloff, Saul 1922- .... **CLC 5**
See also CA 33-36R

Malone, Louis
See MacNeice, (Frederick) Louis

Malone, Michael (Christopher) 1942- **CLC 43**
See also CA 77-80; CANR 14, 32, 57

Malory, (Sir) Thomas 1410(?)-1471(?) **LC 11; DA; DAB; DAC; DAM MST; WLCS**
See also CDBLB Before 1660; DLB 146; SATA 59; SATA-Brief 33

Malouf, (George Joseph) David 1934- **CLC 28, 86**
See also CA 124; CANR 50

Malraux, (Georges-)Andre 1901-1976 **CLC 1, 4, 9, 13, 15, 57; DAM NOV**
See also CA 21-22; 69-72; CANR 34, 58; CAP 2; DLB 72; MTCW 1

Malzberg, Barry N(athaniel) 1939-.... **CLC 7**
See also CA 61-64; CAAS 4; CANR 16; DLB 8

Mamet, David (Alan) 1947-**CLC 9, 15, 34, 46, 91; DAM DRAM; DC 4**
See also AAYA 3; CA 81-84; CABS 3; CANR 15, 41, 67, 72; DLB 7; MTCW 1

Mamoulian, Rouben (Zachary) 1897-1987 **CLC 16**
See also CA 25-28R; 124

Mandelstam, Osip (Emilievich) 1891(?)-1938(?) .... **TCLC 2, 6; PC 14**
See also CA 104; 150

Mander, (Mary) Jane 1877-1949 **TCLC 31**
See also CA 162

Mandeville, John fl. 1350- .... **CMLC 19**
See also DLB 146

Mandiargues, Andre Pieyre de .... **CLC 41**
See also Pieyre de Mandiargues, Andre
See also DLB 83

Mandrake, Ethel Belle
See Thurman, Wallace (Henry)

Mangan, James Clarence 1803-1849 **NCLC 27**

Maniere, J.-E.
See Giraudoux, (Hippolyte) Jean

Mankiewicz, Herman (Jacob) 1897-1953 **TCLC 85**
See also CA 120; 169; DLB 26

Manley, (Mary) Delariviere 1672(?)-1724 **LC 1, 42**
See also DLB 39, 80

Mann, Abel
See Creasey, John

Mann, Emily 1952- .... **DC 7**
See also CA 130; CANR 55

Mann, (Luiz) Heinrich 1871-1950 **TCLC 9**
See also CA 106; 164; DLB 66

Mann, (Paul) Thomas 1875-1955...**TCLC 2, 8, 14, 21, 35, 44, 60; DA; DAB; DAC; DAM MST, NOV; SSC 5; WLC**
See also CA 104; 128; DLB 66; MTCW 1

Mannheim, Karl 1893-1947 ..... **TCLC 65**

Manning, David
See Faust, Frederick (Schiller)

Manning, Frederic 1887(?)-1935 ... **TCLC 25**
See also CA 124

Manning, Olivia 1915-1980 .... **CLC 5, 19**
See also CA 5-8R; 101; CANR 29; MTCW 1

Mano, D. Keith 1942- .... **CLC 2, 10**
See also CA 25-28R; CAAS 6; CANR 26, 57; DLB 6

Mansfield, Katherine .... **TCLC 2, 8, 39; DAB; SSC 9, 23; WLC**
See also Beauchamp, Kathleen Mansfield
See also DLB 162

Manso, Peter 1940- .... **CLC 39**
See also CA 29-32R; CANR 44

Mantecon, Juan Jimenez
See Jimenez (Mantecon), Juan Ramon

Manton, Peter
See Creasey, John

Man Without a Spleen, A
See Chekhov, Anton (Pavlovich)

Manzoni, Alessandro 1785-1873 **NCLC 29**

Mapu, Abraham (ben Jekutiel) 1808-1867 **NCLC 18**

Mara, Sally
See Queneau, Raymond

Marat, Jean Paul 1743-1793 .... **LC 10**

Marcel, Gabriel Honore 1889-1973 **CLC 15**
See also CA 102; 45-48; MTCW 1

Marchbanks, Samuel
See Davies, (William) Robertson

Marchi, Giacomo
See Bassani, Giorgio

Maupassant, (Henri Rene Albert) Guy de 1850-1893 .... NCLC 1, 42; DA; DAB; DAC; DAM MST; SSC 1; WLC
See also DLB 123

Maupin, Armistead 1944- ...... CLC 95; DAM POP
See also CA 125; 130; CANR 58; INT 130

Maurhut, Richard
See Traven, B.

Mauriac, Claude 1914-1996 .... CLC 9
See also CA 89-92; 152; DLB 83

Mauriac, Francois (Charles) 1885-1970 CLC 4, 9, 56; SSC 24
See also CA 25-28; CAP 2; DLB 65; MTCW 1

Mavor, Osborne Henry 1888-1951
See Bridie, James
See also CA 104

Maxwell, William (Keepers, Jr.) 1908- CLC 19
See also CA 93-96; CANR 54; DLBY 80; INT 93-96

May, Elaine 1932- .... CLC 16
See also CA 124; 142; DLB 44

Mayakovski, Vladimir (Vladimirovich) 1893-1930 .... TCLC 4, 18
See also CA 104; 158

Mayhew, Henry 1812-1887 .... NCLC 31
See also DLB 18, 55, 190

Mayle, Peter 1939(?)- .... CLC 89
See also CA 139; CANR 64

Maynard, Joyce 1953- .... CLC 23
See also CA 111; 129; CANR 64

Mayne, William (James Carter) 1928- CLC 12
See also AAYA 20; CA 9-12R; CANR 37; CLR 25; JRDA; MAICYA; SAAS 11; SATA 6, 68

Mayo, Jim
See L'Amour, Louis (Dearborn)

Maysles, Albert 1926- .... CLC 16
See also CA 29-32R

Maysles, David 1932- .... CLC 16

Mazer, Norma Fox 1931- .... CLC 26
See also AAYA 5; CA 69-72; CANR 12, 32, 66; CLR 23; JRDA; MAICYA; SAAS 1; SATA 24, 67

Mazzini, Guiseppe 1805-1872 ... NCLC 34

McAuley, James Phillip 1917-1976 CLC 45
See also CA 97-100

McBain, Ed
See Hunter, Evan

McBrien, William Augustine 1930- . CLC 44
See also CA 107

McCaffrey, Anne (Inez) 1926- ... CLC 17; DAM NOV, POP
See also AAYA 6; AITN 2; BEST 89:2; CA 25-28R; CANR 15, 35, 55; CLR 49; DLB 8; JRDA; MAICYA; MTCW 1; SAAS 11; SATA 8, 70

McCall, Nathan 1955(?)- .... CLC 86
See also CA 146

McCann, Arthur
See Campbell, John W(ood, Jr.)

McCann, Edson
See Pohl, Frederik

McCarthy, Charles, Jr. 1933-
See McCarthy, Cormac
See also CANR 42, 69; DAM POP

McCarthy, Cormac 1933- ... CLC 4, 57, 59, 101
See also McCarthy, Charles, Jr.
See also DLB 6, 143

McCarthy, Mary (Therese) 1912-1989 CLC 1, 3, 5, 14, 24, 39, 59; SSC 24
See also CA 5-8R; 129; CANR 16, 50, 64; DLB 2; DLBY 81; INT CANR-16; MTCW 1

McCartney, (James) Paul 1942- ... CLC 12, 35
See also CA 146

McCauley, Stephen (D.) 1955- .... CLC 50
See also CA 141

McClure, Michael (Thomas) 1932- ... CLC 6, 10
See also CA 21-24R; CANR 17, 46; DLB 16

McCorkle, Jill (Collins) 1958- .... CLC 51
See also CA 121; DLBY 87

McCourt, Frank 1930- .... CLC 109
See also CA 157

McCourt, James 1941- .... CLC 5
See also CA 57-60

McCoy, Horace (Stanley) 1897-1955 TCLC 28
See also CA 108; 155; DLB 9

McCrae, John 1872-1918 .... TCLC 12
See also CA 109; DLB 92

McCreigh, James
See Pohl, Frederik

McCullers, (Lula) Carson (Smith) 1917-1967 . CLC 1, 4, 10, 12, 48, 100; DA; DAB; DAC; DAM MST, NOV; SSC 9, 24; WLC
See also AAYA 21; CA 5-8R; 25-28R; CABS 1, 3; CANR 18; CDALB 1941-1968; DLB 2, 7, 173; MTCW 1; SATA 27

McCulloch, John Tyler
See Burroughs, Edgar Rice

McCullough, Colleen 1938(?)- ... CLC 27, 107; DAM NOV, POP
See also CA 81-84; CANR 17, 46, 67; MTCW 1

McDermott, Alice 1953- .... CLC 90
See also CA 109; CANR 40

McElroy, Joseph 1930- .... CLC 5, 47
See also CA 17-20R

McEwan, Ian (Russell) 1948- ... CLC 13, 66; DAM NOV
See also BEST 90:4; CA 61-64; CANR 14, 41, 69; DLB 14, 194; MTCW 1

McFadden, David 1940- .... CLC 48
See also CA 104; DLB 60; INT 104

McFarland, Dennis 1950- .... CLC 65
See also CA 165

McGahern, John 1934- ... CLC 5, 9, 48; SSC 17
See also CA 17-20R; CANR 29, 68; DLB 14; MTCW 1

McGinley, Patrick (Anthony) 1937- ... CLC 41
See also CA 120; 127; CANR 56; INT 127

McGinley, Phyllis 1905-1978 .... CLC 14
See also CA 9-12R; 77-80; CANR 19; DLB 11, 48; SATA 2, 44; SATA-Obit 24

McGinniss, Joe 1942- .... CLC 32
See also AITN 2; BEST 89:2; CA 25-28R; CANR 26, 70; DLB 185; INT CANR-26

McGivern, Maureen Daly
See Daly, Maureen

McGrath, Patrick 1950- .... CLC 55
See also CA 136; CANR 65

McGrath, Thomas (Matthew) 1916-1990 CLC 28, 59; DAM POET
See also CA 9-12R; 132; CANR 6, 33; MTCW 1; SATA 41; SATA-Obit 66

McGuane, Thomas (Francis III) 1939- CLC 3, 7, 18, 45
See also AITN 2; CA 49-52; CANR 5, 24, 49; DLB 2; DLBY 80; INT CANR-24; MTCW 1

McGuckian, Medbh 1950- ...... CLC 48; DAM POET
See also CA 143; DLB 40

McHale, Tom 1942(?)-1982 .... CLC 3, 5
See also AITN 1; CA 77-80; 106

McIlvanney, William 1936- .... CLC 42
See also CA 25-28R; CANR 61; DLB 14

McIlwraith, Maureen Mollie Hunter
See Hunter, Mollie
See also SATA 2

McInerney, Jay 1955- ..... CLC 34, 112; DAM POP
See also AAYA 18; CA 116; 123; CANR 45, 68; INT 123

McIntyre, Vonda N(eel) 1948- ... CLC 18
See also CA 81-84; CANR 17, 34, 69; MTCW 1

McKay, Claude .... TCLC 7, 41; BLC 3; DAB; PC 2
See also McKay, Festus Claudius
See also DLB 4, 45, 51, 117

McKay, Festus Claudius 1889-1948
See McKay, Claude
See also BW 1; CA 104; 124; CANR 73; DA; DAC; DAM MST, MULT, NOV, POET; MTCW 1; WLC

McKuen, Rod 1933- .... CLC 1, 3
See also AITN 1; CA 41-44R; CANR 40

McLoughlin, R. B.
See Mencken, H(enry) L(ouis)

McLuhan, (Herbert) Marshall 1911-1980 CLC 37, 83
See also CA 9-12R; 102; CANR 12, 34, 61; DLB 88; INT CANR-12; MTCW 1

McMillan, Terry (L.) 1951- ... CLC 50, 61, 112; BLCS; DAM MULT, NOV, POP
See also AAYA 21; BW 2; CA 140; CANR 60

McMurtry, Larry (Jeff) 1936- ... CLC 2, 3, 7, 11, 27, 44; DAM NOV, POP
See also AAYA 15; AITN 2; BEST 89:2; CA 5-8R; CANR 19, 43, 64; CDALB 1968-1988; DLB 2, 143; DLBY 80, 87; MTCW 1

McNally, T. M. 1961- .... CLC 82

McNally, Terrence 1939- ... CLC 4, 7, 41, 91; DAM DRAM
See also CA 45-48; CANR 2, 56; DLB 7

McNamer, Deirdre 1950- .... CLC 70

McNeile, Herman Cyril 1888-1937
See Sapper
See also DLB 77

McNickle, (William) D'Arcy 1904-1977 CLC 89; DAM MULT
See also CA 9-12R; 85-88; CANR 5, 45; DLB 175; NNAL; SATA-Obit 22

McPhee, John (Angus) 1931- .... CLC 36
See also BEST 90:1; CA 65-68; CANR 20, 46, 64, 69; DLB 185; MTCW 1

McPherson, James Alan 1943- .. CLC 19, 77; BLCS
See also BW 1; CA 25-28R; CAAS 17; CANR 24, 74; DLB 38; MTCW 1

McPherson, William (Alexander) 1933- CLC 34
See also CA 69-72; CANR 28; INT CANR-28

Mead, George Herbert 1873-1958 ... TCLC 89

Morgenstern, Christian 1871-1914
  TCLC 8
  See also CA 105
Morgenstern, S.
  See Goldman, William (W.)
Moricz, Zsigmond 1879-1942 .. **TCLC 33**
  See also CA 165
Morike, Eduard (Friedrich) 1804-1875
  NCLC 10
  See also DLB 133
Moritz, Karl Philipp 1756-1793 ...... **LC 2**
  See also DLB 94
Morland, Peter Henry
  See Faust, Frederick (Schiller)
Morley, Christopher (Darlington) 1890-
  1957 .... **TCLC 87**
  See also CA 112; DLB 9
Morren, Theophil
  See Hofmannsthal, Hugo von
Morris, Bill 1952- .... **CLC 76**
Morris, Julian
  See West, Morris L(anglo)
Morris, Steveland Judkins 1950(?)-
  See Wonder, Stevie
  See also CA 111
Morris, William 1834-1896 .... **NCLC 4**
  See also CDBLB 1832-1890; DLB 18, 35, 57,
  156, 178, 184
Morris, Wright 1910-1998...**CLC 1, 3, 7,**
  18, 37
  See also CA 9-12R; 167; CANR 21; DLB 2;
  DLBY 81; MTCW 1
Morrison, Arthur 1863-1945 .... **TCLC 72**
  See also CA 120; 157; DLB 70, 135, 197
Morrison, Chloe Anthony Wofford
  See Morrison, Toni
Morrison, James Douglas 1943-1971
  See Morrison, Jim
  See also CA 73-76; CANR 40
Morrison, Jim .... **CLC 17**
  See also Morrison, James Douglas
Morrison, Toni 1931-...**CLC 4, 10, 22, 55,**
  81, 87; BLC 3; DA; DAB; DAC; DAM
  MST, MULT, NOV, POP
  See also AAYA 1, 22; BW 2; CA 29-32R;
  CANR 27, 42, 67; CDALB 1968-1988;
  DLB 6, 33, 143; DLBY 81; MTCW 1;
  SATA 57
Morrison, Van 1945- .... **CLC 21**
  See also CA 116; 168
Morrissy, Mary 1958-.................... **CLC 99**
Mortimer, John (Clifford) 1923-**CLC 28,**
  43; DAM DRAM, POP
  See also CA 13-16R; CANR 21, 69; CDBLB
  1960 to Present; DLB 13; INT CANR-21;
  MTCW 1
Mortimer, Penelope (Ruth) 1918- .... **CLC 5**
  See also CA 57-60; CANR 45
Morton, Anthony
  See Creasey, John
Mosca, Gaetano 1858-1941 .... **TCLC 75**
Mosher, Howard Frank 1943- .... **CLC 62**
  See also CA 139; CANR 65
Mosley, Nicholas 1923- .... **CLC 43, 70**
  See also CA 69-72; CANR 41, 60; DLB 14
Mosley, Walter 1952-...**CLC 97; BLCS;**
  DAM MULT, POP
  See also AAYA 17; BW 2; CA 142; CANR 57
Moss, Howard 1922-1987...**CLC 7, 14, 45,**
  50; DAM POET
  See also CA 1-4R; 123; CANR 1, 44; DLB 5
Mossgiel, Rab
  See Burns, Robert

Motion, Andrew (Peter) 1952-... **CLC 47**
  See also CA 146; DLB 40
Motley, Willard (Francis) 1909-1965
  CLC 18
  See also BW 1; CA 117; 106; DLB 76, 143
Motoori, Norinaga 1730-1801...**NCLC 45**
Mott, Michael (Charles Alston) 1930-
  CLC 15, 34
  See also CA 5-8R; CAAS 7; CANR 7, 29
Mountain Wolf Woman 1884-1960
  CLC 92
  See also CA 144; NNAL
Moure, Erin 1955- .... **CLC 88**
  See also CA 113; DLB 60
Mowat, Farley (McGill) 1921- . **CLC 26;**
  DAC; DAM MST
  See also AAYA 1; CA 1-4R; CANR 4, 24, 42,
  68; CLR 20; DLB 68; INT CANR-24; JRDA;
  MAICYA; MTCW 1; SATA 3, 55
Mowatt, Anna Cora 1819-1870...**NCLC 74**
Moyers, Bill 1934- .... **CLC 74**
  See also AITN 2; CA 61-64; CANR 31, 52
Mphahlele, Es'kia
  See Mphahlele, Ezekiel
  See also DLB 125
Mphahlele, Ezekiel 1919-1983...**CLC 25;**
  BLC 3; DAM MULT
  See also Mphahlele, Es'kia
  See also BW 2; CA 81-84; CANR 26
Mqhayi, S(amuel) E(dward) K(rune Loliwe)
  1875-1945 .... **TCLC 25; BLC 3; DAM**
  MULT
  See also CA 153
Mrozek, Slawomir 1930- .... **CLC 3, 13**
  See also CA 13-16R; CAAS 10; CANR 29;
  MTCW 1
Mrs. Belloc-Lowndes
  See Lowndes, Marie Adelaide (Belloc)
Mtwa, Percy (?)- .... **CLC 47**
Mueller, Lisel 1924-............. **CLC 13, 51**
  See also CA 93-96; DLB 105
Muir, Edwin 1887-1959 .... **TCLC 2, 87**
  See also CA 104; DLB 20, 100, 191
Muir, John 1838-1914 .... **TCLC 28**
  See also CA 165; DLB 186
Mujica Lainez, Manuel 1910-1984...**CLC**
  31
  See also Lainez, Manuel Mujica
  See also CA 81-84; 112; CANR 32; HW
Mukherjee, Bharati 1940-...**CLC 53, 115;**
  DAM NOV
  See also BEST 89:2; CA 107; CANR 45, 72;
  DLB 60; MTCW 1
Muldoon, Paul 1951-...**CLC 32, 72; DAM**
  POET
  See also CA 113; 129; CANR 52; DLB 40;
  INT 129
Mulisch, Harry 1927-......................**CLC 42**
  See also CA 9-12R; CANR 6, 26, 56
Mull, Martin 1943- .... **CLC 17**
  See also CA 105
Muller, Wilhelm .... **NCLC 73**
Mulock, Dinah Maria
  See Craik, Dinah Maria (Mulock)
Munford, Robert 1737(?)-1783 .... **LC 5**
  See also DLB 31
Mungo, Raymond 1946- .... **CLC 72**
  See also CA 49-52; CANR 2
Munro, Alice 1931-.... **CLC 6, 10, 19, 50, 95;**
  DAC; DAM MST, NOV; SSC 3; WLCS
  See also AITN 2; CA 33-36R; CANR 33, 53,
  75; DLB 53; MTCW 1; SATA 29

Munro, H(ector) H(ugh) 1870-1916
  See Saki
  See also CA 104; 130; CDBLB 1890-1914;
  DA; DAB; DAC; DAM MST, NOV; DLB
  34, 162; MTCW 1; WLC
Murdoch, (Jean) Iris 1919-...**CLC 1, 2, 3,**
  4, 6, 8, 11, 15, 22, 31, 51; DAB; DAC;
  DAM MST, NOV
  See also CA 13-16R; CANR 8, 43, 68; CDBLB
  1960 to Present; DLB 14, 194; INT CANR-
  8; MTCW 1
Murfree, Mary Noailles 1850-1922
  SSC 22
  See also CA 122; DLB 12, 74
Murnau, Friedrich Wilhelm
  See Plumpe, Friedrich Wilhelm
Murphy, Richard 1927- .... **CLC 41**
  See also CA 29-32R; DLB 40
Murphy, Sylvia 1937-.................. **CLC 34**
  See also CA 121
Murphy, Thomas (Bernard) 1935- .. **CLC 51**
  See also CA 101
Murray, Albert L. 1916- .... **CLC 73**
  See also BW 2; CA 49-52; CANR 26, 52;
  DLB 38
Murray, Judith Sargent 1751-1820
  NCLC 63
  See also DLB 37, 200
Murray, Les(lie) A(llan) 1938-...**CLC 40;**
  DAM POET
  See also CA 21-24R; CANR 11, 27, 56
Murry, J. Middleton
  See Murry, John Middleton
Murry, John Middleton 1889-1957
  TCLC 16
  See also CA 118; DLB 149
Musgrave, Susan 1951- .... **CLC 13, 54**
  See also CA 69-72; CANR 45
Musil, Robert (Edler von) 1880-1942
  TCLC 12, 68; SSC 18
  See also CA 109; CANR 55; DLB 81, 124
Muske, Carol 1945- .... **CLC 90**
  See also Muske-Dukes, Carol (Anne)
Muske-Dukes, Carol (Anne) 1945-
  See Muske, Carol
  See also CA 65-68; CANR 32, 70
Musset, (Louis Charles) Alfred de 1810-
  1857 .... **NCLC 7**
  See also DLB 192
My Brother's Brother
  See Chekhov, Anton (Pavlovich)
Myers, L(eopold) H(amilton) 1881-1944
  TCLC 59
  See also CA 157; DLB 15
Myers, Walter Dean 1937-**CLC 35; BLC**
  3; DAM MULT, NOV
  See also AAYA 4, 23; BW 2; CA 33-36R;
  CANR 20, 42, 67; CLR 4, 16, 35; DLB 33;
  INT CANR-20; JRDA; MAICYA; SAAS 2;
  SATA 41, 71; SATA-Brief 27
Myers, Walter M.
  See Myers, Walter Dean
Myles, Symon
  See Follett, Ken(neth Martin)
Nabokov, Vladimir (Vladimirovich) 1899-
  1977...**CLC 1, 2, 3, 6, 8, 11, 15, 23, 44,**
  46, 64; DA; DAB; DAC; DAM MST,
  NOV; SSC 11; WLC
  See also CA 5-8R; 69-72; CANR 20; CDALB
  1941-1968; DLB 2; DLBD 3; DLBY 80, 91;
  MTCW 1

Nagai Kafu 1879-1959 .... **TCLC 51**
See also Nagai Sokichi
See also DLB 180
Nagai Sokichi 1879-1959
See Nagai Kafu
See also CA 117
Nagy, Laszlo 1925-1978 ....**CLC 7**
See also CA 129; 112
Naidu, Sarojini 1879-1943 .... **TCLC 80**
Naipaul, Shiva(dhar Srinivasa) 1945-1985
CLC 32, 39; DAM NOV
See also CA 110; 112; 116; CANR 33; DLB
157; DLBY 85; MTCW 1
Naipaul, V(idiadhar) S(urajprasad) 1932-
**CLC 4, 7, 9, 13, 18, 37, 105; DAB; DAC;
DAM MST, NOV**
See also CA 1-4R; CANR 1, 33, 51; CDBLB
1960 to Present; DLB 125; DLBY 85;
MTCW 1
Nakos, Lilika 1899(?)- .... **CLC 29**
Narayan, R(asipuram) K(rishnaswami)
1906-...**CLC 7, 28, 47; DAM NOV; SSC
25**
See also CA 81-84; CANR 33, 61; MTCW 1;
SATA 62
Nash, (Frediric) Ogden 1902-1971...**C L C
23; DAM POET; PC 21**
See also CA 13-14; 29-32R; CANR 34, 61; CAP
1; DLB 11; MAICYA; MTCW 1; SATA 2, 46
Nashe, Thomas 1567-1601(?) ....**LC 41**
See also DLB 167
Nashe, Thomas 1567-1601 ....**LC 41**
Nathan, Daniel
See Dannay, Frederic
Nathan, George Jean 1882-1958 .... **TCLC 18**
See also Hatteras, Owen
See also CA 114; 169; DLB 137
Natsume, Kinnosuke 1867-1916
See Natsume, Soseki
See also CA 104
Natsume, Soseki 1867-1916 .... **TCLC 2, 10**
See also Natsume, Kinnosuke
See also DLB 180
Natti, (Mary) Lee 1919-
See Kingman, Lee
See also CA 5-8R; CANR 2
Naylor, Gloria 1950-...**CLC 28, 52; BLC
3; DA; DAC; DAM MST, MULT, NOV,
POP; WLCS**
See also AAYA 6; BW 2; CA 107; CANR 27,
51, 74; DLB 173; MTCW 1
Neihardt, John Gneisenau 1881-1973
CLC 32
See also CA 13-14; CANR 65; CAP 1; DLB
9, 54
Nekrasov, Nikolai Alekseevich 1821-1878
NCLC 11
Nelligan, Emile 1879-1941 .... **TCLC 14**
See also CA 114; DLB 92
Nelson, Willie 1933- .... **CLC 17**
See also CA 107
Nemerov, Howard (Stanley) 1920-1991
CLC 2, 6, 9, 36; DAM POET; PC 24
See also CA 1-4R; 134; CABS 2; CANR 1,
27, 53; DLB 5, 6; DLBY 83; INT CANR-
27; MTCW 1
Neruda, Pablo 1904-1973...**CLC 1, 2, 5, 7,
9, 28, 62; DA; DAB; DAC; DAM MST,
MULT, POET; HLC; PC 4; WLC**
See also CA 19-20; 45-48; CAP 2; HW;
MTCW 1
Nerval, Gerard de 1808-1855...**NCLC 1,
67; PC 13; SSC 18**

Nervo, (Jose) Amado (Ruiz de) 1870-1919
TCLC 11
See also CA 109; 131; HW
Nessi, Pio Baroja y
See Baroja (y Nessi), Pio
Nestroy, Johann 1801-1862 ..... **NCLC 42**
See also DLB 133
Netterville, Luke
See O'Grady, Standish (James)
Neufeld, John (Arthur) 1938- .... **CLC 17**
See also AAYA 11; CA 25-28R; CANR 11, 37,
56; CLR 52; MAICYA; SAAS 3; SATA 6,
81
Neville, Emily Cheney 1919 ..... **CLC 12**
See also CA 5-8R; CANR 3, 37; JRDA;
MAICYA; SAAS 2; SATA 1
Newbound, Bernard Slade 1930-
See Slade, Bernard
See also CA 81-84; CANR 49; DAM DRAM
Newby, P(ercy) H(oward) 1918-1997
CLC 2, 13; DAM NOV
See also CA 5-8R; 161; CANR 32, 67; DLB
15; MTCW 1
Newlove, Donald 1928- ....**CLC 6**
See also CA 29-32R; CANR 25
Newlove, John (Herbert) 1938-..........**CLC 14**
See also CA 21-24R; CANR 9, 25
Newman, Charles 1938- .... **CLC 2, 8**
See also CA 21-24R
Newman, Edwin (Harold) 1919- ....**CLC 14**
See also AITN 1; CA 69-72; CANR 5
Newman, John Henry 1801-1890
NCLC 38
See also DLB 18, 32, 55
Newton, (Sir)Isaac 1642-1727 .... **LC 35**
Newton, Suzanne 1936-..................**CLC 35**
See also CA 41-44R; CANR 14; JRDA; SATA
5, 77
Nexo, Martin Andersen 1869-1954...**TCLC
43**
Nezval, Vitezslav 1900-1958 .... **TCLC 44**
See also CA 123
Ng, Fae Myenne 1957(?)- ....**CLC 81**
See also CA 146
Ngema, Mbongeni 1955- ....**CLC 57**
See also BW 2; CA 143
Ngugi, James T(hiong'o) ..... **CLC 3, 7, 13**
See also Ngugi wa Thiong'o
Ngugi wa Thiong'o 1938-...**CLC 36; BLC
3; DAM MULT, NOV**
See also Ngugi, James T(hiong'o)
See also BW 2; CA 81-84; CANR 27, 58; DLB
125; MTCW 1
Nichol, B(arrie) P(hillip) 1944-1988
CLC 18
See also CA 53-56; DLB 53; SATA 66
Nichols, John (Treadwell) 1940-...**CLC 38**
See also CA 9-12R; CAAS 2; CANR 6, 70;
DLBY 82
Nichols, Leigh
See Koontz, Dean R(ay)
Nichols, Peter (Richard) 1927-...**CLC 5,
36, 65**
See also CA 104; CANR 33; DLB 13; MTCW
1
Nicolas, F. R. E.
See Freeling, Nicolas
Niedecker, Lorine 1903-1970...**CLC 10, 42;
DAM POET**
See also CA 25-28; CAP 2; DLB 48
Nietzsche, Friedrich (Wilhelm) 1844-1900
TCLC 10, 18, 55
See also CA 107; 121; DLB 129

Nievo, Ippolito 1831-1861 .... **NCLC 22**
Nightingale, Anne Redmon 1943-
See Redmon, Anne
See also CA 103
Nightingale, Florence 1820-1910
TCLC 85
See also DLB 166
Nik. T. O.
See Annensky, Innokenty (Fyodorovich)
Nin, Anais 1903-1977...**CLC 1, 4, 8, 11, 14,
60; DAM NOV, POP; SSC 10**
See also AITN 2; CA 13-16R; 69-72; CANR
22, 53; DLB 2, 4, 152; MTCW 1
Nishida, Kitaro 1870-1945 .... **TCLC 83**
See also CA 107
Nishiwaki, Junzaburo 1894-1982 .... **PC 15**
See also CA 107
Nissenson, Hugh 1933- .... **CLC 4, 9**
See also CA 17-20R; CANR 27; DLB 28
Niven, Larry ....**CLC 8**
See also Niven, Laurence Van Cott
See also AAYA 27; DLB 8
Niven, Laurence Van Cott 1938-
See Niven, Larry
See also CA 21-24R; CAAS 12; CANR 14,
44, 66; DAM POP; MTCW 1; SATA 95
Nixon, Agnes Eckhardt 1927- ....**CLC 21**
See also CA 110
Nizan, Paul 1905-1940 ....**TCLC 40**
See also CA 161; DLB 72
Nkosi, Lewis 1936-...**CLC 45; BLC 3; DAM
MULT**
See also BW 1; CA 65-68; CANR 27; DLB 157
Nodier, (Jean) Charles (Emmanuel) 1780-
1844 .... **NCLC 19**
See also DLB 119
Noguchi, Yone 1875-1947 .... **TCLC 80**
Nolan, Christopher 1965- .... **CLC 58**
See also CA 111
Noon, Jeff 1957-..................................**CLC 91**
See also CA 148
Norden, Charles
See Durrell, Lawrence (George)
Nordhoff, Charles (Bernard) 1887-1947
TCLC 23
See also CA 108; DLB 9; SATA 23
Norfolk, Lawrence 1963- ....**CLC 76**
See also CA 144
Norman, Marsha 1947- ...**CLC 28; DAM
DRAM; DC 8**
See also CA 105; CABS 3; CANR 41; DLBY
84
Normyx
See Douglas, (George) Norman
Norris, Frank 1870-1902 ....**SSC 28**
See also Norris, (Benjamin) Frank(lin, Jr.)
See also CDALB 1865-1917; DLB 12, 71, 186
Norris, (Benjamin) Frank(lin, Jr.) 1870-
1902 .... **TCLC 24**
See also Norris, Frank
See also CA 110; 160
Norris, Leslie 1921-...........................**CLC 14**
See also CA 11-12; CANR 14; CAP 1; DLB
27
North, Andrew
See Norton, Andre
North, Anthony
See Koontz, Dean R(ay)
North, Captain George
See Stevenson, Robert Louis (Balfour)
North, Milou
See Erdrich, Louise
Northrup, B. A.
See Hubbard, L(afayette) Ron(ald)

North Staffs
    See Hulme, T(homas) E(rnest)
Norton, Alice Mary
    See Norton, Andre
    See also MAICYA; SATA 1, 43
Norton, Andre 1912- .... **CLC 12**
    See also Norton, Alice Mary
    See also AAYA 14; CA 1-4R; CANR 68; CLR
    50; DLB 8, 52; JRDA; MTCW 1; SATA
    91
Norton, Caroline 1808-1877 ... **NCLC 47**
    See also DLB 21, 159, 199
Norway, Nevil Shute 1899-1960
    See Shute, Nevil
    See also CA 102; 93-96
Norwid, Cyprian Kamil 1821-1883
    NCLC 17
Nosille, Nabrah
    See Ellison, Harlan (Jay)
Nossack, Hans Erich 1901-1978 .. **CLC 6**
    See also CA 93-96; 85-88; DLB 69
Nostradamus 1503-1566 .... **LC 27**
Nosu, Chuji
    See Ozu, Yasujiro
Notenburg, Eleanora (Genrikhovna) von
    See Guro, Elena
Nova, Craig 1945- .... **CLC 7, 31**
    See also CA 45-48; CANR 2, 53
Novak, Joseph
    See Kosinski, Jerzy (Nikodem)
Novalis 1772-1801 .... **NCLC 13**
    See also DLB 90
Novis, Emile
    See Weil, Simone (Adolphine)
Nowlan, Alden (Albert) 1933-1983
    CLC 15; DAC; DAM MST
    See also CA 9-12R; CANR 5; DLB 53
Noyes, Alfred 1880-1958 .... **TCLC 7**
    See also CA 104; DLB 20
Nunn, Kem .... **CLC 34**
    See also CA 159
Nye, Robert 1939- ... **CLC 13, 42; DAM NOV**
    See also CA 33-36R; CANR 29, 67; DLB 14;
    SATA 6
Nyro, Laura 1947- .... **CLC 17**
Oates, Joyce Carol 1938-...**CLC 1, 2, 3, 6,
    9, 11, 15, 19, 33, 52, 108; DA; DAB;
    DAC; DAM MST, NOV, POP; SSC 6;
    WLC**
    See also AAYA 15; AITN 1; BEST 89:2; CA 5-
    8R; CANR 25, 45, 74; CDALB 1968-1988;
    DLB 2, 5, 130; DLBY 81; INT CANR-25;
    MTCW 1
O'Brien, Darcy 1939-1998 .... **CLC 11**
    See also CA 21-24R; 167; CANR 8, 59
O'Brien, E. G.
    See Clarke, Arthur C(harles)
O'Brien, Edna 1936-...**CLC 3, 5, 8, 13, 36,
    65, 116; DAM NOV; SSC 10**
    See also CA 1-4R; CANR 6, 41, 65; CDBLB
    1960 to Present; DLB 14; MTCW 1
O'Brien, Fitz-James 1828-1862 ..... **NCLC 21**
    See also DLB 74
O'Brien, Flann .... **CLC 1, 4, 5, 7, 10, 47**
    See also O Nuallain, Brian
O'Brien, Richard 1942- .... **CLC 17**
    See also CA 124
O'Brien, (William) Tim(othy) 1946-...**CLC
    7, 19, 40, 103; DAM POP**
    See also AAYA 16; CA 85-88; CANR 40, 58;
    DLB 152; DLBD 9; DLBY 80
Obstfelder, Sigbjoern 1866-1900**TCLC 23**
    See also CA 123

O'Casey, Sean 1880-1964...**CLC 1, 5, 9,
    11, 15, 88; DAB; DAC; DAM DRAM,
    MST; WLCS**
    See also CA 89-92; CANR 62; CDBLB 1914-
    1945; DLB 10; MTCW 1
O'Cathasaigh, Sean
    See O'Casey, Sean
Ochs, Phil 1940-1976 ....**CLC 17**
    See also CA 65-68
O'Connor, Edwin (Greene) 1918-1968
    CLC 14
    See also CA 93-96; 25-28R
O'Connor, (Mary) Flannery 1925-1964
    **CLC 1, 2, 3, 6, 10, 13, 15, 21, 66, 104;
    DA; DAB; DAC; DAM MST, NOV; SSC
    1, 23; WLC**
    See also AAYA 7; CA 1-4R; CANR 3, 41;
    CDALB 1941-1968; DLB 2, 152; DLBD 12;
    DLBY 80; MTCW 1
O'Connor, Frank .... **CLC 23; SSC 5**
    See also O'Donovan, Michael John
    See also DLB 162
O'Dell, Scott 1898-1989 .... **CLC 30**
    See also AAYA 3; CA 61-64; 129; CANR 12,
    30; CLR 1, 16; DLB 52; JRDA; MAICYA;
    SATA 12, 60
Odets, Clifford 1906-1963...**CLC 2, 28, 98;
    DAM DRAM; DC 6**
    See also CA 85-88; CANR 62; DLB 7, 26;
    MTCW 1
O'Doherty, Brian 1934- ....**CLC 76**
    See also CA 105
O'Donnell, K. M.
    See Malzberg, Barry N(athaniel)
O'Donnell, Lawrence
    See Kuttner, Henry
O'Donovan, Michael John 1903-1966
    CLC 14
    See also O'Connor, Frank
    See also CA 93-96
Oe, Kenzaburo 1935-.... **CLC 10, 36, 86;
    DAM NOV; SSC 20**
    See also CA 97-100; CANR 36, 50, 74; DLB
    182; DLBY 94; MTCW 1
O'Faolain, Julia 1932- .... **CLC 6, 19, 47, 108**
    See also CA 81-84; CAAS 2; CANR 12, 61;
    DLB 14; MTCW 1
O'Faolain, Sean 1900-1991...**CLC 1, 7, 14,
    32, 70; SSC 13**
    See also CA 61-64; 134; CANR 12, 66; DLB
    15, 162; MTCW 1
O'Flaherty, Liam 1896-1984...**CLC 5, 34;
    SSC 6**
    See also CA 101; 113; CANR 35; DLB 36,
    162; DLBY 84; MTCW 1
Ogilvy, Gavin
    See Barrie, J(ames) M(atthew)
O'Grady, Standish (James) 1846-1928
    TCLC 5
    See also CA 104; 157
O'Grady, Timothy 1951- .... **CLC 59**
    See also CA 138
O'Hara, Frank 1926-1966...**CLC 2, 5, 13,
    78; DAM POET**
    See also CA 9-12R; 25-28R; CANR 33; DLB
    5, 16, 193; MTCW 1
O'Hara, John (Henry) 1905-1970...**CLC
    1, 2, 3, 6, 11, 42; DAM NOV; SSC 15**
    See also CA 5-8R; 25-28R; CANR 31, 60;
    CDALB 1929-1941; DLB 9, 86; DLBD 2;
    MTCW 1
O Hehir, Diana 1922- ....**CLC 41**
    See also CA 93-96

Okigbo, Christopher (Ifenayichukwu)
    1932-1967...**CLC 25, 84; BLC 3; DAM
    MULT, POET; PC 7**
    See also BW 1; CA 77-80; CANR 74; DLB 125;
    MTCW 1
Okri, Ben 1959- .... **CLC 87**
    See also BW 2; CA 130; 138; CANR 65; DLB
    157; INT 138
Olds, Sharon 1942-...**CLC 32, 39, 85; DAM
    POET; PC 22**
    See also CA 101; CANR 18, 41, 66; DLB 120
Oldstyle, Jonathan
    See Irving, Washington
Olesha, Yuri (Karlovich) 1899-1960**C L C
    8**
    See also CA 85-88
Oliphant, Laurence 1829(?)-1888
    NCLC 47
    See also DLB 18, 166
Oliphant, Margaret (Oliphant Wilson) 1828-
    1897 .... **NCLC 11, 61; SSC 25**
    See also DLB 18, 159, 190
Oliver, Mary 1935- .... **CLC 19, 34, 98**
    See also CA 21-24R; CANR 9, 43; DLB 5, 193
Olivier, Laurence (Kerr) 1907-1989
    CLC 20
    See also CA 111; 150; 129
Olsen, Tillie 1912-...**CLC 4, 13, 114; DA;
    DAB; DAC; DAM MST; SSC 11**
    See also CA 1-4R; CANR 1, 43, 74; DLB 28;
    DLBY 80; MTCW 1
Olson, Charles (John) 1910-1970**CLC 1,
    2, 5, 6, 9, 11, 29; DAM POET; PC 19**
    See also CA 13-16; 25-28R; CABS 2; CANR
    35, 61; CAP 1; DLB 5, 16, 193; MTCW 1
Olson, Toby 1937- .... **CLC 28**
    See also CA 65-68; CANR 9, 31
Olyesha, Yuri
    See Olesha, Yuri (Karlovich)
Ondaatje, (Philip) Michael 1943-..**C L C
    14, 29, 51, 76; DAB; DAC; DAM MST**
    See also CA 77-80; CANR 42, 74; DLB 60
Oneal, Elizabeth 1934-
    See Oneal, Zibby
    See also CA 106; CANR 28; MAICYA; SATA
    30, 82
Oneal, Zibby .... **CLC 30**
    See also Oneal, Elizabeth
    See also AAYA 5; CLR 13; JRDA
O'Neill, Eugene (Gladstone) 1888-1953
    **TCLC 1, 6, 27, 49; DA; DAB; DAC;
    DAM DRAM, MST; WLC**
    See also AITN 1; CA 110; 132; CDALB
    1929-1941; DLB 7; MTCW 1
Onetti, Juan Carlos 1909-1994 ... **CLC 7, 10;
    DAM MULT, NOV; SSC 23**
    See also CA 85-88; 145; CANR 32, 63; DLB
    113; HW; MTCW 1
O Nuallain, Brian 1911-1966
    See O'Brien, Flann
    See also CA 21-22; 25-28R; CAP 2
Ophuls, Max 1902-1957 .... **TCLC 79**
    See also CA 113
Opie, Amelia 1769-1853 .... **NCLC 65**
    See also DLB 116, 159
Oppen, George 1908-1984 ...... **CLC 7, 13, 34**
    See also CA 13-16R; 113; CANR 8; DLB 5,
    165
Oppenheim, E(dward) Phillips 1866-1946
    TCLC 45
    See also CA 111; DLB 70
Opuls, Max
    See Ophuls, Max

Origen c. 185-c. 254 .... **CMLC 19**
Orlovitz, Gil 1918-1973 .... **CLC 22**
See also CA 77-80; 45-48; DLB 2, 5
Orris
See Ingelow, Jean
Ortega y Gasset, Jose 1883-1955
TCLC 9; DAM MULT; HLC
See also CA 106; 130; HW; MTCW 1
Ortese, Anna Maria 1914- .... **CLC 89**
See also DLB 177
Ortiz, Simon J(oseph) 1941-... **CLC 45;**
DAM MULT, POET; PC 17
See also CA 134; CANR 69; DLB 120, 175;
NNAL
Orton, Joe .... **CLC 4, 13, 43; DC 3**
See also Orton, John Kingsley
See also CDBLB 1960 to Present; DLB 13
Orton, John Kingsley 1933-1967
See Orton, Joe
See also CA 85-88; CANR 35, 66; DAM
DRAM; MTCW 1
Orwell, George ...**TCLC 2, 6, 15, 31, 51;**
DAB; WLC
See also Blair, Eric (Arthur)
See also CDBLB 1945-1960; DLB 15, 98, 195
Osborne, David
See Silverberg, Robert
Osborne, George
See Silverberg, Robert
Osborne, John (James) 1929-1994
CLC 1, 2, 5, 11, 45; DA; DAB; DAC;
DAM DRAM, MST; WLC
See also CA 13-16R; 147; CANR 21, 56;
CDBLB 1945-1960; DLB 13; MTCW 1
Osborne, Lawrence 1958- .... **CLC 50**
Oshima, Nagisa 1932- .... **CLC 20**
See also CA 116; 121
Oskison, John Milton 1874-1947
TCLC 35; DAM MULT
See also CA 144; DLB 175; NNAL
Ossian c. 3rd cent. - .... **CMLC 28**
See also Macpherson, James
Ossoli, Sarah Margaret (Fuller marchesa
d') 1810-1850
See Fuller, Margaret
See also SATA 25
Ostrovsky, Alexander 1823-1886
NCLC 30, 57
Otero, Blas de 1916-1979 .... **CLC 11**
See also CA 89-92; DLB 134
Otto, Rudolf 1869-1937 .... **TCLC 85**
Otto, Whitney 1955- .... **CLC 70**
See also CA 140
Ouida .... **TCLC 43**
See also De La Ramee, (Marie) Louise
See also DLB 18, 156
Ousmane, Sembene 1923- .... **CLC 66; BLC 3**
See also BW 1; CA 117; 125; MTCW 1
Ovid 43B.C.-18(?)...**CMLC 7; DAM POET;**
PC 2
Owen, Hugh
See Faust, Frederick (Schiller)
Owen, Wilfred (Edward Salter) 1893-1918
TCLC 5, 27; DA; DAB; DAC; DAM MST,
POET; PC 19; WLC
See also CA 104; 141; CDBLB 1914-1945;
DLB 20
Owens, Rochelle 1936- .... **CLC 8**
See also CA 17-20R; CAAS 2; CANR 39
Oz, Amos 1939-...**CLC 5, 8, 11, 27, 33, 54;**
DAM NOV
See also CA 53-56; CANR 27, 47, 65; MTCW
1

Ozick, Cynthia 1928-...**CLC 3, 7, 28, 62;**
DAM NOV, POP; SSC 15
See also BEST 90:1; CA 17-20R; CANR 23,
58; DLB 28, 152; DLBY 82; INT CANR-
23; MTCW 1
Ozu, Yasujiro 1903-1963 .... **CLC 16**
See also CA 112
Pacheco, C.
See Pessoa, Fernando (Antonio Nogueira)
Pa Chin .... **CLC 18**
See also Li Fei-kan
Pack, Robert 1929- .... **CLC 13**
See also CA 1-4R; CANR 3, 44; DLB 5
Padgett, Lewis
See Kuttner, Henry
Padilla (Lorenzo), Heberto 1932-
CLC 38
See also AITN 1; CA 123; 131; HW
Page, Jimmy 1944- .... **CLC 12**
Page, Louise 1955- .... **CLC 40**
See also CA 140
Page, P(atricia) K(athleen) 1916-...**CLC**
7, 18; DAC; DAM MST; PC 12
See also CA 53-56; CANR 4, 22, 65; DLB 68;
MTCW 1
Page, Thomas Nelson 1853-1922 .... **SSC 23**
See also CA 118; DLB 12, 78; DLBD 13
Pagels, Elaine Hiesey 1943- .... **CLC 104**
See also CA 45-48; CANR 2, 24, 51
Paget, Violet 1856-1935
See Lee, Vernon
See also CA 104; 166
Paget-Lowe, Henry
See Lovecraft, H(oward) P(hillips)
Paglia, Camille (Anna) 1947-... **CLC 68**
See also CA 140; CANR 72
Paige, Richard
See Koontz, Dean R(ay)
Paine, Thomas 1737-1809 .... **NCLC 62**
See also CDALB 1640-1865; DLB 31, 43,
73, 158
Pakenham, Antonia
See Fraser, (Lady) Antonia (Pakenham)
Palamas, Kostes 1859-1943 .... **TCLC 5**
See also CA 105
Palazzeschi, Aldo 1885-1974 .... **CLC 11**
See also CA 89-92; 53-56; DLB 114
Paley, Grace 1922-... **CLC 4, 6, 37; DAM**
POP; SSC 8
See also CA 25-28R; CANR 13, 46, 74; DLB
28; INT CANR-13; MTCW 1
Palin, Michael (Edward) 1943- .... **CLC 21**
See also Monty Python
See also CA 107; CANR 35; SATA 67
Palliser, Charles 1947- .... **CLC 65**
See also CA 136
Palma, Ricardo 1833-1919 .... **TCLC 29**
See also CA 168
Pancake, Breece Dexter 1952-1979
See Pancake, Breece D'J
See also CA 123; 109
Pancake, Breece D'J .... **CLC 29**
See also Pancake, Breece Dexter
See also DLB 130
Panko, Rudy
See Gogol, Nikolai (Vasilyevich)
Papadiamantis, Alexandros 1851-1911
TCLC 29
See also CA 168
Papadiamantopoulos, Johannes 1856-1910
See Moreas, Jean
See also CA 117

Papini, Giovanni 1881-1956 .... **TCLC 22**
See also CA 121
Paracelsus 1493-1541 .... **LC 14**
See also DLB 179
Parasol, Peter
See Stevens, Wallace
Pardo Bazan, Emilia 1851-1921...**SSC 30**
Pareto, Vilfredo 1848-1923 ...... **TCLC 69**
Parfenie, Maria
See Codrescu, Andrei
Parini, Jay (Lee) 1948- .... **CLC 54**
See also CA 97-100; CAAS 16; CANR 32
Park, Jordan
See Kornbluth, C(yril) M.; Pohl, Frederik
Park, Robert E(zra) 1864-1944 ...... **TCLC 73**
See also CA 122; 165
Parker, Bert
See Ellison, Harlan (Jay)
Parker, Dorothy (Rothschild) 1893-1967
CLC 15, 68; DAM POET; SSC 2
See also CA 19-20; 25-28R; CAP 2; DLB 11,
45, 86; MTCW 1
Parker, Robert B(rown) 1932-...**CLC 27;**
DAM NOV, POP
See also BEST 89:4; CA 49-52; CANR 1, 26,
52; INT CANR-26; MTCW 1
Parkin, Frank 1940- .... **CLC 43**
See also CA 147
Parkman, Francis, Jr. 1823-1893 ... **NCLC 12**
See also DLB 1, 30, 186
Parks, Gordon (Alexander Buchanan)
1912-...**CLC 1, 16; BLC 3; DAM MULT**
See also AITN 2; BW 2; CA 41-44R; CANR
26, 66; DLB 33; SATA 8
Parmenides c. 515B.C.-c. 450B.C....**CMLC**
22
See also DLB 176
Parnell, Thomas 1679-1718 .... **LC 3**
See also DLB 94
Parra, Nicanor 1914-...**CLC 2, 102; DAM**
MULT; HLC
See also CA 85-88; CANR 32; HW; MTCW 1
Parrish, Mary Frances
See Fisher, M(ary) F(rances) K(ennedy)
Parson
See Coleridge, Samuel Taylor
Parson Lot
See Kingsley, Charles
Partridge, Anthony
See Oppenheim, E(dward) Phillips
Pascal, Blaise 1623-1662 .... **LC 35**
Pascoli, Giovanni 1855-1912 .... **TCLC 45**
See also CA 170
Pasolini, Pier Paolo 1922-1975 . **CLC 20, 37,**
106; PC 17
See also CA 93-96; 61-64; CANR 63; DLB 128,
177; MTCW 1
Pasquini
See Silone, Ignazio
Pastan, Linda (Olenik) 1932- . **CLC 27;**
DAM POET
See also CA 61-64; CANR 18, 40, 61; DLB 5
Pasternak, Boris (Leonidovich) 1890-1960
CLC 7, 10, 18, 63; DA; DAB; DAC; DAM
MST, NOV, POET; PC 6; SSC 31; WLC
See also CA 127; 116; MTCW 1
Patchen, Kenneth 1911-1972...**CLC 1, 2,**
18; DAM POET
See also CA 1-4R; 33-36R; CANR 3, 35; DLB
16, 48; MTCW 1
Pater, Walter (Horatio) 1839-1894
NCLC 7
See also CDBLB 1832-1890; DLB 57, 156

Paterson, A(ndrew) B(arton) 1864-1941
TCLC 32
See also CA 155; SATA 97
Paterson, Katherine (Womeldorf) 1932-
CLC 12, 30
See also AAYA 1; CA 21-24R; CANR 28, 59;
CLR 7, 50; DLB 52; JRDA; MAICYA;
MTCW 1; SATA 13, 53, 92
Patmore, Coventry Kersey Dighton 1823-
1896 .... **NCLC 9**
See also DLB 35, 98
Paton, Alan (Stewart) 1903-1988...**CLC 4,
10, 25, 55, 106; DA; DAB; DAC; DAM
MST, NOV; WLC**
See also AAYA 26; CA 13-16; 125; CANR 22;
CAP 1; DLBD 17; MTCW 1; SATA 11;
SATA-Obit 56
Paton Walsh, Gillian 1937-
See Walsh, Jill Paton
See also CANR 38; JRDA; MAICYA; SAAS 3;
SATA 4, 72
Patton, George S. 1885-1945 .... **TCLC 79**
Paulding, James Kirke 1778-1860 ... **NCLC 2**
See also DLB 3, 59, 74
Paulin, Thomas Neilson 1949-
See Paulin, Tom
See also CA 123; 128
Paulin, Tom .... **CLC 37**
See also Paulin, Thomas Neilson
See also DLB 40
Paustovsky, Konstantin (Georgievich)
1892-1968 .... **CLC 40**
See also CA 93-96; 25-28R
Pavese, Cesare 1908-1950 ... **TCLC 3; PC 13;
SSC 19**
See also CA 104; 169; DLB 128, 177
Pavic, Milorad 1929- .... **CLC 60**
See also CA 136; DLB 181
Payne, Alan
See Jakes, John (William)
Paz, Gil
See Lugones, Leopoldo
Paz, Octavio 1914-1998...**CLC 3, 4, 6, 10,
19, 51, 65; DA; DAB; DAC; DAM MST,
MULT, POET; HLC; PC 1; WLC**
See also CA 73-76; 165; CANR 32, 65; DLBY
90; HW; MTCW 1
p'Bitek, Okot 1931-1982 .... **CLC 96; BLC 3;
DAM MULT**
See also BW 2; CA 124; 107; DLB 125; MTCW
1
Peacock, Molly 1947- .... **CLC 60**
See also CA 103; CAAS 21; CANR 52; DLB
120
Peacock, Thomas Love 1785-1866...**NCLC
22**
See also DLB 96, 116
Peake, Mervyn 1911-1968 .... **CLC 7, 54**
See also CA 5-8R; 25-28R; CANR 3; DLB 15,
160; MTCW 1; SATA 23
Pearce, Philippa .... **CLC 21**
See also Christie, (Ann) Philippa
See also CLR 9; DLB 161; MAICYA; SATA 1,
67
Pearl, Eric
See Elman, Richard (Martin)
Pearson, T(homas) R(eid) 1956- ...... **CLC 39**
See also CA 120; 130; INT 130
Peck, Dale 1967-........................... **CLC 81**
See also CA 146; CANR 72
Peck, John 1941- .... **CLC 3**
See also CA 49-52; CANR 3

Peck, Richard (Wayne) 1934-.... **CLC 21**
See also AAYA 1, 24; CA 85-88; CANR 19,
38; CLR 15; INT CANR-19; JRDA;
MAICYA; SAAS 2; SATA 18, 55, 97
Peck, Robert Newton 1928-...**CLC 17; DA;
DAC; DAM MST**
See also AAYA 3; CA 81-84; CANR 31, 63;
CLR 45; JRDA; MAICYA; SAAS 1; SATA
21, 62
Peckinpah, (David) Sam(uel) 1925-1984
CLC 20
See also CA 109; 114
Pedersen, Knut 1859-1952
See Hamsun, Knut
See also CA 104; 119; CANR 63; MTCW 1
Peeslake, Gaffer
See Durrell, Lawrence (George)
Peguy, Charles Pierre 1873-1914...**TCLC
10**
See also CA 107
Peirce, Charles Sanders 1839-1914
TCLC 81
Pena, Ramon del Valle y
See Valle-Inclan, Ramon (Maria) del
Pendennis, Arthur Esquir
See Thackeray, William Makepeace
Penn, William 1644-1718 .... **LC 25**
See also DLB 24
PEPECE
See Prado (Calvo), Pedro
Pepys, Samuel 1633-1703...**LC 11; DA;
DAB; DAC; DAM MST; WLC**
See also CDBLB 1660-1789; DLB 101
Percy, Walker 1916-1990...**CLC 2, 3, 6, 8,
14, 18, 47, 65; DAM NOV, POP**
See also CA 1-4R; 131; CANR 1, 23, 64; DLB
2; DLBY 80, 90; MTCW 1
Percy, William Alexander 1885-1942
TCLC 84
See also CA 163
Perec, Georges 1936-1982 .... **CLC 56, 116**
See also CA 141; DLB 83
Pereda (y Sanchez de Porrua), Jose Maria
de 1833-1906 .... **TCLC 16**
See also CA 117
Pereda y Porrua, Jose Maria de
See Pereda (y Sanchez de Porrua), Jose Maria
de
Peregoy, George Weems
See Mencken, H(enry) L(ouis)
Perelman, S(idney) J(oseph) 1904-1979
**CLC 3, 5, 9, 15, 23, 44, 49; DAM
DRAM; SSC 32**
See also AITN 1, 2; CA 73-76; 89-92; CANR
18; DLB 11, 44; MTCW 1
Peret, Benjamin 1899-1959 .... **TCLC 20**
See also CA 117
Peretz, Isaac Loeb 1851(?)-1915 .. **TCLC 16;
SSC 26**
See also CA 109
Peretz, Yitzkhok Leibush
See Peretz, Isaac Loeb
Perez Galdos, Benito 1843-1920 .... **TCLC 27**
See also CA 125; 153; HW
Perrault, Charles 1628-1703 .... **LC 2**
See also MAICYA; SATA 25
Perry, Brighton
See Sherwood, Robert E(mmet)
Perse, St.-John
See Leger, (Marie-Rene Auguste) Alexis Saint-
Leger
Perutz, Leo 1882-1957 .... **TCLC 60**
See also DLB 81

Peseenz, Tulio F.
See Lopez y Fuentes, Gregorio
Pesetsky, Bette 1932- .... **CLC 28**
See also CA 133; DLB 130
Peshkov, Alexei Maximovich 1868-1936
See Gorky, Maxim
See also CA 105; 141; DA; DAC; DAM
DRAM, MST, NOV
Pessoa, Fernando (Antonio Nogueira) 1898-
1935 .... **TCLC 27; HLC; PC 20**
See also CA 125
Peterkin, Julia Mood 1880-1961..**CLC 31**
See also CA 102; DLB 9
Peters, Joan K(aren) 1945-.............. **CLC 39**
See also CA 158
Peters, Robert L(ouis) 1924- ....**CLC 7**
See also CA 13-16R; CAAS 8; DLB 105
Petofi, Sandor 1823-1849 .... **NCLC 21**
Petrakis, Harry Mark 1923- ....**CLC 3**
See also CA 9-12R; CANR 4, 30
Petrarch 1304-1374 ...... **CMLC 20; DAM
POET; PC 8**
Petrov, Evgeny .... **TCLC 21**
See also Kataev, Evgeny Petrovich
Petry, Ann (Lane) 1908-1997 ... **CLC 1, 7, 18**
See also BW 1; CA 5-8R; 157; CAAS 6; CANR
4, 46; CLR 12; DLB 76; JRDA; MAICYA;
MTCW 1; SATA 5; SATA-Obit 94
Petursson, Halligrimur 1614-1674 .... **LC 8**
Peychinovich
See Vazov, Ivan (Minchov)
Phaedrus 18(?)B.C.-55(?) .... **CMLC 25**
Philips, Katherine 1632-1664 .... **LC 30**
See also DLB 131
Philipson, Morris H. 1926- .... **CLC 53**
See also CA 1-4R; CANR 4
Phillips, Caryl 1958-...**CLC 96; BLCS;
DAM MULT**
See also BW 2; CA 141; CANR 63; DLB 157
Phillips, David Graham 1867-1911
TCLC 44
See also CA 108; DLB 9, 12
Phillips, Jack
See Sandburg, Carl (August)
Phillips, Jayne Anne 1952-...**CLC 15, 33;
SSC 16**
See also CA 101; CANR 24, 50; DLBY 80; INT
CANR-24; MTCW 1
Phillips, Richard
See Dick, Philip K(indred)
Phillips, Robert (Schaeffer) 1938- ... **CLC 28**
See also CA 17-20R; CAAS 13; CANR 8; DLB
105
Phillips, Ward
See Lovecraft, H(oward) P(hillips)
Piccolo, Lucio 1901-1969 .... **CLC 13**
See also CA 97-100; DLB 114
Pickthall, Marjorie L(owry) C(hristie)
1883-1922 .... **TCLC 21**
See also CA 107; DLB 92
Pico della Mirandola, Giovanni 1463-1494
LC 15
Piercy, Marge 1936-...**CLC 3, 6, 14, 18, 27,
62**
See also CA 21-24R; CAAS 1; CANR 13, 43,
66; DLB 120; MTCW 1
Piers, Robert
See Anthony, Piers
Pieyre de Mandiargues, Andre 1909-1991
See Mandiargues, Andre Pieyre de
See also CA 103; 136; CANR 22
Pilnyak, Boris .... **TCLC 23**
See also Vogau, Boris Andreyevich

Radnoti, Miklos 1909-1944 ...... **TCLC 16**
See also CA 118
Rado, James 1939- .... **CLC 17**
See also CA 105
Radvanyi, Netty 1900-1983
See Seghers, Anna
See also CA 85-88; 110
Rae, Ben
See Griffiths, Trevor
Raeburn, John (Hay) 1941- .... **CLC 34**
See also CA 57-60
Ragni, Gerome 1942-1991 .... **CLC 17**
See also CA 105; 134
Rahv, Philip 1908-1973 .... **CLC 24**
See also Greenberg, Ivan
See also DLB 137
Raimund, Ferdinand Jakob 1790-1836
NCLC 69
See also DLB 90
Raine, Craig 1944- .... **CLC 32, 103**
See also CA 108; CANR 29, 51; DLB 40
Raine, Kathleen (Jessie) 1908-...**CLC 7, 45**
See also CA 85-88; CANR 46; DLB 20;
MTCW 1
Rainis, Janis 1865-1929 .... **TCLC 29**
See also CA 170
Rakosi, Carl 1903- .... **CLC 47**
See also Rawley, Callman
See also CAAS 5; DLB 193
Raleigh, Richard
See Lovecraft, H(oward) P(hillips)
Raleigh, Sir Walter 1554(?)-1618...**LC 31, 39**
See also CDBLB Before 1660; DLB 172
Rallentando, H. P.
See Sayers, Dorothy L(eigh)
Ramal, Walter
See de la Mare, Walter (John)
Ramana Maharshi 1879-1950...**TCLC 84**
Ramon, Juan
See Jimenez (Mantecon), Juan Ramon
Ramos, Graciliano 1892-1953 .... **TCLC 32**
See also CA 167
Rampersad, Arnold 1941-........... **CLC 44**
See also BW 2; CA 127; 133; DLB 111; INT
133
Rampling, Anne
See Rice, Anne
Ramsay, Allan 1684(?)-1758 .... **LC 29**
See also DLB 95
Ramuz, Charles-Ferdinand 1878-1947
TCLC 33
See also CA 165
Rand, Ayn 1905-1982...**CLC 3, 30, 44, 79;
DA; DAC; DAM MST, NOV, POP;
WLC**
See also AAYA 10; CA 13-16R; 105; CANR
27, 73; MTCW 1
Randall, Dudley (Felker) 1914-...**CLC 1;
BLC 3; DAM MULT**
See also BW 1; CA 25-28R; CANR 23; DLB
41
Randall, Robert
See Silverberg, Robert
Ranger, Ken
See Creasey, John
Ransom, John Crowe 1888-1974... **C L C
2, 4, 5, 11, 24; DAM POET**
See also CA 5-8R; 49-52; CANR 6, 34; DLB
45, 63; MTCW 1
Rao, Raja 1909- ...... **CLC 25, 56; DAM NOV**
See also CA 73-76; CANR 51; MTCW 1

Raphael, Frederic (Michael) 1931-
CLC 2, 14
See also CA 1-4R; CANR 1; DLB 14
Ratcliffe, James P.
See Mencken, H(enry) L(ouis)
Rathbone, Julian 1935- .... **CLC 41**
See also CA 101; CANR 34, 73
Rattigan, Terence (Mervyn) 1911-1977
CLC 7; DAM DRAM
See also CA 85-88; 73-76; CDBLB 1945-
1960; DLB 13; MTCW 1
Ratushinskaya, Irina 1954- .... **CLC 54**
See also CA 129; CANR 68
Raven, Simon (Arthur Noel) 1927-...**CLC 14**
See also CA 81-84
Ravenna, Michael
See Welty, Eudora
Rawley, Callman 1903-
See Rakosi, Carl
See also CA 21-24R; CANR 12, 32
Rawlings, Marjorie Kinnan 1896-1953
TCLC 4
See also AAYA 20; CA 104; 137; CANR 74;
DLB 9, 22, 102; DLBD 17; JRDA; MAICYA;
SATA 100; YABC 1
Ray, Satyajit 1921-1992 ...**CLC 16, 76; DAM
MULT**
See also CA 114; 137
Read, Herbert Edward 1893-1968 ..... **CLC 4**
See also CA 85-88; 25-28R; DLB 20, 149
Read, Piers Paul 1941- .... **CLC 4, 10, 25**
See also CA 21-24R; CANR 38; DLB 14; SATA
21
Reade, Charles 1814-1884 .... **NCLC 2, 74**
See also DLB 21
Reade, Hamish
See Gray, Simon (James Holliday)
Reading, Peter 1946- .... **CLC 47**
See also CA 103; CANR 46; DLB 40
Reaney, James 1926-...**CLC 13; DAC;
DAM MST**
See also CA 41-44R; CAAS 15; CANR 42; DLB
68; SATA 43
Rebreanu, Liviu 1885-1944 ...... **TCLC 28**
See also CA 165
Rechy, John (Francisco) 1934-...**CLC 1, 7,
14, 18, 107; DAM MULT; HLC**
See also CA 5-8R; CAAS 4; CANR 6, 32, 64;
DLB 122; DLBY 82; HW; INT CANR-6
Redcam, Tom 1870-1933 .... **TCLC 25**
Reddin, Keith .... **CLC 67**
Redgrove, Peter (William) 1932-...**CLC 6,
41**
See also CA 1-4R; CANR 3, 39; DLB 40
Redmon, Anne .... **CLC 22**
See also Nightingale, Anne Redmon
See also DLBY 86
Reed, Eliot
See Ambler, Eric
Reed, Ishmael 1938-...**CLC 2, 3, 5, 6, 13,
32, 60; BLC 3; DAM MULT**
See also BW 2; CA 21-24R; CANR 25, 48, 74;
DLB 2, 5, 33, 169; DLBD 8; MTCW 1
Reed, John (Silas) 1887-1920 .... **TCLC 9**
See also CA 106
Reed, Lou .... **CLC 21**
See also Firbank, Louis
Reeve, Clara 1729-1807 .... **NCLC 19**
See also DLB 39
Reich, Wilhelm 1897-1957 .... **TCLC 57**
Reid, Christopher (John) 1949- .... **CLC 33**
See also CA 140; DLB 40

Reid, Desmond
See Moorcock, Michael (John)
Reid Banks, Lynne 1929-
See Banks, Lynne Reid
See also CA 1-4R; CANR 6, 22, 38; CLR 24;
JRDA; MAICYA; SATA 22, 75
Reilly, William K.
See Creasey, John
Reiner, Max
See Caldwell, (Janet Miriam) Taylor (Hol-
land)
Reis, Ricardo
See Pessoa, Fernando (Antonio Nogueira)
Remarque, Erich Maria 1898-1970...**CLC
21; DA; DAB; DAC; DAM MST, NOV**
See also AAYA 27; CA 77-80; 29-32R; DLB
56; MTCW 1
Remington, Frederic 1861-1909 .... **TCLC 89**
See also CA 108; 169; DLB 12, 186, 188;
SATA 41
Remizov, A.
See Remizov, Aleksei (Mikhailovich)
Remizov, A. M.
See Remizov, Aleksei (Mikhailovich)
Remizov, Aleksei (Mikhailovich) 1877-
1957 .... **TCLC 27**
See also CA 125; 133
Renan, Joseph Ernest 1823-1892
NCLC 26
Renard, Jules 1864-1910 .... **TCLC 17**
See also CA 117
Renault, Mary .... **CLC 3, 11, 17**
See also Challans, Mary
See also DLBY 83
Rendell, Ruth (Barbara) 1930-...**CLC 28,
48; DAM POP**
See also Vine, Barbara
See also CA 109; CANR 32, 52, 74; DLB 87;
INT CANR-32; MTCW 1
Renoir, Jean 1894-1979 .... **CLC 20**
See also CA 129; 85-88
Resnais, Alain 1922- .... **CLC 16**
Reverdy, Pierre 1889-1960 .... **CLC 53**
See also CA 97-100; 89-92
Rexroth, Kenneth 1905-1982...**CLC 1, 2,
6, 11, 22, 49, 112; DAM POET; PC 20**
See also CA 5-8R; 107; CANR 14, 34, 63;
CDALB 1941-1968; DLB 16, 48, 165;
DLBY 82; INT CANR-14; MTCW 1
Reyes, Alfonso 1889-1959 .... **TCLC 33**
See also CA 131; HW
Reyes y Basoalto, Ricardo Eliecer Neftali
See Neruda, Pablo
Reymont, Wladyslaw (Stanislaw) 1868(?)-1925
TCLC 5
See also CA 104
Reynolds, Jonathan 1942- .... **CLC 6, 38**
See also CA 65-68; CANR 28
Reynolds, Joshua 1723-1792 ....**LC 15**
See also DLB 104
Reynolds, Michael Shane 1937- ....**CLC 44**
See also CA 65-68; CANR 9
Reznikoff, Charles 1894-1976 .... **CLC 9**
See also CA 33-36; 61-64; CAP 2; DLB 28, 45
Rezzori (d'Arezzo), Gregor von 1914-1998
CLC 25
See also CA 122; 136; 167
Rhine, Richard
See Silverstein, Alvin
Rhodes, Eugene Manlove 1869-1934
TCLC 53

Rhodius, Apollonius c. 3rd cent. B.C.-
CMLC 28
See also DLB 176

R'hoone
See Balzac, Honore de

Rhys, Jean 1890(?)-1979...**CLC 2, 4, 6, 14, 19, 51; DAM NOV; SSC 21**
See also CA 25-28R; 85-88; CANR 35, 62; CDBLB 1945-1960; DLB 36, 117, 162; MTCW 1

Ribeiro, Darcy 1922-1997 .... **CLC 34**
See also CA 33-36R; 156

Ribeiro, Joao Ubaldo (Osorio Pimentel) 1941- .... **CLC 10, 67**
See also CA 81-84

Ribman, Ronald (Burt) 1932- .... **CLC 7**
See also CA 21-24R; CANR 46

Ricci, Nino 1959- .... **CLC 70**
See also CA 137

Rice, Anne 1941- .... **CLC 41; DAM POP**
See also AAYA 9; BEST 89:2; CA 65-68; CANR 12, 36, 53, 74

Rice, Elmer (Leopold) 1892-1967...**CLC 7, 49; DAM DRAM**
See also CA 21-22; 25-28R; CAP 2; DLB 4, 7; MTCW 1

Rice, Tim(othy Miles Bindon) 1944-
CLC 21
See also CA 103; CANR 46

Rich, Adrienne (Cecile) 1929-...**CLC 3, 6, 7, 11, 18, 36, 73, 76; DAM POET; PC 5**
See also CA 9-12R; CANR 20, 53, 74; DLB 5, 67; MTCW 1

Rich, Barbara
See Graves, Robert (von Ranke)

Rich, Robert
See Trumbo, Dalton

Richard, Keith .... **CLC 17**
See also Richards, Keith

Richards, David Adams 1950-...**CLC 59; DAC**
See also CA 93-96; CANR 60; DLB 53

Richards, I(vor) A(rmstrong) 1893-1979
CLC 14, 24
See also CA 41-44R; 89-92; CANR 34, 74; DLB 27

Richards, Keith 1943-
See Richard, Keith
See also CA 107

Richardson, Anne
See Roiphe, Anne (Richardson)

Richardson, Dorothy Miller 1873-1957
TCLC 3
See also CA 104; DLB 36

Richardson, Ethel Florence (Lindesay) 1870-1946
See Richardson, Henry Handel
See also CA 105

Richardson, Henry Handel .... **TCLC 4**
See also Richardson, Ethel Florence (Lindesay)
See also DLB 197

Richardson, John 1796-1852...**NCLC 55; DAC**
See also DLB 99

Richardson, Samuel 1689-1761 .. **LC 1, 44; DA; DAB; DAC; DAM MST, NOV; WLC**
See also CDBLB 1660-1789; DLB 39

Richler, Mordecai 1931-...**CLC 3, 5, 9, 13, 18, 46, 70; DAC; DAM MST, NOV**
See also AITN 1; CA 65-68; CANR 31, 62; CLR 17; DLB 53; MAICYA; MTCW 1; SATA 44, 98; SATA-Brief 27

Richter, Conrad (Michael) 1890-1968
CLC 30
See also AAYA 21; CA 5-8R; 25-28R; CANR 23; DLB 9; MTCW 1; SATA 3

Ricostranza, Tom
See Ellis, Trey

Riddell, Charlotte 1832-1906 .. **TCLC 40**
See also CA 165; DLB 156

Riding, Laura .... **CLC 3, 7**
See also Jackson, Laura (Riding)

Riefenstahl, Berta Helene Amalia 1902-
See Riefenstahl, Leni
See also CA 108

Riefenstahl, Leni .... **CLC 16**
See also Riefenstahl, Berta Helene Amalia

Riffe, Ernest
See Bergman, (Ernst) Ingmar

Riggs, (Rolla) Lynn 1899-1954 .... **TCLC 56; DAM MULT**
See also CA 144; DLB 175; NNAL

Riis, Jacob A(ugust) 1849-1914 ..... **TCLC 80**
See also CA 113; 168; DLB 23

Riley, James Whitcomb 1849-1916
TCLC 51; DAM POET
See also CA 118; 137; MAICYA; SATA 17

Riley, Tex
See Creasey, John

Rilke, Rainer Maria 1875-1926...**TCLC 1, 6, 19; DAM POET; PC 2**
See also CA 104; 132; CANR 62; DLB 81; MTCW 1

Rimbaud, (Jean Nicolas) Arthur 1854-1891
NCLC 4, 35; DA; DAB; DAC; DAM MST, POET; PC 3; WLC

Rinehart, Mary Roberts 1876-1958
TCLC 52
See also CA 108; 166

Ringmaster, The
See Mencken, H(enry) L(ouis)

Ringwood, Gwen(dolyn Margaret) Pharis 1910-1984 .... **CLC 48**
See also CA 148; 112; DLB 88

Rio, Michel 19(?)- .... **CLC 43**

Ritsos, Giannes
See Ritsos, Yannis

Ritsos, Yannis 1909-1990 .... **CLC 6, 13, 31**
See also CA 77-80; 133; CANR 39, 61; MTCW 1

Ritter, Erika 1948(?)- .... **CLC 52**

Rivera, Jose Eustasio 1889-1928
TCLC 35
See also CA 162; HW

Rivers, Conrad Kent 1933-1968...**CLC 1**
See also BW 1; CA 85-88; DLB 41

Rivers, Elfrida
See Bradley, Marion Zimmer

Riverside, John
See Heinlein, Robert A(nson)

Rizal, Jose 1861-1896 .... **NCLC 27**

Roa Bastos, Augusto (Antonio) 1917-
CLC 45; DAM MULT; HLC
See also CA 131; DLB 113; HW

Robbe-Grillet, Alain 1922-...**CLC 1, 2, 4, 6, 8, 10, 14, 43**
See also CA 9-12R; CANR 33, 65; DLB 83; MTCW 1

Robbins, Harold 1916-1997...**CLC 5; DAM NOV**
See also CA 73-76; 162; CANR 26, 54; MTCW 1

Robbins, Thomas Eugene 1936-
See Robbins, Tom
See also CA 81-84; CANR 29, 59; DAM NOV, POP; MTCW 1

Robbins, Tom .... **CLC 9, 32, 64**
See also Robbins, Thomas Eugene
See also BEST 90:3; DLBY 80

Robbins, Trina 1938- .... **CLC 21**
See also CA 128

Roberts, Charles G(eorge) D(ouglas) 1860-1943 .... **TCLC 8**
See also CA 105; CLR 33; DLB 92; SATA 88; SATA-Brief 29

Roberts, Elizabeth Madox 1886-1941
TCLC 68
See also CA 111; 166; DLB 9, 54, 102; SATA 33; SATA-Brief 27

Roberts, Kate 1891-1985 .... **CLC 15**
See also CA 107; 116

Roberts, Keith (John Kingston) 1935-
CLC 14
See also CA 25-28R; CANR 46

Roberts, Kenneth (Lewis) 1885-1957**TCLC 23**
See also CA 109; DLB 9

Roberts, Michele (B.) 1949- .... **CLC 48**
See also CA 115; CANR 58

Robertson, Ellis
See Ellison, Harlan (Jay); Silverberg, Robert

Robertson, Thomas William 1829-1871
NCLC 35; DAM DRAM

Robeson, Kenneth
See Dent, Lester

Robinson, Edwin Arlington 1869-1935
TCLC 5; DA; DAC; DAM MST, POET; PC 1
See also CA 104; 133; CDALB 1865-1917; DLB 54; MTCW 1

Robinson, Henry Crabb 1775-1867
NCLC 15
See also DLB 107

Robinson, Jill 1936- .... **CLC 10**
See also CA 102; INT 102

Robinson, Kim Stanley 1952-.......... **CLC 34**
See also AAYA 26; CA 126

Robinson, Lloyd
See Silverberg, Robert

Robinson, Marilynne 1944- .... **CLC 25**
See also CA 116

Robinson, Smokey .... **CLC 21**
See also Robinson, William, Jr.

Robinson, William, Jr. 1940-
See Robinson, Smokey
See also CA 116

Robison, Mary 1949- .... **CLC 42, 98**
See also CA 113; 116; DLB 130; INT 116

Rod, Edouard 1857-1910 .... **TCLC 52**

Roddenberry, Eugene Wesley 1921-1991
See Roddenberry, Gene
See also CA 110; 135; CANR 37; SATA 45; SATA-Obit 69

Roddenberry, Gene .... **CLC 17**
See also Roddenberry, Eugene Wesley
See also AAYA 5; SATA-Obit 69

Rodgers, Mary 1931- .... **CLC 12**
See also CA 49-52; CANR 8, 55; CLR 20; INT CANR-8; JRDA; MAICYA; SATA 8

Rodgers, W(illiam) R(obert) 1909-1969**CLC 7**
See also CA 85-88; DLB 20

Rodman, Eric
See Silverberg, Robert

Rodman, Howard 1920(?)-1985 .... **CLC 65**
See also CA 118

Rodman, Maia
See Wojciechowska, Maia (Teresa)
Rodriguez, Claudio 1934- .... **CLC 10**
See also DLB 134
Roelvaag, O(le) E(dvart) 1876-1931
TCLC 17
See also CA 117; 171; DLB 9
Roethke, Theodore (Huebner) 1908-1963
CLC 1, 3, 8, 11, 19, 46, 101; DAM POET; PC 15
See also CA 81-84; CABS 2; CDALB 1941-1968; DLB 5; MTCW 1
Rogers, Samuel 1763-1855 .... **NCLC 69**
See also DLB 93
Rogers, Thomas Hunton 1927-...**CLC 57**
See also CA 89-92; INT 89-92
Rogers, Will(iam Penn Adair) 1879-1935
TCLC 8, 71; DAM MULT
See also CA 105; 144; DLB 11; NNAL
Rogin, Gilbert 1929- .... **CLC 18**
See also CA 65-68; CANR 15
Rohan, Koda .... **TCLC 22**
See also Koda Shigeyuki
Rohlfs, Anna Katharine Green
See Green, Anna Katharine
Rohmer, Eric .... **CLC 16**
See also Scherer, Jean-Marie Maurice
Rohmer, Sax .... **TCLC 28**
See also Ward, Arthur Henry Sarsfield
See also DLB 70
Roiphe, Anne (Richardson) 1935-
CLC 3, 9
See also CA 89-92; CANR 45, 73; DLBY 80; INT 89-92
Rojas, Fernando de 1465-1541 .... **LC 23**
Rolfe, Frederick (William Serafino Austin Lewis Mary) 1860-1913 .... **TCLC 12**
See also CA 107; DLB 34, 156
Rolland, Romain 1866-1944 .... **TCLC 23**
See also CA 118; DLB 65
Rolle, Richard c. 1300-c. 1349...**CMLC 21**
See also DLB 146
Rolvaag, O(le) E(dvart)
See Roelvaag, O(le) E(dvart)
Romain Arnaud, Saint
See Aragon, Louis
Romains, Jules 1885-1972 .... **CLC 7**
See also CA 85-88; CANR 34; DLB 65; MTCW 1
Romero, Jose Ruben 1890-1952 ..... **TCLC 14**
See also CA 114; 131; HW
Ronsard, Pierre de 1524-1585 ..**LC 6; PC 11**
Rooke, Leon 1934- ... **CLC 25, 34; DAM POP**
See also CA 25-28R; CANR 23, 53
Roosevelt, Theodore 1858-1919 ..... **TCLC 69**
See also CA 115; 170; DLB 47, 186
Roper, William 1498-1578 .... **LC 10**
Roquelaure, A. N.
See Rice, Anne
Rosa, Joao Guimaraes 1908-1967 ... **CLC 23**
See also CA 89-92; DLB 113
Rose, Wendy 1948-...**CLC 85; DAM MULT; PC 13**
See also CA 53-56; CANR 5, 51; DLB 175; NNAL; SATA 12
Rosen, R. D.
See Rosen, Richard (Dean)
Rosen, Richard (Dean) 1949- .... **CLC 39**
See also CA 77-80; CANR 62; INT CANR-30
Rosenberg, Isaac 1890-1918 .... **TCLC 12**
See also CA 107; DLB 20

Rosenblatt, Joe .... **CLC 15**
See also Rosenblatt, Joseph
Rosenblatt, Joseph 1933-
See Rosenblatt, Joe
See also CA 89-92; INT 89-92
Rosenfeld, Samuel
See Tzara, Tristan
Rosenstock, Sami
See Tzara, Tristan
Rosenstock, Samuel
See Tzara, Tristan
Rosenthal, M(acha) L(ouis) 1917-1996
CLC 28
See also CA 1-4R; 152; CAAS 6; CANR 4, 51; DLB 5; SATA 59
Ross, Barnaby
See Dannay, Frederic
Ross, Bernard L.
See Follett, Ken(neth Martin)
Ross, J. H.
See Lawrence, T(homas) E(dward)
Ross, John Hume
See Lawrence, T(homas) E(dward)
Ross, Martin
See Martin, Violet Florence
See also DLB 135
Ross, (James) Sinclair 1908-...**CLC 13; DAC; DAM MST; SSC 24**
See also CA 73-76; DLB 88
Rossetti, Christina (Georgina) 1830-1894
NCLC 2, 50, 66; DA; DAB; DAC; DAM MST, POET; PC 7; WLC
See also DLB 35, 163; MAICYA; SATA 20
Rossetti, Dante Gabriel 1828-1882
NCLC 4; DA; DAB; DAC; DAM MST, POET; WLC
See also CDBLB 1832-1890; DLB 35
Rossner, Judith (Perelman) 1935-...**CLC 6, 9, 29**
See also AITN 2; BEST 90:3; CA 17-20R; CANR 18, 51, 73; DLB 6; INT CANR-18; MTCW 1
Rostand, Edmond (Eugene Alexis) 1868-1918
TCLC 6, 37; DA; DAB; DAC; DAM DRAM, MST; DC 10
See also CA 104; 126; DLB 192; MTCW 1
Roth, Henry 1906-1995 ..... **CLC 2, 6, 11, 104**
See also CA 11-12; 149; CANR 38, 63; CAP 1; DLB 28; MTCW 1
Roth, Philip (Milton) 1933-...**CLC 1, 2, 3, 4, 6, 9, 15, 22, 31, 47, 66, 86; DA; DAB; DAC; DAM MST, NOV, POP; SSC 26; WLC**
See also BEST 90:3; CA 1-4R; CANR 1, 22, 36, 55; CDALB 1968-1988; DLB 2, 28, 173; DLBY 82; MTCW 1
Rothenberg, Jerome 1931- .... **CLC 6, 57**
See also CA 45-48; CANR 1; DLB 5, 193
Roumain, Jacques (Jean Baptiste) 1907-1944
TCLC 19; BLC 3; DAM MULT
See also BW 1; CA 117; 125
Rourke, Constance (Mayfield) 1885-1941
TCLC 12
See also CA 107; YABC 1
Rousseau, Jean-Baptiste 1671-1741 ..... **LC 9**
Rousseau, Jean-Jacques 1712-1778
LC 14, 36; DA; DAB; DAC; DAM MST; WLC
Roussel, Raymond 1877-1933 .... **TCLC 20**
See also CA 117
Rovit, Earl (Herbert) 1927-.................**CLC 7**
See also CA 5-8R; CANR 12

Rowe, Elizabeth Singer 1674-1737
LC 44
See also DLB 39, 95
Rowe, Nicholas 1674-1718................**LC 8**
See also DLB 84
Rowley, Ames Dorrance
See Lovecraft, H(oward) P(hillips)
Rowson, Susanna Haswell 1762(?)-1824
NCLC 5, 69
See also DLB 37, 200
Roy, Arundhati 1960(?)-...........**CLC 109**
See also CA 163; DLBY 97
Roy, Gabrielle 1909-1983 ...**CLC 10, 14; DAB; DAC; DAM MST**
See also CA 53-56; 110; CANR 5, 61; DLB 68; MTCW 1
Royko, Mike 1932-1997 .... **CLC 109**
See also CA 89-92; 157; CANR 26
Rozewicz, Tadeusz 1921-...**CLC 9, 23; DAM POET**
See also CA 108; CANR 36, 66; MTCW 1
Ruark, Gibbons 1941- ....**CLC 3**
See also CA 33-36R; CAAS 23; CANR 14, 31, 57; DLB 120
Rubens, Bernice (Ruth) 1923- .... **CLC 19, 31**
See also CA 25-28R; CANR 33, 65; DLB 14; MTCW 1
Rubin, Harold
See Robbins, Harold
Rudkin, (James) David 1936- .... **CLC 14**
See also CA 89-92; DLB 13
Rudnik, Raphael 1933- ....**CLC 7**
See also CA 29-32R
Ruffian, M.
See Hasek, Jaroslav (Matej Frantisek)
Ruiz, Jose Martinez.....................**CLC 11**
See also Martinez Ruiz, Jose
Rukeyser, Muriel 1913-1980...**CLC 6, 10, 15, 27; DAM POET; PC 12**
See also CA 5-8R; 93-96; CANR 26, 60; DLB 48; MTCW 1; SATA-Obit 22
Rule, Jane (Vance) 1931- ....**CLC 27**
See also CA 25-28R; CAAS 18; CANR 12; DLB 60
Rulfo, Juan 1918-1986 .... **CLC 8, 80; DAM MULT; HLC; SSC 25**
See also CA 85-88; 118; CANR 26; DLB 113; HW; MTCW 1
Rumi, Jalal al-Din 1297-1373...**CMLC 20**
Runeberg, Johan 1804-1877 ... **NCLC 41**
Runyon, (Alfred) Damon 1884(?)-1946
TCLC 10
See also CA 107; 165; DLB 11, 86, 171
Rush, Norman 1933- ....**CLC 44**
See also CA 121; 126; INT 126
Rushdie, (Ahmed) Salman 1947-....**CLC 23, 31, 55, 100; DAB; DAC; DAM MST, NOV, POP; WLCS**
See also BEST 89:3; CA 108; 111; CANR 33, 56; DLB 194; INT 111; MTCW 1
Rushforth, Peter (Scott) 1945- .... **CLC 19**
See also CA 101
Ruskin, John 1819-1900 .... **TCLC 63**
See also CA 114; 129; CDBLB 1832-1890; DLB 55, 163, 190; SATA 24
Russ, Joanna 1937- ....**CLC 15**
See also CANR 11, 31, 65; DLB 8; MTCW 1
Russell, George William 1867-1935
See Baker, Jean H.
See also CA 104; 153; CDBLB 1890-1914; DAM POET

Russell, (Henry) Ken(neth Alfred) 1927-
CLC 16
See also CA 105
Russell, William Martin 1947-...**CLC 60**
See also CA 164
Rutherford, Mark .... **TCLC 25**
See also White, William Hale
See also DLB 18
Ruyslinck, Ward 1929- .... **CLC 14**
See also Belser, Reimond Karel Maria de
Ryan, Cornelius (John) 1920-1974 ..... **CLC 7**
See also CA 69-72; 53-56; CANR 38
Ryan, Michael 1946- .... **CLC 65**
See also CA 49-52; DLBY 82
Ryan, Tim
See Dent, Lester
Rybakov, Anatoli (Naumovich) 1911-
CLC 23, 53
See also CA 126; 135; SATA 79
Ryder, Jonathan
See Ludlum, Robert
Ryga, George 1932-1987 **CLC 14; DAC;**
DAM MST
See also CA 101; 124; CANR 43; DLB 60
S. H.
See Hartmann, Sadakichi
S. S.
See Sassoon, Siegfried (Lorraine)
Saba, Umberto 1883-1957 .... **TCLC 33**
See also CA 144; DLB 114
Sabatini, Rafael 1875-1950 ...... **TCLC 47**
See also CA 162
Sabato, Ernesto (R.) 1911-..**CLC 10, 23;**
DAM MULT; HLC
See also CA 97-100; CANR 32, 65; DLB 145;
HW; MTCW 1
Sa-Carniero, Mario de 1890-1916
TCLC 83
Sacastru, Martin
See Bioy Casares, Adolfo
Sacher-Masoch, Leopold von 1836(?)-1895
NCLC 31
Sachs, Marilyn (Stickle) 1927-.**CLC 35**
See also AAYA 2; CA 17-20R; CANR 13, 47;
CLR 2; JRDA; MAICYA; SAAS 2; SATA 3,
68
Sachs, Nelly 1891-1970 .... **CLC 14, 98**
See also CA 17-18; 25-28R; CAP 2
Sackler, Howard (Oliver) 1929-1982
CLC 14
See also CA 61-64; 108; CANR 30; DLB 7
Sacks, Oliver (Wolf) 1933- .... **CLC 67**
See also CA 53-56; CANR 28, 50; INT
CANR-28; MTCW 1
Sadakichi
See Hartmann, Sadakichi
Sade, Donatien Alphonse Francois, Comte
de 1740-1814 .... **NCLC 47**
Sadoff, Ira 1945- .... **CLC 9**
See also CA 53-56; CANR 5, 21; DLB 120
Saetone
See Camus, Albert
Safire, William 1929- .... **CLC 10**
See also CA 17-20R; CANR 31, 54
Sagan, Carl (Edward) 1934-1996
CLC 30, 112
See also AAYA 2; CA 25-28R; 155; CANR
11, 36, 74; MTCW 1; SATA 58; SATA-
Obit 94
Sagan, Francoise .... **CLC 3, 6, 9, 17, 36**
See also Quoirez, Francoise
See also DLB 83

Sahgal, Nayantara (Pandit) 1927-...**CLC 41**
See also CA 9-12R; CANR 11
Saint, H(arry) F. 1941- .... **CLC 50**
See also CA 127
St. Aubin de Teran, Lisa 1953-
See Teran, Lisa St. Aubin de
See also CA 118; 126; INT 126
Saint Birgitta of Sweden c. 1303-1373
CMLC 24
Sainte-Beuve, Charles Augustin 1804-
1869 .... **NCLC 5**
Saint-Exupery, Antoine (Jean Baptiste
Marie Roger) de 1900-1944...**TCLC**
2, 56; DAM NOV; WLC
See also CA 108; 132; CLR 10; DLB 72;
MAICYA; MTCW 1; SATA 20
St. John, David
See Hunt, E(verette) Howard, (Jr.)
Saint-John Perse
See Leger, (Marie-Rene Auguste) Alexis Saint-
Leger
Saintsbury, George (Edward Bateman)
1845-1933 .... **TCLC 31**
See also CA 160; DLB 57, 149
Sait Faik .... **TCLC 23**
See also Abasiyanik, Sait Faik
Saki .... **TCLC 3; SSC 12**
See also Munro, H(ector) H(ugh)
Sala, George Augustus .... **NCLC 46**
Salama, Hannu 1936- .... **CLC 18**
Salamanca, J(ack) R(ichard) 1922-
CLC 4, 15
See also CA 25-28R
Sale, J. Kirkpatrick
See Sale, Kirkpatrick
Sale, Kirkpatrick 1937- ....**CLC 68**
See also CA 13-16R; CANR 10
Salinas, Luis Omar 1937-...**CLC 90; DAM**
MULT; HLC
See also CA 131; DLB 82; HW
Salinas (y Serrano), Pedro 1891(?)-1951
TCLC 17
See also CA 117; DLB 134
Salinger, J(erome) D(avid) 1919-...**CLC 1,**
3, 8, 12, 55, 56; DA; DAB; DAC; DAM
MST, NOV, POP; SSC 2, 28; WLC
See also AAYA 2; CA 5-8R; CANR 39;
CDALB 1941-1968; CLR 18; DLB 2, 102,
173; MAICYA; MTCW 1; SATA 67
Salisbury, John
See Caute, (John) David
Salter, James 1925- .... **CLC 7, 52, 59**
See also CA 73-76; DLB 130
Saltus, Edgar (Everton) 1855-1921
TCLC 8
See also CA 105; DLB 202
Saltykov, Mikhail Evgrafovich 1826-1889
NCLC 16
Samarakis, Antonis 1919- .... **CLC 5**
See also CA 25-28R; CAAS 16; CANR 36
Sanchez, Florencio 1875-1910 .... **TCLC 37**
See also CA 153; HW
Sanchez, Luis Rafael 1936- .... **CLC 23**
See also CA 128; DLB 145; HW
Sanchez, Sonia 1934-...**CLC 5, 116; BLC**
3; DAM MULT; PC 9
See also BW 2; CA 33-36R; CANR 24, 49, 74;
CLR 18; DLB 41; DLBD 8; MAICYA;
MTCW 1; SATA 22
Sand, George 1804-1876...**NCLC 2, 42, 57;**
DA; DAB; DAC; DAM MST, NOV;
WLC
See also DLB 119, 192

Sandburg, Carl (August) 1878-1967
CLC 1, 4, 10, 15, 35; DA; DAB; DAC;
DAM MST, POET; PC 2; WLC
See also AAYA 24; CA 5-8R; 25-28R; CANR
35; CDALB 1865-1917; DLB 17, 54;
MAICYA; MTCW 1; SATA 8
Sandburg, Charles
See Sandburg, Carl (August)
Sandburg, Charles A.
See Sandburg, Carl (August)
Sanders, (James) Ed(ward) 1939- ... **CLC 53**
See also CA 13-16R; CAAS 21; CANR 13, 44;
DLB 16
Sanders, Lawrence 1920-1998...**CLC 41;**
DAM POP
See also BEST 89:4; CA 81-84; 165; CANR
33, 62; MTCW 1
Sanders, Noah
See Blount, Roy (Alton), Jr.
Sanders, Winston P.
See Anderson, Poul (William)
Sandoz, Mari(e Susette) 1896-1966
CLC 28
See also CA 1-4R; 25-28R; CANR 17, 64;
DLB 9; MTCW 1; SATA 5
Saner, Reg(inald Anthony) 1931- ....**CLC 9**
See also CA 65-68
Sannazaro, Jacopo 1456(?)-1530 .... **LC 8**
Sansom, William 1912-1976...**CLC 2, 6;**
DAM NOV; SSC 21
See also CA 5-8R; 65-68; CANR 42; DLB 139;
MTCW 1
Santayana, George 1863-1952 .... **TCLC 40**
See also CA 115; DLB 54, 71; DLBD 13
Santiago, Danny .... **CLC 33**
See also James, Daniel (Lewis)
See also DLB 122
Santmyer, Helen Hoover 1895-1986
CLC 33
See also CA 1-4R; 118; CANR 15, 33; DLBY
84; MTCW 1
Santoka, Taneda 1882-1940 .... **TCLC 72**
Santos, Bienvenido N(uqui) 1911-1996...**CLC**
22; DAM MULT
See also CA 101; 151; CANR 19, 46
Sapper .... **TCLC 44**
See also McNeile, Herman Cyril
Sapphire
See Sapphire, Brenda
Sapphire, Brenda 1950- .... **CLC 99**
Sappho fl. 6th cent. B.C.- ..... **CMLC 3; DAM**
POET; PC 5
See also DLB 176
Sarduy, Severo 1937-1993 .... **CLC 6, 97**
See also CA 89-92; 142; CANR 58; DLB 113;
HW
Sargeson, Frank 1903-1982 .... **CLC 31**
See also CA 25-28R; 106; CANR 38
Sarmiento, Felix Ruben Garcia
See Dario, Ruben
Saro-Wiwa, Ken(ule Beeson) 1941-1995
CLC 114
See also BW 2; CA 142; 150; CANR 60;
DLB 157
Saroyan, William 1908-1981...**CLC 1, 8,**
10, 29, 34, 56; DA; DAB; DAC; DAM
DRAM, MST, NOV; SSC 21; WLC
See also CA 5-8R; 103; CANR 30; DLB 7, 9,
86; DLBY 81; MTCW 1; SATA 23, 24
Sarraute, Nathalie 1900-...**CLC 1, 2, 4, 8,**
10, 31, 80
See also CA 9-12R; CANR 23, 66; DLB 83;
MTCW 1

Sarton, (Eleanor) May 1912-1995...**CLC 4, 14, 49, 91; DAM POET**
See also CA 1-4R; 149; CANR 1, 34, 55; DLB 48; DLBY 81; INT CANR-34; MTCW 1; SATA 36; SATA-Obit 86

Sartre, Jean-Paul 1905-1980...**CLC 1, 4, 7, 9, 13, 18, 24, 44, 50, 52; DA; DAB; DAC; DAM DRAM, MST, NOV; DC 3; SSC 32; WLC**
See also CA 9-12R; 97-100; CANR 21; DLB 72; MTCW 1

Sassoon, Siegfried (Lorraine) 1886-1967 **CLC 36; DAB; DAM MST, NOV, POET; PC 12**
See also CA 104; 25-28R; CANR 36; DLB 20, 191; DLBD 18; MTCW 1

Satterfield, Charles
See Pohl, Frederik

Saul, John (W. III) 1942-...**CLC 46; DAM NOV, POP**
See also AAYA 10; BEST 90:4; CA 81-84; CANR 16, 40; SATA 98

Saunders, Caleb
See Heinlein, Robert A(nson)

Saura (Atares), Carlos 1932- .... **CLC 20**
See also CA 114; 131; HW

Sauser-Hall, Frederic 1887-1961...**CLC 18**
See Cendrars, Blaise
See also CA 102; 93-96; CANR 36, 62; MTCW 1

Saussure, Ferdinand de 1857-1913 **TCLC 49**

Savage, Catharine
See Brosman, Catharine Savage

Savage, Thomas 1915- .... **CLC 40**
See also CA 126; 132; CAAS 15; INT 132

Savan, Glenn 19(?)-........................ **CLC 50**

Sayers, Dorothy L(eigh) 1893-1957 **TCLC 2, 15; DAM POP**
See also CA 104; 119; CANR 60; CDBLB 1914-1945; DLB 10, 36, 77, 100; MTCW 1

Sayers, Valerie 1952- .... **CLC 50**
See also CA 134; CANR 61

Sayles, John (Thomas) 1950-...**CLC 7, 10, 14**
See also CA 57-60; CANR 41; DLB 44

Scammell, Michael 1935-................. **CLC 34**
See also CA 156

Scannell, Vernon 1922- .... **CLC 49**
See also CA 5-8R; CANR 8, 24, 57; DLB 27; SATA 59

Scarlett, Susan
See Streatfeild, (Mary) Noel

Scarron
See Mikszath, Kalman

Schaeffer, Susan Fromberg 1941-...**C L C 6, 11, 22**
See also CA 49-52; CANR 18, 65; DLB 28; MTCW 1; SATA 22

Schary, Jill
See Robinson, Jill

Schell, Jonathan 1943-..................... **CLC 35**
See also CA 73-76; CANR 12

Schelling, Friedrich Wilhelm Joseph von 1775-1854 .... **NCLC 30**
See also DLB 90

Schendel, Arthur van 1874-1946 **TCLC 56**

Scherer, Jean-Marie Maurice 1920-
See Rohmer, Eric
See also CA 110

Schevill, James (Erwin) 1920- .....**CLC 7**
See also CA 5-8R; CAAS 12

Schiller, Friedrich 1759-1805...**NCLC 39, 69; DAM DRAM**
See also DLB 94

Schisgal, Murray (Joseph) 1926- .... **CLC 6**
See also CA 21-24R; CANR 48

Schlee, Ann 1934-........................**CLC 35**
See also CA 101; CANR 29; SATA 44; SATA-Brief 36

Schlegel, August Wilhelm von 1767-1845 **NCLC 15**
See also DLB 94

Schlegel, Friedrich 1772-1829 .... **NCLC 45**
See also DLB 90

Schlegel, Johann Elias (von) 1719(?)-1749 **LC 5**

Schlesinger, Arthur M(eier), Jr. 1917- **CLC 84**
See also AITN 1; CA 1-4R; CANR 1, 28, 58; DLB 17; INT CANR-28; MTCW 1; SATA 61

Schmidt, Arno (Otto) 1914-1979 ...... **CLC 56**
See also CA 128; 109; DLB 69

Schmitz, Aron Hector 1861-1928
See Svevo, Italo
See also CA 104; 122; MTCW 1

Schnackenberg, Gjertrud 1953-...**CLC 40**
See also CA 116; DLB 120

Schneider, Leonard Alfred 1925-1966
See Bruce, Lenny
See also CA 89-92

Schnitzler, Arthur 1862-1931 . **TCLC 4; SSC 15**
See also CA 104; DLB 81, 118

Schoenberg, Arnold 1874-1951 ...... **TCLC 75**
See also CA 109

Schonberg, Arnold
See Schoenberg, Arnold

Schopenhauer, Arthur 1788-1860 **NCLC 51**
See also DLB 90

Schor, Sandra (M.) 1932(?)-1990 ...... **CLC 65**
See also CA 132

Schorer, Mark 1908-1977 .... **CLC 9**
See also CA 5-8R; 73-76; CANR 7; DLB 103

Schrader, Paul (Joseph) 1946- .... **CLC 26**
See also CA 37-40R; CANR 41; DLB 44

Schreiner, Olive (Emilie Albertina) 1855-1920 **TCLC 9**
See also CA 105; 154; DLB 18, 156, 190

Schulberg, Budd (Wilson) 1914-.. **CLC 7, 48**
See also CA 25-28R; CANR 19; DLB 6, 26, 28; DLBY 81

Schulz, Bruno 1892-1942... **TCLC 5, 51; SSC 13**
See also CA 115; 123

Schulz, Charles M(onroe) 1922- ....**CLC 12**
See also CA 9-12R; CANR 6; INT CANR-6; SATA 10

Schumacher, E(rnst) F(riedrich) 1911-1977 **CLC 80**
See also CA 81-84; 73-76; CANR 34

Schuyler, James Marcus 1923-1991 **CLC 5, 23; DAM POET**
See also CA 101; 134; DLB 5, 169; INT 101

Schwartz, Delmore (David) 1913-1966 **CLC 2, 4, 10, 45, 87; PC 8**
See also CA 17-18; 25-28R; CANR 35; CAP 2; DLB 28, 48; MTCW 1

Schwartz, Ernst
See Ozu, Yasujiro

Schwartz, John Burnham 1965-...**CLC 59**
See also CA 132

Schwartz, Lynne Sharon 1939-...**CLC 31**
See also CA 103; CANR 44

Schwartz, Muriel A.
See Eliot, T(homas) S(tearns)

Schwarz-Bart, Andre 1928- .... **CLC 2, 4**
See also CA 89-92

Schwarz-Bart, Simone 1938-...**CLC 7; BLCS**
See also BW 2; CA 97-100

Schwob, Marcel (Mayer Andre) 1867-1905 **TCLC 20**
See also CA 117; 168; DLB 123

Sciascia, Leonardo 1921-1989...**CLC 8, 9, 41**
See also CA 85-88; 130; CANR 35; DLB 177; MTCW 1

Scoppettone, Sandra 1936- .... **CLC 26**
See also AAYA 11; CA 5-8R; CANR 41, 73; SATA 9, 92

Scorsese, Martin 1942- .... **CLC 20, 89**
See also CA 110; 114; CANR 46

Scotland, Jay
See Jakes, John (William)

Scott, Duncan Campbell 1862-1947 **TCLC 6; DAC**
See also CA 104; 153; DLB 92

Scott, Evelyn 1893-1963 .... **CLC 43**
See also CA 104; 112; CANR 64; DLB 9, 48

Scott, F(rancis) R(eginald) 1899-1985 **CLC 22**
See also CA 101; 114; DLB 88; INT 101

Scott, Frank
See Scott, F(rancis) R(eginald)

Scott, Joanna 1960-.......................**CLC 50**
See also CA 126; CANR 53

Scott, Paul (Mark) 1920-1978...**CLC 9, 60**
See also CA 81-84; 77-80; CANR 33; DLB 14; MTCW 1

Scott, Sarah 1723-1795 .... **LC 44**
See also DLB 39

Scott, Walter 1771-1832.. **NCLC 15, 69; DA; DAB; DAC; DAM MST, NOV, POET; PC 13; SSC 32; WLC**
See also AAYA 22; CDBLB 1789-1832; DLB 93, 107, 116, 144, 159; YABC 2

Scribe, (Augustin) Eugene 1791-1861 **NCLC 16; DAM DRAM; DC 5**
See also DLB 192

Scrum, R.
See Crumb, R(obert)

Scudery, Madeleine de 1607-1701 .. **LC 2**

Scum
See Crumb, R(obert)

Scumbag, Little Bobby
See Crumb, R(obert)

Seabrook, John
See Hubbard, L(afayette) Ron(ald)

Sealy, I. Allan 1951-..................... **CLC 55**

Search, Alexander
See Pessoa, Fernando (Antonio Nogueira)

Sebastian, Lee
See Silverberg, Robert

Sebastian Owl
See Thompson, Hunter S(tockton)

Sebestyen, Ouida 1924-.............. **CLC 30**
See also AAYA 8; CA 107; CANR 40; CLR 17; JRDA; MAICYA; SAAS 10; SATA 39

Secundus, H. Scriblerus
See Fielding, Henry

Sedges, John
See Buck, Pearl S(ydenstricker)

Shiel, M(atthew) P(hipps) 1865-1947 **TCLC 8**
See also Holmes, Gordon
See also CA 106; 160; DLB 153
Shields, Carol 1935-...**CLC 91, 113; DAC**
See also CA 81-84; CANR 51, 74
Shields, David 1956- .... **CLC 97**
See also CA 124; CANR 48
Shiga, Naoya 1883-1971... **CLC 33; SSC 23**
See also CA 101; 33-36R; DLB 180
Shikibu, Murasaki c. 978-c. 1014 ... **CMLC 1**
Shilts, Randy 1951-1994 .... **CLC 85**
See also AAYA 19; CA 115; 127; 144; CANR 45; INT 127

Shimazaki, Haruki 1872-1943
See Shimazaki Toson
See also CA 105; 134

Shimazaki Toson 1872-1943 ...... **TCLC 5**
See also Shimazaki, Haruki
See also DLB 180

Sholokhov, Mikhail (Aleksandrovich) 1905-1984 ....**CLC 7, 15**
See also CA 101; 112; MTCW 1; SATA-Obit 36
Shone, Patric
See Hanley, James
Shreve, Susan Richards 1939-.......... **CLC 23**
See also CA 49-52; CAAS 5; CANR 5, 38, 69; MAICYA; SATA 46, 95; SATA-Brief 41
Shue, Larry 1946-1985 .. **CLC 52; DAM DRAM**
See also CA 145; 117

Shu-Jen, Chou 1881-1936
See Lu Hsun
See also CA 104

Shulman, Alix Kates 1932-....**CLC 2, 10**
See also CA 29-32R; CANR 43; SATA 7
Shuster, Joe 1914-............................ **CLC 21**
Shute, Nevil .... **CLC 30**
See also Norway, Nevil Shute
Shuttle, Penelope (Diane) 1947-.......... **CLC 7**
See also CA 93-96; CANR 39; DLB 14, 40
Sidney, Mary 1561-1621 .... **LC 19, 39**
Sidney, Sir Philip 1554-1586...**LC 19, 39; DA; DAB; DAC; DAM MST, POET**
See also CDBLB Before 1660; DLB 167
Siegel, Jerome 1914-1996 .... **CLC 21**
See also CA 116; 169; 151

Siegel, Jerry
See Siegel, Jerome
Sienkiewicz, Henryk (Adam Alexander Pius) 1846-1916 .... **TCLC 3**
See also CA 104; 134
Sierra, Gregorio Martinez
See Martinez Sierra, Gregorio
Sierra, Maria (de la O'LeJarraga) Martinez
See Martinez Sierra, Maria (de la O'LeJarraga)
Sigal, Clancy 1926-............................**CLC 7**
See also CA 1-4R
Sigourney, Lydia Howard (Huntley) 1791-1865 **NCLC 21**
See also DLB 1, 42, 73
Siguenza y Gongora, Carlos de 1645-1700 **LC 8**
Sigurjonsson, Johann 1880-1919 **TCLC 27**
See also CA 170
Sikelianos, Angelos 1884-1951 .... **TCLC 39**
Silkin, Jon 1930- .... **CLC 2, 6, 43**
See also CA 5-8R; CAAS 5; DLB 27

Silko, Leslie (Marmon) 1948-...**CLC 23, 74, 114; DA; DAC; DAM MST, MULT, POP; WLCS**
See also AAYA 14; CA 115; 122; CANR 45, 65; DLB 143, 175; NNAL
Sillanpaa, Frans Eemil 1888-1964 ....**CLC 19**
See also CA 129; 93-96; MTCW 1
Sillitoe, Alan 1928-...**CLC 1, 3, 6, 10, 19, 57**
See also AITN 1; CA 9-12R; CAAS 2; CANR 8, 26, 55; CDBLB 1960 to Present; DLB 14, 139; MTCW 1; SATA 61
Silone, Ignazio 1900-1978.............**CLC 4**
See also CA 25-28; 81-84; CANR 34; CAP 2; MTCW 1
Silver, Joan Micklin 1935-.................**CLC 20**
See also CA 114; 121; INT 121
Silver, Nicholas
See Faust, Frederick (Schiller)
Silverberg, Robert 1935- ..**CLC 7; DAM POP**
See also AAYA 24; CA 1-4R; CAAS 3; CANR 1, 20, 36; DLB 8; INT CANR-20; MAICYA; MTCW 1; SATA 13, 91
Silverstein, Alvin 1933-..............**CLC 17**
See also CA 49-52; CANR 2; CLR 25; JRDA; MAICYA; SATA 8, 69
Silverstein, Virginia B(arbara Opshelor) 1937-**CLC 17**
See also CA 49-52; CANR 2; CLR 25; JRDA; MAICYA; SATA 8, 69
Sim, Georges
See Simenon, Georges (Jacques Christian)
Simak, Clifford D(onald) 1904-1988 **CLC 1, 55**
See also CA 1-4R; 125; CANR 1, 35; DLB 8; MTCW 1; SATA-Obit 56
Simenon, Georges (Jacques Christian) 1903-1989...**CLC 1, 2, 3, 8, 18, 47; DAM POP**
See also CA 85-88; 129; CANR 35; DLB 72; DLBY 89; MTCW 1
Simic, Charles 1938-...**CLC 6, 9, 22, 49, 68; DAM POET**
See also CA 29-32R; CAAS 4; CANR 12, 33, 52, 61; DLB 105
Simmel, Georg 1858-1918 .... **TCLC 64**
See also CA 157
Simmons, Charles (Paul) 1924-...**CLC 57**
See also CA 89-92; INT 89-92
Simmons, Dan 1948-.......**CLC 44; DAM POP**
See also AAYA 16; CA 138; CANR 53
Simmons, James (Stewart Alexander) 1933-**CLC 43**
See also CA 105; CAAS 21; DLB 40
Simms, William Gilmore 1806-1870 **NCLC 3**
See also DLB 3, 30, 59, 73
Simon, Carly 1945- ....**CLC 26**
See also CA 105
Simon, Claude 1913-1984 ..**CLC 4, 9, 15, 39; DAM NOV**
See also CA 89-92; CANR 33; DLB 83; MTCW 1
Simon, (Marvin) Neil 1927-...**CLC 6, 11, 31, 39, 70; DAM DRAM**
See also AITN 1; CA 21-24R; CANR 26, 54; DLB 7; MTCW 1
Simon, Paul (Frederick) 1941(?)-......**CLC 17**
See also CA 116; 153
Simonon, Paul 1956(?)- ....**CLC 30**
Simpson, Harriette
See Arnow, Harriette (Louisa) Simpson

Simpson, Louis (Aston Marantz) 1923-**CLC 4, 7, 9, 32; DAM POET**
See also CA 1-4R; CAAS 4; CANR 1, 61; DLB 5; MTCW 1
Simpson, Mona (Elizabeth) 1957-**CLC 44**
See also CA 122; 135; CANR 68
Simpson, N(orman) F(rederick) 1919-**CLC 29**
See also CA 13-16R; DLB 13
Sinclair, Andrew (Annandale) 1935-**CLC 2, 14**
See also CA 9-12R; CAAS 5; CANR 14, 38; DLB 14; MTCW 1
Sinclair, Emil
See Hesse, Hermann
Sinclair, Iain 1943- .... **CLC 76**
See also CA 132
Sinclair, Iain MacGregor
See Sinclair, Iain
Sinclair, Irene
See Griffith, D(avid Lewelyn) W(ark)
Sinclair, Mary Amelia St. Clair 1865(?)-1946
See Sinclair, May
See also CA 104
Sinclair, May 1863-1946 .... **TCLC 3, 11**
See also Sinclair, Mary Amelia St. Clair
See also CA 166; DLB 36, 135
Sinclair, Roy
See Griffith, D(avid Lewelyn) W(ark)
Sinclair, Upton (Beall) 1878-1968...**CLC 1, 11, 15, 63; DA; DAB; DAC; DAM MST, NOV; WLC**
See also CA 5-8R; 25-28R; CANR 7; CDALB 1929-1941; DLB 9; INT CANR-7; MTCW 1; SATA 9
Singer, Isaac
See Singer, Isaac Bashevis
Singer, Isaac Bashevis 1904-1991 **CLC 1, 3, 6, 9, 11, 15, 23, 38, 69, 111; DA; DAB; DAC; DAM MST, NOV; SSC 3; WLC**
See also AITN 1, 2; CA 1-4R; 134; CANR 1, 39; CDALB 1941-1968; CLR 1; DLB 6, 28, 52; DLBY 91; JRDA; MAICYA; MTCW 1; SATA 3, 27; SATA-Obit 68
Singer, Israel Joshua 1893-1944 **TCLC 33**
See also CA 169
Singh, Khushwant 1915-....................**CLC 11**
See also CA 9-12R; CAAS 9; CANR 6
Singleton, Ann
See Benedict, Ruth (Fulton)
Sinjohn, John
See Galsworthy, John
Sinyavsky, Andrei (Donatevich) 1925-1997 **CLC 8**
See also CA 85-88; 159
Sirin, V.
See Nabokov, Vladimir (Vladimirovich)
Sissman, L(ouis) E(dward) 1928-1976 **CLC 9, 18**
See also CA 21-24R; 65-68; CANR 13; DLB 5
Sisson, C(harles) H(ubert) 1914-...**CLC 8**
See also CA 1-4R; CAAS 3; CANR 3, 48; DLB 27
Sitwell, Dame Edith 1887-1964...**CLC 2, 9, 67; DAM POET; PC 3**
See also CA 9-12R; CANR 35; CDBLB 1945-1960; DLB 20; MTCW 1
Siwaarmill, H. P.
See Sharp, William

Spark, Muriel (Sarah) 1918-...**CLC 2, 3, 5, 8, 13, 18, 40, 94; DAB; DAC; DAM MST, NOV; SSC 10**
See also CA 5-8R; CANR 12, 36; CDBLB 1945-1960; DLB 15, 139; INT CANR-12; MTCW 1

Spaulding, Douglas
See Bradbury, Ray (Douglas)

Spaulding, Leonard
See Bradbury, Ray (Douglas)

Spence, J. A. D.
See Eliot, T(homas) S(tearns)

Spencer, Elizabeth 1921- .... **CLC 22**
See also CA 13-16R; CANR 32, 65; DLB 6; MTCW 1; SATA 14

Spencer, Leonard G.
See Silverberg, Robert

Spencer, Scott 1945-.................... **CLC 30**
See also CA 113; CANR 51; DLBY 86

Spender, Stephen (Harold) 1909-1995 **CLC 1, 2, 5, 10, 41, 91; DAM POET**
See also CA 9-12R; 149; CANR 31, 54; CDBLB 1945-1960; DLB 20; MTCW 1

Spengler, Oswald (Arnold Gottfried) 1880-1936 **TCLC 25**
See also CA 118

Spenser, Edmund 1552(?)-1599...**LC 5, 39; DA; DAB; DAC; DAM MST, POET; PC 8; WLC**
See also CDBLB Before 1660; DLB 167

Spicer, Jack 1925-1965...**CLC 8, 18, 72; DAM POET**
See also CA 85-88; DLB 5, 16, 193

Spiegelman, Art 1948- .... **CLC 76**
See also AAYA 10; CA 125; CANR 41, 55, 74

Spielberg, Peter 1929-....................**CLC 6**
See also CA 5-8R; CANR 4, 48; DLBY 81

Spielberg, Steven 1947-..................... **CLC 20**
See also AAYA 8, 24; CA 77-80; CANR 32; SATA 32

Spillane, Frank Morrison 1918-
See Spillane, Mickey
See also CA 25-28R; CANR 28, 63; MTCW 1; SATA 66

Spillane, Mickey .... **CLC 3, 13**
See also Spillane, Frank Morrison

Spinoza, Benedictus de 1632-1677...**LC 9**

Spinrad, Norman (Richard) 1940- **CLC 46**
See also CA 37-40R; CAAS 19; CANR 20; DLB 8; INT CANR-20

Spitteler, Carl (Friedrich Georg) 1845-1924 **TCLC 12**
See also CA 109; DLB 129

Spivack, Kathleen (Romola Drucker) 1938- **CLC 6**
See also CA 49-52

Spoto, Donald 1941-.......................... **CLC 39**
See also CA 65-68; CANR 11, 57

Springsteen, Bruce (F.) 1949-........... **CLC 17**
See also CA 111

Spurling, Hilary 1940- .... **CLC 34**
See also CA 104; CANR 25, 52

Spyker, John Howland
See Elman, Richard (Martin)

Squires, (James) Radcliffe 1917-1993 **CLC 51**
See also CA 1-4R; 140; CANR 6, 21

Srivastava, Dhanpat Rai 1880(?)-1936
See Premchand
See also CA 118

Stacy, Donald
See Pohl, Frederik

Stael, Germaine de 1766-1817
See Stael-Holstein, Anne Louise Germaine Necker Baronn
See also DLB 119

Stael-Holstein, Anne Louise Germaine Necker Baronn 1766-1817 .... **NCLC 3**
See also Stael, Germaine de
See also DLB 192

Stafford, Jean 1915-1979...**CLC 4, 7, 19, 68; SSC 26**
See also CA 1-4R; 85-88; CANR 3, 65; DLB 2, 173; MTCW 1; SATA-Obit 22

Stafford, William (Edgar) 1914-1993 **CLC 4, 7, 29; DAM POET**
See also CA 5-8R; 142; CAAS 3; CANR 5, 22; DLB 5; INT CANR-22

Stagnelius, Eric Johan 1793-1823 **NCLC 61**

Staines, Trevor
See Brunner, John (Kilian Houston)

Stairs, Gordon
See Austin, Mary (Hunter)

Stannard, Martin 1947- .... **CLC 44**
See also CA 142; DLB 155

Stanton, Elizabeth Cady 1815-1902 **TCLC 73**
See also CA 171; DLB 79

Stanton, Maura 1946- .... **CLC 9**
See also CA 89-92; CANR 15; DLB 120

Stanton, Schuyler
See Baum, L(yman) Frank

Stapledon, (William) Olaf 1886-1950 **TCLC 22**
See also CA 111; 162; DLB 15

Starbuck, George (Edwin) 1931-1996 **CLC 53; DAM POET**
See also CA 21-24R; 153; CANR 23

Stark, Richard
See Westlake, Donald E(dwin)

Staunton, Schuyler
See Baum, L(yman) Frank

Stead, Christina (Ellen) 1902-1983 **CLC 2, 5, 8, 32, 80**
See also CA 13-16R; 109; CANR 33, 40; MTCW 1

Stead, William Thomas 1849-1912...**TCLC 48**
See also CA 167

Steele, Richard 1672-1729 ....**LC 18**
See also CDBLB 1660-1789; DLB 84, 101

Steele, Timothy (Reid) 1948- .... **CLC 45**
See also CA 93-96; CANR 16, 50; DLB 120

Steffens, (Joseph) Lincoln 1866-1936...**TCLC 20**
See also CA 117

Stegner, Wallace (Earle) 1909-1993 **CLC 9, 49, 81; DAM NOV; SSC 27**
See also AITN 1; BEST 90:3; CA 1-4R; 141; CAAS 9; CANR 1, 21, 46; DLB 9; DLBY 93; MTCW 1

Stein, Gertrude 1874-1946...**TCLC 1, 6, 28, 48; DA; DAB; DAC; DAM MST, NOV, POET; PC 18; WLC**
See also CA 104; 132; CDALB 1917-1929; DLB 4, 54, 86; DLBD 15; MTCW 1

Steinbeck, John (Ernst) 1902-1968 **CLC 1, 5, 9, 13, 21, 34, 45, 75; DA; DAB; DAC; DAM DRAM, MST, NOV; SSC 11; WLC**
See also AAYA 12; CA 1-4R; 25-28R; CANR 1, 35; CDALB 1929-1941; DLB 7, 9; DLBD 2; MTCW 1; SATA 9

Steinem, Gloria 1934- ....**CLC 63**
See also CA 53-56; CANR 28, 51; MTCW 1

Steiner, George 1929- ..... **CLC 24; DAM NOV**
See also CA 73-76; CANR 31, 67; DLB 67; MTCW 1; SATA 62

Steiner, K. Leslie
See Delany, Samuel R(ay, Jr.)

Steiner, Rudolf 1861-1925 .... **TCLC 13**
See also CA 107

Stendhal 1783-1842...**NCLC 23, 46; DA; DAB; DAC; DAM MST, NOV; SSC 27; WLC**
See also DLB 119

Stephen, Adeline Virginia
See Woolf, (Adeline) Virginia

Stephen, SirLeslie 1832-1904 .... **TCLC 23**
See also CA 123; DLB 57, 144, 190

Stephen, Sir Leslie
See Stephen, SirLeslie

Stephen, Virginia
See Woolf, (Adeline) Virginia

Stephens, James 1882(?)-1950...**TCLC 4**
See also CA 104; DLB 19, 153, 162

Stephens, Reed
See Donaldson, Stephen R.

Steptoe, Lydia
See Barnes, Djuna

Sterchi, Beat 1949- .... **CLC 65**

Sterling, Brett
See Bradbury, Ray (Douglas); Hamilton, Edmond

Sterling, Bruce 1954- .... **CLC 72**
See also CA 119; CANR 44

Sterling, George 1869-1926 ..... **TCLC 20**
See also CA 117; 165; DLB 54

Stern, Gerald 1925- .... **CLC 40, 100**
See also CA 81-84; CANR 28; DLB 105

Stern, Richard (Gustave) 1928- ... **CLC 4, 39**
See also CA 1-4R; CANR 1, 25, 52; DLBY 87; INT CANR-25

Sternberg, Josef von 1894-1969...**CLC 20**
See also CA 81-84

Sterne, Laurence 1713-1768 ... **LC 2, 48; DA; DAB; DAC; DAM MST, NOV; WLC**
See also CDBLB 1660-1789; DLB 39

Sternheim, (William Adolf) Carl 1878-1942 **TCLC 8**
See also CA 105; DLB 56, 118

Stevens, Mark 1951- .... **CLC 34**
See also CA 122

Stevens, Wallace 1879-1955...**TCLC 3, 12, 45; DA; DAB; DAC; DAM MST, POET; PC 6; WLC**
See also CA 104; 124; CDALB 1929-1941; DLB 54; MTCW 1

Stevenson, Anne (Katharine) 1933- **CLC 7, 33**
See also CA 17-20R; CAAS 9; CANR 9, 33; DLB 40; MTCW 1

Stevenson, Robert Louis (Balfour) 1850-1894 **NCLC 5, 14, 63; DA; DAB; DAC; DAM MST, NOV; SSC 11; WLC**
See also AAYA 24; CDBLB 1890-1914; CLR 10, 11; DLB 18, 57, 141, 156, 174; DLBD 13; JRDA; MAICYA; SATA 100; YABC 2

Stewart, J(ohn) I(nnes) M(ackintosh) 1906-1994 .... **CLC 7, 14, 32**
See also CA 85-88; 147; CAAS 3; CANR 47; MTCW 1

Stewart, Mary (Florence Elinor) 1916- **CLC 7, 35, 117; DAB**
See also CA 1-4R; CANR 1, 59; SATA 12

Stewart, Mary Rainbow
See Stewart, Mary (Florence Elinor)

Swift, Jonathan 1667-1745...**LC 1, 42; DA; DAB; DAC; DAM MST, NOV, POET; PC 9; WLC**
See also CDBLB 1660-1789; CLR 53; DLB 39, 95, 101; SATA 19

Swinburne, Algernon Charles 1837-1909 **TCLC 8, 36; DA; DAB; DAC; DAM MST, POET; PC 24; WLC**
See also CA 105; 140; CDBLB 1832-1890; DLB 35, 57

Swinfen, Ann......**CLC 34**

Swinnerton, Frank Arthur 1884-1982 **CLC 31**
See also CA 108; DLB 34

Swithen, John
See King, Stephen (Edwin)

Sylvia
See Ashton-Warner, Sylvia (Constance)

Symmes, Robert Edward
See Duncan, Robert (Edward)

Symonds, John Addington 1840-1893 **NCLC 34**
See also DLB 57, 144

Symons, Arthur 1865-1945 ...... **TCLC 11**
See also CA 107; DLB 19, 57, 149

Symons, Julian (Gustave) 1912-1994 **CLC 2, 14, 32**
See also CA 49-52; 147; CAAS 3; CANR 3, 33, 59; DLB 87, 155; DLBY 92; MTCW 1

Synge, (Edmund) J(ohn) M(illington) 1871-1909 .. **TCLC 6, 37; DAM DRAM; DC 2**
See also CA 104; 141; CDBLB 1890-1914; DLB 10, 19

Syruc, J.
See Milosz, Czeslaw

Szirtes, George 1948- ...... **CLC 46**
See also CA 109; CANR 27, 61

Szymborska, Wislawa 1923- ..... **CLC 99**
See also CA 154; DLBY 96

T. O., Nik
See Annensky, Innokenty (Fyodorovich)

Tabori, George 1914- ...... **CLC 19**
See also CA 49-52; CANR 4, 69

Tagore, Rabindranath 1861-1941 **TCLC 3, 53; DAM DRAM, POET; PC 8**
See also CA 104; 120; MTCW 1

Taine, Hippolyte Adolphe 1828-1893 **NCLC 15**

Talese, Gay 1932- ...... **CLC 37**
See also AITN 1; CA 1-4R; CANR 9, 58; DLB 185; INT CANR-9; MTCW 1

Tallent, Elizabeth (Ann) 1954- ...... **CLC 45**
See also CA 117; CANR 72; DLB 130

Tally, Ted 1952- ...... **CLC 42**
See also CA 120; 124; INT 124

Talvik, Heiti 1904-1947 ...... **TCLC 87**

Tamayo y Baus, Manuel 1829-1898 **NCLC 1**

Tammsaare, A(nton) H(ansen) 1878-1940 **TCLC 27**
See also CA 164

Tam'si, Tchicaya U
See Tchicaya, Gerald Felix

Tan, Amy (Ruth) 1952-... **CLC 59; DAM MULT, NOV, POP**
See also AAYA 9; BEST 89:3; CA 136; CANR 54; DLB 173; SATA 75

Tandem, Felix
See Spitteler, Carl (Friedrich Georg)

Tanizaki, Jun'ichiro 1886-1965...**CLC 8, 14, 28; SSC 21**
See also CA 93-96; 25-28R; DLB 180

Tanner, William
See Amis, Kingsley (William)

Tao Lao
See Storni, Alfonsina

Tarassoff, Lev
See Troyat, Henri

Tarbell, Ida M(inerva) 1857-1944 **TCLC 40**
See also CA 122; DLB 47

Tarkington, (Newton) Booth 1869-1946 **TCLC 9**
See also CA 110; 143; DLB 9, 102; SATA 17

Tarkovsky, Andrei (Arsenyevich) 1932-1986 **CLC 75**
See also CA 127

Tartt, Donna 1964(?)- ...... **CLC 76**
See also CA 142

Tasso, Torquato 1544-1595 ...... **LC 5**

Tate, (John Orley) Allen 1899-1979 **CLC 2, 4, 6, 9, 11, 14, 24**
See also CA 5-8R; 85-88; CANR 32; DLB 4, 45, 63; DLBD 17; MTCW 1

Tate, Ellalice
See Hibbert, Eleanor Alice Burford

Tate, James (Vincent) 1943-...**CLC 2, 6, 25**
See also CA 21-24R; CANR 29, 57; DLB 5, 169

Tavel, Ronald 1940- ...... **CLC 6**
See also CA 21-24R; CANR 33

Taylor, C(ecil) P(hilip) 1929-1981 ....**CLC 27**
See also CA 25-28R; 105; CANR 47

Taylor, Edward 1642(?)-1729 ..... **LC 11; DA; DAB; DAC; DAM MST, POET**
See also DLB 24

Taylor, Eleanor Ross 1920- ......**CLC 5**
See also CA 81-84; CANR 70

Taylor, Elizabeth 1912-1975 ..... **CLC 2, 4, 29**
See also CA 13-16R; CANR 9, 70; DLB 139; MTCW 1; SATA 13

Taylor, Frederick Winslow 1856-1915 **TCLC 76**

Taylor, Henry (Splawn) 1942- .... **CLC 44**
See also CA 33-36R; CAAS 7; CANR 31; DLB 5

Taylor, Kamala (Purnaiya) 1924-
See Markandaya, Kamala
See also CA 77-80

Taylor, Mildred D. ...... **CLC 21**
See also AAYA 10; BW 1; CA 85-88; CANR 25; CLR 9; DLB 52; JRDA; MAICYA; SAAS 5; SATA 15, 70

Taylor, Peter (Hillsman) 1917-1994 **CLC 1, 4, 18, 37, 44, 50, 71; SSC 10**
See also CA 13-16R; 147; CANR 9, 50; DLBY 81, 94; INT CANR-9; MTCW 1

Taylor, Robert Lewis 1912-1998 ...... **CLC 14**
See also CA 1-4R; 170; CANR 3, 64; SATA 10

Tchekhov, Anton
See Chekhov, Anton (Pavlovich)

Tchicaya, Gerald Felix 1931-1988...**CLC 101**
See also CA 129; 125

Tchicaya U Tam'si
See Tchicaya, Gerald Felix

Teasdale, Sara 1884-1933 ...... **TCLC 4**
See also CA 104; 163; DLB 45; SATA 32

Tegner, Esaias 1782-1846 ...... **NCLC 2**

Teilhard de Chardin, (Marie Joseph) Pierre 1881-1955 ...... **TCLC 9**
See also CA 105

Temple, Ann
See Mortimer, Penelope (Ruth)

Tennant, Emma (Christina) 1937- **CLC 13, 52**
See also CA 65-68; CAAS 9; CANR 10, 38, 59; DLB 14

Tenneshaw, S. M.
See Silverberg, Robert

Tennyson, Alfred 1809-1892...**NCLC 30, 65; DA; DAB; DAC; DAM MST, POET; PC 6; WLC**
See also CDBLB 1832-1890; DLB 32

Teran, Lisa St. Aubin de ...... **CLC 36**
See also St. Aubin de Teran, Lisa

Terence 195(?)B.C.-159B.C....**CMLC 14; DC 7**

Teresa de Jesus, St. 1515-1582 ...... **LC 18**

Terkel, Louis 1912-
See Terkel, Studs
See also CA 57-60; CANR 18, 45, 67; MTCW 1

Terkel, Studs ...... **CLC 38**
See also Terkel, Louis
See also AITN 1

Terry, C. V.
See Slaughter, Frank G(ill)

Terry, Megan 1932- ...... **CLC 19**
See also CA 77-80; CABS 3; CANR 43; DLB 7

Tertullian c. 155-c. 245 ...... **CMLC 29**

Tertz, Abram
See Sinyavsky, Andrei (Donatevich)

Tesich, Steve 1943(?)-1996 ...... **CLC 40, 69**
See also CA 105; 152; DLBY 83

Tesla, Nikola 1856-1943 ...... **TCLC 88**

Teternikov, Fyodor Kuzmich 1863-1927
See Sologub, Fyodor
See also CA 104

Tevis, Walter 1928-1984 ...... **CLC 42**
See also CA 113

Tey, Josephine ...... **TCLC 14**
See also Mackintosh, Elizabeth
See also DLB 77

Thackeray, William Makepeace 1811-1863 **NCLC 5, 14, 22, 43; DA; DAB; DAC; DAM MST, NOV; WLC**
See also CDBLB 1832-1890; DLB 21, 55, 159, 163; SATA 23

Thakura, Ravindranatha
See Tagore, Rabindranath

Tharoor, Shashi 1956- ...... **CLC 70**
See also CA 141

Thelwell, Michael Miles 1939-...**CLC 22**
See also BW 2; CA 101

Theobald, Lewis, Jr.
See Lovecraft, H(oward) P(hillips)

Theodorescu, Ion N. 1880-1967
See Arghezi, Tudor
See also CA 116

Theriault, Yves 1915-1983 .... **CLC 79; DAC; DAM MST**
See also CA 102; DLB 88

Theroux, Alexander (Louis) 1939- **CLC 2, 25**
See also CA 85-88; CANR 20, 63

Theroux, Paul (Edward) 1941-...**CLC 5, 8, 11, 15, 28, 46; DAM POP**
See also BEST 89:4; CA 33-36R; CANR 20, 45, 74; DLB 2; MTCW 1; SATA 44

Thesen, Sharon 1946- ...... **CLC 56**
See also CA 163

Thevenin, Denis
See Duhamel, Georges

Thibault, Jacques Anatole Francois 1844-1924
See France, Anatole
See also CA 106; 127; DAM NOV; MTCW 1

Tremblay, Michel 1942- .....**CLC 29, 102; DAC; DAM MST**
See also CA 116; 128; DLB 60; MTCW 1

Trevanian .... **CLC 29**
See also Whitaker, Rod(ney)

Trevor, Glen
See Hilton, James

Trevor, William 1928-...**CLC 7, 9, 14, 25, 71, 116; SSC 21**
See also Cox, William Trevor
See also DLB 14, 139

Trifonov, Yuri (Valentinovich) 1925-1981
CLC 45
See also CA 126; 103; MTCW 1

Trilling, Lionel 1905-1975 ...... **CLC 9, 11, 24**
See also CA 9-12R; 61-64; CANR 10; DLB 28, 63; INT CANR-10; MTCW 1

Trimball, W. H.
See Mencken, H(enry) L(ouis)

Tristan
See Gomez de la Serna, Ramon

Tristram
See Housman, A(lfred) E(dward)

Trogdon, William (Lewis) 1939-
See Heat-Moon, William Least
See also CA 115; 119; CANR 47; INT 119

Trollope, Anthony 1815-1882...**NCLC 6, 33; DA; DAB; DAC; DAM MST, NOV; SSC 28; WLC**
See also CDBLB 1832-1890; DLB 21, 57, 159; SATA 22

Trollope, Frances 1779-1863 .... **NCLC 30**
See also DLB 21, 166

Trotsky, Leon 1879-1940............ **TCLC 22**
See also CA 118; 167

Trotter (Cockburn), Catharine 1679-1749
LC 8
See also DLB 84

Trout, Kilgore
See Farmer, Philip Jose

Trow, George W. S. 1943- .... **CLC 52**
See also CA 126

Troyat, Henri 1911- .... **CLC 23**
See also CA 45-48; CANR 2, 33, 67; MTCW 1

Trudeau, G(arretson) B(eekman) 1948-
See Trudeau, Garry B.
See also CA 81-84; CANR 31; SATA 35

Trudeau, Garry B. .... **CLC 12**
See also Trudeau, G(arretson) B(eekman)
See also AAYA 10; AITN 2

Truffaut, Francois 1932-1984...**CLC 20, 101**
See also CA 81-84; 113; CANR 34

Trumbo, Dalton 1905-1976............... **CLC 19**
See also CA 21-24R; 69-72; CANR 10; DLB 26

Trumbull, John 1750-1831 ...... **NCLC 30**
See also DLB 31

Trundlett, Helen B.
See Eliot, T(homas) S(tearns)

Tryon, Thomas 1926-1991**CLC 3, 11; DAM POP**
See also AITN 1; CA 29-32R; 135; CANR 32; MTCW 1

Tryon, Tom
See Tryon, Thomas

Ts'ao Hsueh-ch'in 1715(?)-1763 ..... **LC 1**

Tsushima, Shuji 1909-1948
See Dazai Osamu
See also CA 107

Tsvetaeva (Efron), Marina (Ivanovna) 1892-1941 .... **TCLC 7, 35; PC 14**
See also CA 104; 128; CANR 73; MTCW 1

Tuck, Lily 1938- .... **CLC 70**
See also CA 139

Tu Fu 712-770 .... **PC 9**
See also DAM MULT

Tunis, John R(oberts) 1889-1975...**CLC 12**
See also CA 61-64; CANR 62; DLB 22, 171; JRDA; MAICYA; SATA 37; SATA-Brief 30

Tuohy, Frank ....**CLC 37**
See also Tuohy, John Francis
See also DLB 14, 139

Tuohy, John Francis 1925-
See Tuohy, Frank
See also CA 5-8R; CANR 3, 47

Turco, Lewis (Putnam) 1934- ......**CLC 11, 63**
See also CA 13-16R; CAAS 22; CANR 24, 51; DLBY 84

Turgenev, Ivan 1818-1883 .... **NCLC 21; DA; DAB; DAC; DAM MST, NOV; DC 7; SSC 7; WLC**

Turgot, Anne-Robert-Jacques 1727-1781
LC 26

Turner, Frederick 1943- .... **CLC 48**
See also CA 73-76; CAAS 10; CANR 12, 30, 56; DLB 40

Tutu, Desmond M(pilo) 1931-...**CLC 80; BLC 3; DAM MULT**
See also BW 1; CA 125; CANR 67

Tutuola, Amos 1920-1997...**CLC 5, 14, 29; BLC 3; DAM MULT**
See also BW 2; CA 9-12R; 159; CANR 27, 66; DLB 125; MTCW 1

Twain, Mark ...**TCLC 6, 12, 19, 36, 48, 59; SSC 6, 26; WLC**
See also Clemens, Samuel Langhorne
See also AAYA 20; DLB 11, 12, 23, 64, 74

Tyler, Anne 1941-...**CLC 7, 11, 18, 28, 44, 59, 103; DAM NOV, POP**
See also AAYA 18; BEST 89:1; CA 9-12R; CANR 11, 33, 53; DLB 6, 143; DLBY 82; MTCW 1; SATA 7, 90

Tyler, Royall 1757-1826 .... **NCLC 3**
See also DLB 37

Tynan, Katharine 1861-1931 .... **TCLC 3**
See also CA 104; 167; DLB 153

Tyutchev, Fyodor 1803-1873 .... **NCLC 34**

Tzara, Tristan 1896-1963 ...... **CLC 47; DAM POET**
See also CA 153; 89-92

Uhry, Alfred 1936-...**CLC 55; DAM DRAM, POP**
See also CA 127; 133; INT 133

Ulf, Haerved
See Strindberg, (Johan) August

Ulf, Harved
See Strindberg, (Johan) August

Ulibarri, Sabine R(eyes) 1919-...**CLC 83; DAM MULT**
See also CA 131; DLB 82; HW

Unamuno (y Jugo), Miguel de 1864-1936
TCLC 2, 9; DAM MULT, NOV; HLC; SSC 11
See also CA 104; 131; DLB 108; HW; MTCW 1

Undercliffe, Errol
See Campbell, (John) Ramsey

Underwood, Miles
See Glassco, John

Undset, Sigrid 1882-1949...**TCLC 3; DA; DAB; DAC; DAM MST, NOV; WLC**
See also CA 104; 129; MTCW 1

Ungaretti, Giuseppe 1888-1970...**CLC 7, 11, 15**
See also CA 19-20; 25-28R; CAP 2; DLB 114

Unger, Douglas 1952- .... **CLC 34**
See also CA 130

Unsworth, Barry (Forster) 1930-...**CLC 76**
See also CA 25-28R; CANR 30, 54; DLB 194

Updike, John (Hoyer) 1932-...**CLC 1, 2, 3, 5, 7, 9, 13, 15, 23, 34, 43, 70; DA; DAB; DAC; DAM MST, NOV, POET, POP; SSC 13, 27; WLC**
See also CA 1-4R; CABS 1; CANR 4, 33, 51; CDALB 1968-1988; DLB 2, 5, 143; DLBD 3; DLBY 80, 82, 97; MTCW 1

Upshaw, Margaret Mitchell
See Mitchell, Margaret (Munnerlyn)

Upton, Mark
See Sanders, Lawrence

Upward, Allen 1863-1926 .... **TCLC 85**
See also CA 117; DLB 36

Urdang, Constance (Henriette) 1922-
CLC 47
See also CA 21-24R; CANR 9, 24

Uriel, Henry
See Faust, Frederick (Schiller)

Uris, Leon (Marcus) 1924-...**CLC 7, 32; DAM NOV, POP**
See also AITN 1, 2; BEST 89:2; CA 1-4R; CANR 1, 40, 65; MTCW 1; SATA 49

Urmuz
See Codrescu, Andrei

Urquhart, Jane 1949- .... **CLC 90; DAC**
See also CA 113; CANR 32, 68

Ustinov, Peter (Alexander) 1921-........**CLC 1**
See also AITN 1; CA 13-16R; CANR 25, 51; DLB 13

U Tam'si, Gerald Felix Tchicaya
See Tchicaya, Gerald Felix

U Tam'si, Tchicaya
See Tchicaya, Gerald Felix

Vachss, Andrew (Henry) 1942-...**CLC 106**
See also CA 118; CANR 44

Vachss, Andrew H.
See Vachss, Andrew (Henry)

Vaculik, Ludvik 1926- ....**CLC 7**
See also CA 53-56; CANR 72

Vaihinger, Hans 1852-1933 .... **TCLC 71**
See also CA 116; 166

Valdez, Luis (Miguel) 1940- ..**CLC 84; DAM MULT; DC 10; HLC**
See also CA 101; CANR 32; DLB 122; HW

Valenzuela, Luisa 1938-...**CLC 31, 104; DAM MULT; SSC 14**
See also CA 101; CANR 32, 65; DLB 113; HW

Valera y Alcala-Galiano, Juan 1824-1905
TCLC 10
See also CA 106

Valery, (Ambroise) Paul (Toussaint Jules) 1871-1945 .... **TCLC 4, 15; DAM POET; PC 9**
See also CA 104; 122; MTCW 1

Valle-Inclan, Ramon (Maria) del 1866-1936 .... **TCLC 5; DAM MULT; HLC**
See also CA 106; 153; DLB 134

Vallejo, Antonio Buero
See Buero Vallejo, Antonio

Vallejo, Cesar (Abraham) 1892-1938
TCLC 3, 56; DAM MULT; HLC
See also CA 105; 153; HW

Valles, Jules 1832-1885 .... **NCLC 71**
See also DLB 123

Vallette, Marguerite Eymery
See Rachilde

Valle Y Pena, Ramon del
See Valle-Inclan, Ramon (Maria) del

von Rezzori (d'Arezzo), Gregor
See Rezzori (d'Arezzo), Gregor von
von Sternberg, Josef
See Sternberg, Josef von
Vorster, Gordon 1924- .... **CLC 34**
See also CA 133
Vosce, Trudie
See Ozick, Cynthia
Voznesensky, Andrei (Andreievich) 1933-
CLC 1, 15, 57; DAM POET
See also CA 89-92; CANR 37; MTCW 1
Waddington, Miriam 1917- .... **CLC 28**
See also CA 21-24R; CANR 12, 30; DLB 68
Wagman, Fredrica 1937- ....**CLC 7**
See also CA 97-100; INT 97-100

Wagner, Linda W.
See Wagner-Martin, Linda (C.)
Wagner, Linda Welshimer
See Wagner-Martin, Linda (C.)
Wagner, Richard 1813-1883 ...... **NCLC 9**
See also DLB 129
Wagner-Martin, Linda (C.) 1936- ... **CLC 50**
See also CA 159
Wagoner, David (Russell) 1926-...**CLC 3, 5, 15**
See also CA 1-4R; CAAS 3; CANR 2, 71;
DLB 5; SATA 14
Wah, Fred(erick James) 1939- .... **CLC 44**
See also CA 107; 141; DLB 60
Wahloo, Per 1926-1975 ....**CLC 7**
See also CA 61-64; CANR 73
Wahloo, Peter
See Wahloo, Per
Wain, John (Barrington) 1925-1994
CLC 2, 11, 15, 46
See also CA 5-8R; 145; CAAS 4; CANR 23,
54; CDBLB 1960 to Present; DLB 15, 27,
139, 155; MTCW 1
Wajda, Andrzej 1926-................. **CLC 16**
See also CA 102
Wakefield, Dan 1932-..........................**CLC 7**
See also CA 21-24R; CAAS 7
Wakoski, Diane 1937-...**CLC 2, 4, 7, 9, 11, 40; DAM POET; PC 15**
See also CA 13-16R; CAAS 1; CANR 9, 60;
DLB 5; INT CANR-9
Wakoski-Sherbell, Diane
See Wakoski, Diane
Walcott, Derek (Alton) 1930-...**CLC 2, 4, 9, 14, 25, 42, 67, 76; BLC 3; DAB; DAC; DAM MST, MULT, POET; DC 7**
See also BW 2; CA 89-92; CANR 26, 47, 75;
DLB 117; DLBY 81; MTCW 1
Waldman, Anne (Lesley) 1945- ....**CLC 7**
See also CA 37-40R; CAAS 17; CANR 34,
69; DLB 16

Waldo, E. Hunter
See Sturgeon, Theodore (Hamilton)
Waldo, Edward Hamilton
See Sturgeon, Theodore (Hamilton)

Walker, Alice (Malsenior) 1944-...**CLC 5, 6, 9, 19, 27, 46, 58, 103; BLC 3; DA; DAB; DAC; DAM MST, MULT, NOV, POET, POP; SSC 5; WLCS**
See also AAYA 3; BEST 89:4; BW 2; CA 37-
40R; CANR 9, 27, 49, 66; CDALB 1968-
1988; DLB 6, 33, 143; INT CANR-27;
MTCW 1; SATA 31
Walker, David Harry 1911-1992...**CLC 14**
See also CA 1-4R; 137; CANR 1; SATA 8;
SATA-Obit 71

Walker, Edward Joseph 1934-
See Walker, Ted
See also CA 21-24R; CANR 12, 28, 53
Walker, George F. 1947- ..... **CLC 44, 61; DAB; DAC; DAM MST**
See also CA 103; CANR 21, 43, 59; DLB 60
Walker, Joseph A. 1935- ....**CLC 19; DAM DRAM, MST**
See also BW 1; CA 89-92; CANR 26; DLB 38
Walker, Margaret (Abigail) 1915-
CLC 1, 6; BLC; DAM MULT; PC 20
See also BW 2; CA 73-76; CANR 26, 54;
DLB 76, 152; MTCW 1
Walker, Ted ....**CLC 13**
See also Walker, Edward Joseph
See also DLB 40
Wallace, David Foster 1962- .....**CLC 50, 114**
See also CA 132; CANR 59
Wallace, Dexter
See Masters, Edgar Lee
Wallace, (Richard Horatio) Edgar 1875-
1932 .... **TCLC 57**
See also CA 115; DLB 70
Wallace, Irving 1916-1990.... **CLC 7, 13; DAM NOV, POP**
See also AITN 1; CA 1-4R; 132; CAAS 1;
CANR 1, 27; INT CANR-27; MTCW 1
Wallant, Edward Lewis 1926-1962
CLC 5, 10
See also CA 1-4R; CANR 22; DLB 2, 28,
143; MTCW 1
Walley, Byron
See Card, Orson Scott
Walpole, Horace 1717-1797 .... **LC 2**
See also DLB 39, 104
Walpole, Hugh (Seymour) 1884-1941
TCLC 5
See also CA 104; 165; DLB 34
Walser, Martin 1927- ....**CLC 27**
See also CA 57-60; CANR 8, 46; DLB 75, 124
Walser, Robert 1878-1956...**TCLC 18; SSC 20**
See also CA 118; 165; DLB 66
Walsh, Jill Paton .... **CLC 35**
See also Paton Walsh, Gillian
See also AAYA 11; CLR 2; DLB 161; SAAS 3
Walter, William Christian
See Andersen, Hans Christian
Wambaugh, Joseph (Aloysius, Jr.) 1937-
CLC 3, 18; DAM NOV, POP
See also AITN 1; BEST 89:3; CA 33-36R;
CANR 42, 65; DLB 6; DLBY 83; MTCW 1
Wang Wei 699(?)-761(?)..................**PC 18**
Ward, Arthur Henry Sarsfield 1883-1959
See Rohmer, Sax
See also CA 108
Ward, Douglas Turner 1930- ....**CLC 19**
See also BW 1; CA 81-84; CANR 27; DLB 7,
38
Ward, Mary Augusta
See Ward, Mrs. Humphry
Ward, Mrs. Humphry 1851-1920**TCLC 55**
See also DLB 18
Ward, Peter
See Faust, Frederick (Schiller)
Warhol, Andy 1928(?)-1987........ **CLC 20**
See also AAYA 12; BEST 89:4; CA 89-92;
121; CANR 34
Warner, Francis (Robert le Plastrier) 1937-
CLC 14
See also CA 53-56; CANR 11
Warner, Marina 1946- .... **CLC 59**
See also CA 65-68; CANR 21, 55; DLB 194

Warner, Rex (Ernest) 1905-1986...**CLC 45**
See also CA 89-92; 119; DLB 15
Warner, Susan (Bogert) 1819-1885
NCLC 31
See also DLB 3, 42
Warner, Sylvia (Constance) Ashton
See Ashton-Warner, Sylvia (Constance)
Warner, Sylvia Townsend 1893-1978
CLC 7, 19; SSC 23
See also CA 61-64; 77-80; CANR 16, 60;
DLB 34, 139; MTCW 1
Warren, Mercy Otis 1728-1814 .....**NCLC 13**
See also DLB 31, 200
Warren, Robert Penn 1905-1989
CLC 1, 4, 6, 8, 10, 13, 18, 39, 53, 59; DA; DAB; DAC; DAM MST, NOV, POET; SSC 4; WLC
See also AITN 1; CA 13-16R; 129; CANR
10, 47; CDALB 1968-1988; DLB 2, 48,
152; DLBY 80, 89; INT CANR-10;
MTCW 1; SATA 46; SATA-Obit 63
Warshofsky, Isaac
See Singer, Isaac Bashevis
Warton, Thomas 1728-1790...**LC 15; DAM POET**
See also DLB 104, 109
Waruk, Kona
See Harris, (Theodore) Wilson
Warung, Price 1855-1911 .... **TCLC 45**
Warwick, Jarvis
See Garner, Hugh
Washington, Alex
See Harris, Mark
Washington, Booker T(aliaferro) 1856-
1915...**TCLC 10; BLC 3; DAM MULT**
See also BW 1; CA 114; 125; SATA 28
Washington, George 1732-1799 .... **LC 25**
See also DLB 31
Wassermann, (Karl) Jakob 1873-1934
TCLC 6
See also CA 104; DLB 66
Wasserstein, Wendy 1950-...**CLC 32, 59, 90; DAM DRAM; DC 4**
See also CA 121; 129; CABS 3; CANR 53; INT
129; SATA 94, 75
Waterhouse, Keith (Spencer) 1929-
CLC 47
See also CA 5-8R; CANR 38, 67; DLB 13,
15; MTCW 1
Waters, Frank (Joseph) 1902-1995
CLC 88
See also CA 5-8R; 149; CAAS 13; CANR 3,
18, 63; DLBY 86
Waters, Roger 1944-...................... **CLC 35**
Watkins, Frances Ellen
See Harper, Frances Ellen Watkins
Watkins, Gerrold
See Malzberg, Barry N(athaniel)
Watkins, Gloria 1955(?)-
See hooks, bell
See also BW 2; CA 143
Watkins, Paul 1964- .... **CLC 55**
See also CA 132; CANR 62
Watkins, Vernon Phillips 1906-1967
CLC 43
See also CA 9-10; 25-28R; CAP 1; DLB
20
Watson, Irving S.
See Mencken, H(enry) L(ouis)
Watson, John H.
See Farmer, Philip Jose
Watson, Richard F.
See Silverberg, Robert

White, Patrick (Victor Martindale) 1912-1990 .... **CLC 3, 4, 5, 7, 9, 18, 65, 69**
See also CA 81-84; 132; CANR 43; MTCW 1

White, Phyllis Dorothy James 1920-
See James, P. D.
See also CA 21-24R; CANR 17, 43, 65; DAM POP; MTCW 1

White, T(erence) H(anbury) 1906-1964 **CLC 30**
See also AAYA 22; CA 73-76; CANR 37; DLB 160; JRDA; MAICYA; SATA 12

White, Terence de Vere 1912-1994 .. **CLC 49**
See also CA 49-52; 145; CANR 3

White, Walter F(rancis) 1893-1955**TCLC 15**
See also White, Walter
See also BW 1; CA 115; 124; DLB 51

White, William Hale 1831-1913
See Rutherford, Mark
See also CA 121

Whitehead, E(dward) A(nthony) 1933- **CLC 5**
See also CA 65-68; CANR 58

Whitemore, Hugh (John) 1936- .... **CLC 37**
See also CA 132; INT 132

Whitman, Sarah Helen (Power) 1803-1878 **NCLC 19**
See also DLB 1

Whitman, Walt(er) 1819-1892 **NCLC 4, 31; DA; DAB; DAC; DAM MST, POET; PC 3; WLC**
See also CDALB 1640-1865; DLB 3, 64; SATA 20

Whitney, Phyllis A(yame) 1903- ..... **CLC 42; DAM POP**
See also AITN 2; BEST 90:3; CA 1-4R; CANR 3, 25, 38, 60; JRDA; MAICYA; SATA 1, 30

Whittemore, (Edward) Reed (Jr.) 1919-**CLC 4**
See also CA 9-12R; CAAS 8; CANR 4; DLB 5

Whittier, John Greenleaf 1807-1892 **NCLC 8, 59**
See also DLB 1

Whittlebot, Hernia
See Coward, Noel (Peirce)

Wicker, Thomas Grey 1926-
See Wicker, Tom
See also CA 65-68; CANR 21, 46

Wicker, Tom ....**CLC 7**
See also Wicker, Thomas Grey

Wideman, John Edgar 1941- **CLC 5, 34, 36, 67; BLC 3; DAM MULT**
See also BW 2; CA 85-88; CANR 14, 42, 67; DLB 33, 143

Wiebe, Rudy (Henry) 1934-**CLC 6, 11, 14; DAC; DAM MST**
See also CA 37-40R; CANR 42, 67; DLB 60

Wieland, Christoph Martin 1733-1813**NCLC 17**
See also DLB 97

Wiene, Robert 1881-1938 .... **TCLC 56**

Wieners, John 1934- ....**CLC 7**
See also CA 13-16R; DLB 16

Wiesel, Elie(zer) 1928- **CLC 3, 5, 11, 37; DA; DAB; DAC; DAM MST, NOV; WLCS**
See also AAYA 7; AITN 1; CA 5-8R; CAAS 4; CANR 8, 40, 65; DLB 83; DLBY 87; INT CANR-8; MTCW 1; SATA 56

Wiggins, Marianne 1947- .... **CLC 57**
See also BEST 89:3; CA 130; CANR 60

Wight, James Alfred 1916-1995
See Herriot, James
See also CA 77-80; SATA 55; SATA-Brief 44

Wilbur, Richard (Purdy) 1921-...**CLC 3, 6, 9, 14, 53, 110; DA; DAB; DAC; DAM MST, POET**
See also CA 1-4R; CABS 2; CANR 2, 29; DLB 5, 169; INT CANR-29; MTCW 1; SATA 9

Wild, Peter 1940- ....**CLC 14**
See also CA 37-40R; DLB 5

Wilde, Oscar (Fingal O'Flahertie Wills) 1854(?)-1900...**TCLC 1, 8, 23, 41; DA; DAB; DAC; DAM DRAM, MST, NOV; SSC 11; WLC**
See also CA 104; 119; CDBLB 1890-1914; DLB 10, 19, 34, 57, 141, 156, 190; SATA 24

Wilder, Billy ....**CLC 20**
See also Wilder, Samuel
See also DLB 26

Wilder, Samuel 1906-
See Wilder, Billy
See also CA 89-92

Wilder, Thornton (Niven) 1897-1975 **CLC 1, 5, 6, 10, 15, 35, 82; DA; DAB; DAC; DAM DRAM, MST, NOV; DC 1; WLC**
See also AITN 2; CA 13-16R; 61-64; CANR 40; DLB 4, 7, 9; DLBY 97; MTCW 1

Wilding, Michael 1942-....................**CLC 73**
See also CA 104; CANR 24, 49

Wiley, Richard 1944-...................**CLC 44**
See also CA 121; 129; CANR 71

Wilhelm, Kate ....**CLC 7**
See also Wilhelm, Katie Gertrude
See also AAYA 20; CAAS 5; DLB 8; INT CANR-17

Wilhelm, Katie Gertrude 1928-
See Wilhelm, Kate
See also CA 37-40R; CANR 17, 36, 60; MTCW 1

Wilkins, Mary
See Freeman, Mary Eleanor Wilkins

Willard, Nancy 1936- ....**CLC 7, 37**
See also CA 89-92; CANR 10, 39, 68; CLR 5; DLB 5, 52; MAICYA; MTCW 1; SATA 37, 71; SATA-Brief 30

Williams, Ben Ames 1889-1953 ...... **TCLC 89**
See also DLB 102

Williams, C(harles) K(enneth) 1936- **CLC 33, 56; DAM POET**
See also CA 37-40R; CAAS 26; CANR 57; DLB 5

Williams, Charles
See Collier, James L(incoln)

Williams, Charles (Walter Stansby) 1886-1945 **TCLC 1, 11**
See also CA 104; 163; DLB 100, 153

Williams, (George) Emlyn 1905-1987 **CLC 15; DAM DRAM**
See also CA 104; 123; CANR 36; DLB 10, 77; MTCW 1

Williams, Hank 1923-1953 .... **TCLC 81**

Williams, Hugo 1942-.........................**CLC 42**
See also CA 17-20R; CANR 45; DLB 40

Williams, J. Walker
See Wodehouse, P(elham) G(renville)

Williams, John A(lfred) 1925-...**CLC 5, 13; BLC 3; DAM MULT**
See also BW 2; CA 53-56; CAAS 3; CANR 6, 26, 51; DLB 2, 33; INT CANR-6

Williams, Jonathan (Chamberlain) 1929- **CLC 13**
See also CA 9-12R; CAAS 12; CANR 8; DLB 5

Williams, Joy 1944- .... **CLC 31**
See also CA 41-44R; CANR 22, 48

Williams, Norman 1952- .... **CLC 39**
See also CA 118

Williams, Sherley Anne 1944-...**CLC 89; BLC 3; DAM MULT, POET**
See also BW 2; CA 73-76; CANR 25; DLB 41; INT CANR-25; SATA 78

Williams, Shirley
See Williams, Sherley Anne

Williams, Tennessee 1911-1983...**CLC 1, 2, 5, 7, 8, 11, 15, 19, 30, 39, 45, 71, 111; DA; DAB; DAC; DAM DRAM, MST; DC 4; WLC**
See also AITN 1, 2; CA 5-8R; 108; CABS 3; CANR 31; CDALB 1941-1968; DLB 7; DLBD 4; DLBY 83; MTCW 1

Williams, Thomas (Alonzo) 1926-1990 **CLC 14**
See also CA 1-4R; 132; CANR 2

Williams, William C.
See Williams, William Carlos

Williams, William Carlos 1883-1963 **CLC 1, 2, 5, 9, 13, 22, 42, 67; DA; DAB; DAC; DAM MST, POET; PC 7; SSC 31**
See also CA 89-92; CANR 34; CDALB 1917-1929; DLB 4, 16, 54, 86; MTCW 1

Williamson, David (Keith) 1942- ......**CLC 56**
See also CA 103; CANR 41

Williamson, Ellen Douglas 1905-1984
See Douglas, Ellen
See also CA 17-20R; 114; CANR 39

Williamson, Jack ....**CLC 29**
See also Williamson, John Stewart
See also CAAS 8; DLB 8

Williamson, John Stewart 1908-
See Williamson, Jack
See also CA 17-20R; CANR 23, 70

Willie, Frederick
See Lovecraft, H(oward) P(hillips)

Willingham, Calder (Baynard, Jr.) 1922-1995 ....**CLC 5, 51**
See also CA 5-8R; 147; CANR 3; DLB 2, 44; MTCW 1

Willis, Charles
See Clarke, Arthur C(harles)

Willy
See Colette, (Sidonie-Gabrielle)

Willy, Colette
See Colette, (Sidonie-Gabrielle)

Wilson, A(ndrew) N(orman) 1950- **C L C 33**
See also CA 112; 122; DLB 14, 155, 194

Wilson, Angus (Frank Johnstone) 1913-1991 ...... **CLC 2, 3, 5, 25, 34; SSC 21**
See also CA 5-8R; 134; CANR 21; DLB 15, 139, 155; MTCW 1

Wilson, August 1945-... **CLC 39, 50, 63; BLC 3; DA; DAB; DAC; DAM DRAM, MST, MULT; DC 2; WLCS**
See also AAYA 16; BW 2; CA 115; 122; CANR 42, 54; MTCW 1

Wilson, Brian 1942- ....**CLC 12**

Wilson, Colin 1931- .... **CLC 3, 14**
See also CA 1-4R; CAAS 5; CANR 1, 22, 33; DLB 14, 194; MTCW 1

Wilson, Dirk
See Pohl, Frederik

Wilson, Edmund 1895-1972...**CLC 1, 2, 3, 8, 24**
See also CA 1-4R; 37-40R; CANR 1, 46; DLB 63; MTCW 1

Wilson, Ethel Davis (Bryant) 1888(?)-1980 **CLC 13; DAC; DAM POET**
See also CA 102; DLB 68; MTCW 1

Author Index

Short Story Criticism
Cumulative Nationality Index

ALGERIAN
Camus, Albert **9**

AMERICAN
Adams, Alice (Boyd) **24**
Aiken, Conrad (Potter) **9**
Alcott, Louisa May **27**
Algren, Nelson **33**
Anderson, Sherwood **1**
Auchincloss, Louis (Stanton) **22**
Baldwin, James (Arthur) **10, 33**
Barnes, Djuna **3**
Barth, John (Simmons) **10**
Barthelme, Donald **2**
Beattie, Ann **11**
Bellow, Saul **14**
Benet, Stephen Vincent **10**
Berriault, Gina **30**
Bierce, Ambrose (Gwinett) **9**
Bowles, Paul (Frederick) **3**
Boyle, Kay **5**
Boyle, T(homas) Coraghessan **16**
Bradbury, Ray (Douglas) **29**
Cable, George Washington **4**
Caldwell, Erskine (Preston) **19**
Calisher, Hortense **15**
Capote, Truman **2**
Carver, Raymond **8**
Cather, Willa Sibert **2**
Chandler, Raymond (Thornton) **23**
Cheever, John **1**
Chesnutt, Charles W(addell) **7**
Chopin, Kate **8**
Cisneros, Sandra **32**
Coover, Robert (Lowell) **15**
Cowan, Peter (Walkinshaw) **28**
Crane, Stephen (Townley) **7**
Davenport, Guy (Mattison Jr.) **16**
Dixon, Stephen **16**
Dreiser, Theodore (Herman Albert) **30**
Dubus, Andre **15**
Dunbar, Paul Laurence **8**
Elkin, Stanley L(awrence) **12**
Ellison, Harlan (Jay) **14**
Ellison, Ralph (Waldo) **26**
Farrell, James T(homas) **28**
Faulkner, William (Cuthbert) **1**
Fisher, Rudolph **25**
Fitzgerald, F(rancis) Scott (Key) **6, 31**
Freeman, Mary Eleanor Wilkins **1**
Gardner, John (Champlin) Jr. **7**
Garland, (Hannibal) Hamlin **18**
Garrett, George (Palmer) **30**
Gass, William H(oward) **12**
Gilchrist, Ellen **14**
Gilman, Charlotte (Anna) Perkins (Stetson) **13**
Gordon, Caroline **15**
Grau, Shirley Ann **15**
Hammett, (Samuel) Dashiell **17**
Harris, Joel Chandler **19**
Harrison, James (Thomas) **19**
Harte, (Francis) Bret(t) **8**
Hawthorne, Nathaniel **3, 29**

Hemingway, Ernest (Miller) **1, 25**
Henderson, Zenna (Chlarson) **29**
Henry, O. **5**
Hughes, (James) Langston **6**
Hurston, Zora Neale **4**
Irving, Washington **2**
Jackson, Shirley **9**
James, Henry **8, 32**
Jewett, (Theodora) Sarah Orne **6**
King, Stephen (Edwin) **17**
Lardner, Ring(gold) W(ilmer) **32**
Le Guin, Ursula K(roeber) **12**
Ligotti, Thomas (Robert) **16**
Lish, Gordon (Jay) **18**
London, Jack **4**
Lovecraft, H(oward) P(hillips) **3**
Maclean, Norman (Fitzroy) **13**
Malamud, Bernard **15**
Marshall, Paule **3**
Mason, Bobbie Ann **4**
McCarthy, Mary (Therese) **24**
McCullers, (Lula) Carson (Smith) **9, 24**
Melville, Herman **1, 17**
Michaels, Leonard **16**
Murfree, Mary Noailles **22**
Nabokov, Vladimir (Vladimirovich) **11**
Nin, Anais **10**
Norris, Frank **28**
Oates, Joyce Carol **6**
O'Connor, (Mary) Flannery **1, 23**
O'Hara, John (Henry) **15**
Olsen, Tillie **11**
Ozick, Cynthia **15**
Page, Thomas Nelson **23**
Paley, Grace **8**
Parker, Dorothy (Rothschild) **2**
Perelman, S(idney) J(oseph) **32**
Phillips, Jayne Anne **16**
Poe, Edgar Allan **1, 22**
Pohl, Frederik **25**
Porter, Katherine Anne **4, 31**
Powers, J(ames) F(arl) **4**
Price, (Edward) Reynolds **22**
Pynchon, Thomas (Ruggles Jr.) **14**
Roth, Philip (Milton) **26**
Salinger, J(erome) D(avid) **2, 28**
Saroyan, William **21**
Selby, Hubert Jr. **20**
Singer, Isaac Bashevis **3**
Stafford, Jean **26**
Stegner, Wallace (Earle) **27**
Steinbeck, John (Ernst) **11**
Stuart, Jesse (Hilton) **31**
Styron, William **25**
Suckow, Ruth **18**
Taylor, Peter (Hillsman) **10**
Thomas, Audrey (Callahan) **20**
Thurber, James (Grover) **1**
Toomer, Jean **1**
Twain, Mark **6, 26**
Updike, John (Hoyer) **13, 27**
Vinge, Joan (Carol) D(ennison) **24**
Vonnegut, Kurt Jr. **8**

Walker, Alice (Malsenior) **5**
Warren, Robert Penn **4**
Welty, Eudora **1, 27**
West, Nathanael **16**
Wharton, Edith (Newbold Jones) **6**
Williams, William Carlos **31**
Wodehouse, P(elham) G(renville) **2**
Wolfe, Thomas (Clayton) **33**
Wright, Richard (Nathaniel) **2**

ARGENTINIAN
Bioy Casares, Adolfo **17**
Borges, Jorge Luis **4**
Cortazar, Julio **7**
Valenzuela, Luisa **14**

AUSTRALIAN
Jolley, (Monica) Elizabeth **19**
Lawson, Henry (Archibald Hertzberg) **18**

AUSTRIAN
Kafka, Franz **5, 29**
Musil, Robert (Edler von) **18**
Schnitzler, Arthur **15**
Stifter, Adalbert **28**

BRAZILIAN
Machado de Assis, Joaquim Maria **24**

CANADIAN
Atwood, Margaret (Eleanor) **2**
Bellow, Saul **14**
Gallant, Mavis **5**
Laurence, (Jean) Margaret (Wemyss) **7**
Munro, Alice **3**
Ross, (James) Sinclair **24**
Thomas, Audrey (Callahan) **20**

CHINESE
Chang, Eileen **28**
Lu Hsun **20**
P'u Sung-ling **31**

COLOMBIAN
Garcia Marquez, Gabriel (Jose) **8**

CUBAN
Calvino, Italo **3**
CZECH
Kafka, Franz **5, 29**
Kundera, Milan **24**

DANISH
Andersen, Hans Christian **6**
Dinesen, Isak **7**

ENGLISH
Ballard, J(ames) G(raham) **1**
Bates, H(erbert) E(rnest) **10**
Bowen, Elizabeth (Dorothea Cole) **3, 28**
Campbell, (John) Ramsey **19**
Carter, Angela (Olive) **13**
Chesterton, G(ilbert) K(eith) **1**

Short Story Criticism
Cumulative Title Index

Title Index

Title Index

Title Index

Title Index

Title Index

Title Index

Title Index

ISBN 0-7876-3079-9

90000